5-11-11

AN ENCYCLOPEDIA OF
HUMAN RIGHTS
IN THE
UNITED STATES

AN ENCYCLOPEDIA OF HUMAN RIGHTS IN THE UNITED STATES

SECOND EDITION
VOLUME 2

H. VICTOR CONDÉ

GREY HOUSE PUBLISHING

PUBLISHER:	Leslie Mackenzie
EDITORIAL DIRECTOR:	Laura Mars
EDITORIAL ASSISTANT:	Diana Delgado
PRODUCTION MANAGER:	Kristen Thatcher
MARKETING DIRECTOR:	Jessica Moody

AUTHOR:	H. Victor Condé

AUTHOR, TIMELINE PEER REVIEW EDITOR, TERMS CONTRIBUTING AUTHOR, DOCUMENT INTRODUCTIONS:	Tina M. Ramirez

Grey House Publishing, Inc.
4919 Route 22
Amenia, NY 12501
518.789.8700 FAX 845.373.6390
www.greyhouse.com
e-mail: books@greyhouse.com

While every effort has been made to ensure the reliability of the information presented in this publication, Grey House Publishing neither guarantees the accuracy of the data contained herein nor assumes any responsibility for errors, omissions or discrepancies. Grey House accepts no payment for listing; inclusion in the publication of any organization, agency, institution, publication, service or individual does not imply endorsement of the editors or publisher.

Errors brought to the attention of the publisher and verified to the satisfaction of the publisher will be corrected in future editions.

Publisher's Cataloging-In-Publication Data
(Prepared by The Donohue Group, Inc.)

Condé, H. Victor, 1947-

 Human rights in the United States: a dictionary and documents / H. Victor Condé.—2nd ed.

 2 v. : ill., forms ; cm.

   Includes bibliographical references and index.
   ISBN: 978-1-59237-290-4

  1. Human rights—United States—Dictionaries. 2. Human rights—United States—History—Sources. I. Title.
KF4747.5.C37 2011
342.73/085/03

Printed in Canada

This book is dedicated to
Jean Grech Condé and Simone Thérèse Condé,
and in memory of Salvina Mifsud Grech,
Charles Grech, Captain Harry Victor Condé
and Marie Thérèse Condé

ACKNOWLEDGMENTS

Special acknowledgment goes to my dear colleagues Rita Cantos Cartwright and Tina M. Ramirez for their valuable help and human rights expertise without which this book would not have happened.

I would also like to thank the following persons for their competent and heartfelt help in making this book possible—Robert Cartwright, Jean Condé, Simone Condé, Heather Dickey, Catherine Ancel, Dr. Bernard Bastian and Communauté Puits de Jacob, Msgr. Silvano Tomasi, and also Diana Delgado at Grey House Publishing. Thanks to Robert Savage JD and William Luke Gilbert, law student, for developing the case law appendix. Thanks to Trezlen Drake JD, MSIL, law librarian, for updating the bibliography. Special thanks to Sir Nigel Rodley for his input and correction.

In recognition of the International Institute of Human Rights in Strasbourg, France for the knowledge of human rights and humanitarian law I have received over the past 26 years. I also gratefully honor the memory of Professor Jean-Francois Flauss, its late Secretary-General.

In recognition of the University of California at Davis Law School, Martin Luther King Hall, for my legal education in international law.

In recognition of the University of Essex, Human Rights Center in England, for my graduate human rights legal education under the best human rights professors in the world.

Your work will make the United States of America a better country.

TABLE OF CONTENTS

VOLUME 1

TERMS

PRIMARY DOCUMENTS

VOLUME 2

APPENDICES

America did not invent human rights. In a very real sense it is the other way around. Human rights invented America. Ours was the first nation in the history of the world to be founded explicitly on such an idea.

President Jimmy Carter
Farewell Address, January 1981

The desire to live freely under a government that would respect and protect human rights was the fundamental motivation of our country's Founders—human rights have not only been part of the United States since the beginning, they were the reason our nation was created.

U.S. Universal Periodic Report, August 2010

Legislation and court orders can only declare rights. They can never thoroughly deliver them. Only when people themselves begin to act are rights on paper given life blood.

Martin Luther King, 1929-1969

HUMAN RIGHTS PRIMARY DOCUMENTS

HUMANITARIAN LAW & INTERNATIONAL CRIMINAL LAW DOCUMENT

DOCUMENT 68

Full Official Title: Draft Code of Offences Against the Peace and Security of Mankind

Short Title/Acronym/Abbreviation: The Draft Code of Crimes

Type of Document: This is not a treaty and therefore not legally binding. These draft codes were adopted by the International Law Commission at its sixth session in 1996 and submitted to the U.N. General Assembly as part of its report to the Assembly.

Subject: Peace, security, accountability, individual criminal responsibility, and international criminal law

Official Citation: Text adopted by the International Law Commission at its forty-eighth session, in 1996, and submitted to the General Assembly as a part of the Commission's report covering the work of that session (at para. 50). The report, which also contains commentaries on the draft articles, appears in *Yearbook of the International Law Commission, 1996*, vol. II (Part Two).

Date of Document: 1996 (with several subsequent amendments and drafts)

Date of Adoption: 1996

Date of General Entry into Force (EIF): Not applicable

Number of States Parties as of this printing: Not applicable

Date of Signature by the United States: Not applicable

Date of Ratification/Accession/Adhesion: Not applicable

Date of Entry into Force as to United States (effective date): Not applicable

Legal Status/Character of the Instrument/Document as to the United States: Arguably binding as declaratory of customary international law on all states

Supervising Body: Not applicable

Comment: In 1982, the General Assembly called on the International Law Commission to review the Draft Code, which was done at several subsequent sessions and presented to the General Assembly, which later developed into the framework for the International Criminal Court.

Caution: The status and applicability of this instrument as to the United States may have changed since the date of this publication.

Web Address: http://untreaty.un.org/ilc/texts/instruments/english/draft%20articles/7_3_1954.pdf

DRAFT CODE OF OFFENCES AGAINST THE PEACE AND SECURITY OF MANKIND

Text adopted by the International Law Commission at its forty-eighth session, in 1996, and submitted to the General Assembly as a part of the Commission's report covering the work of that session (at para. 50). The report, which also contains commentaries on the draft articles, appears in *Yearbook of the International Law*

Draft Code of Crimes against the Peace and Security of Mankind (1996)

PART ONE

GENERAL PROVISIONS

Article 1

Scope and application of the present Code

1. The present Code applies to the crimes against the peace and security of mankind set out in part two.

2. Crimes against the peace and security of mankind are crimes under international law and punishable as such, whether or not they are punishable under national law.

Article 2

Individual responsibility

1. A crime against the peace and security of mankind entails individual responsibility.

2. An individual shall be responsible for the crime of aggression in accordance with Article 16.

3. An individual shall be responsible for a crime set out in Article 17, 18, 19 or 20 if that individual:

(*a*) Intentionally commits such a crime;

(*b*) Orders the commission of such a crime which in fact occurs or is attempted;

(*c*) Fails to prevent or repress the commission of such a crime in the circumstances set out in Article 6;

(*d*) Knowingly aids, abets or otherwise assists, directly and substantially, in the commission of such a crime, including providing the means for its commission;

(*e*) Directly participates in planning or conspiring to commit such a crime which in fact occurs;

(*f*) Directly and publicly incites another individual to commit such a crime which in fact occurs;

(*g*) Attempts to commit such a crime by taking action commencing the execution of a crime which does not in fact occur because of circumstances independent of his intentions.

Article 3

Punishment

An individual who is responsible for a crime against the peace and security of mankind shall be liable to punishment. The punishment shall be commensurate with the character and gravity of the crime.

Article 4

Responsibility of States

The fact that the present Code provides for the responsibility of individuals for crimes against the peace and security of mankind is without prejudice to any question of the responsibility of States under international law.

Article 5

Order of a Government or a superior

The fact that an individual charged with a crime against the peace and security of mankind acted pursuant to an order of a Government or a superior does not relieve him of criminal responsibility, but may be considered in mitigation of punishment if justice so requires.

Article 6

Responsibility of the superior

The fact that a crime against the peace and security of mankind was committed by a subordinate does not relieve his superiors of criminal responsibility, if they knew or had reason to know, in the circumstances at the time, that the subordinate was committing or was going to commit such a crime and if they did not take all necessary measures within their power to prevent or repress the crime.

Article 7

Official position and responsibility

The official position of an individual who commits a crime against the peace and security of mankind, even if he acted as head of State or Government, does not relieve him of criminal responsibility or mitigate punishment.

Article 8

Establishment of jurisdiction

Without prejudice to the jurisdiction of an international criminal court, each State Party shall take such measures as may be necessary to establish its jurisdiction over the crimes set out in articles 17, 18, 19 and 20, irrespective of where or by whom those crimes were committed. Jurisdiction over the crime set out in Article 16 shall rest with an international criminal court. However, a State referred to in Article 16 is not precluded from trying its nationals for the crime set out in that article.

Article 9

Obligation to extradite or prosecute

Without prejudice to the jurisdiction of an international criminal court, the State Party in the territory of which an individual alleged to have committed a crime set out in Article 17, 18, 19 or 20 is found shall extradite or prosecute that individual.

Article 10

Extradition of alleged offenders

1. To the extent that the crimes set out in articles 17, 18, 19 and 20 are not extraditable offences in any extradition treaty existing between States Parties, they shall be deemed to be included as such therein. States

Parties undertake to include those crimes as extraditable offences in every extradition treaty to be concluded between them.

2. If a State Party which makes extradition conditional on the existence of a treaty receives a request for extradition from another State Party with which it has no extradition treaty, it may at its option consider the present Code as the legal basis for extradition in respect of those crimes. Extradition shall be subject to the conditions provided in the law of the requested State.

3. States Parties which do not make extradition conditional on the existence of a treaty shall recognize those crimes as extraditable offences between themselves subject to the conditions provided in the law of the requested State.

4. Each of those crimes shall be treated, for the purpose of extradition between States Parties, as if it had been committed not only in the place in which it occurred but also in the territory of any other State Party.

Article 11

Judicial guarantees

1. An individual charged with a crime against the peace and security of mankind shall be presumed innocent until proved guilty and shall be entitled without discrimination to the minimum guarantees due to all human beings with regard to the law and the facts and shall have the rights:

(*a*) In the determination of any charge against him, to have a fair and public hearing by a competent, independent and impartial tribunal duly established by law;

(*b*) To be informed promptly and in detail in a language which he understands of the nature and cause of the charge against him;

(*c*) To have adequate time and facilities for the preparation of his defence and to communicate with counsel of his own choosing;

(*d*) To be tried without undue delay;

(*e*) To be tried in his presence, and to defend himself in person or through legal assistance of his own choosing; to be informed, if he does not have legal assistance, of this right; and to have legal assistance assigned to him and without payment by him if he does not have sufficient means to pay for it;

(*f*) To examine, or have examined, the witnesses against him and to obtain the attendance and examination of witnesses on his behalf under the same conditions as witnesses against him;

(*g*) To have the free assistance of an interpreter if he cannot understand or speak the language used in court;

(*h*) Not to be compelled to testify against himself or to confess guilt.

2. An individual convicted of a crime shall have the right to his conviction and sentence being reviewed according to law.

Article 12

Non bis in idem

1. No one shall be tried for a crime against the peace and security of mankind of which he has already been finally convicted or acquitted by an international criminal court.

2. An individual may not be tried again for a crime of which he has been finally convicted or acquitted by a national court except in the following cases:

(*a*) By an international criminal court, if:

(i) The act which was the subject of the judgement in the national court was characterized by that court as an ordinary crime and not as a crime against the peace and security of mankind; or

(ii) The national court proceedings were not impartial or independent or were designed to shield the accused from international criminal responsibility or the case was not diligently prosecuted;

(*b*) By a national court of another State, if:

(i) The act which was the subject of the previous judgement took place in the territory of that State; or

(ii) That State was the main victim of the crime.

3. In the case of a subsequent conviction under the present Code, the court, in passing sentence, shall take into account the extent to which any penalty imposed by a national court on the same person for the same act has already been served.

Article 13

Non-retroactivity

1. No one shall be convicted under the present Code for acts committed before its entry into force.

2. Nothing in this article precludes the trial of anyone for any act which, at the time when it was committed, was criminal in accordance with international law or national law.

Article 14

Defences

The competent court shall determine the admissibility of defences in accordance with the general principles of law, in the light of the character of each crime.

Article 15

Extenuating circumstances

In passing sentence, the court shall, where appropriate, take into account extenuating circumstances in accordance with the general principles of law.

PART TWO
CRIMES AGAINST THE PEACE AND SECURITY OF MANKIND

Article 16

Crime of aggression

An individual who, as leader or organizer, actively participates in or orders the planning, preparation, initiation or waging of aggression committed by a State shall be responsible for a crime of aggression.

Article 17

Crime of genocide

A crime of genocide means any of the following acts committed with intent to destroy, in whole or in part, a national, ethnic, racial or religious group, as such:

(a) Killing members of the group;

(b) Causing serious bodily or mental harm to members of the group;

(c) Deliberately inflicting on the group conditions of life calculated to bring about its physical destruction in whole or in part;

(d) Imposing measures intended to prevent births within the group;

(e) Forcibly transferring children of the group to another group.

Article 18

Crimes against humanity

A crime against humanity means any of the following acts, when committed in a systematic manner or on a large scale and instigated or directed by a Government or by any organization or group:

(a) Murder;

(b) Extermination;

(c) Torture;

(d) Enslavement;

(e) Persecution on political, racial, religious or ethnic grounds;

(f) Institutionalized discrimination on racial, ethnic or religious grounds involving the violation of fundamental human rights and freedoms and resulting in seriously disadvantaging a part of the population;

(g) Arbitrary deportation or forcible transfer of population;

(h) Arbitrary imprisonment;

(i) Forced disappearance of persons;

(j) Rape, enforced prostitution and other forms of sexual abuse;

(k) Other inhumane acts which severely damage physical or mental integrity, health or human dignity, such as mutilation and severe bodily harm.

Article 19

Crimes against United Nations and associated personnel

1. The following crimes constitute crimes against the peace and security of mankind when committed intentionally and in a systematic manner or on a large scale against United Nations and associated personnel involved in a United Nations operation with a view to preventing or impeding that operation from fulfilling its mandate:

(a) Murder, kidnapping or other attack upon the person or liberty of any such personnel;

(b) Violent attack upon the official premises, the private accommodation or the means of transportation of any such personnel likely to endanger his or her person or liberty.

2. This article shall not apply to a United Nations operation authorized by the Security Council as an enforcement action under Chapter VII of the Charter of the United Nations in which any of the personnel are engaged as combatants against organized armed forces and to which the law of international armed conflict applies.

Article 20

War crimes

Any of the following war crimes constitutes a crime against the peace and security of mankind when committed in a systematic manner or on a large scale:

(*a*) Any of the following acts committed in violation of international humanitarian law:

(i) Wilful killing;

(ii) Torture or inhuman treatment, including biological experiments;

(iii) Wilfully causing great suffering or serious injury to body or health;

(iv) Extensive destruction and appropriation of property, not justified by military necessity and carried out unlawfully and wantonly;

(v) Compelling a prisoner of war or other protected person to serve in the forces of a hostile Power;

(vi) Wilfully depriving a prisoner of war or other protected person of the rights of fair and regular trial;

(vii) Unlawful deportation or transfer of unlawful confinement of protected persons;

(viii) Taking of hostages;

(*b*) Any of the following acts committed wilfully in violation of international humanitarian law and causing death or serious injury to body or health:

(i) Making the civilian population or individual civilians the object of attack;

(ii) Launching an indiscriminate attack affecting the civilian population or civilian objects in the knowledge that such attack will cause excessive loss of life, injury to civilians or damage to civilian objects;

(iii) Launching an attack against works or installations containing dangerous forces in the knowledge that such attack will cause excessive loss of life, injury to civilians or damage to civilian objects;

(iv) Making a person the object of attack in the knowledge that he is hors de combat;

(v) The perfidious use of the distinctive emblem of the red cross, red crescent or red lion and sun or of other recognized protective signs;

(*c*) Any of the following acts committed wilfully in violation of international humanitarian law:

(i) The transfer by the Occupying Power of parts of its own civilian population into the territory it occupies;

(ii) Unjustifiable delay in the repatriation of prisoners of war or civilians;

(*d*) Outrages upon personal dignity in violation of international humanitarian law, in particular humiliating and degrading treatment, rape, enforced prostitution and any form of indecent assault;

(*e*) Any of the following acts committed in violation of the laws or customs of war:

(i) Employment of poisonous weapons or other weapons calculated to cause unnecessary suffering;

(ii) Wanton destruction of cities, towns or villages, or devastation not justified by military necessity;

(iii) Attack, or bombardment, by whatever means, of undefended towns, villages, dwellings or buildings or of demilitarized zones;

(iv) Seizure of, destruction of or wilful damage done to institutions dedicated to religion, charity and education, the arts and sciences, historic monuments and works of art and science;

(v) Plunder of public or private property;

(*f*) Any of the following acts committed in violation of international humanitarian law applicable in armed conflict not of an international character:

(i) Violence to the life, health and physical or mental well-being of persons, in particular murder as well as cruel treatment such as torture, mutilation or any form of corporal punishment;

(ii) Collective punishments;

(iii) Taking of hostages;

(iv) Acts of terrorism;

(v) Outrages upon personal dignity, in particular humiliating and degrading treatment, rape, enforced prostitution and any form of indecent assault;

(vi) Pillage;

(vii) The passing of sentences and the carrying out of executions without previous judgement pronounced by a regularly constituted court, affording all the judicial guarantees which are generally recognized as indispensable;

(*g*) In the case of armed conflict, using methods or means of warfare not justified by military necessity with the intent to cause widespread, long-term and severe damage to the natural environment and thereby gravely prejudice the health or survival of the population and such damage occurs.

DOCUMENT 69

Full Official Title: [Hague] Convention (IV) respecting the Laws and Customs of War on Land and its Annex: Regulations concerning the Laws and Customs of War on Land. The Hague, 18 October 1907

Short Title/Acronym/Abbreviation: Hague IV Convention and Hague Regulations/Rules

Subject: The limitation of the methods and means of combat by armed forces in armed conflict in a multilateral treaty.

Official Citation: Not applicable

Date of Document: Not applicable

Date of Adoption: October 18, 1907

Date of General Entry into Force (EIF): Not applicable

Number of States Parties to this Treaty as of this printing: Ratified by a few European states, but now binding as customary international law

Date of Signature by United States: Not applicable

Date of United States Ratification/Accession/Adhesion: Not applicable

Date of Entry into Force (effective date) as to United States: When it became customary international law, around WWII.

Type of Document: An international treaty which codified much of the existing law of armed conflict, but which was signed and ratified by only a few European countries. By the end of World War II it became considered as binding on all states, as a matter of customary international law. This treaty was also read along with an 1899 Hague Convention, which it amplified.

Legal Status/Character of the Instrument/Document as to the United States: Binding the United States as a matter of customary international law.

Comments: This Treaty and its annexed Regulations served as the major source of international legal norms used in the Nuremberg Trials after the Second World War. They stand for the international rule of law that military combatants are not unlimited in what methods or means of combat they use; that there is a certain minimum standard of conduct which soldiers must obey. These Regulations are now considered the basis of customary international law binding on all states in international armed conflicts, and, some say, non-international armed conflicts. They served as one of the legal bases for the prosecution of war criminals from the Bosnia conflict of the early 1990s, being prosecuted by the U.N. International Criminal Tribunal for the Former Yugoslavia (ICTY). The Statute of the ICTY is set forth below, Document 75. U.S. military combat activity can be judged according to these standards today. These standards have been translated into the military handbooks used by American armed forces and its basics are supposed to be taught to all military personnel, along with the basic principles of the Geneva Conventions.

The U.S. military is subject to International Humanitarian Law. These Regulations must also be looked at in conjunction with the 1949 Geneva Conventions and some other international humanitarian norms which are also binding on the United States.

Since very few civilians are knowledgeable about this field of law applicable to U.S. military activities there is little public use of them in judging U.S. military activity.

Caution: The status and applicability of this instrument as to the United States may have changed since date of publication. The above information may be updated by referring to the following site:

Web address: http://www.icrc.org/ihl.nsf/73cb71d18dc4372741256739003e6372/4d47f92df3966a7ec12563cd002d6788?OpenDocument

[HAGUE] CONVENTION (IV) RESPECTING THE LAWS AND CUSTOMS OF WAR ON LAND AND ITS ANNEX: REGULATIONS CONCERNING THE LAWS AND CUSTOMS OF WAR ON LAND. (EXCERPTS)

(List of Contracting Parties)

Seeing that while seeking means to preserve peace and prevent armed conflicts between nations, it is likewise necessary to bear in mind the case where the appeal to arms has been brought about by events which their care was unable to avert;

Animated by the desire to serve, even in this extreme case, the interests of humanity and the ever progressive needs of civilization;

Thinking it important, with this object, to revise the general laws and customs of war, either with a view to defining them with greater precision or to confining them within such limits as would mitigate their severity as far as possible;

868

Have deemed it necessary to complete and explain in certain particulars the work of the First Peace Conference, which, following on the Brussels Conference of 1874, and inspired by the ideas dictated by a wise and generous forethought, adopted provisions intended to define land govern the usages of war on land.

According to the views of the High Contracting Parties, these provisions, the wording of which has been inspired by the desire to diminish the evils of war, as far as military requirements permit, are intended to serve as a general rule of conduct for the belligerents in their mutual relations and in their relations with the inhabitants.

It has not, however, been found possible at present to concert regulations covering all the circumstances which arise in practice;

On the other hand, the High Contracting Parties clearly do not intend that unforeseen cases should, in the absence of a written undertaking, be left to the arbitrary judgment of military commanders.

Until a more complete code of the laws of war has been issued, the High Contracting Parties deem it expedient to declare that, in cases not included in the Regulations adopted by them, the inhabitants and the belligerents remain under the protection and the rule of the principles of the law of nations, as they result from the usages established among civilized peoples, from the laws of humanity, and the dictates of the public conscience.

They declare that it is in this sense especially that Articles 1 and 2 of the Regulations adopted must be understood.

The High Contracting Parties, wishing to conclude a fresh Convention to this effect, have appointed the following as their Plenipotentiaries:

(Here follow the names of Plenipotentiaries)

Who, after having deposited their full powers, found in good and due form, have agreed upon the following:

Article 1. The Contracting Powers shall issue instructions to their armed land forces which shall be in conformity with the Regulations respecting the laws and customs of war on land, annexed to the present Convention.

Article 2. The provisions contained in the Regulations referred to in Article 1, as well as in the present Convention, do not apply except between Contracting powers, and then only if all the belligerents are parties to the Convention.

Article 3. A belligerent party which violates the provisions of the said Regulations shall, if the case demands, be liable to pay compensation. It shall be responsible for all acts committed by persons forming part of its armed forces.

Article 4. The present Convention, duly ratified, shall as between the Contracting Powers, be substituted for the Convention of 29 July 1899, respecting the laws land customs of war on land.

The Convention of 1899 remains in force as between the Powers which signed it, and which do not also ratify the present Convention.

Annex to the Convention—Regulations Respecting the Laws and Customs of War on Land

Section I—On Belligerents

Chapter I—The qualifications of belligerents

Article 1. The laws, rights, and duties of war apply not only to armies, but also to militia and volunteer corps fulfilling the following conditions:

1. To be commanded by a person responsible for his subordinates;
2. To have a fixed distinctive emblem recognizable at a distance;
3. To carry arms openly; and
4. To conduct their operations in accordance with the laws and customs of war.

In countries where militia or volunteer corps constitute the army, or form part of it, they are included under the denomination "army."

Chapter II—Prisoners of war

Article 4. Prisoners of war are in the power of the hostile Government, but not of the individuals or corps who capture them.

They must be humanely treated.

All their personal belongings, except arms, horses, and military papers, remain their property.

Article 5. Prisoners of war may be interned in a town, fortress, camp, or other place, and bound not to go beyond certain fixed limits; but they cannot be confined except as in indispensable measure of safety land only while the circumstances which necessitate the measure continue to exist.

. . .

Article 7. The Government into whose hands prisoners of war have fallen is charged with their maintenance.

In the absence of a special agreement between the belligerents, prisoners of war shall be treated as regards board, lodging, and clothing on the same footing as the troops of the Government who captured them.

Article 8. Prisoners of war shall be subject to the laws, regulations, and orders in force in the army of the State in whose power they are. Any act of insubordination justifies the adoption towards them of such measures of severity as may be considered necessary.

Escaped prisoners who are retaken before being able to rejoin their own army or before leaving the territory occupied by the army which captured them are liable to disciplinary punishment.

Prisoners who, after succeeding in escaping, are again taken prisoners, are not liable to any punishment on account of the previous flight.

Article 9. Every prisoner of war is bound to give, if he is questioned on the subject, his true name and rank, and if he infringes this rule, he is liable to have the advantages given to prisoners of his class curtailed.

. . .

Article 16. Inquiry offices enjoy the privilege of free postage. Letters, money orders, and valuables, as well as parcels by post, intended for prisoners of war, or dispatched by them, shall be exempt from all postal duties in the countries of origin and destination, as well as in the countries they pass through.

Presents and relief in kind for prisoners of war shall be admitted free of all import or other duties, as well as of payments for carriage by the State railways.

. . .

Article 18. Prisoners of war shall enjoy complete liberty in the exercise of their religion, including attendance at the services of whatever church they may belong to, on the sole condition that they comply with the measures of order and police issued by the military authorities.

. . .

Article 20. After the conclusion of peace, the repatriation of prisoners of war shall be carried out as quickly as possible.

Chapter III—The sick and wounded

Article 21. The obligations of belligerents with regard to the sick and wounded are governed by the Geneva Convention.

Section II—Hostilities

Chapter I—Means of injuring the enemy, sieges, and bombardments

Article 22. The right of belligerents to adopt means of injuring the enemy is not unlimited.

Article 23. In addition to the prohibitions provided by special Conventions, it is especially forbidden

(a) To employ poison or poisoned weapons;

(b) To kill or wound treacherously individuals belonging to the hostile nation or army;

(c) To kill or wound an enemy who, having laid down his arms, or having no longer means of defence, has surrendered at discretion;

(d) To declare that no quarter will be given;

(e) To employ arms, projectiles, or material calculated to cause unnecessary suffering;

(f) To make improper use of a flag of truce, of the national flag or of the military insignia and uniform of the enemy, as well as the distinctive badges of the Geneva Convention;

(g) To destroy or seize the enemy's property, unless such destruction or seizure be imperatively demanded by the necessities of war;

(h) To declare abolished, suspended, or inadmissible in a court of law the rights and actions of the nationals of the hostile party. A belligerent is likewise forbidden to compel the nationals of the hostile party to take part in the operations of war directed against their own country, even if they were in the belligerent's service before the commencement of the war.

. . .

Article 25. The attack or bombardment, by whatever means, of towns, villages, dwellings, or buildings which are undefended is prohibited.

Article 26. The officer in command of an attacking force must, before commencing a bombardment, except in cases of assault, do all in his power to warn the authorities.

Article 27. In sieges and bombardments all necessary steps must be taken to spare, as far as possible, buildings dedicated to religion, art, science, or charitable purposes, historic monuments, hospitals, and places where the sick and wounded are collected, provided they are not being used at the time for military purposes.

It is the duty of the besieged to indicate the presence of such buildings or places by distinctive and visible signs, which shall be notified to the enemy beforehand.

Article 28. The pillage of a town or place, even when taken by assault, is prohibited.

Chapter II—Spies

Article 29. A person can only be considered a spy when, acting clandestinely or on false pretences, he obtains or endeavours to obtain information in the zone of operations of a belligerent, with the intention of communicating it to the hostile party.

Thus, soldiers not wearing a disguise who have penetrated into the zone of operations of the hostile army, for the purpose of obtaining information, are not considered spies.

...

Section III—Military Authority over the Territory of the Hostile State

Article 42. Territory is considered occupied when it is actually placed under the authority of the hostile army.

The occupation extends only to the territory where such authority has been established and can be exercised.

Article 43. The authority of the legitimate power having in fact passed into the hands of the occupant, the latter shall take all the measures in his power to restore, and ensure, as far as possible, public order and safety, while respecting, unless absolutely prevented, the laws in force in the country.

Article 44. A belligerent is forbidden to force the inhabitants of territory occupied by it to furnish information about the army of the other belligerent, or about its means of defense.

Article 45. It is forbidden to compel the inhabitants of occupied territory to swear allegiance to the hostile Power.

Article 46. Family honour and rights, the lives of persons, and private property, as well as religious convictions and practice, must be respected. Private property cannot be confiscated.

Article 47. Pillage is formally forbidden.

...

Article 50. No general penalty, pecuniary or otherwise, shall be inflicted upon the population on account of the acts of individuals for which they cannot be regarded as jointly and severally responsible.

DOCUMENT 70

Full Official Title: Principles of International Law Recognized in the Charter of the Nüremberg Tribunal and in the Judgment of the Tribunal, 1950.

Short Title/Acronym/Abbreviation: Nuremberg Principles

Subject: Legal principles applicable to the limitation of the methods and means of combat by armed forces in armed conflict

Official Citation: Not applicable

Date of Document: 1950

Date of Adoption: 1950

Date of General Entry into Force (EIF): Not applicable

Number of States Parties to this Treaty as of November, 1999: Not a treaty

Date of Signature by United States: Not applicable

Date of United States Ratification/Accession/Adhesion: Not applicable

Date of Entry into Force (effective date)as to United States: Became binding as a matter of customary international law when adopted as so by U.N. Resolution in 1950

Type of Document: These are legal principles extracted from the legal process of the Nuremberg Trials against Nazi war criminals after WWI. They were adopted by U.N. resolution as declaratory of customary international law by the United Nations.

Legal Status/Character of the Instrument/Document as to the United States: Binding on the United States as a matter of customary international law.

Comments: This still serves as the major source of international legal norms used in prosecutions of those who commit international crimes such as war crimes, genocide and crimes against humanity. They stand for the international rule of law that no one, whether military or civilian, soldier or government official, is above the law, and that regardless of one's official status or the fact of following a superior's orders, everyone is legally accountable for such crimes. They create individual criminal responsibility for the commission of certain international crimes. Under these and other principles of humanitarian law, military combatants and their government superiors are not unlimited in what methods or means of combat they use; there is a certain minimum standard of conduct which soldiers must obey. Moreover, superiors can be responsible for the criminal acts of their subordinates under certain circumstances.

These principles are now considered the basis of customary international law binding on all states in international armed conflicts, and, some say, non international armed conflicts. They are also being applied in the prosecution of war criminals from the Bosnia conflict of the early 1990s, being prosecuted by the U.N. International Criminal Tribunal for the Forner Yugoslavia (ICTY). They are also reflected in the Statute of the (proposed) International Criminal Court (ICC). (See Statute of the ICC, Document 76 below.) See also Appendix J, case of *Kadic v. Karadzic*).

All U.S. military and civilians are subject to these principles today. The U.S. military and all civilians are subject to International Humanitarian Law.

As a contemporary example of how these principles are applied, in 1999 Slobodan Milosevic, the President of Yugoslavia, was indicted by the ICTY for war crimes and crimes against humanity for the acts which his military and police forces were committing in Kosovo in 1998–1999. The fact that he was a sitting head of state did not matter. Applying these Nuremberg principles, he was subjected to individual criminal responsibility for the crimes of those under his command, as well as for any crimes which he helped plan or ordered.

Web site addresses:
http://www.icrc.org/ihl.nsf/52d68d14de6160e0c12563da005fdb1b/648ff02b73cde729c125641e004064ac?
OpenDocument;
http://www.icrc.org/ihl.nsf/73cb71d18dc4372741256739003e6372/87b0bb4a50a64deac12563cd002d6aae?
OpenDocument

PRINCIPLES OF INTERNATIONAL LAW RECOGNIZED IN THE CHARTER OF THE NÜREMBERG TRIBUNAL AND IN THE JUDGMENT OF THE TRIBUNAL, 1950

Principle I
Any person who commits an act which constitutes a crime under international law is responsible therefore and liable to punishment.

Principle II
The fact that international law does not impose a penalty for an act which constitutes a crime under international law does not relieve the person who committed the act from responsibility under international law.

Principle III
The fact that a person who committed an act which constitutes a crime under international law acted as Head of State or responsible Government official does not relieve him from responsibility under international law.

Principle IV
The fact that a person acted pursuant to order of his Government or of a superior does not relieve him from responsibility under international law, provided a moral choice was in fact possible to him.

Principle V
Any person charged with a crime under international law has the right to a fair trial on the facts and law.

Principle VI
The crimes hereinafter set out are punishable as crimes under international law:

(a) Crimes against peace:

(i) Planning, preparation, initiation or waging of a war of aggression or a war in violation of international treaties, agreements or assurances;

(ii) Participation in a common plan or conspiracy for the accomplishment of any of the acts mentioned under (i).

(b) War crimes:

Violations of the laws or customs of war include, but are not limited to, murder, ill-treatment or deportation to slave-labour or for any other purpose of civilian population of or in occupied territory, murder or ill-treatment of prisoners of war, of persons on the seas, killing of hostages, plunder of public or private property, wanton destruction of cities, towns, or villages, or devastation not justified by military necessity.

(c) Crimes against humanity:

Murder, extermination, enslavement, deportation and other inhuman acts done against any civilian population, or persecutions on political, racial or religious grounds, when such acts are done or such persecutions are carried on in execution of or in connexion with any crime against peace or any war crime.

Principle VII

Complicity in the commission of a crime against peace, a war crime, or a crime against humanity as set forth in Principle VI is a crime under international law.

DOCUMENT 71

Full Official Title: Basic rules of the Geneva Conventions and their Additional Protocols

Short Title/Acronym/Abbreviation: Basic Rules of Armed Conflict

Subject: Basic legal principles applicable to armed conflicts under the Geneva Conventions of 1949 and their Protocols

Official Citation: Nothing official

Date of Document: Not applicable

Date of Adoption: Not applicable

Date of General Entry into Force (EIF): Not applicable

Number of States Parties to this Treaty as of this printing: Not a treaty

Date of Signature by United States: Not applicable

Date of United States Ratification/Accession/Adhesion: Not applicable

Date of Entry into Force (effective date) as to United States: Not applicable

Type of Document: A statement of basic rules which summarize the whole of the legal obligations held by state parties to the Geneva Conventions and Protocols.

Legal Status/Character of the Instrument/Document as to the United States: Not legally binding

Comments: The Geneva Conventions of 1949 and its two amending Protocols of 1977 form the main part of International Humanitarian Law, the international law applicable to armed conflict. The United States has not ratified the two Protocols. Because the United States has ratified the four Geneva Conventions of 1949, all U.S. military and civilians are subject to these rules today.

The International Committee of the Red Cross (ICRC) is an international organization whose history and principle work has been about the establishment of international legal standards limiting the effects of armed conflicts, international and otherwise, and monitoring compliance with these standards. It was the body responsible for the creation of the Geneva Conventions and Protocols and largely responsible for the development of all humanitarian law since the late 1860s, when it was founded, along with the first Geneva Convention.

These basic rules were drafted by the ICRC. The text of the Geneva Conventions and of their additional Protocols, which are set forth in following documents, is very complex and not always easily understood by the layman. A simplified work became necessary to present and explain these international law treaties to an ever-increasing number of readers. The following is a basic summary of the basic rules which apply to all armed conflicts which are subject to the Geneva Conventions and Protocols. Every human being should become familiar with them. They are the minimum standard of humanity for armed conflicts, whether between two or more countries, or purely internal, such as civil wars.

Caution: The status and applicability of this instrument as to the United States may have changed since date of publication. The above information may be updated by referring to any of the following sites:

Web address: http://www.icrc.org/icrceng.nsf/5845147e46836989c12561740044a4f7/26674b4e54f4953341256237003a3ae0?OpenDocument#2

INTERNATIONAL COMMITTEE OF THE RED CROSS—BASIC RULES OF THE GENEVA CONVENTIONS AND THEIR ADDITIONAL PROTOCOLS

The text of the Geneva Conventions and of their Additional Protocols, which follow, is very complex and not always easily understood by the layman. A simplified work became necessary to present and explain these international law treaties to an ever-increasing number of readers. The following is a basic summary of the basic rules which apply to all armed conflicts which are subject to the Geneva Conventions and Protocols. Every human being should become familiar with them. They are the minimum standard of humanity for armed conflicts, whether between two or more countries, or purely internal, such as civil wars.

Summary : Basic rules of international humanitarian law in armed conflicts

1. Persons *hors de combat* (incapable of engaging in combat, such as a POW) and those who do not take a direct part in hostilities are entitled to respect for their lives and their moral and physical integrity. They shall in all circumstances be protected and treated humanely without any adverse distinction.

2. It is forbidden to kill or injure an enemy who surrenders or who is hors de combat.

3. The wounded and sick shall be collected and cared for by the party to the conflict which has them in its power. Protection also covers medical personnel, establishments, transports and equipment. The emblem of the Red Cross or the red crescent is the sign of such protection and must be respected.

4. Captured combatants and civilians under the authority of an adverse party are entitled to respect for their lives, dignity, personal rights and convictions. They shall be protected against all acts of violence and reprisals. They shall have the right to correspond with their families and to receive relief.

5. Everyone shall be entitled to benefit from fundamental judicial guarantees. No one shall be held responsible for an act he has not committed. No one shall be subjected to physical or mental torture, corporal punishment or cruel or degrading treatment.

6. Parties to a conflict and members of their armed forces do not have an unlimited choice of methods and means of warfare. It is prohibited to employ weapons or methods of warfare of a nature to cause unnecessary losses or excessive suffering.

7. Parties to a conflict shall at all times distinguish between the civilian population and combatants in order to spare civilian population and property. Neither the civilian population as such nor civilian persons shall be the object of attack. Attacks shall be directed solely against military objectives.

Note:

1. This text constitutes the quintessence of the provisions of international humanitarian law. It does not have the force of an international legal instrument and is in no way intended to replace the treaties in force. It is designed to facilitate dissemination and a basic understanding of international humanitarian law.

DOCUMENT 72

Full Official Title: [Geneva] Convention (IV) relative to the Protection of Civilian Persons in Time of War. Geneva, 12 August 1949

Short Title/Acronym/Abbreviation: The Fourth Geneva Convention /Geneva Convention IV/ The Geneva Civilians' Convention/GC IV.

Subject: Establishing international legal protection for victims of armed conflicts (military and civilian) in a multilateral treaty.

Official Citation: 6 U.S.T. 3516, T.I.A.S. No. 3365; 75 U.N.T.S. 287

Date of Document: Not applicable

Date of Adoption: August 12, 1949

Date of General Entry into Force (EIF): October 21, 1950

Number of States Parties to this Treaty as of this printing: 194

Date of Signature by United States: Aug. 12, 1949

Date of United States Ratification/Accession/Adhesion: Feb. 2, 1956

Date of Entry into Force (effective date) as to United States: Feb. 2, 1956

Type of Document: An international legal instrument, a treaty

Legal Status/Character of the Instrument/Document as to the United States: Legally binding on the United States as a matter of International Law

Comments: The Geneva Conventions were negotiated and adopted under the auspices of the International Committee of the Red Cross. The Geneva Conventions of 1949 and their two amending Protocols of 1977 form the main part of International Humanitarian Law, the international law applicable to armed conflict. The four Geneva Conventions, ratified by almost every state in the world, are arguable also legally binding as a matter of customary international law. Because the United States has ratified the four Geneva Conventions of 1949, all U.S. military and civilians are subject to these rules today. The United States has not ratified the two Protocols. It accepts Protocol I as constituting customary international law.

The four Geneva Conventions cover: 1) soldiers in the field; 2) wounded sick and shipwrecked at sea; 3) prisoners of war; and 4) civilians. The two Protocols of 1977 (much reflecting the experience of the Vietnam War) had the following effect as regards the 1949 Geneva Conventions: Protocol I expanded the scope of the four Conventions to cover certain non-international armed conflicts involving alien occupation, against racist/apartheid regimes, against colonial powers, and expanded many of the protections in the Four Conventions, making more acts as constituting war crimes; Protocol II applies certain minimum humanitarian standards to non international armed conflicts in parties which ratify it.

This Fourth Geneva Convention was the first instrument of international humanitarian law to grant extensive protection to civilians who are somehow victims of a covered armed conflict. This reflected and responded to the history of World War II, which saw over twelve million civilians, i.e., non combatants, killed by the war. Today the rate of casualties for armed conflicts is about 10–20% military casualties, and 80–90% civilian casualties. Thus, nowadays four to five time more casualties from armed conflicts are innocent civilians. Thus, civilians need extensive legal protection in times of armed conflicts.

This Convention would apply to situations and places of armed military occupation and to situations of internment of civilians, such as happened here in World War II, regarding Japanese internment by and in the United States.

The Geneva Civilians' Convention is included here because of the need of U.S. civilians to know their rights in the event of being subjected to an armed conflict. Americans can also use these standards in judging how U.S. military comply with this law as to civilians states in which they are engaged in armed conflicts.

Note Article 144 of this Convention which states:

The High Contracting Parties undertake, in time of peace as in time of war, to disseminate the text of the present Convention as widely as possible in their respective countries, and, in particular, to include the study thereof in their programmes of military and, if possible, civil instruction, so that the principles thereof may become known to the entire population.

Caution: The status and applicability of this instrument as to the United States may have changed since date of publication. The above information may be updated by referring to any of the following sites.

Web address: http://www.icrc.org/ihl.nsf/7c4d08d9b287a42141256739003e636b/6756482d86146898c125641e004aa3c5?OpenDocument

[Geneva] Convention (IV) Relative to the Protection of Civilian Persons in Time of War. Geneva, 12 August 1949 (The "Civilians' Convention")

Adopted Aug. 12, 1949

Entry into Force Oct. 22, 1950

Part I. General Provisions

Article 1. The High Contracting Parties undertake to respect and to ensure respect for the present Convention in all circumstances.

Article 2. In addition to the provisions which shall be implemented in peace-time, the present Convention shall apply to all cases of declared war or of any other armed conflict which may arise between two or more of the High Contracting Parties, even if the state of war is not recognized by one of them.

The Convention shall also apply to all cases of partial or total occupation of the territory of a High Contracting Party, even if the said occupation meets with no armed resistance.

Although one of the Powers in conflict may not be a party to the present Convention, the Powers who are parties thereto shall remain bound by it in their mutual relations. They shall furthermore be bound by the Convention in relation to the said Power, if the latter accepts and applies the provisions thereof.

[The following Article is known as "Common Article 3" of the Geneva Conventions because it is the same in all four Geneva Conventions. It sets forth minimum humanitarian law standards applicable in purely internal, national (noninternational) armed conflicts of a state party to the Geneva Conventions.]

Article 3. In the case of armed conflict not of an international character occurring in the territory of one of the High Contracting Parties, each Party to the conflict shall be bound to apply, as a minimum, the following provisions:

(1) Persons taking no active part in the hostilities, including members of armed forces who have laid down their arms and those placed hors de combat by sickness, wounds, detention, or any other cause, shall in all circumstances be treated humanely, without any adverse distinction founded on race, colour, religion or faith, sex, birth or wealth, or any other similar criteria.

To this end the following acts are and shall remain prohibited at any time and in any place whatsoever with respect to the above-mentioned persons:

(a) violence to life and person, in particular murder of all kinds, mutilation, cruel treatment and torture;

(b) taking of hostages;

(c) outrages upon personal dignity, in particular humiliating and degrading treatment;

(d) the passing of sentences and the carrying out of executions without previous judgment pronounced by a regularly constituted court, affording all the judicial guarantees which are recognized as indispensable by civilized peoples.

(2) The wounded and sick shall be collected and cared for.

An impartial humanitarian body, such as the International Committee of the Red Cross, may offer its services to the Parties to the conflict.

The Parties to the conflict should further endeavour to bring into force, by means of special agreements, all or part of the other provisions of the present Convention.

The application of the preceding provisions shall not affect the legal status of the Parties to the conflict.

Article 4. Persons protected by the Convention are those who, at a given moment and in any manner whatsoever, find themselves, in case of a conflict or occupation, in the hands of a Party to the conflict or Occupying Power of which they are not nationals.

Nationals of a State which is not bound by the Convention are not protected by it. Nationals of a neutral State who find themselves in the territory of a belligerent State, and nationals of a co-belligerent State, shall not be regarded as protected persons while the State of which they are nationals has normal diplomatic representation in the State in whose hands they are.

The provisions of Part II are, however, wider in application, as defined in Article 13.

Persons protected by the Geneva Convention for the Amelioration of the Condition of the Wounded and Sick in Armed Forces in the Field of 12 August 1949, or by the Geneva Convention for the Amelioration of the Condition of Wounded, Sick and Shipwrecked Members of Armed Forces at Sea of 12 August 1949, or by the Geneva Convention relative to the Treatment of Prisoners of War of 12 August 1949, shall not be considered as protected persons within the meaning of the present Convention.

Article 5. Where in the territory of a Party to the conflict, the latter is satisfied that an individual protected person is definitely suspected of or engaged in activities hostile to the security of the State, such individual person shall not be entitled to claim such rights and privileges under the present Convention as would, if exercised in the favour of such individual person, be prejudicial to the security of such State.

Where in occupied territory an individual protected person is detained as a spy or saboteur, or as a person under definite suspicion of activity hostile to the security of the Occupying Power, such person shall, in those cases where absolute military security so requires, be regarded as having forfeited rights of communication under the present Convention.

In each case, such persons shall nevertheless be treated with humanity and, in case of trial, shall not be deprived of the rights of fair and regular trial prescribed by the present Convention. They shall also be granted the full rights and privileges of a protected person under the present Convention at the earliest date consistent with the security of the State or Occupying Power, as the case may be.

Article 6. The present Convention shall apply from the outset of any conflict or occupation mentioned in Article 2.

In the territory of Parties to the conflict, the application of the present Convention shall cease on the general close of military operations.

In the case of occupied territory, the application of the present Convention shall cease one year after the general close of military operations; however, the Occupying Power shall be bound, for the duration of the occupation, to the extent that such Power exercises the functions of government in such territory, by the provisions of the following Articles of the present Convention: 1 to 12, 27, 29 to 34, 47, 49, 51, 52, 53, 59, 61 to 77, 143.

Protected persons whose release, repatriation or re-establishment may take place after such dates shall meanwhile continue to benefit by the present Convention.

Article 7. In addition to the agreements expressly provided for in Articles 11, 14, 15, 17, 36, 108, 109, 132, 133 and 149, the High Contracting Parties may conclude other special agreements for all matters concerning which they may deem it suitable to make separate provision. No special agreement shall adversely affect the situation of protected persons, as defined by the present Convention, not restrict the rights which it confers upon them.

Protected persons shall continue to have the benefit of such agreements as long as the Convention is applicable to them, except where express provisions to the contrary are contained in the aforesaid or in subsequent agreements, or where more favourable measures have been taken with regard to them by one or other of the Parties to the conflict.

Article 8. Protected persons may in no circumstances renounce in part or in entirety the rights secured to them by the present Convention, and by the special agreements referred to in the foregoing Article, if such there be.

Article 9. The present Convention shall be applied with the cooperation and under the scrutiny of the Protecting Powers whose duty it is to safeguard the interests of the Parties to the conflict. For this purpose, the Protecting Powers may appoint, apart from their diplomatic or consular staff, delegates from amongst their own nationals or the nationals of other neutral Powers. The said delegates shall be subject to the approval of the Power with which they are to carry out their duties.

The Parties to the conflict shall facilitate to the greatest extent possible the task of the representatives or delegates of the Protecting Powers.

The representatives or delegates of the Protecting Powers shall not in any case exceed their mission under the present Convention.

They shall, in particular, take account of the imperative necessities of security of the State wherein they carry out their duties.

Article 10. The provisions of the present Convention constitute no obstacle to the humanitarian activities which the International Committee of the Red Cross or any other impartial humanitarian organization may, subject to the consent of the Parties to the conflict concerned, undertake for the protection of civilian persons and for their relief.

Article 11. The High Contracting Parties may at any time agree to entrust to an international organization which offers all guarantees of impartiality and efficacy the duties incumbent on the Protecting Powers by virtue of the present Convention.

When persons protected by the present Convention do not benefit or cease to benefit, no matter for what reason, by the activities of a Protecting Power or of an organization provided for in the first paragraph above, the Detaining Power shall request a neutral State, or such an organization, to undertake the functions performed under the present Convention by a Protecting Power designated by the Parties to a conflict.

If protection cannot be arranged accordingly, the Detaining Power shall request or shall accept, subject to the provisions of this Article, the offer of the services of a humanitarian organization, such as the International Committee of the Red Cross, to assume the humanitarian functions performed by Protecting Powers under the present Convention.

Any neutral Power or any organization invited by the Power concerned or offering itself for these purposes, shall be required to act with a sense of responsibility towards the Party to the conflict on which persons protected by the present Convention depend, and shall be required to furnish sufficient assurances that it is in a position to undertake the appropriate functions and to discharge them impartially.

No derogation from the preceding provisions shall be made by special agreements between Powers one of which is restricted, even temporarily, in its freedom to negotiate with the other Power or its allies by reason of military events, more particularly where the whole, or a substantial part, of the territory of the said Power is occupied.

Whenever in the present Convention mention is made of a Protecting Power, such mention applies to substitute organizations in the sense of the present Article.

The provisions of this Article shall extend and be adapted to cases of nationals of a neutral State who are in occupied territory or who find themselves in the territory of a belligerent State in which the State of which they are nationals has not normal diplomatic representation.

Article 12. In cases where they deem it advisable in the interest of protected persons, particularly in cases of disagreement between the Parties to the conflict as to the application or interpretation of the provisions of the present Convention, the Protecting Powers shall lend their good offices with a view to settling the disagreement.

For this purpose, each of the Protecting Powers may, either at the invitation of one Party or on its own initiative, propose to the Parties to the conflict a meeting of their representatives, and in particular of the authorities responsible for protected persons, possibly on neutral territory suitably chosen. The Parties to the conflict shall be bound to give effect to the proposals made to them for this purpose. The Protecting Powers may, if necessary, propose for approval by the Parties to the conflict a person belonging to a neutral Power, or delegated by the International Committee of the Red Cross, who shall be invited to take part in such a meeting.

Part II. General Protection of Populations against Certain Consequences of War

Article 13. The provisions of Part II cover the whole of the populations of the countries in conflict, without any adverse distinction based, in particular, on race, nationality, religion or political opinion, and are intended to alleviate the sufferings caused by war.

Article 14. In time of peace, the High Contracting Parties and, after the outbreak of hostilities, the Parties thereto, may establish in their own territory and, if the need arises, in occupied areas, hospital and safety zones and localities so organized as to protect from the effects of war, wounded, sick and aged persons, children under fifteen, expectant mothers and mothers of children under seven.

Article 15. Any Party to the conflict may, either direct or through a neutral State or some humanitarian organization, propose to the adverse Party to establish, in the regions where fighting is taking place, neutralized zones intended to shelter from the effects of war the following persons, without distinction:

(a) wounded and sick combatants or non-combatants;

(b) civilian persons who take no part in hostilities, and who, while they reside in the zones, perform no work of a military character.

When the Parties concerned have agreed upon the geographical position, administration, food supply and supervision of the proposed neutralized zone, a written agreement shall be concluded and signed by the representatives of the Parties to the conflict. The agreement shall fix the beginning and the duration of the neutralization of the zone.

Article 16. The wounded and sick, as well as the infirm, and expectant mothers, shall be the object of particular protection and respect.

As far as military considerations allow, each Party to the conflict shall facilitate the steps taken to search for the killed and wounded, to assist the shipwrecked and other persons exposed to grave danger, and to protect them against pillage and ill-treatment.

Article 17. The Parties to the conflict shall endeavour to conclude local agreements for the removal from besieged or encircled areas, of wounded, sick, infirm, and aged persons, children and maternity cases, and for the passage of ministers of all religions, medical personnel and medical equipment on their way to such areas.

Article 18. Civilian hospitals organized to give care to the wounded and sick, the infirm and maternity cases, may in no circumstances be the object of attack but shall at all times be respected and protected by the Parties to the conflict.

States which are Parties to a conflict shall provide all civilian hospitals with certificates showing that they are civilian hospitals and that the buildings which they occupy are not used for any purpose which would deprive these hospitals of protection in accordance with Article 19.

Civilian hospitals shall be marked by means of the emblem provided for in Article 38 of the Geneva Convention for the Amelioration of the Condition of the Wounded and Sick in Armed Forces in the Field of 12 August 1949, but only if so authorized by the State.

The Parties to the conflict shall, in so far as military considerations permit, take the necessary steps to make the distinctive emblems indicating civilian hospitals clearly visible to the enemy land, air and naval forces in order to obviate the possibility of any hostile action.

In view of the dangers to which hospitals may be exposed by being close to military objectives, it is recommended that such hospitals be situated as far as possible from such objectives.

Article 19. The protection to which civilian hospitals are entitled shall not cease unless they are used to commit, outside their humanitarian duties, acts harmful to the enemy. Protection may, however, cease only after due warning has been given, naming, in all appropriate cases, a reasonable time limit and after such warning has remained unheeded. The fact that sick or wounded members of the armed forces are nursed in these hospitals, or the presence of small arms and ammunition taken from such combatants which have not yet been handed to the proper service, shall not be considered to be acts harmful to the enemy.

Article 20. Persons regularly and solely engaged in the operation and administration of civilian hospitals, including the personnel engaged in the search for, removal and transporting of and caring for wounded and sick civilians, the infirm and maternity cases shall be respected and protected.

Article 21. Convoys of vehicles or hospital trains on land or specially provided vessels on sea, conveying wounded and sick civilians, the infirm and maternity cases, shall be respected and protected in the same manner as the hospitals provided for in Article 18, and shall be marked, with the consent of the State, by the display of the distinctive emblem provided for in Article 38 of the Geneva Convention for the Amelioration of the Condition of the Wounded and Sick in Armed Forces in the Field of 12 August 1949.

. . .

Article 23. Each High Contracting Party shall allow the free passage of all consignments of medical and hospital stores and objects necessary for religious worship intended only for civilians of another High Contracting Party, even if the latter is its adversary. It shall likewise permit the free passage of all consignments of essential foodstuffs, clothing and tonics intended for children under fifteen, expectant mothers and maternity cases.

The obligation of a High Contracting Party to allow the free passage of the consignments indicated in the preceding paragraph is subject to the condition that this Party is satisfied that there are no serious reasons for fearing:

(a) that the consignments may be diverted from their destination,

(b) that the control may not be effective, or

(c) that a definite advantage may accrue to the military efforts or economy of the enemy through the substitution of the above-mentioned consignments for goods which would otherwise be provided or produced by the enemy or through the release of such material, services or facilities as would otherwise be required for the production of such goods.

The Power which allows the passage of the consignments indicated in the first paragraph of this Article may make such permission conditional on the distribution to the persons benefited thereby being made under the local supervision of the Protecting Powers.

Such consignments shall be forwarded as rapidly as possible, and the Power which permits their free passage shall have the right to prescribe the technical arrangements under which such passage is allowed.

Article 24. The Parties to the conflict shall take the necessary measures to ensure that children under fifteen, who are orphaned or are separated from their families as a result of the war, are not left to their own resources, and that their maintenance, the exercise of their religion and their education are facilitated in all circumstances. Their education shall, as far as possible, be entrusted to persons of a similar cultural tradition.

The Parties to the conflict shall facilitate the reception of such children in a neutral country for the duration of the conflict with the consent of the Protecting Power, if any, and under due safeguards for the observance of the principles stated in the first paragraph.

They shall, furthermore, endeavour to arrange for all children under twelve to be identified by the wearing of identity discs, or by some other means.

Article 25. All persons in the territory of a Party to the conflict, or in a territory occupied by it, shall be enabled to give news of a strictly personal nature to members of their families, wherever they may be, and to receive news from them. This correspondence shall be forwarded speedily and without undue delay.

If, as a result of circumstances, it becomes difficult or impossible to exchange family correspondence by the ordinary post, the Parties to the conflict concerned shall apply to a neutral intermediary, such as the Central Agency provided for in Article 140, and shall decide in consultation with it how to ensure the fulfilment of their obligations under the best possible conditions, in particular with the co-operation of the National Red Cross (Red Crescent, Red Lion and Sun) Societies.

If the Parties to the conflict deem it necessary to restrict family correspondence, such restrictions shall be confined to the compulsory use of standard forms containing twenty-five freely chosen words, and to the limitation of the number of these forms despatched to one each month.

Article 26. Each Party to the conflict shall facilitate enquiries made by members of families dispersed owing to the war, with the object of renewing contact with one another and of meeting, if possible. It shall encourage, in particular, the work of organizations engaged on this task provided they are acceptable to it and conform to its security regulations.

Part III. Status and Treatment of Protected Persons

Section I. Provisions common to the territories of the parties to the conflict and to occupied territories

Article 27. Protected persons are entitled, in all circumstances, to respect for their persons, their honour, their family rights, their religious convictions and practices, and their manners and customs. They shall at all times be humanely treated, and shall be protected especially against all acts of violence or threats thereof and against insults and public curiosity.

Women shall be especially protected against any attack on their honour, in particular against rape, enforced prostitution, or any form of indecent assault.

Without prejudice to the provisions relating to their state of health, age and sex, all protected persons shall be treated with the same consideration by the Party to the conflict in whose power they are, without any adverse distinction based, in particular, on race, religion or political opinion.

However, the Parties to the conflict may take such measures of control and security in regard to protected persons as may be necessary as a result of the war.

Article 28. The presence of a protected person may not be used to render certain points or areas immune from military operations.

Article 29. The Party to the conflict in whose hands protected persons may be, is responsible for the treatment accorded to them by its agents, irrespective of any individual responsibility which may be incurred.

Article 30. Protected persons shall have every facility for making application to the Protecting Powers, the International Committee of the Red Cross, the National Red Cross (Red Crescent, Red Lion and Sun) Society of the country where they may be, as well as to any organization that might assist them.

These several organizations shall be granted all facilities for that purpose by the authorities, within the bounds set by military or security considerations.

Apart from the visits of the delegates of the Protecting Powers and of the International Committee of the Red Cross, provided for by Article 143, the Detaining or Occupying Powers shall facilitate, as much as possible, visits to protected persons by the representatives of other organizations whose object is to give spiritual aid or material relief to such persons.

Article 31. No physical or moral coercion shall be exercised against protected persons, in particular to obtain information from them or from third parties.

Article 32. The High Contracting Parties specifically agree that each of them is prohibited from taking any measure of such a character as to cause the physical suffering or extermination of protected persons in their hands. This prohibition applies not only to murder, torture, corporal punishments, mutilation and medical or scientific experiments not necessitated by the medical treatment of a protected person, but also to any other measures of brutality whether applied by civilian or military agents.

Article 33. No protected person may be punished for an offence he or she has not personally committed. Collective penalties and likewise all measures of intimidation or of terrorism are prohibited.

Pillage is prohibited.

Reprisals against protected persons and their property are prohibited.

Article 34. The taking of hostages is prohibited.

Section II. Aliens in the territory of a party to the conflict

Article 35. All protected persons who may desire to leave the territory at the outset of, or during a conflict, shall be entitled to do so, unless their departure is contrary to the national interests of the State. The applications of such persons to leave shall be decided in accordance with regularly established procedures and the decision shall be taken as rapidly as possible. Those persons permitted to leave may provide themselves with the necessary funds for their journey and take with them a reasonable amount of their effects and articles of personal use.

If any such person is refused permission to leave the territory, he shall be entitled to have refusal reconsidered, as soon as possible by an appropriate court or administrative board designated by the Detaining Power for that purpose.

. . .

Article 37. Protected persons who are confined pending proceedings or subject to a sentence involving loss of liberty, shall during their confinement be humanely treated.

As soon as they are released, they may ask to leave the territory in conformity with the foregoing Articles.

Article 38. With the exception of special measures authorized by the present Convention, in particularly by Article 27 and 41 thereof, the situation of protected persons shall continue to be regulated, in principle, by the provisions concerning aliens in time of peace. In any case, the following rights shall be granted to them:

(1) they shall be enabled to receive the individual or collective relief that may be sent to them.

(2) they shall, if their state of health so requires, receive medical attention and hospital treatment to the same extent as the nationals of the State concerned.

(3) they shall be allowed to practise their religion and to receive spiritual assistance from ministers of their faith.

(4) if they reside in an area particularly exposed to the dangers of war, they shall be authorized to move from that area to the same extent as the nationals of the State concerned.

(5) children under fifteen years, pregnant women and mothers of children under seven years shall benefit by any preferential treatment to the same extent as the nationals of the State concerned.

Article 39. Protected persons who, as a result of the war, have lost their gainful employment, shall be granted the opportunity to find paid employment. That opportunity shall, subject to security considerations and to the provisions of Article 40, be equal to that enjoyed by the nationals of the Power in whose territory they are.

Where a Party to the conflict applies to a protected person methods of control which result in his being unable to support himself, and especially if such a person is prevented for reasons of security from finding paid employment on reasonable conditions, the said Party shall ensure his support and that of his dependents.

Protected persons may in any case receive allowances from their home country, the Protecting Power, or the relief societies referred to in Article 30.

Article 40. Protected persons may be compelled to work only to the same extent as nationals of the Party to the conflict in whose territory they are.

If protected persons are of enemy nationality, they may only be compelled to do work which is normally necessary to ensure the feeding, sheltering, clothing, transport and health of human beings and which is not directly related to the conduct of military operations.

In the cases mentioned in the two preceding paragraphs, protected persons compelled to work shall have the benefit of the same working conditions and of the same safeguards as national workers in particular as regards wages, hours of labour, clothing and equipment, previous training and compensation for occupational accidents and diseases.

If the above provisions are infringed, protected persons shall be allowed to exercise their right of complaint in accordance with Article 30.

Article 41. Should the Power, in whose hands protected persons may be, consider the measures of control mentioned in the present Convention to be inadequate, it may not have recourse to any other measure of control more severe than that of assigned residence or internment, in accordance with the provisions of Articles 42 and 43.

In applying the provisions of Article 39, second paragraph, to the cases of persons required to leave their usual places of residence by virtue of a decision placing them in assigned residence, by virtue of a decision placing them in assigned residence, elsewhere, the Detaining Power shall be guided as closely as possible by the standards of welfare set forth in Part III, Section IV of this Convention.

Article 42. The internment or placing in assigned residence of protected persons may be ordered only if the security of the Detaining Power makes it absolutely necessary.

If any person, acting through the representatives of the Protecting Power, voluntarily demands internment, and if his situation renders this step necessary, he shall be interned by the Power in whose hands he may be.

Article 43. Any protected person who has been interned or placed in assigned residence shall be entitled to have such action reconsidered as soon as possible by an appropriate court or administrative board designated by the Detaining Power for that purpose. If the internment or placing in assigned residence is maintained, the court or administrative board shall periodically, and at least twice yearly, give consideration to his or her case, with a view to the favourable amendment of the initial decision, if circumstances permit.

Unless the protected persons concerned object, the Detaining Power shall, as rapidly as possible, give the Protecting Power the names of any protected persons who have been interned or subjected to assigned residence, or who have been released from internment or assigned residence. The decisions of the courts or boards mentioned in the first paragraph of the present Article shall also, subject to the same conditions, be notified as rapidly as possible to the Protecting Power.

Article 44. In applying the measures of control mentioned in the present Convention, the Detaining Power shall not treat as enemy aliens exclusively on the basis of their nationality de jure of an enemy State, refugees who do not, in fact, enjoy the protection of any government.

Article 45. Protected persons shall not be transferred to a Power which is not a party to the Convention.

This provision shall in no way constitute an obstacle to the repatriation of protected persons, or to their return to their country of residence after the cessation of hostilities.

Protected persons may be transferred by the Detaining Power only to a Power which is a party to the present Convention and after the Detaining Power has satisfied itself of the willingness and ability of such transferee Power to apply the present Convention. If protected persons are transferred under such circumstances, responsibility for the application of the present Convention rests on the Power accepting them, while they are in its custody. Nevertheless, if that Power fails to carry out the provisions of the present Convention in any important respect, the Power by which the protected persons were transferred shall, upon being so notified by the Protecting Power, take effective measures to correct the situation or shall request the return of the protected persons. Such request must be complied with.

In no circumstances shall a protected person be transferred to a country where he or she may have reason to fear persecution for his or her political opinions or religious beliefs.

Article 46. Insofar as they have not been previously withdrawn, restrictive measures taken regarding protected persons shall be cancelled as soon as possible after the close of hostilities.

Restrictive measures affecting their property shall be cancelled, in accordance with the law of the Detaining Power, as soon as possible after the close of hostilities.

Section III. Occupied territories

Article 47. Protected persons who are in occupied territory shall not be deprived, in any case or in any manner whatsoever, of the benefits of the present Convention by any change introduced, as the result of the occupation of a territory, into the institutions or government of the said territory, nor by any agreement concluded between the authorities of the occupied territories and the Occupying Power, nor by any annexation by the latter of the whole or part of the occupied territory.

Article 48. Protected persons who are not nationals of the Power whose territory is occupied, may avail themselves of the right to leave the territory subject to the provisions of Article 35, and decisions thereon shall be taken in accordance with the procedure which the Occupying Power shall establish in accordance with the said Article.

Article 49. Individual or mass forcible transfers, as well as deportations of protected persons from occupied territory to the territory of the Occupying Power or to that of any other country, occupied or not, are prohibited, regardless of their motive.

Nevertheless, the Occupying Power may undertake total or partial evacuation of a given area if the security of the population or imperative military reasons so demand. Such evacuations may not involve the displacement of protected persons outside the bounds of the occupied territory except when for material reasons it is impossible to avoid such displacement. Persons thus evacuated shall be transferred back to their homes as soon as hostilities in the area in question have ceased.

The Occupying Power undertaking such transfers or evacuations shall ensure, to the greatest practicable extent, that proper accommodation is provided to receive the protected persons, that the removals are effected in satisfactory conditions of hygiene, health, safety and nutrition, and that members of the same family are not separated.

The Protecting Power shall be informed of any transfers and evacuations as soon as they have taken place.

The Occupying Power shall not detain protected persons in an area particularly exposed to the dangers of war unless the security of the population or imperative military reasons so demand.

The Occupying Power shall not deport or transfer parts of its own civilian population into the territory it occupies.

Article 50. The Occupying Power shall, with the cooperation of the national and local authorities, facilitate the proper working of all institutions devoted to the care and education of children.

The Occupying Power shall take all necessary steps to facilitate the identification of children and the registration of their parentage. It may not, in any case, change their personal status, nor enlist them in formations or organizations subordinate to it.

Should the local institutions be inadequate for the purpose, the Occupying Power shall make arrangements for the maintenance and education, if possible by persons of their own nationality, language and religion, of children who are orphaned or separated from their parents as a result of the war and who cannot be adequately cared for by a near relative or friend.

A special section of the Bureau set up in accordance with Article 136 shall be responsible for taking all necessary steps to identify children whose identity is in doubt. Particulars of their parents or other near relatives should always be recorded if available.

The Occupying Power shall not hinder the application of any preferential measures in regard to food, medical care and protection against the effects of war which may have been adopted prior to the occupation in favour of children under fifteen years, expectant mothers, and mothers of children under seven years.

Article 51. The Occupying Power may not compel protected persons to serve in its armed or auxiliary forces. No pressure or propaganda which aims at securing voluntary enlistment is permitted.

The Occupying Power may not compel protected persons to work unless they are over eighteen years of age, and then only on work which is necessary either for the needs of the army of occupation, or for the public utility services, or for the feeding, sheltering, clothing, transportation or health of the population of the occupied country. Protected persons may not be compelled to undertake any work which would involve them in the obligation of taking part in military operations. The Occupying Power may not compel protected persons to employ forcible means to ensure the security of the installations where they are performing compulsory labour.

The work shall be carried out only in the occupied territory where the persons whose services have been requisitioned are. Every such person shall, so far as possible, be kept in his usual place of employment. Workers shall be paid a fair wage and the work shall be proportionate to their physical and intellectual capacities. The legislation in force in the occupied country concerning working conditions, and safeguards as regards, in particular, such matters as wages, hours of work, equipment, preliminary training and compensation for occupational accidents and diseases, shall be applicable to the protected persons assigned to the work referred to in this Article.

In no case shall requisition of labour lead to a mobilization of workers in an organization of a military or semi-military character.

Article 52. No contract, agreement or regulation shall impair the right of any worker, whether voluntary or not and wherever he may be, to apply to the representatives of the Protecting Power in order to request the said Power's intervention.

All measures aiming at creating unemployment or at restricting the opportunities offered to workers in an occupied territory, in order to induce them to work for the Occupying Power, are prohibited.

Article 53. Any destruction by the Occupying Power of real or personal property belonging individually or collectively to private persons, or to the State, or to other public authorities, or to social or cooperative organizations, is prohibited, except where such destruction is rendered absolutely necessary by military operations.

Article 54. The Occupying Power may not alter the status of public officials or judges in the occupied territories, or in any way apply sanctions to or take any measures of coercion or discrimination against them, should they abstain from fulfilling their functions for reasons of conscience.

This prohibition does not prejudice the application of the second paragraph of Article 51. It does not affect the right of the Occupying Power to remove public officials from their posts.

Article 55. To the fullest extent of the means available to it, the Occupying Power has the duty of ensuring the food and medical supplies of the population; it should, in particular, bring in the necessary foodstuffs, medical stores and other articles if the resources of the occupied territory are inadequate.

The Occupying Power may not requisition foodstuffs, articles or medical supplies available in the occupied territory, except for use by the occupation forces and administration personnel, and then only if the requirements of the civilian population have been taken into account. Subject to the provisions of other international Conventions, the Occupying Power shall make arrangements to ensure that fair value is paid for any requisitioned goods.

The Protecting Power shall, at any time, be at liberty to verify the state of the food and medical supplies in occupied territories, except where temporary restrictions are made necessary by imperative military requirements.

Article 56. To the fullest extent of the means available to it, the public Occupying Power has the duty of ensuring and maintaining, with the cooperation of national and local authorities, the medical and hospital establishments and services, public health and hygiene in the occupied territory, with particular reference to the adoption and application of the prophylactic and preventive measures necessary to combat the spread of contagious diseases and epidemics. Medical personnel of all categories shall be allowed to carry out their duties.

If new hospitals are set up in occupied territory and if the competent organs of the occupied State are not operating there, the occupying authorities shall, if necessary, grant them the recognition provided for in

Article 18. In similar circumstances, the occupying authorities shall also grant recognition to hospital personnel and transport vehicles under the provisions of Articles 20 and 21.

In adopting measures of health and hygiene and in their implementation, the Occupying Power shall take into consideration the moral and ethical susceptibilities of the population of the occupied territory.

Article 57. The Occupying Power may requisition civilian hospitals of hospitals only temporarily and only in cases of urgent necessity for the care of military wounded and sick, and then on condition that suitable arrangements are made in due time for the care and treatment of the patients and for the needs of the civilian population for hospital accommodation.

The material and stores of civilian hospitals cannot be requisitioned so long as they are necessary for the needs of the civilian population.

Article 58. The Occupying Power shall permit ministers of religion to give spiritual assistance to the members of their religious communities.

The Occupying Power shall also accept consignments of books and articles required for religious needs and shall facilitate their distribution in occupied territory.

Article 59. If the whole or part of the population of an occupied territory is inadequately supplied, the Occupying Power shall agree to relief schemes on behalf of the said population, and shall facilitate them by all the means at its disposal.

Such schemes, which may be undertaken either by States or by impartial humanitarian organizations such as the International Committee of the Red Cross, shall consist, in particular, of the provision of consignments of foodstuffs, medical supplies and clothing.

All Contracting Parties shall permit the free passage of these consignments and shall guarantee their protection.

A Power granting free passage to consignments on their way to territory occupied by an adverse Party to the conflict shall, however, have the right to search the consignments, to regulate their passage according to prescribed times and routes, and to be reasonably satisfied through the Protecting Power that these consignments are to be used for the relief of the needy population and are not to be used for the benefit of the Occupying Power.

Article 60. Relief consignments shall in no way relieve the Occupying Power of any of its responsibilities under Articles 55, 56 and 59. The Occupying Power shall in no way whatsoever divert relief consignments from the purpose for which they are intended, except in cases of urgent necessity, in the interests of the population of the occupied territory and with the consent of the Protecting Power.

Article 61. The distribution of the relief consignments referred to in the foregoing Articles shall be carried out with the cooperation and under the supervision of the Protecting Power. This duty may also be delegated, by agreement between the Occupying Power and the Protecting Power, to a neutral Power, to the International Committee of the Red Cross or to any other impartial humanitarian body.

Such consignments shall be exempt in occupied territory from all charges, taxes or customs duties unless these are necessary in the interests of the economy of the territory. The Occupying Power shall facilitate the rapid distribution of these consignments.

All Contracting Parties shall endeavour to permit the transit and transport, free of charge, of such relief consignments on their way to occupied territories.

Article 62. Subject to imperative reasons of security, protected persons in occupied territories shall be permitted to receive the individual relief consignments sent to them.

Article 63. Subject to temporary and exceptional measures imposed for urgent reasons of security by the Occupying Power:

(a) recognized National Red Cross (Red Crescent, Red Lion and Sun) Societies shall be able to pursue their activities in accordance with Red Cross principles, as defined by the International Red Cross Conferences. Other relief societies shall be permitted to continue their humanitarian activities under similar conditions;

(b) the Occupying Power may not require any changes in the personnel or structure of these societies, which would prejudice the aforesaid activities.

The same principles shall apply to the activities and personnel of special organizations of a non-military character, which already exist or which may be established, for the purpose of ensuring the living conditions of the civilian population by the maintenance of the essential public utility services, by the distribution of relief and by the organization of rescues.

Article 64. The penal laws of the occupied territory shall remain in force, with the exception that they may be repealed or suspended by the Occupying Power in cases where they constitute a threat to its security or an obstacle to the application of the present Convention.

Subject to the latter consideration and to the necessity for ensuring the effective administration of justice, the tribunals of the occupied territory shall continue to function in respect of all offences covered by the said laws.

The Occupying Power may, however, subject the population of the occupied territory to provisions which are essential to enable the Occupying Power to fulfil its obligations under the present Convention, to maintain the orderly government of the territory, and to ensure the security of the Occupying Power, of the members and property of the occupying forces or administration, and likewise of the establishments and lines of communication used by them.

Article 65. The penal provisions enacted by the Occupying Power shall not come into force before they have been published and brought to the knowledge of the inhabitants in their own language. The effect of these penal provisions shall not be retroactive.

Article 66. In case of a breach of the penal provisions promulgated by it by virtue of the second paragraph of Article 64 the Occupying Power may hand over the accused to its properly constituted, non-political military courts, on condition that the said courts sit in the occupied country. Courts of appeal shall preferably sit in the occupied country.

Article 67. The courts shall apply only those provisions of law which were applicable prior to the offence, and which are in accordance with general principles of law, in particular the principle that the penalty shall be proportionate to the offence. They shall take into consideration the fact the accused is not a national of the Occupying Power.

Article 68. Protected persons who commit an offence which is solely intended to harm the Occupying Power, but which does not constitute an attempt on the life or limb of members of the occupying forces or administration, nor a grave collective danger, nor seriously damage the property of the occupying forces or administration or the installations used by them, shall be liable to internment or simple imprisonment, provided the duration of such internment or imprisonment is proportionate to the offence committed. Furthermore, internment or imprisonment shall, for such offences, be the only measure adopted for depriving protected persons of liberty. The courts provided for under Article 66 of the present Convention may at their discretion convert a sentence of imprisonment to one of internment for the same period.

The penal provisions promulgated by the Occupying Power in accordance with Articles 64 and 65 may impose the death penalty on a protected person only in cases where the person is guilty of espionage, of serious acts of sabotage against the military installations of the Occupying Power or of intentional offences which have caused the death of one or more persons, provided that such offences were punishable by death under the law of the occupied territory in force before the occupation began.

The death penalty may not be pronounced on a protected person unless the attention of the court has been particularly called to the fact that since the accused is not a national of the Occupying Power, he is not bound to it by any duty of allegiance.

In any case, the death penalty may not be pronounced on a protected person who was under eighteen years of age at the time of the offence.

Article 69. In all cases the duration of the period during which a protected person accused of an offence is under arrest awaiting trial or punishment shall be deducted from any period of imprisonment of awarded.

Article 70. Protected persons shall not be arrested, prosecuted or convicted by the Occupying Power for acts committed or for opinions expressed before the occupation, or during a temporary interruption thereof, with the exception of breaches of the laws and customs of war.

Nationals of the occupying Power who, before the outbreak of hostilities, have sought refuge in the territory of the occupied State, shall not be arrested, prosecuted, convicted or deported from the occupied territory, except for offences committed after the outbreak of hostilities, or for offences under common law committed before the outbreak of hostilities which, according to the law of the occupied State, would have justified extradition in time of peace.

Article 71. No sentence shall be pronounced by the competent courts of the Occupying Power except after a regular trial.

Accused persons who are prosecuted by the Occupying Power shall be promptly informed, in writing, in a language which they understand, of the particulars of the charges preferred against them, and shall be brought to trial as rapidly as possible. The Protecting Power shall be informed of all proceedings instituted by the Occupying Power against protected persons in respect of charges involving the death penalty or imprisonment for two years or more; it shall be enabled, at any time, to obtain information regarding the state of such proceedings. Furthermore, the Protecting Power shall be entitled, on request, to be furnished with all particulars of these and of any other proceedings instituted by the Occupying Power against protected persons.

The notification to the Protecting Power, as provided for in the second paragraph above, shall be sent immediately, and shall in any case reach the Protecting Power three weeks before the date of the first hearing. Unless, at the opening of the trial, evidence is submitted that the provisions of this Article are fully complied with, the trial shall not proceed. The notification shall include the following particulars:

(a) description of the accused;

(b) place of residence or detention;

(c) specification of the charge or charges (with mention of the penal provisions under which it is brought);

(d) designation of the court which will hear the case;

(e) place and date of the first hearing.

Article 72. Accused persons shall have the right to present evidence necessary to their defence and may, in particular, call witnesses. They shall have the right to be assisted by a qualified advocate or counsel of their own choice, who shall be able to visit them freely and shall enjoy the necessary facilities for preparing the defence.

Failing a choice by the accused, the Protecting Power may provide him with an advocate or counsel. When an accused person has to meet a serious charge and the Protecting Power is not functioning, the Occupying Power, subject to the consent of the accused, shall provide an advocate or counsel.

Accused persons shall, unless they freely waive such assistance, be aided by an interpreter, both during preliminary investigation and during the hearing in court. They shall have at any time the right to object to the interpreter and to ask for his replacement.

Article 73. A convicted person shall have the right of appeal provided for by the laws applied by the court. He shall be fully informed of his right to appeal or petition and of the time limit within which he may do so.

The penal procedure provided in the present Section shall apply, as far as it is applicable, to appeals. Where the laws applied by the Court make no provision for appeals, the convicted person shall have the right to petition against the finding and sentence to the competent authority of the Occupying Power.

Article 74. Representatives of the Protecting Power shall have the right to attend the trial of any protected person, unless the hearing has, as an exceptional measure, to be held in camera in the interests of the security of the Occupying Power, which shall then notify the Protecting Power. A notification in respect of the date and place of trial shall be sent to the Protecting Power.

Any judgement involving a sentence of death, or imprisonment for two years or more, shall be communicated, with the relevant grounds, as rapidly as possible to the Protecting Power. The notification shall contain a reference to the notification made under Article 71 and, in the case of sentences of imprisonment, the name of the place where the sentence is to be served. A record of judgements other than those referred to above shall be kept by the court and shall be open to inspection by representatives of the Protecting Power. Any period allowed for appeal in the case of sentences involving the death penalty, or imprisonment of two years or more, shall not run until notification of judgement has been received by the Protecting Power.

Article 75. In no case shall persons condemned to death be deprived of the right of petition for pardon or reprieve.

No death sentence shall be carried out before the expiration of a period of a least six months from the date of receipt by the Protecting Power of the notification of the final judgment confirming such death sentence, or of an order denying pardon or reprieve.

The six months period of suspension of the death sentence herein prescribed may be reduced in individual cases in circumstances of grave emergency involving an organized threat to the security of the Occupying Power or its forces, provided always that the Protecting Power is notified of such reduction and is given reasonable time and opportunity to make representations to the competent occupying authorities in respect of such death sentences.

Article 76. Protected persons accused of offences shall be detained in the occupied country, and if convicted they shall serve their sentences therein. They shall, if possible, be separated from other detainees and shall enjoy conditions of food and hygiene which will be sufficient to keep them in good health, and which will be at least equal to those obtaining in prisons in the occupied country.

They shall receive the medical attention required by their state of health.

They shall also have the right to receive any spiritual assistance which they may require.

Women shall be confined in separate quarters and shall be under the direct supervision of women.

Proper regard shall be paid to the special treatment due to minors.

Protected persons who are detained shall have the right to be visited by delegates of the Protecting Power and of the International Committee of the Red Cross, in accordance with the provisions of Article 143.

Such persons shall have the right to receive at least one relief parcel monthly.

Article 77. Protected persons who have been accused of offences or convicted by the courts in occupied territory, shall be handed over at the close of occupation, with the relevant records, to the authorities of the liberated territory.

Article 78. If the Occupying Power considers it necessary, for imperative reasons of security, to take safety measures concerning protected persons, it may, at the most, subject them to assigned residence or to internment.

Decisions regarding such assigned residence or internment shall be made according to a regular procedure to be prescribed by the Occupying Power in accordance with the provisions of the present Convention. This procedure shall include the right of appeal for the parties concerned. Appeals shall be decided with the least possible delay. In the event of the decision being upheld, it shall be subject to periodical review, if possible every six months, by a competent body set up by the said Power.

Protected persons made subject to assigned residence and thus required to leave their homes shall enjoy the full benefit of Article 39 of the present Convention.

Section IV. Regulations for the treatment of internees
Chapter I. General provisions

Article 79. The Parties to the conflict shall not intern protected persons, except in accordance with the provisions of Articles 41, 42, 43, 68 and 78.

Article 80. Internees shall retain their full civil capacity and shall exercise such attendant rights as may be compatible with their status.

Article 81. Parties to the conflict who intern protected persons shall be bound to provide free of charge for their maintenance, and to grant them also the medical attention required by their state of health.

No deduction from the allowances, salaries or credits due to the internees shall be made for the repayment of these costs.

The Detaining Power shall provide for the support of those dependent on the internees, if such dependents are without adequate means of support or are unable to earn a living.

Article 82. The Detaining Power shall, as far as possible, accommodate the internees according to their nationality, language and customs. Internees who are nationals of the same country shall not be separated merely because they have different languages.

Throughout the duration of their internment, members of the same family, and in particular parents and children, shall be lodged together in the same place of internment, except when separation of a temporary nature is necessitated for reasons of employment or health or for the purposes of enforcement of the provisions of Chapter IX of the present Section. Internees may request that their children who are left at liberty without parental care shall be interned with them.

Wherever possible, interned members of the same family shall be housed in the same premises and given separate accommodation from other internees, together with facilities for leading a proper family life.

Chapter II. Places of Internment

Article 83. The Detaining Power shall not set up places of internment in areas particularly exposed to the dangers of war.

The Detaining Power shall give the enemy Powers, through the intermediary of the Protecting Powers, all useful information regarding the geographical location of places of internment.

Whenever military considerations permit, internment camps shall be indicated by the letters IC, placed so as to be clearly visible in the daytime from the air. The Powers concerned may, however, agree upon any other system of marking. No place other than an internment camp shall be marked as such.

Article 84. Internees shall be accommodated and administered separately from prisoners of war and from persons deprived of liberty for any other reason.

Article 85. The Detaining Power is bound to take all necessary and possible measures to ensure that protected persons shall, from the outset of their internment, be accommodated in buildings or quarters which afford every possible safeguard as regards hygiene and health, and provide efficient protection against the rigours of the climate and the effects of the war. In no case shall permanent places of internment be situated in unhealthy areas or in districts, the climate of which is injurious to the internees. In all cases where the district, in which a protected person is temporarily interned, is an unhealthy area or has a climate which is harmful to his health, he shall be removed to a more suitable place of internment as rapidly as circumstances permit.

The premises shall be fully protected from dampness, adequately heated and lighted, in particular between dusk and lights out. The sleeping quarters shall be sufficiently spacious and well ventilated, and the internees shall have suitable bedding and sufficient blankets, account being taken of the climate, and the age, sex, and state of health of the internees.

Internees shall have for their use, day and night, sanitary conveniences which conform to the rules of hygiene, and are constantly maintained in a state of cleanliness. They shall be provided with sufficient water and soap for their daily personal toilet and for washing their personal laundry; installations and facilities necessary for this purpose shall be granted to them. Showers or baths shall also be available. The necessary time shall be set aside for washing and for cleaning.

Whenever it is necessary, as an exceptional and temporary measure, to accommodate women internees who are not members of a family unit in the same place of internment as men, the provision of separate sleeping quarters and sanitary conveniences for the use of such women internees shall be obligatory.

Article 86. The Detaining Power shall place at the disposal of interned persons, of whatever denomination, premises suitable for the holding of their religious services.

Article 87. Canteens shall be installed in every place of internment, except where other suitable facilities are available. Their purpose shall be to enable internees to make purchases, at prices not higher than local market prices, of foodstuffs and articles of everyday use, including soap and tobacco, such as would increase their personal well-being and comfort.

Profits made by canteens shall be credited to a welfare fund to be set up for each place of internment, and administered for the benefit of the internees attached to such place of internment. The Internee Committee provided for in Article 102 shall have the right to check the management of the canteen and of the said fund.

When a place of internment is closed down, the balance of the welfare fund shall be transferred to the welfare fund of a place of internment for internees of the same nationality, or, if such a place does not exist, to a central welfare fund which shall be administered for the benefit of all internees remaining in the custody of the Detaining Power. In case of a general release, the said profits shall be kept by the Detaining Power, subject to any agreement to the contrary between the Powers concerned.

Article 88. In all places of internment exposed to air raids and other hazards of war, shelters adequate in number and structure to ensure the necessary protection shall be installed. In case of alarms, the measures internees shall be free to enter such shelters as quickly as possible, excepting those who remain for the protection of their quarters against the aforesaid hazards. Any protective measures taken in favour of the population shall also apply to them.

All due precautions must be taken in places of internment against the danger of fire.

Chapter III. Food and Clothing

Article 89. Daily food rations for internees shall be sufficient in quantity, quality and variety to keep internees in a good state of health and prevent the development of nutritional deficiencies. Account shall also be taken of the customary diet of the internees.

Internees shall also be given the means by which they can prepare for themselves any additional food in their possession.

Sufficient drinking water shall be supplied to internees. The use of tobacco shall be permitted.

Internees who work shall receive additional rations in proportion to the kind of labour which they perform.

Expectant and nursing mothers and children under fifteen years of age, shall be given additional food, in proportion to their physiological needs.

Article 90. When taken into custody, internees shall be given all facilities to provide themselves with the necessary clothing, footwear and change of underwear, and later on, to procure further supplies if required.

Should any internees not have sufficient clothing, account being taken of the climate, and be unable to procure any, it shall be provided free of charge to them by the Detaining Power.

The clothing supplied by the Detaining Power to internees and the outward markings placed on their own clothes shall not be ignominious nor expose them to ridicule.

Workers shall receive suitable working outfits, including protective clothing, whenever the nature of their work so requires.

Chapter IV. Hygiene and Medical Attention

Article 91. Every place of internment shall have an adequate infirmary, under the direction of a qualified doctor, where internees may have the attention they require, as well as appropriate diet. Isolation wards shall be set aside for cases of contagious or mental diseases.

Maternity cases and internees suffering from serious diseases, or whose condition requires special treatment, a surgical operation or hospital care, must be admitted to any institution where adequate treatment can be given and shall receive care not inferior to that provided for the general population.

Internees shall, for preference, have the attention of medical personnel of their own nationality.

Internees may not be prevented from presenting themselves to the medical authorities for examination. The medical authorities of the Detaining Power shall, upon request, issue to every internee who has undergone treatment an official certificate showing the nature of his illness or injury, and the duration and nature of the treatment given. A duplicate of this certificate shall be forwarded to the Central Agency provided for in Article 140.

Treatment, including the provision of any apparatus necessary for the maintenance of internees in good health, particularly dentures and other artificial appliances and spectacles, shall be free of charge to the internee.

Article 92. Medical inspections of internees shall be made at least once a month. Their purpose shall be, in particular, to supervise the general state of health, nutrition and cleanliness of internees, and to detect contagious diseases, especially tuberculosis, malaria, and venereal diseases. Such inspections shall include, in particular, the checking of weight of each internee and, at least once a year, radioscopic examination.

Chapter V. Religious, Intellectual and Physical Activities

Article 93. Internees shall enjoy complete latitude in the exercise of their religious duties, including attendance at the services of their faith, on condition that they comply with the disciplinary routine prescribed by the detaining authorities.

Ministers of religion who are interned shall be allowed to minister freely to the members of their community. For this purpose the Detaining Power shall ensure their equitable allocation amongst the various places of internment in which there are internees speaking the same language and belonging to the same religion. Should such ministers be too few in number, the Detaining Power shall provide them with the necessary facilities, including means of transport, for moving from one place to another, and they shall be authorized to visit any internees who are in hospital. Ministers of religion shall be at liberty to correspond on matters concerning their ministry with the religious authorities in the country of detention and, as far as possible, with the international religious organizations of their faith. Such correspondence shall not be considered as forming a part of the quota mentioned in Article 107. It shall, however, be subject to the provisions of Article 112.

When internees do not have at their disposal the assistance of ministers of their faith, or should these latter be too few in number, the local religious authorities of the same faith may appoint, in agreement with the Detaining Power, a minister of the internees' faith or, if such a course is feasible from a denominational point of view, a minister of similar religion or a qualified layman. The latter shall enjoy the facilities granted to the ministry he has assumed. Persons so appointed shall comply with all regulations laid down by the Detaining Power in the interests of discipline and security.

Article 94. The Detaining Power shall encourage intellectual, educational and recreational pursuits, sports and games amongst internees, whilst leaving them free to take part in them or not. It shall take all practicable measures to ensure the exercise thereof, in particular by providing suitable premises.

All possible facilities shall be granted to internees to continue their studies or to take up new subjects. The education of children and young people shall be ensured; they shall be allowed to attend schools either within the place of internment or outside.

Internees shall be given opportunities for physical exercise, sports and outdoor games. For this purpose, sufficient open spaces shall be set aside in all places of internment. Special playgrounds shall be reserved for children and young people.

Article 95. The Detaining Power shall not employ internees as workers, unless they so desire. Employment which, if undertaken under compulsion by a protected person not in internment, would involve a breach of Articles 40 or 51 of the present Convention, and employment on work which is of a degrading or humiliating character are in any case prohibited.

After a working period of six weeks, internees shall be free to give up work at any moment, subject to eight days' notice.

These provisions constitute no obstacle to the right of the Detaining Power to employ interned doctors, dentists and other medical personnel in their professional capacity on behalf of their fellow internees, or to employ internees for administrative and maintenance work in places of internment and to detail such persons for work in the kitchens or for other domestic tasks, or to require such persons to undertake duties connected with the protection of internees against aerial bombardment or other war risks. No internee may, however, be required to perform tasks for which he is, in the opinion of a medical officer, physically unsuited.

The Detaining Power shall take entire responsibility for all working conditions, for medical attention, for the payment of wages, and for ensuring that all employed internees receive compensation for occupational accidents and diseases. The standards prescribed for the said working conditions and for compensation shall be in accordance with the national laws and regulations, and with the existing practice; they shall in no case be inferior to those obtaining for work of the same nature in the same district. Wages for work done shall be determined on an equitable basis by special agreements between the internees, the Detaining Power, and, if the case arises, employers other than the Detaining Power to provide for free maintenance of internees and for the medical attention which their state of health may require. Internees permanently detailed for categories of work mentioned in the third paragraph of this Article, shall be paid fair wages by the Detaining Power. The working conditions and the scale of compensation for occupational accidents and diseases to internees, thus detailed, shall not be inferior to those applicable to work of the same nature in the same district.

Article 96. All labour detachments shall remain part of and dependent upon a place of internment. The competent authorities of the Detaining Power and the commandant of a place of internment shall be responsible for the observance in a labour detachment of the provisions of the present Convention. The commandant shall keep an up-to-date list of the labour detachments subordinate to him and shall communicate it to the delegates of the Protecting Power, of the International Committee of the Red Cross and of other humanitarian organizations who may visit the places of internment.

Chapter VI. Personal Property and Financial Resources

Article 97. Internees shall be permitted to retain articles of personal use. Monies, cheques, bonds, etc., and valuables in their possession may not be taken from them except in accordance with established procedure. Detailed receipts shall be given therefore.

The amounts shall be paid into the account of every internee as provided for in Article 98. Such amounts may not be converted into any other currency unless legislation in force in the territory in which the owner is interned so requires or the internee gives his consent.

Articles which have above all a personal or sentimental value may not be taken away.

A woman internee shall not be searched except by a woman.

On release or repatriation, internees shall be given all articles, monies or other valuables taken from them during internment and shall receive in currency the balance of any credit to their accounts kept in accordance with Article 98, with the exception of any articles or amounts withheld by the Detaining Power by virtue of its legislation in force. If the property of an internee is so withheld, the owner shall receive a detailed receipt.

Family or identity documents in the possession of internees may not be taken away without a receipt being given. At no time shall internees be left without identity documents. If they have none, they shall be issued with special documents drawn up by the detaining authorities, which will serve as their identity papers until the end of their internment.

Internees may keep on their persons a certain amount of money, in cash or in the shape of purchase coupons, to enable them to make purchases.

Article 98. All internees shall receive regular allowances, sufficient to enable them to purchase goods and articles, such as tobacco, toilet requisites, etc. Such allowances may take the form of credits or purchase coupons.

Furthermore, internees may receive allowances from the Power to which they owe allegiance, the Protecting Powers, the organizations which may assist them, or their families, as well as the income on their property in accordance with the law of the Detaining Power. The amount of allowances granted by the Power to which they owe allegiance shall be the same for each category of internees (infirm, sick, pregnant women, etc.) but may not be allocated by that Power or distributed by the Detaining Power on the basis of discriminations between internees which are prohibited by Article 27 of the present Convention.

The Detaining Power shall open a regular account for every internee, to which shall be credited the allowances named in the present Article, the wages earned and the remittances received, together with such sums taken from him as may be available under the legislation in force in the territory in which he is interned. Internees shall be granted all facilities consistent with the legislation in force in such territory to make remittances to their families and to other dependants. They may draw from their accounts the amounts necessary for their personal expenses, within the limits fixed by the Detaining Power. They shall at all times be afforded reasonable facilities for consulting and obtaining copies of their accounts. A statement of accounts shall be furnished to the Protecting Power, on request, and shall accompany the internee in case of transfer.

Chapter VII. Administration and Discipline

Article 99. Every place of internment shall be put under the authority of a responsible officer, chosen from the regular military forces or the regular civil administration of the Detaining Power. The officer in charge of the place of internment must have in his possession a copy of the present Convention in the official language, or one of the official languages, of his country and shall be responsible for its application. The staff in control of internees shall be instructed in the provisions of the present Convention and of the administrative measures adopted to ensure its application.

The text of the present Convention and the texts of special agreements concluded under the said Convention shall be posted inside the place of internment, in a language which the internees understand, or shall be in the possession of the Internee Committee.

Regulations, orders, notices and publications of every kind shall be communicated to the internees and posted inside the places of internment, in a language which they understand.

Every order and command addressed to internees individually must, likewise, be given in a language which they understand.

Article 100. The disciplinary regime in places of internment shall be consistent with humanitarian principles, and shall in no circumstances include regulations imposing on internees any physical exertion dangerous to their health or involving physical or moral victimization. Identification by tattooing or imprinting signs or markings on the body, is prohibited.

In particular, prolonged standing and roll-calls, punishment drill, military drill and manoeuvres, or the reduction of food rations, are prohibited.

Article 101. Internees shall have the right to present to the authorities in whose power they are, any petition with regard to the conditions of internment to which they are subjected.

They shall also have the right to apply without restriction through the Internee Committee or, if they consider it necessary, direct to the representatives of the Protecting Power, in order to indicate to them any points on which they may have complaints to make with regard to the conditions of internment.

Such petitions and complaints shall be transmitted forthwith and without alteration, and even if the latter are recognized to be unfounded, they may not occasion any punishment.

Periodic reports on the situation in places of internment and as to the needs of the internees may be sent by the Internee Committees to the representatives of the Protecting Powers.

Article 102. In every place of internment, the internees shall freely elect by secret ballot every six months, the members of a Committee empowered to represent them before the Detaining and the Protecting Powers, the International Committee of the Red Cross and any other organization which may assist them. The members of the Committee shall be eligible for re-election.

Internees so elected shall enter upon their duties after their election has been approved by the detaining authorities. The reasons for any refusals or dismissals shall be communicated to the Protecting Powers concerned.

Article 103. The Internee Committees shall further the physical, spiritual and intellectual well-being of the internees.

In case the internees decide, in particular, to organize a system of mutual assistance amongst themselves, this organization would be within the competence of the Committees in addition to the special duties entrusted to them under other provisions of the present Convention.

Article 104. Members of Internee Committees shall not be required to perform any other work, if the accomplishment of their duties is rendered more difficult thereby.

Members of Internee Committees may appoint from amongst the internees such assistants as they may require. All material facilities shall be granted to them, particularly a certain freedom of movement necessary for the accomplishment of their duties (visits to labour detachments, receipt of supplies, etc.).

All facilities shall likewise be accorded to members of Internee Committees for communication by post and telegraph with the detaining authorities, the Protecting Powers, the International Committee of the Red Cross and their delegates, and with the organizations which give assistance to internees. Committee members in labour detachments shall enjoy similar facilities for communication with their Internee Committee in the principal place of internment. Such communications shall not be limited, nor considered as forming a part of the quota mentioned in Article 107.

Members of Internee Committees who are transferred shall be allowed a reasonable time to acquaint their successors with current affairs.

Chapter VIII. Relations with the Exterior

Article 105. Immediately upon interning protected persons, the Detaining Powers shall inform them, the Power to which they owe allegiance and their Protecting Power of the measures taken for executing the provisions of the present Chapter. The Detaining Powers shall likewise inform the Parties concerned of any subsequent modifications of such measures.

Article 106. As soon as he is interned, or at the latest not more than one week after his arrival in a place of internment, and likewise in cases of sickness or transfer to another place of internment or to a hospital, every internee shall be enabled to send direct to his family, on the one hand, and to the Central Agency provided for by Article 140, on the other, an internment card similar, if possible, to the model annexed to the present Convention, informing his relatives of his detention, address and state of health. The said cards shall be forwarded as rapidly as possible and may not be delayed in any way.

Article 107. Internees shall be allowed to send and receive letters and cards. If the Detaining Power deems it necessary to limit the number of letters and cards sent by each internee, the said number shall not be less than two letters and four cards monthly; these shall be drawn up so as to conform as closely as possible to the models annexed to the present Convention. If limitations must be placed on the correspondence addressed to internees, they may be ordered only by the Power to which such internees owe allegiance, possibly at the request of the Detaining Power. Such letters and cards must be conveyed with reasonable dispatch; they may not be delayed or retained for disciplinary reasons.

Internees who have been a long time without news, or who find it impossible to receive news from their relatives, or to give them news by the ordinary postal route, as well as those who are at a considerable distance from their homes, shall be allowed to send telegrams, the charges being paid by them in the currency at their disposal. They shall likewise benefit by this provision in cases which are recognized to be urgent.

As a rule, internees' mail shall be written in their own language. The Parties to the conflict may authorize correspondence in other languages.

Article 108. Internees shall be allowed to receive, by post or by any other means, individual parcels or collective shipments containing in particular foodstuffs, clothing, medical supplies, as well as books and objects of a devotional, educational or recreational character which may meet their needs. Such shipments shall in no way free the Detaining Power from the obligations imposed upon it by virtue of the present Convention.

Should military necessity require the quantity of such shipments to be limited, due notice thereof shall be given to the Protecting Power and to the International Committee of the Red Cross, or to any other organization giving assistance to the internees and responsible for the forwarding of such shipments.

The conditions for the sending of individual parcels and collective shipments shall, if necessary, be the subject of special agreements between the Powers concerned, which may in no case delay the receipt by the internees of relief supplies. Parcels of clothing and foodstuffs may not include books. Medical relief supplies shall, as a rule, be sent in collective parcels.

Article 109. In the absence of special agreements between Parties to the conflict regarding the conditions for the receipt and distribution of collective relief shipments, the regulations concerning collective relief which are annexed to the present Convention shall be applied.

The special agreements provided for above shall in no case restrict the right of Internee Committees to take possession of collective relief shipments intended for internees, to undertake their distribution and to dispose of them in the interests of the recipients. Nor shall such agreements restrict the right of representatives of the Protecting Powers, the International Committee of the Red Cross, or any other organization giving assistance to internees and responsible for the forwarding of collective shipments, to supervise their distribution to the recipients.

Article 110. An relief shipments for internees shall be exempt from import, customs and other dues.

All matter sent by mail, including relief parcels sent by parcel post and remittances of money, addressed from other countries to internees or dispatched by them through the post office, either direct or through the Information Bureaux provided for in Article 136 and the Central Information Agency provided for in Article 140, shall be exempt from all postal dues both in the countries of origin and destination and in intermediate countries. ...

...

Costs connected with the transport of such shipments, which are not covered by the above paragraphs, shall be charged to the senders.

The High Contracting Parties shall endeavour to reduce, so far as possible, the charges for telegrams sent by internees, or addressed to them.

Article 111. Should military operations prevent the Powers concerned from fulfilling their obligation to ensure the conveyance of the mail and relief shipments provided for in Articles 106, 107, 108 and 113, the Protecting Powers concerned, the International Committee of the Red Cross or any other organization duly approved by the Parties to the conflict may undertake to ensure the conveyance of such shipments by suitable means (rail, motor vehicles, vessels or aircraft, etc.). For this purpose, the High Contracting Parties shall endeavour to supply them with such transport, and to allow its circulation, especially by granting the necessary safe-conducts.

Such transport may also be used to convey:

(a) correspondence, lists and reports exchanged between the Central Information Agency referred to in Article 140 and the National Bureaux referred to in Article 136;

(b) correspondence and reports relating to internees which the Protecting Powers, the International Committee of the Red Cross or any other organization assisting the internees exchange either with their own delegates or with the Parties to the conflict.

These provisions in no way detract from the right of any Party to the conflict to arrange other means of transport if it should so prefer, nor preclude the granting of safe-conducts, under mutually agreed conditions, to such means of transport.

The costs occasioned by the use of such means of transport shall be borne, in proportion to the importance of the shipments, by the Parties to the conflict whose nationals are benefited thereby.

Article 112. The censoring of correspondence addressed to internees or dispatched by them shall be done as quickly as possible.

The examination of consignments intended for internees shall not be carried out under conditions that will expose the goods contained in them to deterioration. It shall be done in the presence of the addressee, or of a fellow-internee duly delegated by him. The delivery to internees of individual or collective consignments shall not be delayed under the pretext of difficulties of censorship.

Any prohibition of correspondence ordered by the Parties to the conflict either for military or political reasons, shall be only temporary and its duration shall be as short as possible.

Article 113. The Detaining Powers shall provide all reasonable execution facilities for the transmission, through the Protecting Power or the Central Agency provided for in Article 140, or as otherwise required, of wills, powers of attorney, letters of authority, or any other documents intended for internees or despatched by them.

In all cases the Detaining Powers shall facilitate the execution and authentication in due legal form of such documents on behalf of internees, in particular by allowing them to consult a lawyer.

Article 114. The Detaining Power shall afford internees all facilities to enable them to manage their property, provided this is not incompatible with the conditions of internment and the law which is applicable. For this purpose, the said Power may give them permission to leave the place of internment in urgent cases and if circumstances allow.

Article 115. In all cases where an internee is a party to proceedings in any court, the Detaining Power shall, if he so requests, cause the court to be informed of his detention and shall, within legal limits, ensure that all necessary steps are taken to prevent him from being in any way prejudiced, by reason of his internment, as regards the preparation and conduct of his case or as regards the execution of any judgment of the court.

Article 116. Every internee shall be allowed to receive visitors, especially near relatives, at regular intervals and as frequently as possible.

As far as is possible, internees shall be permitted to visit their homes in urgent cases, particularly in cases of death or serious illness of relatives.

Chapter IX. Penal and Disciplinary Sanctions

Article 117. Subject to the provisions of the present Chapter, the laws in force in the territory in which they are detained will continue to apply to internees who commit offences during internment.

If general laws, regulations or orders declare acts committed by internees to be punishable, whereas the same acts are not punishable when committed by persons who are not internees, such acts shall entail disciplinary punishments only.

No internee may be punished more than once for the same act, or on the same count.

Article 118. The courts or authorities shall in passing sentence take as far as possible into account the fact that the defendant is not a national of the Detaining Power. They shall be free to reduce the penalty prescribed for the offence with which the internee is charged and shall not be obliged, to this end, to apply the minimum sentence prescribed.

Imprisonment in premises without daylight, and, in general, all forms of cruelty without exception are forbidden.

Internees who have served disciplinary or judicial sentences shall not be treated differently from other internees.

The duration of preventive detention undergone by an internee shall be deducted from any disciplinary or judicial penalty involving confinement to which he may be sentenced.

Internee Committees shall be informed of all judicial proceedings instituted against internees whom they represent, and of their result.

Article 119. The disciplinary punishments applicable to internees shall be the following:

(1) a fine which shall not exceed 50 per cent of the wages which the internee would otherwise receive under the provisions of Article 95 during a period of not more than thirty days.

(2) discontinuance of privileges granted over and above the treatment provided for by the present Convention

(3) fatigue duties, not exceeding two hours daily, in connection with the maintenance of the place of internment.

(4) confinement.

In no case shall disciplinary penalties be inhuman, brutal or dangerous for the health of internees. Account shall be taken of the internee's age, sex and state of health.

The duration of any single punishment shall in no case exceed a maximum of thirty consecutive days, even if the internee is answerable for several breaches of discipline when his case is dealt with, whether such breaches are connected or not.

Article 120. Internees who are recaptured after having escaped or when attempting to escape, shall be liable only to disciplinary punishment in respect of this act, even if it is a repeated offence.

Article 118, paragraph 3, notwithstanding, internees punished as a result of escape or attempt to escape, may be subjected to special surveillance, on condition that such surveillance does not affect the state of their health, that it is exercised in a place of internment and that it does not entail the abolition of any of the safeguards granted by the present Convention.

Internees who aid and abet an escape or attempt to escape, shall be liable on this count to disciplinary punishment only.

Article 121. Escape, or attempt to escape, even if it is a repeated offence, shall not be deemed an aggravating circumstance in cases where an internee is prosecuted for offences committed during his escape.

The Parties to the conflict shall ensure that the competent authorities exercise leniency in deciding whether punishment inflicted for an offence shall be of a disciplinary or judicial nature, especially in respect of acts committed in connection with an escape, whether successful or not.

Article 122. Acts which constitute offences against discipline shall be investigated immediately. This rule shall be applied, in particular, in cases of escape or attempt to escape. Recaptured internees shall be handed over to the competent authorities as soon as possible.

In cases of offences against discipline, confinement awaiting trial shall be reduced to an absolute minimum for all internees, and shall not exceed fourteen days. Its duration shall in any case be deducted from any sentence of confinement.

The provisions of Articles 124 and 125 shall apply to internees who are in confinement awaiting trial for offences against discipline.

Article 123. Without prejudice to the competence of courts and higher authorities, disciplinary punishment may be ordered only by the commandant of the place of internment, or by a responsible officer or official who replaces him, or to whom he has delegated his disciplinary powers.

Before any disciplinary punishment is awarded, the accused internee shall be given precise information regarding the offences of which he is accused, and given an opportunity of explaining his conduct and of defending himself. He shall be permitted, in particular, to call witnesses and to have recourse, if necessary, to the services of a qualified interpreter. The decision shall be announced in the presence of the accused and of a member of the Internee Committee.

The period elapsing between the time of award of a disciplinary punishment and its execution shall not exceed one month.

When an internee is awarded a further disciplinary punishment, a period of at least three days shall elapse between the execution of any two of the punishments, if the duration of one of these is ten days or more.

A record of disciplinary punishments shall be maintained by the commandant of the place of internment and shall be open to inspection by representatives of the Protecting Power.

Article 124. Internees shall not in any case be transferred to penitentiary establishments (prisons, penitentiaries, convict prisons, etc.) to undergo disciplinary punishment therein.

The premises in which disciplinary punishments are undergone shall conform to sanitary requirements: they shall in particular be provided with adequate bedding. Internees undergoing punishment shall be enabled to keep themselves in a state of cleanliness.

Women internees undergoing disciplinary punishment shall be confined in separate quarters from male internees and shall be under the immediate supervision of women.

Article 125. Internees awarded disciplinary punishment shall be allowed to exercise and to stay in the open air at least two hours daily.

They shall be allowed, if they so request, to be present at the daily medical inspections. They shall receive the attention which their state of health requires and, if necessary, shall be removed to the infirmary of the place of internment or to a hospital.

They shall have permission to read and write, likewise to send and receive letters. Parcels and remittances of money, however, may be withheld from them until the completion of their punishment; such consignments shall meanwhile be entrusted to the Internee Committee, who will hand over to the infirmary the perishable goods contained in the parcels.

No internee given a disciplinary punishment may be deprived of the benefit of the provisions of Articles 107 and 143 of the present Convention.

Article 126. The provisions of Articles 71 to 76 inclusive shall apply, by analogy, to proceedings against internees who are in the national territory of the Detaining Power.

Chapter X. Transfers of Internees

Article 127. The transfer of internees shall always be effected humanely. As a general rule, it shall be carried out by rail or other means of transport, and under conditions at least equal to those obtaining for the forces of the Detaining Power in their changes of station. If, as an exceptional measure, such removals have to be effected on foot, they may not take place unless the internees are in a fit state of health, and may not in any case expose them to excessive fatigue.

The Detaining Power shall supply internees during transfer with drinking water and food sufficient in quantity, quality and variety to maintain them in good health, and also with the necessary clothing, adequate shelter and the necessary medical attention. The Detaining Power shall take all suitable precautions to ensure their safety during transfer, and shall establish before their departure a complete list of all internees transferred.

Sick, wounded or infirm internees and maternity cases shall not be transferred if the journey would be seriously detrimental to them, unless their safety imperatively so demands.

If the combat zone draws close to a place of internment, the internees in the said place shall not be transferred unless their removal can be carried out in adequate conditions of safety, or unless they are exposed to greater risks by remaining on the spot than by being transferred.

When making decisions regarding the transfer of internees, the Detaining Power shall take their interests into account and, in particular, shall not do anything to increase the difficulties of repatriating them or returning them to their own homes.

Article 128. In the event of transfer, internees shall be officially advised of their departure and of their new postal address. Such notification shall be given in time for them to pack their luggage and inform their next of kin.

They shall be allowed to take with them their personal effects, and the correspondence and parcels which have arrived for them. The weight of such baggage may be limited if the conditions of transfer so require, but in no case to less than twenty-five kilograms per internee.

Mail and parcels addressed to their former place of internment shall be forwarded to them without delay.

The commandant of the place of internment shall take, in agreement with the Internee Committee, any measures needed to ensure the transport of the internees' community property and of the luggage the internees are unable to take with them in consequence of restrictions imposed by virtue of the second paragraph.

...

Chapter XIII. Release, Repatriation and Accommodation in Neutral Countries

Article 132. Each interned person shall be released by the Detaining Power as soon as the reasons which necessitated his internment no longer exist.

The Parties to the conflict shall, moreover, endeavour during the course of hostilities, to conclude agreements for the release, the repatriation, the return to places of residence or the accommodation in a neutral country of certain classes of internees, in particular children, pregnant women and mothers with infants and young children, wounded and sick, and internees who have been detained for a long time.

Article 133. Internment shall cease as soon as possible after the close of hostilities.

Internees in the territory of a Party to the conflict against whom penal proceedings are pending for offences not exclusively subject to disciplinary penalties, may be detained until the close of such proceedings and, if circumstances require, until the completion of the penalty. The same shall apply to internees who have been previously sentenced to a punishment depriving them of liberty.

By agreement between the Detaining Power and the Powers concerned, committees may be set up after the close of hostilities, or of the occupation of territories, to search for dispersed internees.

Article 134. The High Contracting Parties shall endeavour, upon the Repatriation close of hostilities or occupation, to ensure the return of all internees to their last place of residence, or to facilitate their residence repatriation.

Article 135. The Detaining Power shall bear the expense of returning released internees to the places where they were residing when interned, or, if it took them into custody while they were in transit or on the high seas, the cost of completing their journey or of their return to their point of departure.

Where a Detaining Power refuses permission to reside in its territory to a released internee who previously had his permanent domicile therein, such Detaining Power shall pay the cost of the said internee's repatriation. If, however, the internee elects to return to his country on his own responsibility or in obedience to the Government of the Power to which he owes allegiance, the Detaining Power need not pay the expenses of his journey beyond the point of his departure from its territory. The Detaining Power need not pay the cost of repatriation of an internee who was interned at his own request.

If internees are transferred in accordance with Article 45, the transferring and receiving Powers shall agree on the portion of the above costs to be borne by each.

The foregoing shall not prejudice such special agreements as may be concluded between Parties to the conflict concerning the exchange and repatriation of their nationals in enemy hands.

Section V. Information Bureaux and Central Agency

Article 136. Upon the outbreak of a conflict and in all cases of occupation, each of the Parties to the conflict shall establish an official Information Bureau responsible for receiving and transmitting information in respect of the protected persons who are in its power.

Each of the Parties to the conflict shall, within the shortest possible period, give its Bureau information of any measure taken by it concerning any protected persons who are kept in custody for more than two weeks, who are subjected to assigned residence or who are interned. It shall, furthermore, require its various departments concerned with such matters to provide the aforesaid Bureau promptly with information concerning all changes pertaining to these protected persons, as, for example, transfers, releases, repatriations, escapes, admittances to hospitals, births and deaths.

Article 137. Each national Bureau shall immediately forward information concerning protected persons by the most rapid means to the Powers in whose territory they resided, through the intermediary of the Protecting Powers and likewise through the Central Agency provided for in Article 140. The Bureaux shall also reply to all enquiries which may be received regarding protected persons.

Information Bureaux shall transmit information concerning a protected person unless its transmission might be detrimental to the person concerned or to his or her relatives. Even in such a case, the information may not be withheld from the Central Agency which, upon being notified of the circumstances, will take the necessary precautions indicated in Article 140.

All communications in writing made by any Bureau shall be authenticated by a signature or a seal.

Article 138. The information received by the national Bureau and transmitted by it shall be of such a character as to make it possible to identify the protected person exactly and to advise his next of kin quickly. The information in respect of each person shall include at least his surname, first names, place and date of birth, nationality last residence and distinguishing characteristics, the first name of the father and the maiden name of the mother, the date, place and nature of the action taken with regard to the individual, the address at which correspondence may be sent to him and the name and address of the person to be informed.

Likewise, information regarding the state of health of internees who are seriously ill or seriously wounded shall be supplied regularly and if possible every week.

Article 139. Each national Information Bureau shall, furthermore, be responsible for collecting all personal valuables left by protected persons mentioned in Article 136, in particular those who have been repatriated or released, or who have escaped or died; it shall forward the said valuables to those concerned, either direct, or, if necessary, through the Central Agency. Such articles shall be sent by the Bureau in sealed packets which shall be accompanied by statements giving clear and full identity particulars of the person to whom the articles belonged, and by a complete list of the contents of the parcel. Detailed records shall be maintained of the receipt and dispatch of all such valuables.

Article 140. A Central Information Agency for protected persons, in particular for internees, shall be created in a neutral country. The International Committee of the Red Cross shall, if it deems necessary, propose to the Powers concerned the organization of such an Agency, which may be the same as that provided for in Article 123 of the Geneva Convention relative to the Treatment of Prisoners of War of 12 August 1949.

The function of the Agency shall be to collect all information of the type set forth in Article 136 which it may obtain through official or private channels and to transmit it as rapidly as possible to the countries of origin or of residence of the persons concerned, except in cases where such transmissions might be detrimental to the persons whom the said information concerns, or to their relatives. It shall receive from the Parties to the conflict all reasonable facilities for effecting such transmissions.

The High Contracting Parties, and in particular those whose nationals benefit by the services of the Central Agency, are requested to give the said Agency the financial aid it may require.

The foregoing provisions shall in no way be interpreted as restricting the humanitarian activities of the International Committee of the Red Cross and of the relief Societies described in Article 142.

Article 141. The national Information Bureaux and the Central Information Agency shall enjoy free postage for all mail, likewise the exemptions provided for in Article 110, and further, so far as possible, exemption from telegraphic charges or, at least, greatly reduced rates.

Part IV. Execution of the Convention

Section I. General Provisions

Article 142. Subject to the measures which the Detaining Powers may consider essential to ensure their security or to meet any other reasonable need, the representatives of religious organizations, relief societies, or any other organizations assisting the protected persons, shall receive from these Powers, for themselves or their duly accredited agents, all facilities for visiting the protected persons, for distributing relief supplies and material from any source, intended for educational, recreational or religious purposes, or for assisting them in organizing their leisure time within the places of internment. Such societies or organizations may be constituted in the territory of the Detaining Power, or in any other country, or they may have an international character.

The Detaining Power may limit the number of societies and organizations whose delegates are allowed to carry out their activities in its territory and under its supervision, on condition, however, that such limitation shall not hinder the supply of effective and adequate relief to all protected persons.

The special position of the International Committee of the Red Cross in this field shall be recognized and respected at all times.

Article 143. Representatives or delegates of the Protecting Powers shall have permission to go to all places where protected persons are, particularly to places of internment, detention and work.

They shall have access to all premises occupied by protected persons and shall be able to interview the latter without witnesses, personally or through an interpreter.

Such visits may not be prohibited except for reasons of imperative military necessity, and then only as an exceptional and temporary measure. Their duration and frequency shall not be restricted.

Such representatives and delegates shall have full liberty to select the places they wish to visit. The Detaining or Occupying Power, the Protecting Power and when occasion arises the Power of origin of the persons to be visited, may agree that compatriots of the internees shall be permitted to participate in the visits.

The delegates of the International Committee of the Red Cross shall also enjoy the above prerogatives. The appointment of such delegates shall be submitted to the approval of the Power governing the territories where they will carry out their duties.

Article 144. The High Contracting Parties undertake, in time of peace as in time of war, to disseminate the text of the present Convention as widely as possible in their respective countries, and, in particular, to include the study thereof in their programmes of military and, if possible, civil instruction, so that the principles thereof may become known to the entire population.

Any civilian, military, police or other authorities, who in time of war assume responsibilities in respect of protected persons, must possess the text of the Convention and be specially instructed as to its provisions.

. . .

Article 146. The High Contracting Parties undertake to enact any legislation necessary to provide effective penal sanctions for persons committing, or ordering to be committed, any of the grave breaches of the present Convention defined in the following Article.

Each High Contracting Party shall be under the obligation to search for persons alleged to have committed, or to have ordered to be committed, such grave breaches, and shall bring such persons, regardless of their nationality, before its own courts. It may also, if it prefers, and in accordance with the provisions of its own legislation, hand such persons over for trial to another High Contracting Party concerned, provided such High Contracting Party has made out a prima facie case.

Each High Contracting Party shall take measures necessary for the suppression of all acts contrary to the provisions of the present Convention other than the grave breaches defined in the following Article.

In all circumstances, the accused persons shall benefit by safeguards of proper trial and defence, which shall not be less favourable than those provided by Article 105 and those following of the Geneva Convention relative to the Treatment of Prisoners of War of 12 August 1949.

Article 147. Grave breaches to which the preceding Article relates shall be those involving any of the following acts, if committed against persons or property protected by the present Convention: wilful killing, torture or inhuman treatment, including biological experiments, wilfully causing great suffering or serious injury to body or health, unlawful deportation or transfer or unlawful confinement of a protected person, compelling a protected person to serve in the forces of a hostile Power, or wilfully depriving a protected person of the rights of fair and regular trial prescribed in the present Convention, taking of hostages and extensive destruction and appropriation of property, not justified by military necessity and carried out unlawfully and wantonly.

Article 148. No High Contracting Party shall be allowed to absolve itself or any other High Contracting Party of any liability incurred by itself or by another High Contracting Party in respect of breaches referred to in the preceding Article.

Article 149. At the request of a Party to the conflict, an enquiry shall be instituted, in a manner to be decided between the interested Parties, concerning any alleged violation of the Convention.

If agreement has not been reached concerning the procedure for the enquiry, the Parties should agree on the choice of an umpire who will decide upon the procedure to be followed.

Once the violation has been established, the Parties to the conflict shall put an end to it and shall repress it with the least possible delay.

Section II. Final Provisions

. . .

Article 154. In the relations between the Powers who are bound by the Hague Conventions respecting the Laws and Customs of War on Land, whether that of 29 July 1899, or that of 18 October 1907, and who are parties to the present Convention, this last Convention shall be supplementary to Sections II and III of the Regulations annexed to the above-mentioned Conventions of The Hague.

Article 158. Each of the High Contracting Parties shall be at liberty to denounce the present Convention.

The denunciation shall be notified in writing to the Swiss Federal Council, which shall transmit it to the Governments of all the High Contracting Parties.

The denunciation shall take effect one year after the notification thereof has been made to the Swiss Federal Council. However, a denunciation of which notification has been made at a time when the denouncing

Power is involved in a conflict shall not take effect until peace has been concluded, and until after operations connected with release, repatriation and re-establishment of the persons protected by the present Convention have been terminated.

The denunciation shall have effect only in respect of the denouncing Power. It shall in no way impair the obligations which the Parties to the conflict shall remain bound to fulfil by virtue of the principles of the law of nations, as they result from the usages established among civilized peoples, from the laws of humanity and the dictates of the public conscience.

...

DOCUMENT 73

Full Official Title: Protocol Additional to the Geneva Conventions of 12 August 1949, and relating to the Protection of Victims of International Armed Conflicts

Short Title/Acronym/Abbreviation: Protocol I

Subject: Establishing and expanding international humanitarian law norms applicable to armed conflicts under the Geneva Conventions of 1949

Official Citation: 1125 U.N.T.S. no. 17512

Date of Document: Not applicable

Date of Adoption: June 8, 1977

Date of General Entry into Force (EIF): Dec. 7, 1978

Number of States Parties to this Treaty as of this printing: 170

Date of Signature by United States: December 12, 1977

Date of United States Ratification/Accession/Adhesion: Not yet ratified by United States

Date of Entry into Force (effective date) as to United States: Not applicable

Type of Document: An international legal instrument, a treaty, which is known by the title "protocol." A protocol is a treaty which amends (modifies or adds to) a prior treaty or set of treaties, here the Geneva Conventions of 1949.

Legal Status/Character of the Instrument/Document as to the United States: Not legally binding upon the United States as a matter of treaty law, but arguably binding, at least as to some of its norms, as a matter of customary international law. This has been officially recognized by the United States.

Comments: The Geneva Conventions of 1949 and its two amending Protocols of 1977 form the main part of International Humanitarian Law, the international law applicable to armed conflict. The United States has not ratified the two Protocols. Because the United States has ratified the four Geneva Conventions of 1949 all U.S. military and civilians are subject to these rules today. Arguably, however, the U.S. military and their civilian commanders/superiors are also bound by certain provisions of this Protocol and so it can be used to judge U.S. military action in conflicts coming under this Protocol.

The International Committee of the Red Cross (ICRC) is an international organization whose history and principle work has been about the establishment of international legal standards limiting the effects of armed conflicts, international and otherwise, and monitoring compliance with these standards. It was the body responsible for the creation of the Geneva Conventions and Protocols and was largely responsible for the development of all humanitarian law since the late 1860s, when it was founded, along with the first Geneva Convention. It monitors compliance with the terms of this Protocol.

One of the major modern phenomena of armed conflict covered by this Protocol is the advent of guerilla wars, such as Vietnam. This 1977 Protocol reflects the need to create legal standards applicable in such conflicts, especially as to protection of civilians, the most frequent victims, from the effects of such hostilities.

Of particular importance are the rules regarding armed attacks against civilians, and when an attack becomes illegal when the damage to civilian persons and objects from an armed attack becomes too great ("disproportionate") in comparison to the military benefit to be achieved. (See Article 48–51). Article 36 on the legality of "new weapons" is also important as to the implications of weapons of mass destruction and other new weapons systems.

Caution: The status and applicability of this instrument as to the United States may have changed since date of publication. The above information may be updated by referring to the following site:

Web address: http://www.icrc.org/ihl.nsf/7c4d08d9b287a42141256739003e636b/f6c8b9fee14a77fdc125 641e0052b079?OpenDocument

1977 PROTOCOL I TO THE GENEVA CONVENTIONS (EXCERPTS)

Preamble

The High Contracting Parties,

Proclaiming their earnest wish to see peace prevail among peoples,

Recalling that every State has the duty, in conformity with the Charter of the United Nations, to refrain in its international relations from the threat or use of force against the sovereignty, territorial integrity or political independence of any State, or in any other manner inconsistent with the purposes of the United Nations,

Believing it necessary nevertheless to reaffirm and develop the provisions protecting the victims of armed conflicts and to supplement measures intended to reinforce their application,

Expressing their conviction that nothing in this Protocol or in the Geneva Conventions of 12 August 1949 can be construed as legitimizing or authorizing any act of aggression or any other use of force inconsistent with the Charter of the United Nations,

Reaffirming further that the provisions of the Geneva Conventions of 12 August 1949 and of this Protocol must be fully applied in all circumstances to all persons who are protected by those instruments, without any adverse distinction based on the nature or origin of the armed conflict or on the causes espoused by or attributed to the Parties to the conflict,

Have agreed on the following:

Part I. General Provisions

Article 1. General principles and scope of application

1. The High Contracting Parties undertake to respect and to ensure respect for this Protocol in all circumstances.

2. In cases not covered by this Protocol or by other international agreements, civilians and combatants remain under the protection and authority of the principles of international law derived from established custom, from the principles of humanity and from dictates of public conscience.

3. This Protocol, which supplements the Geneva Conventions of 12 August 1949 for the protection of war victims, shall apply in the situations referred to in Article 2 common to those Conventions.

4. The situations referred to in the preceding paragraph include armed conflicts which peoples are fighting against colonial domination and alien occupation and against racist regimes in the exercise of their right of self-determination, as enshrined in the Charter of the United Nations and the Declaration on Principles of International Law concerning Friendly Relations and Co-operation among States in accordance with the Charter of the United Nations.

Article 2. Definitions

For the purposes of this Protocol

(a) "First Convention," "Second Convention," "Third Convention" and "Fourth Convention" mean, respectively, the Geneva Convention for the Amelioration of the Condition of the Wounded and Sick in Armed Forces in the Field of 12 August 1949; the Geneva Convention for the Amelioration of the Condition of Wounded, Sick and Ship-wrecked Members of Armed Forces at Sea of 12 August 1949; the Geneva Convention relative to the Treatment of Prisoners of War of 12 August 1949; the Geneva Convention relative to the Protection of Civilian Persons in Time of War of 12 August 1949; "the Conventions" means the four Geneva Conventions of 12 August 1949 for the protection of war victims;

(b) "Rules of international law applicable in armed conflict" means the rules applicable in armed conflict set forth in international agreements to which the Parties to the conflict are Parties and the generally recognized principles and rules of international law which are applicable to armed conflict;

(c) "Protecting Power" means a neutral or other State not a Party to the conflict which has been designated by a Party to the conflict and accepted by the adverse Party and has agreed to carry out the functions assigned to a Protecting Power under the Conventions and this Protocol;

(d) "Substitute" means an organization acting in place of a Protecting Power in accordance with Article 5.

Article 3. Beginning and end of application

Without prejudice to the provisions which are applicable at all times:

(a) the Conventions and this Protocol shall apply from the beginning of any situation referred to in Article 1 of this Protocol.

(b) the application of the Conventions and of this Protocol shall cease, in the territory of Parties to the conflict, on the general close of military operations and, in the case of occupied territories, on the termination of the occupation, except, in either circumstance, for those persons whose final release, repatriation or re-establishment takes place thereafter. These persons shall continue to benefit from the relevant provisions of the Conventions and of this Protocol until their final release repatriation or re-establishment.

Article 4. Legal status of the Parties to the conflict

The application of the Conventions and of this Protocol, as well as the conclusion of the agreements provided for therein, shall not affect the legal status of the Parties to the conflict. Neither the occupation of a territory nor the application of the Conventions and this Protocol shall affect the legal status of the territory in question.

Article 5. Appointment of Protecting Powers and of their substitute

1. It is the duty of the Parties to a conflict from the beginning of that conflict to secure the supervision and implementation of the Conventions and of this Protocol by the application of the system of Protecting Powers, including inter alia the designation and acceptance of those Powers, in accordance with the following paragraphs. Protecting Powers shall have the duty of safeguarding the interests of the Parties to the conflict.

2. From the beginning of a situation referred to in Article 1, each Party to the conflict shall without delay designate a Protecting Power for the purpose of applying the Conventions and this Protocol and shall, likewise without delay and for the same purpose, permit the activities or a Protecting Power which has been accepted by it as such after designation by the adverse Party.

3. If a Protecting Power has not been designated or accepted from the beginning of a situation referred to in Article 1, the International Committee of the Red Cross, without prejudice to the right of any other impartial humanitarian organization to do likewise, shall offer its good offices to the Parties to the conflict with a view to the designation without delay of a Protecting Power to which the Parties to the conflict consent. For that purpose it may inter alia ask each Party to provide it with a list of at least five States which that Party considers acceptable to act as Protecting Power on its behalf in relation to an adverse Party and ask each adverse Party to provide a list or at least five States which it would accept as the Protecting Power of the first Party; these lists shall be communicated to the Committee within two weeks after the receipt or the request; it shall compare them and seek the agreement of any proposed State named on both lists.

4. If, despite the foregoing, there is no Protecting Power, the Parties to the conflict shall accept without delay an offer which may be made by the International Committee of the Red Cross or by any other organization which offers all guarantees of impartiality and efficacy, after due consultations with the said Parties and taking into account the result of these consultations, to act as a substitute. The functioning of such a substitute is subject to the consent of the Parties to the conflict; every effort shall be made by the Parties to the conflict to facilitate the operations of the substitute in the performance of its tasks under the Conventions and this Protocol.

5. In accordance with Article 4, the designation and acceptance of Protecting Powers for the purpose of applying the Conventions and this Protocol shall not affect the legal status of the Parties to the conflict or of any territory, including occupied territory.

6. The maintenance of diplomatic relations between Parties to the conflict or the entrusting of the protection of a Party's interests and those of its nationals to a third State in accordance with the rules of international law relating to diplomatic relations is no obstacle to the designation of Protecting Powers for the purpose of applying the Conventions and this Protocol.

7. Any subsequent mention in this Protocol of a Protecting Power includes also a substitute.

. . .

Part II. Wounded, Sick and Shipwrecked
Section I: General Protection
Article 8. Terminology

For the purposes of this Protocol:

(1) "Wounded" and "sick" mean persons, whether military or civilian, who, because of trauma, disease or other physical or mental disorder or disability, are in need of medical assistance or care and who refrain from any act of hostility. These terms also cover maternity cases, new-born babies and other persons who may be in need of immediate medical assistance or care, such as the infirm or expectant mothers, and who refrain from any act of hostility;

(2) "Shipwrecked" means persons, whether military or civilian, who are in peril at sea or in other waters as a result of misfortune affecting them or the vessel or aircraft carrying them and who refrain from any act of hostility. These persons, provided that they continue to refrain from any act of hostility, shall continue to

be considered shipwrecked during their rescue until they acquire another status under the Conventions or this Protocol;

(3) "Medical personnel" means those persons assigned, by a Party to the conflict, exclusively to the medical purposes enumerated under (5) or to the administration of medical units or to the operation or administration of medical transports. Such assignments may be either permanent or temporary. The term includes:

(a) medical personnel of a Party to the conflict, whether military or civilian, including those described in the First and Second Conventions, and those assigned to civil defence organizations;

(b) medical personnel of national Red Cross (Red Crescent, Red Lion and Sun) Societies and other national voluntary aid societies duly recognized and authorized by a Party to the conflict;

(c) medical personnel or medical units or medical transports described in Article 9, paragraph 2.

(4) "Religious personnel" means military or civilian persons, such as chaplains, who are exclusively engaged in the work of their ministry and attached:

(a) to the armed forces of a Party to the conflict;

(b) to medical units or medical transports of a Party to the conflict;

(c) to medical units or medical transports described in Article 9, Paragraph 2; or

(d) to civil defence organizations of a Party to the conflict.

The attachment of religious personnel may be either permanent or temporary, and the relevant provisions mentioned under (11) apply to them;

(5) "Medical units" means establishments and other units, whether military or civilian, organized for medical purposes, namely the search for, collection, transportation, diagnosis or treatment—including first-aid treatment—of the wounded, sick and shipwrecked, or for the prevention of disease. The term includes for example, hospitals and other similar units, blood transfusion centres, preventive medicine centres and institutes, medical depots and the medical and pharmaceutical stores of such units. Medical units may be fixed or mobile, permanent or temporary;

(6) "Medical transportation" means the conveyance by land, water or air of the wounded, sick, shipwrecked, medical personnel, religious personnel, medical equipment or medical supplies protected by the Conventions and by this Protocol;

(7) "Medical transports" means any means of transportation, whether military or civilian, permanent or temporary, assigned exclusively to medical transportation and under the control of a competent authority of a Party to the conflict;

(8) "Medical vehicles" means any medical transports by land;

(9) "Medical ships and craft" means any medical transports by water;

(10) "Medical aircraft" means any medical transports by air;

(11) "Permanent medical personnel," "permanent medical units" and "permanent medical transports" mean those assigned exclusively to medical purposes for an indeterminate period. "Temporary medical personnel" "temporary medical-units" and "temporary medical transports" mean those devoted exclusively to medical purposes for limited periods during the whole of such periods. Unless otherwise specified, the terms "medical personnel," "medical units" and "medical transports" cover both permanent and temporary categories;

(12) "Distinctive emblem" means the distinctive emblem of the red cross, red crescent or red lion and sun on a white ground when used for the protection of medical units and transports, or medical and religious personnel, equipment or supplies;

(13) "Distinctive signal" means any signal or message specified for the identification exclusively of medical units or transports in Chapter III of Annex I to this Protocol.

Article 9. Field of application

1. This Part, the provisions of which are intended to ameliorate the condition of the wounded, sick and shipwrecked, shall apply to all those affected by a situation referred to in Article 1, without any adverse distinction founded on race, colour, sex, language, religion or belief political or other opinion, national or social origin, wealth, birth or other status, or on any other similar criteria.

2. The relevant provisions of Articles 27 and 32 of the First Convention shall apply to permanent medical units and transports (other than hospital ships, to which Article 25 of the Second Convention applies) and their personnel made available to a Party to the conflict for humanitarian purposes:

(a) by a neutral or other State which is not a Party to that conflict;

(b) by a recognized and authorized aid society of such a State;

(c) by an impartial international humanitarian organization.

Article 10. Protection and care

1. All the wounded, sick and shipwrecked, to whichever Party they belong, shall be respected and protected.

2. In all circumstances they shall be treated humanely and shall receive, to the fullest extent practicable and with the least possible delay, the medical care and attention required by their condition. There shall be no distinction among them founded on any grounds other than medical ones.

Article 11. Protection of persons

1. The physical or mental health and integrity of persons who are in the power of the adverse Party or who are interned, detained or otherwise deprived of liberty as a result of a situation referred to in Article 1 shall not be endangered by any unjustified act or omission. Accordingly, it is prohibited to subject the persons described in this Article to any medical procedure which is not indicated by the state of health of the person concerned and which is not consistent with generally accepted medical standards which would be applied under similar medical circumstances to persons who are nationals of the Party conducting the procedure and who are in no way deprived of liberty.

2. It is, in particular, prohibited to carry out on such persons, even with their consent:

(a) physical mutilations;

(b) medical or scientific experiments;

(c) removal of tissue or organs for transplantation, except where these acts are justified in conformity with the conditions provided for in paragraph 1.

3. Exceptions to the prohibition in paragraph 2 (c) may be made only in the case of donations of blood for transfusion or of skin for grafting, provided that they are given voluntarily and without any coercion or inducement, and then only for therapeutic purposes, under conditions consistent with generally accepted medical standards and controls designed for the benefit of both the donor and the recipient.

4. Any wilfull act or omission which seriously endangers the physical or mental health or integrity of any person who is in the power of a Party other than the one on which he depends and which either violates any of the prohibitions in paragraphs 1 and 2 or fails to comply with the requirements of paragraph 3 shall be a grave breach of this Protocol.

5. The persons described in paragraph 1 have the right to refuse any surgical operation. In case of refusal, medical personnel shall endeavour to obtain a written statement to that effect, signed or acknowledged by the patient.

6. Each Party to the conflict shall keep a medical record for every donation of blood for transfusion or skin for grafting by persons referred to in paragraph 1, if that donation is made under the responsibility of that Party. In addition, each Party to the conflict shall endeavour to keep a record of all medical procedures undertaken with respect to any person who is interned, detained or otherwise deprived of liberty as a result of a situation referred to in Article 1. These records shall be available at all times for inspection by the Protecting Power.

Article 12. Protection of medical units

1. Medical units shall be respected and protected at all times and shall not be the object of attack.

2. Paragraph 1 shall apply to civilian medical units, provided that they:

(a) belong to one of the Parties to the conflict;

(b) are recognized and authorized by the competent authority of one of the Parties to the conflict; or

(c) are authorized in conformity with Article 9, paragraph 2, of this Protocol or Article 27 of the First Convention.

3. The Parties to the conflict are invited to notify each other of the location of their fixed medical units. The absence of such notification shall not exempt any of the Parties from the obligation to comply with the provisions of paragraph 1.

4. Under no circumstances shall medical units be used in an attempt to shield military objectives from attack. Whenever possible, the Parties to the conflict shall ensure that medical units are so sited that attacks against military objectives do not imperil their safety.

Article 13. Discontinuance of protection of civilian medical units

1. The protection to which civilian medical units are entitled shall not cease unless they are used to commit, outside their humanitarian function, acts harmful to the enemy. Protection may, however, cease only

after a warning has been given setting, whenever appropriate, a reasonable time-limit, and after such warning has remained unheeded.

2. The following shall not be considered as acts harmful to the enemy:

(a) that the personnel of the unit are equipped with light individual weapons for their own defence or for that of the wounded and sick in their charge;

(b) that the unit is guarded by a picket or by sentries or by an escort;

(c) that small arms and ammunition taken from the wounded and sick, and not yet handed to the proper service, are found in the units;

(d) that members of the armed forces or other combatants are in the unit for medical reasons.

Article 14. Limitations on requisition of civilian medical units

1. The Occupying Power has the duty to ensure that the medical needs of the civilian population in occupied territory continue to be satisfied.

2. The Occupying Power shall not, therefore, requisition civilian medical units, their equipment, their materiel or the services of their personnel, so long as these resources are necessary for the provision of adequate medical services for the civilian population and for the continuing medical care of any wounded and sick already under treatment.

. . .

Article 15. Protection of civilian medical and religious personnel

1. Civilian medical personnel shall be respected and protected.

2. If needed, all available help shall be afforded to civilian medical personnel in an area where civilian medical services are disrupted by reason of combat activity.

3. The Occupying Power shall afford civilian medical personnel in occupied territories every assistance to enable them to perform, to the best of their ability, their humanitarian functions. The Occupying Power may not require that, in the performance of those functions, such personnel shall give priority to the treatment of any person except on medical grounds. They shall not be compelled to carry out tasks which are not compatible with their humanitarian mission.

4. Civilian medical personnel shall have access to any place where their services are essential, subject to such supervisory and safety measures as the relevant Party to the conflict may deem necessary.

5. Civilian religious personnel shall be respected and protected. The provisions of the Conventions and of this Protocol concerning the protection and identification of medical personnel shall apply equally to such persons.

Article 16. General protection of medical duties

1. Under no circumstances shall any person be punished for carrying out medical activities compatible with medical ethics, regardless of the person benefiting therefrom.

2. Persons engaged in medical activities shall not be compelled to perform acts or to carry out work contrary to the rules of medical ethics or to other medical rules designed for the benefit of the wounded and sick or to the provisions of the Conventions or of this Protocol, or to refrain from performing acts or from carrying out work required by those rules and provisions.

3. No person engaged in medical activities shall be compelled to give to anyone belonging either to an adverse Party, or to his own Party except as required by the law of the latter Party, any information concerning the wounded and sick who are, or who have been, under his care, if such information would, in his opinion, prove harmful to the patients concerned or to their families. Regulations for the compulsory notification of communicable diseases shall, however, be respected.

Article 17. Role of the civilian population and of aid societies

1. The civilian population shall respect the wounded, sick and shipwrecked, even if they belong to the adverse Party, and shall commit no act of violence against them. The civilian population and aid societies, such as national Red Cross (Red Crescent, Red Lion and Sun) Societies, shall be permitted, even on their own initiative, to collect and care for the wounded, sick and shipwrecked, even in invaded or occupied areas. No one shall be harmed, prosecuted, convicted or punished for such humanitarian acts.

2. The Parties to the conflict may appeal to the civilian population and the aid societies referred to in paragraph 1 to collect and care for the wounded, sick and shipwrecked, and to search for the dead and report their location; they shall grant both protection and the necessary facilities to those who respond to this appeal. If the adverse Party gains or regains control of the area, that Party also shall afford the same protection and facilities for as long as they are needed.

Article 18. Identification

1. Each Party to the conflict shall endeavour to ensure that medical and religious personnel and medical units and transports are identifiable.

2. Each Party to the conflict shall also endeavour to adopt and to implement methods and procedures which will make it possible to recognize medical units and transports which use the distinctive emblem and distinctive signals.

3. In occupied territory and in areas where fighting is taking place or is likely to take place, civilian medical personnel and civilian religious personnel should be recognizable by the distinctive emblem and an identity card certifying their status.

. . .

8. The provisions of the Conventions and of this Protocol relating to supervision of the use of the distinctive emblem and to the prevention and repression of any misuse thereof shall be applicable to distinctive signals.

Article 19. Neutral and other States not Parties to the conflict

Neutral and other States not Parties to the conflict shall apply the relevant provisions of this Protocol to persons protected by this Part who may be received or interned within their territory, and to any dead of the Parties to that conflict whom they may find.

Article 20. Prohibition of reprisals

Reprisals against the persons and objects protected by this Part are prohibited.

Section II. Medical Transportation

Article 21. Medical vehicles

Medical vehicles shall be respected and protected in the same way as mobile medical units under the Conventions and this Protocol.

. . .

Article 23. Other medical ships and craft

1. Medical ships and craft other than those referred to in Article 22 of this Protocol and Article 38 of the Second Convention shall, whether at sea or in other waters, be respected and protected in the same way as mobile medical units under the Conventions and this Protocol. Since this protection can only be effective if they can be identified and recognized as medical ships or craft, such vessels should be marked with the distinctive emblem and as far as possible comply with the second paragraph of Article 43 of the Second Convention.

2. The ships and craft referred to in paragraph 1 shall remain subject to the laws of war. Any warship on the surface able immediately to enforce its command may order them to stop, order them off, or make them take a certain course, and they shall obey every such command. Such ships and craft may not in any other way be diverted from their medical mission so long as they are needed for the wounded, sick and shipwrecked on board.

Article 24. Protection of medical Aircraft

Medical aircraft shall be respected and protected, subject to the provisions of this Part.

. . .

Article 27. Medical aircraft in areas controlled by an adverse Party

1. The medical aircraft of a Party to the conflict shall continue to be protected while flying over land or sea areas physically controlled by an adverse Party, provided that prior agreement to such flights has been obtained from the competent authority of that adverse Party.

2. A medical aircraft which flies over an area physically controlled by an adverse Party without, or in deviation from the terms of, an agreement provided for in paragraph 1, either through navigational error or because of an emergency affecting the safety of the flight, shall make every effort to identify itself and to inform the adverse Party of the circumstances. As soon as such medical aircraft has been recognized by the adverse Party, that Party shall make all reasonable efforts to give the order to land or to alight on water, referred to in Article 30, paragraph 1, or to take other measures to safeguard its own interests, and, in either case, to allow the aircraft time for compliance, before resorting to an attack against the aircraft.

Article 28. Restrictions on operations of medical aircraft

1. The Parties to the conflict are prohibited from using their medical aircraft to attempt to acquire any military advantage over an adverse Party. The presence of medical aircraft shall not be used in an attempt to render military objectives immune from attack.

2. Medical aircraft shall not be used to collect or transmit intelligence data and shall not carry any equipment intended for such purposes. They are prohibited from carrying any persons or cargo not included within the definition in Article 8 (6). The carrying on board of the personal effects of the occupants or of equipment intended solely to facilitate navigation, communication or identification shall not be considered as prohibited,

3. Medical aircraft shall not carry any armament except small arms and ammunition taken from the wounded, sick and shipwrecked on board and not yet handed to the proper service, and such light individual weapons as may be necessary to enable the medical personnel on board to defend themselves and the wounded, sick and shipwrecked in their charge.

4. While carrying out the flights referred to in Articles 26 and 27, medical aircraft shall not, except by prior agreement with the adverse Party, be used to search for the wounded, sick and shipwrecked.

. . .

Article 30. Landing and inspection of medical aircraft

1. Medical aircraft flying over areas which are physically controlled by an adverse Party, or over areas the physical control of which is not clearly established, may be ordered to land or to alight on water, as appropriate, to permit inspection in accordance with the following paragraphs. Medical aircraft shall obey any such order.

Article 31. Neutral or other States not Parties to the conflict

1. Except by prior agreement, medical aircraft shall not fly over or land in the territory of a neutral or other State not a Party to the conflict. However, with such an agreement, they shall be respected throughout their flight and also for the duration of any calls in the territory. Nevertheless they shall obey any summons to land or to alight on water, as appropriate.

. . .

Section III Missing and Dead Persons
Article 32. General principle

In the implementation of this Section, the activities of the High Contracting Parties, of the Parties to the conflict and of the international humanitarian organizations mentioned in the Conventions and in this Protocol shall be prompted mainly by the right of families to know the fate of their relatives.

Article 33. Missing persons

1. As soon as circumstances permit, and at the latest from the end of active hostilities, each Party to the conflict shall search for the persons who have been reported missing by an adverse Party. Such adverse Party shall transmit all relevant information concerning such persons in order to facilitate such searches.

2. In order to facilitate the gathering of information pursuant to the preceding paragraph, each Party to the conflict shall, with respect to persons who would not receive more favourable consideration under the Conventions and this Protocol:

(a) record the information specified in Article 138 of the Fourth Convention in respect of such persons who have been detained, imprisoned or otherwise held in captivity for more than two weeks as a result of hostilities or occupation, or who have died during any period of detention;

(b) to the fullest extent possible, facilitate and, if need be, carry out the search for and the recording of information concerning such persons if they have died in other circumstances as a result of hostilities or occupation.

3. Information concerning persons reported missing pursuant to paragraph 1 and requests for such information shall be transmitted either directly or through the Protecting Power or the Central Tracing Agency of the International Committee of the Red Cross or national Red Cross (Red Crescent, Red Lion and Sun) Societies. Where the information is not transmitted through the International Committee of the Red Cross and its Central Tracing Agency, each Party to the conflict shall ensure that such information is also supplied to the Central Tracing Agency.

4. The Parties to the conflict shall endeavour to agree on arrangements for teams to search for, identify and recover the dead from battlefield areas, including arrangements, if appropriate, for such teams to be accompanied by personnel of the adverse Party while carrying out these missions in areas controlled by the adverse Party. Personnel of such teams shall be respected and protected while exclusively carrying out these duties.

Article 34. Remains of deceased

1. The remains of persons who have died for reasons related to occupation or in detention resulting from occupation or hostilities and those or persons not nationals of the country in which they have died as a result

of hostilities shall be respected, and the grave sites of all such persons shall be respected, maintained and marked as provided for in Article 130 of the Fourth Convention, where their remains or grave sites would not receive more favourable consideration under the Conventions and this Protocol.

. . .

Part III. Methods and Means of Warfare Combatant and Prisoners-Of-War
Section I. Methods and Means of Warfare
Article 35. Basic rules

1. In any armed conflict, the right of the Parties to the conflict to choose methods or means of warfare is not unlimited.

2. It is prohibited to employ weapons, projectiles and material and methods of warfare of a nature to cause superfluous injury or unnecessary suffering.

3. It is prohibited to employ methods or means of warfare which are intended, or may be expected, to cause widespread, long-term and severe damage to the natural environment.

Article 36. New weapons

In the study, development, acquisition or adoption of a new weapon, means or method of warfare, a High Contracting Party is under an obligation to determine whether its employment would, in some or all circumstances, be prohibited by this Protocol or by any other rule of international law applicable to the High Contracting Party.

Article 37. Prohibition of Perfidy

1. It is prohibited to kill, injure or capture an adversary by resort to perfidy. Acts inviting the confidence of an adversary to lead him to believe that he is entitled to, or is obliged to accord, protection under the rules of international law applicable in armed conflict, with intent to betray that confidence, shall constitute perfidy. The following acts are examples of perfidy:

(a) the feigning of an intent to negotiate under a flag of truce or of a surrender;

(b) the feigning of an incapacitation by wounds or sickness;

(c) the feigning of civilian, non-combatant status; and

(d) the feigning of protected status by the use of signs, emblems or uniforms of the United Nations or of neutral or other States not Parties to the conflict.

2. Ruses of war are not prohibited. Such ruses are acts which are intended to mislead an adversary or to induce him to act recklessly but which infringe no rule of international law applicable in armed conflict and which are not perfidious because they do not invite the confidence of an adversary with respect to protection under that law. The following are examples of such ruses: the use of camouflage, decoys, mock operations and misinformation.

Article 38. Recognized emblems

1. It is prohibited to make improper use of the distinctive emblem of the red cross, red crescent or red lion and sun or of other emblems, signs or signals provided for by the Conventions or by this Protocol. It is also prohibited to misuse deliberately in an armed conflict other internationally recognized protective emblems, signs or signals, including the flag of truce, and the protective emblem of cultural property.

2. It is prohibited to make use of the distinctive emblem of the United Nations, except as authorized by that Organization.

Article 39. Emblems of nationality

1. It is prohibited to make use in an armed conflict of the flags or military emblems, insignia or uniforms of neutral or other States not Parties to the conflict.

2. It is prohibited to make use of the flags or military emblems, insignia or uniforms of adverse Parties while engaging in attacks or in order to shield, favour, protect or impede military operations.

3. Nothing in this Article or in Article 37, paragraph 1 (d), shall affect the existing generally recognized rules of international law applicable to espionage or to the use of flags in the conduct of armed conflict at sea.

Article 40. Quarter

It is prohibited to order that there shall be no survivors, to threaten an adversary therewith or to conduct hostilities on this basis.

Article 41. Safeguard of an enemy hors de combat

1. A person who is recognized or who, in the circumstances should be recognized to be hors de combat shall not be made the object of attack.

2. A person is hors de combat if:

(a) he is in the power of an adverse Party;

(b) he clearly expresses an intention to surrender; or

(c) he has been rendered unconscious or is otherwise incapacitated by wounds or sickness, and therefore is incapable of defending himself; provided that in any of these cases he abstains from any hostile act and does not attempt to escape.

3. When persons entitled to protection as prisoners of war have fallen into the power or an adverse Party under unusual conditions of combat which prevent their evacuation as provided for in Part III, Section I, of the Third Convention, they shall be released and all feasible precautions shall be taken to ensure their safety.

Article 42. Occupants of aircraft

1. No person parachuting from an aircraft in distress shall be made the object of attack during his descent.

2. Upon reaching the ground in territory controlled by an adverse Party, a person who has parachuted from an aircraft in distress shall be given an opportunity to surrender before being made the object of attack, unless it is apparent that he is engaging in a hostile act.

3. Airborne troops are not protected by this Article.

Section II. Combatants and Prisoners of War

Article 43. Armed forces

1. The armed forces of a Party to a conflict consist of all organized armed forces, groups and units which are under a command responsible to that Party for the conduct or its subordinates, even if that Party is represented by a government or an authority not recognized by an adverse Party. Such armed forces shall be subject to an internal disciplinary system which, inter alia, shall enforce compliance with the rules of international law applicable in armed conflict.

2. Members of the armed forces of a Party to a conflict (other than medical personnel and chaplains covered by Article 33 of the Third Convention) are combatants, that is to say, they have the right to participate directly in hostilities.

3. Whenever a Party to a conflict incorporates a paramilitary or armed law enforcement agency into its armed forces it shall so notify the other Parties to the conflict.

Article 44. Combatants and prisoners of war

1. Any combatant, as defined in Article 43, who falls into the power of an adverse Party shall be a prisoner of war.

2. While all combatants are obliged to comply with the rules of international law applicable in armed conflict, violations of these rules shall not deprive a combatant of his right to be a combatant or, if he falls into the power of an adverse Party, of his right to be a prisoner of war, except as provided in paragraphs 3 and 4.

3. In order to promote the protection of the civilian population from the effects of hostilities, combatants are obliged to distinguish themselves from the civilian population while they are engaged in an attack or in a military operation preparatory to an attack. Recognizing, however, that there are situations in armed conflicts where, owing to the nature of the hostilities an armed combatant cannot so distinguish himself, he shall retain his status as a combatant, provided that, in such situations, he carries his arms openly:

(a) during each military engagement, and

(b) during such time as he is visible to the adversary while he is engaged in a military deployment preceding the launching of an attack in which he is to participate.

Acts which comply with the requirements of this paragraph shall not be considered as perfidious within the meaning of Article 37, paragraph 1 (c).

4. A combatant who falls into the power of an adverse Party while failing to meet the requirements set forth in the second sentence of paragraph 3 shall forfeit his right to be a prisoner of war, but he shall, nevertheless, be given protections equivalent in all respects to those accorded to prisoners of war by the Third Convention and by this Protocol. This protection includes protections equivalent to those accorded to prisoners of war by the Third Convention in the case where such a person is tried and punished for any offences he has committed.

5. Any combatant who falls into the power of an adverse Party while not engaged in an attack or in a military operation preparatory to an attack shall not forfeit his rights to be a combatant and a prisoner of war by virtue of his prior activities.

6. This Article is without prejudice to the right of any person to be a prisoner of war pursuant to Article 4 of the Third Convention.

7. This Article is not intended to change the generally accepted practice of States with respect to the wearing of the uniform by combatants assigned to the regular, uniformed armed units of a Party to the conflict.

8. In addition to the categories of persons mentioned in Article 13 of the First and Second Conventions, all members of the armed forces of a Party to the conflict, as defined in Article 43 of this Protocol, shall be entitled to protection under those Conventions if they are wounded or sick or, in the case of the Second Convention, shipwrecked at sea or in other waters.

Article 45. Protection of persons who have taken part in hostilities

1. A person who takes part in hostilities and falls into the power of an adverse Party shall be presumed to be a prisoner of war, and therefore shall be protected by the Third Convention, if he claims the status of prisoner of war, or if he appears to be entitled to such status, or if the Party on which he depends claims such status on his behalf by notification to the detaining Power or to the Protecting Power. Should any doubt arise as to whether any such person is entitled to the status of prisoner of war, he shall continue to have such status and, therefore, to be protected by the Third Convention and this Protocol until such time as his status has been determined by a competent tribunal.

2. If a person who has fallen into the power of an adverse Party is not held as a prisoner of war and is to be tried by that Party for an offence arising out of the hostilities, he shall have the right to assert his entitlement to prisoner-of-war status before a judicial tribunal and to have that question adjudicated. Whenever possible under the applicable procedure, this adjudication shall occur before the trial for the offence. The representatives of the Protecting Power shall be entitled to attend the proceedings in which that question is adjudicated, unless, exceptionally, the proceedings are held in camera in the interest of State security. In such a case the detaining Power shall advise the Protecting Power accordingly.

3. Any person who has taken part in hostilities, who is not entitled to prisoner-of-war status and who does not benefit from more favourable treatment in accordance with the Fourth Convention shall have the right at all times to the protection of Article 75 of this Protocol. In occupied territory, any such person, unless he is held as a spy, shall also be entitled, notwithstanding Article 5 of the Fourth Convention, to his rights of communication under that Convention.

Article 46. Spies

1. Notwithstanding any other provision of the Conventions or of this Protocol, any member of the armed forces of a Party to the conflict who falls into the power of an adverse Party while engaging in espionage shall not have the right to the status of prisoner of war and may be treated as a spy.

2. A member of the armed forces of a Party to the conflict who, on behalf of that Party and in territory controlled by an adverse Party, gathers or attempts to gather information shall not be considered as engaging in espionage if, while so acting, he is in the uniform of his armed forces.

3. A member of the armed forces of a Party to the conflict who is a resident of territory occupied by an adverse Party and who, on behalf of the Party on which he depends, gathers or attempts to gather information of military value within that territory shall not be considered as engaging in espionage unless he does so through an act of false pretences or deliberately in a clandestine manner. Moreover, such a resident shall not lose his right to the status of prisoner of war and may not be treated as a spy unless he is captured while engaging in espionage.

4. A member of the armed forces of a Party to the conflict who is not a resident of territory occupied by an adverse Party and who has engaged in espionage in that territory shall not lose his right to the status of prisoner of war and may not be treated as a spy unless he is captured before he has rejoined the armed forces to which he belongs.

Article 47. Mercenaries

1. A mercenary shall not have the right to be a combatant or a prisoner of war.

2. A mercenary is any person who:

(a) is specially recruited locally or abroad in order to fight in an armed conflict;

(b) does, in fact, take a direct part in the hostilities;

(c) is motivated to take part in the hostilities essentially by the desire for private gain and, in fact, is promised, by or on behalf of a Party to the conflict, material compensation substantially in excess of that promised or paid to combatants of similar ranks and functions in the armed forces of that Party;

(d) is neither a national of a Party to the conflict nor a resident of territory controlled by a Party to the conflict;

(e) is not a member of the armed forces of a Party to the conflict; and

(f) has not been sent by a State which is not a Party to the conflict on official duty as a member of its armed forces.

Part IV. Civilian Population
Section I. General Protection Against Effects of Hostilities
Chapter I. Basic rule and field of application
Article 48. Basic rule

In order to ensure respect for and protection of the civilian population and civilian objects, the Parties to the conflict shall at all times distinguish between the civilian population and combatants and between civilian objects and military objectives and accordingly shall direct their operations only against military objectives.

Article 49. Definition of attacks and scope of application

1. "Attacks" means acts of violence against the adversary, whether in offence or in defence.

2. The provisions of this Protocol with respect to attacks apply to all attacks in whatever territory conducted, including the national territory belonging to a Party to the conflict but under the control of an adverse Party.

3. The provisions of this section apply to any land, air or sea warfare which may affect the civilian population, individual civilians or civilian objects on land. They further apply to all attacks from the sea or from the air against objectives on land but do not otherwise affect the rules of international law applicable in armed conflict at sea or in the air.

4. The provisions of this section are additional to the rules concerning humanitarian protection contained in the Fourth Convention, particularly in part II thereof, and in other international agreements binding upon the High Contracting Parties, as well as to other rules of international law relating to the protection of civilians and civilian objects on land, at sea or in the air against the effects of hostilities.

Chapter II. Civilians and civilian population
Article 50. Definition of civilians and civilian population

1. A civilian is any person who does not belong to one of the categories of persons referred to in Article 4 (A) (1), (2), (3) and (6) of the Third Convention and in Article 43 of this Protocol. In case of doubt whether a person is a civilian, that person shall be considered to be a civilian.

2. The civilian population comprises all persons who are civilians.

3. The presence within the civilian population of individuals who do not come within the definition of civilians does not deprive the population of its civilian character.

Article 51. Protection of the civilian population

1. The civilian population and individual civilians shall enjoy general protection against dangers arising from military operations. To give effect to this protection, the following rules, which are additional to other applicable rules of international law, shall be observed in all circumstances.

2. The civilian population as such, as well as individual civilians, shall not be the object of attack. Acts or threats of violence the primary purpose of which is to spread terror among the civilian population are prohibited.

3. Civilians shall enjoy the protection afforded by this section, unless and for such time as they take a direct part in hostilities.

4. Indiscriminate attacks are prohibited. Indiscriminate attacks are:

(a) those which are not directed at a specific military objective;

(b) those which employ a method or means of combat which cannot be directed at a specific military objective; or

(c) those which employ a method or means of combat the effects of which cannot be limited as required by this Protocol; and consequently, in each such case, are of a nature to strike military objectives and civilians or civilian objects without distinction.

5. Among others, the following types of attacks are to be considered as indiscriminate:

(a) an attack by bombardment by any methods or means which treats as a single military objective a number of clearly separated and distinct military objectives located in a city, town, village or other area containing a similar concentration of civilians or civilian objects; and

(b) an attack which may be expected to cause incidental loss of civilian life, injury to civilians, damage to civilian objects, or a combination thereof, which would be excessive in relation to the concrete and direct military advantage anticipated.

6. Attacks against the civilian population or civilians by way of reprisals are prohibited.

7. The presence or movements of the civilian population or individual civilians shall not be used to render certain points or areas immune from military operations, in particular in attempts to shield military objectives from attacks or to shield, favour or impede military operations. The Parties to the conflict shall not direct the movement of the civilian population or individual civilians in order to attempt to shield military objectives from attacks or to shield military operations.

8. Any violation of these prohibitions shall not release the Parties to the conflict from their legal obligations with respect to the civilian population and civilians, including the obligation to take the precautionary measures provided for in Article 57.

Chapter III. Civilian objects
Article 52. General Protection of civilian objects
1. Civilian objects shall not be the object of attack or of reprisals. Civilian objects are all objects which are not military objectives as defined in paragraph 2.

2. Attacks shall be limited strictly to military objectives. In so far as objects are concerned, military objectives are limited to those objects which by their nature, location, purpose or use make an effective contribution to military action and whose total or partial destruction, capture or neutralization, in the circumstances ruling at the time, offers a definite military advantage.

3. In case of doubt whether an object which is normally dedicated to civilian purposes, such as a place of worship, a house or other dwelling or a school, is being used to make an effective contribution to military action, it shall be presumed not to be so used.

Article 53. Protection of cultural objects and of places of worship
Without prejudice to the provisions of the Hague Convention for the Protection of Cultural Property in the Event of Armed Conflict of 14 May 1954, and of other relevant international instruments, it is prohibited:

(a) to commit any acts of hostility directed against the historic monuments, works of art or places of worship which constitute the cultural or spiritual heritage of peoples;

(b) to use such objects in support of the military effort;

(c) to make such objects the object of reprisals.

Article 54. Protection of objects indispensable to the survival of the civilian population
1. Starvation of civilians as a method of warfare is prohibited.

2. It is prohibited to attack, destroy, remove or render useless objects indispensable to the survival of the civilian population, such as food-stuffs, agricultural areas for the production of food-stuffs, crops, livestock, drinking water installations and supplies and irrigation works, for the specific purpose of denying them for their sustenance value to the civilian population or to the adverse Party, whatever the motive, whether in order to starve out civilians, to cause them to move away, or for any other motive.

3. The prohibitions in paragraph 2 shall not apply to such of the objects covered by it as are used by an adverse Party:

(a) as sustenance solely for the members of its armed forces; or

(b) if not as sustenance, then in direct support of military action, provided, however, that in no event shall actions against these objects be taken which may be expected to leave the civilian population with such inadequate food or water as to cause its starvation or force its movement.

4. These objects shall not be made the object of reprisals.

5. In recognition of the vital requirements of any Party to the conflict in the defence of its national territory against invasion, derogation from the prohibitions contained in paragraph 2 may be made by a Party to the conflict within such territory under its own control where required by imperative military necessity.

Article 55. Protection of the natural environment
1. Care shall be taken in warfare to protect the natural environment against widespread, long-term and severe damage. This protection includes a prohibition of the use of methods or means of warfare which are intended or may be expected to cause such damage to the natural environment and thereby to prejudice the health or survival of the population.

2. Attacks against the natural environment by way of reprisals are prohibited.

Article 56. Protection of works and installations containing dangerous forces

1. Works or installations containing dangerous forces, namely dams, dykes and nuclear electrical generating stations, shall not be made the object of attack, even where these objects are military objectives, if such attack may cause the release of dangerous forces and consequent severe losses among the civilian population. Other military objectives located at or in the vicinity of these works or installations shall not be made the object of attack if such attack may cause the release of dangerous forces from the works or installations and consequent severe losses among the civilian population.

2. The special protection against attack provided by paragraph 1 shall cease:

(a) for a dam or a dyke only if it is used for other than its normal function and in regular, significant and direct support of military operations and if such attack is the only feasible way to terminate such support;

(b) for a nuclear electrical generating station only if it provides electric power in regular, significant and direct support of military operations and if such attack is the only feasible way to terminate such support;

(c) for other military objectives located at or in the vicinity of these works or installations only if they are used in regular, significant and direct support of military operations and if such attack is the only feasible way to terminate such support.

3. In all cases, the civilian population and individual civilians shall remain entitled to all the protection accorded them by international law, including the protection of the precautionary measures provided for in Article 57. If the protection ceases and any of the works, installations or military objectives mentioned in paragraph 1 is attacked, all practical precautions shall be taken to avoid the release of the dangerous forces.

4. It is prohibited to make any of the works, installations or military objectives mentioned in paragraph 1 the object of reprisals.

5. The Parties to the conflict shall endeavour to avoid locating any military objectives in the vicinity of the works or installations mentioned in paragraph 1. Nevertheless, installations erected for the sole purpose of defending the protected works or installations from attack are permissible and shall not themselves be made the object of attack, provided that they are not used in hostilities except for defensive actions necessary to respond to attacks against the protected works or installations and that their armament is limited to weapons capable only of repelling hostile action against the protected works or installations.

6. The High Contracting Parties and the Parties to the conflict are urged to conclude further agreements among themselves to provide additional protection for objects containing dangerous forces.

7. In order to facilitate the identification of the objects protected by this article, the Parties to the conflict may mark them with a special sign consisting of a group of three bright orange circles placed on the same axis, as specified in Article 16 of Annex I to this Protocol. The absence of such marking in no way relieves any Party to the conflict of its obligations under this Article.

Chapter IV. Precautionary measures

Article 57. Precautions in attack

1. In the conduct of military operations, constant care shall be taken to spare the civilian population, civilians and civilian objects.

2. With respect to attacks, the following precautions shall be taken:

(a) those who plan or decide upon an attack shall:

(i) do everything feasible to verify that the objectives to be attacked are neither civilians nor civilian objects and are not subject to special protection but are military objectives within the meaning of paragraph 2 of Article 52 and that it is not prohibited by the provisions of this Protocol to attack them;

(ii) take all feasible precautions in the choice of means and methods of attack with a view to avoiding, and in any event to minimizing, incidental loss or civilian life, injury to civilians and damage to civilian objects;

(iii) refrain from deciding to launch any attack which may be expected to cause incidental loss of civilian life, injury to civilians, damage to civilian objects, or a combination thereof, which would be excessive in relation to the concrete and direct military advantage anticipated;

(b) an attack shall be cancelled or suspended if it becomes apparent that the objective is not a military one or is subject to special protection or that the attack may be expected to cause incidental loss of civilian life, injury to civilians, damage to civilian objects, or a combination thereof, which would be excessive in relation to the concrete and direct military advantage anticipated;

(c) effective advance warning shall be given of attacks which may affect the civilian population, unless circumstances do not permit.

3. When a choice is possible between several military objectives for obtaining a similar military advantage, the objective to be selected shall be that the attack on which may be expected to cause the least danger to civilian lives and to civilian objects.

4. In the conduct of military operations at sea or in the air, each Party to the conflict shall, in conformity with its rights and duties under the rules of international law applicable in armed conflict, take all reasonable precautions to avoid losses of civilian lives and damage to civilian objects.

5. No provision of this article may be construed as authorizing any attacks against the civilian population, civilians or civilian objects.

Article 58. Precautions against the effects of attacks

The Parties to the conflict shall, to the maximum extent feasible:

(a) without prejudice to Article 49 of the Fourth Convention, endeavour to remove the civilian population, individual civilians and civilian objects under their control from the vicinity of military objectives;

(b) avoid locating military objectives within or near densely populated areas;

(c) take the other necessary precautions to protect the civilian population, individual civilians and civilian objects under their control against the dangers resulting from military operations.

Chapter V. Localities and zones under special protection

Article 59. Non-defended localities

1. It is prohibited for the Parties to the conflict to attack, by any means whatsoever, non-defended localities.

2. The appropriate authorities of a Party to the conflict may declare as a non-defended locality any inhabited place near or in a zone where armed forces are in contact which is open for occupation by an adverse Party.

Such a locality shall fulfil the following conditions:

(a) all combatants, as well as mobile weapons and mobile military equipment must have been evacuated;

(b) no hostile use shall be made of fixed military installations or establishments;

(c) no acts of hostility shall be committed by the authorities or by the population; and

(d) no activities in support of military operations shall be undertaken.

3. The presence, in this locality, of persons specially protected under the Conventions and this Protocol, and of police forces retained for the sole purpose of maintaining law and order, is not contrary to the conditions laid down in paragraph 2.

4. The declaration made under paragraph 2 shall be addressed to the adverse Party and shall define and describe, as precisely as possible, the limits of the non-defended locality. The Party to the conflict to which the declaration is addressed shall acknowledge its receipt and shall treat the locality as a non-defended locality unless the conditions laid down in paragraph 2 are not in fact fulfilled, in which event it shall immediately so inform the Party making the declaration. Even if the conditions laid down in paragraph 2 are not fulfilled, the locality shall continue to enjoy the protection provided by the other provisions of this Protocol and the other rules of international law applicable in armed conflict.

5. The Parties to the conflict may agree on the establishment of non-defended localities even if such localities do not fulfil the conditions laid down in paragraph 2. The agreement should define and describe, as precisely as possible, the limits of the non-defended locality; if necessary, it may lay down the methods of supervision.

6. The Party which is in control of a locality governed by such an agreement shall mark it, so far as possible, by such signs as may be agreed upon with the other Party, which shall be displayed where they are clearly visible, especially on its perimeter and limits and on highways.

7. A locality loses its status as a non-defended locality when its ceases to fulfil the conditions laid down in paragraph 2 or in the agreement referred to in paragraph 5. In such an eventuality, the locality shall continue to enjoy the protection provided by the other provisions of this Protocol and the other rules of international law applicable in armed conflict.

Article 60. Demilitarized zones

1. It is prohibited for the Parties to the conflict to extend their military operations to zones on which they have conferred by agreement the status of demilitarized zone, if such extension is contrary to the terms of this agreement.

2. The agreement shall be an express agreement, may be concluded verbally or in writing, either directly or through a Protecting Power or any impartial humanitarian organization, and may consist of reciprocal and concordant declarations. The agreement may be concluded in peacetime, as well as after the outbreak of hostilities, and should define and describe, as precisely as possible, the limits of the demilitarized zone and, if necessary, lay down the methods of supervision.

3. The subject of such an agreement shall normally be any zone which fulfils the following conditions:

(a) all combatants, as well as mobile weapons and mobile military equipment, must have been evacuated;

(b) no hostile use shall be made of fixed military installations or establishments;

(c) no acts of hostility shall be committed by the authorities or by the population; and

(d) any activity linked to the military effort must have ceased.

The Parties to the conflict shall agree upon the interpretation to be given to the condition laid down in subparagraph (d) and upon persons to be admitted to the demilitarized zone other than those mentioned in paragraph 4.

4. The presence, in this zone, of persons specially protected under the Conventions and this Protocol, and of police forces retained for the sole purpose of maintaining law and order, is not contrary to the conditions laid down in paragraph 3.

5. The Party which is in control of such a zone shall mark it, so far as possible, by such signs as may be agreed upon with the other Party, which shall be displayed where they are clearly visible, especially on its perimeter and limits and on highways.

6. If the fighting draws near to a demilitarized zone, and if the Parties to the conflict have so agreed, none of them may use the zone for purposes related to the conduct of military operations or unilaterally revoke its status.

7. If one of the Parties to the conflict commits a material breach of the provisions of paragraphs 3 or 6, the other Party shall be released from its obligations under the agreement conferring upon the zone the status of demilitarized zone. In such an eventuality, the zone loses its status but shall continue to enjoy the protection provided by the other provisions of this Protocol and the other rules of international law applicable in armed conflict.

Chapter VI. Civil defence

Article 61. Definitions and scope

For the purpose of this Protocol:

(1) "Civil defence" means the performance of some or all of the undermentioned humanitarian tasks intended to protect the civilian population against the dangers, and to help it to recover from the immediate effects, of hostilities or disasters and also to provide the conditions necessary for its survival. These tasks are:

(a) warning;

(b) evacuation;

(c) management of shelters;

(d) management of blackout measures;

(e) rescue;

(f) medical services, including first aid, and religious assistance;

(g) fire-fighting;

(h) detection and marking of danger areas;

(i) decontamination and similar protective measures;

(j) provision of emergency accommodation and supplies;

(k) emergency assistance in the restoration and maintenance of order in distressed areas;

(l) emergency repair of indispensable public utilities;

(m) emergency disposal of the dead;

(n) assistance in the preservation of objects essential for survival;

(o) complementary activities necessary to carry out any of the tasks mentioned above, including, but not limited to, planning and organization;

(2) "Civil defence organizations" means those establishments and other units which are organized or authorized by the competent authorities of a Party to the conflict to perform any of the tasks mentioned under (1), and which are assigned and devoted exclusively to such tasks;

(3) "Personnel" of civil defence organizations means those persons assigned by a Party to the conflict exclusively to the performance of the tasks mentioned under (1), including personnel assigned by the competent authority of that Party exclusively to the administration of these organizations;

(4) "Matériel" of civil defence organizations means equipment, supplies and transports used by these organizations for the performance of the tasks mentioned under (1).

Article 62. General protection

1. Civilian civil defence organizations and their personnel shall be respected and protected, subject to the provisions of this Protocol, particularly the provisions of this section. They shall be entitled to perform their civil defence tasks except in case of imperative military necessity.

2. The provisions of paragraph 1 shall also apply to civilians who, although not members of civilian civil defence organizations, respond to an appeal from the competent authorities and perform civil defence tasks under their control.

3. Buildings and matériel used for civil defence purposes and shelters provided for the civilian population are covered by Article 52. Objects used for civil defence purposes may not be destroyed or diverted from their proper use except by the Party to which they belong.

Article 63. Civil defence in occupied territories

1. In occupied territories, civilian civil defence organizations shall receive from the authorities the facilities necessary for the performance of their tasks. In no Circumstances shall their personnel be compelled to perform activities which would interfere with the proper performance of these tasks. The Occupying Power shall not change the structure or personnel of such organizations in any way which might jeopardize the efficient performance of their mission. These organizations shall not be required to give priority to the nationals or interests of that Power.

2. The Occupying Power shall not compel, coerce or induce civilian civil defence organizations to perform their tasks in any manner prejudicial to the interests of the civilian population.

3. The Occupying Power may disarm civil defence personnel for reasons of security.

4. The Occupying Power shall neither divert from their proper use nor requisition buildings or matériel belonging to or used by civil defence organizations if such diversion or requisition would be harmful to the civilian population.

5. Provided that the general rule in paragraph 4 continues to be observed, the Occupying Power may requisition or divert these resources, subject to the following particular conditions:

(a) that the buildings or matériel are necessary for other needs of the civilian population; and

(b) that the requisition or diversion continues only while such necessity exists.

6. The Occupying Power shall neither divert nor requisition shelters provided for the use of the civilian population or needed by such population.

. . .

Article 65. Cessation of protection

1. The protection to which civilian civil defence organizations, their personnel, buildings, shelters and matériel are entitled shall not cease unless they commit or are used to commit, outside their proper tasks, acts harmful to the enemy. Protection may, however, cease only after a warning has been given setting, whenever appropriate, a reasonable time-limit, and after such warning has remained unheeded.

2. The following shall not be considered as acts harmful to the enemy:

(a) that civil defence tasks are carried out under the direction or control of military authorities;

(b) that civilian civil defence personnel co-operate with military personnel in the performance of civil defence tasks, or that some military personnel are attached to civilian civil defence organizations;

(c) that the performance of civil defence tasks may incidentally benefit military victims, particularly those who are hors de combat.

3. It shall also not be considered as an act harmful to the enemy that civilian civil defence personnel bear light individual weapons for the purpose of maintaining order or for self-defence. However, in areas where land fighting is taking place or is likely to take place, the Parties to the conflict shall undertake the appropriate measures to limit these weapons to handguns, such as pistols or revolvers, in order to assist in distinguishing between civil defence personnel and combatants. Although civil defence personnel bear other light individual weapons in such areas, they shall nevertheless be respected and protected as soon as they have been recognized as such.

4. The formation of civilian civil defence organizations along military lines, and compulsory service in them, shall also not deprive them of the protection conferred by this Chapter.

Article 66. Identification

1. Each Party to the conflict shall endeavour to ensure that its civil defence organizations, their personnel, buildings and matériel are identifiable while they are exclusively devoted to the performance of civil defence tasks. Shelters provided for the civilian population should be similarly identifiable.

2. Each Party to the conflict shall also endeavour to adopt and implement methods and procedures which will make it possible to recognize civilian shelters as well as civil defence personnel, buildings and matériel on which the international distinctive sign of civil defence is displayed.

3. In occupied territories and in areas where fighting is taking place or is likely to take place, civilian civil defence personnel should be recognizable by the international distinctive sign of civil defence and by an identity card certifying their status.

4. The international distinctive sign of civil defence is an equilateral blue triangle on an orange ground when used for the protection of civil defence organizations, their personnel, buildings and matériel and for civilian shelters.

5. In addition to the distinctive sign, Parties to the conflict may agree upon the use of distinctive signals for civil defence identification purposes.

6. The application of the provisions of paragraphs 1 to 4 is governed by Chapter V of Annex I to this Protocol.

7. In time of peace, the sign described in paragraph 4 may, with the consent of the competent national authorities, be used for civil defence identification purposes.

8. The High Contracting Parties and the Parties to the conflict shall take the measures necessary to supervise the display of the international distinctive sign of civil defence and to prevent and repress any misuse thereof.

9. The identification of civil defence medical and religious personnel, medical units and medical transports is also governed by Article 18.

Article 67. Members of the armed forces and military units assigned to civil defence organizations

1. Members of the armed forces and military units assigned to civil defence organizations shall be respected and protected, provided that:

(a) such personnel and such units are permanently assigned and exclusively devoted to the performance of any of the tasks mentioned in Article 61;

(b) if so assigned, such personnel do not perform any other military duties during the conflict;

(c) such personnel are clearly distinguishable from the other members of the armed forces by prominently displaying the international distinctive sign of civil defence, which shall be as large as appropriate, and such personnel are provided with the identity card referred to in Chapter V of Annex I to this Protocol certifying their status;

(d) such personnel and such units are equipped only with light individual weapons for the purpose of maintaining order or for self-defence. The provisions of Article 65, paragraph 3 shall also apply in this case;

(e) such personnel do not participate directly in hostilities, and do not commit, or are not used to commit, outside their civil defence tasks, acts harmful to the adverse Party;

(f) such personnel and such units perform their civil defence tasks only within the national territory of their Party.

The non-observance of the conditions stated in (e) above by any member of the armed forces who is bound by the conditions prescribed in (a) and (b) above is prohibited.

2. Military personnel serving within civil defence organizations shall, if they fall into the power of an adverse Party, be prisoners of war. In occupied territory they may, but only in the interest of the civilian population of that territory, be employed on civil defence tasks in so far as the need arises, provided however that, if such work is dangerous, they volunteer for such tasks.

3. The buildings and major items of equipment and transports of military units assigned to civil defence organizations shall be clearly marked with the international distinctive sign of civil defence. This distinctive sign shall be as large as appropriate.

4. The matériel and buildings of military units permanently assigned to civil defence organizations and exclusively devoted to the performance of civil defence tasks shall, if they fall into the hands of an adverse Party, remain subject to the laws of war. They may not be diverted from their civil defence purpose so long as they are required for the performance of civil defence tasks, except in case of imperative military necessity, unless previous arrangements have been made for adequate provision for the needs of the civilian population.

Section II. Relief in Favour of the Civilian Population
Article 68. Field of application
The provisions of this Section apply to the civilian population as defined in this Protocol and are supplementary to Articles 23, 55, 59, 60, 61 and 62 and other relevant provisions of the Fourth Convention.
Article 69. Basic needs in occupied territories
1. In addition to the duties specified in Article 55 of the Fourth Convention concerning food and medical supplies, the Occupying Power shall, to the fullest extent of the means available to it and without any adverse distinction, also ensure the provision of clothing, bedding, means of shelter, other supplies essential to the survival of the civilian population of the occupied territory and objects necessary for religious worship.

2. Relief actions for the benefit of the civilian population of occupied territories are governed by Articles 59, 60, 61, 62, 108, 109, 110 and 111 of the Fourth Convention, and by Article 71 of this Protocol, and shall be implemented without delay.
Article 70. Relief actions
1. If the civilian population of any territory under the control of a Party to the conflict, other than occupied territory, is not adequately provided with the supplies mentioned in Article 69, relief actions which are humanitarian and impartial in character and conducted without any adverse distinction shall be undertaken, subject to the agreement of the Parties concerned in such relief actions. Offers of such relief shall not be regarded as interference in the armed conflict or as unfriendly acts. In the distribution of relief consignments, priority shall be given to those persons, such as children, expectant mothers, maternity cases and nursing mothers, who, under the Fourth Convention or under this Protocol, are to be accorded privileged treatment or special protection.

2. The Parties to the conflict and each High Contracting Party shall allow and facilitate rapid and unimpeded passage of all relief consignments, equipment and personnel provided in accordance with this Section, even if such assistance is destined for the civilian population of the adverse Party.

3. The Parties to the conflict and each High Contracting Party which allows the passage of relief consignments, equipment and personnel in accordance with paragraph 2:

(a) shall have the right to prescribe the technical arrangements, including search, under which such passage is permitted;

(b) may make such permission conditional on the distribution of this assistance being made under the local supervision of a Protecting Power;

(c) shall, in no way whatsoever, divert relief consignments from the purpose for which they are intended nor delay their forwarding, except in cases of urgent necessity in the interest of the civilian population concerned.

4. The Parties to the conflict shall protect relief consignments and facilitate their rapid distribution.

5. The Parties to the conflict and each High Contracting Party concerned shall encourage and facilitate effective international co-ordination of the relief actions referred to in paragraph 1.
Article 71. Personnel participating in relief actions
1. Where necessary, relief personnel may form part of the assistance provided in any relief action, in particular for the transportation and distribution of relief consignments; the participation of such personnel shall be subject to the approval of the Party in whose territory they will carry out their duties.

2. Such personnel shall be respected and protected.

3. Each Party in receipt of relief consignments shall, to the fullest extent practicable, assist the relief personnel referred to in paragraph 1 in carrying out their relief mission. Only in case of imperative military necessity may the activities of the relief personnel be limited or their movements temporarily restricted.

4. Under no circumstances may relief personnel exceed the terms of their mission under this Protocol. In particular they shall take account of the security requirements of the Party in whose territory they are carrying out their duties. The mission of any of the personnel who do not respect these conditions may be terminated.
Section III. Treatment of Persons in the Power of a Party to the Conflict
Chapter I. Field of application and protection of persons and objects
Article 72. Field of application
The provisions of this Section are additional to the rules concerning humanitarian protection of civilians and civilian objects in the power of a Party to the conflict contained in the Fourth Convention, particularly Parts I and III thereof, as well as to other applicable rules of international law relating to the protection of fundamental human rights during international armed conflict.

. . .

Article 74. Reunion of dispersed families

The High Contracting Parties and the Parties to the conflict shall facilitate in every possible way the reunion of families dispersed as a result of armed conflicts and shall encourage in particular the work of the humanitarian organizations engaged in this task in accordance with the provisions of the Conventions and of this Protocol and in conformity with their respective security regulations.

Article 75. Fundamental guarantees

1. In so far as they are affected by a situation referred to in Article 1 of this Protocol, persons who are in the power of a Party to the conflict and who do not benefit from more favourable treatment under the Conventions or under this Protocol shall be treated humanely in all circumstances and shall enjoy, as a minimum, the protection provided by this Article without any adverse distinction based upon race, colour, sex, language, religion or belief, political or other opinion, national or social origin, wealth, birth or other status, or on any other similar criteria. Each Party shall respect the person, honour, convictions and religious practices of all such persons.

2. The following acts are and shall remain prohibited at any time and in any place whatsoever, whether committed by civilian or by military agents:

(a) violence to the life, health, or physical or mental well-being of persons, in particular:

(i) murder;

(ii) torture of all kinds, whether physical or mental;

(iii) corporal punishment; and

(iv) mutilation;

(b) outrages upon personal dignity, in particular humiliating and degrading treatment, enforced prostitution and any form or indecent assault;

(c) the taking of hostages;

(d) collective punishments; and

(e) threats to commit any of the foregoing acts.

3. Any person arrested, detained or interned for actions related to the armed conflict shall be informed promptly, in a language he understands, of the reasons why these measures have been taken. Except in cases of arrest or detention for penal offences, such persons shall be released with the minimum delay possible and in any event as soon as the circumstances justifying the arrest, detention or internment have ceased to exist.

4. No sentence may be passed and no penalty may be executed on a person found guilty of a penal offence related to the armed conflict except pursuant to a conviction pronounced by an impartial and regularly constituted court respecting the generally recognized principles of regular judicial procedure, which include the following:

(a) the procedure shall provide for an accused to be informed without delay of the particulars of the offence alleged against him and shall afford the accused before and during his trial all necessary rights and means of defence;

(b) no one shall be convicted of an offence except on the basis of individual penal responsibility;

(c) no one shall be accused or convicted of a criminal offence on account or any act or omission which did not constitute a criminal offence under the national or international law to which he was subject at the time when it was committed; nor shall a heavier penalty be imposed than that which was applicable at the time when the criminal offence was committed; if, after the commission of the offence, provision is made by law for the imposition of a lighter penalty, the offender shall benefit thereby;

(d) anyone charged with an offence is presumed innocent until proved guilty according to law;

(e) anyone charged with an offence shall have the right to be tried in his presence;

(f) no one shall be compelled to testify against himself or to confess guilt;

(g) anyone charged with an offence shall have the right to examine, or have examined, the witnesses against him and to obtain the attendance and examination of witnesses on his behalf under the same conditions as witnesses against him;

(h) no one shall be prosecuted or punished by the same Party for an offence in respect of which a final judgement acquitting or convicting that person has been previously pronounced under the same law and judicial procedure;

(i) anyone prosecuted for an offence shall have the right to have the judgement pronounced publicly; and

(j) a convicted person shall be advised on conviction or his judicial and other remedies and of the time-limits within which they may be exercised.

5. Women whose liberty has been restricted for reasons related to the armed conflict shall be held in quarters separated from men's quarters. They shall be under the immediate supervision of women. Nevertheless, in cases where families are detained or interned, they shall, whenever possible, be held in the same place and accommodated as family units.

6. Persons who are arrested, detained or interned for reasons related to the armed conflict shall enjoy the protection provided by this Article until their final release, repatriation or re-establishment, even after the end of the armed conflict.

7. In order to avoid any doubt concerning the prosecution and trial of persons accused of war crimes or crimes against humanity, the following principles shall apply:

(a) persons who are accused or such crimes should be submitted for the purpose of prosecution and trial in accordance with the applicable rules of international law; and

(b) any such persons who do not benefit from more favourable treatment under the Conventions or this Protocol shall be accorded the treatment provided by this Article, whether or not the crimes of which they are accused constitute grave breaches of the Conventions or of this Protocol.

8. No provision of this Article may be construed as limiting or infringing any other more favourable provision granting greater protection, under any applicable rules of international law, to persons covered by paragraph 1

Chapter II. Measures in favour of women and children
Article 76. Protection of women

1. Women shall be the object of special respect and shall be protected in particular against rape, forced prostitution and any other form of indecent assault.

2. Pregnant women and mothers having dependent infants who are arrested, detained or interned for reasons related to the armed conflict, shall have their cases considered with the utmost priority.

3. To the maximum extent feasible, the Parties to the conflict shall endeavour to avoid the pronouncement of the death penalty on pregnant women or mothers having dependent infants, for an offence related to the armed conflict. The death penalty for such offences shall not be executed on such women.

Article 77. Protection of children

1. Children shall be the object of special respect and shall be protected against any form of indecent assault. The Parties to the conflict shall provide them with the care and aid they require, whether because of their age or for any other reason.

2. The Parties to the conflict shall take all feasible measures in order that children who have not attained the age of fifteen years do not take a direct part in hostilities and, in particular, they shall refrain from recruiting them into their armed forces. In recruiting among those persons who have attained the age of fifteen years but who have not attained the age of eighteen years the Parties to the conflict shall endeavour to give priority to those who are oldest.

3. If, in exceptional cases, despite the provisions of paragraph 2, children who have not attained the age of fifteen years take a direct part in hostilities and fall into the power of an adverse Party, they shall continue to benefit from the special protection accorded by this Article, whether or not they are prisoners of war.

4. If arrested, detained or interned for reasons related to the armed conflict, children shall be held in quarters separate from the quarters of adults, except where families are accommodated as family units as provided in Article 75, paragraph 5.

5. The death penalty for an offence related to the armed conflict shall not be executed on persons who had not attained the age of eighteen years at the time the offence was committed.

Article 78. Evacuation of children

1. No Party to the conflict shall arrange for the evacuation of children, other than its own nationals, to a foreign country except for a temporary evacuation where compelling reasons of the health or medical treatment of the children or, except in occupied territory, their safety, so require. Where the parents or legal guardians can be found, their written consent to such evacuation is required. If these persons cannot be found, the written consent to such evacuation of the persons who by law or custom are primarily responsible for the care of the children is required. Any such evacuation shall be supervised by the Protecting Power in agreement with the Parties concerned, namely, the Party arranging for the evacuation, the Party receiving the children and any Parties whose nationals are being evacuated. In each case, all Parties to the conflict shall take all feasible precautions to avoid endangering the evacuation.

2. Whenever an evacuation occurs pursuant to paragraph 1, each child's education, including his religious and moral education as his parents desire, shall be provided while he is away with the greatest possible continuity.

3. With a view to facilitating the return to their families and country of children evacuated pursuant to this Article, the authorities of the Party arranging for the evacuation and, as appropriate, the authorities of the receiving country shall establish for each child a card with photographs, which they shall send to the Central Tracing Agency of the International Committee of the Red Cross. Each card shall bear, whenever possible, and whenever it involves no risk of harm to the child, the following information:

(a) surname(s) of the child;
(b) the child's first name(s);
(c) the child's sex;
(d) the place and date of birth (or, if that date is not known, the approximate age);
(e) the father's full name;
(f) the mother's full name and her maiden name;
(g) the child's next-of-kin;
(h) the child's nationality;
(i) the child's native language, and any other languages he speaks;
(j) the address of the child's family;
(k) any identification number for the child;
(l) the child's state of health;
(m) the child's blood group;
(n) any distinguishing features;
(o) the date on which and the place where the child was found;
(p) the date on which and the place from which the child left the country;
(q) the child's religion, if any;
(r) the child's present address in the receiving country;
(s) should the child die before his return, the date, place and circumstances of death and place of interment.

. . .

Chapter III. Journalists
Part V. Execution of the Conventions and of its Protocols
Section I. General Provisions
Article 80. Measures for execution

1. The High Contracting Parties and the Parties to the conflict shall without delay take all necessary measures for the execution of their obligations under the Conventions and this Protocol.

2. The High Contracting Parties and the Parties to the conflict shall give orders and instructions to ensure observance of the Conventions and this Protocol, and shall supervise their execution.

Article 81. Activities of the Red Cross and other humanitarian organizations

1. The Parties to the conflict shall grant to the International Committee of the Red Cross all facilities, within their power so as to enable it to carry out the humanitarian functions assigned to it by the Conventions and this Protocol in order to ensure protection and assistance to the victims of conflicts; the International Committee of the Red Cross may also carry out any other humanitarian activities in favour of these victims, subject to the consent of the Parties to the conflict concerned.

2. The Parties to the conflict shall grant to their respective Red Cross (Red Crescent, Red Lion and Sun) organizations the facilities necessary for carrying out their humanitarian activities in favour of the victims of the conflict, in accordance with the provisions of the Conventions and this Protocol and the fundamental principles of the Red Cross as formulated by the International Conferences of the Red Cross.

3. The High Contracting Parties and the Parties to the conflict shall facilitate in every possible way the assistance which Red Cross (Red Crescent, Red Lion and Sun) organizations and the League of Red Cross Societies extend to the victims of conflicts in accordance with the provisions of the Conventions and this Protocol and with the fundamental principles of the red Cross as formulated by the International Conferences of the Red Cross.

4. The High Contracting Parties and the Parties to the conflict shall, as far as possible, make facilities similar to those mentioned in paragraphs 2 and 3 available to the other humanitarian organizations referred to in the Conventions and this Protocol which are duly authorized by the respective Parties to the conflict

and which perform their humanitarian activities in accordance with the provisions of the Conventions and this Protocol.

Article 82. Legal advisers in armed forces

The High Contracting Parties at all times, and the Parties to the conflict in time of armed conflict, shall ensure that legal advisers are available, when necessary, to advise military commanders at the appropriate level on the application of the Conventions and this Protocol and on the appropriate instruction to be given to the armed forces on this subject.

Article 83. Dissemination

1. The High Contracting Parties undertake, in time of peace as in time of armed conflict, to disseminate the Conventions and this Protocol as widely as possible in their respective countries and, in particular, to include the study thereof in their programmes of military instruction and to encourage the study thereof by the civilian population, so that those instruments may become known to the armed forces and to the civilian population.

2. Any military or civilian authorities who, in time of armed conflict, assume responsibilities in respect of the application of the Conventions and this Protocol shall be fully acquainted with the text thereof.

Article 84. Rules of application

The High Contracting Parties shall communicate to one another, as soon as possible, through the depositary and, as appropriate, through the Protecting Powers, their official translations of this Protocol, as well as the laws and regulations which they may adopt to ensure its application.

Section II. Repression of Breaches of the Conventions and of this Protocol

Article 85. Repression of breaches of this Protocol

1. The provisions of the Conventions relating to the repression of breaches and grave breaches, supplemented by this Section, shall apply to the repression of breaches and grave breaches of this Protocol.

2. Acts described as grave breaches in the Conventions are grave breaches of this Protocol if committed against persons in the power of an adverse Party protected by Articles 44, 45 and 73 of this Protocol, or against the wounded, sick and shipwrecked of the adverse Party who are protected by this Protocol, or against those medical or religious personnel, medical units or medical transports which are under the control of the adverse Party and are protected by this Protocol.

3. In addition to the grave breaches defined in Article 11, the following acts shall be regarded as grave breaches of this Protocol, when committed wilfully, in violation of the relevant provisions of this Protocol, and causing death or serious injury to body or health:

(a) making the civilian population or individual civilians the object of attack;

(b) launching an indiscriminate attack affecting the civilian population or civilian objects in the knowledge that such attack will cause excessive loss of life, injury to civilians or damage to civilian objects, as defined in Article 57, paragraph 2 (a)(iii);

(c) launching an attack against works or installations containing dangerous forces in the knowledge that such attack will cause excessive loss of life, injury to civilians or damage to civilian objects, as defined in Article 57, paragraph 2 (a)(iii);

(d) making non-defended localities and demilitarized zones the object of attack;

(e) making a person the object of attack in the knowledge that he is hors de combat;

(f) the perfidious use, in violation of Article 37, of the distinctive emblem of the red cross, red crescent or red lion and sun or of other protective signs recognized by the Conventions or this Protocol.

4. In addition to the grave breaches defined in the preceding paragraphs and in the Conventions, the following shall be regarded as grave breaches of this Protocol, when committed wilfully and in violation of the Conventions or the Protocol:

(a) the transfer by the occupying Power of parts of its own civilian population into the territory it occupies, or the deportation or transfer of all or parts of the population of the occupied territory within or outside this territory, in violation of Article 49 of the Fourth Convention;

(b) unjustifiable delay in the repatriation of prisoners of war or civilians;

(c) practices of apartheid and other inhuman and degrading practices involving outrages upon personal dignity, based on racial discrimination;

(d) making the clearly-recognized historic monuments, works of art or places of worship which constitute the cultural or spiritual heritage of peoples and to which special protection has been given by special arrangement, for example, within the framework of a competent international organization, the object of attack, causing as a result extensive destruction thereof, where there is no evidence of the violation by the adverse Party of Article 53, subparagraph (b), and when such historic monuments, works of art and places of worship are not located in the immediate proximity of military objectives;

(e) depriving a person protected by the Conventions or referred to in paragraph 2 or this Article of the rights of fair and regular trial.

5. Without prejudice to the application of the Conventions and of this Protocol, grave breaches of these instruments shall be regarded as war crimes.

Article 86. Failure to act

1. The High Contracting Parties and the Parties to the conflict shall repress grave breaches, and take measures necessary to suppress all other breaches, of the Conventions or of this Protocol which result from a failure to act when under a duty to do so.

2. The fact that a breach of the Conventions or of this Protocol was committed by a subordinate does not absolve his superiors from penal disciplinary responsibility, as the case may be, if they knew, or had information which should have enabled them to conclude in the circumstances at the time, that he was committing or was going to commit such a breach and if they did not take all feasible measures within their power to prevent or repress the breach.

Article 87. Duty of commanders

1. The High Contracting Parties and the Parties to the conflict shall require military commanders, with respect to members of the armed forces under their command and other persons under their control, to prevent and, where necessary, to suppress and to report to competent authorities breaches of the Conventions and of this Protocol.

2. In order to prevent and suppress breaches, High Contracting Parties and Parties to the conflict shall require that, commensurate with their level of responsibility, commanders ensure that members of the armed forces under their command are aware of their obligations under the Conventions and this Protocol.

3. The High Contracting Parties and Parties to the conflict shall require any commander who is aware that subordinates or other persons under his control are going to commit or have committed a breach of the Conventions or of this Protocol, to initiate such steps as are necessary to prevent such violations of the Conventions or this Protocol, and, where appropriate, to initiate disciplinary or penal action against violators thereof.

Article 88. Mutual assistance in criminal matters

1. The High Contracting Parties shall afford one another the greatest measure of assistance in connection with criminal proceedings brought in respect of grave breaches of the Conventions or of this Protocol.

2. Subject to the rights and obligations established in the Conventions and in Article 85, paragraph 1 of this Protocol, and when circumstances permit, the High Contracting Parties shall co-operate in the matter of extradition. They shall give due consideration to the request of the State in whose territory the alleged offence has occurred.

3. The law of the High Contracting Party requested shall apply in all cases. The provisions of the preceding paragraphs shall not, however, affect the obligations arising from the provisions of any other treaty of a bilateral or multilateral nature which governs or will govern the whole or part of the subject of mutual assistance in criminal matters.

Article 89. Co-operation

In situations of serious violations or the Conventions or of this Protocol, the High Contracting Parties undertake to act jointly or individually, in co-operation with the United Nations and in conformity with the United Nations Charter.

Article 90. International Fact-Finding Commission

1. (a) An International Fact-Finding Commission (hereinafter referred to as "the Commission") consisting of 15 members of high moral standing and acknowledged impartiality shall be established;

(b) When not less than 20 High Contracting Parties have agreed to accept the competence of the Commission pursuant to paragraph 2, the depositary shall then, and at intervals of five years thereafter, convene a meeting of representatives of those High Contracting Parties for the purpose of electing the members of the Commission. At the meeting, the representatives shall elect the members of the Commission by secret ballot from a list of persons to which each of those High Contracting Parties may nominate one person;

. . .

(c) The Commission shall be competent to:

(i) inquire into any facts alleged to be a grave breach as defined in the Conventions and this Protocol or other serious violation of the Conventions or of this Protocol;

(ii) facilitate, through its good offices, the restoration of an attitude of respect for the Conventions and this Protocol;

(d) In other situations, the Commission shall institute an inquiry at the request of a Party to the conflict only with the consent of the other Party or Parties concerned;

(e) Subject to the foregoing provisions or this paragraph, the provisions of Article 52 of the First Convention, Article 53 of the Second Convention, Article 132 or the Third Convention and Article 149 of the Fourth Convention shall continue to apply to any alleged violation of the Conventions and shall extend to any alleged violation of this Protocol.

3. (a) Unless otherwise agreed by the Parties concerned, all inquiries shall be undertaken by a Chamber consisting of seven members appointed as follows:

(i) five members of the Commission, not nationals of any Party to the conflict, appointed by the President of the Commission on the basis of equitable representation of the geographical areas, after consultation with the Parties to the conflict;

(ii) two ad hoc members, not nationals of any Party to the conflict, one to be appointed by each side;

(b) Upon receipt of the request for an inquiry, the President of the Commission shall specify an appropriate time-limit for setting up a Chamber. If any ad hoc member has not been appointed within the time-limit, the President shall immediately appoint such additional member or members of the Commission as may be necessary to complete the membership of the Chamber.

4. (a) The Chamber set up under paragraph 3 to undertake an inquiry shall invite the Parties to the conflict to assist it and to present evidence. The Chamber may also seek such other evidence as it deems appropriate and may carry out an investigation of the situation in loco;

(b) All evidence shall be fully disclosed to the Parties, which shall have the right to comment on it to the Commission;

(c) Each Party shall have the right to challenge such evidence.

5. (a) The Commission shall submit to the Parties a report on the findings of fact of the Chamber, with such recommendations as it may deem appropriate;

(b) If the Chamber is unable to secure sufficient evidence for factual and impartial findings, the Commission shall state the reasons for that inability;

(c) The Commission shall not report its findings publicly, unless all the Parties to the conflict have requested the Commission to do so.

. . .

Article 91. Responsibility

A Party to the conflict which violates the provisions of the Conventions or of this Protocol shall, if the case demands, be liable to pay compensation. It shall be responsible for all acts committed by persons forming part of its armed forces.

Part IV. Final Resolutions

. . .

Article 95. Entry into force

1. This Protocol shall enter into force six months after two instruments of ratification or accession have been deposited.

2. For each Party to the Conventions thereafter ratifying or acceding to this Protocol, it shall enter into force six months after the deposit by such Party of its instrument of ratification or accession.

Article 96. Treaty relations upon entry into force or this Protocol

1. When the Parties to the Conventions are also Parties to this Protocol, the Conventions shall apply as supplemented by this Protocol.

2. When one of the Parties to the conflict is not bound by this Protocol, the Parties to the Protocol shall remain bound by it in their mutual relations. They shall furthermore be bound by this Protocol in relation to each of the Parties which are not bound by it, if the latter accepts and applies the provisions thereof.

3. The authority representing a people engaged against a High Contracting Party in an armed conflict of the type referred to in Article 1, paragraph 4, may undertake to apply the Conventions and this Protocol in relation to that conflict by means of a unilateral declaration addressed to the depositary. Such declaration shall, upon its receipt by the depositary, have in relation to that conflict the following effects:

(a) the Conventions and this Protocol are brought into force for the said authority as a Party to the conflict with immediate effect;

(b) the said authority assumes the same rights and obligations as those which have been assumed by a High Contracting Party to the Conventions and this Protocol; and

(c) the Conventions and this Protocol are equally binding upon all Parties to the conflict.

Article 97. Amendment

1. Any High Contracting Party may propose amendments to this Protocol. The text of any proposed amendment shall be communicated to the depositary, which shall decide, after consultation with all the High Contracting Parties and the International Committee of the Red Cross, whether a conference should be convened to consider the proposed amendment.

2. The depositary shall invite to that conference all the High Contracting Parties as well as the Parties to the Conventions, whether or not they are signatories or this Protocol.

. . .

Article 99. Denunciation

1. In case a High Contracting Party should denounce this Protocol, the denunciation shall only take effect one year after receipt of the instrument of denunciation. If, however, on the expiry of that year the denouncing Party is engaged in one of the situations referred to in Article I, the denunciation shall not take effect before the end of the armed conflict or occupation and not, in any case, before operations connected with the final release, repatriation or re-establishment of the persons protected by the Convention or this Protocol have been terminated.

2. The denunciation shall be notified in writing to the depositary, which shall transmit it to all the High Contracting Parties.

3. The denunciation shall have effect only in respect of the denouncing Party.

4. Any denunciation under paragraph 1 shall not affect the obligations already incurred, by reason of the armed conflict, under this Protocol by such denouncing Party in respect of any act committed before this denunciation becomes effective.

. . .

DOCUMENT 74

Full Official Title: Protocol Additional to the Geneva Conventions of 12 August 1949, and relating to the Protection of Victims of Non-International Armed Conflicts ("Protocol II")

Short Title/Acronym/Abbreviation: Protocol II

Subject: Establishing basic humanitarian law norms for non international armed conflicts such as civil wars and revolutions in a multilateral treaty.

Official Citation: 1125 U.N.T.S. no. 17513

Date of Document: Not applicable

Date of Adoption: June 8, 1977

Date of General Entry into Force (EIF): Dec. 7, 1978

Number of States Parties to this Treaty as of this printing: 165

Date of Signature by United States: December 12, 1977

Date of United States Ratification/Accession/Adhesion: Not applicable

Date of Entry into Force (effective date) as to United States: Not applicable

Type of Document: An international legal instrument, a treaty, which is known by the title "protocol." A protocol is a treaty which amends (modifies or adds to) a prior treaty or set of treaties, here the Geneva Conventions of 1949.

Legal Status/Character of the Instrument/Document as to the United States: Not legally binding upon the United States as a matter of treaty law, but some scholars argue that it is binding at least as to some of its norms, as a matter of customary international law. This is not well settled, but in evolution.

Comments: The Geneva Conventions of 1949 and its two amending Protocols of 1977 form the main part of International Humanitarian Law, the international law applicable to armed conflict. The United States has not ratified the two Protocols. Because the United States has ratified the four Geneva Conventions of 1949 all U.S. military and civilians are subject to these rules today.

The International Committee of the Red Cross (ICRC) is an international organization whose history and principle work has been about the establishment of international legal standards limiting the effects of armed conflicts, international and otherwise, and monitoring compliance with these standards. It was the body responsible for the creation of the Geneva Conventions and Protocols and largely responsible for the development of all humanitarian law since the late 1860s, when it was founded, along with the first Geneva Convention. It monitors compliance with the terms of this Protocol.

This Protocol is a radical instrument of international law because it creates international legal obligations for states parties over civil wars and revolutions and other internal armed conflicts which are wholly within their own territory and otherwise subject to their exclusive sovereignty. But so far 165 states have accepted those legal obligations. This is mostly so because most of the human rights violations occurring today are happening in the context of an internal armed conflict, not an international war. In fact, this Protocol is actually an amendment amplifying "common Article 3" of the four Geneva Conventions of 1948. (See Geneva Convention IV, Document 72, art. 3, above) That article is the only one in the four Geneva Conventions of 1948 applying to non international armed conflicts.

Ratification of Protocol II gives the international community, at least the states parties to this Protocol, legal right to seek compliance of both the government and the belligerent non governmental forces.

If the United States ratifies this Protocol it would then apply to a civil war or revolution in the United States, if it meets the threshold criteria. (See art. 1)

Caution: The status and applicability of this instrument as to the United States may have changed since date of publication. The above information may be updated by referring to any of the following sites:

Web address: http://www.icrc.org/ihl.nsf/7c4d08d9b287a42141256739003e636b/d67c3971bcff1c10c12 5641e0052b545?OpenDocument

1977 PROTOCOL II TO THE GENEVA CONVENTIONS (EXCERPTS)
Preamble

The High Contracting Parties, Recalling that the humanitarian principles enshrined in Article 3 common to the Geneva Conventions of 12 August 1949, constitute the foundation of respect for the human person in cases of armed conflict not of an international character,

Recalling furthermore that international instruments relating to human rights offer a basic protection to the human person,

Emphasizing the need to ensure a better protection for the victims of those armed conflicts,

Recalling that, in cases not covered by the law in force, the human person remains under the protection of the principles of humanity and the dictates or the public conscience,

Have agreed on the following:

Part I. Scope of this Protocol
Article 1. Material field of application

1. This Protocol, which develops and supplements Article 3 common to the Geneva Conventions of 12 August 1949 without modifying its existing conditions or application, shall apply to all armed conflicts which are not covered by Article 1 of the Protocol Additional to the Geneva Conventions of 12 August 1949, and relating to the Protection of Victims of International Armed Conflicts (Protocol I) and which take place in the territory of a High Contracting Party between its armed forces and dissident armed forces or other organized armed groups which, under responsible command, exercise such control over a part of its territory as to enable them to carry out sustained and concerted military operations and to implement this Protocol.

2. This Protocol shall not apply to situations of internal disturbances and tensions, such as riots, isolated and sporadic acts of violence and other acts of a similar nature, as not being armed conflicts.
Article 2. Personal field of application

1. This Protocol shall be applied without any adverse distinction founded on race, colour, sex, language, religion or belief, political or other opinion, national or social origin, wealth, birth or other status, or on any other similar criteria (hereinafter referred to as "adverse distinction") to all persons affected by an armed conflict as defined in Article 1.

2. At the end of the armed conflict, all the persons who have been deprived of their liberty or whose liberty has been restricted for reasons related to such conflict, as well as those deprived of their liberty or whose liberty is restricted after the conflict for the same reasons, shall enjoy the protection of Articles 5 and 6 until the end of such deprivation or restriction of liberty.
Article 3. Non-intervention

1. Nothing in this Protocol shall be invoked for the purpose of affecting the sovereignty of a State or the responsibility of the government, by all legitimate means, to maintain or re-establish law and order in the State or to defend the national unity and territorial integrity of the State.

2. Nothing in this Protocol shall be invoked as a justification for intervening, directly or indirectly, for any reason whatever, in the armed conflict or in the internal or external affairs of the High Contracting Party in the territory of which that conflict occurs.

Part II. Humane Treatment

Article 4 Fundamental guarantees

1. All persons who do not take a direct part or who have ceased to take part in hostilities, whether or not their liberty has been restricted, are entitled to respect for their person, honour and convictions and religious practices. They shall in all circumstances be treated humanely, without any adverse distinction. It is prohibited to order that there shall be no survivors.

2. Without prejudice to the generality of the foregoing, the following acts against the persons referred to in paragraph I are and shall remain prohibited at any time and in any place whatsoever:

(a) violence to the life, health and physical or mental well-being of persons, in particular murder as well as cruel treatment such as torture, mutilation or any form of corporal punishment;

(b) collective punishments;

(c) taking of hostages;

(d) acts of terrorism;

(e) outrages upon personal dignity, in particular humiliating and degrading treatment, rape, enforced prostitution and any form or indecent assault;

(f) slavery and the slave trade in all their forms;

(g) pillage;

(h) threats to commit any or the foregoing acts.

3. Children shall be provided with the care and aid they require, and in particular:

(a) they shall receive an education, including religious and moral education, in keeping with the wishes of their parents, or in the absence of parents, of those responsible for their care;

(b) all appropriate steps shall be taken to facilitate the reunion of families temporarily separated;

(c) children who have not attained the age of fifteen years shall neither be recruited in the armed forces or groups nor allowed to take part in hostilities;

(d) the special protection provided by this Article to children who have not attained the age of fifteen years shall remain applicable to them if they take a direct part in hostilities despite the provisions of subparagraph (c) and are captured;

(e) measures shall be taken, if necessary, and whenever possible with the consent of their parents or persons who by law or custom are primarily responsible for their care, to remove children temporarily from the area in which hostilities are taking place to a safer area within the country and ensure that they are accompanied by persons responsible for their safety and well-being.

Article 5. Persons whose liberty has been restricted

1. In addition to the provisions of Article 4 the following provisions shall be respected as a minimum with regard to persons deprived of their liberty for reasons related to the armed conflict, whether they are interned or detained;

(a) the wounded and the sick shall be treated in accordance with Article 7;

(b) the persons referred to in this paragraph shall, to the same extent as the local civilian population, be provided with food and drinking water and be afforded safeguards as regards health and hygiene and protection against the rigours of the climate and the dangers of the armed conflict;

(c) they shall be allowed to receive individual or collective relief;

(d) they shall be allowed to practise their religion and, if requested and appropriate, to receive spiritual assistance from persons, such as chaplains, performing religious functions;

(e) they shall, if made to work, have the benefit of working conditions and safeguards similar to those enjoyed by the local civilian population.

2. Those who are responsible for the internment or detention of the persons referred to in paragraph 1 shall also, within the limits of their capabilities, respect the following provisions relating to such persons:

(a) except when men and women of a family are accommodated together, women shall be held in quarters separated from those of men and shall be under the immediate supervision of women;

(b) they shall be allowed to send and receive letters and cards, the number of which may be limited by competent authority if it deems necessary;

(c) places of internment and detention shall not be located close to the combat zone. The persons referred to in paragraph 1 shall be evacuated when the places where they are interned or detained become particularly exposed to danger arising out of the armed conflict, if their evacuation can be carried out under adequate conditions of safety;

(d) they shall have the benefit of medical examinations;

(e) their physical or mental health and integrity shall not be endangered by any unjustified act or omission. Accordingly, it is prohibited to subject the persons described in this Article to any medical procedure which is not indicated by the state of health of the person concerned, and which is not consistent with the generally accepted medical standards applied to free persons under similar medical circumstances.

3. Persons who are not covered by paragraph 1 but whose liberty has been restricted in any way whatsoever for reasons related to the armed conflict shall be treated humanely in accordance with Article 4 and with paragraphs 1 (a), (c) and (d), and 2 (b) of this Article.

4. If it is decided to release persons deprived of their liberty, necessary measures to ensure their safety shall be taken by those so deciding.

Article 6. Penal prosecutions

1. This Article applies to the prosecution and punishment of criminal offences related to the armed conflict.

2. No sentence shall be passed and no penalty shall be executed on a person found guilty of an offence except pursuant to a conviction pronounced by a court offering the essential guarantees of independence and impartiality.

In particular:

(a) the procedure shall provide for an accused to be informed without delay of the particulars of the offence alleged against him and shall afford the accused before and during his trial all necessary rights and means of defence;

(b) no one shall be convicted of an offence except on the basis of individual penal responsibility;

(c) no one shall be held guilty of any criminal offence on account of any act or omission which did not constitute a criminal offence, under the law, at the time when it was committed; nor shall a heavier penalty be imposed than that which was applicable at the time when the criminal offence was committed; if, after the commission of the offence, provision is made by law for the imposition of a lighter penalty, the offender shall benefit thereby;

(d) anyone charged with an offence is presumed innocent until proved guilty according to law;

(e) anyone charged with an offence shall have the right to be tried in his presence;

(f) no one shall be compelled to testify against himself or to confess guilt.

3. A convicted person shall be advised on conviction of his judicial and other remedies and of the time-limits within which they may be exercised.

4. The death penalty shall not be pronounced on persons who were under the age of eighteen years at the time of the offence and shall not be carried out on pregnant women or mothers of young children.

5. At the end of hostilities, the authorities in power shall endeavour to grant the broadest possible amnesty to persons who have participated in the armed conflict, or those deprived of their liberty for reasons related to the armed conflict, whether they are interned or detained.

Part III. Wounded, Sick and Shipwrecked

Article 7. Protection and care

1. All the wounded, sick and shipwrecked, whether or not they have taken part in the armed conflict, shall be respected and protected.

2. In all circumstances they shall be treated humanely and shall receive to the fullest extent practicable and with the least possible delay, the medical care and attention required by their condition. There shall be no distinction among them founded on any grounds other than medical ones.

Article 8. Search

Whenever circumstances permit and particularly after an engagement, all possible measures shall be taken, without delay, to search for and collect the wounded, sick and shipwrecked, to protect them against pillage and ill-treatment, to ensure their adequate care, and to search for the dead, prevent their being despoiled, and decently dispose of them.

Article 9. Protection of medical and religious personnel

1. Medical and religious personnel shall be respected and protected and shall be granted all available help for the performance of their duties. They shall not be compelled to carry out tasks which are not compatible with their humanitarian mission.

2. In the performance of their duties medical personnel may not be required to give priority to any person except on medical grounds.

Article 10. General protection of medical duties

1. Under no circumstances shall any person be punished for having carried out medical activities compatible with medical ethics, regardless of the person benefiting therefrom.

2. Persons engaged in medical activities shall neither be compelled to perform acts or to carry out work contrary to, nor be compelled to refrain from acts required by, the rules of medical ethics or other rules designed for the benefit of the wounded and sick, or this Protocol.

3. The professional obligations of persons engaged in medical activities regarding information which they may acquire concerning the wounded and sick under their care shall, subject to national law, be respected.

4. Subject to national law, no person engaged in medical activities may be penalized in any way for refusing or failing to give information concerning the wounded and sick who are, or who have been, under his care.

Article 11. Protection of medical units and transports

1. Medical units and transports shall be respected and protected at all times and shall not be the object of attack.

2. The protection to which medical units and transports are entitled shall not cease unless they are used to commit hostile acts, outside their humanitarian function. Protection may, however, cease only after a warning has been given, setting, whenever appropriate, a reasonable time-limit, and after such warning has remained unheeded.

Article 12. The distinctive emblem

Under the direction of the competent authority concerned, the distinctive emblem of the red cross, red crescent or red lion and sun on a white ground shall be displayed by medical and religious personnel and medical units, and on medical transports. It shall be respected in all circumstances. It shall not be used improperly.

Part IV. Civilian Population

Article 13. Protection of the civilian population

1. The civilian population and individual civilians shall enjoy general protection against the dangers arising from military operations. To give effect to this protection, the following rules shall be observed in all circumstances.

2. The civilian population as such, as well as individual civilians, shall not be the object of attack. Acts or threats of violence the primary purpose of which is to spread terror among the civilian population are prohibited.

3. Civilians shall enjoy the protection afforded by this part, unless and for such time as they take a direct part in hostilities.

Article 14. Protection of objects indispensable to the survival of the civilian population

Starvation of civilians as a method of combat is prohibited. It is therefore prohibited to attack, destroy, remove or render useless for that purpose, objects indispensable to the survival of the civilian population such as food-stuffs, agricultural areas for the production of food-stuffs, crops, livestock, drinking water installations and supplies and irrigation works.

Article 15. Protection of works and installations containing dangerous forces

Works or installations containing dangerous forces, namely dams, dykes and nuclear electrical generating stations, shall not be made the object of attack, even where these objects are military objectives, if such attack may cause the release of dangerous forces and consequent severe losses among the civilian population.

Article 16. Protection of cultural objects and of places of worship

Without prejudice to the provisions of the Hague Convention for the Protection of Cultural Property in the Event of Armed Conflict of 14 May 1954, it is prohibited to commit any acts of hostility directed against historic monuments, works of art or places of worship which constitute the cultural or spiritual heritage of peoples, and to use them in support of the military effort.

Article 17. Prohibition of forced movement of civilians

1. The displacement of the civilian population shall not be ordered for reasons related to the conflict unless the security of the civilians involved or imperative military reasons so demand. Should such displace-

ments have to be carried out, all possible measures shall be taken in order that the civilian population may be received under satisfactory conditions of shelter, hygiene, health, safety and nutrition.

2. Civilians shall not be compelled to leave their own territory for reasons connected with the conflict.

Article 18. Relief societies and relief actions

1. Relief societies located in the territory of the High Contracting Party, such as Red Cross (Red Crescent, Red Lion and Sun) organizations may offer their services for the performance of their traditional functions in relation to the victims of the armed conflict. The civilian population may, even on its own initiative, offer to collect and care for the wounded, sick and shipwrecked.

2. If the civilian population is suffering undue hardship owing to a lack of the supplies essential for its survival, such as food-stuffs and medical supplies, relief actions for the civilian population which are of an exclusively humanitarian and impartial nature and which are conducted without any adverse distinction shall be undertaken subject to the consent of the High Contracting Party concerned.

Part V. Final Provisions

Article 19. Dissemination

This Protocol shall be disseminated as widely as possible.

. . .

Article 28. Authentic texts

The original of this Protocol, of which the Arabic, Chinese, English, French, Russian and Spanish texts are equally authentic shall be deposited with the depositary, which shall transmit certified true copies thereof to all the Parties to the Conventions.

DOCUMENT 75

Full Official Title: Convention on Prohibitions or Restrictions on the Use of Certain Conventional Weapons Which May be Deemed to be Excessively Injurious or to Have Indiscriminate Effects. ("Conv.")

Protocol on Prohibitions or Restrictions on the Use of Mines, Booby-Traps and Other Devices ("Prot. II").

Protocol on Prohibitions or Restrictions on the Use of Mines, Booby-Traps and Other Devices as amended on 3 May 1996 (Protocol II to the 1980 Convention as amended on 3 May 1996) ("1996")

Short Title/Acronym/Abbreviation: the CCW; 1980 Conventional Weapons Conventions and Protocols
Official Citation:
Date of Document: Convention and Prot. II: Not applicable
Date of Adoption: Conv. and Prot II: Oct. 10, 1980; 1996
Date of General Entry into Force (EIF): Conv.: Feb. 12, 1983; Prot. II: unknown
Number of States Parties to this treaty as of this printing: 113
Date of Signature by United States: Conv.: Apr. 8, 1982; Prot II: March 24, 1995; 1996: May 24, 1999
Date of Ratification/Accession/Adhesion: Conv.: March 24, 1995; Prot. II: Apr. 24, 1995; 1996 Prot.
Date of Entry into Force as to United States (effective date): Conv.: Aug. 23, 1995: Prot. II: Sept. 24, 1995.; 1996: no EIF
Type of Document: Humanitarian Law treaties and protocols. International legal instruments
Legal Status/Character of the Instrument/Document as to the United States: The Convention and Protocol II have been signed and ratified by the United States and are legally binding upon the United States. The United States filed reservations, declarations and understandings with its ratification and thus these documents must be read in light of those RDUs. The United States is not bound by the 1996 Protocol.

Comments: This treaty was very politically controversial because the United States used the various weapons which this treaty and its protocols sought to prohibit. The world was disappointed in 1996 when the United States would not go along with a ban on anti personnel land mines and so the international community set up another process and proceeded to pass a land mine treaty without the United States. This movement to ban land mines was greatly helped by the work of Princess Diana and Jody Williams, and the fact that it became known that 26,000 people, many of them children, were killed every year by land mines and many were wounded. There are an estimated 26 million land mines in place around the world, most of them leftover from wars that were over long ago.

Caution: The status and applicability of this instrument as to the United States may have changed since date of publication. The above information may be updated by referring to any of the following sites:

DOCUMENT **75**

Web address: http://www.icrc.org/ihl.nsf/385ec082b509e76c41256739003e636d/05e54e8fb1a42782c12 5641f002d5ee5?OpenDocument

CONVENTION ON PROHIBITIONS OR RESTRICTIONS ON THE USE OF CERTAIN CONVENTIONAL WEAPONS (WITH LAND MINE PROTOCOL) (EXCERPTS)

[This convention deals with the international legal standard for the use of certain conventional weapons, including weapons with undetectable fragments, flammable weapons (such as napalm), and mines and booby traps,. It does this by offering states the choice of ratifying any or all of three optional protocols on each of these three areas. Protocol II covers mines and booby traps. In 1996 an international conference was called to try to redraft Protocol II so as to completely ban land mines. Due to strong resistance by the United States the 1996 Protocol which was adopted from this conference did not ban land mines as most countries had hoped. Protocol II of 1996, which follows this Convention, was as far as the United States would go. The bulk of countries then decided to avoid the U.S. opposition and called a conference a year later in Ottawa, Canada and there drafted and adopted a much stronger land mine ban treaty, without the United States. The 1980 Convention and Protocol II on Land mines, and the 1996 Land mine Protocol are included here. The Ottawa Convention, which the United States has not signed, is not included here.]

Geneva, 10 October 1980.

The High Contracting Parties,

'Recalling' that every State has the duty, in conformity with the Charter of the United Nations, to refrain in its international relations from the threat or use of force against the sovereignty, territorial integrity or political independence of any State, or in any other manner inconsistent with the purposes of the United Nations.

'Desiring' to contribute to international détente, the ending of the arms race and the building of confidence among States, and hence to the realization of the aspiration of all peoples to live in peace,

'Recognizing' the importance of pursuing every effort which may contribute to progress towards general and complete disarmament under strict and effective international control,

'Reaffirming' the need to continue the codification and progressive development of the rules of international law applicable in armed conflict,

'Wishing' to prohibit or restrict further the use of certain conventional weapons and believing that the positive results achieved in this area may facilitate the main talks on disarmament with a view to putting an end to the production, stockpiling and proliferation of such weapons,

'Further bearing in mind' that the Committee on Disarmament may decide to consider the question of adopting further measures to prohibit or restrict the use of certain conventional weapons,

Have agreed as follows:

Article 1. Scope of application

This Convention and its annexed Protocols shall apply in the situations referred to in Article 2 common to the Geneva Conventions of 12 August 1949 for the Protection of War Victims, including any situation described in paragraph 4 of Article 1 of Additional Protocol I to these Conventions.

Article 2. Relations with other international agreements

Nothing in this Convention or its annexed Protocols shall be interpreted as detracting from other obligations imposed upon the High Contracting Parties by international humanitarian law applicable in armed conflict.

. . .

Article 6. Dissemination

The High Contracting Parties undertake, in time of peace as in time of armed conflict, to disseminate this Convention and those of its annexed Protocols by which they are bound as widely as possible in their respective countries and, in particular, to include the study thereof in their programmes of military instruction, so that those instruments may become known to their armed forces.

Article 7. Treaty relations upon entry into force of this Convention

1. When one of the parties to a conflict is not bound by an annexed Protocol, the parties bound by this Convention and that annexed Protocol shall remain bound by them in their mutual relations.

2. Any High Contracting Party shall be bound by this Convention and any Protocol annexed thereto which is in force for it, in any situation contemplated by Article 1, in relation to any State which is not a party to this Convention or bound by the relevant annexed Protocol, if the latter accepts and applies this Convention or the relevant Protocol, and so notifies the Depository.

CONVENTION ON PROHIBITIONS OR RESTRICTIONS ON THE USE OF CERTAIN CONVENTIONAL WEAPONS

3. The Depository shall immediately inform the High Contracting Parties concerned of any notification received under paragraph 2 of this Article.

4. This Convention, and the annexed Protocols by which a High Contracting Party is bound, shall apply with respect to an armed conflict against that High Contracting Party of the type referred to in Article 1, paragraph 4, of Additional Protocol I to the Geneva Conventions of 12 August 1949 for the Protection of War Victims: (a) where the High Contracting Party is also a party to Additional Protocol I and an authority referred to in Article 96, paragraph 3, of that Protocol has undertaken to apply the Geneva Conventions and Additional Protocol I in accordance with Article 96, paragraph 3, of the said Protocol, and undertakes to apply this Convention and the relevant annexed Protocols in relation to that conflict; or (b) where the High Contracting Party is not a party to Additional Protocol I and an authority of the type referred to in subparagraph (a) above accepts and applies the obligations of the Geneva Conventions and of this Convention and the relevant annexed Protocols in relation to that conflict. Such an acceptance and application shall have in relation to that conflict the following effects:

(i) the Geneva Conventions and this Convention and its relevant annexed Protocols are brought into force for the parties to the conflict with immediate effect;

(ii) the said authority assumes the same rights and obligations as those which have been assumed by a High Contracting Party to the Geneva Conventions, this Convention and its relevant annexed Protocols; and

(iii) the Geneva Conventions, this Convention and its relevant annexed Protocols are equally binding upon all parties to the conflict. The High Contracting Party and the authority may also agree to accept and apply the obligations of Additional Protocol I to the Geneva Conventions on a reciprocal basis.

Article 8. Review and amendments

1. (a) At any time after the entry into force of this Convention any High Contracting Party may propose amendments to this Convention or any annexed Protocol by which it is bound. Any proposal for an amendment shall be communicated to the Depository, who shall notify it to all the High Contracting Parties and shall seek their views on whether a conference should be convened to consider the proposal. If a majority, that shall not be less than eighteen of the High Contracting Parties so agree, he shall promptly convene a conference to which all High Contracting Parties shall be invited. States not parties to this Convention shall be invited to the conference as observers.

(b) Such a conference may agree upon amendments which shall be adopted and shall enter into force in the same manner as this Convention and the annexed Protocols, provided that amendments to this Convention may be adopted only by the High Contracting Parties and that amendments to a specific annexed Protocol may be adopted only by the High Contracting Parties which are bound by that Protocol.

2. (a) At any time after the entry into force of this Convention any High Contracting Party may propose additional protocols relating to other categories of conventional weapons not covered by the existing annexed Protocols. Any such proposal for an additional protocol shall be communicated to the Depository, who shall notify it to all the High Contracting Parties in accordance with subparagraph 1 (a) of this Article. If a majority, that shall not be less than eighteen of the High Contracting Parties so agree, the Depository shall promptly convene a conference to which all States shall be invited.

(b) Such a conference may agree, with the full participation of all States represented at the conference, upon additional protocols which shall be adopted in the same manner as this Convention, shall be annexed thereto and shall enter into force as provided in paragraphs 3 and 4 of Article 5 of this Convention.

3. (a) If, after a period of ten years following the entry into force of this Convention, no conference has been convened in accordance with subparagraph 1 (a) or 2 (a) of this Article, any High Contracting Party may request the Depository to convene a conference to which all High Contracting Parties shall be invited to review the scope and operation of this Convention and the Protocols annexed thereto and to consider any proposal for amendments of this Convention or of the existing Protocols. States not parties to this Convention shall be invited as observers to the conference. The conference may agree upon amendments which shall be adopted and enter into force in accordance with subparagraph 1 (b) above.

(b) At such conference consideration may also be given to any proposal for additional protocols relating to other categories of conventional weapons not covered by the existing annexed Protocols. All States represented at the conference may participate fully in such consideration. Any additional protocols shall be adopted in the same manner as this Convention, shall be annexed thereto and shall enter into force as provided in paragraphs 3 and 4 of Article 5 of this Convention.

(c) Such a conference may consider whether provision should be made for the convening of a further conference at the request of any High Contracting Party if, after a similar period to that referred to in subparagraph 3 (a) of this Article, no conference has been convened in accordance with subparagraph 1 (a) or 2 (a) of this Article.

Article 9. Denunciation

1. Any High Contracting Party may denounce this Convention or any of its annexed Protocols by so notifying the Depository.

2. Any such denunciation shall only take effect one year after receipt by the Depository of the notification of denunciation. If, however, on the expiry of that year the denouncing High Contracting Party is engaged in one of the situations referred to in Article 1, the Party shall continue to be bound by the obligations of this Convention and of the relevant annexed Protocols until the end of the armed conflict or occupation and, in any case, until the termination of operations connected with the final release, repatriation or re-establishment of the person protected by the rules of international law applicable in armed conflict, and in the case of any annexed Protocol containing provisions concerning situations in which peace-keeping, observation or similar functions are performed by United Nations forces or missions in the area concerned, until the termination of those functions.

3. Any denunciation of this Convention shall be considered as also applying to all annexed Protocols by which the denouncing High Contracting Party is bound.

4. Any denunciation shall have effect only in respect of the denouncing High Contracting Party.

5. Any denunciation shall not affect the obligations already incurred, by reason of an armed conflict, under this Convention and its annexed Protocols by such denouncing High Contracting Party in respect of any act committed before this denunciation becomes effective.

Article 10. Depository

1. The Secretary-General of the United Nations shall be the Depository of this Convention and of its annexed Protocols.

2. In addition to his usual functions, the Depository shall inform all States of: (a) signatures affixed to this Convention under Article 3; (b) deposits of instruments of ratification, acceptance or approval of or accession to this Convention deposited under Article 4; (c) notifications of consent to be bound by annexed Protocols under Article 4; (d) the dates of entry into force of this Convention and of each of its annexed Protocols under Article 5; and (e) notifications of denunciation received under Article 9, and their effective date.

Article 11. Authentic texts

The original of this Convention with the annexed Protocols, of which the Arabic, Chinese, English, French, Russian and Spanish texts are equally authentic, shall be deposited with the Depository, who shall transmit certified true copies thereof to all States.

1980 Protocol on Land Mines etc.
Protocol on Prohibitions or Restrictions on the Use of Mines, Booby-Traps and Other Devices (Protocol II). Geneva, 10 October 1980

Article 1. Material scope of application

This Protocol relates to the use on land of the mines, booby-traps and other devices defined herein, including mines laid to interdict beaches, waterway crossings or river crossings, but does not apply to the use of anti-ship mines at sea or in inland waterways.

Article 2. Definitions

For the purpose of this Protocol:

1. "Mine" means any munition placed under, on or near the ground or other surface area and designed to be detonated or exploded by the presence, proximity or contact of a person or vehicle, and "remotely delivered mine" means any mine so defined delivered by artillery, rocket, mortar or similar means or dropped from an aircraft.

2. "Booby-trap" means any device or material which is designed, constructed or adapted to kill or injure and which functions unexpectedly when a person disturbs or approaches an apparently harmless object or performs an apparently safe act.

3. "Other devices" means manually-emplaced munitions and devices designed to kill, injure or damage and which are actuated by remote control or automatically after a lapse of time.

4. "Military objective" means, so far as objects are concerned, any object which by its nature, location, purpose or use makes an effective contribution to military action and whose total or partial destruction, capture or neutralization, in the circumstances ruling at the time, offers a definite military advantage.

5. "Civilian objects" are all objects which are not military objectives as defined in paragraph 4.

6. "Recording" means a physical, administrative and technical operation designed to obtain, for the purpose of registration in the official records, all available information facilitating the location of minefields, mines and booby-traps.

Article 3. General restrictions on the use of mines, booby-traps and other devices

1. This Article applies to: (a) mines (b) booby-traps; and (c) other devices.

2. It is prohibited in all circumstances to direct weapons to which this Article applies, either in offence, defence or by way of reprisals, against the civilian population as such or against individual civilians.

3. The indiscriminate use of weapons to which this Article applies is prohibited.

Indiscriminate use is any placement of such weapons: (a) which is not on, or directed against, a military objective; or (b) which employs a method or means of delivery which cannot be directed at a specific military objective; or (c) which may be expected to cause incidental loss of civilian life, injury to civilians, damage to civilian objects, or a combination thereof, which would be excessive in relation to the concrete and direct military advantage anticipated.

4. All feasible precautions shall be taken to protect civilians from the effects of weapons to which this Article applies. Feasible precautions are those precautions which are practicable or practically possible taking into account all circumstances ruling at the time, including humanitarian and military considerations.

Article 4. Restrictions on the use of mines other than remotely delivered mines, booby-traps and other devices in populated areas

1. This Article applies to: (a) mines other than remotely delivered mines; (b) booby-traps; and (c) other devices.

2. It is prohibited to use weapons to which this Article applies in any city, town, village or other area containing a similar concentration of civilians in which combat between ground forces is not taking place or does not appear to be imminent, unless either:

(a) they are placed on or in the close vicinity of a military objective belonging to or under the control of an adverse party; or

(b) measures are taken to protect civilians from their effects, for example, the posting of warning signs, the posting of sentries, the issue of warnings or the provision of fences.

Article 5. Restrictions on the use of remotely delivered mines

1. The use of remotely delivered mines is prohibited unless such mines are only used within an area which is itself a military objective or which contains military objectives, and unless:

(a) their location can be accurately recorded in accordance with Article 7(1)(a); or

(b) an effective neutralizing mechanism is used on each such mine, that is to say, a self-actuating mechanism which is designed to render a mine harmless or cause it to destroy itself when it is anticipated that the mine will no longer serve the military purpose for which it was placed in position, or a remotely-controlled mechanism which is designed to render harmless or destroy a mine when the mine no longer serves the military purpose for which it was placed in position.

2. Effective advance warning shall be given of any delivery or dropping of remotely delivered mines which may affect the civilian population, unless circumstances do not permit.

Article 6. Prohibition on the use of certain booby-traps

1. Without prejudice to the rules of international law applicable in armed conflict relating to treachery and perfidy, it is prohibited in all circumstances to use:

(a) any booby-trap in the form of an apparently harmless portable object which is specifically designed and constructed to contain explosive material and to detonate when it is disturbed or approached, or

(b) booby-traps which are in any way attached to or associated with:

(i) internationally recognized protective emblems, signs or signals;

(ii) sick, wounded or dead persons;

(iii) burial or cremation sites or graves;

(iv) medical facilities, medical equipment, medical supplies or medical transportation;

(v) children's toys or other portable objects or products specially designed for the feeding, health, hygiene, clothing or education of children

(vi) food or drink;

(vii) kitchen utensils or appliances except in military establishments, military locations or military supply depots;

(viii) objects clearly of a religious nature;

(ix) historic monuments, works of art or places or worship which constitute the cultural or spiritual heritage of peoples;

(x) animals or their carcasses.

2. It is prohibited in all circumstances to use any booby-trap which is designed to cause superfluous injury or unnecessary suffering.

Article 7. Recording and publication of the location of minefields, mines and booby- traps

1. The parties to a conflict shall record the location of:

(a) all pre-planned minefields laid by them; and

(b) all areas in which they have made large-scale and pre-planned use of booby-traps.

2. The parties shall endeavour to ensure the recording of the location of all other minefields, mines and booby-traps which they have laid or placed in position.

3. All such records shall be retained by the parties who shall: a) immediately after the cessation of active hostilities

(i) take all necessary and civilians from the effects of minefields, mines and booby-traps; and either

(ii) in cases where the forces of neither party are in the territory of the adverse party, make available to each other and to the Secretary-General of the United Nations all information in their possession concerning the location of minefields, mines and booby-traps in the territory of the adverse party; or

(iii) once complete withdrawal of the forces of the parties from the territory of the adverse party has taken place, make available to the adverse party and to the Secretary-General of the United Nations all information in their possession concerning the location of minefields, mines and booby traps in the territory of the adverse party;

(b) when a United Nations force or mission performs functions in any area, make available to the authority mentioned in Article 8 such information as is required by that Article;

(c) whenever possible, by mutual agreement, provide for the release of information concerning the location of minefields, mines and booby traps, particularly in agreements governing the cessation of hostilities.

Article 8. Protection of United Nations forces and missions from the effects of minefields, mines and booby-traps

1. When a United Nations force or mission performs functions of peacekeeping, observation or similar functions in any area, each party to the conflict shall, if requested by the head of the United Nations force or mission in that area, as far as it is able:

(a) remove or render harmless all mines or booby traps in that area; (b) take such measures as may be necessary to protect the force or mission from the effects of minefields, mines and booby traps while carrying out its duties; and (c) make available to the head of the United Nations force or mission in that area, all information in the party's possession concerning the location of minefields, mines and booby traps in that area.

2. When a United Nations fact-finding mission performs functions in any area, any party to the conflict concerned shall provide protection to that mission except where, because of the size of such mission, it cannot adequately provide such protection. In that case it shall make available to the head of the mission the information in its possession concerning the location of minefields, mines and booby-traps in that area.

Article 9. International co-operation in the removal of minefields, mines and booby-traps

After the cessation of active hostilities, the parties shall endeavour to reach agreement, both among themselves and, where appropriate, with other States and with international organizations, on the provision of information and technical and material assistance—including, in appropriate circumstances, joint operations—necessary to remove or otherwise render ineffective minefields, mines and booby-traps placed in position during the conflict.

Technical Annex to the Protocol on Prohibitions or Restrictions on the Use of Mines, Booby-Traps and Other Devices (Protocol II)

Guidelines on Recording

Whenever an obligation for the recording of the location of minefields, mines and booby traps arises under the Protocol, the following guidelines shall be taken into account. With regard to pre-planned minefields and large-scale and pre-planned use of booby traps:

(a) maps, diagrams or other records should be made in such a way as to indicate the extent of the minefield or booby-trapped area; and (b) the location of the minefield or booby-trapped area should be specified by relation to the co-ordinates of a single reference point and by the estimated dimensions of the area containing mines and booby traps in relation to that single reference point.

2. With regard to other minefields, mines and booby traps laid or placed in position: In so far as possible, the relevant information specified in paragraph I above should be recorded so as to enable the areas containing minefields, mines and booby traps to be identified.

LAND MIND PROTOCOL

Article I. Scope of application

1. This Protocol relates to the use on land of the mines, booby-traps and other devices, defined herein, including mines laid to interdict beaches, waterway crossings or river crossings, but does not apply to the use of anti-ship mines at sea or in inland waterways.

Article 2. Definitions

For the purpose of this Protocol:

1. "Mine" means a munition placed under, on or near the ground or other surface area and designed to be exploded by the presence, proximity or contact of a person or vehicle.

2. "Remotely-delivered mine" means a mine not directly emplaced but delivered by artillery, missile, rocket, mortar, or similar means, or dropped from an aircraft. Mines delivered from a land-based system from less than 500 metres are not considered to be "remotely delivered," provided that they are used in accordance with Article 5 and other relevant Articles of this Protocol.

3. "Anti-personnel mine" means a mine primarily designed to be exploded by the presence, proximity or contact of a person and that will incapacitate, injure or kill one or more persons.

4. "Booby-trap" means any device or material which is designed, constructed or adapted to kill or injure, and which functions unexpectedly when a person disturbs or approaches an apparently harmless object or performs an apparently safe act.

5. "Other devices" means manually-emplaced munitions and devices including improvised explosive devices designed to kill, injure or damage and which are actuated manually, by remote control or automatically after a lapse of time.

6. "Military objective" means, so far as objects are concerned, any object which by its nature, location, purpose or use makes an effective contribution to military action and whose total or partial destruction, capture or neutralization, in the circumstances ruling at the time, offers a definite military advantage.

7. "Civilian objects" are all objects which are not military objectives as defined in paragraph 6 of this Article.

8. "Minefield" is a defined area in which mines have been emplaced and "mined area" is an area which is dangerous due to the presence of mines. "Phoney minefield" means an area free of mines that simulates a minefield. The term "minefield" includes phoney minefields.

9. "Recording" means a physical, administrative and technical operation designed to obtain, for the purpose of registration in official records, all available information facilitating the location of minefields, mined areas, mines, booby-traps and other devices.

10. "Self-destruction mechanism" means an incorporated or externally attached automatically-functioning mechanism which secures the destruction of the munition into which it is incorporated or to which it is attached.

11. "Self-neutralization mechanism" means an incorporated automatically-functioning mechanism which renders inoperable the munition into which it is incorporated.

12. "Self-deactivating" means automatically rendering a munition inoperable by means of the irreversible exhaustion of a component, for example, a battery, that is essential to the operation of the munition.

13. "Remote control" means control by commands from a distance.

14. "Anti-handling device" means a device intended to protect a mine and which is part of, linked to, attached to or placed under the mine and which activates when an attempt is made to tamper with the mine.

15. "Transfer" involves, in addition to the physical movement of mines into or from national territory, the transfer of title to and control over the mines, but does not involve the transfer of territory containing emplaced mines.

Article 3. General restrictions on the use, of mines, booby-traps and other devices

1. This Article applies to:

(a) mines;

(b) booby-traps; and

(c) other devices.

2. Each High Contracting Party or party to a conflict is, in accordance with the provisions of this Protocol, responsible for all mines, booby-traps, and other devices employed by it and undertakes to clear, remove, destroy or maintain them as specified in Article 10 of this Protocol.

3. It is prohibited in all circumstances to use any mine, booby-trap or other device which is designed or of a nature to cause superfluous injury or unnecessary suffering.

4. Weapons to which this Article applies shall strictly comply with the standards and limitations specified in the Technical Annex with respect to each particular category.

5. It is prohibited to use mines, booby-traps or other devices which employ a mechanism or device specifically designed to detonate the munition by the presence of commonly available mine detectors as a result of their magnetic or other non-contact influence during normal use in detection operations.

6. It is prohibited to use a self-deactivating mine equipped with an anti-handling device that is designed in such a manner that the anti-handling device is capable of functioning after the mine has ceased to be capable of functioning.

7. It is prohibited in all circumstances to direct weapons to which this Article applies, either in offence, defence or by way of reprisals, against the civilian population as such or against individual civilians or civilian objects.

8. The indiscriminate use of weapons to which this Article applies is prohibited. Indiscriminate use is any placement of such weapons:

(a) which is not on, or directed against, a military objective. In case of doubt as to whether an object which is normally dedicated to civilian purposes, such as a place of worship, a house or other dwelling or a school, is being used to make an effective contribution to military action, it shall be presumed not to be so used; or

(b) which employs a method or means of delivery which cannot be directed at a specific military objective; or

(c) which may be expected to cause incidental loss of civilian life, injury to civilians, damage to civilian objects, or a combination thereof, which would be excessive in relation to the concrete and direct military advantage anticipated.

9. Several clearly separated and distinct military objectives located in a city, town, village or other area containing a similar concentration of civilians or civilian objects are not to be treated as a single military objective.

10. All feasible precautions shall be taken to protect civilians from the effects of weapons to which this Article applies. Feasible precautions are those precautions which are practicable or practically possible taking into account all circumstances ruling at the time, including humanitarian and military considerations.

11. Effective advance warning shall be given of any emplacement of mines, booby-traps and other devices which may affect the civilian population, unless circumstances do not permit.

Article 4. Restrictions on the use of anti-personnel mines

It is prohibited to use anti-personnel mines which are not detectable, as specified in paragraph 2 of the Technical Annex.

Article 5. Restrictions on the use of anti-personnel mines other than remotely-delivered mines

1. This Article applies to anti-personnel mines other than remotely-delivered mines.

2. It is prohibited to use weapons to which this Article applies which are not in compliance with the provisions on self-destruction and self-deactivation in the Technical Annex, unless:

(a) such weapons are placed within a perimeter-marked area which is monitored by military personnel and protected by fencing or other means, to ensure the effective exclusion of civilians from the area. The marking must be of a distinct and durable character and must at least be visible to a person who is about to enter the meter-marked area; and

(b) such weapons are cleared before the area is abandoned, unless the area is turned over to the forces of another State which accept responsibility for the maintenance of the protections required by this Article and the subsequent clearance of those weapons.

Article 6. Restrictions on the use of remotely-delivered mines

1. It is prohibited to use remotely-delivered mines unless they are recorded in accordance with sub-paragraph I (b) of the Technical Annex.

2. It is prohibited to use remotely-delivered anti-personnel mines which are not in compliance with the provisions on self-destruction and self-deactivation in the Technical Annex.

3. It is prohibited to use remotely-delivered mines other than anti-personnel mines, unless, to the extent feasible, they are equipped with an effective self-destruction or self-neutralization mechanism and have a back-up self-deactivation feature, which is designed so that the mine will no longer function as a mine when the mine no longer serves the military purpose for which it was placed in position.

4. Effective advance warning shall be given of any delivery or dropping of remotely-delivered mines which may affect the civilian population, unless circumstances do not permit.

Article 7. Prohibitions on the use of booby-traps and other devices

1. Without prejudice to the rules of international law applicable in armed conflict relating to treachery and perfidy, it is prohibited in all circumstances to use booby-traps and other devices which are in any way attached to or associated with:

(a) internationally recognized protective emblems, signs or signals;

(b) sick, wounded or dead persons;

(c) burial or cremation sites or graves;

(d) medical facilities, medical equipment, medical supplies or medical transportation;

(e) children's toys or other portable objects or products specially designed for the feeding, health;

(g) kitchen utensils or appliances except in military establishments, military locations or military supply depots;

(h) objects clearly of a religious nature;

(i) historic peoples; or

(j) animals or their carcasses.

2. It is prohibited to use booby-traps or other devices in the form of apparently harmless portable objects which are specifically designed and constructed to contain explosive material.

3. Without prejudice to the provisions of Article 3, it is prohibited to use weapons to which this Article applies in any city, town, village or other area containing a similar concentration of civilians in which combat between ground forces is not taking place or does not appear to be imminent, unless either:

(a) they are placed on or in the close vicinity of a military objective; or

(b) measures are taken to protect civilians from their effects, for example, the posting of warning sentries, the issuing of warnings or the provision of fences.

. . .

Article 9. Recording and use of information on minefields, mined areas,
mines, booby-traps and other devices

1. All information concerning minefields, mined areas, mines, booby-traps and other devices shall be recorded in accordance with the provisions of the Technical Annex.

2. All such records shall be retained by the parties to a conflict, who shall, without delay after the cessation of active hostilities, take all necessary and appropriate measures, including the use of such information, to protect civilians from the effects of minefields, mined areas, mines, booby-traps and other devices in areas under their control. At the same time, they shall also make available to the other party or parties to the conflict and to the Secretary-General of the United Nations all such information in their possession concerning minefields, mined areas, Mines, booby-traps and other devices laid by them in areas no longer under their control; provided, however, subject to reciprocity, where the forces of a party to a conflict are in the territory of an adverse party, either party may withhold such information from the Secretary-General and the other party, to the extent that security interests require such withholding, until neither party is in the territory of the other. In the latter case, the information withheld shall be disclosed as soon as those security interests permit. Wherever possible, the parties to the conflict shall seek, by mutual agreement, to provide for the release of such information at the earliest possible time in a manner consistent with the security interests of each party.

Article 10. Removal of minefields, mined areas, mines, booby-traps
and other devices and international cooperation

1. Without delay after the cessation of active hostilities, all minefields, mined areas, mines, booby-traps and other devices shall be cleared, removed, destroyed or maintained in accordance with Article 3 and paragraph 2 of Article 5 of this Protocol.

2. High Contracting Parties and parties to a conflict bear such responsibility with respect to minefields, mined areas, mines, booby-traps and other devices in areas under their control.

3. With respect to minefields, mined areas, mines, booby-traps and other devices laid by a party in areas over which it no longer exercises control, such party shall provide to the party in control of the area pursuant to paragraph 2 of this Article, to the extent permitted by such party, technical and material assistance necessary to fulfil such responsibility.

4. At all times necessary, the parties shall endeavour to reach agreement, both among themselves and, where appropriate, with other States and with international organizations, on the provision of technical and

material assistance, including, in appropriate circumstances, the undertaking of joint operations necessary to fulfill such responsibilities.

. . .

Article 12. Protection from the effects of minefields, mined areas, mines, booby-traps and other devices

1. Application

(a) With the exception of the forces and missions referred to in sub-paragraph 2(a) (i) of this Article, this Article applies only to missions which are performing functions in an area with the consent of the High Contracting Party on whose territory the functions are performed.

(b) The application of the provisions of this Article to parties to a conflict which are not High Contracting Parties shall not change their legal status or the legal status of a disputed territory, either explicitly or implicitly.

(c) The provisions of this Article are without prejudice to existing international humanitarian law, or other international instruments as applicable, or decisions by the Security Council of the United Nations, which provide for a higher level of protection to personnel functioning in accordance with this Article.

2. Peace-keeping and certain other forces and missions

(a) This paragraph applies to:

(i) any United Nations force or mission performing peace-keeping, observation or similar functions in any area in accordance with the Charter of the United Nations;

(ii) any mission established pursuant to Chapter VIII of the Charter of the United Nations and performing its functions in the area of a conflict.

(b) Each High Contracting Party or party to a conflict, if so requested by the head of a force or mission to which this paragraph applies, shall:

(i) so far as it is able, take such measures as are necessary to protect the force or mission from the effects of mines, booby-traps and other devices in any area under its control;

(ii) if necessary in order effectively to protect such personnel, remove or render harmless, so far as it is able, all mines, booby-traps and other devices in that area; and

(iii) inform the head of the force or mission of the location of all known minefields, mined areas, mines, booby-traps and other devices in the area in which the force or mission is performing its functions and, so far as is feasible, make available to the head of the force or mission all information in its session concerning such minefields, mined areas, mines, booby-traps and other devices.

3. Humanitarian and fact-finding missions of the United Nations System

(a) This paragraph applies to any humanitarian or fact-finding mission of the United Nations System.

(b) Each High Contracting Party or party to a conflict, if so requested by the head of a mission to which this paragraph applies, shall:

(i) provide the personnel of the mission with the protections set out in sub-paragraph 2(b) (i) of this Article; and

(ii) if access to or through any place under its control is necessary for the performance of the mission's functions and in order to provide the personnel of the mission with safe passage to or through that place:

(aa) unless on-going hostilities prevent, inform the head of the mission of a safe route to that place if such information is available; or

(bb) if information identifying a safe route is not provided in accordance with sub-paragraph (aa), so far as is necessary and feasible, clear a lane through minefields.

4. Respect for laws and regulations

Without prejudice to such privileges and immunities as they may enjoy or to the requirements of their duties, personnel participating in the forces and missions referred to in this Article shall:

(a) respect the laws and regulations of the host State; and

(b) refrain from any action or activity incompatible with the impartial and international nature of their duties. . . .

Article 13. Consultations of the High Contracting Parties

5. The cost of the Conference of High Contracting Parties shall be borne by the High Contracting Parties and States not parties participating in the work of the Conference, in accordance with the United Nations scale of assessment adjusted appropriately.

Technical Annex

1. Recording

(a) Recording of the location of mines other than remotely-delivered mines, minefields, mined areas, booby-traps and other devices shall be carried out in accordance with the following provisions:

(i) the location of the minefields, mined areas and areas of booby-traps and other devices shall be specified accurately by relation to the coordinates of at least two reference points and the estimated dimensions of the area containing these weapons in relation to those reference points;

(ii) maps, diagrams or other records shall be made in such a way as to indicate the location of minefields, mined areas, booby-traps and other devices in relation to reference points, and these records shall also indicate their perimeters and extent;

(iii) for purposes of detection and clearance of mines, booby-traps and other devices, maps, diagrams or other records shall contain complete information on the type, number, emplacing method, type of fuse and life time, date and time of laying, anti- handling devices (if any) and other relevant information on all these weapons laid. Whenever feasible the minefield record shall show the exact location of every mine, except in row minefields where the row location is sufficient. The precise location and operating mechanism of each booby-trap laid shall be individually recorded.

(b) The estimated location and area of remotely-delivered mines shall be specified by coordinates of reference points (normally corner points) and shall be ascertained and when feasible marked on the ground at the earliest opportunity. The total number and types of mines laid, the date and time of laying and the self-destruction time periods shall also be recorded.

(c) Copies of records shall be held at a level of command sufficient to guarantee their safety as far as possible.

(d) The use of mines produced after the entry into force of this Protocol is prohibited unless they are marked in English or in the respective national language or languages with the following information:

(i) name of the country of origin;

(ii) month and year of production; and

(iii) serial number or lot number. The marking should be visible, legible, durable and resistant to environmental effects, as far as possible.

2. Specifications on detectability

(a) With respect to anti-personnel mines produced after 1 January 1997, such mines shall incorporate in their construction a material or device that enables the mine to be detected by commonly-available technical mine detection equipment and provides a response signal equivalent to a signal from 8 grammes or more of iron in a single coherent mass.

(b) With respect to anti-personnel mines produced before 1 January 1997, such mines shall either incorporate in their construction, or have attached prior to their emplacement, in a manner not easily removable, a material or device that enables the mine to be detected by commonly-available technical mine detection equipment and provides a response signal equivalent to a signal from 8 grammes or more of iron in a single coherent mass.

(c) In the event that a High Contracting Party determines that it cannot immediately comply with sub-paragraph (b), it may declare at the time of its notification of consent to be bound by this Protocol that it will defer compliance with sub-paragraph (b) for a period not to exceed 9 years from the entry into force of this Protocol. In the meantime it shall, to the extent feasible, minimize the use of anti-personnel mines that do not so comply.

3. Specifications on self-destruction and self-deactivation

(a) All remotely-delivered anti-personnel mines shall be designed and constructed so that no more than 10% of activated mines will fail to self-destruct within 30 days after emplacement, and each mine shall have a back-up self-deactivation feature designed and constructed so that, in combination with the self-destruction mechanism, no more than one in one thousand activated mines will function as a mine 120 days after emplacement.

(b) All non-remotely delivered anti-personnel mines, used outside marked areas, as defined in Article 5 of this Protocol, shall comply with the requirements for self-destruction and self-deactivation stated in sub-paragraph (a).

(c) In the event that a High Contracting Party determines that it cannot immediately comply with sub-paragraphs (a) and/or (b), it may declare at the time of its notification of consent to be bound by this Protocol, that it will, with respect to mines produced prior to the entry into force of this Protocol defer compliance with sub-paragraphs (a) and/or (b) for a period not to exceed 9 years from the entry into force of this Protocol. During this period of deferral, the High Contracting Party shall:

(i) undertake to minimize, to the extent feasible, the use of anti-personnel mines that do not so comply, and

(ii) with respect to remotely-delivered anti-personnel mines, comply with either the requirements for self-destruction or the requirements for self-deactivation and, with respect to other anti-personnel mines comply with at least the requirements for self-deactivation.

4. International signs for minefields and mined areas

Signs similar to the example attached [1] and as specified below shall be utilized in the marking of minefields and mined areas to ensure their visibility and recognition by the civilian population:

(a) size and shape: a triangle or square no smaller than 28 centimetres (11 inches) by 20 centimetres (7.9 inches) for a triangle, and 15 centimetres (6 inches) per side for a square;

(b) colour: red or orange with a yellow reflecting border.

DOCUMENT 76

Full Official Title: Rome Statute of the International Criminal Court

Short Title/Acronym/Abbreviation: International Criminal Court Statute/ICC Statute/The Rome ICC Statute

Subject: Creation of a permanent international criminal court to prosecute the worse crimes under international law, such as war crimes, crimes against humanity, genocide and aggression in a multilateral treaty.

Official Citation: A/Conf. 183/9

Date of Document: As amended by process verbale10 November 1998 and 12 July 1999

Date of Adoption: July 17, 1998

Date of General Entry into Force (EIF): July 1, 2002

Number of States Parties to this Treaty as of this printing: 111

Date of Signature by United States: December 31, 2000

Date of United States Ratification/Accession/Adhesion: Not applicable

Date of Entry into Force (effective date) as to United States: Not applicable

Type of Document: An international legal instrument, a treaty, under the title "Statute," which is a term usually signifying a legal basis for establishment of a court. A treaty which, when signed and ratified by sixty states, will cause the formal creation of the permanent International Criminal Court. The Court has been established and is in operation.

Legal Status/Character of the Instrument/Document as to the United States: The United States voted against the adoption of this Statute (120 states voted in favor, 7 against, 21 abstained). The adoption of the text created no legal obligation on the United States. It did express the intent of the United States not to become a party to the Statute as it was. But on December 31, 2000, the last day of his presidency, President Clinton signed the ICC Statute on behalf of the U.S. This had the effect of indicating that the U.S. did intend to ratify the Rome Statute. Also, under the Vienna Conventions on the Law of Treaties this created an "interim" obligation on the U.S. not to do anything incompatible with the object and purpose of the Statute. But as soon as President George W. Bush became President he immediately indicated that the U.S. was "unsigning" the treaty, a function that does not exist in international law. That arguably did have the effect of neutralizing the Vienna Convention "interim" obligation, as it indicated would never ratify the ICC Statute. The Administration proceeded to take several steps to undermine the ICC and protect U.S military and government personnel from ever having to face the ICC. See entry for International Criminal Court in definitions, and introduction section on ICC. At the time of the writing of this book, the Obama Administration has snot taken a clear stand on the ICC, as to whether the U.S. will move towards ratification or not. The U.S. is still a signatory to the ICC Statute.

In 2010 the Assembly of States Parties to the ICC came up with a definition of the crime of Aggression. This crime could not be defined in 1998 when the Statute was adopted. It will become a crime within the scope of the ICC Statue as of 2017. The U.S. actively participated from the outside in that process of negotiating that definition of aggression.

Comments: Since the 1950s the international community has been attempting through the United Nations to establish a permanent international criminal court to deter future holocausts. Such Court was referred to in the Genocide Convention of 1948. In the early 1950s The United Nations started the process of drafting a Statute for such a court. This process was interrupted by the Cold War and sat on the back burner. In 1994 the process was restarted in earnest, and a statute was adopted at a diplomatic conference ending July 17, 1998, in Rome. The United States had been a key proponent of such a court, but had very serious reservations about what cases it should handle and how and by whom cases were referred to the Court.

The Statute was adopted over U.S. objections and the process aimed at the eventual creation of this Court continues with periodic Preparatory Commission meetings, the second of which took place in August 1999. The United States has been allowed to participate on the sidelines because it is such an important party for the success of this court. Its main concerns center around the possible exposure of U.S. soldiers to the jurisdiction of this court and the role of the U.N. Security Council in relation to the Court. The Court will be a judicial body independent from the United Nations, but will have a relation to it by formal agreement.

The few articles given here from this Statute are just a taste of the whole Statute. They reflect the state of the art in international criminal law aimed at deterring the worse human rights violations. They reflect the convergence of international humanitarian law and human rights law. This piece of the Statute may give the reader an idea of the legal text at the center of the political process and controversy aimed at creating this court and fulfilling the dream of the international community, spawned by the Nuremberg Trials, to set up such tribunal to deter such crimes every where and always.

Caution: The status and applicability of this instrument as to the United States may have changed since date of publication. The above information may be updated by referring to the following site:

Web site addresses: http://www.icrc.org/ihl.nsf/385ec082b509e76c41256739003e636d/fb2c5995d7cbf8 46412566900039e535?OpenDocument

Rome Statute of the International Criminal Court (Excerpts)
Adopted July 17, 1998
[* as corrected by the procés-verbaux of 10 November 1998 and 12 July 1999]
Preamble

The States Parties to this Statute,

Conscious that all peoples are united by common bonds, their cultures pieced together in a shared heritage, and concerned that this delicate mosaic may be shattered at any time,

Mindful that during this century millions of children, women and men have been victims of unimaginable atrocities that deeply shock the conscience of humanity,

Recognizing that such grave crimes threaten the peace, security and well-being of the world,

Affirming that the most serious crimes of concern to the international community as a whole must not go unpunished and that their effective prosecution must be ensured by taking measures at the national level and by enhancing international cooperation,

Determined to put an end to impunity for the perpetrators of these crimes and thus to contribute to the prevention of such crimes,

Recalling that it is the duty of every State to exercise its criminal jurisdiction over those responsible for international crimes,

Reaffirming the Purposes and Principles of the Charter of the United Nations, and in particular that all States shall refrain from the threat or use of force against the territorial integrity or political independence of any State, or in any other manner inconsistent with the Purposes of the United Nations,

Emphasizing in this connection that nothing in this Statute shall be taken as authorizing any State Party to intervene in an armed conflict or in the internal affairs of any State,

Determined to these ends and for the sake of present and future generations, to establish an independent permanent International Criminal Court in relationship with the United Nations system, with jurisdiction over the most serious crimes of concern to the international community as a whole,

Emphasizing that the International Criminal Court established under this Statute shall be complementary to national criminal jurisdictions,

Resolved to guarantee lasting respect for and the enforcement of international justice,

Have agreed as follows

Part 1. Establishment of the Court

Article 1. The Court

An International Criminal Court ("the Court") is hereby established. It shall be a permanent institution and shall have the power to exercise its jurisdiction over persons for the most serious crimes of international concern, as referred to in this Statute, and shall be complementary to national criminal jurisdictions. The jurisdiction and functioning of the Court shall be governed by the provisions of this Statute.

Article 2. Relationship of the Court with the United Nations

The Court shall be brought into relationship with the United Nations through an agreement to be approved by the Assembly of States Parties to this Statute and thereafter concluded by the President of the Court on its behalf.

Article 3. Seat of the Court

1. The seat of the Court shall be established at The Hague in the Netherlands ("the host State").

2. The Court shall enter into a headquarters agreement with the host State, to be approved by the Assembly of States Parties and thereafter concluded by the President of the Court on its behalf.

3. The Court may sit elsewhere, whenever it considers it desirable, as provided in this Statute.

Article 4. Legal status and powers of the Court

1. The Court shall have international legal personality. It shall also have such legal capacity as may be necessary for the exercise of its functions and the fulfilment of its purposes.

2. The Court may exercise its functions and powers, as provided in this Statute, on the territory of any State Party and, by special agreement, on the territory of any other State.

Part 2. Jurisdiction, Admissibility and Applicable Law

Article 5. Crimes within the jurisdiction of the Court

1. The jurisdiction of the Court shall be limited to the most serious crimes of concern to the international community as a whole. The Court has jurisdiction in accordance with this Statute with respect to the following crimes:

(a) The crime of genocide;

(b) Crimes against humanity;

(c) War crimes;

(d) The crime of aggression.

2. The Court shall exercise jurisdiction over the crime of aggression once a provision is adopted in accordance with articles 121 and 123 defining the crime and setting out the conditions under which the Court shall exercise jurisdiction with respect to this crime. Such a provision shall be consistent with the relevant provisions of the Charter of the United Nations.

Article 6. Genocide

For the purpose of this Statute, "genocide" means any of the following acts committed with intent to destroy, in whole or in part, a national, ethnical, racial or religious group, as such:

(a) Killing members of the group;

(b) Causing serious bodily or mental harm to members of the group;

(c) Deliberately inflicting on the group conditions of life calculated to bring about its physical destruction in whole or in part;

(d) Imposing measures intended to prevent births within the group;

(e) Forcibly transferring children of the group to another group.

Article 7. Crimes against humanity

1. For the purpose of this Statute, "crime against humanity" means any of the following acts when committed as part of a widespread or systematic attack directed against any civilian population, with knowledge of the attack:

(a) Murder;

(b) Extermination;

(c) Enslavement;

(d) Deportation or forcible transfer of population;

(e) Imprisonment or other severe deprivation of physical liberty in violation of fundamental rules of international law;

(f) Torture;

(g) Rape, sexual slavery, enforced prostitution, forced pregnancy, enforced sterilization, or any other form of sexual violence of comparable gravity;

(h) Persecution against any identifiable group or collectivity on political, racial, national, ethnic, cultural, religious, gender as defined in paragraph 3, or other grounds that are universally recognized as impermissible under international law, in connection with any act referred to in this paragraph or any crime within the jurisdiction of the Court;

(i) Enforced disappearance of persons;

(j) The crime of apartheid;

(k) Other inhumane acts of a similar character intentionally causing great suffering, or serious injury to body or to mental or physical health.

2. For the purpose of paragraph 1:

(a) "Attack directed against any civilian population" means a course of conduct involving the multiple commission of acts referred to in paragraph 1 against any civilian population, pursuant to or in furtherance of a State or organizational policy to commit such attack;

(b) "Extermination" includes the intentional infliction of conditions of life, inter alia the deprivation of access to food and medicine, calculated to bring about the destruction of part of a population;

(c) "Enslavement" means the exercise of any or all of the powers attaching to the right of ownership over a person and includes the exercise of such power in the course of trafficking in persons, in particular women and children;

(d) "Deportation or forcible transfer of population" means forced displacement of the persons concerned by expulsion or other coercive acts from the area in which they are lawfully present, without grounds permitted under international law;

(e) "Torture" means the intentional infliction of severe pain or suffering, whether physical or mental, upon a person in the custody or under the control of the accused; except that torture shall not include pain or suffering arising only from, inherent in or incidental to, lawful sanctions;

(f) "Forced pregnancy" means the unlawful confinement of a woman forcibly made pregnant, with the intent of affecting the ethnic composition of any population or carrying out other grave violations of international law. This definition shall not in any way be interpreted as affecting national laws relating to pregnancy;

(g) "Persecution" means the intentional and severe deprivation of fundamental rights contrary to international law by reason of the identity of the group or collectivity;

(h) "The crime of apartheid" means inhumane acts of a character similar to those referred to in paragraph 1, committed in the context of an institutionalized regime of systematic oppression and domination by one racial group over any other racial group or groups and committed with the intention of maintaining that regime;

(i) "Enforced disappearance of persons" means the arrest, detention or abduction of persons by, or with the authorization, support or acquiescence of, a State or a political organization, followed by a refusal to acknowledge that deprivation of freedom or to give information on the fate or whereabouts of those persons, with the intention of removing them from the protection of the law for a prolonged period of time.

3. For the purpose of this Statute, it is understood that the term "gender" refers to the two sexes, male and female, within the context of society. The term "gender" does not indicate any meaning different from the above.

Article 8. War crimes

1. The Court shall have jurisdiction in respect of war crimes in particular when committed as part of a plan or policy or as part of a large-scale commission of such crimes.

2. For the purpose of this Statute, "war crimes" means:

(a) Grave breaches of the Geneva Conventions of 12 August 1949, namely, any of the following acts against persons or property protected under the provisions of the relevant Geneva Convention:

(i) Wilful killing;

(ii) Torture or inhuman treatment, including biological experiments;

(iii) Wilfully causing great suffering, or serious injury to body or health;

(iv) Extensive destruction and appropriation of property, not justified by military necessity and carried out unlawfully and wantonly;

(v) Compelling a prisoner of war or other protected person to serve in the forces of a hostile Power;

(vi) Wilfully depriving a prisoner of war or other protected person of the rights of fair and regular trial;

(vii) Unlawful deportation or transfer or unlawful confinement;

(viii) Taking of hostages.

(b) Other serious violations of the laws and customs applicable in international armed conflict, within the established framework of international law, namely, any of the following acts:

(i) Intentionally directing attacks against the civilian population as such or against individual civilians not taking direct part in hostilities;

(ii) Intentionally directing attacks against civilian objects, that is, objects which are not military objectives;

(iii) Intentionally directing attacks against personnel, installations, material, units or vehicles involved in a humanitarian assistance or peacekeeping mission in accordance with the Charter of the United Nations, as long as they are entitled to the protection given to civilians or civilian objects under the international law of armed conflict;

(iv) Intentionally launching an attack in the knowledge that such attack will cause incidental loss of life or injury to civilians or damage to civilian objects or widespread, long-term and severe damage to the natural environment which would be clearly excessive in relation to the concrete and direct overall military advantage anticipated;

(v) Attacking or bombarding, by whatever means, towns, villages, dwellings or buildings which are undefended and which are not military objectives;

(vi) Killing or wounding a combatant who, having laid down his arms or having no longer means of defence, has surrendered at discretion;

(vii) Making improper use of a flag of truce, of the flag or of the military insignia and uniform of the enemy or of the United Nations, as well as of the distinctive emblems of the Geneva Conventions, resulting in death or serious personal injury;

(viii) The transfer, directly or indirectly, by the Occupying Power of parts of its own civilian population into the territory it occupies, or the deportation or transfer of all or parts of the population of the occupied territory within or outside this territory;

(ix) Intentionally directing attacks against buildings dedicated to religion, education, art, science or charitable purposes, historic monuments, hospitals and places where the sick and wounded are collected, provided they are not military objectives;

(x) Subjecting persons who are in the power of an adverse party to physical mutilation or to medical or scientific experiments of any kind which are neither justified by the medical, dental or hospital treatment of the person concerned nor carried out in his or her interest, and which cause death to or seriously endanger the health of such person or persons;

(xi) Killing or wounding treacherously individuals belonging to the hostile nation or army;

(xii) Declaring that no quarter will be given;

(xiii) Destroying or seizing the enemy's property unless such destruction or seizure be imperatively demanded by the necessities of war;

(xiv) Declaring abolished, suspended or inadmissible in a court of law the rights and actions of the nationals of the hostile party;

(xv) Compelling the nationals of the hostile party to take part in the operations of war directed against their own country, even if they were in the belligerent's service before the commencement of the war;

(xvi) Pillaging a town or place, even when taken by assault;

(xvii) Employing poison or poisoned weapons;

(xviii) Employing asphyxiating, poisonous or other gases, and all analogous liquids, materials or devices;

(xix) Employing bullets which expand or flatten easily in the human body, such as bullets with a hard envelope which does not entirely cover the core or is pierced with incisions;

(xx) Employing weapons, projectiles and material and methods of warfare which are of a nature to cause superfluous injury or unnecessary suffering or which are inherently indiscriminate in violation of the international law of armed conflict, provided that such weapons, projectiles and material and methods of warfare are the subject of a comprehensive prohibition and are included in an annex to this Statute, by an amendment in accordance with the relevant provisions set forth in articles 121 and 123;

(xxi) Committing outrages upon personal dignity, in particular humiliating and degrading treatment;

(xxii) Committing rape, sexual slavery, enforced prostitution, forced pregnancy, as defined in Article 7, paragraph 2 (f), enforced sterilization, or any other form of sexual violence also constituting a grave breach of the Geneva Conventions;

(xxiii) Utilizing the presence of a civilian or other protected person to render certain points, areas or military forces immune from military operations;

(xxiv) Intentionally directing attacks against buildings, material, medical units and transport, and personnel using the distinctive emblems of the Geneva Conventions in conformity with international law;

(xxv) Intentionally using starvation of civilians as a method of warfare by depriving them of objects indispensable to their survival, including wilfully impeding relief supplies as provided for under the Geneva Conventions;

(xxvi) Conscripting or enlisting children under the age of fifteen years into the national armed forces or using them to participate actively in hostilities.

(c) In the case of an armed conflict not of an international character, serious violations of Article 3 common to the four Geneva Conventions of 12 August 1949, namely, any of the following acts committed against persons taking no active part in the hostilities, including members of armed forces who have laid down their arms and those placed hors de combat by sickness, wounds, detention or any other cause:

(i) Violence to life and person, in particular murder of all kinds, mutilation, cruel treatment and torture;

(ii) Committing outrages upon personal dignity, in particular humiliating and degrading treatment;

(iii) Taking of hostages;

(iv) The passing of sentences and the carrying out of executions without previous judgement pronounced by a regularly constituted court, affording all judicial guarantees which are generally recognized as indispensable.

(d) Paragraph 2 (c) applies to armed conflicts not of an international character and thus does not apply to situations of internal disturbances and tensions, such as riots, isolated and sporadic acts of violence or other acts of a similar nature.

(e) Other serious violations of the laws and customs applicable in armed conflicts not of an international character, within the established framework of international law, namely, any of the following acts:

(i) Intentionally directing attacks against the civilian population as such or against individual civilians not taking direct part in hostilities;

(ii) Intentionally directing attacks against buildings, material, medical units and transport, and personnel using the distinctive emblems of the Geneva Conventions in conformity with international law;

(iii) Intentionally directing attacks against personnel, installations, material, units or vehicles involved in a humanitarian assistance or peacekeeping mission in accordance with the Charter of the United Nations, as long as they are entitled to the protection given to civilians or civilian objects under the international law of armed conflict;

(iv) Intentionally directing attacks against buildings dedicated to religion, education, art, science or charitable purposes, historic monuments, hospitals and places where the sick and wounded are collected, provided they are not military objectives;

(v) Pillaging a town or place, even when taken by assault;

(vi) Committing rape, sexual slavery, enforced prostitution, forced pregnancy, as defined in Article 7, paragraph 2 (f), enforced sterilization, and any other form of sexual violence also constituting a serious violation of Article 3 common to the four Geneva Conventions;

(vii) Conscripting or enlisting children under the age of fifteen years into armed forces or groups or using them to participate actively in hostilities;

(viii) Ordering the displacement of the civilian population for reasons related to the conflict, unless the security of the civilians involved or imperative military reasons so demand;

(ix) Killing or wounding treacherously a combatant adversary;

(x) Declaring that no quarter will be given;

(xi) Subjecting persons who are in the power of another party to the conflict to physical mutilation or to medical or scientific experiments of any kind which are neither justified by the medical, dental or hospital treatment of the person concerned nor carried out in his or her interest, and which cause death to or seriously endanger the health of such person or persons;

(xii) Destroying or seizing the property of an adversary unless such destruction or seizure be imperatively demanded by the necessities of the conflict;

(f) Paragraph 2 (e) applies to armed conflicts not of an international character and thus does not apply to situations of internal disturbances and tensions, such as riots, isolated and sporadic acts of violence or other acts of a similar nature. It applies to armed conflicts that take place in the territory of a State when there is pro-tracted armed conflict between governmental authorities and organized armed groups or between such groups.

3. Nothing in paragraph 2 (c) and (e) shall affect the responsibility of a Government to maintain or re-establish law and order in the State or to defend the unity and territorial integrity of the State, by all legitimate means.

Article 9. Elements of Crimes

1. Elements of Crimes shall assist the Court in the interpretation and application of articles 6, 7 and 8. They shall be adopted by a two-thirds majority of the members of the Assembly of States Parties.

2. Amendments to the Elements of Crimes may be proposed by:

(a) Any State Party;

(b) The judges acting by an absolute majority;

(c) The Prosecutor.

Such amendments shall be adopted by a two-thirds majority of the members of the Assembly of States Parties.

3. The Elements of Crimes and amendments thereto shall be consistent with this Statute.

Article 10

Nothing in this Part shall be interpreted as limiting or prejudicing in any way existing or developing rules of international law for purposes other than this Statute.

Article 11. Jurisdiction ratione temporis

1. The Court has jurisdiction only with respect to crimes committed after the entry into force of this Statute.

2. If a State becomes a Party to this Statute after its entry into force, the Court may exercise its jurisdiction only with respect to crimes committed after the entry into force of this Statute for that State, unless that State has made a declaration under Article 12, paragraph 3.

Article 12. Preconditions to the exercise of jurisdiction

1. A State which becomes a Party to this Statute thereby accepts the jurisdiction of the Court with respect to the crimes referred to in Article 5.

2. In the case of Article 13, paragraph (a) or (c), the Court may exercise its jurisdiction if one or more of the following States are Parties to this Statute or have accepted the jurisdiction of the Court in accordance with paragraph 3:

(a) The State on the territory of which the conduct in question occurred or, if the crime was committed on board a vessel or aircraft, the State of registration of that vessel or aircraft;

(b) The State of which the person accused of the crime is a national.

3. If the acceptance of a State which is not a Party to this Statute is required under paragraph 2, that State may, by declaration lodged with the Registrar, accept the exercise of jurisdiction by the Court with respect to the crime in question. The accepting State shall cooperate with the Court without any delay or exception in accordance with Part 9.

Article 13. Exercise of jurisdiction

The Court may exercise its jurisdiction with respect to a crime referred to in Article 5 in accordance with the provisions of this Statute if:

(a) A situation in which one or more of such crimes appears to have been committed is referred to the Prosecutor by a State Party in accordance with Article 14;

(b) A situation in which one or more of such crimes appears to have been committed is referred to the Prosecutor by the Security Council acting under Chapter VII of the Charter of the United Nations; or

(c) The Prosecutor has initiated an investigation in respect of such a crime in accordance with Article 15.

Article 14. Referral of a situation by a State Party

1. A State Party may refer to the Prosecutor a situation in which one or more crimes within the jurisdic-tion of the Court appear to have been committed requesting the Prosecutor to investigate the situation for

the purpose of determining whether one or more specific persons should be charged with the commission of such crimes.

2. As far as possible, a referral shall specify the relevant circumstances and be accompanied by such supporting documentation as is available to the State referring the situation.

Article 15. Prosecutor

1. The Prosecutor may initiate investigations proprio motu on the basis of information on crimes within the jurisdiction of the Court.

2. The Prosecutor shall analyse the seriousness of the information received. For this purpose, he or she may seek additional information from States, organs of the United Nations, intergovernmental or non-governmental organizations, or other reliable sources that he or she deems appropriate, and may receive written or oral testimony at the seat of the Court.

3. If the Prosecutor concludes that there is a reasonable basis to proceed with an investigation, he or she shall submit to the Pre-Trial Chamber a request for authorization of an investigation, together with any supporting material collected. Victims may make representations to the Pre-Trial Chamber, in accordance with the Rules of Procedure and Evidence.

4. If the Pre-Trial Chamber, upon examination of the request and the supporting material, considers that there is a reasonable basis to proceed with an investigation, and that the case appears to fall within the jurisdiction of the Court, it shall authorize the commencement of the investigation, without prejudice to subsequent determinations by the Court with regard to the jurisdiction and admissibility of a case.

5. The refusal of the Pre-Trial Chamber to authorize the investigation shall not preclude the presentation of a subsequent request by the Prosecutor based on new facts or evidence regarding the same situation.

6. If, after the preliminary examination referred to in paragraphs 1 and 2, the Prosecutor concludes that the information provided does not constitute a reasonable basis for an investigation, he or she shall inform those who provided the information. This shall not preclude the Prosecutor from considering further information submitted to him or her regarding the same situation in the light of new facts or evidence.

Article 16. Deferral of investigation or prosecution

No investigation or prosecution may be commenced or proceeded with under this Statute for a period of 12 months after the Security Council, in a resolution adopted under Chapter VII of the Charter of the United Nations, has requested the Court to that effect; that request may be renewed by the Council under the same conditions.

Article 17. Issues of admissibility

1. Having regard to paragraph 10 of the Preamble and Article 1, the Court shall determine that a case is inadmissible where:

(a) The case is being investigated or prosecuted by a State which has jurisdiction over it, unless the State is unwilling or unable genuinely to carry out the investigation or prosecution;

(b) The case has been investigated by a State which has jurisdiction over it and the State has decided not to prosecute the person concerned, unless the decision resulted from the unwillingness or inability of the State genuinely to prosecute;

(c) The person concerned has already been tried for conduct which is the subject of the complaint, and a trial by the Court is not permitted under Article 20, paragraph 3;

(d) The case is not of sufficient gravity to justify further action by the Court.

2. In order to determine unwillingness in a particular case, the Court shall consider, having regard to the principles of due process recognized by international law, whether one or more of the following exist, as applicable:

(a) The proceedings were or are being undertaken or the national decision was made for the purpose of shielding the person concerned from criminal responsibility for crimes within the jurisdiction of the Court referred to in Article 5;

(b) There has been an unjustified delay in the proceedings which in the circumstances is inconsistent with an intent to bring the person concerned to justice;

(c) The proceedings were not or are not being conducted independently or impartially, and they were or are being conducted in a manner which, in the circumstances, is inconsistent with an intent to bring the person concerned to justice.

3. In order to determine inability in a particular case, the Court shall consider whether, due to a total or substantial collapse or unavailability of its national judicial system, the State is unable to obtain the accused or the necessary evidence and testimony or otherwise unable to carry out its proceedings.

Article 18. Preliminary rulings regarding admissibility

1. When a situation has been referred to the Court pursuant to Article 13 (a) and the Prosecutor has determined that there would be a reasonable basis to commence an investigation, or the Prosecutor initiates an investigation pursuant to articles 13 (c) and 15, the Prosecutor shall notify all States Parties and those States which, taking into account the information available, would normally exercise jurisdiction over the crimes concerned. The Prosecutor may notify such States on a confidential basis and, where the Prosecutor believes it necessary to protect persons, prevent destruction of evidence or prevent the absconding of persons, may limit the scope of the information provided to States.

2. Within one month of receipt of that notification, a State may inform the Court that it is investigating or has investigated its nationals or others within its jurisdiction with respect to criminal acts which may constitute crimes referred to in Article 5 and which relate to the information provided in the notification to States. At the request of that State, the Prosecutor shall defer to the State's investigation of those persons unless the Pre-Trial Chamber, on the application of the Prosecutor, decides to authorize the investigation.

3. The Prosecutor's deferral to a State's investigation shall be open to review by the Prosecutor six months after the date of deferral or at any time when there has been a significant change of circumstances based on the State's unwillingness or inability genuinely to carry out the investigation.

4. The State concerned or the Prosecutor may appeal to the Appeals Chamber against a ruling of the Pre-Trial Chamber, in accordance with Article 82. The appeal may be heard on an expedited basis.

5. When the Prosecutor has deferred an investigation in accordance with paragraph 2, the Prosecutor may request that the State concerned periodically inform the Prosecutor of the progress of its investigations and any subsequent prosecutions. States Parties shall respond to such requests without undue delay.

6. Pending a ruling by the Pre-Trial Chamber, or at any time when the Prosecutor has deferred an investigation under this article, the Prosecutor may, on an exceptional basis, seek authority from the Pre-Trial Chamber to pursue necessary investigative steps for the purpose of preserving evidence where there is a unique opportunity to obtain important evidence or there is a significant risk that such evidence may not be subsequently available.

7. A State which has challenged a ruling of the Pre-Trial Chamber under this article may challenge the admissibility of a case under Article 19 on the grounds of additional significant facts or significant change of circumstances.

. . .

Article 98. *Cooperation with respect to waiver of immunity and consent to surrender:*

Article 98(2) The Court may not proceed with a request for surrender which would require the requested State to act inconsistently with its obligations under international agreements pursuant to which the consent of a sending State is required to surrender a person of that State to the Court, unless the Court can first obtain the cooperation of the sending State for the giving of consent for the surrender.

DOCUMENT **77**

Full Official Title: International Criminal Court Resolution on the Crime of Aggression

Short Title/Acronym/Abbreviation: The Kampala Resolution on Aggression

Type of Document: This is an International Criminal Court resolution.

Subject: War, crime of aggression; definition of aggression for purposes of the jurisdiction of the ICC over that crime

Official Citation: ICC Resolution 6, June 2010

Date of Document: Not applicable

Date of Adoption: June 11, 2010

Date of General Entry into Force (EIF): It should become one of the crimes prosecuted under the ICC as of 2017.

Number of States Parties as of this printing: Not applicable

Date of Signature by the United States: Not applicable

Date of Ratification/Accession/Adhesion: Not applicable

Date of Entry into Force as to United States (effective date): Not applicable

Legal Status/Character of the Instrument/Document as to the United States: Not a treaty and therefore not legally binding upon the United States. Moreover, the United States is not a party to the International Criminal Court and therefore may hold an opinion other than the one expressed by this body.

Comments: This instrument adopted by the International Criminal Court in 2010 adds the crime of aggression to the list of crimes over which the Court has jurisdiction and which may be prosecuted. The resolution is very controversial. The U.S. participated in the negotiations for this definition, which was a compromise.

Caution: The status and applicability of this instrument as to the United States may have changed since the date of this publication. The above information may be updated by referring to the following site:

Web Address: http://www.icc-cpi.int/iccdocs/asp_docs/Resolutions/RC-Res.6-ENG.pdf

ICC Resolution RC/Res.4, June 2010—the Crime of Aggression

The Review Conference,

Recalling paragraph 1 of Article 12 of the Rome Statute,

Recalling paragraph 2 of Article 5 of the Rome Statute,

Recalling also paragraph 7 of resolution F, adopted by the United Nations Diplomatic Conference of Plenipotentiaries on the Establishment of an International Criminal Court on 17 July 1998,

Recalling further resolution ICC-ASP/1/Res.1 on the continuity of work in respect of the crime of aggression, and *expressing its appreciation* to the Special Working Group on the Crime of Aggression for having elaborated proposals on a provision on the crime of aggression,

Taking note of resolution ICC-ASP/8/Res.6, by which the Assembly of States Parties forwarded proposals on a provision on the crime of aggression to the Review Conference for its consideration,

Resolved to activate the Court's jurisdiction over the crime of aggression as early as possible,

1. *Decides* to adopt, in accordance with Article 5, paragraph 2, of the Rome Statute of the International Criminal Court (hereinafter: "the Statute") the amendments to the Statute contained in annex I of the present resolution, which are subject to ratification or acceptance and shall enter into force in accordance with Article 121, paragraph 5; and notes that any State Party may lodge a declaration referred to in Article 15 *bis* prior to ratification or acceptance.

2. *Also decides* to adopt the amendments to the Elements of Crimes contained in annex II of the present resolution.

3. *Also decides* to adopt the understandings regarding the interpretation of the above-mentioned amendments contained in annex III of the present resolution.

4. *Further decides* to review the amendments on the crime of aggression seven years after the beginning of the Court's exercise of jurisdiction.

5. *Calls upon* all States Parties to ratify or accept the amendments contained in annex I.

Annex I

Amendments to the Rome Statute of the International Criminal Court on the Crime of Aggression

1. Article 5, paragraph 2, of the Statute is deleted.

2. The following text is inserted after Article 8 of the Statute:

Article 8 *bis*

Crime of aggression

1. For the purpose of this Statute, "crime of aggression" means the planning, preparation, initiation or execution, by a person in a position effectively to exercise control over or to direct the political or military action of a State, of an act of aggression which, by its character, gravity and scale, constitutes a manifest violation of the Charter of the United Nations.

2. For the purpose of paragraph 1, "act of aggression" means the use of armed force by a State against the sovereignty, territorial integrity or political independence of another State, or in any other manner inconsistent with the Charter of the United Nations. Any of the following acts, regardless

of a declaration of war, shall, in accordance with United Nations General Assembly resolution 3314 (XXIX) of 14

December 1974, qualify as an act of aggression:

a) The invasion or attack by the armed forces of a State of the territory of another State, or any military occupation, however temporary, resulting from such invasion or attack, or any annexation by the use of force of the territory of another State or part thereof;

b) Bombardment by the armed forces of a State against the territory of another State or the use of any weapons by a State against the territory of another State;

c) The blockade of the ports or coasts of a State by the armed forces of another State;

d) An attack by the armed forces of a State on the land, sea or air forces, or marine and air fleets of another State;

e) The use of armed forces of one State which are within the territory of another State with the agreement of the receiving State, in contravention of the conditions provided for in the agreement or any extension of their presence in such territory beyond the termination of the agreement;

f) The action of a State in allowing its territory, which it has placed at the disposal of another State, to be used by that other State for perpetrating an act of aggression against a third State;

g) The sending by or on behalf of a State of armed bands, groups, irregulars or mercenaries, which carry out acts of armed force against another State of such gravity as to amount to the acts listed above, or its substantial involvement therein.

3. The following text is inserted after Article 15 of the Statute:

Article 15 *bis*

Exercise of jurisdiction over the crime of aggression

(State referral, *proprio motu*)

1. The Court may exercise jurisdiction over the crime of aggression in accordance with Article 13, paragraphs (a) and (c), subject to the provisions of this article.

2. The Court may exercise jurisdiction only with respect to crimes of aggression committed one year after the ratification or acceptance of the amendments by thirty States Parties.

3. The Court shall exercise jurisdiction over the crime of aggression in accordance with this article, subject to a decision to be taken after 1 January 2017 by the same majority of States Parties as is required for the adoption of an amendment to the Statute;

4. The Court may, in accordance with Article 12, exercise jurisdiction over a crime of aggression, arising from an act of aggression committed by a State Party, unless that State Party has previously declared that it does not accept such jurisdiction by lodging a declaration with the Registrar. The withdrawal of such a declaration may be effected at any time and shall be considered by the State Party within three years.

5. In respect of a State that is not a party to this Statute, the Court shall not exercise its jurisdiction over the crime of aggression when committed by that State's nationals or on its territory.

6. Where the Prosecutor concludes that there is a reasonable basis to proceed with an investigation in respect of a crime of aggression, he or she shall first ascertain whether the Security Council has made a determination of an act of aggression committed by the State concerned. The Prosecutor shall notify the Secretary-General of the United Nations of the situation before the Court, including any relevant information and documents.

7. Where the Security Council has made such a determination, the Prosecutor may proceed with the investigation in respect of a crime of aggression.

8. Where no such determination is made within six months after the date of notification, the Prosecutor may proceed with the investigation in respect of a crime of aggression, provided that the Pre-Trial Division has authorized the commencement of the investigation in respect of a crime of aggression in accordance with the procedure contained in Article 15, and the Security Council has not decided otherwise in accordance with Article 16.

9. A determination of an act of aggression by an organ outside the Court shall be without prejudice to the Court's own findings under this Statute.

10. This article is without prejudice to the provisions relating to the exercise of jurisdiction with respect to other crimes referred to in Article 5.

4. The following text is inserted after Article 15 bis of the Statute:

Article 15 *ter*
Exercise of jurisdiction over the crime of aggression
(Security Council referral)

1. The Court may exercise jurisdiction over the crime of aggression in accordance with Article 13, paragraph (b), subject to the provisions of this article.

2. The Court may exercise jurisdiction only with respect to crimes of aggression committed one year after the ratification or acceptance of the amendments by thirty States Parties.

3. The Court shall exercise jurisdiction over the crime of aggression in accordance with this article, subject to a decision to be taken after 1 January 2017 by the same majority of States Parties as is required for the adoption of an amendment to the Statute;

4. A determination of an act of aggression by an organ outside the Court shall be without prejudice to the Court's own findings under this Statute.

5. This article is without prejudice to the provisions relating to the exercise of jurisdiction with respect to other crimes referred to in Article 5.

5. The following text is inserted after Article 25, paragraph 3 of the Statute:

3 *bis* In respect of the crime of aggression, the provisions of this article shall apply only to persons in a position effectively to exercise control over or to direct the political or military action of a State.

6. The first sentence of Article 9, paragraph 1 of the Statute is replaced by the following sentence:

1. Elements of Crimes shall assist the Court in the interpretation and application of articles 6, 7, 8 and 8 *bis*.

7. The chapeau of Article 20, paragraph 3, of the Statute is replaced by the following paragraph; the rest of the paragraph remains unchanged:

3. No person who has been tried by another court for conduct also proscribed under Article 6, 7, 8 or 8 *bis* shall be tried by the Court with respect to the same conduct unless the proceedings in the other court:

Annex II
Amendments to the Elements of Crimes
Article 8 *bis*
Crime of aggression
Introduction

1. It is understood that any of the acts referred to in Article 8 *bis*, paragraph 2, qualify as an act of aggression.

2. There is no requirement to prove that the perpetrator has made a legal evaluation as to whether the use of armed force was inconsistent with the Charter of the United Nations.

3. The term "manifest" is an objective qualification.

4. There is no requirement to prove that the perpetrator has made a legal evaluation as to the "manifest" nature of the violation of the Charter of the United Nations.

Elements

1. The perpetrator planned, prepared, initiated or executed an act of aggression.

2. The perpetrator was a person[1] in a position effectively to exercise control over or to direct the political or military action of the State which committed the act of aggression.

3. The act of aggression—the use of armed force by a State against the sovereignty, territorial integrity or political independence of another State, or in any other manner inconsistent with the Charter of the United Nations—was committed.

4. The perpetrator was aware of the factual circumstances that established that such a use of armed force was inconsistent with the Charter of the United Nations.

5. The act of aggression, by its character, gravity and scale, constituted a manifest violation of the Charter of the United Nations.

6. The perpetrator was aware of the factual circumstances that established such a manifest violation of the Charter of the United Nations.

Annex III
Understandings regarding the amendments to the Rome Statute of the International Criminal Court on the Crime of Aggression

Referrals by the Security Council

1. It is understood that the Court may exercise jurisdiction on the basis of a Security Council referral in accordance with Article 13, paragraph (b), of the Statute only with respect to crimes of aggression committed after a decision in accordance with Article 15 *ter*, paragraph 3, is taken, and one year after the ratification or acceptance of the amendments by thirty States Parties, whichever is later.

2. It is understood that the Court shall exercise jurisdiction over the crime of aggression on the basis of a Security Council referral in accordance with Article 13, paragraph (b), of the Statute irrespective of whether the State concerned has accepted the Court's jurisdiction in this regard.

Jurisdiction *ratione temporis*

3. It is understood that in case of Article 13, paragraph (a) or (c), the Court may exercise its jurisdiction only with respect to crimes of aggression committed after a decision in accordance with Article 15 *bis*, paragraph 3, is taken, and one year after the ratification or acceptance of the amendments by thirty States Parties, whichever is later.

Domestic jurisdiction over the crime of aggression

4. It is understood that the amendments that address the definition of the act of aggression and the crime of aggression do so for the purpose of this Statute only. The amendments shall, in accordance with Article 10 of the Rome Statute, not be interpreted as limiting or prejudicing in any way existing or developing rules of international law for purposes other than this Statute.

5. It is understood that the amendments shall not be interpreted as creating the right or obligation to exercise domestic jurisdiction with respect to an act of aggression committed by another State.

Other understandings

6. It is understood that aggression is the most serious and dangerous form of the illegal use of force; and that a determination whether an act of aggression has been committed requires consideration of all the circumstances of each particular case, including the gravity of the acts concerned and their consequences, in accordance with the Charter of the United Nations.

7. It is understood that in establishing whether an act of aggression constitutes a manifest violation of the Charter of the United Nations, the three components of character, gravity and scale must be sufficient to justify a "manifest" determination. No one component can be significant enough to satisfy the manifest standard by itself.

---

[1] With respect to an act of aggression, more than one person may be in a position that meets these criteria.

U.S. GENERATED DOCUMENTS

DOCUMENT 78

Full Official Title: President George W. Bush's Speech following the attacks on September 11, 2001
Short Title/Acronym/Abbreviation: Nothing official
Type of Document: Presidential Address
Subject: 9/11 and Justice
Official Citation: Not applicable
Date of Document: September 20, 2001
Date of Adoption: Not applicable
Date of General Entry into Force (EIF): Not applicable
Number of States Parties as of this printing: Not applicable
Date of Signature by the United States: Not applicable
Date of Ratification/Accession/Adhesion: Not applicable
Date of Entry into Force as to United States (effective date): Not applicable
Legal Status/Character of the Instrument/Document as to the United States: President Bush gave this speech to a joint session of Congress, to express his commitment to bring the perpetrators of the attacks on September 11, 2001 to justice, and to assure the American people that freedom will prevail.
Website: http://articles.cnn.com/2001-09-20/us/gen.bush.transcript_1_joint-session-national-anthem-citizens?_s=PM:US

TRANSCRIPT OF PRESIDENT BUSH'S ADDRESS

Transcript of President Bush's address to a joint session of Congress on Thursday night, September 20, 2001.

Mr. Speaker, Mr. President Pro Tempore, members of Congress, and fellow Americans, in the normal course of events, presidents come to this chamber to report on the state of the union. Tonight, no such report is needed; it has already been delivered by the American people.

We have seen it in the courage of passengers who rushed terrorists to save others on the ground. Passengers like an exceptional man named Todd Beamer. And would you please help me welcome his wife Lisa Beamer here tonight?

(APPLAUSE)

We have seen the state of our union in the endurance of rescuers working past exhaustion.

We've seen the unfurling of flags, the lighting of candles, the giving of blood, the saying of prayers in English, Hebrew and Arabic.

We have seen the decency of a loving and giving people who have made the grief of strangers their own.

My fellow citizens, for the last nine days, the entire world has seen for itself the state of union, and it is strong.

(APPLAUSE)

Tonight, we are a country awakened to danger and called to defend freedom. Our grief has turned to anger and anger to resolution. Whether we bring our enemies to justice or bring justice to our enemies, justice will be done.

(APPLAUSE)

I thank the Congress for its leadership at such an important time.

All of America was touched on the evening of the tragedy to see Republicans and Democrats joined together on the steps of this Capitol singing "God Bless America."

And you did more than sing. You acted, by delivering $40 billion to rebuild our communities and meet the needs of our military. Speaker Hastert, Minority Leader Gephardt, Majority Leader Daschle and Senator Lott, I thank you for your friendship, for your leadership and for your service to our country.

(APPLAUSE)

And on behalf of the American people, I thank the world for its outpouring of support.

America will never forget the sounds of our national anthem playing at Buckingham Palace, on the streets of Paris and at Berlin's Brandenburg Gate.

We will not forget South Korean children gathering to pray outside our embassy in Seoul, or the prayers of sympathy offered at a mosque in Cairo.

We will not forget moments of silence and days of mourning in Australia and Africa and Latin America.

Nor will we forget the citizens of 80 other nations who died with our own. Dozens of Pakistanis, more than 130 Israelis, more than 250 citizens of India, men and women from El Salvador, Iran, Mexico and Japan, and hundreds of British citizens.

America has no truer friend than Great Britain. (APPLAUSE) Once again, we are joined together in a great cause.

I'm so honored the British prime minister has crossed an ocean to show his unity with America.

Thank you for coming, friend.

(APPLAUSE)

On September the 11th, enemies of freedom committed an act of war against our country. Americans have known wars, but for the past 136 years they have been wars on foreign soil, except for one Sunday in 1941. Americans have known the casualties of war, but not at the center of a great city on a peaceful morning.

Americans have known surprise attacks, but never before on thousands of civilians. All of this was brought upon us in a single day, and night fell on a different world, a world where freedom itself is under attack.

Americans have many questions tonight. Americans are asking, "Who attacked our country?"

The evidence we have gathered all points to a collection of loosely affiliated terrorist organizations known as al Qaeda. They are some of the murderers indicted for bombing American embassies in Tanzania and Kenya and responsible for bombing the USS Cole.

Al Qaeda is to terror what the Mafia is to crime. But its goal is not making money, its goal is remaking the world and imposing its radical beliefs on people everywhere.

The terrorists practice a fringe form of Islamic extremism that has been rejected by Muslim scholars and the vast majority of Muslim clerics; a fringe movement that perverts the peaceful teachings of Islam.

The terrorists' directive commands them to kill Christians and Jews, to kill all Americans and make no distinctions among military and civilians, including women and children. This group and its leader, a person named Osama bin Laden, are linked to many other organizations in different countries, including the Egyptian Islamic Jihad, the Islamic Movement of Uzbekistan.

There are thousands of these terrorists in more than 60 countries.

They are recruited from their own nations and neighborhoods and brought to camps in places like Afghanistan where they are trained in the tactics of terror. They are sent back to their homes or sent to hide in countries around the world to plot evil and destruction. The leadership of al Qaeda has great influence in Afghanistan and supports the Taliban regime in controlling most of that country. In Afghanistan we see al Qaeda's vision for the world. Afghanistan's people have been brutalized, many are starving and many have fled.

Women are not allowed to attend school. You can be jailed for owning a television. Religion can be practiced only as their leaders dictate. A man can be jailed in Afghanistan if his beard is not long enough. The United States respects the people of Afghanistan—after all, we are currently its largest source of humanitarian aid—but we condemn the Taliban regime.

(APPLAUSE)

It is not only repressing its own people, it is threatening people everywhere by sponsoring and sheltering and supplying terrorists.

By aiding and abetting murder, the Taliban regime is committing murder. And tonight the United States of America makes the following demands on the Taliban:

— Deliver to United States authorities all of the leaders of Al Qaeda who hide in your land.

— Release all foreign nationals, including American citizens you have unjustly imprisoned.

— Protect foreign journalists, diplomats and aid workers in your country.

— Close immediately and permanently every terrorist training camp in Afghanistan. And hand over every terrorist and every person and their support structure to appropriate authorities.

— Give the United States full access to terrorist training camps, so we can make sure they are no longer operating.

These demands are not open to negotiation or discussion.

(APPLAUSE)

The Taliban must act and act immediately.

They will hand over the terrorists or they will share in their fate. I also want to speak tonight directly to Muslims throughout the world. We respect your faith. It's practiced freely by many millions of Americans and by millions more in countries that America counts as friends. Its teachings are good and peaceful, and those who commit evil in the name of Allah blaspheme the name of Allah.

(APPLAUSE)

The terrorists are traitors to their own faith, trying, in effect, to hijack Islam itself.

The enemy of America is not our many Muslim friends. It is not our many Arab friends. Our enemy is a radical network of terrorists and every government that supports them.

(APPLAUSE)

Our war on terror begins with al Qaeda, but it does not end there.

It will not end until every terrorist group of global reach has been found, stopped and defeated.

(APPLAUSE)

Americans are asking "Why do they hate us?"

They hate what they see right here in this chamber: a democratically elected government. Their leaders are self-appointed. They hate our freedoms: our freedom of religion, our freedom of speech, our freedom to vote and assemble and disagree with each other.

They want to overthrow existing governments in many Muslim countries such as Egypt, Saudi Arabia and Jordan. They want to drive Israel out of the Middle East. They want to drive Christians and Jews out of vast regions of Asia and Africa.

These terrorists kill not merely to end lives, but to disrupt and end a way of life. With every atrocity, they hope that America grows fearful, retreating from the world and forsaking our friends. They stand against us because we stand in their way.

We're not deceived by their pretenses to piety.

We have seen their kind before. They're the heirs of all the murderous ideologies of the 20th century. By sacrificing human life to serve their radical visions, by abandoning every value except the will to power, they follow in the path of fascism, Nazism and totalitarianism. And they will follow that path all the way to where it ends in history's unmarked grave of discarded lies. Americans are asking, "How will we fight and win this war?"

We will direct every resource at our command—every means of diplomacy, every tool of intelligence, every instrument of law enforcement, every financial influence, and every necessary weapon of war—to the destruction and to the defeat of the global terror network.

Now, this war will not be like the war against Iraq a decade ago, with a decisive liberation of territory and a swift conclusion. It will not look like the air war above Kosovo two years ago, where no ground troops were used and not a single American was lost in combat.

Our response involves far more than instant retaliation and isolated strikes. Americans should not expect one battle, but a lengthy campaign unlike any other we have ever seen. It may include dramatic strikes visible on TV and covert operations secret even in success.

We will starve terrorists of funding, turn them one against another, drive them from place to place until there is no refuge or no rest.

And we will pursue nations that provide aid or safe haven to terrorism. Every nation in every region now has a decision to make: Either you are with us or you are with the terrorists.

From this day forward, any nation that continues to harbor or support terrorism will be regarded by the United States as a hostile regime. Our nation has been put on notice, we're not immune from attack. We will take defensive measures against terrorism to protect Americans. Today, dozens of federal departments and agencies, as well as state and local governments, have responsibilities affecting homeland security.

These efforts must be coordinated at the highest level. So tonight, I announce the creation of a Cabinet-level position reporting directly to me, the Office of Homeland Security. And tonight, I also announce a distinguished American to lead this effort, to strengthen American security: a military veteran, an effective governor, a true patriot, a trusted friend, Pennsylvania's Tom Ridge.

He will lead, oversee and coordinate a comprehensive national strategy to safeguard our country against terrorism and respond to any attacks that may come. These measures are essential. The only way to defeat terrorism as a threat to our way of life is to stop it, eliminate it and destroy it where it grows.

Many will be involved in this effort, from FBI agents, to intelligence operatives, to the reservists we have called to active duty. All deserve our thanks, and all have our prayers. And tonight a few miles from the damaged Pentagon, I have a message for our military: Be ready. I have called the armed forces to alert, and there is a reason.

The hour is coming when America will act, and you will make us proud.

This is not, however, just America's fight. And what is at stake is not just America's freedom. This is the world's fight. This is civilization's fight. This is the fight of all who believe in progress and pluralism, tolerance and freedom.

We ask every nation to join us.

We will ask and we will need the help of police forces, intelligence service and banking systems around the world. The United States is grateful that many nations and many international organizations have already responded with sympathy and with support—nations from Latin America to Asia to Africa to Europe to the Islamic world.

Perhaps the NATO charter reflects best the attitude of the world: An attack on one is an attack on all. The civilized world is rallying to America's side.

They understand that if this terror goes unpunished, their own cities, their own citizens may be next. Terror unanswered can not only bring down buildings, it can threaten the stability of legitimate governments.

And you know what? We're not going to allow it.

(APPLAUSE)

Americans are asking, "What is expected of us?"

I ask you to live your lives and hug your children. I know many citizens have fears tonight, and I ask you to be calm and resolute, even in the face of a continuing threat.

I ask you to uphold the values of America and remember why so many have come here.

We're in a fight for our principles, and our first responsibility is to live by them. No one should be singled out for unfair treatment or unkind words because of their ethnic background or religious faith.

I ask you to continue to support the victims of this tragedy with your contributions. Those who want to give can go to a central source of information, Libertyunites.org, to find the names of groups providing direct help in New York, Pennsylvania and Virginia. The thousands of FBI agents who are now at work in this investigation may need your cooperation, and I ask you to give it. I ask for your patience with the delays and inconveniences that may accompany tighter security and for your patience in what will be a long struggle.

I ask your continued participation and confidence in the American economy. Terrorists attacked a symbol of American prosperity; they did not touch its source.

America is successful because of the hard work and creativity and enterprise of our people. These were the true strengths of our economy before September 11, and they are our strengths today.

And finally, please continue praying for the victims of terror and their families, for those in uniform and for our great country. Prayer has comforted us in sorrow and will help strengthen us for the journey ahead. Tonight I thank my fellow Americans for what you have already done and for what you will do.

And ladies and gentlemen of the Congress, I thank you, their representatives, for what you have already done and for what we will do together.

Tonight we face new and sudden national challenges. We will come together to improve air safety, to dramatically expand the number of air marshals on domestic flights and take new measures to prevent hijacking.

We will come together to promote stability and keep our airlines flying with direct assistance during this emergency.

(APPLAUSE)

We will come together to give law enforcement the additional tools it needs to track down terror here at home.

We will come together to strengthen our intelligence capabilities to know the plans of terrorists before they act and to find them before they strike.

(APPLAUSE)

We will come together to take active steps that strengthen America's economy and put our people back to work.

Tonight, we welcome two leaders who embody the extraordinary spirit of all New Yorkers, Governor George Pataki and Mayor Rudolph Giuliani.

As a symbol of America's resolve, my administration will work with Congress and these two leaders to show the world that we will rebuild New York City.

After all that has just passed, all the lives taken and all the possibilities and hopes that died with them, it is natural to wonder if America's future is one of fear.

Some speak of an age of terror. I know there are struggles ahead and dangers to face. But this country will define our times, not be defined by them.

As long as the United States of America is determined and strong, this will not be an age of terror. This will be an age of liberty here and across the world.

Great harm has been done to us. We have suffered great loss. And in our grief and anger we have found our mission and our moment.

Freedom and fear are at war. The advance of human freedom, the great achievement of our time and the great hope of every time, now depends on us.

Our nation, this generation, will lift the dark threat of violence from our people and our future. We will rally the world to this cause by our efforts, by our courage. We will not tire, we will not falter and we will not fail.
(APPLAUSE)

It is my hope that in the months and years ahead life will return almost to normal. We'll go back to our lives and routines and that is good.

Even grief recedes with time and grace.

But our resolve must not pass. Each of us will remember what happened that day and to whom it happened. We will remember the moment the news came, where we were and what we were doing.

Some will remember an image of a fire or story or rescue. Some will carry memories of a face and a voice gone forever.

And I will carry this. It is the police shield of a man named George Howard who died at the World Trade Center trying to save others.

It was given to me by his mom, Arlene, as a proud memorial to her son. It is my reminder of lives that ended and a task that does not end.

I will not forget the wound to our country and those who inflicted it. I will not yield, I will not rest, I will not relent in waging this struggle for freedom and security for the American people. The course of this conflict is not known, yet its outcome is certain. Freedom and fear, justice and cruelty, have always been at war, and we know that God is not neutral between them.
(APPLAUSE)

Fellow citizens, we'll meet violence with patient justice, assured of the rightness of our cause and confident of the victories to come.

In all that lies before us, may God grant us wisdom and may he watch over the United States of America. Thank you.
(APPLAUSE)

Document 79

Full Official Title: President Barack Obama's Remarks "On a New Beginning" in Cairo, Egypt
Short Title/Acronym/Abbreviation: Obama's Cairo Speech
Type of Document: Presidential Speech
Subject: Human rights, relations between the U.S. and the Muslim world
Official Citation: Not applicable
Date of Document: June 4, 2009
Date of Adoption: Not applicable
Date of General Entry into Force (EIF): Not applicable
Number of States Parties as of this printing: Not applicable
Date of Signature by the United States: Not applicable
Date of Ratification/Accession/Adhesion: Not applicable
Date of Entry into Force as to United States (effective date): Not applicable
Legal Status/Character of the Instrument/Document as to the United States: President Obama gave this speech in Cairo, Egypt shortly after he took office. In his speech, he highlighted the need for a new relationship between America and Muslims throughout the world, in six key priorities. These included addressing violent extremism, the Middle East peace process, a shared concern over nuclear weapons, democracy, religious freedom, and women's rights. This speech was intended to mark a shift in U.S. policy with the Middle East by adopting a less confrontational approach. However, the way the policy has been implemented has received sharp criticism from many divergent human rights advocates in the United States.

PRESIDENT BARAK OBAMA CAIRO SPEECH
Remarks by the President
On A New Beginning
Cairo University
Cairo, Egypt
1:10 P.M. (Local)

PRESIDENT OBAMA: Thank you very much. Good afternoon. I am honored to be in the timeless city of Cairo, and to be hosted by two remarkable institutions. For over a thousand years, Al-Azhar has stood as a beacon of Islamic learning; and for over a century, Cairo University has been a source of Egypt's advancement. And together, you represent the harmony between tradition and progress. I'm grateful for your hospitality, and the hospitality of the people of Egypt. And I'm also proud to carry with me the goodwill of the American people, and a greeting of peace from Muslim communities in my country: Assalaamu alaykum. (Applause.)

We meet at a time of great tension between the United States and Muslims around the world—tension rooted in historical forces that go beyond any current policy debate. The relationship between Islam and the West includes centuries of coexistence and cooperation, but also conflict and religious wars. More recently, tension has been fed by colonialism that denied rights and opportunities to many Muslims, and a Cold War in which Muslim-majority countries were too often treated as proxies without regard to their own aspirations. Moreover, the sweeping change brought by modernity and globalization led many Muslims to view the West as hostile to the traditions of Islam.

Violent extremists have exploited these tensions in a small but potent minority of Muslims. The attacks of September 11, 2001 and the continued efforts of these extremists to engage in violence against civilians has led some in my country to view Islam as inevitably hostile not only to America and Western countries, but also to human rights. All this has bred more fear and more mistrust.

So long as our relationship is defined by our differences, we will empower those who sow hatred rather than peace, those who promote conflict rather than the cooperation that can help all of our people achieve justice and prosperity. And this cycle of suspicion and discord must end.

I've come here to Cairo to seek a new beginning between the United States and Muslims around the world, one based on mutual interest and mutual respect, and one based upon the truth that America and Islam are not exclusive and need not be in competition. Instead, they overlap, and share common principles—principles of justice and progress; tolerance and the dignity of all human beings.

I do so recognizing that change cannot happen overnight. I know there's been a lot of publicity about this speech, but no single speech can eradicate years of mistrust, nor can I answer in the time that I have this afternoon all the complex questions that brought us to this point. But I am convinced that in order to move forward, we must say openly to each other the things we hold in our hearts and that too often are said only behind closed doors. There must be a sustained effort to listen to each other; to learn from each other; to respect one another; and to seek common ground. As the Holy Koran tells us, "Be conscious of God and speak always the truth." (Applause.) That is what I will try to do today—to speak the truth as best I can, humbled by the task before us, and firm in my belief that the interests we share as human beings are far more powerful than the forces that drive us apart.

Now part of this conviction is rooted in my own experience. I'm a Christian, but my father came from a Kenyan family that includes generations of Muslims. As a boy, I spent several years in Indonesia and heard the call of the azaan at the break of dawn and at the fall of dusk. As a young man, I worked in Chicago communities where many found dignity and peace in their Muslim faith.

As a student of history, I also know civilization's debt to Islam. It was Islam—at places like Al-Azhar—that carried the light of learning through so many centuries, paving the way for Europe's Renaissance and Enlightenment. It was innovation in Muslim communities—(applause)—it was innovation in Muslim communities that developed the order of algebra; our magnetic compass and tools of navigation; our mastery of pens and printing; our understanding of how disease spreads and how it can be healed. Islamic culture has given us majestic arches and soaring spires; timeless poetry and cherished music; elegant calligraphy and places of peaceful contemplation. And throughout history, Islam has demonstrated through words and deeds the possibilities of religious tolerance and racial equality. (Applause.)

I also know that Islam has always been a part of America's story. The first nation to recognize my country was Morocco. In signing the Treaty of Tripoli in 1796, our second President, John Adams, wrote, "The United States has in itself no character of enmity against the laws, religion or tranquility of Muslims." And since our founding, American Muslims have enriched the United States. They have fought in our wars, they have served in our government, they have stood for civil rights, they have started businesses, they have taught at our universities, they've excelled in our sports arenas, they've won Nobel Prizes, built our tallest building, and lit the Olympic Torch. And when the first Muslim American was recently elected to Congress, he took the oath to defend our Constitution using the same Holy Koran that one of our Founding Fathers—Thomas Jefferson—kept in his personal library. (Applause.)

So I have known Islam on three continents before coming to the region where it was first revealed. That experience guides my conviction that partnership between America and Islam must be based on what Islam is, not what it isn't. And I consider it part of my responsibility as President of the United States to fight against negative stereotypes of Islam wherever they appear. (Applause.)

But that same principle must apply to Muslim perceptions of America. (Applause.) Just as Muslims do not fit a crude stereotype, America is not the crude stereotype of a self-interested empire. The United States has been one of the greatest sources of progress that the world has ever known. We were born out of revolution against an empire. We were founded upon the ideal that all are created equal, and we have shed blood and struggled for centuries to give meaning to those words—within our borders, and around the world. We are shaped by every culture, drawn from every end of the Earth, and dedicated to a simple concept: E pluribus unum—"Out of many, one."

Now, much has been made of the fact that an African American with the name Barack Hussein Obama could be elected President. (Applause.) But my personal story is not so unique. The dream of opportunity for all people has not come true for everyone in America, but its promise exists for all who come to our shores—and that includes nearly 7 million American Muslims in our country today who, by the way, enjoy incomes and educational levels that are higher than the American average. (Applause.)

Moreover, freedom in America is indivisible from the freedom to practice one's religion. That is why there is a mosque in every state in our union, and over 1,200 mosques within our borders. That's why the United States government has gone to court to protect the right of women and girls to wear the hijab and to punish those who would deny it. (Applause.)

So let there be no doubt: Islam is a part of America. And I believe that America holds within her the truth that regardless of race, religion, or station in life, all of us share common aspirations—to live in peace and security; to get an education and to work with dignity; to love our families, our communities, and our God. These things we share. This is the hope of all humanity.

Of course, recognizing our common humanity is only the beginning of our task. Words alone cannot meet the needs of our people. These needs will be met only if we act boldly in the years ahead; and if we understand that the challenges we face are shared, and our failure to meet them will hurt us all.

For we have learned from recent experience that when a financial system weakens in one country, prosperity is hurt everywhere. When a new flu infects one human being, all are at risk. When one nation pursues a nuclear weapon, the risk of nuclear attack rises for all nations. When violent extremists operate in one stretch of mountains, people are endangered across an ocean. When innocents in Bosnia and Darfur are slaughtered, that is a stain on our collective conscience. (Applause.) That is what it means to share this world in the 21st century. That is the responsibility we have to one another as human beings.

And this is a difficult responsibility to embrace. For human history has often been a record of nations and tribes—and, yes, religions—subjugating one another in pursuit of their own interests. Yet in this new age, such attitudes are self-defeating. Given our interdependence, any world order that elevates one nation or group of people over another will inevitably fail. So whatever we think of the past, we must not be prisoners to it. Our problems must be dealt with through partnership; our progress must be shared. (Applause.)

Now, that does not mean we should ignore sources of tension. Indeed, it suggests the opposite: We must face these tensions squarely. And so in that spirit, let me speak as clearly and as plainly as I can about some specific issues that I believe we must finally confront together.

The first issue that we have to confront is violent extremism in all of its forms.

In Ankara, I made clear that America is not—and never will be—at war with Islam. (Applause.) We will, however, relentlessly confront violent extremists who pose a grave threat to our security—because we reject the same thing that people of all faiths reject: the killing of innocent men, women, and children. And it is my first duty as President to protect the American people.

The situation in Afghanistan demonstrates America's goals, and our need to work together. Over seven years ago, the United States pursued al Qaeda and the Taliban with broad international support. We did not go by choice; we went because of necessity. I'm aware that there's still some who would question or even justify the events of 9/11. But let us be clear: Al Qaeda killed nearly 3,000 people on that day. The victims were innocent men, women and children from America and many other nations who had done nothing to harm anybody. And yet al Qaeda chose to ruthlessly murder these people, claimed credit for the attack, and even now states their determination to kill on a massive scale. They have affiliates in many countries and are trying to expand their reach. These are not opinions to be debated; these are facts to be dealt with.

Now, make no mistake: We do not want to keep our troops in Afghanistan. We see no military—we seek no military bases there. It is agonizing for America to lose our young men and women. It is costly and politically difficult to continue this conflict. We would gladly bring every single one of our troops home if we could be confident that there were not violent extremists in Afghanistan and now Pakistan determined to kill as many Americans as they possibly can. But that is not yet the case.

And that's why we're partnering with a coalition of 46 countries. And despite the costs involved, America's commitment will not weaken. Indeed, none of us should tolerate these extremists. They have killed in many countries. They have killed people of different faiths—but more than any other, they have killed Muslims. Their actions are irreconcilable with the rights of human beings, the progress of nations, and with Islam. The Holy Koran teaches that whoever kills an innocent is as—it is as if he has killed all mankind. (Applause.) And the Holy Koran also says whoever saves a person, it is as if he has saved all mankind. (Applause.) The enduring faith of over a billion people is so much bigger than the narrow hatred of a few. Islam is not part of the problem in combating violent extremism—it is an important part of promoting peace.

Now, we also know that military power alone is not going to solve the problems in Afghanistan and Pakistan. That's why we plan to invest $1.5 billion each year over the next five years to partner with Pakistanis to build schools and hospitals, roads and businesses, and hundreds of millions to help those who've been displaced. That's why we are providing more than $2.8 billion to help Afghans develop their economy and deliver services that people depend on.

Let me also address the issue of Iraq. Unlike Afghanistan, Iraq was a war of choice that provoked strong differences in my country and around the world. Although I believe that the Iraqi people are ultimately better off without the tyranny of Saddam Hussein, I also believe that events in Iraq have reminded America of the need to use diplomacy and build international consensus to resolve our problems whenever possible. (Applause.) Indeed, we can recall the words of Thomas Jefferson, who said: "I hope that our wisdom will grow with our power, and teach us that the less we use our power the greater it will be."

Today, America has a dual responsibility: to help Iraq forge a better future—and to leave Iraq to Iraqis. And I have made it clear to the Iraqi people—(applause)—I have made it clear to the Iraqi people that we pursue no bases, and no claim on their territory or resources. Iraq's sovereignty is its own. And that's why I ordered the removal of our combat brigades by next August. That is why we will honor our agreement with Iraq's democratically elected government to remove combat troops from Iraqi cities by July, and to remove all of our troops from Iraq by 2012. (Applause.) We will help Iraq train its security forces and develop its economy. But we will support a secure and united Iraq as a partner, and never as a patron.

And finally, just as America can never tolerate violence by extremists, we must never alter or forget our principles. Nine-eleven was an enormous trauma to our country. The fear and anger that it provoked was understandable, but in some cases, it led us to act contrary to our traditions and our ideals. We are taking concrete actions to change course. I have unequivocally prohibited the use of torture by the United States, and I have ordered the prison at Guantánamo Bay closed by early next year. (Applause.)

So America will defend itself, respectful of the sovereignty of nations and the rule of law. And we will do so in partnership with Muslim communities which are also threatened. The sooner the extremists are isolated and unwelcome in Muslim communities, the sooner we will all be safer.

The second major source of tension that we need to discuss is the situation between Israelis, Palestinians and the Arab world.

America's strong bonds with Israel are well known. This bond is unbreakable. It is based upon cultural and historical ties, and the recognition that the aspiration for a Jewish homeland is rooted in a tragic history that cannot be denied.

Around the world, the Jewish people were persecuted for centuries, and anti-Semitism in Europe culminated in an unprecedented Holocaust. Tomorrow, I will visit Buchenwald, which was part of a network of camps where Jews were enslaved, tortured, shot and gassed to death by the Third Reich. Six million Jews were killed—more than the entire Jewish population of Israel today. Denying that fact is baseless, it is ignorant, and it is hateful. Threatening Israel with destruction—or repeating vile stereotypes about Jews—is deeply wrong, and only serves to evoke in the minds of Israelis this most painful of memories while preventing the peace that the people of this region deserve.

On the other hand, it is also undeniable that the Palestinian people—Muslims and Christians—have suffered in pursuit of a homeland. For more than 60 years they've endured the pain of dislocation. Many wait in refugee camps in the West Bank, Gaza, and neighboring lands for a life of peace and security that they have never been able to lead. They endure the daily humiliations—large and small—that come with occupation. So let there be no doubt: The situation for the Palestinian people is intolerable. And America will not turn our backs on the legitimate Palestinian aspiration for dignity, opportunity, and a state of their own. (Applause.)

For decades then, there has been a stalemate: two peoples with legitimate aspirations, each with a painful history that makes compromise elusive. It's easy to point fingers—for Palestinians to point to the displacement brought about by Israel's founding, and for Israelis to point to the constant hostility and attacks throughout its history from within its borders as well as beyond. But if we see this conflict only from one side or the other, then we will be blind to the truth: The only resolution is for the aspirations of both sides to be met through two states, where Israelis and Palestinians each live in peace and security. (Applause.)

That is in Israel's interest, Palestine's interest, America's interest, and the world's interest. And that is why I intend to personally pursue this outcome with all the patience and dedication that the task requires. (Applause.) The obligations—the obligations that the parties have agreed to under the road map are clear. For peace to come, it is time for them—and all of us—to live up to our responsibilities.

Palestinians must abandon violence. Resistance through violence and killing is wrong and it does not succeed. For centuries, black people in America suffered the lash of the whip as slaves and the humiliation of segregation. But it was not violence that won full and equal rights. It was a peaceful and determined insistence upon the ideals at the center of America's founding. This same story can be told by people from South Africa to South Asia; from Eastern Europe to Indonesia. It's a story with a simple truth: that violence is a dead end. It is a sign neither of courage nor power to shoot rockets at sleeping children, or to blow up old women on a bus. That's not how moral authority is claimed; that's how it is surrendered.

Now is the time for Palestinians to focus on what they can build. The Palestinian Authority must develop its capacity to govern, with institutions that serve the needs of its people. Hamas does have support among some Palestinians, but they also have to recognize they have responsibilities. To play a role in fulfilling Palestinian aspirations, to unify the Palestinian people, Hamas must put an end to violence, recognize past agreements, recognize Israel's right to exist.

At the same time, Israelis must acknowledge that just as Israel's right to exist cannot be denied, neither can Palestine's. The United States does not accept the legitimacy of continued Israeli settlements. (Applause.) This construction violates previous agreements and undermines efforts to achieve peace. It is time for these settlements to stop. (Applause.)

And Israel must also live up to its obligation to ensure that Palestinians can live and work and develop their society. Just as it devastates Palestinian families, the continuing humanitarian crisis in Gaza does not serve Israel's security; neither does the continuing lack of opportunity in the West Bank. Progress in the daily lives of the Palestinian people must be a critical part of a road to peace, and Israel must take concrete steps to enable such progress.

And finally, the Arab states must recognize that the Arab Peace Initiative was an important beginning, but not the end of their responsibilities. The Arab-Israeli conflict should no longer be used to distract the people of Arab nations from other problems. Instead, it must be a cause for action to help the Palestinian people develop the institutions that will sustain their state, to recognize Israel's legitimacy, and to choose progress over a self-defeating focus on the past.

America will align our policies with those who pursue peace, and we will say in public what we say in private to Israelis and Palestinians and Arabs. (Applause.) We cannot impose peace. But privately, many Muslims recognize that Israel will not go away. Likewise, many Israelis recognize the need for a Palestinian state. It is time for us to act on what everyone knows to be true.

Too many tears have been shed. Too much blood has been shed. All of us have a responsibility to work for the day when the mothers of Israelis and Palestinians can see their children grow up without fear; when the Holy Land of the three great faiths is the place of peace that God intended it to be; when Jerusalem is a secure and lasting home for Jews and Christians and Muslims, and a place for all of the children of Abraham to mingle peacefully together as in the story of Isra—(applause)—as in the story of Isra, when Moses, Jesus, and Mohammed, peace be upon them, joined in prayer. (Applause.)

The third source of tension is our shared interest in the rights and responsibilities of nations on nuclear weapons.

This issue has been a source of tension between the United States and the Islamic Republic of Iran. For many years, Iran has defined itself in part by its opposition to my country, and there is in fact a tumultuous history between us. In the middle of the Cold War, the United States played a role in the overthrow of a democratically elected Iranian government. Since the Islamic Revolution, Iran has played a role in acts of hostage-taking and violence against U.S. troops and civilians. This history is well known. Rather than remain trapped in the past, I've made it clear to Iran's leaders and people that my country is prepared to move forward. The question now is not what Iran is against, but rather what future it wants to build.

I recognize it will be hard to overcome decades of mistrust, but we will proceed with courage, rectitude, and resolve. There will be many issues to discuss between our two countries, and we are willing to move forward without preconditions on the basis of mutual respect. But it is clear to all concerned that when it comes to nuclear weapons, we have reached a decisive point. This is not simply about America's interests. It's about preventing a nuclear arms race in the Middle East that could lead this region and the world down a hugely dangerous path.

I understand those who protest that some countries have weapons that others do not. No single nation should pick and choose which nation holds nuclear weapons. And that's why I strongly reaffirmed America's commitment to seek a world in which no nations hold nuclear weapons. (Applause.) And any nation—including Iran—should have the right to access peaceful nuclear power if it complies with its responsibilities under the nuclear Non-Proliferation Treaty. That commitment is at the core of the treaty, and it must be kept for all who fully abide by it. And I'm hopeful that all countries in the region can share in this goal.

The fourth issue that I will address is democracy. (Applause.)

I know—I know there has been controversy about the promotion of democracy in recent years, and much of this controversy is connected to the war in Iraq. So let me be clear: No system of government can or should be imposed by one nation by any other.

That does not lessen my commitment, however, to governments that reflect the will of the people. Each nation gives life to this principle in its own way, grounded in the traditions of its own people. America does not presume to know what is best for everyone, just as we would not presume to pick the outcome of a peaceful election. But I do have an unyielding belief that all people yearn for certain things: the ability to speak your mind and have a say in how you are governed; confidence in the rule of law and the equal administration of justice; government that is transparent and doesn't steal from the people; the freedom to live as you choose. These are not just American ideas; they are human rights. And that is why we will support them everywhere. (Applause.)

Now, there is no straight line to realize this promise. But this much is clear: Governments that protect these rights are ultimately more stable, successful and secure. Suppressing ideas never succeeds in making them go away. America respects the right of all peaceful and law-abiding voices to be heard around the world, even if we disagree with them. And we will welcome all elected, peaceful governments—provided they govern with respect for all their people.

This last point is important because there are some who advocate for democracy only when they're out of power; once in power, they are ruthless in suppressing the rights of others. (Applause.) So no matter where it takes hold, government of the people and by the people sets a single standard for all who would hold power: You must maintain your power through consent, not coercion; you must respect the rights of minorities, and participate with a spirit of tolerance and compromise; you must place the interests of your people and the legitimate workings of the political process above your party. Without these ingredients, elections alone do not make true democracy.

AUDIENCE MEMBER: Barack Obama, we love you!

PRESIDENT OBAMA: Thank you. (Applause.) The fifth issue that we must address together is religious freedom.

Islam has a proud tradition of tolerance. We see it in the history of Andalusia and Cordoba during the Inquisition. I saw it firsthand as a child in Indonesia, where devout Christians worshiped freely in an overwhelmingly Muslim country. That is the spirit we need today. People in every country should be free to choose and live their faith based upon the persuasion of the mind and the heart and the soul. This tolerance is essential for religion to thrive, but it's being challenged in many different ways.

Among some Muslims, there's a disturbing tendency to measure one's own faith by the rejection of somebody else's faith. The richness of religious diversity must be upheld—whether it is for Maronites in Lebanon or the Copts in Egypt. (Applause.) And if we are being honest, fault lines must be closed among Muslims, as well, as the divisions between Sunni and Shia have led to tragic violence, particularly in Iraq.

Freedom of religion is central to the ability of peoples to live together. We must always examine the ways in which we protect it. For instance, in the United States, rules on charitable giving have made it harder for Muslims to fulfill their religious obligation. That's why I'm committed to working with American Muslims to ensure that they can fulfill zakat.

Likewise, it is important for Western countries to avoid impeding Muslim citizens from practicing religion as they see fit—for instance, by dictating what clothes a Muslim woman should wear. We can't disguise hostility towards any religion behind the pretence of liberalism.

In fact, faith should bring us together. And that's why we're forging service projects in America to bring together Christians, Muslims, and Jews. That's why we welcome efforts like Saudi Arabian King Abdullah's interfaith dialogue and Turkey's leadership in the Alliance of Civilizations. Around the world, we can turn dialogue into interfaith service, so bridges between peoples lead to action—whether it is combating malaria in Africa, or providing relief after a natural disaster.

The sixth issue—the sixth issue that I want to address is women's rights. (Applause.) I know—I know—and you can tell from this audience, that there is a healthy debate about this issue. I reject the view of some in the West that a woman who chooses to cover her hair is somehow less equal, but I do believe that a woman who is denied an education is denied equality. (Applause.) And it is no coincidence that countries where women are well educated are far more likely to be prosperous.

Now, let me be clear: Issues of women's equality are by no means simply an issue for Islam. In Turkey, Pakistan, Bangladesh, Indonesia, we've seen Muslim-majority countries elect a woman to lead. Meanwhile, the struggle for women's equality continues in many aspects of American life, and in countries around the world.

I am convinced that our daughters can contribute just as much to society as our sons. (Applause.) Our common prosperity will be advanced by allowing all humanity—men and women—to reach their full potential. I do not believe that women must make the same choices as men in order to be equal, and I respect those women who choose to live their lives in traditional roles. But it should be their choice. And that is why the United States will partner with any Muslim-majority country to support expanded literacy for girls, and to help young women pursue employment through micro-financing that helps people live their dreams. (Applause.)

Finally, I want to discuss economic development and opportunity.

I know that for many, the face of globalization is contradictory. The Internet and television can bring knowledge and information, but also offensive sexuality and mindless violence into the home. Trade can bring new wealth and opportunities, but also huge disruptions and change in communities. In all nations—including America—this change can bring fear. Fear that because of modernity we lose control over our economic choices, our politics, and most importantly our identities—those things we most cherish about our communities, our families, our traditions, and our faith.

But I also know that human progress cannot be denied. There need not be contradictions between development and tradition. Countries like Japan and South Korea grew their economies enormously while maintaining distinct cultures. The same is true for the astonishing progress within Muslim-majority countries from Kuala Lumpur to Dubai. In ancient times and in our times, Muslim communities have been at the forefront of innovation and education.

And this is important because no development strategy can be based only upon what comes out of the ground, nor can it be sustained while young people are out of work. Many Gulf states have enjoyed great wealth as a consequence of oil, and some are beginning to focus it on broader development. But all of us must recognize that education and innovation will be the currency of the 21st century—(applause)—and in too many Muslim communities, there remains underinvestment in these areas. I'm emphasizing such investment within my own country. And while America in the past has focused on oil and gas when it comes to this part of the world, we now seek a broader engagement.

On education, we will expand exchange programs, and increase scholarships, like the one that brought my father to America. (Applause.) At the same time, we will encourage more Americans to study in Muslim communities. And we will match promising Muslim students with internships in America; invest in online learning for teachers and children around the world; and create a new online network, so a young person in Kansas can communicate instantly with a young person in Cairo.

On economic development, we will create a new corps of business volunteers to partner with counterparts in Muslim-majority countries. And I will host a Summit on Entrepreneurship this year to identify how we can deepen ties between business leaders, foundations and social entrepreneurs in the United States and Muslim communities around the world.

On science and technology, we will launch a new fund to support technological development in Muslim-majority countries, and to help transfer ideas to the marketplace so they can create more jobs. We'll open centers of scientific excellence in Africa, the Middle East and Southeast Asia, and appoint new science envoys to collaborate on programs that develop new sources of energy, create green jobs, digitize records, clean water, grow new crops. Today I'm announcing a new global effort with the Organization of the Islamic Conference to eradicate polio. And we will also expand partnerships with Muslim communities to promote child and maternal health.

All these things must be done in partnership. Americans are ready to join with citizens and governments; community organizations, religious leaders, and businesses in Muslim communities around the world to help our people pursue a better life.

The issues that I have described will not be easy to address. But we have a responsibility to join together on behalf of the world that we seek—a world where extremists no longer threaten our people, and American troops have come home; a world where Israelis and Palestinians are each secure in a state of their own, and nuclear energy is used for peaceful purposes; a world where governments serve their citizens, and the rights of all God's children are respected. Those are mutual interests. That is the world we seek. But we can only achieve it together.

I know there are many—Muslim and non-Muslim—who question whether we can forge this new beginning. Some are eager to stoke the flames of division, and to stand in the way of progress. Some suggest that it isn't worth the effort—that we are fated to disagree, and civilizations are doomed to clash. Many more are simply skeptical that real change can occur. There's so much fear, so much mistrust that has built up over the years. But if we choose to be bound by the past, we will never move forward. And I want to particularly say this to young people of every faith, in every country—you, more than anyone, have the ability to reimagine the world, to remake this world.

All of us share this world for but a brief moment in time. The question is whether we spend that time focused on what pushes us apart, or whether we commit ourselves to an effort—a sustained effort—to find common ground, to focus on the future we seek for our children, and to respect the dignity of all human beings.

It's easier to start wars than to end them. It's easier to blame others than to look inward. It's easier to see what is different about someone than to find the things we share. But we should choose the right path, not just the easy path. There's one rule that lies at the heart of every religion—that we do unto others as we would have them do unto us. (Applause.) This truth transcends nations and peoples—a belief that isn't new; that isn't black or white or brown; that isn't Christian or Muslim or Jew. It's a belief that pulsed in the cradle of civilization, and that still beats in the hearts of billions around the world. It's a faith in other people, and it's what brought me here today.

We have the power to make the world we seek, but only if we have the courage to make a new beginning, keeping in mind what has been written.

The Holy Koran tells us: "O mankind! We have created you male and a female; and we have made you into nations and tribes so that you may know one another."

The Talmud tells us: "The whole of the Torah is for the purpose of promoting peace."

The Holy Bible tells us: "Blessed are the peacemakers, for they shall be called sons of God." (Applause.)

The people of the world can live together in peace. We know that is God's vision. Now that must be our work here on Earth.

Thank you. And may God's peace be upon you. Thank you very much. Thank you. (Applause.)
END
2:05 P.M. (Local)

DOCUMENT **80**
Full Official Title: Remarks on the Human Rights Agenda for the 21st Century, by Secretary of State Hilary Clinton

Short Title/Acronym/Abbreviation: Nothing official

Type of Document: A speech by the Secretary of State

Subject: Georgetown University Speech on the Human Rights Agenda of the Obama Administration and the course of U.S. foreign policy

Official Citation: Not applicable

Date of Document: December 14, 2009
Date of Adoption: Not applicable
Date of General Entry into Force (EIF): Not applicable
Number of States Parties as of this printing: Not applicable
Date of Signature by United States: Not applicable
Date of Ratification/Accession/Adhesion: Not applicable
Date of Entry into Force as to United States (effective date): Not applicable
Legal Status/Character of the Instrument/Document as to the United States: Not binding. A statement of U.S. Government Administration policy.
Web Address: www.state.gov/secretary/rm/2009a/12/133544/html

SECRETARY OF STATE HILARY CLINTON, GEORGETOWN UNIVERSITY SPEECH ON THE HUMAN RIGHTS AGENDA OF THE OBAMA ADMINISTRATION

SECRETARY CLINTON: Thank you. It is wonderful being back here at Georgetown in this magnificent Gaston Hall, and to give you something to do during exam week. … It's one of those quasi-legitimate reasons for taking a break—which I'm very happy to have provided.

I want to thank Jas for his introductory remarks, and clearly, those of you who are in the Foreign Service School heard reflections of the extraordinary opportunity you've been given to study here as he spoke about the culture of human rights. It is also a real honor for me to be delivering this speech at Georgetown, because there is no better place than this university to talk about human rights. And President DeGioia, the administration, and the faculty embody the university's long tradition of supporting free expression and free inquiry and the cause of human rights around the world.

I know that President DeGioia himself has taught a course on human rights, as well as on the ethics of international development with one of my longtime colleagues, Carol Lancaster, the acting dean of the School of Foreign Service. And I want to commend the faculty here who are helping to shape our thinking on human rights, on conflict resolution, on development and related subjects. It is important to be at this university because the students here, the faculty, every single year add to the interreligious dialogue. You give voice to many advocates and activists who are working on the front lines of the global human rights movement, through the Human Rights Institute here at the law school and other programs. And the opportunities that you provide your students to work in an international women's rights clinic are especially close to my heart.

All of these efforts reflect the deep commitment of the Georgetown administration, faculty, and students to this cause. So first and foremost, I am here to say thank you. Thank you for keeping human rights front and center. Thank you for training the next generation of human rights advocates, and more generally, introducing students who may never be an activist, may never work for Amnesty International or any other organization specifically devoted to human rights, but who will leave this university with it imbued in their hearts and minds. So thank you, President DeGioia, for all that you do and all that Georgetown has done.

Today, I want to speak to you about the Obama Administration's human rights agenda for the 21st century. It is a subject on the minds of many people who are eager to hear our approach, and understandably so, because it is a critical issue that warrants our energy and our attention. My comments today will provide an overview of our thinking on human rights and democracy and how they fit into our broader foreign policy, as well as the principles and policies that guide our approach.

But let me also say that what this is not. It could not be a comprehensive accounting of abuses or nations with whom we have raised human rights concerns. It could not be and is not a checklist or a scorecard. We issue a Human Rights Report every year and that goes into great detail on the concerns we have for many countries. But I hope that we can use this opportunity to look at this important issue in a broader light and appreciate its full complexity, moral weight, and urgency. And with that, let me turn to the business at hand.

In his acceptance speech for the Nobel Peace Prize last week, President Obama said that while war is never welcome or good, it will sometimes be right and necessary, because, in his words, "Only a just peace based upon the inherent rights and dignity of every individual can be truly lasting." Throughout history and in our own time, there have been those who violently deny that truth. Our mission is to embrace it, to work for lasting peace through a principled human rights agenda, and a practical strategy to implement it.

President Obama's speech also reminded us that our basic values, the ones enshrined in our Declaration of Independence—the rights to life, liberty, and the pursuit of happiness—are not only the source of our strength and endurance; they are the birthright of every woman, man, and child on earth. That is also the promise of the Universal Declaration of Human Rights, the prerequisite for building a world in which every person has the opportunity to live up to his or her God-given potential, and the power behind every movement for freedom, every campaign for democracy, every effort to foster development, and every struggle against oppression.

The potential within every person to learn, discover and embrace the world around them, the potential to join freely with others to shape their communities and their societies so that every person can find fulfillment and self-sufficiency, the potential to share life's beauties and tragedies, laughter and tears with the people we love—that potential is sacred. That, however, is a dangerous belief to many who hold power and who construct their position against an "other"—another tribe or religion or race or gender or political party. Standing up against that false sense of identity and expanding the circle of rights and opportunities to all people—advancing their freedoms and possibilities—is why we do what we do.

This week we observe Human Rights Week. At the State Department, though, every week is Human Rights Week. Sixty-one years ago this month, the world's leaders proclaimed a new framework of rights, laws, and institutions that could fulfill the vow of "never again." They affirmed the universality of human rights through the Universal Declaration and legal agreements including those aimed at combating genocide, war crimes and torture, and challenging discrimination against women and racial and religious minorities. Burgeoning civil society movements and nongovernmental organizations became essential partners in advancing the principle that every person counts, and in exposing those who violate that standard.

As we celebrate that progress, though, our focus must be on the work that remains to be done. The preamble of the Universal Declaration of Human Rights encourages us to use it as a, quote, "standard of achievement." And so we should. But we cannot deny the gap that remains between its eloquent promises and the life experiences of so many of our fellow human beings. Now, we must finish the job.

Our human rights agenda for the 21st century is to make human rights a human reality, and the first step is to see human rights in a broad context. Of course, people must be free from the oppression of tyranny, from torture, from discrimination, from the fear of leaders who will imprison or "disappear" them. But they also must be free from the oppression of want—want of food, want of health, want of education, and want of equality in law and in fact.

To fulfill their potential, people must be free to choose laws and leaders; to share and access information, to speak, criticize, and debate. They must be free to worship, associate, and to love in the way that they choose. And they must be free to pursue the dignity that comes with self-improvement and self-reliance, to build their minds and their skills, to bring their goods to the marketplace, and participate in the process of innovation. Human rights have both negative and positive requirements. People should be free from tyranny in whatever form, and they should also be free to seize the opportunities of a full life. That is why supporting democracy and fostering development are cornerstones of our 21st century human rights agenda.

This Administration, like others before us, will promote, support, and defend democracy. We will relinquish neither the word nor the idea to those who have used it too narrowly, or to justify unwise policies. We stand for democracy not because we want other countries to be like us, but because we want all people to enjoy the consistent protection of the rights that are naturally theirs, whether they were born in Tallahassee or Tehran. Democracy has proven the best political system for making human rights a human reality over the long term.

But it is crucial that we clarify what we mean when we talk about democracy, because democracy means not only elections to choose leaders, but also active citizens and a free press and an independent judiciary and transparent and responsive institutions that are accountable to all citizens and protect their rights equally and fairly. In democracies, respecting rights isn't a choice leaders make day by day; it is the reason they govern. Democracies protect and respect citizens every day, not just on Election Day. And democracies demonstrate their greatness not by insisting they are perfect, but by using their institutions and their principles to make themselves and their union more perfect, just as our country continues to do after 233 years.

At the same time, human development must also be part of our human rights agenda. Because basic levels of well-being—food, shelter, health, and education—and of public common goods like environmental sustainability, protection against pandemic disease, provisions for refugees—are necessary for people to exercise their rights, and because human development and democracy are mutually reinforcing. Democratic governments are not likely to survive long if their citizens do not have the basic necessities of life. The desperation caused by poverty and disease often leads to violence that further imperils the rights of people and threatens the stability of governments. Democracies that deliver on rights, opportunities, and development for their people are stable, strong, and most likely to enable people to live up to their potential.

So human rights, democracy, and development are not three separate goals with three separate agendas. That view doesn't reflect the reality we face. To make a real and long-term difference in people's lives, we have to tackle all three simultaneously with a commitment that is smart, strategic, determined, and long-term. We should measure our success by asking this question: Are more people in more places better able to exercise their universal rights and live up to their potential because of our actions?

Our principles are our North Star, but our tools and tactics must be flexible and reflect the reality on the ground wherever we are trying to have a positive impact. Now, in some cases, governments are willing but unable without support to establish strong institutions and protections for citizens—for example, the nascent democracies in Africa. And we can extend our hand as a partner to help them try to achieve authority and build the progress they desire. In other cases, like Cuba or Nigeria, governments are able but unwilling to make the changes their citizens deserve. There, we must vigorously press leaders to end repression, while supporting those within societies who are working for change. And in cases where governments are both unwilling and unable—places like the eastern Congo—we have to support those courageous individuals and organizations who try to protect people and who battle against the odds to plant seeds for a more hopeful future.

Now, I don't need to tell you that challenges we face are diverse and complicated. And there is not one approach or formula, doctrine or theory that can be easily applied to every situation. But I want to outline four elements of the Obama Administration's approach to putting our principles into action, and share with you some of the challenges we face in doing so.

First, a commitment to human rights starts with universal standards and with holding everyone accountable to those standards, including ourselves. On his second full day in office, President Obama issued an executive order prohibiting the use of torture or official cruelty by any U.S. official and ordered the closure of Guantánamo Bay. Next year, we will report on human trafficking, as we do every year, but this time, not only just on other countries, but also on our own. And we will participate through the United Nations in the Universal Periodic Review of our own human rights record, just as we encourage other nations to do.

By holding ourselves accountable, we reinforce our moral authority to demand that all governments adhere to obligations under international law; among them, not to torture, arbitrarily detain and persecute dissenters, or engage in political killings. Our government and the international community must counter the pretensions of those who deny or abdicate their responsibilities and hold violators to account.

Sometimes, we will have the most impact by publicly denouncing a government action, like the coup in Honduras or violence in Guinea. Other times, we will be more likely to help the oppressed by engaging in tough negotiations behind closed doors, like pressing China and Russia as part of our broader agenda. In every instance, our aim will be to make a difference, not to prove a point.

Calling for accountability doesn't start or stop, however, at naming offenders. Our goal is to encourage—even demand—that governments must also take responsibility by putting human rights into law and embedding them in government institutions; by building strong, independent courts, competent and disciplined police and law enforcement. And once rights are established, governments should be expected to resist the temptation to restrict freedom of expression when criticism arises, and to be vigilant in preventing law from becoming an instrument of oppression, as bills like the one under consideration in Uganda would do to criminalize homosexuality.

We know that all governments and all leaders sometimes fall short. So there have to be internal mechanisms of accountability when rights are violated. Often the toughest test for governments, which is essential to the protection of human rights, is absorbing and accepting criticism. And here too, we should lead by example. In the last six decades we have done this—imperfectly at times but with significant outcomes—from making amends for the internment of our own Japanese American citizens in World War II, to establishing legal recourse for victims of discrimination in the Jim Crow South, to passing hate crimes legislation to include attacks against gays and lesbians. When injustice anywhere is ignored, justice everywhere is denied. Acknowledging and remedying mistakes does not make us weaker, it reaffirms the strength of our principles and institutions.

Second, we must be pragmatic and agile in pursuit of our human rights agenda—not compromising on our principles, but doing what is most likely to make them real. And we will use all the tools at our disposal, and when we run up against a wall, we will not retreat with resignation or recriminations, or repeatedly run up against the same well, but respond with strategic resolve to find another way to effect change and improve people's lives.

We acknowledge that one size does not fit all. And when old approaches aren't working, we won't be afraid to attempt new ones, as we have this year by ending the stalemate of isolation and instead pursuing measured engagement with Burma. In Iran, we have offered to negotiate directly with the government on nuclear issues, but have at the same time expressed solidarity with those inside Iran struggling for democratic change. As President Obama said in his Nobel speech, "They have us on their side."

And we will hold governments accountable for their actions, as we have just recently by terminating Millennium Challenge Corporation grants this year for Madagascar and Niger in the wake of government behavior. As the President said last week, "we must try as best we can to balance isolation and engagement; pressure and incentives, so that human rights and dignity are advanced over time."

We are also working for positive change within multilateral institutions. They are valuable tools that, when in their best, leverage the efforts of many countries around a common purpose. So we have rejoined the U.N. Human Rights Council not because we don't see its flaws, but because we think that participating gives us the best chance to be a constructive influence.

In our first session, we cosponsored the successful resolution on Freedom of Expression, a forceful declaration of principle at a time when that freedom is jeopardized by new efforts to constrain religious practice, including recently in Switzerland, and by efforts to criminalize the defamation of religion—a false solution which exchanges one wrong for another. And in the United Nations Security Council, I was privileged to chair the September session where we passed a resolution mandating protections against sexual violence in armed conflict.

Principled pragmatism informs our approach on human rights with all countries, but particularly with key countries like China and Russia. Cooperation with each of those is critical to the health of the global economy and the nonproliferation agenda we seek, also to managing security issues like North Korea and Iran, and addressing global problems like climate change.

The United States seeks positive relationships with China and Russia, and that means candid discussions of divergent views. In China, we call for protection of rights of minorities in Tibet and Xinxiang; for the rights to express oneself and worship freely; and for civil society and religious organizations to advocate their positions within a framework of the rule of law. And we believe strongly that those who advocate peacefully for reform within the constitution, such as Charter 2008 signatories, should not be prosecuted.

With Russia, we deplore the murders of journalists and activists and support the courageous individuals who advocate at great peril for democracy. With China, Russia, and others, we are engaging on issues of mutual interest while also engaging societal actors in these same countries who are working to advance human rights and democracy. The assumption that we must either pursue human rights or our "national interests" is wrong. The assumption that only coercion and isolation are effective tools for advancing democratic change is also wrong.

Across our diplomacy and development efforts, we keep striving for innovative ways to achieve results. That's why I commissioned the first-ever Quadrennial Diplomacy and Development Review to develop a forward-looking strategy built on analysis of our objectives, our challenges, our tools, and our capacities to achieve America's foreign policy and national security objectives. And make no mistake, issues of Democracy and Governance—D&G as they are called at USAID—are central to this review.

The third element of our approach is that we support change driven by citizens and their communities. The project of making human rights a human reality cannot be just one for governments. It requires cooperation among individuals and organizations within communities and across borders. It means that we work with others who share our commitment to securing lives of dignity for all who share the bonds of humanity.

Six weeks ago, in Morocco, I met with civil society activists from across the Middle East and North Africa. They exemplify how lasting change comes from within and how it depends on activists who create the space in which engaged citizens and civil society can build the foundations for rights-respecting development and democracy. Outside governments and global civil society cannot impose change, but we can promote and bolster it and defend it. We can encourage and provide support for local grassroots leaders, providing a lifeline of protection to human rights and democracy activists when they get in trouble, as they often do, for raising sensitive issues and voicing dissent. This means using tools like our Global Human Rights Defenders Fund, which in the last year has provided targeted legal and relocation assistance to 170 human rights defenders around the world.

And we can stand with these defenders publicly, as we have by sending a high-level diplomatic mission to meet with Aung San Suu Kyi, and as I have done around the world, from Guatemala to Kenya to Egypt, speaking out for civil society and political leaders who are working to try to change their societies from within, and also working through the backchannels for the safety of dissidents and protecting them from persecution.

We can amplify the voices of activists and advocates working on these issues by shining a spotlight on their progress. They often pursue their mission in isolation, often so marginalized within their own societies. And we can endorse the legitimacy of their efforts. We recognize these with honors like the Women of Courage awards that First Lady Michelle Obama and I presented earlier this year and the Human Rights Defenders award I will present next month, and we can applaud others like Vital Voices, the RFK Center for Justice and Human Rights, and the Lantos Foundation, that do the same.

We can give them access to public forums that lend visibility to their ideas, and continue to press for a role for nongovernmental organizations in multilateral institutions like the United Nations and the OSCE. And we can enlist other allies like international labor unions who were instrumental in the Solidarity movement in Poland or religious organizations who are championing the rights of people living with HIV/AIDS in Africa.

We can help change agents, gain access to and share information through the internet and mobile phones so that they can communicate and organize. With camera phones and Facebook pages, thousands of protestors in Iran have broadcast their demands for rights denied, creating a record for all the world, including Iran's leaders, to see. I've established a special unit inside the State Department to use technology for 21st century statecraft.

In virtually every country I visit—from Indonesia to Iraq, from South Korea to the Dominican Republic—I conduct a town hall or roundtable discussion with groups outside of government to learn from them, and to provide a platform for their voices, ideas, and opinions. When I was recently in Russia, I visited an independent radio station to give an interview, and express through word and deed our support for independent media at a time when free expression is under threat.

On my visits to China, I have made a point of meeting with women activists. The U.N. Conference on Women in Beijing in 1995 inspired a generation of women civil society leaders who have become rights defenders for today's China. In 1998, I met with a small group of lawyers in a crowded apartment on the fifth floor of a walk-up building. They described for me their efforts to win rights for women to own property, have a say in marriage and divorce, and be treated as equal citizens.

When I visited China again earlier this year, I met with some of the same women, but this group had grown and expanded its scope. Now there were women working not just for legal rights, but for environmental, health, and economic rights as well.

Yet one of them, Dr. Gao Yaojie, has been harassed for speaking out about AIDS in China. She should instead be applauded by her government for helping to confront the crisis. NGOs and civil society leaders need the financial, technical and political support we provide. Many repressive regimes have tried to limit the independence and effectiveness of activists and NGOs by restricting their activities, including more than 25 governments that have recently adopted new restrictions. But our funding and support can give a foothold to local organizations, training programs, and independent media. And of course, one of the most important ways that we and others in the international community can lay the foundation for change from the bottom up is through targeted assistance to those in need, and through partnerships that foster broad-based economic development.

To build success for the long run, our development assistance needs to be as effective as possible at delivering results and paving the way for broad-based growth and long-term self-reliance. Beyond giving people the capacity to meet their material needs for today, economic empowerment should give them a stake in securing their own futures, in seeing their societies become the kind of democracies that protect rights and govern fairly. So we will pursue a rights-respecting approach to development—consulting with local communities, ensuring transparency, midwife-ing accountable institutions—so our development activities act in concert with our efforts to support democratic governance. That is the pressing challenge we face in Afghanistan and Pakistan today.

The fourth element of our approach is that we will widen our focus. We will not forget that positive change must be reinforced and strengthened where hope is on the rise, and we will not ignore or overlook places of seemingly intractable tragedy and despair. Where human lives hang in the balance, we must do what we can to tilt that balance toward a better future.

Our efforts to support those working for human rights, economic empowerment, and democratic governance are driven by commitment, not convenience. But they have to be sustained. They cannot be subject to the whims or the wins of political change in our own country. Democratic progress is urgent but it is not quick, and we should never take for granted its permanence. Backsliding is always a threat, as we've learned in places like Kenya where the perpetrators of post-election violence have thus far escaped justice; and in the Americas where we are worried about leaders who have seized property, trampled rights, and abused justice to enhance personal rule.

And when democratic change occurs, we cannot afford to become complacent. Instead, we have to continue reinforcing NGOs and the fledgling institutions of democracy. Young democracies like Liberia, East Timor, Moldova and Kosovo need our help to secure improvements in health, education and welfare. We must stay engaged to nurture democratic development in places like Ukraine and Georgia, which experienced democratic breakthroughs earlier this decade but have struggled to consolidate their democratic gains because of both internal and external factors.

So we stand ready—both in our bilateral relationships and through international institutions—to help governments that have committed to improving themselves by assisting them in fighting corruption and helping train police forces and public servants. And we will support regional organizations and institutions like the Organization of American States, the African Union, and the Association of Southeast Asian Nations, where they take their own steps to defend democratic principles and institutions.

Success stories deserve our attention so they continue to make progress and also serve as a model for others. And even as we reinforce the successes, conscience demands that we are not cowed by the overwhelming difficulty of making inroads against misery in the hard places like Sudan, Congo, North Korea, Zimbabwe, or on the hard issues like ending gender inequality and discrimination against gays and lesbians, from the Middle East to Latin America, Africa to Asia.

Now, we have to continue to press for solutions in Sudan where ongoing tensions threaten to add to the devastation wrought by genocide in Darfur and an overwhelming refugee crisis. We will work to identify ways that we and our partners can enhance human security, while at the same time focusing greater attention on efforts to prevent genocide elsewhere.

And of course, we have to remain focused on women—women's rights, women's roles, and women's responsibilities. As I said in Beijing in 1995, "human rights are women's rights, and women's rights are human rights," but oh, I wish it could be so easily translated into action and changes. That ideal is far from being realized in so many places around our world, but there is no place that so epitomizes the very difficult, tragic circumstances confronting women than in eastern Congo.

I was in Goma last August, the epicenter of one of the most violent and chaotic regions on earth. And when I was there, I met with victims of horrific gender and sexual violence, and I met with refugees driven from their homes by the many military forces operating there. I heard from those working to end the conflicts and to protect the victims in such dire circumstances. I saw the best and the worst of humanity in a single day, the unspeakable acts of violence that have left women physically and emotionally brutalized, and the heroism of the women and men themselves, of the doctors, nurses and volunteers working to repair bodies and spirits.

They are on the front lines of the struggle for human rights. Seeing firsthand their courage and tenacity of they and the Congolese people and the internal fortitude that keeps them going is not only humbling, but inspires me every day to keep working.

So those four aspects of our approach—accountability, principled pragmatism, partnering from the bottom up, keeping a wide focus where rights are at stake—will help build a foundation that enables people to stand and rise above poverty, hunger, and disease and that secures their rights under democratic governance. We must lift the ceiling of oppression, corruption, and violence.

And we must light a fire of human potential through access to education and economic opportunity. Build the foundation, lift the ceiling, and light the fire all together, all at once. Because when a person has food and education but not the freedom to discuss and debate with fellow citizens, he is denied the life he deserves. And when a person is too hungry or sick to work or vote or worship, she is denied a life she deserves. Freedom doesn't come in half measures, and partial remedies cannot redress the whole problem.

But we know that the champions of human potential have never had it easy. We may call rights inalienable, but making them so has always been hard work. And no matter how clearly we see our ideals, taking action to make them real requires tough choices. Even if everyone agrees that we should do whatever is most likely to improve the lives of people on the ground, we will not always agree on what course of action fits that description in every case. That is the nature of governing. We all know examples of good intentions that did not produce results, some that even produced unintended consequences that led to greater violations of human rights. And we can learn from the instances in which we have fallen short in the past, because those past difficulties are proof of how difficult progress is, but we do not accept the argument by some that progress in certain places is impossible, because we know progress happens.

Ghana emerged from an era of coups to one of stable democratic governance. Indonesia moved from repressive rule to a dynamic democracy that is Islamic and secular. Chile exchanged dictatorship for democracy and an open economy. Mongolia's constitutional reforms successfully ushered in multiparty democracy without violence. And there is no better example than the progress made in Central and Eastern Europe since the fall of the Berlin Wall 20 years ago, an event I was privileged to help celebrate last month at the Brandenburg Gate.

While the work in front of us is daunting and vast, we face the future together with partners on every continent, partners in faith-based organizations, NGOs, and socially responsible corporations, and partners in governments. From India, the world's largest democracy, and one that continues to use democratic processes and principles to perfect its union of 1.1 billion people, to Botswana where the new president in Africa's oldest democracy has promised to govern according to what he calls the "5 Ds"—democracy, dignity, development, discipline, and delivery—providing a recipe for responsible governance that contrasts starkly with the unnecessary and manmade tragedy in neighboring Zimbabwe.

In the end, this isn't just about what we do; it is about who we are. And we cannot be the people we are—people who believe in human rights—if we opt out of this fight. Believing in human rights means committing ourselves to action, and when we sign up for the promise of rights that apply everywhere, to everyone, that rights will be able to protect and enable human dignity, we also sign up for the hard work of making that promise a reality.

Those of you here at this great university spend time studying the cases of what we've tried to do in human rights, or as Jas said, the culture of human rights. You see the shortcomings and the shortfalls. You see the fact that, as Mario Cuomo famously said about politics here in the United States, we campaign in poetry and we govern in prose. Well, that's true internationally as well. But we need your ideas, we need your criticism, we need your support, we need your intelligent analysis of how together we can slowly, steadily expand that circle of opportunity and rights to every single person.

It is work that we take so seriously. It is work that we know we don't have all the answers for. But it is the work that America signed up to do. And we will continue, day by day, inch by inch, to try to make whatever progress is humanly possible. Thank you all very much. (Applause.)

MODERATOR: Thank you, Secretary Clinton, for an inspiring, comprehensive, and wonderful speech. It made me proud to be an American.

SECRETARY CLINTON: Thank you so much.

MODERATOR: And proud to be at Georgetown, too. (Laughter.)

The Secretary has time for three questions, and we thought because so many of you have abandoned your final papers to be here—the students, that is—that we would take those questions from our students. So let me ask you—we have several people along the sides with microphones. Let—okay, here's somebody with a microphone. Have we got one more? Okay.

So let's have a first question from a student. That doesn't look like a student. (Laughter.) Let's get—here, let's get a young person here. We're not discriminating. We just want a calm approach to things.

QUESTION: Hello, Secretary Clinton. Thank you so much for speaking to us today. You spoke about the situation in Uganda. Could you please talk to us a little bit more about how the United States can protect the rights of LGBT people in areas where those rights are not respected?

SECRETARY CLINTON: Yes. And first let me say that over this past year, we have elevated into our human rights dialogues and our public statements a very clear message about protecting the rights of the LGBT community worldwide. And we are particularly concerned about some of the specific cases that have come to our attention around the world. There have been organized efforts to kill and maim gays and lesbians in some countries that we have spoken out about, and also conveyed our very strong concerns about to their governments—not that they were governmentally implemented or even that the government was aware of them, but that the governments need to pay much greater attention to the kinds of abuses that we've seen in Iraq, for example.

We are deeply concerned about some of the stories coming out of Iran. In large measure, in reaction, we think, to the response to the elections back in June, there have been abuses committed within the detention facilities and elsewhere that we are deeply concerned about. And then the example that I used of a piece of legislation in Uganda which would not only criminalize homosexuality but attach the death penalty to it. We have expressed our concerns directly, indirectly, and we will continue to do so. The bill has not gone through the Ugandan legislature, but it has a lot of public support by various groups, including religious leaders in Uganda. And we view it as a very serious potential violation of human rights.

So it is clear that across the world this is a new frontier in the minds of many people about how we protect the LGBT community, but it is at the top of our list because we see many instances where there is a very serious assault on the physical safety and an increasing effort to marginalize people. And we think it's important for the United States to stand against that and to enlist others to join us in doing so.

MODERATOR: Right here.

QUESTION: Good morning, Secretary Clinton. Thank you so much for being here at Georgetown. You brought up Iran today, and I really appreciate that as an Iranian American. I'm a graduate student here and had the pleasure of being in Iran this summer for my first trip, and to witness really what happened after the election was an incredible moment in history.

Now that six months has passed after the election, what can the United States do to balance our support of the human rights activists and demonstrators in the streets of Iran with our agenda regarding the broader international security issues with Iran's proposed nuclear program? So how do we balance those two issues?

SECRETARY CLINTON: Right. Well, it is a balancing act. But the more important balancing act is to make sure that our very strong opposition to what is going on inside Iran doesn't in any way undermine the legitimacy of the protest movement that has taken hold. Now, this is one of those very good examples of a hard call. After the election and the reaction that began almost immediately by people who felt that the election was invalid, put us in a position of seriously considering what is the best way we can support those who are putting their lives on the line by going into the streets. We wanted to convey clear support, but we didn't want the attention shifted from the legitimate concerns to the United States, because we had nothing to do with the spontaneous reaction that grew up in response to the behavior of the Iranian Government.

So it's been a delicate walk, but I think that the activists inside Iran know that we support them. We have certainly encouraged their continuing communication of what's going on inside Iran. One of the calls that we made shortly after the election in the midst of the demonstrations is this unit of these very tech-savvy young people that we've created inside the State Department knew that there was a lot of communication going on about demonstrations and sharing information on Twitter, and that totally unconnected to what was going on in Iran, Twitter had planned some kind of lapse in service to do something on their system—you can tell I have no idea what they were doing. (Laughter.) I mean, you know, I don't know Twitter from Tweeter, so—(laughter)—to be honest with you.

So these young tech people in the State Department called Twitter and said don't take Twitter down right now. Whatever you're going to do to reboot or whatever it is—(laughter)—don't take Twitter down because people in Iran are dependent upon Twitter. So we have done that careful balancing.

Now, clearly, we think that pursuing an agenda of nonproliferation is a human rights issue. I mean, what would be worse than nuclear material or even a nuclear weapon being in the hands of either a state or a non-state actor that would be used to intimidate and threaten and even, in the worst-case scenario, destroy?

So we see a continuum. So pursuing what we think is in the national security interest not only of the United States but countries in Europe and in the Middle East is also a human rights issue. So we do not want to be in an either/or position: Are we going to pursue nonproliferation with Iran or are we going to support the demonstrators inside Iran? We're going to do both to the best of our ability to get a result that will further the cause we are seeking to support.

MODERATOR: One final question in the back. Right there, with the red. Right. Christmas red.

QUESTION: Thank you. I am wondering what you see the role of artists doing in helping to promote human rights. I had the privilege earlier this summer to hear the playwright Lynn Nottage speak in one of the Senate buildings after she advocated for women's rights in the Congo, and I wonder how you see creative practice accompanying and amplifying policy.

SECRETARY CLINTON: That is a wonderful question because I think the arts and artists are one of our most effective tools in reaching beyond and through repressive regimes, in giving hope to people. It was a very effective tool during the Cold War. I've had so many Eastern Europeans tell me that it was American music, it was American literature, it was American poetry that kept them going. I remember when Vaclav Havel came to the White House during my husband's administration, and we were having a state dinner for him. And I said, "Well, who would you like to entertain at the state dinner?" And I didn't know what he was going to say. And he said, "Lou Reed." (Laughter.) "It was his music that was just so important for us—in prison, out of prison."

Well, you could name many other American artists who have traveled. We're going to try to increase the number of artistic exchanges we do so that we can get people into settings where they will be able to directly communicate. Now, with communication being what it is today, you can download them and all the rest, but there's something about the American Government sending somebody to make that case which I think is very important to our commitment.

Also, artists can bright to light in a gripping, dramatic way some of the challenges we face. You mentioned the play about women in the Congo. I remember some years ago seeing a play about women in Bosnia during the conflict there. It was so gripping. I still see the faces of those women who were pulled from their homes, separated from their husbands, often raped and left just as garbage on the side of the road. So I think that artists both individually and through their works can illustrate better than any speech I can give or any government policy we can promulgate that the spirit that lives within each of us, the right to think and dream and expand our boundaries, is not confined, no matter how hard they try, by any regime anywhere in the world. There is no way that you can deprive people from feeling those stirrings inside their soul. And artists can give voice to that. They can give shape and movement to it. And it is so important in places where people feel forgotten and marginalized and depressed and hopeless to have that glimmer that there is a better future, that there is a better way that they just have to hold onto.

So I'm going to do what I can to continue to increase and enhance our artistic outreach, but this is also a great area for private foundations, for NGOs, for artists themselves, for universities like Georgetown to be engaged in. It's interesting, in today's world we are deluged with so much information. I mean, we are living in information overload time. And so we need ways of cutting through all of that. We're also living in an on-the-one-hand-this and on-another-hand-that sort of media environment. I always joke that if a television station or a newspaper interviews somebody who is claiming that the earth is round, they have to put on somebody from the Flat Earth Society because that's balance, fair and balanced coverage. (Laughter and applause.)

And so part of what we have to do is look for those ways of breaking through all of that. And I think that the power of the arts to do that is so enormous, and we can't ever forget about the role that it must play in giving life to the aspirations of people around the world.

Thank you all very much. (Applause.)

DOCUMENT 81

Full Official Title: Human Rights Commitments and Pledges of the United States of America

Short Title/Acronym/Abbreviation: The U.S. Human Rights Pledge

Type of Document: This is a statement submitted by the U.S. to the U.N. Human Rights Council and its member states to highlight U.S. commitment to human rights as it sought a seat on the Council.

Subject: U.S. policy towards human rights and international inter-governmental organizations, particularly the Human Rights Council

Official Citation: Not applicable

Date of Document: April 27, 2009

Date of Adoption: Not applicable

Date of General Entry into Force (EIF): Not applicable

Number of States Parties as of this printing: Not applicable

Date of Signature by the United States: Not applicable

Date of Ratification/Accession/Adhesion: Not applicable

Date of Entry into Force as to United States (effective date): Not applicable

Legal Status/Character of the Instrument/Document as to the United States: This is not a legal instrument but a document that is expected to be filed by all states seeking a seat on the U.N. Human Rights Council.

Comments: All states seeking a seat on the Council are expected to submit a statement regarding their commitment to human rights. The U.S. sought a seat on the Council in 2009 and this is the first official

U.S. document allowing the international community to scrutinize its human rights record. The U.S. had largely absented itself from the Human Rights Council almost from the beginning in 2006 until the Obama Administration came into office. This pledge constituted somewhat of a "we're back" announcement to the Human Rights Council and the world. The pledge does not bind succeeding administrations.

Web Address: http://www.state.gov/documents/organization/122476.pdf

USA HUMAN RIGHTS PLEDGE

COMMITMENT TO ADVANCING HUMAN RIGHTS, FUNDAMENTAL FREEDOMS AND HUMAN DIGNITY AND PROSPERITY INTERNATIONALLY COMMITMENT TO CONTINUE SUPPORT TO HUMAN RIGHTS ACTIVITIES IN THE U.N. SYSTEM COMMITMENT TO ADVANCING HUMAN RIGHTS IN THE U.N. SYSTEM

The deep commitment of the United States to championing the human rights enshrined in the Universal Declaration of Human Rights is driven by the founding values of our nation and the conviction that international peace, security, and prosperity are strengthened when human rights and fundamental freedoms are respected and protected. As the United States seeks to advance human rights and fundamental freedoms around the world, we do so cognizant of our own commitment to live up to our ideals at home and to meet our international human rights obligations. We therefore make the following pledges:

COMMITMENT TO ADVANCING HUMAN RIGHTS IN THE U.N. SYSTEM

1. The United States commits to continuing its efforts in the U.N. system to be a strong advocate for all people around the world who suffer from abuse and oppression, and to be a stalwart defender of courageous individuals across the globe who work, often at great personal risk, on behalf of the rights of others.

2. The United States commits to working with principled determination for a balanced, credible, and effective U.N. Human Rights Council to advance the purpose of the Universal Declaration of Human Rights. To that same end, in partnership with the international community, we fully intend to promote universality, transparency, and objectivity in all of the Council's endeavors. The United States commits to participating fully in the Universal Periodic Review process and looks forward to the review in 2010 of its own record in promoting and protecting human rights and fundamental freedoms in the United States.

3. The United States is committed to advancing the promotion and protection of human rights and fundamental freedoms in the U.N. General Assembly and Third Committee, and in this vein intends to actively participate in the U.N. General Assembly 2011 review of the Human Rights Council.

4. The United States is also committed to the promotion and protection of human rights through regional organizations. Through our membership in the Organization for Security and Cooperation in Europe and the Organization for American States, the United States commits to continuing efforts to uphold human rights and fundamental freedoms, and to strengthening and developing institutions and mechanisms for their protection. In particular recognition of its human rights commitments within the Inter-American system, the United States strongly supports the work of the Inter-American Commission on Human Rights.

5. The United States recognizes and upholds the vital role of civil society and human rights defenders in the promotion and protection of human rights and commits to promoting the effective involvement of non-governmental organizations in the work of the United Nations, including the Council, and other international organizations.

6. As part of our commitment to the principle of universality of human rights, the United States commits to working with our international partners in the spirit of openness, consultation, and respect and reaffirms that expressions of concern about the human rights situation in any country, our own included, are appropriate matters for international discussion.

COMMITMENT TO CONTINUE SUPPORT TO HUMAN RIGHTS ACTIVITIES IN THE U.N. SYSTEM

1. The United States is committed to continuing its support for the Office of the U.N. High Commissioner for Human Rights. In 2009, the United States intends to pledge $8 million to the OHCHR and its efforts to address violations of human rights worldwide, as well as an additional $1.4 million to the U.N. Voluntary Fund for Technical Cooperation in the Field of Human Rights, and more than $7 million to other funds.

2. The United States is also committed to continuing its support of other U.N. bodies whose work contributes to the promotion of human rights. In 2008–2009, the United States has contributed funding to support human rights efforts such as through UNICEF ($130 million), UNDEF ($7.9 million), and UNIFEM

($4.5 million). The United States also supports the U.N. Population Fund (UNFPA), and is providing $50 million for the 2009 fiscal year as provided in the 2009 Omnibus Appropriations Act.

COMMITMENT TO ADVANCING HUMAN RIGHTS, FUNDAMENTAL FREEDOMS AND HUMAN DIGNITY AND PROSPERITY INTERNATIONALLY

1. The United States commits to continue supporting states in their implementation of human rights obliga-tions, as appropriate, through human rights dialogue, exchange of experts, technical and inter-regional cooperation, and programmatic support of the work of non-governmental organizations.

2. The United States commits to continue its efforts to strengthen mechanisms in the international system to advance the rights, protection, and empowerment of women through, for example, supporting the full imple- Bureau of International Organization Affairs April 27, 2009 implementation of Security Council Resolutions 1325 and 1820 on Women, Peace and Security, and all relevant General Assembly Resolutions, particularly 61/143 and 63/155, on the intensification of efforts to eliminate all forms of violence against women; supporting the work of the U.N. Commission on the Status of Women; and supporting the work of the Inter-American Commission on Women.

3. The United States commits to continuing to promote respect for workers rights worldwide, including by working with other governments and the International Labor Organization to adopt and enforce regula-tions and laws to promote respect for internationally recognized worker rights and by providing funding for technical assistance projects to build the capacity of worker organizations, employers, and governments to address labor issues including forced labor and the worst forms of child labor, such as child soldiering, work-place discrimination, and sweatshop and exploitative working conditions.

4. The United States commits to continuing to advocate a victim-centered and multi-disciplinary approach to combating all forms of trafficking in persons and to restoring the dignity, human rights, and fundamental freedoms of human trafficking victims.

5. The United States commits to continuing to promote freedom of religion for individuals of all beliefs, particularly members of minority and vulnerable religious groups, through dedicated outreach, advocacy, training and programmatic efforts.

6. The United States is committed to continuing to promote human rights in the fight against HIV/AIDS in a variety of ways, including through promoting the rights of people living with HIV/AIDS, fight-ing against stigma and discrimination, and supporting women's rights. The United States is committed to preventing suffering and saving lives by confronting global health challenges through improving the quality, availability, and use of essential health services.

7. The United States is committed to continuing its leadership role in promoting voluntary corporate social responsibility and business and human rights initiatives globally. The United States intends to convene government, civil society and business stake-holders to seek joint solutions on business and human rights, and to serve as an active participant in key multi-stakeholder initiatives such as the Voluntary Principles on Security and Human Rights.

8. Recognizing the essential contributions of independent media in promoting the fundamental freedom of expression, exposing human rights abuses and promoting accountability and transparency in governance, the United States commits to continuing to champion freedom of expression and to promote media freedom and the protection of journalists worldwide.

9. We are dedicated to combating both overt and subtle forms of racism and discrimination internation-ally. The United States is party to the International Covenant on the Elimination of All Forms of Racial Discrimination, and is committed to seeing the goals of this covenant fully realized. Particular emphasis should be placed not only on eliminating any remaining legal barriers to equality, but also on confronting the reality of continuing discrimination and inequality within institutions and societies.

COMMITMENT TO ADVANCING HUMAN RIGHTS AND FUNDAMENTAL FREEDOMS IN THE UNITED STATES

1. The United States executive branch is committed to working with its legislative branch to con-sider the possible ratification of human rights treaties, including but not limited to the Convention on the Elimination of Discrimination Against Women and ILO Convention 111 Concerning Discrimination in Respect of Employment and Occupation.

2. The United States is committed to meeting its U.N. treaty obligations and participating in a meaning-ful dialogue with treaty body members.

3. The United States is committed to cooperating with the UN's human rights mechanisms, as well as the Inter-American Commission on Human Rights and other regional human rights bodies, by responding to inquiries, engaging in dialogues, and hosting visits.

4. The United States is also strongly committed to fighting racism and discrimination, and acts of violence committed because of racial or ethnic hatred. Despite the achievements of the civil rights movement and many years of striving to achieve equal rights for all, racism still exists in our country and we continue to fight it.

5. The United States is committed to continuing to promote human prosperity and human rights and fundamental freedoms of all persons within the United States, including enforcement of the Americans with Disabilities Act and its amendments, engaging religious and community leaders to uphold religious freedom and pluralism, and encouraging the private sector to serve as good corporate citizens both in the United States and overseas.

COMMITMENT TO ADVANCING HUMAN RIGHTS AND FUNDAMENTAL FREEDOMS IN THE UNITED STATES

Produced in support of the United States candidacy for membership in the U.N. Human Rights Council. Bureau of International Organization Affairs April 27, 2009

DOCUMENT 82

Full Official Title: U.S. Department of State Under Secretary for Democracy and Global Affairs, Bureau of Democracy, Human Rights, and Labor, Releases, Human Rights Reports, 2009 Country Reports on Human Rights Practices, Overview and Acknowledgements, and Introduction

Short Title/Acronym/Abbreviation: 2009 Country Reports Overview and Introduction

Type of Document: Human Rights reports prepared yearly by the U.S. Dept. of State, Bureau of Democracy, Human Rights, and Labor on the status of human rights in other countries

Subject: Report on the Human Rights record of (A) countries that receive assistance under the Foreign Assistance Act of 1961, and (B) all other foreign countries which are members of the United Nations and not otherwise the subject of a human rights report under this (Foreign Assistance) Act.

Official Citation: Not applicable

Date of Document: 11 March 2010

Date of Adoption: Not applicable

Date of General Entry into Force (EIF): Not applicable

Number of States Parties as of this printing: Not applicable

Date of Signature by United States: Not applicable

Date of Ratification/Accession/Adhesion: Not applicable

Date of Entry into Force as to United States (effective date): Not applicable

Legal Status/Character of the Instrument/Document as to the United States: Report was prepared pursuant to U.S. Law, the Foreign Assistance Act of 1961, to assist the U.S. Congress in determining foreign aid based on a state's human rights record.

Web Address: www.state.gov/g/drl/hrrpt/2009/frontmatter/135935.html

2009 COUNTRY REPORTS OVERVIEW AND INTRODUCTION

Overview and Acknowledgements U.S. Department of State Under Secretary for Democracy and Global Affairs » Bureau of Democracy,

Human Rights, and Labor » Releases » Human Rights Reports » 2009 Country Reports on Human Rights Practices » Preface, Overview and Acknowledgements, and Introduction » Overview and Acknowledgements

2009 Human Rights Report: Overview and Acknowledgements

Bureau of Democracy, Human Rights, and Labor 2009 Country Reports on Human Rights Practices March 11, 2010

HUMAN RIGHTS REPORTS

Why the Reports Are Prepared

This report is submitted to the Congress by the Department of State in compliance with Sections 116(d) and 502B(b) of the Foreign Assistance Act of 1961 (FAA), as amended. The law provides that the

Secretary of State shall transmit to the Speaker of the House of Representatives and the Committee on Foreign Relations of the Senate by February 25 "a full and complete report regarding the status of internationally recognized human rights, within the meaning of subsection (A) in countries that receive assistance under this part, and (B) in all other foreign countries which are members of the United Nations and which are not otherwise the subject of a human rights report under this Act." We have also included reports on several countries that do not fall into the categories established by these statutes and thus are not covered by the congressional requirement.

In the early 1970s the United States formalized its responsibility to speak out on behalf of international human rights standards. In 1976 Congress enacted legislation creating a Coordinator of Human Rights in the Department of State, a position later upgraded to Assistant Secretary. Legislation also requires that U.S. foreign and trade policy take into account countries' human rights and worker rights performance and that country reports be submitted to the Congress on an annual basis.

How the Reports Are Prepared

The Department of State prepared this report using information from U.S. embassies and consulates abroad, foreign government officials, non governmental and international organizations, and published reports. The initial drafts of the individual country reports were prepared by U.S. diplomatic missions abroad, drawing on information they gathered throughout the year from a variety of sources, including government officials, jurists, the armed forces, journalists, human rights monitors, academics, and labor activists. This information gathering can be hazardous, and U.S. Foreign Service personnel regularly go to great lengths, under trying and sometimes dangerous conditions, to investigate reports of human rights abuse, monitor elections, and come to the aid of individuals at risk, such as political dissidents and human rights defenders whose rights are threatened by their governments. Once the initial drafts of the individual country reports were completed, the Bureau of Democracy, Human Rights and Labor, in cooperation with other Department of State offices, worked to corroborate, analyze, and edit the reports, drawing on their own sources of information. These sources included reports provided by U.S. and other human rights groups, foreign government officials, representatives from the United Nations and other international and regional organizations and institutions, experts from academia, and the media. Bureau officers also consulted experts on worker rights, refugee issues, military and police topics, women's issues, and legal matters. The guiding principle was to ensure that all information was assessed objectively, thoroughly, and fairly.

The reports in this volume will be used as a resource for shaping policy, conducting diplomacy, and making assistance, training, and other resource allocations. They also will serve as a basis for the U.S. Government's cooperation with private groups to promote the observance of internationally recognized human rights.

The Country Reports on Human Rights Practices cover internationally recognized civil, political and worker rights, as set forth in the Universal Declaration of Human Rights. These rights include freedom from torture or other cruel, inhuman or degrading treatment or punishment, from prolonged detention without charges, from disappearance or clandestine detention, and from other flagrant violations of the right to life, liberty and the security of the person.

Universal human rights seek to incorporate respect for human dignity into the processes of government and law. All persons have the right to nationality, the inalienable right to change their government by peaceful means and to enjoy basic freedoms, such as freedom of expression, association, assembly, movement, and religion, without discrimination on the basis of race, religion, national origin, or sex. The right to join a free trade union is a necessary condition of a free society and economy. Thus the reports assess key internationally recognized worker rights, including the right of association, the right to organize and bargain collectively, the prohibition of forced or compulsory labor, the status of child labor practices, the minimum age for employment of children, and acceptable work conditions.

Introduction

BUREAU OF DEMOCRACY, HUMAN RIGHTS AND LABOR

2009 Country Reports on Human Rights Practices

March 11, 2010

Introduction to the 2009 Country Reports

2009 was a year of contrasts. It was a year in which ethnic, racial, and religious tensions led to violent conflicts and serious human rights violations and fueled or exacerbated more than 30 wars or internal armed conflicts. At the same time, it was a year in which the United States and other governments devoted greater attention to finding ways to acknowledge and combat these underlying tensions through showing leadership in advancing respect for universal human rights, promoting tolerance, combating violent extremism, and pursuing peaceful solutions to long-standing conflicts in the Middle East and elsewhere. As President Obama said in his June speech at Cairo University, we should be defined not by our differences but rather by our common humanity, and we should find ways to work in partnership with other nations so that all people achieve justice and prosperity.

2009 also was a year in which more people gained greater access than ever before to more information about human rights through the Internet, cell phones, and other forms of connective technologies. Yet at the same time it was a year in which governments spent more time, money, and attention finding regulatory and technical means to curtail freedom of expression on the Internet and the flow of critical information and to infringe on the personal privacy rights of those who used these rapidly evolving technologies.

Today, all governments grapple with the difficult questions of what are appropriate policies and practices in response to legitimate national security concerns and how to strike the balance between respecting human rights and fundamental freedoms and ensuring the safety of their citizens. That said, during the past year, many governments applied overly broad interpretations of terrorism and emergency powers as a basis for limiting the rights of detainees and curtailing other basic human rights and humanitarian law protections. They did so even as the international community continued to make tangible progress in isolating and weakening the leadership in violent extremist and terrorist groups such as al-Qa'ida.

This report explores these and other trends and developments and provides a specific, detailed picture of human rights conditions in 194 countries around the world. The U.S. Government has compiled these reports for the past 34 years pursuant to a requirement placed on the U.S. executive by law in part to help the U.S. Congress inform its work in assessing requests for U.S. foreign military and economic assistance, as well as to set trade policies and U.S. participation in the multilateral development banks and other financial institutions. The reason for publishing this report is to develop a full, factual record that can help U.S. policymakers to make intelligent and well-informed policy decisions. It has also been increasingly used by policymakers abroad and has become a core reference document for governments, intergovernmental organizations, and concerned citizens throughout the world.

Many have questioned the reason the U.S. Government compiles this report, rather than the United Nations or some other intergovernmental body. One answer is that we believe it is imperative for countries, including our own, to ensure that respect for human rights is an integral component of foreign policy. These reports provide an overview of the human rights situation around the world as a means to raise awareness about human rights conditions, in particular as these conditions impact the well-being of women, children, racial minorities, trafficking victims, members of indigenous groups and ethnic communities, persons with disabilities, sexual minorities, and members of other vulnerable groups. Also, we provide these reports as a form of comprehensive review and analysis. While some nongovernmental organizations (NGOs) do extensive and excellent reporting on some countries, none cover the world as we do. And while we have encouraged more detailed and comprehensive reporting from the U.N. and other intergovernmental bodies, thus far these organizations have not met this need. Because of this unmet need, the U.S. Congress has mandated this report. Even as we continue this reporting exercise, we encourage the U.N. to take up this type of thorough and comprehensive reporting, and we stand ready to work with them to meet the challenge. We will continue to press for enhanced U.N. reporting, for example through the U.N. Human Rights Council as part of its review of its own operations in 2011.

Some critics, in the United States and elsewhere, also have challenged our practice of reviewing every other country's human rights record but not our own. In fact, the U.S. Government reports on and assesses our own human rights record in many other fora pursuant to our treaty obligations (e.g., we file reports on our implementation of the two Optional Protocols to the Convention on the Rights of the Child, the International Covenant on Civil and Political Rights, the International Covenant on the Elimination of Racial Discrimination, and the Convention Against Torture). We are reviewing our reporting, consistent with President Obama and Secretary Clinton's pledge that we will apply a single universal human rights standard to all, including ourselves. Later this year, the U.S. *Trafficking in Persons Report*, for the first time, will rank the United States as it does foreign governments by applying the minimum standards for the elimination of trafficking in persons set forth in the Trafficking Victims Protection Act of 2000 as amended. And in the fall the U.S. Government will appear before the United Nations Human Rights Council for the first Universal Periodic Review of our domestic human rights situation.

These country reports are written to provide an accurate, factual record of human rights conditions around the world, not to examine U.S. policy responses or options or to assess diplomatic alternatives. Yet in a broader sense these reports are a part of the Obama Administration's overall approach to human rights and an essential component of that effort. As outlined above, the administration's approach, as articulated by President Obama and Secretary Clinton, is guided by broad principles, the first of which is a commitment to universal human rights. In preparing this report, we have endeavored to hold all governments accountable to uphold universal human rights in the Universal Declaration of Human Rights and to their human rights treaty obligations. As Secretary Clinton stated in December, all governments, including our own, must "adhere to obligations under international law: among them not to torture, arbitrarily detain and persecute dissenters, or engage in political killings. Our government and the international community must consider the pretentions of those who deny or abdicate their responsibilities and hold violators to account." The first step in that process is to tell the truth and to identify specific instances where such violations are occurring and where governments are failing to take responsibility for holding violators accountable.

A second element of our approach is a principled and pragmatic engagement with other countries on these issues. This means that we will pursue steps that are most likely to make human rights a human reality. This principled pragmatism starts with an honest assessment of human rights conditions and whether violations are the result of deliberate government repression, governmental unwillingness or inability to confront the problems, or a combination of all three. As Secretary Clinton has said, "With China, Russia, and others, we are engaging on issues of mutual interest while also engaging societal actors in the same countries who are working to advance human rights and democracy. The assumption that we must either pursue human rights or our 'national interests' is wrong. The assumption that only coercion and isolation are effective tools for advancing democratic change is also wrong." These reports provide an essential, factual predicate upon which we can shape current and future polices.

A third element is our belief that although foreign governments and global civil society cannot impose change from outside, we can and should encourage and provide support to members of local civil society and other peaceful change agents within each country. As part of such efforts, these reports can and often do amplify these voices, by making reference to their findings, publicly reinforcing their concerns, and by widely disseminating this information to opinion makers, both internationally and within affected countries.

A fourth element of our approach is to keep a wide focus where rights are at stake and to adopt a broad approach to democracy and human rights. As Secretary Clinton stated, "Democracy means not only elections to choose leaders, but also active citizens and a free press and an independent judiciary and transparent and responsive institutions that are accountable to all citizens and protect their rights equally and fairly." President Obama has also highlighted the crucial linkages between development, democracy, and human rights, noting the centrality of issues such as corruption to the realization of basic rights. Consistent with that approach, these reports cover a wide range of topics and trends, providing a detailed and comprehensive picture of human rights and democracy in each country.

The fifth and final element of our approach has been to pursue progress on these issues through multilateral processes and institutions. As President Obama has acknowledged, we live in an increasingly interdependent and multipolar world, and to achieve our international goals, we need to collaborate with other governments and international actors. That is the reason we have joined the U.N. Human Rights Council, have actively supported human rights initiatives in the General Assembly, and have more thoroughly engaged in regional bodies like the Organization of American States and the Organization for Security and Cooperation in Europe in promoting democracy and human rights.

In preparing these reports, we relied on information collected by officials in U.S. embassies around the world and on information from other governments and multilateral organizations. We also solicited and relied on useful information from nongovernmental human rights groups, both those operating internationally and those that work at a national level. We also collected information from academics, lawyers, trade unions, religious leaders, and the media. While we benefited from these many inputs, the U.S. Government alone bears responsibility for the content of these reports. The preparation of these reports involves a major commitment of time and energy by hundreds of people, and includes a lengthy process of fact-checking and editing to ensure high standards of accuracy and objectivity.

The Year in Review

In 2009, governments across the globe continued to commit serious violations of human rights. As we survey the world, there still are an alarming number of reports of torture, extrajudicial killings, and other violations of universal human rights. Often these violations relating to the integrity of the person are in countries where conflicts are occurring. These violent attacks are a central concern wherever they take place.

In a significant number of countries, governments have imposed new and often draconian restrictions on NGOs. Since 2008, no fewer than 25 governments have imposed new restrictions on the ability of these organizations to register, to operate freely, or to receive foreign funding, adversely impacting freedom of association. In many countries, human rights defenders are singled out for particularly harsh treatment, and in the most egregious cases, they are imprisoned or even attacked or killed in reaction to their advocacy.

These restrictions and repressive measures are part of a larger pattern of governmental efforts to control dissenting or critical voices. This pattern also extends to the media and to new forms of electronic communications through the Internet and other new technologies. Restrictions on freedom of expression, including on members of the media, are increasing and becoming more severe. In many cases, such restrictions are applied subtly by autocrats aiming to avoid attention from human rights groups and donor countries, such as through the threat of criminal penalties and administrative or economic obstacles, rather than through violence or imprisonment; the end result is still a chilling effect on freedom of expression. A third trend we observed is the continuing and escalating discrimination and persecution of members of vulnerable groups—often racial, religious, or ethnic minorities, but also women, members of indigenous communities, children, persons with disabilities, and other vulnerable groups that lack the political power in their societies to defend their own interests.

These key trends are discussed in the subsequent sections, illustrated by thumbnail sketches of selected countries (ordered alphabetically) that were chosen for notable developments—positive, negative, or mixed—chronicled during calendar year 2009. For more comprehensive, detailed information, the individual country reports themselves should be consulted.

Specific Human Rights Trends

Human Rights Abuses in Countries in Conflict

In many countries where conflicts were raging during the year, noncombatant civilians faced human rights abuses and violations of international humanitarian law. In many of these conflict zones, insurgents, terrorist organizations, paramilitary forces, and government security forces used murder, rape, and inhumane tactics to assert control over territory, silence opponents, and coerce the cooperation of civilian communities in conflict zones. Throughout the world, thousands of men, women, and children died or were mistreated not only in conflicts, but also in campaigns to intimidate civilian populations.

The security situation in **Afghanistan** deteriorated significantly because of increased insurgent attacks, with civilians bearing the brunt of the violence. Armed conflict spread to almost one-third of the country, hindering the government's ability to govern effectively, extend its influence, and provide services, especially in rural areas. As a result of the insurgency, 1,448 Afghan military personnel, 1,954 government employees, and 2,412 civilians were killed. Approximately five million of the 15 million registered voters participated in the August elections that were marked by serious allegations of widespread fraud, insufficient conditions for participation by women, and a concerted effort by the Taliban to disrupt the voting. Nevertheless, more polling stations opened than in previous elections, the media and public debated political alternatives, and the election followed the constitutional process.

The government in **Burma** continued its egregious human rights violations and abuses during the year, including increased military attacks in ethnic minority regions, such as in the Karen and Shan state. In August, government soldiers attacked the Kokang cease-fire group, the Myanmar National Democratic Alliance Army, which the government claimed was launched in order to shut down narcotics and arms factories. Tens of thousands of civilians reportedly fled across the border to China as a result of the fighting. Government soldiers destroyed several villages in Shan territory, and some media estimates suggested the army razed up to 500 homes in Kokang territory. The regime continued to rule by decree and was not bound by any constitutional provisions guaranteeing any fundamental freedoms. The regime continued to commit other serious abuses, including extrajudicial killings, custodial deaths, disappearances, rape, torture, forcible relocation of persons, the use of forced labor, and conscription of child soldiers. The government detained civic activists indefinitely and without charges.

In the **Democratic Republic of the Congo (DRC)**, conflict in mineral-rich parts of the east, including counterinsurgency operations by government security forces, resulted in the killing of more than 1,000 civilians; the displacement of hundreds of thousands whose government did not adequately protect or assist them; the rapes of tens of thousands of women, children, and men; the burning of hundreds of homes; the unlawful recruitment or use of thousands of children as soldiers by the DRC military and various armed groups; and abductions of numerous persons for forced labor and sexual exploitation, both domestically and internationally.

Despite substantial improvements in the general security situation in **Iraq**, human rights abuses continued. There were reports that the government or its agents committed arbitrary or unlawful killings in connection with the ongoing conflict, and insurgent and terrorist bombings, executions, and killings continued to affect all regions and sectors of society. Due to the continuing conflict, violence against the media was common, and media workers reported that they engaged in self-censorship. Although the government publicly called for tolerance and acceptance for all religious minorities and took steps to increase security at places of worship, frequent attacks by insurgent and extremist groups on places of worship and religious leaders, as well as sectarian violence, hampered the ability of individuals to practice their religion freely.

In response to a sharp increase in the number and frequency of rocket attacks from Gaza against civilians in **Israel** shortly prior to and following the expiration of Hamas's agreed period of "calm" on December 19, 2008, the Israeli Defense Forces launched Operation Cast Lead on December 27, which consisted initially of airstrikes targeted against Hamas security installations, personnel, and other facilities in the Gaza Strip, and later ground operations. Hostilities between Israeli forces and Hamas fighters continued through January 18, and the Israeli withdrawal of troops was completed on January 21. Human rights organizations estimated that close to 1,400 Palestinians died, including more than 1,000 civilians, and that more than 5,000 were wounded. According to Israeli government figures, Palestinian deaths totaled 1,166, including 295 noncombatant deaths. There were 13 Israelis killed, including three civilians. In the West Bank, the Israel Defense Forces relaxed restrictions at several checkpoints during the year that had constituted significant barriers to the movement of Palestinians, yet remaining barriers limited Palestinian access to places of worship, employment, agricultural lands, schools, hospitals, and the conduct of journalism and NGO activities. In Gaza, which remained under the control of Hamas, there were reports of corruption, abuse of prisoners, and failure to provide fair trials to those accused. Hamas also strictly restricted the freedom of expression, religion, and movement of Gaza residents, and promoted gender discrimination against women. Killings by Hamas-controlled security forces remained a problem. There were reports of torture by Gaza Hamas Executive Force and victims were not only security detainees but also included persons associated with the Fatah political party and those held on suspicion of "collaboration" with Israel. Hamas authorities in Gaza often interfered arbitrarily with personal privacy, family, and home.

National police, army, and other security forces in **Nigeria** committed extrajudicial killings and used lethal and excessive force to apprehend criminals and suspects. Violence in the form of killings, kidnappings, and forced disappearances; mass rape; and displacement of civilians attributed to both government and non-government actors continued in the Niger Delta, despite the formation of the Joint Task Force in 2003 that sought to restore stability to the region. Reports of incidents attributed to militant groups in the Niger Delta decreased upon the president's offer of amnesty, although violence remained pervasive in the south. Between July 26 and July 29, police and militant members of Boko Haram, an extremist Islamic group, clashed violently in four northern states, resulting in the displacement of approximately 4,000 people and more than 700 deaths, although this figure is not definitive because quick burials in mass graves precluded an accurate count. Sect leader Muhammad Yusuf; Yusuf's father-in-law, Baba Mohammed; and suspected Boko Haram founder Buji Fai reportedly were killed while in custody of the security forces.

Although **Pakistan**'s civilian authorities took some positive steps, significant human rights challenges remain. Major problems included extrajudicial killings, torture, and disappearances. Militant attacks in the Federally Administered Tribal Areas (FATA) and the North West Frontier Province (NWFP) killed 825 civilians; security operations to repel the militants from Malakand Division and parts of the FATA displaced almost three million persons at the peak of the crisis (although by year's end, approximately 1.66 million had returned to their home areas). The Human Rights Commission of Pakistan, the *New York Times*, and several local publications reported that security forces allegedly committed 300 to 400 extrajudicial killings during counterinsurgency operations in NWFP and Swat. There were widespread accusations that insurgents conducted terror- and revenge killings to intimidate local populations and law enforcement officials. Sectarian violence killed approximately 1,125 persons, and more than 76 suicide bombings killed 1,037 persons.

The situation in the North Caucasus region of **Russia** worsened as the government fought insurgents, Islamist militants, and criminal forces. Local government and insurgent forces in the region reportedly engaged in killings, torture, abuse, violence, politically motivated abductions, and other brutal or humiliating treatment. In Chechnya, Ingushetia, and Dagestan, the number of extrajudicial killings increased markedly, as did the number of attacks on law enforcement personnel (in actions involving insurgents, 342 members of law enforcement were killed and 680 were injured.) Some authorities in the North Caucasus acted with impunity and appeared to act independently of the federal government, in some cases, allegedly targeting families of suspected insurgents for reprisal and engaging in kidnapping, torture, and extrajudicial punishment.

Before the 33-year conflict in **Sri Lanka** came to an end in May, government security forces, progovernment paramilitary groups, and the Liberation Tigers of Tamil Eelam (LTTE) used excessive force and committed abuses against civilians. Several hundred thousand ethnic Tamil civilians were not allowed freedom of movement by the LTTE from LTTE-controlled areas Artillery shelling and mortar fire by both sides occurred close to and among civilian encampments, resulting in thousands of civilian deaths during the last months of the conflict. From January to May, the LTTE dramatically increased its forced recruitment of child soldiers. Although the number of children recruited and killed in fighting is unknown, the government reported 527 ex-LTTE child soldiers in custody several months after the end of the war. The confinement in camps of nearly 300,000 persons displaced by the end of the conflict called into question the government's postconflict commitment to human rights, although the government began to make significant progress on the treatment of internally displaced persons and other human rights improvements toward the end of 2009, in the run up to the January 2010 presidential election.

Conflict and human rights abuses in the Darfur region of **Sudan** continued despite the 2006 Darfur Peace Agreement between the government and a faction of the Sudan Liberation Movement/Army. Government-sponsored forces bombed villages, killed civilians, and supported Chadian rebel groups. Women and children continued to experience gender-based violence. Since the conflict in Darfur began in 2003, nearly 2.7 million civilians have been internally displaced, approximately 253,000 have sought refuge in eastern Chad, and more than 300,000 have died. Tensions also persisted between the north and south over the 2005 Comprehensive Peace Agreement. Interethnic conflict and violence perpetrated by the Lord's Resistance Army in southern Sudan resulted in the deaths of approximately 2,500 and the displacement of 359,000 persons during the year.

Restrictions on Freedom of Expression, Assembly, and Association (including NGOs)

Many governments continued to exert control over information that came into and was produced within their countries. This was accomplished by hindering the ability to organize in public, online, or through use of new technologies; by restricting the dissemination of information on the Internet, radio, or television or through print media; and constructing legal barriers that made it difficult for NGOs to establish themselves. According to the National Endowment for Democracy, 26 laws in 25 countries have been introduced or adopted since January 2008 that impede civil society.

In **Belarus**, the government's human rights record remained very poor. Civil liberties, including freedoms of expression, assembly, association, and religion, continued to be restricted. The government limited distribution of independent print and broadcast media outlets. Authorities used unreasonable force and intimidation to discourage participation in demonstrations and to disperse peaceful protesters. NGOs, opposition activists, and political parties were subjected to persistent harassment, fines, and prosecution, and several leading NGOs were again denied registration, forcing them to operate under threat of criminal prosecution. Following a few positive steps taken by authorities in 2008, the absence of reform during 2009 was disappointing.

The government of **China** increased its efforts to monitor Internet use, control content, restrict information, block access to foreign and domestic Web sites, encourage self-censorship, and punish those who violated regulations. The government employed thousands of persons at the national, provincial, and local levels to monitor electronic communications. In January the government began an "anti-vulgarity" campaign that resulted that same month in the closure of 1,250 Web sites and the deletion of more than 3.2 million items of information. The government at times blocked access to selected sites operated by major foreign news outlets, health organizations, foreign governments, educational institutions, and social networking sites, as well as search engines, that allow rapid communication or organization of users. During the year, particularly around sensitive events such as the 20th anniversary of the Tiananmen crackdown, authorities maintained tight control over Internet news and information. The government also automatically censored e-mail and Web chats based on an ever-changing list of sensitive key words. Despite official monitoring and censorship, dissidents and political activists continued to use the Internet to advocate and call attention to political causes such as prisoner advocacy, political reform, ethnic discrimination, corruption, and foreign policy concerns.

Independent media in **Colombia** were active and expressed a wide variety of views without restriction, and all privately owned radio and television stations broadcast freely. However, members of illegal armed groups intimidated, threatened, kidnapped, or killed journalists, which, according to national and international NGOs, caused many to practice self-censorship and others, 171 to be specific, received protection from the government. The official Administrative Department of Security monitored journalists, trade unionists, the political opposition, and human rights organizations and activists—physically, as well as their phone and email communications and personal and financial data. According to some NGOs, the government allegedly detained arbitrarily hundreds of persons, particularly social leaders, labor activists, and human rights defenders (HRDs), although a key NGO reported that such detentions in 2009 were half the 2008 level. HRDs were also persecuted and accused of supporting terrorism in an effort to discredit their work. Prominent NGOs reported that eight human rights activists and 39 trade unionists were killed during the year. However, the government also worked to protect thousands of union members, human rights activists, and other such groups.

Authorities in **Cuba** interfered with privacy and engaged in pervasive monitoring of private communications. There was no ability to change the government. There were also severe limitations on freedom of expression and no authorized press apart from official media; denial of peaceful assembly and association; restrictions on freedom of religion; and refusal to recognize domestic human rights groups or independent journalists or to permit them to function legally. The law allows for punishment of any unauthorized assembly of more than three persons, including those for private religious services in private homes. The law also provides for imprisonment for vaguely defined crimes such as "dangerousness" and "peaceful sedition." The government did not grant permission to any antigovernment demonstrators or approve any public meeting by a human rights group. Authorities held numerous opposition leaders pursuant to sentences ranging up to 25 years for peaceful political activities and detained activists for short periods to prevent them from attending meetings, demonstrations, or ceremonies. Although unauthorized, the organization Damas de Blanco (Ladies in White) generally was allowed to assemble and walk to church each Sunday demanding freedom for their imprisoned family members. However, the organization reported that its activities beyond the traditional weekly marches to church were disrupted on several occasions during the year. In addition, a prominent blogger and her colleague were detained and beaten while en route to a peaceful protest. Human rights activists also reported frequent government monitoring and disruption of cell phone and landline services prior to planned events or key anniversaries related to human rights. Authorities have never approved the establishment of a human rights group; however, a number of professional associations operated as NGOs without legal recognition.

The government's poor human rights record degenerated during the year, particularly after the disputed June presidential elections. Freedom of expression and association and lack of due process continued to be problems within **Iran**, and the government severely limited individuals' right to change their government peacefully through free and fair elections. Following the June 13 announcement of President Ahmadi-Nejad's reelection, hundreds of thousands of citizens took to the streets to protest. Police and the paramilitary Basij violently suppressed demonstrations. The official death count was 37, although opposition groups report the number may have reached 70. By August, authorities had detained at least 4,000 individuals, and arrests continued throughout the year. A massive show trial involving many of the more prominent detainees was undertaken in September. On June 20, according to eyewitnesses, Basij militia killed Neda Agha-Soltan in Tehran. The video of her death appeared on YouTube and became a symbol of the opposition movement. Ahead of the June presidential election, on the actual day of election, and during the December 27 Ashura protests, when authorities detained 1,000 individuals and at least eight persons were killed in street clashes, the government blocked access to Facebook, Twitter, and other social networking sites. After the June election, there was a major drop in bandwidth, which experts posited the government caused to prevent activists involved in the protests from accessing the Internet and uploading large video files. The government continued to restrict freedom of religion severely, particularly against Baha'is and, increasingly, Christians.

The government of **North Korea** continued to subject citizens to rigid controls over many aspects of their lives, specifically denying citizens freedoms of expression, assembly, and association. Reports by defectors and NGOs of extrajudicial killings, disappearances, and arbitrary detention, including of political prisoners, continued to paint a grim picture of life there. The government sought to control virtually all information: there were no independent media, Internet access was limited to high-ranking officials and other elites, and academic freedom was repressed. Domestic media censorship continued to be strictly enforced and no deviation from the official government line was tolerated. Similarly, the government prohibited all but the political elite from listening to foreign media broadcasts, and violators were subject to severe punishment. There was no genuine freedom of religion. Reports continued that religious believers, their families, and even their descendents were imprisoned, tortured, or simply relegated to a lower status. Indoctrination was carried out systematically through the mass media, schools, and worker and neighborhood associations and continued to involve mass marches, rallies, and staged performances, sometimes including hundreds of thousands of persons.

Government actions weakened freedom of expression and media independence within **Russia** by directing the editorial policies of government-owned media outlets, pressuring major independent outlets to abstain from critical coverage, and harassing and intimidating some journalists into practicing self-censorship. During the year, unknown persons killed a number of human rights activists and eight journalists, including prominent journalist and human rights activist Natalia Estemirova, who spent more than 10 years documenting cases of killings, torture, and disappearances that she linked to the Chechen authorities. President Medvedev stated it was "obvious" that the killings were connected to Estemirova's work and ordered an immediate investigation to find the perpetrators, but there have been no arrests or prosecutions in this case. The government increasingly attempted to restrict media freedom to cover sensitive issues such as the conduct of federal forces in Chechnya, human rights abuses, and criticism of some government leaders. Likewise, many observers noted a selective pattern of officials encouraging government-friendly rallies while attempting to prevent politically sensitive demonstrations. The government also attempted to restrict the activities of some NGOs, making it difficult for some to continue operations. Upon hearing criticism of the 2006 NGO law at a meeting with the Presidential Council on Human Rights, President Medvedev called existing regulations a "burden" and announced that some regulations would be eased. None of the amendments to the law applied to foreign NGOs.

Government officials in **Venezuela**, including the president, used government-controlled media outlets to accuse private media owners and reporters of fomenting antigovernment destabilization campaigns and coup attempts. Senior federal and state government leaders also actively harassed privately owned and opposition-oriented television stations, media outlets, and journalists throughout the year, using administrative sanctions, fines, and threats of closure to prevent or respond to any perceived criticism of the government. The government's harassment of Globovision, the largest private television network, included raiding the home of the company's president and publicly calling for the company's closure. At year's end, 32 radio stations and two television stations had been closed, and 29 other radio stations remained under threat of closure. One domestic media watchdog reported that 191 journalists either were attacked or had their individual rights violated during the year. NGOs expressed concern over official political discrimination against, and the firing of, state employees whose views differed from those of the government. Private groups also alleged that the government was pursuing 45 persons as "political objectives" using various legal and administrative means. The Organization of American States's Inter-American Commission on Human Rights recently noted "a troubling trend of punishments, intimidation, and attacks on individuals in reprisal for expressing their dissent with official policy."

The human rights record of the government of **Vietnam** remained problematic. The government increased its suppression of dissent, arresting and convicting several political activists. Several editors and reporters from prominent newspapers were fired for reporting on official corruption and outside blogging on political topics. Bloggers were detained and arrested under vague national security provisions for criticizing the government and were prohibited from posting material the government saw as sensitive or critical. The government also monitored e-mail and regulated or suppressed Internet content, such as Facebook and other Web sites operated by overseas Vietnamese political groups. The government utilized or tolerated the use of force to resolve disputes with a Buddhist order in Lam Dong and Catholic groups with unresolved property claims. Workers were not free to organize independent unions, and independent labor activists faced arrest and harassment.

The government of **Uzbekistan** tightly controlled the media and did not permit the publication of views critical of the government. Government security officials regularly gave publishers articles and letters to publish under fictitious bylines, as well as explicit instructions about the types of stories permitted for publication. In July, a court convicted independent journalist Dilmurod Sayid to 12 and one-half years in prison on charges of extortion and bribery soon after he published articles regarding the corruption of local government officials. The government requires all NGOs and religious organizations to register in order to operate, and the activities of international human rights NGOs are severely restricted because the government suspects them of participating in an international "information war" against the country. Any religious service conducted by an unregistered religious organization is illegal, and police frequently broke up the meetings of unregistered groups, generally held in private homes. Reportedly, in some regions, universities and schools closed to send students to work in cotton fields; students who refused were expelled or threatened with expulsion.

Discrimination and Harassment of Vulnerable Groups

Members of vulnerable groups—racial, ethnic and religious minorities; the disabled; women and children; migrant workers; and lesbian, gay, bisexual, and transgender individuals—often were marginalized and targets of societal and/or government-sanctioned abuse.

China continued to exert tight control over activities and peoples that the government perceived as a threat to the Chinese Communist Party. For example, public interest lawyers who took on cases deemed sensitive by the government increasingly were harassed or disbarred, and their law firms often were closed. The government also increased repression of Tibetans and Uighurs. The government tightened controls on Uighurs expressing peaceful dissent and on independent Muslim religious leaders, often citing counterterrorism as the reason for taking action. Following the July riots that broke out in Urumqi, the provincial capital of XUAR, officials cracked down on religious extremism, "splittism," and terrorism in an attempt to maintain public order. In the aftermath of the violence, Uighurs were sentenced to long prison terms and in some cases were executed, without due process, on charges of separatism. At year's end, Urumqi remained under a heavy police presence and most Internet and international phone communication remained cut off. In the Tibetan areas of China, the government's human rights record remained poor as authorities committed extrajudicial killings, torture, arbitrary arrests, and extrajudicial detentions. Authorities sentenced Tibetans for alleged support of Tibetan independence, regardless of whether their activities involved violence. The preservation and development of Tibet's unique religious, cultural, and linguistic heritage also remained a concern.

The government of **Egypt** failed to respect the freedom of association and restricted freedom of expression, and its respect for freedom of religion remained very poor. Sectarian attacks on Coptic Christians mounted during the year. The government failed to redress laws and government practices that discriminate against Christians. The government sponsored "reconciliation sessions" following sectarian attacks, which generally prevented the prosecution of perpetrators of crimes against Copts and precluded their recourse to the judicial system for restitution. This practice contributed to a climate of impunity and may have encouraged further assaults. Members of non-Muslim religious minorities that the government officially recognized generally worshipped without harassment; however, Christians and members of the Baha'i faith, which the government does not recognize, faced personal and collective discrimination in many areas. In a step forward, the government promulgated procedures for members of unrecognized religions, including the Baha'i faith, to obtain national identification documents and reportedly issued 17 such documents and 70 birth certificates to Baha'i during the year.

As a growing number of people cross borders to find work, migrant workers have become particularly vulnerable to exploitation and discrimination. In **Malaysia,** foreign workers were subject to exploitative conditions and generally did not have access to the system of labor adjudication. However, the government investigated complaints of abuses, attempted to inform workers of their rights, encouraged workers to come forward with their complaints, and warned employers to end abuses. The law did not effectively prevent employers from holding employees' passports, and it was common practice for employers to do so. Some domestic workers alleged that their employers subjected them to inhuman living conditions, withheld their salaries, confiscated their travel documents, and physically assaulted them.

Violence against women, violations of the rights of children, and discrimination on the basis of gender, religion, sect, and ethnicity were common in many countries in the Middle East region. In **Saudi Arabia**, for example, Muslim religious practices that conflict with the government's interpretation of Sunni Islam are discriminated against and public religious expression by non-Muslims is prohibited. Human rights activists reported more progress in women's rights than in other areas, and the government made efforts to integrate women into mainstream society, for example, through the founding of the Kingdom's first coeducational university in September. However, discrimination against women was a significant problem, demonstrated by the lack of women's autonomy, freedom of movement, and economic independence; discriminatory practices surrounding divorce and child custody; the absence of a law criminalizing violence against women; and difficulties preventing women from escaping abusive environments. There are no laws specifically prohibiting domestic violence. Under the country's interpretation of Shari'a (Islamic law), rape is a punishable criminal offense with a wide range of penalties from flogging to execution. Statistics on incidents of rape were not available, but press reports and observers indicated rape against women and boys was a serious problem.

Lesbian, gay, bisexual, and transgender (LGBT) persons in **Uganda** faced arbitrary legal restrictions. It is illegal to engage in homosexual acts, based on a 1950 legal provision from the colonial era criminalizing "carnal acts against the order of nature" and prescribing a penalty of life imprisonment. No persons have been charged under the law. The September introduction in parliament of a bill providing the death penalty for "aggravated homosexuality" and for homosexual "serial offenders" resulted in increased harassment and intimidation of LGBT persons during the year; the proposed legislation also provides for a fine and three years' imprisonment for persons who fail to report acts of homosexual conduct to authorities within 24 hours. Public resentment of homosexual conduct sparked significant public debate during the year, and the government took a strong position against such conduct despite a December 2008 ruling by the High Court that constitutional rights apply to all persons, regardless of sexual orientation. The local NGO Sexual Minorities Uganda protested alleged police harassment of several members for their vocal stand against sexual discrimination.

Traditional and new forms of anti-Semitism continued to arise, and a spike in such activity followed the Gaza conflict in the winter of 2008–2009. Often despite official efforts to combat the problem, societal anti-Semitism persisted across Europe, South America, and beyond and manifested itself in classic forms (including physical attacks on Jewish individuals, synagogue bombings, cemetery desecrations; the theft of the "Arbeit Macht Frei" sign from the Auschwitz Death Camp; and accusations of blood libel, dual loyalty, and undue influence of Jews on government policy and media.) New forms of anti-Semitism took the form of criticism of Zionism or Israeli policy that crossed the line into demonizing all Jews, and, in some cases, translated into violence against Jewish individuals in general. Instead of combating anti-Semitism, some governments fueled it, most notably **Iran**'s President Ahmadi-Nejad. Anti-Semitic propaganda, including Holocaust denial, was circulated widely by satellite television, radio, and the Internet. A television show in **Egypt** that was widely aired throughout the region did not deny the Holocaust, but instead glorified it, praising the slaughter and humiliation of Jews and calling for future Holocausts.

In several countries with generally strong records of respecting human rights, there were nevertheless some notable examples of members of vulnerable groups facing discrimination and harassment. Discrimination against Muslims in Europe has been an increasing concern. A recent case that received international attention was the passage on November 29 in **Switzerland** of a constitutional amendment banning the construction of minarets. A provision in the Swiss constitution enables direct citizen involvement. The amendment passed with 57.5 percent of the vote despite opposition from both parliament and the Federal Council and public statements by many of the country's leaders describing such a ban as contradicting basic values in the country's constitution and violating its international obligations. Proponents of the initiative to ban minarets contended the construction of minarets symbolized a religious and political claim to power.

In the wake of the economic downturn, there have been a number of killings and incidents of violence against Roma, including in **Italy**, **Hungary**, **Romania**, **Slovakia**, and the **Czech Republic**. Roma are the largest and most vulnerable minority in Europe; they suffer racial profiling, violence, and discrimination. There were also reports of mistreatment of Romani suspects by police officers during arrest and while in custody. Roma faced high levels of poverty, unemployment, and illiteracy, as well as widespread discrimination in education, employment, and housing.

Document 83

Full Official Title: U.S. Department of State Under Secretary for Democracy and Global Affairs, Bureau of Democracy, Human Rights, and Labor, Releases, Human Rights Reports, 2009 Country Reports on Human Rights Practices, Preface

Short Title/Acronym/Abbreviation: 2009 Human Rights Report: Preface

Type of Document: Preface to human rights reports prepared by the U.S. Dept. of State, Bureau of Democracy, Human Rights, and Labor every year on the status of human rights in other countries

Subject: Human Rights record of (A) countries that receive assistance under the Foreign Assistance Act of 1961, and (B) in all other foreign countries which are members of the United Nations and which are not otherwise the subject of a human rights report under this (Foreign Assistance) Act.

Official Citation: Not applicable

Date of Document: 11 March 2010

Date of Adoption: Not applicable

Date of General Entry into Force (EIF): Not applicable

Number of States Parties as of this printing: Not applicable
Date of Signature by United States: Not applicable
Date of Ratification/Accession/Adhesion: Not applicable
Date of Entry into Force as to United States (effective date): Not applicable
Legal Status/Character of the Instrument/Document as to the United States: Non-binding Preface to
Dept. of State Report which was prepared pursuant to U.S. Law, the Foreign Assistance Act of 1961, to assist
the U.S. Congress in determining foreign aid based on a state's human rights record.
Web Address: www.state.gov/g/drl/rls/2009/frontmatter/135934.html

2009 Human Rights Report: Preface
BUREAU OF DEMOCRACY, HUMAN RIGHTS, AND LABOR
2009 Country Reports on Human Rights Practices
March 11, 2010

The idea of human rights begins with a fundamental commitment to the dignity that is the birthright of every man, woman and child. Progress in advancing human rights begins with the facts. And for the last 34 years, the United States has produced the Country Reports on Human Rights Practices, providing the most comprehensive record available of the condition of human rights around the world.

These reports are an essential tool—for activists who courageously struggle to protect rights in communities around the world; for journalists and scholars who document rights violations and who report on the work of those who champion the vulnerable; and for governments, including our own, as they work to craft strategies to encourage protection of the human rights of more individuals in more places.

The principle that each person possesses equal moral value is a simple, self-evident truth; but securing a world in which all can exercise the rights that are naturally theirs is an immense practical challenge. To craft effective human rights policy, we need good assessments of the situation on the ground in the places we want to make a difference. We need a sophisticated, strategic understanding of how democratic governance and economic development can each contribute to creating an environment in which human rights are secured. We need to recognize that rights-protecting democracy and rights-respecting development reinforce each other. And we need the right tools and the right partners to implement our policies.

Human rights are timeless, but our efforts to protect them must be grounded in the here-and-now. We find ourselves in a moment when an increasing number of governments are imposing new and crippling restrictions on the non governmental organizations working to protect rights and enhance accountability. New technologies have proven useful both to oppressors and to those who struggle to expose the failures and cowardice of those oppressors. And global challenges of our time—like food security and climate change; pandemic disease; economic crises; and violent extremism—impact the enjoyment of human rights today, and shape the global political context in which we must advance human rights over the long term.

Human rights are universal, but their experience is local. This is why we are committed to hold everyone to the same standard, including ourselves. And this is why we remember that human rights begin, as Eleanor Roosevelt said, "in small places close to home." When we work to secure human rights, we are working to protect the experiences that make life meaningful, to preserve each person's ability to fulfill his or her God-given potential. The potential within every person to learn, discover and embrace the world around them; the potential to join freely with others to shape their communities and their societies so that every person can find fulfillment and self-sufficiency; the potential to share life's beauties and tragedies, laughter and tears with the people they love.

The reports released today are a record of where we are. They provide a fact-base that will inform the United States's diplomatic, economic and strategic policies toward other countries in the coming year. These reports are not intended to prescribe such policies, but they provide essential data points for everyone in the U.S. Government working on them. I view the these reports not as ends in themselves, but as an important tool in the development of practical and effective human rights strategy by the United States Government. That is a process to which I am deeply committed.

The timeless principles enshrined in the Universal Declaration of Human Rights are a North Star guiding us toward the world we want to inhabit: a just world where, as President Obama has put it, peace rests on the "inherent rights and dignity of every individual." With the facts in hand, and the goals clear in

our hearts and heads, we recommit ourselves to continue the hard work of making human rights a human reality.
Hillary Rodham Clinton
Secretary of State

DOCUMENT 84

Document Full Official Title: U.S. Department of State Under Secretary for Democracy and Global Affairs » Bureau of Democracy, Human Rights, and Labor website on the U.N. Universal Periodic Review
Short Title/Acronym/Abbreviation: State Department UPR website
Type of Document: Front page of Website on a particular topic, the Universal Periodic Review process
Subject: The Universal Periodic Review Process and the U.S. government
Official Citation: Not applicable
Date of Document: Not applicable
Date of Adoption: Not applicable
Date of General Entry into Force (EIF): Not applicable
Number of States Parties as of this printing: Not applicable
Date of Signature by United States: Not applicable
Date of Ratification/Accession/Adhesion: Not applicable
Date of Entry into Force as to United States (effective date): Not applicable
Legal Status/Character of the Instrument/Document as to the United States: This is only a Department of State website introduction for someone looking for information on the U.S. and the U.N. Human Rights Council Universal Periodic Review Process, which the U.S. was preparing for in November 2010 at the time this book was written.
Web Address: www.state.gov/intex.html

STATE DEPARTMENT UPR WEBSITE

Home » Under Secretary for Democracy and Global Affairs » Bureau of Democracy, Human Rights, and Labor » Universal Periodic Review
* **Schedule of UPR Civil Society Consultations**
* **Universal Periodic Review**
* **Technical Guide for the UPR**
* **Basic facts about the UPR**
* **Universal Periodic Review (UPR) Frequently Asked Questions**

UNIVERSAL PERIODIC REVIEW

WELCOME to the Department of State's website for the Universal Periodic Review (UPR)! Here, you can find all you need to know about the United States' efforts to prepare for our review at the 2010 United Nations Human Rights Council. In addition, you can help us by providing feedback on human rights issues *you* feel are important for the United States to address in your community.
U.S. Government Officials Coming Your Way
As part of its preparation, the Department of State, with other federal agencies, will conduct consultations in selected cities across the United States. Please check back on our webpage for upcoming events.

In the pursuit of a transparent and effective UPR process, the Department of State is encouraging the American public, including non-governmental organizations and civil society more broadly to provide input regarding human rights in the United States directly to the Department of State. Those interested in providing their views, comments, proposals and recommendations to the Department of State can send an email to **upr_info@state.gov**.

DOCUMENT 85

Document Full Official Title: U.S. Department of State Under Secretary for Democracy and Global Affairs, Bureau of Democracy, Human Rights, and Labor, website on the U.N. Universal Periodic Review, Frequently Asked Questions.

Short Title/Acronym/Abbreviation: State Department UPR FAQs
Type of Document: FAQ page of Website on a particular topic, the Universal Periodic Review process
Subject: The Universal Periodic Review Process and the U.S. government, frequently asked questions
Official Citation: Not applicable
Date of Document: Not applicable
Date of Adoption: Not applicable
Date of General Entry into Force (EIF): Not applicable
Number of States Parties as of this printing: Not applicable
Date of Signature by United States: Not applicable
Date of Ratification/Accession/Adhesion: Not applicable
Date of Entry into Force as to United States (effective date): Not applicable
Legal Status/Character of the Instrument/Document as to the United States: This is only a Department of State website FAQ section for someone looking for info on the U.S. and the U.N. Human Rights Council Universal Periodic Review Process which the U.S. was preparing for in November 2010 at the time this book was written.

Caution: (If this is a legal instrument) The status and applicability of this instrument as to the United States may have changed since the date of this publication. The above information may be updated by referring to the following site:

Web Address: http://www1.umn.edu/humanrts/instree/ ....

UNIVERSAL PERIODIC REVIEW (UPR) FREQUENTLY ASKED QUESTIONS

Q: What is the Universal Periodic Review?

A: According to the UN's Office of the High Commissioner of Human Rights (OHCHR), "The Universal Periodic Review (UPR) is a unique process which involves a review of the human rights records of all 192 U.N. Member States once every four years. The UPR is a significant innovation of the Human Rights Council which is based on equal treatment for all countries. It provides an opportunity for all States to declare what actions they have taken to improve the human rights situations in their countries and to overcome challenges to the enjoyment of human rights. The UPR also includes a sharing of best human rights practices around the globe. Currently, no other mechanism of this kind exists."

Q: When is the United States' review?

A: The United States' review will be in November 2010.

Q: Who conducts the review?

A: As the OHCHR states, "The reviews are conducted by the UPR Working Group which consists of the 47 members of the Council; however any U.N. Member State can take part in the discussion/dialogue with the reviewed States. Each State review is assisted by groups of three States, known as "troikas," who serve as rapporteurs. The selection of the troikas for each State review is done through a drawing of lots prior to each Working Group session."

Q: What human rights obligations are addressed? A: "The UPR will assess the extent to which States respect their human rights obligations set out in: (1) the U.N. Charter; (2) the Universal Declaration of Human Rights; (3) human rights instruments to which the State is party (human rights treaties ratified by the State concerned); (4) voluntary pledges and commitments made by the State (e.g. national human rights policies and/or programs implemented); and, (5) applicable international humanitarian law."

Q: To which human rights instruments are the United States a party?

A: There are a number of multilateral human rights treaties that the U.S. is a party to, including:

- International Covenant on Civil and Political Rights
- International Convention on the Elimination of Racial Discrimination
- Convention Against Torture and Other Cruel, Inhuman, or Degrading Treatment
- Optional Protocol to the Convention on the Rights of the Child on the Involvement of Children in Armed Conflict
- Optional Protocol to the Convention on the Rights of the Child on the Sale of Children, Child Prostitution and Child Pornography
- Convention on the Prevention and Punishment of the Crime of Genocide
- Protocol Relating to the Status of Refugees
- Convention to Suppress the Slave Trade and Slavery
- Supplementary convention on the abolition of slavery, the slave trade and institutions and practices similar to slavery

- Inter-American convention on the granting of political rights to women
- Convention on the political rights of women
- Agreement for the suppression of the white slave traffic
- Trafficking in Persons Protocol
- International Labor Organization Convention on Forced Labor

Q: Can I provide feedback to the United States on the human rights situation where I live?

A: Yes! An active component of the UPR includes seeking input from non-governmental organizations and other domestic civil society groups, state and local authorities, tribal governments, universities, and individuals on the status of respect for human rights in the United States today. Your feedback is vital for us to better gauge the U.S. human rights situation now, and how protection of human rights can be improved in our country and around the world. We look forward to receiving your comments.

Q: When can I submit information to the Department of State?

A: The Department of State will accept feedback from now until June 15, 2010. At that point, we will take the information gathered from the community and begin to compile our report, which will be submitted to the U.N. for the review of the United States.

Q: How long is the United States submission to the UPR?

A: The United States' submission to the UPR is limited to 20 pages. In light of that (and because we expect submissions from a large number of groups and individuals), we kindly request that submissions from all stakeholders be as succinct as possible.

Again, the email address where you can send your questions, comments, and concerns is: upr_info@state.gov. The Department of State will continue to update the site periodically with announcements about domestic consultations regarding human rights in the United States. Check our calendar page with upcoming events.

DOCUMENT 86

Full Official Title: Report of the United States of America to High Commissioner for Human Rights on the Universal Periodic Review Process

Short Title: U.S. national UPR report to the Human Rights Council

Type of Document: This is a state general human rights report submitted by the U.S. to a U.N. Charter based body, the Human Rights Council.

Subject: Human rights record of the U.S.

Date of Document: August 20, 2010

Date of Adoption: Not applicable

Date of General Entry into Force (EIF): Not applicable

Number of Signatory States as of this Printing: Not applicable

Date of Signature by the United States: Not applicable

Date of Ratification/Accession/Adhesion: Not applicable

Date of Entry into Force as to United States (effective date): Not applicable

Legal Status/Character of the Instrument/Document as to the United States: This is not a legal instrument but a document that is required to be filed by all state parties to fulfill their obligations as member states of the U.N. and under the Human Rights Council mandate.

Comments: Under the U.N. Human Rights Council the U.S. as a Council member and U.N. member state has to participate in the Universal Periodic Review by first submitting a national report to the Office of the High Commissioner of Human Rights. Each state is required to undergo a review of their human rights record during the first year they are on the Council. The Council meets every few months to review states as part of the Universal Periodic Review (UPR) process and issues its observations and comments on the report and makes recommendations. The state may then respond to those recommendations in a subsequent report.

This is the United States' first national UPR report and it was reviewed by the Human Rights Council in open session, along with interactive dialogue on November 5, 2010, in Geneva. The final Outcome Report was issued January 4, 2011. See Document 87. The U.S. responded to this Report May 10, 2011. See Appendix K, #4. The final Outcome Report was adopted by the HRC on March 18, 2011. The report is an important tool to reiterate the U.S. position on its treaty obligations and any differences of opinion it may have with the Council over how they interpret specific obligations and get feedback and recommendations from the HRC, nonmember states and NGOs.

Web Address: http://www.state.gov/documents/organization/146379.pdf

REPORT OF THE UNITED STATES OF AMERICA TO HIGH COMMISSIONER FOR HUMAN RIGHTS ON THE UNIVERSAL PERIODIC REVIEW PROCESS

I. Introduction

I.1 A more perfect union, a more perfect world

1. The story of the United States of America is one guided by universal values shared the world over—that all are created equal and endowed with inalienable rights. In the United States, these values have grounded our institutions and motivated the determination of our citizens to come ever closer to realizing these ideals. Our Founders, who proclaimed their ambition "to form a more perfect Union," bequeathed to us not a static condition but a perpetual aspiration and mission.

2. We present our first Universal Periodic Review (UPR) report in the context of our commitment to help to build a world in which universal rights give strength and direction to the nations, partnerships, and institutions that can usher us toward a more perfect world, a world characterized by, as President Obama has said, "a just peace based on the inherent rights and dignity of every individual."

3. The U.S. has long been a cornerstone of the global economy and the global order. However, the most enduring contribution of the United States has been as a political experiment. The principles that all are created equal and endowed with inalienable rights were translated into promises and, with time, encoded into law. These simple but powerful principles have been the foundation upon which we have built the institutions of a modern state that is accountable to its citizens and whose laws are both legitimated by and limited by an enduring commitment to respect the rights of individuals. It is our political system that enables our economy and undergirds our global influence. As President Obama wrote in the preface to the recently published National Security Strategy, "democracy does not merely represent our better angels, it stands in opposition to aggression and injustice, and our support for universal rights is both fundamental to American leadership and a source of our strength in the world." Part of that strength derives from our democracy's capacity to adopt improvements based upon the firm foundation of our principled commitments. Our democracy is what allows us to acknowledge the realities of the world we live in, to recognize the opportunities to progress toward the fulfillment of an ideal, and to look to the future with pride and hope.

4. The ideas that informed and inform the American experiment can be found all over the world, and the people who have built it over centuries have come from every continent. The American experiment is a human experiment; the values on which it is based, including a commitment to human rights, are clearly engrained in our own national conscience, but they are also universal.

5. Echoing Eleanor Roosevelt, whose leadership was crucial to the adoption of the Universal Declaration of Human Rights (UDHR), Secretary of State Hillary Clinton has reaffirmed that "[h]uman rights are universal, but their experience is local. This is why we are committed to holding everyone to the same standard, including ourselves." From the UDHR to the ensuing Covenants and beyond, the United States has played a central role in the internationalization of human rights law and institutions. We associate ourselves with the many countries on all continents that are sincerely committed to advancing human rights, and we hope this UPR process will help us to strengthen our own system of human rights protections and encourage others to strengthen their commitments to human rights.

I.2 The United States and the Universal Periodic Review: approach and methodology

6. The ultimate objective of the UPR process, and of the U.N. Human Rights Council, is to enhance the protections for and enjoyment of human rights. Our participation signifies our commitment to that end, and we hope to contribute to it by sharing how we have made and will continue to make progress toward it. Some may say that by participating we acknowledge commonality with states that systematically abuse human rights. We do not. There is no comparison between American democracy and repressive regimes. Others will say that our participation, and our assessment of certain areas where we seek continued progress, reflects doubt in the ability of the American political system to deliver progress for its citizens. It does not. As Secretary Clinton said in a speech on human rights last year, "democracies demonstrate their greatness not by insisting they are perfect, but by using their institutions and their principles to make themselves ... more perfect." Progress is our goal, and our expectation thereof is justified by the proven ability of our system of government to deliver the progress our people demand and deserve.

7. This document gives a partial snapshot of the current human rights situation in the United States, including some of the areas where problems persist in our society. In addressing those areas, we use this report to explore opportunities to make further progress and also to share some of our recent progress. For us, the

primary value of this report is not as a diagnosis, but rather as a roadmap for our ongoing work within our democratic system to achieve lasting change. We submit this report with confidence that the legacy of our past efforts to embrace and actualize universal rights foreshadows our continued success.

8. This report is the product of collaboration between the U.S. Government and representatives of civil society from across the United States. Over the last year, senior representatives from more than a dozen federal departments and agencies traveled the country to attend a series of UPR consultations hosted by a wide range of civil society organizations. At these gatherings, individuals presented their concerns and recommendations and often shared stories or reports as they interacted with government representatives. Those conversations shaped the substance and structure of this report. Nearly a thousand people, representing a diversity of communities and viewpoints, and voicing a wide range of concerns, attended these gatherings in New Orleans, Louisiana; New York, New York; El Paso, Texas; Albuquerque, New Mexico; Window Rock, Arizona; the San Francisco Bay Area; Detroit, Michigan; Chicago, Illinois; Birmingham, Alabama; and Washington, D.C. Information about the process was also posted on the website of the U.S. Department of State (www.state.gov/g/drl/upr). Members of the public were encouraged to contribute questions, comments, and recommendations via that site, and many did so. The consultation process followed a familiar tradition of collaboration and discussion between government and civil society that is vital to the strength of our democracy. The U.S. Government is grateful to all those who hosted meetings and shared their views both in those consultations and online. We also welcome constructive comments and recommendations from other governments and non-governmental organizations through the UPR process.

II. The United States and human rights: normative and institutional background

II.1 Human Rights as the ends of government and the means of progress

9. The desire to live freely under a government that would respect and protect human rights was the fundamental motivation of our country's Founders—human rights have not only been part of the United States since the beginning, they were the reason our nation was created. From its adoption in 1789, the U.S. Constitution has been the central legal instrument of government and the supreme law of the land. The Constitution establishes the structure of government in the United States, starting with the fundamental principle that the will of the people is the basis of the legitimacy of government. The Constitution's first ten amendments, adopted in 1791 and known as the Bill of Rights, along with the Thirteenth, Fourteenth, and Fifteenth Amendments, adopted in the wake of the Civil War, protect many rights that, in the twentieth century, became recognized and protected under international human rights law. The principles enshrined in the Constitution and the system of government that it prescribes—including the checks and balances between the legislative, executive, and judicial branches, as well as the reservation of significant authority and autonomy for the fifty states joined together in a federal system—have been the basic building blocks of a government of the people, by the people, and for the people throughout U.S. history.

10. Since our founding, we have made tremendous progress in strengthening the protection of rights and in enhancing and expanding equal opportunities for their enjoyment. Just as the legitimacy of our government is grounded in the will of the people, the credit for progress accrues not only to our Constitution and the government it created, but also to the determination and commitment of our people. Throughout our history, our citizens have used the freedoms provided in the Constitution as a foundation upon which to advocate for changes that would create a more just society. The Constitution provided the means for its own amelioration and revision: its glaring original flaw of tolerating slavery, as well as denying the vote to women, have both been corrected through constitutional reform, judicial review and our democratic processes. Human rights—including the freedoms of speech, association, and religion—have empowered our people to be the engine of our progress.

II.2 Enduring commitments

11. As we look to the future, the United States stands committed to the enduring promises of protecting individual freedoms, fairness and equality before the law, and human dignity—promises that reflect the inalienable rights of each person. Our commitment to the rights protected in our Constitution is matched by a parallel commitment to foster a society characterized by shared prosperity. Finally, we are committed to the idea that the values behind the domestic promises articulated in our Constitution should also guide and inform our engagement with the world. Below, we address these commitments in turn.

III. A commitment to freedom, equality, and dignity

12. Article 1 of the Universal Declaration of Human Rights declares that "all human beings are born free and equal in dignity and rights" and that they are "endowed with reason and conscience." This basic

truth suggests the kinds of obligations—both positive and negative—that governments have with regard to their citizens.

13. People should be free and should have a say in how they are governed. Governments have an obligation not to restrict fundamental freedoms unjustifiably, and governments need to create the laws and institutions that secure those freedoms.

14. People should enjoy fair treatment reflected in due process and equality before the law. Governments have an obligation not to discriminate or persecute and should establish mechanisms for protection and redress.

15. People should be treated with dignity. Governments have an obligation to protect the security of the person and to respect human dignity.

16. These obligations are what enable people to claim "life, liberty, and the pursuit of happiness" as their just entitlements. These same rights are encoded in international human rights law and in our own Constitution.

III.1 Freedom of expression, religion, association, and political participation

Freedom of expression

17. The United States maintains robust protections for freedom of expression. As a general matter, the government does not punish or penalize those who peacefully express their views in the public sphere, even when those views are critical of the government. Indeed, dissent is a valuable and valued part of our politics: democracy provides a marketplace for ideas, and in order to function as such, new ideas must be permitted, even if they are unpopular or potentially offensive. The United States has a free, thriving, and diverse independent press—a feature that existed before the advent of electronic and digital media and that continues today.

18. We also recognize that privacy is linked to free expression, in that individuals need to feel that they can control the boundaries of their self-disclosure and self-expression in order to be able to express themselves freely: surveillance, especially when practiced by a government, can lead to self-censorship. Although protecting the security of all citizens means that no individual can have an absolute right to privacy or expression, any limitations on these rights are determined in a public process, by representatives of the people in the legislature and by the courts.

Freedom of thought, conscience, and religion

19. The desire for freedom from religious persecution has brought millions to our shores. Today, freedom of religion protects each individual's ability to participate in and share the traditions of his or her chosen faith, to change his or her religion, or to choose not to believe or participate in religious practice.

20. Citizens continue to avail themselves of freedom of religion protections in the Constitution and in state and federal law. For example, in a case this year, a Native American primary school student's right to wear his hair in a braid, in accordance with his family's religious beliefs, was upheld pursuant to a Texas religious freedom law.[1]

21. The constitutional prohibition on the establishment of a religion by the government, along with robust protections for freedom of speech and association, have helped to create a multi-religious society in which the freedom to choose and practice one's faith, or to have no faith at all, is secure.

Freedom of association

22. In the United States, our vibrant civil society exists because people freely come together to meet and share interests and to advocate for political and other causes. In some cases, this takes the form of public gatherings, marches, or protests. In others, people establish or join organizations with a sustained purpose or agenda—today, there are more than 1.5 million non-profit organizations in the United States.

23. Freedom of association also protects workers and their right to organize. The labor movement in the United States has a rich history, and the right to organize and bargain collectively under the protection of the law is the bedrock upon which workers are able to form or join a labor union. Workers regularly use legal mechanisms to address complaints such as threats, discharges, interrogations, surveillance, and wages-and-benefits cuts for supporting a union. These legal regimes are continuously assessed and evolving in order to keep pace with a modern work environment. Our UPR consultations included workers from a variety of sectors, including domestic workers who spoke about the challenges they face in organizing effectively. Currently there are several bills in our Congress that seek to strengthen workers' rights—ensuring that workers can continue to associate freely, organize, and practice collective bargaining as the U.S. economy continues to change.

Freedom of political participation

24. Every person should have a say in how he or she is governed, and representative democracy has always been the essential foundation of our country's political system. When the United States was founded,

only white men who owned property could vote. In the subsequent centuries, barriers fell for women, African Americans, Hispanics, Asian Americans, and Native Americans, and we continue to work to ensure universal enfranchisement in both law and fact.

25. After decades of work by women's rights groups and others, women obtained a constitutionally protected right to vote in 1920. Real protection of the right to vote for racial and ethnic minorities came many decades later with the enactment of the Voting Rights Act of 1965, a watershed moment in the fight for fairness in our election system. Nearly a century earlier, in the wake of the Civil War, the Fifteenth Amendment to the Constitution had granted the right to vote to African-American men, although in practice that right continued to be obstructed and denied. Since the Voting Rights Act's passage, the United States has made substantial progress in breaking down racial barriers to voting, resulting in greater participation in elections and significant increases in the election of members of diverse racial and ethnic groups to public office.

26. The Voting Rights Act prohibits racial discrimination in voting, allowing the Department of Justice or a private citizen to challenge a voting practice as discriminatory in federal court. Under the Act, certain jurisdictions with histories of racial discrimination in voting require federal approval to implement any change affecting voting. The Act also ensures meaningful access to the franchise for non-English speaking citizens. In recent months, the Department of Justice has worked to strengthen enforcement of federal voting rights laws. The Department recently obtained consent decrees against some jurisdictions and concluded a settlement with another, and it is preparing to review thousands of redistricting plans that will be submitted after release of the 2010 Census results to ensure that voting districts are not drawn with the purpose or effect of marginalizing minority voters.

27. Other laws, such as the National Voter Registration Act of 1993 and the Help America Vote Act of 2002, help increase historically low registration rates of minorities and persons with disabilities that have resulted from discrimination, and protect the equal rights of all by facilitating complete and accurate voter rolls.

28. Several Members of Congress and other policymakers and advocates have promoted changes to our election administration system including proposals to establish a national mandate for universal voter registration; combat "deceptive practices" designed to deter legitimate voters from voting; require "permanent voter registration" systems; and require fail-safe procedures, so that eligible voters can correct inaccurate voter rolls and vote on the same day. Work continues toward having these proposals enacted into federal law.

III.2 Fairness and equality

29. The United States has always been a multi-racial, multi-ethnic, multi-religious society. Although we have made great strides, work remains to meet our goal of ensuring equality before the law for all. Thirty years ago, the idea of having an African-American president would not have seemed possible; today it is our reality. Our Attorney General, the nation's top law enforcement officer, is also African-American. Three of the last four Secretaries of State have been women, and two of the last three have been African-American. We have recently appointed our first Hispanic Supreme Court Justice, as well as several LGBT individuals to senior positions in the Executive Branch. And while individual stories do not prove the absence of enduring challenges, they demonstrate the presence of possibilities.

30. In 1947, W.E.B. DuBois testified before the U.N. General Assembly on the continued pervasive discrimination against African Americans in the United States. In the ensuing decades the U.S. civil rights movement emerged as a quintessential example of citizens using principles of non-violence, law, protest, and public debate to hold their government accountable and to demand that it deliver on their right to equal and fair treatment. The movement led to critical new laws prohibiting discrimination and seeking to ensure equal opportunity for all individuals. The progress in the decades since is a source of pride to our government and to our people. Indeed, our nation's struggle to banish the legacy of slavery and our long and continuing journey toward racial equality have become the central and emblematic narrative in our quest for a fair and just society that reflects the equality of all.

31. The United States aspires to foster a society in which, as Dr. Martin Luther King, Jr. put it, the success of our children is determined by the "content of their character." We are not satisfied with a situation where the unemployment rate for African Americans is 15.8%, for Hispanics 12.4%, and for whites 8.8%, as it was in February 2010. We are not satisfied that a person with disabilities is only one fourth as likely to be employed as a person without disabilities. We are not satisfied when fewer than half of African-American

---

[1] A.A. v. Needville Indep. Sch. Dist., No. 09-20091 (5th Cir, July 9, 2010)

and Hispanic families own homes while three quarters of white families do. We are not satisfied that whites are twice as likely as Native Americans to have a college degree. The United States continues to address such disparities by working to ensure that equal opportunity is not only guaranteed in law but experienced in fact by all Americans.

32. In addition to our continuing quest to achieve fairness and equality for racial and ethnic minorities across our society, we wish to call attention to the following groups and issues.

Fairness, equality, and persons with disabilities

33. United States law and practice provide broad and effective protections against, and remedies for, disability-based discrimination. The most notable of these is the Americans with Disabilities Act of 1990 (ADA), the first national civil rights legislation in the world to unequivocally prohibit discrimination against persons with disabilities, which was amended in 2008 to ensure broader protections. The intent of these laws is to prohibit discrimination on the basis of disability and remove barriers to the full and equal inclusion of people with disabilities in U.S. society. These laws cover areas of life including education, health care, transportation, housing, employment, technology, information and communication, the judicial system, and political participation. To ensure implementation of these laws, a variety of technical assistance and remedies have been supported with federal funds. For example, training has been provided to the public and private sectors on implementation of the ADA; parent training information centers empower families to understand and claim their rights; and federally funded centers for independent living support the empowerment of individuals with disabilities to live where and with whom they choose in their communities. The Department of Justice and other federal departments and agencies have the authority to enforce these laws and, in this regard, receive complaints and utilize mediation and litigation as appropriate. On July 30, 2009, the United States signed the U.N. Convention on the Rights of Persons with Disabilities and is pursuing the necessary steps toward ratification, which the Administration strongly supports. Upon the 20th anniversary of the ADA, President Obama further demonstrated the nation's commitment to continued vigilance and improvement by announcing new regulations that increase accessibility in a variety of contexts and commit the federal government to hiring more persons with disabilities. Although we recognize that discrimination and access problems persist, which we are actively striving to address, the substantive equality of persons with disabilities in the United States has improved enormously in the past few decades.

Fairness, equality, and Lesbian, Gay, Bisexual and Transgender (LGBT) persons

34. In each era of our history there tends to be a group whose experience of discrimination illustrates the continuing debate among citizens about how we can build a more fair society. In this era, one such group is LGBT Americans. In 2003, reversing a prior decision, the Supreme Court struck down a state criminal law against sodomy, holding that criminalizing consensual private sexual practices between adults violates their rights under the Constitution.[2] With the recent passage of the Matthew Shepard and James Byrd, Jr. Hate Crimes Prevention Act of 2009, the United States has bolstered its authority to prosecute hate crimes, including those motivated by animus based on sexual orientation, gender identity, or disability. Since 1998, employment discrimination based on sexual orientation has been prohibited in federal employment. Earlier this year, the Administration extended many benefits to the same-sex partners of federal employees, and supports the pending Domestic Partnership Benefits and Obligations Act, a law that would extend additional benefits currently accorded to married couples to same sex partners. Furthermore, President Obama is committed to the repeal of the "Don't Ask, Don't Tell" statute, which prevents gays and lesbians from serving openly in the military, and both the Chairman of the Joint Chiefs of Staff and the Secretary of Defense have testified at congressional hearings in support of its repeal. The President has also supported passage of the Employment Non-Discrimination Act, which would prohibit discrimination in employment based on sexual orientation or gender identity. Debate continues over equal rights to marriage for LGBT Americans at the federal and state levels, and several states have reformed their laws to provide for same-sex marriages, civil unions, or domestic partnerships. At the federal level, the President supports repeal of the Defense of Marriage Act.

Fairness, equality, and Muslim, Arab-American and South Asian American persons

35. We have worked to ensure fair treatment of members of Muslim, Arab-American, and South Asian communities. The U.S. Government is committed to protecting the rights of members of these groups, and to combating discrimination and intolerance against them. Examples of such measures include the Justice Department's formation of the 9/11 Backlash Taskforce and civil rights work on religious freedom (e.g., bringing a case on behalf of a Muslim school girl to protect her right to wear a hijab); the civil rights outreach

efforts of the Department of Homeland Security; and the Equal Employment Opportunity Commission's enforcement efforts to combat backlash-related employment discrimination which resulted in over $5 million for victims from 2001–2006.

36. At our UPR consultations, including the meeting in Detroit, Michigan, Muslim, Arab-American, and South Asian citizens shared their experiences of intolerance and pressed for additional efforts to challenge misperceptions and discriminatory stereotypes, to prevent acts of vandalism, and to combat hate crimes. The federal government is committed to ongoing efforts to combat discrimination: the Attorney General's review of the 2003 Guidance Regarding the Use of Race by Federal Law Enforcement Agencies (discussed below), as well as efforts to limit country-specific travel bans, are examples.

Fairness, equality, and women

37. As one of President Obama's first official acts, he signed into law the Lilly Ledbetter Fair Pay Act of 2009, which helps women who face wage discrimination recover their lost wages. Shortly thereafter, the President created the White House Council on Women and Girls to seek to ensure that American women and girls are treated fairly and equally in all matters of public policy. Thus, for instance, the Administration supports the Paycheck Fairness Act, which will help ensure that women receive equal pay for equal work. Our recent health care reform bill also lowers costs and offers greater choices for women, and ends insurance company discrimination against them. Moreover, the Administration established the first White House Advisor on Violence Against Women, appointed two women to the U.S. Supreme Court, and created an unprecedented position of Ambassador-at-Large for Global Women's Issues to mobilize support for women around the world. The Obama Administration strongly supports U.S. ratification of the Convention on the Elimination of all forms of Discrimination Against Women and is working with our Senate toward this end.

Fairness, equality, and Native Americans

38. The U.S. took the UPR process to "Indian Country". One of our UPR consultations was hosted on tribal land in Arizona, the New Mexico consultation addressed American Indian and Alaska Native issues, and other consultations included tribal representatives. The United States has a unique legal relationship with federally recognized tribes. By virtue of their status as sovereigns that pre-date the federal Union, as well as subsequent treaties, statutes, executive orders, and judicial decisions, Indian tribes are recognized as political entities with inherent powers of self-government. The U.S. government therefore has a government-to-government relationship with 564 federally recognized Indian tribes and promotes tribal self-governance over a broad range of internal and local affairs. The United States also recognizes past wrongs and broken promises in the federal government's relationship with American Indians and Alaska Natives, and recognizes the need for urgent change. Some reservations currently face unemployment rates of up to 80 percent; nearly a quarter of Native Americans live in poverty; American Indians and Alaska Natives face significant health care disparities; and some reservations have crime rates up to 10 times the national average. Today we are helping tribes address the many issues facing their communities.

39. In November of last year, President Obama hosted a historic summit with nearly 400 tribal leaders to develop a policy agenda for Native Americans where he emphasized his commitment to regular and meaningful consultation with tribal officials regarding federal policy decisions that have tribal implications. In March, the President signed into law important health provisions for American Indians and Alaska Natives. In addition, President Obama recognizes the importance of enhancing the role of tribes in Indian education and supports Native language immersion and Native language restoration programs.

40. Addressing crimes involving violence against women and children on tribal lands is a priority. After extensive consultations with tribal leaders, Attorney General Eric Holder announced significant reform to increase prosecution of crimes committed on tribal lands. He hired more Assistant U.S. Attorneys and more victim-witness specialists. He created a new position, the National Indian Country Training Coordinator, who will work with prosecutors and law enforcement officers in tribal communities. The Attorney General is establishing a Tribal Nations Leadership Council to provide ongoing advice on issues critical to tribal communities.

41. On July 29, 2010, President Obama signed the Tribal Law and Order Act, requiring the Justice Department to disclose data on cases in Indian Country that it declines to prosecute and granting tribes greater authority to prosecute and punish criminals. The Act also expands support for Bureau of Indian

---

[2] *Lawrence v. Texas*, 539 U.S. 558 (2003).

Affairs and Tribal officers. It includes new provisions to prevent counterfeiting of Indian-produced crafts and new guidelines and training for domestic violence and sex crimes, and it strengthens tribal courts and police departments and enhances programs to combat drug and alcohol abuse and help at-risk youth. These are significant measures that will empower tribal governments and make a difference in people's lives.

42. In April 2010, at the U.N. Permanent Forum on Indigenous Issues, U.S. Ambassador to the U.N. Susan Rice announced that the United States would undertake a review of its position on the U.N. Declaration on the Rights of Indigenous Peoples. That multi-agency review is currently underway in consultation with tribal leaders and with outreach to other stakeholders.

Fairness and equality at work

43. The United States is committed to continuing to root out discrimination in the workplace, and the federal government is committed to vigorously enforcing laws to that end. The Justice Department and the Equal Employment Opportunity Commission have reinvigorated efforts to enforce Title VII of the Civil Rights Act of 1964, which prohibits employment discrimination based on race, color, sex, national origin, and religion, and the Age Discrimination in Employment Act, which prohibits employment discrimination based on age. Both laws also prohibit retaliation against employees who bring charges of discrimination in the workplace.

44. In recognition of discrimination's long-term effects, for 45 years, working through the Department of Labor and other agencies, the federal government has required private companies with which it conducts significant business to take proactive steps to increase the participation of minorities and women in the workplace when they are underrepresented, and to ensure fairness in recruiting, hiring, promotion, and compensation. In May 2010, the Department of Labor chaired the first meeting since 2000 of the President's Committee on the International Labor Organization (ILO), which coordinates U.S. policy toward the ILO. The Committee agreed to work toward the successful ratification of ILO Convention No. 111 (to combat discrimination at work) and directed a subgroup to resume work on reviewing the feasibility of other conventions for ratification.

Fairness and equality in housing

45. The United States protects citizens from discrimination in housing through the Fair Housing Act of 1968, which prohibits discrimination in housing on the basis of race, color, religion, sex, national origin, familial status, or disability. Housing providers, both public and private, as well as other entities, such as municipalities, banks, and homeowners' insurance companies, are all covered by the Act. There is also a robust legal infrastructure in place for the investigation and prosecution of housing discrimination claims brought under the Act. Additionally, the 1974 Equal Credit Opportunity Act prohibits discrimination in the extension of credit, encompassing the actions of mortgage lenders and banks.

46. Following the recent economic crisis, the issue of predatory lending, and particularly discriminatory lending, is an area of enforcement focus. The recession in the United States was fueled largely by a housing crisis, which coincided with some discriminatory lending practices. The subsequent foreclosure crisis has disproportionately affected communities of color, and the federal government has focused resources and efforts to determine whether and where discrimination took place, as well as to ensure greater oversight going forward to prevent similar crises in the future. In this respect President Obama signed major financial reform legislation in 2010 that includes a new consumer protection bureau, among other provisions.

Fairness and equality in education

47. The United States is committed to providing equal educational opportunities to all children, regardless of their individual circumstances, race, national origin, ethnicity, gender, or disability. Consistent with this commitment, the federal government uses educational programs to ensure that federal dollars assist underserved students and develop strategies that will help such students succeed. The federal government has also taken steps to ensure that students with disabilities have access to technology, and to provide low-income students and students of color with increased access to early learning and college. In addition, the Department of Education administers and promotes programs that seek to provide financial aid to all students in need; promotes educational equity for women and students of color; assists school districts in offering educational opportunities to Native Hawaiians, American Indians, and Alaska Natives; and provides grants to strengthen historically Black colleges and universities and other institutions serving previously underserved populations.

48. Additionally, the Departments of Justice and Education enforce numerous laws, including the Civil Rights Act of 1964, the Americans with Disabilities Act of 1990, the Patsy T. Mink Equal Opportunity

in Education Act of 1972 (Title IX), and the Rehabilitation Act of 1973, that prohibit discrimination on the basis of race, color, national origin, sex, disability, and age with regard to education. In this capacity, the Justice Department is a party to more than 200 court cases addressing equal opportunities for students, and is involved in numerous out-of-court investigations, many of which have led to settlement agreements. The Department of Education investigates and resolves civil rights complaints filed by individuals, resolving 6,150 such complaints in the most recent fiscal year, and initiates compliance reviews where information suggests widespread discrimination. The Individuals with Disabilities Education Act (IDEA) requires public schools to make available to all eligible children with disabilities a free appropriate public education in the least restrictive environment appropriate to their individual needs.

49. The federal government is working closely with civil society groups–the representatives of which frequently raised the issue of education in our UPR consultations—and with state and local education authorities in our fifty states to address the factors that contribute to the education "achievement gap," and to ensure equality and excellence for all children in public schools, and particularly African-American and Hispanic children and children for whom English is a second language, who, like others, find linguistic discrimination a barrier to full participation.

Fairness and equality in law enforcement

50. The United States recognizes that racial or ethnic profiling is not effective law enforcement and is not consistent with our commitment to fairness in our justice system. For many years, concerns about racial profiling arose mainly in the context of motor vehicle or street stops related to enforcement of drug or immigration laws. Since the September 11, 2001 terrorist attacks, the debate has also included an examination of law enforcement conduct in the context of the country's effort to combat terrorism. Citizens and civil society have advocated forcefully that efforts by law enforcement to prevent future terrorist attacks must be consistent with the government's goal to end racial and ethnic profiling.

51. In addition to the U.S. Constitution, there are several federal statutes and regulations that impose limits on the use of race or ethnicity by law enforcement in their decision-making and enforcement activities. In particular, title VI of the Civil Rights Act of 1964, prohibits discrimination based on race, color or national origin in all federally assisted programs or activities, and 42 U.S.C. §14141 provides the Department of Justice with a cause of action to sue police departments for injunctive relief if they are engaging in a pattern or practice of unlawful conduct, including violations of non-discrimination mandates.

52. The U.S. Government's efforts to combat racial and ethnic profiling include increasing enforcement of federal anti-profiling statutes, as well as an examination of federal law enforcement policies and practices. In late 2009, the Attorney General initiated an internal review of the Justice Department's 2003 Guidance Regarding the Use of Race by Federal Law Enforcement Agencies to determine whether it is effective, and will recommend any changes that may be warranted.

53. On August 3, 2010, President Obama signed a law that reduces sentencing disparities between powder cocaine and crack cocaine offenses, capping a long effort—one discussed at our UPR consultations—that arose out of the fact that those convicted of crack cocaine offenses are more likely to be members of a racial minority.

54. The Administration is also committed to ensuring that the United States complies with its international obligations to provide consular notification and access for foreign nationals in U.S. custody, including the obligations arising from the *Avena* decision of the International Court of Justice.

III.3 Dignity

Safeguards for dignity in law enforcement and criminal justice

55. Law enforcement is one of the fundamental duties of any state. Our commitment to the inalienable rights of each person guides our efforts to ensure that our law enforcement system reflects and respects those rights.

56. The U.S. Constitution, as well as federal and state statutes, provides a number of substantive and procedural protections for individuals accused of committing crimes, those being held for trial, and those who are held in prisons or jails. These include the right to be protected from unreasonable search and seizures, the right to due process under the law, the right to equal protection under the law, the right to an attorney, the right to remain silent during a criminal proceeding, the right to be protected from excessive bail in federal prosecutions, the right to be informed of the nature of the charges filed and of potential punishments, the right to a speedy and public trial, the right to cross-examine witnesses at trial, the right to an impartial jury of peers before someone can be sentenced to a year or more in prison, the right to be protected against being

tried for the same crime twice, and the right to be free from cruel and unusual punishment in all prosecutions. (These constitutional rights are generally reflected, at times with different terminology, in international human rights law instruments to which the U.S. is party. In some respects, our constitutional rights go beyond those guaranteed in international law.)

57. These protections help to ensure that our process for determining criminal sanctions, including those that deprive individuals of their liberty, is fairly designed and implemented. Nonetheless many in civil society continue to raise concerns about our nation's criminal justice system at federal and state levels, including in the areas of capital punishment, juvenile justice, racial profiling, and racial disparities in sentencing. We are committed to continued vigilance in our effort to enforce the law in a manner consistent with the Constitution and with the rights and dignity of all citizens.

Dignity and incarceration

58 The United States is committed to protecting the rights of incarcerated persons, and we regularly investigate, monitor compliance, and, where necessary, take legal action to secure the constitutional rights of incarcerated people, including the right to practice their religion.

59. We have also taken action to prevent assaults on the dignity of prisoners that may come from other prisoners. The independent National Prison Rape Elimination Commission, established by Congress under the Prison Rape Elimination Act, was charged with studying the impact of sexual assault in correction and detention facilities and developing national standards for the detection, prevention, reduction, and punishment of prison rape. In 2009, the Commission released its report which detailed progress made in improving the safety and security in these facilities as well as areas still in need of reform. The United States is working to address these issues. The Department of Justice is in the process of developing comprehensive regulations to effectively reduce rape in our nation's prisons.

60. In addition to working to ensure that prisons and jails meet constitutional standards, alternatives to incarceration are being utilized by states, including intensive probation supervision, boot camps, house arrest, and diversion to drug treatment.

Dignity and criminal sanctions

61. The United States may impose the death penalty for the most serious crimes and subject to exacting procedural safeguards. Federal laws providing for the death penalty most often involve serious crimes in which death results. Several non-homicide crimes may also result in the imposition of a death sentence, e.g., espionage, treason, and several carefully circumscribed capital offenses intended to target the threat of terrorist attacks resulting in widespread loss of life.

62. The federal government utilizes a system for carefully examining each potential federal death penalty case. This system operates to help ensure that the death penalty is not applied in an arbitrary, capricious, or discriminatory manner, and to promote indigent defendants receiving competent representation by qualified attorneys. Many of our states have adopted procedures of their own to provide experienced counsel for indigent defendants. In addition, existing federal law permits DNA testing in relevant federal and state cases.

63. In 2009, the death penalty was applied in 52 cases in the United States, about half the number of a decade earlier. The death penalty is authorized by 35 states, the federal government, and the U.S. military. There are currently 16 jurisdictions without the death penalty. While state governments retain primary responsibility for establishing procedures and policies that govern state capital prosecutions, the Supreme Court has excluded from application of the death penalty those offenders who, at the time of the offense, were under age 18[3] or had intellectual disabilities.[4]

Dignity and juvenile offenders

64. In 1974, Congress enacted the Juvenile Justice and Delinquency Prevention Act (JJDPA), to ensure that youth were not treated merely as "little adults," and that they received necessary and appropriate rehabilitative services in the least restrictive environment consistent with public safety. The JJDPA created an office within the Justice Department dedicated to supporting federal, state, and local efforts to prevent juvenile crime, improving the juvenile justice system, and addressing the needs of juvenile crime victims. This office provides funding to states for system improvement, as well as funding for research to identify optimal prevention and intervention strategies for youth in the juvenile justice system or at risk of entering it. Our UPR consultations included direct testimony from juvenile offenders who underscored the importance of intervention strategies and programs to help juvenile offenders find education and employment so that they can become self-sufficient.

65. The Department of Justice also has a robust program to protect the rights of juveniles in juvenile justice facilities. For example, in July 2010, the Department entered an agreement with the State of New York regarding unconstitutional conditions in four upstate facilities. The agreement, in addition to limiting the kinds of restraints that can be used, mandates adequate mental health and substance abuse services.

66. In May 2010, the Supreme Court ruled that sentences of life imprisonment without the possibility of parole for juveniles who commit non-homicide offenses violate the Constitution's prohibition against cruel and unusual punishment.[5]

IV. A commitment to foster a society where citizens are empowered to exercise their rights

67. The paradigm elucidated in Franklin Roosevelt's 1941 "Four Freedoms" speech became a reference point for many in the international human rights movement. On subjects such as "freedom from want," the United States has focused on democratic solutions and civil society initiatives while the U.S. courts have defined our federal constitutional obligations narrowly and primarily by focusing on procedural rights to due process and equal protection of the law. But as a matter of public policy, our citizens have taken action through their elected representatives to help create a society in which prosperity is shared, including social benefits provided by law, so that all citizens can live what Roosevelt called "a healthy peacetime life." Often this has included safeguards for the most vulnerable in our society—including the young, the old, the poor, and the infirm. In the wake of the Civil War, legislation was passed to support the well-being of widows and veterans, and to provide land to former slaves. By the early 20th century, all of our states had recognized that children needed schooling in order to become free and engaged citizens and had instituted free education for all. During the Great Depression, new programs were introduced to ensure the security of those who could no longer work. In the 1960s, several administrations announced a "war on poverty," and programs were established to provide health care for seniors and the very poor. And this year saw the passage of major legislation that will greatly expand the number of Americans who have health insurance. In every case, the creation of these programs has reflected a popular sense that the society in which we want to live is one in which each person has the opportunity to live a full and fulfilling life. That begins, but does not end, with the exercise of their human rights.

IV.1 Education

68. Through the American Recovery and Reinvestment Act of 2009, the current Administration has made an unprecedented financial commitment of almost $100 billion to education. In November 2009, the Administration announced the Race to the Top program, a $4.35 billion fund that is the largest competitive education grant program in U.S. history. It is designed to provide incentives to states to implement large-scale, system-changing reforms that improve student achievement, narrow achievement gaps, and increase graduation and college enrollment rates. Additionally, Recovery Act funds are being used to promote high-quality early childhood education, provide an increase in available financial aid and loans for post-secondary school, and provide $12 billion for community colleges to give access to workers who need more education and training.

IV.2 Health

69. The United States has been the source of many significant innovations in modern medicine that have alleviated suffering and cured disease for millions in our own country and around the world. This year, we also made significant progress by enacting major legislation that expands access to health care for our citizens.

70. On March 23, 2010, President Obama signed the Affordable Care Act into law. The Act makes great strides toward the goal that all Americans have access to quality, affordable health care. The law is projected to expand health insurance coverage to 32 million Americans who would otherwise lack health insurance, significantly reduces disparities in accessing high-quality care, and includes substantial new investments in prevention and wellness activities to improve public health. The law also includes important consumer protections, such as prohibiting insurance companies from denying coverage to people based on pre-existing conditions or medical history, which disproportionately impacts older and sicker populations.

71. The law increases access to care for underserved populations by expanding community health centers that deliver preventive and primary care services. The law will also help our nation reduce disparities and discrimination in access to care that have contributed to poor health. For example, African Americans are 29 percent more likely to die from heart disease than non-Hispanic whites. Asian American men suffer from stomach cancer 114 percent more often than non-Hispanic white men. Hispanic women

are 2.2 times more likely to be diagnosed with cervical cancer than non-Hispanic white women. American Indians and Alaska Natives are 2.2 times as likely to have diabetes as non-Hispanic whites. Additionally, these racial and ethnic groups accounted for almost 70 percent of the newly diagnosed cases of HIV and AIDS in 2003.[6]

72. The Act will reduce disparities like these through access to preventive services; investment in chronic disease control and prevention; enhanced data collection to support population-specific epidemiological research; and recruitment of health professionals from diverse backgrounds.

73. Implementation of the Affordable Care Act will help more Americans get the care they need to live healthy lives and ensure more Americans are free to learn, work, and contribute to their communities.

IV.3 Housing

74. The ability to access quality and affordable housing has a substantial impact on a person's health, education, and economic opportunities. Although we are fortunate to have a high-quality housing stock and a high percentage of homeownership, meeting our nation's housing needs will require continued effort, particularly in expanding the availability of affordable housing in all communities as our population grows. This was a topic frequently raised by citizens in our consultations, and our meetings in New York and New Orleans, included visits to public housing facilities and discussions with residents.

75. Federal housing assistance programs play an important role in covering the difference between the rents that low-income families are able to afford and the cost of rental housing. The main federal assistance programs to help households access affordable housing are the Housing Choice Voucher Program (Section 8), project-based Section 8 rental assistance, and public housing. These programs are intended to reduce housing costs to about 30 percent of household income.

76. We are creating new solutions to address the challenge of homelessness, which often coincides with other vulnerabilities such as mental illness. $190 million in new funding announced in July, 2010, will provide support to 550 local projects that will offer critically needed housing and support services to nearly 20,000 homeless individuals and families. This comes on top of the nearly $1.4 billion awarded last December to renew funding to more than 6,400 existing local programs. Moreover, the Homeless Prevention and Rapid Re-Housing Program, part of the Recovery Act, has helped prevent and end homelessness for nearly a half million people since it became law last year.

V. A commitment to values in our engagement across borders

77. The United States understands its role as a cornerstone in an international system of cooperation to preserve global security, support the growth of global prosperity, and progress toward world peace based on respect for the human rights and dignity of every person.

78. Our own efforts to build such a world include our role as the world's largest donor of development aid—including our commitment to disaster relief as seen recently in Haiti and Pakistan. And they include a commitment to using "smart power" in our foreign policy, including a focus on honest, determined diplomacy and on harnessing the full potential of international institutions to facilitate cooperation.

79. We also know that although we never welcome the use of force, wisdom and necessity will sometimes require it. As President Obama said in his Nobel Lecture, "To say that force may sometimes be necessary is not a call to cynicism—it is a recognition of history; the imperfections of man and the limits of reason."

80. The fundamental truth which grounds the principles of government enshrined in our Constitution—that each person is created with equal value from which flows inalienable rights—is not an exclusively American truth; it is a universal one. It is the truth that anchors the Universal Declaration of Human Rights, it is the truth that underpins the legitimate purposes and obligations not just of our government, but of all governments.

81. We are committed to that universal truth, and so we are committed to principled engagement across borders and with foreign governments and their citizens. This commitment includes, in the words of our Declaration of Independence, according "decent respect to the opinions of mankind," and seeking always to preserve and protect the dignity of all persons, because the values that we cherish apply everywhere and to everyone.

V.1 Values and National Security

82. The United States is currently at war with Al Qaeda and its associated forces. President Obama has made clear that the United States is fully committed to complying with the Constitution and with all

[3] *Roper v. Simmons*, 543 U.S. 551, 578 (2005).
[4] *Atkins v. Virginia*, 536 U.S. 304 (2002).
[5] *Graham v. Florida*, __ U.S. __ (May 17, 2010).

applicable domestic and international law, including the laws of war, in all aspects of this or any armed conflict. We start from the premise that there are no law-free zones, and that everyone is entitled to protection under law. In his Nobel Lecture, the President made clear that "[w]here force is necessary, we have a moral and strategic interest in binding ourselves to certain rules of conduct ... [E]ven as we confront a vicious adversary that abides by no rules ... the United States of America must remain a standard bearer in the conduct of war."

Detention and treatment of detainees

83. On his second full day in office, President Obama acted to implement this vision by issuing three Executive Orders relating to U.S. detention, interrogation, and transfer policies and the Guantánamo Bay detention facility.

84. Executive Order 13491, *Ensuring Lawful Interrogations*, directed that individuals detained in any armed conflict shall in all circumstances be treated humanely and shall not be subjected to violence to life and person, nor to outrages upon personal dignity, whenever such individuals are in the custody or under the effective control of the United States Government or detained within a facility owned, operated, or controlled by the United States. Such individuals shall not be subjected to any interrogation technique or approach that is not authorized by and listed in Army Field Manural 2-22.3, which explicitly prohibits threats, coercion, physical abuse, and water boarding. The Order further directed the Central Intelligence Agency to close any detention facilities it operated, and not to oerate any such detention facilities in the future. Individuals detained in armed conflict must be treated in conformity with all applicable laws, including Common Article 3 of the 1949 Geneva Conventions, which the President and the Supreme Court have recognized as providing "minimum" standards of protection in all non-international armed conflicts, including in the conflict with Al Qaeda.[7]

85. The Executive Order also directed a review of all U.S. transfer policies to ensure that they do not result in the transfer of individuals to other nations to face torture or otherwise for the purpose, or with the effect, of undermining or circumventing the commitments or obligations of the United States to ensure the humane treatment of individuals in its custody or control. The resulting Task Force on transfer practices issued recommendations to the President regarding ways to strengthen existing safeguards in transfer policies, including that the State Department be involved in evaluating all diplomatic assurances; that mechanisms for monitoring treatment in the receiving country be further developed; and that the inspectors general of three key U.S. government Departments involved in transfers prepare annually a coordinated report on transfers conducted by each of their agencies in reliance on assurances. The United States is developing practices and procedures that will ensure the implementation of Task Force recommendations.

86. Thus, the United States prohibits torture and cruel, inhuman, or degrading treatment or punishment of persons in the custody or control of the U.S. Government, regardless of their nationality or physical location. It takes vigilant action to prevent such conduct and to hold those who commit acts of official cruelty accountable for their wrongful acts. The United States is a party to the Convention Against Torture, and U.S. law prohibits torture at both the federal and state levels. On June 26, 2010, on the anniversary of adoption of the Convention Against Torture, President Obama issued a statement unequivocally reaffirming U.S. support for its principles, and committing the United States to continue to cooperate in international efforts to eradicate torture.

87. In issuing Executive Order 13492, *Review and Disposition of Individuals Detained at the Guantánamo Bay Naval Base and Closure of Detention Facilities*, the President announced the Administration's intention to close the Guantánamo Bay detention facilities. The President also created a task force to recommend the appropriate disposition of each detainee held at Guantánamo. The Task Force assembled large volumes of information from across the government to determine the proper disposition of each detainee. The Task Force examined this information critically, giving careful consideration to, among other things, the threat posed by the detainee, the reliability of the underlying information, any concerns about the post-transfer humane treatment of the detainee, and the interests of national security. Based on the Task Force's evaluations and recommendations, senior officials representing each agency responsible for the review reached unanimous determinations on the appropriate disposition for all detainees. Since January 2009, 38 detainees have resettled successfully in third countries, an additional 26 detainees have been repatriated, and one has

---

[6] U.S. Department of Health and Human Services, Office of Minority Health "Protecting the Health of Minority Communities" (2006), available at: www.hhs.gov/news/factsheet/minorityhealth.html

been transferred to the United States for prosecution. The Administration remains committed to closure of the Guantánamo detention facility.

88. Executive Order 13493, *Review of Detention Policy Options*, established a task force to review and facilitate significant policy decisions regarding broader detention questions. This Special Task Force on Detention Policy has reviewed available options for the apprehension, detention, trial, transfer, release, or other disposition of individuals captured or apprehended in connection with armed conflicts and counterterrorism operations. As a matter of domestic law, the Obama Administration has not based its claim of authority to detain individuals at Guantánamo and in Afghanistan on the President's inherent constitutional powers, but rather on legislative authority expressly granted to the President by Congress in 2001. The Administration has expressly acknowledged that international law informs the scope of our detention authority. The President has also made clear that we have a national security interest in prosecuting terrorists, either before Article III courts or military commissions, and that we would exhaust all available avenues to prosecute Guantánamo detainees before deciding whether it would be appropriate to continue detention under the laws of war. Working with our Congress, we have revised our military commissions to enhance their procedural protections, including prohibiting introduction of any statements taken as a result of cruel, inhuman, or degrading treatment.
Privacy

89. Freedom from arbitrary and unlawful interference with privacy is protected under the Fourth Amendment to the Constitution and federal statutes. In addition, state and local laws and regulations provide robust protections of individuals' right to privacy and rigorous processes to ensure that investigative authorities are undertaken consistent with the Constitution.

90. Protecting our national interests may involve new arrangements to confronting threats like terrorism, but these structures and practices must always be in line with our Constitution and preserve the rights and freedoms of our people. Although the departments and agencies of the U.S. Government involved in surveillance and the collection of foreign intelligence information comply with a robust regime of laws, rules, regulations, and policies designed to protect national security and privacy, significant concerns in these areas have been raised by civil society, including concerns that relevant laws have been made outdated by technological changes, and that privacy protections need to be applied more broadly and methodically to surveillance.

91. The 2001 USA PATRIOT Act expanded intelligence collection authorities under the Foreign Intelligence Surveillance Act (FISA), which regulates electronic surveillance and physical searches conducted to acquire foreign intelligence information. The U.S. Executive Branch acknowledged in 2005 that the U.S. National Security Agency had been intercepting without a court order certain international communications where the government had a reasonable basis to conclude that one person was a member of, or affiliated with, Al Qaeda or a member of an organization affiliated with Al Qaeda and where one party was outside the United States. In response, considerable congressional and public attention focused on issues regarding the authorization, review, and oversight of electronic surveillance programs designed to acquire foreign intelligence information or to address international terrorism. Congress held hearings and enacted new legislation, including the 2007 Protect America Act and a series of amendments to FISA.

V.2 *Values and Immigration*

92. That immigrants have been consistently drawn to our shores throughout our history is both a testament to and a source of the strength and appeal of our vibrant democracy. As he left office, President Reagan remarked that the United States is "still a beacon, still a magnet for all who must have freedom, for all the pilgrims from all the lost places who are hurtling through the darkness, toward home." Over the last 50 years, the U.S. has accepted several million refugees fleeing persecution from all corners of the globe as well as many millions of immigrants seeking a better life or joining family. Today, the United States and other countries to which a significant number of people seek to emigrate face challenges in developing and enforcing immigration laws and policies that reflect economic, social, and national security realities. In addressing these issues we seek to build a system of immigration enforcement that is both effective and fair.

93. In 2009, the Department of Homeland Security (DHS) began a major overhaul of the U.S. immigration detention system in an effort to improve detention center management and prioritize health, safety, and uniformity among immigration detention facilities, while ensuring security and efficiency. As part of this effort, in conjunction with ongoing consultations with non-governmental organizations and outside experts, DHS issued revised parole guidelines, effective January 2010, for arriving aliens in expedited removal found

---

[7] Executive Order 13491 § 3(a) (Jan 22, 2009); *Hamdan v Rumsfeld*, 548 U.S. 557, 631 (2006

to have a credible fear of persecution or torture. The new guidelines firmly establish that it is not in the public interest to detain those arriving aliens found to have a credible fear who establish their identities, and that they pose neither a flight risk nor a danger to the community.

94. Under section 287(g) of the Immigration and Nationality Act, DHS may delegate authority to state and local officers to enforce federal immigration law. DHS has made improvements to the 287(g) program, including implementing a new, standardized Memorandum of Agreement with state and local partners that strengthens program oversight and provides uniform guidelines for DHS supervision of state and local agency officer operations; information reporting and tracking; complaint procedures; and implementation measures. DHS continues to evaluate the program, incorporating additional safeguards as necessary to aid in the prevention of racial profiling and civil rights violations and improve accountability for protecting human rights.

95. A recent Arizona law, S.B. 1070, has generated significant attention and debate at home and around the world. The issue is being addressed in a court action that argues that the federal government has the authority to set and enforce immigration law. That action is ongoing; parts of the law are currently enjoined.

96. President Obama remains firmly committed to fixing our broken immigration system, because he recognizes that our ability to innovate, our ties to the world, and our economic prosperity depend on our capacity to welcome and assimilate immigrants. The Administration will continue its efforts to work with the U.S. Congress and affected communities toward this end.

V.3 Values and Trafficking

97. In June 2010, the United States issued its 10th annual Trafficking in Persons Report outlining the continuing challenges posed by human trafficking across the globe and, for the first time, included a ranking and full narrative of the United States. The narrative includes detailed information about U.S. anti-trafficking efforts undertaken by more than 10 federal agencies and its pursuit of policies, partnerships, and practices aimed at protecting victims, preventing trafficking, and prosecuting traffickers.

98. Hallmarks of the U.S. approach to combating human trafficking include a) vigorous prosecution of traffickers, and funding task forces throughout the nation comprised of local, state and federal law enforcement and a non-governmental victim service provider; b) a victim-centered approach that recognizes victims require specialized care and are an integral part of any investigation and/or prosecution; c) comprehensive victim services such as shelter, health care, mental health care, food, safety, legal services, interpretation, victim advocacy, immigration relief, education, job skills, employment placement, family reunification, and reintegration; d) temporary immigration relief and work authorization for victims assisting investigations and prosecutions and longer term immigration relief for certain victims and their family members which may then lead to permanent residence and citizenship; e) a coordinated identification and enforcement approach among labor, border, and criminal enforcement; and f) an expansive view of prevention activities that includes strengthening labor protections and enforcement, addressing demand for commercial sex, and working with civil society to rid corporate supply chains of forced labor.

99. The U.S. stands out in terms of the sophistication and breadth of its anti-trafficking efforts. Furthermore, we provide substantial international assistance aimed at preventing trafficking in persons, protecting victims, and prosecuting traffickers.

VI. Conclusion

100. The United States views participation in this UPR process as an opportunity to discuss with our citizenry and with fellow members of the Human Rights Council our accomplishments, challenges, and vision for the future on human rights. We welcome observations and recommendations that can help us on that road to a more perfect union. Delivering on human rights has never been easy, but it is work we will continue to undertake with determination, for human rights will always undergird our national identity and define our national aspirations.

Annex 1: Human Rights Treaty Ratification and Reporting

The United States is at present Party to the following multilateral human rights related treaties:

- Slavery Convention and its amending Protocol;
- Supplementary Convention on the Abolition of Slavery, the Slave Trade and Institutions and Practices Similar to Slavery;
- Protocol Relating to the Status of Refugees;
- Inter-American Convention on the Granting of Political Rights to Women;
- Convention on the Political Rights of Women;

- Convention on the Prevention and Punishment of the Crime of Genocide;
- ILO Convention No. 105 concerning the Abolition of Forced Labor;
- International Covenant on Civil and Political Rights;
- Convention against Torture and Other Cruel, Inhuman or Degrading Treatment or Punishment;
- International Convention on the Elimination of All Forums of Racial Discrimination;
- ILO Convention 182 Concerning the Prohibition and Immediate Action for the Elimination of the Worst Forms of Child Labor;
- Optional Protocol to the Convention on the Rights of the Child on the Involvement of Children in Armed Conflict; and
- Optional Protocol to the Convention on the Rights of the Child on the Sale of Children, Child Prostitution, and Child Pornography.

The United States has signed but not ratified the following multilateral human rights treaties:

- International Covenant on Economic, Social and Cultural Rights;
- American Convention on Human Rights;
- Convention on the Elimination of All Forms of Discrimination Against Women;
- Convention on the Rights of the Child; and
- International Convention on the Rights of Persons with Disabilities.

In addition, the United States has entered into many bilateral treaties (including consular treaties and treaties of friendship, commerce and navigation) that contain provisions guaranteeing various rights and protections to nationals of foreign countries on a reciprocal basis. In some cases, these may be invoked directly in United States courts for that purpose.

Note that shorter forms of these complete treaty names are used in the UPR report, e.g., "Convention Against Torture."

In addition to accepting human rights obligations under the above-referenced treaties to which it is a party, the United States has made human rights commitments through numerous other instruments, including the 1948 Universal Declaration of Human Rights and the 1948 American Declaration of the Rights and Duties of Man.

The United States regularly submits lengthy and detailed reports on its implementation of several of the human rights treaties listed above, specifically the International Covenant on Civil and Political Rights, the Convention against Torture, the Convention on the Elimination of All Forums of Racial Discrimination, and the two Optional Protocols to the Convention on the Rights of the Child. A compilation of that reporting is posted on the State Department's website, at http://www.state.gov/g/drl/hr/treaties/index.htm

Annex 2: Abbreviations

ADA	American with Disabilities Act of 1990
AIDS	Acquired immune deficiency syndrome
DHS	Department of Homeland Security
DNA	Deoxyribonucleic acid
FISA	Foreign Intelligence Surveillance Act
HIV	Human immunodeficiency virus
IDEA	Individuals with Disabilities Education Act
ILO	International Labor Organization
JJDPA	Juvenile Justice and Delinquency Prevention Act
LGBT	Lesbian, gay, bisexual and transgender
UDHR	Universal Declaration of Human Rights
UPR	Universal Periodic Review
USA PATRIOT	Uniting and Strengthening America by Providing Appropriate Tools Required to

Intercept and Obstruct Terrorism Act of 2001.

DOCUMENT 87

Full Official Title: Report of the Working Group on the Universal Periodic Review, United States of America

Short Title: U.S. Final UPR Outcome Report/ Document

Type of Document: Written record of the U.S. UPR process and recommendations submitted to the Human Rights Council for its informal adoption, then submitted at HRC session for formal adoption. This is not a legal document as such, but a report by a UPR working group called a troika. The UPR process is about how the United States is complying with human rights and humanitarian law norms, and receiving recommendations by other states on how it could improve.

Subject: Outcome of the U.S. Universal Periodic Review by the U.N. Human Rights Council
Official Citation: UN Doc A/HRC/16/11, previously issued under A/HRC/WG.6/9/L.9.
Date of Document: January 04, 2010
Date of Adoption: March 18, 2011
Date of General Entry into Force (EIF): Not applicable
Number of Signatory States as of this Printing: Not applicable
Date of Signature by the United States: Not applicable
Date of Ratification/Accession/Adhesion: Not applicable
Date of Entry into Force as to United States (effective date): Not applicable
Legal Status/Character of the Instrument/Document as to the United States: Not legally binding. The Outcome Document should be seriously considered.
Supervising Body: United Nations, Human Rights Council
Comments: On November 5, 2010 the U.S. had its interactive dialogue session at the U.N as part of the Universal Periodic Review Process. After that session, the randomly selected "Troika" of three countries (France, Cameroon and Japan) helped prepare a draft Outcome Document in November 2010, which summarized all the documentation and proceedings to that time and included all the recommendations of states to the U.S. for the U.S to consider accepting and agreeing to put into effect. This was the most recommendations made of any of the states which had done the UPR process.

This Document was issued January 4, 2011, and is the Working Group's final Outcome report from the prepared draft. The U.S. needed to decide how to respond to this document and on March 10, 2011, the US submitted its written response to the HRC. See Appendix K, #4. The US decided which recommendations to accept and agree to put into practice.

The final Outcome document was presented and voted on by the Council and formally adopted on March 18, 2011. It should help guide the United States as to how to comply better with its human rights and humanitarian law obligations. The US will be expected to exert its good faith efforts to put those accepted recommendations into practice. What it does will be considered at its next UPR in four years.

Web Address: http://www.ohchr.org/EN/HRBodies/UPR/PAGES/USSession9.aspx, and http://www.state.gov/documents

REPORT OF THE WORKING GROUP ON THE UNIVERSAL PERIODIC REVIEW, UNITED STATES OF AMERICA

* Previously issued as document A/HRC/WG.6/9/L.9. The annex to the present report is circulated as received.

Introduction

1. The Working Group on the Universal Periodic Review (UPR), established in accordance with Human Rights Council resolution 5/1, held its ninth session from 1 to 12 November 2010. The review of the United States of America was held at the 9th meeting, on 5 November 2010. The delegation of the United States of America was headed jointly by the Honourable Esther Brimmer, Assistant Secretary, Bureau of International Organizations, Department of State; the Honourable Harold Hongju Koh, Legal Adviser, Office of the Legal Adviser, Department of State; and the Honourable Michael Posner, Assistant Secretary, Democracy, Human Rights and Labour, Department of State. At its13th meeting, held on 9 November 2010, the Working Group adopted the report on the United States of America.

2. On 21 June 2010, the Human Rights Council selected the following group of rapporteurs (troika) to facilitate the review of the United States of America: Cameroon, France and Japan.

3. In accordance with paragraph 15 of the annex to resolution 5/1, the following documents were issued for the review of the United States of America:

(a) A national report submitted/written presentation made in accordance with paragraph 15 (a) (A/HRC/WG.6/9/USA/1);

(b) A compilation prepared by the Office of the United Nations High Commissioner for Human Rights (OHCHR) in accordance with paragraph 15 (b)(A/HRC/WG.6/9/USA/2);

(c) A summary prepared by OHCHR in accordance with paragraph 15 (c) (A/HRC/WG.6/9/USA/3/Rev.1).

4. A list of questions prepared in advance by Plurinational State of Bolivia, the Czech Republic, Denmark, Germany, Japan, Latvia, Mexico, the Netherlands, Norway, the Russian Federation, Slovenia, Sweden, Switzerland and the United Kingdom of Great Britain and Northern Ireland was transmitted to the United States of America through the troika. Those questions are available on the extranet of the universal periodic review.

I. Summary of the proceedings of the review process

5. During the interactive dialogue, 56 delegations made statements. Additional statements, which could not be delivered during the interactive dialogue owing to time constraints, will be posted on the extranet of the universal periodic review when available. Recommendations made during the dialogue are found in section II of the present report.

A. Presentation by the State under review

6. The delegation expressed its pleasure at presenting its first UPR report and noted President Obama's and Secretary Clinton's deep commitment to multilateral engagement, human rights, and the rule of law. The story of the United States has been one of striving for a more perfect union. By admitting the possibility of imperfection, new opportunities to improve are revealed—the ability to do this has been and continues to be a source of national strength.

7. The United States explained that it encourages the involvement of its civil society, and works through law-abiding executives, democratic legislatures and independent courts to make progress. The United States expressed pride in its accomplishments, recognized that there remains room for further progress and reiterated its commitment to principled engagement with the international system to advance human rights at home and abroad.

B. Interactive dialogue and responses by the State under review

8. Cuba made recommendations.

9. The Bolivarian Republic of Bolivarian Republic of Venezuela expressed the hope that President Obama would make a commitment to human rights.

10. The Islamic Republic of Islamic Republic of Iran expressed concern over the situation of human rights and systematic violations committed by the United States at both the national and international levels.

11. The Russian Federation positively assessed the current Government's efforts to eliminate a number of human rights violations that had been committed in the course of the "fight against terrorism" and to join in the work of the Human Rights Council. On the other hand, in a number of areas, including, first of all, acceding to the international human rights treaties and ensuring human rights in the process of the fight against terrorism, additional efforts by the United States were required.

12. Nicaragua stated that the United States had made the use of force the cornerstone of its expansionist policy and that Latin America was one of its victims. It stated that the United States had violated human rights while pretending to be the world's guardian of human rights.

13. Indonesia noted positively the United States' commitment to freedom and equality, and welcomed the country's engagement with the Human Rights Council. It expressed its belief that the United States needed to make efforts to protect human rights in a balanced manner and to promote tolerance. Indonesia acknowledged the United States' contribution to the development of the United Nations norms.

14. The Plurinational State of Bolivia made recommendations.

15. Ecuador noted the Government's efforts to improve human rights, although the results had been limited.

16. The Democratic People's Republic of Korea remained concerned about the persistent reports of human rights violations committed by the United States at home and abroad.

17. Algeria stated that the election of a President of African descent had spoken louder than any statement about the United States' commitment to civil and political rights.

Algeria noted that prison overcrowding was the norm and that prisons housed 60 per cent more inmates than they had been designed for.

18. Qatar welcomed the United States' efforts in combating racial and religious discrimination, providing social services and ensuring the enjoyment of economic, social and cultural rights.

19. Mexico recognized the robust institutional infrastructure for the protection of human rights.

20. Egypt expressed the hope of seeing concrete steps undertaken by the United States to ensure the protection of the human rights of the members of Muslim, Arab, African-American and South Asian communities. It remained concerned about certain policies and practices in the human rights field.

21. China noted the Government's efforts in past years to promote and protect human rights and to make progress in health care and education. However, China expressed concern about the gaps in human rights legislation and the fact that the United States had not become a party to a number of core international human rights instruments. It was also concerned, inter alia, that the law enforcement agencies tended to use excessive force and that the incidence of poverty was higher among Afro-Americans, Latinos and Native Americans.

22. India commended the United States for its commitment to human rights and its acknowledgment of the remaining challenges. India was concerned about human rights abuses by business corporations and inquired about the United States' position on its Alien Tort Claims Act. It was concerned at the sexual harassment of women in the United States military and the disproportionately high conviction rates for African-Americans, as well as their low access to education, health and employment.

23. Bangladesh stated that, while progress had been made in the protection of civil and political rights, the protection of social and economic rights had not been fully recognized. It stated that the United States played a positive role internationally in supporting many countries' development efforts. Bangladesh was concerned at the recent enactment of an immigration law that might encourage discriminatory attitudes and ill treatment against migrants.

24. Malaysia appreciated the renewed commitment expressed by the Government to reengage on the full range of human rights, including through United States membership of the Human Rights Council. Malaysia stated that several issues, such as racial discrimination, racial profiling, religious intolerance and widening income equality, could be given more attention.

25. Brazil welcomed the measures announced by the United States to address violations of human rights that had been committed under its counter-terrorism policy. It noted with concern the rise in the number of persons living in poverty. Brazil encouraged the United States to investigate and address situations of forced labour against migrants.

26. Switzerland noted with satisfaction that several states had abolished the death penalty. Switzerland also noted, inter alia, that thousands of migrants had been detained in harsh conditions and without access to legal counselling for violations of immigration laws.

27. The Republic of Korea commended the Government's decision to close the Guantánamo Bay detention facility and to ban methods of interrogation that might not be in compliance with international law. It welcomed the adoption of legislation to expand access to health care for its citizens.

28. In addressing a number of observations and recommendations related to ratification of treaties, the delegation noted that its practice was to ensure that it could fully implement a treaty before it became a party to it and not to ratify unless it could do so. Under its Constitution, such ratification required approval of two thirds of the United States Senate.

The United States was strongly committed to ratifying the CEDAW and the Convention on the Rights of Persons with Disabilities.

29. In response to questions regarding the creation of a national human rights institution, the U.S. delegation noted that this was an issue currently under consideration in the United States. The United States believed that multiple levels of complementary work at the federal and sub-federal levels and by different branches of government (executive, legislative and judicial) provided multiple and reinforcing protections for individual rights.

30. The United States then discussed other points raised by several countries: torture and the closing of the detention facility at Guantánamo Bay.

31. The delegation explained that the United States is unequivocally committed to the humane treatment of all individuals in detention, whether criminal detention or detainees in United States custody in armed conflict. Through Executive Orders, the President affirmed the United States commitment to abiding by the ban on torture and inhumane treatment, ordered CIA "black sites" closed, and instructed that any interrogations must be conducted consistent with United States treaty obligations and the revised Army Field Manual.

President Obama also ordered a review to ensure that the detention facility at Guantánamo Bay fully complied with Common Article 3, and established a special interagency task force to review United States interrogation and transfer policies and to ensure that all United States transfer practices comply with United States law, policy and international obligations and never result in the transfer of any individual to face torture.

32. The United States reaffirmed the President's commitment to closing the Guantánamo detention facility as quickly as possible, noting that the task has proven enormously complex and also involves United States allies, the courts, and the United States Congress. The United States expressed its gratitude to those countries that had accepted detainees for resettlement.

33. The delegation addressed questions related to its work to combat discrimination. The United States is committed to ensuring political participation by all qualified voters through enforcement of voting rights laws. The Justice Department will review redistricting plans after the 2010 Census to ensure that voting districts are not drawn with the purpose or effect of discriminating against minority voters. The United States explained its enforcement of laws to ensure equal access to housing, lending, credit, educational opportunities, and environmental justice. Although still grappling with the legacy of slavery and addressing problems of racial discrimination, the United States remains mindful of the need to address other inequalities as well.

34. The United States is committed to promoting equal rights for women. The delegation discussed the passage of the Lilly Ledbetter Fair Pay Act, the creation of an Ambassador-at-Large for Global Women's Issues, and other measures.

35. The delegation also noted important initiatives to ensure more robust protections for lesbian, gay, bisexual and transgender individuals. In addition to several non-legislative measures, the United States is seeking the legislative repeal of the Defence of Marriage Act and the "Don't Ask, Don't Tell law" and policy.

36. The United States continues to be a world leader in protecting disability rights. In addition to signing the Disabilities Convention, it vigorously enforces laws against architectural barriers and unnecessary institutionalization. In the past year, the United States filed or participated in more than a dozen lawsuits to promote full inclusion of persons with disabilities.

37. The delegation then addressed questions regarding the Arizona immigration law. The Justice Department had challenged this law on grounds that it unconstitutionally interferes with the federal Government's authority to set and enforce immigration policy, and litigation is ongoing in which a federal judge has enjoined the law. The United States expressed its commitment to advancing comprehensive immigration reform.

38. Thailand noted with appreciation that the United States had initiated the ratification process relating to a number of human rights instruments. It also welcomed the Government's efforts to address discrimination on various grounds and to promote equality before the law for all.

39. The Libyan Arab Jamahiriya was concerned at, inter alia, the racial discrimination and intolerance against persons with African, Arab Islamic and Latin American origins, the denial of the indigenous community of their rights, human rights violations resulting from its policies of occupation and invasion and the imposition of blockades. It was concerned over the large number of prisoners at Guantánamo, deprived of their right to a fair trial.

40. The United Kingdom noted that the United States had a strong record in human rights protection. However, it was concerned by evidence that the death penalty could sometimes be administered in a discriminatory manner and encouraged the United States to address those systematic issues. It asked about the steps that the United States had taken towards the ratification of ICESCR, CEDAW, CRC, OP-CAT and Optional Protocols to the Geneva Conventions of 1949 that the United States had already signed. The United Kingdom also encouraged the United States to redouble its efforts to ensure the closure of the Guantánamo detention facilities in a timely manner.

41. France welcomed the United States' pledge to ratify CEDAW and its intention to close the Guantánamo detention centre. It asked what measures had been taken in that regard and when the closure was expected.

42. Australia noted that the United States, in many ways, led by example in promoting human rights standards around the world. It expressed concern, however, at the country's continued use of the death penalty. It remained concerned about reports of violent crimes against persons of minority sexual orientation. Australia welcomed the United States' efforts to address the gap between the rights of Native and other Americans. Australia encouraged the United States to become a party to CRPD.

43. Belgium noted with regret that the death penalty was still applied by some 35 states. It expressed concern at the situation in the prison system, including violence against detainees; prison overpopulation

and overrepresentation of some ethnic groups; and imprisonment, sometimes for life, without any possible reprieve for those who were minors when the acts were carried out.

44. The Sudan commended the United States' efforts to promote and protect human rights on its territory and globally. It commended the United States for its efforts to create the conditions necessary for the ratification of international conventions.

45. Austria stated that the United States had set positive examples in the protection of human rights at the national and international levels.

46. Bahrain noted the adoption of legislation on health care. Bahrain referred to the recommendations made by CAT on CAT's applicability in times of war and peace, and asked on the steps taken to implement that recommendation. It also referred to the recommendation made by CERD on the establishment of a national human rights institution.

47. Vietnam noted the United States' commitment to strengthening its system of human rights protection. It expressed concern about the reported discrimination against migrants and foreigners, including Vietnamese migrants and students, and the lack of Government commitment to support many core international human rights instruments.

48. Ireland welcomed progressive developments in the United States including the Hate Crimes Prevention Act of 2009 and the work that is being conducted towards the ratification of the ILO Convention No. 111. Ireland noted that the United States remains one of the few countries in the world that continue to apply the death penalty. Ireland asked whether the United States intends to proceed to the introduction of a nation-wide moratorium on the death penalty. Ireland regretted that an increasing number of states within the United States have lifted moratoria on the death penalty and urged the United States to introduce a nation-wide moratorium. Ireland welcomed the United States' exclusion of the death penalty for crimes committed by minors and persons with an intellectual disability.

49. Morocco expressed appreciation for the United States' commitment to development assistance and referred to a number of programmes and innovative solutions concerning housing rights.

50. Cyprus noted with appreciation that the U.S. had signed the Rome Statute of ICC. It was concerned about use of the death penalty and referred to the concerns of a number of treaty bodies related to allegations of brutality and the use of excessive force by law enforcement officials against migrants.

51. Spain asked questions about the closing of Guantánamo prison, the new regulations on military commissions and the right to a fair trial, the guarantees for the remaining detainees, and the United States' obligations related to consular access to foreign detainees, particularly in relation to the *Avena* ruling.

52. The delegation addressed issues raised by a number of states, including the relationship between human rights and national security, the death penalty, and indigenous issues. The United States was committed to establishing national security policies that respect the rule of law. It has redoubled its efforts over the past two years to ensure that all armed conflict operations comply fully with all applicable domestic and international law. Torture and cruel treatment are crimes in the United States and steps are taken to prosecute those who commit such acts. All individuals held in armed conflict are held lawfully. In response to a question from Spain, the United States said that all detainees in the U.S. and Guantánamo have robust access to habeas review by its federal courts.

53. U.S. targeting practices, including lethal operations conducted with the use of unmanned aerial vehicles, comply with all applicable law. To the extent that human rights law may apply in armed conflict or national actions taken in self-defence, in all cases, the U.S. works to ensure that its actions are lawful. The delegation noted first, that international human rights law and international humanitarian law are complementary, reinforcing, and animated by humanitarian principles designed to protect innocent life.

Second, while the United States complied with human rights law wherever applicable, the applicable rules for the protection of individuals and the conduct of hostilities in armed conflict outside a nation's territory are typically found in international humanitarian law, which apply to government and non-government actors. Third, determining which international law rules apply to any particular government action during an armed conflict is highly fact-specific.

54. In answer to a number of questions regarding detainee treatment, the Defence Department has well-established procedures for reporting detainee abuse and investigates all credible allegations of abuse by United States forces. Between Iraq, Afghanistan, and Guantánamo, the United States has conducted hundreds of investigations regarding detainee abuse allegations, which have led to hundreds of disciplinary actions. All credible allegations of detainee abuse by United States forces have been thoroughly investigated and appropriate corrective action has been taken. The United States further noted its commitment to ensuring that it does not transfer individuals to torture in Iraq and elsewhere.

55. In response to comments from a number of countries regarding capital punishment, the delegation noted that while the matter is a subject of earnest debate in the United States, as a matter of law that punishment is permitted for the most serious crimes with appropriate safeguards. Recently, the United States Supreme Court has narrowed the class of individuals that can be executed, the types of crimes subject to the penalty, and the manner by which the punishment is administered so that it is not cruel and unusual. In response to questions from Mexico and the United Kingdom about consular notification and foreign nationals on death row, the United States noted its commitment, and pending federal legislation, to comply with the *Avena* ICJ judgment.

56. Turning to indigenous issues, the delegation noted the many challenges faced by Native Americans—poverty, unemployment, health care gaps, violent crime, and discrimination—and the laws and programmes it has in place to address these problems.

The United States stated its belief that tribes and their members will flourish if they are empowered to deal with the challenges they face. This conclusion is reflected in law and policy regarding tribal self-determination. President Obama hosted the White House Tribal Nations Conference at which he directed all agencies to submit plans for and progress reports on implementation of the Executive Order on Consultation and Coordination with Indian Tribal Governments. As a result, the level of tribal consultations is now at an historic high.

57. In response to questions from Australia, Cyprus, Finland, and Norway, the delegation noted the considerable attention that has been paid to the interagency consultations with tribal leaders as a part of the United States review of its position on the United Nations Declaration on the Rights of Indigenous Peoples. The decision to review its position was made in response to calls from tribes and other indigenous groups and individuals.

58. The United States has also taken numerous steps to address particular challenges faced by indigenous communities. These include health care reform, the settlement of certain claims, and improvements in criminal justice issues.

59. Denmark urged the Government to follow the recommendations of the international community that it ensure that state and federal authorities applied a moratorium on executions with a view to ultimately abolishing the death penalty nationwide. It would like to see the United States join the vast majority of States that adhered to ICESCR, CEDAW, CRC and OP-CAT.

60. Finland, while welcoming the progress made by the United States in enhancing the rights of indigenous peoples, including the ongoing review of its position on the United Nations Declaration on the Rights of Indigenous Peoples, asked how the Government was conducting the review and about the current situation with respect to the process. Finland also asked about measures undertaken to combat discrimination against women.

61. Ghana commended the United States for, inter alia, efforts that had transformed the country into a multi-racial, multi-ethnic and multi-religious society. It noted with appreciation that the Government continued to work to ensure that equal opportunity was not only guaranteed in law, but experienced by all Americans. Ghana, however, referred to the concerns expressed by several special procedures concerning ongoing structural discriminations.

62. Hungary recognized that the United States had a well-developed system of domestic human rights laws. However, the United States had limited obligations under the international human rights treaties. Hungary welcomed the change in the country's attitude towards ICC, and hoped for further steps to deepen relations with it.

63. Slovakia stated that the United States had been one of the prominent global defenders and promoters of human rights, dedicating significant resources to that commitment.

64. The Netherlands, while noting the Government's support for the ratification of CEDAW by the United States, noted with concern that no specific steps had been taken thus far to that end. The Netherlands also expressed concern at the use of death penalty in 35 states. The Netherlands commended the United States for having received many visits by Special Rapporteurs.

65. Turkey welcomed the decision of the United States to become a member of the Human Rights Council. Turkey expressed its belief that the increasing multilateral cooperation and engagement that the United States had embraced would contribute to global peace and stability and constitute an important factor for the protection of the human rights of those belonging to minority groups, in particular Muslims and immigrants.

66. Norway noted with appreciation the role that the United States played in the international human rights arena. It welcomed the answers provided by the United States to advance questions that it had posed. Norway stated that it looked forward to the transparent and inclusive follow-up in the universal periodic review implementation phase.

67. Sweden welcomed the repeal of the use of capital punishment in some states, but regretted the recurring sentencing to the death penalty and executions in many states. Sweden asked the United States to elaborate on the status of the death penalty and about the plans to impose an official moratorium on executions towards the complete abolition of the death penalty. It also asked about the measures taken by the United States to ensure the full enjoyment of the human rights of persons deprived of their liberty.

68. The Holy See noted that "Operation Streamline" against irregular migrants should be suspended and asked for information about the Government's decision to review its position on the United Nations Declaration on the Rights of Indigenous Peoples.

69. Italy noted with appreciation the Government's efforts to fight economic, social gender and ethnic discrimination. It noted that the death penalty was still in force in 35 states, even though some states had applied a de facto moratorium.

70. Uruguay made recommendations.

71. The United States delegation noted that the United States criminal justice system is based on the protection of individual rights. The United States has acted to address a history of racially based law enforcement, through, among other things, enactment and enforcement of laws that prohibit discrimination based on race, colour or national origin by police departments that receive federal funds. The United States was working actively to study and address persistent racial and ethnic disparities in the U.S. criminal justice system and to implement appropriate corrective measures.

72. The United States assured delegations that it condemns racial and ethnic profiling in all of its forms, and is conducting a thorough review of policies and procedures to ensure that none of its law enforcement practices improperly target individuals based on race or ethnicity. With regard to Switzerland's concern for juveniles, the United States delegation noted that the United States Supreme Court recently decided that juvenile offenders convicted of crimes other than homicide may no longer be sentenced to life imprisonment without parole. The United States is committed to meeting its obligations under both international and domestic law for proper treatment of persons detained or incarcerated in the criminal justice system, including those in maximum security facilities. In response to inquiries from the Netherlands and Sweden about prison conditions, the United States appropriately secure, and in response to questions from the Netherlands, Latvia and Denmark, noted that the United States has hosted visits from eight Special Procedures during the past three years.

73. The United States addressed additional questions regarding immigration. Over the last five years, it welcomed over 5.5 million new permanent residents and over 3.5 million new naturalized citizens, and resettled or granted asylum to nearly 425,000 refugees. It is committed to improving its immigration system. The Departments of Homeland Security(DHS) and Labour are working together to improve protections for migrants. In response to concerns from civil society regarding immigration detention and the removal process, DHS has undertaken major reforms to improve detention center management, health, safety, and uniformity among facilities. DHS's reforms are designed to ensure that detention was used only when appropriate, in light of legal requirements and the need to ensure public safety. In 2010 the United States lifted a 22-year ban on travel to the country by HIV-infected individuals. The United States delegation discussed recent programmes to combat international trafficking in persons.

74. In consultation with civil society and the United Nation High Commissioner for Refugees, the United States established that each arriving alien with a credible fear of persecution or torture would be considered for release; and that those who established their identity and did not pose a flight risk or a danger to the community would not be detained pending completion of their immigration proceedings. For detained aliens, the United States recognizes the need to improve conditions of confinement, medical care, and the ability to exercise their human rights. DHS is revising standards governing immigration detention conditions, implemented a new detainee locator system, and assigned new oversight personnel nationwide. In the context of immigration enforcement, the United States recognized concerns regarding racial and ethnic profiling by local law enforcement officials and reaffirmed its commitment and recent actions to combat profiling through significantly strengthened protections and training against such discrimination.

75. The Republic of Moldova underlined the important involvement of the United States in countering human trafficking. It noted with appreciation the fact that the number of applied death penalties had been decreasing and that the death penalty as a punishment was excluded for those offenders who were under the age of 18 at the time of the offence.

76. Trinidad and Tobago noted the Government's efforts to respect human rights, including those to eliminate all forms of racial discrimination, and the enactment of legislation in 2009 to combat gender-based wage discrimination.

77. New Zealand stated that the United States had demonstrated leadership in the promotion of human rights. It noted with appreciation that the United States had excluded the death penalty for those under 18 years of age at the time of the offence, and those with intellectual disabilities. However, it noted that significant numbers of people continued to be executed. New Zealand welcomed the signing by the United States of CPRD.

78. Haiti deplored the difficulties encountered by persons of African descent who, for example, faced a high rate of unemployment and had lower income. Haiti asked about the Government's intention to set up a national human rights institution.

79. Israel expressed appreciation for the United States' significant contribution and commitment to the advancement and protection of human rights throughout the world. It also noted with appreciation the United States' engagement with stakeholders in a comprehensive consultation process.

80. Japan praised the United States for its efforts to tackle human rights issues in the unique context of its multi-racial, multi-national and multi-religious society. Japan was concerned about the alleged use of excessive force by law enforcement officials, especially against Latino and African-American persons.

81. Canada welcomed reinvigorated United States efforts to enforce its Civil Rights Act of 1964, which prohibited discrimination based on race, colour, sex, national origin and religion. It recognized the anti-human-trafficking efforts of the United States. Canada noted with appreciation the active re-engagement in the Human Rights Council by the United States.

82. Germany asked how the United States was following up the recommendations of the treaty bodies on the ratification of CRC, Additional Protocols I and II to the Geneva Conventions and the Rome Statue of ICC. Germany noted that the United States did not have a national human rights institution.

83. Guatemala made recommendations.

84. Costa Rica acknowledged the United States' openness and commitment to the protection and promotion of the human rights of its people. Costa Rica noted with appreciation the constructive contribution of the United States in the formulation of international law and mechanisms. However, it noted the gap between the Government's ratification and contribution to international law.

85. The United States delegation responded to a number of questions and concerns regarding discrimination against Muslims, Arab Americans, and South Asians. The United States is committed to addressing negative stereotypes, discrimination and hate crimes through measures such as the creation of a 9/11 backlash taskforce, litigation to protect religious freedom including the right of school girls to wear the hijab, nationwide community outreach, and enforcement of employment discrimination laws. The United States is taking concrete measures to make border and aviation security measures more effective and targeted to eliminate profiling based on race, religion, or ethnicity.

86. Regarding online privacy, the United States recognized that new technologies like the Internet demand legitimate and effective law enforcement as well as protection of privacy, free expression, and the rule of law. Secretary Clinton was deeply committed to Internet freedom at home and around the world, and to ensuring that the rights of free expression and association through the Internet were protected and defended.

87. Regarding questions related to economic, social and cultural rights, what Franklin Roosevelt described as "freedom from want," the United States has focused on democratic solutions and civil society initiatives while courts have defined constitutional obligations primarily by focusing on procedural rights to due process and equal protection of the law. As a matter of broader public policy, the United States is committed to help create a society in which prosperity is shared, including social benefits provided by law.

88. The United States is committed to working to pursue laws and policies that will build an economy and society that lifts up all Americans. The Government is taking on the structural inequalities that have too often held back some citizens. The United States is taking significant measures to ensure equal opportunities and access to areas including housing, education, and health care. The Government is actively responding to the foreclosure crisis by helping millions of families restructure or refinance their mortgages

to avoid foreclosure. The United States has taken important measures to help lift up every child in every school in the country, particularly those most disadvantaged. Recent legislation allowed schools to invest in technology, teacher development, and other measures. In 2010, President Obama signed into law the Affordable Care Act, which is projected to expand health insurance to 32 million Americans who would otherwise lack coverage.

89. The United States is also committed to enforcing employment and labor laws to protect workers' rights, has revitalized its engagement with ILO, and is renewing work on ratification of ILO conventions.

90. In closing, the United States delegation expressed its deep appreciation to civil society—not only for helping in the preparation of its report and presentation, but also in continuing to push the government to do better. United States civil society has been invaluable to the United States' Universal Periodic Review, and commended to other states active engagement with civil society throughout the process.

91. It is a testament to the steady erosion of barriers of race, gender, sexual orientation, religion, disability, and ethnicity that United States delegation members of such diversity were present to speak for the United States today. The United States is proud of its record of accomplishments, humbled by the recognition that more work remains, and remains committed to improvement and to continuing this dialogue going forward.

II. Conclusions and/or recommendations

92. In the course of the discussion, the following recommendations were made to the United States of America:

92.1. Ratify without reservations the following conventions and protocols:

CEDAW; the ICESCR; the Convention on the Rights of the Child; the Convention on the Rights of Persons with Disabilities; the International Convention on the Protection of the Rights of All Migrant Workers and Members of Their Families; the International Convention for the Protection of All Persons from Enforced Disappearance; the Statute of the International Criminal Court; those of the ILO; the United Nations Declaration on Indigenous Peoples, and all those from the Inter-American Human Rights System (Bolivarian Republic of Venezuela);

92.2. Continue the process to ratify CEDAW and adhere to the other human rights fundamental instruments, such as the Statute of Rome of the International Criminal Court, the Convention on the Rights of the Child, the Optional Protocol to the Convention against Torture and the International Convention for the Protection of all Persons against Enforced Disappearance (France);

92.3. Ratify, until the next universal periodic review, ICESCR, the Convention on the Rights of the Child, Protocols I and II of the Geneva Conventions of 12 August 1949, ILO Conventions no. 87 (on freedom of association) and no. 98 (on the right to collective bargaining) as well as withdraw the reservation made to Article 4 of the International Convention on the Elimination of Racial Discrimination (Russian Federation);

92.4. Ratify ICESCR and its Optional Protocol; the first Optional Protocol to the International Covenant of Civil and Political Rights, CEDAW, the Convention on the Rights of the Child, the Optional Protocol to the Convention against Torture, the Convention on the Rights of Persons with Disabilities, the Convention for the Protection of All Persons from Enforced Disappearance(Spain);

92.5. Continue its efforts to realize universal human rights by

a) ratifying CEDAW;

b) becoming a party to the United Nations Convention on the Rights of the Child;

c) acceding to ICESCR;

d) ratifying the United Nations Convention on the Rights of Persons with Disabilities (Canada);

92.6. Ratify the core human rights treaties, particularly the CRC, ICESCR, CEDAW and its Optional Protocol, the OP-CAT and the CMW and the CRPD with its Optional Protocol (Sudan);

92.7. Ratify the ICESCR, CEDAW and the Convention of the Rights of the Child at an early stage together with other important human rights conventions (Japan);

92.8. Ratify CEDAW, ICESCR, and CRC in token of its commitment to their implementation worldwide, as well as become party to other international human rights conventions as referred to in the OHCHR report (Indonesia);

92.9. Ratify all core international instruments on human rights, in particular ICESCR, CEDAW, the Convention on the Rights of the Child (Vietnam);

92.10. Consider ratifying ICESCR, CEDAW and CRC at the earliest (India);

92.11. Consider undertaking necessary steps leading to ratification of the parent/umbrella United Nations Convention on the Rights of the Child and CEDAW respectively (Malaysia);

92.12. Ratify ICESCR (Democratic People's Republic of Korea, Ghana); Become a party to the ICESCR (Australia);

92.13. Proceed with ratifying the CRPD and CRC (Qatar);

92.14. Ratify, and ensure implementation into domestic law of CEDAW and CRC (Turkey);

92.15. Ratify the Convention on the Rights of the Child and the International Convention on the Protection of the Rights of All Migrant Workers and Members of Their Families (Haiti);

92.16. Endeavour to ratify international instruments that USA is not party, in particular among others the CRC, OP-CAT; CEDAW; and Rome Statute of the International Criminal Court (Costa Rica);

92.17. Ratify ICESCR, CEDAW, the Convention on the Rights of the Child; the Convention on the Rights of Persons with Disabilities and other core human rights treaties as soon as possible (China);

92.18. Ratify additional human rights treaties such as the ICESCR; the Convention of the Rights of the Child; the International Convention for the Protection of All Persons from Enforced Disappearances and the Convention on Rights of Persons with Disabilities in order to further strengthen their support to the United Nations Human Rights mechanisms (Netherlands);

92.19. Ratify the pending core international human rights instruments, in particular CRC, ICESCR, and its OP, CEDAW and its OP as well as CRPD, and others, and ensure their due translation into the domestic legislation and review existing ratifications with a view to withdraw all reservations and declarations (Slovakia);

92.20. Consider ratifying the treaties to which it is not a party, including the CEDAW, CRC, ICESCR, and CRPD (Republic of Korea);

92.21. Consider ratifying CEDAW, the Convention on the Rights of the Child, and the Convention on the Rights of Persons with Disabilities (Austria);

92.22. Consider prioritizing acquiescence to the Convention of the Rights of the Child, CEDAW, the ILO Convention No. 111 on Discrimination in Respect of Employment and Occupation so as to further strengthen its national framework for human rights, but also to assist in achieving their universality (Trinidad and Tobago);

92.23. Proceed with the ratification of Additional Protocols I and II of the Geneva Conventions of 1949, of the Convention on the Rights of the Child, of CEDAW as well as the Optional Protocol to the Convention against Torture (Cyprus);

92.24. Ratify at its earliest opportunity other core human rights instruments, particularly, those to which it is already a signatory, namely CEDAW, Convention on the Rights of the Child, ICESCR, and the Convention on the Rights of Persons with Disabilities (Thailand);

92.25. Ratify the ICESCR, CEDAW, CRC the CRPD, the Additional Protocol I and II (1977), to the Geneva Conventions, the ICC Statute, as well as the 1st and 2nd Protocol to the Hague Convention 1954 (Hungary);

92.26. Consider ratifying ILO Convention 100 on equal remuneration for men and women for work of equal value, and ILO Convention 111 on discrimination in employment and occupation (India);

92.27. Accede to ICESCR, the CRC and ILO convention No. 111 (Islamic Republic of Iran);

92.28. Consider ratifying the Rome Statute of the International Criminal Court and the Additional Protocols I and II of the Geneva Conventions (Austria);

92.29. Ratify the Convention on the Protection of the Rights of All Migrant Workers and Members of their Families and observe international standards in this regard (Egypt);

92.30. Consider signing the International Convention on the Protection of the Rights of All Migrant Workers and Members of Their Families (Turkey);

92.31. Accede to the International Convention on the Protection of the Rights of All Migrant Workers and Members of Their Families (Guatemala);

92.32. Complement its signature of ICESCR by ratifying it and recognizing the justiciability of these rights in its domestic legal systems (Egypt);

92.33. Swiftly ratify CEDAW (Finland); Ratify CEDAW (Democratic People's Republic of Korea, Ghana, Netherlands, New Zealand); Become a party to CEDAW (Australia);

92.34. Ratify the Convention on the Rights of the Child (Democratic People's Republic of Korea, New Zealand); Become a party to the Convention on the Rights of the Child (Australia);

92.35. Ratify the Convention on the Rights of Persons with Disabilities as a matter of priority (New Zealand); become a party to the Convention on the Rights of Persons with Disabilities (Australia);

92.36. Proceed with the ratification process of the Rome Statute of the International Criminal Court at the earliest possible (Cyprus);

92.37. Ratify the 12 international human rights instruments to which it is not a party (Nicaragua);

92.38. Implement a program of ratification of all international human right s instruments, and then proceed to the incorporation of these in its internal legal system (Plurinational State of Bolivia);

92.39. Examine the possibility of ratifying the core human rights treaties to which the country is not yet a party and raising its reservations on those which it has ratified (Algeria);

92.40. Accede to international human rights instruments which is not yet acceded to (Libyan Arab Jamahiriya);

92.41. Continue the process to ratify and implement into domestic law the several international human rights instruments that still wait for this formal acceptance (Holy See);

92.42. Accede to the universal core treaties on human rights and those of inter-American system, in particular the recognition of the jurisdiction of the Inter-American Court on Human Rights (Brazil);

92.43. Consider the signing, ratification or accession, as corresponds, of the main international and Inter-American human rights instruments, especially the Convention on the Rights of the Child (Uruguay);

92.44. Withdraw all reservations and declarations on the international instruments to which it is a party that undermine its obligations or the purpose of the treaty (Spain);

92.45. Withdraw reservations, denunciations, and interpretations of the Covenant on Civil and Political Rights; the International Convention on the Elimination of All Forms of Racial Discrimination and the Convention against Torture, that undermine their compliance, and accept their individual procedures (Bolivarian Republic of Venezuela);

92.46. Withdraw reservations to the Convention against Torture (Brazil);

92.47. Consider lifting reservations to a number of ICCPR articles (Indonesia);

92.48. Take the necessary measures to consider lifting the United States reservation to Article 5, paragraph 6 of the International Covenant on Civil and Political Rights that bans the imposition of the death penalty for crimes committed by persons under 18 (France);

92.49. Consider the withdrawal of all reservations and declarations that undermine the objective and spirit of the human rights instruments, in particular reservation to Article 6 paragraph 5 of the International Covenant on Civil and Political Rights that bans the imposition of the death penalty to those who committed a crime when they were minors (Uruguay);

92.50. Withdraw the reservation to Article 6, paragraph 5 of the International Covenant of Civil and Political Rights and consider further to abolish the death penalty in all cases (Austria);

92.51. Comply with its international obligations for the effective mitigation of greenhouse gas emissions, because of their impact in climate change (Bolivarian Republic of Venezuela);

92.52. Ensure the implementation of its obligations under international humanitarian law vis-à-vis Palestinian people (Islamic Republic of Iran);

92.53. Respect the ruling of the International Court of Justice of the Hague, of 27 June 1986, which orders the United States Government to compensate Nicaragua for the terrorist acts that the people of Nicaragua suffered on those years from the part of the American President Ronald Reagan (Nicaragua);

92.54. Take appropriate action to resolve the obstacles that prevent the full implementation of the *Avena* Judgment of the International Court of Justice and, until this occurs, avoid the execution of the individuals covered in said judgment (Mexico);

92.55. Repeal the amendment which allows for slavery as a punishment (Bolivarian Republic of Venezuela);

92.56. Repeal the norms that limit freedom of expression and require journalists to reveal their sources, under penalty of imprisonment (Bolivarian Republic of Venezuela);

92.57. Abolish its extrajudicial and extraterritorial laws and refrain from the application of unilateral measures against other countries (Islamic Republic of Iran);

92.58. Make fully consistent all domestic anti-terrorism legislation and action with human rights standards (Islamic Republic of Iran);

92.59. Legislate appropriate regulations to prevent the violations of individual privacy, constant intrusion in and control of cyberspace as well as eavesdropping of communications, by its intelligence and security organizations (Islamic Republic of Iran);

92.60. Take effective legal steps to halt human rights violations by its military forces and private security firms in Afghanistan and other States (Islamic Republic of Iran);

92.61. Unconditionally abolish its extraterritorial legislation on human rights and other related matters against other countries including the 'North Korea Human Rights Act', as these legislations represent flagrant breach of their sovereignty and insulting violations of the dignity and the rights of the people (Democratic People's Republic of Korea);

92.62. Review, reform and adequate its federal and state laws, in consultation with civil society, to comply with the protection of the right to nondiscrimination established by the Convention on the Elimination of all Forms of Racial Discrimination, especially in the areas of employment, housing, health, education and justice (Plurinational State of Bolivia);

92.63. Modify the definition of the discrimination in the law to bring it in line with the ICERD and other international standards (China);

92.64. Review, with a view to their amendment and elimination, all laws and practices that discriminate against African, Arab and Muslim Americans, as well as migrants, in the administration of justice, including racial and religious profiling (Egypt);

92.65. Review its laws at the Federal and State levels with a view to bringing them in line with its international human rights obligations (Egypt);

92.66. Enact a federal crime of torture, consistent with the Convention, and also encompassing acts described as 'enhanced interrogation techniques' (Austria);

92.67. Take legislative and administrative measures to address a wide range of racial discrimination and inequalities in housing, employment and education (Democratic People's Republic of Korea);

92.68. Take legislative and administrative measures to ban racial profiling in law enforcement (Democratic People's Republic of Korea);

92.69. Take legislative and administrative measures to end defamation of religion (Democratic People's Republic of Korea);

92.70. Take appropriate legislative and practical measures to improve living conditions through its prisons systems, in particular with regard to access to health care and education (Austria);

92.71. Consider raising to 18 years the minimum age for the voluntary recruitment to the armed forces, and explicitly define as a crime the violation of the provisions of the Optional Protocol to the Convention on the Rights of the Child on the involvement of children in armed conflict (Uruguay);

92.72. Establish a national human rights institution, in accordance with the Paris Principles (Egypt, Germany, Ghana, Sudan, Bolivarian Republic of Venezuela);

92.73. Implement recommendations of the United Nations human rights bodies concerning the establishment of an independent national human rights institute in line with the Paris Principles (Russian Federation); Taking necessary steps to establish an independent national human rights institution, in accordance with Paris Principles, in order to strengthen human rights at federal and state level in addition to the local level (Qatar); Establish an independent national human rights institution in accordance with Paris Principles, to monitor compliance with international standards and to ensure coordination in implementing its human rights obligations between federal, state and local governments (Republic of Korea); Establishment of an independent national human rights institution compliant with Paris Principles at federal level with appropriate affiliated structures at state level (Ireland);

92.74. That a human rights institution at the federal level be considered in order to ensure implementation of human rights in all states (Norway);

92.75. End the blockade against Cuba (Cuba); Put an end to the infamous blockade against Cuba (Bolivarian Republic of Venezuela); Lift the economic, financial and commercial blockade against Cuba, which affects the enjoyment of the human rights of more than 11 million people (Plurinational State of Bolivia);

92.76. Lift the infamous economic, commercial and financial blockade as well as liberate immediately the five Cubans held in prison for 12 years (Nicaragua);

92.77. Put an end to the economic financial and commercial embargo against Cuba and Sudan (Sudan);

92.78. Unconditionally lift its measures of economic embargoes and sanctions unilaterally and coercively imposed upon other countries, as these measures are inflicting severe and negative impact on the human rights of the peoples (Democratic People's Republic of Korea);

92.79. Attempt to restrain any state initiative which approaches immigration issues in a repressive way towards the migrant community and that violates its rights by applying racial profiling, criminalizing undocumented immigration and violating the human and civil rights of persons (Guatemala);

92.80. Spare no efforts to constantly evaluate the enforcement of the immigration federal legislation, with a vision of promoting and protecting human rights (Guatemala);

92.81. Take the necessary measures in favor of the right to work and fair conditions of work so that workers belonging to minorities, in particular women and undocumented migrant workers, do not become victims of discriminatory treatment and abuse in the work place and enjoy the full protection of the labour legislation, regardless of their migratory status (Guatemala);

92.82. Adopt a fair immigration policy, and cease xenophobia, racism and intolerance to ethnic, religious and migrant minorities (Bolivarian Republic of Venezuela);

92.83. Implement concrete measures consistent with the Covenant on Civil and Political Rights, to ensure the participation of indigenous peoples in the decisions affecting their natural environment, measures of subsistence, culture and spiritual practices (Plurinational State of Bolivia);

92.84. Include and rank the human rights situation in the United States in the United States Annual Country Reports on Human Rights as was done for the annual report on trafficking of persons (Algeria);

92.85. Formulate goals and policy guidelines for the promotion of the rights of indigenous peoples and cooperation between government and indigenous peoples (Finland);

92.86. Undertake awareness-raising campaigns for combating stereo types and violence against gays, lesbians, bisexuals and transsexuals, and ensure access to public services paying attention to the special vulnerability of sexual workers to violence and human rights abuses (Uruguay);

92.87. Incorporate human rights training and education strategies in their public policies (Costa Rica);

92.88. Invite United Nations Special Rapporteurs to visit and investigate Guantánamo Bay prison and United States secret prisons and to subsequently close them (Islamic Republic of Iran);

92.89. Consider the possibility of inviting relevant mandate holders as follow-up to the 2006 joint-study by the 5 special procedures, in view of the decision of the current Administration to close the Guantánamo Bay detention facility (Malaysia);

92.90. Respond and follow-up appropriately the recommendations formulated to the United States by the Special Rapporteur for the Protection of Human Rights and Fundamental Freedoms while Countering Terrorism (Mexico);

92.91. Accept individual applications procedures provided for in human rights instruments (Denmark);

92.92. In view of its positive cooperation with special procedures of the Human Rights Council, extend an open standing invitation to these procedures (Costa Rica); Issue a standing invitation to the Special Procedures of the Human Rights Council (Austria); Issue an open and standing invitation to the Special Procedures (Spain); Extend a standing invitation to all special procedures (Netherlands);

92.93. Consider extending a standing invitation to special procedures (Cyprus); (Denmark); (Republic of Korea);

92.94. End the discrimination against persons of African descent (Cuba);

92.95. Undertake studies to determine the factors of racial disparity in the application of the death penalty, to prepare effective strategies aimed at ending possible discriminatory practices (France);

92.96. Take appropriate legislative and practical measures to prevent racial bias in the criminal justice system (Austria);

92.97. Review the minimum mandatory sentences in order to assess their disproportionate impact on the racial and ethnic minorities (Haiti);

92.98. Devise specific programs aimed at countering growing Islamophobic and xenophobic trends in society (Egypt);

92.99. Eliminate discrimination against migrants and religious and ethnic minorities and ensure equal opportunity for enjoyment of their economic, social and cultural rights (Bangladesh);

92.100. End all forms of racial discrimination in terms of housing, education, health care, social security and labor (Libyan Arab Jamahiriya);

92.101. Ban, at the federal and state levels, the use of racial profiling by police and immigration officers (Plurinational State of Bolivia); Prohibit expressly the use of racial profiling in the enforcement of immigration legislation (Mexico);

92.102. Revoke the national system to register the entry and exit of citizens of 25 countries from the Middle-East, South Asia and North Africa, and eliminate racial and other forms of profiling and stereotyping of Arabs, Muslims and South Asians as recommended by CERD. (Sudan);

92.103. Ensure the prosecution and punishment, according to the law, of those responsible of racial hate and xenophobic criminal acts, as well as guarantee a fair compensation to the victims, such as the case of the Ecuadoreans Marcelo Lucero and Jose Sucuzhañay, murdered in the United States (Ecuador);

92.104. Make further efforts in order to eliminate all forms of discrimination and the abuse of authority by police officers against migrants and foreigners, especially the community of Vietnamese origin people in the United States (Vietnam);

92.105. Avoid the criminalization of migrants and ensure the end of police brutality, through human rights training and awareness-raising campaigns, especially to eliminate stereotypes and guarantee that the incidents of excessive use of force be investigated and the perpetrators prosecuted (Uruguay);

92.106. Take administrative and legal measures against perpetrators of racially motivated acts, targeting migrants and minority communities (Bangladesh);

92.107. Adopt effective measures and an anti-discrimination Act to address racial problems (Ghana);

92.108. Prohibit and punish the use of racial profiling in all programs that enable local authorities with the enforcement of immigration legislation and provide effective and accessible recourse to remedy human rights violations occurred under these programs (Mexico);

92.109. Promote equal socio-economic as well as educational opportunities for all both in law and in fact, regardless of their ethnicity, race, religion, national origin, gender or disability (Thailand);

92.110. Repeal and do not enforce discriminatory and racial laws such as Law SB 1070 of the State of Arizona (Ecuador);

92.111. Adopt a comprehensive national work-plan to combat racial discrimination (Qatar);

92.112. Take measures to comprehensively address discrimination against individuals on the basis of their sexual orientation or gender identity (Australia);

92.113. That further measures be taken in the areas of economic and social rights for women and minorities, including providing equal access to decent work and reducing the number of homeless people (Norway);

92.114. Increase its efforts to effectively guarantee human rights of persons with disabilities, while welcoming the signing of the Convention and urging their prompt implementation (Costa Rica);

92.115. Consider taking further action to better ensure gender equality at work (Finland);

92.116. Continue its intense efforts to undertake all necessary measures to ensure fair and equal treatment of all persons, without regard to sex, race, religion, colour, creed, sexual orientation, gender identity or disability, and encourage further steps in this regard (Israel);

92.117. Respect the Cuban people's right to self-determination and cease its actions of interference and hostility against Cuba (Cuba);

92.118. A national moratorium on the death penalty is introduced with a view to completely abolish the penalty and, before such a moratorium is introduced, to take all necessary measures to ensure that any use of the death penalty complies with minimum standards under international law relating to the death penalty such as under Article 6 and 14 of the International Covenant on Civil and Political Rights (Sweden);

92.119. Consider the possibility of announcing moratorium on the use of the death penalty (Russian Federation);

92.120. Establish a moratorium on the use of the death penalty at the federal and state level as a first step towards abolition (United Kingdom); Establish a moratorium on executions on the entire American territory, with a view to a definitive abolition of the death penalty (Belgium); Establish, at all levels, a moratorium on executions with a view to completely abolish the death penalty(Switzerland); Adopt a moratorium on the use of the death penalty with a view to abolishing capital punishment in federal and national legislations (Italy); Establish a moratorium to the death penalty with a view to its abolition (Uruguay); Impose a moratorium on executions with a view to abolishing the death penalty nationwide (New Zealand); Work towards a moratorium on executions with the view to abolishing the death penalty, in conformity with General Assembly resolution 62/149, adopted on 18 December 2007 (Netherlands);

92.121. Take all necessary measures in order to impose a moratorium on the use of the death penalty, with a view to abolishing it both at the federal and State levels (Cyprus);

92.122. Abolish the death penalty and in any event, establish a moratorium as an interim measure towards full abolition (Australia); Abolish capital punishment and, as a first step on that road, introduce as soon as practicable a moratorium on the execution of death sentences (Hungary); That steps be taken to set federal and state-level moratoria on executions with a view to abolish the death penalty nationwide (Norway);

92.123. Impose a nationwide moratorium on executions and commute existing death sentences to imprisonment term with a view to abolish the capital punishment entirely (Slovakia);

92.124. Consider abolishing death penalty (Turkey);

92.125. Abolish the death penalty (Germany);

92.126. Implement at the federal level a moratorium on executions (France);

92.127. Begin a process leading to the ending of the death penalty punishment (Ireland); pursuing the process to abolishing the death penalty (Holy See);

92.128. Abolish as soon as possible the death penalty in the 35 Federal States where this brutal practice is authorized (Nicaragua);

92.129. Study the possibility for the Federal Government of campaigning in favour of applying the United Nations Moratorium on the death penalty (Algeria);

92.130. Establish a de jure moratorium of the death penalty at the federal level and in the military justice, in view of its abolition and as an example for the States that still retain it (Spain);

92.131. That, until a moratorium is applied, steps be taken to restrict the number of offences carrying the death penalty (Denmark);

92.132. A review of federal and state legislation with a view to restricting the number of offences carrying the death penalty (Norway);

92.133. Abolish the death penalty, which is also applied to persons with mental disabilities and commute those which have already been imposed (Bolivarian Republic of Venezuela);

92.134. End the prosecution and execution of mentally-ill persons and minors; (Cuba);

92.135. Extend the exclusion of death penalty to all crimes committed by persons with mental illness (Ireland);

92.136. Take legal and administrative measures to address civilian killings by the U.S. military troops during and after its invasion of Afghanistan and Iraq by investigating and bringing perpetrators to justice and remedying the victims and to close its detention facilities in foreign territories like Guantánamo, including CIA secret camps (Democratic People's Republic of Korea);

92.137. Prosecute the perpetrators of tortures, extrajudicial executions and other serious violations of human rights committed in Guantánamo, Abu Ghraib, Bagram, the NAMA and BALAD camps, and those carried out by the Joint Special Operations Command and the CIA (Cuba);

92.138. Heed the call of the High Commissioner to launch credible independent investigations into all reliable allegations made to date of violations of international human rights law committed by American forces in Iraq, including extrajudicial killings, summary executions, and other abuses (Egypt);

92.139. That measures be taken to eradicate all forms of torture and ill treatment of detainees by military or civilian personnel, in any territory of jurisdiction, and that any such acts be thoroughly investigated (Norway);

92.140. Stop the war crimes committed by its troops abroad, including the killings of innocent civilians and prosecute those who are responsible (Cuba);

92.141. Halt immediately the unjustified arms race and bring to justice those responsible for all war crimes and massacres against unarmed civilians, women, children as well as acts of torture carried-out in prisons such as Abu Ghraib, Bagram and Guantánamo (Nicaragua);

92.142. Halt selective assassinations committed by contractors, and the privatization of conflicts with the use of private military companies (Bolivarian Republic of Venezuela);

92.143. End the use of military technology and weaponry that have proven to be indiscriminate and cause excessive and disproportionate damage to civilian life (Egypt);

92.144. Increases its efforts to eliminate alleged brutality and use of excessive force by law enforcement officials against, inter alia, Latino and African American persons and undocumented migrants, and to ensure that relevant allegations are investigated and that perpetrators are prosecuted (Cyprus);

92.145. Guarantee the complete prohibition of torture in all prisons under its control (Islamic Republic of Iran);

92.146. Define torture as a federal offense in line with the Convention against Torture and investigate, prosecute and punish those responsible of crimes of extraterritorial torture (Plurinational State of Bolivia);

92.147. Conduct thorough and objective investigation of facts concerning use of torture against imprisoned persons in the secret prisons of United States of America and detainees of the detention centres in Bagram and Guantánamo, bring those who are responsible for these violations to justice, and undertake all necessary measures to provide redress to those whose rights were violated, including payment of necessary compensation (Russian Federation);

92.148. Take measures to ensure reparation to victims of acts of torture committed under United States' control and allow access to the International Committee of the Red Cross to detention facilities under the control of the United States (Brazil);

92.149. Observe the Amnesty International 12 points program to prevent torture perpetrated by government agents (Ecuador);

92.150. Take measures with a view to prohibiting and punishing the brutality and the use of excessive or deadly force by the law enforcement officials and to banning torture and other ill-treatment in its detention facilities at home and abroad (Democratic People's Republic of Korea);

92.151. Strengthen oversight with a view to ending excessive use of force by law enforcement bodies, particularly when it is directed to the racial minorities and bring those responsible for violation of laws to justice (China);

92.152. Prevent and repress the illegitimate use of violence against detainees (Belgium);

92.153. Release the five Cuban political prisoners—arbitrarily detained, as acknowledged by the Working Group on Arbitrary Detentions in its Opinion No. 19/2005, serving unjust sentences that resulted from a politically manipulated trial in open disregard for the rules of due process (Cuba);

92.154. End the unjust incarceration of political prisoners, including Leonard Peltier and Mumia Abu-Jamal (Cuba);

92.155. Close Guantánamo and secret centers of detention in the world, punish agents that torture, disappear and execute persons who have been arbitrarily detained, and compensate victims (Bolivarian Republic of Venezuela);

92.156. Expedite efforts aimed at closing the detention facility at Guantánamo Bay and ensure that all remaining detainees are tried, without delay, in accordance with the relevant international standards (Egypt); Proceed with the closure of Guantánamo at the earliest possible date and bring to trial promptly in accordance with the applicable rules of international law the detainees held there or release them (Ireland);

92.157. Quickly close down Guantánamo prison and follow the provision of the United Nations Charter and the Security Council Resolution by expatriating the terrorist suspect to their country of origin (China);

92.158. The closure of Guantánamo prison as the detention conditions violate the UDHR and ICCPR and the European Convention on Human Rights (ECHR) and all other related human rights instruments (Sudan);

92.159. Close without any delay all detention facilities at the Guantánamo Bay as President Barack Obama has promised (Vietnam);

92.160. Find for all persons still detained in the Guantánamo Bay detention center a solution in line with the United States obligations regarding the foundations of international and human rights law, in particular with the International Covenant on Civil and Political Rights (Switzerland);

92.161. Halt all transfer detainees to third countries unless there are adequate safeguards to ensure that they will be treated in accordance with international law requirements (Ireland);

92.162. Redouble its efforts to address sexual violence in correction and detention facilities as well as to address the problem of prison conditions, with a view to preserving the rights and dignity of all those deprived of their liberty (Thailand);

92.163. Reduce overcrowding in prisons by enlarging existing facilities or building new ones and/or making more use of alternative penalties (Belgium);

92.164. Ensure that detention centers for migrants and the treatment they receive meet the basic conditions and universal human rights law (Guatemala);

92.165. Further foster its measures in relation to migrant women and foreign adopted children that are exposed to domestic violence (Republic of Moldova);

92.166. Take effective measures to put an end to gross human rights abuses including violence against women, committed for decades by the United States military personnel stationed in foreign bases (Democratic People's Republic of Korea);

92.167. Take effective steps to put an end to child prostitution, and effectively combat violence against women and gun violence (Islamic Republic of Iran);

92.168. Define, prohibit and punish the trafficking of persons and child prostitution (Bolivarian Republic of Venezuela);

92.169. Insist more on measures aiming to combat the demand and provide information and services to victims of trafficking (Republic of Moldova);

92.170. Guarantee civilians to be tried by their natural judge and not by military commissions (Bolivarian Republic of Venezuela);

92.171. Prosecute or extradite for trial Luis Posada Carriles and dozens of other well-known terrorists living in impunity in the United States (Cuba);

92.172. Extradite the confessed terrorist Luis Posada Carriles (Bolivarian Republic of Venezuela);

92.173. Comply with the principles of international cooperation, as defined in Resolution 3074 of the General Assembly, for the extradition of persons accused of crimes against humanity and proceed to extradite former Bolivian authorities that are legally accused of such crimes, in order to be brought to trial in their country of origin (Plurinational State of Bolivia);

92.174. Make those responsible for gross violations of human rights in American prisons and prisons under the jurisdiction of America outside its territory accountable, compensate victims and provide them with remedies (Libyan Arab Jamahiriya);

92.175. Put on trial its gross violators of human rights and its war criminals and accede to ICC (Islamic Republic of Iran);

92.176. Respect the human rights of prisoners of war, guaranteed by the penal norms (Nicaragua);

92.177. Ensure the full enjoyment of human rights by persons deprived of their liberty, including by way of ensuring treatment in maximum-security prisons inconformity with international law (Sweden);

92.178. Ensure the enjoyment of the right to vote both by persons deprived of their liberty and of persons who have completed their prison sentences (Sweden);

92.179. Review of alternative ways to handle petty crime and of measures to improve the situation of inmates in prisons (Algeria);

92.180. Incorporate in its legal system the possibility of granting parole to offenders under 18 sentenced to life imprisonment for murder (Switzerland); Renounce to life in prison without parole sentences for minors at the moment of the actions for which they were charged and introduce for those who have already been sentenced in these circumstances the possibility of a remission (Belgium); Prohibit sentencing of juvenile offenders under the age of 18 without the possibility of parole at the federal and state level (Austria); Cease application of life imprisonment without parole for juvenile offenders and to review all existing sentences to provide for a possibility of parole (Slovakia);

92.181. Enact legislation to ensure that imprisonment is only used as a last resort when sentencing all juvenile offenders and provide systematic re-socialisation support (Austria);

92.182. Incarcerate immigrants only exceptionally (Switzerland); human rights law (Switzerland);

92.183. Investigate carefully each case of immigrants' incarceration (Switzerland);

92.184. Adapt the detention conditions of immigrants in line with international human rights law (Switzerland);

92.185. Ensure that migrants in detention, subject to a process of expulsion are entitled to counsel, a fair trial and fully understand their rights, even in their own language (Guatemala);

92.186. Ensure the right to habeas corpus in all cases of detention (Austria);

92.187. Guarantee the right to privacy and stop spying on its citizens without judicial authorization (Bolivarian Republic of Venezuela);

92.188. Adopt a set of legislative and administrative measures aimed at ensuring prohibition of the use by state and local authorities of modern technology for excessive and unjustified intervention in citizens' private life (Russian Federation);

92.189. Consider discontinuing measures that curtail human rights and fundamental freedoms (Bangladesh);

92.190. Take effective measures to counter insults against Islam and Holy Quran, as well as Islamophobia and violence against Moslems, and adopt necessary legislation (Islamic Republic of Iran);

92.191. Continue to create an enabling climate for religious and cultural tolerance and understanding at the grass roots level (Indonesia);

92.192. Recognize the right to association as established by ILO, for migrant, agricultural workers and domestic workers (Plurinational State of Bolivia);

92.193. Prevent slavery of agriculture workers, in particular children and women (Bolivarian Republic of Venezuela);

92.194. Decree maternity leave as mandatory (Bolivarian Republic of Venezuela);

92.195. Ensure the realization of the rights to food and health of all who live in its territory (Cuba);

92.196. Expand its social protection coverage (Brazil);

92.197. Continue its efforts in the domain of access to housing, vital for the realization of several other rights, in order to meet the needs for adequate housing at an affordable price for all segments of the American society (Morocco);

92.198. Reinforce the broad range of safeguards in favour of the most vulnerable groups such as persons with disabilities and the homeless to allow them the full enjoyment of their rights and dignity (Morocco);

92.199. End the violation of the rights of indigenous peoples (Cuba);

92.200. Guarantee the rights of indigenous Americans, and to fully implement the United Nations Declaration on the Rights of Indigenous Peoples (Islamic Republic of Iran);

92.201. Recognize the United Nations Declaration on the Rights of Indigenous Peoples without conditions or reservations, and implement it at the federal and state levels (Plurinational State of Bolivia);

92.202. Adopt and implement the United Nations Declaration on the Rights of Indigenous Peoples (Libyan Arab Jamahiriya);

92.203. Endorse the United Nations Declaration on the Rights of Indigenous Peoples when completing its national review process (Finland);

92.204. That the United Nations Declaration on the Rights of Indigenous People be used as a guide to interpret the State obligations under the Convention relating to indigenous peoples (Ghana);

92.205. Continue its forward movement on the Declaration of the Rights of Indigenous Peoples (New Zealand);

92.206. Guarantee the full enjoyment of the rights on natives of America in line with the United Nations Declaration on the Rights of Indigenous Peoples (Nicaragua);

92.207. End violence and discrimination against migrants (Cuba);

92.208. Prohibit, prevent and punish the use of lethal force in carrying out immigration control activities (Mexico);

92.209. Guarantee the prohibition of use of cruelty and excessive or fatal force by law enforcement officials against people of Latin American or African origin as well as illegal migrants and to investigate such cases of excessive use of force (Sudan);

92.210. Protect the human rights of migrants, regardless of their migratory status (Ecuador);

92.211. Reconsider restrictions on undocumented migrants' access to publicly supported healthcare (Brazil);

92.212. Reconsider alternatives to the detention of migrants (Brazil);

92.213. Ensure access of migrants to consular assistance (Brazil);

92.214. Make greater efforts to guarantee the access of migrants to basic services, regardless of their migratory status (Uruguay);

92.215. Put an end to its actions against the realization of the rights of peoples to a healthy environment, peace, development and self-determination (Cuba);

92.216. Raise the level of official development assistance to achieve the United Nations target of 0.7 percent of GDP and allow duty free-quota-free access to all products of all LDCs (Bangladesh);

92.217. Halt serious violations of human rights and humanitarian law including covert external operations by the CIA, carried out on the pretext of combating terrorism (Islamic Republic of Iran);

92.218. Do not prosecute those arrested for terrorist crimes or any other crime in exceptional tribunals or jurisdictions, but bring them to judicial instances legally established, with the protection of due process and under all the guarantees of the American Constitution (Ecuador);

92.219. Enact a national legislation that prohibits religious, racial and colour profiling particularly in context of the fight against terrorism (Qatar);

92.220. Smarten security checks so as to take into account the frequent homonymy specific to Moslem names so as to avoid involuntary discrimination against innocent people with such names because of namesakes listed as members of terrorist groups (Algeria);

92.221. Take positive steps in regard to climate change, by assuming the responsibilities arising from capitalism that have generated major natural disasters particularly in the most impoverished countries (Nicaragua);

92.222. Implement the necessary reforms to reduce their greenhouse gas emissions and cooperate with the international community to mitigate threats against human rights resulting from climate change (Plurinational State of Bolivia);

92.223. Inform Foreign Missions regularly of efforts to ensure compliance with consular notification and access for foreign nationals in United States custody at all levels of law enforcement (United Kingdom);

92.224. Abandon the State Department practice of qualifying other States according to its interpretation of human rights and contribute to the strengthening and effectiveness of the Universal Periodic Review as a fair and appropriate mechanism of the international community to evaluate the situation of human rights between States (Ecuador);

92.225. Continue consultations with non-governmental organisations and civil society in the follow up (Austria);

92.226. Persevere in the strengthening of its aid to development, considered as fundamental, in particular the assistance and relief in case of natural disasters (Morocco);

92.227. That the model legal framework expressed by the Leahy Laws be applied with respect to all countries receiving US's security assistance, and that the human rights records of all units receiving such assistance be documented, evaluated, made available and followed up upon in cases of abuse (Norway);

92.228. The removal of blanket abortion restrictions on humanitarian aid covering medical care given women and girls who are raped and impregnated in situations of armed conflict (Norway);

93. The response of the United States of America to these recommendations will be included in the outcome report adopted by the Council at its sixteenth session.

94. All conclusions and/or recommendations contained in the present report reflect the position of the submitting State(s) and/or the State under review. They should not be construed as endorsed by the Working Group as a whole.

Annex
Composition of the delegation
The delegation of the United States of America was headed jointly by the Honourable Esther Brimmer, Assistant Secretary, Bureau of International Organizations, Department of State; the Honourable Harold Hongju Koh, Legal Adviser, Office of the Legal Adviser, Department of State; and the Honourable Michael Posner, Assistant Secretary, Democracy, Human Rights, and Labor, Department of State and was composed of the following members:

Advisers
• Ambassador Eileen Chamberlain Donahoe, United States Representative to the Human Rights Council;

• Honourable Larry Echo Hawk, Assistant Secretary Bureau of Indian Affairs Department of the Interior;

[see website for other advisers]

Notes:
1 Colombia, Panama, Argentina, Chile, Paraguay, Slovenia, Nepal, Rwanda, Chad, Bhutan, Kuwait, Belarus, Peru, Timor-Leste, Latvia, Jordan, South Africa, Iraq, Ukraine, Nigeria, Burkina Faso, Cameroon, Afghanistan, Burundi, the former Yugoslav Republic of Macedonia, Mauritius and Namibia.
2 The original recommendation as read during the interactive dialogue: "End the blockade against Cuba, which qualifies as the crime of genocide and which seriously violates the human rights of the Cuban people, as well as fundamental freedoms of American and third states citizens."
3 The original recommendation as read during the interactive dialogue: "Prosecute or extradite for trial Luis Posada Carriles and dozens of other well-known terrorists living in impunity in the United States, who are responsible for the deaths of more than 3,000 Cubans and for causing disabilities to over 2,000."

DOCUMENT 88

Full Official Title: Uniting and Strengthening America by Providing Appropriate Tools Required to Intercept and Obstruct Terrorism (USA Patriot Act) Act of 2001.

Short Title/Acronym/Abbreviation: The PATRIOT Act

Type of Document: This is a bill passed by the U.S. Congress and signed into law by the president.

Subject: To deter and punish terrorist acts in the United States and around the world, to enhance law enforcement investigatory tools, and for other purposes.

Official Citation: Public Law 107-56 107th Congress

Date of Document: Not applicable

Date of Adoption: Signed October 26, 2001

Date of General Entry into Force (EIF): Not applicable

Number of States Parties as of this printing: Not applicable

Date of Signature by the United States: Not applicable

Date of Ratification/Accession/Adhesion: Not applicable

Date of Entry into Force as to United States (effective date): Not applicable

Legal Status/Character of the Instrument/Document as to the United States: This bill was signed by President George W. Bush and is legally binding. Some of the provisions have expired under the sunset provision and are no longer in force.

Comments: The Patriot Act amended the Federal Intelligence Surveillance Act (FISA) to make it easier for government officials and agencies to obtain foreign intelligence and respond more rapidly to the particular needs in countering acts of terrorism following the attacks on the United States on September 11, 2001. Changes included permitting the use of "roving" wiretaps, expanding the type of materials sought under FISA to "any tangible thing" and limiting requirements needed to obtain a court order, and expanding the authority of various agencies to issue national security letters. These changes apply to intelligence on individuals that are not U.S. citizens and for the purpose of protecting against lone terrorist agents or international terrorist groups.

The bill relates to the surveillance of foreigners, but may indirectly include American citizens if they are in contact with the foreigners under surveillance. This had led to some concerns regarding how American citizens' right to "unreasonable search and seizures" under the fourth amendment to the Constitution would be protected in this bill. According to the bill and government statements about it, this bill does not change or threaten existing privacy protections of American citizens in the United States. Several provisions of the Patriot Act are set to sunset or expire on February 28, 2011 if they are not renewed with legislation currently under consideration in the House and Senate.

Some technical and other amendments were made to the bill following its adoption; however, all amendments will expire with the bill if it is not renewed by Congress. There is a grandfather clause in the bill that allows for the continued surveillance of individuals who may have committed a crime before the expiration date or in cases that began before the bill expired.

Many lawsuits were filed against specific provisions of the Act and decisions have come down both ways.

Caution: The status and applicability of this instrument as to the United States may have changed since the date of this publication.

Web Address: http://thomas.loc.gov/cgi-bin/query/z?c107:H.R.3162.ENR:
http://www1.umn.edu/humanrts/instree/

Uniting And Strengthening America By Providing Appropriate Tools Required to Intercept And Obstruct Terrorism (USA Patriot Act) Act Of 2001 (Excerpts)

Public Law 107–56

107th Congress

An Act

To deter and punish terrorist acts in the United States and around the world, to enhance law enforcement investigatory tools, and for other purposes.

Be it enacted by the Senate and House of Representatives of the United States of America in Congress assembled,

SECTION 1. SHORT TITLE AND TABLE OF CONTENTS.

(a) SHORT TITLE.—This Act may be cited as the "Uniting and Strengthening America by Providing Appropriate Tools Required to Intercept and Obstruct Terrorism (USA PATRIOT ACT) Act of 2001".

(b) TABLE OF CONTENTS.—The table of contents for this Act has been omitted.

Sec. 1. Short title and table of contents.

Sec. 2. Construction; severability.

...

SEC. 2. CONSTRUCTION; SEVERABILITY. ...
TITLE I—ENHANCING DOMESTICSECURITY AGAINST TERRORISM
SEC. 101. COUNTERTERRORISM FUND.

(a) ESTABLISHMENT; AVAILABILITY.—There is hereby established in the Treasury of the United States a separate fund to be known as the "Counterterrorism Fund", amounts in which shall remain available without fiscal year limitation—

(1) to reimburse any Department of Justice component for any costs incurred in connection with—

(A) reestablishing the operational capability of an office or facility that has been damaged or destroyed as the result of any domestic or international terrorism incident;

(B) providing support to counter, investigate, or prosecute domestic or international terrorism, including, without limitation, paying rewards in connection with these activities; and

(C) conducting terrorism threat assessments of Federal agencies and their facilities; and

(2) to reimburse any department or agency of the Federal Government for any costs incurred in connection with detaining in foreign countries individuals accused of acts of terrorism that violate the laws of the United States.

(b) NO EFFECT ON PRIOR APPROPRIATIONS.—Subsection (a) shall not be construed to affect the amount or availability of any appropriation to the Counterterrorism Fund made before the date of the enactment of this Act.

SEC. 102. SENSE OF CONGRESS CONDEMNING DISCRIMINATION AGAINST ARAB AND MUSLIM AMERICANS.

(a) FINDINGS.—Congress makes the following findings:

(1) Arab Americans, Muslim Americans, and Americans from South Asia play a vital role in our Nation and are entitled to nothing less than the full rights of every American.

(2) The acts of violence that have been taken against Arab and Muslim Americans since the September 11, 2001, attacks against the United States should be and are condemned by all Americans who value freedom.

(3) The concept of individual responsibility for wrongdoing is sacrosanct in American society, and applies equally to all religious, racial, and ethnic groups.

(4) When American citizens commit acts of violence against those who are, or are perceived to be, of Arab or Muslim descent, they should be punished to the full extent of the law.

(5) Muslim Americans have become so fearful of harassment that many Muslim women are changing the way they dress to avoid becoming targets.

(6) Many Arab Americans and Muslim Americans have acted heroically during the attacks on the United States, including Mohammed Salman Hamdani, a 23-year-old New Yorker of Pakistani descent, who is believed to have gone to the World Trade Center to offer rescue assistance and is now missing.

(b) SENSE OF CONGRESS.—It is the sense of Congress that—

(1) the civil rights and civil liberties of all Americans, including Arab Americans, Muslim Americans, and Americans from South Asia, must be protected, and that every effort must be taken to preserve their safety;

(2) any acts of violence or discrimination against any Americans be condemned; and

(3) the Nation is called upon to recognize the patriotism of fellow citizens from all ethnic, racial, and religious backgrounds.

. . .

SEC. 105. EXPANSION OF NATIONAL ELECTRONIC CRIME TASK FORCE INITIATIVE.

The Director of the United States Secret Service shall take appropriate actions to develop a national network of electronic crime task forces, based the New York Electronic Crimes Task

Force model, throughout the United States, for the purpose of preventing, detecting, and investigating various forms of electronic crimes, including potential terrorist attacks against critical infrastructure and financial payment systems.

SEC. 106. PRESIDENTIAL AUTHORITY.

Section 203 of the International Emergency Powers Act (50U.S.C. 1702) is amended—

(1) in subsection (a)(1)—

(A) at the end of subparagraph (A) (flush to that sub paragraph), by striking "; and" and inserting a comma and the following:

"by any person, or with respect to any property, subject to the jurisdiction of the United States;";

(B) in subparagraph (B)—

(i) by inserting ", block during the pendency of an investigation" after "investigate"; and

(ii) by striking "interest;" and inserting "interest by any person, or with respect to any property, subject to the jurisdiction of the United States; and";

(C) by striking "by any person, or with respect to any property, subject to the jurisdiction of the United States"; and

(D) by inserting at the end the following:

"(C) when the United States is engaged in armed hostilities or has been attacked by a foreign country or foreign nationals, confiscate any property, subject to the jurisdiction of the United States, of any foreign person, foreign organization, or foreign country that he determines has planned, authorized, aided, or engaged in such hostilities or attacks against the United States; and all right, title, and interest in any property so confiscated shall vest, when, as, and upon the terms directed by the President, in such agency or person as the President may designate from time to time, and upon such terms and conditions as the President may prescribe, such interest or property shall be held, used, administered, liquidated, sold, or otherwise dealt with in the interest of and for the benefit of the United States, and such designated agency or person may perform any and all acts incident to the accomplishment or furtherance of these purposes."; and

(2) by inserting at the end the following:

"(c) CLASSIFIED INFORMATION. —In any judicial review of a determination made under this section, if the determination was based on classified information (as defined in section 1(a) of the Classified Information Procedures Act) such information may be submitted to the reviewing court ex parte and in camera. This subsection does not confer or imply any right to judicial review".

TITLE II—ENHANCED SURVEILLANCE PROCEDURES
SEC. 201. AUTHORITY TO INTERCEPT WIRE, ORAL, AND ELECTRONIC COMMUNICATIONS RELATING TO TERRORISM.

Section 2516(1) of title 18, United States Code, is amended—

(1) by redesignating paragraph (p), as so redesignated by section 434(2) of the Antiterrorism and Effective Death Penalty Act of 1996 (Public Law 104–132; 110 Stat. 1274), as paragraph(r); and

(2) by inserting after paragraph (p), as so redesignated by section 201(3) of the Illegal Immigration Reform and Immigrant Responsibility Act of 1996 (division C of Public Law 104–208; 110 Stat. 3009–565), the following new paragraph:

"(q) any criminal violation of section 229 (relating to chemical weapons); or sections 2332, 2332a, 2332b, 2332d, 2339A, or 2339B of this title (relating to terrorism); or".

SEC. 202. AUTHORITY TO INTERCEPT WIRE, ORAL, AND ELECTRONIC COMMUNICATIONS RELATING TO COMPUTER FRAUD AND ABUSE OFFENSES.

Section 2516(1)(c) of title 18, United States Code, is amended by striking "and section 1341 (relating to mail fraud)," and inserting "section 1341 (relating to mail fraud), a felony violation of section1030 (relating to computer fraud and abuse),".

SEC. 203. AUTHORITY TO SHARE CRIMINAL INVESTIGATIVE INFORMATION.

(a) AUTHORITY TO SHARE GRAND JURY INFORMATION.—

(1) IN GENERAL.—Rule 6(e)(3)(C) of the Federal Rules of Criminal Procedure is amended to read as follows:

"(C)(i) Disclosure otherwise prohibited by this rule of matters occurring before the grand jury may also be made—

"(I) when so directed by a court preliminarily to or in connection with a judicial proceeding;

"(II) when permitted by a court at the request of the defendant, upon a showing that grounds may exist for a motion to dismiss the indictment because of matters occurring before the grand jury;

"(III) when the disclosure is made by an attorney for the government to another Federal grand jury;

"(IV) when permitted by a court at the request of an attorney for the government, upon a showing that such matters may disclose a violation of State criminal law, to an appropriate official of a State or subdivision of a State for the purpose of enforcing such law; or

"(V) when the matters involve foreign intelligence or counterintelligence (as defined in section 3 of the National Security Act of 1947 (50 U.S.C. 401a)), or foreign intelligence information (as defined in clause (iv) of this subparagraph), to any Federal law enforcement, intelligence, protective, immigration, national defense, or national security official in order to assist the official receiving that information in the performance of his official duties.

"(ii) If the court orders disclosure of matters occurring before the grand jury, the disclosure shall be made in such manner, at such time, and under such conditions as the court may direct.

"(iii) Any Federal official to whom information is disclosed pursuant to clause (i)(V) of this subparagraph may use that information only as necessary in the conduct of that person's official duties subject to any limitations on the unauthorized disclosure of such information. Within a reasonable time after such disclosure, an attorney for the government shall file under seal a notice with the court stating the fact that such information was disclosed and the departments, agencies, or entities to which the disclosure was made.

"(iv) In clause (i)(V) of this subparagraph, the term 'foreign intelligence information' means—

"(I) information, whether or not concerning a United States person, that relates to the ability of the United States to protect against—

"(aa) actual or potential attack or other grave hostile acts of a foreign power or an agent of a foreign power;

"(bb) sabotage or international terrorism by a foreign power or an agent of a foreign power; or

"(cc) clandestine intelligence activities by an intelligence service or network of a foreign power or by an agent of foreign power; or

"(II) information, whether or not concerning a United States person, with respect to a foreign power or foreign territory that relates to—

"(aa) the national defense or the security of the United States; or

"(bb) the conduct of the foreign affairs of the United States."

(2) CONFORMING AMENDMENT.—Rule 6(e)(3)(D) of the Federal Rules of Criminal Procedure is amended by striking "(e)(3)(C)(i)" and inserting "(e)(3)(C)(i)(I)".

(b) AUTHORITY TO SHARE ELECTRONIC, WIRE, AND ORAL INTERCEPTION INFORMATION.—

(1) LAW ENFORCEMENT.—Section 2517 of title 18, United States Code, is amended by inserting at the end the following:

"(6) Any investigative or law enforcement officer, or attorney for the Government, who by any means authorized by this chapter, has obtained knowledge of the contents of any wire, oral, or electronic communication, or evidence derived therefrom, may disclose such contents to any other Federal law enforcement, intelligence, protective, immigration, national defense, or national security official to the extent that such contents include foreign intelligence or counterintelligence (as defined in section 3 of the National Security Act of 1947 (50 U.S.C. 401a)), or foreign intelligence information(as defined in subsection (19) of section 2510 of this title), to assist the official who is to receive that information in the performance of his official duties. Any Federal official who receives information pursuant to this provision may use that information only as necessary in the conduct of that person's official duties subject to any limitations on the unauthorized disclosure of such information".

(2) DEFINITION.—Section 2510 of title 18, United States Code, is amended by—

(A) in paragraph (17), by striking "and" after the semicolon;

(B) in paragraph (18), by striking the period and inserting "; and"; and

(C) by inserting at the end the following:"(19) 'foreign intelligence information' means—

"(A) information, whether or not concerning a United States person, that relates to the ability of the United States to protect against—

"(i) actual or potential attack or other grave hostile acts of a foreign power or an agent of a foreign power;

"(ii) sabotage or international terrorism by a foreign power or an agent of a foreign power; or

"(iii) clandestine intelligence activities by an intelligence service or network of a foreign power or by an agent of a foreign power; or

"(B) information, whether or not concerning a United States person, with respect to a foreign power or foreign territory that relates to—

"(i) the national defense or the security of the United States; or

"(ii) the conduct of the foreign affairs of the United States."

(c) PROCEDURES.—The Attorney General shall establish procedures for the disclosure of information pursuant to section 2517(6) and Rule 6(e)(3)(C)(i)(V) of the Federal Rules of Criminal Procedure that identifies a United States person, as defined in section 101of the Foreign Intelligence Surveillance Act of 1978 (50 U.S.C.1801).

(d) FOREIGN INTELLIGENCE INFORMATION.—

(1) IN GENERAL.—Notwithstanding any other provision of law, it shall be lawful for foreign intelligence or counterintelligence(as defined in section 3 of the National Security Act of 1947 (50 U.S.C. 401a)) or foreign intelligence information obtained as part of a criminal investigation to be disclosed to any Federal

law enforcement, intelligence, protective, immigration, national defense, or national security official in order to assist the official receiving that information in the performance of his official duties. Any Federal official who receives information pursuant to this provision may use that information only as necessary in the conduct of that person's official duties subject to any limitations on the unauthorized disclosure of such information.

(2) DEFINITION.—In this subsection, the term "foreign intelligence information" means—

(A) information, whether or not concerning a United States person, that relates to the ability of the United States to protect against—(i) actual or potential attack or other grave hostile acts of a foreign power or an agent of a foreign power; (ii) sabotage or international terrorism by a foreign power or an agent of a foreign power; or (iii) clandestine intelligence activities by an intelligence service or network of a foreign power or by an agent of a foreign power; or

(B) information, whether or not concerning a United States person, with respect to a foreign power or foreign territory that relates to—

(i) the national defense or the security of the United States; or

(ii) the conduct of the foreign affairs of the United States.

SEC. 204. CLARIFICATION OF INTELLIGENCE EXCEPTIONS FROM LIMITATIONS ON INTERCEPTION AND DISCLOSURE OFWIRE, ORAL, AND ELECTRONIC COMMUNICATIONS.

Section 2511(2)(f) of title 18, United States Code, is amended—

(1) by striking "this chapter or chapter 121" and inserting "this chapter or chapter 121 or 206 of this title"; and (2) by striking "wire and oral" and inserting "wire, oral, and electronic".

SEC. 205. EMPLOYMENT OF TRANSLATORS BY THE FEDERAL BUREAU OF INVESTIGATION.

(a) AUTHORITY.—The Director of the Federal Bureau of Investigation is authorized to expedite the employment of personnel as translators to support counter terrorism investigations and operations without regard to applicable Federal personnel requirements and limitations.

(b) SECURITY REQUIREMENTS.—The Director of the Federal Bureau of Investigation shall establish such security requirements as are necessary for the personnel employed as translators under subsection (a).

(c) REPORT.—The Attorney General shall report to the Committees on the Judiciary of the House of Representatives and the Senate on—

(1) the number of translators employed by the FBI and other components of the Department of Justice;

(2) any legal or practical impediments to using translators employed by other Federal, State, or local agencies, on a full, part-time, or shared basis; and

(3) the needs of the FBI for specific translation services in certain languages, and recommendations for meeting those needs.

SEC. 206. ROVING SURVEILLANCE AUTHORITY UNDER THE FOREIGN INTELLIGENCE SURVEILLANCE ACT OF 1978.

Section 105(c)(2)(B) of the Foreign Intelligence Surveillance Act of 1978 (50 U.S.C. 1805(c)(2)(B)) is amended by inserting ", or in circumstances where the Court finds that the actions of the target of the application may have the effect of thwarting the identification of a specified person, such other persons," after "specified person."

SEC. 207. DURATION OF FISA SURVEILLANCE OF NON-UNITED STATESPERSONS WHO ARE AGENTS OF A FOREIGN POWER.

(a) DURATION.—

(1) SURVEILLANCE.—Section 105(e)(1) of the Foreign Intelligence Surveillance Act of 1978 (50 U.S.C. 1805(e)(1)) is amended by—

(A) inserting "(A)" after "except that"; and

(B) inserting before the period the following: ", and

(B) an order under this Act for a surveillance targeted against an agent of a foreign power, as defined in section101(b)(1)(A) may be for the period specified in the application or for 120 days, whichever is less".

(2) PHYSICAL SEARCH.—Section 304(d)(1) of the Foreign Intelligence Surveillance Act of 1978 (50 U.S.C. 1824(d)(1)) is amended by—

(A) striking "forty-five" and inserting "90";

(B) inserting "(A)" after "except that"; and

(C) inserting before the period the following: ", and (B)an order under this section for a physical search targeted against an agent of a foreign power as defined in section101(b)(1)(A) may be for the period specified in the application or for 120 days, whichever is less".

(b) EXTENSION.—

(1) IN GENERAL.—Section 105(d)(2) of the Foreign Intelligence Surveillance Act of 1978 (50 U.S.C. 1805(d)(2)) is amended by—

(A) inserting "(A)" after "except that"; and

(B) inserting before the period the following: ", and

(B) an extension of an order under this Act for a surveillance targeted against an agent of a foreign power as defined in section 101(b)(1)(A) may be for a period not to exceed 1 year".

(2) DEFINED TERM.—Section 304(d)(2) of the Foreign Intelligence Surveillance Act of 1978 (50 U.S.C. 1824(d)(2) is amended by inserting after "not a United States person," the following: "or against an agent of a foreign power as defined in section 101(b)(1)(A),".

SEC. 208. DESIGNATION OF JUDGES.

Section 103(a) of the Foreign Intelligence Surveillance Act of1978 (50 U.S.C. 1803(a)) is amended by—

(1) striking "seven district court judges" and inserting "11district court judges"; and

(2) inserting "of whom no fewer than 3 shall reside within 20 miles of the District of Columbia" after "circuits".

SEC. 209. SEIZURE OF VOICE-MAIL MESSAGES PURSUANT TO WARRANTS.

Title 18, United States Code, is amended—

(1) in section 2510—

(A) in paragraph (1), by striking beginning with "and such" and all that follows through "communication"; and

(B) in paragraph (14), by inserting "wire or" after "transmission of"; and

(2) in subsections (a) and (b) of section 2703—

(A) by striking "CONTENTS OF ELECTRONIC" and inserting "CONTENTS OF WIRE OR ELECTRONIC" each place it appears;

(B) by striking "contents of an electronic" and inserting "contents of a wire or electronic" each place it appears; and

(C) by striking "any electronic" and inserting "any wire or electronic" each place it appears.

SEC. 210. SCOPE OF SUBPOENAS FOR RECORDS OF ELECTRONICCOMMUNICATIONS.

Section 2703(c)(2) of title 18, United States Code, as redesignated by section 212, is amended—

(1) by striking "entity the name, address, local and long distance telephone toll billing records, telephone number or other subscriber number or identity, and length of service of a subscriber" and inserting the following: "entity the—

"(A) name;

"(B) address;

"(C) local and long distance telephone connection records, or records of session times and durations;

"(D) length of service (including start date) and types of service utilized;

"(E) telephone or instrument number or other subscriber number or identity, including any temporarily assigned network address; and

"(F) means and source of payment for such service(including any credit card or bank account number), of a subscriber"; and

(2) by striking "and the types of services the subscriber or customer utilized."

SEC. 211. CLARIFICATION OF SCOPE.

Section 631 of the Communications Act of 1934 (47 U.S.C.551) is amended—

(1) in subsection (c)(2)—

(A) in subparagraph (B), by striking "or";

(B) in subparagraph (C), by striking the period at the end and inserting "; or"; and

(C) by inserting at the end the following:

"(D) to a government entity as authorized under chapters 119, 121, or 206 of title 18, United States Code, except that such disclosure shall not include records revealing cable subscribers election of video programming from a cable operator."; and

(2) in subsection (h), by striking "A governmental entity" and inserting "Except as provided in subsection (c)(2)(D), a governmental entity".

SEC. 212. EMERGENCY DISCLOSURE OF ELECTRONIC COMMUNICATIONS TO PROTECT LIFE AND LIMB.

(a) DISCLOSURE OF CONTENTS.—

(1) IN GENERAL.—Section 2702 of title 18, United States Code, is amended—

(A) by striking the section heading and inserting the following:

"§ 2702. Voluntary disclosure of customer communications or records";

(B) in subsection (a)—

(i) in paragraph (2)(A), by striking "and" at the end;

(ii) in paragraph (2)(B), by striking the period and inserting "; and"; and

(iii) by inserting after paragraph (2) the following:

"(3) a provider of remote computing service or electronic communication service to the public shall not knowingly divulge a record or other information pertaining to a subscriber to or customer of such service (not including the contents of communications covered by paragraph (1) or (2)) to any governmental entity.";

(C) in subsection (b), by striking "EXCEPTIONS.—A person or entity" and inserting "EXCEPTIONS FOR DISCLOSUREOF COMMUNICATIONS.— A provider described in subsection (a)";

(D) in subsection (b)(6)—

(i) in subparagraph (A)(ii), by striking "or";

(ii) in subparagraph (B), by striking the period and inserting "; or"; and

(iii) by adding after subparagraph (B) the following:

"(C) if the provider reasonably believes that an emergency involving immediate danger of death or serious physical injury to any person requires disclosure of the information without delay."; and

(E) by inserting after subsection (b) the following:

"(c) EXCEPTIONS FOR DISCLOSURE OF CUSTOMER RECORDS.—

A provider described in subsection (a) may divulge a record or other information pertaining to a subscriber to or customer of such service (not including the contents of communications covered by subsection (a)(1) or (a)(2))—

"(1) as otherwise authorized in section 2703;

"(2) with the lawful consent of the customer or subscriber;

"(3) as may be necessarily incident to the rendition of the service or to the protection of the rights or property of the provider of that service;

"(4) to a governmental entity, if the provider reasonably believes that an emergency involving immediate danger of death or serious physical injury to any person justifies disclosure of the information; or

"(5) to any person other than a governmental entity."

(2) TECHNICAL AND CONFORMING AMENDMENT.—The table of sections for chapter 121 of title 18, United States Code, is amended by striking the item relating to section 2702 and inserting the following: "2702. Voluntary disclosure of customer communications or records."

(b) REQUIREMENTS FOR GOVERNMENT ACCESS.—

(1) IN GENERAL.—Section 2703 of title 18, United State Code, is amended—

(A) by striking the section heading and inserting the following:

"§ 2703. Required disclosure of customer communications or records";

(B) in subsection (c) by redesignating paragraph (2) as paragraph (3);

(C) in subsection (c)(1)—

(i) by striking "(A) Except as provided in subparagraph (B), a provider of electronic communication service or remote computing service may" and inserting

"A governmental entity may require a provider of electronic communication service or remote computing service to";

(ii) by striking "covered by subsection (a) or (b) of this section) to any person other than a governmental entity.

"(B) A provider of electronic communication service or remote computing service shall disclose a record or other information pertaining to a subscriber to or customer of such service (not including the contents of communications covered by subsection (a) or (b) of this section) to a governmental entity" and inserting ")";

(iii) by redesignating subparagraph (C) as paragraph (2);

(iv) by redesignating clauses (i), (ii), (iii), and (iv) as subparagraphs (A), (B), (C), and (D), respectively;

(v) in subparagraph (D) (as redesignated) by striking the period and inserting "; or"; and

(vi) by inserting after subparagraph (D) (as redesignated) the following:

"(E) seeks information under paragraph (2)."; and

(D) in paragraph (2) (as redesignated) by striking "subparagraph (B)" and insert "paragraph (1)".

(2) TECHNICAL AND CONFORMING AMENDMENT.—The table of sections for chapter 121 of title 18, United States Code, is amended by striking the item relating to section 2703 and inserting the following:

"2703. Required disclosure of customer communications or records."

SEC. 213. AUTHORITY FOR DELAYING NOTICE OF THE EXECUTION OF A WARRANT.

Section 3103a of title 18, United States Code, is amended—

115 STAT. 286 PUBLIC LAW 107–56—OCT. 26, 2001

(1) by inserting "(a) IN GENERAL.—" before "In addition"; and

(2) by adding at the end the following:

"(b) DELAY.—With respect to the issuance of any warrant or court order under this section, or any other rule of law, to search for and seize any property or material that constitutes evidence of a criminal offense in violation of the laws of the United States, any notice required, or that may be required, to be given may be delayed if—

"(1) the court finds reasonable cause to believe that providing immediate notification of the execution of the warrant may have an adverse result (as defined in section 2705);

"(2) the warrant prohibits the seizure of any tangible property, any wire or electronic communication (as defined in section 2510), or, except as expressly provided in chapter 121, any stored wire or electronic information, except where the court finds reasonable necessity for the seizure; and

"(3) the warrant provides for the giving of such notice within a reasonable period of its execution, which period may thereafter be extended by the court for good cause shown."

SEC. 214. PEN REGISTER AND TRAP AND TRACE AUTHORITY UNDER FISA.

(a) APPLICATIONS AND ORDERS.—Section 402 of the Foreign Intelligence Surveillance Act of 1978 (50 U.S.C. 1842) is amended—

(1) in subsection (a)(1), by striking "for any investigation to gather foreign intelligence information or information concerning international terrorism" and inserting "for any investigation to obtain foreign intelligence information not concerning a United States person or to protect against international terrorism or clandestine intelligence activities, provided that such investigation of a United States person is not conducted solely upon the basis of activities protected by the first amendment to the Constitution";

(2) by amending subsection (c)(2) to read as follows:

"(2) a certification by the applicant that the information likely to be obtained is foreign intelligence information not concerning a United States person or is relevant to an ongoing investigation to protect against international terrorism or clandestine intelligence activities, provided that such investigation of a United States person is not conducted solely upon the basis of activities protected by the first amendment to the Constitution.";

(3) by striking subsection (c)(3); and

(4) by amending subsection (d)(2)(A) to read as follows:

"(A) shall specify—

"(i) the identity, if known, of the person who is the subject of the investigation;

"(ii) the identity, if known, of the person to whom is leased or in whose name is listed the telephone line or other facility to which the pen register or trap and trace device is to be attached or applied;

"(iii) the attributes of the communications to which the order applies, such as the number or other identifier, and, if known, the location of the telephone line or other facility to which the pen register or trap and trace device is to be attached or applied and, in the case of a trap and trace device, the geographic limits of the trap and trace order."

(b) AUTHORIZATION DURING EMERGENCIES.—Section 403 of the Foreign Intelligence Surveillance Act of 1978 (50 U.S.C. 1843) is amended—

(1) in subsection (a), by striking "foreign intelligence information or information concerning international terrorism" and inserting "foreign intelligence information not concerning a United States person or

information to protect against international terrorism or clandestine intelligence activities, provided that such investigation of a United States person is not conducted solely upon the basis of activities protected by the first amendment to the Constitution"; and

(2) in subsection (b)(1), by striking "foreign intelligence information or information concerning international terrorism" and inserting "foreign intelligence information not concerning a United States person or information to protect against international terrorism or clandestine intelligence activities, provided that such investigation of a United States person is not conducted solely upon the basis of activities protected by the first amendment to the Constitution."

SEC. 215. ACCESS TO RECORDS AND OTHER ITEMS UNDER THE FOREIGN INTELLIGENCE SURVEILLANCE ACT.

Title V of the Foreign Intelligence Surveillance Act of 1978 (50 U.S.C. 1861 et seq.) is amended by striking sections 501 through 503 and inserting the following:

"SEC. 501. ACCESS TO CERTAIN BUSINESS RECORDS FOR FOREIGN INTELLIGENCE AND INTERNATIONAL TERRORISM INVESTIGATIONS.

"(a)(1) The Director of the Federal Bureau of Investigation or a designee of the Director (whose rank shall be no lower than Assistant Special Agent in Charge) may make an application for an order requiring the production of any tangible things (including books, records, papers, documents, and other items) for an investigation to protect against international terrorism or clandestine intelligence activities, provided that such investigation of a United States person is not conducted solely upon the basis of activities protected by the first amendment to the Constitution.

"(2) An investigation conducted under this section shall—

"(A) be conducted under guidelines approved by the Attorney General under Executive Order 12333 (or a successor order); and

"(B) not be conducted of a United States person solely upon the basis of activities protected by the first amendment to the Constitution of the United States.

"(b) Each application under this section—

"(1) shall be made to—

"(A) a judge of the court established by section 103(a); or

"(B) a United States Magistrate Judge under chapter 43 of title 28, United States Code, who is publicly designated by the Chief Justice of the United States to have the power to hear applications and grant orders for the production of tangible things under this section on behalf of a judge of that court; and

"(2) shall specify that the records concerned are sought for an authorized investigation conducted in accordance with subsection (a)(2) to obtain foreign intelligence information not concerning a United States person or to protect against international terrorism or clandestine intelligence activities.

"(c)(1) Upon an application made pursuant to this section, the judge shall enter an ex parte order as requested, or as modified, approving the release of records if the judge finds that the application meets the requirements of this section.

"(2) An order under this subsection shall not disclose that it is issued for purposes of an investigation described in subsection (a).

"(d) No person shall disclose to any other person (other than those persons necessary to produce the tangible things under this section) that the Federal Bureau of Investigation has sought or obtained tangible things under this section.

"(e) A person who, in good faith, produces tangible things under an order pursuant to this section shall not be liable to any other person for such production. Such production shall not be deemed to constitute a waiver of any privilege in any other proceeding or context.

"SEC. 502. CONGRESSIONAL OVERSIGHT.

"(a) On a semiannual basis, the Attorney General shall fully inform the Permanent Select Committee on Intelligence of the House of Representatives and the Select Committee on Intelligence of the Senate concerning all requests for the production of tangible things under section 402.

"(b) On a semiannual basis, the Attorney General shall provide to the Committees on the Judiciary of the House of Representatives and the Senate a report setting forth with respect to the preceding 6-month period—

"(1) the total number of applications made for orders approving requests for the production of tangible things under section 402; and

"(2) the total number of such orders either granted, modified, or denied."

SEC. 216. MODIFICATION OF AUTHORITIES RELATING TO USE OF PEN REGISTERS AND TRAP AND TRACE DEVICES.

(a) GENERAL LIMITATIONS.—Section 3121(c) of title 18, United States Code, is amended—

(1) by inserting "or trap and trace device" after "pen register";

(2) by inserting ", routing, addressing," after "dialing"; and

(3) by striking "call processing" and inserting "the processing and transmitting of wire or electronic communications so as not to include the contents of any wire or electronic communications".

(b) ISSUANCE OF ORDERS.—

(1) IN GENERAL.—Section 3123(a) of title 18, United States Code, is amended to read as follows:

"(a) IN GENERAL.—

"(1) ATTORNEY FOR THE GOVERNMENT.—Upon an application made under section 3122(a)(1), the court shall enter an ex parte order authorizing the installation and use of a pen register or trap and trace device anywhere within the United States, if the court finds that the attorney for the Government has certified to the court that the information likely to be obtained by such installation and use is relevant to an ongoing criminal investigation. The order, upon service of that order, shall apply to any person or entity providing wire or electronic communication service in the United States whose assistance may facilitate the execution of the order. Whenever such an order is served on any person or entity not specifically named in the order, upon request of such person or entity, the attorney for the Government or law enforcement or investigative officer that is serving the order shall provide written or electronic certification that the order applies to the person or entity being served.

"(2) STATE INVESTIGATIVE OR LAW ENFORCEMENT OFFICER.—Upon an application made under section 3122(a)(2), the court shall enter an ex parte order authorizing the installation and use of a pen register or trap and trace device within the jurisdiction of the court, if the court finds that the State law enforcement or investigative officer has certified to the court that the information likely to be obtained by such installation and use is relevant to an ongoing criminal investigation.

"(3)(A) Where the law enforcement agency implementing an ex parte order under this subsection seeks to do so by installing and using its own pen register or trap and trace device on a packet-switched data network of a provider of electronic communication service to the public, the agency shall ensure that a record will be maintained which will identify—

"(i) any officer or officers who installed the device and any officer or officers who accessed the device to obtain information from the network;

"(ii) the date and time the device was installed, the date and time the device was uninstalled, and the date, time, and duration of each time the device is accessed to obtain information;

"(iii) the configuration of the device at the time of its installation and any subsequent modification thereof; and

"(iv) any information which has been collected by the device. To the extent that the pen register or trap and trace device can be set automatically to record this information electronically, the record shall be maintained electronically throughout the installation and use of such device.

"(B) The record maintained under subparagraph (A) shall be provided ex parte and under seal to the court which entered the ex parte order authorizing the installation and use of the device within 30 days after termination of the order (including any extensions thereof)."

(2) CONTENTS OF ORDER.—Section 3123(b)(1) of title 18, United States Code, is amended—

(A) in subparagraph (A)—

(i) by inserting "or other facility" after "telephone line"; and

(ii) by inserting before the semicolon at the end "or applied"; and

(B) by striking subparagraph (C) and inserting the following:

"(C) the attributes of the communications to which the order applies, including the number or other identifier and, if known, the location of the telephone line or other facility to which the pen register or trap and trace device is to be attached or applied, and, in the case of an order authorizing installation and use of a trap and trace device under subsection (a)(2), the geographic limits of the order; and".

(3) NONDISCLOSURE REQUIREMENTS.—Section 3123(d)(2) of title 18, United States Code, is amended—

(A) by inserting "or other facility" after "the line"; and

(B) by striking ", or who has been ordered by the court" and inserting "or applied, or who is obligated by the order".

(c) DEFINITIONS.—

(1) COURT OF COMPETENT JURISDICTION.—Section 3127(2) of title 18, United States Code, is amended by striking subparagraph (A) and inserting the following:

"(A) any district court of the United States (including a magistrate judge of such a court) or any United States court of appeals having jurisdiction over the offense being investigated; or".

(2) PEN REGISTER.—Section 3127(3) of title 18, United States Code, is amended—

(A) by striking "electronic or other impulses" and all that follows through "is attached" and inserting "dialing, routing, addressing, or signaling information transmitted by an instrument or facility from which a wire or electronic communication is transmitted, provided, however, that such information shall not include the contents of any communication"; and

(B) by inserting "or process" after "device" each place it appears.

(3) TRAP AND TRACE DEVICE.—Section 3127(4) of title 18, United States Code, is amended—

(A) by striking "of an instrument" and all that follows through the semicolon and inserting "or other dialing, routing, addressing, and signaling information reasonably likely to identify the source of a wire or electronic communication, provided, however, that such information shall not include the contents of any communication;"; and

(B) by inserting "or process" after "a device".

(4) CONFORMING AMENDMENT.—Section 3127(1) of title 18, United States Code, is amended—

(A) by striking "and"; and

(B) by inserting ", and 'contents' " after "electronic communication service".

(5) TECHNICAL AMENDMENT.—Section 3124(d) of title 18, United States Code, is amended by striking "the terms of".

(6) CONFORMING AMENDMENT.—Section 3124(b) of title 18, United States Code, is amended by inserting "or other facility" after "the appropriate line".

SEC. 217. INTERCEPTION OF COMPUTER TRESPASSER COMMUNICATIONS.

Chapter 119 of title 18, United States Code, is amended—

(1) in section 2510—

(A) in paragraph (18), by striking "and" at the end;

(B) in paragraph (19), by striking the period and inserting a semicolon; and

(C) by inserting after paragraph (19) the following:

"(20) 'protected computer' has the meaning set forth in section 1030; and

"(21) 'computer trespasser'—

"(A) means a person who accesses a protected computer without authorization and thus has no reasonable expectation of privacy in any communication transmitted to, through, or from the protected computer; and

"(B) does not include a person known by the owner or operator of the protected computer to have an existing contractual relationship with the owner or operator of the protected computer for access to all or part of the protected computer."; and

(2) in section 2511(2), by inserting at the end the following:

"(i) It shall not be unlawful under this chapter for a person acting under color of law to intercept the wire or electronic communications of a computer trespasser transmitted to, through, or from the protected computer, if—

"(I) the owner or operator of the protected computer authorizes the interception of the computer trespasser's communications on the protected computer;

"(II) the person acting under color of law is lawfully engaged in an investigation;

"(III) the person acting under color of law has reasonable grounds to believe that the contents of the computer trespasser's communications will be relevant to the investigation; and

"(IV) such interception does not acquire communications other than those transmitted to or from the computer trespasser".

SEC. 218. FOREIGN INTELLIGENCE INFORMATION.

Sections 104(a)(7)(B) and section 303(a)(7)(B) (50 U.S.C.1804(a)(7)(B) and 1823(a)(7)(B)) of the Foreign Intelligence Surveillance of 1978 are each amended by striking "the purpose" and inserting "a significant purpose".

SEC. 219. SINGLE-JURISDICTION SEARCH WARRANTS FOR TERRORISM.

Rule 41(a) of the Federal Rules of Criminal Procedure is amended by inserting after "executed" the following: "and (3) in an investigation of domestic terrorism or international terrorism (as defined in section 2331 of title 18, United States Code), by a Federal magistrate judge in any district in which activities related to the terrorism may have occurred, for a search of property or for a person within or outside the district."

SEC. 220. NATIONWIDE SERVICE OF SEARCH WARRANTS FOR ELECTRONIC EVIDENCE.

(a) IN GENERAL.—Chapter 121 of title 18, United States Code, is amended—

(1) in section 2703, by striking "under the Federal Rules of Criminal Procedure" every place it appears and inserting "using the procedures described in the Federal Rules of Criminal Procedure by a court with jurisdiction over the offense under investigation"; and

(2) in section 2711—

(A) in paragraph (1), by striking "and";

(B) in paragraph (2), by striking the period and inserting "; and"; and

(C) by inserting at the end the following:

"(3) the term 'court of competent jurisdiction' has the meaning assigned by section 3127, and includes any Federal court within that definition, without geographic limitation."

(b) CONFORMING AMENDMENT.—Section 2703(d) of title 18, United States Code, is amended by striking "described in section 3127(2)(A)."

. . .

SEC. 222. ASSISTANCE TO LAW ENFORCEMENT AGENCIES.

Nothing in this Act shall impose any additional technical obligation or requirement on a provider of a wire or electronic communication service or other person to furnish facilities or technical assistance. A provider of a wire or electronic communication service, landlord, custodian, or other person who furnishes facilities or technical assistance pursuant to section 216 shall be reasonably compensated for such reasonable expenditures incurred in providing such facilities or assistance.

SEC. 223. CIVIL LIABILITY FOR CERTAIN UNAUTHORIZED DISCLOSURES.

(a) Section 2520 of title 18, United States Code, is amended—

(1) in subsection (a), after "entity", by inserting ", other than the United States,";

(2) by adding at the end the following:

"(f) ADMINISTRATIVE DISCIPLINE.—If a court or appropriate department or agency determines that the United States or any of its departments or agencies has violated any provision of this chapter, and the court or appropriate department or agency finds that the circumstances surrounding the violation raise serious questions about whether or not an officer or employee of the United States acted willfully or intentionally with respect to the violation, the department or agency shall, upon receipt of a true and correct copy of the decision and findings of the court or appropriate department or agency promptly initiate a proceeding to determine whether disciplinary action against the officer or employee is warranted. If the head of the department or agency involved determines that disciplinary action is not warranted, he or she shall notify the Inspector General with jurisdiction over the department or agency concerned and shall provide the Inspector General with the reasons for such determination."; and

(3) by adding a new subsection (g), as follows:

"(g) IMPROPER DISCLOSURE IS VIOLATION.—Any willful disclosure or use by an investigative or law enforcement officer or governmental entity of information beyond the extent permitted by section 2517 is a violation of this chapter for purposes of section 2520(a)."

(b) Section 2707 of title 18, United States Code, is amended—

(1) in subsection (a), after "entity", by inserting ", other than the United States,";

(2) by striking subsection (d) and inserting the following:

"(d) ADMINISTRATIVE DISCIPLINE.—If a court or appropriate department or agency determines that the United States or any of its departments or agencies has violated any provision of this chapter, and the court or appropriate department or agency finds that the circumstances surrounding the violation raise serious questions about whether or not an officer or employee of the United States acted willfully or intentionally with respect to the violation, the department or agency shall, upon receipt of a true and correct copy of the decision and findings of the court or appropriate department or agency promptly initiate a proceeding to determine whether disciplinary action against the officer or employee is warranted. If the head of the department or agency involved determines that disciplinary action is not warranted, he or she shall notify the Inspector General with jurisdiction over the department or agency concerned and shall provide the Inspector General with the reasons for such determination."; and

(3) by adding a new subsection (g), as follows:

"(g) IMPROPER DISCLOSURE.—Any willful disclosure of a 'record', as that term is defined in section 552a(a) of title 5, United States Code, obtained by an investigative or law enforcement officer, or a governmental entity, pursuant to section 2703 of this title, or from a device installed pursuant to section 3123 or 3125 of this title, that is not a disclosure made in the proper performance of the official functions of the officer or governmental entity making the disclosure, is a violation of this chapter. This provision shall not apply to information previously lawfully disclosed (prior to the commencement of any civil or administrative proceeding under this chapter) to the public by a Federal, State, or local governmental entity or by the plaintiff in a civil action under this chapter."

(c)(1) Chapter 121 of title 18, United States Code, is amended by adding at the end the following:

"§ 2712. Civil actions against the United States

"(a) IN GENERAL.—Any person who is aggrieved by any willful violation of this chapter or of chapter 119 of this title or of sections 106(a), 305(a), or 405(a) of the Foreign Intelligence Surveillance Act of 1978 (50 U.S.C. 1801 et seq.) may commence an action in United States District Court against the United States to recover money damages. In any such action, if a person who is aggrieved successfully establishes such a violation of this chapter or of chapter 119 of this title or of the above specific provisions of title 50, the Court may assess as damages—

"(1) actual damages, but not less than $10,000, which ever amount is greater; and

"(2) litigation costs, reasonably incurred.

"(b) PROCEDURES.—(1) Any action against the United States under this section may be commenced only after a claim is presented to the appropriate department or agency under the procedures of the Federal Tort Claims Act, as set forth in title 28, United States Code.

"(2) Any action against the United States under this section shall be forever barred unless it is presented in writing to the appropriate Federal agency within 2 years after such claim accrues or unless action is begun within 6 months after the date of mailing, by certified or registered mail, of notice of final denial of the claim by the agency to which it was presented. The claim shall accrue on the date upon which the claimant first has a reasonable opportunity to discover the violation.

"(3) Any action under this section shall be tried to the court without a jury.

"(4) Notwithstanding any other provision of law, the procedures set forth in section 106(f), 305(g), or 405(f) of the Foreign Intelligence Surveillance Act of 1978 (50 U.S.C. 1801 et seq.) shall be the exclusive means by which materials governed by those sections may be reviewed.

"(5) An amount equal to any award against the United States under this section shall be reimbursed by the department or agency concerned to the fund described in section 1304 of title 31, United States Code, out of any appropriation, fund, or other account (excluding any part of such appropriation, fund, or account that is available for the enforcement of any Federal law) that is available for the operating expenses of the department or agency concerned.

"(c) ADMINISTRATIVE DISCIPLINE.—If a court or appropriate department or agency determines that the United States or any of its departments or agencies has violated any provision of this chapter, and the court or appropriate department or agency finds that the circumstances surrounding the violation raise serious questions about whether or not an officer or employee of the United States acted willfully or intentionally with respect to the violation, the department or agency shall, upon receipt of a true and correct copy of the decision and findings of the court or appropriate department or agency promptly initiate a proceeding to determine whether disciplinary action against the officer or employee is warranted. If the head of the department or agency involved determines that disciplinary action is not warranted, he or she shall notify the Inspector General with jurisdiction over the department or agency concerned and shall provide the Inspector General with the reasons for such determination.

"(d) EXCLUSIVE REMEDY.—Any action against the United States under this subsection shall be the exclusive remedy against the United States for any claims within the purview of this section.

"(e) STAY OF PROCEEDINGS.—(1) Upon the motion of the United States, the court shall stay any action commenced under this section if the court determines that civil discovery will adversely affect the ability of the Government to conduct a related investigation or the prosecution of a related criminal case. Such a stay shall toll the limitations periods of paragraph (2) of subsection (b)

"(2) In this subsection, the terms 'related criminal case' and 'related investigation' mean an actual prosecution or investigation in progress at the time at which the request for the stay or any subsequent motion to lift the stay is made. In determining whether an investigation or a criminal case is related to an action commenced under this section, the court shall consider the degree of similarity between the parties, witnesses, facts, and circumstances involved in the 2 proceedings, without requiring that any one or more factors be identical.

"(3) In requesting a stay under paragraph (1), the Government may, in appropriate cases, submit evidence ex parte in order to avoid disclosing any matter that may adversely affect a related investigation or a related criminal case. If the Government makes such an ex parte submission, the plaintiff shall be given an opportunity to make a submission to the court, not ex parte, and the court may, in its discretion, request further information from either party."

(2) The table of sections at the beginning of chapter 121 is amended to read as follows:

"2712. Civil action against the United States."

SEC. 224. SUNSET.

(a) IN GENERAL.—Except as provided in subsection (b), this title and the amendments made by this title (other than sections 203(a), 203(c), 205, 208, 210, 211, 213, 216, 219, 221, and 222, and the amendments made by those sections) shall cease to have effect on December 31, 2005.

(b) EXCEPTION.—With respect to any particular foreign intelligence investigation that began before the date on which the provisions referred to in subsection (a) cease to have effect, or with respect to any particular offense or potential offense that began or occurred before the date on which such provisions cease to have effect, such provisions shall continue in effect.

SEC. 225. IMMUNITY FOR COMPLIANCE WITH FISA WIRETAP.

Section 105 of the Foreign Intelligence Surveillance Act of 1978 (50 U.S.C. 1805) is amended by inserting after subsection (g) the following:

"(h) No cause of action shall lie in any court against any provider of a wire or electronic communication service, landlord, custodian, or other person (including any officer, employee, agent, or other specified person thereof) that furnishes any information, facilities, or technical assistance in accordance with a court order or request for emergency assistance under this Act."

TITLE III—INTERNATIONAL MONEY LAUNDERING ABATEMENT AND ANTITERRORIST FINANCING ACT OF 2001

SEC. 301. SHORT TITLE.

This title may be cited as the "International Money Laundering Abatement and Financial Anti-Terrorism Act of 2001."

SEC. 302. FINDINGS AND PURPOSES.

(a) FINDINGS.—The Congress finds that—

(1) money laundering, estimated by the International Monetary Fund to amount to between 2 and 5 percent of global gross domestic product, which is at least $600,000,000,000 annually, provides the financial fuel that permits transnational criminal enterprises to conduct and expand their operations to the detriment of the safety and security of American citizens;

(2) money laundering, and the defects in financial transparency on which money launderers rely, are critical to the financing of global terrorism and the provision of funds for terrorist attacks;

(3) money launderers subvert legitimate financial mechanisms and banking relationships by using them as protective covering for the movement of criminal proceeds and the financing of crime and terrorism, and, by so doing, can threaten the safety of United States citizens and undermine the integrity of United States financial institutions and of the global financial and trading systems upon which prosperity and growth depend;

(4) certain jurisdictions outside of the United States that offer "offshore" banking and related facilities designed to provide anonymity, coupled with weak financial supervisory and enforcement regimes, provide essential tools to disguise ownership and movement of criminal funds, derived from, or used to commit, offenses ranging from narcotics trafficking, terrorism, arms smuggling, and trafficking in human beings, to financial frauds that prey on law-abiding citizens;

(5) transactions involving such offshore jurisdictions make it difficult for law enforcement officials and regulators to follow the trail of money earned by criminals, organized international criminal enterprises, and global terrorist organizations;

(6) correspondent banking facilities are one of the banking mechanisms susceptible in some circumstances to manipulation by foreign banks to permit the laundering of funds by hiding the identity of real parties in interest to financial transactions;

(7) private banking services can be susceptible to manipulation by money launderers, for example corrupt foreign government officials, particularly if those services include the creation of offshore accounts and facilities for large personal funds transfers to channel funds into accounts around the globe;

(8) United States anti-money laundering efforts are impeded by outmoded and inadequate statutory provisions that make investigations, prosecutions, and forfeitures more difficult, particularly in cases in which money laundering involves foreign persons, foreign banks, or foreign countries;

(9) the ability to mount effective counter-measures to international money launderers requires national, as well as bilateral and multilateral action, using tools specially designed for that effort; and (10) the Basle Committee on Banking Regulation and Supervisory Practices and the Financial Action Task Forceey Laundering, of both of which the United States is a member, have each adopted international anti-money laundering principles and recommendations.

(b) PURPOSES.—The purposes of this title are—

(1) to increase the strength of United States measures to prevent, detect, and prosecute international money laundering and the financing of terrorism;

(2) to ensure that—

(A) banking transactions and financial relationships and the conduct of such transactions and relationships, do not contravene the purposes of subchapter II of chapter 53 of title 31, United States Code, section 21 of the Federal Deposit Insurance Act, or chapter 2 of title I of Public Law 91–508 (84 Stat. 1116), or facilitate the evasion of any such provision; and

(B) the purposes of such provisions of law continue to be fulfilled, and such provisions of law are effectively and efficiently administered;

(3) to strengthen the provisions put into place by the Money Laundering Control Act of 1986 (18 U.S.C. 981 note), especially on-United States nationals and foreign financial institutions;

(4) to provide a clear national mandate for subjecting to special scrutiny those foreign jurisdictions, financial institutions operating outside of the United States, and classes of international transactions or types of accounts that pose particular, identifiable opportunities for criminal abuse;

(5) to provide the Secretary of the Treasury (in this title referred to as the "Secretary") with broad discretion, subject to the safeguards provided by the Administrative Procedure Act under title 5, United States Code, to take measures tailored to the particular money laundering problems presented by specific foreign jurisdictions, financial institutions operating outside of the United States, and classes of international transactions or types of accounts;

(6) to ensure that the employment of such measures by the Secretary permits appropriate opportunity for comment by affected financial institutions;

(7) to provide guidance to domestic financial institutions on particular foreign jurisdictions, financial institutions operating outside of the United States, and classes of international transactions that are of primary money laundering concern to the United States Government;

(8) to ensure that the forfeiture of any assets in connection with the anti-terrorist efforts of the United States permits for adequate challenge consistent with providing due process rights;

(9) to clarify the terms of the safe harbor from civil liability for filing suspicious activity reports;

(10) to strengthen the authority of the Secretary to issue and administer geographic targeting orders, and to clarify that violations of such orders or any other requirement imposed under the authority contained in chapter 2 of title I of Public Law 91–508 and subchapters II and III of chapter 53 of title 31, United States Code, may result in criminal and civil penalties;

(11) to ensure that all appropriate elements of the financial services industry are subject to appropriate requirements to report potential money laundering transactions to proper authorities, and that jurisdictional disputes do not hinder examination of compliance by financial institutions with relevant reporting requirements;

(12) to strengthen the ability of financial institutions to maintain the integrity of their employee population; and

(13) to strengthen measures to prevent the use of the United States financial system for personal gain by corrupt foreign officials and to facilitate the repatriation of any stolen assets to the citizens of countries to whom such assets belong.

SEC. 303. 4-YEAR CONGRESSIONAL REVIEW; EXPEDITED CONSIDERATION.

(a) IN GENERAL.—Effective on and after the first day of fiscal year 2005, the provisions of this title and the amendments made by this title shall terminate if the Congress enacts a joint resolution, the text after the resolving clause of which is as follows: "That provisions of the International Money Laundering Abatement and Anti-Terrorist Financing Act of 2001, and the amendments made thereby, shall no longer have the force of law."

(b) EXPEDITED CONSIDERATION.—Any joint resolution submitted pursuant to this section should be considered by the Congress expeditiously. In particular, it shall be considered in the Senate in accordance with the provisions of section 601(b) of the International Security Assistance and Arms Control Act of 1976.

Subtitle A—International Counter Money Laundering and Related Measures

SEC. 311. SPECIAL MEASURES FOR JURISDICTIONS, FINANCIAL INSTITUTIONS, OR INTERNATIONAL TRANSACTIONS OF PRIMARY MONEY LAUNDERING CONCERN.

(a) IN GENERAL.—Subchapter II of chapter 53 of title 31, United States Code, is amended by inserting after section 5318 the following new section:

"§ 5318A. Special measures for jurisdictions, financial institutions, or international transactions of primary money laundering concern

"(a) INTERNATIONAL COUNTER-MONEY LAUNDERING REQUIREMENTS.—

"(1) IN GENERAL.—The Secretary of the Treasury may require domestic financial institutions and domestic financial agencies to take 1 or more of the special measures described in subsection (b) if the Secretary finds that reasonable grounds exist for concluding that a jurisdiction outside of the United States, 1 or more financial institutions operating outside of the United States, 1 or more classes of transactions within, or involving, a jurisdiction outside of the United States, or 1 or more types of accounts is of primary money laundering concern, in accordance with subsection (c).

"(2) FORM OF REQUIREMENT.—The special measures described in—

"(A) subsection (b) may be imposed in such sequence or combination as the Secretary shall determine;

"(B) paragraphs (1) through (4) of subsection (b) may be imposed by regulation, order, or otherwise as permitted by law; and

"(C) subsection (b)(5) may be imposed only by regulation.

"(3) DURATION OF ORDERS; RULEMAKING.—Any order by which a special measure described in paragraphs (1) through (4) of subsection (b) is imposed (other than an order described in section 5326)—

"(A) shall be issued together with a notice of proposed rulemaking relating to the imposition of such special measure; and

"(B) may not remain in effect for more than 120 days, except pursuant to a rule promulgated on or before the end of the 120-day period beginning on the date of issuance of such order.

"(4) PROCESS FOR SELECTING SPECIAL MEASURES.—In selecting which special measure or measures to take under this subsection, the Secretary of the Treasury—

"(A) shall consult with the Chairman of the Board of Governors of the Federal Reserve System, any other appropriate Federal banking agency, as defined in section 3 of the Federal Deposit Insurance Act, the Secretary of State, the Securities and Exchange Commission, the Commodity Futures Trading Commission, the National Credit Union Administration Board, and in the sole discretion of the Secretary, such other agencies and interested parties as the Secretary may find to be appropriate; and

"(B) shall consider—

"(i) whether similar action has been or is being taken by other nations or multilateral groups;

"(ii) whether the imposition of any particular special measure would create a significant competitive disadvantage, including any undue cost or burden associated with compliance, for financial institutions organized or licensed in the United States;

"(iii) the extent to which the action or the timing of the action would have a significant adverse systemic impact on the international payment, clearance, and settlement system, or on legitimate business activities involving the particular jurisdiction, institution, or class of transactions; and

"(iv) the effect of the action on United States national security and foreign policy.

"(5) NO LIMITATION ON OTHER AUTHORITY.—This section shall not be construed as superseding or otherwise restricting any other authority granted to the Secretary, or to any other agency, by this subchapter or otherwise.

"(b) SPECIAL MEASURES.—The special measures referred to in subsection (a), with respect to a jurisdiction outside of the United States, financial institution operating outside of the United States, class of transaction within, or involving, a jurisdiction outside of the United States, or 1 or more types of accounts are as follows:

"(1) RECORDKEEPING AND REPORTING OF CERTAIN FINANCIAL TRANSACTIONS.—

"(A) IN GENERAL.—The Secretary of the Treasury may require any domestic financial institution or domestic financial agency to maintain records, file reports, or both, concerning the aggregate amount of transactions, or concerning each transaction, with respect to a jurisdiction outside of the United States, 1 or more financial institutions operating outside of the United States, 1 or more classes of transactions within, or involving, a jurisdiction outside of the United States, or 1 or more types of accounts if the Secretary finds any such jurisdiction, institution, or class of transactions to be of primary money laundering concern.

"(B) FORM OF RECORDS AND REPORTS.—Such records and reports shall be made and retained at such time, in such manner, and for such period of time, as the Secretary shall determine, and shall include such information as the Secretary may determine, including—

"(i) the identity and address of the participants in a transaction or relationship, including the identity of the originator of any funds transfer;

"(ii) the legal capacity in which a participant in any transaction is acting;

"(iii) the identity of the beneficial owner of the funds involved in any transaction, in accordance with such procedures as the Secretary determines to be reasonable and practicable to obtain and retain the information; and

"(iv) a description of any transaction.

"(2) INFORMATION RELATING TO BENEFICIAL OWNERSHIP.—
In addition to any other requirement under any other provision of law, the Secretary may require any domestic financial institution or domestic financial agency to take such steps as the Secretary may determine to be reasonable and practicable to obtain and retain information concerning the beneficial ownership of any account opened or maintained in the United States by a foreign person (other than a foreign entity whose shares are subject to public reporting requirements or are listed and traded on a regulated exchange or trading market), or a representative of such a foreign person, that involves a jurisdiction outside of the United States, 1 or more financial institutions operating outside of the United States, 1 or more classes of transactions within, or involving, a jurisdiction outside of the United States, or 1 or more types of accounts if the Secretary finds any such jurisdiction, institution, or transaction or type of account to be of primary money laundering concern.

"(3) INFORMATION RELATING TO CERTAIN PAYABLE-THROUGH ACCOUNTS.—If the Secretary finds a jurisdiction outside of the United States, 1 or more financial institutions operating outside of the United States, or 1 or more classes of transactions within, or involving, a jurisdiction outside of the United States to be of primary money laundering concern, the Secretary may require any domestic financial institution or domestic financial agency that opens or maintains a payable-through account in the United States for a foreign financial institution involving any such jurisdiction or any such financial institution operating outside of the United States, or a payable through account through which any such transaction may be conducted, as a condition of opening or maintaining such account—

"(A) to identify each customer (and representative of such customer) of such financial institution who is permitted to use, or whose transactions are routed through, such payable-through account; and

"(B) to obtain, with respect to each such customer (and each such representative), information that is substantially comparable to that which the depository institution obtains in the ordinary course of business with respect to its customers residing in the United States.

"(4) INFORMATION RELATING TO CERTAIN CORRESPONDENT ACCOUNTS.—If the Secretary finds a jurisdiction outside of the United States, 1 or more financial institutions operating outside of the United States, or 1 or more classes of transactions within, or involving, a jurisdiction outside of the United States to be of primary money laundering concern, the Secretary may require any domestic financial institution or domestic financial agency that opens or maintains a correspondent account in the United States for a foreign financial institution involving any such jurisdiction or any such financial institution operating outside of the United States, or a correspondent account through which any such transaction may be conducted, as a condition of opening or maintaining such account—

"(A) to identify each customer (and representative of such customer) of any such financial institution who is permitted to use, or whose transactions are routed through, such correspondent account; and

"(B) to obtain, with respect to each such customer (and each such representative), information that is substantially comparable to that which the depository institution obtains in the ordinary course of business with respect to its customers residing in the United States.

"(5) PROHIBITIONS OR CONDITIONS ON OPENING OR MAINTAINING CERTAIN CORRESPONDENT OR PAYABLE-THROUGH ACCOUNTS.—If the Secretary finds a jurisdiction outside of the United States, 1 or more financial institutions operating outside of the United States, or 1 or more classes of transactions within, or involving, a jurisdiction outside of the United States to be of primary money laundering concern, the Secretary, in consultation with the Secretary of State, the Attorney General, and the Chairman of the Board of Governors of the Federal Reserve System, may prohibit, or impose conditions upon, the opening or maintaining in the United States of a correspondent account or payable-through account by any domestic financial institution or domestic financial agency for or on behalf a foreign banking institution, if such correspondent account or payable-through account involves any such jurisdiction or institution, or if any such transaction may be conducted through such correspondent account or payable-through account.

"(c) CONSULTATIONS AND INFORMATION TO BE CONSIDERED IN FINDING JURISDICTIONS, INSTITUTIONS, TYPES OF ACCOUNTS, OR TRANSACTIONS TO BE OF PRIMARY MONEY LAUNDERING CONCERN.—

"(1) IN GENERAL.—In making a finding that reasonable grounds exist for concluding that a jurisdiction outside of the United States, 1 or more financial institutions operating outside of the United States, 1 or more classes of transactions within, or involving, a jurisdiction outside of the United States, or 1 or more types of accounts is of primary money laundering concern so as to authorize the Secretary of the Treasury to take 1 or more of the special measures described in subsection (b), the Secretary shall consult with the Secretary of State and the Attorney General.

"(2) ADDITIONAL CONSIDERATIONS.—In making a finding described in paragraph (1), the Secretary shall consider in addition such information as the Secretary determines to be relevant, including the following potentially relevant factors:

"(A) JURISDICTIONAL FACTORS.—In the case of a particular jurisdiction—

"(i) evidence that organized criminal groups, international terrorists, or both, have transacted business in that jurisdiction;

"(ii) the extent to which that jurisdiction or financial institutions operating in that jurisdiction offer bank secrecy or special regulatory advantages to nonresidents or nondomiciliaries of that jurisdiction;

"(iii) the substance and quality of administration of the bank supervisory and counter-money laundering laws of that jurisdiction;

"(iv) the relationship between the volume of financial transactions occurring in that jurisdiction and the size of the economy of the jurisdiction;

"(v) the extent to which that jurisdiction is characterized as an offshore banking or secrecy haven by credible international organizations or multilateral expert groups;

"(vi) whether the United States has a mutual legal assistance treaty with that jurisdiction, and the experience of United States law enforcement officials and regulatory officials in obtaining information about transactions originating in or routed through or to such jurisdiction; and

"(vii) the extent to which that jurisdiction is characterized by high levels of official or institutional corruption.

"(B) INSTITUTIONAL FACTORS.—In the case of a decision to apply 1 or more of the special measures described in subsection (b) only to a financial institution or institutions, or to a transaction or class of transactions, or to a type of account, or to all 3, within or involving a particular jurisdiction—

"(i) the extent to which such financial institutions, transactions, or types of accounts are used to facilitate or promote money laundering in or through the jurisdiction;

"(ii) the extent to which such institutions, transactions, or types of accounts are used for legitimate business purposes in the jurisdiction; and "(iii) the extent to which such action is sufficient to ensure, with respect to transactions involving the jurisdiction and institutions operating in the jurisdiction, that the purposes of this subchapter continue to be fulfilled, and to guard against international money laundering and other financial crimes.

"(d) NOTIFICATION OF SPECIAL MEASURES INVOKED BY THE SECRETARY.—

Not later than 10 days after the date of any action taken by the Secretary of the Treasury under subsection (a)(1), the Secretary shall notify, in writing, the Committee on Financial Services of the House of Representatives and the Committee on Banking, Housing, and Urban Affairs of the Senate of any such action.

"(e) DEFINITIONS.—Notwithstanding any other provision of this subchapter, for purposes of this section and subsections (i) and (j) of section 5318, the following definitions shall apply:

"(1) BANK DEFINITIONS.—The following definitions shall apply with respect to a bank:

"(A) ACCOUNT.—The term 'account'—

"(i) means a formal banking or business relationship established to provide regular services, dealings, and other financial transactions; and

"(ii) includes a demand deposit, savings deposit, or other transaction or asset account and a credit account or other extension of credit.

"(B) CORRESPONDENT ACCOUNT.—The term 'correspondent account' means an account established to receive deposits from, make payments on behalf of a foreign financial institution, or handle other financial transactions related to such institution.

"(C) PAYABLE-THROUGH ACCOUNT.—The term 'payable through account' means an account, including a transaction account (as defined in section 19(b)(1)(C) of the Federal Reserve Act), opened at a depository institution by a foreign financial institution by means of which the foreign financial institution permits its customers to engage, either directly or through a subaccount, in banking activities usual in connection with the business of banking in the United States.

"(2) DEFINITIONS APPLICABLE TO INSTITUTIONS OTHER THAN BANKS.—With respect to any financial institution other than a bank, the Secretary shall, after consultation with the appropriate Federal functional regulators (as defined in section 509 of the Gramm-Leach-Bliley Act), define by regulation the term 'account', and shall include within the meaning of that term, to the extent, if any, that the Secretary deems appropriate, arrangements similar to payable-through and correspondent accounts.

"(3) REGULATORY DEFINITION OF BENEFICIAL OWNERSHIP.—

The Secretary shall promulgate regulations defining beneficial ownership of an account for purposes of this section and subsections (i) and (j) of section 5318. Such regulations shall address issues related to an individual's authority to fund, direct, or manage the account (including, without limitation, the power to direct payments into or out of the account), and an individual's material interest in the income or corpus of the account, and shall ensure that the identification of individuals under this section does not extend to any individual whose beneficial interest in the income or corpus of the account is immaterial.

"(4) OTHER TERMS.—The Secretary may, by regulation, further define the terms in paragraphs (1), (2), and (3), and define other terms for the purposes of this section, as the Secretary deems appropriate."

(b) CLERICAL AMENDMENT.—The table of sections for subchapter II of chapter 53 of title 31, United States Code, is amended by inserting after the item relating to section 5318 the following new item:

"5318A. Special measures for jurisdictions, financial institutions, or international transactions of primary money laundering concern."

SEC. 312. SPECIAL DUE DILIGENCE FOR CORRESPONDENT ACCOUNTS AND PRIVATE BANKING ACCOUNTS.

(a) IN GENERAL.—Section 5318 of title 31, United States Code, is amended by adding at the end the following:

"(i) DUE DILIGENCE FOR UNITED STATES PRIVATE BANKING AND CORRESPONDENT BANK ACCOUNTS INVOLVING FOREIGN PERSONS.—

"(1) IN GENERAL.—Each financial institution that establishes, maintains, administers, or manages a private banking account or a correspondent account in the United States for a non-United States person, including a foreign individual visiting the United States, or a representative of a non-United States person shall establish appropriate, specific, and, where necessary, enhanced, due diligence policies, procedures, and controls that are reasonably designed to detect and report instances of money laundering through those accounts.

"(2) ADDITIONAL STANDARDS FOR CERTAIN CORRESPONDENT ACCOUNTS.—

"(A) IN GENERAL.—Subparagraph (B) shall apply if a correspondent account is requested or maintained by, or on behalf of, a foreign bank operating—

"(i) under an offshore banking license; or

"(ii) under a banking license issued by a foreign country that has been designated—

"(I) as noncooperative with international antimoney laundering principles or procedures by an intergovernmental group or organization of which the United States is a member, with which designation the United States representative to the group or organization concurs; or

"(II) by the Secretary of the Treasury as warranting special measures due to money laundering concerns.

"(B) POLICIES, PROCEDURES, AND CONTROLS.—The enhanced due diligence policies, procedures, and controls required under paragraph (1) shall, at a minimum, ensure that the financial institution in the United States takes reasonable steps—

"(i) to ascertain for any such foreign bank, the shares of which are not publicly traded, the identity of each of the owners of the foreign bank, and the nature and extent of the ownership interest of each such owner;

"(ii) to conduct enhanced scrutiny of such account to guard against money laundering and report any suspicious transactions under subsection (g); and

"(iii) to ascertain whether such foreign bank provides correspondent accounts to other foreign banks and, if so, the identity of those foreign banks and related due diligence information, as appropriate under paragraph (1).

"(3) MINIMUM STANDARDS FOR PRIVATE BANKING ACCOUNTS.—If a private banking account is requested or maintained by, or on behalf of, a non-United States person, then the due diligence policies, procedures, and controls required under paragraph (1) shall, at a minimum, ensure that the financial institution takes reasonable steps—

"(A) to ascertain the identity of the nominal and beneficial owners of, and the source of funds deposited into, such account as needed to guard against money laundering and report any suspicious transactions under subsection (g); and

"(B) to conduct enhanced scrutiny of any such account that is requested or maintained by, or on behalf of, a senior foreign political figure, or any immediate family member or close associate of a senior foreign political figure that is reasonably designed to detect and report transactions that may involve the proceeds of foreign corruption.

"(4) DEFINITION.—For purposes of this subsection, the following definitions shall apply:

"(A) OFFSHORE BANKING LICENSE.—The term 'offshore banking license' means a license to conduct banking activities which, as a condition of the license, prohibits the licensed entity from conducting banking activities with the citizens of, or with the local currency of, the country which issued the license.

"(B) PRIVATE BANKING ACCOUNT.—The term 'private banking account' means an account (or any combination of accounts) that—

"(i) requires a minimum aggregate deposits of funds or other assets of not less than $1,000,000;

"(ii) is established on behalf of 1 or more individuals who have a direct or beneficial ownership interest in the account; and

"(iii) is assigned to, or is administered or managed by, in whole or in part, an officer, employee, or agent of a financial institution acting as a liaison between the financial institution and the direct or beneficial owner of the account."

(b) REGULATORY AUTHORITY AND EFFECTIVE DATE.—

(1) REGULATORY AUTHORITY.—Not later than 180 days after the date of enactment of this Act, the Secretary, in consultation with the appropriate Federal functional regulators (as defined in section 509 of the Gramm-Leach-Bliley Act) of the affected financial institutions, shall further delineate, by regulation, the due diligence policies, procedures, and controls required under section 5318(i)(1) of title 31, United States Code, as added by this section.

(2) EFFECTIVE DATE.—Section 5318(i) of title 31, United States Code, as added by this section, shall take effect 270 days after the date of enactment of this Act, whether or not final regulations are issued under paragraph (1), and the failure to issue such regulations shall in no way affect the enforceability of this section or the amendments made by this section. Section 5318(i) of title 31, United States Code, as added by this

section, shall apply with respect to accounts covered by that section 5318(i), that are opened before, on, or after the date of enactment of this Act.

SEC. 313. PROHIBITION ON UNITED STATES CORRESPONDENT ACCOUNTS WITH FOREIGN SHELL BANKS.

(a) IN GENERAL.—Section 5318 of title 31, United States Code, as amended by this title, is amended by adding at the end the following:

"(j) PROHIBITION ON UNITED STATES CORRESPONDENT ACCOUNTS WITH FOREIGN SHELL BANKS.—

"(1) IN GENERAL.—A financial institution described in subparagraphs (A) through (G) of section 5312(a)(2) (in this subsection referred to as a 'covered financial institution') shall not establish, maintain, administer, or manage a correspondent account in the United States for, or on behalf of, a foreign bank that does not have a physical presence in any country.

"(2) PREVENTION OF INDIRECT SERVICE TO FOREIGN SHELL BANKS.—A covered financial institution shall take reasonable steps to ensure that any correspondent account established, maintained, administered, or managed by that covered financial institution in the United States for a foreign bank is not being used by that foreign bank to indirectly provide banking services to another foreign bank that does not have a physical presence in any country. The Secretary of the Treasury shall, by regulation, delineate the reasonable steps necessary to comply with this paragraph.

"(3) EXCEPTION.—Paragraphs (1) and (2) do not prohibit a covered financial institution from providing a correspondent account to a foreign bank, if the foreign bank—

"(A) is an affiliate of a depository institution, credit union, or foreign bank that maintains a physical presence in the United States or a foreign country, as applicable; and

"(B) is subject to supervision by a banking authority in the country regulating the affiliated depository institution, credit union, or foreign bank described in subparagraph (A), as applicable.

"(4) DEFINITIONS.—For purposes of this subsection—

"(A) the term 'affiliate' means a foreign bank that is controlled by or is under common control with a depository institution, credit union, or foreign bank; and

"(B) the term 'physical presence' means a place of business that—

"(i) is maintained by a foreign bank;

"(ii) is located at a fixed address (other than solely an electronic address) in a country in which the foreign bank is authorized to conduct banking activities, at which location the foreign bank—

"(I) employs 1 or more individuals on a fulltime basis; and

"(II) maintains operating records related to its banking activities; and

"(iii) is subject to inspection by the banking authority which licensed the foreign bank to conduct banking activities."

(b) EFFECTIVE DATE.—The amendment made by subsection (a) shall take effect at the end of the 60-day period beginning on the date of enactment of this Act.

SEC. 314. COOPERATIVE EFFORTS TO DETER MONEY LAUNDERING.

(a) COOPERATION AMONG FINANCIAL INSTITUTIONS, REGULATORY AUTHORITIES, AND LAW ENFORCEMENT AUTHORITIES.—

(1) REGULATIONS.—The Secretary shall, within 120 days after the date of enactment of this Act, adopt regulations to encourage further cooperation among financial institutions, their regulatory authorities, and law enforcement authorities, with the specific purpose of encouraging regulatory authorities and law enforcement authorities to share with financial institutions information regarding individuals, entities, and organizations engaged in or reasonably suspected based on credible evidence of engaging in terrorist acts or money laundering activities.

(2) COOPERATION AND INFORMATION SHARING PROCEDURES.—The regulations adopted under paragraph (1) may include or create procedures for cooperation and information sharing focusing on—

(A) matters specifically related to the finances of terrorist groups, the means by which terrorist groups transfer funds around the world and within the United States, including through the use of charitable organizations, nonprofit organizations, and nongovernmental organizations, and the extent to which financial institutions in the United States are unwittingly involved in such finances and the extent to which such institutions are at risk as a result;

B) the relationship, particularly the financial relationship, between international narcotics traffickers and foreign terrorist organizations, the extent to which their memberships overlap and engage in joint activities, and the extent to which they cooperate with each other in raising and transferring funds for their respective purposes; and

(C) means of facilitating the identification of accounts and transactions involving terrorist groups and facilitating the exchange of information concerning such accounts and transactions between financial institutions and law enforcement organizations.

(3) CONTENTS.—The regulations adopted pursuant to paragraph (1) may—

(A) require that each financial institution designate 1 or more persons to receive information concerning, and to monitor accounts of individuals, entities, and organizations identified, pursuant to paragraph (1); and

(B) further establish procedures for the protection of the shared information, consistent with the capacity, size, and nature of the institution to which the particular procedures apply.

(4) RULE OF CONSTRUCTION.—The receipt of information by a financial institution pursuant to this section shall not relieve or otherwise modify the obligations of the financial institution with respect to any other person or account.

(5) USE OF INFORMATION.—Information received by a financial institution pursuant to this section shall not be used for any purpose other than identifying and reporting on activities that may involve terrorist acts or money laundering activities.

(b) COOPERATION AMONG FINANCIAL INSTITUTIONS.—Upon notice provided to the Secretary, 2 or more financial institutions and any association of financial institutions may share information with one another regarding individuals, entities, organizations, and countries suspected of possible terrorist or money laundering activities. A financial institution or association that transmits, receives, or shares such information for the purposes of identifying and reporting activities that may involve terrorist acts or money laundering activities shall not be liable to any person under any law or regulation of the United States, any constitution, law, or regulation of any State or political subdivision thereof, or under any contract or other legally enforceable agreement (including any arbitration agreement), for such disclosure or for any failure to provide notice of such disclosure to the person who is the subject of such disclosure, or any other person identified in the disclosure, except where such transmission, receipt, or sharing violates this section or regulations promulgated pursuant to this section.

(c) RULE OF CONSTRUCTION.—Compliance with the provisions of this title requiring or allowing financial institutions and any association of financial institutions to disclose or share information regarding individuals, entities, and organizations engaged in or suspected of engaging in terrorist acts or money laundering activities shall not constitute a violation of the provisions of title V of the Gramm-Leach-Bliley Act (Public Law 106–102).

(d) REPORTS TO THE FINANCIAL SERVICES INDUSTRY ON SUSPICIOUS FINANCIAL ACTIVITIES.—At least semiannually, the Secretary shall—

(1) publish a report containing a detailed analysis identifying patterns of suspicious activity and other investigative insights derived from suspicious activity reports and investigations conducted by Federal, State, and local law enforcement agencies to the extent appropriate; and

(2) distribute such report to financial institutions (as defined in section 5312 of title 31, United States Code).

SEC. 315. INCLUSION OF FOREIGN CORRUPTION OFFENSES AS MONEY LAUNDERING CRIMES.

Section 1956(c)(7) of title 18, United States Code, is amended—

(1) in subparagraph (B)—

(A) in clause (ii), by striking "or destruction of property by means of explosive or fire" and inserting "destruction of property by means of explosive or fire, or a crime of violence (as defined in section 16)";

(B) in clause (iii), by striking "1978" and inserting "1978)"; and

(C) by adding at the end the following:

"(iv) bribery of a public official, or the misappropriation, theft, or embezzlement of public funds by or for the benefit of a public official;

"(v) smuggling or export control violations involving—

"(I) an item controlled on the United States Munitions List established under section 38 of the Arms Export Control Act (22 U.S.C. 2778); or

"(II) an item controlled under regulations under the Export Administration Regulations (15 C.F.R. Parts 730–774); or

"(vi) an offense with respect to which the United States would be obligated by a multilateral treaty, either to extradite the alleged offender or to submit the case for prosecution, if the offender were found within the territory of the United States;"; and

(2) in subparagraph (D)—

(A) by inserting "section 541 (relating to goods falsely classified)," before "section 542";

(B) by inserting "section 922(1) (relating to the unlawful importation of firearms), section 924(n) (relating to firearms trafficking)," before "section 956";

(C) by inserting "section 1030 (relating to computer fraud and abuse)," before "1032"; and

(D) by inserting "any felony violation of the Foreign Agents Registration Act of 1938," before "or any felony violation of the Foreign Corrupt Practices Act".

SEC. 316. ANTI-TERRORIST FORFEITURE PROTECTION.

(a) RIGHT TO CONTEST.—An owner of property that is confiscated under any provision of law relating to the confiscation of assets of suspected international terrorists, may contest that confiscation by filing a claim in the manner set forth in the Federal Rules of Civil Procedure (Supplemental Rules for Certain Admiralty and Maritime Claims), and asserting as an affirmative defense that—

(1) the property is not subject to confiscation under such provision of law; or

(2) the innocent owner provisions of section 983(d) of title 18, United States Code, apply to the case.

(b) EVIDENCE.—In considering a claim filed under this section, a court may admit evidence that is otherwise inadmissible under the Federal Rules of Evidence, if the court determines that the evidence is reliable, and that compliance with the Federal Rules of Evidence may jeopardize the national security interests of the United States.

(c) CLARIFICATIONS.—

(1) PROTECTION OF RIGHTS.—The exclusion of certain provisions of Federal law from the definition of the term "civil forfeiture statute" in section 983(i) of title 18, United States Code, shall not be construed to deny an owner of property the right to contest the confiscation of assets of suspected international terrorists under—

(A) subsection (a) of this section;

(B) the Constitution; or

(C) subchapter II of chapter 5 of title 5, United States Code (commonly known as the "Administrative Procedure Act").

(2) SAVINGS CLAUSE.—Nothing in this section shall limit or otherwise affect any other remedies that may be available to an owner of property under section 983 of title 18, United States Code, or any other provision of law.

(d) TECHNICAL CORRECTION.—Section 983(i)(2)(D) of title 18, United States Code, is amended by inserting "or the International Emergency Economic Powers Act (IEEPA) (50 U.S.C. 1701 et seq.)" before the semicolon.

. . .

Subtitle B—Bank Secrecy Act Amendments and Related Improvements
SEC. 351. AMENDMENTS RELATING TO REPORTING OF SUSPICIOUS ACTIVITIES.

(a) AMENDMENT RELATING TO CIVIL LIABILITY IMMUNITY FOR DISCLOSURES.—Section 5318(g)(3) of title 31, United States Code, is amended to read as follows:

"(3) LIABILITY FOR DISCLOSURES.—

"(A) IN GENERAL.—Any financial institution that makes a voluntary disclosure of any possible violation of law or regulation to a government agency or makes a disclosure pursuant to this subsection or any other authority, and any director, officer, employee, or agent of such institution who makes, or requires another to make any such disclosure, shall not be liable to any person under any law or regulation of the United States, any constitution, law, or regulation of any State or political subdivision of any State, or under any contract or other legally enforceable agreement (including any arbitration agreement), for such disclosure or for any failure to provide notice of such disclosure to the person who is the subject of such disclosure or any other person identified in the disclosure.

"(B) RULE OF CONSTRUCTION.—Subparagraph (A) shall not be construed as creating—

"(i) any inference that the term 'person', as used in such subparagraph, may be construed more broadly than its ordinary usage so as to include any government or agency of government; or

"(ii) any immunity against, or otherwise affecting, any civil or criminal action brought by any government or agency of government to enforce any constitution, law, or regulation of such government or agency."

(b) PROHIBITION ON NOTIFICATION OF DISCLOSURES.—Section 5318(g)(2) of title 31, United States Code, is amended to read as follows:

"(2) NOTIFICATION PROHIBITED.—

"(A) IN GENERAL.—If a financial institution or any director, officer, employee, or agent of any financial institution, voluntarily or pursuant to this section or any other authority, reports a suspicious transaction to a government agency—

"(i) the financial institution, director, officer, employee, or agent may not notify any person involved in the transaction that the transaction has been reported; and

"(ii) no officer or employee of the Federal Government or of any State, local, tribal, or territorial government within the United States, who has any knowledge that such report was made may disclose to any person involved in the transaction that the transaction has been reported, other than as necessary to fulfill the official duties of such officer or employee.

"(B) DISCLOSURES IN CERTAIN EMPLOYMENT REFERENCES.—

"(i) RULE OF CONSTRUCTION.—Notwithstanding the application of subparagraph (A) in any other context, subparagraph (A) shall not be construed as prohibiting any financial institution, or any director, officer, employee, or agent of such institution, from including information that was included in a report to which subparagraph (A) applies—

"(I) in a written employment reference that is provided in accordance with section 18(w) of the Federal Deposit Insurance Act in response to a request from another financial institution; or

"(II) in a written termination notice or employment reference that is provided in accordance with the rules of a self-regulatory organization registered with the Securities and Exchange Commission or the Commodity Futures Trading Commission, except that such written reference or notice may not disclose that such information was also included in any such report, or that such report was made.

"(ii) INFORMATION NOT REQUIRED.—Clause (i) shall not be construed, by itself, to create any affirmative duty to include any information described in clause (i) in any employment reference or termination notice referred to in clause (i)."

...

TITLE IV—PROTECTING THE BORDER
Subtitle A—Protecting the Northern Border

...

SEC. 403. ACCESS BY THE DEPARTMENT OF STATE AND THE INS TO CERTAIN IDENTIFYING INFORMATION IN THE CRIMINAL HISTORY RECORDS OF VISA APPLICANTS AND APPLICANTS FOR ADMISSION TO THE UNITED STATES.

(a) AMENDMENT OF THE IMMIGRATION AND NATIONALITY ACT.—

Section 105 of the Immigration and Nationality Act (8 U.S.C. 1105) is amended—

(1) in the section heading, by inserting "; DATA EXCHANGE" after "SECURITY OFFICERS";

(2) by inserting "(a)" after "SEC. 105.";

(3) in subsection (a), by inserting "and border" after "internal" the second place it appears; and

(4) by adding at the end the following:

"(b)(1) The Attorney General and the Director of the Federal Bureau of Investigation shall provide the Department of State and the Service access to the criminal history record information contained in the National Crime Information Center's Interstate Identification Index (NCIC-III), Wanted Persons File, and to any other files maintained by the National Crime Information Center that may be mutually agreed upon by the Attorney General and the agency receiving the access, for the purpose of determining whether or not a visa applicant or applicant for admission has a criminal history record indexed in any such file.

"(2) Such access shall be provided by means of extracts of the records for placement in the automated visa lookout or other appropriate database, and shall be provided without any fee or charge.

"(3) The Federal Bureau of Investigation shall provide periodic updates of the extracts at intervals mutually agreed upon with the agency receiving the access. Upon receipt of such updated extracts, the receiving agency shall make corresponding updates to its database and destroy previously provided extracts.

"(4) Access to an extract does not entitle the Department of State to obtain the full content of the corresponding automated criminal history record. To obtain the full content of a criminal history record, the Department of State shall submit the applicant's fingerprints and any appropriate fingerprint processing fee authorized by law to the Criminal Justice Information Services Division of the Federal Bureau of Investigation.

"(c) The provision of the extracts described in subsection (b) may be reconsidered by the Attorney General and the receiving agency upon the development and deployment of a more cost-effective and efficient means of sharing the information.

"(d) For purposes of administering this section, the Department of State shall, prior to receiving access to NCIC data but not later than 4 months after the date of enactment of this subsection, promulgate final regulations—

"(1) to implement procedures for the taking of fingerprints; and

"(2) to establish the conditions for the use of the information received from the Federal Bureau of Investigation, in order—

"(A) to limit the redissemination of such information;

"(B) to ensure that such information is used solely to determine whether or not to issue a visa to an alien or to admit an alien to the United States;

"(C) to ensure the security, confidentiality, and destruction of such information; and

"(D) to protect any privacy rights of individuals who are subjects of such information."

(b) REPORTING REQUIREMENT.—Not later than 2 years after the date of enactment of this Act, the Attorney General and the Secretary of State jointly shall report to Congress on the implementation of the amendments made by this section.

(c) TECHNOLOGY STANDARD TO CONFIRM IDENTITY.—

(1) IN GENERAL.—The Attorney General and the Secretary of State jointly, through the National Institute of Standards and Technology (NIST), and in consultation with the Secretary of the Treasury and other Federal law enforcement and intelligence agencies the Attorney General or Secretary of State deems appropriate and in consultation with Congress, shall within 2 years after the date of the enactment of this section, develop and certify a technology standard that can be used to verify the identity of persons applying for a United States visa or such persons seeking to enter the United States pursuant to a visa for the purposes of conducting background checks, confirming identity, and ensuring that a person has not received a visa under a different name or such person seeking to enter the United States pursuant to a visa.

(2) INTEGRATED.—The technology standard developed pursuant to paragraph (1), shall be the technological basis for a cross-agency, cross-platform electronic system that is a cost-effective, efficient, fully integrated means to share law enforcement and intelligence information necessary to confirm the identity of such persons applying for a United States visa or such person seeking to enter the United States pursuant to a visa.

(3) ACCESSIBLE.—The electronic system described in paragraph (2), once implemented, shall be readily and easily accessible to—

(A) all consular officers responsible for the issuance of visas;

(B) all Federal inspection agents at all United States border inspection points; and

(C) all law enforcement and intelligence officers as determined by regulation to be responsible for investigation or identification of aliens admitted to the United States pursuant to a visa.

(4) REPORT.—Not later than 18 months after the date of the enactment of this Act, and every 2 years thereafter, the Attorney General and the Secretary of State shall jointly, in consultation with the Secretary of Treasury, report to Congress describing the development, implementation, efficacy, and privacy implications of the technology standard and electronic database system described in this subsection.

(5) FUNDING.—There is authorized to be appropriated to the Secretary of State, the Attorney General, and the Director of the National Institute of Standards and Technology such sums as may be necessary to carry out the provisions of this subsection.

(d) STATUTORY CONSTRUCTION.—Nothing in this section, or in any other law, shall be construed to limit the authority of the Attorney General or the Director of the Federal Bureau of Investigation to provide access to the criminal history record information contained in the National Crime Information Center's (NCIC) Interstate Identification Index (NCIC-III), or to any other information maintained by the NCIC, to any Federal agency or officer authorized to enforce or administer the immigration laws of the United States, for the purpose of such enforcement or administration, upon terms that are consistent with the National Crime Prevention and Privacy Compact Act of 1998 (subtitle A of title II of Public Law 105–251; 42 U.S.C. 14611–16) and section 552a of title 5, United States Code.

SEC. 404. LIMITED AUTHORITY TO PAY OVERTIME.

The matter under the headings "Immigration And Naturalization Service: Salaries and Expenses, Enforcement And Border Affairs" and "Immigration And Naturalization Service: Salaries and Expenses, Citizenship And Benefits, Immigration And Program Direction" in the Department of Justice Appropriations Act, 2001 (as enacted into law by Appendix B (H.R. 5548) of Public Law 106–553 (114 Stat. 2762A–58 to 2762A–59)) is amended by striking the following each place it occurs: "*Provided*, That none of the funds available to the Immigration and Naturalization Service shall be available to pay any employee overtime pay in an amount in excess of $30,000 during the calendar year beginning January 1, 2001:".

SEC. 405. REPORT ON THE INTEGRATED AUTOMATED FINGERPRINT IDENTIFICATION SYSTEM FOR PORTS OF ENTRY AND OVERSEAS CONSULAR POSTS.

(a) IN GENERAL.—The Attorney General, in consultation with the appropriate heads of other Federal agencies, including the Secretary of State, Secretary of the Treasury, and the Secretary of Transportation, shall report to Congress on the feasibility of enhancing the Integrated Automated Fingerprint Identification System (IAFIS) of the Federal Bureau of Investigation and other identification systems in order to better identify a person who holds a foreign passport or a visa and may be wanted in connection with a criminal investigation in the United States or abroad, before the issuance of a visa to that person or the entry or exit from the United States by that person.

(b) AUTHORIZATION OF APPROPRIATIONS.—There is authorized to be appropriated not less than $2,000,000 to carry out this section.

Subtitle B—Enhanced Immigration Provisions

SEC. 411. DEFINITIONS RELATING TO TERRORISM.

(a) GROUNDS OF INADMISSIBILITY.—Section 212(a)(3) of the Immigration and Nationality Act (8 U.S.C. 1182(a)(3)) is amended—

(1) in subparagraph (B)—

(A) in clause (i)—

(i) by amending subclause (IV) to read as follows:

"(IV) is a representative (as defined in clause (v)) of—

"(aa) a foreign terrorist organization, as designated by the Secretary of State under section 219, or

"(bb) a political, social or other similar group whose public endorsement of acts of terrorist activity the Secretary of State has determined undermines United States efforts to reduce or eliminate terrorist activities,";

(ii) in subclause (V), by inserting "or" after "section 219,"; and

(iii) by adding at the end the following new subclauses:

"(VI) has used the alien's position of prominence within any country to endorse or espouse terrorist activity, or to persuade others to support terrorist activity or a terrorist organization, in a way that the Secretary of State has determined undermines United States efforts to reduce or eliminate terrorist activities, or

"(VII) is the spouse or child of an alien who is inadmissible under this section, if the activity causing the alien to be found inadmissible occurred within the last 5 years,";

(B) by redesignating clauses (ii), (iii), and (iv) as clauses (iii), (iv), and (v), respectively;

(C) in clause (i)(II), by striking "clause (iii)" and inserting "clause (iv)";

(D) by inserting after clause (i) the following:

"(ii) EXCEPTION.—Subclause (VII) of clause (i) does not apply to a spouse or child—

"(I) who did not know or should not reasonably have known of the activity causing the alien to be found inadmissible under this section; or

"(II) whom the consular officer or Attorney General has reasonable grounds to believe has renounced the activity causing the alien to be found inadmissible under this section.";

(E) in clause (iii) (as redesignated by subparagraph (B))—

(i) by inserting "it had been" before "committed in the United States"; and

(ii) in subclause (V)(b), by striking "or firearm" and inserting ", firearm, or other weapon or dangerous device";

(F) by amending clause (iv) (as redesignated by subparagraph (B)) to read as follows:

"(iv) ENGAGE IN TERRORIST ACTIVITY DEFINED.—

As used in this chapter, the term 'engage in terrorist activity' means, in an individual capacity or as a member of an organization—

"(I) to commit or to incite to commit, under circumstances indicating an intention to cause death or serious bodily injury, a terrorist activity;

"(II) to prepare or plan a terrorist activity;

"(III) to gather information on potential targets for terrorist activity;

"(IV) to solicit funds or other things of value for—

"(aa) a terrorist activity;

"(bb) a terrorist organization described in clause (vi)(I) or (vi)(II); or

"(cc) a terrorist organization described in clause (vi)(III), unless the solicitor can demonstrate that he did not know, and should not reasonably have known, that the solicitation would further the organization's terrorist activity;

"(V) to solicit any individual—

"(aa) to engage in conduct otherwise described in this clause;

"(bb) for membership in a terrorist organization described in clause (vi)(I) or (vi)(II); or

"(cc) for membership in a terrorist organization described in clause (vi)(III), unless the solicitor can demonstrate that he did not know, and should not reasonably have known, that the solicitation would further the organization's terrorist activity; or

"(VI) to commit an act that the actor knows, or reasonably should know, affords material support, including a safe house, transportation, communications, funds, transfer of funds or other material financial benefit, false documentation or identification, weapons (including chemical, biological, or radiological weapons), explosives, or training—

"(aa) for the commission of a terrorist activity;

"(bb) to any individual who the actor knows, or reasonably should know, has committed or plans to commit a terrorist activity;

"(cc) to a terrorist organization described in clause (vi)(I) or (vi)(II); or

"(dd) to a terrorist organization described in clause (vi)(III), unless the actor can demonstrate that he did not know, and should not reasonably have known, that the act would further the organization's terrorist activity. This clause shall not apply to any material support the alien afforded to an organization or individual that has committed terrorist activity, if the Secretary of State, after consultation with the Attorney General, or the Attorney General, after consultation with the Secretary of State, concludes in his sole unreviewable discretion, that this clause should not apply."; and

(G) by adding at the end the following new clause:

"(vi) TERRORIST ORGANIZATION DEFINED.—As used in clause (i)(VI) and clause (iv), the term 'terrorist organization' means an organization—

"(I) designated under section 219;

"(II) otherwise designated, upon publication in the Federal Register, by the Secretary of State in consultation with or upon the request of the Attorney General, as a terrorist organization, after finding that the organization engages in the activities described in subclause (I), (II), or (III) of clause (iv), or that the organization provides material support to further terrorist activity; or

"(III) that is a group of two or more individuals, whether organized or not, which engages in the activities described in subclause (I), (II), or (III) of clause (iv)."; and

(2) by adding at the end the following new subparagraph:

"(F) ASSOCIATION WITH TERRORIST ORGANIZATIONS.—

Any alien who the Secretary of State, after consultation with the Attorney General, or the Attorney General, after consultation with the Secretary of State, determines has been associated with a terrorist organization and intends while in the United States to engage solely, principally, or incidentally in activities that could endanger the welfare, safety, or security of the United States is inadmissible."

(b) CONFORMING AMENDMENTS.—

(1) Section 237(a)(4)(B) of the Immigration and Nationality Act (8 U.S.C. 1227(a)(4)(B)) is amended by striking "section 212(a)(3)(B)(iii)" and inserting "section 212(a)(3)(B)(iv)".

(2) Section 208(b)(2)(A)(v) of the Immigration and Nationality Act (8 U.S.C. 1158(b)(2)(A)(v)) is amended by striking "or (IV)" and inserting "(IV), or (VI)".

. . .

(c) DESIGNATION OF FOREIGN TERRORIST ORGANIZATIONS.—Section 219(a) of the Immigration and Nationality Act (8 U.S.C. 1189(a)) is amended—

(1) in paragraph (1)(B), by inserting "or terrorism (as defined in section 140(d)(2) of the Foreign Relations Authorization Act, Fiscal Years 1988 and 1989 (22 U.S.C. 2656f(d)(2)), or retains the capability and intent to engage in terrorist activity or terrorism" after "212(a)(3)(B)";

(2) in paragraph (1)(C), by inserting "or terrorism" after "terrorist activity";

(3) by amending paragraph (2)(A) to read as follows:

"(A) NOTICE.—

"(i) TO CONGRESSIONAL LEADERS.—Seven days before making a designation under this subsection, the Secretary shall, by classified communication, notify the Speaker and Minority Leader of the House of Representatives, the President pro tempore, Majority Leader, and Minority Leader of the Senate, and the members of the relevant committees of the House of Representatives and the Senate, in writing, of the intent to designate an organization under this subsection, together with the findings made under paragraph (1) with respect to that organization, and the factual basis therefor.

"(ii) PUBLICATION IN FEDERAL REGISTER.—The Secretary shall publish the designation in the Federal Register seven days after providing the notification under clause (i).";

(4) in paragraph (2)(B)(i), by striking "subparagraph (A)" and inserting "subparagraph (A)(ii)";

(5) in paragraph (2)(C), by striking "paragraph (2)" and inserting "paragraph (2)(A)(i)";

(6) in paragraph (3)(B), by striking "subsection (c)" and inserting "subsection (b)";

(7) in paragraph (4)(B), by inserting after the first sentence the following: "The Secretary also may redesignate such organization at the end of any 2-year redesignation period (but not sooner than 60 days prior to the termination of such period) for an additional 2-year period upon a finding that the relevant circumstances described in paragraph (1) still exist. Any redesignation shall be effective immediately following the end of the prior 2-year designation or redesignation period unless a different effective date is provided in such redesignation.";

(8) in paragraph (6)(A)—

(A) by inserting "or a redesignation made under paragraph (4)(B)" after "paragraph (1)";

(B) in clause (i)—

(i) by inserting "or redesignation" after "designation" the first place it appears; and

(ii) by striking "of the designation"; and

(C) in clause (ii), by striking "of the designation"; (9) in paragraph (6)(B)—

(A) by striking "through (4)" and inserting "and (3)"; and

(B) by inserting at the end the following new sentence:

"Any revocation shall take effect on the date specified in the revocation or upon publication in the Federal Register if no effective date is specified.";

(10) in paragraph (7), by inserting ", or the revocation of a redesignation under paragraph (6)," after "paragraph (5) or (6)"; and

(11) in paragraph (8)—

(A) by striking "paragraph (1)(B)" and inserting "paragraph (2)(B), or if a redesignation under this subsection has become effective under paragraph (4)(B)";

(B) by inserting "or an alien in a removal proceeding" after "criminal action"; and

(C) by inserting "or redesignation" before "as a defense."

SEC. 412. MANDATORY DETENTION OF SUSPECTED TERRORISTS; HABEAS CORPUS; JUDICIAL REVIEW.

(a) IN GENERAL.—The Immigration and Nationality Act (8 U.S.C. 1101 et seq.) is amended by inserting after section 236 the following:

"MANDATORY DETENTION OF SUSPECTED TERRORISTS; HABEAS CORPUS; JUDICIAL REVIEW

"SEC. 236A. (a) DETENTION OF TERRORIST ALIENS.—

"(1) CUSTODY.—The Attorney General shall take into custody any alien who is certified under paragraph (3).

"(2) RELEASE.—Except as provided in paragraphs (5) and (6), the Attorney General shall maintain custody of such an alien until the alien is removed from the United States. Except as provided in paragraph (6), such custody shall be maintained irrespective of any relief from removal for which the alien may be eligible, or any relief from removal granted the alien, until the Attorney General determines that the alien is no longer an alien who may be certified under paragraph (3). If the alien is finally determined not to be removable, detention pursuant to this subsection shall terminate.

"(3) CERTIFICATION.—The Attorney General may certify an alien under this paragraph if the Attorney General has reasonable grounds to believe that the alien—

"(A) is described in section 212(a)(3)(A)(i), 212(a)(3)(A)(iii), 212(a)(3)(B), 237(a)(4)(A)(i), 237(a)(4)(A)(iii), or 237(a)(4)(B); or

"(B) is engaged in any other activity that endangers the national security of the United States.

"(4) NONDELEGATION.—The Attorney General may delegate the authority provided under paragraph (3) only to the Deputy Attorney General. The Deputy Attorney General may not delegate such authority.

"(5) COMMENCEMENT OF PROCEEDINGS.—The Attorney General shall place an alien detained under paragraph (1) in removal proceedings, or shall charge the alien with a criminal offense, not later than 7 days after the commencement of such detention. If the requirement of the preceding sentence is not satisfied, the Attorney General shall release the alien.

"(6) LIMITATION ON INDEFINITE DETENTION.—An alien detained solely under paragraph (1) who has not been removed under section 241(a)(1)(A), and whose removal is unlikely in the reasonably foreseeable future, may be detained for additional periods of up to six months only if the release of the alien will threaten the national security of the United States or the safety of the community or any person.

"(7) REVIEW OF CERTIFICATION.—The Attorney General shall review the certification made under paragraph (3) every 6 months. If the Attorney General determines, in the Attorney General's discretion, that the certification should be revoked, the alien may be released on such conditions as the Attorney General deems appropriate, unless such release is otherwise prohibited by law. The alien may request each 6 months in writing that the Attorney General reconsider the certification and may submit documents or other evidence in support of that request.

"(b) HABEAS CORPUS AND JUDICIAL REVIEW.—

"(1) IN GENERAL.—Judicial review of any action or decision relating to this section (including judicial review of the merits of a determination made under subsection (a)(3) or (a)(6)) is available exclusively in habeas corpus proceedings consistent with this subsection. Except as provided in the preceding sentence, no court shall have jurisdiction to review, by habeas corpus petition or otherwise, any such action or decision.

"(2) APPLICATION.—

"(A) IN GENERAL.—Notwithstanding any other provision of law, including section 2241(a) of title 28, United States Code, habeas corpus proceedings described in paragraph (1) may be initiated only by an application filed with—

"(i) the Supreme Court;

"(ii) any justice of the Supreme Court;

"(iii) any circuit judge of the United States Court of Appeals for the District of Columbia Circuit; or

"(iv) any district court otherwise having jurisdiction to entertain it.

"(B) APPLICATION TRANSFER.—Section 2241(b) of title 28, United States Code, shall apply to an application for a writ of habeas corpus described in subparagraph (A).

"(3) APPEALS.—Notwithstanding any other provision of law, including section 2253 of title 28, in habeas corpus proceedings described in paragraph (1) before a circuit or district judge, the final order shall be subject to review, on appeal, by the United States Court of Appeals for the District of Columbia Circuit. There shall be no right of appeal in such proceedings to any other circuit court of appeals.

"(4) RULE OF DECISION.—The law applied by the Supreme Court and the United States Court of Appeals for the District of Columbia Circuit shall be regarded as the rule of decision in habeas corpus proceedings described in paragraph (1).

"(c) STATUTORY CONSTRUCTION.—The provisions of this section shall not be applicable to any other provision of this Act."

(b) CLERICAL AMENDMENT.—The table of contents of the Immigration and Nationality Act is amended by inserting after the item relating to section 236 the following:
"Sec. 236A. Mandatory detention of suspected terrorist; habeas corpus; judicial review."

(c) REPORTS.—Not later than 6 months after the date of the enactment of this Act, and every 6 months thereafter, the Attorney General shall submit a report to the Committee on the Judiciary of the House of Representatives and the Committee on the Judiciary of the Senate, with respect to the reporting period, on—

(1) the number of aliens certified under section 236A(a)(3) of the Immigration and Nationality Act, as added by subsection (a);

(2) the grounds for such certifications;

(3) the nationalities of the aliens so certified;

(4) the length of the detention for each alien so certified; and

(5) the number of aliens so certified who—

(A) were granted any form of relief from removal;

(B) were removed;

(C) the Attorney General has determined are no longer aliens who may be so certified; or

(D) were released from detention.

SEC. 413. MULTILATERAL COOPERATION AGAINST TERRORISTS.

Section 222(f) of the Immigration and Nationality Act (8 U.S.C. 1202(f)) is amended—

(1) by striking "except that in the discretion of" and inserting the following: "except that—

"(1) in the discretion of"; and

(2) by adding at the end the following:

"(2) the Secretary of State, in the Secretary's discretion and on the basis of reciprocity, may provide to a foreign government information in the Department of State's computerized visa lookout database and, when necessary and appropriate, other records covered by this section related to information in the database—

"(A) with regard to individual aliens, at any time on a case-by-case basis for the purpose of preventing, investigating, or punishing acts that would constitute a crime in the United States, including, but not limited to, terrorism or trafficking in controlled substances, persons, or illicit weapons; or

"(B) with regard to any or all aliens in the database, pursuant to such conditions as the Secretary of State shall establish in an agreement with the foreign government in which that government agrees to use such information and records for the purposes described in subparagraph (A) or to deny visas to persons who would be inadmissible to the United States."

SEC. 414. VISA INTEGRITY AND SECURITY.

(a) SENSE OF CONGRESS REGARDING THE NEED TO EXPEDITE IMPLEMENTATION OF INTEGRATED ENTRY AND EXIT DATA SYSTEM.—

(1) SENSE OF CONGRESS.—In light of the terrorist attacks perpetrated against the United States on September 11, 2001, it is the sense of the Congress that—

(A) the Attorney General, in consultation with the Secretary of State, should fully implement the integrated entry and exit data system for airports, seaports, and land border ports of entry, as specified in section 110 of the Illegal Immigration Reform and Immigrant Responsibility Act of 1996 (8 U.S.C. 1365a), with all deliberate speed and as expeditiously as practicable; and

(B) the Attorney General, in consultation with the Secretary of State, the Secretary of Commerce, the Secretary of the Treasury, and the Office of Homeland Security, should immediately begin establishing the Integrated Entry and Exit Data System Task Force, as described in section 3 of the Immigration and Naturalization Service Data Management Improvement Act of 2000 (Public Law 106–215).

(2) AUTHORIZATION OF APPROPRIATIONS.—There is authorized to be appropriated such sums as may be necessary to fully implement the system described in paragraph (1)(A).

(b) DEVELOPMENT OF THE SYSTEM.—In the development of the integrated entry and exit data system under section 110 of the Illegal Immigration Reform and Immigrant Responsibility Act of 1996 (8 U.S.C. 1365a), the Attorney General and the Secretary of State shall particularly focus on—

(1) the utilization of biometric technology; and

(2) the development of tamper-resistant documents readable at ports of entry.

(c) INTERFACE WITH LAW ENFORCEMENT DATABASES.—The entry and exit data system described in this section shall be able to interface with law enforcement databases for use by Federal law enforcement to identify and detain individuals who pose a threat to the national security of the United States.

(d) REPORT ON SCREENING INFORMATION.—Not later than 12 months after the date of enactment of this Act, the Office of Homeland Security shall submit a report to Congress on the information that is needed from any United States agency to effectively screen visa applicants and applicants for admission to the United States to identify those affiliated with terrorist organizations or those that pose any threat to the safety or security of the United States, including the type of information currently received by United States agencies and the regularity with which such information is transmitted to the Secretary of State and the Attorney General.

. . .

SEC. 416. FOREIGN STUDENT MONITORING PROGRAM.

(a) FULL IMPLEMENTATION AND EXPANSION OF FOREIGN STUDENT VISA MONITORING PROGRAM REQUIRED.—The Attorney General, in consultation with the Secretary of State, shall fully implement and expand the program established by section 641(a) of the Illegal Immigration Reform and Immigrant Responsibility Act of 1996 (8 U.S.C. 1372(a)).

. . .

SEC. 417. MACHINE READABLE PASSPORTS.

(a) AUDITS.—The Secretary of State shall, each fiscal year until September 30, 2007—

(1) perform annual audits of the implementation of section 217(c)(2)(B) of the Immigration and Nationality Act (8 U.S.C. 1187(c)(2)(B));

(2) check for the implementation of precautionary measures to prevent the counterfeiting and theft of passports; and

(3) ascertain that countries designated under the visa waiver program have established a program to develop tamper resistant passports.

. . .

SEC. 428. DEFINITIONS.

(a) APPLICATION OF IMMIGRATION AND NATIONALITY ACT PROVISIONS.—

Except as otherwise specifically provided in this subtitle, the definitions used in the Immigration and Nationality Act (excluding the definitions applicable exclusively to title III of such Act) shall apply in the administration of this subtitle.

(b) SPECIFIED TERRORIST ACTIVITY.—For purposes of this subtitle, the term "specified terrorist activity" means any terrorist activity conducted against the Government or the people of the United States on September 11, 2001.

TITLE V—REMOVING OBSTACLES TO INVESTIGATING TERRORISM SEC. 501. ATTORNEY GENERAL'S AUTHORITY TO PAY REWARDS TO COMBAT TERRORISM.

(a) PAYMENT OF REWARDS TO COMBAT TERRORISM.—Funds available to the Attorney General may be used for the payment of rewards pursuant to public advertisements for assistance to the Department of Justice to combat terrorism and defend the Nation against terrorist acts, in accordance with procedures and regulations established or issued by the Attorney General.

(b) CONDITIONS.—In making rewards under this section—

(1) no such reward of $250,000 or more may be made or offered without the personal approval of either the Attorney General or the President;

(2) the Attorney General shall give written notice to the Chairmen and ranking minority members of the Committees on Appropriations and the Judiciary of the Senate and of the House of Representatives not later than 30 days after the approval of a reward under paragraph (1);

(3) any executive agency or military department (as defined, respectively, in sections 105 and 102 of title 5, United States Code) may provide the Attorney General with funds for the payment of rewards;

(4) neither the failure of the Attorney General to authorize a payment nor the amount authorized shall be subject to judicial review; and

(5) no such reward shall be subject to any per- or aggregate reward spending limitation established by law, unless that law expressly refers to this section, and no reward paid pursuant to any such offer shall count toward any such aggregate reward spending limitation.

...

SEC. 503. DNA IDENTIFICATION OF TERRORISTS AND OTHER VIOLENT OFFENDERS.

Section 3(d)(2) of the DNA Analysis Backlog Elimination Act of 2000 (42 U.S.C. 14135a(d)(2)) is amended to read as follows:

"(2) In addition to the offenses described in paragraph (1), the following offenses shall be treated for purposes of this section as qualifying Federal offenses, as determined by the Attorney General:

"(A) Any offense listed in section 2332b(g)(5)(B) of title 18, United States Code.

"(B) Any crime of violence (as defined in section 16 of title 18, United States Code).

"(C) Any attempt or conspiracy to commit any of the above offenses."

SEC. 504. COORDINATION WITH LAW ENFORCEMENT.

(a) INFORMATION ACQUIRED FROM AN ELECTRONIC SURVEILLANCE.—Section 106 of the Foreign Intelligence Surveillance Act of 1978 (50 U.S.C. 1806), is amended by adding at the end the following:

"(k)(1) Federal officers who conduct electronic surveillance to acquire foreign intelligence information under this title may consult with Federal law enforcement officers to coordinate efforts to investigate or protect against—

"(A) actual or potential attack or other grave hostile acts of a foreign power or an agent of a foreign power;

"(B) sabotage or international terrorism by a foreign power or an agent of a foreign power; or

"(C) clandestine intelligence activities by an intelligence service or network of a foreign power or by an agent of a foreign power.

"(2) Coordination authorized under paragraph (1) shall not preclude the certification required by section 104(a)(7)(B) or the entry of an order under section 105."

(b) INFORMATION ACQUIRED FROM A PHYSICAL SEARCH.—Section 305 of the Foreign Intelligence Surveillance Act of 1978 (50 U.S.C.1825) is amended by adding at the end the following:

"(k)(1) Federal officers who conduct physical searches to acquire foreign intelligence information under this title may consult with Federal law enforcement officers to coordinate efforts to investigate or protect against—

"(A) actual or potential attack or other grave hostile acts of a foreign power or an agent of a foreign power;

"(B) sabotage or international terrorism by a foreign power or an agent of a foreign power; or

"(C) clandestine intelligence activities by an intelligence service or network of a foreign power or by an agent of a foreign power.

"(2) Coordination authorized under paragraph (1) shall not preclude the certification required by section 303(a)(7) or the entry of an order under section 304."

SEC. 505. MISCELLANEOUS NATIONAL SECURITY AUTHORITIES.

(a) TELEPHONE TOLL AND TRANSACTIONAL RECORDS.—Section 2709(b) of title 18, United States Code, is amended—

(1) in the matter preceding paragraph (1), by inserting "at Bureau headquarters or a Special Agent in Charge in a Bureau field office designated by the Director" after "Assistant Director";

(2) in paragraph (1)—

(A) by striking "in a position not lower than Deputy Assistant Director"; and

(B) by striking "made that" and all that follows and inserting the following: "made that the name, address, length of service, and toll billing records sought are relevant to an authorized investigation to protect against international terrorism or clandestine intelligence activities, provided that such an investigation of a United States person is not conducted solely on the basis of activities protected by the first amendment to the Constitution of the United States; and"; and

(3) in paragraph (2)—

(A) by striking "in a position not lower than Deputy Assistant Director"; and

(B) by striking "made that" and all that follows and inserting the following: "made that the information sought is relevant to an authorized investigation to protect against international terrorism or clandestine intelligence activities, provided that such an investigation of a United States person is not conducted solely upon the basis of activities protected by the first amendment to the Constitution of the United States."

(b) FINANCIAL RECORDS.—Section 1114(a)(5)(A) of the Right to Financial Privacy Act of 1978 (12 U.S.C. 3414(a)(5)(A)) is amended—

(1) by inserting "in a position not lower than Deputy Assistant Director at Bureau headquarters or a Special Agent in Charge in a Bureau field office designated by the Director" after "designee"; and

(2) by striking "sought" and all that follows and inserting "sought for foreign counter intelligence purposes to protect against international terrorism or clandestine intelligence activities, provided that such an investigation of a United States person is not conducted solely upon the basis of activities protected by the first amendment to the Constitution of the United States."

(c) CONSUMER REPORTS.—Section 624 of the Fair Credit Reporting Act (15 U.S.C. 1681u) is amended—

(1) in subsection (a)—

(A) by inserting "in a position not lower than Deputy Assistant Director at Bureau headquarters or a Special Agent in Charge of a Bureau field office designated by the Director" after "designee" the first place it appears; and

(B) by striking "in writing that" and all that follows through the end and inserting the following: "in writing, that such information is sought for the conduct of an authorized investigation to protect against international terrorism or clandestine intelligence activities, provided that such an investigation of a United States person is not conducted solely upon the basis of activities protected by the first amendment to the Constitution of the United States.";

(2) in subsection (b)—

(A) by inserting "in a position not lower than Deputy Assistant Director at Bureau headquarters or a Special Agent in Charge of a Bureau field office designated by the Director" after "designee" the first place it appears; and

(B) by striking "in writing that" and all that follows through the end and inserting the following: "in writing that such information is sought for the conduct of an authorized investigation to protect against international terrorism or clandestine intelligence activities, provided that such an investigation of a United States person is not conducted solely upon the basis of activities protected by the first amendment to the Constitution of the United States."; and

(3) in subsection (c)—

(A) by inserting "in a position not lower than Deputy Assistant Director at Bureau headquarters or a Special Agent in Charge in a Bureau field office designated by the Director" after "designee of the Director"; and

(B) by striking "in camera that" and all that follows through "States." and inserting the following: "in camera that the consumer report is sought for the conduct of an authorized investigation to protect against international terrorism or clandestine intelligence activities, provided that such an investigation of a United States person is not conducted solely upon the basis of activities protected by the first amendment to the Constitution of the United States."

...

SEC. 507. DISCLOSURE OF EDUCATIONAL RECORDS.

Section 444 of the General Education Provisions Act (20 U.S.C. 1232g), is amended by adding after subsection (i) a new subsection (j) to read as follows:

"(j) INVESTIGATION AND PROSECUTION OF TERRORISM.—

"(1) IN GENERAL.—Notwithstanding subsections (a) through (i) or any provision of State law, the Attorney General (or any Federal officer or employee, in a position not lower than an Assistant Attorney General, designated by the Attorney General) may submit a written application to a court of competent jurisdiction for an ex parte order requiring an educational agency or institution to permit the Attorney General (or his designee) to—

"(A) collect education records in the possession of the educational agency or institution that are relevant to an authorized investigation or prosecution of an offense listed in section 2332b(g)(5)(B) of title 18 United States Code, or an act of domestic or international terrorism as defined in section 2331 of that title; and

"(B) for official purposes related to the investigation or prosecution of an offense described in paragraph (1)(A), retain, disseminate, and use (including as evidence at trial or in other administrative or judicial proceedings) such records, consistent with such guidelines as the Attorney General, after consultation with the Secretary, shall issue to protect confidentiality.

"(2) APPLICATION AND APPROVAL.—

"(A) IN GENERAL.—An application under paragraph (1) shall certify that there are specific and articulable facts giving reason to believe that the education records are likely to contain information described in paragraph (1)(A).

"(B) The court shall issue an order described in paragraph (1) if the court finds that the application for the order includes the certification described in subparagraph (A).

"(3) PROTECTION OF EDUCATIONAL AGENCY OR INSTITUTION.—

An educational agency or institution that, in good faith, produces education records in accordance with an order issued under this subsection shall not be liable to any person for that production.

"(4) RECORD-KEEPING.—Subsection (b)(4) does not apply to education records subject to a court order under this subsection."

SEC. 508. DISCLOSURE OF INFORMATION FROM NCES SURVEYS.

Section 408 of the National Education Statistics Act of 1994 (20 U.S.C. 9007), is amended by adding after subsection (b) a new subsection (c) to read as follows:

"(c) INVESTIGATION AND PROSECUTION OF TERRORISM.—

"(1) IN GENERAL.—Notwithstanding subsections (a) and (b), the Attorney General (or any Federal officer or employee, in a position not lower than an Assistant Attorney General, designated by the Attorney General) may submit a written application to a court of competent jurisdiction for an ex parte order requiring the Secretary to permit the Attorney General (or his designee) to—

"(A) collect reports, records, and information (including individually identifiable information) in the possession of the center that are relevant to an authorized investigation or prosecution of an offense listed in section 2332b(g)(5)(B) of title 18, United States Code, or an act of domestic or international terrorism as defined in section 2331 of that title; and

"(B) for official purposes related to the investigation or prosecution of an offense described in paragraph (1)(A), retain, disseminate, and use (including as evidence at trial or in other administrative or judicial proceedings) such information, consistent with such guidelines as the Attorney General, after consultation with the Secretary, shall issue to protect confidentiality.

"(2) APPLICATION AND APPROVAL.—

"(A) IN GENERAL.—An application under paragraph (1) shall certify that there are specific and articulable facts giving reason to believe that the information sought is described in paragraph (1)(A).

"(B) The court shall issue an order described in paragraph (1) if the court finds that the application for the order includes the certification described in subparagraph (A).

"(3) PROTECTION.—An officer or employee of the Department who, in good faith, produces information in accordance with an order issued under this subsection does not violate subsection (b)(2) and shall not be liable to any person for that production."

TITLE VI—PROVIDING FOR VICTIMS OF TERRORISM, PUBLIC SAFETY OFFICERS, AND THEIR FAMILIES

Subtitle A—Aid to Families of Public Safety Officers

...

TITLE VII—INCREASED INFORMATION SHARING FOR CRITICAL INFRASTRUCTURE PROTECTION

SEC. 701. EXPANSION OF REGIONAL INFORMATION SHARING SYSTEM TO FACILITATE FEDERAL-STATE-LOCAL LAW ENFORCEMENT RESPONSE RELATED TO TERRORIST ATTACKS.

...

TITLE VIII—STRENGTHENING THE CRIMINAL LAWS AGAINST TERRORISM

SEC. 801. TERRORIST ATTACKS AND OTHER ACTS OF VIOLENCE AGAINST MASS TRANSPORTATION SYSTEMS.

Chapter 97 of title 18, United States Code, is amended by adding at the end the following:

"**§ 1993. Terrorist attacks and other acts of violence against mass transportation systems**

"(a) GENERAL PROHIBITIONS.—Whoever willfully—

"(1) wrecks, derails, sets fire to, or disables a mass transportation vehicle or ferry;

"(2) places or causes to be placed any biological agent or toxin for use as a weapon, destructive substance, or destructive device in, upon, or near a mass transportation vehicle or ferry, without previously obtaining the permission of the mass transportation provider, and with intent to endanger the safety of any passenger or employee of the mass transportation provider, or with a reckless disregard for the safety of human life;

"(3) sets fire to, or places any biological agent or toxin for use as a weapon, destructive substance, or destructive device in, upon, or near any garage, terminal, structure, supply, or facility used in the operation of, or in support of the operation of, a mass transportation vehicle or ferry, without previously obtaining the permission of the mass transportation provider, and knowing or having reason to know such activity would likely derail, disable, or wreck a mass transportation vehicle or ferry used, operated, or employed by the mass transportation provider;

"(4) removes appurtenances from, damages, or otherwise impairs the operation of a mass transportation signal system, including a train control system, centralized dispatching system, or rail grade crossing warning signal without authorization from the mass transportation provider;

"(5) interferes with, disables, or incapacitates any dispatcher, driver, captain, or person while they are employed in dispatching, operating, or maintaining a mass transportation vehicle or ferry, with intent to endanger the safety of any passenger or employee of the mass transportation provider, or with a reckless disregard for the safety of human life;

"(6) commits an act, including the use of a dangerous weapon, with the intent to cause death or serious bodily injury to an employee or passenger of a mass transportation provider or any other person while any of the foregoing are on the property of a mass transportation provider;

"(7) conveys or causes to be conveyed false information, knowing the information to be false, concerning an attempt or alleged attempt being made or to be made, to do any act which would be a crime prohibited by this subsection; or

"(8) attempts, threatens, or conspires to do any of the aforesaid acts, shall be fined under this title or imprisoned not more than twenty years, or both, if such act is committed, or in the case of a threat or conspiracy such act would be committed, on, against, or affecting a mass transportation provider engaged in or affecting interstate or foreign commerce, or if in the course of committing such act, that person travels or communicates across a State line in order to commit such act, or transports materials across a State line in aid of the commission of such act.

"(b) AGGRAVATED OFFENSE.—Whoever commits an offense under subsection (a) in a circumstance in which—

"(1) the mass transportation vehicle or ferry was carrying a passenger at the time of the offense; or

"(2) the offense has resulted in the death of any person, shall be guilty of an aggravated form of the offense and shall be fined under this title or imprisoned for a term of years or for life, or both.

"(c) DEFINITIONS.—In this section—

"(1) the term 'biological agent' has the meaning given to that term in section 178(1) of this title;

"(2) the term 'dangerous weapon' has the meaning given to that term in section 930 of this title;

"(3) the term 'destructive device' has the meaning given to that term in section 921(a)(4) of this title;

"(4) the term 'destructive substance' has the meaning given to that term in section 31 of this title;

"(5) the term 'mass transportation' has the meaning given to that term in section 5302(a)(7) of title 49, United States Code, except that the term shall include school bus, charter, and sightseeing transportation;

"(6) the term 'serious bodily injury' has the meaning given to that term in section 1365 of this title;

"(7) the term 'State' has the meaning given to that term in section 2266 of this title; and

"(8) the term 'toxin' has the meaning given to that term in section 178(2) of this title."

(f) CONFORMING AMENDMENT.—The analysis of chapter 97 of title 18, United States Code, is amended by adding at the end:

"1993. Terrorist attacks and other acts of violence against mass transportation systems."

SEC. 802. DEFINITION OF DOMESTIC TERRORISM.

(a) DOMESTIC TERRORISM DEFINED.—Section 2331 of title 18, United States Code, is amended—

(1) in paragraph (1)(B)(iii), by striking "by assassination or kidnapping" and inserting "by mass destruction, assassination, or kidnapping";

(2) in paragraph (3), by striking "and";

(3) in paragraph (4), by striking the period at the end and inserting "; and"; and

(4) by adding at the end the following:

"(5) the term 'domestic terrorism' means activities that—

"(A) involve acts dangerous to human life that are a violation of the criminal laws of the United States or of any State;

"(B) appear to be intended—

"(i) to intimidate or coerce a civilian population;

"(ii) to influence the policy of a government by intimidation or coercion; or

"(iii) to affect the conduct of a government by mass destruction, assassination, or kidnapping; and

"(C) occur primarily within the territorial jurisdiction of the United States."

(b) CONFORMING AMENDMENT.—Section 3077(1) of title 18, United States Code, is amended to read as follows:

"(1) 'act of terrorism' means an act of domestic or international terrorism as defined in section 2331;".

SEC. 803. PROHIBITION AGAINST HARBORING TERRORISTS.

(a) IN GENERAL.—Chapter 113B of title 18, United States Code, is amended by adding after section 2338 the following new section:

"§ 2339. Harboring or concealing terrorists

"(a) Whoever harbors or conceals any person who he knows, or has reasonable grounds to believe, has committed, or is about to commit, an offense under section 32 (relating to destruction of aircraft or aircraft facilities), section 175 (relating to biological weapons), section 229 (relating to chemical weapons), section 831 (relating to nuclear materials), paragraph (2) or (3) of section 844(f) (relating to arson and bombing of government property risking or causing injury or death), section 1366(a) (relating to the destruction of an energy facility), section 2280 (relating to violence against maritime navigation), section 2332a (relating to weapons of mass destruction), or section 2332b (relating to acts of terrorism transcending national boundaries) of this title, section 236(a) (relating to sabotage of nuclear facilities or fuel) of the Atomic Energy Act of 1954 (42 U.S.C. 2284(a)), or section 46502 (relating to aircraft piracy) of title 49, shall be fined under this title or imprisoned not more than ten years, or both."

"(b) A violation of this section may be prosecuted in any Federal judicial district in which the underlying offense was committed, or in any other Federal judicial district as provided by law."

(b) TECHNICAL AMENDMENT.—The chapter analysis for chapter 113B of title 18, United States Code, is amended by inserting after the item for section 2338 the following:

"2339. Harboring or concealing terrorists."

SEC. 804. JURISDICTION OVER CRIMES COMMITTED AT U.S. FACILITIES ABROAD.

Section 7 of title 18, United States Code, is amended by adding at the end the following:

"(9) With respect to offenses committed by or against a national of the United States as that term is used in section 101 of the Immigration and Nationality Act—

"(A) the premises of United States diplomatic, consular, military or other United States Government missions or entities in foreign States, including the buildings, parts of buildings, and land appurtenant or ancillary thereto or used for purposes of those missions or entities, irrespective of ownership; and

"(B) residences in foreign States and the land appurtenant or ancillary thereto, irrespective of ownership, used for purposes of those missions or entities or used by United States personnel assigned to those missions or entities.

Nothing in this paragraph shall be deemed to supersede any treaty or international agreement with which this paragraph conflicts. This paragraph does not apply with respect to an offense committed by a person described in section 3261(a) of this title."

SEC. 805. MATERIAL SUPPORT FOR TERRORISM.

(a) IN GENERAL.—Section 2339A of title 18, United States Code, is amended—

(1) in subsection (a)—

(A) by striking ", within the United States,";

(B) by inserting "229," after "175,";

(C) by inserting "1993," after "1992,";

(D) by inserting ", section 236 of the Atomic Energy Act of 1954 (42 U.S.C. 2284)," after "of this title";

(E) by inserting "or 60123(b)" after "46502"; and

(F) by inserting at the end the following: "A violation of this section may be prosecuted in any Federal judicial district in which the underlying offense was committed, or in any other Federal judicial district as provided by law."; and

(2) in subsection (b)—

(A) by striking "or other financial securities" and inserting "or monetary instruments or financial securities"; and

(B) by inserting "expert advice or assistance," after "training,".

(b) TECHNICAL AMENDMENT.—Section 1956(c)(7)(D) of title 18, United States Code, is amended by inserting "or 2339B" after "2339A".

SEC. 806. ASSETS OF TERRORIST ORGANIZATIONS.

Section 981(a)(1) of title 18, United States Code, is amended by inserting at the end the following:

"(G) All assets, foreign or domestic—

"(i) of any individual, entity, or organization engaged in planning or perpetrating any act of domestic or international terrorism (as defined in section 2331) against the United States, citizens or residents of the United States, or their property, and all assets, foreign or domestic, affording any person a source of influence over any such entity or organization;

"(ii) acquired or maintained by any person with the intent and for the purpose of supporting, planning, conducting, or concealing an act of domestic or international terrorism (as defined in section 2331) against the United States, citizens or residents of the United States, or their property; or

"(iii) derived from, involved in, or used or intended to be used to commit any act of domestic or international terrorism (as defined in section 2331) against the United States, citizens or residents of the United States, or their property."

SEC. 807. TECHNICAL CLARIFICATION RELATING TO PROVISION OF MATERIAL SUPPORT TO TERRORISM.

No provision of the Trade Sanctions Reform and Export Enhancement Act of 2000 (title IX of Public Law 106–387) shall be construed to limit or otherwise affect section 2339A or 2339B of title 18, United States Code.

SEC. 808. DEFINITION OF FEDERAL CRIME OF TERRORISM.

Section 2332b of title 18, United States Code, is amended—

(1) in subsection (f), by inserting "and any violation of section 351(e), 844(e), 844(f)(1), 956(b), 1361, 1366(b), 1366(c), 1751(e), 2152, or 2156 of this title," before "and the Secretary"; and

(2) in subsection (g)(5)(B), by striking clauses (i) through (iii) and inserting the following:

"(i) section 32 (relating to destruction of aircraft or aircraft facilities), 37 (relating to violence at international airports), 81 (relating to arson within special maritime and territorial jurisdiction), 175 or 175b (relating to biological weapons), 229 (relating to chemical weapons), subsection (a), (b), (c), or (d) of section 351 (relating to congressional, cabinet, and Supreme Court assassination and kidnapping), 831 (relating to nuclear materials), 842(m) or (n) (relating to plastic explosives), 844(f)(2) or (3) (relating to arson and bombing of Government property risking or causing death), 844(i) (relating to arson and bombing of property used in interstate commerce), 930(c) (relating to killing or attempted killing during an attack on a Federal facility with a dangerous weapon), 956(a)(1) (relating to conspiracy to murder, kidnap, or maim persons abroad), 1030(a)(1) (relating to protection of computers), 1030(a)(5)(A)(i) resulting in damage as defined in 1030(a)(5)(B)(ii) through (v) (relating to protection of computers), 1114 (relating to killing or attempted killing of officers and employees of the United States), 1116 (relating to murder or manslaughter of foreign officials, official guests, or internationally protected persons), 1203 (relating to hostage taking), 1362 (relating to destruction of communication lines, stations, or systems), 1363 (relating to injury to buildings or property within special maritime and territorial jurisdiction of the United States), 1366(a) (relating to destruction of an energy facility), 1751(a), (b), (c), or (d) (relating to Presidential and Presidential staff assassination and kidnapping), 1992 (relating to wrecking trains), 1993 (relating to terrorist attacks and other acts of violence against mass transportation systems), 2155 (relating to destruction of national defense materials, premises, or utilities), 2280 (relating to violence against maritime navigation), 2281 (relating to violence against maritime fixed platforms), 2332 (relating to certain homicides and other violence against United States nationals occurring outside of the United States), 2332a (relating to use of weapons of mass destruction), 2332b (relating to acts of terrorism transcending national boundaries), 2339 (relating to harboring terrorists), 2339A (relating to providing material support to terrorists), 2339B (relating to providing material support to terrorist organizations), or 2340A (relating to torture) of this title;

"(ii) section 236 (relating to sabotage of nuclear facilities or fuel) of the Atomic Energy Act of 1954 (42 U.S.C. 2284); or "(iii) section 46502 (relating to aircraft piracy), the second sentence of section 46504 (relating to assault on a flight crew with a dangerous weapon), section 46505(b)(3) or (c) (relating to explosive or incendiary devices, or endangerment of human life by means of weapons, on aircraft), section 46506 if homicide or attempted homicide is involved (relating to application of certain criminal laws to acts on aircraft), or section 60123(b) (relating to destruction of interstate gas or hazardous liquid pipeline facility) of title 49."

SEC. 809. NO STATUTE OF LIMITATION FOR CERTAIN TERRORISM OFFENSES.

(a) IN GENERAL.—Section 3286 of title 18, United States Code, is amended to read as follows:

"§ 3286. Extension of statute of limitation for certain terrorism offenses

"(a) EIGHT-YEAR LIMITATION.—Notwithstanding section 3282, no person shall be prosecuted, tried, or punished for any noncapital offense involving a violation of any provision listed in section 2332b(g)(5)(B), or a violation of section 112, 351(e), 1361, or 1751(e) of this title, or section 46504, 46505, or 46506 of title 49, unless the indictment is found or the information is instituted within 8 years after the offense was committed. Notwithstanding the preceding sentence, offenses listed in section 3295 are subject to the statute of limitations set forth in that section.

"(b) NO LIMITATION.—Notwithstanding any other law, an indictment may be found or an information instituted at any time without limitation for any offense listed in section 2332b(g)(5)(B), if the commission of such offense resulted in, or created a foreseeable risk of, death or serious bodily injury to another person."

(b) APPLICATION.—The amendments made by this section shall apply to the prosecution of any offense committed before, on, or after the date of the enactment of this section.

SEC. 810. ALTERNATE MAXIMUM PENALTIES FOR TERRORISM OFFENSES.

(a) ARSON.—Section 81 of title 18, United States Code, is amended in the second undesignated paragraph by striking "not more than twenty years" and inserting "for any term of years or for life."

(b) DESTRUCTION OF AN ENERGY FACILITY.—Section 1366 of title 18, United States Code, is amended—

(1) in subsection (a), by striking "ten" and inserting "20"; and

(2) by adding at the end the following:

"(d) Whoever is convicted of a violation of subsection (a) or (b) that has resulted in the death of any person shall be subject to imprisonment for any term of years or life."

(c) MATERIAL SUPPORT TO TERRORISTS.—Section 2339A(a) of title 18, United States Code, is amended—

(1) by striking "10" and inserting "15"; and

(2) by striking the period and inserting ", and, if the death of any person results, shall be imprisoned for any term of years or for life."

(d) MATERIAL SUPPORT TO DESIGNATED FOREIGN TERRORIST ORGANIZATIONS.—Section 2339B(a)(1) of title 18, United States Code, is amended—

(1) by striking "10" and inserting "15"; and

(2) by striking the period after "or both" and inserting ", and, if the death of any person results, shall be imprisoned for any term of years or for life."

(e) DESTRUCTION OF NATIONAL-DEFENSE MATERIALS.—Section 2155(a) of title 18, United States Code, is amended—

(1) by striking "ten" and inserting "20"; and

(2) by striking the period at the end and inserting ", and, if death results to any person, shall be imprisoned for any term of years or for life."

(f) SABOTAGE OF NUCLEAR FACILITIES OR FUEL.—Section 236 of the Atomic Energy Act of 1954 (42 U.S.C. 2284), is amended—

(1) by striking "ten" each place it appears and inserting "20";

(2) in subsection (a), by striking the period at the end and inserting ", and, if death results to any person, shall be imprisoned for any term of years or for life."; and

(3) in subsection (b), by striking the period at the end and inserting ", and, if death results to any person, shall be imprisoned for any term of years or for life."

(g) SPECIAL AIRCRAFT JURISDICTION OF THE UNITED STATES.—

Section 46505(c) of title 49, United States Code, is amended—

(1) by striking "15" and inserting "20"; and

(2) by striking the period at the end and inserting ", and, if death results to any person, shall be imprisoned for any term of years or for life."

(h) DAMAGING OR DESTROYING AN INTERSTATE GAS OR HAZARDOUS LIQUID PIPELINE FACILITY.—Section 60123(b) of title 49,

United States Code, is amended—

(1) by striking "15" and inserting "20"; and

(2) by striking the period at the end and inserting ", and, if death results to any person, shall be imprisoned for any term of years or for life."

SEC. 811. PENALTIES FOR TERRORIST CONSPIRACIES.

(a) ARSON.—Section 81 of title 18, United States Code, is amended in the first undesignated paragraph—

(1) by striking ", or attempts to set fire to or burn"; and

(2) by inserting "or attempts or conspires to do such an act," before "shall be imprisoned."

(b) KILLINGS IN FEDERAL FACILITIES.—Section 930(c) of title 18, United States Code, is amended—

(1) by striking "or attempts to kill";

(2) by inserting "or attempts or conspires to do such an act," before "shall be punished"; and

(3) by striking "and 1113" and inserting "1113, and 1117".

(c) COMMUNICATIONS LINES, STATIONS, OR SYSTEMS.—Section 1362 of title 18, United States Code, is amended in the first undesignated paragraph—

(1) by striking "or attempts willfully or maliciously to injure or destroy"; and

(2) by inserting "or attempts or conspires to do such an act," before "shall be fined."

(d) BUILDINGS OR PROPERTY WITHIN SPECIAL MARITIME AND TERRITORIAL JURISDICTION.—Section 1363 of title 18, United States Code, is amended—

(1) by striking "or attempts to destroy or injure"; and

(2) by inserting "or attempts or conspires to do such an act," before "shall be fined" the first place it appears.

(e) WRECKING TRAINS.—Section 1992 of title 18, United States Code, is amended by adding at the end the following:

"(c) A person who conspires to commit any offense defined in this section shall be subject to the same penalties (other than the penalty of death) as the penalties prescribed for the offense, the commission of which was the object of the conspiracy."

(f) MATERIAL SUPPORT TO TERRORISTS.—Section 2339A of title 18, United States Code, is amended by inserting "or attempts or conspires to do such an act," before "shall be fined".

(g) TORTURE.—Section 2340A of title 18, United States Code, is amended by adding at the end the following:

"(c) CONSPIRACY.—A person who conspires to commit an offense under this section shall be subject to the same penalties (other than the penalty of death) as the penalties prescribed for the offense, the commission of which was the object of the conspiracy."

(h) SABOTAGE OF NUCLEAR FACILITIES OR FUEL.—Section 236 of the Atomic Energy Act of 1954 (42 U.S.C. 2284), is amended—

(1) in subsection (a)—

(A) by striking ", or who intentionally and willfully attempts to destroy or cause physical damage to";

(B) in paragraph (4), by striking the period at the end and inserting a comma; and

(C) by inserting "or attempts or conspires to do such an act," before "shall be fined"; and

(2) in subsection (b)—

(A) by striking "or attempts to cause"; and

(B) by inserting "or attempts or conspires to do such an act," before "shall be fined."

(i) INTERFERENCE WITH FLIGHT CREW MEMBERS AND ATTENDANTS.—Section 46504 of title 49, United States Code, is amended by inserting "or attempts or conspires to do such an act," before "shall be fined."

(j) SPECIAL AIRCRAFT JURISDICTION OF THE UNITED STATES.—Section 46505 of title 49, United States Code, is amended by adding at the end the following:

"(e) CONSPIRACY.—If two or more persons conspire to violate subsection (b) or (c), and one or more of such persons do any act to effect the object of the conspiracy, each of the parties to such conspiracy shall be punished as provided in such subsection."

(k) DAMAGING OR DESTROYING AN INTERSTATE GAS OR HAZARDOUS LIQUID PIPELINE FACILITY.—Section 60123(b) of title 49, United States Code, is amended—

(1) by striking ", or attempting to damage or destroy,"; and

(2) by inserting ", or attempting or conspiring to do such an act," before "shall be fined."

SEC. 812. POST-RELEASE SUPERVISION OF TERRORISTS.

Section 3583 of title 18, United States Code, is amended by adding at the end the following:

"(j) SUPERVISED RELEASE TERMS FOR TERRORISM PREDICATES.—Notwithstanding subsection (b), the authorized term of supervised release for any offense listed in section 2332b(g)(5)(B), the commission of which resulted in, or created a foreseeable risk of, death or serious bodily injury to another person, is any term of years or life."

SEC. 813. INCLUSION OF ACTS OF TERRORISM AS RACKETEERING ACTIVITY.

Section 1961(1) of title 18, United States Code, is amended—

(1) by striking "or (F)" and inserting "(F)"; and

(2) by inserting before the semicolon at the end the following: ", or (G) any act that is indictable under any provision listed in section 2332b(g)(5)(B)".

SEC. 814. DETERRENCE AND PREVENTION OF CYBERTERRORISM.

(a) CLARIFICATION OF PROTECTION OF PROTECTED COMPUTERS.—Section 1030(a)(5) of title 18, United States Code, is amended—

(1) by inserting "(i)" after "(A)";

(2) by redesignating subparagraphs (B) and (C) as clauses (ii) and (iii), respectively;

(3) by adding "and" at the end of clause (iii), as so redesignated; and

(4) by adding at the end the following:

"(B) by conduct described in clause (i), (ii), or (iii) of subparagraph (A), caused (or, in the case of an attempted offense, would, if completed, have caused)—

"(i) loss to 1 or more persons during any 1-year period (and, for purposes of an investigation, prosecution, or other proceeding brought by the United States only, loss resulting from a related course of conduct affecting 1 or more other protected computers) aggregating at least $5,000 in value;

"(ii) the modification or impairment, or potential modification or impairment, of the medical examination, diagnosis, treatment, or care of 1 or more individuals;

"(iii) physical injury to any person;

"(iv) a threat to public health or safety; or

"(v) damage affecting a computer system used by or for a government entity in furtherance of the administration of justice, national defense, or national security;".

(b) PROTECTION FROM EXTORTION.—Section 1030(a)(7) of title 18, United States Code, is amended by striking ", firm, association, educational institution, financial institution, government entity, or other legal entity,".

(c) PENALTIES.—Section 1030(c) of title 18, United States Code, is amended—

(1) in paragraph (2)—

(A) in subparagraph (A) —

(i) by inserting "except as provided in subparagraph (B)," before "a fine";

(ii) by striking "(a)(5)(C)" and inserting "(a)(5)(A)(iii)"; and

(iii) by striking "and' at the end;

(B) in subparagraph (B), by inserting "or an attempt to commit an offense punishable under this subparagraph," after "subsection (a)(2)," in the matter preceding clause (i); and

(C) in subparagraph (C), by striking "and" at the end; (2) in paragraph (3)—

(A) by striking ", (a)(5)(A), (a)(5)(B)," both places it appears; and

(B) by striking "(a)(5)(C)" and inserting "(a)(5)(A)(iii)"; and

(3) by adding at the end the following:

"(4)(A) a fine under this title, imprisonment for not more than 10 years, or both, in the case of an offense under subsection (a)(5)(A)(i), or an attempt to commit an offense punishable under that subsection;

"(B) a fine under this title, imprisonment for not more than 5 years, or both, in the case of an offense under subsection (a)(5)(A)(ii), or an attempt to commit an offense punishable under that subsection;

"(C) a fine under this title, imprisonment for not more than 20 years, or both, in the case of an offense under subsection (a)(5)(A)(i) or (a)(5)(A)(ii), or an attempt to commit an offense punishable under either subsection, that occurs after a conviction for another offense under this section."

(d) DEFINITIONS.—Section 1030(e) of title 18, United States Code is amended—

(1) in paragraph (2)(B), by inserting ", including a computer located outside the United States that is used in a manner that affects interstate or foreign commerce or communication of the United States" before the semicolon;

(2) in paragraph (7), by striking "and" at the end;

(3) by striking paragraph (8) and inserting the following:

"(8) the term 'damage' means any impairment to the integrity or availability of data, a program, a system, or information;";

(4) in paragraph (9), by striking the period at the end and inserting a semicolon; and

(5) by adding at the end the following:

"(10) the term 'conviction' shall include a conviction under the law of any State for a crime punishable by imprisonment for more than 1 year, an element of which is unauthorized access, or exceeding authorized access, to a computer;

"(11) the term 'loss' means any reasonable cost to any victim, including the cost of responding to an offense, conducting a damage assessment, and restoring the data, program, system, or information to its condition prior to the offense, and any revenue lost, cost incurred, or other consequential damages incurred because of interruption of service; and

"(12) the term 'person' means any individual, firm, corporation, educational institution, financial institution, governmental entity, or legal or other entity."

(e) DAMAGES IN CIVIL ACTIONS.—Section 1030(g) of title 18, United States Code is amended—

(1) by striking the second sentence and inserting the following:

"A civil action for a violation of this section may be brought only if the conduct involves 1 of the factors set forth in clause (i), (ii), (iii), (iv), or (v) of subsection (a)(5)(B). Damages for a violation involving only conduct described in subsection (a)(5)(B)(i) are limited to economic damages."; and

(2) by adding at the end the following: "No action may be brought under this subsection for the negligent design or manufacture of computer hardware, computer software, or firmware."

(f) AMENDMENT OF SENTENCING GUIDELINES RELATING TO CERTAIN COMPUTER FRAUD AND ABUSE.—Pursuant to its authority under section 994(p) of title 28, United States Code, the United States Sentencing Commission shall amend the Federal sentencing guidelines to ensure that any individual convicted of a violation of section 1030 of title 18, United States Code, can be subjected to appropriate penalties, without regard to any mandatory minimum term of imprisonment.

SEC. 815. ADDITIONAL DEFENSE TO CIVIL ACTIONS RELATING TO PRESERVING RECORDS IN RESPONSE TO GOVERNMENT REQUESTS.

Section 2707(e)(1) of title 18, United States Code, is amended by inserting after "or statutory authorization" the following: "(including a request of a governmental entity under section 2703(f) of this title)."

SEC. 816. DEVELOPMENT AND SUPPORT OF CYBERSECURITY FORENSIC CAPABILITIES.

(a) IN GENERAL.—The Attorney General shall establish such regional computer forensic laboratories as the Attorney General considers appropriate, and provide support to existing computer forensic laboratories, in order that all such computer forensic laboratories have the capability—

(1) to provide forensic examinations with respect to seized or intercepted computer evidence relating to criminal activity (including cyberterrorism);

(2) to provide training and education for Federal, State, and local law enforcement personnel and prosecutors regarding investigations, forensic analyses, and prosecutions of computer-related crime (including cyberterrorism);

(3) to assist Federal, State, and local law enforcement in enforcing Federal, State, and local criminal laws relating to computer-related crime;

(4) to facilitate and promote the sharing of Federal law enforcement expertise and information about the investigation, analysis, and prosecution of computer-related crime with State and local law enforcement personnel and prosecutors, including the use of multijurisdictional task forces; and

(5) to carry out such other activities as the Attorney General considers appropriate.

(b) AUTHORIZATION OF APPROPRIATIONS.—

(1) AUTHORIZATION.—There is hereby authorized to be appropriated in each fiscal year $50,000,000 for purposes of carrying out this section.

(2) AVAILABILITY.—Amounts appropriated pursuant to the authorization of appropriations in paragraph (1) shall remain available until expended.

SEC. 817. EXPANSION OF THE BIOLOGICAL WEAPONS STATUTE.

Chapter 10 of title 18, United States Code, is amended—

(1) in section 175—

(A) in subsection (b)—

(i) by striking "does not include" and inserting "includes";

(ii) by inserting "other than" after "system for"; and

(iii) by inserting "bona fide research" after "protective";

(B) by redesignating subsection (b) as subsection (c); and

(C) by inserting after subsection (a) the following:

"(b) ADDITIONAL OFFENSE.—Whoever knowingly possesses any biological agent, toxin, or delivery system of a type or in a quantity that, under the circumstances, is not reasonably justified by a prophylactic, protective, bona fide research, or other peaceful purpose, shall be fined under this title, imprisoned not more than 10 years, or both. In this subsection, the terms 'biological agent' and 'toxin' do not encompass any biological agent or toxin that is in its naturally occurring environment, if the biological agent or toxin has not been cultivated, collected, or otherwise extracted from its natural source.";

(2) by inserting after section 175a the following:

"SEC. 175B. POSSESSION BY RESTRICTED PERSONS.

"(a) No restricted person described in subsection (b) shall ship or transport interstate or foreign commerce, or possess in or affecting commerce, any biological agent or toxin, or receive any biological agent or toxin that has been shipped or transported in interstate or foreign commerce, if the biological agent or toxin is listed as a select agent in subsection (j) of section 72.6 of title 42, Code of Federal Regulations, pursuant to section 511(d)(l) of the Antiterrorism and Effective Death Penalty Act of 1996 (Public Law 104–132), and is not exempted under subsection (h) of such section 72.6, or appendix A of part 72 of the Code of Regulations.

"(b) In this section:

"(1) The term 'select agent' does not include any such biological agent or toxin that is in its naturally-occurring environment, if the biological agent or toxin has not been cultivated, collected, or otherwise extracted from its natural source.

"(2) The term 'restricted person' means an individual who—

"(A) is under indictment for a crime punishable by imprisonment for a term exceeding 1 year;

"(B) has been convicted in any court of a crime punishable by imprisonment for a term exceeding 1 year;

"(C) is a fugitive from justice;

"(D) is an unlawful user of any controlled substance (as defined in section 102 of the Controlled Substances Act (21 U.S.C. 802));

"(E) is an alien illegally or unlawfully in the United States;

"(F) has been adjudicated as a mental defective or has been committed to any mental institution;

"(G) is an alien (other than an alien lawfully admitted for permanent residence) who is a national of a country as to which the Secretary of State, pursuant to section 6(j) of the Export Administration Act of 1979 (50 U.S.C. App. 2405(j)), section 620A of chapter 1 of part M of the Foreign Assistance Act of 1961 (22 U.S.C. 2371), or section 40(d) of chapter 3 of the Arms Export Control Act (22 U.S.C. 2780(d)), has made a determination (that remains in effect) that such country has repeatedly provided support for acts of international terrorism; or

"(H) has been discharged from the Armed Services of the United States under dishonorable conditions.

"(3) The term 'alien' has the same meaning as in section 1010(a)(3) of the Immigration and Nationality Act (8 U.S.C. 1101(a)(3)).

"(4) The term 'lawfully admitted for permanent residence' has the same meaning as in section 101(a)(20) of the Immigration and Nationality Act (8 U.S.C. 1101(a)(20)).

"(c) Whoever knowingly violates this section shall be fined as provided in this title, imprisoned not more than 10 years, or both, but the prohibition contained in this section shall not apply with respect to any duly authorized United States governmental activity."; and

(3) in the chapter analysis, by inserting after the item relating to section 175a the following:
"175b. Possession by restricted persons."

TITLE IX—IMPROVED INTELLIGENCE

SEC. 901. RESPONSIBILITIES OF DIRECTOR OF CENTRAL INTELLIGENCE REGARDING FOREIGN INTELLIGENCE COLLECTED UNDER FOREIGN INTELLIGENCE SURVEILLANCE ACT OF 1978.

Section 103(c) of the National Security Act of 1947 (50 U.S.C. 403–3(c)) is amended—

(1) by redesignating paragraphs (6) and (7) as paragraphs (7) and (8), respectively; and

(2) by inserting after paragraph (5) the following new paragraph (6):

"(6) establish requirements and priorities for foreign intelligence information to be collected under the Foreign Intelligence Surveillance Act of 1978 (50 U.S.C. 1801 et seq.), and provide assistance to the Attorney General to ensure that information derived from electronic surveillance or physical searches under that Act is disseminated so it may be used efficiently and effectively for foreign intelligence purposes, except that the Director shall have no authority to direct, manage, or undertake electronic surveillance or physical search operations pursuant to that Act unless otherwise authorized by statute or Executive order;".

SEC. 902. INCLUSION OF INTERNATIONAL TERRORIST ACTIVITIES WITHIN SCOPE OF FOREIGN INTELLIGENCE UNDER NATIONAL SECURITY ACT OF 1947.

Section 3 of the National Security Act of 1947 (50 U.S.C. 401a) is amended—

(1) in paragraph (2), by inserting before the period the following: ", or international terrorist activities"; and

(2) in paragraph (3), by striking "and activities conducted" and inserting ", and activities conducted,".

SEC. 903. SENSE OF CONGRESS ON THE ESTABLISHMENT AND MAINTENANCE OF INTELLIGENCE RELATIONSHIPS TO ACQUIRE INFORMATION ON TERRORISTS AND TERRORIST ORGANIZATIONS.

It is the sense of Congress that officers and employees of the intelligence community of the Federal Government, acting within the course of their official duties, should be encouraged, and should make every effort, to establish and maintain intelligence relationships with any person, entity, or group for the purpose of engaging in lawful intelligence activities, including the acquisition of information on the identity, location, finances, affiliations, capabilities, plans, or intentions of a terrorist or terrorist organization, or information on any other person, entity, or group (including a foreign government) engaged in harboring, comforting, financing, aiding, or assisting a terrorist or terrorist organization.

SEC. 904. TEMPORARY AUTHORITY TO DEFER SUBMITTAL TO CONGRESS OF REPORTS ON INTELLIGENCE AND INTELLIGENCE-RELATED MATTERS.

(a) AUTHORITY TO DEFER.—The Secretary of Defense, Attorney General, and Director of Central Intelligence each may, during the effective period of this section, defer the date of submittal to Congress of any covered intelligence report under the jurisdiction of such official until February 1, 2002.

(b) COVERED INTELLIGENCE REPORT.—Except as provided in subsection (c), for purposes of subsection (a), a covered intelligence report is as follows:

(1) Any report on intelligence or intelligence-related activities of the United States Government that is required to be submitted to Congress by an element of the intelligence community during the effective period of this section.

(2) Any report or other matter that is required to be submitted to the Select Committee on Intelligence of the Senate and Permanent Select Committee on Intelligence of the House of Representatives by the Department of Defense or the Department of Justice during the effective period of this section.

(c) EXCEPTION FOR CERTAIN REPORTS.—For purposes of subsection (a), any report required by section 502 or 503 of the National Security Act of 1947 (50 U.S.C. 413a, 413b) is not a covered intelligence report.

(d) NOTICE TO CONGRESS.—Upon deferring the date of submittal to Congress of a covered intelligence report under subsection (a), the official deferring the date of submittal of the covered intelligence report shall submit to Congress notice of the deferral. Notice of deferral of a report shall specify the provision of law, if any, under which the report would otherwise be submitted to Congress.

(e) EXTENSION OF DEFERRAL.—(1) Each official specified in subsection (a) may defer the date of submittal to Congress of a covered intelligence report under the jurisdiction of such official to a date after

February 1, 2002, if such official submits to the committees of Congress specified in subsection (b)(2) before February 1, 2002, a certification that preparation and submittal of the covered intelligence report on February 1, 2002, will impede the work of officers or employees who are engaged in counterterrorism activities.

(2) A certification under paragraph (1) with respect to a covered intelligence report shall specify the date on which the covered intelligence report will be submitted to Congress.

(f) EFFECTIVE PERIOD.—The effective period of this section is the period beginning on the date of the enactment of this Act and ending on February 1, 2002.

(g) ELEMENT OF THE INTELLIGENCE COMMUNITY DEFINED.—In this section, the term "element of the intelligence community"means any element of the intelligence community specified or designated under section 3(4) of the National Security Act of 1947 (50 U.S.C. 401a(4)).

SEC. 905. DISCLOSURE TO DIRECTOR OF CENTRAL INTELLIGENCE OF FOREIGN INTELLIGENCE-RELATED INFORMATION WITH RESPECT TO CRIMINAL INVESTIGATIONS.

(a) IN GENERAL.—Title I of the National Security Act of 1947 (50 U.S.C. 402 et seq.) is amended—

(1) by redesignating subsection 105B as section 105C; and

(2) by inserting after section 105A the following new section 105B:

"DISCLOSURE OF FOREIGN INTELLIGENCE ACQUIRED IN CRIMINAL INVESTIGATIONS; NOTICE OF CRIMINAL INVESTIGATIONS OF FOREIGN INTELLIGENCE SOURCES

"SEC. 105B. (a) DISCLOSURE OF FOREIGN INTELLIGENCE.—(1) Except as otherwise provided by law and subject to paragraph (2), the Attorney General, or the head of any other department or agency of the Federal Government with law enforcement responsibilities, shall expeditiously disclose to the Director of Central Intelligence, pursuant to guidelines developed by the Attorney General in consultation with the Director, foreign intelligence acquired by an element of the Department of Justice or an element of such department or agency, as the case may be, in the course of a criminal investigation.

"(2) The Attorney General by regulation and in consultation with the Director of Central Intelligence may provide for exceptions to the applicability of paragraph (1) for one or more classes of foreign intelligence, or foreign intelligence with respect to one or more targets or matters, if the Attorney General determines that disclosure of such foreign intelligence under that paragraph would jeopardize an ongoing law enforcement investigation or impair other significant law enforcement interests.

"(b) PROCEDURES FOR NOTICE OF CRIMINAL INVESTIGATIONS.— Not later than 180 days after the date of enactment of this section, the Attorney General, in consultation with the Director of Central Intelligence, shall develop guidelines to ensure that after receipt of a report from an element of the intelligence community of activity of a foreign intelligence source or potential foreign intelligence source that may warrant investigation as criminal activity, the Attorney General provides notice to the Director of Central Intelligence, within a reasonable period of time, of his intention to commence, or decline to commence, a criminal investigation of such activity.

"(c) PROCEDURES.—The Attorney General shall develop procedures for the administration of this section, including the disclosure of foreign intelligence by elements of the Department of Justice, and elements of other departments and agencies of the Federal Government, under subsection (a) and the provision of notice with respect to criminal investigations under subsection (b)."

(b) CLERICAL AMENDMENT.—The table of contents in the first section of that Act is amended by striking the item relating to section 105B and inserting the following new items:

"Sec. 105B. Disclosure of foreign intelligence acquired in criminal investigations; notice of criminal investigations of foreign intelligence sources.

"Sec. 105C. Protection of the operational files of the National Imagery and Mapping Agency."

SEC. 906. FOREIGN TERRORIST ASSET TRACKING CENTER.

(a) REPORT ON RECONFIGURATION.—Not later than February 1, 2002, the Attorney General, the Director of Central Intelligence, and the Secretary of the Treasury shall jointly submit to Congress a report on the feasibility and desirability of reconfiguring the Foreign Terrorist Asset Tracking Center and the Office of Foreign Assets Control of the Department of the Treasury in order to establish a capability to provide for the effective and efficient analysis and dissemination of foreign intelligence relating to the financial capabilities and resources of international terrorist organizations.

(b) REPORT REQUIREMENTS.—(1) In preparing the report under subsection (a), the Attorney General, the Secretary, and the Director shall consider whether, and to what extent, the capacities and resources of the Financial Crimes Enforcement Center of the Department of the Treasury may be integrated into the capability contemplated by the report.

(2) If the Attorney General, Secretary, and the Director determine that it is feasible and desirable to undertake the reconfiguration described in subsection (a) in order to establish the capability described in that subsection, the Attorney General, the Secretary, and the Director shall include with the report under that subsection a detailed proposal for legislation to achieve the reconfiguration.

SEC. 907. NATIONAL VIRTUAL TRANSLATION CENTER.

(a) REPORT ON ESTABLISHMENT.—(1) Not later than February 1, 2002, the Director of Central Intelligence shall, in consultation with the Director of the Federal Bureau of Investigation, submit to the appropriate committees of Congress a report on the establishment and maintenance within the intelligence community of an element for purposes of providing timely and accurate translations of foreign intelligence for all other elements of the intelligence community. In the report, the element shall be referred to as the "National Virtual Translation Center."

(2) The report on the element described in paragraph (1) shall discuss the use of state-of-the-art communications technology, the integration of existing translation capabilities in the intelligence community, and the utilization of remote-connection capacities so as to minimize the need for a central physical facility for the element.

(b) RESOURCES.—The report on the element required by subsection (a) shall address the following:

(1) The assignment to the element of a staff of individuals possessing a broad range of linguistic and translation skills appropriate for the purposes of the element.

(2) The provision to the element of communications capabilities and systems that are commensurate with the most current and sophisticated communications capabilities and systems available to other elements of intelligence community.

(3) The assurance, to the maximum extent practicable, that the communications capabilities and systems provided to the element will be compatible with communications capabilities and systems utilized by the Federal Bureau of Investigation in securing timely and accurate translations of foreign language materials for law enforcement investigations.

(4) The development of a communications infrastructure to ensure the efficient and secure use of the translation capabilities of the element.

(c) SECURE COMMUNICATIONS.—The report shall include a discussion of the creation of secure electronic communications between the element described by subsection (a) and the other elements of the intelligence community.

(d) DEFINITIONS.—In this section:

(1) FOREIGN INTELLIGENCE.—The term "foreign intelligence" has the meaning given that term in section 3(2) of the National Security Act of 1947 (50 U.S.C. 401a(2)).

(2) ELEMENT OF THE INTELLIGENCE COMMUNITY.—The term "element of the intelligence community" means any element of the intelligence community specified or designated under section 3(4) of the National Security Act of 1947 (50 U.S.C.401a(4)).

SEC. 908. TRAINING OF GOVERNMENT OFFICIALS REGARDING IDENTIFICATION AND USE OF FOREIGN INTELLIGENCE.

(a) PROGRAM REQUIRED.—The Attorney General shall, in consultation with the Director of Central Intelligence, carry out a program to provide appropriate training to officials described in subsection (b) in order to assist such officials in—

(1) identifying foreign intelligence information in the course of their duties; and

(2) utilizing foreign intelligence information in the course of their duties, to the extent that the utilization of such information is appropriate for such duties.

(b) OFFICIALS.—The officials provided training under subsection (a) are, at the discretion of the Attorney General and the Director, the following:

(1) Officials of the Federal Government who are not ordinarily engaged in the collection, dissemination, and use of foreign intelligence in the performance of their duties.

(2) Officials of State and local governments who encounter, or may encounter in the course of a terrorist event, foreign intelligence in the performance of their duties.

(c) AUTHORIZATION OF APPROPRIATIONS.—There is hereby authorized to be appropriated for the Department of Justice such sums as may be necessary for purposes of carrying out the program required by subsection (a).

TITLE X—MISCELLANEOUS
SEC. 1001. REVIEW OF THE DEPARTMENT OF JUSTICE.

The Inspector General of the Department of Justice shall designate one official who shall—

(1) review information and receive complaints alleging abuses of civil rights and civil liberties by employees and officials of the Department of Justice;

(2) make public through the Internet, radio, television, and newspaper advertisements information on the responsibilities and functions of, and how to contact, the official; and

(3) submit to the Committee on the Judiciary of the House of Representatives and the Committee on the Judiciary of the Senate on a semi-annual basis a report on the implementation of this subsection and detailing any abuses described in paragraph (1), including a description of the use of funds appropriations used to carry out this subsection.

SEC. 1002. SENSE OF CONGRESS.

(a) FINDINGS.—Congress finds that—

(1) all Americans are united in condemning, in the strongest possible terms, the terrorists who planned and carried out the attacks against the United States on September 11, 2001, and in pursuing all those responsible for those attacks and their sponsors until they are brought to justice;

(2) Sikh-Americans form a vibrant, peaceful, and law-abiding part of America's people;

(3) approximately 500,000 Sikhs reside in the United States and are a vital part of the Nation;

(4) Sikh-Americans stand resolutely in support of the commitment of our Government to bring the terrorists and those that harbor them to justice;

(5) the Sikh faith is a distinct religion with a distinct religious and ethnic identity that has its own places of worship and a distinct holy text and religious tenets;

(6) many Sikh-Americans, who are easily recognizable by their turbans and beards, which are required articles of their faith, have suffered both verbal and physical assaults as a result of misguided anger toward Arab-Americans and Muslim-Americans in the wake of the September 11, 2001 terrorist attack;

(7) Sikh-Americans, as do all Americans, condemn acts of prejudice against any American; and

(8) Congress is seriously concerned by the number of crimes against Sikh-Americans and other Americans all across the Nation that have been reported in the wake of the tragic events that unfolded on September 11, 2001.

(b) SENSE OF CONGRESS.—Congress—

(1) declares that, in the quest to identify, locate, and bring to justice the perpetrators and sponsors of the terrorist attacks on the United States on September 11, 2001, the civil rights and civil liberties of all Americans, including Sikh-Americans, should be protected;

(2) condemns bigotry and any acts of violence or discrimination against any Americans, including Sikh-Americans;

(3) calls upon local and Federal law enforcement authorities to work to prevent crimes against all Americans, including Sikh-Americans; and

(4) calls upon local and Federal law enforcement authorities to prosecute to the fullest extent of the law all those who commit crimes.

. . .

SEC. 1009. STUDY OF ACCESS.

(a) IN GENERAL.—Not later than 120 days after enactment of this Act, the Federal Bureau of Investigation shall study and report to Congress on the feasibility of providing to airlines access via computer to the names of passengers who are suspected of terrorist activity by Federal officials.

. . .

DOCUMENT 89

Full Official Title: An Act to express United States foreign policy with respect to, and to strengthen United States advocacy on behalf of, individuals persecuted in foreign countries on account of religion; to authorize United States actions in response to violations of religious freedom in foreign countries; to establish an Ambassador at Large for International Religious Freedom within the Department of State, a Commission on International Religious Freedom, and a Special Adviser on International Religious Freedom within the National Security Council; and for other purposes.

Short Title/Acronym/Abbreviation: International Religious Freedom Act of 1998, or IRFA
Type of Document: U.S. Statute
Subject: International religious freedom, human rights and U.S. Foreign Policy
Official Citation: International Religious Freedom Act of 1998, USC Title 22, Sec. 6401.
Public Law 105-292, as amended by Public Law 106-55, Public Law 106-113, Public Law 107-228, Public Law 108-332, and Public Law 108-458
Date of Document: Signed into law October 27, 1998
Date of Adoption: Passed in House, May 14, 1998; October 9, 1998, passed in Senate.
Date of General Entry into Force (EIF): Not applicable
Number of States Parties as of this printing: Not applicable
Date of Signature by United States: Not applicable
Date of Ratification/Accession/Adhesion: Not applicable
Date of Entry into Force as to United States (effective date): Not applicable
Legal Status/Character of the Instrument/Document as to the United States: Binding U.S. law found at 22 U.S. Code section 6401, as amended. http://www.state.gov/documents/organization/2297.pdf

Comment: This Act ties U.S. foreign policy and certain aid to respect for religious freedom according to international human rights legal standards, establishes the Commission on International Religious Freedom (CIRF), which produces an annual report of the state of religious freedom in almost every other country in the world. CIRF establishes a list of "Countries of Particular Concern" (CPCs), which are the most egregious violators of religious freedom. An excerpt taken from the 2010 annual report of CIRF on China can be found in Appendix L.

Caution: (If this is a legal instrument) The status and applicability of this instrument as to the United States may have changed since the date of this publication. The above information may be updated by referring to the following site:
Web Address: http://www.uscirf.gov/

INTERNATIONAL RELIGIOUS FREEDOM ACT OF 1998

USC Title 22, Secs. 6401 and following:
Chapter 73—International Religious Freedom
Current through P.L. 106–55, approved 8-17-99
Sec. 6401. Findings; policy
(a) Findings
Congress makes the following findings:

(1) The right to freedom of religion undergirds the very origin and existence of the United States. Many of our Nation's founders fled religious persecution abroad, cherishing in their hearts and minds the ideal of religious freedom. They established in law, as a fundamental right and as a pillar of our Nation, the right to freedom of religion. From its birth to this day, the United States has prized this legacy of religious freedom and honored this heritage by standing for religious freedom and offering refuge to those suffering religious persecution.

(2) Freedom of religious belief and practice is a universal human right and fundamental freedom articulated in numerous international instruments, including the Universal Declaration of Human Rights, the International Covenant on Civil and Political Rights, the Helsinki Accords, the Declaration on the Elimination of All Forms of Intolerance and Discrimination Based on Religion or Belief, the United Nations Charter, and the European Convention for the Protection of Human Rights and Fundamental Freedoms.

(3) Article 18 of the Universal Declaration of Human Rights recognizes that "Everyone has the right to freedom of thought, conscience, and religion. This right includes freedom to change his religion or belief, and freedom, either alone or in community with others and in public or private, to manifest his religion or belief in teaching, practice, worship, and observance." Article 18(1) of the International Covenant on Civil and Political Rights recognizes that "Everyone shall have the right to freedom of thought, conscience, and religion. This right shall include freedom to have or to adopt a religion or belief of his choice, and freedom, either individually or in community with others and in public or private, to manifest his religion or belief in worship, observance, practice, and teaching." Governments have the responsibility to protect the fundamental rights of their citizens and to pursue justice for all. Religious freedom is a fundamental right of every individual, regardless of race, sex, country, creed, or nationality, and should never be arbitrarily abridged by any government.

(4) The right to freedom of religion is under renewed and, in some cases, increasing assault in many countries around the world. More than one-half of the world's population lives under regimes that severely restrict or prohibit the freedom of their citizens to study, believe, observe, and freely practice the religious faith of their choice. Religious believers and communities suffer both government-sponsored and government-tolerated violations of their rights to religious freedom. Among the many forms of such violations are state-sponsored slander campaigns, confiscations of property, surveillance by security police, including by special divisions of "religious police," severe prohibitions against construction and repair of places of worship, denial of the right to assemble and relegation of religious communities to illegal status through arbitrary registration laws, prohibitions against the pursuit of education or public office, and prohibitions against publishing, distributing, or possessing religious literature and materials.

(5) Even more abhorrent, religious believers in many countries face such severe and violent forms of religious persecution as detention, torture, beatings, forced marriage, rape, imprisonment, enslavement, mass resettlement, and death merely for the peaceful belief in, change of or practice of their faith. In many countries, religious believers are forced to meet secretly, and religious leaders are targeted by national security forces and hostile mobs.

(6) Though not confined to a particular region or regime, religious persecution is often particularly widespread, systematic, and heinous under totalitarian governments and in countries with militant, politicized religious majorities.

(7) Congress has recognized and denounced acts of religious persecution through the adoption of the following resolutions:

(A) House Resolution 515 of the One Hundred Fourth Congress, expressing the sense of the House of Representatives with respect to the persecution of Christians worldwide.

(B) Senate Concurrent Resolution 71 of the One Hundred Fourth Congress, expressing the sense of the Senate regarding persecution of Christians worldwide.

(C) House Concurrent Resolution 102 of the One Hundred Fourth Congress, expressing the sense of the House of Representatives concerning the emancipation of the Iranian Baha'i community.

(b) Policy

It shall be the policy of the United States, as follows:

(1) To condemn violations of religious freedom, and to promote, and to assist other governments in the promotion of, the fundamental right to freedom of religion.

(2) To seek to channel United States security and development assistance to governments other than those found to be engaged in gross violations of the right to freedom of religion, as set forth in the Foreign Assistance Act of 1961, in the International Financial Institutions Act of 1977, and in other formulations of United States human rights policy.

(3) To be vigorous and flexible, reflecting both the unwavering commitment of the United States to religious freedom and the desire of the United States for the most effective and principled response, in light of the range of violations of religious freedom by a variety of persecuting regimes, and the status of the relations of the United States with different nations.

(4) To work with foreign governments that affirm and protect religious freedom, in order to develop multilateral documents and initiatives to combat violations of religious freedom and promote the right to religious freedom abroad.

(5) Standing for liberty and standing with the persecuted, to use and implement appropriate tools in the United States foreign policy apparatus, including diplomatic, political, commercial, charitable, educational, and cultural channels, to promote respect for religious freedom by all governments and peoples.

. . .

Sec. 6402. Definitions

(9) Human Rights Reports

The term "Human Rights Reports" means all reports submitted by the Department of State to Congress under sections 2151n and 2304 of this title.

. . .

(11) Particularly severe violations of religious freedom

The term "particularly severe violations of religious freedom" means systematic, ongoing, egregious violations of religious freedom, including violations such as—

(A) torture or cruel, inhuman, or degrading treatment or punishment;

(B) prolonged detention without charges;

(C) causing the disappearance of persons by the abduction or clandestine detention of those persons; or

(D) other flagrant denial of the right to life, liberty, or the security of persons.

(12) Special Adviser

The term "Special Adviser" means the Special Adviser to the President on International Religious Freedom described in section 402(i) of Title 50, as added by section 301 of this Act.

(13) Violations of religious freedom

The term "violations of religious freedom" means violations of the internationally recognized right to freedom of religion and religious belief and practice, as set forth in the international instruments referred to in section 6401(a)(2) of this title and as described in section 6401(a)(3) of this title, including violations such as—

(A) arbitrary prohibitions on, restrictions of, or punishment for—

(i) assembling for peaceful religious activities such as worship, preaching, and prayer, including arbitrary registration requirements;

(ii) speaking freely about one's religious beliefs;

(iii) changing one's religious beliefs and affiliation;

(iv) possession and distribution of religious literature, including Bibles; or

(v) raising one's children in the religious teachings and practices of one's choice; or

(B) any of the following acts if committed on account of an individual's religious belief or practice: detention, interrogation, imposition of an onerous financial penalty, forced labor, forced mass resettlement, imprisonment, forced religious conversion, beating, torture, mutilation, rape, enslavement, murder, and execution.

. . .

Subchapter I—Department of State Activities
Sec. 6412. Reports

(a) Portions of annual Human Rights Reports

The Ambassador at Large shall assist the Secretary of State in preparing those portions of the Human Rights Reports that relate to freedom of religion and freedom from discrimination based on religion and those portions of other information provided Congress under sections 116 and 502B of the Foreign Assistance Act of 1961 (22 U.S.C. 2151m, 2304) that relate to the right to freedom of religion.

(b) Annual Report on International Religious Freedom

(1) Deadline for submission

. . .

Each Annual Report shall contain the following:

(A) Status of religious freedom

A description of the status of religious freedom in each foreign country, including—

(i) trends toward improvement in the respect and protection of the right to religious freedom and trends toward deterioration of such right;

(ii) violations of religious freedom engaged in or tolerated by the government of that country; and

(iii) particularly severe violations of religious freedom engaged in or tolerated by the government of that country.

(B) Violations of religious freedom

An assessment and description of the nature and extent of violations of religious freedom in each foreign country, including persecution of one religious group by another religious group, religious persecution by governmental and non governmental entities, persecution targeted at individuals or particular denominations or entire religions, the existence of government policies violating religious freedom, and the existence of government policies concerning—

(i) limitations or prohibitions on, or lack of availability of, openly conducted, organized religious services outside of the premises of foreign diplomatic missions or consular posts; and

(ii) the forced religious conversion of minor United States citizens who have been abducted or illegally removed from the United States, and the refusal to allow such citizens to be returned to the United States.

(C) United States policies

A description of United States actions and policies in support of religious freedom in each foreign country engaging in or tolerating violations of religious freedom. . . .

(D) International agreements in effect

A description of any binding agreement with a foreign government entered into by the United States under section 6441(b) or 6442(c) of this title.

...

Sec. 6417. Prisoner lists and issue briefs on religious freedom concerns

(a) Sense of the Congress

To encourage involvement with religious freedom concerns at every possible opportunity and by all appropriate representatives of the United States Government, it is the sense of the Congress that officials of the executive branch of Government should promote increased advocacy on such issues during meetings between foreign dignitaries and executive branch officials or Members of Congress.

(b) Prisoner lists and issue briefs on religious freedom concerns

The Secretary of State, in consultation with the Ambassador at Large, the Assistant Secretary of State for Democracy, Human Rights and Labor, United States chiefs of mission abroad, regional experts, and non governmental human rights and religious groups, shall prepare and maintain issue briefs on religious freedom, on a country-by-country basis, consisting of lists of persons believed to be imprisoned, detained, or placed under house arrest for their religious faith, together with brief evaluations and critiques of the policies of the respective country restricting religious freedom. In considering the inclusion of names of prisoners on such lists, the Secretary of State shall exercise appropriate discretion, including concerns regarding the safety, security, and benefit to such prisoners.

(c) Availability of information

The Secretary shall, as appropriate, provide religious freedom issue briefs under subsection (b) to executive branch officials and Members of Congress in anticipation of bilateral contacts with foreign leaders, both in the United States and abroad.

...

Subchapter II—Commission on International Religious Freedom

Sec. 6431. Establishment and composition

(a) In general

There is established the United States Commission on International Religious Freedom.

(b) Membership

(1) Appointment

The Commission shall be composed of—

(A) the Ambassador at Large, who shall serve ex officio as a nonvoting member of the Commission; and

(B) Nine other members, who shall be United States citizens who are not being paid as officers or employees of the United States, and who shall be appointed as follows:

(i) Three members of the Commission shall be appointed by the President.

(ii) Three members of the Commission shall be appointed by the President pro tempore of the Senate, of which two of the members shall be appointed upon the recommendation of the leader in the Senate of the political party that is not the political party of the President, and of which one of the members shall be appointed upon the recommendation of the leader in the Senate of the other political party.

(iii) Three members of the Commission shall be appointed by the Speaker of the House of Representatives, of which two of the members shall be appointed upon the recommendation of the leader in the House of the political party that is not the political party of the President, and of which one of the members shall be appointed upon the recommendation of the leader in the House of the other political party.

(c) Terms

(1) In general

The term of office of each member of the Commission shall be 2 years. Members of the Commission shall be eligible for reappointment to a second term....

...

(e) Quorum

Six voting members of the Commission shall constitute a quorum for purposes of transacting business.

Sec. 6432. Duties of the Commission

(a) In general

The Commission shall have as its primary responsibility—

(1) the annual and ongoing review of the facts and circumstances of violations of religious freedom presented in the Country Reports on Human Rights Practices, the Annual Report, and the Executive Summary, as well as information from other sources as appropriate; and

(2) the making of policy recommendations to the President, the Secretary of State, and Congress with respect to matters involving international religious freedom.

Sec. 6432a. Powers of the Commission

...

(d) Administrative procedures

The Commission may adopt such rules and regulations, relating to administrative procedure, as may be reasonably necessary to enable it to carry out the provisions of this title.

(e) Views of the Commission

The Members of the Commission may speak in their capacity as private citizens....

Sec. 6433. Report of the Commission

(a) In general

Not later than May 1 of each year, the Commission shall submit a report to the President, the Secretary of State, and Congress setting forth its recommendations for United States policy options based on its evaluations under section 6432 of this title.

Sec. 6434. Applicability of other laws

The Federal Advisory Committee Act (5 U.S.C. App.) shall not apply to the Commission.

...

Sec. 6441. Presidential actions in response to violations of religious freedom

(a) Response to violations of religious freedom

(1) In general

(A) United States policy

It shall be the policy of the United States—

(i) to oppose violations of religious freedom that are or have been engaged in or tolerated by the governments of foreign countries; and

(ii) to promote the right to freedom of religion in those countries through the actions described in subsection (b).

...

Sec. 6445. Description of Presidential actions

(a) Description of Presidential actions

Except as provided in subsection (d), the Presidential actions referred to in this subsection are the following:

(1) A private demarche.

(2) An official public demarche.

(3) A public condemnation.

(4) A public condemnation within one or more multilateral fora.

(5) The delay or cancellation of one or more scientific exchanges.

(6) The delay or cancellation of one or more cultural exchanges.

(7) The denial of one or more working, official, or state visits.

(8) The delay or cancellation of one or more working, official, or state visits.

(9) The withdrawal, limitation, or suspension of United States development assistance in accordance with section 2151n of this title.

(10) Directing the Export-Import Bank of the United States, the Overseas Private Investment Corporation, or the Trade and Development Agency not to approve the issuance of any (or a specified number of) guarantees, insurance, extensions of credit, or participations in the extension of credit with respect to the specific government, agency, instrumentality, or official found or determined by the President to be responsible for violations under section 6441 or 6442 of this title.

(11) The withdrawal, limitation, or suspension of United States security assistance in accordance with section 2304 of this title.

(12) Consistent with section 262d of this title, directing the United States executive directors of international financial institutions to oppose and vote against loans primarily benefiting the specific foreign

government, agency, instrumentality, or official found or determined by the President to be responsible for violations under section 6441 or 6442 of this title.

(13) Ordering the heads of the appropriate United States agencies not to issue any (or a specified number of) specific licenses, and not to grant any other specific authority (or a specified number of authorities), to export any goods or technology to the specific foreign government, agency, instrumentality, or official found or determined by the President to be responsible for violations under section 6441 or 6442 of this title, under—

(A) the Export Administration Act of 1979;

(B) the Arms Export Control Act;

(C) the Atomic Energy Act of 1954; or

(D) any other statute that requires the prior review and approval of the United States Government as a condition for the export or re-export of goods or services.

(14) Prohibiting any United States financial institution from making loans or providing credits totaling more than $10,000,000 in any 12-month period to the specific foreign government, agency, instrumentality, or official found or determined by the President to be responsible for violations under section 6441 or 6442 of this title.

(15) Prohibiting the United States Government from procuring, or entering into any contract for the procurement of, any goods or services from the foreign government, entities, or officials found or determined by the President to be responsible for violations under section 6441 or 6442 of this title.

Sec. 6446. Effects on existing contracts

The President shall not be required to apply or maintain any Presidential action under this part—

(1) in the case of procurement of defense articles or defense services—

(A) under existing contracts or subcontracts, including the exercise of options for production quantities, to satisfy requirements essential to the national security of the United States....

. . .

Sec. 6450. Preclusion of judicial review

No court shall have jurisdiction to review any Presidential determination or agency action under this chapter or any amendment made by this chapter.

. . .

Part B—Strengthening Existing LaW
Sec. 6461. Exports of certain items used in particularly severe violations of religious freedom

(a) Mandatory licensing

Notwithstanding any other provision of law, the Secretary of Commerce, with the concurrence of the Secretary of State, shall include on the list of crime control and detection instruments or equipment controlled for export and re-export under section 6(n) of the Export Administration Act of 1979 (22 U.S.C. App. 2405(n)), or under any other provision of law, items being exported or re-exported to countries of particular concern for religious freedom that the Secretary of Commerce, with the concurrence of the Secretary of State, and in consultation with appropriate officials including the Assistant Secretary of State for Democracy, Human Rights and Labor and the Ambassador at Large, determines are being used or are intended for use directly and in significant measure to carry out particularly severe violations of religious freedom.

(b) Licensing ban

The prohibition on the issuance of a license for export of crime control and detection instruments or equipment under section 502B(a)(2) of the Foreign Assistance Act of 1961 (22 U.S.C. 2304(a)(2)) shall apply to the export and re-export of any item included pursuant to subsection (a) on the list of crime control instruments.

. . .

Subchapter IV—Refugee, Asylum, and Consular Matters
Sec. 6471. Use of annual report

The Annual Report, together with other relevant documentation, shall serve as a resource for immigration judges and consular, refugee, and asylum officers in cases involving claims of persecution on the grounds of religion. Absence of reference by the Annual Report to conditions described by the alien shall not constitute the sole grounds for a denial of the alien's claim.

Sec. 6472. Reform of refugee policy

(a),(b) Omitted

(d) Annual consultation

The President shall include in each annual report on proposed refugee admissions under section 207(d) of the Immigration and Nationality Act (8 U.S.C. 1157(d)) information about religious persecution of refugee populations eligible for consideration for admission to the United States. The Secretary of State shall include information on religious persecution of refugee populations in the formal testimony presented to the Committees on the Judiciary of the House of Representatives and the Senate during the consultation process under section 207(e) of the Immigration and Nationality Act (8 U.S.C. 1157(e)).

...

Subchapter V—Miscellaneous Provisions
Sec. 6481. Business codes of conduct
(a) Congressional finding
Congress recognizes the increasing importance of transitional corporations as global actors, and their potential for providing positive leadership in their host countries in the area of human rights.
(b) Sense of the Congress
It is the sense of the Congress that transitional corporations operating overseas, particularly those corporations operating in countries the governments of which have engaged in or tolerated violations of religious freedom, as identified in the Annual Report, should adopt codes of conduct—
(1) upholding the right to freedom of religion of their employees; and
(2) ensuring that a worker's religious views and peaceful practices of belief in no way affect, or be allowed to affect, the status or terms of his or her employment.

DOCUMENT 90

Full Official Title: Review and Disposition of Individuals Detained at the Guantánamo Bay Naval Base and Closure of Detention Facilities

Short Title/Acronym/Abbreviation: Not applicable

Type of Document: This is an executive order issued by the president. Executive orders are policy statements by the president directing government agencies under his authority to particular actions.

Subject: Disposition of Detainees of Guantánamo Detention Center and closing this facility.

Official Citation: Executive Order 13492 of January 22, 2009

Federal Register/Vol. 74, No. 16/Tuesday, January 27, 2009/Presidential Documents 4897

Date of Document: January 22, 2009

Date of Adoption: Not applicable

Date of General Entry into Force (EIF): Not applicable. This EO went into effect upon President Obama signing it.

Number of States Parties as of this printing: Not applicable

Date of Signature by the United States: Not applicable

Date of Ratification/Accession/Adhesion: Not applicable

Date of Entry into Force as to United States (effective date): Not applicable

Legal Status/Character of the Instrument/Document as to the United States: These orders can be challenged by the Supreme Court if they are deemed unconstitutional, and they can be reversed by subsequent Administrations. Moreover, the president can amend his order at any time, and Congress may limit its application with subsequent legislation.

Comments: This E.O. expressed fulfillment of a campaign promise of President Obama. At the time of writing this book, approximately one year and eight months after this E.O. was issued the facilities at Guantánamo have still not been closed and all detainees have not been reviewed and processed for transition.

Caution: The status and applicability of this instrument as to the United States may have changed since the date of this publication.

REVIEW AND DISPOSITION OF INDIVIDUALS DETAINED AT THE GUANTÁNAMO BAY NAVAL BASE AND CLOSURE OF DETENTION FACILITIES

Presidential Documents
Federal Register/Vol. 74, No. 16/Tuesday, January 27, 2009/Presidential Documents 4897
Executive Order 13492 of January 22, 2009
Review and Disposition of Individuals Detained at the Guantánamo Bay Naval Base and Closure of Detention Facilities

By the authority vested in me as President by the Constitution and the laws of the United States of America, in order to effect the appropriate disposition of individuals currently detained by the Department of Defenseat the Guantánamo Bay Naval Base (Guantánamo) and promptly to close detention facilities at Guantánamo, consistent with the national security and foreign policy interests of the United States and the interests of justice, I hereby order as follows:

Section 1. Definitions. As used in this order:

(a) "Common Article 3" means Article 3 of each of the Geneva Conventions.

(b) "Geneva Conventions" means:

(i) the Convention for the Amelioration of the Condition of the Wounded and Sick in Armed Forces in the Field, August 12, 1949 (6 UST 3114);

(ii) the Convention for the Amelioration of the Condition of Wounded, Sick and Shipwrecked Members of Armed Forces at Sea, August 12, 1949 (6 UST 3217);

(iii) the Convention Relative to the Treatment of Prisoners of War, August 12, 1949 (6 UST 3316); and

(iv) the Convention Relative to the Protection of Civilian Persons in Time of War, August 12, 1949 (6 UST 3516).

(c) "Individuals currently detained at Guantánamo" and "individuals covered by this order" mean individuals currently detained by the Department of Defense in facilities at the Guantánamo Bay Naval Base whom the Department of Defense has ever determined to be, or treated as, enemy combatants.

Section 2. Findings.

(a) Over the past 7 years, approximately 800 individuals whom the Department of Defense has ever determined to be, or treated as, enemy combatants have been detained at Guantánamo. The Federal Government has moved more than 500 such detainees from Guantánamo, either by returning them to their home country or by releasing or transferring them to a third country. The Department of Defense has determined that a number of the individuals currently detained at Guantánamo are eligible for such transfer or release.

(b) Some individuals currently detained at Guantánamo have been there for more than 6 years, and most have been detained for at least 4 years. In view of the significant concerns raised by these detentions, both within the United States and internationally, prompt and appropriate disposition of the individuals currently detained at Guantánamo and closure of the facilities in which they are detained would further the national security and foreign policy interests of the United States and the interests of justice.

Merely closing the facilities without promptly determining the appropriate disposition of the individuals detained would not adequately serve those interests. To the extent practicable, the prompt and appropriate disposition of the individuals detained at Guantánamo should precede the closure of the detention facilities at Guantánamo. (c) The individuals currently detained at Guantánamo have the constitutional privilege of the writ of habeas corpus. Most of those individuals have filed petitions for a writ of habeas corpus in Federal court challenging the lawfulness of their detention.

(d) It is in the interests of the United States that the executive branch undertake a prompt and thorough review of the factual and legal bases for the continued detention of all individuals currently held at Guantánamo, and of whether their continued detention is in the national security and foreign policy interests of the United States and in the interests of justice.

The unusual circumstances associated with detentions at Guantánamo require a comprehensive interagency review.

(e) New diplomatic efforts may result in an appropriate disposition of a substantial number of individuals currently detained at Guantánamo.

(f) Some individuals currently detained at Guantánamo may have committed offenses for which they should be prosecuted. It is in the interests of the United States to review whether and how any such individuals can and should be prosecuted.

(g) It is in the interests of the United States that the executive branch conduct a prompt and thorough review of the circumstances of the individuals currently detained at Guantánamo who have been charged with offenses before military commissions pursuant to the Military Commissions Act of 2006, Public Law 109–366, as well as of the military commission process more generally.

Section 3. Closure of Detention Facilities at Guantánamo. The detention facilities at Guantánamo for individuals covered by this order shall be closed as soon as practicable, and no later than 1 year from the date of this order.

If any individuals covered by this order remain in detention at Guantánamo at the time of closure of those detention facilities, they shall be returned to their home country, released, transferred to a third country, or transferred to another United States detention facility in a manner consistent with law and the national security and foreign policy interests of the United States.

Section 4. Immediate Review of All Guantánamo Detentions.

(a) **Scope and Timing of Review.** A review of the status of each individual currently detained at Guantánamo (Review) shall commence immediately.

(b) **Review Participants.** The Review shall be conducted with the full cooperation and participation of the following officials:

(1) the Attorney General, who shall coordinate the Review;

(2) the Secretary of Defense;

(3) the Secretary of State;

(4) the Secretary of Homeland Security;

(5) the Director of National Intelligence;

(6) the Chairman of the Joint Chiefs of Staff; and

(7) other officers or full-time or permanent part-time employees of the United States, including employees with intelligence, counterterrorism, military, and legal expertise, as determined by the Attorney General, with the concurrence of the head of the department or agency concerned.

(c) **Operation of Review.** The duties of the Review participants shall include the following:

(1) **Consolidation of Detainee Information.** The Attorney General shall, to the extent reasonably practicable, and in coordination with the other Review participants, assemble all information in the possession of the Federal Government that pertains to any individual currently detained at Guantánamo and that is relevant to determining the proper disposition of any such individual. All executive branch departments and agencies shall promptly comply with any request of the Attorney General to provide information in their possession or control pertaining to any such individual.

The Attorney General may seek further information relevant to the Review from any source.

(2) **Determination of Transfer.** The Review shall determine, on a rolling basis and as promptly as possible with respect to the individuals currently detained at Guantánamo, whether it is possible to transfer or release the individuals consistent with the national security and foreign policy interests of the United States and, if so, whether and how the Secretary of Defense may effect their transfer or release. The Secretary of Defense, the Secretary of State, and, as appropriate, other Review participants shall work to effect promptly the release or transfer of all individuals for whom release or transfer is possible.

(3) **Determination of Prosecution.** In accordance with United States law, the cases of individuals detained at Guantánamo not approved for release or transfer shall be evaluated to determine whether the Federal Government should seek to prosecute the detained individuals for any offenses they may have committed, including whether it is feasible to prosecute such individuals before a court established pursuant to Article III of the United States Constitution, and the Review participants shall in turn take the necessary and appropriate steps based on such determinations.

(4) **Determination of Other Disposition.** With respect to any individuals currently detained at Guantánamo whose disposition is not achieved under paragraphs (2) or (3) of this subsection, the Review shall select lawful means, consistent with the national security and foreign policy interests of the United States and the interests of justice, for the disposition of such individuals. The appropriate authorities shall promptly implement such dispositions.

(5) **Consideration of Issues Relating to Transfer to the United States.** The Review shall identify and consider legal, logistical, and security issues relating to the potential transfer of individuals currently detained at Guantánamo to facilities within the United States, and the Review participants shall work with the Congress on any legislation that may be appropriate.

Section 5. Diplomatic Efforts. The Secretary of State shall expeditiously pursue and direct such negotiations and diplomatic efforts with foreign governments as are necessary and appropriate to implement this order.

Section 6. Humane Standards of Confinement. No individual currently detained at Guantánamo shall be held in the custody or under the effective control of any officer, employee, or other agent of the United States Government, or at a facility owned, operated, or controlled by a department or agency of the United States, except in conformity with all applicable laws governing the conditions of such confinement, including Common Article 3 of the Geneva Conventions. The Secretary of Defense shall immediately undertake a review of the conditions of detention at Guantánamo to ensure full compliance with this directive. Such review shall be completed within 30 days and any necessary corrections shall be implemented immediately thereafter.

Section 7. Military Commissions. The Secretary of Defense shall immediately take steps sufficient to ensure that during the pendency of the Review described in section 4 of this order, no charges are sworn, or referred to a military commission under the Military Commissions Act of 2006 and the Rules for Military Commissions, and that all proceedings of such military commissions to which charges have been referred but in which no judgment has been rendered, and all proceedings pending in the United States Court of Military Commission Review, are halted.

Section 8. General Provisions.

(a) Nothing in this order shall prejudice the authority of the Secretary of Defense to determine the disposition of any detainees not covered by this order.

(b) This order shall be implemented consistent with applicable law and subject to the availability of appropriations.

(c) This order is not intended to, and does not, create any right or benefit, substantive or procedural, enforceable at law or in equity by any party against the United States, its departments, agencies, or entities, its officers, employees, or agents, or any other person.

THE WHITE HOUSE,

January 22, 2009.

DOCUMENT **91**

Full Official Title: Memorandum for John Rizzo, acting General Counsel for the Central Intelligence Agency- Interrogation of Al Qaeda Operative

Short Title/Acronym/Abbreviation: The 2002 Torture Memo

Type of Document: TOP SECRET Legal memorandum from the U.S. Department of Justice Office of the Attorney general, to the acting General Legal Counsel of the CIA.

Subject: Answering a legal inquiry presented by the CIA to the Attorney General's office concerning the legality of certain acts of the CIA in interrogating Al Qaeda suspects.

Official Citation: U.S. Department of Justice, Office of the Legal Council, Washington D.C., Memorandum for John Rizzo, acting General Counsel for the Central Intelligence Agency-Interrogation of Al Qaeda Operative, by Jay S. Bybee, Assistant Attorney General

Date of Document: August 1, 2002

Date of Adoption: Not applicable

Date of General Entry into Force (EIF): Not applicable

Number of States Parties as of this printing: Not applicable

Date of Signature by United States: Not applicable

Date of Ratification/Accession/Adhesion: Not applicable

Date of Entry into Force as to United States (effective date): Not applicable

Legal Status/Character of the Instrument/Document as to the United States: An inter-office legal opinion as to how the Administration's Attorney General views the legality of the acts committed or proposed by the CIA for interrogating terrorist suspects. An 18-page memo.

Comment: This is one of least four so-called "Torture Memos" issued by the DOJ to the Bush Administration from 2002 to 2005. They give a legal opinion as to whether certain intelligence gathering techniques are legal under U.S. and International Law, particularly Constitution and the Torture Convention A, dated August 1, 2002, from Jay Bybee, Assistant Attorney General, OLC, to John A. Rizzo, General Counsel CIA.

The other three so-called "Torture Memos" are as follows:

• A 46-page memo, dated May 10, 2005, from Steven Bradbury, Acting Assistant Attorney General, OLC, to John A. Rizzo, General Counsel CIA.

• A 20-page memo, dated May 10, 2005, from Steven Bradbury, Acting Assistant Attorney General, OLC, to John A. Rizzo, General Counsel CIA.

• A 40-page memo, dated May 30, 2005, from Steven Bradbury, Acting Assistant Attorney General, OLC, to John A. Rizzo, General Counsel CIA.

These and other Torture Memo documents (e.g. Yoo, Gonzalez) can be found at http://www.aclu.org/accountability/olc.html and www.texscience.org/reform/torture

When these memos came to public knowledge there was a strong opposition to their conclusions by many scholars and legal authorities in the U.S. and in the international community, such as the ICRC. The 2009 Obama Executive Order of January 22, 2009, caused the process of rescission of those Torture Memos and the techniques found in them were ordered stopped. See Document 92.

MEMORANDUM FOR JOHN RIZZO, ACTING GENERAL COUNSEL FOR THE CENTRAL INTELLIGENCE AGENCY-INTERROGATION OF AL QAEDA OPERATIVE

U.S. Department of Justice
Office of Legal Counsel
Office of the Assistant Attorney General
Washington, D.C. 20530
August 1, 2002
Interrogation of al Qaeda Operative

You have asked for this Office's views on whether certain proposed conduct would violate the prohibition against torture found at Section 2340A of title 18 of the United States Code. You have asked for this advice in the course of conducting interrogations of Abu Zubaydah. As we understand it, Zubaydah is one of the highest ranking members of the al Qaeda terrorist organization, with which the United States is currently engaged in an international armed conflict following the attacks on the World Trade Center and the Pentagon on September 11, 2001. This letter memorializes our previous oral advice, given on July 24, 2002 and July 26, 2002, that the proposed conduct would not violate this prohibition.

I.

Our advice is based upon the following facts, which you have provided to us. We also understand that you do not have any facts in your possession contrary to the facts outlined here, and this opinion is limited to these facts. If these facts were to change, this advice would not necessarily apply. Zubaydah is currently being held by the United States. The interrogation team is certain that he has additional information that he refuses to divulge. Specifically, he is withholding information regarding terrorist networks in the United States or in Saudi Arabia and information regarding plans to conduct attacks within the United States or against our interests overseas. Zubaydah has become accustomed to a certain level of treatment and displays no signs of willingness to disclose further information. Moreover, your intelligence indicates that there is currently a level of "chatter" equal to that which preceded the September 11 attacks. In light of the information you believe Zubaydah has and the high level of threat you believe now exists, you wish to move the interrogations into what you have described as an "increased pressure phase."

As part of this increased pressure phase, Zubaydah will have contact only with a new interrogation specialist, whom he has not met previously, and the Survival, Evasion, Resistance, Escape ("SERE") training psychologist who has been involved with the interrogations since they began. This phase will likely last no more than several days but could last up to thirty days. In this phase, you would like to employ ten techniques that you believe will dislocate his expectations regarding the treatment he believes he will receive and encourage him to disclose the crucial information mentioned above. These ten techniques are: (1) attention grasp, (2) walling, (3) facial hold, (4) facial slap (insult slap), (5) cramped confinement, (6) wall standing, (7) stress positions, (8) sleep deprivation, (9) insects placed in a confinement box, and (10) the waterboard. You have informed us that the use of these techniques would be on an as-needed basis and that not all of these techniques will necessarily be used. The interrogation team would use these techniques in some combination to convince Zubaydah that the only way he can influence his surrounding environment is through cooperation. You have, however, informed us that you expect these techniques to be used in some sort of escalating fashion, culminating with the waterboard, though not necessarily ending with this technique. Moreover, you have also orally informed us that although some of these techniques may be used with more than once, that repetition will not be substantial because the techniques generally lose their effectiveness after several repetitions. You have also informed us that Zabaydah sustained a wound during his capture, which is being treated.

Based on the facts you have given us, we understand each of these techniques to be as follows. The attention grasp consists of grasping the individual with both hands, one hand on each side of the collar opening, in a controlled and quick motion. In the same motion as the grasp, the individual is drawn toward the interrogator.

For walling, a flexible false wall will be constructed. The individual is placed with his heels touching the wall. The interrogator pulls the individual forward and then quickly and firmly pushes the individual into the wall. It is the individual's shoulder blades that hit the wall. During this motion, the head and neck are supported with a rolled hood or towel that provides a c-collar effect to help prevent whiplash. To further reduce the probability of injury, the individual is allowed to rebound from the flexible wall. You have orally informed us that the false wall is in part constructed to create a loud sound when the individual hits it, which will further shock or surprise in the individual. In part, the idea is to create a sound that will make the impact seem far worse than it is and that will be far worse than any injury that might result from the action.

The facial hold is used to hold the head immobile. One open palm is placed on either side of the individual's face. The fingertips are kept well away from the individual's eyes.

With the facial slap or insult slap, the interrogator slaps the individual's face with fingers slightly spread. The hand makes contact with the area directly between the tip of the individual's chin and the bottom of the corresponding earlobe. The interrogator invades the individual's personal space. The goal of the facial slap is not to inflict physical pain that is severe or lasting. Instead, the purpose of the facial slap is to induce shock, surprise, and/or humiliation.

Cramped confinement involves the placement of the individual in a confined space, the dimensions of which restrict the individual's movement. The confined space is usually dark. The duration of confinement varies based upon the size of the container. For the larger confined space, the individual can stand up or sit down; the smaller space is large enough for the subject to sit down. Confinement in the larger space can last up to eighteen hours; for the smaller space, confinement lasts for no more than two hours.

Wall standing is used to induce muscle fatigue. The individual stands about four to five feet from a wall, with his feet spread approximately to shoulder width. His arms are stretched out in front of him, with his fingers resting on the wall. His fingers support all of his body weight. The individual is not permitted to move or reposition his hands or feet.

A variety of stress positions may be used. You have informed us that these positions are not designed to produce the pain associated with contortions or twisting of the body. Rather, somewhat like walling, they are designed to produce the physical discomfort associated with muscle fatigue. Two particular stress positions are likely to be used on Zubaydah: (1) sitting on the floor with legs extended straight out in front of him with his arms raised above his head; and (2) kneeling on the floor while leaning back at a 45 degree angle. You have also orally informed us that through observing Zubaydah in captivity, you have noted that he appears to be quite flexible despite his wound.

Sleep deprivation may be used. You have indicated that your purpose in using this technique is to reduce the individual's ability to think on his feet and, through the discomfort associated with lack of sleep, to motivate him to cooperate. The effect of such sleep deprivation will generally remit after one or two nights of uninterrupted sleep. You have informed us that your research has revealed that, in rare instances, some individuals who are already predisposed to psychological problems may experience abnormal reactions to sleep deprivation. Even in those cases, however, reactions abate after the individual is permitted to sleep. Moreover, personnel with medical training are available to and will intervene in the unlikely event of an abnormal reaction. You have orally informed us that you would not deprive Zubaydah of sleep for more than eleven days at a time and that you have previously kept him awake for 72 hours, from which no mental or physical harm resulted.

You would like to place Zubaydah in a cramped confinement box with an insect. You have informed us that he appears to have a fear of insects. In particular, you would like to tell Zubaydah that you intend to place a stinging insect into the box with him. You would, however, place a harmless insect in the box. You have orally informed us that you would in fact place a harmless insect such as a caterpillar in the box with him.

Finally, you would like to use a technique called the "waterboard." In this procedure, the individual is bound securely to an inclined bench, which is approximately four feet by seven feet. The individual's feet are generally elevated. A cloth is placed over the forehead and eyes. Water is then applied to the cloth in a controlled manner. As this is done, the cloth is lowered until it covers both the nose and mouth. Once the cloth is saturated and completely covers the mouth and nose, air flow is slightly restricted for 20 to 40 seconds due to the presence of the cloth. This causes an increase in carbon dioxide level in the individual's blood. This increase in the carbon dioxide level stimulates increased effort to breathe. This effort plus the cloth produces the perception of "suffocation and incipient panic," i.e., the perception of drowning. The individual does not breathe any water into his lungs. During those 20 to 40 seconds, water is continuously applied from a height of twelve to twenty-four inches. After this period, the cloth is lifted, and the individual is allowed to breathe unimpeded for three or four full breaths. The sensation of drowning is immediately relieved by the removal of the cloth. The procedure may then be repeated. The water is usually applied from a canteen cup or small watering can, with a spout. You have orally informed us that this procedure triggers an automatic physiological sensation of drowning that the individual cannot control even though he may be aware that he is in fact not drowning. You have also orally informed us that it is likely that this procedure would not last more than 20 minutes in any one application.

We also understand that a medical expert with SERE experience will be present throughout this phase and that the procedures will be stopped if deemed medically necessary to prevent severe mental or physical harm to Zubaydah. As mentioned above. Zubaydah suffered an injury during his capture. You have informed us that steps will be taken to ensure that this injury is not in any way exacerbated by the use of these methods and that adequate medical attention will be given to ensure that it-will heal properly.

II.

In this part, we review the context within which these procedures will be applied. You have informed us that you have taken various steps to ascertain what effect, if any, these techniques would have on Zubaydah's mental health. These same techniques, with, the exception of the insect in the cramped confined space, have been used and continue to he used on some members of our military personnel during their SERE training. Because of the use of these procedures in training our own military personnel to resist interrogations, you have consulted with various individuals who have extensive experience in the use of these techniques. You have done so in order to ensure that no prolonged mental harm would result from the use of these proposed procedures.

Through your consultation with various individuals responsible for such training, you have learned that these techniques have been used as elements of a course of conduct without any reported incident of prolonged mental harm. ████████████████ of the SERE school, ████████████████ has reported that, during the seven-year period that he spent in those positions, there were two requests from Congress for information concerning alleged injuries resulting from the training. One of these inquiries was prompted by the temporary physical injury a trainee sustained as result of being placed in a confinement box. The other inquiry involved claims that the SERE training caused two individuals to engage, in criminal behavior, namely, felony shoplifting and downloading child pornography onto a military computer. According to this official, these claims were found to be baseless. Moreover, he has indicated that during the three and a half years he spent as of the SERE program, ████████████████ he trained 10,000 students. Of those students, only two dropped out of the training following the use of these techniques. Although on rare occasions some students temporarily postponed the remainder of their training and received psychological counseling, those students were able to finish the program without any indication of subsequent mental health effects.

You have informed us that you have consulted with ████████████████ who has ten years of experience with SERE training. ██

████████████████████████ He stated that, during those ten years, insofar as he is aware, none of the individuals who completed the program suffered any adverse mental health effects. He informed you that there was one person who did not complete the training. That person experienced an adverse mental health reaction that lasted, only two hours. After those two hours, the individual's symptoms spontaneously, dissipated without requiring treatment or counseling and no other symptoms were ever reported by this individual According to the information you have provided to us, this assessment of the use of these procedures includes the use of the waterboard.

Additionally you received a memorandum from the ████████████████████████ ████████████████ which you supplied to us. ████████████████ has experience, with the use of all of these procedures in a course of conduct, with the exception of the insect in the confinement box and the waterboard. This memorandum confirms that the use of these procedures has not resulted in any reported instances of prolonged mental harm, and very few instances of immediate and temporary adverse psychological responses to the training. ████████████████ Reported that a small minority of students have had temporary adverse psychological reactions during training. Of the 26,829 students trained from 1992 through

2001 in the Air Force SERE training, 4.3 percent of those students had contact with psychology services. Of those 4.3 percent, only 3.2 percent were pulled from the program for psychological reasons. Thus, out of the students trained overall, only 0.14 percent were pulled from the program for psychological reasons. Furthermore, although ██████████████ indicated that surveys of students having completed this training are not done, he expressed confidence that the training did not cause any long-term psychological impact. He based his conclusion on the debriefing of students that is done after the training. More importantly, be based this assessment on the fact that although training is required to be extremely stressful in order to be effective, very few complaints have been made regarding die training. During his tenure, in which 10.000 students were trained, no congressional complaints have been made. While there was one Inspector General complaint, it was not due to psychological concerns. Moreover, he was aware of only one letter inquiring about the long-term impact of these techniques from an individual trained over twenty years ago. He found that it was impossible to attribute this individual's symptoms to his training. ██████████████ concluded that if there are any long-term psychological effects of die United States Air Force training using the procedures outlined above they "are certainly minimal."

With respect to the waterboard, you have also orally informed us that the Navy continues to use it in training. You have informed us that your on-site psychologists, who have extensive experience with tire use of the waterboard in Navy training, have not encountered any significant long-term mental health consequences from its use. Your on-site-psychologists have also indicated that JPKA has likewise not reported any significant long-term, mental health consequences from the use of the waterboard. You have informed us that other services ceased use of the waterboard because it was so successful as an interrogation technique, but not because of any concerns over any harm, physical or mental, caused by it. It was also reported to be almost 100 percent effective in producing cooperation among the trainees. ██████████████ also indicated that he had observed the use of the waterboard in Navy training some ten to twelve times. Each time it resulted in cooperation but it did not result in any physical harm to the student.

You have also reviewed the relevant literature and found no empirical data on the effect of these techniques, with the exception of sleep deprivation. With respect to sleep deprivation, you have informed us that is not uncommon for someone to be deprived of sleep for 72 hours and still perform excellently en visual-spatial motor tasks and short-term memory tests. Although some individuals may experience hallucinations, according to the literature you surveyed, those who experience such psychotic symptoms have almost always had such episodes prior to the sleep deprivation. You have indicated the studies of lengthy sleep deprivation showed no psychosis, loosening of thoughts, flattening of emotions, delusions, or paranoid ideas. In one case, even after eleven days of deprivation, no psychosis or permanent brain damaged, occurred. In fact the individual reported feeling almost back to normal after one night's sleep. Further, based on the experiences with its use in military training (where it is induced for up to 48 hours), you found that rarely, if ever, will the individual suffer harm after the sleep deprivation is discontinued. Instead, the effects remit after a few good nights of sleep.

You have taken the additional step of consulting with U.S. interrogations experts, and other individuals with oversight over the SERE training process. None of these individuals was aware of any prolonged psychological effect caused by the use of any of the above techniques either separately or as a course of conduct. Moreover, you consulted with outside psychologists who reported that they were unaware of any cases where long-term problems have occurred as a result of these techniques.

Moreover, in consulting with a number of mental health experts, you have learned that the effect of any of these procedures will be dependant on the individual's personal history, cultural history and psychological tendencies. To that end, you have informed us that you have completed a psychological assessment of Zubadyah. This assessment is based on interviews with Zubaydah, observations of him, and information collected from other sources such as intelligence and press reports. Our understanding of Zubaydah's psychological profile, which we set forth below, is based on that assessment.

According to this assessment, Zubaydah, though only 31, rose quickly from very low level mujahedin to third or fourth man in al Qaeda. He has served as Osama Bin Laden's senior lieutenant. In that capacity, he has managed a network of training camps. He has been instrumental in the training of operatives for al Qaeda, the Egyptian Islamic Jihad, and other terrorist elements inside Pakistan and Afghanistan. He acted as the Deputy Camp Commander for al Qaeda training camp in Afghanistan, personally approving entry and graduation of all trainees during 1999–2000. From 1996 until 1999, he approved all individuals going in and out of Afghanistan to the training camps. Further, no one went in and out of Peshawar, Pakistan without his knowledge and approval. He also acted as al Qaeda's coordinator of external contacts and foreign communications. Additionally, he has acted as al Qaeda's counterintelligence officer and has been trusted to find spies within the organization.

Zubaydah has been involved in every major terrorist operation carried out by al Qaeda. He was a planner for the Millennium plot to attack U.S. and Israeli targets during the Millennium celebrations in Jordan. Two of the central figures in tins plot who were arrested have identified Zubaydah as the supporter of their cell and the plot. He also served as a planner for the Paris Embassy plot in 2001. Moreover, be was one of the planners of the September 11 attacks. Prior to his capture, he was engaged in planning future terrorist attacks against U.S. interests.

Your psychological assessment indicates that it is believed Zubaydah wrote al Qaeda's manual on resistance techniques. You also believe that his experiences in al Qaeda make him well-acquainted with and well-versed in such techniques. As part of his role in al Qaeda, Zubaydah visited individuals in prison and helped them upon their release. Through tins contact and activities with other al Qaeda mujahedin, you believe that he knows many stories off capture, interrogation, and resistance to such interrogation. Additionally, he has spoken with Ayman al-Zawahiri, and you believe it is likely that the two discussed Zawahiri's experiences as a prisoner of the Russians and the Egyptians.

Zubaydah stated during interviews that he thinks of any activity outside of jihad as "silly." He has indicated that his heart and mind are devoted to serving Allah, and Islam through jihad and he has stated that lie has no doubts or regrets about committing himself to jihad. Zubaydah believes that the global victory of Islam, is inevitable. You have, informed us that he continues to express his unabated desire to kill Americans and Jews.

Your psychological assessment describes his personality as follows. He is "a highly self-directed individual who prizes his independence," He has "narcissistic features," which are evidenced in the attention he pays to his personal appearance and his "obvious 'efforts' to demonstrate that he is really a rather 'humble and regular guy.'" He is "somewhat compulsive" in how he organizes his environment and business. He is confident, self-assured, and possesses an air of authority. While he admits to at times wrestling with how to determine who is an "innocent," he has acknowledged celebrating the destruction of the World Trade Center. He is intelligent and intellectually curious. He displays "excellent self-discipline." The assessment describes him as a perfectionist, persistent, private, and highly capable in his social interactions. He is very guarded about opening up to others and your assessment repeatedly emphasizes that he tends not to trust others easily. He is also "quick to recognize and assess the moods and motivations of others." Furthermore, he is proud of his ability to lie and deceive others successfully. Through his deception he has, among other things, prevented the location of al Qaeda safehouses and even acquired a United Nations refugee identification card.

According to your reports, Zubaydah does not have any pre-existing mental conditions or problems that would make him likely to suffer prolonged mental harm from your proposed interrogation methods. Through reading his diaries and interviewing him, you have found no history of "mood disturbance or other psychiatric pathology[,]" "thought disorder[,] ... enduring mood or mental health problems." He is in fact "remarkably resilient and confident that he can overcome adversity." When he encounters stress or low mood, this appears to last only for a short time. He deals with stress by assessing its source, evaluating the coping resources available to him, and then taking action. Your assessment notes that he is "generally self-sufficient and relies on his understanding and application of religious and psychological principles, intelligence and discipline to avoid and overcome problems." Moreover, you have found that he has a "reliable and durable support system" in his faith, "the blessings of religious leaders, and camaraderie of like-minded mujahedin brothers." During detention, Zubaydah has managed his mood, remaining at most points "circumspect, calm, controlled, and deliberate." He has maintained this demeanor during aggressive interrogations and reductions in sleep. You describe that in an initial confrontational incident, Zubaydah showed signs of sympathetic nervous system arousal, which you think was possibly fear. Although this incident led him to disclose intelligence information, he was able to quickly regain his composure, his air of confidence, and his "strong resolve" not to reveal any information.

Overall, you summarize his primary strengths as the following: ability to focus, goal-directed discipline, intelligence, emotional resilience, street savvy, ability to organize and manage people, keen observation skills, fluid adaptability (can anticipate and adapt under duress and with minimal resources), capacity to assess and exploit the needs of others, and ability to adjust goals to emerging opportunities.

You anticipate that he will draw upon his vast knowledge of interrogation techniques to cope with the interrogation. Your assessment indicates that Zubaydah may be willing to die to protect the most important information that he holds. Nonetheless, you are of the view that his belief that Islam will ultimately dominate the world and that this victory is inevitable may provide the chance that Zubaydah will give information and rationalize it solely as a temporary setback. Additionally, you believe be may be willing to disclose some information, particularly information he deems to not be critical, but which may ultimately be useful to us when pieced together with other intelligence information you have gained.

III.

Section 2340A makes it a criminal offense for any person "outside of the United States [to] commit[] or attempt[] to commit torture." Section 2340(1) defines torture as:

> an act committed by a person acting under the color of law specifically intended to inflict severe physical or mental pain or suffering (other than pain or suffering incidental to lawful sanctions) upon another person within his custody of physical control.

18 U.S.C. § 2340(1). As we outlined in our opinion on standards of conduct under Section 2340A, a violation of 2340A requires a showing that: (1) the torture occurred outside the United States: (2) the defendant acted under the color of law; (3) the victim was within, the defendant's custody or control; (4) the defendant specifically intended to inflict severe pain or suffering; and (5) that the acted inflicted severe pain or suffering. *See* Memorandum for John Rizzo, Acting General Counsel for the Central Intelligence Agency, from Jay S. Bybee, Assistant Attorney General, Office of Legal Counsel *Re: Standards of Conduct far Interrogation under 18 U.S.C. §§ 2340–2340A* at 3 (.August 1, 2002) ("Section 2340A Memorandum"). You have asked us to assume that Zubayadah is being held outside the United Slates, Zubayadah is within U.S. custody, and the interrogators are acting under the color of law. At issue is whether the last two elements would be met by the use of the proposed procedures, namely, whether those using these procedures would have the requisite mental state and whether these procedures would inflict severe pain or suffering within the meaning of the statute.

<u>Severe Pain or Suffering.</u> In order for pain or suffering to rise to the level of torture, the statute requires that it be severe. As we have previously explained, this reaches only extreme acts. *See id.* at 13. Nonetheless, drawing upon cases under the Torture Victim Protection Act (TVPA), which has a definition of torture that is similar to Section 2340's definition, we found that a single event of sufficiently intense pain may fall within this prohibition. *See id.* at 26. As a result, we have analyzed each of these techniques separately, [and] further drawing upon those cases, we also have found that courts tend to take a totality-of-the-circumstances approach and consider an entire course of conduct to determine whether torture has occurred. *See id.* at 27. Therefore, in addition to considering each technique separately, we consider them together as a course of conduct.

Section 2340 defines torture as the infliction of severe physical or mental pain or suffering. We will consider physical pain and mental pain separately. *See* 18 U.S.C. § 2340(1). With respect to *physical* pain, we previously concluded that "severe pain" within the meaning of Section 2340 is pain that is difficult for the individual to endure and is of an intensity akin to the pain accompanying serious physical injury. *See* Section 2340A Memorandum at 6. Drawing upon the TVPA precedent, we have noted that examples of acts inflicting severe pain that typify torture are, among other things, severe beatings with weapons such as clubs, and the burning of prisoners. *See id.* at 24. We conclude below that none of the proposed techniques inflicts such pain.

The facial hold and the attention grasp involve no physical pain. In the absence of such pain it is obvious that they cannot be said to inflict severe physical pain or suffering. The stress positions and wall standing both may result in muscle fatigue. Each involves the sustained holding of a position. In wall standing, it will be holding a position in which all of the individual's body weight is placed on his finger tips. The stress positions will likely include sitting on the floor with legs extended straight out in front and arms raised above the head, and kneeling on the floor and leaning back at a 45 degree angle. Any pain associated with muscle fatigue is not of the intensity sufficient to amount to "severe physical pain or suffering" under the statute, nor, despite its discomfort, can it be said to be difficult to endure. Moreover, you have orally Informed us that no stress position will be used that could interfere with the healing of Zubaydah's wound. Therefore, we conclude that these techniques involve discomfort that falls far below the threshold of severe physical pain.

Similarly, although the confinement boxes (both small and large) are physically uncomfortable because their size restricts movement, they are not so small as to require the individual to contort his body to sit (small box) or stand (large box). You have also orally informed us that despite his wound, Zubaydah remains quite flexible, which would substantially reduce any pain associated with being placed in the box. We have no information from the medical experts you have consulted that the limited duration for which the individual is kept in the boxes causes any substantial physical pain. As a result, we do not think the use of these boxes can be said to cause pain that is of the intensity associated with serious physical injury.

The use of one of these boxes with the introduction of an insect does not alter this assessment. As we understand it, no actually harmful insect will be placed in the box. Thus, though the introduction of an insect may produce trepidation in Zubaydah (which we discuss below), it certainly does not cause physical pain.

As for sleep deprivation, it is clear that depriving someone of sleep does not involve severe physical pain within the meaning of the statute. While sleep deprivation may involve some physical discomfort, such as the fatigue or the discomfort experienced in the difficulty of keeping one's eyes open, these effects remit after the individual is permitted to sleep. Based on the facts you have provided us, we are not aware of any evidence that sleep deprivation results in severe physical pain or suffering. As a result, its use does not violate Section 2340A.

Even those techniques that involve physical contact between the interrogator and the individual do lete not result in severe pain. The facial slap and walling contain precautions to ensure that no pain even approaching this level results. The slap is delivered with fingers slightly spread, which you have explained to us is designed to be less painful than a closed-hand slap. The slap is also delivered to the fleshy part of the face, further reducing any risk of physical damage or serious pain. The facial slap does not produce pain that is difficult to endure. Likewise, walling involves quickly pulling the person forward and then thrusting him against a flexible false wall. You have informed us that the sound of hitting the wall will actually be far worse than any possible injury to the individual. The use of the roiled towel around the neck also reduces any risk of injury. While it may hurt to be pushed against the wall, any pain experienced is not of the intensity associated with serious physical injury.

As we understand it, when the waterboard is used, the subject's body responds as if the subject were drowning—even though the subject may he well aware that he is in fact not drowning. You have informed us that this procedure does not inflict actual physical harm. Thus, although the subject may experience the fear or panic associated with the feeling of drowning, the waterboard does not inflict physical pain. As we explained in the Section 2340A Memorandum, "pain and suffering" as used in Section 2340 is best understood as a single concept, not distinct concepts of "pain" as distinguished from "suffering." See Section 2340A Memorandum at 6 n.3. The waterboard, which inflicts no pain or actual harm whatsoever, does not, in our view inflict "severe pain or suffering." Even if one were to parse the statute more finely to attempt to treat "suffering" as a distinct concept, the waterboard could not be said to inflict severe suffering. The waterboard is simply a controlled acute episode, lacking the connotation of a protracted period of time generally given to suffering.

Finally, as we discussed above, you have informed us that in determining which procedures to use and how you will use them, you have selected techniques that will not harm Zubaydah's wound. You have also indicated that numerous steps will be taken to ensure that none of these procedures in any way interferes with the proper healing of Zubaydah's wound. You have also indicated that, should it appear at any time that Zubaydah is experiencing severe pain or suffering, the medical personnel on hand will stop the use of any technique.

Even when all of these methods are considered combined in an overall course of conduct, they still would not inflict severe physical pain or suffering. As discussed above, a number of these acts result in no physical pain, others produce only physical discomfort. You have indicated that these acts will not be used with substantial repetition, so that there is no possibility that severe physical pain could arise from such repetition. Accordingly, we conclude that these acts neither separately nor as part of a course of conduct would inflict severe physical pain or suffering within the meaning of the statute.

We next consider whether the use of these techniques would inflict severe *mental* pain or suffering within the meaning of Section 2340. Section 2340 defines severe mental pain or suffering as "the prolonged mental harm caused by or resulting from" one of several predicate acts. 18 U.S.C. § 2340(2). Those predicate acts are: (1) the intentional infliction or threatened infliction of severe physical pain or suffering; (2) the administration or application, or threatened administration or application of mind-altering substances or other procedures calculated to disrupt profoundly the senses or the personality; (3) the threat of imminent death; or (4) the threat that any of the preceding acts will be done to another person. See 18 U.S.C. § 2340(2)(A)–(D). As we have explained, this list of predicate acts is exclusive. See Section 2340A Memorandum at 8. No other acts can support a charge under Section 2340A based on die infliction of severe mental pain or suffering. See id. Thus, if the methods that you have described do not either in and of themselves constitute one of these acts or as a course of conduct fulfill the predicate act requirement, the prohibition has not been violated. *See id.* Before addressing these techniques, we note that it is plain that none of these procedures involves a threat to any third party, the use of any kind of drugs, or for the reasons described above, the infliction of severe physical pain. Thus, the question is whether any of these acts, separately or as a course of conduct, constitutes a threat of severe physical pain or suffering, a procedure designed to disrupt profoundly the senses, or a threat of imminent death. As we previously explained, whether an action constitutes a threat must be assessed from the standpoint of a reasonable person in the subject's position. *See id:* at 9.

No argument can be made that the attention grasp or the facial hold constitute threats of imminent death or are procedures designed to disrupt profoundly the senses or personality. In general the grasp and the facial hold will startle the subject, produce fear, or even insult him. As you have informed us, the use of these techniques is not accompanied by a specific verbal/threat of severe physical pain or suffering. To the extent that these techniques could be considered a threat of severe physical pain or suffering, such a threat would have to be inferred from the acts themselves. Because these actions themselves involve no pain, neither could be interpreted by a reasonable, person in Zubaydah's position to constitute a threat of severe pain or suffering. Accordingly, these two techniques are not predicate acts within the meaning of Section 2340.

The facial slap likewise falls outside the set of predicate acts. It plainly is not a threat of imminent death, under Section 2340(2)(C), or a procedure designed to disrupt profoundly the senses or personality, under Section 2340(2)(B). Though it may hurt, as discussed above, the effect is one of smarting or stinging and surprise or humiliation, but not severe pain. Nor does it alone constitute a threat of severe pain or suffering, under Section 2340(2)(A). Like the facial hold and the attention grasp, the use of this slap is not accompanied by a specific verbal threat of further escalating violence. Additionally, you have informed us that in one use this technique will typically involve almost two slaps. Certainly, the use of this slap may dislodge any expectation that Zubaydah bad that lie would not be touched in a physically aggressive manner. Nonetheless, this alteration in his expectations could hardly be construed by a reasonable person in his situation to be tantamount to a threat of severe physical pain or suffering. At most, this technique suggests that the circumstances of his confinement and interrogation have changed. Therefore, the facial slap is not within the statute's exclusive list of predicate acts.

Walling plainly is not a procedure calculated to disrupt profoundly the senses or personality. While walling involves what might be characterized as rough handling, it does not involve the threat of imminent death or, as discussed above, the infliction of severe physical pain. Moreover, once again we understand that use of this technique will not be accompanied by any specific verbal threat that violence will ensue absent cooperation. Thus, like the facial slap, walling can only constitute a threat of severe physical pain if a reasonable person would infer such a threat from the use of the technique itself. Walling does not in and of itself inflict severe pain or suffering. Like the facial slap, walling may alter the subject's expectation as to the treatment he believes he will receive. Nonetheless, the character of the action falls so far short of inflicting severe pain or suffering within the meaning of the statute that even if he inferred that greater aggressiveness was to follow, the type of actions that could be reasonably be anticipated would still fall below anything sufficient to inflict severe physical pain or suffering under the statute. Thus, we conclude that this technique falls outside the proscribed predicate acts.

Like walling, stress positions and wall-standing are not procedures calculated to disrupt profoundly the senses, nor are they threats of imminent death. These procedures, as discussed above, involve the use of muscle fatigue to encourage cooperation and do not themselves constitute the infliction of severe physical pain or suffering. Moreover, there is no aspect of violence to either technique that remotely suggests future severe pain or suffering from which such a threat of future harm could be inferred. They simply involve forcing the subject to remain in uncomfortable positions. While these acts may indicate to the subject that he may be placed in these positions again if he does not disclose information, the use of these techniques would not suggest to a reasonable person in the subject's position that he is being threatened with severe pain or suffering. Accordingly, we conclude that these two procedures do not constitute any of the predicate acts set forth in Section 2340(2).

As with the other techniques discussed so far, cramped confinement is not a threat of imminent death. It may be argued that, focusing in part on the fact that the boxes will be without light, placement in these boxes would constitute a procedure designee to disrupt profoundly the senses. As we explained in our recent opinion, however, to "disrupt profoundly the senses" a technique must produce an extreme effect in the subject. *See* Section 2340A Memorandum at 10–12. We have previously concluded that this requires that the procedure cause substantial interference with the individual's cognitive abilities or fundamentally alter his personality. *See id.* at 11. Moreover, the statute requires that such procedures must be calculated to produce this effect. *See id.* at 10; 18 U.S.C. § 2340(2)(B).

With respect to the small confinement box, you have informed us that he would spend at most two hours in this box. You have informed us that your purpose in using these boxes is not to interfere with his senses or his personality, but to cause him physical discomfort that will encourage him to disclose critical information. Moreover, your imposition of time limitations on the use of either of the boxes also indicates that the use of these boxes is not designed or calculated to disrupt profoundly the senses or personality. For the larger box, in which he can both stand and sit, he may be placed in this box for up to eighteen hours at a time, while you have informed us that he will never spend more than an hour at time in the smaller box. These time limits further ensure that no profound disruption of the senses or personality, were it even possible, would result. As such, the use of the confinement boxes does not constitute a procedure calculated to disrupt profoundly the senses or personality.

Nor does the use of the boxes threaten Zubaydah with severe physical pain or suffering. While additional time spent in the boxes may be threatened, their use is not accompanied by any express threats of severe physical pain or suffering. Like the stress positions and walling, placement in the boxes is physically uncomfortable but any such discomfort does not rise to the level of severe physical pain or suffering. Accordingly, a reasonable person in the subject's position would not infer from die use of this technique that severe physical, pain is the next step in his interrogator's treatment of him. Therefore, we conclude that the use of the confinement boxes does not fall within the statute's required predicate acts.

In addition to using the confinement boxes alone, you also would like to introduce an insect into one of the boxes with Zubaydah. As we understand it, you plan to inform Zubaydah that you are going to place a stinging insect into the box, but you will actually place a harmless insect in the box, such as a caterpillar. If you do so, to ensure that you are outside the predicate act requirement, you must inform him that the insects will not have a sting that would produce death or severe pain. If, however, you were to place the insect in the box without informing him that you are doing so, then, in order to not commit a predicate act, you should not affirmatively lead him to believe that any insect is present which has a sting what could produce severe pain or suffering or even cause his death. ████████████████████████████████████ ████████████████████████████████ so long as you take either of the approaches we have described, the insect's placement in the box would not constitute a threat of severe physical pain or suffering to a reasonable person in his position. An individual placed in a box, even an individual, with a fear of insects, would not reasonably feel threatened with severe physical pain or suffering if a caterpillar was placed in the box. Further, you have informed us that you are not aware that Zubaydah has any allergies to insects, and you have not informed us of any other factors that would cause a reasonable person in that same situation to believe that an unknown insect would cause him severe physical pain nr death. Thus, we conclude that the placement of the insect in the confinement box with Zubaydah would not constitute a predicate act.

Sleep deprivation also clearly does not involve a threat of imminent death. Although it produces physical discomfort, it cannot be said to constitute a threat of severe physical, pain or suffering from the perspective of a reasonable person in Zubaydah's position. Nor could sleep deprivation constitute a procedure calculated to disrupt profoundly the senses, so long as sleep deprivation (as you have informed us is your intent) is used for limited periods, before hallucinations or other profound disruptions of the senses would occur. To be sure, sleep deprivation may reduce the subject's ability to think on his feet. Indeed, you indicate that this is the intended result. His mere reduced ability to evade your questions and resist answering does not, however, rise to the level of disruption required by the statute. As explained above, a disruption within the meaning of the statute is an extreme one, substantially interfering with an individual's cognitive abilities, for example, inducing hallucinations, or driving him to engage in uncharacteristic self-destructive behavior. *See infra* 13; Section 2340A Memorandum at 11. Therefore, the limited use of sleep deprivation does not constitute one of the required predicate acts.

We find that the use of the waterboard constitutes a threat of imminent death. As you have explained the waterboard procedure to us, it creates in the subject the uncontrollable physiological sensation that the subject is drowning. Although the procedure will be monitored by personnel with medical training and extensive SERE school experience with this procedure who will ensure the subject's mental and physical safety, the subject is not aware of any of these precautions. From the vantage point of any reasonable person undergoing this procedure in such circumstances, he would feel as if he is drowning at very moment of the procedure due to the uncontrollable physiological sensation he is experiencing. Thus, this procedure cannot be viewed as too uncertain to satisfy the imminence requirement. Accordingly, it constitutes a threat of imminent death and fulfills the predicate act requirement under the statute.

Although the waterboard constitutes a threat of imminent, death, prolonged mental harm must nonetheless result to violate the statutory prohibition on infliction of severe mental pain or suffering. *See* Section 2340A Memorandum at 7. We have previously concluded that prolonged mental harm is mental harm of some lasting duration, e.g., mental harm lasting months or years. *See id.* Prolonged mental harm is not simply the stress experienced in. for example, an interrogation by state police. *See id.* Based on your research into the use of these methods at the SERE school and consultation with others with expertise in the field of psychology and interrogation, you do not anticipate that any prolonged mental harm would result, from the use of the waterboard. Indeed, you have advised us that the relief is almost immediate when the cloth is removed from the nose and mouth. In the absence of prolonged mental harm, no severe mental pain or suffering would have been inflicted, and the use of these procedures would not constitute torture within the meaning of the statute.

When these acts are considered as a course of conduct, we are unsure whether these acts may constitute a threat of severe physical pain or suffering. You have indicated to us that you have not determined either the order or the precise timing for implementing these procedures. It is conceivable that these procedures could be used in a course of escalating conduct, moving incrementally and rapidly from least physically intrusive, e.g., facial hold, to the most physical contact, e.g., walling or the waterboard. As we understand it, based on his treatment so far, Zubaydah has come to expect that no physical harm will be done to him. By using these techniques in increasing intensity and in rapid succession, the goal would be to dislodge this expectation. Based on the facts you have provided to us, we cannot say definitively that the entire course of conduct would cause a reasonable person to believe that he is being threatened with severe pain or suffering within the meaning of section 2340. On the other hand, however, under certain circumstances—for example, rapid escalation in the use of these techniques culminating in the waterboard (which we acknowledge constitutes a threat of imminent death) accompanied by verbal, or other suggestions that physical violence will follow— might cause a reasonable person to believe that they arc faced with such a threat. Without more information, we are uncertain whether the course of conduct would constitute a predicate act under Section 2340(2).

Even if the course of conduct were thought to pose a threat of physical pain or suffering, it would nevertheless—on the facts before us—not constitute a violation of Section 2340A. Not only must the course of conduct be a predicate act, but also those who use the procedure must actually cause prolonged mental harm. Based or; the information that you have provided to us, indicating that no evidence exists that, this course of conduct produces any prolonged mental harm, we conclude mat a course of conduct using these procedures and culminating in the waterboard would not violate Section 2340A.

<u>Specific Intent.</u> To violate the statute, an individual must have the specific intent to inflict severe pain or suffering. Because specific intent is an element of the offense, the absence of specific intent negates the charge of torture. As we previously opined, to have the required specific intent, an individual must expressly intend to cause such severe pain or suffering. *See* Section 2340A Memorandum at 3 citing *Carter v. United States*, 530 U.S. 255, 267 (2000). We have further found that if a defendant acts with the good faith belief that his actions will not cause such suffering, he has not acted with specific intent. *See id.* at 4 citing *South Ad. Lmtd. Ptrshp. of Tenn. v. Reise*, 218 F.3d 518, 531 (4th Cir. 2002). A defendant acts in good faith when lie has an honest belief that his actions will not result in severe pain or suffering. *See id.* citing *Cheek v. United States*, 498 U.S. 192, 202 (1991). Although an honest belief need not be reasonable, such a belief is easier to establish where there is a reasonable basis for it. *See id.* at 5 Good faith may be established by, among other things, the reliance on the advice of experts. *See id.* at 8.

Based on the information you have provided us, we believe that those carrying out these procedures would not have the specific intent to inflict severe physical pain or suffering. The objective of these techniques is not to cause severe physical pain. First, the constant presence of personnel with medical training who have the authority to stop the interrogation should it appear it is medically necessary indicates that it is not your intent to cause severe physical pain. The personnel on site have extensive experience with these specific techniques as they are used in SERE school training. Second, you have informed, us that you are taking steps to ensure that Zubaydah's injury is not worsened or his recovery impeded by the use of these techniques.

Third, as you have described them to us, the proposed techniques involving physical contact between the interrogator and Zubaydah actually contain precautions to prevent any serious physical harm to Zubaydah. In "walling," a rolled hood or towel will be used to prevent whiplash and he will be permitted to rebound from the flexible wail to reduce the likelihood of injury. Similarly, in the "facial hold," the fingertips will be kept well away from the his eyes to ensure that there is no injury to them. The purpose of that facial hold is not injure him but to hold the head immobile. Additionally, while the stress positions and wall standing will undoubtedly result in physical discomfort by tiring the muscles, it is obvious that these positions are not intended to produce the kind of extreme pain required by the statute.

Furthermore, no specific intent to cause severe mental pain or suffering appears to be present. As we explained in our recent opinion, an individual must have the specific intent to cause prolonged mental harm in order to have the specific intent to inflict severe mental pain or suffering. See Section 2340A Memorandum at 8. Prolonged mental harm is substantial mental harm of a sustained duration, e.g., harm lasting months or even years after the acts were inflicted upon the prisoner. As we indicated above, a good faith belief can negate this element. Accordingly, if an individual conducting the interrogation has a good faith belief that the procedures he will apply, separately or together, would not result in prolonged mental harm, that individual lacks the requisite specific intent. This conclusion concerning specific intent is further bolstered by the due diligence that has been conducted concerning the effects of these interrogation procedures.

The mental health experts that you have consulted have indicated that the psychological impact of a course of conduct must be assessed with reference to the subject's psychological history and current mental health status. The healthier the individual, the less likely that the use of any one procedure or set of procedures as a course of conduct will result hi prolonged mental harm. A comprehensive psychological profile of Zubaydah has been created. In creating this profile, your personnel drew on direct interviews, Zubaydah's diaries, observation of Zubaydah since his capture, and information from other sources such as other intelligence and press reports.

As we indicated above, you have informed us that your proposed interrogation methods have been used and continue to be used in SERE training. It is our understanding that these techniques are not used one by one in isolation, but as a full course of conduct to resemble a real interrogation. Thus, the information derived from SERE training bears both upon the impact of the use of the individual techniques and upon their use as a course of conduct. You have found that the use of these methods together or separately, including the use of the waterboard, has not resulted in any negative long-term mental health consequences. The continued use of these methods without mental health consequences to the trainees indicates that it is highly improbable that such consequences would result here. Because you have conducted due diligence to determine that these procedures, either alone or in combination, do not produce prolonged mental harm, we believe that you do not meet the specific intent requirement necessary to violate Section 2340A.

You have also informed us that you have reviewed the relevant literature on the subject, and consulted with outside psychologists. Your review of the literature uncovered no empirical data on the use of these procedures, with the exception of sleep deprivation for which no long-term health consequences resulted. The outside psychologists with whom you consulted indicated were unaware of any cases where long-term problems have occurred as a result of these techniques.

As described above, it appears you have conducted an extensive inquiry to ascertain what impact, if any, these procedures individually and as a course of conduct would have on Zubaydah. You have consulted with interrogation experts, including those with substantial SERE school experience, consulted with outside psychologists, completed a psychological assessment and reviewed the relevant literature on this topic. Based on this inquiry, you believe that the use of these procedures, including the waterboard, and as a course of conduct would not result in prolonged mental harm. Reliance on this information about Zubaydah and about the effect of the use of these techniques more generally demonstrates the presence of a good faith belief that no prolonged mental harm will result from using these methods in the interrogation of Zubaydah. Moreover, we think that this represents not only an honest belief but also a reasonable belief based on the information that you have supplied to us. Thus, we believe that the specific intent to inflict prolonged mental is not present, and consequently, there is no specific intent to inflict severe mental pain or suffering. Accordingly, we conclude that on the facts in this case the use of these methods separately or a course of conduct would not violate Section 2340A.

Based on the foregoing, and based on the facts that you have provided, we conclude that the interrogation procedures that you propose would not violate Section 2340A. We wish to emphasize that this is our best reading of the law; however, you should be aware that there are no cases construing this statute, just as there have been no prosecutions brought under it.

Please let us know if we can be of further assistance.

Jay S. Bybee

Assistant Attorney General

DOCUMENT 92

Full Official Title: President Obama Executive Order on Ensuring Lawful Interrogations

Short Title/Acronym/Abbreviation: Nothing official

Type of Document: This is an executive order issued by the president. Executive orders are policy statements by the president directing government agencies under his authority to particular actions.

Subject: Torture, interrogation of terrorist suspects

Official Citation: Not applicable

Date of Document: January 22, 2009

Date of Adoption: Not applicable

Date of General Entry into Force (EIF): Not applicable

Number of Signatory States: Not applicable

Date of Signature by the United States: Not applicable

Date of Ratification/Accession/Adhesion: Not applicable

Date of Entry into Force as to United States (effective date): Not applicable

Legal Status/Character of the Instrument/Document as to the United States: These orders can be challenged by the Supreme Court if they are deemed unconstitutional, and they can be reversed by subsequent Administrations. Moreover, the president can amend his order at any time, and Congress may limit its application with subsequent legislation.

Comments: This executive order revoked Executive Order 13440 related to the treatment of detainees and called for an end to all interrogations of detainees inconsistent with the Army Field Manual. There was an exception made for the FBI but the CIA was also called upon to immediately close any detention facilities it was currently operating without opening any in the future as well.

Caution: The status and applicability of this instrument as to the United States may have changed since the date of this publication.

PRESIDENT OBAMA EXECUTIVE ORDER ON ENSURING LAWFUL INTERROGATIONS

Tuesday,

January 27, 2009

Part V

The President

Executive Order 13491—Ensuring Lawful Interrogations

Executive Order 13492—Review and Disposition of Individuals Detained at the Guantánamo Bay Naval Base and Closure of Detention Facilities

Executive Order 13493—Review of Detention Policy Options

Presidential Documents

4893

Federal Register

Vol. 74, No. 16

Tuesday, January 27, 2009

Title 3—

The President

Executive Order 13491 of January 22, 2009

Ensuring Lawful Interrogations

By the authority vested in me by the Constitution and the laws of the United States of America, in order to improve the effectiveness of human intelligence-gathering, to promote the safe, lawful, and humane treatment of individuals in United States custody and of United States personnel who are detained in armed conflicts, to ensure compliance with the treaty obligations of the United States, including the Geneva Conventions, and to take care that the laws of the United States are faithfully executed,

I hereby order as follows:

Section 1. *Revocation*. Executive Order 13440 of July 20, 2007, is revoked.

All executive directives, orders, and regulations inconsistent with this order, including but not limited to those issued to or by the Central Intelligence Agency (CIA) from September 11, 2001, to January 20, 2009, concerning detention or the interrogation of detained individuals, are revoked to the extent of their inconsistency with this order. Heads of departments and agencies shall take all necessary steps to ensure that all directives, orders, and regulations of their respective departments or agencies are consistent with this order. Upon request, the Attorney General shall provide guidance about which directives, orders, and regulations are inconsistent with this order.

Section 2. *Definitions*. As used in this order:

(a) "Army Field Manual 2–22.3" means FM 2–22.3, Human Intelligence Collector Operations, issued by the Department of the Army on September 6, 2006.

(b) "Army Field Manual 34–52" means FM 34–52, Intelligence Interrogation, issued by the Department of the Army on May 8, 1987.

(c) "Common Article 3" means Article 3 of each of the Geneva Conventions.

(d) "Convention Against Torture" means the Convention Against Torture and Other Cruel, Inhuman or Degrading Treatment or Punishment, December 10, 1984, 1465 U.N.T.S. 85, S. Treaty Doc. No. 100–20 (1988).

(e) "Geneva Conventions" means:

(i) the Convention for the Amelioration of the Condition of the Wounded and Sick in Armed Forces in the Field, August 12, 1949 (6 UST 3114);

(ii) the Convention for the Amelioration of the Condition of Wounded, Sick and Shipwrecked Members of Armed Forces at Sea, August 12, 1949 (6 UST 3217);

(iii) the Convention Relative to the Treatment of Prisoners of War, August 12, 1949 (6 UST 3316); and

(iv) the Convention Relative to the Protection of Civilian Persons in Time of War, August 12, 1949 (6 UST 3516).

(f) "Treated humanely," "violence to life and person," "murder of all kinds," "mutilation," "cruel treatment," "torture," "outrages upon personal dignity," and "humiliating and degrading treatment" refer to, and have the same meaning as, those same terms in Common Article 3.

(g) The terms "detention facilities" and "detention facility" in section 4(a) of this order do not refer to facilities used only to hold people on a short-term, transitory basis.

Section 3. *Standards and Practices for Interrogation of Individuals in the Custody or Control of the United States in Armed Conflicts*.

(a) **Common Article 3 Standards as a Minimum Baseline.** Consistent with the requirements of the Federal torture statute, 18 U.S.C. 2340–2340A, section 1003 of the Detainee Treatment Act of 2005, 42 U.S.C. 2000dd, the Convention Against Torture, Common Article 3, and other laws regulating the treatment and interrogation of individuals detained in any armed conflict, such persons shall in all circumstances be treated humanely and shall not be subjected to violence to life and person (including murder of all kinds, mutilation, cruel treatment, and torture), nor to outrages upon personal dignity (including humiliating and degrading treatment), whenever such individuals are in the custody or under the effective control of an officer, employee, or other agent of the United States Government or detained within a facility owned, operated, or controlled by a department or agency of the United States.

(b) **Interrogation Techniques and Interrogation-Related Treatment.** Effective immediately, an individual in the custody or under the effective control of an officer, employee, or other agent of the United States Government, or detained within a facility owned, operated, or controlled by a department or agency of the United States, in any armed conflict, shall not be subjected to any interrogation technique or approach, or any treatment related to interrogation, that is not authorized by and listed in Army Field Manual 2–22.3 (Manual). Interrogation techniques, approaches, and treatments described in the Manual shall be implemented strictly in accord with the principles, processes, conditions, and limitations the Manual prescribes.

Where processes required by the Manual, such as a requirement of approval by specified Department of Defense officials, are inapposite to a department or an agency other than the Department of Defense, such a department or agency shall use processes that are substantially equivalent to the processes the Manual prescribes for the Department of Defense. Nothing in this section shall preclude the Federal Bureau of Investigation, or other Federal law enforcement agencies, from continuing to use authorized, non-coercive techniques of interrogation that are designed to elicit voluntary statements and do not involve the use of force, threats, or promises.

(c) **Interpretations of Common Article 3 and the Army Field Manual.** From this day forward, unless the Attorney General with appropriate consultation provides further guidance, officers, employees, and other agents of the United States Government may, in conducting interrogations, act in reliance upon Army Field Manual 2–22.3, but may not, in conducting interrogations, rely upon any interpretation of the law governing interrogation—including interpretations of Federal criminal laws, the Convention Against Torture, Common Article 3, Army Field Manual 2–22.3, and its predecessor document, Army Field Manual 34–52—issued by the Department of Justice between September 11, 2001, and January 20, 2009.

Section 4. *Prohibition of Certain Detention Facilities, and Red Cross Access to Detained Individuals.*

(a) **CIA Detention.** The CIA shall close as expeditiously as possible any detention facilities that it currently operates and shall not operate any such detention facility in the future.

(b) **International Committee of the Red Cross Access to Detained Individuals.** All departments and agencies of the Federal Government shall provide the International Committee of the Red Cross with notification of, and timely access to, any individual detained in any armed conflict in the custody or under the effective control of an officer, employee, or other agent of the United States Government or detained within a facility owned, operated, or controlled by a department or agency of the United States Government, consistent with Department of Defense regulations and policies.

Section 5. *Special Interagency Task Force on Interrogation and Transfer Policies.*

(a) **Establishment of Special Interagency Task Force.** There shall be established a Special Task Force on Interrogation and Transfer Policies (Special Task Force) to review interrogation and transfer policies.

(b) **Membership.** The Special Task Force shall consist of the following members, or their designees:

(i) the Attorney General, who shall serve as Chair;

(ii) the Director of National Intelligence, who shall serve as Co-Vice- Chair;

(iii) the Secretary of Defense, who shall serve as Co-Vice-Chair;

(iv) the Secretary of State;

(v) the Secretary of Homeland Security;

(vi) the Director of the Central Intelligence Agency;

(vii) the Chairman of the Joint Chiefs of Staff; and

(viii) other officers or full-time or permanent part-time employees of the United States, as determined by the Chair, with the concurrence of the head of the department or agency concerned.

(c) **Staff.** The Chair may designate officers and employees within the Department of Justice to serve as staff to support the Special Task Force. At the request of the Chair, officers and employees from other departments or agencies may serve on the Special Task Force with the concurrence of the head of the department or agency that employ such individuals.

Such staff must be officers or full-time or permanent part-time employees of the United States. The Chair shall designate an officer or employee of the Department of Justice to serve as the Executive Secretary of the Special Task Force.

(d) **Operation.** The Chair shall convene meetings of the Special Task Force, determine its agenda, and direct its work. The Chair may establish and direct subgroups of the Special Task Force, consisting exclusively of members of the Special Task Force, to deal with particular subjects.

(e) **Mission.** The mission of the Special Task Force shall be:

(i) to study and evaluate whether the interrogation practices and techniques in Army Field Manual 2–22.3, when employed by departments or agencies outside the military, provide an appropriate means of acquiring the intelligence necessary to protect the Nation, and, if warranted, to recommend any additional or different guidance for other departments or agencies; and

(ii) to study and evaluate the practices of transferring individuals to other nations in order to ensure that such practices comply with the domestic laws, international obligations, and policies of the United States and do not result in the transfer of individuals to other nations to face torture or otherwise for the purpose, or with the effect, of undermining or circumventing the commitments or obligations of the United States to ensure the humane treatment of individuals in its custody or control.

(f) **Administration.** The Special Task Force shall be established for administrative purposes within the Department of Justice and the Department of Justice shall, to the extent permitted by law and subject to the availability of appropriations, provide administrative support and funding for the Special Task Force.

(g) **Recommendations.** The Special Task Force shall provide a report to the President, through the Assistant to the President for National Security Affairs and the Counsel to the President, on the matters set forth in subsection (d) within 180 days of the date of this order, unless the Chair determines that an extension is necessary.

(h) **Termination.** The Chair shall terminate the Special Task Force upon the completion of its duties.

Section 6. *Construction with Other Laws.* Nothing in this order shall be construed to affect the obligations of officers, employees, and other agents of the United States Government to comply with all pertinent laws and treaties of the United States governing detention and interrogation, including but not limited to: the Fifth and Eighth Amendments to the United States Constitution; the Federal torture statute, 18 U.S.C. 2340–2340A; the War Crimes Act, 18 U.S.C. 2441; the Federal assault statute, 18 U.S.C. 113; the Federal maiming statute, 18 U.S.C. 114; the Federal "stalking" statute, 18 U.S.C. 2261A; articles 93, 124, 128, and 134 of the Uniform Code of Military Justice, 10 U.S.C. 893, 924, 928, and 934; section 1003 of the Detainee Treatment Act of 2005, 42 U.S.C. 2000dd; section 6(c) of the Military Commissions Act of 2006, Public Law 109–366; the Geneva Conventions; and the Convention Against Torture. Nothing in this order shall be construed to diminish any rights that any individual may have under these or other laws and treaties. This order is not intended to, and does not, create any right or benefit, substantive or procedural, enforceable at law or in equity against the United States, its departments, agencies, or other entities, its officers or employees, or any other person.

THE WHITE HOUSE,

January 22, 2009.

[FR Doc. E9–1885

Filed 1–26–09; 11:15 am]

Billing code 3195–W9–P

DOCUMENT 93

Full Official Title: U.S. Department of State recognizing acceptance of U.N. Statement on "Human Rights, Sexual Orientation, and Gender Identity"

Short Title/Acronym/Abbreviation: U.S. Statement to U.N. on "Human Rights, Sexual Orientation and Gender Identity"

Type of Document: Press Release on U.S. Department of State website; dissemination of an official statement made by the U.S. government to the U.N. General Assembly and Human Rights Council

Subject: U.S expressing to U.N. its approval of a Statement on Sexual Orientation and Identity that had previously been made to the U.N.

Official Citation: Website announcement made by U.S. Department of State, Acting Department Spokesman, Bureau of Public Affairs, Office of the Spokesman, Washington, DC, March 18, 2009. http://www.state.gov/r/pa/prs/ps/2009/ 03/ 120509.htm.

Date of Document: March 18, 2009

Date of Adoption: Not applicable

Date of General Entry into Force (EIF): Not applicable

Number of States Parties as of this printing: N/A

Date of Signature by United States: Not applicable

Date of Ratification/Accession/Adhesion: Not applicable

Date of Entry into Force as to United States (effective date): Not applicable

Legal Status/Character of the Instrument/Document as to the United States: a non-binding statement by the U.S. A foreign policy and human rights statement of the Obama Administration on behalf of the U.S. on sexual orientation, gender identity and human rights.

Comment: This statement is the product of an initiative of several countries who drafted the statement and invited other states to voluntarily sign onto it indicating their informal acceptance. This was outside of the normal international institutional processes but has gained some stature within the U.N. particularly the GA and HRC, as more and more states have signed on. It has become a part of the UPR process in that one of the recommendations often made to states undergoing the UPR process is that they sign on to this Statement if they have not already done so. It was the first statement at the United Nations General Assembly on sexual orientation and identity. It is only a statement of approval of a non binding statement previously submitted to the U.N. by several other states.

The Department of State says: The United States supports the U.N. Statement on "Human Rights, Sexual Orientation, and Gender Identity," and is pleased to join the other 66 U.N. member states who have declared their support of this Statement that condemns human rights violations based on sexual orientation and gender identity wherever they occur.

Caution: (If this is a legal instrument) The status and applicability of this instrument as to the United States may have changed since the date of this publication. The above information may be updated by referring to the following site: http://www1.umn.edu/humanrts/instree/

Web Address: http://www.state.gov/r/pa/prs/ps/2009/03/120509.htm.

Test of the Statement was found at http://en. wikisource.org/ wiki/UN_ declaration_on_sexual_orientation_and_gender_identity.

DEPARTMENT OF STATE: U.N. STATEMENT ON "HUMAN RIGHTS, SEXUAL ORIENTATION, AND GENDER IDENTITY"

Acting Department Spokesman, Bureau of Public Affairs, Office of the Spokesman
Washington, DC
March 18, 2009

The United States supports the U.N. Statement on "Human Rights, Sexual Orientation, and Gender Identity," and is pleased to join the other 66 U.N. member states who have declared their support of this Statement that condemns human rights violations based on sexual orientation and gender identity wherever they occur.

The United States is an outspoken defender of human rights and critic of human rights abuses around the world. As such, we join with the other supporters of this Statement and we will continue to remind countries of the importance of respecting the human rights of all people in all appropriate international fora.

First ever statement on sexual orientation and gender identity at the U.N. General Assembly

The statement read by Argentina and the counterstatement read by the Syrian Arab Republic that immediately followed can be seen respectively at 2:25:00 and at 2:32:00 in the video archived on the U.N. website and marked as "18 December 08 General Assembly: 70th and 71st plenary meeting—Morning session".

We have the honour to make this statement on human rights, sexual orientation and gender identity on behalf of Albania, Andorra, Argentina, Armenia, Australia, Austria, Belgium, Bolivia, Bosnia and Herzegovina, Brazil, Bulgaria, Canada, Cape Verde, Central African Republic, Chile, Colombia, Croatia, Cuba, Cyprus, Czech Republic, Denmark, Ecuador, Estonia, Finland, France, Gabon, Georgia, Germany, Greece, Guinea-Bissau, Hungary, Iceland, Ireland, Israel, Italy, Japan, Latvia, Liechtenstein, Lithuania, Luxembourg, Malta, Mauritius, Mexico, Montenegro, Nepal, Netherlands, New Zealand, Nicaragua, Norway, Paraguay, Poland, Portugal, Romania, San Marino, Sao Tome and Principe, Serbia, Slovakia, Slovenia, Spain, Sweden, Switzerland, the former Yugoslav Republic of Macedonia, Timor-Leste, United Kingdom, Uruguay, and Venezuela.

Text of the draft declaration

1. We reaffirm the principle of universality of human rights, as enshrined in the Universal Declaration of Human Rights whose 60th anniversary is celebrated this year, Article 1 of which proclaims that "all human beings are born free and equal in dignity and rights";

2. We reaffirm that everyone is entitled to the enjoyment of human rights without distinction of any kind, such as race, colour, sex, language, religion, political or other opinion, national or social origin, property, birth or other status, as set out in Article 2 of the Universal Declaration of Human Rights and Article 2 of the International Covenants on Civil and Political, Economic, Social and Cultural

Rights, as well as in Article 26 of the International Covenant on Civil and Political Rights;

3. We reaffirm the principle of non-discrimination which requires that human rights apply equally to every human being regardless of sexual orientation or gender identity;

4. We are deeply concerned by violations of human rights and fundamental freedoms based on sexual orientation or gender identity;

5. We are also disturbed that violence, harassment, discrimination, exclusion, stigmatisation and prejudice are directed against persons in all countries in the world because of sexual orientation or gender identity, and that these practices undermine the integrity and dignity of those subjected to these abuses;

6. We condemn the human rights violations based on sexual orientation or gender identity wherever they occur, in particular the use of the death penalty on this ground, extrajudicial, summary or arbitrary executions, the practice of torture and other cruel, inhuman and degrading treatment or punishment, arbitrary arrest or detention and deprivation of economic, social and cultural rights, including the right to health;

7. We recall the statement in 2006 before the Human Rights Council by fifty four countries requesting the President of the Council to provide an opportunity, at an appropriate future session of the Council, for discussing these violations;

8. We commend the attention paid to these issues by special procedures of the Human Rights Council and treaty bodies and encourage them to continue to integrate consideration of human rights violations based on sexual orientation or gender identity within their relevant mandates;

9. We welcome the adoption of Resolution AG/RES. 2435 (XXXVIII-O/08) on "Human Rights, Sexual Orientation, and Gender Identity" by the General Assembly of the Organization of American States during its 38th session in 3 June 2008;

10. We call upon all States and relevant international human rights mechanisms to commit to promote and protect human rights of all persons, regardless of sexual orientation and gender identity;

11. We urge States to take all the necessary measures, in particular legislative or administrative, to ensure that sexual orientation or gender identity may under no circumstances be the basis for criminal penalties, in particular executions, arrests or detention.

12. We urge States to ensure that human rights violations based on sexual orientation or gender identity are investigated and perpetrators held accountable and brought to justice;

13. We urge States to ensure adequate protection of human rights defenders, and remove obstacles which prevent them from carrying out their work on issues of human rights and sexual orientation and gender identity.

DOCUMENT 94

Full Official Title: Defense of Marriage Act
Short Title/Acronym/Abbreviation: DOMA
Type of Document: This is a bill passed by the U.S. Congress and signed into law by the president.
Subject: Marriage
Official Citation: Public Law 104-199
Date of Document: Not applicable
Date of Adoption: Not applicable
Date of General Entry into Force (EIF): Not applicable
Number of States Parties as of this printing: Not applicable
Date of Signature by the United States: September 21, 1996
Date of Ratification/Accession/Adhesion: Not applicable
Date of Entry into Force as to United States (effective date): Not applicable
Legal Status/Character of the Instrument/Document as to the United States: This bill is legally binding.
Comments: The federal government passed legislation defending the traditional definition of marriage as a legal union between one man and one woman as husband and wife. This bill ensured that no state, territory or possession of the United States would have to recognize any marriage between individuals of the same sex despite any claims they may have to such a relationship. It was signed into law by President Bill

Clinton in 1996. Federal courts in Massachusetts and California have since challenged the constitutionality of DOMA and the Justice Department is reviewing the recent decisions.

Caution: The status and applicability of this instrument as to the United States may have changed since the date of this publication.

DEFENSE OF MARRIAGE ACT
UNITED STATES CODE
Definition of Marriage

"In determining the meaning of any Act of Congress, or of any ruling, regulation, or interpretation of the various administrative bureaus and agencies of the United States, the word 'marriage' means only a legal union between one man and one woman as husband and wife, and the word 'spouse' refers only to a person of the opposite sex who is a husband or a wife." 1 U.S.C. §7(3)."

(Federal Limitation on States' Respect for Marriages of Same-Sex Couples (aka DOMA section 2)
28 U.S.C. § 1738C. Certain acts, records, and proceedings and the effect thereof

"No State, territory, or possession of the United States, or Indian tribe, shall be required to give effect to any public act, record, or judicial proceeding of any other State, territory, possession, or tribe respecting a relationship between persons of the same sex that is treated as a marriage under the laws of such other State, territory, possession, or tribe, or a right or claim arising from such relationship." 28 U.S.C. § 1738C.

DOCUMENT 95
Full Official Title: Federal Intelligence Surveillance Act
Short Title/Acronym/Abbreviation: FISA
Type of Document: This is a bill passed by the U.S. Congress and signed into law by the president.
Subject: Surveillance, terrorism
Official Citation: Not applicable
Date of Document: 1978 and later amendments
Date of Adoption: Not applicable
Date of General Entry into Force (EIF): Not applicable
Number of States Parties as of this printing: Not applicable
Date of Signature by the United States: Not applicable
Date of Ratification/Accession/Adhesion: Not applicable
Date of Entry into Force as to United States (effective date): Not applicable
Legal Status/Character of the Instrument/Document as to the United States: This bill is legally binding.

Comments: The Federal Intelligence Surveillance Act (FISA) was first passed by the U.S. Congress in 1978 to establish clear procedures for how government officials and agencies may legally obtain authorization to gather foreign intelligence. FISA covers several types of foreign intelligence gathering such as electronic surveillance, physical searches, pen registers, and trap and trace devices, as well as accessing certain business records. All such authorizations must be obtained by a Foreign Intelligence Surveillance Court. However, the FISA was amended in response to the changing needs of intelligence gathering, following the attacks on the United States on September 11, 2001, in order to respond more rapidly to the particular needs in countering acts of terrorism.

Caution: The status and applicability of this instrument as to the United States may have changed since the date of this publication.

FOREIGN INTELLIGENCE SURVEILLANCE ACT
1801. Definitions
As used in this subchapter:
(a) "Foreign power" means—
(1) a foreign government or any component thereof, whether or not recognized by the United States;
(2) a faction of a foreign nation or nations, not substantially composed of United States persons;
(3) an entity that is openly acknowledged by a foreign government or governments to be directed and controlled by such foreign government or governments;

(4) a group engaged in international terrorism or activities in preparation therefor;

(5) a foreign-based political organization, not substantially composed of United States persons;

(6) an entity that is directed and controlled by a foreign government or governments; or

(7) an entity not substantially composed of United States persons that is engaged in the international proliferation of weapons of mass destruction.

(b) "Agent of a foreign power" means—

(1) any person other than a United States person, who—

(A) acts in the United States as an officer or employee of a foreign power, or as a member of a foreign power as defined in subsection (a)(4) of this section;

(B) acts for or on behalf of a foreign power which engages in clandestine intelligence activities in the United States contrary to the interests of the United States, when the circumstances of such person's presence in the United States indicate that such person may engage in such activities in the United States, or when such person knowingly aids or abets any person in the conduct of such activities or knowingly conspires with any person to engage in such activities;

(C) engages in international terrorism or activities in preparation therefore;

(D) engages in the international proliferation of weapons of mass destruction, or activities in preparation therefor; or

(E) engages in the international proliferation of weapons of mass destruction, or activities in preparation therefor for or on behalf of a foreign power; or

(2) any person who—

(A) knowingly engages in clandestine intelligence gathering activities for or on behalf of a foreign power, which activities involve or may involve a violation of the criminal statutes of the United States;

(B) pursuant to the direction of an intelligence service or network of a foreign power, knowingly engages in any other clandestine intelligence activities for or on behalf of such foreign power, which activities involve or are about to involve a violation of the criminal statutes of the United States;

(C) knowingly engages in sabotage or international terrorism, or activities that are in preparation therefor, for or on behalf of a foreign power;

(D) knowingly enters the United States under a false or fraudulent identity for or on behalf of a foreign power or, while in the United States, knowingly assumes a false or fraudulent identity for or on behalf of a foreign power; or

(E) knowingly aids or abets any person in the conduct of activities described in subparagraph (A), (B), or (C) or knowingly conspires with any person to engage in activities described in subparagraph (A), (B), or (C).

(c) "International terrorism" means activities that—

(1) involve violent acts or acts dangerous to human life that are a violation of the criminal laws of the United States or of any State, or that would be a criminal violation if committed within the jurisdiction of the United States or any State;

(2) appear to be intended—

(A) to intimidate or coerce a civilian population;

(B) to influence the policy of a government by intimidation or coercion; or

(C) to affect the conduct of a government by assassination or kidnapping; and

(3) occur totally outside the United States, or transcend national boundaries in terms of the means by which they are accomplished, the persons they appear intended to coerce or intimidate, or the locale in which their perpetrators operate or seek asylum.

(d) "Sabotage" means activities that involve a violation of chapter 105 of title 18, or that would involve such a violation if committed against the United States.

(e) "Foreign intelligence information" means—

(1) information that relates to, and if concerning a United States person is necessary to, the ability of the United States to protect against—

(A) actual or potential attack or other grave hostile acts of a foreign power or an agent of a foreign power;

(B) sabotage, international terrorism, or the international proliferation of weapons of mass destruction by a foreign power or an agent of a foreign power; or

(C) clandestine intelligence activities by an intelligence service or network of a foreign power or by an agent of a foreign power; or

(2) information with respect to a foreign power or foreign territory that relates to, and if concerning a United States person is necessary to—

(A) the national defense or the security of the United States; or

(B) the conduct of the foreign affairs of the United States.

(f) "Electronic surveillance" means—

(1) the acquisition by an electronic, mechanical, or other surveillance device of the contents of any wire or radio communication sent by or intended to be received by a particular, known United States person who is in the United States, if the contents are acquired by intentionally targeting that United States person, under circumstances in which a person has a reasonable expectation of privacy and a warrant would be required for law enforcement purposes;

(2) the acquisition by an electronic, mechanical, or other surveillance device of the contents of any wire communication to or from a person in the United States, without the consent of any party thereto, if such acquisition occurs in the United States, but does not include the acquisition of those communications of computer trespassers that would be permissible under section 2511 (2)(i) of title 18;

(3) the intentional acquisition by an electronic, mechanical, or other surveillance device of the contents of any radio communication, under circumstances in which a person has a reasonable expectation of privacy and a warrant would be required for law enforcement purposes, and if both the sender and all intended recipients are located within the United States; or

(4) the installation or use of an electronic, mechanical, or other surveillance device in the United States for monitoring to acquire information, other than from a wire or radio communication, under circumstances in which a person has a reasonable expectation of privacy and a warrant would be required for law enforcement purposes.

(g) "Attorney General" means the Attorney General of the United States (or Acting Attorney General), the Deputy Attorney General, or, upon the designation of the Attorney General, the Assistant Attorney General designated as the Assistant Attorney General for National Security under section 507A of title 28.

(h) "Minimization procedures", with respect to electronic surveillance, means—

(1) specific procedures, which shall be adopted by the Attorney General, that are reasonably designed in light of the purpose and technique of the particular surveillance, to minimize the acquisition and retention, and prohibit the dissemination, of nonpublicly available information concerning unconsenting United States persons consistent with the need of the United States to obtain, produce, and disseminate foreign intelligence information;

(2) procedures that require that nonpublicly available information, which is not foreign intelligence information, as defined in subsection (e)(1) of this section, shall not be disseminated in a manner that identifies any United States person, without such person's consent, unless such person's identity is necessary to understand foreign intelligence information or assess its importance;

(3) notwithstanding paragraphs (1) and (2), procedures that allow for the retention and dissemination of information that is evidence of a crime which has been, is being, or is about to be committed and that is to be retained or disseminated for law enforcement purposes; and

(4) notwithstanding paragraphs (1), (2), and (3), with respect to any electronic surveillance approved pursuant to section 1802 (a) of this title, procedures that require that no contents of any communication to which a United States person is a party shall be disclosed, disseminated, or used for any purpose or retained for longer than 72 hours unless a court order under section 1805 of this title is obtained or unless the Attorney General determines that the information indicates a threat of death or serious bodily harm to any person.

(i) "United States person" means a citizen of the United States, an alien lawfully admitted for permanent residence (as defined in section 1101 (a)(20) of title 8), an unincorporated association a substantial number of members of which are citizens of the United States or aliens lawfully admitted for permanent residence, or a corporation which is incorporated in the United States, but does not include a corporation or an association which is a foreign power, as defined in subsection (a)(1), (2), or (3) of this section.

(j) "United States", when used in a geographic sense, means all areas under the territorial sovereignty of the United States and the Trust Territory of the Pacific Islands.

(k) "Aggrieved person" means a person who is the target of an electronic surveillance or any other person whose communications or activities were subject to electronic surveillance.

(l) "Wire communication" means any communication while it is being carried by a wire, cable, or other like connection furnished or operated by any person engaged as a common carrier in providing or operating such facilities for the transmission of interstate or foreign communications.

(m) "Person" means any individual, including any officer or employee of the Federal Government, or any group, entity, association, corporation, or foreign power.

(n) "Contents", when used with respect to a communication, includes any information concerning the identity of the parties to such communication or the existence, substance, purport, or meaning of that communication.

(o) "State" means any State of the United States, the District of Columbia, the Commonwealth of Puerto Rico, the Trust Territory of the Pacific Islands, and any territory or possession of the United States.

(p) "Weapon of mass destruction" means—

(1) any explosive, incendiary, or poison gas device that is designed, intended, or has the capability to cause a mass casualty incident;

(2) any weapon that is designed, intended, or has the capability to cause death or serious bodily injury to a significant number of persons through the release, dissemination, or impact of toxic or poisonous chemicals or their precursors;

(3) any weapon involving a biological agent, toxin, or vector (as such terms are defined in section 178 of title 18) that is designed, intended, or has the capability to cause death, illness, or serious bodily injury to a significant number of persons; or

(4) any weapon that is designed, intended, or has the capability to release radiation or radioactivity causing death, illness, or serious bodily injury to a significant number of persons.

§ 1802. Electronic surveillance authorization without court order; certification by Attorney General; reports to Congressional committees; transmittal under seal; duties and compensation of communication common carrier; applications; jurisdiction of court

(a)

(1) Notwithstanding any other law, the President, through the Attorney General, may authorize electronic surveillance without a court order under this subchapter to acquire foreign intelligence information for periods of up to one year if the Attorney General certifies in writing under oath that—

(A) the electronic surveillance is solely directed at—

(i) the acquisition of the contents of communications transmitted by means of communications used exclusively between or among foreign powers, as defined in section 1801 (a)(1), (2), or (3) of this title; or

(ii) the acquisition of technical intelligence, other than the spoken communications of individuals, from property or premises under the open and exclusive control of a foreign power, as defined in section 1801 (a)(1), (2), or (3) of this title;

(B) there is no substantial likelihood that the surveillance will acquire the contents of any communication to which a United States person is a party; and

(C) the proposed minimization procedures with respect to such surveillance meet the definition of minimization procedures under section 1801 (h) of this title; and if the Attorney General reports such minimization procedures and any changes thereto to the House Permanent Select Committee on Intelligence and the Senate Select Committee on Intelligence at least thirty days prior to their effective date, unless the Attorney General determines immediate action is required and notifies the committees immediately of such minimization procedures and the reason for their becoming effective immediately.

(2) An electronic surveillance authorized by this subsection may be conducted only in accordance with the Attorney General's certification and the minimization procedures adopted by him. The Attorney General shall assess compliance with such procedures and shall report such assessments to the House Permanent Select Committee on Intelligence and the Senate Select Committee on Intelligence under the provisions of section 1808 (a) of this title.

(3) The Attorney General shall immediately transmit under seal to the court established under section 1803 (a) of this title a copy of his certification. Such certification shall be maintained under security measures established by the Chief Justice with the concurrence of the Attorney General, in consultation with the Director of National Intelligence, and shall remain sealed unless—

(A) an application for a court order with respect to the surveillance is made under sections 1801 (h)(4) and 1804 of this title; or

(B) the certification is necessary to determine the legality of the surveillance under section 1806 (f) of this title.

(4) With respect to electronic surveillance authorized by this subsection, the Attorney General may direct a specified communication common carrier to—

(A) furnish all information, facilities, or technical assistance necessary to accomplish the electronic surveillance in such a manner as will protect its secrecy and produce a minimum of interference with the services that such carrier is providing its customers; and

(B) maintain under security procedures approved by the Attorney General and the Director of National Intelligence any records concerning the surveillance or the aid furnished which such carrier wishes to retain.

The Government shall compensate, at the prevailing rate, such carrier for furnishing such aid.

(b) Applications for a court order under this subchapter are authorized if the President has, by written authorization, empowered the Attorney General to approve applications to the court having jurisdiction under section 1803 of this title, and a judge to whom an application is made may, notwithstanding any other law, grant an order, in conformity with section 1805 of this title, approving electronic surveillance of a foreign power or an agent of a foreign power for the purpose of obtaining foreign intelligence information, except that the court shall not have jurisdiction to grant any order approving electronic surveillance directed solely as described in paragraph (1)(A) of subsection (a) of this section unless such surveillance may involve the acquisition of communications of any United States person.

...

§ 1822. Authorization of physical searches for foreign intelligence purposes

(a) **Presidential authorization**

(1) Notwithstanding any other provision of law, the President, acting through the Attorney General, may authorize physical searches without a court order under this subchapter to acquire foreign intelligence information for periods of up to one year if—

(A) the Attorney General certifies in writing under oath that—

(i) the physical search is solely directed at premises, information, material, or property used exclusively by, or under the open and exclusive control of, a foreign power or powers (as defined in section 1801 (a)(1), (2), or (3) of this title);

(ii) there is no substantial likelihood that the physical search will involve the premises, information, material, or property of a United States person; and

(iii) the proposed minimization procedures with respect to such physical search meet the definition of minimization procedures under paragraphs (1) through (4) of section 1821 (4) of this title; and

(B) the Attorney General reports such minimization procedures and any changes thereto to the Permanent Select Committee on Intelligence of the House of Representatives and the Select Committee on Intelligence of the Senate at least 30 days before their effective date, unless the Attorney General determines that immediate action is required and notifies the committees immediately of such minimization procedures and the reason for their becoming effective immediately.

(2) A physical search authorized by this subsection may be conducted only in accordance with the certification and minimization procedures adopted by the Attorney General. The Attorney General shall assess compliance with such procedures and shall report such assessments to the Permanent Select Committee on Intelligence of the House of Representatives and the Select Committee on Intelligence of the Senate under the provisions of section 1826 of this title.

(3) The Attorney General shall immediately transmit under seal to the Foreign Intelligence Surveillance Court a copy of the certification. Such certification shall be maintained under security measures established by the Chief Justice of the United States with the concurrence of the Attorney General, in consultation with the Director of National Intelligence, and shall remain sealed unless—

(A) an application for a court order with respect to the physical search is made under section 1821 (4) of this title and section 1823 of this title; or

(B) the certification is necessary to determine the legality of the physical search under section 1825 (g) of this title.

(4) (A) With respect to physical searches authorized by this subsection, the Attorney General may direct a specified landlord, custodian, or other specified person to—

(i) furnish all information, facilities, or assistance necessary to accomplish the physical search in such a manner as will protect its secrecy and produce a minimum of interference with the services that such landlord, custodian, or other person is providing the target of the physical search; and

(ii) maintain under security procedures approved by the Attorney General and the Director of National Intelligence any records concerning the search or the aid furnished that such person wishes to retain.

(B) The Government shall compensate, at the prevailing rate, such landlord, custodian, or other person for furnishing such aid.

(b) Application for order; authorization

Applications for a court order under this subchapter are authorized if the President has, by written authorization, empowered the Attorney General to approve applications to the Foreign Intelligence Surveillance Court. Notwithstanding any other provision of law, a judge of the court to whom application is made may grant an order in accordance with section 1824 of this title approving a physical search in the United States of the premises, property, information, or material of a foreign power or an agent of a foreign power for the purpose of collecting foreign intelligence information.

(c) Jurisdiction of Foreign Intelligence Surveillance Court

The Foreign Intelligence Surveillance Court shall have jurisdiction to hear applications for and grant orders approving a physical search for the purpose of obtaining foreign intelligence information anywhere within the United States under the procedures set forth in this subchapter, except that no judge (except when sitting en banc) shall hear the same application which has been denied previously by another judge designated under section 1803 (a) of this title. If any judge so designated denies an application for an order authorizing a physical search under this subchapter, such judge shall provide immediately for the record a written statement of each reason for such decision and, on motion of the United States, the record shall be transmitted, under seal, to the court of review established under section 1803 (b) of this title.

(d) Court of review; record; transmittal to Supreme Court

The court of review established under section 1803 (b) of this title shall have jurisdiction to review the denial of any application made under this subchapter. If such court determines that the application was properly denied, the court shall immediately provide for the record a written statement of each reason for its decision and, on petition of the United States for a writ of certiorari, the record shall be transmitted under seal to the Supreme Court, which shall have jurisdiction to review such decision.

(e) Expeditious conduct of proceedings; security measures for maintenance of records

Judicial proceedings under this subchapter shall be concluded as expeditiously as possible. The record of proceedings under this subchapter, including applications made and orders granted, shall be maintained under security measures established by the Chief Justice of the United States in consultation with the Attorney General and the Director of National Intelligence.

...

§ 1825. Use of information

(a) Compliance with minimization procedures; lawful purposes

Information acquired from a physical search conducted pursuant to this subchapter concerning any United States person may be used and disclosed by Federal officers and employees without the consent of the United States person only in accordance with the minimization procedures required by this subchapter. No information acquired from a physical search pursuant to this subchapter may be used or disclosed by Federal officers or employees except for lawful purposes.

(b) Notice of search and identification of property seized, altered, or reproduced

Where a physical search authorized and conducted pursuant to section 1824 of this title involves the residence of a United States person, and, at any time after the search the Attorney General determines there is no national security interest in continuing to maintain the secrecy of the search, the Attorney General shall provide notice to the United States person whose residence was searched of the fact of the search conducted pursuant to this chapter and shall identify any property of such person seized, altered, or reproduced during such search.

(c) Statement for disclosure

No information acquired pursuant to this subchapter shall be disclosed for law enforcement purposes unless such disclosure is accompanied by a statement that such information, or any information derived therefrom, may only be used in a criminal proceeding with the advance authorization of the Attorney General.

(d) Notification by United States

Whenever the United States intends to enter into evidence or otherwise use or disclose in any trial, hearing, or other proceeding in or before any court, department, officer, agency, regulatory body, or other authority of the United States, against an aggrieved person, any information obtained or derived from a physical search pursuant to the authority of this subchapter, the United States shall, prior to the trial, hearing, or the other proceeding or at a reasonable time prior to an effort to so disclose or so use that information or submit it in evidence, notify the aggrieved person and the court or other authority in which the information is to be disclosed or used that the United States intends to so disclose or so use such information.

(e) Notification by States or political subdivisions

Whenever any State or political subdivision thereof intends to enter into evidence or otherwise use or disclose in any trial, hearing, or other proceeding in or before any court, department, officer, agency, regulatory body, or other authority of a State or a political subdivision thereof against an aggrieved person any information obtained or derived from a physical search pursuant to the authority of this subchapter, the State or political subdivision thereof shall notify the aggrieved person, the court or other authority in which the information is to be disclosed or used, and the Attorney General that the State or political subdivision thereof intends to so disclose or so use such information.

(f) Motion to suppress

(1) Any person against whom evidence obtained or derived from a physical search to which he is an aggrieved person is to be, or has been, introduced or otherwise used or disclosed in any trial, hearing, or other proceeding in or before any court, department, officer, agency, regulatory body, or other authority of the United States, a State, or a political subdivision thereof, may move to suppress the evidence obtained or derived from such search on the grounds that—

(A) the information was unlawfully acquired; or

(B) the physical search was not made in conformity with an order of authorization or approval.

(2) Such a motion shall be made before the trial, hearing, or other proceeding unless there was no opportunity to make such a motion or the person was not aware of the grounds of the motion.

(g) In camera and ex parte review by district court

Whenever a court or other authority is notified pursuant to subsection (d) or (e) of this section, or whenever a motion is made pursuant to subsection (f) of this section, or whenever any motion or request is made by an aggrieved person pursuant to any other statute or rule of the United States or any State before any court or other authority of the United States or any State to discover or obtain applications or orders or other materials relating to a physical search authorized by this subchapter or to discover, obtain, or suppress evidence or information obtained or derived from a physical search authorized by this subchapter, the United States district court or, where the motion is made before another authority, the United States district court in the same district as the authority shall, notwithstanding any other provision of law, if the Attorney General files an affidavit under oath that disclosure or any adversary hearing would harm the national security of the United States, review in camera and ex parte the application, order, and such other materials relating to the physical search as may be necessary to determine whether the physical search of the aggrieved person was lawfully authorized and conducted. In making this determination, the court may disclose to the aggrieved person, under appropriate security procedures and protective orders, portions of the application, order, or other materials relating to the physical search, or may require the Attorney General to provide to the aggrieved person a summary of such materials, only where such disclosure is necessary to make an accurate determination of the legality of the physical search.

(h) Suppression of evidence; denial of motion

If the United States district court pursuant to subsection (g) of this section determines that the physical search was not lawfully authorized or conducted, it shall, in accordance with the requirements of law, suppress the evidence which was unlawfully obtained or derived from the physical search of the aggrieved person or otherwise grant the motion of the aggrieved person. If the court determines that the physical search was lawfully authorized or conducted, it shall deny the motion of the aggrieved person except to the extent that due process requires discovery or disclosure.

(i) Finality of orders

Orders granting motions or requests under subsection (h) of this section, decisions under this section that a physical search was not lawfully authorized or conducted, and orders of the United States district court requiring review or granting disclosure of applications, orders, or other materials relating to the physical search shall be final orders and binding upon all courts of the United States and the several States except a United States Court of Appeals or the Supreme Court.

(j) Notification of emergency execution of physical search; contents; postponement, suspension, or elimination

(1) If an emergency execution of a physical search is authorized under section 1824 (d) of this title and a subsequent order approving the search is not obtained, the judge shall cause to be served on any United States person named in the application and on such other United States persons subject to the search as the judge may determine in his discretion it is in the interests of justice to serve, notice of—

(A) the fact of the application;

(B) the period of the search; and

(C) the fact that during the period information was or was not obtained.

(2) On an ex parte showing of good cause to the judge, the serving of the notice required by this subsection may be postponed or suspended for a period not to exceed 90 days. Thereafter, on a further ex parte showing of good cause, the court shall forego ordering the serving of the notice required under this subsection.

(k) Coordination with law enforcement on national security matters

(1) Federal officers who conduct physical searches to acquire foreign intelligence information under this subchapter may consult with Federal law enforcement officers or law enforcement personnel of a State or political subdivision of a State (including the chief executive officer of that State or political subdivision who has the authority to appoint or direct the chief law enforcement officer of that State or political subdivision) to coordinate efforts to investigate or protect against—

(A) actual or potential attack or other grave hostile acts of a foreign power or an agent of a foreign power;

(B) sabotage, international terrorism, or the international proliferation of weapons of mass destruction by a foreign power or an agent of a foreign power; or

(C) clandestine intelligence activities by an intelligence service or network of a foreign power or by an agent of a foreign power.

(2) Coordination authorized under paragraph (1) shall not preclude the certification required by section 1823 (a)(6) of this title or the entry of an order under section 1824 of this title.

§ 1826. Congressional oversight

On a semiannual basis the Attorney General shall fully inform the Permanent Select Committee on Intelligence of the House of Representatives and the Select Committee on Intelligence of the Senate, and the Committee on the Judiciary of the Senate, concerning all physical searches conducted pursuant to this subchapter. On a semiannual basis the Attorney General shall also provide to those committees and the Committee on the Judiciary of the House of Representatives a report setting forth with respect to the preceding six-month period—

(1) the total number of applications made for orders approving physical searches under this subchapter;

(2) the total number of such orders either granted, modified, or denied;

(3) the number of physical searches which involved searches of the residences, offices, or personal property of United States persons, and the number of occasions, if any, where the Attorney General provided notice pursuant to section 1825 (b) of this title; and

(4) the total number of emergency physical searches authorized by the Attorney General under section 1824 (e) of this title and the total number of subsequent orders approving or denying such physical searches.

...

§ 1861. Access to certain business records for foreign intelligence and international terrorism investigations

(a) Application for order; conduct of investigation generally

(1) Subject to paragraph (3), the Director of the Federal Bureau of Investigation or a designee of the Director (whose rank shall be no lower than Assistant Special Agent in Charge) may make an application for an order requiring the production of any tangible things (including books, records, papers, documents, and other items) for an investigation to obtain foreign intelligence information not concerning a United States

person or to protect against international terrorism or clandestine intelligence activities, provided that such investigation of a United States person is not conducted solely upon the basis of activities protected by the first amendment to the Constitution.

(2) An investigation conducted under this section shall—

(A) be conducted under guidelines approved by the Attorney General under Executive Order 12333 (or a successor order); and

(B) not be conducted of a United States person solely upon the basis of activities protected by the first amendment to the Constitution of the United States.

(3) In the case of an application for an order requiring the production of library circulation records, library patron lists, book sales records, book customer lists, firearms sales records, tax return records, educational records, or medical records containing information that would identify a person, the Director of the Federal Bureau of Investigation may delegate the authority to make such application to either the Deputy Director of the Federal Bureau of Investigation or the Executive Assistant Director for National Security (or any successor position). The Deputy Director or the Executive Assistant Director may not further delegate such authority.

(b) Recipient and contents of application

Each application under this section—

(1) shall be made to—

(A) a judge of the court established by section 1803 (a) of this title; or

(B) a United States Magistrate Judge under chapter 43 of title 28, who is publicly designated by the Chief Justice of the United States to have the power to hear applications and grant orders for the production of tangible things under this section on behalf of a judge of that court; and

(2) shall include—

(A) a statement of facts showing that there are reasonable grounds to believe that the tangible things sought are relevant to an authorized investigation (other than a threat assessment) conducted in accordance with subsection (a)(2) to obtain foreign intelligence information not concerning a United States person or to protect against international terrorism or clandestine intelligence activities, such things being presumptively relevant to an authorized investigation if the applicant shows in the statement of the facts that they pertain to—

(i) a foreign power or an agent of a foreign power;

(ii) the activities of a suspected agent of a foreign power who is the subject of such authorized investigation; or

(iii) an individual in contact with, or known to, a suspected agent of a foreign power who is the subject of such authorized investigation; and

(B) an enumeration of the minimization procedures adopted by the Attorney General under subsection (g) that are applicable to the retention and dissemination by the Federal Bureau of Investigation of any tangible things to be made available to the Federal Bureau of Investigation based on the order requested in such application.

(c) Ex parte judicial order of approval

(1) Upon an application made pursuant to this section, if the judge finds that the application meets the requirements of subsections (a) and (b), the judge shall enter an ex parte order as requested, or as modified, approving the release of tangible things. Such order shall direct that minimization procedures adopted pursuant to subsection (g) be followed.

(2) An order under this subsection—

(A) shall describe the tangible things that are ordered to be produced with sufficient particularity to permit them to be fairly identified;

(B) shall include the date on which the tangible things must be provided, which shall allow a reasonable period of time within which the tangible things can be assembled and made available;

(C) shall provide clear and conspicuous notice of the principles and procedures described in subsection (d);

(D) may only require the production of a tangible thing if such thing can be obtained with a subpoena duces tecum issued by a court of the United States in aid of a grand jury investigation or with any other order issued by a court of the United States directing the production of records or tangible things; and

(E) shall not disclose that such order is issued for purposes of an investigation described in subsection (a).

(d) Nondisclosure

(1) No person shall disclose to any other person that the Federal Bureau of Investigation has sought or obtained tangible things pursuant to an order under this section, other than to—

(A) those persons to whom disclosure is necessary to comply with such order;

(B) an attorney to obtain legal advice or assistance with respect to the production of things in response to the order; or

(C) other persons as permitted by the Director of the Federal Bureau of Investigation or the designee of the Director.

(2) (A) A person to whom disclosure is made pursuant to paragraph (1) shall be subject to the nondisclosure requirements applicable to a person to whom an order is directed under this section in the same manner as such person.

(B) Any person who discloses to a person described in subparagraph (A), (B), or (C) of paragraph (1) that the Federal Bureau of Investigation has sought or obtained tangible things pursuant to an order under this section shall notify such person of the nondisclosure requirements of this subsection.

(C) At the request of the Director of the Federal Bureau of Investigation or the designee of the Director, any person making or intending to make a disclosure under subparagraph (A) or (C) of paragraph (1) shall identify to the Director or such designee the person to whom such disclosure will be made or to whom such disclosure was made prior to the request.

(e) Liability for good faith disclosure; waiver

A person who, in good faith, produces tangible things under an order pursuant to this section shall not be liable to any other person for such production. Such production shall not be deemed to constitute a waiver of any privilege in any other proceeding or context.

(f) Judicial review of FISA orders

(1) In this subsection—

(A) the term "production order" means an order to produce any tangible thing under this section; and

(B) the term "nondisclosure order" means an order imposed under subsection (d).

(2) (A) (i) A person receiving a production order may challenge the legality of that order by filing a petition with the pool established by section 1803 (e)(1) of this title. Not less than 1 year after the date of the issuance of the production order, the recipient of a production order may challenge the nondisclosure order imposed in connection with such production order by filing a petition to modify or set aside such nondisclosure order, consistent with the requirements of subparagraph (C), with the pool established by section 1803 (e)(1) of this title.

(ii) The presiding judge shall immediately assign a petition under clause (i) to 1 of the judges serving in the pool established by section 1803 (e)(1) of this title. Not later than 72 hours after the assignment of such petition, the assigned judge shall conduct an initial review of the petition. If the assigned judge determines that the petition is frivolous, the assigned judge shall immediately deny the petition and affirm the production order or nondisclosure order. If the assigned judge determines the petition is not frivolous, the assigned judge shall promptly consider the petition in accordance with the procedures established under section 1803 (e)(2) of this title.

(iii) The assigned judge shall promptly provide a written statement for the record of the reasons for any determination under this subsection. Upon the request of the Government, any order setting aside a nondisclosure order shall be stayed pending review pursuant to paragraph (3).

(B) A judge considering a petition to modify or set aside a production order may grant such petition only if the judge finds that such order does not meet the requirements of this section or is otherwise unlawful. If the judge does not modify or set aside the production order, the judge shall immediately affirm such order, and order the recipient to comply therewith.

(C) (i) A judge considering a petition to modify or set aside a nondisclosure order may grant such petition only if the judge finds that there is no reason to believe that disclosure may endanger the national security of the United States, interfere with a criminal, counterterrorism, or counterintelligence investigation, interfere with diplomatic relations, or endanger the life or physical safety of any person.

(ii) If, upon filing of such a petition, the Attorney General, Deputy Attorney General, an Assistant Attorney General, or the Director of the Federal Bureau of Investigation certifies that disclosure may endanger the national security of the United States or interfere with diplomatic relations, such certification shall be treated as conclusive, unless the judge finds that the certification was made in bad faith.

(iii) If the judge denies a petition to modify or set aside a nondisclosure order, the recipient of such order shall be precluded for a period of 1 year from filing another such petition with respect to such nondisclosure order.

(D) Any production or nondisclosure order not explicitly modified or set aside consistent with this subsection shall remain in full effect.

(3) A petition for review of a decision under paragraph (2) to affirm, modify, or set aside an order by the Government or any person receiving such order shall be made to the court of review established under section 1803 (b) of this title, which shall have jurisdiction to consider such petitions. The court of review shall provide for the record a written statement of the reasons for its decision and, on petition by the Government or any person receiving such order for writ of certiorari, the record shall be transmitted under seal to the Supreme Court of the United States, which shall have jurisdiction to review such decision.

(4) Judicial proceedings under this subsection shall be concluded as expeditiously as possible. The record of proceedings, including petitions filed, orders granted, and statements of reasons for decision, shall be maintained under security measures established by the Chief Justice of the United States, in consultation with the Attorney General and the Director of National Intelligence.

(5) All petitions under this subsection shall be filed under seal. In any proceedings under this subsection, the court shall, upon request of the Government, review ex parte and in camera any Government submission, or portions thereof, which may include classified information.

(g) Minimization procedures

(1) In general

Not later than 180 days after March 9, 2006, the Attorney General shall adopt specific minimization procedures governing the retention and dissemination by the Federal Bureau of Investigation of any tangible things, or information therein, received by the Federal Bureau of Investigation in response to an order under this subchapter.

(2) Defined

In this section, the term "minimization procedures" means—

(A) specific procedures that are reasonably designed in light of the purpose and technique of an order for the production of tangible things, to minimize the retention, and prohibit the dissemination, of nonpublicly available information concerning unconsenting United States persons consistent with the need of the United States to obtain, produce, and disseminate foreign intelligence information;

(B) procedures that require that nonpublicly available information, which is not foreign intelligence information, as defined in section 1801 (e)(1) of this title, shall not be disseminated in a manner that identifies any United States person, without such person's consent, unless such person's identity is necessary to understand foreign intelligence information or assess its importance; and

(C) notwithstanding subparagraphs (A) and (B), procedures that allow for the retention and dissemination of information that is evidence of a crime which has been, is being, or is about to be committed and that is to be retained or disseminated for law enforcement purposes.

(h) Use of information

Information acquired from tangible things received by the Federal Bureau of Investigation in response to an order under this subchapter concerning any United States person may be used and disclosed by Federal officers and employees without the consent of the United States person only in accordance with the minimization procedures adopted pursuant to subsection (g). No otherwise privileged information acquired from tangible things received by the Federal Bureau of Investigation in accordance with the provisions of this subchapter shall lose its privileged character. No information acquired from tangible things received by the Federal Bureau of Investigation in response to an order under this subchapter may be used or disclosed by Federal officers or employees except for lawful purposes.

DOCUMENT **96**

Full Official Title: An Act to authorize trial by military commission for violations of the law of war, and for other purposes. PL 109-366

Short Title/Acronym/Abbreviation: Military Commission Act of 2006. MCA 2006

Type of Document: This is a bill passed by the U.S. Congress and signed into law by the president.

Subject: procedures governing the use of military commissions, detainees, humanitarian law

Official Citation: Not applicable

Date of Document: Not applicable

Date of Adoption: signed October 17, 2006, with later amendments

Date of General Entry into Force (EIF): Not applicable

Number of States Parties as of this printing: Not applicable

Date of Signature by the United States: Not applicable

Date of Ratification/Accession/Adhesion: Not applicable

Date of Entry into Force as to United States (effective date): Not applicable

Legal Status/Character of the Instrument/Document: This was a legislative Act that created the legal basis for the military commission to try certain war-on-terrorism detainees on Guantánamo. As law, it was binding until amended by the Military Commission Act of 2009, after the U.S. Supreme Court found some of its provisions unconstitutional. See Appendix. J, case law.

Comments: The Military Commission Act of 2006 was passed by the U.S. Congress "to authorize trial by military commission for violations of the law of war, and for other purposes." The MCA of 2006 was drafted and passed following the Supreme Court's decision in *Hamdan v. Rumsfeld* in which the court decided that military commission established by the president in an executive order were invalid under the Uniform Code of Military Justice. The MCA of 2006 provided a legal framework for the president to try detainees, also known as "alien unlawful enemy combatants", in military rather than civilian courts. The MCA of 2006 amended the Detainee Treatment Act and established clear rules for military commissions to try suspected terrorists detained in Guantánamo Bay. It included provisions to prevent the judiciary from providing habeas jurisdiction to persons brought before the commissions, but these provisions were later declared unconstitutional. The MCA was amended in 2009 under the Obama Administration.

For the text of the Military Commissions Act of 2009 see Appendix M, or visit: http://www.defense.gov/news/2009%20MCA%20Pub%20%20Law%20111-84.pdf

MILITARY COMMISSION ACT OF 2006 (EXCERPTS)
PUBLIC LAW 109–366—OCT. 17, 2006

MILITARY COMMISSIONS ACT OF 2006

109th Congress

An Act To authorize trial by military commission for violations of the law of war, and for other purposes.

Be it enacted by the Senate and House of Representatives of the United States of America in Congress assembled,

SECTION 1. SHORT TITLE; TABLE OF CONTENTS.

(a) SHORT TITLE.—This Act may be cited as the "Military Commissions Act of 2006".

(b) TABLE OF CONTENTS.—The table of contents for this Act is as follows:

SEC. 2. CONSTRUCTION OF PRESIDENTIAL AUTHORITY TO ESTABLISH MILITARY COMMISSIONS.

The authority to establish military commissions under chapter 47A of title 10, United States Code, as added by section 3(a), may not be construed to alter or limit the authority of the President under the Constitution of the United States and laws of the United States to establish military commissions for areas declared to be under martial law or in occupied territories should circumstances so require.

SEC. 3. MILITARY COMMISSIONS.

(a) MILITARY COMMISSIONS.—

(1) IN GENERAL.—Subtitle A of title 10, United States Code, is amended by inserting after chapter 47 the following new chapter:

CHAPTER 47A—MILITARY COMMISSIONS

"SUBCHAPTER I—GENERAL PROVISIONS

Sec. 948a. Definitions.
948b. Military commissions generally.
948c. Persons subject to military commissions.
948d. Jurisdiction of military commissions.
948e. Annual report to congressional committees.

§ 948a. Definitions

In this chapter:

(1) UNLAWFUL ENEMY COMBATANT.—(A) The term 'unlawful enemy combatant' means—

(i) a person who has engaged in hostilities or who has purposefully and materially supported hostilities against the United States or its co-belligerents who is not a lawful enemy combatant (including a person who is part of the Taliban, al Qaeda, or associated forces); or

(ii) a person who, before, on, or after the date of the enactment of the Military Commissions Act of 2006, has been determined to be an unlawful enemy combatant by a Combatant Status Review Tribunal or another competent tribunal established under the authority of the President or the Secretary of Defense.

(B) CO-BELLIGERENT.—In this paragraph, the term 'cobelligerent', with respect to the United States, means any State or armed force joining and directly engaged with the United States in hostilities or directly supporting hostilities against a common enemy.

(2) LAWFUL ENEMY COMBATANT.—The term 'lawful enemy combatant' means a person who is—

(A) a member of the regular forces of a State party engaged in hostilities against the United States;

(B) a member of a militia, volunteer corps, or organized resistance movement belonging to a State party engaged in such hostilities, which are under responsible command, wear a fixed distinctive sign recognizable at a distance, carry their arms openly, and abide by the law of war; or

(C) a member of a regular armed force who professes allegiance to a government engaged in such hostilities, but not recognized by the United States.

(3) ALIEN.—The term 'alien' means a person who is not a citizen of the United States.

(4) CLASSIFIED INFORMATION.—The term 'classified information' means the following:

(A) Any information or material that has been determined by the United States Government pursuant to statute, Executive order, or regulation to require protection against unauthorized disclosure for reasons of national security.

(B) Any restricted data, as that term is defined in section 11 y. of the Atomic Energy Act of 1954 (42 U.S.C. 2014(y)).

(5) GENEVA CONVENTIONS.—The term 'Geneva Conventions' means the international conventions signed at Geneva on August 12, 1949.

"§ 948b. Military commissions generally

(a) PURPOSE.—This chapter establishes procedures governing the use of military commissions to try alien unlawful enemy combatants engaged in hostilities against the United States for violations of the law of war and other offenses triable by military commission.

(b) AUTHORITY FOR MILITARY COMMISSIONS UNDER THIS CHAPTER.—The President is authorized to establish military commissions under this chapter for offenses triable by military commission as provided in this chapter.

(c) CONSTRUCTION OF PROVISIONS.—The procedures for military commissions set forth in this chapter are based upon the procedures for trial by general courts-martial under chapter 47of this title (the

Uniform Code of Military Justice). Chapter 47 of this title does not, by its terms, apply to trial by military commission except as specifically provided in this chapter. The judicial construction and application of that chapter are not binding on military commissions established under this chapter.

. . . .

(e) TREATMENT OF RULINGS AND PRECEDENTS.—The findings, holdings, interpretations, and other precedents of military commissions under this chapter may not be introduced or considered in any hearing, trial, or other proceeding of a court-martial convened under chapter 47 of this title. The findings, holdings, interpretations, and other precedents of military commissions under this chapter may not form the basis of any holding, decision, or other determination of a court-martial convened under that chapter.

(f) STATUS OF COMMISSIONS UNDER COMMON ARTICLE 3.—A military commission established under this chapter is a regularly constituted court, affording all the necessary 'judicial guarantees which are recognized as indispensable by civilized peoples' for purposes of common Article 3 of the Geneva Conventions.

(g) GENEVA CONVENTIONS NOT ESTABLISHING SOURCE OF RIGHTS.—No alien unlawful enemy combatant subject to trial by military commission under this chapter may invoke the Geneva Conventions as a source of rights.

§ 948c. Persons subject to military commissions

Any alien unlawful enemy combatant is subject to trial by military commission under this chapter.

§ 948d. Jurisdiction of military commissions

(a) JURISDICTION.—A military commission under this chapter shall have jurisdiction to try any offense made punishable by this chapter or the law of war when committed by an alien unlawful enemy combatant before, on, or after September 11, 2001.

(b) LAWFUL ENEMY COMBATANTS.—Military commissions under this chapter shall not have jurisdiction over lawful enemy combatants.

Lawful enemy combatants who violate the law of war are subject to chapter 47 of this title. Courts-martial established under that chapter shall have jurisdiction to try a lawful enemy combatant for any offense made punishable under this chapter.

(c) DETERMINATION OF UNLAWFUL ENEMY COMBATANT STATUS DISPOSITIVE.—A finding, whether before, on, or after the date of the enactment of the Military Commissions Act of 2006, by a Combatant Status Review Tribunal or another competent tribunal established under the authority of the President or the Secretary of Defense that a person is an unlawful enemy combatant is dispositive for purposes of jurisdiction for trial by military commission under this chapter.

(d) PUNISHMENTS.—A military commission under this chapter may, under such limitations as the Secretary of Defense may prescribe, adjudge any punishment not forbidden by this chapter, including the penalty of death when authorized under this chapter or the law of war.

§ 948e. Annual report to congressional committees

(a) ANNUAL REPORT REQUIRED.—. . . .

"SUBCHAPTER II—COMPOSITION OF MILITARY COMMISSIONS

Sec.
948h. Who may convene military commissions.
948i. Who may serve on military commissions.
948j. Military judge of a military commission.
948k. Detail of trial counsel and defense counsel.
948l. Detail or employment of reporters and interpreters.
948m. Number of members; excuse of members; absent and additional members.

§ 948h. Who may convene military commissions

Military commissions under this chapter may be convened by the Secretary of Defense or by any officer or official of the United States designated by the Secretary for that purpose.

§ 948i. Who may serve on military commissions

(a) IN GENERAL.—Any commissioned officer of the armed forces on active duty is eligible to serve on a military commission under this chapter.

(b) DETAIL OF MEMBERS.—When convening a military commission under this chapter, the convening authority shall detail as members of the commission such members of the armed forces eligible under subsection (a), as in the opinion of the convening authority, are best qualified for the duty by reason of age, education, training, experience, length of service, and judicial temperament.

....

§ 948j. Military judge of a military commission

(a) DETAIL OF MILITARY JUDGE.—A military judge shall be detailed to each military commission under this chapter. The Secretary of Defense shall prescribe regulations providing for the manner in which military judges are so detailed to military commissions. The military judge shall preside over each military commission to which he has been detailed.

(b) QUALIFICATIONS.—A military judge shall be a commissioned officer of the armed forces who is a member of the bar of a Federal court, or a member of the bar of the highest court of a State, and who is certified to be qualified for duty under section 826 of this title (Article 26 of the Uniform Code of Military Justice) as a military judge in general courts-martial by the Judge Advocate General of the armed force of which such military judge is a member.

....

§ 948k. Detail of trial counsel and defense counsel

(a) DETAIL OF COUNSEL GENERALLY.—(1) Trial counsel and military defense counsel shall be detailed for each military commission under this chapter.

(2) Assistant trial counsel and assistant and associate defense counsel may be detailed for a military commission under this chapter.

(3) Military defense counsel for a military commission under this chapter shall be detailed as soon as practicable after the swearing of charges against the accused.

(4) The Secretary of Defense shall prescribe regulations providing for the manner in which trial counsel and military defense counsel are detailed for military commissions under this chapter and for the persons who are authorized to detail such counsel for such commissions.

(b) TRIAL COUNSEL.—Subject to subsection (e), trial counsel detailed for a military commission under this chapter must be—

(1) a judge advocate (as that term is defined in section 801 of this title (Article 1 of the Uniform Code of Military Justice) who—"(A) is a graduate of an accredited law school or is a member of the bar of a Federal court or of the highest court of a State; and

(B) is certified as competent to perform duties as trial counsel before general courts-martial by the Judge Advocate General of the armed force of which he is a member; or

(2) a civilian who—

(A) is a member of the bar of a Federal court or of the highest court of a State; and

(B) is otherwise qualified to practice before the military commission pursuant to regulations prescribed by the Secretary of Defense.

(c) MILITARY DEFENSE COUNSEL.—Subject to subsection (e), military defense counsel detailed for a military commission under this chapter must be a judge advocate (as so defined) who is—

(1) a graduate of an accredited law school or is a member of the bar of a Federal court or of the highest court of a State; and "(2) certified as competent to perform duties as defense counsel before general courts-martial by the Judge Advocate General of the armed force of which he is a member.

....

SUBCHAPTER III—PRE-TRIAL PROCEDURE

Sec.

948q. Charges and specifications.

948r. Compulsory self-incrimination prohibited; treatment of statements obtained by torture and other statements.

948s. Service of charges.

§ 948q. Charges and specifications

(a) CHARGES AND SPECIFICATIONS.—Charges and specifications against an accused in a military commission under this chapter shall be signed by a person subject to chapter 47 of this title under oath before a commissioned officer of the armed forces authorized to administer oaths and shall state—

(1) that the signer has personal knowledge of, or reason to believe, the matters set forth therein; and

(2) that they are true in fact to the best of the signer's knowledge and belief.

(b) NOTICE TO ACCUSED.—Upon the swearing of the charges and specifications in accordance with subsection (a), the accused shall be informed of the charges against him as soon as practicable.

§ 948r. Compulsory self-incrimination prohibited; treatment of statements obtained by torture and other statements

(a) IN GENERAL.—No person shall be required to testify against himself at a proceeding of a military commission under this chapter.

(b) EXCLUSION OF STATEMENTS OBTAINED BY TORTURE.—A statement obtained by use of torture shall not be admissible in a military commission under this chapter, except against a person accused of torture as evidence that the statement was made.

(c) STATEMENTS OBTAINED BEFORE ENACTMENT OF DETAINEE TREATMENT ACT OF 2005.—A statement obtained before December 30, 2005 (the date of the enactment of the Defense Treatment Act of 2005) in which the degree of coercion is disputed may be admitted only if the military judge finds that—

(1) the totality of the circumstances renders the statement reliable and possessing sufficient probative value; and

(2) the interests of justice would best be served by admission of the statement into evidence.

(d) STATEMENTS OBTAINED AFTER ENACTMENT OF DETAINEE TREATMENT ACT OF 2005.—A statement obtained on or after December 30, 2005 (the date of the enactment of the Defense Treatment Act of 2005) in which the degree of coercion is disputed may be admitted only if the military judge finds that—

(1) the totality of the circumstances renders the statement reliable and possessing sufficient probative value;

(2) the interests of justice would best be served by admission of the statement into evidence; and

(3) the interrogation methods used to obtain the statement do not amount to cruel, inhuman, or degrading treatment prohibited by section 1003 of the Detainee Treatment Act of 2005.

§ 948s. Service of charges

The trial counsel assigned to a case before a military commission under this chapter shall cause to be served upon the accused and military defense counsel a copy of the charges upon which trial is to be had. Such charges shall be served in English and, if appropriate, in another language that the accused understands. Such service shall be made sufficiently in advance of trial to prepare a defense.

SUBCHAPTER IV—TRIAL PROCEDURE

§ 949a. Rules

(a) PROCEDURES AND RULES OF EVIDENCE.—Pretrial, trial, and post-trial procedures, including elements and modes of proof, for cases triable by military commission under this chapter may be prescribed by the Secretary of Defense, in consultation with the Attorney General. Such procedures shall, so far as the Secretary considers practicable or consistent with military or intelligence activities, apply the principles of law and the rules of evidence in trial by general courts-martial. Such procedures and rules of evidence may not be contrary to or inconsistent with this chapter.

(b) RULES FOR MILITARY COMMISSION.—(1) Notwithstanding any departures from the law and the rules of evidence in trial by general courts-martial authorized by subsection (a), the procedures and rules of evidence in trials by military commission under this chapter shall include the following:

(A) The accused shall be permitted to present evidence in his defense, to cross-examine the witnesses who testify against him, and to examine and respond to evidence admitted against him on the issue of guilt or innocence and for sentencing, as provided for by this chapter.

(B) The accused shall be present at all sessions of the military commission (other than those for deliberations or voting), except when excluded under section 949d of this title.

(C) The accused shall receive the assistance of counsel as provided for by section 948k.

(D) The accused shall be permitted to represent himself, as provided for by paragraph (3).

(2) In establishing procedures and rules of evidence for military commission proceedings, the Secretary of Defense may prescribe the following provisions:

(A) Evidence shall be admissible if the military judge determines that the evidence would have probative value to a reasonable person.

(B) Evidence shall not be excluded from trial by military commission on the grounds that the evidence was not seized pursuant to a search warrant or other authorization.

(C) A statement of the accused that is otherwise admissible shall not be excluded from trial by military commission on grounds of alleged coercion or compulsory self-incrimination so long as the evidence complies with the provisions of section 948r of this title.

(D) Evidence shall be admitted as authentic so long as—

(i) the military judge of the military commission determines that there is sufficient basis to find that the evidence is what it is claimed to be; and

(ii) the military judge instructs the members that they may consider any issue as to authentication or identification of evidence in determining the weight, if any, to be given to the evidence.

(E)(i) Except as provided in clause (ii), hearsay evidence not otherwise admissible under the rules of evidence applicable in trial by general courts-martial may be admitted in a trial by military commission if the proponent of the evidence makes known to the adverse party, sufficiently in advance to provide the adverse party with a fair opportunity to meet the evidence, the intention of the proponent to offer the evidence, and the particulars of the evidence (including information on the general circumstances under which the evidence was obtained).The disclosure of evidence under the preceding sentence is subject to the requirements and limitations applicable to the disclosure of classified information in section 949j(c) of this title.

(ii) Hearsay evidence not otherwise admissible under the rules of evidence applicable in trial by general courts-martial shall not be admitted in a trial by military commission if the party opposing the admission of the evidence demonstrates that the evidence is unreliable or lacking in probative value.

(F) The military judge shall exclude any evidence the probative value of which is substantially outweighed—

(i) by the danger of unfair prejudice, confusion of the issues, or misleading the commission; or

(ii) by considerations of undue delay, waste of time, or needless presentation of cumulative evidence.

(3)(A) The accused in a military commission under this chapter who exercises the right to self-representation under paragraph (1)(D) shall conform his deportment and the conduct of the defense to the rules of evidence, procedure, and decorum applicable to trials by military commission.

(B) Failure of the accused to conform to the rules described in subparagraph (A) may result in a partial or total revocation by the military judge of the right of self-representation under paragraph (1)(D). In such case, the detailed defense counsel of the accused or an appropriately authorized civilian counsel shall perform the functions necessary for the defense.

. . . .

§ 949b. Unlawfully influencing action of military commission

(a) IN GENERAL.—(1) No authority convening a military commission under this chapter may censure, reprimand, or admonish the military commission, or any member, military judge, or counsel thereof, with respect to the findings or sentence adjudged by the military commission, or with respect to any other exercises of its or his functions in the conduct of the proceedings.

(2) No person may attempt to coerce or, by any unauthorized means, influence—

(A) the action of a military commission under this chapter, or any member thereof, in reaching the findings or sentence in any case;

(B) the action of any convening, approving, or reviewing authority with respect to his judicial acts; or

(C) the exercise of professional judgment by trial counsel or defense counsel.

. . . .

§ 949c. Duties of trial counsel and defense counsel

(a) TRIAL COUNSEL.—The trial counsel of a military commission under this chapter shall prosecute in the name of the United States.

(b) DEFENSE COUNSEL.—(1) The accused shall be represented in his defense before a military commission under this chapter as provided in this subsection.

(2) The accused shall be represented by military counsel detailed under section 948k of this title.

(3) The accused may be represented by civilian counsel if retained by the accused, but only if such civilian counsel—

(A) is a United States citizen;

(B) is admitted to the practice of law in a State, district, or possession of the United States or before a Federal court;

(C) has not been the subject of any sanction of disciplinary action by any court, bar, or other competent governmental authority for relevant misconduct;

(D) has been determined to be eligible for access to classified information that is classified at the level Secret or higher; and

(E) has signed a written agreement to comply with all applicable regulations or instructions for counsel, including any rules of court for conduct during the proceedings.

(4) Civilian defense counsel shall protect any classified information received during the course of representation of the accused in accordance with all applicable law governing the protection of classified information and may not divulge such information to any person not authorized to receive it.

(5) If the accused is represented by civilian counsel, detailed military counsel shall act as associate counsel.

(6) The accused is not entitled to be represented by more than one military counsel. However, the person authorized under regulations prescribed under section 948k of this title to detail counsel, in that person's sole discretion, may detail additional military counsel to represent the accused.

(7) Defense counsel may cross-examine each witness for the prosecution who testifies before a military commission under this chapter.

§ 949d. Sessions

(a) SESSIONS WITHOUT PRESENCE OF MEMBERS.—(1) At any time after the service of charges which have been referred for trial by military commission under this chapter, the military judge may call the military commission into session without the presence of the members for the purpose of—

(A) hearing and determining motions raising defenses or objections which are capable of determination without trial of the issues raised by a plea of not guilty;

(B) hearing and ruling upon any matter which may be ruled upon by the military judge under this chapter, whether or not the matter is appropriate for later consideration or decision by the members;

(C) if permitted by regulations prescribed by the Secretary of Defense, receiving the pleas of the accused; and

(D) performing any other procedural function which may be performed by the military judge under this chapter or under rules prescribed pursuant to section 949a of this title and which does not require the presence of the members.

(2) Except as provided in subsections (c) and (e), any proceedings under paragraph (1) shall—

(A) be conducted in the presence of the accused, defense counsel, and trial counsel; and

(B) be made part of the record.

(b) PROCEEDINGS IN PRESENCE OF ACCUSED.—Except as provided in subsections (c) and (e), all proceedings of a military commission under this chapter, including any consultation of the members with the military judge or counsel, shall—

(1) be in the presence of the accused, defense counsel, and trial counsel; and

(2) be made a part of the record.

(c) DELIBERATION OR VOTE OF MEMBERS.—When the members of a military commission under this chapter deliberate or vote, only the members may be present.

(d) CLOSURE OF PROCEEDINGS.—(1) The military judge may close to the public all or part of the proceedings of a military commission under this chapter, but only in accordance with this subsection.

(2) The military judge may close to the public all or a portion of the proceedings under paragraph (1) only upon making a specific finding that such closure is necessary to—

(A) protect information the disclosure of which could reasonably be expected to cause damage to the national security, including intelligence or law enforcement sources, methods, or activities; or

(B) ensure the physical safety of individuals.

(3) A finding under paragraph (2) may be based upon a presentation, including a presentation ex parte or in camera, by either trial counsel or defense counsel.

(e) EXCLUSION OF ACCUSED FROM CERTAIN PROCEEDINGS.—The military judge may exclude the accused from any portion of a proceeding upon a determination that, after being warned by the military judge, the accused persists in conduct that justifies exclusion from the courtroom—

(1) to ensure the physical safety of individuals; or

(2) to prevent disruption of the proceedings by the accused.

(f) PROTECTION OF CLASSIFIED INFORMATION.—

(1) NATIONAL SECURITY PRIVILEGE.—(A) Classified information shall be protected and is privileged from disclosure if disclosure would be detrimental to the national security.

The rule in the preceding sentence applies to all stages of the proceedings of military commissions under this chapter.

(B) The privilege referred to in subparagraph (A) may be claimed by the head of the executive or military department or government agency concerned based on a finding by the head of that department or agency that—

(i) the information is properly classified; and "(ii) disclosure of the information would be detrimental to the national security.

(C) A person who may claim the privilege referred to in subparagraph (A) may authorize a representative, witness, or trial counsel to claim the privilege and make the finding described in subparagraph (B) on behalf of such person. The authority of the representative, witness, or trial counsel to do so is presumed in the absence of evidence to the contrary.

(2) INTRODUCTION OF CLASSIFIED INFORMATION.—

(A) ALTERNATIVES TO DISCLOSURE.—To protect classified information from disclosure, the military judge, upon motion of trial counsel, shall authorize, to the extent practicable—

(i) the deletion of specified items of classified information from documents to be introduced as evidence before the military commission;

(ii) the substitution of a portion or summary of the information for such classified documents; or

(iii) the substitution of a statement of relevant facts that the classified information would tend to prove.

(B) PROTECTION OF SOURCES, METHODS, OR ACTIVITIES.—The military judge, upon motion of trial counsel, shall permit trial counsel to introduce otherwise admissible evidence before the military commission, while protecting from disclosure the sources, methods, or activities by which the United States acquired the evidence if the military judge finds that (i) the sources, methods, or activities by which the United States acquired the evidence are classified, and (ii) the evidence is reliable. The military judge may require trial counsel to present to the military commission and the defense, to the extent practicable and consistent with national security, an unclassified summary of the sources, methods, or activities by which the United States acquired the evidence.

(C) ASSERTION OF NATIONAL SECURITY PRIVILEGE AT TRIAL.—During the examination of any witness, trial counsel may object to any question, line of inquiry, or motion to admit evidence that would require the disclosure of classified information. Following such an objection, the military judge shall take suitable action to safeguard such classified information. Such action may include the review of trial counsel's claim of privilege by the military judge in camera and on an ex parte basis, and the delay of proceedings to permit trial counsel to consult with the department or agency concerned as to whether the national security privilege should be asserted.

(3) CONSIDERATION OF PRIVILEGE AND RELATED MATERIALS.—A claim of privilege under this subsection, and any materials submitted in support thereof, shall, upon request of the Government, be considered by the military judge in camera and shall not be disclosed to the accused.

. . . .

§ 949f. Challenges

(a) CHALLENGES AUTHORIZED.—The military judge and members of a military commission under this chapter may be challenged by the accused or trial counsel for cause stated to the commission. The military judge shall determine the relevance and validity of challenges for cause. The military judge may not receive a challenge to more than one person at a time. Challenges by trial counsel shall ordinarily be presented and decided before those by the accused are offered.

(b) PEREMPTORY CHALLENGES.—Each accused and the trial counsel are entitled to one peremptory challenge. The military judge may not be challenged except for cause.

(c) CHALLENGES AGAINST ADDITIONAL MEMBERS.—Whenever additional members are detailed to a military commission under this chapter, and after any challenges for cause against such additional members are presented and decided, each accused and the trial counsel are entitled to one peremptory challenge against members not previously subject to peremptory challenge.

§ 949g. Oaths

(a) IN GENERAL.—(1) Before performing their respective duties in a military commission under this chapter, military judges, members, trial counsel, defense counsel, reporters, and interpreters shall take an oath to perform their duties faithfully.....

(b) WITNESSES.—Each witness before a military commission under this chapter shall be examined on oath.

§ 949h. Former jeopardy

(a) IN GENERAL.—No person may, without his consent, be tried by a military commission under this chapter a second time for the same offense.

....

§ 949i. Pleas of the accused

(a) ENTRY OF PLEA OF NOT GUILTY.—If an accused in a military commission under this chapter after a plea of guilty sets up matter inconsistent with the plea, or if it appears that the accused has entered the plea of guilty through lack of understanding of its meaning and effect, or if the accused fails or refuses to plead, a plea of not guilty shall be entered in the record, and the military commission shall proceed as though the accused had pleaded not guilty.

(b) FINDING OF GUILT AFTER GUILTY PLEA.—With respect to any charge or specification to which a plea of guilty has been made by the accused in a military commission under this chapter and accepted by the military judge, a finding of guilty of the charge or specification may be entered immediately without a vote. The finding shall constitute the finding of the commission unless the plea of guilty is withdrawn prior to announcement of the sentence, in which event the proceedings shall continue as though the accused had pleaded not guilty.

§ 949j. Opportunity to obtain witnesses and other evidence

(a) RIGHT OF DEFENSE COUNSEL.—Defense counsel in a military commission under this chapter shall have a reasonable opportunity to obtain witnesses and other evidence as provided in regulations prescribed by the Secretary of Defense.

(b) PROCESS FOR COMPULSION.—Process issued in a military commission under this chapter to compel witnesses to appear and testify and to compel the production of other evidence—

(1) shall be similar to that which courts of the United States having criminal jurisdiction may lawfully issue; and

(2) shall run to any place where the United States shall have jurisdiction thereof.

(c) PROTECTION OF CLASSIFIED INFORMATION.—(1) With respect to the discovery obligations of trial counsel under this section, the military judge, upon motion of trial counsel, shall authorize, to the extent practicable—

(A) the deletion of specified items of classified information from documents to be made available to the accused;

(B) the substitution of a portion or summary of the information for such classified documents; or Regulations.

(C) the substitution of a statement admitting relevant facts that the classified information would tend to prove.

(2) The military judge, upon motion of trial counsel, shall authorize trial counsel, in the course of complying with discovery obligations under this section, to protect from disclosure the sources, methods, or activities by which the United States acquired evidence if the military judge finds that the sources, methods, or activities by which the United States acquired such evidence are classified. The military judge may require trial counsel to provide, to the extent practicable, an unclassified summary of the sources, methods, or activities by which the United States acquired such evidence.

(d) EXCULPATORY EVIDENCE.—(1) As soon as practicable, trial counsel shall disclose to the defense the existence of any evidence known to trial counsel that reasonably tends to exculpate the accused. Where exculpatory evidence is classified, the accused shall be provided with an adequate substitute in accordance with the procedures under subsection (c).

(2) In this subsection, the term 'evidence known to trial counsel', in the case of exculpatory evidence, means exculpatory evidence that the prosecution would be required to disclose in a trial by general court-martial under chapter 47 of this title.

§ 949k. Defense of lack of mental responsibility

(a) AFFIRMATIVE DEFENSE.—It is an affirmative defense in a trial by military commission under this chapter that, at the time of the commission of the acts constituting the offense, the accused, as a result of a severe mental disease or defect, was unable to appreciate the nature and quality or the wrongfulness of the acts. Mental disease or defect does not otherwise constitute a defense.

(b) BURDEN OF PROOF.—The accused in a military commission under this chapter has the burden of proving the defense of lack of mental responsibility by clear and convincing evidence.

. . . .

§ 949l. Voting and rulings

(a) VOTE BY SECRET WRITTEN BALLOT.—Voting by members of a military commission under this chapter on the findings and on the sentence shall be by secret written ballot.

(b) RULINGS.—(1) The military judge in a military commission under this chapter shall rule upon all questions of law, including the admissibility of evidence and all interlocutory questions arising during the proceedings.

(2) Any ruling made by the military judge upon a question of law or an interlocutory question (other than the factual issue of mental responsibility of the accused) is conclusive and constitutes the ruling of the military commission. However, a military judge may change his ruling at any time during the trial.

(c) INSTRUCTIONS PRIOR TO VOTE.—Before a vote is taken of the findings of a military commission under this chapter, the military judge shall, in the presence of the accused and counsel, instruct the members as to the elements of the offense and charge the members—

(1) that the accused must be presumed to be innocent until his guilt is established by legal and competent evidence beyond a reasonable doubt;

(2) that in the case being considered, if there is a reasonable doubt as to the guilt of the accused, the doubt must be resolved in favor of the accused and he must be acquitted;

(3) that, if there is reasonable doubt as to the degree of guilt, the finding must be in a lower degree as to which there is no reasonable doubt; and

(4) that the burden of proof to establish the guilt of the accused beyond a reasonable doubt is upon the United States.

§ 949m. Number of votes required

(a) CONVICTION.—No person may be convicted by a military commission under this chapter of any offense, except as provided in section 949i(b) of this title or by concurrence of two-thirds of the members present at the time the vote is taken.

(b) SENTENCES.—(1) No person may be sentenced by a military commission to suffer death, except insofar as—

(A) the penalty of death is expressly authorized under this chapter or the law of war for an offense of which the accused has been found guilty;

(B) trial counsel expressly sought the penalty of death by filing an appropriate notice in advance of trial;

(C) the accused is convicted of the offense by the concurrence of all the members present at the time the vote is taken; and

(D) all the members present at the time the vote is taken concur in the sentence of death.

(2) No person may be sentenced to life imprisonment, or to confinement for more than 10 years, by a military commission under this chapter except by the concurrence of three-fourths of the members present at the time the vote is taken.

(3) All other sentences shall be determined by a military commission by the concurrence of two-thirds of the members present at the time the vote is taken.

(c) NUMBER OF MEMBERS REQUIRED FOR PENALTY OF DEATH.—(1) Except as provided in paragraph (2), in a case in which the penalty of death is sought, the number of members of the military commission under this chapter shall be not less than 12.

(2) In any case described in paragraph (1) in which 12 members are not reasonably available because of physical conditions or military exigencies, the convening authority shall specify a lesser number of members for the military commission (but not fewer than 9 members), and the military commission may be assembled, and the trial held, with not fewer than the number of members so specified. In such a case, the convening authority shall make a detailed written statement, to be appended to the record, stating why a greater number of members were not reasonably available.

§ 949n. Military commission to announce action

A military commission under this chapter shall announce its findings and sentence to the parties as soon as determined.

§ 949o. Record of trial

(a) RECORD AUTHENTICATION.—Each military commission under this chapter shall keep a separate, verbatim, record of the proceedings in each case brought before it, and the record shall be authenticated by the signature of the military judge.....

SUBCHAPTER V—SENTENCES

Sec.

949s. Cruel or unusual punishments prohibited.

949t. Maximum limits.

949u. Execution of confinement.

§ 949s. Cruel or unusual punishments prohibited

Punishment by flogging, or by branding, marking, or tattooing on the body, or any other cruel or unusual punishment, may not be adjudged by a military commission under this chapter or inflicted under this chapter upon any person subject to this chapter. The use of irons, single or double, except for the purpose of safe custody, is prohibited under this chapter.

§ 949t. Maximum limits

The punishment which a military commission under this chapter may direct for an offense may not exceed such limits as the President or Secretary of Defense may prescribe for that offense.

§ 949u. Execution of confinement

(a) IN GENERAL.—Under such regulations as the Secretary of Defense may prescribe, a sentence of confinement adjudged by a military commission under this chapter may be carried into execution by confinement—

(1) in any place of confinement under the control of any of the armed forces; or Regulations.

(2) in any penal or correctional institution under the control of the United States or its allies, or which the United States may be allowed to use.

(b) TREATMENT DURING CONFINEMENT BY OTHER THAN THE ARMED FORCES.— Persons confined under subsection (a)(2) in a penal or correctional institution not under the control of an armed force are subject to the same discipline and treatment as persons confined or committed by the courts of the United States or of the State, District of Columbia, or place in which the institution is situated.

SUBCHAPTER VI—POST-TRIAL PROCEDURE AND REVIEW OF MILITARY COMMISSIONS

Sec.

950a. Error of law; lesser included offense.

950b. Review by the convening authority.

950c. Appellate referral; waiver or withdrawal of appeal.

950d. Appeal by the United States.

950e. Rehearings.

950f. Review by Court of Military Commission Review.

950g. Review by the United States Court of Appeals for the District of Columbia Circuit and the Supreme Court.

950h. Appellate counsel.

950i. Execution of sentence; procedures for execution of sentence of death.

950j. Finality or proceedings, findings, and sentences.

§ 950a. Error of law; lesser included offense

(a) ERROR OF LAW.—A finding or sentence of a military commission under this chapter may not be held incorrect on the ground of an error of law unless the error materially prejudices the substantial rights of the accused.

(b) LESSER INCLUDED OFFENSE.—Any reviewing authority with the power to approve or affirm a finding of guilty by a military commission under this chapter may approve or affirm, instead, so much of the finding as includes a lesser included offense.

§ 950b. Review by the convening authority

(a) NOTICE TO CONVENING AUTHORITY OF FINDINGS AND SENTENCE.— The findings and sentence of a military commission under this chapter shall be reported in writing promptly to the convening authority after the announcement of the sentence.

. . . .

§ 950c. Appellate referral; waiver or withdrawal of appeal

(a) AUTOMATIC REFERRAL FOR APPELLATE REVIEW.—Except as provided under subsection (b), in each case in which the final decision of a military commission (as approved by the convening authority) includes a finding of guilty, the convening authority shall refer the case to the Court of Military Commission Review. Any such referral shall be made in accordance with procedures prescribed under regulations of the Secretary.

. . . .

(c) WITHDRAWAL OF APPEAL.—Except in a case in which the sentence as approved under section 950b of this title extends to death, the accused may withdraw an appeal at any time.

. . . .

(b) NOTICE OF APPEAL.—The United States shall take an appeal of an order or ruling under subsection (a) by filing a notice of appeal with the military judge within five days after the date of such order or ruling.

(c) APPEAL.—An appeal under this section shall be forwarded, by means specified in regulations prescribed the Secretary of Defense, directly to the Court of Military Commission Review. In ruling on an appeal under this section, the Court may act only with respect to matters of law.

. . . .

§ 950f. Review by Court of Military Commission Review

(a) ESTABLISHMENT.—The Secretary of Defense shall establish a Court of Military Commission Review which shall be composed of one or more panels, and each such panel shall be composed of not less than three appellate military judges. For the purpose of reviewing military commission decisions under this chapter, the court may sit in panels or as a whole in accordance with rules prescribed by the Secretary.

. . . .

§ 950g. Review by the United States Court of Appeals for the District of Columbia Circuit and the Supreme Court

(a) EXCLUSIVE APPELLATE JURISDICTION.—(1)(A) Except as provided in subparagraph (B), the United States Court of Appeals for the District of Columbia Circuit shall have exclusive jurisdiction to determine the validity of a final judgment rendered by a military commission (as approved by the convening authority) under this chapter.

. . . .

(b) STANDARD FOR REVIEW.—In a case reviewed by it under this section, the Court of Appeals may act only with respect to matters of law.

(c) SCOPE OF REVIEW.—The jurisdiction of the Court of Appeals on an appeal under subsection (a) shall be limited to the consideration of—

(1) whether the final decision was consistent with the standards and procedures specified in this chapter; and

(2) to the extent applicable, the Constitution and the laws of the United States.

(d) SUPREME COURT.—The Supreme Court may review by writ of certiorari the final judgment of the Court of Appeals pursuant to section 1257 of title 28.

§ 950h. Appellate counsel

(a) APPOINTMENT.—The Secretary of Defense shall, by regulation, establish procedures for the appointment of appellate counsel for the United States and for the accused in military commissions under this chapter. Appellate counsel shall meet the qualifications for counsel appearing before military commissions under this chapter.

. . . .

(c) REPRESENTATION OF ACCUSED.—The accused shall be represented by appellate counsel appointed under subsection (a) before the Court of Military Commission Review, the United States Court of Appeals for the District of Columbia Circuit, and the Supreme Court, and by civilian counsel if retained by the accused. Any such civilian counsel shall meet the qualifications under paragraph (3) of section 949c(b) of this title for civilian counsel appearing before military commissions under this chapter and shall be subject to the requirements of paragraph (4) of that section.

§ 950i. Execution of sentence; procedures for execution of sentence of death

(a) IN GENERAL.—The Secretary of Defense is authorized to carry out a sentence imposed by a military commission under this chapter in accordance with such procedures as the Secretary may prescribe.

(b) EXECUTION OF SENTENCE OF DEATH ONLY UPON APPROVAL BY THE PRESIDENT.—If the sentence of a military commission under this chapter extends to death, that part of the sentence providing for death may not be executed until approved by the President. In such a case, the President may commute, remit, or suspend the sentence, or any part thereof, as he sees fit.

(c) EXECUTION OF SENTENCE OF DEATH ONLY UPON FINAL JUDGMENT OF LEGALITY OF PROCEEDINGS.—(1) If the sentence of a military commission under this chapter extends to death, the sentence may not be executed until there is a final judgment as to the legality of the proceedings (and with respect to death, approval under subsection (b)).

. . . .

(d) SUSPENSION OF SENTENCE.—The Secretary of the Defense, or the convening authority acting on the case (if other than the Secretary), may suspend the execution of any sentence or part thereof in the case, except a sentence of death.

§ 950j. Finality or proceedings, findings, and sentences

(a) FINALITY.—The appellate review of records of trial provided by this chapter, and the proceedings, findings, and sentences of military commissions as approved, reviewed, or affirmed as required by this chapter, are final and conclusive. Orders publishing the proceedings of military commissions under this chapter are binding upon all departments, courts, agencies, and officers of the United States, except as otherwise provided by the President.

(b) PROVISIONS OF CHAPTER SOLE BASIS FOR REVIEW OF MILITARY COMMISSION PROCEDURES AND ACTIONS.— Except as otherwise provided in this chapter and notwithstanding any other provision of law (including section 2241 of title 28 or any other habeas corpus provision), no court, justice, or judge shall have jurisdiction to hear or consider any claim or cause of action whatsoever, including any action pending on or filed after the date of the enactment of the Military Commissions Act of 2006, relating to the prosecution, trial, or judgment of a military commission under this chapter, including challenges to the lawfulness of procedures of military commissions under this chapter.

SUBCHAPTER VII—PUNITIVE MATTERS

Sec.

950p. Statement of substantive offenses.

950q. Principals.

950r. Accessory after the fact.

950s. Conviction of lesser included offense.

950t. Attempts.

950u. Solicitation."

950v. Crimes triable by military commissions.

950w. Perjury and obstruction of justice; contempt.

§ 950p. Statement of substantive offenses

(a) PURPOSE.—The provisions of this subchapter codify offenses that have traditionally been triable by military commissions. This chapter does not establish new crimes that did not exist before its enactment, but rather codifies those crimes for trial by military commission.

(b) EFFECT.—Because the provisions of this subchapter(including provisions that incorporate definitions in other provisions of law) are declarative of existing law, they do not preclude trial for crimes that occurred before the date of the enactment of this chapter.

§ 950q. Principals

Any person is punishable as a principal under this chapter who—

(1) commits an offense punishable by this chapter, or aids, abets, counsels, commands, or procures its commission;

(2) causes an act to be done which if directly performed by him would be punishable by this chapter; or

(3) is a superior commander who, with regard to acts punishable under this chapter, knew, had reason to know, or should have known, that a subordinate was about to commit such acts or had done so and who failed to take the necessary and reasonable measures to prevent such acts or to punish the perpetrators thereof.

§ 950r. Accessory after the fact

Any person subject to this chapter who, knowing that an offense punishable by this chapter has been committed, receives, comforts, or assists the offender in order to hinder or prevent his apprehension, trial, or Punishment shall be punished as a military commission under this chapter may direct.

§ 950s. Conviction of lesser included offense

An accused may be found guilty of an offense necessarily included in the offense charged or of an attempt to commit either the offense charged or an attempt to commit either the offense charged or an offense necessarily included therein.

§ 950t. Attempts

(a) IN GENERAL.—Any person subject to this chapter who attempts to commit any offense punishable by this chapter shall be punished as a military commission under this chapter may direct.

(b) SCOPE OF OFFENSE.—An act, done with specific intent to commit an offense under this chapter, amounting to more than mere preparation and tending, even though failing, to effect its commission, is an attempt to commit that offense.

(c) EFFECT OF CONSUMMATION.—Any person subject to this chapter may be convicted of an attempt to commit an offense although it appears on the trial that the offense was consummated.

§ 950u. Solicitation

Any person subject to this chapter who solicits or advises another or others to commit one or more substantive offenses triable by military commission under this chapter shall, if the offense solicited or advised is attempted or committed, be punished with the punishment provided for the commission of the offense, but, if the offense solicited or advised is not committed or attempted, he shall be punished as a military commission under this chapter may direct.

§ 950v. Crimes triable by military commissions

(a) DEFINITIONS AND CONSTRUCTION.—In this section:

(1) MILITARY OBJECTIVE.—The term 'military objective' means—

(A) combatants; and"(B) those objects during an armed conflict—

(i) which, by their nature, location, purpose, or use, effectively contribute to the opposing force's war fighting or war-sustaining capability; and"(ii) the total or partial destruction, capture, or neutralization of which would constitute a definite military advantage to the attacker under the circumstances at the time of the attack.

(2) PROTECTED PERSON.—The term 'protected person' means any person entitled to protection under one or more of the Geneva Conventions, including—

(A) civilians not taking an active part in hostilities;

(B) military personnel placed hors de combat by sickness, wounds, or detention; and

(C) military medical or religious personnel;

(3) PROTECTED PROPERTY.—The term 'protected property' means property specifically protected by the law of war (such as buildings dedicated to religion, education, art, science or charitable purposes, historic monuments, hospitals, or places where the sick and wounded are collected), if such property is not being used for military purposes or is not otherwise a military objective. Such term includes objects properly identified by one of the distinctive emblems of the Geneva Conventions, but does not include civilian property that is a military objective.

(4) CONSTRUCTION.—The intent specified for an offense under paragraph (1), (2), (3), (4), or (12) of subsection (b) precludes the applicability of such offense with regard to—

(A) collateral damage; or

(B) death, damage, or injury incident to a lawful attack.

(b) OFFENSES.—The following offenses shall be triable by military commission under this chapter at any time without limitation:

(1) MURDER OF PROTECTED PERSONS.—Any person subject to this chapter who intentionally kills one or more protected persons shall be punished by death or such other punishment as a military commission under this chapter may direct.

(2) ATTACKING CIVILIANS.—Any person subject to this chapter who intentionally engages in an attack upon a civilian population as such, or individual civilians not taking active part in hostilities, shall be punished, if death results to one or more of the victims, by death or such other punishment as a military commission under this chapter may direct, and, if death does not result to any of the victims, by such punishment, other than death, as a military commission under this chapter may direct.

(3) ATTACKING CIVILIAN OBJECTS.—Any person subject to this chapter who intentionally engages in an attack upon a civilian object that is not a military objective shall be punished as a military commission under this chapter may direct.

(4) ATTACKING PROTECTED PROPERTY.—Any person subject to this chapter who intentionally engages in an attack upon protected property shall be punished as a military commission under this chapter may direct.

(5) PILLAGING.—Any person subject to this chapter who intentionally and in the absence of military necessity appropriates or seizes property for private or personal use, without the consent of a person with authority to permit such appropriation or seizure, shall be punished as a military commission under this chapter may direct.

(6) DENYING QUARTER.—Any person subject to this chapter who, with effective command or control over subordinate groups, declares, orders, or otherwise indicates to those groups that there shall be no survivors or surrender accepted, with the intent to threaten an adversary or to conduct hostilities such that there would be no survivors or surrender accepted, shall be punished as a military commission under this chapter may direct.

(7) TAKING HOSTAGES.—Any person subject to this chapter who, having knowingly seized or detained one or more persons, threatens to kill, injure, or continue to detain such person or persons with the intent of compelling any nation, person other than the hostage, or group of persons to act or refrain from acting as an explicit or implicit condition for the safety or release of such person or persons, shall be punished, if death results to one or more of the victims, by death or such other punishment as a military commission under this chapter may direct, and, if death does not result to any of the victims, by such punishment, other than death, as a military commission under this chapter may direct.

(8) EMPLOYING POISON OR SIMILAR WEAPONS.—Any person subject to this chapter who intentionally, as a method of warfare, employs a substance or weapon that releases a substance that causes death or serious and lasting damage to health in the ordinary course of events, through its asphyxiating, bacteriological, or toxic properties, shall be punished, if death results to one or more of the victims, by death or such other punishment as a military commission under this chapter may direct, and, if death does not result to any of the victims, by such punishment, other than death, as a military commission under this chapter may direct.

(9) USING PROTECTED PERSONS AS A SHIELD.—Any person subject to this chapter who positions, or otherwise takes advantage of, a protected person with the intent to shield a military objective from attack, or to shield, favor, or impede military operations, shall be punished, if death results to one or more of the victims, by death or such other punishment as a military commission under this chapter may direct, and, if death does not result to any of the victims, by such punishment, other than death, as a military commission under this chapter may direct.

(10) USING PROTECTED PROPERTY AS A SHIELD.—Any person subject to this chapter who positions, or otherwise takes advantage of the location of, protected property with the intent to shield a military objective from attack, or to shield, favor, or impede military operations, shall be punished as a military commission under this chapter may direct.

(11) TORTURE.—

(A) OFFENSE.—Any person subject to this chapter who commits an act specifically intended to inflict severe physical or mental pain or suffering (other than pain or suffering incidental to lawful sanctions) upon another person within his custody or physical control for the purpose of obtaining information or a confession, punishment, intimidation, coercion, or any reason based on discrimination of any kind, shall be punished, if death results to one or more of the victims, by death or such other punishment as a military commission under this chapter may direct, and, if death does not result to any of the victims, by such punishment, other than death, as a military commission under this chapter may direct.

(B) SEVERE MENTAL PAIN OR SUFFERING DEFINED.—In this section, the term 'severe mental pain or suffering' has the meaning given that term in section 2340(2) of title 18.

(12) CRUEL OR INHUMAN TREATMENT.—

(A) OFFENSE.—Any person subject to this chapter who commits an act intended to inflict severe or serious physical or mental pain or suffering (other than pain or suffering incidental to lawful sanctions), including serious physical abuse, upon another within his custody or control shall be punished, if death results to the victim, by death or such other punishment as a military commission under this chapter may direct, and, if death does not result to the victim, by such punishment, other than death, as a military commission under this chapter may direct.

(B) DEFINITIONS.—In this paragraph:

(i) The term 'serious physical pain or suffering' means bodily injury that involves—"(I) a substantial risk of death;"(II) extreme physical pain; "(III) a burn or physical disfigurement of a serious nature (other than cuts, abrasions, or bruises); or"(IV) significant loss or impairment of the function of a bodily member, organ, or mental faculty.

(ii) The term 'severe mental pain or suffering' has the meaning given that term in section 2340(2) of title 18.

(iii) The term 'serious mental pain or suffering' has the meaning given the term 'severe mental pain or suffering' in section 2340(2) of title 18, except that—(I) the term 'serious' shall replace the term 'severe' where it appears; and

(II) as to conduct occurring after the date of the enactment of the Military Commissions Act of 2006, the term 'serious and non-transitory mental harm (which need not be prolonged)' shall replace the term 'prolonged mental harm' where it appears.

(13) INTENTIONALLY CAUSING SERIOUS BODILY INJURY.—

(A) OFFENSE.—Any person subject to this chapter who intentionally causes serious bodily injury to one or more persons, including lawful combatants, in violation of the law of war shall be punished, if death results to one or more of the victims, by death or such other punishment as a military commission under this chapter may direct, and, if death does not result to any of the victims, by such punishment, other than death, as a military commission under this chapter may direct.

(B) SERIOUS BODILY INJURY DEFINED.—In this paragraph, the term 'serious bodily injury' means bodily injury which involves—

(i) a substantial risk of death;

(ii) extreme physical pain;

(iii) protracted and obvious disfigurement; or

(iv) protracted loss or impairment of the function of a bodily member, organ, or mental faculty.

(14) MUTILATING OR MAIMING.—Any person subject to this chapter who intentionally injures one or more protected persons by disfiguring the person or persons by any mutilation of the person or persons, or by permanently disabling any member, limb, or organ of the body of the person or persons, without any legitimate medical or dental purpose, shall be punished, if death results to one or more of the victims, by death or such other punishment as a military commission under this chapter may direct, and, if death does not result to any of the victims, by such punishment, other than death, as a military commission under this chapter may direct.

(15) MURDER IN VIOLATION OF THE LAW OF WAR.—Any person subject to this chapter who intentionally kills one or more persons, including lawful combatants, in violation of the law of war shall be punished by death or such other punishment as a military commission under this chapter may direct.

(16) DESTRUCTION OF PROPERTY IN VIOLATION OF THE LAW OF WAR.—Any person subject to this chapter who intentionally destroys property belonging to another person in violation of the law of war shall punished as a military commission under this chapter may direct.

(17) USING TREACHERY OR PERFIDY.—Any person subject to this chapter who, after inviting the confidence or belief of one or more persons that they were entitled to, or obliged to accord, protection under the law of war, intentionally makes use of that confidence or belief in killing, injuring, or capturing such person or persons shall be punished, if death results to one or more of the victims, by death or such other

punishment as a military commission under this chapter may direct, and, if death does not result to any of the victims, by such punishment, other than death, as a military commission under this chapter may direct.

(18) IMPROPERLY USING A FLAG OF TRUCE.—Any person subject to this chapter who uses a flag of truce to feign an intention to negotiate, surrender, or otherwise suspend hostilities when there is no such intention shall be punished as a military commission under this chapter may direct.

(19) IMPROPERLY USING A DISTINCTIVE EMBLEM.—Any person subject to this chapter who intentionally uses a distinctive emblem recognized by the law of war for combatant purposes in a manner prohibited by the law of war shall be punished as a military commission under this chapter may direct.

(20) INTENTIONALLY MISTREATING A DEAD BODY.—Any person subject to this chapter who intentionally mistreats the body of a dead person, without justification by legitimate military necessity, shall be punished as a military commission under this chapter may direct.

(21) RAPE.—Any person subject to this chapter who forcibly or with coercion or threat of force wrongfully invades the body of a person by penetrating, however slightly, the anal or genital opening of the victim with any part of the body of the accused, or with any foreign object, shall be punished as a military commission under this chapter may direct.

(22) SEXUAL ASSAULT OR ABUSE.—Any person subject to this chapter who forcibly or with coercion or threat of force engages in sexual contact with one or more persons, or causes one or more persons to engage in sexual contact, shall be punished as a military commission under this chapter may direct.

(23) HIJACKING OR HAZARDING A VESSEL OR AIRCRAFT.— Any person subject to this chapter who intentionally seizes, exercises unauthorized control over, or endangers the safe navigation of a vessel or aircraft that is not a legitimate military objective shall be punished, if death results to one or more of the victims, by death or such other punishment as a military commission under this chapter may direct, and, if death does not result to any of the victims, by such punishment, other than death, as a military commission under this chapter may direct.

(24) TERRORISM.—Any person subject to this chapter who intentionally kills or inflicts great bodily harm on one or more protected persons, or intentionally engages in an act that evinces a wanton disregard for human life, in a manner calculated to influence or affect the conduct of government or civilian population by intimidation or coercion, or to retaliate against government conduct, shall be punished, if death results to one or more of the victims, by death or such other punishment as a military commission under this chapter may direct, and, if death does not result to any of the victims, by such punishment, other than death, as a military commission under this chapter may direct.

(25) PROVIDING MATERIAL SUPPORT FOR TERRORISM.—

(A) OFFENSE.—Any person subject to this chapter who provides material support or resources, knowing or intending that they are to be used in preparation for, or in carrying out, an act of terrorism (as set forth in paragraph (24)), or who intentionally provides material support or resources to an international terrorist organization engaged in hostilities against the United States knowing that such organization has engaged or engages in terrorism (as so set forth), shall be punished as a military commission under this chapter may direct.

(B) MATERIAL SUPPORT OR RESOURCES DEFINED.—In this paragraph, the term 'material support or resources' has the meaning given that term in section 2339A(b) of title 18.

(26) WRONGFULLY AIDING THE ENEMY.—Any person subject to this chapter who, in breach of an allegiance or duty to the United States, knowingly and intentionally aids an enemy of the United States, or one of the co-belligerents of the enemy, shall be punished as a military commission under this chapter may direct.

(27) SPYING.—Any person subject to this chapter who with intent or reason to believe that it is to be used to the injury of the United States or to the advantage of a foreign power, collects or attempts to collect information by clandestine means or while acting under false pretenses, for the purpose of conveying such information to an enemy of the United States, or one of the co-belligerents of the enemy, shall be punished by death or such other punishment as a military commission under this chapter may direct.

(28) CONSPIRACY.—Any person subject to this chapter who conspires to commit one or more substantive offenses triable by military commission under this chapter, and who knowingly does any overt act to effect the object of the conspiracy, shall be punished, if death results to one or more of the victims, by death or such other punishment as a military commission under this chapter may direct, and, if death does

not result to any of the victims, by such punishment, other than death, as a military commission under this chapter may direct.

§ 950w. Perjury and obstruction of justice; contempt

(a) PERJURY AND OBSTRUCTION OF JUSTICE.—A military commission under this chapter may try offenses and impose such punishment as the military commission may direct for perjury, false testimony, or obstruction of justice related to military commissions under this chapter.

(b) CONTEMPT.—A military commission under this chapter may punish for contempt any person who uses any menacing word sign, or gesture in its presence, or who disturbs its proceedings by any riot or disorder."

....

SEC. 5. TREATY OBLIGATIONS NOT ESTABLISHING GROUNDS FOR CERTAIN CLAIMS.

(a) IN GENERAL.—No person may invoke the Geneva Conventions or any protocols thereto in any habeas corpus or other civil action or proceeding to which the United States, or a current or former officer, employee, member of the Armed Forces, or other agent of the United States is a party as a source of rights in any court of the United States or its States or territories.

(b) GENEVA CONVENTIONS DEFINED.—In this section, the term "Geneva Conventions" means—

(1) the Convention for the Amelioration of the Condition of the Wounded and Sick in Armed Forces in the Field, done at Geneva August 12, 1949 (6 UST 3114);

(2) the Convention for the Amelioration of the Condition of the Wounded, Sick, and Shipwrecked Members of the Armed Forces at Sea, done at Geneva August 12, 1949 (6 UST 3217);

(3) the Convention Relative to the Treatment of Prisoners of War, done at Geneva August 12, 1949 (6 UST 3316); and

(4) the Convention Relative to the Protection of Civilian Persons in Time of War, done at Geneva August 12, 1949(6 UST 3516).

SEC. 6. IMPLEMENTATION OF TREATY OBLIGATIONS

(a) IMPLEMENTATION OF TREATY OBLIGATIONS.—

(1) IN GENERAL.—The acts enumerated in subsection (d)of section 2441 of title 18, United States Code, as added by subsection (b) of this section, and in subsection (c) of this section, constitute violations of common Article 3 of the Geneva Conventions prohibited by United States law.

(2) PROHIBITION ON GRAVE BREACHES.—The provisions of section 2441 of title 18, United States Code, as amended by this section, fully satisfy the obligation under Article 129 of the Third Geneva Convention for the United States to provide effective penal sanctions for grave breaches which are encompassed in common Article 3 in the context of an armed conflict not of an international character. No foreign or international source of law shall supply a basis for a rule of decision in the courts of the United States in interpreting the prohibitions enumerated in subsection (d) of such section 2441.

(3) INTERPRETATION BY THE PRESIDENT.—

(A) As provided by the Constitution and by this section, the President has the authority for the United States to interpret the meaning and application of the Geneva Conventions and to promulgate higher standards and administrative regulations for violations of treaty obligations which are not grave breaches of the Geneva Conventions.

....

(b) REVISION TO WAR CRIMES OFFENSE UNDER FEDERAL CRIMINAL CODE.—

(1) IN GENERAL.—Section 2441 of title 18, United States Code, is amended—

(A) in subsection (c), by striking paragraph (3) and inserting the following new paragraph (3):

(3) which constitutes a grave breach of common Article3 (as defined in subsection (d)) when committed in the context of and in association with an armed conflict not of an international character; or"; and

(B) by adding at the end the following new subsection:

(d) COMMON ARTICLE 3 VIOLATIONS.—

(1) PROHIBITED CONDUCT.— In subsection (c)(3), the term 'grave breach of common Article 3' means any conduct (such conduct constituting a grave breach of common Article 3 of the international conventions done at Geneva August 12, 1949), as follows:

(A) TORTURE.—The act of a person who commits, or conspires or attempts to commit, an act specifically intended to inflict severe physical or mental pain or suffering (other than pain or suffering incidental to lawful sanctions) upon another person within his custody or physical control for the purpose of obtaining information or a confession, punishment, intimidation, coercion, or any reason based on discrimination of any kind.

(B) CRUEL OR INHUMAN TREATMENT.—The act of a person who commits, or conspires or attempts to commit, an act intended to inflict severe or serious physical or mental pain or suffering (other than pain or suffering incidental to lawful sanctions), including serious physical abuse, upon another within his custody or control.

(C) PERFORMING BIOLOGICAL EXPERIMENTS.—The act of a person who subjects, or conspires or attempts to subject, one or more persons within his custody or physical control to biological experiments without a legitimate medical or dental purpose and in so doing endangers the body or health of such person or persons.

(D) MURDER.—The act of a person who intentionally kills, or conspires or attempts to kill, or kills whether intentionally or unintentionally in the course of committing any other offense under this subsection, one or more persons taking no active part in the hostilities, including those placed out of combat by sickness, wounds, detention, or any other cause.

(E) MUTILATION OR MAIMING.—The act of a person who intentionally injures, or conspires or attempts to injure, or injures whether intentionally or unintentionally in the course of committing any other offense under this subsection, one or more persons taking no active part in the hostilities, including those placed out of combat by sickness, wounds, detention, or any other cause, by disfiguring the person or persons by any mutilation thereof or by permanently disabling any member, limb, or organ of his body, without any legitimate medical or dental purpose.

(F) INTENTIONALLY CAUSING SERIOUS BODILY INJURY.—

The act of a person who intentionally causes, or conspires or attempts to cause, serious bodily injury to one or more persons, including lawful combatants, in violation of the law of war.

(G) RAPE.—The act of a person who forcibly or with coercion or threat of force wrongfully invades, or conspires or attempts to invade, the body of a person by penetrating, however slightly, the anal or genital opening of the victim with any part of the body of the accused, or with any foreign object.

(H) SEXUAL ASSAULT OR ABUSE.—The act of a person who forcibly or with coercion or threat of force engages, or conspires or attempts to engage, in sexual contact with one or more persons, or causes, or conspires or attempts to cause, one or more persons to engage in sexual contact.

(I) TAKING HOSTAGES.—The act of a person who, having knowingly seized or detained one or more persons, threatens to kill, injure, or continue to detain such person or persons with the intent of compelling any nation, person other than the hostage, or group of persons to act or refrain from acting as an explicit or implicit condition for the safety or release of such person or persons.

(2) DEFINITIONS.—In the case of an offense under subsection (a) by reason of subsection (c)(3)—

(A) the term 'severe mental pain or suffering' shall be applied for purposes of paragraphs (1)(A) and (1)(B)in accordance with the meaning given that term in section2340(2) of this title;

(B) the term 'serious bodily injury' shall be applied for purposes of paragraph (1)(F) in accordance with the meaning given that term in section 113(b)(2) of this title;

(C) the term 'sexual contact' shall be applied for purposes of paragraph (1)(G) in accordance with the meaning given that term in section 2246(3) of this title;

(D) the term 'serious physical pain or suffering' shall be applied for purposes of paragraph (1)(B) as meaning bodily injury that involves—"(i) a substantial risk of death;"(ii) extreme physical pain;"(iii) a burn or physical disfigurement of a serious nature (other than cuts, abrasions, or bruises); or"(iv) significant loss or impairment of the function of a bodily member, organ, or mental faculty; and

(E) the term 'serious mental pain or suffering' shall be applied for purposes of paragraph (1)(B) in accordance with the meaning given the term 'severe mental pain or suffering' (as defined in section 2340(2) of this title), except that—"(i) the term 'serious' shall replace the term 'severe' where it appears; and"(ii) as to conduct occurring after the date of the enactment of the Military Commissions Act of 2006,the term 'serious and non-transitory mental harm(which need not be prolonged)' shall replace the term' prolonged mental harm' where it appears.

. . . .

(5) DEFINITION OF GRAVE BREACHES.—The definitions in this subsection are intended only to define the grave breaches of common Article 3 and not the full scope of United States obligations under that Article."

....

(c) ADDITIONAL PROHIBITION ON CRUEL, INHUMAN, OR DEGRADING TREATMENT OR PUNISHMENT.—

(1) IN GENERAL.—No individual in the custody or under the physical control of the United States Government, regardless of nationality or physical location, shall be subject to cruel, inhuman, or degrading treatment or punishment.

(2) CRUEL, INHUMAN, OR DEGRADING TREATMENT OR PUNISHMENT DEFINED.—In this subsection, the term "cruel, inhuman, or degrading treatment or punishment" means cruel, unusual, and inhumane treatment or punishment prohibited by the Fifth, Eighth, and Fourteenth Amendments to the Constitution of the United States, as defined in the United States Reservations, Declarations and Understandings to the United Nations Convention Against Torture and Other Forms of Cruel, Inhuman or Degrading Treatment or Punishment done at New York, December 10, 1984.

(3) COMPLIANCE.—The President shall take action to ensure compliance with this subsection, including through the establishment of administrative rules and procedures.

SEC. 7. HABEAS CORPUS MATTERS.

(a) IN GENERAL.—Section 2241 of title 28, United States Code, is amended by striking both the subsection (e) added by section109–163 (119 Stat. 3477) and inserting the following new subsection:

(e)(1) No court, justice, or judge shall have jurisdiction to hear or consider an application for a writ of habeas corpus filed by or on behalf of an alien detained by the United States who has been determined by the United States to have been properly detained as an enemy combatant or is awaiting such determination.

(2) Except as provided in paragraphs (2) and (3) of section 1005(e) of the Detainee Treatment Act of 2005 (10 U.S.C. 801note), no court, justice, or judge shall have jurisdiction to hear or consider any other action against the United States or its agents relating to any aspect of the detention, transfer, treatment, trial, or conditions of confinement of an alien who is or was detained by the United States and has been determined by the United States to have been properly detained as an enemy combatant or is awaiting such determination."

....

DOCUMENT 97

Full Official Title: War Crimes Act of 1996

Short Title/Acronym/Abbreviation: Not applicable

Type of Document: This is a bill passed by the U.S. Congress and signed into law by the president.

Subject: Common Article Three, war

Official Citation: 18 U.S.C. § 2441 (as amended)

Date of Document: January 3, 1996

Date of Adoption: Not applicable

Date of General Entry into Force (EIF): Not applicable

Number of States Parties as of this printing: Not applicable

Date of Signature by the United States: Not applicable

Date of Ratification/Accession/Adhesion: Not applicable

Date of Entry into Force as to United States (effective date): Not applicable

Legal Status/Character of the Instrument/Document as to the United States: This bill is legally binding.

Comments: The War Crimes Act of 1996 was passed by the U.S. Congress to "amend title 18, United States Code, to carry out the international obligations of the United States under the Geneva Conventions to provide criminal penalties for certain war crimes." The bill implemented a provision of the Geneva Convention to which the U.S. is a party providing criminal penalties to anyone who commits a "grave breach" of one of the Conventions equating to a "war crime." This bill was amended by the Military Commissions Act of 2006 to limit the ability of U.S. military personnel to be tried for violating the full scope of "grave breaches" and "war crimes" under the Geneva Convention in their treatment of detainees.

Caution: The status and applicability of this instrument as to the United States may have changed since the date of this publication.

THE WAR CRIMES ACT OF 1996, USC TITLE 18, SEC. 2441
Title 18—Crimes and Criminal Procedure
Part I—Crimes, Chapter 118—War Crimes
Sec. 2441. War Crimes

(a) Offense.—Whoever, whether inside or outside the United States, commits a war crime, in any of the circumstances described in subsection (b), shall be fined under this title or imprisoned for life or any term of years, or both, and if death results to the victim, shall also be subject to the penalty of death.

(b) Circumstances.—The circumstances referred to in subsection (a) are that the person committing such war crime or the victim of such war crime is a member of the Armed Forces of the United States or a national of the United States (as defined in section 101 of the Immigration and Nationality Act).

(c) Definition.—As used in this section the term "war crime" means any conduct

(1) defined as a grave breach in any of the international conventions signed at Geneva 12 August 1949, or any protocol to such convention to which the United States is a party;

(2) prohibited by Article 23, 25, 27, or 28 of the Annex to the Hague Convention IV, Respecting the Laws and Customs of War on Land, signed 18 October 1907;

(3) which constitutes a violation of common Article 3 of the international Conventions signed at Geneva, 12 August 1949, or any protocol to such convention to which the United States is a party and which deals with non-international armed conflict; or

(4) of a person who, in relation to an armed conflict and contrary to the provisions of the Protocol on Prohibitions or Restrictions on the Use of Mines, Booby-Traps and Other Devices as amended at Geneva on 3 May 1996 (Protocol II as amended on 3 May 1996), when the United States is a party to such Protocol, willfully kills or causes serious injury to civilians.

DOCUMENT 98

Full Official Title: Detainee Treatment Act of 2005
Short Title/Acronym/Abbreviation: DTA
Type of Document: This is a bill passed by the U.S. Congress and signed into law by the president.
Subjects: Detainees, war
Official Citation: Not applicable
Date of Document: December 30, 2005
Date of Adoption: Not applicable
Date of General Entry into Force (EIF): Not applicable
Number of States Parties as of this printing: Not applicable
Date of Signature by the United States: December 30, 2005
Date of Ratification/Accession/Adhesion: Not applicable
Date of Entry into Force as to United States (effective date): Not applicable
Legal Status/Character of the Instrument/Document as to the United States: This bill is legally binding.
Comments: The Detainee Treatment Act of 2005 was passed by Congress as part of the Department of Defense (DOD) Appropriations bill for 2006, for the purpose of ensuring that DOD personnel utilized the U.S. Army Field Manual guidelines when interrogating detainees, and to clarify the treatment of prisoners being held in an ambiguous state. Moreover, it prohibited "cruel, inhuman and degrading treatment or punishment of persons under the detention, custody, or control of the United States Government." The DTA was drafted in response to criticism of the U.S. interrogation of detainees, and reported cases of misconduct by U.S. military personnel in Iraq, Afghanistan and other locations, following the military actions taken as a result of the attacks on September 11, 2001.
Caution: The status and applicability of this instrument as to the United States may have changed since the date of this publication.

DETAINEE TREATMENT ACT OF 2005
The **Detainee Treatment Act of 2005 (DTA)** is an Act of the United States Congress that prohibits inhumane treatment of prisoners, including prisoners at Guantánamo Bay; requires military interrogations to be performed according to the U.S. Army Field Manual for Human Intelligence Collector Operations; and

strips federal courts of jurisdiction to consider habeas corpus petitions filed by prisoners in Guantánamo, or other claims asserted by Guantánamo detainees against the U.S. government, as well as limiting appellate review of decisions of the Combatant Status Review Tribunals and Military Commissions. On June 12, 2008, the Supreme Court, in the case of *Boumediene v. Bush*, ruled 5-4 that the Military Commissions Act of 2006 unconstitutionally limited detainee's access to judicial review and that detainees have the right to challenge their detention in conventional civilian courts.

Legislative details

The amendment affected the United States Senate Department of Defense Appropriations Act, 2006 (DOD Act); the amendment is commonly referred to as the *Amendment on (1) the Army Field Manual and (2) Cruel, Inhumane, Degrading Treatment, amendment #1977* and also known as the *McCain Amendment 1977*. It became the **Detainee Treatment Act of 2005** (DTA) as Division A, Title X of the DOD Act. The amendment prohibits inhumane treatment of prisoners, including prisoners at Guantánamo Bay, by confining interrogations to the techniques in FM 34-52 Intelligence Interrogation. Also, section 1005(e) of the DTA prohibits aliens detained in Guantánamo Bay from applying for a writ of habeas corpus. Certain portions of the amendment were enacted as 42 U.S.C. § 2000dd.

Amendment 1977 amended the Defense Appropriations Bill for 2005 (H.R.2863) passed by the United States House of Representatives. The amendment was introduced to the Senate by Senator John McCain (R-Arizona) on October 3, 2005 as S.Amdt.1977.

The amendment was co-sponsored by Senators Lindsey Graham, Chuck Hagel, Gordon H. Smith, Susan M. Collins, Lamar Alexander, Richard Durbin, Carl Levin, John Warner, Lincoln Chafee, John E. Sununu, and Ken Salazar.

On October 5, 2005, the United States Senate voted 90-9 to support the amendment.

The Senators who voted against the amendment were Wayne Allard (R-CO), Christopher Bond (R-MO), Tom Coburn (R-OK), Thad Cochran (R-MS), John Cornyn (R-TX), James Inhofe (R-OK), Pat Roberts (R-KS), Jeff Sessions (R-AL), and Ted Stevens (R-AK).

Signing statement by President Bush

After approving the bill President Bush issued a signing statement: an official document in which a president lays out his interpretation of a new law. In it Bush said:

"The executive branch shall construe Title X in Division A of the Act, relating to detainees, in a manner consistent with the constitutional authority of the President to supervise the unitary executive branch and as Commander in Chief and consistent with the constitutional limitations on the judicial power, which will assist in achieving the shared objective of the Congress and the President, evidenced in Title X, of protecting the American people from further terrorist attacks."

The *Boston Globe* quoted an anonymous senior administration official saying, "Of course the president has the obligation to follow this law, (but) he also has the obligation to defend and protect the country as the commander in chief, and he will have to square those two responsibilities in each case. We are not expecting that those two responsibilities will come into conflict, but it's possible that they will".

Criticism

The Act sets the Army's standards of interrogation as the standard for all agencies in the Department of Defense. It further prohibits all other agencies of the U.S. government, such as the CIA, from subjecting any person in their custody to "cruel, inhuman, or degrading treatment or punishment." However, the Act does not provide detailed guidelines that spell out the meaning of that phrase. In an effort to provide clarification, Congress passed legislation in 2008 to similarly constrain the intelligence community to the Field Manual's techniques. McCain voted against this bill and recommended that President Bush follow through on his threat to veto it, arguing that the CIA already could not engage in torture but should have more options than afforded to military interrogators. That bill was passed by both chambers of Congress but, once vetoed, failed to pass with sufficient votes to override the executive veto.

The Detainee Treatment Act cited the U.S. Army's Field Manual on interrogation as the authoritative guide to interrogation techniques, but did not cite a specific edition of the Manual. The contents of the Manual are controlled by the Department of Defense, and thus the executive branch controls whether a given technique will be permitted or banned. The Manual has been revised since the Amendment became law. The Department of Defense has claimed that none of the techniques permitted by the new Field Manual 2-22.3 are classified.

Also, the Detainee Treatment Act's anti-torture provisions were modified by the Graham-Levin Amendment, which was also attached to the $453-billion 2006 Defense Budget Bill. The Graham-

Levin Amendment permits the Department of Defense to consider evidence obtained through torture of Guantánamo Bay detainees, and expands the prohibition of *habeas corpus* for redetainees, which subsequently leaves detainees no legal recourse if they are tortured.

Critics say these two actions deflate the Detainee Treatment Act from having any real power in stopping torture by the United States government, and these were the true reasons why President Bush and McCain "conceded" to Congressional demands. The mainstream media credited their concession to "overwhelming Congressional support" for the measure.

Amnesty International claims that the amendment's loopholes actually signal that torture is now official U.S. policy.

Criticisms have also been directed at Senators Lindsey Graham and Jon Kyl for their *amicus curiae* brief filed in the *Hamdan v. Rumsfeld* case, in which they argued that the Detainee Treatment Act's passage sufficed to deny the Supreme Court jurisdiction over the case. Language in the Congressional Record that the majority opinion cites was inserted into the Record for the day on which the amendment passed by Graham and Kyl *after the legislation had already been enacted*, and furthermore that the language in question was worded in such a manner as to imply it had been recorded in live debate. The revised Record contains such phrasing as Kyl's "Mr. President, I see that we are nearing the end of our allotted time" and Sen. Sam Brownback's "If I might interrupt". Brownback has not responded to press inquiries. Justice Scalia's dissent noted this as an example of Scalia's longstanding hostility to the use of legislative history. Scalia wrote:

Worst of all is the Court's reliance on the legislative history of the DTA to buttress its implausible reading ... These statements were made when Members of Congress were fully aware that our continuing jurisdiction *over this very case* was at issue. ... The question was divisive, and floor statements made on both sides were undoubtedly opportunistic and crafted *solely* for use in the briefs in this very litigation. ... [T]he handful of floor statements that the Court treats as authoritative do not "reflec[t] any general agreement[,]" [t] hey reflect the now-common tactic—which the Court once again rewards—of pursuing through floor-speech ipse dixit what could not be achieved through the constitutionally prescribed method of putting language into a bill that a majority of both Houses vote for and the President signs.

—(Emphases in original)

DOCUMENT 99

Full Official Title: Religious Land Use and Institutionalized Persons Act
Short Title/Acronym/Abbreviation: RLUIPA
Type of Document: This is a bill passed by the U.S. Congress and signed into law by the president.
Subject: Religious freedom, property rights
Official Citation: Public Law 106-274; 42 U.S.C. § 2000cc
Date of Document: Not applicable
Date of Adoption: Not applicable
Date of General Entry into Force (EIF): Not applicable
Number of States Parties as of this printing: Not applicable
Date of Signature by the United States: September 22, 2000
Date of Ratification/Accession/Adhesion: Not applicable
Date of Entry into Force as to United States (effective date): January 24, 2002
Legal Status/Character of the Instrument/Document as to the United States: This bill is legally binding.

Comments: Congress passed the Religious Land Use and Institutionalized Persons Act in order to ensure that land use regulations, such as zoning and landmarking laws, not be imposed in such a way that they would place any undue burden on the ability of individuals and religious assemblies or institutions to exercise their religion. The government must demonstrate that any burden imposed on such individuals or groups meets certain criteria established in this act. RLUIPA passed unanimously in both houses of Congress before being sent to the President for signature. President Clinton and Congress both reaffirmed the fundamental importance of religious freedom in adopting this bill.

Caution: The status and applicability of this instrument as to the United States may have changed since the date of this publication. For more information on the impact of this law please see the following website.

Website: http://www.justice.gov/crt/rluipa_report_092210.pdf

Religious Land Use and Institutionalized Persons Act

Public Law 106–274

106th Congress

An Act

To protect religious liberty, and for other purposes.

Be it enacted by the Senate and House of Representatives of the United States of America in Congress assembled,

SECTION 1. SHORT TITLE.

This Act may be cited as the "Religious Land Use and Institutionalized Persons Act of 2000".

SEC. 2. PROTECTION OF LAND USE AS RELIGIOUS EXERCISE.

(a) SUBSTANTIAL BURDENS.—

(1) GENERAL RULE.—No government shall impose or implement a land use regulation in a manner that imposes a substantial burden on the religious exercise of a person, including a religious assembly or institution, unless the government demonstrates that imposition of the burden on that person, assembly, or institution—

(A) is in furtherance of a compelling governmental interest; and

(B) is the least restrictive means of furthering that compelling governmental interest.

(2) SCOPE OF APPLICATION.—This subsection applies in any case in which—

(A) the substantial burden is imposed in a program or activity that receives Federal financial assistance, even if the burden results from a rule of general applicability;

(B) the substantial burden affects, or removal of that substantial burden would affect, commerce with foreign nations, among the several States, or with Indian tribes, even if the burden results from a rule of general applicability; or

(C) the substantial burden is imposed in the implementation of a land use regulation or system of land use regulations, under which a government makes, or has in place formal or informal procedures or practices that permit the government to make, individualized assessments of the proposed uses for the property involved.

(b) DISCRIMINATION AND EXCLUSION.—

(1) EQUAL TERMS.—No government shall impose or implement a land use regulation in a manner that treats a religious assembly or institution on less than equal terms with a nonreligious assembly or institution.

(2) NONDISCRIMINATION.—No government shall impose or implement a land use regulation that discriminates against any assembly or institution on the basis of religion or religious denomination.

(3) EXCLUSIONS AND LIMITS.—No government shall impose or implement a land use regulation that—

(A) totally excludes religious assemblies from a jurisdiction; or

(B) unreasonably limits religious assemblies, institutions, or structures within a jurisdiction.

SEC. 3. PROTECTION OF RELIGIOUS EXERCISE OF INSTITUTIONALIZED PERSONS.

(a) GENERAL RULE.—No government shall impose a substantial burden on the religious exercise of a person residing in or confined to an institution, as defined in section 2 of the Civil Rights of Institutionalized Persons Act (42 U.S.C. 1997), even if the burden results from a rule of general applicability, unless the government demonstrates that imposition of the burden on that person—

(1) is in furtherance of a compelling governmental interest; and

(2) is the least restrictive means of furthering that compelling governmental interest.

(b) SCOPE OF APPLICATION.—This section applies in any case in which—

(1) the substantial burden is imposed in a program or activity that receives Federal financial assistance; or

(2) the substantial burden affects, or removal of that substantial burden would affect, commerce with foreign nations, among the several States, or with Indian tribes.

SEC. 4. JUDICIAL RELIEF.

(a) CAUSE OF ACTION.—A person may assert a violation of this Act as a claim or defense in a judicial proceeding and obtain appropriate relief against a government. Standing to assert a claim or defense under this section shall be governed by the general rules of standing under article III of the Constitution.

(b) BURDEN OF PERSUASION.—If a plaintiff produces prima facie evidence to support a claim alleging a violation of the Free Exercise Clause or a violation of section 2, the government shall bear the burden of persuasion on any element of the claim, except that the plaintiff shall bear the burden of persuasion on whether the law (including a regulation) or government practice that is challenged by the claim substantially burdens the plaintiff's exercise of religion.

(c) FULL FAITH AND CREDIT.—Adjudication of a claim of a violation of section 2 in a non-Federal forum shall not be entitled to full faith and credit in a Federal court unless the claimant had a full and fair adjudication of that claim in the non-Federal forum.

(d) ATTORNEYS' FEES.—Section 722(b) of the Revised Statutes (42 U.S.C. 1988(b)) is amended—

(1) by inserting "the Religious Land Use and Institutionalized Persons Act of 2000," after "Religious Freedom Restoration Act of 1993,"; and

(2) by striking the comma that follows a comma.

(e) PRISONERS.—Nothing in this Act shall be construed to amend or repeal the Prison Litigation Reform Act of 1995 (including provisions of law amended by that Act).

(f) AUTHORITY OF UNITED STATES TO ENFORCE THIS ACT.—The United States may bring an action for injunctive or declaratory relief to enforce compliance with this Act. Nothing in this subsection shall be construed to deny, impair, or otherwise affect any right or authority of the Attorney General, the United States, or any agency, officer, or employee of the United States, acting under any law other than this subsection, to institute or intervene in any proceeding.

(g) LIMITATION.—If the only jurisdictional basis for applying a provision of this Act is a claim that a substantial burden by a government on religious exercise affects, or that removal of that substantial burden would affect, commerce with foreign nations, among the several States, or with Indian tribes, the provision shall not apply if the government demonstrates that all substantial burdens on, or the removal of all substantial burdens from, similar religious exercise throughout the Nation would not lead in the aggregate to a substantial effect on commerce with foreign nations, among the several States, or with Indian tribes.

SEC. 5. RULES OF CONSTRUCTION.

(a) RELIGIOUS BELIEF UNAFFECTED.—Nothing in this Act shall be construed to authorize any government to burden any religious belief.

(b) RELIGIOUS EXERCISE NOT REGULATED.—Nothing in this Act shall create any basis for restricting or burdening religious exercise or for claims against a religious organization including any religiously affiliated school or university, not acting under color of law.

(c) CLAIMS TO FUNDING UNAFFECTED.—Nothing in this Act shall create or preclude a right of any religious organization to receive funding or other assistance from a government, or of any person to receive government funding for a religious activity, but this Act may require a government to incur expenses in its own operations to avoid imposing a substantial burden on religious exercise.

(d) OTHER AUTHORITY TO IMPOSE CONDITIONS ON FUNDING UNAFFECTED.—Nothing in this Act shall—

(1) authorize a government to regulate or affect, directly or indirectly, the activities or policies of a person other than a government as a condition of receiving funding or other assistance; or

(2) restrict any authority that may exist under other law to so regulate or affect, except as provided in this Act.

(e) GOVERNMENTAL DISCRETION IN ALLEVIATING BURDENS ON RELIGIOUS EXERCISE.—A government may avoid the preemptive force of any provision of this Act by changing the policy or practice that results in a substantial burden on religious exercise, by retaining the policy or practice and exempting the substantially burdened religious exercise, by providing exemptions from the policy or practice for applications that substantially burden religious exercise, or by any other means that eliminates the substantial burden.

(f) EFFECT ON OTHER LAW.—With respect to a claim brought under this Act, proof that a substantial burden on a person's religious exercise affects, or removal of that burden would affect, commerce with foreign nations, among the several States, or with Indian tribes, shall not establish any inference or presumption that Congress intends that any religious exercise is, or is not, subject to any law other than this Act.

(g) BROAD CONSTRUCTION.—This Act shall be construed in favor of a broad protection of religious exercise, to the maximum extent permitted by the terms of this Act and the Constitution.

(h) NO PREEMPTION OR REPEAL.—Nothing in this Act shall be construed to preempt State law, or repeal Federal law, that is equally as protective of religious exercise as, or more protective of religious exercise than, this Act.

(i) SEVERABILITY.—If any provision of this Act or of an amendment made by this Act, or any application of such provision to any person or circumstance, is held to be unconstitutional, the remainder of this Act, the amendments made by this Act, and the application of the provision to any other person or circumstance shall not be affected.

SEC. 6. ESTABLISHMENT CLAUSE UNAFFECTED.

Nothing in this Act shall be construed to affect, interpret, or in any way address that portion of the first amendment to the Constitution prohibiting laws respecting an establishment of religion (referred to in this section as the "Establishment Clause"). Granting government funding, benefits, or exemptions, to the extent permissible under the Establishment Clause, shall not constitute a violation of this Act. In this section, the term "granting", used with respect to government funding, benefits, or exemptions, does not include the denial of government funding, benefits, or exemptions.

SEC. 7. AMENDMENTS TO RELIGIOUS FREEDOM RESTORATION ACT.

(a) DEFINITIONS.—Section 5 of the Religious Freedom Restoration Act of 1993 (42 U.S.C. 2000bb–2) is amended—

(1) in paragraph (1), by striking "a State, or a subdivision of a State" and inserting "or of a covered entity";

(2) in paragraph (2), by striking "term" and all that follows through "includes" and inserting "term 'covered entity' means"; and

(3) in paragraph (4), by striking all after "means" and inserting "religious exercise, as defined in section 8 of the Religious Land Use and Institutionalized Persons Act of 2000."

(b) CONFORMING AMENDMENT.—Section 6(a) of the Religious Freedom Restoration Act of 1993 (42 U.S.C. 2000bb–3(a)) is amended by striking "and State".

SEC. 8. DEFINITIONS.

In this Act:

(1) CLAIMANT.—The term "claimant" means a person raising a claim or defense under this Act.

(2) DEMONSTRATES.—The term "demonstrates" means meets the burdens of going forward with the evidence and of persuasion.

(3) FREE EXERCISE CLAUSE.—The term "Free Exercise Clause" means that portion of the first amendment to the Constitution that proscribes laws prohibiting the free exercise of religion.

(4) GOVERNMENT.—The term "government"—

(A) means—

(i) a State, county, municipality, or other governmental entity created under the authority of a State;

(ii) any branch, department, agency, instrumentality, or official of an entity listed in clause (i); and

(iii) any other person acting under color of State law; and

(B) for the purposes of sections 4(b) and 5, includes the United States, a branch, department, agency, instrumentality, or official of the United States, and any other person acting under color of Federal law.

(5) LAND USE REGULATION.—The term "land use regulation" means a zoning or landmarking law, or the application of such a law, that limits or restricts a claimant's use or development of land (including a structure affixed to land), if the claimant has an ownership, leasehold, easement, servitude, or other property interest in the regulated land or a contract or option to acquire such an interest.

(6) PROGRAM OR ACTIVITY.—The term "program or activity" means all of the operations of any entity as described in paragraph (1) or (2) of section 606 of the Civil Rights Act of 1964 (42 U.S.C. 2000d–4a).

(7) RELIGIOUS EXERCISE.—

(A) IN GENERAL.—The term "religious exercise" includes any exercise of religion, whether or not compelled by, or central to, a system of religious belief.

(B) RULE.—The use, building, or conversion of real property for the purpose of religious exercise shall be considered to be religious exercise of the person or entity that uses or intends to use the property for that purpose.

Approved September 22, 2000.

LEGISLATIVE HISTORY—S. 2869:
CONGRESSIONAL RECORD, Vol. 146 (2000):
    July 27, considered and passed Senate and House.
WEEKLY COMPILATION OF PRESIDENTIAL DOCUMENTS, Vol. 36 (2000):
    Sept. 22, Presidential statement.

DOCUMENT 100

Full Official Title: The Matthew Shepherd and James Byrd, Jr. Hate Crimes Prevention Act

Short Title/Acronym/Abbreviation: The Hate Crimes Bill

Type of Document: This is a bill passed by the U.S. Congress and signed into law by the president.

Subject: Hate crimes

Official Citation: Public Law 111-84 at 18 U.S.C. §249

Date of Document: Not applicable

Date of Adoption: Not applicable

Date of General Entry into Force (EIF): Not applicable

Number of States Parties as of this printing: Not applicable

Date of Signature by the United States: October 28, 2009

Date of Ratification/Accession/Adhesion: Not applicable

Date of Entry into Force as to United States (effective date): Not applicable

Legal Status/Character of the Instrument/Document as to the United States: This bill is legally binding.

Comments: The U.S. Congress passed the Hate Crimes Prevention Act as part of the Department of Defense authorization for 2010. The bill establishes gender identity and sexual orientation as protected classes under the U.S. criminal code, thereby expanding the current class of persons provided preferred protection when victims of a hate crime. The bill included an amendment by Senator Sam Brownback (R-KS) to offer some protection for religious organizations but there is concern that this provision doesn't offer any assurances of such protection. The main concern opponents of this bill have is its lack of protection for religious speech, and the possible chilling effect this may have on individuals who engage in self-censorship, in order to avoid potential prosecution on the basis of their words. There is concern of prosecution for words that victims may claim associate the speaker with acts of violence by others even though the words may not have been intended to do so.

Caution: The status and applicability of this instrument as to the United States may have changed since the date of this publication.

MATTHEW SHEPARD AND JAMES BYRD, JR. HATE CRIMES PREVENTION ACT

Sec. 4701. Short title.

Sec. 4702. Findings.

Sec. 4703. Definitions.

Sec. 4704. Support for criminal investigations and prosecutions by State, local, and tribal law enforcement officials.

Sec. 4705. Grant program.

Sec. 4706. Authorization for additional personnel to assist State, local, and tribal law enforcement.

Sec. 4707. Prohibition of certain hate crime acts.

Sec. 4708. Statistics.

Sec. 4709. Severability.

Sec. 4710. Rule of construction.

Sec. 4711. Guidelines for hate-crimes offenses.

Sec. 4712. Attacks on United States servicemen.

Sec. 4713. Report on mandatory minimum sentencing provisions.

SEC. 4701. SHORT TITLE.

This division may be cited as the 'Matthew Shepard and James Byrd, Jr. Hate Crimes Prevention Act'.

SEC. 4702. FINDINGS.

Congress makes the following findings:

(1) The incidence of violence motivated by the actual or perceived race, color, religion, national origin, gender, sexual orientation, gender identity, or disability of the victim poses a serious national problem.

(2) Such violence disrupts the tranquility and safety of communities and is deeply divisive.

(3) State and local authorities are now and will continue to be responsible for prosecuting the overwhelming majority of violent crimes in the United States, including violent crimes motivated by bias. These authorities can carry out their responsibilities more effectively with greater Federal assistance.

(4) Existing Federal law is inadequate to address this problem.

(5) A prominent characteristic of a violent crime motivated by bias is that it devastates not just the actual victim and the family and friends of the victim, but frequently savages the community sharing the traits that caused the victim to be selected.

(6) Such violence substantially affects interstate commerce in many ways, including the following:

(A) The movement of members of targeted groups is impeded, and members of such groups are forced to move across State lines to escape the incidence or risk of such violence.

(B) Members of targeted groups are prevented from purchasing goods and services, obtaining or sustaining employment, or participating in other commercial activity.

(C) Perpetrators cross State lines to commit such violence.

(D) Channels, facilities, and instrumentalities of interstate commerce are used to facilitate the commission of such violence.

(E) Such violence is committed using articles that have traveled in interstate commerce.

(7) For generations, the institutions of slavery and involuntary servitude were defined by the race, color, and ancestry of those held in bondage. Slavery and involuntary servitude were enforced, both prior to and after the adoption of the 13th amendment to the Constitution of the United States, through widespread public and private violence directed at persons because of their race, color, or ancestry, or perceived race, color, or ancestry. Accordingly, eliminating racially motivated violence is an important means of eliminating, to the extent possible, the badges, incidents, and relics of slavery and involuntary servitude.

(8) Both at the time when the 13th, 14th, and 15th amendments to the Constitution of the United States were adopted, and continuing to date, members of certain religious and national origin groups were and are perceived to be distinct 'races'. Thus, in order to eliminate, to the extent possible, the badges, incidents, and relics of slavery, it is necessary to prohibit assaults on the basis of real or perceived religions or national origins, at least to the extent such religions or national origins were regarded as races at the time of the adoption of the 13th, 14th, and 15th amendments to the Constitution of the United States.

(9) Federal jurisdiction over certain violent crimes motivated by bias enables Federal, State, and local authorities to work together as partners in the investigation and prosecution of such crimes.

(10) The problem of crimes motivated by bias is sufficiently serious, widespread, and interstate in nature as to warrant Federal assistance to States, local jurisdictions, and Indian tribes.

SEC. 4703. DEFINITIONS.

(a) Amendment—Section 280003(a) of the Violent Crime Control and Law Enforcement Act of 1994 (Public Law 103-322; 108 Stat. 2096) is amended by inserting 'gender identity,' after 'gender,'.

(b) This Division—In this division—

(1) the term 'crime of violence' has the meaning given that term in section 16 of title 18, United States Code;

(2) the term 'hate crime' has the meaning given that term in section 280003(a) of the Violent Crime Control and Law Enforcement Act of 1994 (Public Law 103-322; 108 Stat. 2096), as amended by this Act;

(3) the term 'local' means a county, city, town, township, parish, village, or other general purpose political subdivision of a State; and

(4) the term 'State' includes the District of Columbia, Puerto Rico, and any other territory or possession of the United States.

SEC. 4704. SUPPORT FOR CRIMINAL INVESTIGATIONS AND PROSECUTIONS BY STATE, LOCAL, AND TRIBAL LAW ENFORCEMENT OFFICIALS.

(a) Assistance Other Than Financial Assistance-

(1) IN GENERAL—At the request of a State, local, or tribal law enforcement agency, the Attorney General may provide technical, forensic, prosecutorial, or any other form of assistance in the criminal investigation or prosecution of any crime that—

(A) constitutes a crime of violence;

(B) constitutes a felony under the State, local, or tribal laws; and

(C) is motivated by prejudice based on the actual or perceived race, color, religion, national origin, gender, sexual orientation, gender identity, or disability of the victim, or is a violation of the State, local, or tribal hate crime laws.

(2) PRIORITY—In providing assistance under paragraph (1), the Attorney General shall give priority to crimes committed by offenders who have committed crimes in more than one State and to rural jurisdictions that have difficulty covering the extraordinary expenses relating to the investigation or prosecution of the crime.

(b) Grants—

(1) IN GENERAL—The Attorney General may award grants to State, local, and tribal law enforcement agencies for extraordinary expenses associated with the investigation and prosecution of hate crimes.

(2) OFFICE OF JUSTICE PROGRAMS- In implementing the grant program under this subsection, the Office of Justice Programs shall work closely with grantees to ensure that the concerns and needs of all affected parties, including community groups and schools, colleges, and universities, are addressed through the local infrastructure developed under the grants.

(3) APPLICATION—

(A) IN GENERAL—Each State, local, and tribal law enforcement agency that desires a grant under this subsection shall submit an application to the Attorney General at such time, in such manner, and accompanied by or containing such information as the Attorney General shall reasonably require.

(B) DATE FOR SUBMISSION—Applications submitted pursuant to subparagraph (A) shall be submitted during the 60-day period beginning on a date that the Attorney General shall prescribe.

(C) REQUIREMENTS—A State, local, and tribal law enforcement agency applying for a grant under this subsection shall—

(i) describe the extraordinary purposes for which the grant is needed;

(ii) certify that the State, local government, or Indian tribe lacks the resources necessary to investigate or prosecute the hate crime;

(iii) demonstrate that, in developing a plan to implement the grant, the State, local, and tribal law enforcement agency has consulted and coordinated with nonprofit, nongovernmental victim services programs that have experience in providing services to victims of hate crimes; and

(iv) certify that any Federal funds received under this subsection will be used to supplement, not supplant, non-Federal funds that would otherwise be available for activities funded under this subsection.

(4) DEADLINE—An application for a grant under this subsection shall be approved or denied by the Attorney General not later than 180 business days after the date on which the Attorney General receives the application.

(5) GRANT AMOUNT—A grant under this subsection shall not exceed $100,000 for any single jurisdiction in any 1-year period.

(6) REPORT—Not later than December 31, 2011, the Attorney General shall submit to Congress a report describing the applications submitted for grants under this subsection, the award of such grants, and the purposes for which the grant amounts were expended.

(7) AUTHORIZATION OF APPROPRIATIONS—There is authorized to be appropriated to carry out this subsection $5,000,000 for each of fiscal years 2010, 2011, and 2012.

SEC. 4705. GRANT PROGRAM.

(a) Authority to Award Grants—The Office of Justice Programs of the Department of Justice may award grants, in accordance with such regulations as the Attorney General may prescribe, to State, local, or tribal programs designed to combat hate crimes committed by juveniles, including programs to train local law enforcement officers in identifying, investigating, prosecuting, and preventing hate crimes.

(b) Authorization of Appropriations—There are authorized to be appropriated such sums as may be necessary to carry out this section.

SEC. 4706. AUTHORIZATION FOR ADDITIONAL PERSONNEL TO ASSIST STATE, LOCAL, AND TRIBAL LAW ENFORCEMENT.

There are authorized to be appropriated to the Department of Justice, including the Community Relations Service, for fiscal years 2010, 2011, and 2012 such sums as are necessary to increase the number of personnel to prevent and respond to alleged violations of section 249 of title 18, United States Code, as added by section 4707 of this division.

SEC. 4707. PROHIBITION OF CERTAIN HATE CRIME ACTS.

(a) In General—Chapter 13 of title 18, United States Code, is amended by adding at the end the following:

-'Sec. 249. Hate crime acts

'(a) In General—

'(1) OFFENSES INVOLVING ACTUAL OR PERCEIVED RACE, COLOR, RELIGION, OR NATIONAL ORIGIN—Whoever, whether or not acting under color of law, willfully causes bodily injury to any person or, through the use of fire, a firearm, a dangerous weapon, or an explosive or incendiary device, attempts to cause bodily injury to any person, because of the actual or perceived race, color, religion, or national origin of any person—

'(A) shall be imprisoned not more than 10 years, fined in accordance with this title, or both; and

'(B) shall be imprisoned for any term of years or for life, fined in accordance with this title, or both, if—

'(i) death results from the offense; or

'(ii) the offense includes kidnapping or an attempt to kidnap, aggravated sexual abuse or an attempt to commit aggravated sexual abuse, or an attempt to kill.

'(2) OFFENSES INVOLVING ACTUAL OR PERCEIVED RELIGION, NATIONAL ORIGIN, GENDER, SEXUAL ORIENTATION, GENDER IDENTITY, OR DISABILITY—

'(A) IN GENERAL—Whoever, whether or not acting under color of law, in any circumstance described in subparagraph (B) or paragraph (3), willfully causes bodily injury to any person or, through the use of fire, a firearm, a dangerous weapon, or an explosive or incendiary device, attempts to cause bodily injury to any person, because of the actual or perceived religion, national origin, gender, sexual orientation, gender identity, or disability of any person—

'(i) shall be imprisoned not more than 10 years, fined in accordance with this title, or both; and

'(ii) shall be imprisoned for any term of years or for life, fined in accordance with this title, or both, if—

'(I) death results from the offense; or

'(II) the offense includes kidnapping or an attempt to kidnap, aggravated sexual abuse or an attempt to commit aggravated sexual abuse, or an attempt to kill.

'(B) CIRCUMSTANCES DESCRIBED—For purposes of subparagraph (A), the circumstances described in this subparagraph are that—

'(i) the conduct described in subparagraph (A) occurs during the course of, or as the result of, the travel of the defendant or the victim—

'(I) across a State line or national border; or

'(II) using a channel, facility, or instrumentality of interstate or foreign commerce;

'(ii) the defendant uses a channel, facility, or instrumentality of interstate or foreign commerce in connection with the conduct described in subparagraph (A);

'(iii) in connection with the conduct described in subparagraph (A), the defendant employs a firearm, dangerous weapon, explosive or incendiary device, or other weapon that has traveled in interstate or foreign commerce; or

'(iv) the conduct described in subparagraph (A)—

'(I) interferes with commercial or other economic activity in which the victim is engaged at the time of the conduct; or

'(II) otherwise affects interstate or foreign commerce.

'(3) OFFENSES OCCURRING IN THE SPECIAL MARITIME OR TERRITORIAL JURISDICTION OF THE UNITED STATES—Whoever, within the special maritime or territorial jurisdiction of the United States, engages in conduct described in paragraph (1) or in paragraph (2)(A) (without regard to whether that conduct occurred in a circumstance described in paragraph (2)(B)) shall be subject to the same penalties as prescribed in those paragraphs.

'(b) Certification Requirement—

'(1) IN GENERAL—No prosecution of any offense described in this subsection may be undertaken by the United States, except under the certification in writing of the Attorney General, or a designee, that—

'(A) the State does not have jurisdiction;

'(B) the State has requested that the Federal Government assume jurisdiction;

'(C) the verdict or sentence obtained pursuant to State charges left demonstratively unvindicated the Federal interest in eradicating bias-motivated violence; or

'(D) a prosecution by the United States is in the public interest and necessary to secure substantial justice.

'(2) RULE OF CONSTRUCTION—Nothing in this subsection shall be construed to limit the authority of Federal officers, or a Federal grand jury, to investigate possible violations of this section.

'(c) Definitions— In this section—

'(1) the term 'bodily injury' has the meaning given such term in section 1365(h)(4) of this title, but does not include solely emotional or psychological harm to the victim;

'(2) the term 'explosive or incendiary device' has the meaning given such term in section 232 of this title;

'(3) the term 'firearm' has the meaning given such term in section 921(a) of this title;

'(4) the term 'gender identity' means actual or perceived gender-related characteristics; and

'(5) the term 'State' includes the District of Columbia, Puerto Rico, and any other territory or possession of the United States.

'(d) Statute of Limitations—

'(1) OFFENSES NOT RESULTING IN DEATH— Except as provided in paragraph (2), no person shall be prosecuted, tried, or punished for any offense under this section unless the indictment for such offense is found, or the information for such offense is instituted, not later than 7 years after the date on which the offense was committed.

'(2) DEATH RESULTING OFFENSES—An indictment or information alleging that an offense under this section resulted in death may be found or instituted at any time without limitation.'

(b) Technical and Conforming Amendment- The table of sections for chapter 13 of title 18, United States Code, is amended by adding at the end the following:

'249. Hate crime acts.'.

SEC. 4708. STATISTICS.

(a) In General- Subsection (b)(1) of the first section of the Hate Crime Statistics Act (28 U.S.C. 534 note) is amended by inserting 'gender and gender identity,' after 'race,'.

(b) Data- Subsection (b)(5) of the first section of the Hate Crime Statistics Act (28 U.S.C. 534 note) is amended by inserting ', including data about crimes committed by, and crimes directed against, juveniles' after 'data acquired under this section'.

SEC. 4709. SEVERABILITY.

If any provision of this division, an amendment made by this division, or the application of such provision or amendment to any person or circumstance is held to be unconstitutional, the remainder of this division, the amendments made by this division, and the application of the provisions of such to any person or circumstance shall not be affected thereby.

SEC. 4710. RULE OF CONSTRUCTION.

For purposes of construing this division and the amendments made by this division the following shall apply:

(1) IN GENERAL—Nothing in this division shall be construed to allow a court, in any criminal trial for an offense described under this division or an amendment made by this division, in the absence of a stipulation by the parties, to admit evidence of speech, beliefs, association, group membership, or expressive conduct unless that evidence is relevant and admissible under the Federal Rules of Evidence. Nothing in this division is intended to affect the existing rules of evidence.

(2) VIOLENT ACTS—This division applies to violent acts motivated by actual or perceived race, color, religion, national origin, gender, sexual orientation, gender identity, or disability of a victim.

(3) CONSTRUCTION AND APPLICATION—Nothing in this division, or an amendment made by this division, shall be construed or applied in a manner that infringes any rights under the first amendment to the Constitution of the United States. Nor shall anything in this division, or an amendment made by this division, be construed or applied in a manner that substantially burdens a person's exercise of religion (regardless of whether compelled by, or central to, a system of religious belief), speech, expression, or association, unless the Government demonstrates that application of the burden to the person is in furtherance of a compelling governmental interest and is the least restrictive means of furthering that compelling governmental interest, if such exercise of religion, speech, expression, or association was not intended to—

(A) plan or prepare for an act of physical violence; or

(B) incite an imminent act of physical violence against another.

(4) FREE EXPRESSION—Nothing in this division shall be construed to allow prosecution based solely upon an individual's expression of racial, religious, political, or other beliefs or solely upon an individual's membership in a group advocating or espousing such beliefs.

(5) FIRST AMENDMENT—Nothing in this division, or an amendment made by this division, shall be construed to diminish any rights under the first amendment to the Constitution of the United States.

(6) CONSTITUTIONAL PROTECTIONS—Nothing in this division shall be construed to prohibit any constitutionally protected speech, expressive conduct or activities (regardless of whether compelled by, or central to, a system of religious belief), including the exercise of religion protected by the first amendment to the Constitution of the United States and peaceful picketing or demonstration. The Constitution of the United States does not protect speech, conduct or activities consisting of planning for, conspiring to commit, or committing an act of violence.

SEC. 4711. GUIDELINES FOR HATE-CRIMES OFFENSES.

Section 249(a) of title 18, United States Code, as added by section 4707 of this Act, is amended by adding at the end the following:

'(4) GUIDELINES—All prosecutions conducted by the United States under this section shall be undertaken pursuant to guidelines issued by the Attorney General, or the designee of the Attorney General, to be included in the United States Attorneys' Manual that shall establish neutral and objective criteria for determining whether a crime was committed because of the actual or perceived status of any person.'.

SEC. 4712. ATTACKS ON UNITED STATES SERVICEMEN.

(a) In General—Chapter 67 of title 18, United States Code, is amended by adding at the end the following:

'Sec. 1389. Prohibition on attacks on United States servicemen on account of service

'(a) In General—Whoever knowingly assaults or batters a United States serviceman or an immediate family member of a United States serviceman, or who knowingly destroys or injures the property of such serviceman or immediate family member, on account of the military service of that serviceman or status of that individual as a United States serviceman, or who attempts or conspires to do so, shall—

'(1) in the case of a simple assault, or destruction or injury to property in which the damage or attempted damage to such property is not more than $500, be fined under this title in an amount not less than $500 nor more than $10,000 and imprisoned not more than 2 years;

'(2) in the case of destruction or injury to property in which the damage or attempted damage to such property is more than $500, be fined under this title in an amount not less than $1000 nor more than $100,000 and imprisoned not more than 5 years; and

'(3) in the case of a battery, or an assault resulting in bodily injury, be fined under this title in an amount not less than $2500 and imprisoned not less than 6 months nor more than 10 years.

'(b) Exception—This section shall not apply to conduct by a person who is subject to the Uniform Code of Military Justice.

'(c) Definitions—In this section—

'(1) the term 'Armed Forces' has the meaning given that term in section 1388;

'(2) the term 'immediate family member' has the meaning given that term in section 115; and

'(3) the term 'United States serviceman'—

'(A) means a member of the Armed Forces; and

'(B) includes a former member of the Armed Forces during the 5-year period beginning on the date of the discharge from the Armed Forces of that member of the Armed Forces.'

(b) Technical and Conforming Amendment—The table of sections for chapter 67 of title 18, United States Code, is amended by adding at the end the following:

'1389. Prohibition on attacks on United States servicemen on account of service.'

SEC. 4713. REPORT ON MANDATORY MINIMUM SENTENCING PROVISIONS.

(a) Report—Not later than 1 year after the date of enactment of this Act, the United States Sentencing Commission shall submit to the Committee on the Judiciary of the Senate and the Committee on the Judiciary of the House of Representatives a report on mandatory minimum sentencing provisions under Federal law.

(b) Contents of Report—The report submitted under subsection (a) shall include—

(1) a compilation of all mandatory minimum sentencing provisions under Federal law;

(2) an assessment of the effect of mandatory minimum sentencing provisions under Federal law on the goal of eliminating unwarranted sentencing disparity and other goals of sentencing;

(3) an assessment of the impact of mandatory minimum sentencing provisions on the Federal prison population;

(4) an assessment of the compatibility of mandatory minimum sentencing provisions under Federal law and the sentencing guidelines system established under the Sentencing Reform Act of 1984 (Public Law

98-473; 98 Stat. 1987) and the sentencing guidelines system in place after Booker v. United States, 543 U.S. 220 (2005);

(5) a description of the interaction between mandatory minimum sentencing provisions under Federal law and plea agreements;

(6) a detailed empirical research study of the effect of mandatory minimum penalties under Federal law;

(7) a discussion of mechanisms other than mandatory minimum sentencing laws by which Congress can take action with respect to sentencing policy; and

(8) any other information that the Commission determines would contribute to a thorough assessment of mandatory minimum sentencing provisions under Federal law.

Speaker of the House of Representatives.

Vice President of the United States and

President of the Senate.

DOCUMENT 101

Full Official Title: Global Anti-Semitism Act of 2004

Short Title/Acronym/Abbreviation: Nothing official

Type of Document: This is a bill passed by the U.S. Congress and signed into law by the president.

Subject: Monitoring and preventing anti-Semitism

Official Citation: Public Law 108-332

Date of Document: Not applicable

Date of Adoption: Not applicable

Date of General Entry into Force (EIF): Not applicable

Number of States Parties as of this printing: Not applicable

Date of Signature by the United States: October 16, 2004

Date of Ratification/Accession/Adhesion: Not applicable

Date of Entry into Force as to United States (effective date): Not applicable

Legal Status/Character of the Instrument/Document as to the United States: This bill is legally binding.

Comments: The U.S. Congress passed the Global Anti-Semitism Review Act of 2004 to require a report on acts of anti-Semitism around the world and continue to combat such acts. The bill recognized an increase in acts of anti-Semitism around the world which prompted them to call for a specific report and action to address these concerns; however the State Department was initially not supportive of this initiative as such acts were already included to a lesser extent in other reports on human rights and religious freedom. The report also called for an Office at the State Department to combat and monitor acts of anti-Semitism to be headed by a special envoy. President George W. Bush signed this bill into law after it passed both houses of Congress.

Caution: The status and applicability of this instrument as to the United States may have changed since the date of this publication.

GLOBAL ANTI-SEMITISM ACT OF 2004

Public Law 108–332

108th Congress

An Act

To require a report on acts of anti-Semitism around the world.

Be it enacted by the Senate and House of Representatives of the United States of America in Congress assembled,

SECTION 1. SHORT TITLE.

This Act may be cited as the "Global Anti-Semitism Review Act of 2004".

SEC. 2. FINDINGS.

Congress makes the following findings:

(1) Acts of anti-Semitism in countries throughout the world, including some of the world's strongest democracies, have increased significantly in frequency and scope over the last several years.

(2) During the last 3 months of 2003 and the first 3 months of 2004, there were numerous instances of anti-Semitic violence around the world, including the following incidents:

(A) In Putrajaya, Malaysia, on October 16, 2003, former Prime Minister Mahatir Mohammad told the 57 national leaders assembled for the Organization of the Islamic Conference that Jews "rule the world by proxy," and called for a "final victory" by the world's 1.3 billion Muslims, who, he said, "cannot be defeated by a few million Jews."

(B) In Istanbul, Turkey, on November 15, 2003, simultaneous car bombs exploded outside two synagogues filled with worshippers, killing 24 people and wounding more than 250 people.

(C) In Australia on January 5, 2004, poison was used to ignite, and burn anti-Semitic slogans into, the lawns of the Parliament House in the state of Tasmania.

(D) In St. Petersburg, Russia, on February 15, 2004, vandals desecrated approximately 50 gravestones in a Jewish cemetery, painting the stones with swastikas and anti-Semitic graffiti.

(E) In Toronto, Canada, over the weekend of March 19 through March 21, 2004, vandals attacked a Jewish school, a Jewish cemetery, and area synagogues, painting swastikas and anti-Semitic slogans on the walls of a synagogue and on residential property in a nearby, predominantly Jewish, neighborhood.

(F) In Toulon, France, on March 23, 2004, a Jewish synagogue and community center were set on fire.

(3) Anti-Semitism in old and new forms is also increasingly emanating from the Arab and Muslim world on a sustained basis, including through books published by government-owned publishing houses in Egypt and other Arab countries.

(4) In November 2002, state-run television in Egypt broadcast the anti-Semitic series entitled "Horseman Without a Horse", which is based upon the fictitious conspiracy theory known as the Protocols of the Elders of Zion. The Protocols have been used throughout the last century by despots such as Adolf Hitler to justify violence against Jews.

(5) In November 2003, Arab television featured an anti-Semitic series, entitled "Ash-Shatat" (or "The Diaspora"), which depicts Jewish people hatching a plot for Jewish control of the world.

(6) The sharp rise in anti-Semitic violence has caused international organizations such as the Organization for Security and Cooperation in Europe (OSCE) to elevate, and bring renewed focus to, the issue, including the convening by the OSCE in June 2003 of a conference in Vienna dedicated solely to the issue of anti-Semitism.

(7) The OSCE convened a conference again on April 28–29, 2004, in Berlin, to address the problem of anti-Semitism with the United States delegation led by former Mayor of New York City, Ed Koch.

(8) The United States Government has strongly supported efforts to address anti-Semitism through bilateral relationships and interaction with international organizations such as the OSCE, the European Union, and the United Nations.

(9) Congress has consistently supported efforts to address the rise in anti-Semitic violence. During the 107th Congress, both the Senate and the House of Representatives passed resolutions expressing strong concern with the sharp escalation of anti-Semitic violence in Europe and calling on the Department of State to thoroughly document the phenomenon.

(10) Anti-Semitism has at times taken the form of vilification of Zionism, the Jewish national movement, and incitement against Israel.

SEC. 3. SENSE OF CONGRESS.

It is the sense of Congress that—

(1) the United States Government should continue to strongly support efforts to combat anti-Semitism worldwide through bilateral relationships and interaction with international organizations such as the OSCE, the European Union, and the United Nations; and

(2) the Department of State should thoroughly document acts of anti-Semitism that occur around the world.

SEC. 4. REPORTS.

Not later than November 15, 2004, the Secretary of State shall submit to the Committee on Foreign Relations of the Senate and the Committee on International Relations of the House of Representatives a one-time report on acts of anti-Semitism around the world, including a description of—

(1) acts of physical violence against, or harassment of, Jewish people, and acts of violence against, or vandalism of, Jewish community institutions, such as schools, synagogues, or cemeteries, that occurred in each country;

(2) the responses of the governments of those countries to such actions;

(3) the actions taken by such governments to enact and enforce laws relating to the protection of the right to religious freedom of Jewish people;

(4) the efforts by such governments to promote anti-bias and tolerance education; and

(5) instances of propaganda in government and nongovernment media that attempt to justify or promote racial hatred or incite acts of violence against Jewish people.

SEC. 5. AUTHORIZATION FOR ESTABLISHMENT OF OFFICE TO MONITOR AND COMBAT ANTI-SEMITISM.

The State Department Basic Authorities Act of 1956 is amended by adding after section 58 (22 U.S.C. 2730) the following new section:

"SEC. 59. MONITORING AND COMBATING ANTI-SEMITISM.

(a) OFFICE TO MONITOR AND COMBAT ANTI-SEMITISM.—

(1) ESTABLISHMENT OF OFFICE.—The Secretary shall establish within the Department of State an Office to Monitor and Combat anti-Semitism (in this section referred to as the 'Office').

(2) HEAD OF OFFICE.—

(A) SPECIAL ENVOY FOR MONITORING AND COMBATING ANTI-SEMITISM.—The head of the Office shall be the Special Envoy for Monitoring and Combating anti-Semitism (in this section referred to as the 'Special Envoy').

(B) APPOINTMENT OF HEAD OF OFFICE.—The Secretary shall appoint the Special Envoy. If the Secretary determines that such is appropriate, the Secretary may appoint the Special Envoy from among officers and employees of the Department. The Secretary may allow such officer or employee to retain the position (and the responsibilities associated with such position) held by such officer or employee prior to the appointment of such officer or employee to the position of Special Envoy under this paragraph.

(b) PURPOSE OF OFFICE.—Upon establishment, the Office shall assume the primary responsibility for—

(1) monitoring and combating acts of anti-Semitism and anti-Semitic incitement that occur in foreign countries;

(2) coordinating and assisting in the preparation of that portion of the report required by sections 116(d)(7) and 502B(b) of the Foreign Assistance Act of 1961 (22 U.S.C. 2151n(d)(7) and 2304(b)) relating to an assessment and description of the nature and extent of acts of anti-Semitism and anti-Semitic incitement for inclusion in the annual Country Reports on Human Rights Practices; and

(3) coordinating and assisting in the preparation of that portion of the report required by section 102(b)(1)(A)(iv) of the International Religious Freedom Act of 1998 (22 U.S.C. 6412(b)(1)(A)(iv)) relating to an assessment and description of the nature and extent of acts of anti-Semitism and anti-Semitic incitement for inclusion in the Annual Report on International Religious Freedom.

(c) CONSULTATIONS.—The Special Envoy shall consult with domestic and international nongovernmental organizations and multilateral organizations and institutions, as the Special Envoy considers appropriate to fulfill the purposes of this section."

SEC. 6. INCLUSION IN DEPARTMENT OF STATE ANNUAL REPORTS OF INFORMATION CONCERNING ACTS OF ANTI-SEMITISM IN FOREIGN COUNTRIES.

(a) INCLUSION IN COUNTRY REPORTS ON HUMAN RIGHTS PRACTICES.—The Foreign Assistance Act of 1961 (22 U.S.C. 2151 et seq.) is amended—

(1) in section 116(d) (22 U.S.C. 2151n(d))—

(A) by redesignating paragraphs (8), (9), and (10), as paragraphs (9), (10), and (11), respectively; and

(B) by inserting after paragraph (7) the following new paragraph:

(8) wherever applicable, a description of the nature and extent of acts of anti-Semitism and anti-Semitic incitement that occur during the preceding year, including descriptions of—

(A) acts of physical violence against, or harassment of Jewish people, and acts of violence against, or vandalism of Jewish community institutions, including schools, synagogues, and cemeteries;

(B) instances of propaganda in government and nongovernment media that attempt to justify or promote racial hatred or incite acts of violence against Jewish people;

(C) the actions, if any, taken by the government of the country to respond to such violence and attacks or to eliminate such propaganda or incitement;

(D) the actions taken by such government to enact and enforce laws relating to the protection of the right to religious freedom of Jewish people; and

(E) the efforts of such government to promote anti-bias and tolerance education;"; and

(2) after the fourth sentence of section 502B(b) (22 U.S.C. 2304(b)), by inserting the following new sentence: "Wherever applicable, a description of the nature and extent of acts of anti-Semitism and anti-Semitic incitement that occur, including the descriptions of such acts required under section 116(d)(8)."

(b) INCLUSION IN ANNUAL REPORT ON INTERNATIONAL RELIGIOUS FREEDOM.—Section 102(b)(1)(A) of the International Religious Freedom Act of 1998 (22 U.S.C. 6412(b)(1)(A)) is amended—

(1) in clause (ii), by striking "and" at the end;

(2) in clause (iii), by striking the period at the end and inserting "; and"; and

(3) by adding after clause (iii) the following new clause:

(iv) wherever applicable, an assessment and description of the nature and extent of acts of anti-Semitism and anti-Semitic incitement that occur in that country during the preceding year, including—

(I) acts of physical violence against, or harassment of, Jewish people, acts of violence against, or vandalism of, Jewish community institutions, and instances of propaganda in government and nongovernment media that incite such acts; and

(II) the actions taken by the government of that country to respond to such violence and attacks or to eliminate such propaganda or incitement, to enact and enforce laws relating to the protection of the right to religious freedom of Jewish people, and to promote anti-bias and tolerance education."

(c) EFFECTIVE DATE OF INCLUSIONS.—The amendments made by subsections (a) and (b) shall apply beginning with the first report under sections 116(d) and 502B(b) of the Foreign Assistance Act of 1961 (22 U.S.C. 2151n(d) and 2304(b)) and section 102(b) of the International Religious Freedom Act of 1998 (22 U.S.C. 6312(b)) submitted more than 180 days after the date of the enactment of this Act.

Approved October 16, 2004.

LEGISLATIVE HISTORY—S. 2292:
CONGRESSIONAL RECORD, Vol. 150 (2004):
    May 7, considered and passed Senate.
    Oct. 8, considered and passed House, amended.
    Oct. 10, Senate concurred in House amendments.

DOCUMENT 102

Full Official Title: An Act to Authorize Appropriations for Fiscal Years 2006 and 2007 for the Trafficking Victim's Protection Reauthorization Act of 2005

    Short Title/Acronym/Abbreviation: Trafficking Victim's Protection Reauthorization Act of 2005
    Type of Document: This is a bill passed by the U.S. Congress and signed into law by the president.
    Subject: Trafficking
    Official Citation: Public Law 106-306
    Date of Document: Not applicable
    Date of Adoption: Not applicable
    Date of General Entry into Force (EIF): Not applicable
    Number of States Parties as of this printing: Not applicable
    Date of Signature by the United States: October 16, 2004
    Date of Ratification/Accession/Adhesion: Not applicable
    Date of Entry into Force as to United States (effective date): Not applicable
    Legal Status/Character of the Instrument/Document as to the United States: This bill is legally binding.
    Comments: The U.S. Congress passed the Protecting Victims of Trafficking Act of 2000 in order to "combat trafficking in persons, especially into the sex trade, slavery, and involuntary servitude, to reauthorize certain Federal programs to prevent violence against women, and for other purposes." Congressman Christopher Smith (R-NJ), a long-time supporter of international human rights drafted and introduced this bill to require a report on trafficking in persons throughout the world in order for the U.S. government to better combat such acts. The reporting requirement also requires states to be designated to various tiers based on the level of protection for victims of trafficking in the country which is then used to determine U.S. policy with that country to help the country improve in this area. The bill recognized trafficking as a form of modern-day slavery. The bill established several mechanisms to address trafficking,

including an Inter-Agency Task Force and an Office in the State Department to monitor and combat trafficking in persons.

Caution: The status and applicability of this instrument as to the United States may have changed since the date of this publication.

TRAFFICKING VICTIM'S PROTECTION REAUTHORIZATION ACT OF 2005

One Hundred Ninth Congress of the United States of America

AT THE FIRST SESSION

Begun and held at the City of Washington on Tuesday, the fourth day of January, two thousand and five

An Act

To authorize appropriations for fiscal years 2006 and 2007 for the Trafficking Victims Protection Act of 2000, and for other purposes.

Be it enacted by the Senate and House of Representatives of the United States of America in Congress assembled,

SECTION 1. SHORT TITLE; TABLE OF CONTENTS.

(a) SHORT TITLE.—This Act may be cited as the "Trafficking Victims Protection Reauthorization Act of 2005".

(b) TABLE OF CONTENTS.—The table of contents for this Act was omitted.

SEC. 2. FINDINGS.

Congress finds the following:

(1) The United States has demonstrated international leadership in combating human trafficking and slavery through the enactment of the Trafficking Victims Protection Act of 2000 (division A of Public Law 106–386; 22 U.S.C. 7101 et seq.) and the Trafficking Victims Protection Reauthorization Act of 2003 (Public Law 108–193).

(2) The United States Government currently estimates that 600,000 to 800,000 individuals are trafficked across international borders each year and exploited through forced labor and commercial sex exploitation. An estimated 80 percent of such individuals are women and girls.

(3) Since the enactment of the Trafficking Victims Protection Act of 2000, United States efforts to combat trafficking in persons have focused primarily on the international trafficking in persons, including the trafficking of foreign citizens into the United States.

(4) Trafficking in persons also occurs within the borders of a country, including the United States.

(5) No known studies exist that quantify the problem of trafficking in children for the purpose of commercial sexual exploitation in the United States. According to a report issued by researchers at the University of Pennsylvania in 2001, as many as 300,000 children in the United States are at risk for commercial sexual exploitation, including trafficking, at any given time.

(6) Runaway and homeless children in the United States are highly susceptible to being domestically trafficked for commercial sexual exploitation. According to the National Runaway Switchboard, every day in the United States, between 1,300,000 and 2,800,000 runaway and homeless youth live on the streets. One out of every seven children will run away from home before the age of 18.

(7) Following armed conflicts and during humanitarian emergencies, indigenous populations face increased security challenges and vulnerabilities which result in myriad forms of violence, including trafficking for sexual and labor exploitation. Foreign policy and foreign aid professionals increasingly recognize the increased activity of human traffickers in post-conflict settings and during humanitarian emergencies.

(8) There is a need to protect populations in post-conflict settings and humanitarian emergencies from being trafficked for sexual or labor exploitation. The efforts of aid agencies to address the protection needs of, among others, internally displaced persons and refugees are useful in this regard. Nonetheless, there is a need for further integrated programs and strategies at the United States Agency for International Development, the Department of State, and the Department of Defense to combat human trafficking, including through protection and prevention methodologies, in post-conflict environments and during humanitarian emergencies.

(9) International and human rights organizations have documented a correlation between international deployments of military and civilian peacekeepers and aid workers and a resulting increase in the number of women and girls trafficked into prostitution in post-conflict regions.

(10) The involvement of employees and contractors of the United States Government and members of the Armed Forces in trafficking in persons, facilitating the trafficking in persons, or exploiting the victims of trafficking in persons is inconsistent with United States laws and policies and undermines the credibility and mission of United States Government programs in post-conflict regions.

(11) Further measures are needed to ensure that United States Government personnel and contractors are held accountable for involvement with acts of trafficking in persons, including by expanding United States criminal jurisdiction to all United States Government contractors abroad.

TITLE I—COMBATTING INTERNATIONAL TRAFFICKING IN PERSONS

SEC. 101. PREVENTION OF TRAFFICKING IN CONJUNCTION WITH POST-CONFLICT AND HUMANITARIAN EMERGENCY ASSISTANCE.

(a) AMENDMENT.—Section 106 of the Trafficking Victims Protection Act of 2000 (22 U.S.C. 7104) is amended by adding at the end the following new subsection:

"(h) PREVENTION OF TRAFFICKING IN CONJUNCTION WITH POST-CONFLICT AND HUMANITARIAN EMERGENCY ASSISTANCE.—The United States Agency for International Development, the Department of State, and the Department of Defense shall incorporate anti-trafficking and protection measures for vulnerable populations, particularly women and children, into their post-conflict and humanitarian emergency assistance and program activities."

(b) STUDY AND REPORT.—

(1) STUDY.—

(A) IN GENERAL.—The Secretary of State and the Administrator of the United States Agency for International Development, in consultation with the Secretary of Defense, shall conduct a study regarding the threat and practice of trafficking in persons generated by postconflict and humanitarian emergencies in foreign countries.

(B) FACTORS.—In carrying out the study, the Secretary of State and the Administrator of the United States Agency for International Development shall examine—

(i) the vulnerabilities to human trafficking of commonly affected populations, particularly women and children, generated by post-conflict and humanitarian emergencies;

(ii) the various forms of trafficking in persons, both internal and trans-border, including both sexual and labor exploitation;

(iii) a collection of best practices implemented to date to combat human trafficking in such areas; and

(iv) proposed recommendations to better combat trafficking in persons in conjunction with post-conflict reconstruction and humanitarian emergencies assistance.

(2) REPORT.—Not later than 180 days after the date of the enactment of this Act, the Secretary of State and the Administrator of the United States Agency for International Development, with the concurrence of the Secretary of Defense, shall transmit to the Committee on International Relations and the Committee on Armed Services of the House of Representatives and the Committee on Foreign Relations and the Committee on Armed Services of the Senate a report that contains the results of the study conducted pursuant to paragraph (1).

SEC. 102. PROTECTION OF VICTIMS OF TRAFFICKING IN PERSONS.

(a) ACCESS TO INFORMATION.—Section 107(c)(2) of the Trafficking Victims Protection Act of 2000 (22 U.S.C. 7105(c)(2)) is amended by adding at the end the following new sentence: "To the extent practicable, victims of severe forms of trafficking shall have access to information about federally funded or administered anti-trafficking programs that provide services to victims of severe forms of trafficking."

(b) ESTABLISHMENT OF PILOT PROGRAM FOR RESIDENTIAL REHABILITATIVE FACILITIES FOR VICTIMS OF TRAFFICKING.—

(1) STUDY.—

(A) IN GENERAL.—Not later than 180 days after the date of the enactment of this Act, the Administrator of the United States Agency for International Development shall carry out a study to identify best practices for the rehabilitation of victims of trafficking in group residential facilities in foreign countries.

(B) FACTORS.—In carrying out the study under subparagraph (A), the Administrator shall—

(i) investigate factors relating to the rehabilitation of victims of trafficking in group residential facilities, such as the appropriate size of such facilities, services to be provided, length of stay, and cost; and

(ii) give consideration to ensure the safety and security of victims of trafficking, provide alternative sources of income for such victims, assess and provide for the educational needs of such victims, including literacy, and assess the psychological needs of such victims and provide professional counseling, as appropriate.

(2) PILOT PROGRAM.—Upon completion of the study carried out pursuant to paragraph (1), the Administrator of the United States Agency for International Development shall establish and carry out a pilot program to establish residential treatment facilities in foreign countries for victims of trafficking based upon the best practices identified in the study.

(3) PURPOSES.—The purposes of the pilot program established pursuant to paragraph (2) are to—

(A) provide benefits and services to victims of trafficking, including shelter, psychological counseling, and assistance in developing independent living skills;

(B) assess the benefits of providing residential treatment facilities for victims of trafficking, as well as the most efficient and cost-effective means of providing such facilities; and

(c) assess the need for and feasibility of establishing additional residential treatment facilities for victims of trafficking.

(4) SELECTION OF SITES.—The Administrator of the United States Agency for International Development shall select 2 sites at which to operate the pilot program established pursuant to paragraph (2).

(5) FORM OF ASSISTANCE.—In order to carry out the responsibilities of this subsection, the Administrator of the United States Agency for International Development shall enter into contracts with, or make grants to, organizations with relevant expertise in the delivery of services to victims of trafficking.

(6) REPORT.—Not later than one year after the date on which the first pilot program is established pursuant to paragraph (2), the Administrator of the United States Agency for international Development shall submit to the committee on International Relations of the House of Representatives and the Committee on Foreign Relations of the Senate a report on the implementation of this subsection.

(7) AUTHORIZATION OF APPROPRIATIONS.—There are authorized to be appropriated to the Administrator of the United States Agency for International Development to carry out this subsection $2,500,000 for each of the fiscal years 2006 and 2007.

SEC. 103. ENHANCING PROSECUTIONS OF TRAFFICKING IN PERSONS OFFENSES.

(a) EXTRATERRITORIAL JURISDICTION OVER CERTAIN TRAFFICKING IN PERSONS OFFENSES.—

(1) IN GENERAL.—Part II of title 18, United States Code, is amended by inserting after chapter 212 the following new chapter:

CHAPTER 212A—EXTRATERRITORIAL JURISDICTION OVER CERTAIN TRAFFICKING IN PERSONS OFFENSES

Sec.

3271. TRAFFICKING IN PERSONS OFFENSES COMMITTED BY PERSONS EMPLOYED BY OR ACCOMPANYING THE FEDERAL GOVERNMENT OUTSIDE THE UNITED STATES.

3272. Definitions.

§3271. Trafficking in persons offenses committed by persons employed by or accompanying the Federal Government outside the United States

(a) Whoever, while employed by or accompanying the Federal Government outside the United States, engages in conduct outside the United States that would constitute an offense under chapter 77 or 117 of this title if the conduct had been engaged in within the United States or within the special maritime and territorial jurisdiction of the United States shall be punished as provided for that offense.

(b) No prosecution may be commenced against a person under this section if a foreign government, in accordance with jurisdiction recognized by the United States, has prosecuted or is prosecuting such person for the conduct constituting such offense, except upon the approval of the Attorney General or the Deputy Attorney General (or a person acting in either such capacity), which function of approval may not be delegated.

§3272. Definitions

As used in this chapter:

(1) The term 'employed by the Federal Government outside the United States' means—

(A) employed as a civilian employee of the Federal Government, as a Federal contractor (including a subcontractor at any tier), or as an employee of a Federal contractor (including a subcontractor at any tier);

(B) present or residing outside the United States in connection with such employment; and

(C) not a national of or ordinarily resident in the host nation.

(2) The term 'accompanying the Federal Government outside the United States' means—

(A) a dependant of—

(i) a civilian employee of the Federal Government; or

(ii) a Federal contractor (including a subcontractor at any tier) or an employee of a Federal contractor (including a subcontractor at any tier);

(B) residing with such civilian employee, contractor, or contractor employee outside the United States; and

"(c) not a national of or ordinarily resident in the host nation."

(2) CLERICAL AMENDMENT.—The table of chapters at the beginning of such part is amended by inserting after the item relating to chapter 212 the following new item:

"212A. Extraterritorial jurisdiction over certain trafficking in persons offenses ... 3271".

(b) LAUNDERING OF MONETARY INSTRUMENTS.—Section 1956(c)(7)(B) of title 18, United States Code, is amended—

(1) in clause (v), by striking "or" at the end;

(2) in clause (vi), by adding "or" at the end; and

(3) by adding at the end the following new clause:

(vii) trafficking in persons, selling or buying of children, sexual exploitation of children, or transporting, recruiting or harboring a person, including a child, for commercial sex acts;".

(c) DEFINITION OF RACKETEERING ACTIVITY.—Section 1961(1)(B) of title 18, United States Code, is amended by striking "1581–1591" and inserting "1581–1592".

(d) CIVIL AND CRIMINAL FORFEITURES.—

(1) IN GENERAL.—Chapter 117 of title 18, United States code, is amended by adding at the end the following new section:

§2428. Forfeitures

(a) IN GENERAL.—The court, in imposing sentence on any person convicted of a violation of this chapter, shall order, in addition to any other sentence imposed and irrespective of any provision of State law, that such person shall forfeit to the United States—

(1) such person's interest in any property, real or personal, that was used or intended to be used to commit or to facilitate the commission of such violation; and

(2) any property, real or personal, constituting or derived from any proceeds that such person obtained, directly or indirectly, as a result of such violation.

(b) PROPERTY SUBJECT TO FORFEITURE.—

(1) IN GENERAL.—The following shall be subject to forfeiture to the United States and no property right shall exist in them:

(A) Any property, real or personal, used or intended to be used to commit or to facilitate the commission of any violation of this chapter.

(B) Any property, real or personal, that constitutes or is derived from proceeds traceable to any violation of this chapter.

(2) APPLICABILITY OF CHAPTER 46.—The provisions of chapter 46 of this title relating to civil forfeitures shall apply to any seizure or civil forfeiture under this subsection."

(2) CLERICAL AMENDMENT.—The table of sections at the beginning of such chapter is amended by adding at the end the following new item: "2428. Forfeitures."

SEC. 104. ENHANCING UNITED STATES EFFORTS TO COMBAT TRAFFICKING IN PERSONS.

(a) APPOINTMENT TO INTERAGENCY TASK FORCE TO MONITOR AND COMBAT TRAFFICKING.—Section 105(b) of the Trafficking Victims Protection Act of 2000 (22 U.S.C. 7103(b)) is amended—

(1) by striking "the Director of Central Intelligence" and inserting "the Director of National Intelligence"; and

(2) by inserting ", the Secretary of Defense, the Secretary of Homeland Security" after "the Director of National Intelligence" (as added by paragraph (1)).

(b) MINIMUM STANDARDS FOR THE ELIMINATION OF TRAFFICKING.—

(1) AMENDMENTS.—Section 108(b) of the Trafficking Victims Protection Act of 2000 (22 U.S.C. 7106(b)) is amended—

(A) in paragraph (3), by adding at the end before the period the following: ", measures to reduce the demand for commercial sex acts and for participation in international sex tourism by nationals of the country, measures to ensure that its nationals who are deployed abroad as part of a peacekeeping or other similar mission do not engage in or facilitate severe forms of trafficking in persons or exploit victims of such trafficking, and measures to prevent the use of forced labor or child labor in violation of international standards"; and

(B) in the first sentence of paragraph (7), by striking "persons," and inserting "persons, including nationals of the country who are deployed abroad as part of a peacekeeping or other similar mission who engage in or facilitate severe forms of trafficking in persons or exploit victims of such trafficking,".

(2) EFFECTIVE DATE.—The amendments made by subparagraphs (A) and (B) of paragraph (1) take effect beginning two years after the date of the enactment of this Act.

(c) RESEARCH.—

(1) AMENDMENTS.—Section 112A of the Trafficking Victims Protection Act of 2000 (22 U.S.C. 7109a) is amended—

(A) in the first sentence of the matter preceding paragraph (1)—

(i) by striking "The President" and inserting "(a) In General.—The President"; and

(ii) by striking "the Director of Central Intelligence" and inserting "the Director of National Intelligence";

(B) in paragraph (3), by adding at the end before the period the following: ", particularly HIV/AIDS";

(C) by adding at the end the following new paragraphs:

(4) Subject to subsection (b), the interrelationship between trafficking in persons and terrorism, including the use of profits from trafficking in persons to finance terrorism.

(5) An effective mechanism for quantifying the number of victims of trafficking on a national, regional, and international basis.

"(6) The abduction and enslavement of children for use as soldiers, including steps taken to eliminate the abduction and enslavement of children for use as soldiers and recommendations for such further steps as may be necessary to rapidly end the abduction and enslavement of children for use as soldiers."; and

(D) by further adding at the end the following new subsections:

(b) ROLE OF HUMAN SMUGGLING AND TRAFFICKING CENTER.—The research initiatives described in subsection (a)(4) shall be carried out by the Human Smuggling and Trafficking center (established pursuant to section 7202 of the intelligence Reform and Terrorism Prevention Act of 2004 (Public Law 108–458)).

(c) DEFINITIONS.—In this section:

(1) AIDS.—The term 'AIDS' means the acquired immune deficiency syndrome.

(2) HIV.—The term 'HIV' means the human immunodeficiency virus, the pathogen that causes AIDS.

(3) HIV/AIDS.—The term 'HIV/AIDS' means, with respect to an individual, an individual who is infected with HIV or living with AIDS."

(2) REPORT.—

(A) IN GENERAL.—Not later than one year after the date of the enactment of this Act, the Human Smuggling and Trafficking center (established pursuant to section 7202 of the Intelligence Reform and Terrorism Prevention Act of 2004 (Public Law 108–458)) shall submit to the appropriate congressional committees a report on the results of the research initiatives carried out pursuant to section 112A(4) of the Trafficking Victims Protection Act of 2000 (as added by paragraph (1)(C) of this subsection).

(B) DEFINITION.—In this paragraph, the term "appropriate congressional committees" means—

(i) the committee on international Relations and the committee on the judiciary of the House of Representatives; and

(ii) the committee on Foreign Relations and the committee on the judiciary of the Senate.

(d) FOREIGN SERVICE OFFICER TRAINING.—Section 708(a) of the Foreign Service Act of 1980 (22 U.S.c. 4028(a)) is amended—

(1) in the matter preceding paragraph (1), by inserting ", the Director of the Office to Monitor and Combat Trafficking," after "the international Religious Freedom Act of 1998";

(2) in paragraph (1), by striking "and" at the end;

(3) in paragraph (2), by striking the period at the end and inserting "; and"; and

(4) by adding at the end the following:

"(3) instruction on international documents and United States policy on trafficking in persons, including provisions of the Trafficking Victims Protection Act of 2000 (division A of Public Law 106–386; 22 U.S.C. 7101 et seq.) which may affect the United States bilateral relationships."

(e) PREVENTION OF TRAFFICKING BY PEACEKEEPERS.—

(1) INCLUSION IN TRAFFICKING IN PERSONS REPORT.—Section 110(b)(1) of the Trafficking Victims Protection Act of 2000 (22 U.S.C. 7107(b)(1)) is amended—

(A) in subparagraph (B), by striking "and" at the end;

(B) in subparagraph (c), by striking the period at the end and inserting "; and"; and

(C) by adding at the end the following new subparagraph:

"(D) information on the measures taken by the United Nations, the Organization for Security and Cooperation in Europe, the North Atlantic Treaty Organization and, as appropriate, other multilateral organizations in which the United States participates, to prevent the involvement of the organization's employees, contractor personnel, and peacekeeping forces in trafficking in persons or the exploitation of victims of trafficking."

(2) REPORT BY SECRETARY OF STATE.—At least 15 days prior to voting for a new or reauthorized peacekeeping mission under the auspices of the United Nations, the North Atlantic Treaty organization, or any other multilateral organization in which the United States participates (or in an emergency, as far in advance as is practicable), the Secretary of State shall submit to the Committee on International Relations of the House of Representatives, the Committee on Foreign Relations of the Senate, and any other appropriate congressional committee a report that contains—

(A) a description of measures taken by the organization to prevent the organization's employees, contractor personnel, and peacekeeping forces serving in the peacekeeping mission from trafficking in persons, exploiting victims of trafficking, or committing acts of sexual exploitation or abuse, and the measures in place to hold accountable any such individuals who engage in any such acts while participating in the peacekeeping mission; and

(B) an analysis of the effectiveness of each of the measures referred to in subparagraph (A).

SEC. 105. ADDITIONAL ACTIVITIES TO MONITOR AND COMBAT FORCED LABOR AND CHILD LABOR.

(a) ACTIVITIES OF THE DEPARTMENT OF STATE.—

(1) FINDING.—Congress finds that in the report submitted to Congress by the Secretary of State in June 2005 pursuant to section 110(b) of the Trafficking Victims Protection Act of 2000 (22 U.S.C. 7107(b)), the list of countries whose governments do not comply with the minimum standards for the elimination of trafficking and are not making significant efforts to bring themselves into compliance was composed of a large number of countries in which the trafficking involved forced labor, including the trafficking of women into domestic servitude.

(2) SENSE OF CONGRESS.—It is the sense of Congress that the Director of the Office to Monitor and Combat Trafficking of the Department of State should intensify the focus of the Office on forced labor in the countries described in paragraph (1) and other countries in which forced labor continues to be a serious human rights concern.

(b) ACTIVITIES OF THE DEPARTMENT OF LABOR.—

(1) IN GENERAL.—The Secretary of Labor, acting through the head of the Bureau of International Labor Affairs of the Department of Labor, shall carry out additional activities to monitor and combat forced labor and child labor in foreign countries as described in paragraph (2).

(2) ADDITIONAL ACTIVITIES DESCRIBED.—The additional activities referred to in paragraph (1) are—

(A) to monitor the use of forced labor and child labor in violation of international standards;

(B) to provide information regarding trafficking in persons for the purpose of forced labor to the office to Monitor and Combat Trafficking of the Department of State for inclusion in trafficking in persons report required by section 110(b) of the Trafficking Victims Protection Act of 2000 (22 U.S.C. 7107(b));

(C) to develop and make available to the public a list of goods from countries that the Bureau of international Labor Affairs has reason to believe are produced by forced labor or child labor in violation of international standards;

(D) to work with persons who are involved in the production of goods on the list described in subparagraph (C) to create a standard set of practices that will reduce the likelihood that such persons will produce goods using the labor described in such subparagraph; and

(E) to consult with other departments and agencies of the United States Government to reduce forced and child labor internationally and ensure that products made by forced labor and child labor in violation of international standards are not imported into the United States.

TITLE II—COMBATTING DOMESTIC TRAFFICKING IN PERSONS
SEC. 201. PREVENTION OF DOMESTIC TRAFFICKING IN PERSONS.

(a) PROGRAM TO REDUCE TRAFFICKING IN PERSONS AND DEMAND FOR COMMERCIAL SEX ACTS IN THE UNITED STATES.—

(1) COMPREHENSIVE RESEARCH AND STATISTICAL REVIEW AND ANALYSIS OF INCIDENTS OF TRAFFICKING IN PERSONS AND COMMERCIAL SEX ACTS.—

(A) IN GENERAL.—The Attorney General shall use available data from State and local authorities as well as research data to carry out a biennial comprehensive research and statistical review and analysis of severe forms of trafficking in persons, and a biennial comprehensive research and statistical review and analysis of sex trafficking and unlawful commercial sex acts in the United States, and shall submit to Congress separate biennial reports on the findings.

(B) CONTENTS.—The research and statistical review and analysis under this paragraph shall consist of two separate studies, utilizing the same statistical data where appropriate, as follows:

(i) The first study shall address severe forms of trafficking in persons in the United States and shall include, but need not be limited to—

(I) the estimated number and demographic characteristics of persons engaged in acts of severe forms of trafficking in persons; and

(II) the number of investigations, arrests, prosecutions, and incarcerations of persons engaged in acts of severe forms of trafficking in persons by States and their political subdivisions.

(ii) The second study shall address sex trafficking and unlawful commercial sex acts in the United States and shall include, but need not be limited to—

(I) the estimated number and demographic characteristics of persons engaged in sex trafficking and commercial sex acts, including purchasers of commercial sex acts;

(II) the estimated value in dollars of the commercial sex economy, including the estimated average annual personal income derived from acts of sex trafficking;

(III) the number of investigations, arrests, prosecutions, and incarcerations of persons engaged in sex trafficking and unlawful commercial sex acts, including purchasers of commercial sex acts, by States and their political subdivisions; and

(IV) a description of the differences in the enforcement of laws relating to unlawful commercial sex acts across the United States.

(2) TRAFFICKING CONFERENCE.—

(A) IN GENERAL.—The Attorney General, in consultation and cooperation with the Secretary of Health and Human Services, shall conduct an annual conference in each of the fiscal years 2006, 2007, and 2008, and thereafter conduct a biennial conference, addressing severe forms of trafficking in persons and commercial sex acts that occur, in whole or in part, within the territorial jurisdiction of the United States. At each such conference, the Attorney General, or his designee, shall—

(i) announce and evaluate the findings contained in the research and statistical reviews carried out under paragraph (1);

(ii) disseminate best methods and practices for enforcement of laws prohibiting acts of severe forms of trafficking in persons and other laws related to acts of trafficking in persons, including, but not limited to, best methods and practices for training State and local law enforcement personnel on the enforcement of such laws;

(iii) disseminate best methods and practices for training State and local law enforcement personnel on the enforcement of laws prohibiting sex trafficking and commercial sex acts, including, but not limited to, best methods for investigating and prosecuting exploiters and persons who solicit or purchase an unlawful commercial sex act; and

(iv) disseminate best methods and practices for training State and local law enforcement personnel on collaborating with social service providers and relevant nongovernmental organizations and establishing trust of persons subjected to commercial sex acts or severe forms of trafficking in persons.

(B) PARTICIPATION.—Each annual conference conducted under this paragraph shall involve the participation of persons with expertise or professional responsibilities with relevance to trafficking in persons, including, but not limited to—

(i) Federal Government officials, including law enforcement and prosecutorial officials;

(ii) State and local government officials, including law enforcement and prosecutorial officials;

(iii) persons who have been subjected to severe forms of trafficking in persons or commercial sex acts;

(iv) medical personnel;

(v) social service providers and relevant nongovernmental organizations; and

(vi) academic experts.

(C) REPORTS.—The Attorney General and the Secretary of Health and Human Services shall prepare and post on the respective Internet Web sites of the Department of Justice and the Department of Health and Human Services reports on the findings and best practices identified and disseminated at the conference described in this paragraph.

(b) TERMINATION OF CERTAIN GRANTS, CONTRACTS, AND COOPERATIVE AGREEMENTS.—Section 106(g) of the Trafficking Victims Protection Act of 2000 (22 U.S.C. 7104) is amended—

(1) by striking "COOPERATIVE AGREEMENTS.—" and all that follows through "The President shall" and inserting "COOPERATIVE AGREEMENTS.—The President shall";

(2) by striking "described in paragraph (2)"; and

(3) by striking paragraph (2).

(c) AUTHORIZATION OF APPROPRIATIONS.—There are authorized to be appropriated—

(1) $2,500,000 for each of the fiscal years 2006 and 2007 to carry out the activities described in subsection (a)(1)(B)(i) and $2,500,000 for each of the fiscal years 2006 and 2007 to carry out the activities described in subsection (a)(1)(B)(ii); and

(2) $1,000,000 for each of the fiscal years 2006 through 2007 to carry out the activities described in subsection (a)(2).

SEC. 202. ESTABLISHMENT OF GRANT PROGRAM TO DEVELOP, EXPAND, AND STRENGTHEN ASSISTANCE PROGRAMS FOR CERTAIN PERSONS SUBJECT TO TRAFFICKING.

(a) GRANT PROGRAM.—The Secretary of Health and Human Services may make grants to States, Indian tribes, units of local government, and nonprofit, nongovernmental victims' service organizations to establish, develop, expand, and strengthen assistance programs for United States citizens or aliens admitted for permanent residence who are the subject of sex trafficking or severe forms of trafficking in persons that occurs, in whole or in part, within the territorial jurisdiction of the United States.

(b) SELECTION FACTOR.—In selecting among applicants for grants under subsection (a), the Secretary shall give priority to applicants with experience in the delivery of services to persons who have been subjected to sexual abuse or commercial sexual exploitation and to applicants who would employ survivors of sexual abuse or commercial sexual exploitation as a part of their proposed project.

(c) LIMITATION ON FEDERAL SHARE.—The Federal share of a grant made under this section may not exceed 75 percent of the total costs of the projects described in the application submitted.

(d) AUTHORIZATION OF APPROPRIATIONS.—There are authorized to be appropriated $10,000,000 for each of the fiscal years 2006 and 2007 to carry out the activities described in this section.

SEC. 203. PROTECTION OF JUVENILE VICTIMS OF TRAFFICKING IN PERSONS.

(a) ESTABLISHMENT OF PILOT PROGRAM.—Not later than 180 days after the date of the enactment of this Act, the Secretary of Health and Human Services shall establish and carry out a pilot program to establish residential treatment facilities in the United States for juveniles subjected to trafficking.

(b) PURPOSES.—The purposes of the pilot program established pursuant to subsection (a) are to—

(1) provide benefits and services to juveniles subjected to trafficking, including shelter, psychological counseling, and assistance in developing independent living skills;

(2) assess the benefits of providing residential treatment facilities for juveniles subjected to trafficking, as well as the most efficient and cost-effective means of providing such facilities; and

(3) assess the need for and feasibility of establishing additional residential treatment facilities for juveniles subjected to trafficking.

(c) SELECTION OF SITES.—The Secretary of Health and Human Services shall select three sites at which to operate the pilot program established pursuant to subsection (a).

(d) FORM OF ASSISTANCE.—In order to carry out the responsibilities of this section, the Secretary of Health and Human Services shall enter into contracts with, or make grants to, organizations that—

(1) have relevant expertise in the delivery of services to juveniles who have been subjected to sexual abuse or commercial sexual exploitation; or

(2) have entered into partnerships with organizations that have expertise as described in paragraph (1) for the purpose of implementing the contracts or grants.

(e) REPORT.—Not later than one year after the date on which the first pilot program is established pursuant to subsection (a), the Secretary of Health and Human Services shall submit to Congress a report on the implementation of this section.

(f) DEFINITION.—In this section, the term "juvenile subjected to trafficking" means a United States citizen, or alien admitted for permanent residence, who is the subject of sex trafficking or severe forms of trafficking in persons that occurs, in whole or in part, within the territorial jurisdiction of the United States and who has not attained 18 years of age at the time the person is identified as having been the subject of sex trafficking or severe forms of trafficking in persons.

(g) AUTHORIZATION OF APPROPRIATIONS.—There are authorized to be appropriated to the Secretary of Health and Human Services to carry out this section $5,000,000 for each of the fiscal years 2006 and 2007.

SEC. 204. ENHANCING STATE AND LOCAL EFFORTS TO COMBAT TRAFFICKING IN PERSONS.

(a) ESTABLISHMENT OF GRANT PROGRAM FOR LAW ENFORCEMENT.—

(1) IN GENERAL.—The Attorney General may make grants to States and local law enforcement agencies to establish, develop, expand, or strengthen programs—

(A) to investigate and prosecute acts of severe forms of trafficking in persons, and related offenses, which involve United States citizens, or aliens admitted for permanent residence, and that occur, in whole or in part, within the territorial jurisdiction of the United States;

(B) to investigate and prosecute persons who engage in the purchase of commercial sex acts;

(C) to educate persons charged with, or convicted of, purchasing or attempting to purchase commercial sex acts; and

(D) to educate and train law enforcement personnel in how to establish trust of persons subjected to trafficking and encourage cooperation with prosecution efforts.

(2) DEFINITION.—In this subsection, the term "related offenses" includes violations of tax laws, transacting in illegally derived proceeds, money laundering, racketeering, and other violations of criminal laws committed in connection with an act of sex trafficking or a severe form of trafficking in persons.

(b) MULTI-DISCIPLINARY APPROACH REQUIRED.—Grants under subsection (a) may be made only for programs in which the State or local law enforcement agency works collaboratively with social service providers and relevant nongovernmental organizations, including organizations with experience in the delivery of services to persons who are the subject of trafficking in persons.

(c) LIMITATION ON FEDERAL SHARE.—The Federal share of a grant made under this section may not exceed 75 percent of the total costs of the projects described in the application submitted.

(d) AUTHORIZATION OF APPROPRIATIONS.—There are authorized to be appropriated to the Attorney General to carry out this section $25,000,000 for each of the fiscal years 2006 and 2007.

SEC. 205. REPORT TO CONGRESS.

Section 105(d)(7) of the Trafficking Victims Protection Act of 2000 (22 U.S.C. 7103(d)(7)) is amended—

(1) in subparagraph (F), by striking "and" at the end;

(2) by redesignating subparagraph (G) as subparagraph (H); and

(3) by inserting after subparagraph (F) the following new subparagraph:

"(G) the amount, recipient, and purpose of each grant under sections 202 and 204 of the Trafficking victims Protection Act of 2005; and".

SEC. 206. SENIOR POLICY OPERATING GROUP.

Each Federal department or agency involved in grant activities related to combatting trafficking or providing services to persons subjected to trafficking inside the United States shall, as the department or agency determines appropriate, apprise the Senior Policy Operating Group established by section 105(f) of the Victims of Trafficking and Violence Protection Act of 2000 (22 U.S.C. 7103(f)), under the procedures established by the Senior Policy Operating Group, of such activities of the department or agency to ensure that the activities are consistent with the purposes of the Trafficking Victims Protection Act of 2000 (22 U.S.C. 7101 et seq.).

SEC. 207. DEFINITIONS.

in this title:

(1) SEVERE FORMS OF TRAFFICKING IN PERSONS.—The term "severe forms of trafficking in persons" has the meaning given the term in section 103(8) of the Trafficking Victims Protection Act of 2000 (22 U.S.C. 7102(8)).

(2) SEX TRAFFICKING.—The term "sex trafficking" has the meaning given the term in section 103(9) of the Trafficking Victims Protection Act of 2000 (22 U.S.C. 7102(9)).

(3) COMMERCIAL SEX ACT.—The term "commercial sex act" has the meaning given the term in section 103(3) of the Trafficking Victims Protection Act of 2000 (22 U.S.C. 7102(3)).

TITLE III—AUTHORIZATIONS OF APPROPRIATIONS
SEC. 301. AUTHORIZATIONS OF APPROPRIATIONS.

Section 113 of the Trafficking Victims Protection Act of 2000 (22 U.S.C. 7110) is amended—

(1) in subsection (a)—

(A) by striking "and $5,000,000" and inserting "$5,000,000";

(B) by adding at the end before the period the following: ", and $5,500,000 for each of the fiscal years 2006 and 2007"; and

(C) by further adding at the end the following new sentence: "in addition, there are authorized to be appropriated to the Office to Monitor and Combat Trafficking for official reception and representation expenses $3,000 for each of the fiscal years 2006 and 2007.";

(2) in subsection (b), by striking "2004 and 2005" and inserting "2004, 2005, 2006, and 2007";

(3) in subsection (c)(1), by striking "2004 and 2005" each place it appears and inserting "2004, 2005, 2006, and 2007";

(4) in subsection (d), by striking "2004 and 2005" each place it appears and inserting "2004, 2005, 2006, and 2007";

(5) in subsection (e)—

(A) in paragraphs (1) and (2), by striking "2003 through 2005" and inserting "2003 through 2007"; and

(B) in paragraph (3), by striking "$300,000 for fiscal year 2004 and $300,000 for fiscal year 2005" and inserting "$300,000 for each of the fiscal years 2004 through 2007";

(6) in subsection (f), by striking "2004 and 2005" and inserting "2004, 2005, 2006, and 2007"; and

(7) by adding at the end the following new subsections:

"(h) AUTHORIZATION OF APPROPRIATIONS TO DIRECTOR OF THE FBI.—There are authorized to be appropriated to the Director of the Federal Bureau of Investigation $15,000,000 for fiscal year 2006, to remain available until expended, to investigate severe forms of trafficking in persons.

"(i) AUTHORIZATION OF APPROPRIATIONS TO THE SECRETARY OF HOMELAND SECURITY.—There are authorized to be appropriated to the Secretary of Homeland Security, $18,000,000 for each of the fiscal years 2006 and 2007, to remain available until expended, for investigations by the Bureau of Immigration and Customs Enforcement of severe forms of trafficking in persons."

Speaker of the House of Representatives.

Vice President of the United States and President of the Senate.

DOCUMENT **103**

Full Official Title: Alien Tort Claims Act of 1789

Short Title/Acronym/Abbreviation: ATCA, ATS

Type of Document: This is a bill passed as part of the Judiciary Act of 1789 by the first U.S. Congress and signed into law by the President at the start of this nation. It established the Federal Court system.

Subject: giving U.S. federal courts subject matter jurisdiction over "torts in violation of international law."

Official Citation: 28 U.S. Code section 1350

Date of Document: Not applicable

Date of Adoption: passed Sept. 24, 1789.

Date of General Entry into Force (EIF): Not applicable
Number of States Parties as of this printing: Not applicable
Date of Signature by United States: Not applicable
Date of Ratification/Accession/Adhesion: Not applicable
Date of Entry into Force as to United States (effective date): Not applicable
Legal Status/Character of the Instrument/Document as to the United States: Binding U.S. law found at 28 U.S. Code section 1350.

Comment: Actions under this statute are referred to as ATCA or ATS or 1350 claims/cases/actions. For the judicial application of this Act in U.S. Courts, up to the U.S. Supreme Court, see Appendix J, the decisions in *Sosa*, *Kiobel*, and *Kadic*. This jurisdictional statute gives the federal courts jurisdiction to hear human rights cases by aliens against other aliens committed outside the U.S. The human rights violations alleged must constitute torts in violation of international law.

Caution: (If this is a legal instrument) The status and applicability of this instrument as to the United States may have changed since the date of this publication. The above information may be updated by referring to the following site:

Web Address: http://thomas.loc.gov/; or http://www1.umn.edu/humanrts/instree/
or
http://www.law.cornell.edu/uscode/html/uscode28/usc_sec_28_00001350____000-.html

THE ALIEN TORT CLAIMS ACT OF 1789 (ACTA), USC TITLE 28, SEC. 1350

Title 28—Judiciary and Judicial Procedure; Part IV—Jurisdiction and Venue; Chapter 85—District Courts; Jurisdiction
Sec. 1350. Alien's action for tort

The district courts shall have original jurisdiction of any civil action by an alien for a tort only, committed in violation of the law of nations or a treaty of the United States.

DOCUMENT 104

Full Official Title: An Act to carry out obligations of the United States under the United Nations Charter and other international agreements pertaining to the protection of human rights by establishing a civil action for recovery of damages from an individual who engages in torture or extrajudicial killing.

Short Title/Acronym/Abbreviation: Torture Victim Protection Act of 1991, or TVPA
Type of Document: This is a bill passed by the U.S. Congress and signed into law by the President
Subject: Federal court cause of action for torture and extrajudicial killing.
Official Citation: Pub. L. 102–256, Mar. 12, 1992, 106 Stat. 73. 28 U.S. Code sec. 1350
Date of Document: Not applicable
Date of Adoption: passed January 3, 1992
Date of General Entry into Force (EIF): Not applicable
Number of States Parties as of this printing: Not applicable
Date of Signature by United States: Not applicable
Date of Ratification/Accession/Adhesion: Not applicable
Date of Entry into Force as to United States (effective date): Not applicable
Legal Status/Character of the Instrument/Document as to the United States: A binding federal statute found at 28 U.S. Code section 1350. It creates a cause of action against "An individual who, under actual or apparent authority, or color of law, of any foreign nation" commits torture or extrajudicial killing.

Caution: (If this is a legal instrument) The status and applicability of this instrument as to the United States may have changed since the date of this publication. The above information may be updated by referring to the following sites:

Web Address: http://www.law.cornell.edu/uscode/uscode28/usc_sec_28_00001350——000-notes.html
http://www1.umn.edu/humanrts/instree/;

or
http://thomas.loc.gov/cgi-bin/query/z?c102:H.R.2092.ENR:

TORTURE VICTIM PROTECTION ACT OF 1991, USC TITLE 28, SEC. 1350

Section 1. Short Title

This Act may be cited as the "Torture Victim Protection Act of 1991."

Section 2. Establishment of Civil Action

(a) Liability. An individual who, under actual or apparent authority, or color of law, of any foreign nation

(1) subjects an individual to torture shall, in a civil action, be liable for damages to that individual; or

(2) subjects an individual to extrajudicial killing shall, in a civil action, be liable for damages to the individual's legal representative, or to any person who may be a claimant in an action for wrongful death.

(b) Exhaustion of Remedies. A court shall decline to hear a claim under this section if the claimant has not exhausted adequate and available remedies in the place in which the conduct giving rise to the claim occurred.

(c) Statute of Limitations. No action shall be maintained under this section unless it is commenced within 10 years after the cause of action arose.

Section 3. Definitions

(a) Extrajudicial Killing. For the purposes of this Act, the term "extrajudicial killing" means a deliberated killing not authorized by a previous judgment pronounced by a regularly constituted court affording all the judicial guarantees which are recognized as indispensable by civilized peoples. Such term, however, does not include any such killing that, under international law, is lawfully carried out under the authority of a foreign nation.

(b) Torture. For the purposes of this Act

(1) the term "torture" means any act, directed against an individual in the offender's custody or physical control, by which severe pain or suffering (other than pain or suffering arising only from or inherent in, or incidental to, lawful sanctions), whether physical or mental, is intentionally inflicted on that individual for such purposes as obtaining from that individual or a third person information or a confession, punishing that individual for an act that individual or a third person has committed or is suspected of having committed, intimidating or coercing that individual or a third person, or for any reason based on discrimination of any kind; and

(2) mental pain or suffering refers to prolonged mental harm caused by or resulting from

(A) the intentional infliction or threatened infliction of severe physical pain or suffering;

(B) the administration or application, or threatened administration or application, of mind altering substances or other procedures calculated to disrupt profoundly the senses or the personality;

(C) the threat of imminent death; or

(D) the threat that another individual will imminently be subjected to death, severe physical pain or suffering, or the administration or application of mind altering substances or other procedures calculated to disrupt profoundly the senses or personality.

DOCUMENT 105

Full Official Title: An Act to define the jurisdiction of United States Courts in suits against foreign states, the circumstances in which foreign states are immune from suit and in which execution may not be levied on their property, and for other purposes.

Short Title/Acronym/Abbreviation: Foreign Sovereign Immunities Act of 1976.

Type of Document: This is a bill passed by the U.S. Congress and signed into law by the President. Public Law 94-583.

Subject: immunity of foreign governments from suits in U.S. Courts and executions on their property, such as would adversely interfere with U.S. foreign relations.

Official Citation: 28 United States Code Sec. 1602-1605

Date of Document: 1976

Date of Adoption: passed October 21, 1976

Date of General Entry into Force (EIF): Not applicable

Number of States Parties as of this printing: Not applicable

Date of Signature by United States: Not applicable

Date of Ratification/Accession/Adhesion: Not applicable

Date of Entry into Force as to United States (effective date): Not applicable

Legal Status/Character of the Instrument/Document as to the United States: a binding U.S. federal law.

Comment: This legislation is meant to protect the Executive branch of government in dealing with foreign relations with other countries. It says that you cannot sue a foreign sovereign in a U.S. Court without our government's approval. This legislation has granted immunity to governments and government officials when they were sued for human rights violations in the past. But in 2010 a very important Supreme Court case was decided which would limit the immunity defense to former government officials accused of such violations. See *Samantar vs Yousuf*, in Appendix J.

Caution: (If this is a legal instrument) The status and applicability of this instrument as to the United States may have changed since the date of this publication. The above information may be updated by referring to the following sites:

Web Address: http://www.law.cornell.edu/uscode/28/usc_sup_01_28_10_IV_20_97.html;

or

http://www1.umn.edu/humanrts/instree/; or http://thomas.loc.gov/

FOREIGN SOVEREIGN IMMUNITIES ACT OF 1976, USC TITLE 28, SEC. 1602–1605

Title 28—Judiciary and Judicial Procedure; Part IV—Jurisdiction and Venue; Chapter 97—Jurisdictional Immunities of Foreign States

Sec. 1602. Findings and declaration of purpose

The Congress finds that the determination by United States courts of the claims of foreign states to immunity from the jurisdiction of such courts would serve the interests of justice and would protect the rights of both foreign states and litigants in United States courts. Under international law, states are not immune from the jurisdiction of foreign courts insofar as their commercial activities are concerned, and their commercial property may be levied upon for the satisfaction of judgments rendered against them in connection with their commercial activities. Claims of foreign states to immunity should henceforth be decided by courts of the United States and of the States in conformity with the principles set forth in this chapter.

Section 1603. Definitions

For purposes of this chapter

(a) A "foreign state," except as used in section 1608 of this title, includes a political subdivision of a foreign state or an agency or instrumentality of a foreign state as defined in subsection (b).

(b) An "agency or instrumentality of a foreign state" means any entity

(1) which is a separate legal person, corporate or otherwise, and

(2) which is an organ of a foreign state or political subdivision thereof, or a majority of whose shares or other ownership interest is owned by a foreign state or political subdivision thereof, and

(3) which is neither a citizen of a State of the United States as defined in section 1332 (c) and (d) of this title, nor created under the laws of any third country.

(c) The "United States" includes all territory and waters, continental or insular, subject to the jurisdiction of the United States.

(d) A "commercial activity" means either a regular course of commercial conduct or a particular commercial transaction or act. The commercial character of an activity shall be determined by reference to the nature of the course of conduct or particular transaction or act, rather than by reference to its purpose.

(e) A "commercial activity carried on in the United States by a foreign state" means commercial activity carried on by such state and having substantial contact with the United States.

Section 1604. Immunity of a foreign state from jurisdiction

Subject to existing international agreements to which the United States is a party at the time of enactment of this Act a foreign state shall be immune from the jurisdiction of the courts of the United States and of the States except as provided in sections 1605 to 1607 of this chapter.

Section 1605. General exceptions to the jurisdictional immunity of a foreign state

(a) A foreign state shall not be immune from the jurisdiction of courts of the United States or of the States in any case

(1) in which the foreign state has waived its immunity either explicitly or by implication, notwithstanding any withdrawal of the waiver which the foreign state may purport to effect except in accordance with the terms of the waiver;

(2) in which the action is based upon a commercial activity carried on in the United States by the foreign state; or upon an act performed in the United States in connection with a commercial activity of the foreign state elsewhere; or upon an act outside the territory of the United States in connection with a commercial activity of the foreign state elsewhere and that act causes a direct effect in the United States;

(3) in which rights in property taken in violation of international law are in issue and that property or any property exchanged for such property is present in the United States in connection with a commercial activity carried on in the United States by the foreign state; or that property or any property exchanged for such property is owned or operated by an agency or instrumentality of the foreign state and that agency or instrumentality is engaged in a commercial activity in the United States;

(4) in which rights in property in the United States acquired by succession or gift or rights in immovable property situated in the United States are in issue;

(5) not otherwise encompassed in paragraph (2) above, in which money damages are sought against a foreign state for personal injury or death, or damage to or loss of property, occurring in the United States and caused by the tortuous act or omission of that foreign state or of any official or employee of that foreign state while acting within the scope of his office or employment; except this paragraph shall not apply to (A) any claim based upon the exercise or performance or the failure to exercise or perform a discretionary function regardless of whether the discretion be abused, or (B) any claim arising out of malicious prosecution, abuse of process, libel, slander, misrepresentation, deceit, or interference with contract rights;

(6) in which the action is brought, either to enforce an agreement made by the foreign state with or for the benefit of a private party to submit to arbitration all or any differences which have arisen or which may arise between the parties with respect to a defined legal relationship, whether contractual or not, concerning a subject matter capable of settlement by arbitration under the laws of the United States, or to confirm an award made pursuant to such an agreement to arbitrate, if (A) the arbitration takes place or is intended to take place in the United States, (B) the agreement or award is or may be governed by a treaty or other international agreement in force for the United States calling for the recognition and enforcement of arbitral awards, (C) the underlying claim, save for the agreement to arbitrate, could have been brought in a United States court under this section or section 1607, or (D) paragraph (1) of this subsection is otherwise applicable; or

(7) not otherwise covered by paragraph (2), in which money damages are sought against a foreign state for personal injury or death that was caused by an act of torture, extrajudicial killing, aircraft sabotage, hostage taking, or the provision of material support or resources (as defined in section 2339A of title 18) for such an act if such act or provision of material support is engaged in by an official, employee, or agent of such foreign state while acting within the scope of his or her office, employment, or agency, except that the court shall decline to hear a claim under this paragraph

(A) if the foreign state was not designated as a state sponsor of terrorism under section 6(j) of the Export Administration Act of 1979 (50 U.S.C. App. 2405(j)) or section 620A of the Foreign Assistance Act of 1961 (22 U.S.C. 2371) at the time the act occurred, unless later so designated as a result of such act; and

(B) even if the foreign state is or was so designated, if (i) the act occurred in the foreign state against which the claim has been brought and the claimant has not afforded the foreign state a reasonable opportunity to arbitrate the claim in accordance with accepted international rules of arbitration; or (ii) neither the claimant nor the victim was a national of the United States (as that term is defined in section 101(a)(22) of the Immigration and Nationality Act) when the act upon which the claim is based occurred.

(b) A foreign state shall not be immune from the jurisdiction of the courts of the United States in any case in which a suit in admiralty is brought to enforce a maritime lien against a vessel or cargo of the foreign state, which maritime lien is based upon a commercial activity of the foreign state: Provided that

(1) notice of the suit is given by delivery of a copy of the summons and of the complaint to the person, or his agent, having possession of the vessel or cargo against which the maritime lien is asserted; and if the vessel or cargo is arrested pursuant to process obtained on behalf of the party bringing the suit, the service of process of arrest shall be deemed to constitute valid delivery of such notice, but the party bringing the suit shall be

liable for any damages sustained by the foreign state as a result of the arrest if the party bringing the suit had actual or constructive knowledge that the vessel or cargo of a foreign state was involved; and

(2) notice to the foreign state of the commencement of suit as provided in section 1608 of this title is initiated within ten days either of the delivery of notice as provided in paragraph (1) of this subsection or, in the case of a party who was unaware that the vessel or cargo of a foreign state was involved, of the date such party determined the existence of the foreign state's interest.

(c) Whenever notice is delivered under subsection (b)(1), the suit to enforce a maritime lien shall thereafter proceed and shall be heard and determined according to the principles of law and rules of practice of suits in rem whenever it appears that, had the vessel been privately owned and possessed, a suit in rem might have been maintained. A decree against the foreign state may include costs of the suit and, if the decree is for a money judgment, interest as ordered by the court, except that the court may not award judgment against the foreign state in an amount greater than the value of the vessel or cargo upon which the maritime lien arose. Such value shall be determined as of the time notice is served under subsection (b)(1). Decrees shall be subject to appeal and revision as provided in other cases of admiralty and maritime jurisdiction. Nothing shall preclude the plaintiff in any proper case from seeking relief in personam in the same action brought to enforce a maritime lien as provided in this section.

(d) A foreign state shall not be immune from the jurisdiction of the courts of the United States in any action brought to foreclose a preferred mortgage, as defined in the Ship Mortgage Act, 1920 (46 U.S.C. 911 and following). Such action shall be brought, heard, and determined in accordance with the provisions of that Act and in accordance to the principles of law and rules of practice of suits in rem, whenever it appears that had the vessel been privately owned and possessed a suit in rem might have been maintained.

(e) For purposes of paragraph (7) of subsection (a)

(1) the terms "torture" and "extrajudicial killing" have the meaning given those terms in section 3 of the Torture Victim Protection Act of 1991;

(2) the term "hostage taking" has the meaning given that term in Article 1 of the International Convention Against the Taking of Hostages; and

(3) the term "aircraft sabotage" has the meaning given that term in Article 1 of the Convention for the Suppression of Unlawful Acts Against the Safety of Civil Aviation.

(f) No action shall be maintained under subsection (a)(7) unless the action is commenced not later than 10 years after the date on which the cause of action arose. All principles of equitable tolling, including the period during which the foreign state was immune from suit, shall apply in calculating this limitation period.

(g) Limitation on Discovery.

(1) In general.

(A) Subject to paragraph (2), if an action is filed that would otherwise be barred by section 1604, but for subsection (a)(7), the court, upon request of the Attorney General, shall stay any request, demand, or order for discovery on the United States that the Attorney General certifies would significantly interfere with a criminal investigation or prosecution, or a national security operation, related to the incident that gave rise to the cause of action, until such time as the Attorney General advises the court that such request, demand, or order will no longer so interfere.

(B) A stay under this paragraph shall be in effect during the 12-month period beginning on the date on which the court issues the order to stay discovery. The court shall renew the order to stay discovery for additional 12-month periods upon motion by the United States if the Attorney General certifies that discovery would significantly interfere with a criminal investigation or prosecution, or a national security operation, related to the incident that gave rise to the cause of action.

(2) Sunset.

(A) Subject to subparagraph (B), no stay shall be granted or continued in effect under paragraph (1) after the date that is 10 years after the date on which the incident that gave rise to the cause of action occurred.

(B) After the period referred to in paragraph (A), the court, upon request of the Attorney General, may stay any request, demand, or order for discovery on the United States that the court finds a substantial likelihood would (i) create a serious threat of death or serious bodily injury to any person; (ii) adversely affect the ability of the United States to work in cooperation with foreign and international law enforcement agencies in investigating violations of United States law; or (iii) obstruct the criminal case related to the incident that gave rise to the cause of action or undermine the potential for a conviction in such case.

(3) Evaluation of evidence. The court's evaluation of any request for a stay under this subsection filed by the Attorney General shall be conducted ex parte and in camera.

(4) Bar on motions to dismiss. A stay of discovery under this subsection shall constitute a bar to the granting of a motion to dismiss under rules 12(b)(6) and 56 of the Federal Rules of Civil Procedure.

(5) Construction. Nothing in this subsection shall prevent the United States from seeking protective orders or asserting privileges ordinarily available to the United States.

DOCUMENT 106

Full Official Title: United States Army Field Manual (Excerpts)
Short Title/Acronym/Abbreviation: Army Field Manual, the Soldiers Guide
Type of Document: Military field manual for soldiers
Subject: Duties, Responsibilities, and Authority of the Soldier
Official Citation: FM 7.21.13 Chapter 3, Sections I and III
Date of Document: October 15, 2003
Date of Adoption: October 15, 2003
Date of General Entry into Force (EIF): Not applicable
Number of States Parties as of this printing: Not applicable
Date of Signature by United States: Not applicable
Date of Ratification/Accession/Adhesion: Not applicable
Date of Entry into Force as to United States (effective date):
Legal Status/Character of the Instrument/Document as to the United States: Administrative manual for all military operations, obligatory for military personnel. This is a sample of one of the manuals, showing some of what rights soldiers have and what they must know about humanitarian law. The full text of the Law of War for the Army is found at FM 27-10.

Caution: (If this is a legal instrument) The status and applicability of this instrument as to the United States may have changed since the date of this publication. The above information may be updated by referring to the following site:

Web Address: http://www1.umn.edu/humanrts/instree/

U.S. ARMY FIELD MANUAL (SELECTED EXCERPTS)

FM 7.21.13 Ch3 sections 1 and III

Chapter 3

Duties, Responsibilities, and Authority of the Soldier

Being an effective part of a team as a soldier means knowing your role and the rules for that team. This chapter explains the meaning of duty, responsibility, and authority and how these apply to every soldier in the Army. You'll find a quick reference to some of the rules soldiers live by in the sections on wear, appearance, and fit and standards of conduct. The discussion of the Uniform Code of Military Justice (UCMJ) explains some of the procedures in the use of military justice. This chapter provides brief overviews of these topics and for additional detailed information refer to the appropriate manuals.

<u>Section IV—Standards of Conduct</u>
<u>Relationships Between Soldiers of Different Rank</u>
<u>Extremist Organizations and Activities</u>
<u>Homosexual Conduct</u>
<u>Hazing</u>
<u>Code of Conduct</u>
<u>Gifts and Donations</u>
<u>Fund-Raising</u>
<u>Lautenberg Amendment</u>

For more information on duties, responsibilities and authority see <u>AR 600-20</u>, *Army Command Policy*, <u>FM 6-0</u>, *Command and Control*, <u>FM 6-22 (22-100)</u>, *Army Leadership*, and <u>FM 7-22.7</u>, *The Army Noncommissioned Officer Guide*.

For more information on the law of land warfare, see <u>FM 1-04.10 (27-10)</u>, *The Law of Land Warfare*.

For more information on Army standards of conduct, see <u>AR 600-20</u> and DOD 5500.7-R, *Joint Ethics Regulation (JER)*.

...

3-1. Every soldier has certain duties, responsibilities, and most have some level of authority. You should know what these are and how they apply to you. One of your obligations as a soldier is to carry out your duties to standard and the best of your ability. Bear your responsibilities knowing that you are part of a great team that only works well when each of its members do their best. If you are in a leadership position, exert authority to build the team and develop your soldiers. Your fellow soldiers are depending on you each and every day to make tough decisions based on your rank and duty position.

...

ARTICLES OF THE MANUAL FOR COURTS-MARTIAL

3-132. The Manual for Courts-Martial (MCM) is a pretty big book. It contains the Uniform Code of Military Justice and instructs military lawyers and judges on how to conduct courts-martial. It is also where nonjudicial punishment (Article 15) is found. There are a total of 140 articles in the MCM. The MCM explains what conduct is in violation of the UCMJ, sets forth rules of evidence, contains a list of maximum punishments for each offense and explains types of court-martials. Articles 1 through 146 are in the following categories:

- General Provisions—Articles 1 through 6.
- Apprehension and Restraint—Articles 7 through 14.
- Nonjudicial Punishment—Article 15.
- Court-Martial Jurisdiction—Articles 16 through 21.
- Composition of Courts-Martial—Articles 22 through 29.
- Courts-Martial Procedures and Sentences—Articles 30 through 58.
- Post-Trial Procedures and Review of Courts-Martial—Articles 59 through 76.
- Punitive Articles—Articles 77 through 133. Also known as the "punitive offenses," these describe specific offenses that can result in punishment by court-martial or nonjudicial punishment.
- Article 134 is a "catch-all" that covers any offenses not specifically named in Articles 77-133.
- Miscellaneous Provisions—Articles 135 through 146.

3-133. Soldiers have rights under the UCMJ. In some ways, the USMJ provides even greater protections of soldiers' rights than under strictly civilian jurisdiction. A soldier has the following rights:

- The right to remain silent.
- The right to counsel.
- The right to demand trial.
- Under Article 15, the right to present his case, in the presence of the imposing commander.
- The right to call witnesses (if they are reasonably available).
- The right to present evidence.
- Under Article 15, the right to request a spokesperson (but not an attorney at the hearing).
- The right to request an open hearing.
- The right to examine all evidence.

3-134. Most courts-martial are preceded by an Article 32 investigation. This is an investigation by an officer, probably from the same installation, that tries to determine if there is enough evidence to go to a court-martial. It can be thought of as a little like a grand jury in the civilian legal system. The Article 32 investigation will also consider if the charges are correct and how to proceed with the case, whether by court-martial, nonjudicial punishment, administrative action, or even no action at all.

3-135. Refer to AR 27-10, *Military Justice*, the *Manual for Courts-Martial (MCM)*, *United States*, or visit your installation legal office for additional information. Also see Chapter 7 for information on the effects of the character of discharge on benefits after separation. Making the right decision is critical for the soldier receiving the punishment as well as the individual administering punishment under the UCMJ.

ARTICLE 15

3-136. Within the UCMJ is a provision for punishing misconduct through judicial proceedings like a court-martial. The UCMJ also gives commanders the authority to impose nonjudicial punishment, described in the UCMJ under Article 15. Article 15 provides commanders an essential tool in maintaining discipline. The Article allows commanders to impose punishment for relatively minor infractions. Only commanders may impose punishment under Article 15. A commander is any warrant officer or commissioned officer that is in command of a unit and has been given authority under AR 600-20, either orally or in writing, to administer nonjudicial punishment.

3-137. When reviewing the circumstances surrounding an incident of misconduct, the commander will ensure that prior to processing an Article 15, an actual offense under the UCMJ was committed. He ensures the alleged offense violated the UCMJ, Army Regulations, Army Policy, a lawful order, local laws or some other rule the soldier had a duty to obey.

3-138. The soldier is informed that the commander has started nonjudicial punishment (Article 15) procedures against him. Once the commander has conducted the hearing and if he decides that the accused is (a) guilty and (b) needs to be punished, he will prescribe punishment that fits the offense(s). Soldiers may present evidence at Article 15 hearings. Evidence would be something that shows a soldier is not guilty of the alleged offense(s). A soldier may also present matters in extenuation and mitigation, which are reasons why he should be punished less or not at all.

3-139. The level of proof is the same at both an Article 15 hearing and a court-martial; the imposing commander must be convinced of the accused soldier's guilt by the evidence presented before the soldier can be found guilty. Whatever the outcome of the hearing, an Article 15 is not considered a conviction and will not appear in your civilian record. On the other hand, if you demand a trial by court-martial and are convicted, this would be a federal conviction that would stay with you even after you leave the Army. No lawyers are involved in the Article 15 hearing however, the soldier has the right to speak with an attorney prior to accepting proceedings under Article 15. There is also no prosecutor at an Article 15 hearing. At a court-martial, a military lawyer may represent the accused at no cost to the soldier, and there would also be a prosecutor present.

3-140. If a soldier thinks he has been punished excessively, or evidence was not properly considered, he may appeal to the next level of command within five days. The soldier is not entitled to a personal appearance in front of the appeal authority (although he may request one) so he should include written statements as to why the appeal should be granted. If the soldier doesn't submit these statements, the appeal authority may never get his side of what happened. The appeal authority can take any action to lessen the punishment but may NOT INCREASE the punishment given by the original commander.

3-141. Article 15 comes in different levels: Summarized, Company Grade and Field Grade. They differ in two main respects: the severity of the punishment and in how the record of it can affect a soldier's future in the Army.

LAW OF LAND WARFARE

3-149. American traditions and morals require us to educate and enforce the laws of war among members of the Armed Forces. Throughout the history of armed conflict, lives have been lost and property destroyed because combatants failed to abide by the laws of war. Some of these violations are caused by a blatant disregard for the international laws of war, and some are a result of pure ignorance. The laws are not new. Some versions of the present laws of war have been around a long time. Over 100 years ago most civilized nations recognized a need to prevent unnecessary destruction of lives and property on the battlefield. Most nations endorse these laws but do not always abide by them. The law of war today, embodied by the Hague and Geneva Conventions, can be generally divided into four categories:

- Conduct of hostilities, forbidden targets, illegal tactics, and unlawful warfare techniques.
- Treatment of wounded and sick on land and sea.
- Treatment of prisoners of war.

- Treatment of civilians.

3-150. The conduct of armed hostilities on land is regulated by the law of land warfare which is both written and unwritten. It is inspired by the desire to diminish the evils of war. The purposes of the law of war are as follows:

- Protect combatants and noncombatants from unnecessary suffering.
- Safeguard certain fundamental human rights of persons who fall into the hands of the enemy, particularly prisoners of war, the wounded and sick, and civilians.
- Facilitate the restoration of peace.

BASIC PRINCIPLES

3-151. The law of war places limits on employing any kind or degree of violence that is not actually necessary for military purposes. The law of war also requires belligerents to conduct hostilities with regard for the principles of humanity. The law of war is binding not only upon states but also upon individuals and the members of their armed forces. American soldiers must know and abide by the law of land warfare—even if the enemy does not.

3-152. Any person, whether a member of the armed forces or a civilian who commits an act which constitutes a crime under international law is responsible and liable for punishment. The term "war crime" is a technical expression for violation of the law of war by any person or persons, military or civilian. Every violation of the law of war is a war crime.

3-153. In some cases, military commanders may be responsible for war crimes committed by subordinate members of the armed forces or other persons subject to their control. For example, if soldiers commit atrocities against prisoners of war, the responsibility may rest not only with the actual perpetrators but also with the commander, especially if the acts occurred by an order of the commander concerned. The commander is also responsible if he has or should have knowledge that soldiers or other persons subject to his control are about to commit or have committed a war crime and he fails to take steps to prevent such crime or to punish violators.

3-154. The United States normally punishes war crimes as such only if they are committed by enemy nationals or by persons serving the interests of the enemy state. Violations of the law of war committed by persons subject to military law of the United States usually constitute violations of the Uniform Code of Military Justice and are prosecuted under the UCMJ. Commanders must insure that war crimes committed by members of their forces against enemy personnel are promptly and adequately punished.

DEFENSE OF SUPERIOR ORDERS

3-155. The fact that the law of war has been violated even if on the order of a superior authority, whether military or civil, does not change the act in question of its character as a war crime. It does not constitute a defense in the trial of an accused individual unless he did not know and could not reasonably have been expected to know that the act was unlawful. In all cases where the order is held not to constitute a defense to an allegation of war crime, the fact that the individual was acting pursuant to orders may be considered in mitigation of punishment.

3-156. In considering the question of whether a superior order constitutes a valid defense, a court-martial takes into consideration the fact that obedience to lawful military orders is the duty of every member of the armed forces. At the same time, remember that members of the armed forces are bound to obey only lawful orders.

...

THE GENEVA CONVENTIONS ON THE LAWS OF WAR

3-157. Noncombatants are persons not taking part in hostilities, including members of armed forces who have laid down their arms and those incapacitated by sickness, wounds, detention, or any other cause. Noncombatants shall in all circumstances be treated humanely without exception. The following acts are and shall remain prohibited at any time and in any place whatsoever with respect to noncombatants:

- Violence to life and person, in particular murder of all kinds, mutilation, cruel treatment, and torture.
- Taking of hostages.
- Outrages upon personal dignity, in particular humiliating and degrading treatment.
- Passing sentences and carrying out executions without previous judgment of a regularly constituted court that affords all the judicial guarantees recognized as indispensable by civilized peoples.

3-158. For more information about the law of land warfare, see FM 1-04.10 (27-10), *The Law of Land Warfare*.

APPENDICES

APPENDIX A: CHRONOLOGY OF HUMAN RIGHTS IN RELATION TO THE U.S.

This Chronology of Human Rights in Relation to the U.S. highlights the major, historical human rights milestones for the U.S. including violations, actions, legislation and landmark court cases.

©Tina M. Ramirez 2010

1215   Magna Carta signed by King John.
1619   First 20 African slaves sold as indentured servants to settlers in Virginia.
1628   British Petition of Rights signed by King Charles I.
1632   Lord Baltimore receives a charter for Maryland as a refuge for Catholics; founded in 1634.
1636   Roger Williams expelled from Massachusetts Bay Colony for religious dissension and establishes Providence Plantation in Rhode Island for religious freedom.
1638   Anne Hutchinson expelled from Massachusetts Bay Colony for religious dissension and establishes colony of Portsmouth.
1649   Maryland passes the Act Concerning Religion.
1654   Jews fleeing Spanish Inquisition arrive in New Amsterdam.
1660   Virginia enacts laws against Quakers.
1660   Mary Dyer hanged on Boston Commons for spreading Quaker principals.
1663   King Charles II grants royal charter recognizing the colony of Rhode Island and religious freedom.
1681   King Charles II grants William Penn charter to establish colony in Pennsylvania.
1682   Penn issues the Frame of Government recognizing religious liberty in Pennsylvania.
1689   John Locke publishes a "Letter of Toleration."
        British Parliament adopts Bill of Rights.
1776   British Colonies issue Declaration of Independence.
1785   Virginia House of Burgesses adopts Statute of Religious Freedom drafted by Thomas Jefferson.
1787   Constitutional Convention adopts U.S. Constitution, enters into force in 1789.
1789   Judiciary Act of 1789 includes Alien Tort Claims Act, 28 USC sec. 1350.
1791   Congress passes Bill of Rights, the first ten amendments to the Constitution.
1807   Congress passes Slave Importation Act prohibiting further importation of slaves.
1830   Congress passes Indian Removal Act forcing Native Americans to relocate.
1831   Nat Turner leads a slave revolt in Virginia.
1848   Seneca Falls Convention drafts Declaration of Sentiments of women's rights.
1857   *Dred Scott v Sandford* decided by Supreme Court.
1863   Civil War begins and President Lincoln signs Instructions for the Government of Armies of the U.S. in the Field or "Lieber Code" to regulate conduct of Union forces.
        President Lincoln issues Emancipation Proclamation
        President Lincoln gives Gettysburg Address
        International Conference meets in Geneva and establishes the Red Cross.
1864   Diplomatic Conference passes First Geneva Convention protecting victims of conflict.
1865   Thirteenth Amendment passes and abolishes slavery; Freedmen's Bureau established.
        Ku Klux Klan established in Pulaski, Tennessee.
1868   Fourteenth Amendment passes protecting equal protection and due process.
1870   Fifteenth Amendment passes protecting voting rights.
        States pass "Jim Crow" laws beginning with Tennessee.
1882   Congress passes Chinese Exclusion Act.
1888   Congress passes the Scott Act restricting immigration by Chinese laborers into the U.S.
1889   First International Conference of American States held in Washington, D.C. established the International Union of American Republics (from October 1889 to April 1890).
1896   Supreme Court rules in *Plessy v Ferguson*, upholding the constitutionality of state laws requiring racial segregation in private businesses, under the doctrine of "separate but equal". This would be the racial standard of the U.S. until *Brown v Board of Education*.

| 1899 | First Hague Peace Conference adopts revised Geneva Convention adding Regulations concerning the Laws and Customs of War on Land. |

1899   First Hague Peace Conference adopts revised Geneva Convention adding Regulations concerning the Laws and Customs of War on Land.

1907   Second Hague Peace Conference adopts revised Geneva Convention governing combatants.

1914   First World War begins.

1915–17 Armenian Genocide

1919   Treaty of Versailles concludes WWI and requires Kaiser Wilhelm II to be tried for a "supreme offense against international morality and the sanctity of treaties."
International Labor Organization (ILO) established.

1920   League of Nations established to maintain international peace.
Nineteenth Amendment passes and is ratified by required states giving women the right to vote.

1922   Supreme Court rules in *Ozawa v U.S.* against Japanese right to naturalization.
Congress passes Cable Act restricting citizenship for women marrying foreigners.

1923   Treaty of Lausanne.

1924   Congress passes The Indian Citizenship or Snyder Act granting Native Americans born in the U.S. citizenship.

1926   Geneva Conference passes the Slavery Convention.

1929   Convention Relative to the Treatment of Prisoners of War adopted as Third Geneva Convention.
U.S. accedes to Slavery Convention.

1930   ILO adopts Convention Concerning Forced or Compulsory Labor (enters into force 1932).

1933   Congress passes President Franklin D. Roosevelt's "New Deal."

1934   Congress passes the Indian Reorganization Act.

1933   Adolph Hitler elected, National Socialist Party of Germany passes Nuremburg Laws against the Jewish population beginning the "Holocaust"; ends 1945.

1941   President Roosevelt gives "Four Freedoms" speech.
President Roosevelt and British Prime Minister Winston Churchill adopt Atlantic Charter.
Pearl Harbor attacked; U.S. enters the Second World War.

1942   At least 120,000 Japanese Americans forcibly moved to internment camps (until 1945).

1943   Congress repeals legislation excluding Chinese in and from the U.S.

1945   Charter of the United Nations adopted recognizing individual human rights and establishing the International Court of Justice.
Nuremburg war crimes tribunals begin under Nuremberg Charter, Rules and Principles.

1946   U.N. Economic and Social Council (ECOSOC) establishes UN Commission on Human Rights and U.N. Commission on the Status of Women.

1948   Charter of the Organization of American States (OAS) signed (enters into force in 1951) and OAS adopts Declaration of the Rights of Man.
U.N. General Assembly adopts Universal Declaration of Human Rights.
ILO adopts Convention on the Freedom of Association and Protection of the Right to Organize.
U.N. adopts Convention on the Prevention and Punishment of the Crime of Genocide (enters into force 1951).
U.S. signs Genocide Convention (ratified in 1988).

1949   Diplomatic Conference adopts four Geneva Conventions as international humanitarian law.
U.S. signs Four Geneva Conventions (ratifies all 1955).
Council of Europe founded.

1950   Council of Europe adopts European Convention on Human Rights (enters into force in 1953) establishing European Court of Human Rights.

1951   U.N. adopts Convention relating to the Status of Refugees (enters into force 1954).

1952   Congress passes the Immigration and Naturalization Act.

1953   U.N. adopts Convention on the Political Rights of Women (enters into force 1954).
U.S. signs Protocol to Slavery Convention (ratifies 1956).

1954   Supreme Court rules in *Brown v Board of Education.*

1955   Rosa Parks refuses to give up her seat on the bus, beginning the Montgomery bus boycott.

1957   "Little Rock Nine" try to attend Little Rock Central High School but are blocked.
U.N. adopts Convention on Nationality of Married Women (enters into force 1958).

ILO adopts Convention Concerning Abolition of Forced Labor and Convention Concerning Indigenous and Tribal Populations.

Congress passes Civil Rights Act of 1957 related to voting rights.

1959   OAS creates Inter-American Commission on Human Rights headquartered in Washington, D.C.

1961   Council of Europe adopts European Social Charter.

1963   Martin Luther King Jr. participates in March on Washington and gives "I Have A Dream" speech.

24th Amendment passes and is ratified by required states ending poll taxes.

1964   Congress passes Civil Rights Act of 1964 protecting against racial or sexual discrimination.

1965   Congress passes Voting rights Act of 1965.

U.N. adopts Convention on the Elimination of All Forms of Racial Discrimination (ICERD enters into force 1969).

1966   U.N. adopts International Covenant on Civil and Political Rights and its First Optional Protocol and the International Covenant on Economic, Social and Cultural Rights (ICCPR, First Optional Protocol and ICESCR enter into force 1976).

U.S. signs ICERD (ratifies 1994).

U.S. Supreme Court rules in *Miranda v Arizona* that law enforcement must give suspects certain procedural rights.

1967   U.N. adopts a Protocol to the 1951 Refugee Convention (enters into force 1967).

U.S. accedes to Supplementary Convention on the Abolition of Slavery, the Slave Trade, and Institutions and Practices Similar to Slavery.

Detroit race riots begin, sparking riots throughout the U.S.

Congress passes Age Discrimination Act of 1967.

1968   U.N. General Assembly Convenes First International Conference on Human Rights in Tehran, Iran.

U.S. accedes to 1961 Protocol to Refugee Convention.

U.N. adopts Convention on the Non-Applicability of Statutory Limitations to War Crimes Against Humanity (enters into force 1970).

Supreme Court rules in *Green v County School Board of New Kent County (Virginia)*.

1969   OAS adopts American Convention on Human Rights (enters into force in 1978) which calls for creation of an Inter-American Court of Human Rights.

1970   U.S. signs International Convention for the Suppression on Unlawful Seizure of Aircraft (ratified 1971).

1972   Equal Rights Amendment to U.S. Constitution passes Congress but fails to be ratified by states.

U.S. Supreme Court decides *Furman v Georgia* requiring national consistency in death penalty determination. Decision resulted in national moratorium on death penalty application.

1973   U.N. adopts Convention on Suppression and Punishment of the Crime of Apartheid (enters into force 1976).

U.S. signs International Convention on the Prevention and Punishment of Crimes Against International Protected Persons (1976).

Supreme Court rules in *Roe v Wade* on privacy and abortion.

1975   Helsinki Conference on Security and Cooperation in Europe adopts Helsinki Final Act.

U.N. adopts Convention on Rights of Disabled Persons.

Congress passes Age Discrimination Act of 1975.

1976   Congress over-rides a presidential veto and passes legislation amending the Foreign Assistance Act of 1961 to require an annual human rights report and Coordinator of Human Rights at the State Department (later to become the Assistant Secretary for the Bureau of Democracy, Human Rights and Labor).

Congress passes Foreign Sovereign Immunity Act ("FSIA"), 28 USC SEC 1330 etc., 1602–1611.

U.S. Supreme Court decides *Gregg v Georgia*, finding state death penalty constitutional under 8th amendment, and setting two necessary criteria. Executions resume in U.S.

1977   U.S. signs American Convention on Human Rights, ICCPR (ratifies 1992) and ICESCR.

1978   U.S. Supreme Court rules in *California v Bakke* limiting affirmative action.

1979   U.N. adopts Convention on the Elimination of All Forms of Discrimination Against Women (CEDAW enters into force 1981).

U.S. signs U.N. Convention Against the Taking of Hostages (ratifies 1984).

1980   U.S. signs Convention on Elimination of Discrimination of Women ("CEDAW").

        Filartiga v Pena-Irala ruled U.S. District Courts could decide cases of human right violations ("torts in violation of international law") by aliens against other aliens found in U.S.

1981   Organization for African Unity (OAU) adopts African Charter on Human and People's Rights.

        U.N. adopts Declaration on the Elimination of All Forms of Intolerance Based on Religion or Belief.

1984   U.N. adopts Convention Against Torture and Other Cruel, Inhuman or Degrading Treatment or Punishment ("CAT") (enters into force 1987).

1986   Congress overrides presidential veto and places economic sanctions on South Africa.

        U.N. adopts Declaration on the Right to Development.

1988   U.S. signs UN Torture Convention (ratifies 1994) and ratifies UN Genocide Convention.

        Congress passes Civil rights Restoration Act over President Ronald Reagan's veto.

        U.S. Supreme Court in *Thompson v Oklahoma* finds that capital punishment on those 15 or under is unconstitutional.

1989   U.N. adopts Convention on the Rights of the Child (CRC enters into force 1990) and the Second Optional Protocol to the ICCPR regarding the death penalty (enters into force 1991).

        U.S. Supreme Court rules in *Sanford v Kentucky* allowing capital punishment of children 16 and over when crime committed.

1990   Congress passes Americans with Disabilities Act.

        U.N. adopts International Convention on the Rights of All Migrant Workers and members of Their Families (enters into force 2003).

1991   U.S. signs Refugee Convention and ratifies Abolition of Forced Labor Convention.

1992   U.N. General Assembly adopts Declaration on the Rights of Persons Belonging to National or Ethnic, Religious or Linguistic Minorities.

1993   U.N. Security Council establishes the International Criminal Tribunal for the Former Yugoslavia.

        Second World Conference on Human Rights adopts Vienna Declaration and Programme of Action.

        U.N. General Assembly establishes the Office of the High Commissioner for Human Rights.

        President Bill Clinton institutes "Don't Ask, Don't Tell" policy regarding homosexuals in military services.

1994   U.N. Security Council establishes the International Criminal Tribunal for Rwanda.

1995   U.S. signs CRC.

        Fourth World Conference on Women occurs in Beijing.

1996   Anti-terrorism and Effective Death Penalty Act, 28 USC Sec. 1605, creates exception to TVPA, allows civil suits by Americans against state sponsors of terrorism causing torture or extrajudicial killing.

1998   Diplomatic Conference on the Establishment of the International Criminal Court adopts Rome Statute Establishing an International Criminal Court (enters into force 2002).

        U.S. signs International Convention for the Suppression of Terrorist Bombing (ratified 2002).

        Congress passes the International Religious Freedom Act.

1999   U.S. ratifies Convention Concerning the Prohibition and Immediate Action for the Elimination of the Worst Forms of Child Labor (entered into force 2000).

2000   U.S. signs Rome Statute of the ICC ("unsigned" in 2001 by President Bush), International Convention for the Suppression of the Financing of Terrorism (ratified 2002), Optional Protocol to the CRC related to children in armed conflict (ratified 2002), UN Convention Against Transnational Crime and its Protocol to Prevent, Suppress and Punish Trafficking in Persons and Protocol Against the Smuggling of Migrants.

        Congress passes the Religious Land Use and Institutionalized Persons Act (RLUIPA).

2001   World Conference Against Racism, Racial Discrimination, Xenophobia and Related Intolerance takes place in South Africa and produces The Durban Declaration and Programme of Action; the U.S. walks out.

        Terrorist attack World Trade Center in New York, President George W. Bush declares "War on Terror."

        Congress passes PATRIOT Act.

2002   U.S. ratifies First Optional Protocol to the CRC related to child soldiers and Second Optional Protocol to CRC related to Child Trafficking and Pornography.

Supreme Court rules in *Atkins v Virginia*, that capital punishment of mentally ill is unconstitutional.

Congress passes American Serviceman's Protection Act.

U.S. opens Guantánamo Bay Detention Camp for suspected terrorist detainees.

2003   U.N. International Convention on the Protection of the Rights of All Migrant Workers and Members of Their Families enters into force. U.S. has not signed as of October 2010.

Iraq Abu Ghraib Prison scandal by U.S. soldiers and CIA breaks and is investigated.

2004   U.S. Supreme Court in *Rasul v Bush* rules that U.S. District Courts have jurisdiction to determine legality of detention of non citizen Guantánamo "enemy combatant" detainees.

U.S. Supreme Court in *Hamdi v Rumsfeld* rules that U.S. citizen enemy combatant in Guantánamo has right to challenge detention before an impartial judge.

2005   U.S. Supreme Court in *Roper v Simmons*, overturning *Stanford v Kentucky*, rules that all capital punishment of juveniles is unconstitutional.

U.N. Security Council adopts resolution referring Sudan to the International Criminal Court for human rights crimes in Darfur.

2006   U.N. Secretary General Kofi Annan leads an effort to reform Human Rights Commission.

U.N. adopts Convention on the Rights of Persons With Disabilities and International Convention for the Protection of All Persons from Enforced Disappearances.

U.S. Supreme Court rules in *Hamdan v Rumsfeld* that military commission set up to try Guantánamo detainees lacked authority to do because of structure and procedure.

2007   UN Human Rights Council established to replace former Commission; U.S. voted against its establishment and withdraws from Council.

U.N. adopts Declaration on the Rights of Indigenous Peoples.

2009   U.S. issues "Human Rights Pledge" and seeks seat on U.N. Human Rights Council; is elected a member.

U.S. signs Convention on the Rights of Persons with Disabilities.

U.N. World Conference Against Racism or Durban II is held in Geneva.

2010   Secretary Clinton announces Obama Administration's four point Human Rights Policy.

U.S. Supreme Court rules in *Samantar v Yousuf* that FSIA does not provide immunity defense to individual torturers from a civil case in U.S. Federal court.

Supreme Court rules in *Graham v Florida* prohibiting juvenile Life Without Possibility of Parole Sentences for non capital offenses.

Congress passes Patient Protection and Affordable Care Act.

U.S. undergoes first Universal Periodic Review in U.N. Human Rights Council.

U.S. Supreme Court hears *Skinner v Switzer*, regarding death row inmate recourse to federal civil rights law to obtain DNA testing from state.

Assembly of States Parties to the International Criminal Court, with U.S. input, establishes the definition of the international crime of aggression for ICC jurisdictional purposes.

U.S. deals with issues of Ground Zero Mosque and threatened burning of Koran.

2011   U.S. completes Universal Periodic Review procedure by U.N. Human Rights Council by HRC vote adopting final Outcome Report.

APPENDIX B: UNIVERSAL DECLARATION OF HUMAN RIGHTS ALTERNATIVE FORMS

Two alternative versions of the Universal Declaration of Human Rights—Children's (Plain Language) Version and Simplified Version. Each of these alternative versions are presented in language and format that is simpler and more accessible than the complete document (Document 6).

A. Children's Plain Language Version of the Universal Declaration of Human Rights

1. When children are born, they are free and each should be treated in the same way. They have reason and conscience and should act towards one another in a friendly manner.
2. Everyone can claim the following rights, despite
   - a different sex
   - a different skin colour
   - speaking a different language
   - thinking different things
   - believing in another religion
   - owning more or less
   - being born in another social group
   - coming from another country
   It also makes no difference whether the country you live in is independent or not.
3. You have the right to live, and to live in freedom and safety
4. Nobody has the right to treat you as his her slave and you should not make anyone your slave.
5. Nobody has the right to torture you.
6. You should be legally protected in the same way everywhere, and like everyone else.
7. The law is the same for everyone; it should be applied in the same way to all.
8. You should be able to ask for legal help when the rights your country grants you are not respected.
9. Nobody has the right to put you in prison, to keep you there, or to send you away from your country unjustly, or without good reason.
10. If you go on trial this should be done in public. The people who try you should not let themselves be influenced by others.
11. You should be considered innocent until it can be proved that you are guilty. If you are accused of a crime, you should always have the right to defend yourself. Nobody has the right to condemn you and punish you for something you have not done.
12. You have the right to ask to be protected if someone tries to harm your good name, enter your house, open your letters, or bother you or your family without a good reason.
13. You have the right to come and go as you wish within your country. You have the right to leave your country to go to another one; and you should be able to return to your country if you want.
14. If someone hurts you, you have the right to go to another country and ask it to protect you. You lose this right if you have killed someone and if you, yourself, do not respect what is written here.
15. You have the right to belong to a country and nobody can prevent you, without a good reason, from belonging country if you wish.
16. As soon as person is legally entitled, he or she has the right to marry and have a family. In doing this, neither the colour of your skin, the country you come from nor your region should be impediments. Men and women have the same rights when they are married and also when they are separated. Nobody should force a person to marry.
    The government of your country should protect your family and its members.
17. You have the right to own things and nobody has the right to take these from you without a good reason.
18. You have the right to profess your religion freely, to change it, and to practise it either on your own or with other people.
19. You have the right to think what you want, to say what you like, and nobody should forbid you from doing so. You should be able to share your ideas also—with people from any other country.

20. You have the right to organize peaceful meetings or to take part in meetings in a peaceful way. It is wrong to force someone to belong to a group.
21. You have the right to take part in your country's political affairs either by belonging to the government yourself or by choosing politicians who have the same ideas as you. Governments should be voted for regularly and voting should be secret. You should get a vote and all votes should be equal. You also have the same right to join the public service as anyone else.
22. The society in which you live should help you to develop and to make the most of all the advantages (culture, work, social welfare) which are offered to you and to you and to all the men and women in your country.
23. You have the right to work, to be free to choose your work, to get a salary which allows you to support your family. If a man and a woman do the same work, they should get the same pay. All people who work have the right to join together to defend their interests.
24. Each workday should not be too long, since everyone has the right to rest and should be able to take regular paid holidays.
25. You have the right to have whatever you need so that you and your family: do not fall ill; go hungry; have clothes and a house; and are helped if you are out of work, if you are ill, if you are old, if your wife or husband is dead, or if you do not earn a living for any other reason you cannot help. The mother who is going is going to have a baby, and her baby should get special help. All children have the same rights, whether or not the mother is married.
26. You have the right to go to school and everyone should go to school. Primary schooling should be free. You should be able to learn a profession or continue your studies as far as wish. At school, you should be able to develop all your talents and you should be taught to get on with others, whatever their race, religion or the country they come from. Your parents have the right to choose how and what you will be taught at school.
27. You have the right to share in your community's arts and sciences, and any good they do. Your works as an artist, writer, or a scientist should be protected, and you should be able to benefit from them.
28. So that your rights will be respected, there must be an 'order' which can protect them. This 'order' should be local and worldwide.
29. You have duties towards the community within which your personality can only fully develop. The law should guarantee human rights. It should allow everyone to respect others and to be respected.
30. In all parts of the world, no society, no human being, should take it upon her or himself to act in such a way as to destroy the rights which you have just been reading about.

(This plain language version is only given as a guide. For an exact rendering of each principle, refer students to the original. This version is based in part on the translation of a text, prepared in 1978, for the World Association for the School as an Instrument of Peace, by a Research Group of the University of Geneva, under the responsibility of Prof. L. Massarenti. In preparing the translation, the Group used a basic vocabulary of 2,500 words in use in the French-speaking part of Switzerland. Teachers may adopt this methodology by translating the text of the Universal Declaration in the language in use in their region.)

This is not an official text.
Source: United Nations Cyber School Bus http://www.un.org/cyberschoolbus/humanrights/resources/plain.asp

B. Simplified Version of the Universal Declaration of Human Rights
Summary of Preamble
The General Assembly recognizes that the inherent dignity and the equal and inalienable rights of all members of the human family is the foundation of freedom, justice and peace in the world, human rights should be protected by the rule of law, friendly relations between nations must be fostered, the peoples of the UN have affirmed their faith in human rights, the dignity and the worth of the human person, the equal rights of men and women and are determined to promote social progress, better standards of life and larger freedom and have promised to promote human rights and a common understanding of these rights.

A summary of the Universal Declaration of Human Rights

1. Everyone is free and we should all be treated in the same way.
2. Everyone is equal despite differences in skin colour, sex, religion, language for example.
3. Everyone has the right to life and to live in freedom and safety.
4. No one has the right to treat you as a slave nor should you make anyone your slave.
5. No one has the right to hurt you or to torture you.
6. Everyone has the right to be treated equally by the law.
7. The law is the same for everyone, it should be applied in the same way to all.
8. Everyone has the right to ask for legal help when their rights are not respected.
9. No one has the right to imprison you unjustly or expel you from your own country.
10. Everyone has the right to a fair and public trial.
11. Everyone should be considered innocent until guilt is proved.
12. Every one has the right to ask for help if someone tries to harm you, but no-one can enter your home, open your letters or bother you or your family without a good reason.
13. Everyone has the right to travel as they wish.
14. Everyone has the right to go to another country and ask for protection if they are being persecuted or are in danger of being persecuted.
15. Everyone has the right to belong to a country. No one has the right to prevent you from belonging to another country if you wish to.
16. Everyone has the right to marry and have a family.
17. Everyone has the right to own property and possessions.
18. Everyone has the right to practise and observe all aspects of their own religion and change their religion if they want to.
19. Everyone has the right to say what they think and to give and receive information.
20. Everyone has the right to take part in meetings and to join associations in a peaceful way.
21. Everyone has the right to help choose and take part in the government of their country.
22. Everyone has the right to social security and to opportunities to develop their skills.
23. Everyone has the right to work for a fair wage in a safe environment and to join a trade union.
24. Everyone has the right to rest and leisure.
25. Everyone has the right to an adequate standard of living and medical help if they are ill.
26. Everyone has the right to go to school.
27. Everyone has the right to share in their community's cultural life.
28. Everyone must respect the 'social order' that is necessary for all these rights to be available.
29. Everyone must respect the rights of others, the community and public property.
30. No one has the right to take away any of the rights in this declaration.

This is not an official text.
Source: HREA.org, from Resource Centre: *First Steps: A manual for starting human rights education*
http://www.hrea.org/index.php?base_id=104&language_id=1&erc_doc_id=5211&category_id=24&category_type=3&group=

Appendix C: Charts of the U.N. System for the Promotion and Observance of Human Rights

This Appendix includes nine elements that show the structure of the United Nations, and its human rights bodies and procedures. This information is important because most of the U.S. human rights activity in the international context happens in the institutional context of the United Nations, especially U.N. Human Rights Council. This Appendix includes:

A. U.N. Organogram

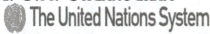

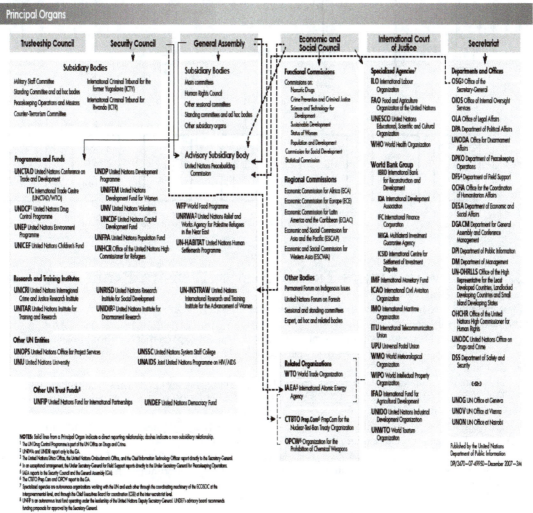

B. CHART ON HUMAN RIGHTS TREATY BODIES

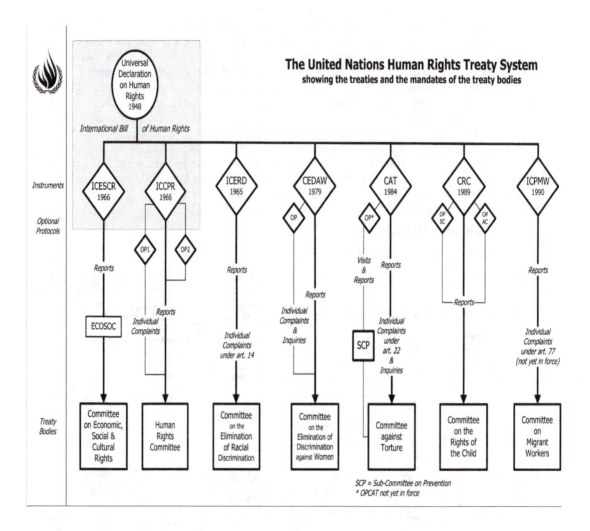

The United Nations Human Rights Treaty System
showing the treaties and the mandates of the treaty bodies

SCP = Sub-Committee on Prevention
* OPCAT not yet in force

C. U.N. HUMAN RIGHTS TREATY SYSTEM WEBSITE PAGE

Human Rights Treaty Bodies

Monitoring the core international human rights treaties

What are the treaty bodies?

The human rights treaty bodies are committees of independent experts that monitor implementation of the core international human rights treaties. They are created in accordance with the provisions of the treaty that they monitor.

There are nine human rights treaty bodies and the Subcommittee on Prevention of Torture (SPT):

The Human Rights Committee (CCPR) monitors implementation of the International Covenant on Civil and Political Rights (1966) and its optional protocols;

The Committee on Economic, Social and Cultural Rights (CESCR) monitors implementation of the International Covenant on Economic, Social and Cultural Rights (1966);

The Committee on the Elimination of Racial Discrimination (CERD) monitors implementation of the International Convention on the Elimination of All Forms of Racial Discrimination (1965);

The Committee on the Elimination of Discrimination Against Women (CEDAW) monitors implementation of the Convention on the Elimination of All Forms of Discrimination against Women (1979) and its optional protocol (1999);

The Committee Against Torture (CAT) monitors implementation of the Convention against Torture and Other Cruel, Inhuman or Degrading Treatment (1984);

The Committee on the Rights of the Child (CRC) monitors implementation of the Convention on the Rights of the Child (1989) and its optional protocols (2000); and

The Committee on Migrant Workers (CMW) monitors implementation of the International Convention on the Protection of the Rights of All Migrant Workers and Members of Their Families (1990).

The Committee on the Right of Persons with Disabilities (CRPD) monitors implementation of the International Convention on the Rights of Persons with Disabilities (2006).

The Committee on Enforced Disappearance (CED) monitors implementation of the International Convention for the Protection of All Persons from Enforced Disappearance (2006)

Each treaty body receives secretariat support from the Human Rights Treaties Branch of OHCHR in Geneva. CEDAW, which was suppported until 31 December 2007 by the Division for the Advancement of Women (DAW), meets once a year in New York at United Nations Headquarters. Similarly, the Human Rights Committee usually holds its session in March/April in New York. The other treaty bodies meet in Geneva, either at Palais Wilson or Palais des Nations.

What do the treaty bodies do?

The treaty bodies perform a number of functions in accordance with the provisions of the treaties that created them. These include:

- Consideration of State parties' reports
- Consideration of individual complaints or communications

They also publish general comments on the treaties and organize discussions on related themes.

Consideration of State parties' reports

When a country ratifies one of these treaties, it assumes a legal obligation to implement the rights recognized in that treaty. But signing up is only the first step, because recognition of rights on paper is not sufficient to guarantee that they will be enjoyed in practice. So the country incurs an additional obligation to submit regular reports to the monitoring committee set up under that treaty on how the rights are being implemented. This system of human rights monitoring is common to most of the UN human rights treaties.

To meet their reporting obligation, States must report submit an initial report usually one year after joining (two years in the case of the CRC) and then periodically in accordance with the provisions of the treaty (usually every four or five years). In addition to the government report, the treaty bodies may receive information on a country's human rights situation from other sources, including non-governmental organizations, UN agencies, other intergovernmental organizations, academic institutions and the press. In the light of all the information available, the Committee examines the report together with government representatives. Based on this dialogue, the Committee publishes its concerns and recommendations, referred to as "concluding observations".

Consideration of individual complaints or communications

In addition to the reporting procedure, some of the treaty bodies may perform additional monitoring functions through three other mechanisms: the inquiry procedure, the examination of inter-state complaints and the examination of individual complaints.

Four of the Committees (CCPR, CERD, CAT and CEDAW) can, under certain conditions, receive petitions from individuals who claim that their rights under the treaties have been violated. More information.

General Comments

The Committees also publish their interpretation of the content of human rights provisions, known as general comments on thematic issues or methods of work.

Meeting of chairpersons and inter-committee meeting

The treaty bodies coordinate their activities through the annual meeting of chairpersons of human rights treaty bodies and through the inter-committee meeting. More information.

The treaty body are continually seeking ways to enhance their effectiveness through streamlining and harmonization of working methods and practices. More information on treaty body reform.

Source: U.N. Office of the High Commissioner for Human Rights
http://www.ohchr.org/en/hrbodies/Pages/HumanRightsBodies.aspx

APPENDIX C

D. OTHER U.N. BODIES DEALING WITH HUMAN RIGHTS
Other United Nations Bodies

Other UN bodies and entities involved in human rights promotion and protection
There are several other important United Nations bodies which are concerned with the promotion and protection of human rights. These bodies are not serviced by OHCHR and include:
United Nations General Assembly Third Committee of the General Assembly Economic and Social Council International Court of Justice
Find Further information about the promotion and protection of human rights on the UN website.
Many United Nations agencies and partners are also involved in the promotion and protection of human rights and interact with the main human rights bodies:

- United Nations High Commissioner for Refugees (UNHCR)
- Office for the Coordination of Humanitarian Affairs (OCHA)
- Inter-Agency Internal Displacement Division
- International Labour Organization
- World Health Organization
- United Nations Educational, Scientific and Cultural Organization (UNESCO)
- Joint United Nations Programme on HIV/AIDS (UNAIDS)
- Inter-Agency Standing Committee (IASC)
- DESA (Department of Economic and Social Affairs)
- Commission on the Status of Women (CSW)
- Office of the Special Adviser on Gender Issues and the Advancement of Women (OSAGI)
- Division for the Advancement of Women (DAW)
- United Nations Population Fund (UNFPA)
- United Nations Children's Fund (UNICEF)
- United Nations Development Fund for Women (UNIFEM)
- United Nations Development Programme (UNDP)
- Food and Agriculture Organization of the United Nations (FAO)
- United Nations Human Settlements Programme (HABITAT)
- United Nations Mine Action

Source: http://www.ohchr.org/EN/HRBodies/Pages/OtherUnitedNationsBodies.aspx

E. HUMAN RIGHTS COUNCIL SPECIAL PROCEDURES (WEBSITE GENERAL INFORMATION—EXCERPTED AND REFORMATTED)
The reader must check with U.N. website below for up-to-date changes in the mandates. They are subject to change.
Source: http://www2.ohchr.org/english/bodies/chr/special/index.htm

Special Procedures
Introduction
Coordination Committee of Special Procedures
Nominations / Public List of Candidates for Special Procedures Mandates
Code of conduct
Contact
Mandates
Country mandates
Thematic mandates
List of all special procedures mandate holders
Activities
Communications Country visits

Special Procedures of the Human Rights Council

United Nations Special Procedures Facts and Figures 2009
English—French—Spanish

"Special procedures" is the general name given to the mechanisms established by the Commission on Human Rights and assumed by the Human Rights Council to address either specific country situations or thematic issues in all parts of the world. Currently, there are 31 thematic and 8 country mandates. The Office of the High Commissioner for Human Rights provides these mechanisms with personnel, policy, research and logistical support for the discharge of their mandates.

Special procedures' mandates usually call on mandate holders to examine, monitor, advise and publicly report on human rights situations in specific countries or territories, known as country mandates, or on major phenomena of human rights violations worldwide, known as thematic mandates. Various activities are undertaken by special procedures, including responding to individual complaints, conducting studies, providing advice on technical cooperation at the country level, and engaging in general promotional activities.

Special procedures are either an individual (called "Special Rapporteur", "Special Representative of the Secretary-General" or "Independent Expert") or a working group usually composed of five members (one from each region). The mandates of the special procedures are established and defined by the resolution creating them. Mandate-holders of the special procedures serve in their personal capacity, and do not receive salaries or any other financial compensation for their work. The independent status of the mandate-holders is crucial in order to be able to fulfill their functions in all impartiality. (See Fact sheet N.27 - under revision).

Most Special Procedures receive information on specific allegations of human rights violations and send urgent appeals or letters of allegation to governments asking for clarification. In 2008, a total of 911 communications were sent to Governments in 118 countries. 66% of these were joint communications of two or more mandate holders.

Mandate holders also carry out country visits to investigate the situation of human rights at the national level. They typically send a letter to the Government requesting to visit the country, and, if the Government agrees, an invitation to visit is extended. Some countries have issued "standing invitations", which means that they are, in principle, prepared to receive a visit from any special procedures mandate holder. As of 30 June 2010, 73 States had extended standing invitations to the special procedures. After their visits, special procedures' mandate-holders issue a mission report containing their findings and recommendations.

Starting June 2006, the Human Rights Council engaged in an institution building process, which included a review of the special procedures system. On 18 June 2007, at the conclusion of its fifth session, the Human Rights Council adopted a Resolution 5/1 entitled "Institution-building of the United Nations Human Rights Council," which included provisions on the selection of mandate holders and the review of all special procedures mandates. The review was conducted throughout 2007 and 2008. All thematic mandates were extended. New thematic mandates have also been established, namely on contemporary forms of slavery (2007), on access to safe drinking water and sanitation (2008) and on cultural rights (2009). Country mandates have been extended with the exception of Belarus, Cuba, the Democratic Republic of the Congo and Liberia. At its 11th session, the Human Right Council created the mandate of independent expert on the situation of human rights in the Sudan which replaced a previous country mandate, for a period of one year. The independent expert was appointed at the 12th session of the Human Rights Council. A mandate-holder's tenure in a given function, whether it is a thematic or country mandate, will be no longer than six years (two terms of three years for thematic mandate-holders).

In June 2007, the Council also adopted Resolution 5/2, containing a Code of Conduct for special procedures mandate holders. At the Annual Meeting of special procedures in June 2008, special procedures mandate holders adopted their Manual, which provides guidelines on the working methods of special procedures. At the same meeting, they also adopted an Internal Advisory Procedure to review practices and working methods, which allows any stakeholder to bring issues relating to working methods and conduct to the attention of the Coordination Committee. The procedure was devised to enhance the independence and effectiveness of special procedures and cooperation by States, and to contribute to the self-regulation of the special procedures system and of individual mandate-holders. At its 8th session, the Human Rights Council adopted a <u>Presidential statement</u> concerning the terms of special procedures mandate holders and their compliance with the Code of Conduct.

Special Procedures reports to the Human Rights Council

Manual of the United Nations Human Rights Special Procedures
English (Word 247 kb) <u>French</u> (181 kb)   <u>Spanish</u> (Word 159 kb)

F. HUMAN RIGHTS COUNCIL SPECIAL PROCEDURES: SPECIAL RAPPORTEURS

Thematic mandates change from time to time. Be sure to update at:
http://www2.ohchr.org/english/bodies/chr/special/themes.htm

Special Procedures assumed by the Human Rights Council

Thematic mandates

(Updated on 1 November 2010)

Title / Mandate	Mandate established		Mandate extended		Name & country of origin of the mandate-holder(s)	Contact us
	in	by	in	by		
Special Rapporteur on <u>adequate housing</u> as a component of the right to an adequate standard of living, and on the right to non-discrimination in this context	2000	Commission on Human Rights resolution 2000/9	2007	Human Rights Council resolution <u>15/8</u>	Ms. Raquel **ROLNIK** (*Brazil*)	srhousing@ ohchr.org
Working Group on people of <u>African descent</u>	2002	Commission on Human Rights resolution 2002/68	2008	Human Rights Council resolution <u>9/14</u>	• Ms. Maya **SAHLI** (*Algeria*) • Ms. Monorama Biswas (*Bangladesh*) • Ms. Verene **SHEPHERD** (*Jamaica*) • Mr. Linos-Alexandros **SICILIANOS**, (*Greece*) • Ms. Mirjana Najcevska Chairperson-Rapporteur (*The Former Yugoslav Republic of Macedonia*)	african descent@ ohchr.org

Title / Mandate	Mandate established		Mandate extended		Name & country of origin of the mandate-holder(s)	Contact us
	in	by	in	by		
Working Group on <u>Arbitrary Detention</u>	1991	Commission on Human Rights resolution 1991/42	2010	Human Rights Council resolution <u>15/18</u>	• Mr. El Hadji Malick SOW (*Senegal*) Chair-Rapporteur • Ms. Shaheen Sardar ALI (*Pakistan*) Vice-Chair • Mr. Roberto GARRETON (*Chile*) • Mr. Vladimir TOCHILOVSKY (*Ukraine*) • Mr. Mads ANDENAS (*Norway*)	<u>wgad@ ohchr.org</u>
Special Rapporteur on the <u>sale of children</u>, child prostitution and child pornography	1990	Commission on Human Rights resolution 1990/68	2008	Human Rights Council resolution <u>7/13</u>	Ms. Najat M'jid MAALLA (*Morocco*)	<u>srsaleof children@ ohchr.org</u>
Independent Expert in the field of <u>cultural rights</u>	2009	Human Rights Council resolution <u>10/23</u>			Ms. Farida Shaheed (*Pakistan*)	<u>iecultur alrights@ ohchr.org</u>
Special Rapporteur on the right to <u>education</u>	1998	Commission on Human Rights resolution 1998/33	2008	Human Rights Council resolution <u>8/4</u>	Mr. Kishore SINGH (*India*)	<u>sreducation@ ohchr.org</u>
Working Group on <u>Enforced or Involuntary Disappearances</u>	1980	Commission on Human Rights resolution 20 (XXXVI)	2007	Human Rights Council resolution <u>7/12</u>	• Mr. Jeremy SARKIN (*South Africa*) Chairperson-Rapporteur • Mr. Ariel DULITZKY (*Argentina/United States of America*) • Ms. Jazminka DZUMHUR (*Bosnia and Herzegovina*)	<u>wgeid@ ohchr.org</u>

(Continued)

Title / Mandate	Mandate established		Mandate extended		Name & country of origin of the mandate-holder(s)	Contact us
	in	by	in	by		
					• Mr. Olivier de FROUVILLE *(France)* • Mr. Osman EL-HAJJE *(Lebanon)*	
Special Rapporteur on <u>extrajudicial, summary or arbitrary executions</u>	1982	Commission on Human Rights resolution 1982/35	2008	Human Rights Council resolution <u>8/3</u>	**Mr. Christof HEYNS** *(South Africa)*	eje@ohchr.org
Independent Expert on the question of human rights and <u>extreme poverty</u>	1998	Commission on Human Rights resolution 1998/25	2008	Human Rights Council resolution <u>8/11</u>	**Ms. Maria Magdalena SEPÚLVEDA CARMONA** *(Chile)*	ieextreme-poverty@ohchr.org
Special Rapporteur on the right to <u>food</u>	2000	Commission on Human Rights resolution 2000/10	2010	Human Rights Council resolution <u>13/4</u>	**Mr. Olivier de SCHUTTER** *(Belgium)*	srfood@ohchr.org
Independent expert on the effects of <u>foreign debt</u> and other related international financial obligations of States on the full enjoyment of human rights, particularly economic, social and cultural rights	2000	Commission on Human Rights resolution 2000/82	2008	Human Rights Council resolution <u>7/4</u>	**Mr. Cephas LUMINA** *(Zambia)*	ieforeign debt@ohchr.org
Special Rapporteur on the rights to freedom of peaceful assembly and of association	2010	Human Rights Council resolution <u>15/21</u>			Mandate holder to be appointed during the sixteenth session of the Human Rights Council (March 2011)	

Title / Mandate	Mandate established		Mandate extended		Name & country of origin of the mandate-holder(s)	Contact us
	in	by	in	by		
Special Rapporteur on the promotion and protection of the right to freedom of opinion and expression	1993	Commission on Human Rights resolution 1993/45	2008	Human Rights Council resolution 7/36	Mr. Frank La Rue (Guatemala)	freedex@ohchr.org
Special Rapporteur on freedom of religion or belief	1986	Commission on Human Rights resolution 1986/20	2010	Human Rights Council resolution 14/11	Mr. Heiner BIELEFELDT (Germany)	freedomof religion@ ohchr.org
Special Rapporteur on the right of everyone to the enjoyment of the highest attainable standard of physical and mental health	2002	Commission on Human Rights resolution 2002/31	2007	Human Rights Council resolution 15/22http://ap.ohchr.org/Documents/E/HRC/resolutions/A HRC RES_6_29.pdf	Mr. Anand GROVER (India)	srhealth@ohchr.org
Special Rapporteur on the situation of human rights defenders	2000	Commission on Human Rights resolution 2000/61	2008	Human Rights Council resolution 7/8	Ms. Margaret SEKAGGYA (Uganda)	defenders@ohchr.orgurgent-action@ohchr.org
Special Rapporteur on the independence of judges and lawyers	1994	Commission on Human Rights resolution 1994/41	2008	Human Rights Council resolution 8/6	Ms. Gabriela KNAUL (Brazil)	srindependencejl@ohchr.org
Special Rapporteur on the situation of human rights and fundamental freedoms of indigenous people	2001	Commission on Human Rights resolution 2001/57	2007	Human Rights Council resolution 15/14	Mr. James ANAYA (United States of America)	indigenous@ohchr.org

Title / Mandate	Mandate established		Mandate extended		Name & country of origin of the mandate-holder(s)	Contact us
	in	by	in	by		
Special Rapporteur on the human rights of <u>internally displaced persons</u>	2004	Commission on Human Rights resolution 2004/55	2010	Human Rights Council resolution <u>14/6</u>	**Mr.Chaloka BEYANI** (*Zambia*)	<u>idp@ohchr.org</u>
Working Group on the use of <u>mercenaries</u> as a means of impeding the exercise of the right of peoples to self-determination	2005	Commission on Human Rights resolution 2005/2	2008	Human Rights Council resolution <u>15/12</u>	• **Ms. Faiza PATEL** (*Pakistan*) • **Mr. Alexander Ivanovich NIKITIN** (*Russian Federation*) : • **Mr. José GÓMEZ DEL PRADO** (*Spain*) • **Ms. Najat AL-HAJJAJI** (*Libyan Arab Jamahiriya*) • **Ms. Amada BENAVIDES DE PÉREZ** (*Colombia*)	<u>mercenaries@ohchr.org</u>
Special Rapporteur on the human rights of <u>migrants</u>	1999	Commission on Human Rights resolution 1999/44	2008	Human Rights Council resolution <u>8/10</u>	**Mr. Jorge A. BUSTAMANTE** (*Mexico*)	<u>migrant@ohchr.org</u>
Independent Expert on <u>minority issues</u>	2005	Commission on Human Rights resolution 2005/79	2008	Human Rights Council resolution <u>7/6</u>	**Ms. Gay MCDOUGALL** (*United States of America*)	<u>minorityissues@ohchr.org</u>
Special Rapporteur on contemporary forms of <u>racism</u>, racial discrimination, xenophobia and related intolerance	1993	Commission on Human Rights resolution 1993/20	2008	Human Rights Council resolution <u>7/34</u>	**Mr. Githu MUIGAI** (*Kenya*)	<u>racism@ohchr.org</u>

Title / Mandate	Mandate established		Mandate extended		Name & country of origin of the mandate-holder(s)	Contact us
	in	by	in	by		
Special Rapporteur on contemporary forms of slavery, including its causes and consequences	2007	Human Rights Council resolution 6/14		Human Rights Council resolution 15/2	Ms. Gulnara SHAHINIAN (*Armenia*)	srslavery@ohchr.org
Independent Expert on human rights and international solidarity	2005	Commission on Human Rights resolution 2005/55	2008	Human Rights Council resolution 7/5	Mr. Rudi Muhammad RIZKI (*Indonesia*)	iesolidarity@ohchr.org
Special Rapporteur on the promotion and protection of human rights while countering terrorism	2005	Commission on Human Rights resolution 2005/80	2007	Human Rights Council resolution 15/15	Mr. Martin SCHEININ (*Finland*)	srct@ohchr.org
Special Rapporteur on torture and other cruel, inhuman or degrading treatment or punishment	1985	Commission on Human Rights resolution 1985/33	2008	Human Rights Council resolution 8/8	Mr. Juan MENDEZ (*Argentina*)	sr-torture@ohchr.org
Special Rapporteur on the adverse effects of the movement and dumping of toxic and dangerous products and wastes on the enjoyment of human rights	1995	Commission on Human Rights resolution 1995/81	2008	Human Rights Council resolution 9/1	Mr. Calin GEORGESCU (*Romania*)	srtox icwaste@ohchr.org
Special Rapporteur on trafficking in persons, especially in women and children	2004	Commission on Human Rights resolution 2004/110	2008	Human Rights Council resolution 8/12	Ms. Joy Ngozi EZEILO (*Nigeria*)	srtraffiking@ohchr.org

Title / Mandate	Mandate established		Mandate extended		Name & country of origin of the mandate-holder(s)	Contact us
	in	by	in	by		
Special Representative of the SG on human rights and transnational corporations and other business enterprises	2005	Commission on Human Rights resolution 2005/69	2008	Human Rights Council resolution 8/7	**Mr. John RUGGIE** (*United States of America*)	lwendland@ ohchr.org
Independent Expert on the issue of human rights obligations related to access to safe drinking water and sanitation	2008	Human Rights Council resolution 7/22			**Ms. Catarina de ALBUQUERQUE** (*Portugal*)	iewater@ ohchr.org
Working Group on the issue of discrimination against women in law and in practice	2010	Human Rights Council resolution 15/23			**Members to be appointed during the sixteenth session of the Human Rights Council (March 2011)**	
Special Rapporteur on violence against women, its causes and consequences	1994	Commission on Human Rights resolution 1994/45	2008	Human Rights Council resolution 7/24	**Ms. Rashida MANJOO** (*South Africa*)	vaw@ohchr. org

G. Human Rights Council Special Procedures: Country Specific Mandates

Country Mandates change from time to time. Be sure to update at:
http://www2.ohchr.org/english/bodies/chr/special/countries.htm

Special Procedures assumed by the Human Rights Council

Country mandates

1 August 2010

Title / Mandate	Mandate established		Mandate extended		Name & country of origin of the mandate-holder	Contact us
	in	by	in	by		
Independent Expert on the situation of human rights in <u>Burundi</u>	2004	Commission on Human Rights resolution 2004/82	2008	Human Rights Council resolution 9/19 (until establishment of an independent national human rights commission)	Mr. Fatsah **OUGUERGOUZ** (Algeria)	
Special Rapporteur on human rights in <u>Cambodia</u>	1993	Commission on Human Rights resolution 1993/6	2009	Human Rights Council resolution 12/25 (for 1 year)	Mr. Surya Prasad **SUBEDI** (Nepal)	
Special Rapporteur on the situation of human rights in the <u>Democratic People's Republic of Korea</u>	2004	Commission on Human Rights resolution 2004/13 (duration of mandate not specified)	2010	Human Rights Council resolution 13/14 (for 1 year)	Mr. Marzuki **DARUSMAN** (Indonesia)	hr-dprk@ohchr.org
Independent Expert on the situation of human rights in <u>Haiti</u>	1995	Commission on Human Rights resolution 1995/70 (duration of mandate not specified)	2008	Human Rights Council PRST/9/1	Mr. Michel **FORST** (France)	ie-haiti@ohchr.org
Special Rapporteur on the situation of human rights in <u>Myanmar</u>	1992	Commission on Human Rights resolution 1992/58	2010	Human Rights Council resolution 13/25 (for 1 year)	Mr. Tomás **OJEA QUINTANA** (Argentina)	sr-myanmar@ohchr.org

(Continued)

Title / Mandate	Mandate established		Mandate extended		Name & country of origin of the mandate-holder	Contact us
	in	by	in	by		
Special Rapporteur on the situation of human rights in the <u>Palestinian territories occupied since 1967</u>	1993	Commission on Human Rights resolution 1993/2 A (*"until the end of the Israeli occupation"*)			**Mr. Richard FALK** (*United States of America*)	sropt@ ohchr.org
Independent Expert on the situation of human rights in <u>Somalia</u>	1993	Commission on Human Rights resolution 1993/86	2009	Human Rights Council resolution <u>12/26</u> (for 1 year)	**Mr. Shamsul BARI** (*Bangladesh*)	ie-somalia@ ohchr.org
Independent Expert on the situation of human rights in the <u>Sudan</u>	2009	Human Rights Council resolution 11/10 (*for 1 year*)	2010	Human Rights Council decision 14/117 (until 15th session of HRC)	**Mr. Mohamed Chande Othman** (*Tanzania*)	sudan@ ohchr.org

H. UN HUMAN RIGHTS COMMITTEE, INTERNATIONAL COVENANT ON CIVIL AND POLITICAL RIGHTS, PROCEDURAL CHART FOR COMMUNICATIONS (COMPLAINTS)

3. International Covenant on Civil and Political Rights, Procedures

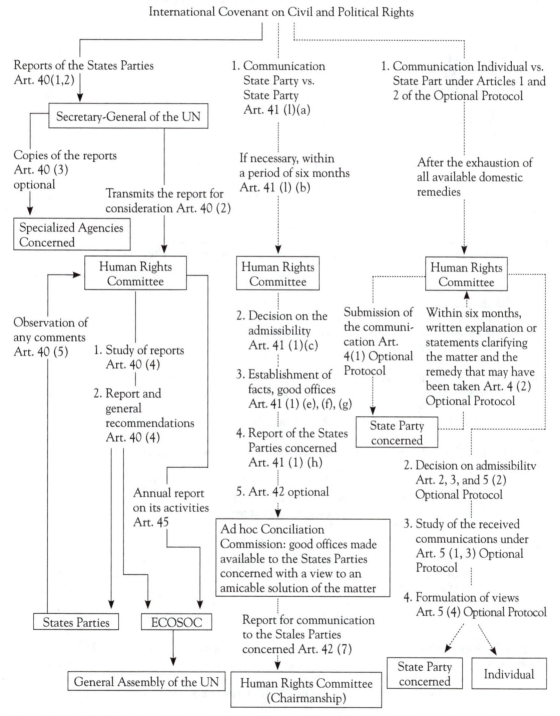

International Covenant on Civil and Political Rights

Reports of the States Parties
Art. 40(1,2)

Secretary-General of the UN

Copies of the reports
Art. 40 (3)
optional

Transmits the report for
consideration Art. 40 (2)

Specialized Agencies
Concerned

Human Rights
Committee

Observation of
any comments
Art. 40 (5)

1. Study of reports
Art. 40 (4)

2. Report and
general
recommendations
Art. 40 (4)

Annual report
on its activities
Art. 45

States Parties

ECOSOC

General Assembly of the UN

1. Communication
State Party vs.
State Party
Art. 41 (l)(a)

If necessary, within
a period of six months
Art. 41 (l) (b)

Human Rights
Committee

2. Decision on the
admissibility
Art. 41 (1)(c)

3. Establishment of
facts, good offices
Art. 41 (1) (e), (f), (g)

4. Report of the States
Parties concerned
Art. 41 (1) (h)

5. Art. 42 optional

Ad hoc Conciliation
Commission: good offices made
available to the States Parties
concerned with a view to an
amicable solution of the matter

Report for communication
to the States Parties
concerned Art. 42 (7)

Human Rights Committee
(Chairmanship)

1. Communication Individual vs.
State Part under Articles 1 and
2 of the Optional Protocol

After the exhaustion of
all available domestic
remedies

Human Rights
Committee

Submission of
the communi-
cation Art.
4(1) Optional
Protocol

Within six months,
written explanation or
statements clarifying
the matter and the
remedy that may have
been taken Art. 4 (2)
Optional Protocol

State Party
concerned

2. Decision on admissibility
Art. 2, 3, and 5 (2)
Optional Protocol

3. Study of the received
communications under
Art. 5 (1, 3) Optional
Protocol

4. Formulation of views
Art. 5 (4) Optional Protocol

State Party
concerned

Individual

I. UN Human Rights Committee Model Communication

4. Model ICCPR Complaint

U.N. Human Rights Committee Model Communication

Date: _____
Communication to:
The Human Rights Committee
c/o OHCHR-UNOG
1211 Geneva 10, Switzerland

Submitted for consideration under the Optional Protocol to the International Covenant on Civil and Political Rights.

1. Information concerning the author of the communication

Name _____ First name(s) _____
Nationality _____ Profession _____
Date and place of birth _____
Present address _____
Address for exchange of confidential correspondence (if other than present address)

_____

Submitting the communication as:
      (a) Victim of the violation or violations set forth below
      (b) Appointed representative/legal counsel of the alleged victim(s)
      (c) Other

If box (c) is marked, the author should explain:
      (i) In what capacity he is acting on behalf of the victim(s) (e.g., family relationship or other personal links with the alleged victim(s)):
      (ii) Why the victim(s) is (are) unable to submit the communication himself (themselves):

An unrelated third party having no link to the victim(s) cannot submit a communication on his (their) behalf.

II. Information concerning the alleged victim(s)
(if other than author)

Name _____ First name(s) _____
Nationality _____ Profession _____
Date and place of birth _____
Present address or whereabouts _____

III. State concerned/articles violated/domestic remedies

Name of the State party (country) to the International Covenant and the Optional Protocol against which the communication is directed: _____

Articles of the International Covenant on Civil and Political Rights allegedly violated:

_____

Steps taken by or on behalf of the alleged victim(s) to exhaust domestic remedies—recourse to the courts or other public authorities, when and with what results (if possible, enclose copies of all relevant judicial or administrative decisions):

If domestic remedies have not been exhausted, explain why:

IV. Other international procedures

Has the same matter been submitted for examination under another procedure of international investigation or settlement (e.g., the Inter-American Commission on Human Rights, the European Commission on Human Rights)? If so, when and with what results'

V. Facts of the claim

Detailed description of the facts of the alleged violation or violations (including relevant dates)*

Author's signature: _____

* Add as many pages as needed for this description.

Printed at United Nations, Geneva
May 1989

APPENDIX D: CHARTS OF THE INTERNATIONAL PROTECTION OF HUMAN RIGHTS AND HUMANITARIAN LAW

States such as the U.S, not international organizations, are the primary protectors of human rights. The international protection of human rights is a backup system in the event that the state system does not succeed in protecting and respecting human rights. This is according to the principal of subsidiarity. States are supposed to be the primary actors in the field of human rights. The international system is subsidiary to the States, who are supposed to form and operate their legislative, executive and judicial branches such that all human rights are respected and protected and all claims of violation are fully handled "at home" in the state. Sometimes states do not get it right. The international human rights system can then be called upon to address the matter because the state has voluntarily chosen to be part of the international institutional system which deals with human rights at the international level.

There exists in this world human rights legal-political systems at both the regional and global levels. There are also non legal human rights institutions in which the U.S. is involved. The most important human rights system of which the U.S. plays a part and where some of its human rights issues are dealt with is the United Nations. The U.N. human rights system sees the U.S. involved in both establishing human rights treaties and treaty bodies, the so-called "treaty based" organs, and working in or dealing with issues before U.N. "charter based" organs. The most important U.N. body in which the U.S. is involved in human rights is the Human Rights Council. In 2009 the U.S. became a member of this 47 member Council. There are many bodies at the U.N. which in some way deal with human rights and which the U.S., as members, participated in, such as the International Labor Organization . Human rights are also dealt with in the Security Council and involved in cases before the International Court of Justice.

The U.N. organogram (Appendix C) and the lists of "special mechanisms" of the Council shows the place of the U.N. Human Rights Council, under the general Assembly, and the Office of the High Commissioner for Human Rights under the Secretary General's office.

This Appendix includes four charts of human rights systems:

   This is included even though humanitarian law norms are juridically different. Some experts do not accept humanitarian law as part of the field of human rights. I recognize the historical and juridical differences between human rights law proper, and humanitarian law, and accept humanitarian law as part of the field of human rights because of its ultimate goals and objectives. There has been an increasing convergence of human rights and humanitarian law ever since the U.N. World Human Rights Conferences in 1968 and 1993. I believe that human rights law is the fulfillment of the so-called de Martens Clause found in the 1907 Hague IV Convention, which reads:

> Until a more complete code of the laws of war has been issued, the High Contracting Parties deem it expedient to declare that, in cases not included in the Regulations adopted by them, the inhabitants and the belligerents remain under the protection and the rule of the principles of the law of nations, as they result from the usages established among civilized peoples, from the laws of humanity, and the dictates of the public conscience.

   This chart of humanitarian law will show that area of international law in relations to human rights law. It is very general and does not purport to be an exact model of the existing system of international law in these areas.

   The U.S. is part of the Organization of American States regional human rights system. It is also a member of another forum called the Organization for Security and Cooperation in Europe, an international, inter-governmental political institution.

1. Inter-Governmental Organizations: Global

United Nations

Instrument: U.N. Charter

| General Assembly | Security Council | International Court Of Justice | Secretariat | ECOSOC |

ICTY/ICTR

Secretary General

Office of the High Commissioner for Human Rights

Universal Declaration of Human Rights

Vienna Declaration & Programme of Action

Treaty Based Organs
(See Appendix C, doc. G)

Human Rights Council (Charter based)

Human Rights Committee: CCPR

HRC Advisory Committee

Committee on Econ., Social and Cultural Rights: CESCR

Committee on Elimination of Discrimination Against Women: CEDAW

Special Mechanisms:

Special Rapporteurs
Special representatives
Independent Experts
Working Groups

Thematic and country based.

Committee Against Torture: CAT

Committee on the Rights of the Child: CRC

Committee on Elimination of Racial Discrimination: CERD

Complaint procedure: Gross and reliably attested violations

Committee on Migrant Workers: CPMW

Committee on Forced Disappearances: CPED

Committee on Rights of Persons with Disabilities: CDRPD

2. International Humanitarian Law in relation to Human Rights norms
   applicable during periods of armed conflict.

International Human Rights And Humanitarian Law Norm Chart

International Human Rights Law Juridical basis: inherent human dignity. (during peacetime and during armed conflict, *except for rights derogated)	International Humanitarian Law Juridical Basis: Humanitarianism. (only during armed conflict)

Universal Declaration of Human Rights

Global and regional human rights treaties, e.g. ICCPR, CAT, CERD, etc.*

And

Customary international human rights norms

Geneva Law
GC I, (Land); GC II, (Sea); GC III, (POW); GC IV, (Civilian); Prot. I; Prot. II. (protection of victims of armed conflict)

Other Treaties: Conventional Weapons, Cluster Munitions Cultural Property, ENMOD etc. (There are about 100 humanitarian law related legal instruments)

Hague Law 1899, 1907 (conduct of hostilities)

Laws and Customs of War (conduct of hostilities)

During armed conflict applicable international humanitarian law applies **and** so do all applicable human rights legal obligations, under customary law and all non derogable human rights treaty obligations, such as right to life, torture, cruel inhuman and degrading treatment or punishment, slavery, due process, freedom of religion. In addition, all derogable human rights which have not been officially derogated are also fully applicable during armed conflict, as if the case in the U.S. in 2010. The U.S. has not declared a period of derogation in the U.S. as a result of the war on terrorism as of December 2010.

STATES ARE EXPECTED TO RESPECT AND ENSURE RESPECT OF HUMANITARIAN LAW LEGAL OBLIGATIONS

Compliance is done by:

Domestic: military/legal system: Courts martial, military commissions, e.g. Army Field Manual, Doc. #106, and AFM 27-10. Suppress and Repress violations. Educate military and civilian populations (GC IV art. 144). Civil Litigation, e.g. ATCA, *see Kadic Case* in Appendix J.

International Committee of the Red Cross ("Promoter and Guardian of Humanitarian Law") monitors and reports on conflict compliance /visits detainees. HAS NO LEGAL ENFORCEMENT POWER.

Protecting Powers under GC s (e.g. GC IV art., Doc. #72)

UN General Assembly
UN Security Council
Human Rights Council
Intl Criminal Tribunals (Ad Hoc and ICC (U.S. Not a Party to ICC Stat.))
ICJ
Somewhat by: regional HR Systems
Civil Society

3. Regional Human Rights Systems: A. North, Central and South America

Organization of American States	Council of Europe (47 states) HQ: Strasbourg, France	
OAS Charter	Human Rights Instruments	Other Instruments (National Minorities, Torture, Minority Languages, Human Trafficking)
Human Rights Instruments:	European Convention for the Protection of Human Rights and Fundamental Freedoms (European Convention on Human Rights) (and Protocols)	
American Declaration on the Rights and Duties of Man		European Social Charter (Revised)
American Convention on Human Rights (and Protocols)	Organs	Organ
	European Court of Human Rights (Chambers and Grand Chambers)	European Committee of Social Rights
Other Human Rights instruments: Cartagena, Torture, Violence against Women, Forced Disappearance, Disabilities	Committee of Ministers	
Organs		Other Organs: Committee for Prevention of Torture (CPT); European Commission against Racism and Intolerance (ECRI)
Inter-American Commission on Human Rights (Washington DC)		Venice Commission (Constitutional Advisory)
Inter- American Court of Human Rights (Costa Rica)		Commissioner for Human Rights (Strasbourg)
OAS Governance		(Elected by COE Parliamentary Assembly
Council of Europe (47 states) HQ: Strasbourg, France		

C. Europe: European Union

European Union (EU)
(27 states)
HQ: Brussels, Strasbourg
EU Treaty (Lisbon)

Organs

Council, Commission,
Parliament, Court
of Justice

Human Rights Instruments
Organs

Charter of Fundamental Rights
(under Lisbon treaty)

Proposed Accession of EU as a
party to the European Convention
on Human Rights (COE)

D. African

African Union
(replaced Organization of African
Unity
AU Constitutive Act

Organs

Assembly, Executive Council,
Commission, Permanent Repre-
sentatives Committee, Court of
Justice, ECOSOCC, PSC Pan
African Parliament

Human Rights Instruments

African Charter on Human and
Peoples Rights (and Protocols)

Other HR instruments: Child
Welfare, Internally Displaced
persons etc.

Organs

African Commission on Human
and Peoples' Rights Instruments

African Court of Justice and
Human Rights

E. League of Arab States

F. South East Asia (ASEAN)

League of Arab State (Arab League) 22 States Charter of the Arab League

Association of South East Asian Nations (ASEAN) Charter Of The Association Of Southeast Asian Nations

Organs

Organs

Council of the Arab League

ASEAN Intergovernmental Commission on the Human Rights (AICHR) (Inaugurated Oct. 2009)

Human Rights Instruments

Arab Charter on Human Rights (Revised)

Human Rights Instruments

No regional instrument as of November 2010. Terms of reference can be found at http://www.aseansec.org/DOC-TOR-AHRB.pdf, "To uphold international human rights standards as prescribed by the Universal Declaration of Human Rights, the Vienna Declaration and Programme of Action, and international human rights instruments to which ASEAN Member States are parties."

4. National Human Rights Institutions, NGOs and Civil Society

National Human Rights Institutions (Not all States have NHRIs)	NGOs: International level (Examples)	NGOs: National Level
National Human Rights institutions (NHRI)	International Committee of the Red Cross (ICRC)	Amnesty International USA
Set up in a state, independent from government. Based on Paris Principles on NHRIs	Amnesty International	Human Rights First
Functions and powers vary from state to state. There is no NHRI in the U.S.	International Commission of Jurists	Human Rights USA
	Freedom House	Minnesota Advocates for human Rights
	Human Rights Watch	NAACP
	International Institute of Human Rights	League of Women Voters
	Carter Center	American Civil Liberties Union

Other Civil Society Actors

State or Local Human Rights Organizations
Community Based Organizations
Ad Hoc Issue Groups Organs
Individual activities

APPENDIX E: TREATY ANALYSIS—INTERPRETATION HELPS

These documents are included to help the reader understand and interpret the meaning of treaties:

A. VIENNA CONVENTION ON THE LAW OF TREATIES (EXCERPTS)

Done at Vienna on 23 May 1969. Entered into force on 27 January 1980.

United Nations, *Treaty Series*, vol. 1155, p. 331

The States Parties to the present Convention,

Considering the fundamental role of treaties in the history of international relations,

Recognizing the ever-increasing importance of treaties as a source of international law and as a means of developing peaceful cooperation among nations, whatever their constitutional and social systems,

Noting that the principles of free consent and of good faith and the *pacta sunt servanda* rule are universally recognized,

Affirming that disputes concerning treaties, like other international disputes, should be settled by peaceful means and in conformity with the principles of justice and international law,

Recalling the determination of the peoples of the United Nations to establish conditions under which justice and respect for the obligations arising from treaties can be maintained,

Having in mind the principles of international law embodied in the Charter of the United Nations, such as the principles of the equal rights and self-determination of peoples, of the sovereign equality and independence of all States, of non-interference in the domestic affairs of States, of the prohibition of the threat or use of force and of universal respect for, and observance of, human rights and fundamental freedoms for all,

Believing that the codification and progressive development of the law of treaties achieved in the present Convention will promote the purposes of the United Nations set forth in the Charter, namely, the maintenance of international peace and security, the development of friendly relations and the achievement of cooperation among nations,

Affirming that the rules of customary international law will continue to govern questions not regulated by the provisions of the present Convention,

Have agreed as follows:

PART I. INTRODUCTION

Article 1 Scope of the present Convention

The present Convention applies to treaties between States.

Article 2 Use of terms

1. For the purposes of the present Convention:

(*a*) "treaty" means an international agreement concluded between States in written form and governed by international law, whether embodied in a single instrument or in two or more related instruments and whatever its particular designation;

(*b*) "ratification", "acceptance", "approval" and "accession" mean in each case the international act so named whereby a State establishes on the international plane its consent to be bound by a treaty;

(*c*) "full powers" means a document emanating from the competent authority of a State designating a person or persons to represent the State for negotiating, adopting or authenticating the text of a treaty, for expressing the consent of the State to be bound by a treaty, or for accomplishing any other act with respect to a treaty;

(*d*) "reservation" means a unilateral statement, however phrased or named, made by a State, when signing, ratifying, accepting, approving or acceding to a treaty, whereby it purports to exclude or to modify the legal effect of certain provisions of the treaty in their application to that State;

(*e*) "negotiating State" means a State which took part in the drawing up and adoption of the text of the treaty;

(*f*) "contracting State" means a State which has consented to be bound by the treaty, whether or not the treaty has entered into force;

(*g*) "party" means a State which has consented to be bound by the treaty and for which the treaty is in force;

(*h*) "third State" means a State not a party to the treaty;

(*i*) "international organization" means an intergovernmental organization.

2. The provisions of paragraph 1 regarding the use of terms in the present Convention are without prejudice to the use of those terms or to the meanings which may be given to them in the internal law of any State.

PART II. CONCLUSION AND ENTRY INTO FORCE OF TREATIES

SECTION 1. CONCLUSION OF TREATIES

Article 6 *Capacity of States to conclude treaties*

Every State possesses capacity to conclude treaties.

Article 7 *Full powers*

1. A person is considered as representing a State for the purpose of adopting or authenticating the text of a treaty or for the purpose of expressing the consent of the State to be bound by a treaty if:

(*a*) he produces appropriate full powers; or

(*b*) it appears from the practice of the States concerned or from other circumstances that their intention was to consider that person as representing the State for such purposes and to dispense with full powers.

2. In virtue of their functions and without having to produce full powers, the following are considered as representing their State:

(*a*) Heads of State, Heads of Government and Ministers for Foreign Affairs, for the purpose of performing all acts relating to the conclusion of a treaty;

(*b*) heads of diplomatic missions, for the purpose of adopting the text of a treaty between the accrediting State and the State to which they are accredited;

(*c*) representatives accredited by States to an international conference or to an international organization or one of its organs, for the purpose of adopting the text of a treaty in that conference, organization or organ.

Article 9 *Adoption of the text*

1. The adoption of the text of a treaty takes place by the consent of all the States participating in its drawing up except as provided in paragraph 2.

2. The adoption of the text of a treaty at an international conference takes place by the vote of two thirds of the States present and voting, unless by the same majority they shall decide to apply a different rule.

Article 11 *Means of expressing consent to be bound by a treaty*

The consent of a State to be bound by a treaty may be expressed by signature, exchange of instruments constituting a treaty, ratification, acceptance, approval or accession, or by any other means if so agreed.

Article 14 *Consent to be bound by a treaty expressed by ratification, acceptance or approval*

1. The consent of a State to be bound by a treaty is expressed by ratification when:

(*a*) the treaty provides for such consent to be expressed by means of ratification;

(*b*) it is otherwise established that the negotiating States were agreed that ratification should be required;

(*c*) the representative of the State has signed the treaty subject to ratification; or

(*d*) the intention of the State to sign the treaty subject to ratification appears from the full powers of its representative or was expressed during the negotiation.

2. The consent of a State to be bound by a treaty is expressed by acceptance or approval under conditions similar to those which apply to ratification.

Article 18 *Obligation not to defeat the object and purpose of a treaty prior to its entry into force*

A State is obliged to refrain from acts which would defeat the object and purpose of a treaty when:

(*a*) it has signed the treaty or has exchanged instruments constituting the treaty subject to ratification, acceptance or approval, until it shall have made its intention clear not to become a party to the treaty; or

(*b*) it has expressed its consent to be bound by the treaty, pending the entry into force of the treaty and provided that such entry into force is not unduly delayed.

....

SECTION 2. RESERVATIONS

Article 19 *Formulation of reservations*

A State may, when signing, ratifying, accepting, approving or acceding to a treaty, formulate a reservation unless:

(*a*) the reservation is prohibited by the treaty;

(b) the treaty provides that only specified reservations, which do not include the reservation in question, may be made; or

(c) in cases not failing under subparagraphs (a) and (b), the reservation is incompatible with the object and purpose of the treaty.

....

PART III. OBSERVANCE, APPLICATION AND INTERPRETATION OF TREATIES
SECTION 1. OBSERVANCE OF TREATIES

Article 26 "Pacta sunt servanda"

Every treaty in force is binding upon the parties to it and must be performed by them in good faith.

Article 27 Internal law and observance of treaties

A party may not invoke the provisions of its internal law as justification for its failure to perform a treaty. This rule is without prejudice to article 46.

....

SECTION 3. INTERPRETATION OF TREATIES

Article 31 General rule of interpretation

1. A treaty shall be interpreted in good faith in accordance with the ordinary meaning to be given to the terms of the treaty in their context and in the light of its object and purpose.

2. The context for the purpose of the interpretation of a treaty shall comprise, in addition to the text, including its preamble and annexes:

(a) any agreement relating to the treaty which was made between all the parties in connection with the conclusion of the treaty;

(b) any instrument which was made by one or more parties in connection with the conclusion of the treaty and accepted by the other parties as an instrument related to the treaty.

3. There shall be taken into account, together with the context:

(a) any subsequent agreement between the parties regarding the interpretation of the treaty or the application of its provisions;

(b) any subsequent practice in the application of the treaty which establishes the agreement of the parties regarding its interpretation;

(c) any relevant rules of international law applicable in the relations between the parties.

4. A special meaning shall be given to a term if it is established that the parties so intended.

Article 32 Supplementary means of interpretation

Recourse may be had to supplementary means of interpretation, including the preparatory work of the treaty and the circumstances of its conclusion, in order to confirm the meaning resulting from the application of article 31, or to determine the meaning when the interpretation according to article 31: (a) leaves the meaning ambiguous or obscure; or (b) leads to a result which is manifestly absurd or unreasonable.

....

SECTION 2. INVALIDITY OF TREATIES

Article 53 Treaties conflicting with a peremptory norm of general international law ("jus cogens")

A treaty is void if, at the time of its conclusion, it conflicts with a peremptory norm of general international law. For the purposes of the present Convention, a peremptory norm of general international law is a norm accepted and recognized by the international community of States as a whole as a norm from which no derogation is permitted and which can be modified only by a subsequent norm of general international law having the same character.

For Full text see: http://www1.umn.edu/humanrts/instree/viennaconvention.html

B. U.N. HUMAN RIGHTS COMMITTEE, SELECTED GENERAL COMMENTS TO THE INTERNATIONAL COVENANT ON CIVIL AND POLITICAL RIGHTS

Because the ICCPR is the most important general human rights instrument to which the U.S. is legally bound the Author has set forth in the Primary Documents a sample of a General Comment by the U.N. Human Rights Committee, General Comment 22. The Committee is the supervising organ of the ICCPR. The General Comments are the expert views of the members of the Committee on the interpretation and application of the articles of the ICCPR. In this Appendix are other selected General Comments.

The reader should be aware that any time one uses the text of the ICCPR one should consult the various General Comments to see if there is one concerning the article being used. Reading the General Comment will help the reader understand the official understanding and scope of application of an ICCPR norm.

In addition to consulting the treaty text and General Comments the reader who seeks to know how the Human Rights Committee has applied the Covenant text should look at the "jurisprudence", the case law, of the Committee taken from petitions filed by individuals against states under the Optional Protocol to the ICCPR. This is expressed in the "Views" of the Committee, which are the decisions in particular cases brought before the Committee. General Comments are largely based on the Views of the Committee.

Other U.N. treaty bodies issue general comments but the author chose to focus on the ICCPR. All footnotes have been omitted. See original for footnotes. General Comments of the Human Rights Committee can be found at *http://www2.ohchr.org/english/bodies/hrc/comments.htm.*

OFFICE OF THE HIGH COMMISSIONER
FOR HUMAN RIGHTS

General Comment No. 06: The right to life (art. 6):. 04/30/1982. CCPR General Comment No. 6.
(General Comments)

Convention Abbreviation: CCPR
GENERAL COMMENT 6
The right to life
(Article 6)
(Sixteenth session, 1982)

1. The right to life enunciated in article 6 of the Covenant has been dealt with in all State reports. It is the supreme right from which no derogation is permitted even in time of public emergency which threatens the life of the nation (art. 4). However, the Committee has noted that quite often the information given concerning article 6 was limited to only one or other aspect of this right. It is a right which should not be interpreted narrowly.

2. The Committee observes that war and other acts of mass violence continue to be a scourge of humanity and take the lives of thousands of innocent human beings every year. Under the Charter of the United Nations the threat or use of force by any State against another State, except in exercise of the inherent right of self-defence, is already prohibited. The Committee considers that States have the supreme duty to prevent wars, acts of genocide and other acts of mass violence causing arbitrary loss of life. Every effort they make to avert the danger of war, especially thermonuclear war, and to strengthen international peace and security would constitute the most important condition and guarantee for the safeguarding of the right to life. In this respect, the Committee notes, in particular, a connection between article 6 and article 20, which states that the law shall prohibit any propaganda for war (para.1) or incitement to violence (para. 2) as therein described.

3. The protection against arbitrary deprivation of life which is explicitly required by the third sentence of article 6 (1) is of paramount importance. The Committee considers that States parties should take measures not only to prevent and punish deprivation of life by criminal acts, but also to prevent arbitrary killing by their own security forces. The deprivation of life by the authorities of the State is a matter of the utmost gravity. Therefore, the law must strictly control and limit the circumstances in which a person may be deprived of his life by such authorities.

4. States parties should also take specific and effective measures to prevent the disappearance of individuals, something which unfortunately has become all too frequent and leads too often to arbitrary deprivation of life. Furthermore, States should establish effective facilities and procedures to investigate thoroughly cases of missing and disappeared persons in circumstances which may involve a violation of the right to life.

5. Moreover, the Committee has noted that the right to life has been too often narrowly interpreted. The expression "inherent right to life" cannot properly be understood in a restrictive manner, and the protection of this right requires that States adopt positive measures. In this connection, the Committee considers that it would be desirable for States parties to take all possible measures to reduce infant mortality and to increase life expectancy, especially in adopting measures to eliminate malnutrition and epidemics.

6. While it follows from article 6 (2) to (6) that States parties are not obliged to abolish the death penalty totally they are obliged to limit its use and, in particular, to abolish it for other than the "most serious crimes".

Accordingly, they ought to consider reviewing their criminal laws in this light and, in any event, are obliged to restrict the application of the death penalty to the "most serious crimes". The article also refers generally to abolition in terms which strongly suggest (paras. 2 (2) and (6)) that abolition is desirable. The Committee concludes that all measures of abolition should be considered as progress in the enjoyment of the right to life within the meaning of article 40, and should as such be reported to the Committee. The Committee notes that a number of States have already abolished the death penalty or suspended its application. Nevertheless, States' reports show that progress made towards abolishing or limiting the application of the death penalty is quite inadequate.

7. The Committee is of the opinion that the expression "most serious crimes" must be read restrictively to mean that the death penalty should be a quite exceptional measure. It also follows from the express terms of article 6 that it can only be imposed in accordance with the law in force at the time of the commission of the crime and not contrary to the Covenant. The procedural guarantees therein prescribed must be observed, including the right to a fair hearing by an independent tribunal, the presumption of innocence, the minimum guarantees for the defence, and the right to review by a higher tribunal. These rights are applicable in addition to the particular right to seek pardon or commutation of the sentence.

GENERAL COMMENT 11
Prohibition of propaganda for war and inciting national, racial or religious hatred
(Article 20)
(Nineteenth session, 1983)

1. Not all reports submitted by States parties have provided sufficient information as to the implementation of article 20 of the Covenant. In view of the nature of article 20, States parties are obliged to adopt the necessary legislative measures prohibiting the actions referred to therein. However, the reports have shown that in some States such actions are neither prohibited by law nor are appropriate efforts intended or made to prohibit them. Furthermore, many reports failed to give sufficient information concerning the relevant national legislation and practice.

2. Article 20 of the Covenant states that any propaganda for war and any advocacy of national, racial or religious hatred that constitutes incitement to discrimination, hostility or violence shall be prohibited by law. In the opinion of the Committee, these required prohibitions are fully compatible with the right of freedom of expression as contained in article 19, the exercise of which carries with it special duties and responsibilities. The prohibition under paragraph 1 extends to all forms of propaganda threatening or resulting in an act of aggression or breach of the peace contrary to the Charter of the United Nations, while paragraph 2 is directed against any advocacy of national, racial or religious hatred that constitutes incitement to discrimination, hostility or violence, whether such propaganda or advocacy has aims which are internal or external to the State concerned. The provisions of article 20, paragraph 1, do not prohibit advocacy of the sovereign right of self-defence or the right of peoples to self-determination and independence in accordance with the Charter of the United Nations. For article 20 to become fully effective there ought to be a law making it clear that propaganda and advocacy as described therein are contrary to public policy and providing for an appropriate sanction in case of violation. The Committee, therefore, believes that States parties which have not yet done so should take the measures necessary to fulfil the obligations contained in article 20, and should themselves refrain from any such propaganda or advocacy.

GENERAL COMMENT 14
Nuclear weapons and the right to life (Article 6)
(Twenty-third session, 1984)

1. In its general comment 6 [16] adopted at its 378th meeting on 27 July 1982, the Human Rights Committee observed that the right to life enunciated in the first paragraph of article 6 of the International Covenant on Civil and Political Rights is the supreme right from which no derogation is permitted even in time of public emergency. The same right to life is enshrined in article 3 of the Universal Declaration of Human Rights adopted by the General Assembly of the United Nations on 10 December 1948. It is basic to all human rights.

2. In its previous general comment, the Committee also observed that it is the supreme duty of States to prevent wars. War and other acts of mass violence continue to be a scourge of humanity and take the lives of thousands of innocent human beings every year.

3. While remaining deeply concerned by the toll of human life taken by conventional weapons in armed conflicts, the Committee has noted that, during successive sessions of the General Assembly, representatives from all geographical regions have expressed their growing concern at the development and proliferation of increasingly awesome weapons of mass destruction, which not only threaten human life but also absorb resources that could otherwise be used for vital economic and social purposes, particularly for the benefit of developing countries, and thereby for promoting and securing the enjoyment of human rights for all.

4. The Committee associates itself with this concern. It is evident that the designing, testing, manufacture, possession and deployment of nuclear weapons are among the greatest threats to the right to life which confront mankind today. This threat is compounded by the danger that the actual use of such weapons may be brought about, not only in the event of war, but even through human or mechanical error or failure.

5. Furthermore, the very existence and gravity of this threat generates a climate of suspicion and fear between States, which is in itself antagonistic to the promotion of universal respect for and observance of human rights and fundamental freedoms in accordance with the Charter of the United Nations and the International Covenants on Human Rights.

6. The production, testing, possession, deployment and use of nuclear weapons should be prohibited and recognized as crimes against humanity.

7. The Committee accordingly, in the interest of mankind, calls upon all States, whether Parties to the Covenant or not, to take urgent steps, unilaterally and by agreement, to rid the world of this menace.

GENERAL COMMENT 15
The position of aliens under the Covenant (Twenty-seventh session, 1986),
Compilation of General Comments and General Recommendations
Adopted by Human Rights Treaty Bodies, U.N. Doc. HRI/GEN/1/Rev.1 at 18 (1994).

1. Reports from States parties have often failed to take into account that each State party must ensure the rights in the Covenant to "all individuals within its territory and subject to its jurisdiction" (art. 2, para. 1). In general, the rights set forth in the Covenant apply to everyone, irrespective of reciprocity, and irrespective of his or her nationality or statelessness.

2. Thus, the general rule is that each one of the rights of the Covenant must be guaranteed without discrimination between citizens and aliens. Aliens receive the benefit of the general requirement of non-discrimination in respect of the rights guaranteed in the Covenant, as provided for in article 2 thereof. This guarantee applies to aliens and citizens alike. Exceptionally, some of the rights recognized in the Covenant are expressly applicable only to citizens (art. 25), while article 13 applies only to aliens. However, the Committee's experience in examining reports shows that in a number of countries other rights that aliens should enjoy under the Covenant are denied to them or are subject to limitations that cannot always be justified under the Covenant.

3. A few constitutions provide for equality of aliens with citizens. Some constitutions adopted more recently carefully distinguish fundamental rights that apply to all and those granted to citizens only, and deal with each in detail. In many States, however, the constitutions are drafted in terms of citizens only when granting relevant rights. Legislation and case law may also play an important part in providing for the rights of aliens. The Committee has been informed that in some States fundamental rights, though not guaranteed to aliens by the Constitution or other legislation, will also be extended to them as required by the Covenant. In certain cases, however, there has clearly been a failure to implement Covenant rights without discrimination in respect of aliens.

4. The Committee considers that in their reports States parties should give attention to the position of aliens, both under their law and in actual practice. The Covenant gives aliens all the protection regarding rights guaranteed therein, and its requirements should be observed by States parties in their legislation and in practice as appropriate. The position of aliens would thus be considerably improved. States parties should ensure that the provisions of the Covenant and the rights under it are made known to aliens within their jurisdiction.

5. The Covenant does not recognize the right of aliens to enter or reside in the territory of a State party. It is in principle a matter for the State to decide who it will admit to its territory. However, in certain circumstances an alien may enjoy the protection of the Covenant even in relation to entry or residence, for example, when considerations of non-discrimination, prohibition of inhuman treatment and respect for family life arise.

6. Consent for entry may be given subject to conditions relating, for example, to movement, residence and employment. A State may also impose general conditions upon an alien who is in transit. However, once aliens are allowed to enter the territory of a State party they are entitled to the rights set out in the Covenant.

7. Aliens thus have an inherent right to life, protected by law, and may not be arbitrarily deprived of life. They must not be subjected to torture or to cruel, inhuman or degrading treatment or punishment; nor may they be held in slavery or servitude. Aliens have the full right to liberty and security of the person. If lawfully deprived of their liberty, they shall be treated with humanity and with respect for the inherent dignity of their person. Aliens may not be imprisoned for failure to ÿractic a contractual obligation. They have the right to liberty of movement and free choice of residence; they shall be free to leave the country. Aliens shall be equal before the courts and tribunals, and shall be entitled to a fair and public hearing by a competent, independent and impartial tribunal established by law in the determination of any criminal charge or of rights and obligations in a suit at law. Aliens shall not be subjected to retrospective penal legislation, and are entitled to recognition before the law. They may not be subjected to arbitrary or unlawful interference with their privacy, family, home or correspondence. They have the right to freedom of thought, conscience and religion, and the right to hold opinions and to express them. Aliens receive the benefit of the right of peaceful assembly and of freedom of association. They may marry when at marriageable age. Their children are entitled to those measures of protection required by their status as minors. In those cases where aliens constitute a minority within the meaning of article 27, they shall not be denied the right, in community with other members of their group, to enjoy their own culture, to profess and practice their own religion and to use their own language. Aliens are entitled to equal protection by the law. There shall be no discrimination between aliens and citizens in the application of these rights. These rights of aliens may be qualified only by such limitations as may be lawfully imposed under the Covenant.

8. Once an alien is lawfully within a territory, his freedom of movement within the territory and his right to leave that territory may only be restricted in accordance with article 12, paragraph 3. Differences in treatment in this regard between aliens and nationals, or between different categories of aliens, need to be justified under article 12, paragraph 3. Since such restrictions must, inter alia, be consistent with the other rights recognized in the Covenant, a State party cannot, by restraining an alien or deporting him to a third country, arbitrarily prevent his return to his own country (art. 12, para. 4).

9. Many reports have given insufficient information on matters relevant to article 13. That article is applicable to all procedures aimed at the obligatory departure of an alien, whether described in national law as expulsion or otherwise. If such procedures entail arrest, the safeguards of the Covenant relating to deprivation of liberty (arts. 9 and 10) may also be applicable. If the arrest is for the particular purpose of extradition, other provisions of national and international law may apply. Normally an alien who is expelled must be allowed to leave for any country that agrees to take him. The particular rights of article 13 only protect those aliens who are lawfully in the territory of a State party. This means that national law concerning the requirements for entry and stay must be taken into account in determining the scope of that protection, and that illegal entrants and aliens who have stayed longer than the law or their permits allow, in particular, are not covered by its provisions. However, if the legality of an alien's entry or stay is in dispute, any decision on this point leading to his expulsion or deportation ought to be taken in accordance with article 13. It is for the competent authorities of the State party, in good faith and in the exercise of their powers, to apply and interpret the domestic law, observing, however, such requirements under the Covenant as equality before the law (art. 26).

10. Article 13 directly regulates only the procedure and not the substantive grounds for expulsion. However, by allowing only those carried out "in pursuance of a decision reached in accordance with law", its purpose is clearly to prevent arbitrary expulsions. On the other hand, it entitles each alien to a decision in his own case and, hence, article 13 would not be satisfied with laws or decisions providing for collective or mass expulsions. This understanding, in the opinion of the Committee, is confirmed by further provisions concerning the right to submit reasons against expulsion and to have the decision reviewed by and to be represented before the competent authority or someone designated by it. An alien must be given full facilities for pursuing his remedy against expulsion so that this right will in all the circumstances of his case be an effective one. The principles of article 13 relating to appeal against expulsion and the entitlement to review by a competent authority may only be departed from when "compelling reasons of national security" so require. Discrimination may not be made between different categories of aliens in the application of article 13.

GENERAL COMMENT 16
The right to respect of privacy, family, home and correspondence,
and protection of honour and reputation
(Article 17)
(Thirty-second session, 1988)

1. Article 17 provides for the right of every person to be protected against arbitrary or unlawful interference with his privacy, family, home or correspondence as well as against unlawful attacks on his honour and reputation. In the view of the Committee this right is required to be guaranteed against all such interferences and attacks whether they emanate from State authorities or from natural or legal persons. The obligations imposed by this article require the State to adopt legislative and other measures to give effect to the prohibition against such interferences and attacks as well as to the protection of this right.

2. In this connection, the Committee wishes to point out that in the reports of States parties to the Covenant the necessary attention is not being given to information concerning the manner in which respect for this right is guaranteed by legislative, administrative or judicial authorities, and in general by the competent organs established in the State. In particular, insufficient attention is paid to the fact that article 17 of the Covenant deals with protection against both unlawful and arbitrary interference. That means that it is precisely in State legislation above all that provision must be made for the protection of the right set forth in that article. At present the reports either say nothing about such legislation or provide insufficient information on the subject.

3. The term "unlawful" means that no interference can take place except in cases envisaged by the law. Interference authorized by States can only take place on the basis of law, which itself must comply with the provisions, aims and objectives of the Covenant.

4. The expression "arbitrary interference" is also relevant to the protection of the right provided for in article 17. In the Committee's view the expression "arbitrary interference" can also extend to interference provided for under the law. The introduction of the concept of arbitrariness is intended to guarantee that even interference provided for by law should be in accordance with the provisions, aims and objectives of the Covenant and should be, in any event, reasonable in the particular circumstances.

5. Regarding the term "family", the objectives of the Covenant require that for purposes of article 17 this term be given a broad interpretation to include all those comprising the family as understood in the society of the State party concerned. The term "home" in English, "manzel" in Arabic, "zhùzhái" in Chinese, "domicile" in French, "zhilische" in Russian and "domicilio" in Spanish, as used in article 17 of the Covenant, is to be understood to indicate the place where a person resides or carries out his usual occupation. In this connection, the Committee invites States to indicate in their reports the meaning given in their society to the terms "family" and "home".

6. The Committee considers that the reports should include information on the authorities and organs set up within the legal system of the State which are competent to authorize interference allowed by the law. It is also indispensable to have information on the authorities which are entitled to exercise control over such interference with strict regard for the law, and to know in what manner and through which organs persons concerned may complain of a violation of the right provided for in article 17 of the Covenant. States should in their reports make clear the extent to which actual practice conforms to the law. State party reports should also contain information on complaints lodged in respect of arbitrary or unlawful interference, and the number of any findings in that regard, as well as the remedies provided in such cases.

7. As all persons live in society, the protection of privacy is necessarily relative. However, the competent public authorities should only be able to call for such information relating to an individual's private life the knowledge of which is essential in the interests of society as understood under the Covenant. Accordingly, the Committee recommends that States should indicate in their reports the laws and regulations that govern authorized interferences with private life.

8. Even with regard to interferences that conform to the Covenant, relevant legislation must specify in detail the precise circumstances in which such interferences may be permitted. A decision to make use of such authorized interference must be made only by the authority designated under the law, and on a case-by-case basis. Compliance with article 17 requires that the integrity and confidentiality of correspondence should be guaranteed de jure and de facto. Correspondence should be delivered to the addressee without interception and without being opened or otherwise read. Surveillance, whether electronic or otherwise, interceptions

of telephonic, telegraphic and other forms of communication, wire-tapping and recording of conversations should be prohibited. Searches of a person's home should be restricted to a search for necessary evidence and should not be allowed to amount to harassment. So far as personal and body search is concerned, effective measures should ensure that such searches are carried out in a manner consistent with the dignity of the person who is being searched. Persons being subjected to body search by State officials, or medical personnel acting at the request of the State, should only be examined by persons of the same sex.

9. States parties are under a duty themselves not to engage in interferences inconsistent with article 17 of the Covenant and to provide the legislative framework prohibiting such acts by natural or legal persons.

10. The gathering and holding of personal information on computers, data banks and other devices, whether by public authorities or private individuals or bodies, must be regulated by law. Effective measures have to be taken by States to ensure that information concerning a person's private life does not reach the hands of persons who are not authorized by law to receive, process and use it, and is never used for purposes incompatible with the Covenant. In order to have the most effective protection of his private life, every individual should have the right to ascertain in an intelligible form, whether, and if so, what personal data is stored in automatic data files, and for what purposes. Every individual should also be able to ascertain which public ÿracticedÿ or private individuals or bodies control or may control their files. If such files contain incorrect personal data or have been collected or processed contrary to the provisions of the law, every individual should have the right to request rectification or elimination.

11. Article 17 affords protection to personal honour and reputation and States are under an obligation to provide adequate legislation to that end. Provision must also be made for everyone effectively to be able to protect himself against any unlawful attacks that do occur and to have an effective remedy against those responsible. States parties should indicate in their reports to what extent the honour or reputation of individuals is protected by law and how this protection is achieved according to their legal system.

GENERAL COMMENT 18
Non-discrimination
(Thirty-seventh session, 1989)

1. Non-discrimination, together with equality before the law and equal protection of the law without any discrimination, constitute a basic and general principle relating to the protection of human rights. Thus, article 2, paragraph 1, of the International Covenant on Civil and Political Rights obligates each State party to respect and ensure to all persons within its territory and subject to its jurisdiction the rights recognized in the Covenant without distinction of any kind, such as race, colour, sex, language, religion, political or other opinion, national or social origin, property, birth or other status. Article 26 not only entitles all persons to equality before the law as well as equal protection of the law but also prohibits any discrimination under the law and guarantees to all persons equal and effective protection against discrimination on any ground such as race, colour, sex, language, religion, political or other opinion, national or social origin, property, birth or other status.

2. Indeed, the principle of non-discrimination is so basic that article 3 obligates each State party to ensure the equal right of men and women to the enjoyment of the rights set forth in the Covenant. While article 4, paragraph 1, allows States parties to take measures derogating from certain obligations under the Covenant in time of public emergency, the same article requires, inter alia, that those measures should not involve discrimination solely on the ground of race, colour, sex, language, religion or social origin. Furthermore, article 20, paragraph 2, obligates States parties to prohibit, by law, any advocacy of national, racial or religious hatred which constitutes incitement to discrimination.

3. Because of their basic and general character, the principle of non-discrimination as well as that of equality before the law and equal protection of the law are sometimes expressly referred to in articles relating to particular categories of human rights. Article 14, paragraph 1, provides that all persons shall be equal before the courts and tribunals, and paragraph 3 of the same article provides that, in the determination of any criminal charge against him, everyone shall be entitled, in full equality, to the minimum guarantees enumerated in subparagraphs (a) to (g) of paragraph 3. Similarly, article 25 provides for the equal participation in public life of all citizens, without any of the distinctions mentioned in article 2.

4. It is for the States parties to determine appropriate measures to implement the relevant provisions. However, the Committee is to be informed about the nature of such measures and their conformity with the principles of non-discrimination and equality before the law and equal protection of the law.

5. The Committee wishes to draw the attention of States parties to the fact that the Covenant sometimes expressly requires them to take measures to guarantee the equality of rights of the persons concerned. For example, article 23, paragraph 4, stipulates that States parties shall take appropriate steps to ensure equality of rights as well as responsibilities of spouses as to marriage, during marriage and at its dissolution. Such steps may take the form of legislative, administrative or other measures, but it is a positive duty of States parties to make certain that spouses have equal rights as required by the Covenant. In relation to children, article 24 provides that all children, without any discrimination as to race, colour, sex, language, religion, national or social origin, property or birth, have the right to such measures of protection as are required by their status as minors, on the part of their family, society and the State.

6. The Committee notes that the Covenant neither defines the term "discrimination" nor indicates what constitutes discrimination. However, article 1 of the International Convention on the Elimination of All Forms of Racial Discrimination provides that the term "racial discrimination" shall mean any distinction, exclusion, restriction or preference based on race, colour, descent, or national or ethnic origin which has the purpose or effect of nullifying or impairing the recognition, enjoyment or exercise, on an equal footing, of human rights and fundamental freedoms in the political, economic, social, cultural or any other field of public life. Similarly, article 1 of the Convention on the Elimination of All Forms of Discrimination against Women provides that "discrimination against women" shall mean any distinction, exclusion or restriction made on the basis of sex which has the effect or purpose of impairing or nullifying the recognition, enjoyment or exercise by women, irrespective of their marital status, on a basis of equality of men and women, of human rights and fundamental freedoms in the political, economic, social, cultural, civil or any other field.

7. While these conventions deal only with cases of discrimination on specific grounds, the Committee believes that the term "discrimination" as used in the Covenant should be understood to imply any distinction, exclusion, restriction or preference which is based on any ground such as race, colour, sex, language, religion, political or other opinion, national or social origin, property, birth or other status, and which has the purpose or effect of nullifying or impairing the recognition, enjoyment or exercise by all persons, on an equal footing, of all rights and freedoms.

8. The enjoyment of rights and freedoms on an equal footing, however, does not mean identical treatment in every instance. In this connection, the provisions of the Covenant are explicit. For example, article 6, paragraph 5, prohibits the death sentence from being imposed on persons below 18 years of age. The same paragraph prohibits that sentence from being carried out on pregnant women. Similarly, article 10, paragraph 3, requires the segregation of juvenile offenders from adults. Furthermore, article 25 guarantees certain political rights, differentiating on grounds of citizenship.

9. Reports of many States parties contain information regarding legislative as well as administrative measures and court decisions which relate to protection against discrimination in law, but they very often lack information which would reveal discrimination in fact. When reporting on articles 2 (1), 3 and 26 of the Covenant, States parties usually cite provisions of their constitution or equal opportunity laws with respect to equality of persons. While such information is of course useful, the Committee wishes to know if there remain any problems of discrimination in fact, which may be practiced either by public authorities, by the community, or by private persons or bodies. The Committee wishes to be informed about legal provisions and administrative measures directed at diminishing or eliminating such discrimination.

10. The Committee also wishes to point out that the principle of equality sometimes requires States parties to take affirmative action in order to diminish or eliminate conditions which cause or help to perpetuate discrimination prohibited by the Covenant. For example, in a State where the general conditions of a certain part of the population prevent or impair their enjoyment of human rights, the State should take specific action to correct those conditions. Such action may involve granting for a time to the part of the population concerned certain preferential treatment in specific matters as compared with the rest of the population. However, as long as such action is needed to correct discrimination in fact, it is a case of legitimate differentiation under the Covenant.

11. Both article 2, paragraph 1, and article 26 enumerate grounds of discrimination such as race, colour, sex, language, religion, political or other opinion, national or social origin, property, birth or other status. The Committee has observed that in a number of constitutions and laws not all the grounds on which discrimination is prohibited, as cited in article 2, paragraph 1, are enumerated. The Committee would therefore like to receive information from States parties as to the significance of such omissions.

12. While article 2 limits the scope of the rights to be protected against discrimination to those provided for in the Covenant, article 26 does not specify such limitations. That is to say, article 26 provides that all persons are equal before the law and are entitled to equal protection of the law without discrimination, and that the law shall guarantee to all persons equal and effective protection against discrimination on any of the enumerated grounds. In the view of the Committee, article 26 does not merely duplicate the guarantee already provided for in article 2 but provides in itself an autonomous right. It prohibits discrimination in law or in fact in any field regulated and protected by public authorities. Article 26 is therefore concerned with the obligations imposed on States parties in regard to their legislation and the application thereof. Thus, when legislation is adopted by a State party, it must comply with the requirement of article 26 that its content should not be discriminatory. In other words, the application of the principle of non-discrimination contained in article 26 is not limited to those rights which are provided for in the Covenant.

13. Finally, the Committee observes that not every differentiation of treatment will constitute discrimination, if the criteria for such differentiation are reasonable and objective and if the aim is to achieve a purpose which is legitimate under the Covenant.

GENERAL COMMENT NO. 19
Convention Abbreviation: CCPR

Protection of the family, the right to marriage and equality of the spouses (Art. 23) : . 07/27/1990.

1. Article 23 of the International Covenant on Civil and Political Rights recognizes that the family is the natural and fundamental group unit of society and is entitled to protection by society and the State. Protection of the family and its members is also guaranteed, directly or indirectly, by other provisions of the Covenant. Thus, article 17 establishes a prohibition on arbitrary or unlawful interference with the family. In addition, article 24 of the Covenant specifically addresses the protection of the rights of the child, as such or as a member of a family. In their reports, States parties often fail to give enough information on how the State and society are discharging their obligation to provide protection to the family and the persons composing it.

2. The Committee notes that the concept of the family may differ in some respects from State to State, and even from region to region within a State, and that it is therefore not possible to give the concept a standard definition. However, the Committee emphasizes that, when a group of persons is regarded as a family under the legislation and practice of a State, it must be given the protection referred to in article 23. Consequently, States parties should report on how the concept and scope of the family is construed or defined in their own society and legal system. Where diverse concepts of the family, "nuclear" and "extended", exist within a State, this should be indicated with an explanation of the degree of protection afforded to each. In view of the existence of various forms of family, such as unmarried couples and their children or single parents and their children, States parties should also indicate whether and to what extent such types of family and their members are recognized and protected by domestic law and practice.

3. Ensuring the protection provided for under article 23 of the Covenant requires that States parties should adopt legislative, administrative or other measures. States parties should provide detailed information concerning the nature of such measures and the means whereby their effective implementation is assured. In fact, since the Covenant also recognizes the right of the family to protection by society, States parties' reports should indicate how the necessary protection is granted to the family by the State and other social institutions, whether and to what extent the State gives financial or other support to the activities of such institutions, and how it ensures that these activities are compatible with the Covenant.

4. Article 23, paragraph 2, of the Covenant reaffirms the right of men and women of marriageable age to marry and to found a family. Paragraph 3 of the same article provides that no marriage shall be entered into without the free and full consent of the intending spouses. States parties' reports should indicate whether there are restrictions or impediments to the exercise of the right to marry based on special factors such as degree of kinship or mental incapacity. The Covenant does not establish a specific marriageable age either for men or for women, but that age should be such as to enable each of the intending spouses to give his or her free and full personal consent in a form and under conditions prescribed by law. In this connection, the Committee wishes to note that such legal provisions must be compatible with the full exercise of the other rights guaranteed by the Covenant; thus, for instance, the right to freedom of thought, conscience and religion implies that the legislation of each State should provide for the possibility of both religious and civil marriages. In the Committee's view, however, for a State to require that a marriage, which is celebrated in

accordance with religious rites, be conducted, affirmed or registered also under civil law is not incompatible with the Covenant. States are also requested to include information on this subject in their reports.

5. The right to found a family implies, in principle, the possibility to procreate and live together. When States parties adopt family planning policies, they should be compatible with the provisions of the Covenant and should, in particular, not be discriminatory or compulsory. Similarly, the possibility to live together implies the adoption of appropriate measures, both at the internal level and as the case may be, in cooperation with other States, to ensure the unity or reunification of families, particularly when their members are separated for political, economic or similar reasons.

6. Article 23, paragraph 4, of the Covenant provides that States parties shall take appropriate steps to ensure equality of rights and responsibilities of spouses as to marriage, during marriage and at its dissolution.

7. With regard to equality as to marriage, the Committee wishes to note in particular that no sex-based discrimination should occur in respect of the acquisition or loss of nationality by reason of marriage. Likewise, the right of each spouse to retain the use of his or her original family name or to participate on an equal basis in the choice of a new family name should be safeguarded.

8. During marriage, the spouses should have equal rights and responsibilities in the family. This equality extends to all matters arising from their relationship, such as choice of residence, running of the household, education of the children and administration of assets. Such equality continues to be applicable to arrangements regarding legal separation or dissolution of the marriage.

9. Thus, any discriminatory treatment in regard to the grounds and procedures for separation or divorce, child custody, maintenance or alimony, visiting rights or the loss or recovery of parental authority must be prohibited, bearing in mind the paramount interest of the children in this connection. States parties should, in particular, include information in their reports concerning the provision made for the necessary protection of any children at the dissolution of a marriage or on the separation of the spouses.

GENERAL COMMENT 20
Replaces general comment 7 concerning prohibition
of torture and cruel treatment or punishment
(Article 7)
(Forty-fourth session, 1992)

1. This general comment replaces general comment 7 (the sixteenth session, 1982) reflecting and further developing it.

2. The aim of the provisions of article 7 of the International Covenant on Civil and Political Rights is to protect both the dignity and the physical and mental integrity of the individual. It is the duty of the State party to afford everyone protection through legislative and other measures as may be necessary against the acts prohibited by article 7, whether inflicted by people acting in their official capacity, outside their official capacity or in a private capacity. The prohibition in article 7 is complemented by the positive requirements of article 10, paragraph 1, of the Covenant, which stipulates that "All persons deprived of their liberty shall be treated with humanity and with respect for the inherent dignity of the human person".

3. The text of article 7 allows of no limitation. The Committee also reaffirms that, even in situations of public emergency such as those referred to in article 4 of the Covenant, no derogation from the provision of article 7 is allowed and its provisions must remain in force. The Committee likewise observes that no justification or extenuating circumstances may be invoked to excuse a violation of article 7 for any reasons, including those based on an order from a superior officer or public authority.

4. The Covenant does not contain any definition of the concepts covered by article 7, nor does the Committee consider it necessary to draw up a list of prohibited acts or to establish sharp distinctions between the different kinds of punishment or treatment; the distinctions depend on the nature, purpose and severity of the treatment applied.

5. The prohibition in article 7 relates not only to acts that cause physical pain but also to acts that cause mental suffering to the victim. In the Committee's view, moreover, the prohibition must extend to corporal punishment, including excessive chastisement ordered as punishment for a crime or as an educative or disciplinary measure. It is appropriate to emphasize in this regard that article 7 protects, in particular, children, pupils and patients in teaching and medical institutions.

6. The Committee notes that prolonged solitary confinement of the detained or imprisoned person may amount to acts prohibited by article 7. As the Committee has stated in its general comment No. 6 (16), article 6 of the Covenant refers generally to abolition of the death penalty in terms that strongly suggest that abolition is desirable. Moreover, when the death penalty is applied by a State party for the most serious crimes, it must not only be strictly limited in accordance with article 6 but it must be carried out in such a way as to cause the least possible physical and mental suffering.

7. Article 7 expressly prohibits medical or scientific experimentation without the free consent of the person concerned. The Committee notes that the reports of States parties generally contain little information on this point. More attention should be given to the need and means to ensure observance of this provision. The Committee also observes that special protection in regard to such experiments is necessary in the case of persons not capable of giving valid consent, and in particular those under any form of detention or imprisonment. Such persons should not be subjected to any medical or scientific experimentation that may be detrimental to their health.

8. The Committee notes that it is not sufficient for the implementation of article 7 to prohibit such treatment or punishment or to make it a crime. States parties should inform the Committee of the legislative, administrative, judicial and other measures they take to prevent and punish acts of torture and cruel, inhuman and degrading treatment in any territory under their jurisdiction.

9. In the view of the Committee, States parties must not expose individuals to the danger of torture or cruel, inhuman or degrading treatment or punishment upon return to another country by way of their extradition, expulsion or refoulement. States parties should indicate in their reports what measures they have adopted to that end.

10. The Committee should be informed how States parties disseminate, to the population at large, relevant information concerning the ban on torture and the treatment prohibited by article 7. Enforcement personnel, medical personnel, police officers and any other persons involved in the custody or treatment of any individual subjected to any form of arrest, detention or imprisonment must receive appropriate instruction and training. States parties should inform the Committee of the instruction and training given and the way in which the prohibition of article 7 forms an integral part of the operational rules and ethical standards to be followed by such persons.

11. In addition to describing steps to provide the general protection against acts prohibited under article 7 to which anyone is entitled, the State party should provide detailed information on safeguards for the special protection of particularly vulnerable persons. It should be noted that keeping under systematic review interrogation rules, instructions, methods and practices as well as arrangements for the custody and treatment of persons subjected to any form of arrest, detention or imprisonment is an effective means of preventing cases of torture and ill-treatment. To guarantee the effective protection of detained persons, provisions should be made for detainees to be held in places officially recognized as places of detention and for their names and places of detention, as well as for the names of persons responsible for their detention, to be kept in registers readily available and accessible to those concerned, including relatives and friends. To the same effect, the time and place of all interrogations should be recorded, together with the names of all those present and this information should also be available for purposes of judicial or administrative proceedings. Provisions should also be made against incommunicado detention. In that connection, States parties should ensure that any places of detention be free from any equipment liable to be used for inflicting torture or ill-treatment. The protection of the detainee also requires that prompt and regular access be given to doctors and lawyers and, under appropriate supervision when the investigation so requires, to family members.

12. It is important for the discouragement of violations under article 7 that the law must prohibit the use of admissibility in judicial proceedings of statements or confessions obtained through torture or other prohibited treatment.

13. States parties should indicate when presenting their reports the provisions of their criminal law which penalize torture and cruel, inhuman and degrading treatment or punishment, specifying the penalties applicable to such acts, whether committed by public officials or other persons acting on behalf of the State, or by private persons. Those who violate article 7, whether by encouraging, ordering, tolerating or perpetrating prohibited acts, must be held responsible. Consequently, those who have refused to obey orders must not be punished or subjected to any adverse treatment.

14. Article 7 should be read in conjunction with article 2, paragraph 3, of the Covenant. In their reports, States parties should indicate how their legal system effectively guarantees the immediate termination of all the

acts prohibited by article 7 as well as appropriate redress. The right to lodge complaints against maltreatment prohibited by article 7 must be recognized in the domestic law. Complaints must be investigated promptly and impartially by competent authorities so as to make the remedy effective. The reports of States parties should provide specific information on the remedies available to victims of maltreatment and the procedure that complainants must follow, and statistics on the number of complaints and how they have been dealt with.

15. The Committee has noted that some States have granted amnesty in respect of acts of torture. Amnesties are generally incompatible with the duty of States to investigate such acts; to guarantee freedom from such acts within their jurisdiction; and to ensure that they do not occur in the future. States may not deprive individuals of the right to an effective remedy, including compensation and such full rehabilitation as may be possible.

GENERAL COMMENT 21
Replaces general comment 9 concerning humane treatment
of persons deprived of liberty
(Article 10)
(Forty-fourth session, 1992)

1. This general comment replaces general comment 9 (the sixteenth session, 1982) reflecting and further developing it.

2. Article 10, paragraph 1, of the International Covenant on Civil and Political Rights applies to any one deprived of liberty under the laws and authority of the State who is held in prisons, hospitals—particularly psychiatric hospitals—detention camps or correctional institutions or elsewhere. States parties should ensure that the principle stipulated therein is observed in all institutions and establishments within their jurisdiction where persons are being held.

3. Article 10, paragraph 1, imposes on States parties a positive obligation towards persons who are particularly vulnerable because of their status as persons deprived of liberty, and complements for them the ban on torture or other cruel, inhuman or degrading treatment or punishment contained in article 7 of the Covenant. Thus, not only may persons deprived of their liberty not be subjected to treatment that is contrary to article 7, including medical or scientific experimentation, but neither may they be subjected to any hardship or constraint other than that resulting from the deprivation of liberty; respect for the dignity of such persons must be guaranteed under the same conditions as for that of free persons. Persons deprived of their liberty enjoy all the rights set forth in the Covenant, subject to the restrictions that are unavoidable in a closed environment.

4. Treating all persons deprived of their liberty with humanity and with respect for their dignity is a fundamental and universally applicable rule. Consequently, the application of this rule, as a minimum, cannot be dependent on the material resources available in the State party. This rule must be applied without distinction of any kind, such as race, colour, sex, language, religion, political or other opinion, national or social origin, property, birth or other status.

5. States parties are invited to indicate in their reports to what extent they are applying the relevant United Nations standards applicable to the treatment of prisoners: the Standard Minimum Rules for the Treatment of Prisoners (1957), the Body of Principles for the Protection of All Persons under Any Form of Detention or Imprisonment (1988), the Code of Conduct for Law Enforcement Officials (1978) and the Principles of Medical Ethics relevant to the Role of Health Personnel, particularly Physicians, in the Protection of Prisoners and Detainees against Torture and Other Cruel, Inhuman or Degrading Treatment or Punishment (1982).

6. The Committee recalls that reports should provide detailed information on national legislative and administrative provisions that have a bearing on the right provided for in article 10, paragraph 1. The Committee also considers that it is necessary for reports to specify what concrete measures have been taken by the competent authorities to monitor the effective application of the rules regarding the treatment of persons deprived of their liberty. States parties should include in their reports information concerning the system for supervising penitentiary establishments, the specific measures to prevent torture and cruel, inhuman or degrading treatment, and how impartial supervision is ensured.

7. Furthermore, the Committee recalls that reports should indicate whether the various applicable provisions form an integral part of the instruction and training of the personnel who have authority over persons

deprived of their liberty and whether they are strictly adhered to by such personnel in the discharge of their duties. It would also be appropriate to specify whether arrested or detained persons have access to such information and have effective legal means enabling them to ensure that those rules are respected, to complain if the rules are ignored and to obtain adequate compensation in the event of a violation.

8. The Committee recalls that the principle set forth in article 10, paragraph 1, constitutes the basis for the more specific obligations of States parties in respect of criminal justice, which are set forth in article 10, paragraphs 2 and 3.

9. Article 10, paragraph 2 (a), provides for the segregation, save in exceptional circumstances, of accused persons from convicted ones. Such segregation is required in order to emphasize their status as unconvicted persons who at the same time enjoy the right to be presumed innocent as stated in article 14, paragraph 2. The reports of States parties should indicate how the separation of accused persons from convicted persons is effected and explain how the treatment of accused persons differs from that of convicted persons.

10. As to article 10, paragraph 3, which concerns convicted persons, the Committee wishes to have detailed information on the operation of the penitentiary system of the State party. No penitentiary system should be only retributory; it should essentially seek the reformation and social rehabilitation of the prisoner. States parties are invited to specify whether they have a system to provide assistance after release and to give information as to its success.

11. In a number of cases, the information furnished by the State party contains no specific reference either to legislative or administrative provisions or to practical measures to ensure the re-education of convicted persons. The Committee requests specific information concerning the measures taken to provide teaching, education and re-education, vocational guidance and training and also concerning work programmes for prisoners inside the penitentiary establishment as well as outside.

12. In order to determine whether the principle set forth in article 10, paragraph 3, is being fully respected, the Committee also requests information on the specific measures applied during detention, e.g., how convicted persons are dealt with individually and how they are categorized, the disciplinary system, solitary confinement and high-security detention and the conditions under which contacts are ensured with the outside world (family, lawyer, social and medical services, non-governmental organizations).

13. Moreover, the Committee notes that in the reports of some States parties no information has been provided concerning the treatment accorded to accused juvenile persons and juvenile offenders. Article 10, paragraph 2 (b), provides that accused juvenile persons shall be separated from adults. The information given in reports shows that some States parties are not paying the necessary attention to the fact that this is a mandatory provision of the Covenant. The text also provides that cases involving juveniles must be considered as speedily as possible. Reports should specify the measures taken by States parties to give effect to that provision. Lastly, under article 10, paragraph 3, juvenile offenders shall be segregated from adults and be accorded treatment appropriate to their age and legal status in so far as conditions of detention are concerned, such as shorter working hours and contact with relatives, with the aim of furthering their reformation and rehabilitation. Article 10 does not indicate any limits of juvenile age. While this is to be determined by each State party in the light of relevant social, cultural and other conditions, the Committee is of the opinion that article 6, paragraph 5, suggests that all persons under the age of 18 should be treated as juveniles, at least in matters relating to criminal justice. States should give relevant information about the age groups of persons treated as juveniles. In that regard, States parties are invited to indicate whether they are applying the United Nations Standard Minimum Rules for the Administration of Juvenile Justice, known as the Beijing Rules (1987).

GENERAL COMMENT 23
The rights of minorities
(Article 27)
(Fiftieth session, 1994)

1. Article 27 of the Covenant provides that, in those States in which ethnic, religious or linguistic minorities exist, persons belonging to these minorities shall not be denied the right, in community with the other members of their group, to enjoy their own culture, to profess and practise their own religion, or to use their own language. The Committee observes that this article establishes and recognizes a right which is conferred on individuals belonging to minority groups and which is distinct from, and additional to, all the other rights which, as individuals in common with everyone else, they are already entitled to enjoy under the Covenant.

2. In some communications submitted to the Committee under the Optional Protocol, the right protected under article 27 has been confused with the right of peoples to self-determination proclaimed in article 1 of the Covenant. Further, in reports submitted by States parties under article 40 of the Covenant, the obligations placed upon States parties under article 27 have sometimes been confused with their duty under article 2.1 to ensure the enjoyment of the rights guaranteed under the Covenant without discrimination and also with equality before the law and equal protection of the law under article 26.

3.1. The Covenant draws a distinction between the right to self-determination and the rights protected under article 27. The former is expressed to be a right belonging to peoples and is dealt with in a separate part (Part I) of the Covenant. Self-determination is not a right cognizable under the Optional Protocol. Article 27, on the other hand, relates to rights conferred on individuals as such and is included, like the articles relating to other personal rights conferred on individuals, in Part III of the Covenant and is cognizable under the Optional Protocol.

3.2. The enjoyment of the rights to which article 27 relates does not prejudice the sovereignty and territorial integrity of a State party. At the same time, one or other aspect of the rights of individuals protected under that article—for example, to enjoy a particular culture—may consist in a way of life which is closely associated with territory and use of its resources. This may particularly be true of members of indigenous communities constituting a minority.

4. The Covenant also distinguishes the rights protected under article 27 from the guarantees under articles 2.1 and 26. The entitlement, under article 2.1, to enjoy the rights under the Covenant without discrimination applies to all individuals within the territory or under the jurisdiction of the State whether or not those persons belong to a minority. In addition, there is a distinct right provided under article 26 for equality before the law, equal protection of the law, and non-discrimination in respect of rights granted and obligations imposed by the States. It governs the exercise of all rights, whether protected under the Covenant or not, which the State party confers by law on individuals within its territory or under its jurisdiction, irrespective of whether they belong to the minorities specified in article 27 or not. Some States parties who claim that they do not discriminate on grounds of ethnicity, language or religion, wrongly contend, on that basis alone, that they have no minorities.

5.1. The terms used in article 27 indicate that the persons designed to be protected are those who belong to a group and who share in common a culture, a religion and/or a language. Those terms also indicate that the individuals designed to be protected need not be citizens of the State party. In this regard, the obligations deriving from article 2.1 are also relevant, since a State party is required under that article to ensure that the rights protected under the Covenant are available to all individuals within its territory and subject to its jurisdiction, except rights which are expressly made to apply to citizens, for example, political rights under article 25. A State party may not, therefore, restrict the rights under article 27 to its citizens alone.

5.2. Article 27 confers rights on persons belonging to minorities which "exist" in a State party. Given the nature and scope of the rights envisaged under that article, it is not relevant to determine the degree of permanence that the term "exist" connotes. Those rights simply are that individuals belonging to those minorities should not be denied the right, in community with members of their group, to enjoy their own culture, to practise their religion and speak their language. Just as they need not be nationals or citizens, they need not be permanent residents. Thus, migrant workers or even visitors in a State party constituting such minorities are entitled not to be denied the exercise of those rights. As any other individual in the territory of the State party, they would, also for this purpose, have the general rights, for example, to freedom of association, of assembly, and of expression. The existence of an ethnic, religious or linguistic minority in a given State party does not depend upon a decision by that State party but requires to be established by objective criteria.

5.3. The right of individuals belonging to a linguistic minority to use their language among themselves, in private or in public, is distinct from other language rights protected under the Covenant. In particular, it should be distinguished from the general right to freedom of expression protected under article 19. The latter right is available to all persons, irrespective of whether they belong to minorities or not. Further, the right protected under article 27 should be distinguished from the particular right which article 14.3 (f) of the Covenant confers on accused persons to interpretation where they cannot understand or speak the language used in the courts. Article 14.3 (f) does not, in any other circumstances, confer on accused persons the right to use or speak the language of their choice in court proceedings.

6.1. Although article 27 is expressed in negative terms, that article, nevertheless, does recognize the existence of a "right" and requires that it shall not be denied. Consequently, a State party is under an obligation to ensure that the existence and the exercise of this right are protected against their denial or violation. Positive measures of protection are, therefore, required not only against the acts of the State party itself, whether through its legislative, judicial or administrative authorities, but also against the acts of other persons within the State party.

6.2. Although the rights protected under article 27 are individual rights, they depend in turn on the ability of the minority group to maintain its culture, language or religion. Accordingly, positive measures by States may also be necessary to protect the identity of a minority and the rights of its members to enjoy and develop their culture and language and to practice their religion, in community with the other members of the group. In this connection, it has to be observed that such positive measures must respect the provisions of articles 2.1 and 26 of the Covenant both as regards the treatment between different minorities and the treatment between the persons belonging to them and the remaining part of the population. However, as long as those measures are aimed at correcting conditions which prevent or impair the enjoyment of the rights guaranteed under article 27, they may constitute a legitimate differentiation under the Covenant, provided that they are based on reasonable and objective criteria.

7. With regard to the exercise of the cultural rights protected under article 27, the Committee observes that culture manifests itself in many forms, including a particular way of life associated with the use of land resources, especially in the case of indigenous peoples. That right may include such traditional activities as fishing or hunting and the right to live in reserves protected by law. The enjoyment of those rights may require positive legal measures of protection and measures to ensure the effective participation of members of minority communities in decisions which affect them.

8. The Committee observes that none of the rights protected under article 27 of the Covenant may be legitimately exercised in a manner or to an extent inconsistent with the other provisions of the Covenant.

9. The Committee concludes that article 27 relates to rights whose protection imposes specific obligations on States parties. The protection of these rights is directed towards ensuring the survival and continued development of the cultural, religious and social identity of the minorities concerned, thus enriching the fabric of society as a whole. Accordingly, the Committee observes that these rights must be protected as such and should not be confused with other personal rights conferred on one and all under the Covenant. States parties, therefore, have an obligation to ensure that the exercise of these rights is fully protected and they should indicate in their reports the measures they have adopted to this end.

GENERAL COMMENT 24
Issues relating to reservations made upon ratification or accession to the Covenant or the Optional Protocols thereto, or in relation to declarations under article 41 of the Covenant
(Fifty-second session, 1994)

1. As of 1 November 1994, 46 of the 127 States parties to the International Covenant on Civil and Political Rights had, between them, entered 150 reservations of varying significance to their acceptance of the obligations of the Covenant. Some of these reservations exclude the duty to provide and guarantee particular rights in the Covenant. Others are couched in more general terms, often directed to ensuring the continued paramountcy of certain domestic legal provisions. Still others are directed at the competence of the Committee. The number of reservations, their content and their scope may undermine the effective implementation of the Covenant and tend to weaken respect for the obligations of States parties. It is important for States parties to know exactly what obligations they, and other States parties, have in fact undertaken. And the Committee, in the performance of its duties under either article 40 of the Covenant or under the Optional Protocols, must know whether a State is bound by a particular obligation or to what extent. This will require a determination as to whether a unilateral statement is a reservation or an interpretative declaration and a determination of its acceptability and effects.

2. For these reasons the Committee has deemed it useful to address in a General Comment the issues of international law and human rights policy that arise. The General Comment identifies the principles of international law that apply to the making of reservations and by reference to which their acceptability is to be tested and their purport to be interpreted. It addresses the role of States parties in relation to the reservations of others. It further addresses the role of the Committee itself in relation to reservations. And it makes certain recommendations to present States parties for a reviewing of reservations and to those States that are not yet parties about legal and human rights policy considerations to be borne in mind should they consider ratifying or acceding with particular reservations.

3. It is not always easy to distinguish a reservation from a declaration as to a State's understanding of the interpretation of a provision, or from a statement of policy. Regard will be had to the intention of the State, rather than the form of the instrument. If a statement, irrespective of its name or title, purports to exclude or modify the legal effect of a treaty in its application to the State, it constitutes a reservation. Conversely, if a so-called reservation merely offers a State's understanding of a provision but does not exclude or modify that provision in its application to that State, it is, in reality, not a reservation.

4. The possibility of entering reservations may encourage States which consider that they have difficulties in guaranteeing all the rights in the Covenant none the less to accept the generality of obligations in that instrument. Reservations may serve a useful function to enable States to adapt specific elements in their laws to the inherent rights of each person as articulated in the Covenant. However, it is desirable in principle that States accept the full range of obligations, because the human rights norms are the legal expression of the essential rights that every person is entitled to as a human being.

5. The Covenant neither prohibits reservations nor mentions any type of permitted reservation. The same is true of the first Optional Protocol. The Second Optional Protocol provides, in article 2, paragraph 1, that "No reservation is admissible to the present Protocol, except for a reservation made at the time of ratification or accession that provides for the application of the death penalty in time of war pursuant to a conviction for a most serious crime of a military nature committed during wartime". Paragraphs 2 and 3 provide for certain procedural obligations.

6. The absence of a prohibition on reservations does not mean that any reservation is permitted. The matter of reservations under the Covenant and the first Optional Protocol is governed by international law. Article 19 (3) of the Vienna Convention on the Law of Treaties provides relevant guidance. It stipulates that where a reservation is not prohibited by the treaty or falls within the specified permitted categories, a State may make a reservation provided it is not incompatible with the object and purpose of the treaty. Even though, unlike some other human rights treaties, the Covenant does not incorporate a specific reference to the object and purpose test, that test governs the matter of interpretation and acceptability of reservations.

7. In an instrument which articulates very many civil and political rights, each of the many articles, and indeed their interplay, secures the objectives of the Covenant. The object and purpose of the Covenant is to create legally binding standards for human rights by defining certain civil and political rights and placing them in a framework of obligations which are legally binding for those States which ratify; and to provide an efficacious supervisory machinery for the obligations undertaken.

8. Reservations that offend peremptory norms would not be compatible with the object and purpose of the Covenant. Although treaties that are mere exchanges of obligations between States allow them to reserve inter se application of rules of general international law, it is otherwise in human rights treaties, which are for the benefit of persons within their jurisdiction. Accordingly, provisions in the Covenant that represent customary international law (and a fortiori when they have the character of peremptory norms) may not be the subject of reservations. Accordingly, a State may not reserve the right to engage in slavery, to torture, to subject persons to cruel, inhuman or degrading treatment or punishment, to arbitrarily deprive persons of their lives, to arbitrarily arrest and detain persons, to deny freedom of thought, conscience and religion, to presume a person guilty unless he proves his innocence, to execute pregnant women or children, to permit the advocacy of national, racial or religious hatred, to deny to persons of marriageable age the right to marry, or to deny to minorities the right to enjoy their own culture, profess their own religion, or use their own language. And while reservations to particular clauses of article 14 may be acceptable, a general reservation to the right to a fair trial would not be.

9. Applying more generally the object and purpose test to the Covenant, the Committee notes that, for example, reservation to article 1 denying peoples the right to determine their own political status and to pursue their economic, social and cultural development, would be incompatible with the object and purpose of the Covenant. Equally, a reservation to the obligation to respect and ensure the rights, and to do so on a non-discriminatory basis (article 2 (1)) would not be acceptable. Nor may a State reserve an entitlement not to take the necessary steps at the domestic level to give effect to the rights of the Covenant (article 2 (2)).

10. The Committee has further examined whether categories of reservations may offend the "object and purpose" test. In particular, it falls for consideration as to whether reservations to the non-derogable provisions of the Covenant are compatible with its object and purpose. While there is no hierarchy of importance of rights under the Covenant, the operation of certain rights may not be suspended, even in times of national emergency. This underlines the great importance of non-derogable rights. But not all

rights of profound importance, such as articles 9 and 27 of the Covenant, have in fact been made non-derogable. One reason for certain rights being made non-derogable is because their suspension is irrelevant to the legitimate control of the state of national emergency (for example, no imprisonment for debt, in article 11). Another reason is that derogation may indeed be impossible (as, for example, freedom of conscience). At the same time, some provisions are non-derogable exactly because without them there would be no rule of law. A reservation to the provisions of article 4 itself, which precisely stipulates the balance to be struck between the interests of the State and the rights of the individual in times of emergency, would fall in this category. And some non-derogable rights, which in any event cannot be reserved because of their status as peremptory norms, are also of this character—the prohibition of torture and arbitrary deprivation of life are examples. While there is no automatic correlation between reservations to non-derogable provisions, and reservations which offend against the object and purpose of the Covenant, a State has a heavy onus to justify such a reservation.

11. The Covenant consists not just of the specified rights, but of important supportive guarantees. These guarantees provide the necessary framework for securing the rights in the Covenant and are thus essential to its object and purpose. Some operate at the national level and some at the international level. Reservations designed to remove these guarantees are thus not acceptable. Thus, a State could not make a reservation to article 2, paragraph 3, of the Covenant, indicating that it intends to provide no remedies for human rights violations. Guarantees such as these are an integral part of the structure of the Covenant and underpin its efficacy. The Covenant also envisages, for the better attainment of its stated objectives, a monitoring role for the Committee. Reservations that purport to evade that essential element in the design of the Covenant, which is also directed to securing the enjoyment of the rights, are also incompatible with its object and purpose. A State may not reserve the right not to present a report and have it considered by the Committee. The Committee's role under the Covenant, whether under article 40 or under the Optional Protocols, necessarily entails interpreting the provisions of the Covenant and the development of a jurisprudence. Accordingly, a reservation that rejects the Committee's competence to interpret the requirements of any provisions of the Covenant would also be contrary to the object and purpose of that treaty.

12. The intention of the Covenant is that the rights contained therein should be ensured to all those under a State party's jurisdiction. To this end certain attendant requirements are likely to be necessary. Domestic laws may need to be altered properly to reflect the requirements of the Covenant; and mechanisms at the domestic level will be needed to allow the Covenant rights to be enforceable at the local level. Reservations often reveal a tendency of States not to want to change a particular law. And sometimes that tendency is elevated to a general policy. Of particular concern are widely formulated reservations which essentially render ineffective all Covenant rights which would require any change in national law to ensure compliance with Covenant obligations. No real international rights or obligations have thus been accepted. And when there is an absence of provisions to ensure that Covenant rights may be sued on in domestic courts, and, further, a failure to allow individual complaints to be brought to the Committee under the first Optional Protocol, all the essential elements of the Covenant guarantees have been removed.

13. The issue arises as to whether reservations are permissible under the first Optional Protocol and, if so, whether any such reservation might be contrary to the object and purpose of the Covenant or of the first Optional Protocol itself. It is clear that the first Optional Protocol is itself an international treaty, distinct from the Covenant but closely related to it. Its object and purpose is to recognize the competence of the Committee to receive and consider communications from individuals who claim to be victims of a violation by a State party of any of the rights in the Covenant. States accept the substantive rights of individuals by reference to the Covenant, and not the first Optional Protocol. The function of the first Optional Protocol is to allow claims in respect of those rights to be tested before the Committee. Accordingly, a reservation to an obligation of a State to respect and ensure a right contained in the Covenant, made under the first Optional Protocol when it has not previously been made in respect of the same rights under the Covenant, does not affect the State's duty to comply with its substantive obligation. A reservation cannot be made to the Covenant through the vehicle of the Optional Protocol but such a reservation would operate to ensure that the State's compliance with that obligation may not be tested by the Committee under the first Optional Protocol. And because the object and purpose of the first Optional Protocol is to allow the rights obligatory for a State under the Covenant to be tested before the Committee, a reservation that seeks to preclude this would be contrary to the object and purpose of the first Optional Protocol, even if not of the Covenant. A reservation to a substantive obligation made for the first time under the first Optional Protocol would seem

to reflect an intention by the State concerned to prevent the Committee from expressing its views relating to a particular article of the Covenant in an individual case.

14. The Committee considers that reservations relating to the required procedures under the first Optional Protocol would not be compatible with its object and purpose. The Committee must control its own procedures as specified by the Optional Protocol and its rules of procedure. Reservations have, however, purported to limit the competence of the Committee to acts and events occurring after entry into force for the State concerned of the first Optional Protocol. In the view of the Committee this is not a reservation but, most usually, a statement consistent with its normal competence ratione temporis. At the same time, the Committee has insisted upon its competence, even in the face of such statements or observations, when events or acts occurring before the date of entry into force of the first Optional Protocol have continued to have an effect on the rights of a victim subsequent to that date. Reservations have been entered which effectively add an additional ground of inadmissibility under article 5, paragraph 2, by precluding examination of a communication when the same matter has already been examined by another comparable procedure. In so far as the most basic obligation has been to secure independent third party review of the human rights of individuals, the Committee has, where the legal right and the subject-matter are identical under the Covenant and under another international instrument, viewed such a reservation as not violating the object and purpose of the first Optional Protocol.

15. The primary purpose of the Second Optional Protocol is to extend the scope of the substantive obligations undertaken under the Covenant, as they relate to the right to life, by prohibiting execution and abolishing the death penalty. It has its own provision concerning reservations, which is determinative of what is permitted. Article 2, paragraph 1, provides that only one category of reservation is permitted, namely one that reserves the right to apply the death penalty in time of war pursuant to a conviction for a most serious crime of a military nature committed during wartime. Two procedural obligations are incumbent upon States parties wishing to avail themselves of such a reservation. Article 2, paragraph 1, obliges such a State to inform the Secretary-General, at the time of ratification or accession, of the relevant provisions of its national legislation during warfare. This is clearly directed towards the objectives of specificity and transparency and in the view of the Committee a purported reservation unaccompanied by such information is without legal effect. Article 2, paragraph 3, requires a State making such a reservation to notify the Secretary-General of the beginning or ending of a state of war applicable to its territory. In the view of the Committee, no State may seek to avail itself of its reservation (that is, have execution in time of war regarded as lawful) unless it has complied with the procedural requirement of article 2, paragraph 3.

16. The Committee finds it important to address which body has the legal authority to make determinations as to whether specific reservations are compatible with the object and purpose of the Covenant. As for international treaties in general, the International Court of Justice has indicated in the Reservations to the Genocide Convention Case (1951) that a State which objected to a reservation on the grounds of incompatibility with the object and purpose of a treaty could, through objecting, regard the treaty as not in effect as between itself and the reserving State. Article 20, paragraph 4, of the Vienna Convention on the Law of Treaties 1969 contains provisions most relevant to the present case on acceptance of and objection to reservations. This provides for the possibility of a State to object to a reservation made by another State. Article 21 deals with the legal effects of objections by States to reservations made by other States. Essentially, a reservation precludes the operation, as between the reserving and other States, of the provision reserved; and an objection thereto leads to the reservation being in operation as between the reserving and objecting State only to the extent that it has not been objected to.

17. As indicated above, it is the Vienna Convention on the Law of Treaties that provides the definition of reservations and also the application of the object and purpose test in the absence of other specific provisions. But the Committee believes that its provisions on the role of State objections in relation to reservations are inappropriate to address the problem of reservations to human rights treaties. Such treaties, and the Covenant specifically, are not a web of inter-State exchanges of mutual obligations. They concern the endowment of individuals with rights. The principle of inter-State reciprocity has no place, save perhaps in the limited context of reservations to declarations on the Committee's competence under article 41. And because the operation of the classic rules on reservations is so inadequate for the Covenant, States have often not seen any legal interest in or need to object to reservations. The absence of protest by States cannot imply that a reservation is either compatible or incompatible with the object and purpose of the Covenant. Objections have been occasional, made by some States but not others, and on grounds not always specified;

when an objection is made, it often does not specify a legal consequence, or sometimes even indicates that the objecting party none the less does not regard the Covenant as not in effect as between the parties concerned. In short, the pattern is so unclear that it is not safe to assume that a non-objecting State thinks that a particular reservation is acceptable. In the view of the Committee, because of the special characteristics of the Covenant as a human rights treaty, it is open to question what effect objections have between States inter se. However, an objection to a reservation made by States may provide some guidance to the Committee in its interpretation as to its compatibility with the object and purpose of the Covenant.

18. It necessarily falls to the Committee to determine whether a specific reservation is compatible with the object and purpose of the Covenant. This is in part because, as indicated above, it is an inappropriate task for States parties in relation to human rights treaties, and in part because it is a task that the Committee cannot avoid in the performance of its functions. In order to know the scope of its duty to examine a State's compliance under article 40 or a communication under the first Optional Protocol, the Committee has necessarily to take a view on the compatibility of a reservation with the object and purpose of the Covenant and with general international law. Because of the special character of a human rights treaty, the compatibility of a reservation with the object and purpose of the Covenant must be established objectively, by reference to legal principles, and the Committee is particularly well placed to perform this task. The normal consequence of an unacceptable reservation is not that the Covenant will not be in effect at all for a reserving party. Rather, such a reservation will generally be severable, in the sense that the Covenant will be operative for the reserving party without benefit of the reservation.

19. Reservations must be specific and transparent, so that the Committee, those under the jurisdiction of the reserving State and other States parties may be clear as to what obligations of human rights compliance have or have not been undertaken. Reservations may thus not be general, but must refer to a particular provision of the Covenant and indicate in precise terms its scope in relation thereto. When considering the compatibility of possible reservations with the object and purpose of the Covenant, States should also take into consideration the overall effect of a group of reservations, as well as the effect of each reservation on the integrity of the Covenant, which remains an essential consideration. States should not enter so many reservations that they are in effect accepting a limited number of human rights obligations, and not the Covenant as such. So that reservations do not lead to a perpetual non-attainment of international human rights standards, reservations should not systematically reduce the obligations undertaken only to those presently existing in less demanding standards of domestic law. Nor should interpretative declarations or reservations seek to remove an autonomous meaning to Covenant obligations, by pronouncing them to be identical, or to be accepted only in so far as they are identical, with existing provisions of domestic law. States should not seek through reservations or interpretative declarations to determine that the meaning of a provision of the Covenant is the same as that given by an organ of any other international treaty body.

20. States should institute procedures to ensure that each and every proposed reservation is compatible with the object and purpose of the Covenant. It is desirable for a State entering a reservation to indicate in precise terms the domestic legislation or practices which it believes to be incompatible with the Covenant obligation reserved; and to explain the time period it requires to render its own laws and practices compatible with the Covenant, or why it is unable to render its own laws and practices compatible with the Covenant. States should also ensure that the necessity for maintaining reservations is periodically reviewed, taking into account any observations and recommendations made by the Committee during examination of their reports. Reservations should be withdrawn at the earliest possible moment. Reports to the Committee should contain information on what action has been taken to review, reconsider or withdraw reservations.

GENERAL COMMENTS ADOPTED BY THE HUMAN RIGHTS COMMITTEE UNDER
ARTICLE 40, PARAGRAPH 4,
OF THE INTERNATIONAL COVENANT ON CIVIL AND POLITICAL RIGHTS
Addendum
GENERAL COMMENT No. 28 (68)
Equality of rights between men and women
(Article 3)

1. The Committee has decided to update its general comment on article 3 of the Covenant and to replace General Comment No. 4 (thirteenth session, 1981), in the light of the experience it has gathered in

its activities over the last 20 years. The present revision seeks to take account of the important impact of this article on the enjoyment by women of the human rights protected under the Covenant.

2. Article 3 implies that all human beings should enjoy the rights provided for in the Covenant, on an equal basis and in their totality. The full effect of this provision is impaired whenever any person is denied the full and equal enjoyment of any right. Consequently, States should ensure to men and women equally the enjoyment of all rights provided for in the Covenant.

3. The obligation to ensure to all individuals the rights recognized in the Covenant, established in articles 2 and 3 of the Covenant, requires that States parties take all necessary steps to enable every person to enjoy those rights. These steps include the removal of obstacles to the equal enjoyment of such rights, the education of the population and of State officials in human rights, and the adjustment of domestic legislation so as to give effect to the undertakings set forth in the Covenant. The State party must not only adopt measures of protection, but also positive measures in all areas so as to achieve the effective and equal empowerment of women. States parties must provide information regarding the actual role of women in society so that the Committee may ascertain what measures, in addition to legislative provisions, have been or should be taken to give effect to these obligations, what progress has been made, what difficulties are encountered and what steps are being taken to overcome them.

4. States parties are responsible for ensuring the equal enjoyment of rights without any discrimination. Articles 2 and 3 mandate States parties to take all steps necessary, including the prohibition of discrimination on the ground of sex, to put an end to discriminatory actions, both in the public and the private sector, which impair the equal enjoyment of rights.

5. Inequality in the enjoyment of rights by women throughout the world is deeply embedded in tradition, history and culture, including religious attitudes. The subordinate role of women in some countries is illustrated by the high incidence of prenatal sex selection and abortion of female foetuses. States parties should ensure that traditional, historical, religious or cultural attitudes are not used to justify violations of women's right to equality before the law and to equal enjoyment of all Covenant rights. States parties should furnish appropriate information on those aspects of tradition, history, cultural practices and religious attitudes which jeopardize, or may jeopardize, compliance with article 3, and indicate what measures they have taken or intend to take to overcome such factors.

6. In order to fulfil the obligation set forth in article 3, States parties should take account of the factors which impede the equal enjoyment by women and men of each right specified in the Covenant. To enable the Committee to obtain a complete picture of the situation of women in each State party as regards the implementation of the rights in the Covenant, this general comment identifies some of the factors affecting the equal enjoyment by women of the rights under the Covenant and spells out the type of information that is required with regard to these rights.

7. The equal enjoyment of human rights by women must be protected during a state of emergency (art. 4). States parties which take measures derogating from their obligations under the Covenant in time of public emergency, as provided in article 4, should provide information to the Committee with respect to the impact on the situation of women of such measures and should demonstrate that they are non-discriminatory.

8. Women are particularly vulnerable in times of internal or international armed conflicts. States parties should inform the Committee of all measures taken during these situations to protect women from rape, abduction and other forms of gender-based violence.

9. In becoming parties to the Covenant, States undertake, in accordance with article 3, to ensure the equal right of men and women to the enjoyment of all civil and political rights set forth in the Covenant, and in accordance with article 5, nothing in the Covenant may be interpreted as implying for any State, group or person any right to engage in any activity or perform any act aimed at the destruction of any of the rights provided for in article 3, or at limitations not covered by the Covenant. Moreover, there shall be no restriction upon or derogation from the equal enjoyment by women of all fundamental human rights recognized or existing pursuant to law, conventions, regulations or customs, on the pretext that the Covenant does not recognize such rights or that it recognizes them to a lesser extent.

10. When reporting on the right to life protected by article 6, States parties should provide data on birth rates and on pregnancy- and childbirth-related deaths of women. Gender-disaggregated data should be provided on infant mortality rates. States parties should give information on any measures taken by the State to help women prevent unwanted pregnancies, and to ensure that they do not have to undergo life-threatening clandestine abortions. States parties should also report on measures to protect women from practices that

violate their right to life, such as female infanticide, the burning of widows and dowry killings. The Committee also wishes to have information on the particular impact on women of poverty and deprivation that may pose a threat to their lives.

11. To assess compliance with article 7 of the Covenant, as well as with article 24, which mandates special protection for children, the Committee needs to be provided information on national laws and practice with regard to domestic and other types of violence against women, including rape. It also needs to know whether the State party gives access to safe abortion to women who have become pregnant as a result of rape. The States parties should also provide the Committee with information on measures to prevent forced abortion or forced sterilization. In States parties where the practice of genital mutilation exists information on its extent and on measures to eliminate it should be provided. The information provided by States parties on all these issues should include measures of protection, including legal remedies, for women whose rights under article 7 have been violated.

12. Having regard to their obligations under article 8, States parties should inform the Committee of measures taken to eliminate trafficking of women and children, within the country or across borders, and forced prostitution. They must also provide information on measures taken to protect women and children, including foreign women and children, from slavery, disguised, *inter alia*, as domestic or other kinds of personal service. States parties where women and children are recruited, and from which they are taken, and States parties where they are received should provide information on measures, national or international, which have been taken in order to prevent the violation of women's and children's rights.

13. States parties should provide information on any specific regulation of clothing to be worn by women in public. The Committee stresses that such regulations may involve a violation of a number of rights guaranteed by the Covenant, such as: article 26, on non-discrimination; article 7, if corporal punishment is imposed in order to enforce such a regulation; article 9, when failure to comply with the regulation is punished by arrest; article 12, if liberty of movement is subject to such a constraint; article 17, which guarantees all persons the right to privacy without arbitrary or unlawful interference; articles 18 and 19, when women are subjected to clothing requirements that are not in keeping with their religion or their right of self-expression; and, lastly, article 27, when the clothing requirements conflict with the culture to which the woman can lay a claim.

14. With regard to article 9, States parties should provide information on any laws or practices which may deprive women of their liberty on an arbitrary or unequal basis, such as by confinement within the house (see General Comment No. 8, para. 1).

15. As regards articles 7 and 10, States parties must provide all information relevant to ensuring that the rights of persons deprived of their liberty are protected on equal terms for men and women. In particular, States parties should report on whether men and women are separated in prisons and whether women are guarded only by female guards. States parties should also report about compliance with the rule that accused juvenile females shall be separated from adults and on any difference in treatment between male and female persons deprived of liberty, such as access to rehabilitation and education programmes and to conjugal and family visits. Pregnant women who are deprived of their liberty should receive humane treatment and respect for their inherent dignity at all times, and in particular during the birth and while caring for their newborn children; States parties should report on facilities to ensure this and on medical and health care for such mothers and their babies.

16. As regards article 12, States parties should provide information on any legal provision or any practice which restricts women's right to freedom of movement, for example the exercise of marital powers over the wife or of parental powers over adult daughters; legal or de facto requirements which prevent women from travelling, such as the requirement of consent of a third party to the issuance of a passport or other type of travel documents to an adult woman. States parties should also report on measures taken to eliminate such laws and practices and to protect women against them, including reference to available domestic remedies (see General Comment No. 27, paras. 6 and 18).

17. States parties should ensure that alien women are accorded on an equal basis the right to submit arguments against their expulsion and to have their case reviewed, as provided in article 13. In this regard, they should be entitled to submit arguments based on gender-specific violations of the Covenant such as those mentioned in paragraphs 10 and 11 above.

18. States parties should provide information to enable the Committee to ascertain whether access to justice and the right to a fair trial, provided for in article 14, are enjoyed by women on equal terms with

men. In particular, States parties should inform the Committee whether there are legal provisions preventing women from direct and autonomous access to the courts (see communication No. 202/1986, *Ato del Avellanal v Peru*, Views of 28 October 1988); whether women may give evidence as witnesses on the same terms as men; and whether measures are taken to ensure women equal access to legal aid, in particular in family matters. States parties should report on whether certain categories of women are denied the enjoyment of the presumption of innocence under article 14, paragraph 2, and on the measures which have been taken to put an end to this situation.

19. The right of everyone under article 16 to be recognized everywhere as a person before the law is particularly pertinent for women, who often see it curtailed by reason of sex or marital status. This right implies that the capacity of women to own property, to enter into a contract or to exercise other civil rights may not be restricted on the basis of marital status or any other discriminatory ground. It also implies that women may not be treated as objects to be given, together with the property of the deceased husband, to his family. States must provide information on laws or practices that prevent women from being treated or from functioning as full legal persons and the measures taken to eradicate laws or practices that allow such treatment.

20. States parties must provide information to enable the Committee to assess the effect of any laws and practices that may interfere with women's right to enjoy privacy and other rights protected by article 17 on the basis of equality with men. An example of such interference arises where the sexual life of a woman is taken into consideration in deciding the extent of her legal rights and protections, including protection against rape. Another area where States may fail to respect women's privacy relates to their reproductive functions, for example, where there is a requirement for the husband's authorization to make a decision in regard to sterilization; where general requirements are imposed for the sterilization of women, such as having a certain number of children or being of a certain age, or where States impose a legal duty upon doctors and other health personnel to report cases of women who have undergone abortion. In these instances, other rights in the Covenant, such as those of articles 6 and 7, might also be at stake. Women's privacy may also be interfered with by private actors, such as employers who request a pregnancy test before hiring a woman. States parties should report on any laws and public or private actions that interfere with the equal enjoyment by women of the rights under article 17, and on the measures taken to eliminate such interference and to afford women protection from any such interference.

21. States parties must take measures to ensure that freedom of thought, conscience and religion, and the freedom to adopt the religion or belief of one's choice—including the freedom to change religion or belief and to express one's religion or belief—will be guaranteed and protected in law and in practice for both men and women, on the same terms and without discrimination. These freedoms, protected by article 18, must not be subject to restrictions other than those authorized by the Covenant and must not be constrained by, *inter alia*, rules requiring permission from third parties, or by interference from fathers, husbands, brothers or others. Article 18 may not be relied upon to justify discrimination against women by reference to freedom of thought, conscience and religion; States parties should therefore provide information on the status of women as regards their freedom of thought, conscience and religion, and indicate what steps they have taken or intend to take both to eliminate and prevent infringements of these freedoms in respect of women and to protect their right not to be discriminated against.

22. In relation to article 19, States parties should inform the Committee of any laws or other factors which may impede women from exercising the rights protected under this provision on an equal basis. As the publication and dissemination of obscene and pornographic material which portrays women and girls as objects of violence or degrading or inhuman treatment is likely to promote these kinds of treatment of women and girls, States parties should provide information about legal measures to restrict the publication or dissemination of such material.

23. States are required to treat men and women equally in regard to marriage in accordance with article 23, which has been elaborated further by General Comment No. 19 (1990). Men and women have the right to enter into marriage only with their free and full consent, and States have an obligation to protect the enjoyment of this right on an equal basis. Many factors may prevent women from being able to make the decision to marry freely. One factor relates to the minimum age for marriage. That age should be set by the State on the basis of equal criteria for men and women. These criteria should ensure women's capacity to make an informed and uncoerced decision. A second factor in some States may be that either by statutory or customary law a guardian, who is generally male, consents to the marriage instead of the woman herself, thereby preventing women from exercising a free choice.

24. Another factor that may affect women's right to marry only when they have given free and full consent is the existence of social attitudes which tend to marginalize women victims of rape and put pressure on them to agree to marriage. A woman's free and full consent to marriage may also be undermined by laws which allow the rapist to have his criminal responsibility extinguished or mitigated if he marries the victim. States parties should indicate whether marrying the victim extinguishes or mitigates criminal responsibility and, in the case in which the victim is a minor, whether the rape reduces the marriageable age of the victim, particularly in societies where rape victims have to endure marginalization from society. A different aspect of the right to marry may be affected when States impose restrictions on remarriage by women that are not imposed on men. Also, the right to choose one's spouse may be restricted by laws or practices that prevent the marriage of a woman of a particular religion to a man who professes no religion or a different religion. States should provide information on these laws and practices and on the measures taken to abolish the laws and eradicate the practices which undermine the right of women to marry only when they have given free and full consent. It should also be noted that equality of treatment with regard to the right to marry implies that polygamy is incompatible with this principle. Polygamy violates the dignity of women. It is an inadmissible discrimination against women. Consequently, it should be definitely abolished wherever it continues to exist.

25. To fulfil their obligations under article 23, paragraph 4, States parties must ensure that the matrimonial regime contains equal rights and obligations for both spouses with regard to the custody and care of children, the children's religious and moral education, the capacity to transmit to children the parent's nationality, and the ownership or administration of property, whether common property or property in the sole ownership of either spouse. States parties should review their legislation to ensure that married women have equal rights in regard to the ownership and administration of such property, where necessary. Also, States parties should ensure that no sex-based discrimination occurs in respect of the acquisition or loss of nationality by reason of marriage, of residence rights, and of the right of each spouse to retain the use of his or her original family name or to participate on an equal basis in the choice of a new family name. Equality during marriage implies that husband and wife should participate equally in responsibility and authority within the family.

26. States parties must also ensure equality in regard to the dissolution of marriage, which excludes the possibility of repudiation. The grounds for divorce and annulment should be the same for men and women, as well as decisions with regard to property distribution, alimony and the custody of children. Determination of the need to maintain contact between children and the non-custodial parent should be based on equal considerations. Women should also have equal inheritance rights to those of men when the dissolution of marriage is caused by the death of one of the spouses.

27. In giving effect to recognition of the family in the context of article 23, it is important to accept the concept of the various forms of family, including unmarried couples and their children and single parents and their children, and to ensure the equal treatment of women in these contexts (see General Comment No. 19, para. 2). Single-parent families frequently consist of a single woman caring for one or more children, and States parties should describe what measures of support are in place to enable her to discharge her parental functions on the basis of equality with a man in a similar position.

28. The obligation of States parties to protect children (art. 24) should be carried out equally for boys and girls. States parties should report on measures taken to ensure that girls are treated equally to boys in education, in feeding and in health care, and provide the Committee with disaggregated data in this respect. States parties should eradicate, both through legislation and any other appropriate measures, all cultural or religious practices which jeopardize the freedom and well-being of female children.

29. The right to participate in the conduct of public affairs is not fully implemented everywhere on an equal basis. States parties must ensure that the law guarantees to women the rights contained in article 25 on equal terms with men and take effective and positive measures to promote and ensure women's participation in the conduct of public affairs and in public office, including appropriate affirmative action. Effective measures taken by States parties to ensure that all persons entitled to vote are able to exercise that right should not be discriminatory on the grounds of sex. The Committee requires States parties to provide statistical information on the percentage of women in publicly elected office, including the legislature, as well as in high-ranking civil service positions and the judiciary.

30. Discrimination against women is often intertwined with discrimination on other grounds such as race, colour, language, religion, political or other opinion, national or social origin, property, birth or

other status. States parties should address the ways in which any instances of discrimination on other grounds affect women in a particular way, and include information on the measures taken to counter these effects.

31. The right to equality before the law and freedom from discrimination, protected by article 26, requires States to act against discrimination by public and private agencies in all fields. Discrimination against women in areas such as social security laws (communications Nos. 172/84, *Broeks v Netherlands*, Views of 9 April 1987; 182/84, *Zwaan de Vries v the Netherlands*, Views of 9 April 1987; 218/1986, *Vos v the Netherlands*, Views of 29 March 1989) as well as in the area of citizenship or rights of non-citizens in a country (communication No. 035/1978, *Aumeeruddy-Cziffra et al. v Mauritius*, Views adopted 9 April 1981) violates article 26. The commission of so-called "honour crimes" which remain unpunished constitutes a serious violation of the Covenant and in particular of articles 6, 14 and 26. Laws which impose more severe penalties on women than on men for adultery or other offences also violate the requirement of equal treatment. The Committee has also often observed in reviewing States parties reports that a large proportion of women are employed in areas which are not protected by labour laws and that prevailing customs and traditions discriminate against women, particularly with regard to access to better paid employment and to equal pay for work of equal value. States parties should review their legislation and practices and take the lead in implementing all measures necessary to eliminate discrimination against women in all fields, for example by prohibiting discrimination by private actors in areas such as employment, education, political activities and the provision of accommodation, goods and services. States parties should report on all these measures and provide information on the remedies available to victims of such discrimination.

32. The rights which persons belonging to minorities enjoy under article 27 of the Covenant in respect of their language, culture and religion do not authorize any State, group or person to violate the right to the equal enjoyment by women of any Covenant rights, including the right to equal protection of the law. States should report on any legislation or administrative practices related to membership in a minority community that might constitute an infringement of the equal rights of women under the Covenant (communication No. 24/1977, *Lovelace v Canada*, Views adopted July 1981) and on measures taken or envisaged to ensure the equal right of men and women to enjoy all civil and political rights in the Covenant. Likewise, States should report on measures taken to discharge their responsibilities in relation to cultural or religious practices within minority communities that affect the rights of women. In their reports, States parties should pay attention to the contribution made by women to the cultural life of their communities.

HUMAN RIGHTS COMMITTE
Eightieth session
General Comment No. 31 [80]

The Nature of the General Legal Obligation Imposed on States Parties to the Covenant
Adopted on 29 March 2004 (2187th meeting)

1. This General Comment replaces General Comment No 3, reflecting and developing its principles. The general non-discrimination provisions of article 2, paragraph 1, have been addressed in General Comment 18 and General Comment 28, and this General Comment should be read together with them.

2. While article 2 is couched in terms of the obligations of State Parties towards individuals as the right-holders under the Covenant, every State Party has a legal interest in the performance by every other State Party of its obligations. This follows from the fact that the ë'rules concerning the basic rights of the human person' are *erga omnes* obligations and that, as indicated in the fourth preambular paragraph of the Covenant, there is a United Nations Charter obligation to promote universal respect for, and observance of, human rights and fundamental freedoms. Furthermore, the contractual dimension of the treaty involves any State Party to a treaty being obligated to every other State Party to comply with its undertakings under the treaty. In this connection, the Committee reminds States Parties of the desirability of making the declaration contemplated in article 41. It further reminds those States Parties already having made the declaration of the potential value of availing themselves of the procedure under that article. However, the mere fact that a formal interstate mechanism for complaints to the Human Rights Committee exists in respect of States Parties that have made the declaration under article 41 does not mean that this procedure is the only method by which States Parties can assert their interest in the performance of other States Parties. On the contrary,

the article 41 procedure should be seen as supplementary to, not diminishing of, States Parties' interest in each others' discharge of their obligations. Accordingly, the Committee commends to States Parties the view that violations of Covenant rights by any State Party deserve their attention. To draw attention to possible breaches of Covenant obligations by other States Parties and to call on them to comply with their Covenant obligations should, far from being regarded as an unfriendly act, be considered as a reflection of legitimate community interest.

3. Article 2 defines the scope of the legal obligations undertaken by States Parties to the Covenant. A general obligation is imposed on States Parties to respect the Covenant rights and to ensure them to all individuals in their territory and subject to their jurisdiction (see paragraph 10 below). Pursuant to the principle articulated in article 26 of the Vienna Convention on the Law of Treaties, States Parties are required to give effect to the obligations under the Covenant in good faith.

4. The obligations of the Covenant in general and article 2 in particular are binding on every State Party as a whole. All branches of government (executive, legislative and judicial), and other public or governmental authorities, at whatever level—national, regional or local—are in a position to engage the responsibility of the State Party. The executive branch that usually represents the State Party internationally, including before the Committee, may not point to the fact that an action incompatible with the provisions of the Covenant was carried out by another branch of government as a means of seeking to relieve the State Party from responsibility for the action and consequent incompatibility. This understanding flows directly from the principle contained in article 27 of the Vienna Convention on the Law of Treaties, according to which a State Party 'may not invoke the provisions of its internal law as justification for its failure to perform a treaty'. Although article 2, paragraph 2, allows States Parties to give effect to Covenant rights in accordance with domestic constitutional processes, the same principle operates so as to prevent States parties from invoking provisions of the constitutional law or other aspects of domestic law to justify a failure to perform or give effect to obligations under the treaty. In this respect, the Committee reminds States Parties with a federal structure of the terms of article 50, according to which the Covenant's provisions 'shall extend to all parts of federal states without any limitations or exceptions'.

5. The article 2, paragraph 1, obligation to respect and ensure the rights recognized by in the Covenant has immediate effect for all States parties. Article 2, paragraph 2, provides the overarching framework within which the rights specified in the Covenant are to be promoted and protected. The Committee has as a consequence previously indicated in its General Comment 24 that reservations to article 2, would be incompatible with the Covenant when considered in the light of its objects and purposes.

6. The legal obligation under article 2, paragraph 1, is both negative and positive in nature. States Parties must refrain from violation of the rights recognized by the Covenant, and any restrictions on any of those rights must be permissible under the relevant provisions of the Covenant. Where such restrictions are made, States must demonstrate their necessity and only take such measures as are proportionate to the pursuance of legitimate aims in order to ensure continuous and effective protection of Covenant rights. In no case may the restrictions be applied or invoked in a manner that would impair the essence of a Covenant right.

7. Article 2 requires that States Parties adopt legislative, judicial, administrative, educative and other appropriate measures in order to fulfill their legal obligations. The Committee believes that it is important to raise levels of awareness about the Covenant not only among public officials and State agents but also among the population at large.

8. The article 2, paragraph 1, obligations are binding on States [Parties] and do not, as such, have direct horizontal effect as a matter of international law. The Covenant cannot be viewed as a substitute for domestic criminal or civil law. However the positive obligations on States Parties to ensure Covenant rights will only be fully discharged if individuals are protected by the State, not just against violations of Covenant rights by its agents, but also against acts committed by private persons or entities that would impair the enjoyment of Covenant rights in so far as they are amenable to application between private persons or entities. There may be circumstances in which a failure to ensure Covenant rights as required by article 2 would give rise to violations by States Parties of those rights, as a result of States Parties' permitting or failing to take appropriate measures or to exercise due diligence to prevent, punish, investigate or redress the harm caused by such acts by private persons or entities. States are reminded of the interrelationship between the positive obligations imposed under article 2 and the need to provide effective remedies in the event of breach under article 2, paragraph 3. The Covenant itself envisages in some articles certain areas where there

are positive obligations on States Parties to address the activities of private persons or entities. For example, the privacy-related guarantees of article 17 must be protected by law. It is also implicit in article 7 that States Parties have to take positive measures to ensure that private persons or entities do not inflict torture or cruel, inhuman or degrading treatment or punishment on others within their power. In fields affecting basic aspects of ordinary life such as work or housing, individuals are to be protected from discrimination within the meaning of article 26.]

9. The beneficiaries of the rights recognized by the Covenant are individuals. Although, with the exception of article 1, the Covenant does not mention he rights of legal persons or similar entities or collectivities, many of the rights recognized by the Covenant, such as the freedom to manifest one's religion or belief (article 18), the freedom of association (article 22) or the rights of members of minorities (article 27), may be enjoyed in community with others. The fact that the competence of the Committee to receive and consider communications is restricted to those submitted by or on behalf of individuals (article 1 of the Optional Protocol) does not prevent such individuals from claiming that actions or omissions that concern legal persons and similar entities amount to a violation of their own rights.

10. States Parties are required by article 2, paragraph 1, to respect and to ensure the Covenant rights to all persons who may be within their territory and to all persons subject to their jurisdiction. This means that a State party must respect and ensure the rights laid down in the Covenant to anyone within the power or effective control of that State Party, even if not situated within the territory of the State Party. As indicated in General Comment 15 adopted at the twenty-seventh session (1986), the enjoyment of Covenant rights is not limited to citizens of States Parties but must also be available to all individuals, regardless of nationality or statelessness, such as asylum seekers, refugees, migrant workers and other persons, who may find themselves in the territory or subject to the jurisdiction of the State Party. This principle also applies to those within the power or effective control of the forces of a State Party acting outside its territory, regardless of the circumstances in which such power or effective control was obtained, such as forces constituting a national contingent of a State Party assigned to an international peace-keeping or peace-enforcement operation.

11. As implied in General Comment 29, the Covenant applies also in situations of armed conflict to which the rules of international humanitarian law are applicable. While, in respect of certain Covenant rights, more specific rules of international humanitarian law may be specially relevant for the purposes of the interpretation of Covenant rights, both spheres of law are complementary, not mutually exclusive.

12. Moreover, the article 2 obligation requiring that States Parties respect and ensure the Covenant rights for all persons in their territory and all persons under their control entails an obligation not to extradite, deport, expel or otherwise remove a person from their territory, where there are substantial grounds for believing that there is a real risk of irreparable harm, such as that contemplated by articles 6 and 7 of the Covenant, either in the country to which removal is to be effected or in any country to which the person may subsequently be removed. The relevant judicial and administrative authorities should be made aware of the need to ensure compliance with the Covenant obligations in such matters.

13. Article 2, paragraph 2, requires that States Parties take the necessary steps to give effect to the Covenant rights in the domestic order. It follows that, unless Covenant rights are already protected by their domestic laws or practices, States Parties are required on ratification to make such changes to domestic laws and practices as are necessary to ensure their conformity with the Covenant. Where there are inconsistencies between domestic law and the Covenant, article 2 requires that the domestic law or practice be changed to meet the standards imposed by the Covenant's substantive guarantees. Article 2 allows a State Party to pursue this in accordance with its own domestic constitutional structure and accordingly does not require that the Covenant be directly applicable in the courts, by incorporation of the Covenant into national law. The Committee takes the view, however, that Covenant guarantees may receive enhanced protection in those States where the Covenant is automatically or through specific incorporation part of the domestic legal order. The Committee invites those States Parties in which the Covenant does not form part of the domestic legal order to consider incorporation of the Covenant to render it part of domestic law to facilitate full realization of Covenant rights as required by article 2.

14. The requirement under article 2, paragraph 2, to take steps to give effect to the Covenant rights is unqualified and of immediate effect. A failure to comply with this obligation cannot be justified by reference to political, social, cultural or economic considerations within the State.

15. Article 2, paragraph 3, requires that in addition to effective protection of Covenant rights States Parties must ensure that individuals also have accessible and effective remedies to vindicate those rights. Such remedies should be appropriately adapted so as to take account of the special vulnerability of certain categories of person, including in particular children. The Committee attaches importance to States Parties' establishing appropriate judicial and administrative mechanisms for addressing claims of rights violations under domestic law. The Committee notes that the enjoyment of the rights recognized under the Covenant can be effectively assured by the judiciary in many different ways, including direct applicability of the Covenant, application of comparable constitutional or other provisions of law, or the interpretive effect of the Covenant in the application of national law. Administrative mechanisms are particularly required to give effect to the general obligation to investigate allegations of violations promptly, thoroughly and effectively through independent and impartial bodies. National human rights institutions, endowed with appropriate powers, can contribute to this end. A failure by a State Party to investigate allegations of violations could in and of itself give rise to a separate breach of the Covenant. Cessation of an ongoing violation is an essential element of the right to an effective remedy.

16. Article 2, paragraph 3, requires that States Parties make reparation to individuals whose Covenant rights have been violated. Without reparation to individuals whose Covenant rights have been violated, the obligation to provide an effective remedy, which is central to the efficacy of article 2, paragraph 3, is not discharged. In addition to the explicit reparation required by articles 9, paragraph 5, and 14, paragraph 6, the Committee considers that the Covenant generally entails appropriate compensation. The Committee notes that, where appropriate, reparation can involve restitution, rehabilitation and measures of satisfaction, such as public apologies, public memorials, guarantees of non-repetition and changes in relevant laws and practices, as well as bringing to justice the perpetrators of human rights violations.

17. In general, the purposes of the Covenant would be defeated without an obligation integral to article 2 to take measures to prevent a recurrence of a violation of the Covenant. Accordingly, it has been a frequent practice of the Committee in cases under the Optional Protocol to include in its Views the need for measures, beyond a victim-specific remedy, to be taken to avoid recurrence of the type of violation in question. Such measures may require changes in the State Party's laws or practices.

18. Where the investigations referred to in paragraph 15 reveal violations of certain Covenant rights, States Parties must ensure that those responsible are brought to justice. As with failure to investigate, failure to bring to justice perpetrators of such violations could in and of itself give rise to a separate breach of the Covenant. These obligations arise notably in respect of those violations recognized as criminal under either domestic or international law, such as torture and similar cruel, inhuman and degrading treatment (article 7), summary and arbitrary killing (article 6) and enforced disappearance (articles 7 and 9 and, frequently, 6). Indeed, the problem of impunity for these violations, a matter of sustained concern by the Committee, may well be an important contributing element in the recurrence of the violations. When committed as part of a widespread or systematic attack on a civilian population, these violations of the Covenant are crimes against humanity (see Rome Statute of the International Criminal Court, article 7).

Accordingly, where public officials or State agents have committed violations of the Covenant rights referred to in this paragraph, the States Parties concerned may not relieve perpetrators from personal responsibility, as has occurred with certain amnesties (see General Comment 20 (44)) and prior legal immunities and indemnities. Furthermore, no official status justifies persons who may be accused of responsibility for such violations being held immune from legal responsibility. Other impediments to the establishment of legal responsibility should also be removed, such as the defence of obedience to superior orders or unreasonably short periods of statutory limitation in cases where such limitations are applicable. States parties should also assist each other to bring to justice persons suspected of having committed acts in violation of the Covenant that are punishable under domestic or international law.

19. The Committee further takes the view that the right to an effective remedy may in certain circumstances require States Parties to provide for and implement provisional or interim measures to avoid continuing violations and to endeavour to repair at the earliest possible opportunity any harm that may have been caused by such violations.

20. Even when the legal systems of States parties are formally endowed with the appropriate remedy, violations of Covenant rights still take place. This is presumably attributable to the failure of the remedies to function effectively in practice. Accordingly, States parties are requested to provide information on the obstacles to the effectiveness of existing remedies in their periodic reports.

HUMAN RIGHTS COMMITTEE
Ninetieth session
Geneva, 9 to 27 July 2007

General Comment No. 32

Article 14: Right to equality before courts and tribunals and to a fair trial

I. GENERAL REMARKS

1. This general comment replaces general comment No. 13 (twenty-first session).

2. The right to equality before the courts and tribunals and to a fair trial is a key element of human rights protection and serves as a procedural means to safeguard the rule of law. Article 14 of the Covenant aims at ensuring the proper administration of justice, and to this end guarantees a series of specific rights.

3. Article 14 is of a particularly complex nature, combining various guarantees with different scopes of application. The first sentence of paragraph 1 sets out a general guarantee of equality before courts and tribunals that applies regardless of the nature of proceedings before such bodies. The second sentence of the same paragraph entitles individuals to a fair and public hearing by a competent, independent and impartial tribunal established by law, if they face any criminal charges or if their rights and obligations are determined in a suit at law. In such proceedings the media and the public may be excluded from the hearing only in the cases specified in the third sentence of paragraph 1. Paragraphs 2–5 of the article contain procedural guarantees available to persons charged with a criminal offence. Paragraph 6 secures a substantive right to compensation in cases of miscarriage of justice in criminal cases. Paragraph 7 prohibits double jeopardy and thus guarantees a substantive freedom, namely the right to remain free from being tried or punished again for an offence for which an individual has already been finally convicted or acquitted. States parties to the Covenant, in their reports, should clearly distinguish between these different aspects of the right to a fair trial.

4. Article 14 contains guarantees that States parties must respect, regardless of their legal traditions and their domestic law. While they should report on how these guarantees are interpreted in relation to their respective legal systems, the Committee notes that it cannot be left to the sole discretion of domestic law to determine the essential content of Covenant guarantees.

5. While reservations to particular clauses of article 14 may be acceptable, a general reservation to the right to a fair trial would be incompatible with the object and purpose of the Covenant.1

6. While article 14 is not included in the list of non-derogable rights of article 4, paragraph 2 of the Covenant, States derogating from normal procedures required under article 14 in circumstances of a public emergency should ensure that such derogations do not exceed those strictly required by the exigencies of the actual situation. The guarantees of fair trial may never be made subject to measures of derogation that would circumvent the protection of non derogable rights. Thus, for example, as article 6 of the Covenant is non-derogable in its entirety, any trial leading to the imposition of the death penalty during a state of emergency must conform to the provisions of the Covenant, including all the requirements of article 14.2 Similarly, as article 7 is also non-derogable in its entirety, no statements or confessions or, in principle, other evidence obtained in violation of this provision may be invoked as evidence in any proceeding is covered by article 14, including during a state of emergency, except if a statement or confession obtained in violation of article 7 is used as evidence that torture or other treatment prohibited by this provision occurred. Deviating from fundamental principles of fair trial, including the presumption of innocence, is prohibited at all times.5

II. EQUALITY BEFORE COURTS AND TRIBUNALS

7. The first sentence of article 14, paragraph 1 guarantees in general terms the right to equality before courts and tribunals. This guarantee not only applies to courts and tribunals addressed in the second sentence of this paragraph of article 14, but must also be respected whenever domestic law entrusts a judicial body with a judicial task.

8. The right to equality before courts and tribunals, in general terms, guarantees, in addition to the principles mentioned in the second sentence of Article 14, paragraph 1, those of equal access and equality of arms, and ensures that the parties to the proceedings in question are treated without any discrimination.

9. Article 14 encompasses the right of access to the courts in cases of determination of criminal charges and rights and obligations in a suit at law. Access to administration of justice must effectively be guaranteed in all such cases to ensure that no individual is deprived, in procedural terms, of his/her right to claim justice. The right of access to courts and tribunals and equality before them is not limited to citizens of States parties, but must also be available to all individuals, regardless of nationality or statelessness, or whatever their

status, whether asylum seekers, refugees, migrant workers, unaccompanied children or other persons, who may find themselves in the territory or subject to the jurisdiction of the State party. A situation in which an individual's attempts to access the competent courts or tribunals are systematically frustrated de jure or de facto runs counter to the guarantee of article 14, paragraph 1, first sentence. This guarantee also prohibits any distinctions regarding access to courts and tribunals that are not based on law and cannot be justified on objective and reasonable grounds. The guarantee is violated if certain persons are barred from bringing suit against any other persons such as by reason of their race, colour, sex, language, religion, political or other opinion, national or social origin, property, birth or other status.

10. The availability or absence of legal assistance often determines whether or not a person can access the relevant proceedings or participate in them in a meaningful way. While article 14 explicitly addresses the guarantee of legal assistance in criminal proceedings in paragraph 3 (d), States are encouraged to provide free legal aid in other cases, for individuals who do not have sufficient means to pay for it. In some cases, they may even be obliged to do so.

For instance, where a person sentenced to death seeks available constitutional review of irregularities in a criminal trial but does not have sufficient means to meet the costs of legal assistance in order to pursue such remedy, the State is obliged to provide legal assistance in accordance with article 14, paragraph 1, in conjunction with the right to an effective remedy as enshrined in article 2, paragraph 3 of the Covenant.

11. Similarly, the imposition of fees on the parties to proceedings that would de facto prevent their access to justice might give rise to issues under article 14, paragraph 1. In particular, a rigid duty under law to award costs to a winning party without consideration of the implications thereof or without providing legal aid may have a deterrent effect on the ability of persons to pursue the vindication of their rights under the Covenant in proceedings available to them.

12. The right of equal access to a court, embodied in article 14, paragraph 1, concerns access to first instance procedures and does not address the issue of the right to appeal or other remedies.

13. The right to equality before courts and tribunals also ensures equality of arms. This means that the same procedural rights are to be provided to all the parties unless distinctions are based on law and can be justified on objective and reasonable grounds, not entailing actual disadvantage or other unfairness to the defendant. There is no equality of arms if, for instance, only the prosecutor, but not the defendant, is allowed to appeal a certain decision. The principle of equality between parties applies also to civil proceedings, and demands, inter alia, that each side be given the opportunity to contest all the arguments and evidence adduced by the other party. In exceptional cases, it also might require that the free assistance of an interpreter be provided where otherwise an indigent party could not participate in the proceedings on equal terms or witnesses produced by it be examined.

14. Equality before courts and tribunals also requires that similar cases are dealt with in similar proceedings. If, for example, exceptional criminal procedures or specially constituted courts or tribunals apply in the determination of certain categories of cases, objective and reasonable grounds must be provided to justify the distinction.

III. FAIR AND PUBLIC HEARING BY A COMPETENT, INDEPENDENT AND IMPARTIAL TRIBUNAL

15. The right to a fair and public hearing by a competent, independent and impartial tribunal established by law is guaranteed, according to the second sentence of article 14, paragraph 1, in cases regarding the determination of criminal charges against individuals or of their rights and obligations in a suit at law. Criminal charges relate in principle to acts declared to be punishable under domestic criminal law. The notion may also extend to acts that are criminal in nature with sanctions that, regardless of their qualification in domestic law, must be regarded as penal because of their purpose, character or severity.

16. The concept of determination of rights and obligations "in a suit at law" (de caractère civil/de carácter civil) is more complex. It is formulated differently in the various languages of the Covenant that, according to article 53 of the Covenant, are equally authentic, and the travaux préparatoires do not resolve the discrepancies in the various language texts. The Committee notes that the concept of a "suit at law" or its equivalents in other language texts is based on the nature of the right in question rather than on the status of one of the parties or the particular forum provided by domestic legal systems for the determination of particular rights. The concept encompasses (a) judicial procedures aimed at determining rights and obligations pertaining to the areas of contract, property and torts in the area of private law, as well as (b) equivalent notions in the area of administrative law such as the termination of employment of civil servants for other than disciplinary reasons,19 the determination of social security benefits or the pension rights of soldiers, or procedures regarding

the use of public land22 or the taking of private property. In addition, it may (c) cover other procedures which, however, must be assessed on a case by case basis in the light of the nature of the right in question.

17. On the other hand, the right to access a court or tribunal as provided for by article 14, paragraph 1, second sentence, does not apply where domestic law does not grant any entitlement to the person concerned. For this reason, the Committee held this provision to be inapplicable in cases where domestic law did not confer any right to be promoted to a higher position in the civil service, to be appointed as a judge or to have a death sentence commuted by an executive body. Furthermore, there is no determination of rights and obligations in a suit at law where the persons concerned are confronted with measures taken against them in their capacity as persons subordinated to a high degree of administrative control, such as disciplinary measures not amounting to penal sanctions being taken against a civil servant, a member of the armed forces, or a prisoner. This guarantee furthermore does not apply to extradition, expulsion and deportation procedures. Although there is no right of access to a court or tribunal as provided for by article 14, paragraph 1, second sentence, in these and similar cases, other procedural guarantees may still apply.

18. The notion of a "tribunal" in article 14, paragraph 1 designates a body, regardless of its denomination, that is established by law, is independent of the executive and legislative branches of government or enjoys in specific cases judicial independence in deciding legal matters in proceedings that are judicial in nature. Article 14, paragraph 1, second sentence, guarantees access to such tribunals to all who have criminal charges brought against them. This right cannot be limited, and any criminal conviction by a body not constituting a tribunal is incompatible with this provision. Similarly, whenever rights and obligations in a suit at law are determined, this must be done at least at one stage of the proceedings by a tribunal within the meaning of this sentence. The failure of a State party to establish a competent tribunal to determine such rights and obligations or to allow access to such a tribunal in specific cases would amount to a violation of article 14 if such limitations are not based on domestic legislation, are not necessary to pursue legitimate aims such as the proper administration of justice, or are based on exceptions from jurisdiction deriving from international law such, for example, as immunities, or if the access left to an individual would be limited to an extent that would undermine the very essence of the right.

19. The requirement of competence, independence and impartiality of a tribunal in the sense of article 14, paragraph 1, is an absolute right that is not subject to any exception. The requirement of independence refers, in particular, to the procedure and qualifications for the appointment of judges, and guarantees relating to their security of tenure until a mandatory retirement age or the expiry of their term of office, where such exist, the conditions governing promotion, transfer, suspension and cessation of their functions, and the actual independence of the judiciary from political interference by the executive branch and legislature. States should take specific measures guaranteeing the independence of the judiciary, protecting judges from any form of political influence in their decision-making through the constitution or adoption of laws establishing clear procedures and objective criteria for the appointment, remuneration, tenure, promotion, suspension and dismissal of the members of the judiciary and disciplinary sanctions taken against them. A situation where the functions and competencies of the judiciary and the executive are not clearly distinguishable or where the latter is able to control or direct the former is incompatible with the notion of an independent tribunal. It is necessary to protect judges against conflicts of interest and intimidation. In order to safeguard their independence, the status of judges, including their term of office, their independence, security, adequate remuneration, conditions of service, pensions and the age of retirement shall be adequately secured by law.

20. Judges may be dismissed only on serious grounds of misconduct or incompetence, in accordance with fair procedures ensuring objectivity and impartiality set out in the constitution or the law. The dismissal of judges by the executive, e.g. before the expiry of the term for which they have been appointed, without any specific reasons given to them and without effective judicial protection being available to contest the dismissal is incompatible with the independence of the judiciary. The same is true, for instance, for the dismissal by the executive of judges alleged to be corrupt, without following any of the procedures provided for by the law.

21. The requirement of impartiality has two aspects. First, judges must not allow their judgement to be influenced by personal bias or prejudice, nor harbour preconceptions about the particular case before them, nor act in ways that improperly promote the interests of one of the parties to the detriment of the other. Second, the tribunal must also appear to a reasonable observer to be impartial. For instance, a trial substantially affected by the participation of a judge who, under domestic statutes, should have been disqualified cannot normally be considered to be impartial.

22. The provisions of article 14 apply to all courts and tribunals within the scope of that article whether ordinary or specialized, civilian or military. The Committee notes the existence, in many countries, of military or special courts which try civilians. While the Covenant does not prohibit the trial of civilians in military or special courts, it requires that such trials are in full conformity with the requirements of article 14 and that its guarantees cannot be limited or modified because of the military or special character of the court concerned. The Committee also notes that the trial of civilians in military or special courts may raise serious problems as far as the equitable, impartial and independent administration of justice is concerned. Therefore, it is important to take all necessary measures to ensure that such trials take place under conditions which genuinely afford the full guarantees stipulated in article 14. Trials of civilians by military or special courts should be exceptional, i.e. limited to cases where the State party can show that resorting to such trials is necessary and justified by objective and serious reasons, and where with regard to the specific class of individuals and offences at issue the regular civilian courts are unable to undertake the trials.

23. Some countries have resorted to special tribunals of "faceless judges" composed of anonymous judges, e.g. within measures taken to fight terrorist activities. Such courts, even if the identity and status of such judges has been verified by an independent authority, often suffer not only from the fact that the identity and status of the judges is not made known to the accused persons but also from irregularities such as exclusion of the public or even the accused or their representatives[38] from the proceedings;[39] restrictions of the right to a lawyer of their own choice; severe restrictions or denial of the right to communicate with their lawyers, particularly when held incommunicado; threats to the lawyers; inadequate time for preparation of the case; or severe restrictions or denial of the right to summon and examine or have examined witnesses, including prohibitions on cross-examining certain categories of witnesses, e.g. police officers responsible for the arrest and interrogation of the defendant. Tribunals with or without faceless judges, in circumstances such as these, do not satisfy basic standards of fair trial and, in particular, the requirement that the tribunal must be independent and impartial.

24. Article 14 is also relevant where a State, in its legal order, recognizes courts based on customary law, or religious courts, to carry out or entrusts them with judicial tasks. It must be ensured that such courts cannot hand down binding judgments recognized by the State, unless the following requirements are met: proceedings before such courts are limited to minor civil and criminal matters, meet the basic requirements of fair trial and other relevant guarantees of the Covenant, and their judgments are validated by State courts in light of the guarantees set out in the Covenant and can be challenged by the parties concerned in a procedure meeting the requirements of article 14 of the Covenant. These principles are notwithstanding the general obligation of the State to protect the rights under the Covenant of any persons affected by the operation of customary and religious courts.

25. The notion of fair trial includes the guarantee of a fair and public hearing. Fairness of proceedings entails the absence of any direct or indirect influence, pressure or intimidation or intrusion from whatever side and for whatever motive. A hearing is not fair if, for instance, the defendant in criminal proceedings is faced with the expression of a hostile attitude from the public or support for one party in the courtroom that is tolerated by the court, thereby impinging on the right to defence, or is exposed to other manifestations of hostility with similar effects. Expressions of racist attitudes by a jury that are tolerated by the tribunal, or a racially biased jury selection are other instances which adversely affect the fairness of the procedure.

26. Article 14 guarantees procedural equality and fairness only and cannot be interpreted as ensuring the absence of error on the part of the competent tribunal. It is generally for the courts of States parties to the Covenant to review facts and evidence, or the application of domestic legislation, in a particular case, unless it can be shown that such evaluation or application was clearly arbitrary or amounted to a manifest error or denial of justice, or that the court otherwise violated its obligation of independence and impartiality.[49] The same standard applies to specific instructions to the jury by the judge in a trial by jury.

27. An important aspect of the fairness of a hearing is its expeditiousness. While the issue of undue delays in criminal proceedings is explicitly addressed in paragraph 3 (c) of article 14, delays in civil proceedings that cannot be justified by the complexity of the case or the behavior of the parties detract from the principle of a fair hearing enshrined in paragraph 1 of this provision. Where such delays are caused by a lack of resources and chronic under-funding, to the extent possible supplementary budgetary resources should be allocated for the administration of justice.

28. All trials in criminal matters or related to a suit at law must in principle be conducted orally and publicly. The publicity of hearings ensures the transparency of proceedings and thus provides an important safeguard for the interest of the individual and of society at large. Courts must make information regarding

the time and venue of the oral hearings available to the public and provide for adequate facilities for the attendance of interested members of the public, within reasonable limits, taking into account, inter alia, the potential interest in the case and the duration of the oral hearing. The requirement of a public hearing does not necessarily apply to all appellate proceedings which may take place on the basis of written presentations, or to pre-trial decisions made by prosecutors and other public authorities.

29. Article 14, paragraph 1, acknowledges that courts have the power to exclude all or part of the public for reasons of morals, public order (*ordre public*) or national security in a democratic society, or when the interest of the private lives of the parties so requires, or to the extent strictly necessary in the opinion of the court in special circumstances where publicity would be prejudicial to the interests of justice. Apart from such exceptional circumstances, a hearing must be open to the general public, including members of the media, and must not, for instance, be limited to a particular category of persons. Even in cases in which the public is excluded from the trial, the judgment, including the essential findings, evidence and legal reasoning must be made public, except where the interest of juvenile persons otherwise requires, or the proceedings concern matrimonial disputes or the guardianship of children.

IV. PRESUMPTION OF INNOCENCE

30. According to article 14, paragraph 2 everyone charged with a criminal offence shall have the right to be presumed innocent until proven guilty according to law. The presumption of innocence, which is fundamental to the protection of human rights, imposes on the prosecution the burden of proving the charge, guarantees that no guilt can be presumed until the charge has been proved beyond reasonable doubt, ensures that the accused has the benefit of doubt, and requires that persons accused of a criminal act must be treated in accordance with this principle.

It is a duty for all public authorities to refrain from prejudging the outcome of a trial, e.g. by abstaining from making public statements affirming the guilt of the accused. Defendants should normally not be shackled or kept in cages during trials or otherwise presented to the court in a manner indicating that they may be dangerous criminals. The media should avoid news coverage undermining the presumption of innocence. Furthermore, the length of pre-trial detention should never be taken as an indication of guilt and its degree. The denial of bail[58] or findings of liability in civil proceedings[59] do not affect the presumption of innocence.

V. RIGHTS OF PERSONS CHARGED WITH A CRIMINAL OFFENCE

31. The right of all persons charged with a criminal offence to be informed promptly and in detail in a language which they understand of the nature and cause of criminal charges brought against them, enshrined in paragraph 3 (a), is the first of the minimum guarantees in criminal proceedings of article 14. This guarantee applies to all cases of criminal charges, including those of persons not in detention, but not to criminal investigations preceding the laying of charges. Notice of the reasons for an arrest is separately guaranteed in article 9, paragraph 2 of the Covenant. The right to be informed of the charge "promptly" requires that information be given as soon as the person concerned is formally charged with a criminal offence under domestic law,[62] or the individual is publicly named as such. The specific requirements of subparagraph 3 (a) may be met by stating the charge either orally—if later confirmed in writing—or in writing, provided that the information indicates both the law and the alleged general facts on which the charge is based. In the case of trials in absentia, article 14, paragraph 3 (a) requires that, notwithstanding the absence of the accused, all due steps have been taken to inform accused persons of the charges and to notify them of the proceedings.

32. Subparagraph 3 (b) provides that accused persons must have adequate time and facilities for the preparation of their defence and to communicate with counsel of their own choosing. This provision is an important element of the guarantee of a fair trial and an application of the principle of equality of arms. In cases of an indigent defendant, communication with counsel might only be assured if a free interpreter is provided during the pre-trial and trial phase. What counts as "adequate time" depends on the circumstances of each case. If counsel reasonably feel that the time for the preparation of the defence is insufficient, it is incumbent on them to request the adjournment of the trial. A State party is not to be held responsible for the conduct of a defence lawyer, unless it was, or should have been, manifest to the judge that the lawyer's behaviour was incompatible with the interests of justice. There is an obligation to grant reasonable requests for adjournment, in particular, when the accused is charged with a serious criminal offence and additional time for preparation of the defence is needed.

33. "Adequate facilities" must include access to documents and other evidence; this access must include all materials that the prosecution plans to offer in court against the accused or that are exculpatory. Exculpatory material should be understood as including not only material establishing innocence but also other evidence

that could assist the defence (e.g. indications that a confession was not voluntary). In cases of a claim that evidence was obtained in violation of article 7 of the Covenant, information about the circumstances in which such evidence was obtained must be made available to allow an assessment of such a claim. If the accused does not speak the language in which the proceedings are held, but is represented by counsel who is familiar with the language, it may be sufficient that the relevant documents in the case file are made available to counsel.

34. The right to communicate with counsel requires that the accused is granted prompt access to counsel. Counsel should be able to meet their clients in private and to communicate with the accused in conditions that fully respect the confidentiality of their communications.

Furthermore, lawyers should be able to advise and to represent persons charged with a criminal offence in accordance with generally recognised professional ethics without restrictions, influence, pressure or undue interference from any quarter.

35. The right of the accused to be tried without undue delay, provided for by article 14, paragraph 3 (c), is not only designed to avoid keeping persons too long in a state of uncertainty about their fate and, if held in detention during the period of the trial, to ensure that such deprivation of liberty does not last longer than necessary in the circumstances of the specific case, but also to serve the interests of justice. What is reasonable has to be assessed in the circumstances of each case, taking into account mainly the complexity of the case, the conduct of the accused, and the manner in which the matter was dealt with by the administrative and judicial authorities. In cases where the accused are denied bail by the court, they must be tried as expeditiously as possible. This guarantee relates not only to the time between the formal charging of the accused and the time by which a trial should commence, but also the time until the final judgement on appeal. All stages, whether in first instance or on appeal must take place "without undue delay."

36. Article 14, paragraph 3 (d) contains three distinct guarantees. First, the provision requires that accused persons are entitled to be present during their trial. Proceedings in the absence of the accused may in some circumstances be permissible in the interest of the proper administration of justice, i.e. when accused persons, although informed of the proceedings sufficiently in advance, decline to exercise their right to be present. Consequently, such trials are only compatible with article 14, paragraph 3 (d) if the necessary steps are taken to summon accused persons in a timely manner and to inform them beforehand about the date and place of their trial and to request their attendance.

37. Second, the right of all accused of a criminal charge to defend themselves in person or through legal counsel of their own choosing and to be informed of this right, as provided for by article 14, paragraph 3 (d), refers to two types of defence which are not mutually exclusive.

Persons assisted by a lawyer have the right to instruct their lawyer on the conduct of their case, within the limits of professional responsibility, and to testify on their own behalf. At the same time, the wording of the Covenant is clear in all official languages, in that it provides for a defence to be conducted in person "or" with legal assistance of one's own choosing, thus providing the possibility for the accused to reject being assisted by any counsel. This right to defend oneself without a lawyer is, however not absolute. The interests of justice may, in the case of a specific trial, require the assignment of a lawyer against the wishes of the accused, particularly in cases of persons substantially and persistently obstructing the proper conduct of trial, or facing a grave charge but being unable to act in their own interests, or where this is necessary to protect vulnerable witnesses from further distress or intimidation if they were to be questioned by the accused. However, any restriction of the wish of accused persons to defend themselves must have an objective and sufficiently serious purpose and not go beyond what is necessary to uphold the interests of justice. Therefore, domestic law should avoid any absolute bar against the right to defend oneself in criminal proceedings without the assistance of counsel.

38. Third, article 14, paragraph 3 (d) guarantees the right to have legal assistance assigned to accused persons whenever the interests of justice so require, and without payment by them in any such case if they do not have sufficient means to pay for it. The gravity of the offence is important in deciding whether counsel should be assigned "in the interest of justice" as is the existence of some objective chance of success at the appeals stage. In cases involving capital punishment, it is axiomatic that the accused must be effectively assisted by a lawyer at all stages of the proceedings. Counsel provided by the competent authorities on the basis of this provision must be effective in the representation of the accused. Unlike in the case of privately retained lawyers, blatant misbehavior or incompetence, for example the withdrawal of an appeal without consultation in a death penalty case, or absence during the hearing of a witness in such cases may entail the responsibility of the State concerned for a violation of article 14, paragraph 3 (d), provided that it was manifest to the judge that

the lawyer's behavior was incompatible with the interests of justice. There is also a violation of this provision if the court or other relevant authorities hinder appointed lawyers from fulfilling their task effectively.

39. Paragraph 3 (e) of article 14 guarantees the right of accused persons to examine, or have examined, the witnesses against them and to obtain the attendance and examination of witnesses on their behalf under the same conditions as witnesses against them. As an application of the principle of equality of arms, this guarantee is important for ensuring an effective defence by the accused and their counsel and thus guarantees the accused the same legal powers of compelling the attendance of witnesses and of examining or cross-examining any witnesses as are available to the prosecution. It does not, however, provide an unlimited right to obtain the attendance of any witness requested by the accused or their counsel, but only a right to have witnesses admitted that are relevant for the defence, and to be given a proper opportunity to question and challenge witnesses against them at some stage of the proceedings. Within these limits, and subject to the limitations on the use of statements, confessions and other evidence obtained in violation of article 7, it is primarily for the domestic legislatures of States parties to determine the admissibility of evidence and how their courts assess it.

40. The right to have the free assistance of an interpreter if the accused cannot understand or speak the language used in court as provided for by article 14, paragraph 3 (f) enshrines another aspect of the principles of fairness and equality of arms in criminal proceedings. This right arises at all stages of the oral proceedings. It applies to aliens as well as to nationals. However, accused persons whose mother tongue differs from the official court language are, in

41. Finally, article 14, paragraph 3 (g), guarantees the right not to be compelled to testify against one-self or to confess guilt. This safeguard must be understood in terms of the absence of any direct or indirect physical or undue psychological pressure from the investigating authorities on the accused, with a view to obtaining a confession of guilt. A fortiori, it is unacceptable to treat an accused person in a manner contrary to article 7 of the Covenant in order to extract a confession. Domestic law must ensure that statements or confessions obtained in violation of article 7 of the Covenant are excluded from the evidence, except if such material is used as evidence that torture or other treatment prohibited by this provision occurred, and that in such cases the burden is on the State to prove that statements made by the accused have been given of their own free will.

VI. JUVENILE PERSONS

42. Article 14, paragraph 4, provides that in the case of juvenile persons, procedures should take account of their age and the desirability of promoting their rehabilitation. Juveniles are to enjoy at least the same guarantees and protection as are accorded to adults under article 14 of the Covenant. In addition, juveniles need special protection. In criminal proceedings they should, in particular, be informed directly of the charges against them and, if appropriate, through their parents or legal guardians, be provided with appropriate assistance in the preparation and presentation of their defence; be tried as soon as possible in a fair hearing in the presence of legal counsel, other appropriate assistance and their parents or legal guardians, unless it is considered not to be in the best interest of the child, in particular taking into account their age or situation. Detention before and during the trial should be avoided to the extent possible.

43. States should take measures to establish an appropriate juvenile criminal justice system, in order to ensure that juveniles are treated in a manner commensurate with their age. It is important to establish a minimum age below which children and juveniles shall not be put on trial for criminal offences; that age should take into account their physical and mental immaturity.

44. Whenever appropriate, in particular where the rehabilitation of juveniles alleged to have committed acts prohibited under penal law would be fostered, measures other than criminal proceedings, such as mediation between the perpetrator and the victim, conferences with the family of the perpetrator, counselling or community service or educational programmes, should be considered, provided they are compatible with the requirements of this Covenant and other relevant human rights standards.

VII. REVIEW BY A HIGHER TRIBUNAL

45. Article 14, paragraph 5 of the Covenant provides that anyone convicted of a crime shall have the right to have their conviction and sentence reviewed by a higher tribunal according to law. As the different language versions (crime, *infraction*, *delito*) show, the guarantee is not confined to the most serious offences. The expression "according to law" in this provision is not intended to leave the very existence of the right of review to the discretion of the States parties, since this right is recognised by the Covenant, and not merely by domestic law. The term according to law rather relates to the determination of the modalities by which the review by a higher tribunal is to be carried out, as well as which court is responsible for carrying out a review in accordance

with the Covenant. Article 14, paragraph 5 does not require States parties to provide for several instances of appeal. However, the reference to domestic law in this provision is to be interpreted to mean that if domestic law provides for further instances of appeal, the convicted person must have effective access to each of them.

46. Article 14, paragraph 5 does not apply to procedures determining rights and obligations in a suit at law95 or any other procedure not being part of a criminal appeal process, such as constitutional motions.96

47. Article 14, paragraph 5 is violated not only if the decision by the court of first instance is final, but also where a conviction imposed by an appeal court97 or a court of final instance, following acquittal by a lower court, according to domestic law, cannot be reviewed by a higher court. Where the highest court of a country acts as first and only instance, the absence of any right to review by a higher tribunal is not offset by the fact of being tried by the supreme tribunal of the State party concerned; rather, such a system is incompatible with the Covenant, unless the State party concerned has made a reservation to this effect.

48. The right to have one's conviction and sentence reviewed by a higher tribunal established under article 14, paragraph 5, imposes on the State party a duty to review substantively, both on the basis of sufficiency of the evidence and of the law, the conviction and sentence, such that the procedure allows for due consideration of the nature of the case. A review that is limited to the formal or legal aspects of the conviction without any consideration whatsoever of the facts is not sufficient under the Covenant. However, article 14, paragraph 5 does not require a full retrial or a "hearing", as long as the tribunal carrying out the review can look at the factual dimensions of the case. Thus, for instance, where a higher instance court looks at the allegations against a convicted person in great detail, considers the evidence submitted at the trial and referred to in the appeal, and finds that there was sufficient incriminating evidence to justify a finding of guilt in the specific case, the Covenant is not violated.

49. The right to have one's conviction reviewed can only be exercised effectively if the convicted person is entitled to have access to a duly reasoned, written judgement of the trial court, and, at least in the court of first appeal where domestic law provides for several instances of appeal, also to other documents, such as trial transcripts, necessary to enjoy the effective exercise of the right to appeal. The effectiveness of this right is also impaired, and article 14, paragraph 5 violated, if the review by the higher instance court is unduly delayed in violation of paragraph 3 (c) of the same provision.

50. A system of supervisory review that only applies to sentences whose execution has commenced does not meet the requirements of article 14, paragraph 5, regardless of whether such review can be requested by the convicted person or is dependent on the discretionary power of a judge or prosecutor.

51. The right of appeal is of particular importance in death penalty cases. A denial of legal aid by the court reviewing the death sentence of an indigent convicted person constitutes not only a violation of article 14, paragraph 3 (d), but at the same time also of article 14, paragraph 5, as in such cases the denial of legal aid for an appeal effectively precludes an effective review of the conviction and sentence by the higher instance court. The right to have one's conviction reviewed is also violated if defendants are not informed of the intention of their counsel not to put any arguments to the court, thereby depriving them of the opportunity to seek alternative representation, in order that their concerns may be ventilated at the appeal level.

VIII. COMPENSATION IN CASES OF MISCARRIAGE OF JUSTICE

52. According to paragraph 6 of article 14 of the Covenant, compensation according to the law shall be paid to persons who have been convicted of a criminal offence by a final decision and have suffered punishment as a consequence of such conviction, if their conviction has been reversed or they have been pardoned on the ground that a new or newly discovered fact shows conclusively that there has been a miscarriage of justice. It is necessary that States parties enact legislation ensuring that compensation as required by this provision can in fact be paid and that the payment is made within a reasonable period of time.

53. This guarantee does not apply if it is proved that the non-disclosure of such a material fact in good time is wholly or partly attributable to the accused; in such cases, the burden of proof rests on the State. Furthermore, no compensation is due if the conviction is set aside upon appeal, i.e. before the judgement becomes final,111 or by a pardon that is humanitarian or discretionary in nature, or motivated by considerations of equity, not implying that there has been a miscarriage of justice.

IX. NE BIS IN IDEM

54. Article 14, paragraph 7 of the Covenant, providing that no one shall be liable to be tried or punished again for an offence of which they have already been finally convicted or acquitted in accordance with the law and penal procedure of each country, embodies the principle of *ne bis in idem*. This provision prohibits bringing a person, once convicted or acquitted of a certain offence, either before the same court again or before another tribunal again for the same offence; thus, for instance, someone acquitted by a civilian court

cannot be tried again for the same offence by a military or special tribunal. Article 14, paragraph 7 does not prohibit retrial of a person convicted in absentia who requests it, but applies to the second conviction.

55. Repeated punishment of conscientious objectors for not having obeyed a renewed order to serve in the military may amount to punishment for the same crime if such subsequent refusal is based on the same constant resolve grounded in reasons of conscience.

56. The prohibition of article 14, paragraph 7, is not at issue if a higher court quashes a conviction and orders a retrial. Furthermore, it does not prohibit the resumption of a criminal trial justified by exceptional circumstances, such as the discovery of evidence which was not available or known at the time of the acquittal.

57. This guarantee applies to criminal offences only and not to disciplinary measures that do not amount to a sanction for a criminal offence within the meaning of article 14.

X. RELATIONSHIP OF ARTICLE 14 WITH OTHER PROVISIONS OF THE COVENANT

58. As a set of procedural guarantees, article 14 of the Covenant often plays an important role in the implementation of the more substantive guarantees of the Covenant that must be taken into account in the context of determining criminal charges and rights and obligations of a person in a suit at law. In procedural terms, the relationship with the right to an effective remedy provided for by article 2, paragraph 3 of the Covenant is relevant. In general, this provision needs to be respected whenever any guarantee of article 14 has been violated. However, as regards the right to have one's conviction and sentence reviewed by a higher tribunal, article 14, paragraph 5 of the Covenant is a *lex specialis* in relation to article 2, paragraph 3 when invoking the right to access a tribunal at the appeals level.

59. In cases of trials leading to the imposition of the death penalty scrupulous respect of the guarantees of fair trial is particularly important. The imposition of a sentence of death upon conclusion of a trial, in which the provisions of article 14 of the Covenant have not been respected, constitutes a violation of the right to life (article 6 of the Covenant).

60. To ill-treat persons against whom criminal charges are brought and to force them to make or sign, under duress, a confession admitting guilt violates both article 7 of the Covenant prohibiting torture and inhuman, cruel or degrading treatment and article 14, paragraph 3 (g) prohibiting compulsion to testify against oneself or confess guilt.

61. If someone suspected of a crime and detained on the basis of article 9 of the Covenant is charged with an offence but not brought to trial, the prohibitions of unduly delaying trials as provided for by articles 9, paragraph 3, and 14, paragraph 3 (c) of the Covenant may be violated at the same time.122

62. The procedural guarantees of article 13 of the Covenant incorporate notions of due process also reflected in article 14 and thus should be interpreted in the light of this latter provision. Insofar as domestic law entrusts a judicial body with the task of deciding about expulsions or deportations, the guarantee of equality of all persons before the courts and tribunals as enshrined in article 14, paragraph 1, and the principles of impartiality, fairness and equality of arms implicit in this guarantee are applicable. All relevant guarantees of article 14, however, apply where expulsion takes the form of a penal sanction or where violations of expulsion orders are punished under criminal law.

63. The way criminal proceedings are handled may affect the exercise and enjoyment of rights and guarantees of the Covenant unrelated to article 14. Thus, for instance, to keep pending, for several years, indictments for the criminal offence of defamation brought against a journalist for having published certain articles, in violation of article 14, paragraph 3 (c), may leave the accused in a situation of uncertainty and intimidation and thus have a chilling effect which unduly restricts the exercise of his right to freedom of expression (article 19 of the Covenant). Similarly, delays of criminal proceedings for several years in contravention of article 14, paragraph 3 (c), may violate the right of a person to leave one's own country as guaranteed in article 12, paragraph 2 of the Covenant, if the accused has to remain in that country as long as proceedings are pending.

64. As regards the right to have access to public service on general terms of equality as provided for in article 25 (c) of the Covenant, a dismissal of judges in violation of this provision may amount to a violation of this guarantee, read in conjunction with article 14, paragraph 1 providing for the independence of the judiciary.

65. Procedural laws or their application that make distinctions based on any of the criteria listed in article 2, paragraph 1 or article 26, or disregard the equal right of men and women, in accordance with article 3, to the enjoyment of the guarantees set forth in article 14 of the Covenant, not only violate the requirement of paragraph 1 of this provision that "all persons shall be equal before the courts and tribunals," but may also amount to discrimination.

Distr.: Restricted
25 November 2010

Distr.: Restricted
25 November 2010
Original: English

NB: THE FOLLOWING GENERAL COMMENT #34 IS ONLY A DRAFT. IT HAS NOT BEEN ADOPTED BY THE HUMAN RIGHTS COMMITTEE AS OF THE TIME OF WRITING THIS BOOK. AS SUCH, IT CANNOT BE USED TO REFLECT THE OFFICIAL POSITION OF THE HUMAN RIGHTS COMMITTEE. THE READER IS ADVISED TO CHECK THE WEBSITE FOLLOWING THIS DRAFT GENERAL COMMENT TO FIND OUT THE STATUS OF THIS DRAFT. ANY REFERENCE OR CITATION TO THIS DRAFT GENERAL COMMENT SHOULD REFLECT THIS STATUS.

CCPR.C.GC.34.CRP.4
Distr.: Restricted
25 November 2010
Original: English

Human Rights Committee
Hundredth session
Geneva, 11-29 October 2010
Draft general comment No. 34 (Upon completion of the first reading by the Human Rights Committee)
Article 19
General remarks

1. This general comment replaces general comment No. 10 (nineteenth session).

2. Freedom of opinion and freedom of expression are indispensable conditions for the full development of the person. They are essential for any society.[1] They constitute the foundation stone for every free and democratic society. The two freedoms are closely related, with freedom of expression providing the vehicle for the exchange and development of opinions.

3. Among the other articles that contain guarantees for freedom of opinion and, or expression, are articles 18, 17, 25 and 27. The freedoms of opinion and expression form a basis for the full enjoyment of a wide range of other human rights. For instance, freedom of expression is integral to the enjoyment of the rights to freedom of assembly and association.

4. Taking account of the specific terms of article 19, paragraph 1, as well as the relationship of opinion and thought (article 18), a reservation to paragraph 1 would be incompatible with the object and purpose of the Covenant.[2] Furthermore, although freedom of opinion is not listed among those rights that may not be derogated from pursuant to the provisions of article 4 of the Covenant, it is recalled that, "in those provisions of the Covenant that are not listed in article 4, paragraph 2, there are elements that in the Committee's opinion cannot be made subject to lawful derogation under article 4".[3] Freedom of opinion is one such element, since it can never become necessary to derogate from it during a state of emergency.[4]

5. Taking account of the relationship of freedom of expression to the other rights in the Covenant, while reservations to particular elements of article 19, paragraph 2 may be acceptable, a general reservation to the rights set out in paragraph 2 would be incompatible with the object and purpose of the Covenant.[5]

6. The obligation to respect freedoms of opinion and expression is binding on every State party as a whole. All branches of the State (executive, legislative and judicial) and other public or governmental authorities, at whatever level—national, regional or local—are in a position to engage the responsibility of the State party.[6] Such responsibility may also be incurred by a State party under some circumstances in respect of acts of semi-State entities.[7] The State party must also ensure that persons are protected from any acts of private persons or entities that would impair the enjoyment of freedoms of opinion and expression in so far as these Covenant rights are amenable to application between private persons or entities.[8]

---

[1]Benhadi v Algeria, No. 1173/2003; Tee-Hoon Park v Republic of Korea, No. 628/1995.

[2]See general Comment 24 on issues relating to reservations made upon ratification or accession to the Covenant or Optional Protocol thereto, or in relation to declarations under article 41 of the Covenant.

[3]General comment No. 29, para. 13.

[4]General comment No. 29, para. 11.

[5]See general comment 24 on issues relating to reservations made upon ratification or accession to the Covenant or the Optional Protocols thereto, or in relation to declarations under article 41 of the Covenant.

[6]General comment No. 31, para. 4.

[7]Hertzberg et al. v Finland, No. 61/1979.

[8]General comment No. 31, para. 8; Gauthier v Canada, No. 633/1995.

7. States parties are required to ensure that the rights contained in article 19 of the Covenant are enshrined in the domestic law of the State, in a manner consistent with the guidance provided by the Committee in its general comment No. 31 on the nature of the general legal obligation imposed on States parties to the Covenant.

8. It is recalled that States parties should provide the Committee in their periodic reports with the relevant domestic legal rules, administrative practices and judicial decisions, as well as relevant policy level and other sectorial practices relating to the rights protected by article 19, taking into account the issues discussed in the present general comment. They must also include information on remedies available if those rights are violated.

Freedom of opinion

9. Paragraph 1 of article 19 requires protection of the right to hold opinions without interference. This is a right to which the Covenant permits no exception or restriction. Freedom of opinion extends to the right to change an opinion whenever and for whatever reason a person so freely chooses. No person may be subjected to any form of discrimination or the impairment of any rights under the Covenant on the basis of his or her actual, perceived or supposed opinions. All forms of opinion are protected, including, but not limited to, opinions of a political, scientific, historic, moral or religious nature. It is incompatible with paragraph 1 to criminalise the holding of an opinion.[9] The harassment, intimidation or stigmatisation of a person, including arrest, detention, trial or imprisonment for reasons of the opinions they may hold, constitutes a violation of article 19, paragraph 1.[10]

10. Any form of coerced effort to shape opinion is prohibited.[11] Since freedom to express one's opinion necessarily includes freedom not to express one's opinions, article 19, paragraph 1, prohibits any action to compel the disclosure of an opinion.

Freedom of expression

11. Paragraph 2 requires guarantees of the right to seek, receive and impart information and ideas of all kinds regardless of frontiers. This right extends to the guarantee of the expression of every form of subjective idea and opinion capable of transmission to others, subject to the provisions in article 19, paragraph 3, and article 20.[12] It includes political discourse,[13] commentary on one's own[14] and on public affairs,[15] canvassing,[16] discussion of human rights,[17] journalism,[18] cultural and artistic expression,[19] teaching,[20] religious discourse[21] [and commercial advertising][22] The scope of paragraph 2 embraces even views that may be regarded as deeply offensive,[23] although such expression may be restricted in accordance with the provisions of article 19, paragraph 3 and article 20.

12. Paragraph 2 protects all forms of expression and the means of their publication. Such forms include, but are not limited to, the spoken and written word and such non-verbal expression as images and objects of art.[24] Means of expression include books, newspapers,[25] pamphlets,[26] posters, banners[27] and legal submissions.[28] They include all forms of audio-visual as well as electronic and internet-based media. Paragraph 2 does not, however, provide a right of free expression in any specific location.[29]

13. A State party may choose one or more national or official languages, but it may not exclude, outside the spheres of public life, the freedom to express oneself in a language of one's own choice,[30] and article 27

---

[9]Faurisson v France, No. 550/93.

[10]Mpaka-Nsusu v Zaire, No. 157/1983; Primo Jose Essono Mika Miha v Equatorial Guinea, No. 414/1990.

[11]Yong-Joo Kang v Republic of Korea, No. 878/1999.

[12]Ballantyne v Canada, Nos. 359/1989 and 385/1989.

[13]Primo Jose Essono Mika Miha v Equatorial Guinea, No. 414/1990.

[14]Fernando v Sri Lanka, No. 1189/2003.

[15]Coleman v Australia, No. 1157/2003.

[16]Concluding observations on Japan (CCPR/C/JPN/CO/5).

[17]Velichkin v Belarus, No. 1022/2001.

[18]Mavlonov et al. v Uzbekistan, No. 1334/2004.

[19]Hak-Chul Sin v Republic of Korea, No. 926/2000.

[20]Ross v Canada, No. 736/97.

[21]Ibid.

[22]Ballantyne et al. v Canada, No. 359, 385/89.

[23]Ross v Canada, No. 736/97.

[24]Hak-Chul Sin v Republic of Korea, No. 926/2000.

[25]Zundel v Canada, No. 1341/2005

[26]Shchetoko et al. v Belarus, No. 1009/2001.

[27]Kivenmaa v Finland, No. 412/1990.

[28]Fernando v Sri Lanka, No. 1189/2003.

[29]Zundel v Canada, No. 1341/2005.

[30]Ballantyne v Canada, Nos. 359/1989 and 385/1989.

of the Covenant expressly provides that persons belonging to ethnic, religious or linguistic minorities shall not be denied the right, in community with other members of their group, to use their own language.

Freedom of expression and the media

14. A free, uncensored and unhindered press or other media is essential in any society for the ensuring of freedom of opinion and expression and the enjoyment of other Covenant rights. It constitutes one of the cornerstones of a democratic society.[31] The Covenant embraces a right to receive information on the part of the media as a basis on which they can carry out their function.[32] The free communication of information and ideas about public and political issues between citizens, candidates and elected representatives is essential. This implies a free press and other media able to comment on public issues without censorship or restraint and to inform public opinion.[33] Pursuant to article 19, the public also has the right to receive information as a corollary to the specific function of any journalist to impart information.[34]

15. States parties must take particular care to encourage an independent and diverse media. They must also promote and protect access to the media for minority groups.

16. [States parties should ensure that public broadcasting services operate in an independent manner.[35] Actions to ensure independence may include the setting out of the mandate of such broadcasters in law and the provision of legislative guarantees of independence and editorial freedom, as well as the provision of funding in a manner that does not undermine independence].

17. Issues concerning the media are discussed further in the section of this general comment that addresses restrictions on freedom of expression.

Access to information

18. Article 19, paragraph 2 embraces a general right of access to information held by public bodies. Such infor—mation includes all records held by a public body, regardless of the form in which the information is stored, its source and the date of production. Public bodies include all levels of State bodies and organs, including the judiciary and with regard to the carrying out of public functions, it may include other bodies.

19. As has already been noted, taken together with article 25 of the Covenant, the right of access to information includes a right of the mass media to have access to information on public affairs[36] and the right of the general public to receive mass media output.[37] The right of access to information is also addressed elsewhere in the Covenant. As the Committee observed in its general comment No. 16, regarding article 17 of the Covenant, "every individual should have the right to ascertain in an intelligible form, whether, and if so, what personal data is stored in automatic data files, and for what purposes. Every individual should also be able to ascertain which public authorities or private individuals or bodies control or may control their files. If such files contain incorrect personal data or have been collected or processed contrary to the provisions of the law, every individual should have the right to request rectification or elimination".[38] Pursuant to article 10 of the Covenant, a prisoner does not lose the entitlement to access to his medical records.[39] The Committee, in general comment No. 32 on article 14, set out the various entitlements to information that are held by those accused with a criminal offence.[40] Pursuant to the provisions of article 2, persons should be in receipt of information regarding their Covenant rights in general.[41] Under article 27, a State party's decision-making that may substantively compromise the way of life and culture of a minority group must be undertaken in a process of information-sharing and consultation with affected communities.[42]

20. To give effect to the right of access to information, States parties should enact the necessary procedures, such as by means of freedom of information legislation.[43] The procedures should provide for the rapid processing of requests for information according to clear rules that are compatible with the Covenant.

---

[31]Marques de Morais v Angola, No. 1128/2002.

[32]Gauthier v Canada, No. 633/95.

[33]See general comment No. 25 on article 25 (Participation in public affairs and the right to vote)

[34]Mavlonov et al v Uzbekistan, No. 1334/2004.

[35]Concluding observations on Republic of Moldova (CCPR/CO/75/MDA).

[36]Gauthier v Canada, No. 633/95.

[37]Mavlonov et al v Uzbekistan, No. 1334/2004.

[38]See also concluding observations on Norway (CCPR/CO/76/D).

[39]Zheludkova v Ukraine, No. 726/1996.

[40]At para. 33.

[41]General comment No. 31 on the nature of the general legal obligation imposed on States parties to the Covenant.

[42]Poma Poma v Peru, No. 1457/2006.

[43]Concluding observations on Azerbaijan (CCPR/C/79/Add.38 (1994)).

Arrangements should be put in place for appeals from refusals to provide access to information. Fees for the processing of requests for information should not be such as to constitute an unreasonable impediment to access to information. Authorities should provide reasons for any refusal to provide access to information. States parties should make every effort to ensure easy, effective and practical access to state-controlled information in the public domain.

Freedom of expression and political rights

21. The Committee, in general comment No. 25 on participation in public affairs and the right to vote, elaborated on the importance of freedom of expression for the conduct of public affairs and the effective exercise of the right to vote. The free communication of information and ideas about public and political issues between citizens, candidates and elected representatives is essential. This implies a free press and other media able to comment on public issues without censorship or restraint and to inform public opinion.[44] The attention of States parties is drawn to the guidance that general comment No. 25 provides with regard to the promotion and the protection of freedom of expression in that context

The application of article 19 (3)

22. Paragraph 3 expressly states that the exercise of the right to freedom of expression carries with it special duties and responsibilities and for this reason two limitative areas of restrictions on the right are permitted which may relate either to respect of the rights or reputations of others or to the protection of national security or of public order (ordre public), or of public health or morals. However, when a State party imposes restrictions on the exercise of freedom of expression, these may not put in jeopardy the right itself. The Committee also recalls the provisions of article 5, paragraph 1 of the Covenant according to which "nothing in the present Covenant may be interpreted as implying for any State, group or person any right to engage in any activity or perform any act aimed at the destruction of any of the rights and freedoms recognized herein or at their limitation to a greater extent than is provided for in the present Covenant". The Committee recalls that the relation between right and restriction and between norm and exception must not be reversed.[45]

23. Paragraph 3 lays down specific conditions and it is only subject to these conditions that restrictions may be imposed: the restrictions must be "provided by law"; they may only be imposed for one of the grounds set out in subparagraphs (a) and (b) of paragraph 3; and they must be justified as being "necessary" for the State party for one of those grounds. Restrictions on freedom of expression must meet a strict test of justification.[46] Restrictions are not allowed on grounds not specified in paragraph 3, even if they would be allowed as restrictions to other rights protected in the Covenant, such as public safety. Restrictions must be applied only for those purposes for which they were prescribed and must be directly related to the specific need on which they are predicated.[47]

24. Paragraph 3 may never be invoked as a justification for the muzzling of any advocacy of multi-party democracy, democratic tenets and human rights.[48] Nor, under any circumstances, can an attack on a person, because of the exercise of his or her freedom of opinion or expression, including such forms of attack as arbitrary arrest, torture, threats to life and killing, be compatible with article 19.[49] Journalists are frequently subjected to such threats, intimidation and attacks because of their activities.[50] So too are persons who engage in the gathering and analysis of information on the human rights situation and who publish human rights-related reports.[51] All allegations of attacks on or other forms of intimidation or harassment of journalists, human rights defenders and others should be vigorously investigated, the perpetrators prosecuted,[52] and the victims, or, in the case of killings, their representatives, be in receipt of appropriate forms of redress.[53]

---

[44]See para. 25 of general comment no. 25 on article 25 of the Covenant.
[45]See general comment No. 27.
[46]Velichkin v Belarus, No. 1022/2001.
[47]See general comment No. 22.
[48]Mukong v Cameroon, No. 458/91.
[49]Njaru v Cameroon, No. 1353/2005.
[50]See, for instance, concluding observations on Algeria (CCPR/C/DZA/CO/3); concluding observations on
[51]Njaru v Cameroon, No. 1353/2005; concluding observations on Nicaragua (CCPR/C/NIC/CO/3); concluding
[52]Ibid. and concluding observations on Georgia (CCPR/C/GEO/CO/3).
[53]Concluding observations on Guyana (CCPR/C/79/Add.121v).

25. Restrictions must be provided by law. "Law" in this regard may include statutory law [and, where appropriate, case law].[54] It may include the law of parliamentary privilege[55] and the law of contempt of court.[56] Since any restriction on freedom of expression constitutes a serious curtailment of human rights, it is not compatible with the Covenant for a restriction to be enshrined in customary law.[57]

26. For purposes of paragraph 3, a norm, to be characterised as a "law", must be formulated with sufficient precision to enable an individual to regulate his or her conduct accordingly[58] and it must be made public. A law may not confer unfettered discretion for the restriction of freedom of expression on those charged with its execution.[59]

27. Laws restricting Covenant rights must themselves be compatible with the provisions, aims and objectives of the Covenant.[60] Laws may not violate the non-discrimination provisions of the Covenant. Laws may not provide for penalties that are incompatible with the Covenant, such as corporal punishment.[61]

28. It is for the State party to demonstrate the legal basis for any restrictions imposed on freedom of expression.[62] If, with regard to a particular State party, the Committee has to consider whether a particular restriction is imposed by law, the State party should provide details of the law and of actions that fall within the scope of the law.[63]

29. The first of the legitimate grounds for restriction listed in paragraph 3 is that of respect for the rights or reputations of others. The term "rights" includes human rights as recognised in the Covenant and more generally in international human rights law. For example, it may be legitimate to restrict freedom of expression in order to protect the Article 25 right to vote, as well as under Article 17 rights (See para. 39).[64] Such restrictions must be constructed with care: while it may be permissible to protect voters from forms of expression that constitute intimidation or coercion, such restrictions must not impede political debate, including, for example, calls for the boycotting of a non-compulsory vote.[65] The term 'others' may relate to other persons individually or as members of a community.[66] Thus, it may, for instance, refer to members of a community defined by its religious faith[67] or ethnicity.[68]

30. The second legitimate ground is that of protection of national security or of public order (ordre public), or of public health or morals.

31. Extreme care must be taken by States parties to ensure that treason laws[69] and similar provisions relating to national security, such as official secrets and sedition laws, are crafted and applied in a manner that conforms to paragraph 3. It is not compatible with paragraph 3, for instance, to invoke treason laws to prosecute journalists, researchers, environmental activists, human rights defenders, or others, for having disseminated information of legitimate public interest.[70] Nor is it generally appropriate to include in the remit of a state secrets law such categories of information as those relating to the commercial sector, banking and scientific progress.[71] The Committee has found in one case that a restriction on the issuing of a statement in support of a labour dispute, including for the convening of a national strike was not permissible on the grounds of national security.[72]

32. On the basis of maintenance of public order it may, for instance, be permissible in certain circumstances to regulate speech-making in a particular public place.[73] Contempt of court proceedings relating to

---

[54]Coleman v Australia, No. 1157/2003.

[55]Gauthier v Canada, No. 633/95. [56]Dissanayake v Sri Lanka, No. 1373/2005.

[57]See general comment No. 32.

[58]Leonardus J.M. de Groot v The Netherlands, No. 578/1994.

[59]See general comment No. 27.

[60]Toonen v Australia, No. 488/1992.

[61]General comment No. 20.

[62]Korneenko et al. v Belarus, No. 1553/2007.

[63]Monja Jaona v Madagascar, No. 132/1982.

[64]Svetik v Belarus, No. 927/2000.

[65]Ibid.

[66]Ross v Canada, No. 736/97.

[67]Faurisson v France, 550/93; concluding observations on Austria (CCPR/C/AUT/CO/4).

[68]Concluding observations on Slovakia (CCPR/CO/78/SVK); concluding observations on Israel (CCPR/CO/78/ISR).

[69]Concluding observations on Hong Kong (CCPR/C/HKG/CO/2).

[70]Concluding observations on the Russian Federation (CCPR/CO/79/RUS).

[71]Concluding observations on Uzbekistan (CCPR/CO/71/UZB).

[72]Jong-Kyu Sohn v Republic of Korea, No. 518/1992.

[73]Coleman v Australia, No. 1157/2003.

forms of expression may be tested against the public order ground. In order to comply with paragraph 3, such proceedings and the penalty imposed must be shown to be warranted in the exercise of a court's power to maintain orderly proceedings.[74]

33. Concerning public morals, it has to be observed that the content of the term may differ widely from society to society—there is no universally applicable common standard.[75] However, as the Committee observed in general comment No. 22, "the concept of morals derives from many social, philosophical and religious traditions; consequently, limitations... for the purpose of protecting morals must be based on principles not deriving exclusively from a single tradition".

34. Restrictions must be "necessary" for a legitimate purpose. Thus, for instance, a prohibition on commercial advertising in one language, with a view to protecting the language of a particular community, violates the test of necessity if the protection could be achieved in other ways that do not restrict freedom of expression.[76] On the other hand, the Committee has considered that a State party complied with the test of necessity when it transferred a teacher who had published materials that expressed hostility to a religious community to a non-teaching position in order to protect the right and freedom of children of that faith in a school district.[77]

35. The Committee observed in general comment No. 27 that "restrictive measures must conform to the principle of proportionality; they must be appropriate to achieve their protective function; they must be the least intrusive instrument amongst those which might achieve their protective function; they must be proportionate to the interest to be protected.... The principle of proportionality has to be respected not only in the law that frames the restrictions but also by the administrative and judicial authorities in applying the law".[78] The principle of proportionality must also take account of the form of expression at issue. For instance, the value placed by the Covenant upon uninhibited expression is particularly high in the circumstances of public debate in a democratic society concerning figures in the public and political domain.[79]

36. When a State party invokes a legitimate ground for restriction of freedom of expression, it must demonstrate in specific and individualised fashion the precise nature of the threat and the necessity of the specific action taken, in particular by establishing a direct and immediate connection between the expression and the threat.[80]

37. The Committee reserves to itself an assessment of whether, in a given situation, there may have been circumstances which made a restriction of freedom of expression necessary.[81] In this regard, the Committee recalls that the scope of this freedom is not to be assessed by reference to a "margin of appreciation"[82] and in order for the Committee to carry out this function, a State party, in any given case, must demonstrate in specific fashion the precise nature of the threat to any of the enumerated grounds listed in paragraph 3 that has caused it to restrict freedom of expression.[83]

Limitative scope of restrictions on freedom of expression in certain specific areas

38. Restrictions on freedom of expression in order to be compatible with paragraph 3, must be enshrined in legal provisions that comply with the conditions indicated in this general comment. They must also comply with the test of necessity and the proportionality principle.

39. Among those restrictions on political discourse that have given the Committee cause for concern are the prohibition of door-to-door canvassing,[84] restrictions on the number and type of written materials that may be distributed during election campaigns,[85] blocking access during election periods to sources, including local and international media, of political commentary,[86] and limiting access of opposition parties and

---

[74]Dissanayake v Sri Lanka, No. 1373/2005.

[75]Hertzberg et al. v Finland, No. 61/79; see Delgado Paez v Colombia, No. 195/85.

[76]Ballantyne et al. v Canada, No. 359, 385/89.

[77]Ross v Canada, No. 736/97.

[78]See also Marques de Morais v Angola, No. 1128/2002; Coleman v Australia, No. 1157/2003.

[79]Bodrozic v Serbia and Montenegro, No. 1180/2003.

[80]Shin v Republic of Korea, No. 926/2000.

[81]Sohn v Republic of Korea, No. 518/1992.

[82]Ilmari Lansman, et al. v Finland, No. 511/1992.

[83]Sohn v Republic of Korea, No. 518/92; Shin v Republic of Korea, No. 926/2000.

[84]Concluding observations on Japan (CCPR/C/JPN/CO/5).

[85]Ibid.

[86]Concluding observations on Tunisia (CCPR/C/TUN/CO/5).

politicians to media outlets.[87] Not every restriction is incompatible with paragraph 3. For instance, it may be legitimate for a State party to restrict political polling in the days preceding an election in order to maintain the integrity of the electoral process.[88]

40. As noted earlier in paragraph (paras. 14 and 21,), concerning the content of political discourse, the Committee has observed that in circumstances of public debate concerning public figures in the political domain, the value placed by the Covenant upon uninhibited expression is particularly high.[89] Thus, the mere fact that forms of expression are considered to be insulting to a public figure is not sufficient to justify the imposition of penalties, albeit, public figures benefit from the provisions of the Covenant.[90] Moreover, all public figures, including those exercising the highest political authority such as heads of state and government, are legitimately subject to criticism and political opposition.[91] Accordingly, the Committee has expressed concern regarding laws on such matters as, *lese majeste*,[92] *desacato*,[93] disrespect for authority,[94] defamation of the head of state[95] and the protection of the honour of public officials,[96] and laws should not provide for more severe penalties solely on the basis of the identity of the person that may have been impugned. State parties should not prohibit criticism of institutions, such as the army or the administration.[97]

41. Legislative and administrative frameworks for the regulation of the mass media should be reviewed to ensure that they are consistent with the provisions of paragraph 3.[98] Regulatory systems should take into account the differences between the print and broadcast sectors and the internet, while also noting the manner in which various media converge. It is incompatible with article 19 to refuse to permit the publication of newspapers and other print media other than in the specific circumstances of the application of paragraph 3. Such circumstances may never include a ban on a particular publication unless specific content, that is not severable, offends paragraph 3. States parties must avoid imposing onerous licensing conditions and fees on the broadcast media, including on community and commercial stations.[99] The criteria for the application of such conditions and licence fees should be reasonable and objective,[100] clear,[101] transparent,[102] non-discriminatory and otherwise in compliance with the Covenant.[103] Licensing regimes for broadcasting via media with limited capacity, such as audiovisual terrestrial and satellite services should provide for an equitable allocation of access and frequencies between public, commercial and community broadcasters. It is recommended that States parties that have not already done so should establish an independent and public broadcasting licensing authority, with the power to examine broadcasting applications and to grant licenses.[104]

42. The Committee reiterates its observation in general comment No. 10 that "because of the development of modern mass media, effective measures are necessary to prevent such control of the media as would interfere with the right of everyone to freedom of expression". The State should avoid having or seeking to have monopoly control over the media.[105] States parties should take appropriate action, consistent with the Covenant, to prevent undue media dominance or concentration by privately controlled media groups in monopolistic situations that may be harmful to a diversity of sources and views.

---

[87]Concluding observations on Togo (CCPR/CO/76/TGO); concluding observations on Moldova (CCPR/CO/75/MDA).

[88]Jung-Cheol Kim v Republic of Korea, No. 968/2001.

[89]Bodrozic v Serbia and Montenegro, No. 1180/2003.

[90]Ibid.

[91]Marques de Morais v Angola, No. 1128/2002.

[92]Aduayom et al. v Togo, Nos. 422-424/1990.

[93]Concluding observations on the Dominican Republic (CCPR/CO/71/DOM).

[94]Concluding observations on Honduras (CCPR/C/HND/CO/1).

[95]Concluding observations on Zambia (CCPR/ZMB/CO/3).

[96]Concluding observations on Costa Rica (CCPR/C/CRI/CO/5).

[97]Concluding observations on Costa Rica (CCPR/C/CRI/CO/5); concluding observations on Tunisia (CCPR/C/TUN/CO/5).

[98]Concluding observations on Vietnam (CCPR/CO/75/VNM); concluding observations on Lesotho (CCPR/CO/ 79/Add. 106).

[99]Concluding observations on Gambia (CCPR/CO/75/GMB).

[100]Concluding observations on Lebanon (CCPR/CO/79/Add.78).

[101]Concluding observations on Kuwait (CCPR/CO/69/KWT); concluding observations on Ukraine (CCPR/CO/73/UKR).

[102]Concluding observations on Kyrgyzstan (CCPR/CO/69/KGZ).

[103]Concluding observations on Ukraine (CCPR/CO/73/UKR).

[104]Concluding observations on Lebanon (CCPR/CO/79/Add.78).

[105]Concluding observations on Guyana (CCPR/CO/79/Add.121); concluding observations on the Russian Federation (CCPR/ CO/79/RUS); concluding observations on Vietnam (CCPR/CO/75/VNM); concluding observations on Italy (CCPR/C/79/ Add. 37).

43. Care must be taken to ensure that systems of government subsidy to media outlets and the placing of govern—ment advertisements[106] are not employed to the effect of impeding freedom of expression.[107] Furthermore, private media must not be put at a disadvantage compared to public media in such matters as access to means of dissemination/distribution and access to news.[108]

44. It is not compatible with paragraph 3 to penalise a media outlet, publishers or journalist solely for being critical of the government or the political social system espoused by the government.[109]

45. Any restrictions on the operation of websites, blogs or any other internet-based, electronic or other such information dissemination system, including systems to support such communication, such as internet service providers or search engines, must be compatible with paragraph 3. Any restrictions must be content-specific. Generic bans on the operation of certain sites and systems are not compatible with paragraph 3. It is also inconsistent with paragraph 3 to prohibit a site or a system from publishing material solely on the basis that it may be critical of the government or the political social system espoused by the government.[110]

46. Since journalism is a function shared by a wide range of actors, including professional full time reporters and analysts, as well as bloggers and others who engage in forms of self-publication in print, on the internet or elsewhere, general systems of registration or licensing of journalists are incompatible with paragraph 3. Limited accreditation schemes are permissible only where necessary to provide journalists with privileged access to certain places and, or events. Such schemes should be applied in a manner that is non-discriminatory and compatible with article 19 and other provisions of the Covenant.

47. It is normally incompatible with paragraph 3 to restrict the freedom of journalists and others who seek to exercise their freedom of expression (such as persons who wish to travel to human rights-related meetings)[111] to travel outside the State party, to restrict the entry into the State party of foreign journalists to those from specified countries[112] or to restrict freedom of movement of journalists and human rights investigators within the State party (including to conflict-affected locations, the sites of natural disasters and locations where there are allegations of human rights abuses). States parties should recognise and respect the limited journalistic privilege not to disclose information sources.[113]

48. States parties should ensure that counter-terrorism measures are compatible with paragraph 3. Such offences as "encouragement of terrorism"[114] and "extremist activity"[115] as well as offences of "praising", "glorifying", or "justifying" terrorism, should be clearly defined to ensure that they do not lead to a disproportionate interference with freedom of expression. Excessive restrictions on freedom of information must also be avoided. The media play a crucial role in informing the public about acts of terrorism and their capacity to operate should not be unduly restricted. In this regard, journalists should not be penalised for carrying out their legitimate activities.

49. Defamation laws must be crafted with care to ensure that they comply with paragraph 3, and that they do not serve, in practice, to stifle freedom of expression.[116] All such laws should include the defence of truth and they should not be applied with regard to the expression of opinions that are not, of their nature, subject to verification. At least with regard to comments about public figures, consideration should be given to avoiding penalising or otherwise rendering unlawful untrue statements that have been published in error but without malice.[117] In any event, a public interest in the subject matter of the criticism should be recognised as a defence. Care should be taken by States parties to avoid excessively punitive measures and penalties. Where relevant, States parties should place reasonable limits on the requirement for a defendant

---

[106]Concluding observations on Lesotho (CCPR/CO/79/Add. 106).

[107]Concluding observations on Ukraine (CCPR/CO/73/UKR).

[108]Concluding observations on Sri Lanka (CCPR/CO/79/LKA); concluding observations on Togo (CCPR/CO/76/TGO).

[109]Concluding observations on Peru (CCPR/CO/70/PER).

[110]Concluding observations on the Syrian Arab Republic (CCPR/CO/84/SYR).

[111]Concluding observations on Uzbekistan (CCPR/CO/83/UZB); concluding observations on Morocco (CCPR/CO/82/MAR).

[112]Concluding observations on Democratic People's Republic of Korea (CCPR/CO/72/PRK).

[113]Concluding observations on Kuwait (CCPR/CO/69/KWT).

[114]Concluding observations on the United Kingdom of Great Britain and Northern Ireland (CCPR/C/GBR/CO/6).

[115]Concluding observations on the Russian Federation (CCPR/CO/79/RUS).

[116]Concluding observations on the United Kingdom of Great Britain and Northern Ireland (CCPR/C/GBR/CO/6).

[117]Ibid.

to reimburse the expenses of the successful party.[118] States parties should consider the decriminalisation of defamation[119] and, in any case, the application of the criminal law should only be countenanced in the most serious of cases and imprisonment is never an appropriate penalty. It is impermissible for a State party to indict a person for criminal defamation but then not to proceed to trial expeditiously—such a practice has a chilling effect that may unduly restrict the person's exercise of freedom of expression of the person concerned and others.[120]

50. Blasphemy prohibitions and other prohibitions of display of disrespect to a religion or other belief system may not be applied in a manner that is incompatible with the paragraph 3 or other provisions of the Covenant, including articles 2, 5, 18 and 26 taking into account relevant general comments including general comment No. 22. Thus, for instance, they may not discriminate in a manner that prefers one or certain religions or belief systems or their adherents over another, or religious believers over non-believers. Blasphemy laws should not be used to prevent or punish criticism of religious leaders or commentary on religious doctrine and tenets of faith. States parties should repeal criminal law provisions on blasphemy and regarding displays of disrespect for religion or other belief system other than in the specific context of compliance with article 20 (discussed below).[121]

51. Laws that penalise the promulgation of specific views about past events, so called "memory-laws",[122] must be reviewed to ensure they violate neither freedom of opinion nor expression. The Covenant does not permit general prohibitions on expression of historical views, nor does it prohibit a person's entitlement to be wrong or to incorrectly interpret past events. Restrictions must never be imposed on the right of freedom of opinion and, with regard to freedom of expression they may not go beyond what is permitted in paragraph 3 or required under article 20. The relationship of articles 19 and 20

52. Articles 19 and 20 are compatible with and complement each other. The acts that are addressed in article 20 are of such an extreme nature that they would all be subject to restriction pursuant to article 19, paragraph 3. As such, a limitation that is justified on the basis of article 20 must also comply with article 19, paragraph 3, which lays down requirements for determining whether restrictions on expression are permissible.[123]

53. What distinguishes the acts addressed in article 20 from other acts that may be subject to restriction under article 19, paragraph 3, is that for the acts addressed in article 20, the Covenant indicates the specific response required from the State: their prohibition by law. It is only to this extent that article 20 may be considered as *lex specialis* with regard to article 19.

54. The Committee is concerned with the many forms of "hate speech" that, although a matter of concern, do not meet the level of seriousness set out in article 20. It also takes account of the many other forms of discriminatory, derogatory and demeaning discourse. However, it is only with regard to the specific forms of expression indicated in article 20 that States parties are obliged to have legal prohibitions. In every other case, while the State is not precluded in general terms from having such prohibitions, it is necessary to justify the prohibitions and their provisions in strict conformity with article 19.

[1]Ross v Canada, No. 736/1997.

All General Comments taken from website of **Office of the United Nations High Commissioner for Human Rights, Geneva, Switzerland:**

http://www2.ohchr.org/english/bodies/hrc/comments.htm

©1996-2001United Nations

---

[118]Concluding observations on the United Kingdom of Great Britain and Northern Ireland (CCPR/C/GBR/CO/6).

[119]Concluding observations on Italy (CCPR/C/ITA/CO/5); concluding observations on the Former Yugoslav Republic of Macedonia (CCPR/C/MKD/CO/2).

[120]Kankanamge v Sri Lanka, No. 909/2000.

[121]Concluding observations on the United Kingdom of Great Britain and Northern Ireland (CCPR/C/79/Add.119).

[122]Faurisson v France, No. 550/93.

C. Siracusa Principles on Limitations and Derogation of Provisions in the ICCPR

The following principles are legally not legally binding but are backed by very strong and credible legal scholarship and are highly respected and generally accepted in the human rights legal community. They should be used in applying the limitations clauses or the derogation clauses of the ICCPR. They have been cited and applied outside of the context of the ICCPR.

The reader is advised to read articles 18 and 19 of the ICCPR in order to read sample human rights norms with limitations clauses in them; and to read article 4 of the ICCPR which is the derogation clause of that treaty.

United Nations, Economic and Social Council, U.N. Sub-Commission on Prevention of Discrimination and Protection of Minorities, Siracusa Principles on the Limitation and Derogation of Provisions in the International Covenant on Civil and Political Rights, Annex, UN Doc E/CN.4/1984/4 (1984).

I. Limitation Clauses
A. General Interpretative Principles Relating to the Justification of Limitations
B. Interpretative Principles Relating to Specific Limitation Clauses†
i.   "prescribed by law"
ii.   "in a democratic society"
iii. "public order (ordre public)"
iv.   "public health"
v.   "public morals"
vi.   "national security"
vii. "public safety"
viii. "rights and freedoms of others," or "rights and reputations of others"
ix.   "restrictions on public trial"

II. Derogations in a Public Emergency
A.   "Public Emergency Which Threatens the Life of the Nation"
B.   Proclamation, Notification, and Termination of a Public Emergency
C.   "Strictly Required by the Exigencies of the Situation"
D.   Non-Derogable Rights
E.   Some General Principles on the Introduction and Application of a Public Emergency and Consequent Derogation Measures
F.   Recommendations Concerning the Functions and Duties of the Human Rights Committee and United Nations Bodies.

I. LIMITATION CLAUSES

A. General Interpretative Principles Relating to the Justification of Limitations*

1. No limitations or grounds for applying them to rights guaranteed by the Covenant are permitted other than those contained in the terms of the Covenant itself.
2. The scope of a limitation referred to in the Covenant shall not be interpreted so as to jeopardize the essence of the right concerned.
3. All limitation clauses shall be interpreted strictly and in favor of the rights at issue.
4. All limitations shall be interpreted in the light and context of the particular right concerned.
5. All limitations on a right recognized by the Covenant shall be provided for by law and be compatible with the objects and purposes of the Covenant.
6. No limitation referred to in the Covenant shall be applied for any purpose other than that for which it has been prescribed.
7. No limitation shall be applied in an arbitrary manner.
8. Every limitation imposed shall be subject to the possibility of challenge to and remedy against its abusive application.
9. No limitation on a right recognized by the Covenant shall discriminate contrary to Article 2, paragraph 1.

---

*The term "limitations" in these principles includes the term "restrictions" as used in the Covenant.

10. Whenever a limitation is required in the terms of the Covenant to be "necessary," this term implies that the limitation:
    (a) is based on one of the grounds justifying limitations recognized by the relevant article of the Covenant,
    (b) responds to a pressing public or social need,
    (c) pursues a legitimate aim, and
    (d) is proportionate to that aim.
    Any assessment as to the necessity of a limitation shall be made on objective considerations.
11. In applying a limitation, a state shall use no more restrictive means than are required for the achievement of the purpose of the limitation.
12. The burden of justifying a limitation upon a right guaranteed under the Covenant lies with the state.
13. The requirement expressed in Article 12 of the Covenant, that any restrictions be consistent with other rights recognized in the Covenant, is implicit in limitations to the other rights recognized in the Covenant.
14. The limitation clauses of the Covenant shall not be interpreted to restrict the exercise of any human rights protected to a greater extent by other international obligations binding upon the state.

B. Interpretative Principles Relating to Specific Limitation Clauses

i. "prescribed by law"

15. No limitation on the exercise of human rights shall be made unless provided for by national law of general application which is consistent with the Covenant and is in force at the time the limitation is applied.
16. Laws imposing limitations on the exercise of human rights shall not be arbitrary or unreasonable.
17. Legal rules limiting the exercise of human rights shall be clear and accessible to everyone.
18. Adequate safeguards and effective remedies shall be provided by law against illegal or abusive imposition or application of limitations on human rights.

ii. "in a democratic society"

19. The expression "in a democratic society" shall be interpreted as imposing a further restriction on the limitation clauses it qualifies.
20. The burden is upon a state imposing limitations so qualified to demonstrate that the limitations do not impair the democratic functioning of the society.
21. While there is no single model of a democratic society, a society which recognizes and respects the human rights set forth in the United Nations Charter and the Universal Declaration of Human Rights may be viewed as meeting this definition.

iii. "public order (ordre public)"

22. The expression "public order (ordre public)" as used in the Covenant may be defined as the sum of rules which ensure the functioning of society or the set of fundamental principles on which society is founded. Respect for human rights is part of public order (ordre public).
23. Public order (ordre public) shall be interpreted in the context of the purpose of the particular human right which is limited on this ground.
24. State organs or agents responsible for the maintenance of public order (ordre public) shall be subject to controls in the exercise of their power through the parliament, courts, or other competent independent bodies.

iv. "public health"

25. Public health may be invoked as a ground for limiting certain rights in order to allow a state to take measures dealing with a serious threat to the health of the population or individual members of the population. These measures must be specifically aimed at preventing disease or injury or providing care for the sick and injured.
26. Due regard shall be had to the international health regulations of the World Health Organization.

v. "public morals"

27. Since public morality varies over time and from one culture to another, a state which invokes public morality as a ground for restricting human rights, while enjoying a certain margin of discretion, shall demonstrate that the limitation in question is essential to the maintenance of respect for fundamental values of the community.

28. The margin of discretion left to states does not apply to the rule of non-discrimination as defined in the Covenant.

vi. "national security"

29. National security may be invoked to justify measures limiting certain rights only when they are taken to protect the existence of the nation or its territorial integrity or political independence against force or threat of force.

30. National security cannot be invoked as a reason for imposing limitations to prevent merely local or relatively isolated threats to law and order.

31. National security cannot be used as a pretext for imposing vague or arbitrary limitations and may only be invoked when there exists adequate safeguards and effective remedies against abuse.

32. The systematic violation of human rights undermines true national security and may jeopardize international peace and security. A state responsible for such violation shall not invoke national security as a justification for measures aimed at suppressing opposition to such violation or at perpetrating repressive practices against its population.

vii. "public safety"

33. Public safety means protection against danger to the safety of persons, to their life or physical integrity, or serious damage to their property.

34. The need to protect public safety can justify limitations provided by law. It cannot be used for imposing vague or arbitrary limitations and may only be invoked when there exist adequate safeguards and effective remedies against abuse.

viii. "rights and freedoms of others" or the "rights or reputations of others"

35. The scope of the rights and freedoms of others that may act as a limitation upon rights in the Covenant extends beyond the rights and freedoms recognized in the Covenant.

36. When a conflict exists between a right protected in the Covenant and one which is not, recognition and consideration should be given to the fact that the Covenant seeks to protect the most fundamental rights and freedoms. In this context especial weight should be afforded to rights not subject to limitations in the Covenant.

37. A limitation to a human right based upon the reputation of others shall not be used to protect the state and its officials from public opinion or criticism.

ix. "restrictions on public trial"

38. All trials shall be public unless the Court determines in accordance with law that:
    (a) the press or the public should be excluded from all or part of a trial on the basis of specific findings announced in open court showing that the interest of the private lives of the parties or their families or of juveniles so requires; or
    (b) the exclusion is strictly necessary to avoid publicity prejudicial to the fairness of the trial or endangering public morals, public order (ordre public), or national security in a democratic society.

II. DEROGATIONS IN A PUBLIC EMERGENCY

A. "Public Emergency which Threatens the Life of the Nation"

39. A state party may take measures derogating from its obligations under the International Covenant on Civil and Political Rights pursuant to Article 4 (hereinafter called "derogation measures") only when faced with a situation of exceptional and actual or imminent danger which threatens the life of the nation. A threat to the life of the nation is one that:
    (a) affects the whole of the population and either the whole or part of the territory of the State, and
    (b) threatens the physical integrity of the population, the political independence or the territorial integrity of the State or the existence or basic functioning of institutions indispensable to ensure and project the rights recognized in the Covenant.

40. Internal conflict and unrest that do not constitute a grave and imminent threat to the life of the nation cannot justify derogations under Article 4.

41. Economic difficulties per se cannot justify derogation measures.

B. Proclamation, Notification, and Termination of a Public Emergency

42. A state party derogating from its obligations under the Covenant shall make an official proclamation of the existence of the public emergency threatening the life of the nation.

43. Procedures under national law for the proclamation of a state of emergency shall be prescribed in advance of the emergency.

44. A state party derogating from its obligations under the Covenant shall immediately notify the other states parties to the Covenant, through the intermediary of the Secretary-General of the United Nations, of the provisions from which it has derogated and the reasons by which it was actuated.

45. The notification shall contain sufficient information to permit the states parties to exercise their rights and discharge their obligations under the Covenant. In particular it shall contain:
(a) the provisions of the Covenant from which it has derogated;
(b) a copy of the proclamation of emergency, together with the constitutional provisions, legislation, or decrees governing the state of emergency in order to assist the states parties to appreciate the scope of the derogation;
(c) the effective date of the imposition of the state of emergency and the period for which it has been proclaimed;
(d) an explanation of the reasons which actuated the government's decision to derogate, including a brief description of the factual circumstances leading up to the proclamation of the state of emergency; and
(e) a brief description of the anticipated effect of the derogation measures on the rights recognized by the Covenant, including copies of decrees derogating from these rights issued prior to the notification.

46. States parties may require that further information necessary to enable them to carry out their role under the Covenant be provided through the intermediary of the Secretary-General.

47. A state party which fails to make an immediate notification in due form of its derogation is in breach of its obligations to other states parties and may be deprived of the defenses otherwise available to it in procedures under the Covenant.

48. A state party availing itself of the right of derogation pursuant to Article 4 shall terminate such derogation in the shortest time required to bring to an end the public emergency which threatens the life of the nation.

49. The state party shall on the date on which it terminates such derogation inform the other state parties, through the intermediary of the Secretary-General of the United Nations, of the fact of the termination.

50. On the termination of a derogation pursuant to Article 4 all rights and freedoms protected by the Covenant shall be restored in full. A review of the continuing consequences of derogation measures shall be made as soon as possible. Steps shall be taken to correct injustices and to compensate those who have suffered injustice during or in consequence of the derogation measures.

C. Strictly Required by the Exigencies of the Situation"

51. The severity, duration, and geographic scope of any derogation measure shall be such only as are strictly necessary to deal with the threat to the life of the nation and are proportionate to its nature and extent.

52. The competent national authorities shall be under a duty to assess individually the necessity of any derogation measure taken or proposed to deal with the specific dangers posed by the emergency.

53. A measure is not strictly required by the exigencies of the situation where ordinary measures permissible under the specific limitations clauses of the Covenant would be adequate to deal with the threat to the life of the nation.

54. The principle of strict necessity shall be applied in an objective manner. Each measure shall be directed to an actual, clear, present, or imminent danger and may not be imposed merely because of an apprehension of potential danger.

55. The national constitution and laws governing states of emergency shall provide for prompt and periodic independent review by the legislature of the necessity for derogation measures.

56. Effective remedies shall be available to persons claiming that derogation measures affecting them are not strictly required by the exigencies of the situation.

57. In determining whether derogation measures are strictly required by the exigencies of the situation the judgment of the national authorities cannot be accepted as conclusive.

D. Non-Derogable Rights

58. No state party shall, even in time of emergency threatening the life of the nation, derogate from the Covenant's guarantees of the right to life; freedom from torture, cruel, inhuman or degrading treatment or punishment, and from medical or scientific experimentation without free consent; freedom from slavery or involuntary servitude; the right not to be imprisoned for contractual debt; the right not to be convicted or sentenced to a heavier penalty by virtue of retroactive criminal legislation; the right to

recognition as a person before the law; and freedom of thought, conscience and religion. These rights are not derogable under any conditions even for the asserted purpose of preserving the life of the nation.

59. State parties to the Covenant, as part of their obligation to ensure the enjoyment of these rights to all persons within their jurisdiction (Art. 2(1)) and to adopt measures to secure an effective remedy for violations (Art. 2(3)), shall take special precautions in time of public emergency to ensure that neither official nor semi-official groups engage in a practice of arbitrary and extra-judicial killings or involuntary disappearances, that persons in detention are protected against torture and other forms of cruel, inhuman or degrading treatment or punishment, and that no persons are convicted or punished under laws or decrees with retroactive effect.

60. The ordinary courts shall maintain their jurisdiction, even in a time of public emergency, to adjudicate any complaint that a non-derogable right has been violated

E. Some General Principles on the Introduction and Application of a Public Emergency and Consequent Derogation Measures

61. Derogation from rights recognized under international law in order to respond to a threat to the life of the nation is not exercised in a legal vacuum. It is authorized by law and as such it is subject to several legal principles of general application.

62. A proclamation of a public emergency shall be made in good faith based upon an objective assessment of the situation in order to determine to what extent, if any, it poses a threat to the life of the nation. A proclamation of a public emergency, and consequent derogations from Covenant obligations, that are not made in good faith are violations of international law.

63. The provisions of the Covenant allowing for certain derogations in a public emergency are to be interpreted restrictively.

64. In a public emergency the rule of law shall still prevail. Derogation is an authorized and limited perogative in order to respond adequately to a threat to the life of the nation. The derogating state shall burden of justifying its actions under law.

65. The Covenant subordinates all procedures to the basic objectives of human rights. Article 5(1) of the Covenant sets definite limits to actions taken under the Covenant:

Nothing in the present Covenant may be interpreted as implying for any State, group or person any right to engage in any activity or perform any act aimed at the destruction of any of the rights and freedoms recognized herein or at their limitation to a greater extent than is provided for in the present Covenant.

Article 29(2) of the Universal Declaration of Human Rights sets out the ultimate purpose of law:

In the exercise of his rights and freedoms, everyone shall be subject only to such limitations as are determined by law solely for the purpose of securing due recognition and respect for the rights and freedoms of others and of meeting the just requirements of morality, public order and the general welfare in a democratic society.

These provisions apply with full force to claims that a situation constitutes a threat to the life of a nation and hence enables authorities to derogate.

66. A bona fide proclamation of the public emergency permits derogation from specified obligations in the Covenant, but does not authorize a general departure from international obligations. The Covenant in Article 4(1) and 5(2) expressly prohibits derogations which are inconsistent with other obligations under international law. In this regard, particular note should be taken of international obligations which apply in a public emergency under the Geneva and I.L.O. Conventions.

67. In a situation of a non-international armed conflict a state party to the 1949 Geneva Conventions for the protection of war victims may under no circumstances suspend the right to a trial by a court offering the essential guarantees of independence and impartiality (Article 3 common to the 1949 Conventions). Under the 1977 additional Protocol II, the following rights with respect to penal prosecution shall be respected under all circumstances by state parties to the Protocol:

(a) the duty to give notice of changes without delay and to grant the necessary rights and means of defense;

(b) conviction only on the basis of individual penal responsibility;

(c) the right not to be convicted, or sentenced to a heavier penalty, by virtue of retroactive criminal legislation;

(d) presumption of innocence;

(e) trial in the presence of the accused;

(f) no obligation on the accused to testify against himself or to confess guilt;

(g) the duty to advise the convicted person on judicial and other remedies.

68. The I.L.O. basic human rights conventions contain a number of rights dealing with such matters as forced labor, freedom of association, equality in employment and trade union and workers' rights which are not subject to derogation during an emergency; others permit derogation, but only to the extent strictly necessary to meet the exigencies of the situation.

69. No state, including those that are not parties to the Covenant, may suspend or violate, even in times of public emergency:
    (a) the right to life;
    (b) freedom from torture or cruel, inhuman or degrading treatment or punishment and from medical or scientific experimentation;
    (c) the right not to be held in slavery or involuntary servitude; and,
    (d) the right not to be subjected to retroactive criminal penalties as defined in the Covenant.
    Customary international law prohibits in all circumstances the denial of such fundamental rights.

70. Although protections against arbitrary arrest and detention (Art. 9) and the right to a fair and public hearing in the determination of a criminal charge (Art. 14) may be subject to legitimate limitations if strictly required by the exigencies of an emergency situation, the denial of certain rights fundamental to human dignity can never be strictly necessary in any conceivable emergency. Respect for these fundamental rights is essential in order to ensure enjoyment of non-derogable rights and to provide an effective remedy against their violation. In particular:
    (a) all arrests and detention and the place of detention shall be recorded, if possible centrally, and make available to the public without delay;
    (b) no person shall be detained for an indefinite period of time, whether detained pending judicial investigation or trial or detained without charge;
    (c) no person shall be held in isolation without communication with his family, friend, or lawyer for longer than a few days, e.g., three to seven days;
    (d) where persons are detained without charge the need of their continued detention shall be considered periodically by an independent review tribunal;
    (e) any person charged with an offense shall be entitled to a fair trial by a competent, independent and impartial court established by law;
    (f) civilians shall normally be tried by the ordinary courts; where it is found strictly necessary to establish military tribunals or special courts to try civilians, their competence, independence and impartiality shall be ensured and the need for them reviewed periodically by the competent authority;
    (g) any person charged with a criminal offense shall be entitled to the presumption of innocence and to at least the following rights to ensure a fair trial:
        — the right to be informed of the charges promptly, in detail and in a language he understands,
        — the right to have adequate time and facilities to prepare the defense including the right to communicate confidentially with his lawyer,
        — the right to a lawyer of his choice, with free legal assistance if he does not have the means to pay for it,
        — the right to be present at the trial,
        — the right not to be compelled to testify against himself or to make a confession,
        — the right to obtain the attendance and examination of defense witnesses,
        — the right to be tried in public save where the court orders otherwise on grounds of security with adequate safeguards to prevent abuse,
        — the right to appeal to a higher court;
    (h) an adequate record of the proceedings shall be kept in all cases; and,
    (i) no person shall be tried or punished again for an offense for which he has already been convicted or acquitted.

F. Recommendations Concerning the Functions and Duties of the Human Rights Committee and United Nations Bodies

71. In the exercise of its power to study, report, and make general comments on states parties' reports under Article 40 of the Covenant, the Human Rights Committee may and should examine the compliance of states parties with the provisions of Article 4. Likewise it may and should do so when exercising its powers in relevant cases under Article 41 and the Optional Protocol relating, respectively, to interstate and individual communications.

72. In order to determine whether the requirements of Article 4(1) and (2) have been met and for the purpose of supplementing information in states parties' reports, members of the Human Rights Committee, as persons of recognized competence in the field of human rights, may and should have regard to information they consider to be reliable provided by other inter-governmental bodies, non-governmental organizations, and individual communications.

73. The Human Rights Committee should develop a procedure for requesting additional reports under Article 40(1)(b) from states parties which have given notification of derogation under Article 4(3) or which are reasonably believed by the Committee to have imposed emergency measures subject to Article 4 constraints. Such additional reports should relate to questions concerning the emergency insofar as it affects the implementation of the Covenant and should be dealt with by the Committee at the earliest possible date.

74. In order to enable the Human Rights Committee to perform its fact-finding functions more effectively, the committee should develop its procedures for the consideration of communications under the Optional Protocol to permit the hearing of oral submissions and evidence as well as visits to states parties alleged to be in violation of the Covenant. If necessary, the states parties to the Optional Protocol should consider amending it to this effect.

75. The United Nations Commission on Human Rights should request its Sub-Commission on Prevention of Discrimination and Protection of Minorities to prepare an annual list if states, whether parties to the Covenant or not, that proclaim, maintain, or terminate a public emergency together with:

    (a) in the case of a state party, the proclamation and notification; and,

    (b) in the case of other states, any available and apparently reliable information concerning the proclamation, threat to the life of the nation, derogation measures and their proportionality, non-discrimination, and respect for non-derogable rights.

76. The United Nations Commission on Human Rights and its Sub-Commission should continue to utilize the technique of appointment of special rapporteurs and investigatory and fact-finding bodies in relation to prolonged public emergencies.

D. Criteria for Determining Whether a Restriction/ Limitation Measure Is Legitimate and Permissible

BY H. VICTOR CONDÉ

In the international arena the battle for human rights is being fought for respect by the U.S. government for express written human rights legal norms, for example ICCPR articles 7 and 19, in such human rights bodies such as the UN Human Rights Committee and Committee against Torture in domestic discussion over whether the U.S. has correctly interpreted and has fully complied with certain human rights treaty norms.

Some human rights norms are absolute and apply always and everywhere the same. Examples are the prohibition against torture and slavery. The only issues that arise with regards to absolute rights are the interpretation of the meaning of the terms. Examples would be whether water boarding is within the meaning of torture, or not. There, at the U.S. domestic level, one applies the rules of interpretation, such as applying the Vienna Convention on Treaties, and one looks to the U.S. reservations, declarations and understandings, RUDs, to see if there are any qualifications on how the member state, the U.S., interprets a norms or the meaning of a term such as "torture." Then one compares that to any Congressional implementing legislation, since the U.S. usually ratifies human rights treaties with RUDs, which among other things, declare that the treaty is non self-executing, requiring implementing legislation. Finally, one compares that to the terms of the U.S. Constitution to determine constitutionality.

At the international law level applying international human rights treaties, the situation of applying legal norms is different. And it is different for absolute and non absolute, or "conditional" human rights norms. While absolute norms apply everywhere and always unconditionally, the same is not true of non-absolute or conditional human rights. Conditional human rights norms are those which have a limitation or restriction clause in them. See ICCPR article 19.3. Article 19.3 is called a limitation clause or restriction cause. The limitation/ restriction clause allows the state to take measures which restrict or limit the exercise of the substantive right, such as freedom of expression, so long as the measure fulfils certain criteria.

The real legal battles over human rights compliance are being fought principally within the context of the limitation/restriction clauses of those norms, such as ICCPR art.19.3. Simply put, where one can establish that the state has in fact interfered with someone's exercise of their right to expression, for example, the state will always try to show that there was a good legal reason, a legal justification, for why it has so interfered. An example would be the state trying to prevent anti war protestors from demonstrating at the funeral of a dead American soldier. If the state tried to prevent such expression would that be a justified limitation on freedom of expression under international human rights law? The international way of analysing that issue is a bit different from the classical U.S. Constitutional analysis. Here one will see the international legal manner of analysing such a limitation/restriction measure. These measures taken by a state which interfere with an exercise of expression and which are claimed to be legally justified are called "limitations" or "restriction." These measures limit or restrict the otherwise free exercise of one's expressions. They are the legal loopholes to human rights obligations of states. They in theory allow a fair balance between the freedom of the individual, on the one hand, versus the needs of state to regulate society in an orderly, harmonious and productive way.

State measures, which interferes as a limitation/restriction with exercise of one's freedom of expression is not necessarily a violation of that human rights norm. These measures are usually claimed by the state to constitute legitimate government aims, such as protection of public safety or health or national security, which can be permissible under the convention norms.

The legitimate aims which are applicable to a particular norm, such as ICCPR article 19 are set forth in what are called limitation or restriction clauses. Again, article 19.3 is known as limitation or restriction clauses. Not all measures taken by states under the claim of legitimate restriction/limitation are valid under the human rights conventions. One must analyze the specific measure taken in order to determine if it is a permissible or legitimate restriction/limitation. If the limitation is not permissible as a matter of law then a violation of the human rights norms of freedom of expression will be normally be found.

There has developed an extensive international jurisprudence, particularly in the European Court of Human Rights, the most advanced system of human rights jurisprudence, about how to analyze and thus determine whether a limitation measure is permissible under a convention article. Under international legal principles the analysis of whether a state measure is a valid limitation/restriction measure is as follows:

The first thing to do is determine whether the state's measure in fact interfered with the exercise of the substantive rights. Was there an "interference"? If one finds an interference one will then ask whether the measure taken or by the state meets the following criteria:

1. Prescribed by Law

Was the measure "prescribed by law"? This means that the measure is consistent with the Principle of Legality in that it meets all the following sub criteria:

a. It was issued by a **proper legal authority** who had the legal power and right to establish or take the measure under domestic (national) law;

b. The measure is "**accessible**" to persons, they can find out what it is and what is required; and

c. It is sufficiently **clear and precise** enough that persons can know the **foreseeable consequences** of compliance or non compliance, so as to be able to regulate their conduct accordingly.

2. Legitimate Aim

By this is meant that the reason for which the state took the measure was to achieve a specific objective beneficial to society, which object or "aim" is expressly listed in the limitation clause (viz. ICCPR art. 19.3: " for the protection of public order";

Human rights limitation/restriction clauses will be interpreted narrowly against the state. Only those aims listed in the limitation/restriction clause will serve to justify a measure of restriction/limitation. Note that not even national security constitutes a legitimate aim to restrict exercise all human rights, for example freedom of religion or belief in article 18.

3. Necessity/Necessary

Exercise of a right is the rule and limitation of the exercise is an exception to the rule.

Assuming it is both prescribed by law and meets a legitimate aim or aims set forth in the limitation/ restriction clause, in order for the measure to be permitted, it still must then pass the test of whether it is "necessary" to pass that measure to fulfill the state's obligations towards respect for and protection of human rights. This issue requires analysis of the measure in light of the following three criteria:

a. The measure meets a "**pressing social need**". Since freedom is the rule and limitation of freedom by the state is the exception, there must be a real and genuine need to take this measure to achieve the legitimate aim.

b. The measure must be "<u>justified in principle</u>". This means that the measure taken is really being taken for the reasons asserted by the state, and the measure is consistent with achieving respect for human rights. They cannot be used in a discriminatory way, nor for discriminatory purposes, nor be used to undermine any other human rights. The result of the limitation/restriction will end up being beneficial for both the society and the person affected.

c. The measure is "**<u>proportionate</u>**" to the goal sought to be achieved. In order to be accepted as a legitimate limit of the exercise of a right the state is authorized to take on interfere with individual freedom only to a degree that is necessary to meet the legitimate aim. There must be a relation of proportionality between the measure taken, such as a criminal punishment or disbanding of a group, and the legitimate aim, for example, control of violence or a threat to the rights and freedoms of others. One must always ask of all measures taken by states to restrict or control expression whether the measures are proportionate. Even if it is prescribed by law and there is a legitimate aim there will be no pressing social need found if the measure taken is disproportionate to the aim. That will render the measure legally invalid and impermissible and a violation will be found.

d. The measures must be **relevant** to the aim to be accomplished and **sufficient** to accomplish the aims.

For a limitation/restriction measure to be legitimate and permissible to justify an interference on behalf of the state the state must show it meets all of these above criteria.

From an International Law perspective this is the method of analysis that applies to U.S. law, policy and practice when judgeing whether the U.S. is incompliance with it internationa human rights law obigations, such as under the ICCPR.

Not all human rights treaties have limitation/restriction clauses. This analysis applies primarily to the ICCPR, which at this time is the most important general human rights treaty which is legally binding on the U.S. because the U.S. ratified it.

The U.S. has told the U.N. Human Rights committee that its law, policy and practice are in harmony with the norms of the ICCPR. The ony way to determine this definitively from a legal perspective is to apply the above criteria to a U.S. law, policy, or practice.

Only when the U.S. law, policy and practice fulfill the above criteria, will they be in compliance with the international legal norms of the ICCPR.

APPENDIX F: HOW AN INTERNATIONAL HUMAN RIGHTS NORM BECOMES U.S. LAW

This Appendix charts the process in the U.S. legal system whereby an international human rights norm is established in international law and gets transformed into or recognized by the legal system for application by our courts. It shows how specific norms in the articles of treaties in the Documents section become either U.S. law, or binding legal obligations, and gives a general description of the various steps from human rights ideal to binding law. There are many variations and exceptions to the general process not identified here.

1. Treaty Norm:
Creation of an International Human Rights Treaty

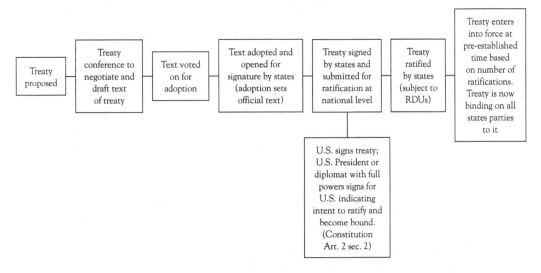

2. U.S. Treaty Ratification Process

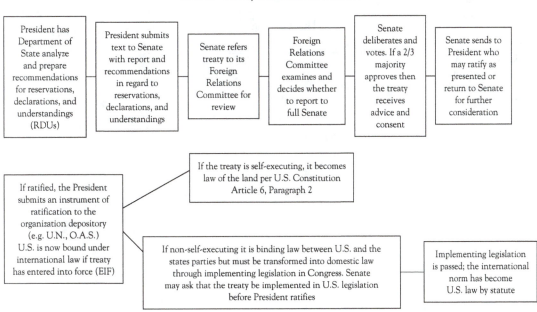

APPENDIX G: SPECTRUM OF
LAW APPLICABLE IN THE U.S.

This Appendix charts the large spectrum of laws that regulate our society, from local municipal ordinances to international laws to international human rights norms applicable to the
U.S. It shows how human rights norms, which constitute a body of law applicable in U.S.,
fit into and influence the U.S. legal system.

U.S. Constitution and Bill of Rights

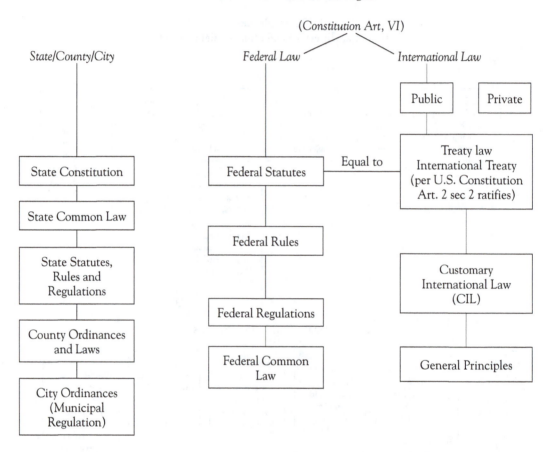

APPENDIX H: STATUS OF TREATIES APPLICABLE TO THE U.S.

This Appendix comprises a chart showing what main human rights treaty instruments the U.S. has signed and ratified or acceded to, a list of other human rights instruments relevant to the U.S. indicating whether the U.S. has ratified/acceded, or just signed, and a list of treaties the U.S. has neither ratified nor signed.

To understand treaty procedures, see definition of the term Ratification and the section on how treaties are created in the Introductory Essay.

The following information on treaty abbreviations and treaty status (scope of legal obligations) was taken from the U.N. document entitled "Compilation prepared by the Office of the High Commissioner for Human Rights in accordance with paragraph 15 (b) of the annex to Human Rights Council resolution 5/1

Document A/HRC/WG.6/9/USA/2 of 12 August 2010. It was the document used for purposes of the U.S. UPR process.

The following abbreviations are used for the following list of treaty status:

ICERD	International Convention on the Elimination of All Forms of Racial Discrimination
ICESCR	International Covenant on Economic, Social and Cultural Rights
OP-ICESCR	Optional Protocol to ICESCR
ICCPR	International Covenant on Civil and Political Rights
ICCPR-OP 1	Optional Protocol to ICCPR
ICCPR-OP 2	Second Optional Protocol to ICCPR, aiming at the abolition of the death penalty
CEDAW	Convention on the Elimination of All Forms of Discrimination against Women
OP-CEDAW	Optional Protocol to CEDAW
CAT	Convention against Torture and Other Cruel, Inhuman or Degrading Treatment or Punishment
OP-CAT	Optional Protocol to CAT
CRC	Convention on the Rights of the Child
OP-CRC-AC	Optional Protocol to CRC on the involvement of children in armed conflict
OP-CRC-SC	Optional Protocol to CRC on the sale of children, child prostitution and child pornography
ICRMW	International Convention on the Protection of the Rights of All Migrant Workers and Members of Their Families
CRPD	Convention on the Rights of Persons with Disabilities
OP-CRPD	Optional Protocol to the Convention on the Rights of Persons with Disabilities
CED	International Convention for the Protection of All Persons from Enforced Disappearance

Universal human rights treaties[2]	Date of ratification, accession or succession	Declarations/reservations	Recognition of specific competences of treaty bodies
ICERD	21 October 1994	Yes (arts. 2, para. 1 (c) and (d), 3, 4, 5, 7 22)[3]	Individual Complaints (art. 14): No
ICCPR	8 June 1992	Yes (arts. 1–27 not self-executing) 5, para. 2; 6; 7; 10, paras. 2 (b) and 3; 14, para. 4; 15, para. 1; 19, para. 3; 20; 47)[4]	Inter-State (arts. complaints (art. 41): Yes
CAT	21 October 1994	Yes (arts. 16 and 30, para. 1)[5]	Inter-State complaints (art. 21): Yes Individual Complaints (art. 22): No Inquiry procedure (art. 20): Yes
OP-CRC-AC	23 December 2002	Binding declaration under art. 3, para. 2: 17 years[6]	–
OP-CRC-SC	23 December 2002	Yes (arts. 3, para. 1, and 4, para. 1)[7]	–

Treaties to which United States of America is not a party:

ICESCR (signature only, 1977),
OP-ICESCR[8],
ICCPR-OP 1,
ICCPR-OP 2,
CEDAW (signature only, 1980),
OP-CEDAW,
OP-CAT, CRC (signature only, 1995),
ICRMW,
CRPD (signature only, 2009),
OP-CRPD and CED.

Other main relevant international instruments[9]	Ratification, accession or succession
Convention on the Prevention and Punishment of the Crime of Genocide	Yes
Rome Statute of the International Criminal Court	No (signature only)
Palermo Protocol[10] Refugees and stateless persons[11]	Yes No, except 1967 Protocol
Geneva Conventions of 12 August 1949 and Additional Protocols thereto[12]	Yes (signatory to Additional Protocols I and II)
ILO fundamental conventions[13]	No, except C.105 and C.182
UNESCO Convention against Discrimination in Education	No

1. In 2008, the Committee on the Rights of the Child (CRC) recommended that the United States of America proceed to become party to the Convention on the Rights of the Child.[14] The Working Group of experts on people of African descent noted that the U.S. has not ratified the Convention or the ILO Convention No. 111 concerning Discrimination in Respect of Employment and Occupation.[15]

2. In 2008, the Special Rapporteur on the human rights of migrants recommended that the U.S. consider ratifying the International Convention on the Protection of the Rights of All Migrant Workers and Members of Their Families.[16]

3. CRC recommended that the State consider ratifying Additional Protocols I and II to the Geneva Conventions of 12 August 1949.[17]

4. The Committee against Torture (CAT) invited the State to reconsider its intention not to become party to the Rome Statute of the International Criminal Court.[18] CRC made a similar recommendation.[19]

5. In 2006, CAT recommended that the State ensure that the Convention applies at all times, whether in peace, war or armed conflict[20] and that the provisions of the Convention expressed as applicable to "territory under the State party's jurisdiction" apply to all persons under the effective control of its authorities.[21]

6. In 2006, the Human Rights Committee (HR Committee) encouraged the State to withdraw its reservation to article 6, paragraph 5, of ICCPR, which forbids imposition of the death penalty on offenders who were under the age of 18 when their crimes were committed.[22] Other committees recommended that reservations and understandings to relevant human rights treaties be withdrawn.[23]

In the U.S. national UPR report submitted to the U.N. Office of the High Commissioner for Human Rights in preparation for the Universal Periodic Review Process, (See Primary Document #86) the U.S. reported in Annex 1 the following human rights treaty status as to the U.S.:

The U.S. is at present Party to the following multilateral human rights related treaties:
- Slavery Convention and its amending Protocol;
- Supplementary Convention on the Abolition of Slavery, the Slave Trade and Institutions and Practices Similar to Slavery;
- Protocol Relating to the Status of Refugees;
- Inter-American Convention on the Granting of Political Rights to Women;
- Convention on the Political Rights of Women;
- Convention on the Prevention and Punishment of the Crime of Genocide;
- ILO Convention No. 105 concerning the Abolition of Forced Labor;
- International Covenant on Civil and Political Rights;
- Convention against Torture and Other Cruel, Inhuman or Degrading Treatment or Punishment;
- International Convention on the Elimination of All Forums of Racial Discrimination;
- ILO Convention 182 Concerning the Prohibition and Immediate Action for the Elimination of the Worst Forms of Child Labor;
- Optional Protocol to the Convention on the Rights of the Child on the Involvement of Children in Armed Conflict; and
- Optional Protocol to the Convention on the Rights of the Child on the Sale of Children, Child Prostitution, and Child Pornography.

The U.S. has signed but not ratified the following multilateral human rights treaties:
- International Covenant on Economic, Social and Cultural Rights;
- American Convention on Human Rights;
- Convention on the Elimination of All Forms of Discrimination Against Women;
- Convention on the Rights of the Child; and
- International Convention on the Rights of Persons with Disabilities.

In addition, the U.S. has entered into many bilateral treaties (including consular treaties and treaties of friendship, commerce and navigation) that contain provisions guaranteeing various rights and protections to nationals of foreign countries on a reciprocal basis. In some cases, these may be invoked directly in U.S. courts for that purpose.

Note that shorter forms of these complete treaty names are used in the UPR report, e.g., "Convention Against Torture."

In addition to accepting human rights obligations under the above-referenced treaties to which it is a party, the U.S. has made human rights commitments through numerous other instruments, including the 1948 Universal Declaration of Human Rights and the 1948 American Declaration of the Rights and Duties of Man.

The U.S. regularly submits lengthy and detailed reports on its implementation of several of the human rights treaties listed above, specifically the International Covenant on Civil and Political Rights, the Convention against Torture, the Convention on the Elimination of All Forums of Racial Discrimination, and the two Optional Protocols to the Convention on the Rights of the Child. A compilation of that reporting is posted on the State Department's website, at http://www.state.gov/g/drl/hr/treaties/index.htm

In addition to the above, the U.S. has not signed or ratified the following human rights related treaties:

Convention related to the Status of Refugees (the U.S. acceded to the Protocol to this treaty and so is bound by the Protocol. See Primary Documents 36–37).

First Optional Protocol to the American Convention on Human Rights, (See Primary Documents 63–64) providing for economic, social and cultural rights.

Second Optional Protocol to the American Convention on Human Rights, (See Primary Documents 63 and 65) providing for abolition of capital punishment.

Inter-American Convention to Prevent and Punish Torture (OAS 1987)

Inter-American Convention on the Prevention, Punishment and Eradication of Violence against Women (OAS 1949) other instruments, including the 1948 Universal Declaration of Human Rights and the 1948 American Declaration of the Rights and Duties of Man.

The U.S. regularly submits lengthy and detailed reports on its implementation of several of the human rights treaties listed above, specifically the International Covenant on Civil and Political Rights, the Convention against Torture, the Convention on the Elimination of All Forums of Racial Discrimination, and the two Optional Protocols to the Convention on the Rights of the Child. A compilation of that reporting is posted on the State Department's website, at http://www.state.gov/g/drl/hr/treaties/index.htm

APPENDIX I: SELECTED U.S. LEGISLATION, RESOLUTIONS, AND THE RESTATEMENT OF LAW

The purpose of this Appendix is to show how international human rights norms have influenced and become a part of American national and even local law. As stated in the Introductory Essay, human rights norms are set into legal standards at the international level becoming part of the body of international law. It is a requirement of that body of law, that states who accept to be bound by those norms then transform or incorporate those international human rights norms into national law, so that they can be implemented at the national level.

Again, under the principle of subsidiarity it is at the national level, not the international level, that the primary protection of human rights lies. States under state law are the primary protectors of human rights. If states fully transform or incorporate human rights norms into the national legal system and provide effective domestic procedures and remedies for violation, then no one needs to go to the international level to seek recourse for violations. That is the theory. But because states don't always get it right, the international system exists to let the states know that there is a place where the whole of the international community, humanity itself, has an interest in seeing how states treat human beings under their jurisdiction or control. The lessons of World War II remind us of that.

This Appendix includes selected U.S. laws, Congressional resolutions, proposed legislation, and information relating to international human rights in U.S. law. Most, but not all, of these have the purpose of legislating in the international context or connecting to international human rights standards.

It must be remembered that there are many U.S. laws that, broadly speaking, seek to protect human beings and advance their fullest individual development. Laws aimed at education, racial and other types of discrimination, environmental protection, medical patients' bills of rights, and consumer protection may all serve to protect human freedom from government overreaching its boundaries. However, only a few of these laws will be mentioned here, as many are outside the scope of this book. This book seeks to inform the reader about "human rights" as they are understood in the international context, even where they are interpreted or applied in a purely domestic, national context.

The examples given here are not exhaustive. Congress proposes and enacts new human rights legislation every year. The examples given here are those that have recently been most important and most frequently seen in the U.S. legal system, especially in judicial decisions. In order for the reader to get a fuller sense of U.S. human rights legislation, the excerpted texts of actual legislation have been provided. These legal texts have been chosen either for their contemporary relevance or controversial nature.

The materials from the Restatement (Third) of the Foreign Relations Law are provided because of the authoritative nature of their work as legal treatises. This work is produced by some of the most competent legal experts in the U.S. in the field of human rights. The Restatement materials were published in the late 1980s and much has happened in the evolution of human rights law since that time. Therefore, other scholarly and more up-to-date sources of information should also be consulted.

Where it is important to know if particular legislation is now binding law or not the reader is advised to research and update the status of the law on the various government websites or through his or her congressional representative's office. I make no representation that any of the following legislation is U.S. law. Any legislation can be modified, amended, or repealed.

The following legislation and resolutions have been included either by brief narrative reference or by setting forth the actual text, in whole or excerpts:

1. Federal Criminal Prohibition of Torture, USC Title 18, Sec. 2340
2. Federal Criminal Prohibition of Genocide, USC Title 18, Sec. 1091
3. Federal Criminal Prohibition of Female Genital Mutilation, USC Title 18, Sec. 116
4. Foreign Affairs Reform and Restructuring Act of 1998, USC Title 22, Sec. 2242(b)
5. The Harkin Amendment—Prohibition of Foreign Assistance to Gross Violators of Human Rights, USC Title 22, Sec. 167; 2151n (1994)
6. Human Rights and Security Assistance, USC Title 22 Section 2304 (1994)
7. Human Rights and U.S. Assistance Policies with International Financial Institutions, USC Title 22 Sec. 262d (1994)
8. Jackson Vanik Amendment, USC Title 19, Sec. 2432
9. Leahy Legislation—Foreign Operations Appropriations Act, Fiscal Year 2001
10. Leahy Legislation— Defense Appropriations Act , Fiscal Year 2001
11. Human Rights Enforcement Act Of 2009
12. American Service-Members' Protection Act of 2003 (Excerpted)
13. Clean Diamond Trade Act (Excerpted)
14. Russian Democracy Act of 2002. (Excerpted)
15. Burmese Freedom And Democracy Act Of 2003 (Excerpted)
16. "North Korean Human Rights Act of 2004" (Excerpted)
17. Hawaii Apology Resolution of 1993
18. Free Speech Protection Act Of 2009 Congressional Resolutions
19. The Armenian Genocide Resolution (Excerpted)
20. Concurrent Resolution Declaring Genocide In Darfur, Sudan. (Excerpted)
21. Resolution Proposing an amendment to the Constitution of the U.S. relating to parental rights. Other Miscellaneous Federal and State Legislation

Restatement (Third) of the Foreign Relations Law

LEGISLATION

1. Federal Criminal Prohibition of Torture, USC Title 18, Sec. 2340a–b

Sec. 2340. Definitions

As used in this chapter [18 U.S.C. Sec. 2340 et seq.]

(1) "torture" means an act committed by a person acting under the color of law specifically intended to inflict severe physical or mental pain or suffering (other than pain or suffering incidental to lawful sanctions) upon another person within his custody or physical control;

(2) "severe mental pain or suffering" means the prolonged mental harm caused by or resulting from-

(A) the intentional infliction or threatened infliction of severe physical pain or suffering;

(B) the administration or application, or threatened administration or application, of mind-altering substances or other procedures calculated to disrupt profoundly the senses or the personality;

(C) the threat of imminent death; or

(D) the threat that another person will imminently be subjected to death, severe physical pain or suffering, or the administration or application of mind-altering substances or other procedures calculated to disrupt profoundly the senses or personality; and

(3) "U.S." includes all areas under the jurisdiction of the U.S. including any of the places described in sections 5 and 7 of this title and section 46501(2) of title 49.

Sec. 2340A. Torture

(a) Offense. Whoever outside the U.S. commits or attempts to commit torture shall be fined under this title or imprisoned not more than 20 years, or both, and if death results to any person from conduct prohibited by this subsection, shall be punished by death or imprisoned for any term of years or for life.

(b) Jurisdiction. There is jurisdiction over the activity prohibited in subsection (a) if

(1) the alleged offender is a national of the U.S.; or

(2) the alleged offender is present in the U.S., irrespective of the nationality of the victim or alleged offender.

2. Federal Criminal Prohibition of Genocide, USC Title 18, Sec. 1091

Part I—Crimes

Chapter 50A—Genocide

Sec. 1091. Genocide

(a) Basic Offense. Whoever, whether in time of peace or in time of war, in a circumstance described in subsection (d) and with the specific intent to destroy, in whole or in substantial part, a national, ethnic, racial, or religious group as such—

(1) kills members of that group;

(2) causes serious bodily injury to members of that group;

(3) causes the permanent impairment of the mental faculties of members of the group through drugs, torture, or similar techniques;

(4) subjects the group to conditions of life that are intended to cause the physical destruction of the group in whole or in part;

(5) imposes measures intended to prevent births within the group; or

(6) transfers by force children of the group to another group; or attempts to do so, shall be punished as provided in subsection (b).

(b) Punishment for Basic Offense. The punishment for an offense under subsection (a) is

(1) in the case of an offense under subsection (a) (1), where death results, by death or imprisonment for life and a fine of not more than $1,000,000, or both; and so in original.

(2) a fine of not more than $1,000,000 or imprisonment for not more than twenty years, or both, in any other case.

(c) Incitement Offense. Whoever in a circumstance described in subsection (d) directly and publicly incites another to violate subsection (a) shall be fined not more than $500,000 or imprisoned not more than five years, or both.

(d) Required Circumstance for Offenses. The circumstance referred to in subsections (a) and (c) is that—(1) the offense is committed within the U.S.; or (2) the alleged offender is a national of the U.S. (as defined in section 101 of the Immigration and Nationality Act (8 U.S.C. 1101)).

(e) Nonapplicability of Certain Limitations. Notwithstanding section 3282 of this title, in the case of an offense under subsection (a) (1), an indictment may be found, or information instituted, at any time without limitation.

Short Title

This act may be cited as the 'Genocide Convention Implementation Act of 1987 (the Proxmire Act)'.

3. Federal Criminal Prohibition of Female Genital Mutilation, USC Title 18, Sec. 116

Title 18—Crimes and Criminal Procedure

Sec. 116. Female genital mutilation

(a) Except as provided in subsection (b), whoever knowingly circumcises, excises, or infibulates the whole or any part of the labia majora or labia minora or clitoris of another person who has not attained the age of 18 years shall be fined under this title or imprisoned not more than 5 years, or both.

(b) A surgical operation is not a violation of this section if the operation is—

(1) necessary to the health of the person on whom it is performed, and is performed by a person licensed in the place of its performance as a medical practitioner; or

(2) performed on a person in labor or who has just given birth and is performed for medical purposes connected with that labor or birth by a person licensed in the place it is performed as a medical practitioner, midwife, or person in training to become such a practitioner or midwife.

(c) In applying subsection (b)(1), no account shall be taken of the effect on the person on whom the operation is to be performed of any belief on the part of that person, or any other person, that the operation is required as a matter of custom or ritual.

4. Foreign Affairs Reform and Restructuring Act of 1998, USC Title 22, Sec. 2242b

Section 2242 (b):

(b) Regulations. Not later than 120 days after the date of enactment of this Act, the heads of the appropriate agencies shall prescribe regulations to implement the obligations of the U.S. under Article 3 of the United Nations Convention Against Torture and Other Forms of Cruel, Inhuman or Degrading Treatment or Punishment, subject to any reservations, understandings, declarations, and provisos contained in the U.S. Senate resolution of ratification of the Convention.

The Harkin Amendment—Prohibition of Foreign Assistance to Gross Violators of Human Rights, USC Title 22, Sec. 167, 2151n (1994)

5. Foreign Assistance Act of 1961, Section 116, as amended

(a) Violations barring assistance; assistance for needy people

No assistance may be provided under subchapter I of this chapter to the government of any country which engages in a consistent pattern of gross violations of internationally recognized human rights, including torture or cruel, inhuman, or degrading treatment or punishment, prolonged detention without charges, causing the disappearance of persons by the abduction and clandestine detention of those persons, or other flagrant denial of the right to life, liberty, and the security of person, unless such assistance will directly benefit the needy people in such country.

(b) Information to Congressional committees for realization of assistance for needy people; concurrent resolution terminating assistance.

In determining whether this standard is being met with regard to funds allocated under subchapter I of this chapter, the Committee on Foreign Relations of the Senate or the Committee on Foreign Affairs of the House of Representatives may require the Administrator primarily responsible for administering subchapter I of this chapter to submit in writing information demonstrating that such assistance will directly benefit the needy people in such country, together with a detailed explanation of the assistance to be provided (including the dollar amounts of such assistance) and an explanation of how such assistance will directly benefit the needy people in such country. If either committee or either House of Congress disagrees with the Administrator's justification it may initiate action to terminate assistance to any country by a concurrent resolution under section 2367 of this title.

(b) Protection of children from exploitation

No assistance may be provided to any government failing to take appropriate and adequate measures, within their means, to protect children from exploitation, abuse or forced conscription into military or paramilitary services.

(c) Factors considered

In determining whether or not a government falls within the provisions of subsection (a) of this section and in formulating development assistance programs under subchapter I of this chapter, the Administrator shall consider, in consultation with the Assistant Secretary for Democracy, Human Rights, and Labor

(1) the extent of cooperation of such government in permitting an unimpeded investigation of alleged violations of internationally recognized human rights by appropriate international organizations, including the International Committee of the Red Cross, or groups or persons acting under the authority of the United Nations or of the Organization of American States; and

(2) specific actions which have been taken by the President or the Congress relating to multilateral or security assistance to a less developed country because of the human rights practices or policies of such country.

(d) Report to Speaker of House and Committee on Foreign Relations of the Senate

The Secretary of State shall transmit to the Speaker of the House of Representatives and the Committee on Foreign Relations of the Senate, by January 31 of each year, a full and complete report regarding (1) the status of internationally recognized human rights, within the meaning of subsection (a) of this section

(A) in countries that receive assistance under subchapter I of this chapter, and

(B) in all other foreign countries which are members of the United Nations and which are not otherwise the subject of a human rights report under this chapter; and

(2) wherever applicable, practices regarding coercion in population control, including coerced abortion and involuntary sterilization; and

(3) the steps the Administrator has taken to alter U.S. programs under subchapter I of this chapter in any country because of human rights considerations.

(e) Promotion of civil and political rights

The President is authorized and encouraged to use not less than $3,000,000 of the funds made available under this part and part IV of subchapter II of this chapter for each fiscal year for studies to identify, and for openly carrying out, programs and activities which will encourage or promote increased adherence to civil and political rights, as set forth in the Universal Declaration of Human Rights, in countries eligible for assistance under this part or under part 10 of this subchapter, except that funds made available under part 10 of this subchapter may only be used under this subsection with respect to countries in sub-Saharan Africa. None of these funds may be used, directly or indirectly, to influence the outcome of any election in any country.

6. Human Rights and Security Assistance, USC Title 22, Sec. 2304 (1994)(Excerpted)

Foreign Assistance Act of 1961, section 502B, as amended

(a) Observance of human rights as principal goal of foreign policy; implementation requirements

(1) The U.S. shall, in accordance with its international obligations as set forth in the Charter of the United Nations and in keeping with the constitutional heritage and traditions of the U.S., promote and encourage increased respect for human rights and fundamental freedoms throughout the world without distinction as to race, sex, language, or religion. Accordingly, a principal goal of the foreign policy of the U.S. shall be to promote the increased observance of internationally recognized human rights by all countries.

(2) Except under circumstances specified in this section, no security assistance may be provided to any country the government of which engages in a consistent pattern of gross violations of internationally recognized human rights. Security assistance may not be provided to the police, domestic intelligence, or similar law enforcement forces of a country, and licenses may not be issued under the Export Administration Act of 1979 for the export of crime control and detection instruments and equipment to a country, the government of which engages in a consistent pattern of gross violations of internationally recognized human rights unless the President certifies in writing to the Speaker of the House of Representatives and the chairman of the Committee on Foreign Relations of the Senate and the chairman of the Committee on Banking, Housing, and Urban Affairs of the Senate (when licenses are to be issued pursuant to the Export Administration Act of 1979) that extraordinary circumstances exist warranting provision of such assistance and issuance of such licenses. Assistance may not be provided under part V of this subchapter to a country the government of which engages in a consistent pattern of gross violations of internationally recognized human rights unless the President certifies in writing to the Speaker of the House of Representatives and the chairman of the Committee on Foreign Relations of the Senate that extraordinary circumstances exist warranting provision of such assistance.

(3) In furtherance of paragraphs (1) and (2), the President is directed to formulate and conduct international security assistance programs of the U.S. in a manner which will promote and advance human rights and avoid identification of the U.S., through such programs, with governments which deny to their people internationally recognized human rights and fundamental freedoms, in violation of international law or in contravention of the policy of the U.S. as expressed in this section or otherwise.

(b) Report by Secretary of State on practices of proposed recipient countries; considerations

The Secretary of State shall transmit to the Congress, as part of the presentation materials for security assistance programs proposed for each fiscal year, a full and complete report, prepared with the assistance of the Assistant Secretary of State for Democracy, Human Rights, and Labor, with respect to practices regarding the observance of and respect for internationally recognized human rights in each country proposed as a recipient of security assistance. Wherever applicable, such report shall include information on practices regarding coercion in population control, including coerced abortion and involuntary sterilization. In determining whether a government falls within the provisions of subsection (a)(3) of this section and in the preparation of any report or statement required under this section, consideration shall be given to

(1) the relevant findings of appropriate international organizations, including non governmental organizations, such as the International Committee of the Red Cross; and

(2) the extent of cooperation by such government in permitting an unimpeded investigation by any such organization of alleged violations of internationally recognized human rights.

(c) Congressional request for information; information required; 30-day period; failure to supply information; termination or restriction of assistance

(1) Upon the request of the Senate or the House of Representatives by resolution of either such House, or upon the request of the Committee on Foreign Relations of the Senate or the Committee on Foreign Affairs of the House of Representatives, the Secretary of State shall, within thirty days after receipt of such request, transmit to both such committees a statement, prepared with the assistance of the Assistant Secretary of State for Democracy, Human Rights, and Labor, with respect to the country designated in such request, setting forth

(A) all the available information about observance of and respect for human rights and fundamental freedom in that country, and a detailed description of practices by the recipient government with respect thereto;

(B) the steps the U.S. has taken to

(i) promote respect for and observance of human rights in that country and discourage any practices which are inimical to internationally recognized human rights, and

(ii) publicly or privately call attention to, and disassociate the U.S. and any security assistance provided for such country from, such practices;

(C) whether, in the opinion of the Secretary of State, notwithstanding any such practices

(i) extraordinary circumstances exist which necessitate a continuation of security assistance for such country, and, if so, a description of such circumstances and the extent to which such assistance should be continued (subject to such conditions as Congress may impose under this section), and

(ii) on all the facts it is in the national interest of the U.S. to provide such assistance; and

(D) such other information as such committee or such House may request.

(2) (A) A resolution of request under paragraph (1) of this subsection shall be considered in the Senate in accordance with the provisions of section 601(b) of the International Security Assistance and Arms Export Control Act of 1976.

...

(d) Definitions. For the purposes of this section

(1) the term "gross violations of internationally recognized human rights" includes torture or cruel, inhuman, or degrading treatment or punishment, prolonged detention without charges and trial, causing the disappearance of persons by the abduction and clandestine detention of those persons, and other flagrant denial of the right to life, liberty, or the security of person; and

(2) the term "security assistance" means

(A) assistance under part II (military assistance) or part IV (economic support fund) or part V (military education and training) or part VI (peacekeeping operations) or part VIII (antiterrorism assistance) of this subchapter;

(B) sales of defense articles or services, extension of credits (including participation in credits, and guaranties of loans under the Arms Export Control Act); or

(C) any license in effect with respect to the export of defense articles or defense services to or for the armed forces, police, intelligence, or other internal security forces of a foreign country under section 38 of the Arms Export Control Act.

(e) Removal of prohibition on assistance

Notwithstanding any other provision of law, funds authorized to be appropriated under subchapter I of this chapter may be made available for the furnishing of assistance to any country with respect to which the President finds that such a significant improvement in its human rights record has occurred as to warrant lifting the prohibition on furnishing such assistance in the national interest of the U.S.

(f) Allocations concerned with performance record of recipient countries without contravention of other provisions.

In allocating the funds authorized to be appropriated by this chapter and the Arms Export Control Act, the President shall take into account significant improvements in the human rights records of recipient countries, except that such allocations may not contravene any other provision of law.

7. Human Rights and U.S. Assistance Policies with International Financial Institutions, USC Title 22, Sec. 262d (1994)

[This Act requires U.S. representatives on the boards of international financial institutions such as the World Bank and International Monetary Fund to vote against giving any loans to countries with bad human rights records and to vote in favor of loans to states with good records.]

(a) Policy goals

The U.S. Government, in connection with its voice and vote in the International Bank for Reconstruction and Development, the International Development Association, the International Finance Corporation, the Inter-American Development Bank, the African Development Fund, the Asian Development Bank, and the African Development Bank, the European Bank for Reconstruction and Development, and the International Monetary Fund, shall advance the cause of human rights, including by seeking to channel assistance toward countries other than those whose governments engage in—

(1) a pattern of gross violations of internationally recognized human rights, such as torture or cruel, inhumane, or degrading treatment or punishment, prolonged detention without charges, or other flagrant denial to life, liberty, and the security of person; or

(2) provide refuge to individuals committing acts of international terrorism by hijacking aircraft.

(b) Policy considerations for Executive Directors of institutions in implementation of duties

Further, the Secretary of the Treasury shall instruct each Executive Director of the above institutions to consider in carrying out his duties:

(1) specific actions by either the executive branch or the Congress as a whole on individual bilateral assistance programs because of human rights considerations;

(2) the extent to which the economic assistance provided by the above institutions directly benefits the needy people in the recipient country;

(3) whether the recipient country—

(A) is seeking to acquire unsafeguarded special nuclear material (as defined in section 830 (8) of the Nuclear Proliferation Prevention Act of 1994) or a nuclear explosive device (as defined in section 830(4) of that Act);

(B) is not a State Party to the Treaty on the Non-Proliferation of Nuclear Weapons; or

(C) has detonated a nuclear explosive device; and

(4) in relation to assistance for the Socialist Republic of Vietnam, the People's Democratic Republic of Laos, Russia and the other independent states of the former Soviet Union (as defined in section 5801 of this title), and Democratic Kampuchea (Cambodia), the responsiveness of the governments of such countries in providing a more substantial accounting of Americans missing in action.

(c) Reporting requirements

(1) Not later than 30 days after the end of each calendar quarter, the Secretary of the Treasury shall report quarterly on all loans considered by the Boards of Executive Directors of the institutions listed in subsection (a) of this section to the Chairman and ranking minority member of the Committee on Banking, Finance and Urban Affairs of the House of Representatives, or the designees of such Chairman and ranking minority member, and the Chairman and ranking minority member of the Committee on Foreign Relations of the Senate.

(2) Each report required by paragraph (1) shall—

(A) include a list of all loans considered by the Board of Executive Directors of the institutions listed in subsection (a) of this section and shall specify with respect to each such loan—

(i) the institution involved;

(ii) the date of final action;

(iii) the borrower;

(iv) the amount;

(v) the project or program;

(vi) the vote of the U.S. Government;

(vii) the reason for U.S. Government opposition, if any;

(viii) the final disposition of the loan; and

(ix) if the U.S. Government opposed the loan, whether the loan meets basic human needs.

(B) indicate whether the U.S. has opposed any loan, financial assistance, or technical assistance to a country on human rights grounds;

(C) indicate whether the U.S. has voted in favor of a loan, financial assistance, or technical assistance to a country with respect to which the U.S. had, in the preceding 2 years, opposed a loan, financial assistance, or technical assistance on human rights grounds; and

(D) in cases where the U.S. changed its voting position from opposition to support or from support to opposition, on human rights grounds—

(i) indicate the policy considerations that were taken into account in the development of the U.S. voting position;

(ii) describe human rights conditions in the country involved;

(iii) indicate how the U.S. voted on all other loans, financial assistance, and technical assistance to such country during the preceding 2 years; and

(iv) contain information as to how the U.S. voting position relates to the overall U.S. Government policy on human rights in such country.

(d) Requirements of U.S. assistance through institutions for projects in recipient countries

The U.S. Government, in connection with its voice and vote in the institutions listed in subsection (a) of this section, shall seek to channel assistance to projects which address basic human needs of the people of the recipient country.

(e) Criteria for determination of gross violations of internationally recognized human rights standards

In determining whether a country is in gross violation of internationally recognized human rights standards, as defined by the provisions of subsection (a) of this section, the U.S. Government shall give consideration to the extent of cooperation of such country in permitting an unimpeded investigation of alleged violations of internationally recognized human rights by appropriate international organizations including, but not limited to, the International Committee of the Red Cross, Amnesty International, the International Commission of Jurists, and groups or persons acting under the authority of the United Nations or the Organization of American States.

(f) Opposition by U.S. Executive Directors of institutions to financial or technical assistance to violating countries

The U.S. Executive Directors of the institutions listed in subsection (a) of this section are authorized and instructed to oppose any loan, any extension of financial assistance, or any technical assistance to any country described in subsection (a) (1) or (2), unless such assistance is directed specifically to programs which serve the basic human needs of the citizens of such country.

(g) Consultative and additional reporting requirements

The Secretary of the Treasury or his delegate shall consult frequently and in a timely manner with the chairmen and ranking minority members of the Committee on Banking, Finance and Urban Affairs of the House of Representatives and of the Committee on Foreign Relations of the Senate to inform them regarding any prospective changes in policy direction toward countries which have or recently have had poor human rights records.

...

This statute mandates that the Secretary of the Treasury will instruct the U.S. representatives of such international financial institutions to vote against loans to countries which have as a cultural practice a history of the practice of female genital mutilation, or failure to educate against such practice, which is the cutting of certain parts of the female genitals.

8. The Jackson Vanik Amendment, USC Title 19, Sec. 2432

Title 19—Customs Duties

Chapter IV—Trade Relations with Countries Not Currently Receiving Nondiscriminatory Treatment

Sec. 2432. Freedom of emigration in East-West trade

(a) Actions of nonmarket economy countries making them ineligible for normal trade relations, programs of credits, credit guarantees, or investment guarantees, or commercial agreements

To assure the continued dedication of the U.S. to fundamental human rights, and notwithstanding any other provision of law, on or after January 3, 1975, products from any nonmarket economy country shall not be eligible to receive nondiscriminatory treatment (normal trade relations), such country shall not participate in any program of the Government of the U.S. which extends credits or credit guarantees or investment guarantees, directly or indirectly, and the President of the U.S. shall not conclude any commercial agreement with any such country, during the period beginning with the date on which the President determines that such country

(1) denies its citizens the right or opportunity to emigrate;

(2) imposes more than a nominal tax on emigration or on the visas or other documents required for emigration, for any purpose or cause whatsoever; or

(3) imposes more than a nominal tax, levy, fine, fee, or other charge on any citizen as a consequence of the desire of such citizen to emigrate to the country of his choice, and ending on the date on which the President determines that such country is no longer in violation of paragraph (1), (2), or (3).

(b) Presidential determination and report to Congress that nation is not violating freedom of emigration

After January 3, 1975, (A) products of a nonmarket economy country may be eligible to receive nondiscriminatory treatment (normal trade relations), (B) such country may participate in any program of the Government of the U.S. which extends credits or credit guarantees or investment guarantees, and (C) the President may conclude a commercial agreement with such country, only after the President has submitted to the Congress a report indicating that such country is not in violation of paragraph (1), (2), or (3) of subsection (a) of this section. Such report with respect to such country shall include information as to the nature and implementation of emigration laws and policies and restrictions or discrimination applied to or against persons wishing to emigrate. The report required by this subsection shall be submitted initially as provided herein and, with current information, on or before each June 30 and December 31 thereafter so long as such treatment is received, such credits or guarantees are extended, or such agreement is in effect.

(c) Waiver authority of President

(1) During the 18-month period beginning on January 3, 1975, the President is authorized to waive by Executive order the application of subsections (a) and (b) of this section with respect to any country, if he reports to the Congress that

(A) he has determined that such waiver will substantially promote the objectives of this section; and

(B) he has received assurances that the emigration practices of that country will henceforth lead substantially to the achievement of the objectives of this section.

(2) During any period subsequent to the 18-month period referred to in paragraph (1), the President is authorized to waive by Executive order the application of subsections (a) and (b) of this section with respect to any country, if the waiver authority granted by this subsection continues to apply to such country pursuant to subsection (d) of this section, and if he reports to the Congress that

(A) he has determined that such waiver will substantially promote the objectives of this section; and

(B) he has received assurances that the emigration practices of that country will henceforth lead substantially to the achievement of the objectives of this section.

9. Leahy Legislation

Leahy Law in Foreign Operations Appropriations Act, Fiscal Year 2001(Excerpt)

(a) None of the funds made available by this Act may be provided to any unit of the security forces of a foreign country if the Secretary of State has credible evidence that such unit has committed gross violations of human rights, unless the Secretary determines and reports to the Committees on Appropriations that the government of such country is taking effective measures to bring the responsible members of the security forces unit to justice.

10. Leahy Law in Defense Appropriations Act, Fiscal Year 2001(Excerpt)

(a) None of the funds made available by this Act may be used to support any training program involving a unit of the security forces of a foreign country if the Secretary of Defense has received credible information from the Department of State that a member of such unit has committed a gross violation of human rights, unless all necessary corrective steps have been taken.

11. Human Rights Enforcement Act Of 2009
123 STAT. 3480 PUBLIC LAW 111–122—DEC. 22, 2009
Public Law 111–122 111th Congress

An Act

To establish a section within the Criminal Division of the Department of Justice to enforce human rights laws, to make technical and conforming amendments to criminal and immigration laws pertaining to human rights violations, and for other purposes.

Be it enacted by the Senate and House of Representatives of the United States of America in Congress assembled,

SECTION 1. SHORT TITLE.

This Act may be cited as the "Human Rights Enforcement Act of 2009".

SEC. 2. SECTION TO ENFORCE HUMAN RIGHTS LAWS.

(a) REPEAL.—Section 103(h) of the Immigration and Nationality Act (8 U.S.C. 1103(h)) is repealed.

(b) SECTION TO ENFORCE HUMAN RIGHTS LAWS.—Chapter 31 of title 28, U.S. Code, is amended by inserting after section 509A the following:"§ 509B. Section to enforce human rights laws

"(a) Not later than 90 days after the date of the enactment of the Human Rights Enforcement Act of 2009, the Attorney General shall establish a section within the Criminal Division of the Department of Justice with responsibility for the enforcement of laws against suspected participants in serious human rights offenses.

"(b) The section established under subsection (a) is authorized to—

"(1) take appropriate legal action against individuals suspected of participating in serious human rights offenses; and "(2) coordinate any such legal action with the U.S. Attorney for the relevant jurisdiction.

"(c) The Attorney General shall, as appropriate, consult with the Secretary of Homeland Security and the Secretary of State.

"(d) In determining the appropriate legal action to take against individuals who are suspected of committing serious human rights offenses under Federal law, the section shall take into consideration the availability of criminal prosecution under the laws of the U.S. for such offenses or in a foreign jurisdiction that is prepared to undertake a prosecution for the conduct that forms the basis for such offenses.

"(e) The term 'serious human rights offenses' includes violations of Federal criminal laws relating to genocide, torture, war crimes, and the use or recruitment of child soldiers under sections 1091, 2340, 2340A, 2441, and 2442 of title 18, U.S. Code."

12. American Service-Members' Protection Act of 2003 (U.S. Dept. of State website)

TITLE II—AMERICAN SERVICE-MEMBERS' PROTECTION ACT
SEC. 2001. SHORT TITLE.
SEC. 2002. FINDINGS.

On July 17, 1998, the United Nations Diplomatic Conference of Plenipotentiaries on the Establishment of an International Criminal Court, meeting in Rome, Italy, adopted the 'Rome Statute of the International Criminal Court'. The vote on whether to proceed with the statute was 120 in favor to 7 against, with 21 countries abstaining. The U.S. voted against final adoption of the Rome Statute.

1. As of April 30, 2001, 139 countries had signed the Rome Statute and 30 had ratified it. Pursuant to Article 126 of the Rome Statute, the statute will enter into force on the first day of the month after the 60th day following the date on which the 60th country deposits an instrument ratifying the statute.

2. Since adoption of the Rome Statute, a Preparatory Commission for the International Criminal Court has met regularly to draft documents to implement the Rome Statute, including Rules of Procedure and Evidence, Elements of Crimes, and a definition of the Crime of Aggression.

3. During testimony before the Congress following the adoption of the Rome Statute, the lead U.S. negotiator, Ambassador David Scheffer stated that the U.S. could not sign the Rome Statute because certain critical negotiating objectives of the U.S. had not been achieved. As a result, he stated: 'We are left with consequences that do not serve the cause of international justice.'.

4. Ambassador Scheffer went on to tell the Congress that: 'Multinational peacekeeping forces operating in a country that has joined the treaty can be exposed to the Court's jurisdiction even if the country of the individual peacekeeper has not joined the treaty. Thus, the treaty purports to establish an arrangement whereby U.S. armed forces operating overseas could be conceivably prosecuted by the international court even if the U.S. has not agreed to be bound by the treaty. Not only is this contrary to the most fundamental principles of treaty law, it could inhibit the ability of the U.S. to use its military to meet alliance obligations and participate in multinational operations, including humanitarian interventions to save civilian lives. Other contributors to peacekeeping operations will be similarly exposed.'.

5. Notwithstanding these concerns, President Clinton directed that the U.S. sign the Rome Statute on December 31, 2000. In a statement issued that day, he stated that in view of the unremedied deficiencies of the Rome Statute, 'I will not, and do not recommend that my successor submit the Treaty to the Senate for advice and consent until our fundamental concerns are satisfied'.

6. Any American prosecuted by the International Criminal Court will, under the Rome Statute, be denied procedural protections to which all Americans are entitled under the Bill of Rights to the U.S. Constitution, such as the right to trial by jury.

7. Members of the Armed Forces of the U.S. should be free from the risk of prosecution by the International Criminal Court, especially when they are stationed or deployed around the world to protect the vital national interests of the U.S. The U.S. Government has an obligation to protect the members of its Armed Forces, to the maximum extent possible, against criminal prosecutions carried out by the International Criminal Court.

8. In addition to exposing members of the Armed Forces of the U.S. to the risk of international criminal prosecution, the Rome Statute creates a risk that the President and other senior elected and appointed officials of the U.S. Government may be prosecuted by the International Criminal Court. Particularly if the Preparatory Commission agrees on a definition of the Crime of Aggression over U.S. objections, senior U.S. officials may be at risk of criminal prosecution for national security decisions involving such matters as responding to acts of terrorism, preventing the proliferation of weapons

of mass destruction, and deterring aggression. No less than members of the Armed Forces of the U.S., senior officials of the U.S. Government should be free from the risk of prosecution by the International Criminal Court, especially with respect to official actions taken by them to protect the national interests of the U.S.

9. Any agreement within the Preparatory Commission on a definition of the Crime of Aggression that usurps the prerogative of the United Nations Security Council under Article 39 of the charter of the United Nations to 'determine the existence of any .... act of aggression' would contravene the charter of the United Nations and undermine deterrence.

10. It is a fundamental principle of international law that a treaty is binding upon its parties only and that it does not create obligations for nonparties without their consent to be bound. The U.S. is not a party to the Rome Statute and will not be bound by any of its terms. The U.S. will not recognize the jurisdiction of the International Criminal Court over U.S. nationals.

Congress makes the following findings:

SEC. 2003. WAIVER AND TERMINATION OF PROHIBITIONS OF THIS TITLE.

a. AUTHORITY TO INITIALLY WAIVE SECTIONS 5 AND 7- The President is authorized to waive the prohibitions and requirements of sections 2005 and 2007 for a single period of 1 year.

...

e. TERMINATION OF PROHIBITIONS OF THIS TITLE- The prohibitions and requirements of sections 2004, 2005, 2006, and 2007 shall cease to apply, and the authority of section 2008 shall terminate, if the U.S. becomes a party to the International Criminal Court pursuant to a treaty made under article II, section 2, clause 2 of the Constitution of the U.S.

SEC. 2004. PROHIBITION ON COOPERATION WITH THE INTERNATIONAL CRIMINAL COURT.

a. APPLICATION- The provisions of this section—

1. apply only to cooperation with the International Criminal Court and shall not apply to cooperation with an ad hoc international criminal tribunal established by the United Nations Security Council before or after the date of the enactment of this Act to investigate and prosecute war crimes committed in a specific country or during a specific conflict; and

2. shall not prohibit—

A. any action permitted under section 2008; or

B. communication by the U.S. of its policy with respect to a matter.

b. PROHIBITION ON RESPONDING TO REQUESTS FOR COOPERATION- Notwithstanding section 1782 of title 28, U.S. Code, or any other provision of law, no U.S. Court, and no agency or entity of any State or local government, including any court, may cooperate with the International Criminal Court in response to a request for cooperation submitted by the International Criminal Court pursuant to the Rome Statute.

c. PROHIBITION ON TRANSMITTAL OF LETTERS ROGATORY FROM THE INTER-NATIONAL CRIMINAL COURT- Notwithstanding section 1781 of title 28, U.S. Code, or any other provision of law, no agency of the U.S. Government may transmit for execution any letter rogatory issued, or other request for cooperation made, by the International Criminal Court to the tribunal, officer, or agency in the U.S. to whom it is addressed.

d. PROHIBITION ON EXTRADITION TO THE INTERNATIONAL CRIMINAL COURT- Notwithstanding any other provision of law, no agency or entity of the U.S. Government or of any State or local government may extradite any person from the U.S. to the International Criminal Court, nor support the transfer of any U.S. citizen or permanent resident alien to the International Criminal Court.

e. PROHIBITION ON PROVISION OF SUPPORT TO THE INTERNATIONAL CRIMINAL COURT- Notwithstanding any other provision of law, no agency or entity of the U.S. Government or of any State or local government, including any court, may provide support to the International Criminal Court.

f. PROHIBITION ON USE OF APPROPRIATED FUNDS TO ASSIST THE INTERNATIONAL CRIMINAL COURT- Notwithstanding any other provision of law, no funds appropriated under any provision of law may be used for the purpose of assisting the investigation, arrest, detention, extradition, or prosecution of any U.S. citizen or permanent resident alien by the International Criminal Court.

g. PROHIBITION ON INVESTIGATIVE ACTIVITIES OF AGENTS- No agent of the International Criminal Court may conduct, in the U.S. or any territory subject to the jurisdiction of the U.S., any investigative activity relating to a preliminary inquiry, investigation, prosecution, or other proceeding at the International Criminal Court.

SEC. 2005. RESTRICTION ON U.S. PARTICIPATION IN CERTAIN UNITED NATIONS PEACEKEEPING OPERATIONS.

a. POLICY- Effective beginning on the date on which the Rome Statute enters into force pursuant to Article 126 of the Rome Statute, the President should use the voice and vote of the U.S. in the United Nations Security Council to ensure that each resolution of the Security Council authorizing any peacekeeping operation under chapter VI of the charter of the United Nations or peace enforcement operation under chapter VII of the charter of the United Nations permanently exempts, at a minimum, members of the Armed Forces of the U.S. participating in such operation from criminal prosecution or other assertion of jurisdiction by the International Criminal Court for actions undertaken by such personnel in connection with the operation.

b. RESTRICTION- Members of the Armed Forces of the U.S. may not participate in any peacekeeping operation under chapter VI of the charter of the United Nations or peace enforcement operation under chapter VII of the charter of the United Nations, the creation of which is authorized by the United Nations Security Council on or after the date that the Rome Statute enters into effect pursuant to Article 126 of the Rome Statute, unless the President has submitted to the appropriate congressional committees a certification described in subsection (c) with respect to such operation.

c. CERTIFICATION- The certification referred to in subsection (b) is a certification by the President that—

1. members of the Armed Forces of the U.S. are able to participate in the peacekeeping or peace enforcement operation without risk of criminal prosecution or other assertion of jurisdiction by the International Criminal Court because, in authorizing the operation, the United Nations Security Council permanently exempted, at a minimum, members of the Armed Forces of the U.S. participating in the operation from criminal prosecution or other assertion of jurisdiction by the International Criminal Court for actions undertaken by them in connection with the operation;

2. members of the Armed Forces of the U.S. are able to participate in the peacekeeping or peace enforcement operation without risk of criminal prosecution or other assertion of jurisdiction by the International Criminal Court because each country in which members of the Armed Forces of the U.S. participating in the operation will be present either is not a party to the International Criminal Court and has not invoked the jurisdiction of the International Criminal Court pursuant to Article 12 of the Rome Statute, or has entered into an agreement in accordance with Article 98 of the Rome Statute preventing the International Criminal Court from proceeding against members of the Armed Forces of the U.S. present in that country; or

3. the national interests of the U.S. justify participation by members of the Armed Forces of the U.S. in the peacekeeping or peace enforcement operation.

SEC. 2006. PROHIBITION ON DIRECT OR INDIRECT TRANSFER OF CLASSIFIED NATIONAL SECURITY INFORMATION AND LAW ENFORCEMENT INFORMATION TO THE INTERNATIONAL CRIMINAL COURT.

a. IN GENERAL- Not later than the date on which the Rome Statute enters into force, the President shall ensure that appropriate procedures are in place to prevent the transfer of classified national security information and law enforcement information to the International Criminal Court for the purpose of facilitating an investigation, apprehension, or prosecution.

b. INDIRECT TRANSFER- The procedures adopted pursuant to subsection (a) shall be designed to prevent the transfer to the United Nations and to the government of any country that is party to the International Criminal Court of classified national security information and law enforcement information that specifically relates to matters known to be under investigation or prosecution by the International Criminal Court, except to the degree that satisfactory assurances are received from the United Nations or that government, as the case may be, that such information will not be made available to the International Criminal Court for the purpose of facilitating an investigation, apprehension, or prosecution.

c. CONSTRUCTION- The provisions of this section shall not be construed to prohibit any action permitted under section 2008.

SEC. 2007. PROHIBITION OF U.S. MILITARY ASSISTANCE TO PARTIES TO THE INTERNATIONAL CRIMINAL COURT.

a. PROHIBITION OF MILITARY ASSISTANCE- Subject to subsections (b) and (c), and effective 1 year after the date on which the Rome Statute enters into force pursuant to Article 126 of the Rome Statute, no U.S. military assistance may be provided to the government of a country that is a party to the International Criminal Court.

b. NATIONAL INTEREST WAIVER- The President may, without prior notice to Congress, waive the prohibition of subsection (a) with respect to a particular country if he determines and reports to the appropriate congressional committees that it is important to the national interest of the U.S. to waive such prohibition.

c. ARTICLE 98 WAIVER- The President may, without prior notice to Congress, waive the prohibition of subsection (a) with respect to a particular country if he determines and reports to the appropriate congressional committees that such country has entered into an agreement with the U.S. pursuant to Article 98 of the Rome Statute preventing the International Criminal court from proceeding against U.S. personnel present in such country.

d. EXEMPTION- The prohibition of subsection (a) shall not apply to the government of—

1. a NATO member country;

2. a major non-NATO ally (including Australia, Egypt, Israel, Japan, Jordan, Argentina, the Republic of Korea, and New Zealand); or

3. Taiwan.

SEC. 2008. AUTHORITY TO FREE MEMBERS OF THE ARMED FORCES OF THE U.S. AND CERTAIN OTHER PERSONS DETAINED OR IMPRISONED BY OR ON BEHALF OF THE INTERNATIONAL CRIMINAL COURT.

a. AUTHORITY- The President is authorized to use all means necessary and appropriate to bring about the release of any person described in subsection (b) who is being detained or imprisoned by, on behalf of, or at the request of the International Criminal Court.

b. PERSONS AUTHORIZED TO BE FREED- The authority of subsection (a) shall extend to the following persons:

1. Covered U.S. persons.

2. Covered allied persons.

3. Individuals detained or imprisoned for official actions taken while the individual was a covered U.S. person or a covered allied person, and in the case of a covered allied person, upon the request of such government.

c. AUTHORIZATION OF LEGAL ASSISTANCE- When any person described in subsection (b) is arrested, detained, investigated, prosecuted, or imprisoned by, on behalf of, or at the request of the International Criminal Court, the President is authorized to direct any agency of the U.S. Government to provide—

1. legal representation and other legal assistance to that person (including, in the case of a person entitled to assistance under section 1037 of title 10, U.S. Code, representation and other assistance in the manner provided in that section);

2. exculpatory evidence on behalf of that person; and

3. defense of the interests of the U.S. through appearance before the International Criminal Court pursuant to Article 18 or 19 of the Rome Statute, or before the courts or tribunals of any country.

d. BRIBES AND OTHER INDUCEMENTS NOT AUTHORIZED- This section does not authorize the payment of bribes or the provision of other such incentives to induce the release of a person described in subsection (b).

SEC. 2009. ALLIANCE COMMAND ARRANGEMENTS.

a. REPORT ON ALLIANCE COMMAND ARRANGEMENTS- Not later than 6 months after the date of the enactment of this Act, the President should transmit to the appropriate congressional committees a report with respect to each military alliance to which the U.S. is party—

1. describing the degree to which members of the Armed Forces of the U.S. may, in the context of military operations undertaken by or pursuant to that alliance, be placed under the command or operational control of foreign military officers subject to the jurisdiction of the International Criminal Court because they are nationals of a party to the International Criminal Court; and

2. evaluating the degree to which members of the Armed Forces of the U.S. engaged in military operations undertaken by or pursuant to that alliance may be exposed to greater risks as a result of being placed under the command or operational control of foreign military officers subject to the jurisdiction of the International Criminal Court.

b. DESCRIPTION OF MEASURES TO ACHIEVE ENHANCED PROTECTION FOR MEMBERS OF THE ARMED FORCES OF THE U.S.- Not later than 1 year after the date of the enactment of this Act, the President should transmit to the appropriate congressional committees a description of modifications to command and operational control arrangements within military alliances to which the U.S. is a party that could be made in order to reduce any risks to members of the Armed Forces of the U.S. identified pursuant to subsection (a)(2).

c. SUBMISSION IN CLASSIFIED FORM- The report under subsection (a), and the description of measures under subsection (b), or appropriate parts thereof, may be submitted in classified form.

...

SEC. 2011. APPLICATION OF SECTIONS 2004 AND 2006 TO EXERCISE OF CONSTITUTIONAL AUTHORITIES.

a. IN GENERAL- Sections 2004 and 2006 shall not apply to any action or actions with respect to a specific matter involving the International Criminal Court taken or directed by the President on a case-by-case basis in the exercise of the President's authority as Commander in Chief of the Armed Forces of the U.S. under article II, section 2 of the U.S. Constitution or in the exercise of the executive power under article II, section 1 of the U.S. Constitution.

b. NOTIFICATION TO CONGRESS-

1. IN GENERAL- Subject to paragraph (2), not later than 15 days after the President takes or directs an action or actions described in subsection (a) that would otherwise be prohibited under section 2004 or 2006, the President shall submit a notification of such action to the appropriate congressional committees. A notification under this paragraph shall include a description of the action, a determination that the action is in the national interest of the U.S., and a justification for the action.

2. EXCEPTION- If the President determines that a full notification under paragraph (1) could jeopardize the national security of the U.S. or compromise a U.S. law enforcement activity, not later than 15 days after the President takes or directs an action or actions referred to in paragraph (1) the President shall notify the appropriate congressional committees that an action has been taken and a determination has been made pursuant to this paragraph. The President shall provide a full notification under paragraph (1) not later than 15 days after the reasons for the determination under this paragraph no longer apply.

c. CONSTRUCTION- Nothing in this section shall be construed as a grant of statutory authority to the President to take any action.

...

SEC. 2013. DEFINITIONS.

As used in this title and in section 706 of the Admiral James W. Nance and Meg Donovan Foreign Relations Authorization Act, Fiscal Years 2000 and 2001:

APPROPRIATE CONGRESSIONAL COMMITTEES- The term 'appropriate congressional committees' means the Committee on International Relations of the House of Representatives and the Committee on Foreign Relations of the Senate.

CLASSIFIED NATIONAL SECURITY INFORMATION- The term 'classified national security information' means information that is classified or classifiable under Executive Order 12958 or a successor Executive order.

COVERED ALLIED PERSONS- The term 'covered allied persons' means military personnel, elected or appointed officials, and other persons employed by or working on behalf of the government of a NATO member country, a major non-NATO ally (including Australia, Egypt, Israel, Japan, Jordan, Argentina, the Republic of Korea, and New Zealand), or Taiwan, for so long as that government is not a party to the International Criminal Court and wishes its officials and other persons working on its behalf to be exempted from the jurisdiction of the International Criminal Court.

COVERED U.S. PERSONS- The term 'covered U.S. persons' means members of the Armed Forces of the U.S., elected or appointed officials of the U.S. Government, and other persons employed by or working on behalf of the U.S. Government, for so long as the U.S. is not a party to the International Criminal Court.

EXTRADITION- The terms 'extradition' and 'extradite' mean the extradition of a person in accordance with the provisions of chapter 209 of title 18, U.S. Code, (including section 3181(b) of such title) and such terms include both extradition and surrender as those terms are defined in Article 102 of the Rome Statute.

INTERNATIONAL CRIMINAL COURT- The term 'International Criminal Court' means the court established by the Rome Statute.

MAJOR NON-NATO ALLY- The term 'major non-NATO ally' means a country that has been so designated in accordance with section 517 of the Foreign Assistance Act of 1961.

1. PARTICIPATE IN ANY PEACEKEEPING OPERATION UNDER CHAPTER VI OF THE CHARTER OF THE UNITED NATIONS OR PEACE ENFORCEMENT OPERATION UNDER CHAPTER VII OF THE CHARTER OF THE UNITED NATIONS- The term 'participate in any peacekeeping operation under chapter VI of the charter of the United Nations or peace enforcement operation under chapter VII of the charter of the United Nations' means to assign members of the Armed Forces of the U.S. to a United Nations military command structure as part of a peacekeeping operation under chapter VI of the charter of the United Nations or peace enforcement operation under chapter VII of the charter of the United Nations in which those members of the Armed Forces of the U.S. are subject to the command or operational control of one or more foreign military officers not appointed in conformity with article II, section 2, clause 2 of the Constitution of the U.S.

2. PARTY TO THE INTERNATIONAL CRIMINAL COURT- The term 'party to the International Criminal Court' means a government that has deposited an instrument of ratification, acceptance, approval, or accession to the Rome Statute, and has not withdrawn from the Rome Statute pursuant to Article 127 thereof.

3. PEACEKEEPING OPERATION UNDER CHAPTER VI OF THE CHARTER OF THE UNITED NATIONS OR PEACE ENFORCEMENT OPERATION UNDER CHAPTER VII OF THE CHARTER OF THE UNITED NATIONS- The term 'peacekeeping operation under chapter VI of the charter of the United Nations or peace enforcement operation under chapter VII of the charter of the United Nations' means any military operation to maintain or restore international peace and security that—

A. is authorized by the United Nations Security Council under chapter VI or VII of the charter of the United Nations; and

B. is paid for from assessed contributions of United Nations members that are made available for peacekeeping or peace enforcement activities.

4. ROME STATUTE- The term 'Rome Statute' means the Rome Statute of the International Criminal Court, adopted by the United Nations Diplomatic Conference of Plenipotentiaries on the Establishment of an International Criminal Court on July 17, 1998.

5. SUPPORT- The term 'support' means assistance of any kind, including financial support, transfer of property or other material support, services, intelligence sharing, law enforcement cooperation, the training or detail of personnel, and the arrest or detention of individuals.

6. U.S. MILITARY ASSISTANCE- The term 'U.S. military assistance' means— assistance provided under chapter 2 or 5 of part II of the Foreign Assistance Act of 1961 (22 U.S.C. 2151 et seq.); or

A. defense articles or defense services furnished with the financial assistance of the U.S. Government, including through loans and guarantees, under section 23 of the Arms Export Control Act (22 U.S.C. 2763).

...

SEC. 2015. ASSISTANCE TO INTERNATIONAL EFFORTS.

Nothing in this title shall prohibit the U.S. from rendering assistance to international efforts to bring to justice Saddam Hussein, Slobodan Milosovic, Osama bin Laden, other members of Al Queda, leaders of Islamic Jihad, and other foreign nationals accused of genocide, war crimes or crimes against humanity. This title may be cited as the 'American Service-members' Protection Act of 2002'.

12. Clean Diamond Trade Act
PUBLIC LAW 108–19—APR. 25, 2003 117 STAT. 631
Public Law 108–19
108th Congress

An Act

To implement effective measures to stop trade in conflict diamonds, and for other purposes.

Be it enacted by the Senate and House of Representatives of the United States of America in Congress assembled,

SECTION 1. SHORT TITLE.

This Act may be cited as the "Clean Diamond Trade Act".

SEC. 2. FINDINGS.

Congress finds the following:

(1) Funds derived from the sale of rough diamonds are being used by rebels and state actors to finance military activities, overthrow legitimate governments, subvert international efforts to promote peace and stability, and commit horrifying atrocities against unarmed civilians. During the past decade, more than 6,500,000 people from Sierra Leone, Angola, and the Democratic Republic of the Congo have been driven from their homes by wars waged in large part for control of diamond mining areas. A million of these are refugees eking out a miserable existence in neighboring countries, and tens of thousands have fled to the U.S. Approximately 3,700,000 people have died during these wars.

(2) The countries caught in this fighting are home to nearly 70,000,000 people whose societies have been torn apart not only by fighting but also by terrible human rights violations.

(3) Human rights and humanitarian advocates, the diamond trade as represented by the World Diamond Council, and the U.S. Government have been working to block the trade in conflict diamonds. Their efforts have helped to build a consensus that action is urgently needed to end the trade in conflict diamonds.

(4) The United Nations Security Council has acted at various times under chapter VII of the Charter of the United Nations to address threats to international peace and security posed by conflicts linked to diamonds. Through these actions, it has prohibited all states from exporting weapons to certain countries affected by such conflicts. It has further required all states to prohibit the direct and indirect import of rough diamonds from Sierra Leone unless the diamonds are controlled under specified certificate of origin regimes and to prohibit absolutely the direct and indirect import of rough diamonds from Liberia.

(5) In response, the U.S. implemented sanctions restricting the importation of rough diamonds from Sierra Leone to those diamonds accompanied by specified certificates of origin and fully prohibiting the importation of rough diamonds from Liberia. The U.S. is now taking further action against trade in conflict diamonds.

(6) Without effective action to eliminate trade in conflict diamonds, the trade in legitimate diamonds faces the threat of a consumer backlash that could damage the economies of countries not involved in the trade in conflict diamonds and penalize members of the legitimate trade and the people they employ. To prevent that, South Africa and more than 30 other countries are involved in working, through the "Kimberley Process", toward devising a solution to this problem. As the consumer of a majority of the world's supply of diamonds, the U.S. has an obligation to help sever the link between diamonds and conflict and press for implementation of an effective solution.

(7) Failure to curtail the trade in conflict diamonds or to differentiate between the trade in conflict diamonds and the trade in legitimate diamonds could have a severe negative impact on the legitimate diamond trade in countries such as Botswana, Namibia, South Africa, and Tanzania.

(8) Initiatives of the U.S. seek to resolve the regional conflicts in sub-Saharan Africa which facilitate the trade in conflict diamonds.

(9) The Interlaken Declaration on the Kimberley Process Certification Scheme for Rough Diamonds of November 5, 2002, states that Participants will ensure that measures taken to implement the Kimberley Process Certification Scheme for Rough Diamonds will be consistent with international trade rules.

SEC. 3. DEFINITIONS.

In this Act:

(1) APPROPRIATE CONGRESSIONAL COMMITTEES.—The term "appropriate congressional committees" means the Committee on Ways and Means and the Committee on International Relations of the House of Representatives, and the Committee on Finance and the Committee on Foreign Relations of the Senate.

(2) CONTROLLED THROUGH THE KIMBERLEY PROCESS CERTIFICATION SCHEME.—An importation or exportation of rough diamonds is "controlled through the Kimberley Process Certification Scheme" if it is an importation from the territory of a Participant or exportation to the territory of a Participant of rough diamonds that is—

(A) carried out in accordance with the Kimberley Process Certification Scheme, as set forth in regulations promulgated by the President; or (B) controlled under a system determined by the President to meet substantially the standards, practices, and procedures of the Kimberley Process Certification Scheme.

. . .

(6) KIMBERLEY PROCESS CERTIFICATION SCHEME.—The term "Kimberley Process Certification Scheme" means those standards, practices, and procedures of the international certification scheme for rough diamonds presented in the document entitled "Kimberley Process Certification Scheme" referred to in the Interlaken Declaration on the Kimberley Process Certification Scheme for Rough Diamonds of November 5, 2002.

. . .

(9) ROUGH DIAMOND.—The term "rough diamond" means any diamond that is unworked or simply sawn, cleaved, or bruted and classifiable under subheading 7102.10, 7102.21, or 7102.31 of the Harmonized Tariff Schedule of the U.S.

. . .

SEC. 4. MEASURES FOR THE IMPORTATION AND EXPORTATION OF ROUGH DIAMONDS.

(a) PROHIBITION.—The President shall prohibit the importation into, or exportation from, the U.S. of any rough diamond, from whatever source, that has not been controlled through the Kimberley Process Certification Scheme.

(b) WAIVER.—The President may waive the requirements set forth in subsection (a) with respect to a particular country for periods of not more than 1 year each, if, with respect to each such waiver—

(1) the President determines and reports to the appropriate congressional committees that such country is taking effective steps to implement the Kimberley Process Certification Scheme;

(2) the President determines that the waiver is in the national interests of the U.S., and reports such determination to the appropriate congressional committees, together with the reasons therefor.

SEC. 5. REGULATORY AND OTHER AUTHORITY.

(a) IN GENERAL.—The President is authorized to and shall as necessary issue such proclamations, regulations, licenses, and orders, and conduct such investigations, as may be necessary to carry out this Act.

. . .

SEC. 6. IMPORTING AND EXPORTING AUTHORITIES.

(a) IN THE U.S.—For purposes of this Act—

(1) the importing authority shall be the U.S. Bureau of Customs and Border Protection or, in the case of a territory or possession of the U.S. with its own customs administration, analogous officials; and

(2) the exporting authority shall be the Bureau of the Census.

(b) OF OTHER COUNTRIES.—The President shall publish in the Federal Register a list of all Participants, and all exporting authorities and importing authorities of Participants. The President shall update the list as necessary.

SEC. 7. STATEMENT OF POLICY.

The Congress supports the policy that the President shall take appropriate steps to promote and facilitate the adoption by the international community of the Kimberley Process Certification Scheme implemented under this Act.

SEC. 8. ENFORCEMENT.

(a) IN GENERAL.—In addition to the enforcement provisions set forth in subsection (b)—

(1) a civil penalty of not to exceed $10,000 may be imposed on any person who violates, or attempts to violate, any license, order, or regulation issued under this Act; and (2) whoever willfully violates, or willfully attempts to violate,

any license, order, or regulation issued under this Act shall, upon conviction, be fined not more than $50,000, or, if a natural person, may be imprisoned for not more than 10 years, or both; and any officer, director, or agent of any corporation who willfully participates in such violation may be punished by a like fine, imprisonment, or both.

(b) IMPORT VIOLATIONS.—Those customs laws of the U.S., both civil and criminal, including those laws relating to seizure and forfeiture, that apply to articles imported in violation of such laws shall apply with respect to rough diamonds imported in violation of this Act.

(c) AUTHORITY TO ENFORCE.—The U.S. Bureau of Customs and Border Protection and the U.S. Bureau of Immigration and Customs Enforcement are authorized, as appropriate, to enforce the provisions of subsection (a) and to enforce the laws and regulations governing exports of rough diamonds, including with respect to the validation of the Kimberley Process Certificate by the exporting authority.

SEC. 9. TECHNICAL ASSISTANCE.

The President may direct the appropriate agencies of the U.S. Government to make available technical assistance to countries seeking to implement the Kimberley Process Certification Scheme.

SEC. 10. SENSE OF CONGRESS.

(a) ONGOING PROCESS.—It is the sense of the Congress that the Kimberley Process Certification Scheme, officially launched on January 1, 2003, is an ongoing process. The President should work with Participants to strengthen the Kimberley Process Certification Scheme through the adoption of measures for the sharing of statisticson the production of and trade in rough diamonds, and for monitoring the effectiveness of the Kimberley Process Certification Scheme in stemming trade in diamonds the importation or exportation of which is not controlled through the Kimberley Process Certification Scheme.

. . .

SEC. 11. KIMBERLEY PROCESS IMPLEMENTATION COORDINATING COMMITTEE.

The President shall establish a Kimberley Process Implementation Coordinating Committee to coordinate the implementation of this Act. The Committee shall be composed of the following individuals or their designees:

(1) The Secretary of the Treasury and the Secretary of State, who shall be co-chairpersons. (2) The Secretary of Commerce. (3) The U.S. Trade Representative. (4) The Secretary of Homeland Security. (5) A representative of any other agency the President deems appropriate.

SEC. 12. REPORTS.

(a) ANNUAL REPORTS.—Not later than 1 year after the date of the enactment of this Act and every 12 months thereafter for such period as this Act is in effect, the President shall transmit to the Congress a report—

(1) describing actions taken by countries that have exported rough diamonds to the U.S. during the preceding 12-month period to control the exportation of the diamonds through the Kimberley Process Certification Scheme; (2) describing whether there is statistical information or other evidence that would indicate efforts to circumvent the Kimberley Process Certification Scheme, including cutting rough diamonds for the purpose of circumventing the Kimberley Process Certification Scheme; (3) identifying each country that, during the preceding12-month period, exported rough diamonds to the U.S. and was exporting rough diamonds not controlled through the Kimberley Process Certification Scheme, if the failure to do so has significantly increased the likelihood that those diamonds not so controlled are being imported into the U.S.; and (4) identifying any problems or obstacles encountered in the implementation of this Act or the Kimberly Process Certification Scheme.

. . .

The President may delegate the duties and authorities under this Act to such officers, officials, departments, or agencies of the U.S. Government as the President deems appropriate.

LEGISLATIVE HISTORY—H.R. 1584:
CONGRESSIONAL RECORD, Vol. 149 (2003):
Æ
Approved April 25, 2003.
N: PUBL019

14. Russian Democracy Act of 2002. (Excerpted)
PUBLIC LAW 107–246—OCT. 23, 2002 116 STAT. 1511
Public Law 107–246 107th Congress

An Act

To make available funds under the Foreign Assistance Act of 1961 to expand democracy, good governance, and anti-corruption programs in the Russian Federation in order to promote and strengthen democratic government and civil society and independent media in that country.

Be it enacted by the Senate and House of Representatives of the United States of America in Congress assembled,

SECTION 1. SHORT TITLE.

This Act may be cited as the "Russian Democracy Act of 2002".

SEC. 2. FINDINGS AND PURPOSES.

(a) FINDINGS.—Congress makes the following findings:

(1) Since the dissolution of the Soviet Union, the leadership of the Russian Federation has publicly committed itself to building—

(A) a society with democratic political institutions and practices, the observance of universally recognized standards of human rights, and religious and press freedom; and

(B) a market economy based on internationally accepted principles of transparency, accountability, and the rule of law.

(2) In order to facilitate this transition, the international community has provided multilateral and bilateral technical assistance, and the U.S.' contribution to these efforts has played an important role in developing new institutions built on democratic and liberal economic foundations and the rule of law.

...

(6) Because the capability of Russian democratic forces and the civil society to organize and defend democratic gains without international support is uncertain, and because the gradual integration of the Russian Federation into the global order of free-market, democratic nations would enhance Russian cooperation with the U.S. on a wide range of political, economic, and security issues, the success of democracy in Russia is in the national security interest of the U.S., and the U.S. Government should develop a far-reaching and flexible strategy aimed at strengthening Russian society's support for democracy and a market economy, particularly by enhancing Russian democratic institutions and education, promoting the rule of law, and supporting Russia's independent media.

(7) Since the tragic events of September 11, 2001, the Russian Federation has stood with the U.S. and the rest of the civilized world in the struggle against terrorism and has cooperated in the war in Afghanistan by sharing intelligence and through other means.

(8) U.S.-Russia relations have improved, leading to a successful summit between President Bush and President Putin in May 2002, resulting in a "Foundation for Cooperation".

(b) PURPOSES.—The purposes of this Act are—

(1) to strengthen and advance institutions of democratic government and of free and independent media, and to sustain the development of an independent civil society in the Russian Federation based on religious and ethnic tolerance, internationally recognized human rights, and an internationally recognized rule of law; and

(2) to focus U.S. foreign assistance programs on using local expertise and to give local organizations a greater role in designing and implementing such programs, while maintaining appropriate oversight and monitoring.

SEC. 3. U.S. POLICY TOWARD THE RUSSIAN FEDERATION.

(a) SENSE OF CONGRESS.—It is the sense of Congress that the U.S. Government should—

(1) recognize that a democratic and economically stable Russian Federation is inherently less confrontational and destabilizing in its foreign policy and therefore that the promotion of democracy in Russia is in the national security interests of the U.S.; and

(2) continue and increase assistance to the democratic forces in the Russian Federation, including the independent media, regional administrations, democratic political parties, and nongovernmental organizations.

(b) STATEMENT OF POLICY.—It shall be the policy of the U.S.—

(1) to facilitate Russia's integration into the Western community of nations, including supporting the establishment of a stable democracy and a market economy within the framework of the rule of law and respect for individual rights, including Russia's membership in the appropriate international institutions;

(2) to engage the Government of the Russian Federation and Russian society in order to strengthen democratic reform and institutions, and to promote transparency and good governance in all aspects of

society, including fair and honest business practices, accessible and open legal systems, freedom of religion, and respect for human rights;

(3) to advance a dialogue among U.S. Government officials, private sector individuals, and representatives of the Government of the Russian Federation regarding Russia's integration into the Western community of nations;

(4) to encourage U.S. Government officials and private sector individuals to meet regularly with democratic activists, human rights activists, representatives of the independent media, representatives of nongovernmental organizations, civic organizers, church officials, and reform-minded politicians from Moscow and all other regions of the Russian Federation;

(5) to incorporate democratic reforms, the promotion of independent media, and economic reforms in a broader U.S. dialogue with the Government of the Russian Federation;

(6) to encourage the Government of the Russian Federation to address, in a cooperative and transparent manner consistent with internationally recognized and accepted principles, cross border issues, including the nonproliferation of weapons of mass destruction, environmental degradation, crime, trafficking, and corruption;

(7) to consult with the Government of the Russian Federation and the Russian Parliament on the adoption of economic and social reforms necessary to sustain Russian economic growth and to ensure Russia's transition to a fully functioning market economy and membership in the World Trade Organization;

(8) to persuade the Government of the Russian Federation to honor its commitments made to the Organization for Security and Cooperation in Europe (OSCE) at the November 1999, Istanbul Conference, and to conduct a genuine good neighbor policy toward the other independent states of the former Soviet Union in the spirit of internationally accepted principles of regional cooperation; and

(9) to encourage the G–8 partners and international financial institutions, including the World Bank, the International Monetary Fund, and the European Bank for Reconstruction and Development, to develop financial safeguards and transparency practices in lending to the Russian Federation.

15. Burmese Freedom And Democracy Act Of 2003
117 STAT. 864 PUBLIC LAW 108–61—JULY 28, 2003
Public Law 108–61
108th Congress

An Act

To sanction the ruling Burmese military junta, to strengthen Burma's democratic forces and support and recognize the National League of Democracy as the legitimate representative of the Burmese people, and for other purposes.

Be it enacted by the Senate and House of Representatives of the United States of America in Congress assembled,

SECTION 1. SHORT TITLE.

This Act may be cited as the "Burmese Freedom and Democracy Act of 2003".

SEC. 2. FINDINGS.

Congress makes the following findings:

(1) The State Peace and Development Council (SPDC) has failed to transfer power to the National League for Democracy (NLD) whose parliamentarians won an overwhelming victory in the 1990 elections in Burma.

(2) The SPDC has failed to enter into meaningful, political dialogue with the NLD and ethnic minorities and has dismissed the efforts of United Nations Special Envoy Razali bin Ismail to further such dialogue.

(3) According to the State Department's "Report to the Congress Regarding Conditions in Burma and U.S. Policy Toward Burma" dated March 28, 2003, the SPDC has become "more confrontational" in its exchanges with the NLD.

(4) On May 30, 2003, the SPDC, threatened by continued support for the NLD throughout Burma, brutally attacked NLD supporters, killed and injured scores of civilians, and arrested democracy advocate Aung San Suu Kyi and other activists.

(5) The SPDC continues egregious human rights violations against Burmese citizens, uses rape as a weapon of intimidation and torture against women, and forcibly conscripts child-soldiers for the use in fighting indigenous ethnic groups.

(6) The SPDC is engaged in ethnic cleansing against minorities within Burma, including the Karen, Karenni, and Shan people, which constitutes a crime against humanity and has directly led to more than 600,000 internally displaced people living within Burma and more than 130,000 people from Burma living in refugee camps along the Thai-Burma border.

...

(13) On April 15, 2003, the American Apparel and Footwear Association expressed its "strong support for a full and immediate ban on U.S. textiles, apparel and footwear imports from Burma" and called upon the U.S. Government to "impose an outright ban on U.S. imports" of these items until Burma demonstrates respect for basic human and labor rights of its citizens.

(14) The policy of the U.S., as articulated by the President on April 24, 2003, is to officially recognize the NLD as the legitimate representative of the Burmese people as determined by the 1990 election.

(15) The U.S. must work closely with other nations, including Thailand, a close ally of the U.S., to highlight attention to the SPDC's systematic abuses of human rights in Burma, to ensure that nongovernmental organizations promoting human rights and political freedom in Burma are allowed to operate freely and without harassment, and to craft a multilateral sanctions regime against Burma in order to pressure the SPDC to meet the conditions identified in section 3(a)(3) of this Act.

SEC. 3. BAN AGAINST TRADE THAT SUPPORTS THE MILITARY REGIME OF BURMA.

(a) GENERAL BAN.—

(1) IN GENERAL.—Notwithstanding any other provision of law, until such time as the President determines and certifies to Congress that Burma has met the conditions described in paragraph (3), beginning 30 days after the date of the enactment of this Act, the President shall ban the importation of any article that is a product of Burma.

(2) BAN ON IMPORTS FROM CERTAIN COMPANIES.—The import restrictions contained in paragraph (1) shall apply to, among other entities—

(A) the SPDC, any ministry of the SPDC, a member of the SPDC or an immediate family member of such member; (B) known narcotics traffickers from Burma or an immediate family member of such narcotics trafficker; (C) the Union of Myanmar Economics Holdings Incorporated (UMEHI) or any company in which the UMEHI has a fiduciary interest; (D) the Myanmar Economic Corporation (MEC) or any company in which the MEC has a fiduciary interest; (E) the Union Solidarity and Development Association (USDA); and (F) any successor entity for the SPDC, UMEHI, MEC, or USDA.

(3) CONDITIONS DESCRIBED.—The conditions described in this paragraph are the following:

(A) The SPDC has made substantial and measurable progress to end violations of internationally recognized human rights including rape, and the Secretary of State, after consultation with the ILO Secretary General and relevant nongovernmental organizations, reports to the appropriate congressional committees that the SPDC no longer systematically violates workers' rights, including the use of forced and child labor, and conscription of child soldiers.

(B) The SPDC has made measurable and substantial progress toward implementing a democratic government including—

(i) releasing all political prisoners; (ii) allowing freedom of speech and the press; (iii) allowing freedom of association; (iv) permitting the peaceful exercise of religion; and

(v) bringing to a conclusion an agreement between the SPDC and the democratic forces led by the NLD and Burma's ethnic nationalities on the transfer of power to a civilian government accountable to the Burmese people through democratic elections under the rule of law. (C) Pursuant to section 706(2) of the Foreign Relations Authorization Act, Fiscal Year 2003 (Public Law 107–228), Burma has not been designated as a country that has failed demonstrably to make substantial efforts to adhere to its obligations under international counter narcotics agreements and to take other effective counter narcotics measures, including, but not limited to (i) the arrest and extradition of all individuals under indictment in the U.S. for narcotics trafficking, (ii) concrete and measurable actions to stem the flow of illicit drug money into Burma's banking system and economic enterprises, and (iii) actions to stop the manufacture and export of methamphetamines.

...

SEC. 4. FREEZING ASSETS OF THE BURMESE REGIME IN THE U.S.

(a) REPORTING REQUIREMENT.—Not later than 60 days after the date of enactment of this Act, the President shall take such action as is necessary to direct, and promulgate regulations to the same, that any U.S. financial institution holding funds belonging to the SPDC or the assets of those individuals who hold senior positions in the SPDC or its political arm, the Union Solidarity Development Association, shall promptly report those funds or assets to the Office of Foreign Assets Control.

(b) ADDITIONAL AUTHORITY.—The President may take such action as may be necessary to impose a sanctions regime to freeze such funds or assets, subject to such terms and conditions as the President determines to be appropriate.

(c) DELEGATION.—The President may delegate the duties and authorities under this section to such Federal officers or other officials as the President deems appropriate.

SEC. 5. LOANS AT INTERNATIONAL FINANCIAL INSTITUTIONS.

The Secretary of the Treasury shall instruct the U.S. executive director to each appropriate international financial institution in which the U.S. participates, to oppose, and vote against the extension by such institution of any loan or financial or technical assistance to Burma until such time as the conditions described in section 3(a)(3) are met.

SEC. 6. EXPANSION OF VISA BAN.

(a) IN GENERAL.—

(1) VISA BAN.—The President is authorized to deny visas and entry to the former and present leadership of the SPDC or the Union Solidarity Development Association.

. . .

(b) PUBLICATION.—The Secretary of State shall post on the Department of State's website the names of individuals whose entry into the U.S. is banned under subsection (a).

SEC. 7. CONDEMNATION OF THE REGIME AND DISSEMINATION OF INFORMATION.

Congress encourages the Secretary of State to highlight the abysmal record of the SPDC to the international community and use all appropriate fora, including the Association of Southeast Asian Nations Regional Forum and Asian Nations Regional Forum, to encourage other states to restrict financial resources to the SPDC and Burmese companies while offering political recognition and support to Burma's democratic movement including the National League for Democracy and Burma's ethnic groups.

SEC. 8. SUPPORT DEMOCRACY ACTIVISTS IN BURMA.

(a) IN GENERAL.—The President is authorized to use all available resources to assist Burmese democracy activists dedicated to nonviolent opposition to the regime in their efforts to promote freedom, democracy, and human rights in Burma, including a listing of constraints on such programming.

(b) REPORTS.—

(1) FIRST REPORT.—Not later than 3 months after the date of enactment of this Act, the Secretary of State shall provide the Committees on Appropriations and Foreign Relations of the Senate and the Committees on Appropriations and International Relations of the House of Representatives a comprehensive report on its short- and long-term programs and activities to support democracy activists in Burma, including a list of constraints on such programming.

(2) REPORT ON RESOURCES.—Not later than 6 months after the date of enactment of this Act, the Secretary of State shall provide the Committees on Appropriations and Foreign Relations of the Senate and the Committees on Appropriations and International Relations of the House of Representatives a report identifying resources that will be necessary for the reconstruction of Burma, after the SPDC is removed from power, including—

(A) the formation of democratic institutions;

(B) establishing the rule of law;

(C) establishing freedom of the press;

(D) providing for the successful reintegration of military officers and personnel into Burmese society; and

(E) providing health, educational, and economic development.

. . .

SEC. 9. DURATION OF SANCTIONS.

(a) TERMINATION BY REQUEST FROM DEMOCRATIC BURMA.—

The President may terminate any provision in this Act upon the request of a democratically elected government in Burma, provided that all the conditions in section 3(a)(3) have been met.

(b) CONTINUATION OF IMPORT SANCTIONS.—

(1) EXPIRATION.—The import restrictions contained in section 3(a)(1) shall expire 1 year from the date of enactment of this Act unless renewed under paragraph (2) of this section.

(2) RESOLUTION BY CONGRESS.—The import restrictions contained in section 3(a)(1) may be renewed annually for a 1-year period if, prior to the anniversary of the date of enactment of this Act, and each year thereafter, a renewal resolution is enacted into law in accordance with subsection (c).

(3) LIMITATION.—The import restrictions contained in section 3(a)(1) may be renewed for a maximum of three years from the date of the enactment of this Act.

...

16. North Korean Human Rights Act Of 2004
PUBLIC LAW 108–333—OCT. 18, 2004 118 STAT. 1287 (EXCERPTED)
Public Law 108–333 108th Congress

An Act

To promote human rights and freedom in the Democratic People's Republic of Korea, and for other purposes.

Be it enacted by the Senate and House of Representatives of the United States of America in Congress assembled,

SECTION 1. SHORT TITLE.

This Act may be cited as the "North Korean Human Rights Act of 2004". ...

SEC. 3. FINDINGS.

Congress makes the following findings:

(1) According to the Department of State, the Government of North Korea is "a dictatorship under the absolute rule of Kim Jong Il" that continues to commit numerous, serious human rights abuses.

(2) The Government of North Korea attempts to control all information, artistic expression, academic works, and media activity inside North Korea and strictly curtails freedom of speech and access to foreign broad casts.

(3) The Government of North Korea subjects all its citizens to systematic, intensive political and ideological indoctrination in support of the cult of personality glorifying Kim Jong Il and the late Kim Il Sung that approaches the level of a state religion.

(4) The Government of North Korea divides its population into categories, based on perceived loyalty to the leadership, which determines access to food, employment, higher education, place of residence, medical facilities, and other resources.

(5) According to the Department of State, "[t]he [North Korean] Penal Code is [d]raconian, stipulating capital punishment and confiscation of assets for a wide variety of 'crimes against the revolution,' including defection, attempted defection, slander of the policies of the Party or State, listening to foreign broadcasts, writing 'reactionary' letters, and possessing reactionary printed matter".

(6) The Government of North Korea executes political prisoners, opponents of the regime, some repatriated defectors, some members of underground churches, and others, sometimes at public meetings attended by workers, students, and schoolchildren.

(7) The Government of North Korea holds an estimated 200,000 political prisoners in camps that its State Security Agency manages through the use of forced labor, beatings, torture, and executions, and in which many prisoners also die from disease, starvation, and exposure.

(8) According to eyewitness testimony provided to the U.S. Congress by North Korean camp survivors, camp inmates have been used as sources of slave labor for the production of export goods, as targets for martial arts practice, and as experimental victims in the testing of chemical and biological poisons.

(9) According to credible reports, including eyewitness testimony provided to the U.S. Congress, North Korean Government officials prohibit live births in prison camps, and forced abortion and the killing of newborn babies are standard prison practices. (10) According to the Department of State, "[g]enuine religious freedom does not exist in North Korea" and, according to the U.S. Commission on International Religious Freedom, "[t]he North Korean state severely represses public and private religious activities" with penalties that reportedly include arrest, imprisonment, torture, and sometimes execution.

(11) More than 2,000,000 North Koreans are estimated to have died of starvation since the early 1990s because of the failure of the centralized agricultural and public distribution systems operated by the Government of North Korea.

(12) According to a 2002 United Nations-European Union survey, nearly one out of every ten children in North Korea suffers from acute malnutrition and four out of every ten children in North Korea are chronically malnourished.

(13) Since 1995, the U.S. has provided more than 2,000,000 tons of humanitarian food assistance to the people of North Korea, primarily through the World Food Program.

(14) Although U.S. food assistance has undoubtedly saved many North Korean lives and there have been minor improvements in transparency relating to the distribution of such assistance in North Korea, the Government of North Korea continues to deny the World Food Program forms of access necessary to properly monitor the delivery of food aid, including the ability to conduct random site visits, the use of native Korean-speaking employees, and travel access throughout North Korea.

(25) In addition to infringing the rights of its own citizens, the Government of North Korea has been responsible in years past for the abduction of numerous citizens of South Korea and Japan, whose condition and whereabouts remain unknown.

SEC. 4. PURPOSES.

The purposes of this Act are—

(1) to promote respect for and protection of fundamental human rights in North Korea;

(2) to promote a more durable humanitarian solution to the plight of North Korean refugees;

(3) to promote increased monitoring, access, and transparency in the provision of humanitarian assistance inside North Korea;

(4) to promote the free flow of information into and out of North Korea; and

(5) to promote progress toward the peaceful reunification of the Korean peninsula under a democratic system of government.

...

TITLE I—PROMOTING THE HUMAN RIGHTS OF NORTH KOREANS

SEC. 101. SENSE OF CONGRESS REGARDING NEGOTIATIONS WITH NORTH KOREA.

It is the sense of Congress that the human rights of North Koreans should remain a key element in future negotiations between the U.S., North Korea, and other concerned parties in Northeast Asia.

SEC. 102. SUPPORT FOR HUMAN RIGHTS AND DEMOCRACY PROGRAMS.

(a) SUPPORT.—The President is authorized to provide grants to private, nonprofit organizations to support programs that promote human rights, democracy, rule of law, and the development of a market economy in North Korea. Such programs may include appropriate educational and cultural exchange programs with North Korean participants, to the extent not otherwise prohibited by law.

17. The Hawaii Apology Resolution,
Public Law 103-150-S.J Res. 19- November 23, 1993
103RD U.S. CONGRESS
1ST SESSION

Joint Resolution

To acknowledge the 100th anniversary of the January 17, 1893 overthrow of the Kingdom of Hawaii, and to offer an apology to Native Hawaiians on behalf of the U.S. for the overthrow of the Kingdom of Hawaii.

Whereas, prior to the arrival of the first Europeans in 1778, the Native Hawaiian people lived in a highly organized, self-sufficient, subsistent social system based on communal land tenure with a sophisticated language, culture, and religion;

Whereas, a unified monarchical government of the Hawaiian Islands was established in 1810 under Kamehameha I, the first King of Hawaii;

Whereas, from 1826 until 1893, the U.S. recognized the independence of the Kingdom of Hawaii, extended full and complete diplomatic recognition to the Hawaiian Government, and entered into treaties and conventions with the Hawaiian monarchs to govern commerce and navigation in 1826, 1842, 1849, 1875, and 1887;

Whereas, the Congregational Church (now known as the United Church of Christ), through its American Board of Commissioners for Foreign Missions, sponsored and sent more than 100 missionaries to the Kingdom of Hawaii between 1820 and 1850;

Whereas, on January 14, 1893, John L. Stevens (hereafter referred to in this Resolution as the "U.S. Minister"), the U.S. Minister assigned to the sovereign and independent Kingdom of Hawaii conspired with a small group of non-Hawaiian residents of the Kingdom of Hawaii, including citizens of the U.S., to overthrow the indigenous and lawful Government of Hawaii;

Whereas, in pursuance of the conspiracy to overthrow the Government of Hawaii, the U.S. Minister and the naval representatives of the U.S. caused armed naval forces of the U.S. to invade the sovereign Hawaiian nation on January 16, 1893, and to position themselves near the Hawaiian Government buildings and the Iolani Palace to intimidate Queen Liliuokalani and her Government;

Whereas, on the afternoon of January 17,1893, a Committee of Safety that represented the American and European sugar planters, descendants of missionaries, and financiers deposed the Hawaiian monarchy and proclaimed the establishment of a Provisional Government;

Whereas, the U.S. Minister thereupon extended diplomatic recognition to the Provisional Government that was formed by the conspirators without the consent of the Native Hawaiian people or the lawful Government of Hawaii and in violation of treaties between the two nations and of international law;

Whereas, soon thereafter, when informed of the risk of bloodshed with resistance, Queen Liliuokalani issued the following statement yielding her authority to the U.S. Government rather than to the Provisional Government:

> *I Liliuokalani, by the Grace of God and under the Constitution of the Hawaiian Kingdom, Queen, do hereby solemnly protest against any and all acts done against myself and the Constitutional Government of the Hawaiian Kingdom by certain persons claiming to have established a Provisional Government of and for this Kingdom.*
>
> *That I yield to the superior force of the United States of America whose Minister Plenipotentiary, His Excellency John L. Stevens, has caused U.S. troops to be landed a Honolulu and declared that he would support the Provisional Government.*
>
> *Now to avoid any collision of armed forces, and perhaps the loss of life, I do this under protest and impelled by said force yield my authority until such time as the Government of the U.S. shall, upon facts being presented to it, undo the action of its representatives and reinstate me in the authority which I claim as the Constitutional Sovereign of the Hawaiian Islands.*
>
> *Done at Honolulu this 17th day of January, A.D. 1893.*

Whereas, without the active support and intervention by the U.S. diplomatic and military representatives, the insurrection against the Government of Queen Liliuokalani would have failed for lack of popular support and insufficient arms;

Whereas, on February 1, 1893, the U.S. Minister raised the American flag and proclaimed Hawaii to be a protectorate of the U.S.;

Whereas, the report of a Presidentially established investigation conducted by former Congressman James Blount into the events surrounding the insurrection and overthrow of January 17, 1893, concluded that the U.S. diplomatic and military representatives had abused their authority and were responsible for the change in government;

Whereas, as a result of this investigation, the U.S. Minister to Hawaii was recalled from his diplomatic post and the military commander of the U.S. armed forces stationed in Hawaii was disciplined and forced to resign his commission;

Whereas, in a message to Congress on December 18, 1893, President Grover Cleveland reported fully and accurately on the illegal acts of the conspirators, described such acts as an "act of war, committed with the participation of a diplomatic representative of the U.S. and without authority of Congress", and acknowledged that by such acts the government of a peaceful and friendly people was overthrown;

Whereas, President Cleveland further concluded that a "substantial wrong has thus been done which a due regard for our national character as well as the rights of the injured people requires we should endeavor to repair" and called for the restoration of the Hawaiian monarchy;

Whereas, the Provisional Government protested President Cleveland's call for the restoration of the monarchy and continued to hold state power and pursue annexation to the U.S.;

Whereas, the Provisional Government successfully lobbied the Committee on Foreign Relations of the Senate (hereafter referred to in this Resolution as the "Committee") to conduct a new investigation into the events surrounding the overthrow of the monarchy;

Whereas, the Committee and its chairman, Senator John Morgan, conducted hearings in Washington, D.C., from December 27,1893, through February 26, 1894, in which members of the Provisional Government justified and condoned the actions of the U.S. Minister and recommended annexation of Hawaii;

Whereas, although the Provisional Government was able to obscure the role of the U.S. in the illegal overthrow of the Hawaiian monarchy, it was unable to rally the support from two-thirds of the Senate needed to ratify a treaty of annexation;

Whereas, on July 4, 1894, the Provisional Government declared itself to be the Republic of Hawaii;

Whereas, on January 24, 1895, while imprisoned in Iolani Palace, Queen Liliuokalani was forced by representatives of the Republic of Hawaii to officially abdicate her throne;

Whereas, in the 1896 U.S. Presidential election, William McKinley replaced Grover Cleveland;

Whereas, on July 7, 1898, as a consequence of the Spanish-American War, President McKinley signed the Newlands Joint Resolution that provided for the annexation of Hawaii;

Whereas, through the Newlands Resolution, the self-declared Republic of Hawaii ceded sovereignty over the Hawaiian Islands to the U.S.;

Whereas, the Republic of Hawaii also ceded 1,800,000 acres [7,280 km²] of crown, government and public lands of the Kingdom of Hawaii, without the consent of or compensation to the Native Hawaiian people of Hawaii or their sovereign government;

Whereas, the Congress, through the Newlands Resolution, ratified the cession, annexed Hawaii as part of the U.S., and vested title to the lands in Hawaii in the U.S.;

Whereas, the Newlands Resolution also specified that treaties existing between Hawaii and foreign nations were to immediately cease and be replaced by U.S. treaties with such nations;

Whereas, the Newlands Resolution effected the transaction between the Republic of Hawaii and the U.S. Government;

Whereas, the indigenous Hawaiian people never directly relinquished their claims to their inherent sovereignty as a people or over their national lands to the U.S., either through their monarchy or through a plebiscite or referendum;

Whereas, on April 30, 1900, President McKinley signed the Organic Act that provided a government for the territory of Hawaii and defined the political structure and powers of the newly established Territorial Government and its relationship to the U.S.;

Whereas, on August 21, 1959, Hawaii became the 50th State of the U.S.;

Whereas, the health and well-being of the Native Hawaiian people is intrinsically tied to their deep feelings and attachment to the land;

Whereas, the long-range economic and social changes in Hawaii over the nineteenth and early twentieth centuries have been devastating to the population and to the health and well-being of the Hawaiian people;

Whereas, the Native Hawaiian people are determined to preserve, develop and transmit to future generations their ancestral territory, and their cultural identity in accordance with their own spiritual and traditional beliefs, customs, practices, language, and social institutions;

Whereas, in order to promote racial harmony and cultural understanding, the Legislature of the State of Hawaii has determined that the year 1993, should serve Hawaii as a year of special reflection on the rights and dignities of the Native Hawaiians in the Hawaiian and the American societies;

Whereas, the Eighteenth General Synod of the United Church of Christ in recognition of the denomination's historical complicity in the illegal overthrow of the Kingdom of Hawaii in 1893 directed the Office of the President of the United Church of Christ to offer a public apology to the Native Hawaiian people and to initiate the process of reconciliation between the United Church of Christ and the Native Hawaiians; and

Whereas, it is proper and timely for the Congress on the occasion of the impending one hundredth anniversary of the event, to acknowledge the historic significance of the illegal overthrow of the Kingdom of Hawaii, to express its deep regret to the Native Hawaiian people, and to support the reconciliation efforts of the State of Hawaii and the United Church of Christ with Native Hawaiians;

Now, therefore, be it resolved by the Senate and House of Representatives of the United States of America in Congress assembled,

Section 1. Acknowledgment and Apology.

The Congress

(1) on the occasion of the 100th anniversary of the illegal overthrow of the Kingdom of Hawaii on January 17, 1893, acknowledges the historical significance of this event which resulted in the suppression of the inherent sovereignty of the Native Hawaiian people;

(2) recognizes and commends efforts of reconciliation initiated by the State of Hawaii and the United Church of Christ with Native Hawaiians;

(3) apologizes to Native Hawaiians on behalf of the people of the U.S. for the overthrow of the Kingdom of Hawaii on January 17, 1893 with the participation of agents and citizens of the U.S., and the deprivation of the rights of Native Hawaiians to self-determination;

(4) expresses its commitment to acknowledge the ramifications of the overthrow of the Kingdom of Hawaii, in order to provide a proper foundation for reconciliation between the U.S. and the Native Hawaiian people; and

(5) urges the President of the U.S. to also acknowledge the ramifications of the overthrow of the Kingdom of Hawaii and to support reconciliation efforts between the U.S. and the Native Hawaiian people.

Section 2. Definitions.

As used in this Joint Resolution, the term "Native Hawaiians" means any individual who is a descendent of the aboriginal people who, prior to 1778, occupied and exercised sovereignty in the area that now constitutes the State of Hawaii.

Section 3. Disclaimer.

Nothing in this Joint Resolution is intended to serve as a settlement of any claims against the U.S.

18. Free Speech Protection Act Of 2009
111TH CONGRESS
1ST SESSION S. 449

To protect free speech.
IN THE SENATE OF THE U.S.
FEBRUARY 13, 2009

Mr. SPECTER (for himself, Mr. LIEBERMAN, and Mr. SCHUMER) introduced the following bill; which was read twice and referred to the Committee on the Judiciary

A BILL

To protect free speech.

Be it enacted by the Senate and House of Representatives of the United States of America in Congress assembled,

SECTION 1. SHORT TITLE.

This Act may be cited as the "Free Speech Protection Act of 2009".

SEC. 2. FINDINGS.

Congress finds the following:

(1) The freedom of speech and the press is enshrined in the first amendment to the Constitution of the U.S.

(2) Free speech, the free exchange of information, and the free expression of ideas and opinions are essential to the functioning of representative democracy in the U.S.

(3) The free expression and publication by journalists, academics, commentators, experts, and others of the information they uncover and develop through research and study is essential to the formation of sound public policy and thus to the security of the people of the U.S.

(4) The first amendment jurisprudence of the Supreme Court of the U.S., articulated in such precedents as New York Times v Sullivan (376 U.S. 254 (1964)), and its progeny, reflects the fun damental value that the people of the U.S. place on promoting the free exchange of ideas and information, requiring in cases involving public figures a demonstration of actual malice, that is, that allegedly defamatory,

libelous, or slanderous statements about public figures are not merely false but made with knowledge of that falsity or with reckless disregard of their truth or falsity.

(5) Some persons are obstructing the free expression rights of U.S. persons, and the vital interest of the people of the U.S. in receiving information on matters of public importance, by first seeking out foreign jurisdictions that3 do not provide the full extent of free-speech protection that is fundamental in the U.S. and then suing U.S. persons in such jurisdictions in defamation actions based on speech uttered or published in the U.S., speech that is fully protected under first amendment jurisprudence in the U.S. and the laws of the several States and the District of Columbia.

(6) Some of these actions are intended not only to suppress the free speech rights of journalists, academics, commentators, experts, and other individuals but to intimidate publishers and other organizations that might otherwise disseminate or support the work of those individuals with the threat of prohibitive foreign lawsuits, litigation expenses, and judgments that provide for money damages and other speech-suppressing relief. Such actions are intentional tortious acts aimed at U.S. persons, even though the harmful conduct may have occurred extraterritorially.

(7) The governments and courts of some foreign countries have failed to curtail this practice, permitting lawsuits filed by persons who are often not citizens of those countries, under circumstances where there is often little or no basis for jurisdiction over the U.S. persons against whom such suits are brought.

(8) Some of the plaintiffs bringing such suits are intentionally and strategically refraining from filing their suits in the U.S., even though the speech at issue was published in the U.S., in order to avoid the Supreme Court's first amendment jurisprudence and frustrate the protections it affords U.S. persons.

(9) The U.S. persons against whom such suits are brought must consequently endure the prohibitive expense, inconvenience, and anxiety attendant to being sued in foreign courts for conduct that is protected under the first amendment, or decline to answer such suits and risk the entry of costly default judgments that may be executed in countries other than the U.S. where those individuals travel or own property.

(10) Journalists, academics, commentators, experts, and others subjected to such suits are suffering concrete and profound financial and professional damage for engaging in conduct that is protected under the Constitution of the U.S. and essential to informing the people of the U.S., their representatives, and other policy makers.

(11) In turn, the people of the U.S. are suffering concrete and profound harm because they, their representatives, and other government policymakers rely on the free expression of information, ideas, and opinions developed by responsible journalists, academics, commentators, experts, and others for the formulation of sound public policy, including national security policy.

(12) The U.S. respects the sovereign right of other countries to enact their own laws regarding speech, and seeks only to protect the first amendment rights of the people of the U.S. in connection with speech that occurs, in whole or in part, in the U.S.

18 SEC. 3. FEDERAL CAUSE OF ACTION.

19 (a) CAUSE OF ACTION.—Any U.S. person against whom a lawsuit is brought in a foreign country for defamation on the basis of the content of any writing, utterance, or other speech by that person that has been published, uttered, or otherwise primarily disseminated in the U.S. may bring an action in a U.S. district court specified in subsection (f) against any person who, or entity which, brought the foreign lawsuit if— (1) the writing, utterance, or other speech at issue in the foreign lawsuit does not constitute defamation under U.S. law; and (2) the person or entity which brought the foreign lawsuit serves or causes to be served any documents in connection with such foreign lawsuit on a U.S. person.

10 (b) JURISDICTION.—The district court shall have personal jurisdiction under this section if, in light of the facts alleged in the complaint, the person or entity bringing the foreign suit described in subsection (a) served or caused to be served any documents in connection with such foreign lawsuit on a U.S. person with assets in the U.S. against which the claimant in the foreign lawsuit could execute if a judgment in the foreign lawsuit were awarded.

CONGRESSIONAL RESOLUTIONS

19. The Armenian Genocide Resolution (Excerpted)
111TH CONGRESS
1ST SESSION H. RES. 252

Calling upon the President to ensure that the foreign policy of the U.S. reflects appropriate understanding and sensitivity concerning issues related to human rights, ethnic cleansing, and genocide documented in the U.S. record relating to the Armenian Genocide, and for other purposes.

IN THE HOUSE OF REPRESENTATIVES

MARCH 17, 2009

Mr. SCHIFF (for himself, Mr. RADANOVICH, ET AL, (Sponsors) submitted the following resolution; which was referred to the Committee on Foreign Affairs.

RESOLUTION

Calling upon the President to ensure that the foreign policy of the U.S. reflects appropriate understanding and sensitivity concerning issues related to human rights, ethnic cleansing, and genocide documented in the U.S. record relating to the Armenian Genocide, and for other purposes.

Resolved,

SHORT TITLE

SEC. 1. This resolution may be cited as the "Affirmation of the U.S. Record on the Armenian Genocide Resolution".

FINDINGS

SEC. 2. The House of Representatives finds the following:

(1) The Armenian Genocide was conceived and carried out by the Ottoman Empire from 1915 to 1923, resulting in the deportation of nearly 2,000,000 Armenians, of whom 1,500,000 men, women, and children were killed, 500,000 survivors were expelled from their homes, and which succeeded in the elimination of the over 2,500-year presence of Armenians in their historic homeland.

(2) On May 24, 1915, the Allied Powers, England, France, and Russia, jointly issued a statement explicitly charging for the first time ever another government of committing "a crime against humanity".

(3) This joint statement stated "the Allied Governments announce publicly to the Sublime Porte that they will hold personally responsible for these crimes all members of the Ottoman Government, as well as those of their agents who are implicated in such massacres".

(4) The post-World War I Turkish Government indicted the top leaders involved in the "organization and execution" of the Armenian Genocide and in the "massacre and destruction of the Armenians".

(5) In a series of courts-martial, officials of the Young Turk Regime were tried and convicted, as charged, for organizing and executing massacres against the Armenian people.

(6) The chief organizers of the Armenian Genocide, Minister of War Enver, Minister of the Interior Talaat, and Minister of the Navy Jemal were all condemned to death for their crimes, however, the verdicts of the courts were not enforced.

(7) The Armenian Genocide and these domestic judicial failures are documented with overwhelming evidence in the national archives of Austria, France, Germany, Great Britain, Russia, the U.S., the Vatican and many other countries, and this vast body of evidence at tests to the same facts, the same events, and the same consequences. \ HR252.IH HR252 wwoods2 on PRODPC68 with BILLS

(8) The U.S. National Archives and Record Administration holds extensive and thorough documentation on the Armenian Genocide, especially in its holdings under Record Group 59 of the U.S. Department of State, files 867.00 and 867.40, which are open and widely available to the public and interested institutions.

(9) The Honorable Henry Morgenthau, U.S. Ambassador to the Ottoman Empire from 1913 to 1916, organized and led protests by officials of many countries, among them the allies of the Ottoman Empire, against the Armenian Genocide.

(10) Ambassador Morgenthau explicitly described to the U.S. Department of State the policy of the Government of the Ottoman Empire as "a campaign of race extermination," and was instructed on July 16, 1915, by U.S. Secretary of State Robert Lansing that the "Department approves your procedure . . . to stop Armenian persecution".

(11) Senate Concurrent Resolution 12 of February 9, 1916, resolved that "the President of the U.S. be respectfully asked to designate a day on which the citizens of this country may give expression to their sympathy by contributing funds now being raised for the relief of the Armenians", who at the time were enduring "starvation, disease, and untold suffering".

1 (12) President Woodrow Wilson concurred and also encouraged the formation of the organization known as Near East Relief, chartered by an Act of Congress, which contributed some $116,000,000 from

1915 to 1930 to aid Armenian Genocide survivors, including 132,000 orphans who became foster children of the American people.

(13) Senate Resolution 359, dated May 11, 1920, stated in part, "the testimony adduced at the hearings conducted by the sub-committee of the Senate Committee on Foreign Relations have clearly established the truth of the reported massacres and other atrocities from which the Armenian people have suffered".

(14) The resolution followed the April 13, 1920, report to the Senate of the American Military Mission to Armenia led by General James Harbord, that stated "[m]utilation, violation, torture, and death have left their haunting memories in a hundred beautiful Armenian valleys, and the traveler in that region is seldom free from the evidence of this most colossal crime of all the ages".

(15) As displayed in the U.S. Holocaust Memorial Museum, Adolf Hitler, on ordering his military commanders to attack Poland without provocation in 1939, dismissed objections by saying "[w]ho, after all, speaks today of the annihilation of the Armenians?" and thus set the stage for the Holocaust.

(16) Raphael Lemkin, who coined the term "genocide" in 1944, and who was the earliest proponent of the United Nations Convention on the Prevention and Punishment of Genocide, invoked the Armenian case as a definitive example of genocide in the 20th century.

(17) The first resolution on genocide adopted by the United Nations at Lemkin's urging, the December 11, 1946, United Nations General Assembly Resolution 96(1) and the United Nations Convention on the Prevention and Punishment of Genocide itself recognized the Armenian Genocide as the type of crime the United Nations intended to prevent and punish by codifying existing standards.

(18) In 1948, the United Nations War Crimes Commission invoked the Armenian Genocide "precisely . . . one of the types of acts which the modern term 'crimes against humanity' is intended to cover" as a precedent for the Nuremberg tribunals.

(19) The Commission stated that "[t]he provisions of Article 230 of the Peace Treaty of Sevres were obviously intended to cover, in conformity with the Allied note of 1915 . . . , offenses which had been committed on Turkish territory against persons of Turkish citizenship, though of Armenian or Greek race. This article constitutes therefore a precedent for Article 6c and 5c of the Nuremberg and Tokyo Charters, and offers an example of one of the categories of 'crimes against humanity' as understood by these enactments".

(20) House Joint Resolution 148, adopted on April 8, 1975, resolved: "[t]hat April 24, 1975, is hereby designated as 'National Day of Remembrance of Man's Inhumanity to Man', and the President of the U.S. is authorized and requested to issue a proclamation calling upon the people of the U.S. to observe such day as a day of remembrance for all the victims of genocide, especially those of Armenian ancestry . . .".

(21) President Ronald Reagan in proclamation number 4838, dated April 22, 1981, stated in part "like the genocide of the Armenians before it, and the genocide of the Cambodians, which followed it—and like too many other persecutions of too many other people—the lessons of the Holocaust must never be forgotten".

(22) House Joint Resolution 247, adopted on September 10, 1984, resolved: "[t]hat April 24, 1985, is hereby designated as 'National Day of Remembrance of Man's Inhumanity to Man', and the President of the U.S. is authorized and requested to issue a proclamation calling upon the people of the U.S. to observe such day as a day of remembrance for all the victims of genocide, especially the one and one-half million people of Armenian ancestry . . .".

(23) In August 1985, after extensive study and deliberation, the United Nations Sub Commission on Prevention of Discrimination and Protection of Minorities voted 14 to 1 to accept a report entitled "Study of the Question of the Prevention and Punishment of the Crime of Genocide," which stated "[t]he Nazi aberration has unfortunately not been the only case of genocide in the 20th century. Among other examples which can be cited as qualifying are . . . the Ottoman massacre of Armenians in 1915–1916".

(24) This report also explained that "[a]t least 1,000,000, and possibly well over half of the Armenian population, are reliably estimated to have been killed or death marched by independent authorities and eye-witnesses. This is corroborated by reports in U.S., German and British archives and of contemporary diplomats in the Ottoman Empire, including those of its ally Germany.".

(25) The U.S. Holocaust Memorial Council, an independent Federal agency, unanimously resolved on 21 April 30, 1981, that the U.S. Holocaust Memorial Museum would include the Armenian Genocide in the Museum and has since done so.

(26) Reviewing an aberrant 1982 expression (later retracted) by the U.S. Department of State asserting that the facts of the Armenian Genocide may be ambiguous, the U.S. Court of Appeals for the District of Columbia in 1993, after a review of documents pertaining to the policy record of the U.S., noted that the assertion on ambiguity in the U.S. record about the Armenian Genocide "contradicted long standing U.S. policy and was eventually retracted".

(27) On June 5, 1996, the House of Representatives adopted an amendment to House Bill 3540 (the Foreign Operations, Export Financing, and Related Programs Appropriations Act, 1997) to reduce aid to Turkey by $3,000,000 (an estimate of its payment of lobbying fees in the U.S.) until the Turkish Government acknowledged the Armenian Genocide and took steps to honor the memory of its victims.

17 (28) President William Jefferson Clinton, on April 24, 1998, stated: "This year, as in the past, we join with 19 Armenian-Americans throughout the nation in commemorating one of the saddest chapters in the history of this century, the deportations and massacres of a million and a half Armenians in the Ottoman Empire in the years 1915–1923.".

(29) President George W. Bush, on April 24, 2004, stated: "On this day, we pause in remembrance of one of the most horrible tragedies of the 20th century, the anihilation of as many as 1,500,000 Armenians through forced exile and murder at the end of the Ottoman Empire.".

(30) Despite the international recognition and affirmation of the Armenian Genocide, the failure of the domestic and international authorities to punish those responsible for the Armenian Genocide is a reason why similar genocides have recurred and may recur in the future, and that a just resolution will help prevent future genocides.

DECLARATION OF POLICY

SEC. 3. The House of Representatives—

(1) calls upon the President to ensure that the foreign policy of the U.S. reflects appropriate understanding and sensitivity concerning issues related to human rights, ethnic cleansing, and genocide documented in the U.S. record relating to the Armenian Genocide and the consequences of the failure to realize a just resolution; and (2) calls upon the President in the President's annual message commemorating the Armenian Genocide issued on or about April 24, to accurately characterize the systematic and deliberate annihilation of 1,500,000 Armenians as genocide and to recall the proud history of U.S. intervention in opposition to the Armenian Genocide.

20. Concurrent Resolution Declaring Genocide In Darfur, Sudan.
108TH CONGRESS
2D SESSION H. CON. RES. 467
CONCURRENT RESOLUTION
Declaring genocide in Darfur, Sudan.

Whereas Article 1 of the Convention on the Prevention and Punishment of the Crime of Genocide (signed at Paris on December 9, 1948) states that "the Contracting Parties confirm that genocide, whether committed in time of peace or in time of war, is a crime under international law which they undertake to prevent and to punish";

Whereas Article 2 of the Convention on the Prevention and Punishment of the Crime of Genocide declares that "in the present Convention, genocide means any of the following acts committed with the intent to destroy, in whole or in part, a national, ethnical, racial or religious group, as such: (a) killing members of the group; (b) Causing serious bodily or mental harm to members of the group; (c) deliberately inflicting on the group conditions of life calculated to bring about its physical destruction in whole or in part; (d) imposing measures intended to prevent births within the group; and (e) forcibly transferring children of the group to another group";

Whereas Article 3 of the Convention on the Prevention and Punishment of the Crime of Genocide affirms that "[the] following acts shall be punishable: (a) genocide; (b) conspiracy to commit genocide; (c) direct and public incitement to commit genocide; (d) attempt to committed genocide; and (e) complicit in genocide";

Whereas in Darfur, Sudan, an estimated 30,000 innocent civilians have been brutally murdered, more than 130,000 people have been forced from their homes and have fled to neighboring Chad, and more than 1,000,000 people have been internally displaced; and

Whereas in March 2004 the United Nations Resident Humanitarian Coordinator stated: "[T]he war in Darfur started off in a small way last year but it has progressively gotten worse. A predominant feature of this is that the brunt is being borne by civilians. This includes vulnerable women and children . . . The violence in Darfur appears to be particularly directed at a specific group based on their ethnic identity and appears to be systemized.": Now, therefore, be it

Resolved by the House of Representatives (the Senate concurring),

That Congress—

(1) declares that the atrocities unfolding in Darfur, Sudan, are genocide;

(2) reminds the Contracting Parties to the Convention on the Prevention and Punishment of the Crime of Genocide (signed at Paris on December 9, 1948), particularly the Government of Sudan, of their legal obligations under the Convention;

(3) declares that the Government of Sudan, as a Contracting Party, has violated the Convention on the Prevention and Punishment of the Crime of Genocide;

(4) deplores the failure of the United Nations Human Rights Commission to take appropriate action with respect to the crisis in Darfur, Sudan, particularly the failure by the Commission to support U.S.-sponsored efforts to strongly condemn gross human rights violations committed in Darfur, and calls upon the United Nations and the United Nations Secretary General to assert leadership by calling the atrocities being committed in Darfur by their rightful name: "genocide";

(5) calls on the member states of the United Nations, particularly member states from the African Union, the Arab League, and the Organization of the Islamic Conference, to undertake measures to prevent the genocide in Darfur, Sudan, from escalating further, including the imposition of targeted sanctions against those responsible for the atrocities;

(6) urges the Administration to call the atrocities being committed in Darfur, Sudan, by their rightful name: "genocide";

(7) commends the Administration's leadership in seeking a peaceful resolution to the conflict in Darfur, Sudan, and in addressing the ensuing humanitarian crisis, including the visit of Secretary of State Colin Powell to Darfur in June 2004 to engage directly in efforts to end the genocide, and the15 provision of nearly $140,000,000 to date in bilateral humanitarian assistance through the U.S. Agency for International Development;

(8) commends the President for appointing former Senator John Danforth as Envoy for Peace in Sudan on September 6, 2001, and further commends the appointment of Senator Danforth as U.S. Ambassador to the United Nations;

(9) calls on the Administration to continue to lead an international effort to stop genocide in Darfur, Sudan;

(10) urges the Administration to seriously consider multilateral or even unilateral intervention to stop genocide in Darfur, Sudan, should the United Nations Security Council fail to act;

(11) calls on the Administration to impose targeted sanctions, including visa bans and the freezing of assets of the Sudanese National Congress and affiliated business and individuals directly responsible for the atrocities in Darfur, Sudan; and

(12) calls on the U.S. Agency for International Development to establish a Darfur Resettlement, Rehabilitation, and Reconstruction Fund so that those individuals driven off their land may return and begin to rebuild their communities.

Passed the House of Representatives July 22, 2004.

Attest: *Clerk.*

21. Resolution Proposing An Amendment To The Constitution Of The U.S. Relating To Parental Rights.
111TH CONGRESS
1ST SESSION H. J. RES. 42
Proposing an amendment to the Constitution of the U.S. relating to parental rights.

IN THE HOUSE OF REPRESENTATIVES
MARCH 31, 2009

Mr. HOEKSTRA (for himself, Mr. WOLF, [et al.] introduced the following joint resolution; which was referred to the Committee on the Judiciary.

JOINT RESOLUTION

Proposing an amendment to the Constitution of the U.S. relating to parental rights.

Resolved by the Senate and House of Representatives of the United States of America in Congress assembled (*two-thirds of each House concurring therein*), That the following article is proposed as an amendment to the Constitution of the U.S., which shall be valid to all intents and purposes as part of the Constitution when ratified by the legislatures of three-fourths of the several States within seven years after the date of its submission for ratification:

"ARTICLE—

"SECTION 1. The liberty of parents to direct the up bringing and education of their children is a fundamental right.

"SECTION 2. Neither the U.S. nor any State shall infringe upon this right without demonstrating that its governmental interest as applied to the person is of the highest order and not otherwise served.

"SECTION 3. No treaty may be adopted nor shall any source of international law be employed to supersede, modify, interpret, or apply to the rights guaranteed by this article.".

Other Miscellaneous Federal and State Legislation

The following laws are also very much in the nature of human rights protections found in U.S. law. The variety of subject matters (e.g., education, civil rights, criminal law) demonstrates how broadly human rights considerations have become an express part of the U.S. legal landscape.

Civil Rights Act of 1964, USC Title 42, Sec. 1981–1988

Civil Rights of Institutionalized Persons Act (CRIPA), USC Title 42, Sec. 1997 (1982)

This act gives the U.S. Attorney General power to protect the mentally handicapped in state mental institutions.

Indian Civil Rights Act (ICRA), USC Title 25, Sec. 1301

This act requires that Native American tribes respect the civil rights of everyone within their jurisdiction.

American Indian Religious Freedom Act (AIRFA), USC Title 42, Sec. 1996

This act ensures religious freedom for all Native Americans, including American Indians, Aleuts, Eskimos, and Native Hawaiians. It requires the U.S. government to respect and promote the religious rights of Native Americans, including rights to practice traditional religious ceremonies and have access to sacred places and use sacred objects.

Americans with Disabilities Act of 1990 (ADA), USC Title 22, Sec. 12101

This act seeks to eliminate discrimination against persons with certain disabilities, with regard to such areas as employment and housing. It also seeks to establish federal standards for dealing with problems of the disabled. It seeks to achieve legal and factual equality of the disabled with all other members of society.

Juvenile Justice and Delinquency Prevention Act (JJDPA), USC Title 42, Sec. 5601–40 (1974)

Congress enacted this to get states that have accepted JJDPA funds to remove juvenile-status offenders from secured facilities, place juveniles in facilities separate from adult offenders, remove juveniles from jails, and make sure children are given procedural due process of law in juvenile proceedings.

California Civil Code Sec. 51.7

[This is a sample of California state law civil code giving individuals or the attorney general or district attorney a right to seek judicial remedies against hate-crime–type activity violating individual rights.]

51.7. (a) All persons within the jurisdiction of this state have the right to be free from any violence, or intimidation by threat of violence, committed against their persons or property because of their race, color, religion, ancestry, national origin, political affiliation, sex, sexual orientation, age, disability, or position in a labor dispute, or because another person perceives them to have one or more of those characteristics. The identification in this subdivision of particular bases of discrimination is illustrative rather than restrictive.

. . .

52.1. (a) Whenever a person or persons, whether or not acting under color of law, interferes by threats, intimidation, or coercion, or attempts to interfere by threats, intimidation, or coercion, with the exercise or enjoyment by any individual or individuals of rights secured by the Constitution or laws of the U.S., or of the rights secured by the Constitution or laws of this state, the Attorney General, or any district attorney or city attorney may bring a civil action for injunctive and other appropriate equitable relief in the name of the people of the State of California, in order to protect the peaceable exercise or enjoyment of the right or rights secured.

(b) Any individual whose exercise or enjoyment of rights secured by the Constitution or laws of the U.S., or of rights secured by the Constitution or laws of this state, has been interfered with, or attempted to be interfered with, as described in subdivision (a), may institute and prosecute in his or her own name and on his or her own behalf a civil action for damages, including, but not limited to, damages under Section 52, injunctive relief, and other appropriate equitable relief to protect the peaceable exercise or enjoyment of the right or rights secured.

(c) An action brought pursuant to subdivision (a) or (b) may be filed either in the superior court for the county in which the conduct complained of occurred or in the superior court for the county in which a person whose conduct complained of resides or has his or her place of business. An action brought by the Attorney General pursuant to subdivision (a) also may be filed in the superior court for any county wherein the Attorney General has an office, and in such a case, the jurisdiction of the court shall extend throughout the state.

[Following is an example of state legislation, a California Education Code Section, mandating the teaching of Human Rights in the curriculum of public schools, grades 7–12.]

California Education Code: Section 51220–51230

Chapter 2. Required Courses of Study

Article 3. Courses of Study, Grades 7 to 12 [51220–51230]

51220. The adopted course of study for grades 7 to 12, inclusive, shall offer courses in the following areas of study:

(b) Social sciences, drawing upon the disciplines of anthropology, economics, geography, history, political science, psychology, and sociology, designed to fit the maturity of the pupils. Instruction shall provide a foundation for understanding the history, resources, development, and government of California and the United States of America; instruction in our American legal system, the operation of the juvenile and adult criminal justice systems, and the rights and duties of citizens under the criminal and civil law and the State and Federal Constitutions; ... *human rights issues, with particular attention to the study of the inhumanity of genocide, slavery, and the Holocaust, and contemporary issues.* (emphasis added)

LEGISLATIVE INTENT

11 (a) The Legislature recognizes and affirms the importance to pupils of learning to appreciate the sanctity of life and the dignity of the individual. Pupils must develop a respect for each person as a unique individual, and understand the importance of a universal concern for ethics and human rights .

(b) The Legislature recognizes the importance of teaching our youth ethical and moral behavior specifically relating to human rights violations, genocide issues, and slavery, as well as the Holocaust. - -

Restatement (Third) of the Foreign Relations Law (Excerpts)

Pt. VII Intro. Note (1986 Main Vol.)

Foreign Relations Law of the U.S. 3d

Part VII. Protection of Persons (Natural and Juridical)

Introductory Note

International law governs primarily relations between states, see sec. 101, and traditional international jurisprudence insisted that the individual was not a "subject" of international law, see Part II, Introductory Note, but customary international law and numerous international agreements have created obligations for states in relation to persons, both natural and juridical. International law has long held states responsible for "denials of justice" and certain other injuries to nationals of other states. Increasingly, international human rights agreements have created obligations and responsibilities for states in respect of all individuals subject to their jurisdiction, including their own nationals, and a customary international law of human rights has developed and has continued to grow.

The traditional law of responsibility for injury to aliens and the contemporary law of human rights have had separate growth and, originally, different jurisprudential underpinnings. Injury by a state to the nationals of another state implicates relations between those states, and responsibility for such injury was established early as a norm of customary international law. The injury to the person has been seen as an offense to the state of his nationality. The offense being to the state, the remedy for the violation also runs to the state, although the injured person may have to exhaust domestic remedies before the state of nationality can formally seek reparation for the offense. See sec. 713, Comments b, c; sec. 902(2) and Comment i to that section. Under this principle, the state is responsible as well for injury to juridical persons of foreign nationality. (As to the nationality of companies, see secs. 213, 414.)

The contemporary international law of human rights has developed largely since the Second World War. It is concerned with natural persons only, and it applies to all human beings, not to aliens alone. It reflects general acceptance that every individual should have rights in his or her society which the state should recognize, respect, and ensure. See sec. 701, Comment a. It reflects general acceptance, too, that how a state treats individual human beings, including its own citizens, in respect of their human rights, is not the state's own business alone and therefore exclusively within its "domestic jurisdiction," but is a matter of international concern and a proper subject for regulation by international law. One of the purposes for which the United Nations was created was "to achieve international co-operation ... in promoting and encouraging respect for human rights and fundamental freedoms for all without distinctions as to race, sex, language, or religion." The Universal Declaration of Human Rights, adopted by the United Nations General Assembly in 1948, proclaimed a series of political, civil, economic, social, and cultural rights as a universal standard, and the Declaration has been incorporated or reflected in national constitutions and has contributed to an international law of human rights. The Declaration was also the basis of two international agreements, the International Covenant on Civil and Political Rights and the International Covenant on Economic, Social and Cultural Rights. (The internationally recognized human rights included in the Declaration and the Covenants are summarized in sec. 701, Reporters' Note 6.) Numerous other international human rights agreements dealing with particular rights have been concluded and have been adhered to by many states. These agreements, and international concern for human rights reflected in other international instruments and in the practice of states, have led also to the development of some customary law of human rights. See sec. 702.

The difference in history and in jurisprudential origins between the older law of responsibility for injury to aliens and the newer law of human rights should not conceal their essential affinity and their increasing convergence. The law of responsibility to aliens posited and invoked an international standard of justice for individuals, even if dogmas of the international system limited the application of that standard to foreign nationals. That standard of justice, like contemporary human rights law, derived from historic conceptions of natural law, as reflected in the conscience of contemporary mankind and the major cultures and legal systems of the world. As the law of human rights developed, the law of responsibility for injury to aliens, as applied to natural persons, began to refer to violation of their "fundamental human rights," and states began to invoke contemporary human rights norms as the basis for claims for injury to their nationals. See sec. 711, Comment c and Reporters' Note 3.

The traditional law of responsibility for injury to aliens, however, retains independent vitality. It provides an additional foundation for protecting the human rights of foreign nationals, and affords protection also for injuries not seen as violations of human rights. The traditional law of responsibility for injury to aliens also continues to protect juridical persons, which do not have "human" rights.

The international law of the rights of aliens. The traditional law of state responsibility for denials of justice to aliens has been a subject of international controversy in recent decades, see sec. 712, Reporters' Note 1, but the principles governing responsibility, including those requiring compensation for economic injury to aliens, have not been undermined by that controversy or by the growth of the law of human rights. A state whose national suffers economic injury or other denial of justice by another state may make a claim against the offending state for that violation, whether or not the state might have claimed under the international law of human rights. The state of nationality may hold an offending state responsible also for injury to a juridical person, whether or not that injury might have constituted denial of human rights if the injured person had been a natural person. See Chapter 2.

The international law of human rights. Virtually all states are members of the United Nations and parties to its Charter, a legally binding international agreement. In Articles 55 and 56 of the Charter, all members "pledge themselves to take joint and separate action in cooperation with the [United Nations] Organization for the achievement of," inter alia, "universal respect for, and observance of, human rights and fundamental freedoms for all without distinction as to race, sex, language, or religion." The language imports legal obligation, but there has been no agreement or authoritative determination as to the character and extent of the obligation. Compare sec. 701, Comment d and Reporters' Note 4. Increasingly, the Charter provisions have been linked to the Universal Declaration of Human Rights, the legal character of which has also been debated. See sec. 701, Reporters' Notes 4 and 5. Few states would agree that any action by a state contrary to any provision of the Declaration is, for that reason alone, a violation of the Charter or of customary international law. On the other hand, almost all states would agree that some infringements of human rights enumerated in the Declaration are violations of the Charter or of customary international law. See sec. 702.

The international law of human rights includes also a number of international human rights agreements, some of which have been adhered to by many states. (As of 1987, the U.S. has adhered to very few. See … sec. 701, Comment e.)

The principal agreements are the International Covenant on Civil and Political Rights and the International Covenant on Economic, Social, and Cultural Rights. There are also numerous conventions dealing with particular rights.

...

International human rights law and agreements have the same status and the same binding character as other international law and agreements. However, international law generally is largely observed because violations directly affect the interests of states, which are alert to deter, prevent, or respond to violations. See Introductory Note to Part I, Chapter 1. Violations of the international law of human rights, on the other hand, generally injure the inhabitants of the violating state; ordinarily, other states are not directly affected by such violations and their concern for human rights in other states has been uneven. Moreover, states are generally reluctant to submit their actions in respect to human rights to scrutiny by other states. Special international "machinery" has been created to monitor compliance with international human rights law, but the effectiveness of those bodies and procedures in helping induce compliance has been variable. (The European Convention regime has had conspicuous success.) The condition of human rights varies widely even among states that have adhered to international human rights agreements.

Human rights in U.S. foreign relations law. The United Nations Charter and the Charter of the Organization of American States, both of which include human rights provisions, are treaties of the U.S. The human rights conventions to which the U.S. is a party (see sec. 701, Comment e …) are also treaties of the U.S. Obligations assumed by the U.S. in these agreements are law of the land, either directly if the provisions are self-executing or upon implementation by Congress. See sec. 111. The customary international law of human rights, sec. 702, is also law of the U.S. sec. 111(1). Federal statutes refer to "internationally recognized human rights" and have legislated national policy toward governments guilty of "consistent patterns of gross violations" of such rights. See sec. 702, Reporters' Note 10. The U.S. has frequently reiterated its acceptance of the Universal Declaration, and whatever legal character it has applies to the U.S.

Several major human rights agreements have been signed by the U.S. but as of 1987 not yet ratified. In 1978, President Carter transmitted to the Senate the International Covenant on Civil and Political Rights, the International Covenant on Economic, Social and Cultural Rights, the Convention on the Elimination of All Forms of Racial Discrimination, and the American Convention on Human Rights. In 1980, President Carter submitted to the Senate the Covenant on the Elimination of All Forms of Discrimination against Women. If the Senate consents and the President proceeds with ratification of these treaties, they will become law of the U.S. Even in the absence of ratification by the U.S., some provisions of these covenants and conventions reflect principles of customary international law and thus are a part of the law of the U.S. See sec. 702. The acts forbidden by the covenants and conventions usually are acts that are prohibited by the U.S. Constitution or by federal or State law; the obligations imposed on the U.S. by those instruments are in fact generally honored pursuant to federal or State law. See sec. 701, Reporters' Note 8. The principal safeguards for individual rights in the U.S. are those provided by the Constitution and laws of the U.S. and of the States. Much of that law is properly part of the foreign relations law of the U.S., since it "has substantial significance for the foreign relations of the U.S. or has other substantial international consequences." See sec. 1. At best, however, it is feasible to restate here only so much of that law as may directly implicate U.S. foreign relations, e.g., the constitutional rights of individuals in foreign relations contexts, the rights of citizens abroad, the rights of aliens. See Chapter 3 of this Part.

(The following texts are the specific statements of the American Law Institute as to what the law was in the U.S. at that time. The reader is advised to check the pocket part of the law book text (at the back of the book) for case law and legislative updates)

Sec. 1. Foreign Relations Law of the U.S.

The foreign relations law of the U.S., as dealt with in this Restatement, consists of

(a) international law as it applies to the U.S.; and

(b) domestic law that has substantial significance for the foreign relations of the U.S. or has other substantial international consequences.

Comment:

a. International law in U.S. foreign relations law. As a state in the international community of states, the U.S. is subject to international law, the law that governs relations between states.

Sec. 111. International law and agreements as law of the U.S.

(1) International law and international agreements of the U.S. are law of the U.S. and supreme over the law of the several States.

(2) Cases arising under international law or international agreements of the U.S. are within the Judicial Power of the U.S. and, subject to Constitutional and statutory limitations and requirements of justiciability, are within the jurisdiction of the federal courts.

(3) Courts in the U.S. are bound to give effect to international law and to international agreements of the U.S., except that a "non-self-executing" agreement will not be given effect as law in the absence of necessary implementation.

(4) An international agreement of the U.S. is "non-self-executing"

(a) if the agreement manifests an intention that it shall not become effective as domestic law without the enactment of implementing legislation,

(b) if the Senate in giving consent to a treaty, or Congress by resolution, requires implementing legislation, or

(c) if implementing legislation is constitutionally required.

Comment:

a. International law and agreements subject to the Constitution. In their character as law of the U.S., rules of international law and provisions of international agreements of the U.S. are subject to the Bill of Rights and other prohibitions, restrictions, and requirements of the Constitution, and cannot be given effect in violation of them. See secs. 115(3), 302(2) and 721. However, failure of the U.S. to carry out an obligation on the ground of its unconstitutionality will not relieve the U.S. of responsibility under international law. See sec. 115, Comment b, and sec. 311(3).

b. U.S. law as result of international obligation. A rule of international law or a provision of an international agreement derives its status as law in the U.S. from its character as an international legal obligation of the U.S. A rule of international law or an international agreement has no status as law of the U.S. if the U.S. is not in fact bound by it: for example, any rule of customary law from which the U.S. may have dissociated itself during the process of its formation (see Introductory Note to Part I, Chapter 1, sec. 102, Comment d, and sec. 103, Comment a), or a provision in a treaty that is invalid or has been terminated or suspended (see Part III, Chapter 4).

c. International law and agreements as law of the U.S. The proposition that international law and agreements are law in the U.S. is addressed largely to the courts. In appropriate cases they apply international law or agreements without the need of enactment by Congress or proclamation by the President. (But see sec. 115, Comment d, as to customary law inconsistent with a prior act of Congress.) Much customary law and many international agreements, however, do not have the quality of law for the courts in that they do not regulate activities, relations, or interests in the U.S. Some international agreements of the U.S. are non-self-executing and will not be applied as law by the courts until they are implemented by necessary legislation.

Subsection (3) and Comment h.

That international law and agreements of the U.S. are law of the U.S. means also that the President has the obligation and the necessary authority to take care that they be faithfully executed. U.S. Constitution, Article II, Section 2. But under the President's constitutional authority, as "sole organ of the nation in its external relations" or as Commander in Chief (s 1, Reporters' Note 2), the President has the power to take various measures including some that might constitute violations of international law by the U.S. See sec. 115, Reporters' Note 3.

d. International law and agreements as supreme federal law. Treaties made under the authority of the U.S., like the Constitution itself and the laws of the U.S., are expressly declared to be "supreme Law of the Land" by Article VI of the Constitution. International agreements of the U.S. other than treaties (see sec. 303), and customary international law, while not mentioned explicitly in the Supremacy Clause, are also federal law and as such are supreme over State law. Interpretations of international agreements by the U.S. Supreme Court are binding on the States. Customary international law is considered to be like common law in the U.S., but it is federal law. A determination of international law by the Supreme Court is binding on the States and on State courts. See sec. 112(2) and Comment a to that section.

Questions under international law or international agreements of the U.S. often arise in State courts. As law of the U.S., international law is also the law of every State, is a basis for the exercise of judicial authority by State courts, and is cognizable in cases in State courts, in the same way as other U.S. law. A final judgment or decree "rendered by the highest court of a State in which a decision could be had ... where the validity of a State statute is drawn in question on the ground of its being repugnant" to a treaty or other international agreement of the U.S., or to a principle of customary international law, is reviewable by the U.S. Supreme Court under 28 U.S.C. sec. 1257. A State "statute," for purposes of such review, includes a constitutional provision, a municipal ordinance, and a judicial or an administrative order of "legislative" character.

Sec. 321. Binding force of agreement

Every international agreement in force is binding upon the parties to it and must be performed by them in good faith.

Sec. 404. Universal jurisdiction to define and punish certain offenses

A state has jurisdiction to define and prescribe punishment for certain offenses recognized by the community of nations as of universal concern, such as piracy, slave trade, attacks on or hijacking of aircraft, genocide, war crimes, and perhaps certain acts of terrorism, even where none of the bases of jurisdiction indicated in sec. 402 is present.

Sec. 701. Obligation to respect human rights

A state is obligated to respect the human rights of persons subject to its jurisdiction

(a) that it has undertaken to respect by international agreement;

(b) that states generally are bound to respect as a matter of customary international law (s 702); and

(c) that it is required to respect under general principles of law common to the major legal systems of the world.

Comment:

a. Human rights defined. "Human rights" refers to freedoms, immunities, and benefits which, according to widely accepted contemporary values, every human being should enjoy in the society in which he or she lives. By international law and agreement states have recognized many specific human rights and assumed the obligation to respect them. The rights protected by customary international law are set forth in sec. 702. Rights protected by the principal international agreements are summarized in Reporters' Note 6.

b. Human rights and sources of international law. The international law of human rights has strong antecedents in natural law, in contemporary moral values, and in the constitutional law of states. Human rights principles come into international law by the same means and from the same sources as other international law, viz., as customary law, by international agreement, or from general principles of law common to the major legal systems of the world. See sec. 102. This chapter specifies human rights obligations deriving from customary law or international agreement; some obligations deriving from those sources may also be regarded as having been absorbed into international law as general principles common to the major legal systems. As of 1986, it has not been authoritatively determined whether any obligations to observe human rights, in addition to those included in clauses (a) and (b), have been absorbed into international law as general principles common to the major legal systems. See sec. 102, Comment b and Reporters' Note 7.

c. Human rights law as obligations between states. Like international agreements generally, international human rights agreements create legal obligations between the states parties, although the agreements are for the benefit of individuals, including nationals, residents, and others subject to the jurisdiction of the promisor state. Human rights obligations in customary international law generally are obligations to all other states. See sec. 702. Remedies for violations of human rights obligations are generally state to state (see sec. 703 and sec. 902(2)), but some international agreements also provide remedies to individuals whose human rights have been violated, or to individuals or non governmental bodies acting on their behalf. See sec. 703(3) and Comment c; sec. 906, Comment a and Reporters' Note 1.

d. Human rights obligations under United Nations Charter. Almost all states are parties to the United Nations Charter, which contains human rights obligations. There has been no authoritative determination of the full content of those obligations, but it is increasingly accepted that states parties to the Charter are legally obligated to respect some of the rights recognized in the Universal Declaration. See Introductory Note to this Part. A violation of the rights protected by customary law, sec. 702, also may be seen as a violation of the Charter. See Reporters' Note 4.

e. International human rights obligations of the U.S. The U.S. is bound by the international customary law of human rights. See sec. 702. It is a party to the United Nations Charter and the Charter of the Organization of American States, both of which include general human rights undertakings. The U.S. has also adhered to the Slavery Convention of 1926 and the Supplementary Convention on the Abolition of Slavery and the Slave Trade, the Convention on the Political Rights of Women, and the Protocol Relating to the Status of Refugees. See Introductory Note to this Part.

Reporters' Notes

1. Human rights law and sources of international law. Ordinarily, international law does not assume restrictions on state autonomy. But the universal acceptance of human rights in principle, and active international concern with human rights, has led to some readiness to conclude that states have assumed human rights obligations. There is a disposition to find legal obligation in indeterminate language about human rights in international agreements, e.g., the United Nations Charter (see Introductory Note to this Part). There is some willingness to find that the practice of states, perhaps under constitutional, political, or moral impetus, is practice with a sense of international legal obligation creating a customary international law of human rights, even though many states sometimes violate these rights, see sec. 102(2). Absorption into international law of principles common to national legal systems generally is only a secondary source of international law (s 102(4)), but there is a willingness to conclude that prohibitions common to the constitutions or laws of many states are general principles that have been absorbed into international law.

2. Practice creating customary human rights law. International human rights law governs relations between a state and its own inhabitants. Other states are only occasionally involved in monitoring such law through ordinary diplomatic practice. Therefore, the practice of states that is accepted as building customary international law of human rights includes some forms of conduct different from those that build customary international law generally. See sec. 102, Comment b. Practice accepted as building customary human rights law includes: virtually universal adherence to the United Nations Charter and its human rights provisions, and virtually universal and frequently reiterated acceptance of the Universal Declaration of Human Rights even if only in principle; virtually universal participation of states in the preparation and adoption of international agreements recognizing human rights principles generally, or particular rights; the adoption of human rights principles by states in regional organizations in Europe, Latin America, and Africa (see Introductory Note to this Part); general support by states for United Nations resolutions declaring, recognizing, invoking, and applying international human rights principles as international law; action by states to conform their national law or practice to standards or principles declared by international bodies, and the incorporation of human rights provisions, directly or by reference, in national constitutions and laws; invocation of human rights principles in national policy, in diplomatic practice, in international organization activities and actions; and other diplomatic communications or action by states reflecting the view that certain practices violate international human rights law, including condemnation and other adverse state reactions to violations by other states. The International Court of Justice and the International Law Commission have recognized the existence of customary human rights law. See Case Concerning the Barcelona Traction, Light & Power Co., Ltd. (Belgium v Spain), [1970] I.C.J. Rep. 32, quoted in sec. 703, Reporters' Note 3; sec. 702, Reporters' Notes 3, 4. See, generally McDougal, Lasswell and Chen, Human Rights and World Public Order 266 et seq., 313 et seq. (1980). Some of these practices may also support the conclusion that particular human rights have been absorbed into international law as general principles common to the major state legal systems. See sec. 702, Reporters' Note 1.

3. Human rights law as obligations among states. Like multilateral agreements generally, an international human rights agreement creates rights and obligations between each party and every other party. Most multilateral agreements, however, are essentially networks of bilateral agreements, creating obligations between each pair of parties as regards their particular interests inter se, e.g., as to trade or communication

between them. In such cases, remedies also are essentially bilateral, by the state victim of a violation against the violating state. Human rights agreements, however, are more genuinely multilateral. The obligations run to all parties equally and do not ordinarily engage the interests of one state more than another; unless otherwise provided, all states parties have the same remedies for violations. See sec. 703.

Ordinarily, customary law, too, creates obligations between particular states; for example, a violation of the immunity of a diplomat (s 464) is effectively an offense to the diplomat's state, not to states generally, and states other than the one directly offended do not ordinarily invoke remedies for such a violation. See sec. 902, Comment a. The customary international law of human rights, however, creates obligations by each state to all other states (erga omnes), so that a violation by a state of the rights of persons subject to its jurisdiction is a breach of obligation to all other states. In practice, states may not see fit to vindicate such norms except on behalf of persons with whom they identify in some way, e.g., their nationals, or minorities with which they have ethnic, cultural, or other links. In principle, however, every state can pursue remedies against any other state that commits a violation of the rights under customary law of persons subject to its jurisdiction. See sec. 703(2) and Reporters' Note 2 to that section.

4. Human rights obligations under United Nations Charter. It has been argued that the general pledge of members in the Charter, Introductory Note to this Part, has been made definite by the Universal Declaration, and that failure by any member to respect the rights recognized in the Declaration is a violation of the Charter. Alternatively, it has been urged, the Charter, the Universal Declaration, other international resolutions and declarations, and other practice of states have combined to create a customary international law of human rights requiring every state to respect the rights set forth in the Declaration. There are indeed numerous United Nations resolutions and statements referring, for example, to "the duty of states to fully and faithfully observe the provisions of the Universal Declaration." Art. 11, G.A. Res. 1904, 18 U.N. GAOR Supp. No. 15, at 35. See, generally, United Nations Action in the Field of Human Rights, U.N. Doc. ST/HR/2/Rev. 1, 8–15 (1983); McDougal, Lasswell and Chen, Reporters' Note 2, 325 et seq.

5. Human rights provisions of United Nations Charter in U.S. law. In Sei Fujii v California, 38 Cal.2d 718, 722–25, 242 P.2d 617, 621–22 (1952), a lower court held that the human rights articles of the United Nations Charter had become supreme law of the land in the U.S. and invalidated State law precluding the ownership of land by certain aliens on account of their race. The Supreme Court of California upheld the judgment on the ground that the State law violated the Equal Protection Clause of the Fourteenth Amendment, but expressly rejected the lower court's reliance on the United Nations Charter provision. The court observed that the Charter provisions "lack the mandatory quality and definiteness which would indicate an intent to create justiciable rights in private persons immediately upon ratification. Instead, they are framed as a promise of future action by the member nation." See also Hitai v Immigration and Naturalization Service, 343 F.2d 466, 468 (2d Cir.) certiorari denied, 382 U.S. 816, 86 S.Ct. 36, 15 L.Ed.2d 63 (1965) (Charter provision not self-executing and does not invalidate provision of immigration law); also Vlissidis v Anadell, 262 F.2d 398, 400 (7th Cir. 1959) (United Nations Charter does not supersede quota system of U.S. immigration law); Spiess v C. Itoh & Co. (America), Inc., 643 F.2d 353, 363 (5th Cir. 1981) vacated, 457 U.S. 1128, 102 S.Ct. 2951, 73 L.Ed.2d 1344 (1982) (Title VII of Civil Rights Act not intended to override treaty provisions permitting New York subsidiary of Japanese corporation to hire only Japanese citizens for managerial and technical positions; United Nations Charter not self-executing and Title VII not designed to implement Charter and does not partake of Charter's character as superior law).

6. Internationally recognized human rights. The binding character of the Universal Declaration of Human Rights continues to be debated, Introductory Note to this Part, and Reporters' Notes 4 and 5, but the Declaration has become the accepted general articulation of recognized rights. With some variations, the same rights are recognized by the two principal covenants, the Covenant on Civil and Political Rights and the Covenant on Economic, Social and Cultural Rights. The particular conventions (Introductory Note to this Part) also protect rights that are recognized in the Universal Declaration.

The rights recognized in the Universal Declaration include: the right to life, liberty, and security of the person; freedom from slavery or servitude; freedom from torture or cruel, inhuman or degrading treatment or punishment; the right to recognition as a person before the law; equality before the law and equal protection of the law; the right to a remedy for violations of fundamental rights, granted by law; freedom from arbitrary arrest, detention or exile; a fair and public trial for persons charged with crime, with guarantees necessary for one's defense; the presumption of innocence; the right to be convicted only according to law and to freedom from the application of ex post facto law; freedom from arbitrary interference with privacy, family, home or correspondence, and legal protection against such interference; freedom of movement and residence within a country; the right to leave any country and the right to seek asylum; the right to a nationality and not to be arbitrarily deprived of one's nationality, and the right to change one's nationality; the right to marry and found a family, and equality of men and women in marriage and its dissolution; the right to own property and not to be arbitrarily deprived of it; freedom of thought, conscience, and religion, freedom of opinion and expression, assembly and association. The Universal Declaration includes some political rights, for example, the right to take part in government and have equal access to the public service, which are accepted as being human rights for every person but only in relation to "his country." Art. 21(1), (2). (Compare the right of everyone to return "to his country." Art. 13(2).) The Declaration also includes certain "economic and social rights," for example, the right to social security; the right to work, to free choice of employment and protection against unemployment, to just remuneration and equal pay for equal work, and the right to join a trade union; the right to rest and leisure; to a standard of living adequate for oneself and one's family; to education, which at elementary levels must be free and compulsory. The rights set forth in the Declaration are not subject to "distinctions of any kind, such as race, colour, sex, language, religion, political or other opinion, national or social origin, property, birth or other status." Art. 2. Article 29(2) provides: "In the exercise of his rights and freedoms, everyone shall be subject only to such limitations as are determined by law solely for the purpose of securing due recognition and respect for the rights and freedoms of others and of meeting the just requirements of morality, public order and the general welfare in a democratic society."

The rights set forth in the Declaration are restated, generally, in greater detail and with legal precision in the Covenant on Civil and Political Rights and the Covenant on Economic, Social and Cultural Rights. In the former, each state party "undertakes to respect and to ensure to all individuals within its territory and subject to its jurisdiction the rights recognized in the present Covenant." Art. 2(1). In the Covenant on Economic, Social and Cultural Rights, each state party "undertakes to take steps ... to the maximum of its available resources, with a view to achieving progressively the full realization of the rights recognized in the present Covenant." Art. 2(1). The Covenants include some rights not mentioned in the Universal Declaration. Both Covenants recognize a right of all peoples to self-determination, and all peoples may "freely dispose of their natural wealth and resources without prejudice to any obligations arising out of international economic cooperation, based upon the principle of mutual benefit, and international law." (Art. 1 of each of the Covenants.) The Covenant on Civil and Political Rights forbids imprisonment for inability to fulfill a contractual obligation, a right not mentioned in the Declaration. On the other hand, the right to own property and not to be arbitrarily deprived of it (Universal Declaration, Art. 17) is not expressly mentioned in either Covenant, but that omission has not been construed to be a rejection of the right. See sec. 711, Comment d; also sec. 702, Comment k. A number of the civil-political rights are expressly made subject to limitations; e.g., the freedom of movement and residence within a country, and the right to leave a country, "shall not be subject to any restrictions except those which are provided by law, are necessary to protect national security, public order (ordre public), public health or morals or the rights and freedoms of others." Art. 12(3). The rights in the Covenant on Economic, Social and Cultural Rights are subject "only to such limitations as are determined by law only in so far as this may be compatible with the nature of these rights and solely for the purpose of promoting the general welfare in a democratic society." Art. 4. Most civil-political rights are subject to derogation during public emergency. For a guide to the interpretation of the Covenant on Civil and Political Rights, see Henkin, ed., The International Bill of Rights: The Covenant on Civil and Political Rights (1981).

International human rights principles generally, the Universal Declaration, and, notably, the International Covenant on Civil and Political Rights address the rights of natural persons only. The Covenant on Economic, Social, and Cultural Rights, however, recognizes some rights for trade unions. Art. 8(1). Compare the European Convention on Human Rights, some of whose provisions would apply to juridical persons also; Article 25 of that Convention expressly accords a right of petition to "any person, non governmental organization or group of individuals claiming to be a victim of a violation." See Buergenthal, "To Respect and to Ensure: State Obligations and Permissible Derogations" in Henkin, ed., The International Bill of Rights, supra, 72, 73.

7. International human rights standards as source of U.S. law. Courts in the U.S. have increasingly looked to international human rights standards as law in the U.S. or as a guide to U.S. law. See cases cited in sec. 702, Reporters' Notes 5 and 6; compare Reporters' Note 5 to this

section. There are numerous references to the Universal Declaration, e.g., Zemel v Rusk, 381 U.S. 1, 14, n. 13, 85 S.Ct. 1271, 1279, n. 13, 14 L.Ed.2d 179 (1963); Kennedy v Mendoza-Martinez, 372 U.S. 144, 161, n. 16, 83 S.Ct. 554, 564, n. 16, 9 L.Ed.2d 644 (1965). Several cases have cited the United Nations Standard Minimum Rules for the Treatment of Prisoners (10 GAOR, U.N. Doc. A/Conf. 6/C.1/ L.1, 1955), to help determine rights under the due process and the cruel and unusual punishment clauses of the U.S. Constitution. See Estelle v Gamble, 429 U.S. 97, 103–104 and n. 8, 97 S.Ct. 285, 290–291 and n. 8, 50 L.Ed.2d 251 (1976); Detainees of Brooklyn House of Detention for Men v Malcolm, 520 F.2d 392, 396 (2d Cir. 1975); Morgan v Lavallee, 526 F.2d 221 (2d Cir. 1975); Lareau v Manson, 507 F.Supp. 1177, 1187, and n. 9 (D.Conn. 1980), affirmed in part, 651 F.2d 96 (2d Cir. 1981); see also U.S. ex rel. Wolfish v Levi, 439 F.Supp. 114, n. 20 (S.D.N.Y. 1977), affirmed in part and reversed in part, 573 F.2d 118 (2d Cir. 1978), reversed, Bell v Wolfish, 441 U.S. 520, 99 S.Ct. 1861, 60 L.Ed.2d 447 (1979). In Sterling v Cupp, 290 Or. 611, 625 P.2d 123 (1981), the Supreme Court of Oregon enjoined prison officials from assigning female guards to certain duties in relation to male prisoners, citing the United Nations standards and other international human rights instruments to support its conclusion that "needlessly harsh, degrading, or dehumanizing treatment of prisoners" violated the Oregon Constitution. 625 P.2d at 131, n. 21.

8. Effect of future U.S. ratification of principal international covenants. Adherence by the U.S. to the principal international covenants would not effect any major change in the rights enjoyed by inhabitants of the U.S. under the U.S. and State constitutions and laws. The International Covenant on Civil and Political Rights requires states parties to the Covenant to respect and ensure rights generally similar to those protected by the U.S. Constitution. Some provisions in the Covenant parallel express constitutional provisions, for example, the freedoms protected by the First Amendment, and the prohibition on double jeopardy. Other provisions in the Covenant parallel rights that the Supreme Court has found to be constitutionally protected, e.g., the right to vote, Harper v Virginia Bd. of Elections, 383

Court Citations for Section 701 (Cumulative Supplement 1999)

Sec. 701. Obligation to Respect Human Rights

...

S.D.Fla. 1992. Cit. in ftn. Foreign leader who was captured during U.S. Armed Forces intervention in Panama and convicted in the U.S. of narcotics-related offenses raised the question during his sentencing hearing of his prisoner of war status as that status related to his confinement. The court held that although defendant was a prisoner of war, he could be incarcerated in a federal penitentiary as long as he was afforded the full benefits of the Geneva Convention Relative to the Treatment of Prisoners of War (Geneva III). The court stated that, were it to decide the matter, it would almost certainly find that Geneva III was self-executing and provided defendant with a right of action in a U.S. court for violation of its provisions and that, even if Geneva III was not self-executing, the U.S. was still obligated to honor its international commitment. U.S. v Noriega, 808 F.Supp. 791, 798.

D.Mass. 1995. Cit. in disc. as secs. 701–702. Nine expatriate citizens of Guatemala and an American citizen brought separate suits against Guatemala's former minister of defense, seeking compensatory and punitive damages for devastating injuries they suffered from conduct of Guatemalan military forces. The complaints were served upon defendant while he was attending graduate school at Harvard. This court entered default judgment for eight of the nine expatriates and for the American plaintiff, holding, inter alia, that the court had jurisdiction under 28 U.S.C. sec. 1350, the Alien Tort Claims Act. The court also determined that because it found jurisdiction over the expatriates' claims under the Alien Tort Statute, and over the American plaintiff's claims under the Torture Victim Protection Act, it need not definitively decide whether their claims would support the exercise of jurisdiction independently under the federal question statute, 28 U.S.C. sec. 1331. Xuncax v Gramajo, 886 F.Supp. 162, 184.

...

Sec. 702. Customary International Law of Human Rights

A state violates international law if, as a matter of state policy, it practices, encourages, or condones

(a) genocide,

(b) slavery or slave trade,

(c) the murder or causing the disappearance of individuals,

(d) torture or other cruel, inhuman, or degrading treatment or punishment,

(e) prolonged arbitrary detention,

(f) systematic racial discrimination, or

(g) a consistent pattern of gross violations of internationally recognized human rights.

Comment:

a. Scope of customary law of human rights. This section includes as customary law only those human rights whose status as customary law is generally accepted (as of 1987) and whose scope and content are generally agreed. See sec. 701, Reporters' Note 6. The list is not necessarily complete, and is not closed: human rights not listed in this section may have achieved the status of customary law, and some rights might achieve that status in the future. See Comments j, k, and l.

b. State policy as violation of customary law. In general, a state is responsible for acts of officials or official bodies, national or local, even if the acts were not authorized by or known to the responsible national authorities, indeed even if expressly forbidden by law, decree or instruction. sec. 207, Comment d. The violations of human rights cited in this section, however, are violations of customary international law only if practiced, encouraged, or condoned by the government of a state as official policy. A state is not responsible under this section for a violation of human rights by an official that was not authorized, encouraged, or condoned by the responsible governmental authorities of the state. (Compare the different rule as to state responsibility for official injuries to nationals of another state, sec. 711, Comment a and sec. 207, Comment d.)

A government may be presumed to have encouraged or condoned acts prohibited by this section if such acts, especially by its officials, have been repeated or notorious and no steps have been taken to prevent them or to punish the perpetrators. That state law prohibits the violation and provides generally effective remedies is strong evidence that the violation is not state policy. A state is not ordinarily responsible under this section for violations of human rights by individuals, such as individual acts of torture or of racial discrimination. A state would be responsible if, as a matter of state policy, it required, encouraged, or condoned such private violations, but mere failure to enact laws prohibiting private violations of human rights would not ordinarily constitute encouragement or condonation. International law requires a state to outlaw genocide, slavery, and the slave trade, and the state would be responsible under this section if it failed to prohibit them or to enforce the prohibition.

Even when a state is not responsible under this section because a violation is not state policy, the state may be responsible under some international agreement that requires the state to prevent the violation. For example, under the Covenant on Civil and Political Rights, a state party is guilty of a violation if any of the acts listed in this section is perpetrated by officials, persons acting under color of law, or other persons for whose acts the state is responsible under sec. 207, even when their acts are contrary to state law or policy. See also sec. 207, Comment a. And see Reporters' Note 2 to this section.

c. Customary law of human rights as U.S. law. The customary law of human rights is part of the law of the U.S. to be applied as such by State as well as federal courts. See sec. 111(1).

. . .

n. Customary law of human rights and jus cogens. Not all human rights norms are peremptory norms (jus cogens), but those in clauses (a) to (f) of this section are, and an international agreement that violates them is void. See sec. 331(2).

o. Responsibility to all states (erga omnes). Violations of the rules stated in this section are violations of obligations to all other states and any state may invoke the ordinary remedies available to a state when its rights under customary law are violated. See sec. 703(2) and Comment b to that section, and sec. 902(2) and Comment a to that section.

Reporters' Notes

1. Customary law of human rights. This section adopts the view that customary international law prohibits the particular human rights violations indicated, if the violations are state policy. This view is accepted by virtually all states; with the exception of the Republic of South Africa in respect of apartheid, no state claims the right to commit the practices set forth in this section as state policy, and few, if any, would deny that they are violations of international law. Other rights may already have become customary law and international law may develop to include additional rights. It has been argued that customary international law is already more comprehensive than here indicated and forbids violation of any of the rights set forth in the Universal Declaration. See sec. 701, Reporters' Note 4; McDougal, Lasswell, and Chen, Human Rights and World Public Order 273–74, 325–27 (1980); Waldock, "Human Rights in Contemporary International Law and the Significance of the European Convention," in The European Convention on Human Rights 15 (1963) (British Inst. Int'l & Comp. L., Int'l L. Ser. No. 11).

The practice of states has established the principles of this section in customary law, as indicated in the following notes. Clauses (a) through (e) (and perhaps (f)) also reflect general principles common to the major legal systems that may have been absorbed into international law. See sec. 102(4). The violations listed in this section are also cited as examples in U.S. legislation denying benefits to states guilty of "consistent patterns of gross violation of internationally recognized human rights." See Reporters' Note 10. See also address of Secretary of State Vance, 76 Dep't State Bull. 505 (1977).

That customary international law protects some human rights was suggested in the Nuremberg Charter, under which the Nazi defendants were charged, inter alia, with crimes against humanity: namely, murder, extermination, enslavement, deportation, and other inhumane acts committed against any civilian population, before or during the war; or persecutions on political, racial or religious grounds in execution of or in connection with any crime within the jurisdiction of the Tribunal, whether or not in violation of the domestic law of the country where perpetrated.

See Charter of the International Military Tribunal, August 8, 1945, 59 Stat. 1546, 1547, 82 U.N.T.S. 279; Jackson, The Nuremberg Case (1947); see generally Taylor, Nuremberg Trials, War Crimes and International Law, International Conciliation No. 450 (1949). The principles of international law recognized in the Nuremberg Charter and Judgment were unanimously affirmed by the United Nations General Assembly in a resolution proposed by the U.S. G.A. Res. 95, 1 GAOR UN Doc. A/64/Add.1, at 188 (1946).

2. State responsibility for private violations of rights. Under customary law, the state is responsible for the acts enumerated in this section when committed by its officials as state policy, or, when committed by private persons, if they were encouraged or condoned as state policy. By contrast, under the Covenant on Civil and Political Rights, a state is required not only to respect but also to "ensure" the rights recognized by the Covenant, suggesting an obligation to act to prevent their violation whether by officials or by private persons. See Art. 2. Article 20 expressly requires parties to the Covenant to prohibit by law war propaganda and advocacy of national, racial, or religious hatred. See sec. 701, Reporters' Note 8.

A violation of rights covered by this section is committed as a matter of state policy when it is required or encouraged by law, clear custom, or usage, or by some official act or statement of a responsible high official. Evidence of condonation might be found in failure to take steps to punish acts of officials that are common or notorious. See Comment b.

Under this section, a state is responsible for the acts of individual officials that violate the indicated human rights only if the acts were in furtherance of state policy. A different formulation asserts that a state is responsible for the acts of its officials in such human rights cases as in other cases even if the action was not state policy (see Comment b), but there is no violation, and therefore no responsibility, where the state provides an effective domestic remedy. The formulation adopted in this Restatement may produce a different result where the state remedy fails or is not effective for reasons of general domestic jurisprudence, rather than as the result of a state policy to cover up the human rights violation.

Court Citations to Restatement, Third

D.N.J. 1998. Aliens who sought asylum and who were detained at a New Jersey facility sued the INS and others, alleging mistreatment while detained at that facility and asserting claims under federal, state, and international law. This court granted in part and denied in part defendants' motions to dismiss, holding, inter alia, that the mental and physical abuses allegedly inflicted upon plaintiffs violated the international human rights norm of the right to be free from cruel, inhuman, and degrading treatment, and that the Alien Tort Claims Act conferred subject matter jurisdiction. Jama v U.S. I.N.S., 22 F.Supp.2d 353, 363.

Sec. 703. Remedies for Violation of Human Rights Obligations

(1) A state party to an international human rights agreement has, as against any other state party violating the agreement, the remedies generally available for violation of an international agreement, as well as any special remedies provided by the agreement.

(2) Any state may pursue international remedies against any other state for a violation of the customary international law of human rights (s 702).

(3) An individual victim of a violation of a human rights agreement may pursue any remedy provided by that agreement or by other applicable international agreements.

Comment:

a. Remedies for violation of international human rights obligations. Under international law, a breach of an international obligation, whether deriving from customary law or from international agreement, gives rise to international remedies against the violating state. These remedies include the right to make an international claim; to resort to the International Court of Justice or other international tribunal to whose jurisdiction the complaining and responding states have submitted; and in some circumstances to some measures of self-help. See secs. 901–905. For this purpose, human rights agreements are no different from other international agreements. Unless the human rights agreement provides or clearly implies otherwise, the ordinary remedies are available to any state party against a state party violating the agreement, even if the violation did not affect nationals of the claimant state or any other particular interest of that state. Whether a state may intercede to provide diplomatic protection to an individual who is not its national, see Comment b and Reporters' Notes 2 and 4.

Some international human rights agreements provide for special "implementing machinery," for example complaint before an international human rights committee. See Reporters' Note 2. Unless the agreement provides or clearly implies the contrary, such special remedies generally supplement rather than replace the traditional remedies between states.

b. Remedies for violation of customary law of human rights. Since the obligations of the customary law of human rights are erga omnes (obligations to all states), sec. 702, Comment o, any state may pursue remedies for their violation, even if the individual victims were not nationals of the complaining state and the violation did not affect any other particular interest of that state. For the remedies available to individual victims against the state or state officials, see Comment c. For remedies against individuals charged with commission of universal crimes, including some that would constitute violations under this section if the state were responsible for them, see sec. 404.

c. Remedies of individual victims. In general, individuals do not have direct international remedies against a state violating their human rights except where such remedies are provided by international agreement. See sec. 906. Whether they have a remedy under the law of a state depends on that state's law. See Reporters' Note 7. International human rights agreements generally require a state party to provide such remedies. See, e.g., International Covenant on Civil and Political Rights, Article 2(3). Failure to provide such remedies would constitute an additional violation of the agreement. Lack of an effective remedy under state law for violation of the customary law of human rights might itself be evidence that a violation of rights is state policy, "systematic," or part of a "consistent pattern of gross violations" for purposes of sec. 702.

d. Exhaustion of domestic remedies. A state may pursue formal, bilateral remedies under Subsections (1) and (2) only after the individual claiming to be a victim of a human rights violation has exhausted available remedies under the domestic law of the accused state. Compare sec. 713, Comment b, as regards remedies for injury to a state's nationals by another state; see sec. 902, Comment i. International agreements providing remedies to individuals, Subsection (3) and Comment c, also generally require that the individual first exhaust domestic remedies. That requirement is met if it is shown that none is available or that it would be futile to pursue them. The individual's failure to exhaust remedies is not an obstacle to informal intercession by a state on behalf of an individual, to unilateral "sanctions" by a state against another for human rights violations, or to multilateral measures against violators by United Nations bodies or international financial institutions. See Comments f and g and Reporters' Note 10, and sec. 702, Reporters' Note 10.

e. Humanitarian intervention to rescue victims or suppress human rights violations. It is increasingly accepted that a state may take steps to rescue victims or potential victims in an action strictly limited to that purpose and not likely to involve disproportionate destruction of life or property in the state where the rescue takes place. Whether a state may intervene with military force in the territory of another state without its consent, not to rescue the victims but to prevent or terminate human rights violations, is not agreed or authoritatively determined. Such intervention might be acceptable if taken pursuant to resolution of a United Nations body or of a regional organization such as the Organization of American States. See sec. 905.

f. State sanctions for human rights violations by another state. A state may criticize another state for failure to abide by recognized international human rights standards, and may shape its trade, aid or other national policies so as to dissociate itself from the violating state or to influence that state to discontinue the violations.

g. Consideration by United Nations bodies. Remedies for violation of human rights include possible consideration by international bodies acting within their jurisdiction, notably the United Nations General Assembly, the Economic and Social Council, the Commission on Human Rights, and even the Security Council when "the continuance of . . . the situation is likely to endanger the maintenance of international peace and security." See United Nations Charter, Articles 34, 36. A charge that a state had violated human rights may be brought to such bodies by any member of the United Nations in accordance with the rules and procedures of the Organization.

. . .

5. Remedies of individual victims. The principal international human rights agreements have optional provisions for individual complaints. Under the Optional Protocol to the International Covenant on Civil and Political Rights, the Human Rights Committee may receive and consider private "communications" alleging violation of rights under the Covenant. See also Art. 14 of the Convention on the Elimination of All Forms of Racial Discrimination; European Convention, Art. 25. In the American Convention, the provision for private complaints is not optional; under Article 44, any person, group of persons, or non governmental entity may lodge complaints with the Inter-American Commission on Human Rights alleging violation by any state party. The African Convention also provides for communications "other than those of States" which the African Commission may decide to consider. Arts. 55-59. See also the procedure for considering individual complaints of a "consistent pattern of gross violations" by a working group of the Sub commission on Prevention of Discrimination and Protection of Minorities of the United Nations Commission on Human Rights, pursuant to Res. 1503 of the U.N. Economic and Social Council, sec. 702, Reporters' Note 10. For discussion of the legal character of the rights of the individual under international human rights law, see Henkin, "International Human Rights as 'Rights,'" 1 Cardozo L.Rev. 425, 438 (1979).

6. Exhaustion of domestic remedies. Exhaustion of remedies is expressly made a precondition for consideration of an interstate complaint under the International Covenant on Civil and Political Rights, Art. 41(c), and the Convention on the Elimination of All Forms of Racial Discrimination, Art. 11. It is a precondition for consideration of private complaints under the Optional Protocol to the Covenant (Art. 5) and Art. 14(7) of the Racial Discrimination Convention. See also the American Convention, Art. 46(a); the European Convention, Art. 26; the African Convention, Arts. 50, 56(b). Cf. Parratt v Taylor, 451 U.S. 527, 101 S.Ct. 1908, 68 L.Ed.2d 420 (1981) (no civil rights action for deprivation of property by State officials where complainant did not avail himself of State remedy). See sec. 713, Comment f and Reporters' Note 5.

7. Individual remedies under U.S. law. Since 1790, the U.S. district courts have had jurisdiction "of a civil action by an alien for a tort only, committed in violation of the law of nations." 28 U.S.C. sec. 1350. In Filartiga v Pena-Irala, 630 F.2d 876 (2d Cir. 1980), the court of appeals held that under that statute the district court had jurisdiction of a suit in tort by an alien against a Paraguayan official alleged to have tortured the plaintiff's brother to death, since such torture was a violation of the law of nations. See sec. 702, Reporters' Note 5. On remand, the district court awarded punitive as well as actual damages, 577 F.Supp. 860 (E.D.N.Y. 1984). But cf. Tel-Oren v Libyan Arab Republic, 517 F.Supp. 542 (D.D.C. 1981), affirmed, 726 F.2d 774 (D.C.Cir. 1984), certiorari denied, 470 U.S. 1003, 105 S.Ct. 1354, 84 L.Ed.2d 377 (1985), dismissing a suit by victims of a terrorist attack on an Israeli bus, the district court ruling, inter alia, that sec. 1350 does not support jurisdiction unless international law or a treaty of the U.S. clearly contemplated an individual remedy for the violation. See also Rodriguez-Fernandez v Wilkinson, 505 F.Supp. 787 (D.Kan. 1980), affirmed, 654 F.2d 1382 (10th Cir. 1981), sec. 702, Reporters' Note 6, which held that prolonged and arbitrary detention was "judicially remediable as a violation of international law," and a detained alien could seek a writ of habeas corpus for his release. (The court of appeals affirmed on the ground that detention in the circumstances was not authorized by Congress.) And see Fernandez-Roque v Smith, sec. 702, Reporters' Note 6, which assumed the right of an individual to object to detention as a violation of international law but refused to enjoin a violation of international law committed under the authority of the Attorney General. See generally Henkin, "The Constitution and U.S. Sovereignty: A Century of Chinese Exclusion and Its Progeny," 100 Harv.L. Rev. 853, 883-85 (1987). Violations of international law were also asserted in cases involving detention of Cubans or Haitians not lawfully admitted to the U.S., but the cases were decided under U.S. domestic law. See, e.g., Jean v Nelson, 727 F.2d 957 (11th Cir. 1984) (en banc), affirmed on other grounds, 472 U.S. 846, 105 S.Ct. 2992, 86 L.Ed.2d 664 (1985); Soroa-Gonzales v Civiletti, 515 F.Supp. 1049, 1054 n. 2 (N.D.Ga. 1981), reversed, 734 F.2d 576 (11th Cir. 1984).

8. Humanitarian intervention. Since 1945, the law as to humanitarian intervention has turned largely on the interpretation of Article 2(4) of the United Nations Charter and its effect on prior customary law. Article 2(4) obligates member states "to refrain in their international relations from the threat or use of force against the territorial integrity or political independence of any state, or in any other manner inconsistent with the Purposes of the United Nations." Missions strictly for rescue, such as that by Belgium and the U.S. in Stanleyville, the Congo, in 1965, or by Israel at Entebbe, Uganda, in 1976, were commonly thought not to violate Article 2(4), either because they did not involve the "use of force," or were not against "the territorial integrity or political independence" of the target state, within the meaning of Article 2(4). It is

far more difficult to justify an implied exception to Article 2(4) that would permit a use of force otherwise contrary to that Article on the ground that the purpose is to suppress or prevent violations of human rights. See Brownlie, International Law and the Use of Force by States 301 (1963); Lillich, ed., Humanitarian Intervention and the United Nations (1973); Lillich, "Humanitarian Intervention: A Reply to Dr. Brownlie and a Plea for Constructive Alternatives," in Moore, ed., Law and Civil War in the Modern World 229 (1974). Of course, if the violation of human rights were itself accomplished or accompanied by a use of armed force in violation of Article 2(4), the Charter would permit the use of force in individual or collective self defense under Article 51, or pursuant to appropriate United Nations authorization. See sec. 905(2) and Comment g to that section.

9. State criticism and sanctions for violations by other states. Although states occasionally reject charges that they are violating human rights as interference in their internal affairs, such charges are not unlawful intervention or other improper interference under international law. Virtually every state has criticized some other state for its human rights practices, both directly and by statement or vote in international bodies. See, e.g., the numerous resolutions condemning apartheid in South Africa, approved by virtually all the members of the United Nations, e.g., G.A. Res. 1761, 17 U.N. GAOR Supp. No. 17, at 9; see also Henkin, "International Human Rights and 'Domestic Jurisdiction,'" Reporters' Note 2.

U.S. legislation requires the Department of State to publish annual reports on the condition of human rights in all countries, and provides for denial of assistance, loans, or trade benefits to countries guilty of a "consistent pattern of gross violations" of human rights.

...

Sec. 721. Applicability of Constitutional Safeguards

The provisions of the U.S. Constitution safeguarding individual rights generally control the U.S. government in the conduct of its foreign relations as well as in domestic matters, and generally limit governmental authority whether it is exercised in the U.S. or abroad, and whether such authority is exercised unilaterally or by international agreement.

Comment:

a. U.S. foreign relations subject to constitutional restraints. Any exercise of authority by the U.S. in the conduct of foreign relations is subject to the Bill of Rights and other constitutional restraints protecting individual rights. That principle applies equally to authority exercised pursuant to powers expressed in the Constitution, for example the power of Congress to regulate commerce with foreign nations (Article I, Section 8), as to foreign affairs powers not enumerated in the Constitution but inherent in the U.S. "as necessary concomitants of nationality." U.S. v Curtiss-Wright Export Corp., 299 U.S. 304, 318, 57 S.Ct. 216, 220, 81 L.Ed. 255 (1936); see sec. 1, Reporters' Note 1. Treaties and other international agreements are also subject to such constitutional restraints. See Reporters' Note 1.

b. Applicability of Constitution outside U.S. territory. The Constitution governs the exercise of authority by the U.S. government over U.S. citizens outside U.S. territory, for example on the high seas, and even on foreign soil. Although the matter has not been definitely adjudicated, the Constitution probably governs also at least some exercises of authority by the U.S. in respect of some aliens abroad. See sec. 722, Reporters' Note 16.

Sec. 722. Rights of Aliens

(1) An alien in the U.S. is entitled to the guarantees of the U.S. Constitution other than those expressly reserved for citizens.

(2) Under Subsection (1), an alien in the U.S. may not be denied the equal protection of the laws, but equal protection does not preclude reasonable distinctions between aliens and citizens, or between different categories of aliens.

Comment:

a. Constitutional rights of aliens. The Bill of Rights of the U.S. Constitution (Amendments I–X) declares the rights of persons, not of citizens only. Aliens in the U.S. therefore enjoy, notably, the freedoms of speech, press, religion, and assembly (Amendment I), the rights of privacy and freedom from unreasonable arrest and search or seizure (Amendment IV), the safeguards for fair trial in criminal process (Amendments V, VI, and VIII), the due process protections for life, liberty, and property (Amendment V), the right to jury trial in civil cases (Amendment VII). Aliens are also protected from slavery (Amendment XIII). Unlike citizens, however, aliens may be subject to deportation, and aliens admitted other than for permanent residence are subject to the conditions of their entry.

APPENDIX J: U.S. CASE LAW AND NON U.S. CASES INVOLVING THE U.S. AND INTERNATIONAL HUMAN RIGHTS LAW

Prepared by H. Victor Condé and Robert Savage, Juris Doctors, International Human Rights Lawyers, with assistance from William Luke Gilbert, Law Student

U.S. Courts have been involved in and often are the center of national attention in struggling with human rights issues since the beginning of this nation. Both federal and state courts have had to research human rights law from a variety of sources and apply it to situations that have occurred both in the U.S. and elsewhere around the globe. In the broadest sense, famous cases such as the *Dred Scott* decision, the *Amistad* case, *Gideon v Wainwright*, *Miranda v Arizona*, and *Brown v Board of Education* all involved human rights, but were decided on the basis of historical U.S. constitutional, statutory, and common law, with no international human rights laws, in the modern sense, being considered.

In the past fifty years, U.S. courts across the land have been confronted with legal issues of international magnitude or with cases in which lawyers have based their claims in whole or part on international human rights law, or U.S. laws implementing international norms. U.S. judges sat on the bench at the Nuremberg Trials after World War II and heard American prosecutors prosecuting Nazi war criminals. A U.S. judge now sits on the International Court of Justice, which sometimes hears cases involving international human rights law. Several judges from the U.S. have sat as judges of the International Criminal Tribunal for the former Yugoslavia seated at the Hague.

But the introduction of modern international human rights law into the American judicial arena has been very difficult for judges. Most judges never studied international law in law school, and almost none had ever studied international human rights law, as presented in this book. Most judges were unaware that there was such law, much less how to interpret and apply it. When a creative American attorney would present legal contentions based on international human rights law, many judges were unprepared to handle them and unreceptive to applying them. They treated these legal claims as though they were based on some body of foreign law outside the U.S. legal system, although many of them were based on legal norms that are legally binding on the U.S. Often if the case were based on norms adopted under the auspices of an international organization such as the United Nations, some judges felt that this was a case of a non-American body trying to tell the U.S. how it should act; a sort of interference with sovereignty in our legal system. Thus, a legal matter could be looked at as a battle of competing legal systems, one American, the other international. Legal xenophobia occurred and human rights lost out. Slowly this is changing. Now, even at the level of the U.S. Supreme Court, there appears to be a more respectful awareness and deepening knowledge of international human rights law and humanitarian law and international criminal law. This is due largely thanks to lawyers and NGOs who have taken the time to learn human rights and humanitarian law and to use it in cases, most often in an amicus briefs submitted in a case, with the intention to educate the court about the pertinent international law issues and authorities.

As stated in the Introductory Essay of this book, most international human rights legal norms are part of U.S. law by virtue of the U.S. Constitution itself. According to the U.S. Supreme Court in the case of the *Paquete Habana*, international law *is* U.S. law, whether treaty or customary. This will be shown by the following cases.

We have chosen to present a small random selection of cases to show the reader how this law has been interpreted and applied by U.S. courts, and also by other legal bodies that decide human rights cases involving the U.S. There are many other cases worthy of coverage in this work but time and space prevent it. The reader is encouraged to peruse one of the textbooks referred to in the bibliography for further reading on cases.

1308

The reader will be introduced to 19 different case decision excerpts or case summaries, and one international level legal case Petition (pleading), 13 from U.S. courts and 7 from non-U.S. legal bodies. The 19 decisions are all excerpted or summarized texts of actual court decisions or the case pleadings, and have been selected because of their legal importance or because they contain or refer to many of the most important issues, principles, treaties, laws, and institutions referred to elsewhere in this text. They are meant to show a variety of issues. They also show how both U.S. law and the body of international law are cross-fertilizing each other. More than ever these days, judicial fora hear references to the laws of other legal systems, or the case law of those systems.

Some of these cases reflect the era since 9/11 and the start of what is called the war on terrorism. These cases show judicial organs are performing their utmost important task of interpreting the law and limiting the power of the other two branches of government in the exercise of check and balances. Limiting the power of the most powerful state in the world is a daunting task. They represent the protection of our rule of law system where we say we are a nation of laws and not of men. Because of the importance and need of checks and balances in the U.S. system during the so-called war on terrorism we have chosen to present four extremely important cases regarding the issue of war on terror detainees and limits on the powers of the executive branch: Rasul, Hamdan, Hamdi and Boumediene. These four cases have shown how the nation's highest court has grappelled with the ultimate issues of the Constitution and national security, with the balance between human freedom and national security.

The one case which is not a decision (Ameziane) sets forth the Petition and correspondence with a Petitioner's lawyer in a pending Guantánamo detainee case in the Inter-American Commission of Human Rights.

The Selected Cases

The following 13 actual U.S. court decisions, in excerpted form, will give readers a deeper look at how a few U.S. courts have decided cases based on or related to this international human rights law:

1. *In re Cincinnati Radiation Litigation.* This was a 1995 decision by the District Court for the Southern District of Ohio, filed by terminally ill, poor, African-American cancer patients against university doctors and scientists and the government for exposing them to massive doses of radiation in 1960–1972. This was a medical experiment about the effects of radiation, but it was done without disclosing the nature of the experiment or getting their free and informed consent. This case shows how human rights norms birthed fifty years ago in the Nuremberg Trials against Nazi medical doctors have now ripened into customary international law binding on all U.S. courts. These norms concerning medical doctors are known as the "Nuremburg Code" and are part of what is known as the "Nuremburg Rules," which grew out of the Nuremburg Trials and related cases.

In mid 2010, it was reported that in Guatemala in the 1960s, the U.S. had engaged in certain high risk medical experiments using Guatemalans who had not given their free and informed consent. This Cincinnati Radiation norm would apply to that situation.

2. *Kadic v Karadzic.*, This was a 1995 decision of the Second Circuit Court of Appeals, in a successful civil case brought by plaintiff Bosnian Croats and Muslims against Radovan Karadzic involving the Bosnia conflict of the early 1990s. The Court upheld the validity of international human rights and humanitarian law, particularly customary international norms law in those fields, which it found were within the subject matter jurisdiction of U.S. courts, in a human rights issue that arose in another country.

3. *U.S. v Roy M. Belfast* ("Chuckie Taylor"). In this 2010 federal criminal law case the U.S. prosecuted a human rights violator from Liberia, the son of Charles Taylor, for the crime of Torture under the U.S. federal criminal code. This crime of torture was the domestic implementation of the U.S obligation under the Convention against Torture (See Doc. 19) to criminalize torture in U.S. law. Roy M. Belfast, aka Chuckie Taylor, was sentenced to 97 years in prison by a U.S. federal Court for acts he committed entirely in Africa. The Court of Appeals in this decision upheld the conviction and application of the Torture Convention.

The Court held that the Convention Against Torture, or CAT, created a floor, not a ceiling, by which to guide signatories in implementing it. Thus, the Congress did not overstep its bounds by passing the more stringent Torture Act, implementing CAT. Furthermore, the CAT (and thus the Torture Act) are not restricted to time of war, to the territorial boundaries of signatory nations, or only intra-territorial conduct of U.S. citizens. The statute has extra territorial application because it deals with an international crime, giving rise to universal jurisdiction, permitting every country in the world to prosecute violators.

4. *Hill v Rincon Band of Louiseno Indians.* This 2007 federal court case involved indigenous rights as part of human rights in the U.S. and is an example of how litigants are asserting international human rights law in U.S. Courts, often unsuccessfully. The Court held that International Law norms set forth in the United Nations Charter and Universal Declaration of Human Rights are not binding legal norms that can support a cause of action for damages in U.S. courts. Looking at international law as primarily the regulation of relationships among states the court found that even if such a cause of action existed, Indian tribes are not "foreign states" for the purposes of international human rights law.

5. *Kiobel v Royal Dutch Petroleum.* In this 2010, case the Court of Appeals decided a very important issue which had a lot to do with environmental racism and cases in U.S federal courts against corporation under the Alien Tort Statute, for damages to people in foreign countries who claim to have been harmed by the aiding and abetting of corporation with a government which violated plaintiffs' human rights. It primarily involved customary international law, and whether such law provided a cause of action against a corporation for aiding and abetting a government to violate human rights. It reflected the use of human rights norms for environmental issues.

A number of similar cases are pending in U.S Courts against corporations for damages in other countries by alien plaintiffs. This case was important for the issue of indirect corporate liability for human rights violations. In this case the court does an excellent job of walking through the process of determining customary international law, and the history of the issue of corporate liability under customary international law.

6. *Graham v Florida.* In this 2010, case the U.S. Supreme Court decided an important issue of criminal sentencing law regarding juvenile offenders. It had to decide whether a U.S. court could sentence a juvenile to life in prison without possibility of parole, for commission of a crime not resulting in death. It looked at U.S. state law and practice looking for a "national consensus." The Supreme Court also looked at the international human rights standard and practice, which was against such sentence. The Court stated that the fact that international human rights consensus was against such a sentence for juveniles, was not controlling in the U.S. court system when analyzing such a punishment under the Cruel and Unusual Punishment Clause of the 8th Amendment. Such consensus was, however, supportive of the Court's conclusion that such a punishment is unconstitutional given the principle of decency underlying the Amendment. The Court stated, regarding looking at human rights law and practice outside the U.S, that "the judgment of the world's nations that a particular sentencing practice is inconsistent with basic principles of decency demonstrates that the Court's rationale has respected reasoning to support it."

7. *Roper v Simmons.* In this 2005 death penalty case the U.S. Supreme Court ruled that imposition of the death penalty on offenders who offended when they were juveniles, violated the 8th amendment to the U.S. Constitution. The Court considered international human rights law and practice. In determining whether or not to impose the death penalty on a minor, the Supreme Court did not find the vast international opinion against such a penalty dispositive, as it is the Supreme Court's job alone to interpret the Constitution. It did, however, consider the international prohibition against such a penalty supportive of its decision that it is unconstitutional.

8. *Rasul v George W. Bush.* In this 2004, U.S. Supreme Court Opinion the Supreme Court had to determine the rights of war on terror detainees held as so called enemy combatants at the U.S. base in Guantánamo, Cuba. The Court held that U.S. district courts are granted jurisdiction over the habeas corpus claims of those held at Guantánamo Bay, Cuba, as granted by the federal habeas corpus statute. Even though Guantánamo is ultimately under the sovereignty of Cuba, as a matter of U.S. and International law it was the same as under U.S. sovereignty and the habeas corpus statute applied there. The Court found that the U.S. government violated Rasul's right to access to U.S. Courts by way of a writ of habeas corpus.

9. *Hamdan v George W. Bush.* In this second 2004 Guantánamo detainee case the U.S. Supreme Court found that despite the fact that the conflict in which Hamdan was captured was not one between High Contracting Parties to the Geneva Convention, the Geneva Convention still applied to him as an enemy combatant and in Guantánamo Cuba. It ruled that even as a so called enemy combatant he was

legally protected by the Geneva Conventions. Furthermore, the Court ruled that the Military Commission convened to try him violated Common Article 3 of the Third Geneva Convention. It concluded that the military commission convened to try Hamdan lacked power to proceed because its structure and procedures violate both the UCMJ and the Geneva Conventions. Four Justices also concluded that the offense with which Hamdan has been charged with (conspiracy, was not even an "offens[e] that by . . . the law of war may be tried by a military commissions."

10. *Hamdi v Donald Rumsfeld.* This is another U.S. Supreme Court case involving a former Guantánamo detainee, decided in 2006. The detainee, Hamdi, was a U.S. citizen born in Louisiana, held as an enemy combatant and moved from Guantánamo to South Carolina. In holding Hamdi indefinitely and without any criminal charges, and preventing him from communication with his family or with access to a legal counsel or a civilian court, the U.S. was not respecting his due process constitutional rights as a citizen. The Court found that even though the Government had a legal right to capture and hold him, as an enemy combatant, Hamdi had a legal right as a U.S. citizen to access to habeas corpus in U.S. civilian courts to challenge the factual basis of his detention. The Supreme Court held that due process demands that a citizen held in the U.S. as an enemy combatant be given a meaningful opportunity to contest the factual basis for that detention before a neutral decision maker. The Government had violated his Constitutional right to due process of law. His Constitutional right to access to the writ of habeas corpus was affirmed. In capturing the critical issue of the balance between freedom and justice on the one hand and protection of national security on the other, the Court stated, citing another case, "the imperative necessity for safeguarding these rights to procedural due process under the gravest of emergencies has existed throughout our constitutional history, for it is then, under the pressing exigencies of crisis, that there is the greatest temptation to dispense with fundamental constitutional guarantees which, it is feared, will inhibit governmental action."

11. *Boumediene v George W. Bush.* This is the fourth important war on terror case before the U.S. Supreme Court. The Court held,. in 2008, that the Guantánamo prisoners held as enemy combatants had a right to file for writs of habeas corpus under the U.S. Constitution. It found that the Military Commission Act of 2006 was an unconstitutional suspension of that right. The Court again found that the fact that the U.S., by virtue of its complete jurisdiction and control, maintains "de facto" sovereignty over this territory, even though Cuba retained ultimate sovereignty over the territory, the aliens detained as enemy combatants on that territory were entitled to the writ of habeas corpus protected in Article I, Section 9 of the U.S. Constitution. This Court's case precedent recognized that fundamental rights afforded by the Constitution extend to Guantánamo. Along with *Rasul v Bush, Hamdi v Rumsfeld,* and *Hamdan v Rumsfeld,* this is a major case in the jurisprudence of the U.S. Courts regarding controversial enemy combatant detainee access to justice in the U.S. As a matter of U.S. Constitutional and statutory law all such detainees have a legal right to access to civilian courts to challenge the legality of their detention.

12. *Sosa v Alvarez-Machain.* This is a 2010 The *Sosa* decision confirms that Alien Tort Claims Act (ATCA or ATS) provides a basis for civil suits by an alien against another alien in federal courts, based upon causes of action for torts in violations of the law of nations. The source of those causes of action is federal common law, rather than ATCA itself. However, ATCA provides the authority for judges to recognize causes of action based on contemporary interpretations of the law of nations. Those causes of action extend to events which occurred entirely in another country. In this case the U.S Drug Enforcement Agency, with the help of Mexican agents, kidnapped a Mexican doctor in Mexico and abducted him into the U.S. regarding the death of a DEA agent in Mexico. The Court ruled that the arrest of Alvarez-Machain in Mexico and his subsequent transportation did not violate any recognized international norms, and thus his Alien Tort Statute claim was invalid. It ruled that the ATCA provided jurisdiction in U.S. courts but does not provide a cause of action, a legal basis, for such civil damages lawsuits. Causes of action under federal common law constituting "torts in violation of international law, based on customary international human rights law were to be narrowly defined.

13. *Samantar v Yousuf.* This 2010 U.S. Supreme Court Case is about who can be sued for violation of human rights under the ATCA. It relates to the principle of sovereign immunity as expressed in U.S. law in the Foreign Sovereign Immunities Act (FSIA). That Act prevented certain lawsuits in U.S. courts against other countries for the acts of their agents, so as not to create problems in the relations between the U.S and the country being sued. This was a case of a torture victim from Somalia suing the Somalia government agent who ordered him to be tortured. The agent, Samantar, raised the issue of sovereign immunity as a defense to being sued. He claimed he committed those acts while an agent of the Somalia government and so they

fell under the U.S. Foreign Sovereign Immunity Act, which was a defense to individual tort liability. The issue here is whether individual foreign government agents sued by other aliens in the U.S. district court can assert the FSIA defense in the U.S. courts. Upon a reading of the statutory text of the Foreign Sovereign Immunities Act, as well as an examination of its history and purpose, the Supreme Court held that FSIA does not govern claims of immunity by a government official acting in his official capacity. This ruling removed on of the major legal defenses raised by foreign human rights violators who come to the U.S. and are discovered here by victims of their human rights violations and sued under the ACTA. The case against Samantar, the defendant, was allowed to proceed without that statutory defense as a shield to his actions.

All of these cases have an international human rights legal dimension, as will become readily apparent. They also show how some U.S. courts are not always very receptive to international human rights law arguments, especially where there appears to be a strong U.S. public opinion contrary to the international legal norm.

The legal phenomenon that is occurring in the world of human rights is that there are now also certain legal bodies outside the U.S. that are dealing with human rights issues directly or indirectly involving the U.S. Sometimes this is because the U.S. is a party to the case in a non-U.S. legal forum. Sometimes it is simply because the human rights practices of the U.S. are at issue in another case outside the U.S. And in others, it is an issue of international concern where human rights law is applicable. We have chosen to include seven cases from other legal systems applying international human rights law in relation to the U.S., or involving issues in which the U.S. has a particular interest. These cases are presented for purposes of showing how other legal systems have viewed the human rights practices of the U.S., or how non-U.S. courts have decided issues directly or indirectly involving the U.S.

The different systems chosen are the Inter-American Commission on Human Rights, the U.N. Human Rights Committee, Council of Europe, and the International Court of Justice (the World Court). The excerpted cases decisions presented in this section are:

14. *Ameziane v U.S.* These documents are not a case decision but some of the legal pleadings and correspondence in a case pending before the Inter-American Commission of Human Rights involving a Guantánamo war on terror detainee. Faced with the denial of access to U.S. Federal Courts and the desire to bring alleged human rights violations to international attention some detainee representatives, have sought recourse before international human rights organs, here the Inter-American Commission on Human Rights, which sits in Washington D.C. The documents here are principally the Petition filed by NGOs, here the Center for Justice and International Law, Washington D.C., and Center for Constitutional Rights, New York, who engage in international human rights litigation and cooperated in bring this case for a Guantánamo detainee before the Organization of American States body known as the Inter-American Commission on Human Rights (See Document 61). These documents show how lawyers write human rights petitions to present to international human rights organs alleging a violation of their client victim petitioner's human rights under an international human rights instrument. Here this case against the U.S. government is based on the human rights norms in the American Declaration of Human Rights (See Document 62)

15. *Cherokee Nation v U.S.* This case before the Inter American Commission of Human Rights involved indigenous rights to former Native American land and claims for damages against the U.S. It shows a petitioner using international human rights law in the only international forum accessible to Americans concerning U.S. human rights violations. It also shows about the concept of and criteria for admissibility of Petitions (Complaints) before such a body. Whether or not the U.S. violated the petitioner's human rights, the Commission decided the case was inadmissible and that it had no authority to decide the merits of the case. This was because the petitioner had not exhausted all her remedies in the U.S. legal system before going to the Commission. This case was also based on the human rights norms in the American Declaration of Human Rights (See Document 62)

16. *Haitian Centre for Human Rights et al. v U.S.* was a case also decided by the Inter-American Commission on Human Rights. This Commission, again, had the right and power to make such decisions because of U.S. membership in the Organization of American States. This case was also based on the American Declaration of Human Rights. It involves the famous U.S. Coast Guard move in the early 1990s to stop and board boats filled with Haitian refugees on the high seas and forcibly return the refugees to Haiti.

17. *Ng v Canada*, a case decided by the U.N. Human Rights Committee under the Optional Protocol to the ICCPR. It involved a petitioner, Charles Ng, a lawful permanent resident of the U.S., who was fighting extradition from Canada to California to face trial for gruesome murders committed in California, for which the death penalty by gas would be imposed. This case was about his attempt to use the international human rights legal obligations of Canada under the ICCPR to keep from being extradited to the U.S. to face a possible death sentence. (Ng was extradited to California in the late 1990s and was convicted by the Orange County Superior Court in mid-1999 for multiple counts of murder. He was given a death sentence.)

18. *Soering v United Kingdom*, a now famous and important decision from the European Court of Human Rights about the extradition of a young man by England to the U.S. to face trial for murder, with a possible death sentence and long death row ordeal. This case is presented to show how the European human rights systems view the U.S. criminal justice system. It involves the issue of the long wait before the imposition of the death penalty and death row prison conditions in the U.S., the so called death row phenomenon. This situation in the U.S. is judged by the European Court in light of Article 3 of the European Convention on Human Rights regarding cruel, inhuman, and degrading treatment and punishment. The U.S. is not a party to this case, nor a state party to the European Convention, but the effect of the deportation of the petitioner to the U.S. to face the death penalty and death row is the focus issue of this case.

19. *Mexico v U.S.A.* (Avena) A 2004 summary of an opinion of the International Court of Justice. It a case by Mexico against the U.S. for what Mexico claims the U.S. did not do for certain Mexican citizens arrested in the U.S. Mexico claimed the U.S breached its obligation under an international treaty, the Vienna Convention on Consular Relations (VCCR), which obligated the U.S. to assure that where Mexican nationals were subject to prosecutions in the U.S for capital crimes, the Mexican defendants had to be advised of their right to contact the Mexican consulate to inform the Consulate of their situation and to seek the assistance of their Consulate, for example, in help in finding effective legal counsel to fight the charges. This case raises the issue of human rights in light of a U.S. federal state system, where most criminal matters are handled at the state level, and the issue of access to effective counsel and criminal due process rights of Mexicans being prosecuted for capital crimes in the U.S. The ICJ found that the U.S. violated its international legal obligations to consular notification under the VCCR, even though such criminal prosecutions are handled exclusively by state courts. The VCCR is not a human rights treaty as such but in its consular notification provision it affects the subject foreign citizen's right to effectively defend themselves by effective counsel fair trial in U.S. courts where their lives are at stake. See discussion of this issue in the Introduction section of this book: International Court Of Justice Cases And The Federalism Issue.

20. **The Advisory Opinion on the Legality of the Threat or Use of Nuclear Weapons** is a 1996 summary of a legal opinion issued by the International Court of Justice, the judicial organ of the United Nations, to the U.N. General Assembly, which had requested this opinion from the Court. (An American judge, Stephen Schwebel, was sitting as one of the judges.) An advisory opinion is a legal opinion issued by a court at the request of an institution or a party to a treaty system where there is no actual adversarial case and controversy between two or more parties. It is a legal opinion wherein the court gives its opinion as to the legal interpretation or application of law. It is given to help the requesting body or state party get an official statement as to how a particular legal norm should be interpreted or applied by all parties bound by that norm. The opinion is given in response to a specific question or issue presented to the court.

The issue presented to the International Court of Justice by the U.N. General Assembly was the compatibility of the use or threat of use of nuclear weapons with existing international law. This case deals with the ultimate issue of whether it is legal under international law to use or even to threaten to use nuclear weapons. The opinion would likely apply equally to other types of weapons of mass destruction. The court analyzes the applicability of international humanitarian law, the branch of human rights law applicable in times of armed conflict. It deals with the effects of nuclear weapons not just between states, but on the human rights of individuals who would be affected by the indiscriminate use of such destructive weapons. This shows the modern trend toward factoring the rights of individual human beings into a legal arena, public international law, which once only involved states and international organizations.

This advisory opinion is, strictly speaking, not legally binding on the U.S. or any other state. It is, however, a very important and authoritative guideline on the legality of the use of nuclear weapons under existing international law, of which international human rights law is a part. The bottom line of this case is that ultimately the use of or threat to use nuclear weapons will only be legally permissible in extremely narrow situations of national self-defense when there is no alternative to save the state, and then only where that use or threat fully complies with international humanitarian law.

Although the case was not directed against the U.S., nor did it even refer to any state as doing anything wrong, it was clear in the minds of the General Assembly and the court that the U.S., the post–Cold War world leader and holder of many nuclear weapons, was the state most interested in and most affected by this decision. Few U.S. citizens even know about this opinion, though it potentially affects the survival of the U.S. and of the whole world.

These cases were not selected because of a perception of the correctness of the decision, nor for purposes of making the U.S., or any other country, seem unjust. They are simply randomly selected, sample international human rights–related cases, directly or indirectly involving the U.S. and its laws, policies, institutions, and practices in today's world.

U.S. Decisions

1. *In re Cincinnati Radiation Litigation* U.S. District Court, S.D. Ohio,
   Western Division (Excerpted)
   Cite as No. C-1–94–126

In re Cincinnati Radiation Litigation
Jan. 11, 1995

Beckwith, District Judge

The Complaint in this much-publicized matter alleges that the Defendants engaged in the design and implementation of experiments from 1960 to 1972 to study the effects of massive doses of radiation on human beings in preparation for a possible nuclear war. The experiments utilized terminal cancer patients who were not informed of the consequences of their participation nor, indeed, informed of the existence or purpose of the experiments. The Complaint alleges that most of the patients selected were African-American and, in the vernacular of the time, charity patients. The Complaint further alleges that the various Defendants actively concealed the nature, purpose and consequences of the experiments. The allegations of the Complaint make out an outrageous tale of government perfidy in dealing with some of its most vulnerable citizens. . . . .

The Plaintiffs are, for the most part, heirs and personal representatives of the patients who were the subjects of the experiments in question, because the patients are deceased. . . .

. . . Plaintiffs allege that they were the unwitting subjects of Human Radiation Experiments conducted at Cincinnati General Hospital ("CGH") between 1960 and 1972. The Complaint alleges that the experiments were conducted under the auspices of the University of Cincinnati College of Medicine with funding and authorization from the U.S. Department of Defense's Nuclear Agency. . . .

Plaintiffs allege that the Human Radiation Experiments were designed to study the effects of radiation on combat troops. Consequently, Plaintiffs allege they were exposed to doses of radiation at levels to be expected on a nuclear battlefield.

It is also alleged that the subjects of the radiation experiments all had inoperable cancer and were told that they were receiving treatment for their cancer. Plaintiffs allege that they were in fact never told that they were part of a medical experiment or that they were receiving radiation in doses ranging from 25 to 300 rads as a means of providing the Defense Department information about the effects of radiation on military personnel in the event of a nuclear attack. Thus, the principal thrust of the Complaint is that none of the subjects gave informed consent to participate in the Human Radiation Experiments.

The Plaintiffs claim they were denied substantive due process, procedural due process, equal protection, and access to courts under the Fourth, Fifth, and Fourteenth Amendments of the U.S. Constitution. The Plaintiffs also claim that the individual Defendants engaged in a conspiracy to deprive Plaintiffs of their constitutional rights and seek recovery under this theory pursuant to 42 U.S.C. 1983 and 1985(3).

. . . the claims against Drs. Kessler and Varon will also be analyzed separately under the Bivens doctrine, which specifically permits claims against federal employees who violate constitutional law. . . .

Patients were selected to be subjects in the experiments because they had cancer. The patients were not, however, in the final stages of their disease, nor were they close to death. Each patient selected was deemed in reasonably good clinical condition. . . . No consent forms were used for the first five years of the Human Radiation Experiments. . . .

The Plaintiffs also allege that the subjects of the experiments were poorly educated and deemed to be of low intelligence, according to standardized tests. In light of the Plaintiffs' lack of sophistication, the Complaint alleges that the information provided by Defendants could not have been sufficient, in any event, to provide a basis for informed consent. In other words, voluntary and informed consent was impossible. . . .

Based upon the foregoing factual allegations, Plaintiffs set forth the following claims for relief:

(1) Plaintiffs' participation in the Human Radiation Experiments without informed consent resulted in a violation of their rights, privileges and immunities secured by the First and Fourteenth Amendments to the U.S. Constitution, including, but not limited to, the right of access to the courts, the rights to procedural and substantive due process of law, the right to equal protection under the law, and the right to privacy under 42 U.S.C. 1983.

(2) The federal Defendants, Drs. Kessler and Varon, have, under color of law, deprived Plaintiffs of rights, privileges and immunities secured by the First and Fourteenth Amendments to the U.S. Constitution, including the right of access to the courts, the rights to procedural and substantive due process of law, the right to equal protection under the law, and the right to privacy under Bivens v Six Unknown Federal Agents. . . .

(3) By conspiring with each other to choose African-Americans as subjects for the Human Radiation Experiments, the Defendants violated 42 U.S.C. 1985 and the U.S. Constitution. . . .

C. The Nuremberg Code

The preceding demonstrates that the constitutional law controlling the invasion of an individual's bodily integrity was clearly established between 1960 and 1972. Indeed, the prevailing law detailing the right was sufficiently clear that a reasonable official would have known that the Human Radiation Experiments violated constitutional law. Accordingly, that law provides an independent basis for the Plaintiffs' Section 1983 action. Nevertheless, it is impossible for the Court to ignore the historical context in which the Human Radiation Experiments were conducted.

After World War II, the U.S. and its allies were involved in a succession of criminal trials. The trials have commonly become known as the Nuremberg trials. Perhaps the best known Nuremberg trial involved the military officers of the Third Reich. The doctors' trial, United States of America v Carl Brandt, et al., I Trials of War Criminals, Vol. 11 at 181 (1949); 6 F.R.D. 305 (1949), also known as the "Medical Case," was tried at the Palace of Justice in postwar Nuremberg, Germany. The trial was conducted under U.S. military auspices according to the Moscow Declaration on German Atrocities (November 1, 1943), Executive Order 9547 (May 2, 1945), and the London Agreement (August 8, 1945).

The judges appointed by President Truman to hear the Medical Case were all American judges and lawyers: Walter Beals, a justice from the Washington Supreme Court; Harold Sebring, a Florida Supreme Court Justice; Johnson Crawford, a judge from the Oklahoma District Court; and Victor Swearingen, an assistant attorney general of the State of Michigan. The case was prosecuted by then Supreme Court Justice Robert Jackson, and a military lawyer, Telford Taylor.

The Nuremberg tribunal was asked to determine the culpability of twenty-three (23) German physicians under "the principles of the law of nations as they result from the usages established among civilized peoples, from the laws of humanity, and from the dictates of public conscience." Id. at 181. The charges against the physicians included human experimentation involving non consenting prisoners. The experiments included studies of the limits of human tolerance to high altitudes and freezing temperatures. Medically-related experiments included inoculation of prisoners with infectious disease pathogens and tests of new antibiotics. Various experiments involving the mutilation of bone, muscle and nerve were also performed on non consenting prisoner subjects.

Throughout the trial, the question of what were or should be the universal standards for justifying human experimentation recurred. "The lack of a universally accepted principle for carrying out human experimentation was the central issue pressed by the defendant physicians throughout their testimony." The Nazi doctors and the Nuremberg Code, Human rights in human experimentation 132–133 (George J. Annas & Michael A. Grodin eds., 1992).

A few of the ethical arguments presented by the defendants during the trial as justification for their participation in the experimentation programs are summarized as follows:

(1) Research is necessary in times of national emergency. Military and civilian survival may depend on the scientific and medical knowledge derived from human experimentation. Extreme circumstances demand extreme action.

(2) There were no universal standards of research ethics.

(3) The state determined the necessity for the human experimentation. The physicians were merely following orders.

(4) Sometimes it is necessary to tolerate a lesser evil, the killing of some, to achieve a greater good, the saving of many.

(5) The prisoners' consent to participation in human experimentation was tacit. Since there were no statements that the subjects did not consent, it should be assumed that valid consent existed. Id. at 133.

The final judgment of the court was delivered on July 19, 1947. The judgment has since become known as the "Nuremberg Code." The first provision of the Code states as follows:

The voluntary consent of the human subject is absolutely essential. This means that the person involved should have legal capacity to give consent; should be so situated as to be able to exercise free power of choice without the intervention of any element of force, fraud, deceit, duress, overreaching, or other ulterior form of constraint or coercion and should have sufficient knowledge and comprehension of the elements of the subject matter involved as to enable him to make an understanding and enlightened decision. This latter element requires that before the acceptance of an affirmative decision by the experimental subject there should be made known to him the nature, duration, and purpose of the experiment; the method and means by which it is to be conducted; all inconveniences and hazards reasonably to be expected; and the effects upon his health and person which may possibly come from his participation in the experiment.

The duty and responsibility for ascertaining the quality of the consent rests upon each individual who initiates, directs, or engages in the experiment. It is a personal duty and responsibility which may not be delegated to another with impunity. United States of America v Brandt (the Medical Case), II Trials of War Criminals Before The Nuremberg Military Tribunals Under Control Council Law No. 10, p. 181 (1949).

Only five years later, in recognition of these principles, the Secretary of Defense directed that human experimentation for the Department of Defense could only be conducted where there was full and voluntary consent of the subject. The directive issued by the Secretary of Defense is a mirror of the Nuremberg Code. See Memorandum for the Secretary of the Army, Navy, Air Force, February 26, 1953. In 1954, the World Medical Association adopted five general principles for those engaged in research and experimentation. Also in the mid-1950's, the Clinical Center of the National Institutes of Health ("NIH") adopted guidelines that applied to the use of human subjects in experimental medical research. The NIH Guidelines state: The rigid safeguards observed at NIH are based on the so-called "ten commandments" of human medical research which were adopted at the Nuremberg War Crimes Trials after the atrocities performed by Nazi doctors had been exposed.

Every subject must give his full consent to any test, and he must be told exactly what it involves so that he goes into it with his eyes open. Among other things, the experiment must be designed to yield "fruitful results for the good of society," unnecessary "physical and mental suffering and injury" must be avoided, the test must be conducted by "scientifically qualified" persons, and the subject must be free to end it at any time he feels unable to go on. See NIH, "Handbook On The Utilization of Normal Volunteers In The Clinical Center," Section 3.06, (1961) p. 10.

Finally, in 1962, the federal government became more formally involved in the regulation of research. The Drug Amendments Act of 1962 was enacted to keep unsafe or useless drugs off the market by requiring proof of safety and efficacy from the drug companies. In the wake of the thalidomide experience, Congress noted that no state required physicians to inform patients that an experimental drug was being used on them. As a result, the final version of the 1962 law contained a provision that required "experts using such drugs for investigational purposes" to inform persons to whom they are to be administered that they are being given drugs for investigational purposes and to obtain the consent of these individuals or their representatives, except "where they deem it not feasible, or in their professional judgment, contrary to the best interest of such human beings." See Federal Food, Drug and Cosmetic Act, Section 505(i), 1962.

The Nuremberg Code is part of the law of humanity. It may be applied in both civil and criminal cases by the federal courts in the U.S. At the very least, by the time the Human Radiation Experiments were designed, the Nuremberg Code served as a tangible example of conduct that "shocked the conscience." . . . Thus, even were the Nuremberg Code not afforded precedential weight in the courts of the U.S., it cannot be readily dismissed from its proper context in this case. The individual and Bivens Defendants, as physicians and other health professionals, must have been aware of the Nuremberg Code, the Hippocratic Oath, and the several pronouncements by both world and American medical organizations adopting the Nuremberg Code. It is inconceivable to the Court that the individual and Bivens Defendants, when allegedly planning to perform radiation experiments on unwitting subjects, were not moved to pause or rethink their procedures in light of the forceful dictates of the Nuremberg Tribunal and the several medical organizations. See U.S. v Stanley, 483 U.S. 669, 710, 107 S.Ct. 3054, 3066, 97 L.Ed.2d 550 (1987) (O'Connor, J. dissenting).

In Stanley, the Army administered LSD to an unwitting enlisted man. Under the Feres doctrine, the Supreme Court held that Mr. Stanley could not obtain money damages from the military for his involvement in the experiment. Writing for a five-four Court, Justice Scalia expressed concern that permitting an enlisted man to sue the Army "would call into serious question military discipline and decision-making." In her forceful dissent, Justice O'Connor relied on the Nuremberg Code for the proposition that due process guarantees the subjects of human experiments the right to voluntary and informed consent. Because Plaintiffs in this case are not military personnel, the Court is convinced that Justice O'Connor's dissent in Stanley controls. . . .

The allegations in this case indicate that the government of the U.S., aided by officials of the City of Cincinnati, treated at least eighty-seven (87) of its citizens as though they were laboratory animals. If the Constitution has not clearly established a right under which these Plaintiffs may attempt to prove their case, then a gaping hole in that document has been exposed. The subject of experimentation who has not volunteered is merely an object. . . . As Justice O'Connor indicated in her dissent from U.S. v Stanley, 483 U.S. 669, 107 S.Ct. 3054, 97 L.Ed.2d 550 (1987), "[t]he U.S. military played an instrumental role in the criminal prosecution of Nazi officials who experimented with human beings during the Second World War . . . and the standards that the Nuremberg Military Tribunals developed to judge the behavior of the defendants stated that the voluntary consent of the human subject is absolutely essential . . . to satisfy moral, ethical, and legal concepts. . . . If this principle is violated, the very least society can do is to see that the victims are compensated, as best they can be, by the perpetrators. I am prepared to say that our Constitution's promise of due process of law guarantees this much." Id. at 710, 107 S.Ct. at 3066.

The doctrine of qualified immunity does not insulate the individual and Bivens Defendants from liability for their deliberate and calculated exposure of cancer patients to harmful medical experimentation without their informed consent. No judicially-crafted rule insulates from examination the state-sponsored involuntary and unknowing human experimentation alleged to have occurred in this case. Accordingly, the individual and Bivens Defendants' motion to dismiss the substantive due process claim is DENIED.

The Plaintiffs assert a substantive due process claim under the right to be free from nonconsensual invasions of bodily integrity and, in the alternative, the right to privacy. In the preceding analysis, the Court has determined that a cause of action is appropriate under the right to bodily integrity. Thus, the Court will not analyze the plaintiffs' assertion that a right to privacy creates a viable cause of action. . . .

Conclusion

For all the reasons set forth herein, the individual and Bivens Defendants' motions to dismiss are GRANTED in part and DENIED in part. Plaintiffs have stated claims for violations of their constitutional rights of substantive due process, procedural due process, access to the courts, and equal protection as well as a claim for a violation of 42 U.S.C. 1985. . . .

2. *Kadic v Karadzic* U.S. Court of Appeals for the Second Circuit (Excerpted)
   Cite as: 70 F.3d 232 (2d Cir. 1995)

KADIC V KARADZIC,
Docket Nos. 94–9035, 94–9069
October 13, 1995

Prior History: Appeals from the judgment entered September 19, 1994, in the Southern District of New York (Peter K. Leisure, Judge) dismissing, for lack of subject matter jurisdiction, two lawsuits by victims of atrocities allegedly committed in Bosnia by the Bosnian-Serb leader, Radovan Karadzic. Doe v Karadzic, 866 F. Supp. 734 (S.D.N.Y. 1994).

Disposition: Judgment reversed and cases remanded.

Counsel: Beth Stephens, New York, N.Y. (Matthew J. Chachere, Jennifer Green, Peter Weiss, Michael Ratner, Jules Lobel, Center for Constitutional Rights, New York, N.Y.; Rhonda Copelon, Celina Romany, International Women's Human Rights Clinic, Flushing, N.Y.; Judith Levin, International League of Human Rights, New York, N.Y.; Harold Hongju Koh, . . . (names of other legal counsel for the parties, and Friends of the Court)

Judges: Before: NEWMAN, Chief Judge, FEINBERG and WALKER, Circuit Judges.

Opinion: JON O. NEWMAN, Chief Judge:

Most Americans would probably be surprised to learn that victims of atrocities committed in Bosnia are suing the leader of the insurgent Bosnian-Serb forces in a U.S. District Court in Manhattan. Their claims seek to build upon the foundation of this Court's decision in Filartiga v Pena-Irala, 630 F.2d 876 (2d Cir. 1980), which recognized the important principle that the venerable Alien Tort Act, 28 U.S.C. sec. 1350 (1988), enacted in 1789 but rarely invoked since then, validly creates federal court jurisdiction for suits alleging torts committed anywhere in the world against aliens in violation of the law of nations. The pending appeals pose additional significant issues as to the scope of the Alien Tort Act: whether some violations of the law of nations may be remedied when committed by those not acting under the authority of a state; if so, whether genocide, war crimes, and crimes against humanity are among the violations that do not require state action; and whether a person, otherwise liable for a violation of the law of nations, is immune from service of process because he is present in the U.S. as an invitee of the United Nations.

These issues arise on appeals by two groups of plaintiffs-appellants from the November 19, 1994, judgment of the U.S. District Court for the Southern District of New York (Peter K. Leisure, Judge), dismissing, for lack of subject matter jurisdiction, their suits against defendant-appellee Radovan Karadzic, President of the self-proclaimed Bosnian-Serb republic of "Srpska." Doe v Karadzic, 866 F. Supp. 734 (S.D.N.Y. 1994) ("Doe"). For reasons set forth below, we hold that subject matter jurisdiction exists, that Karadzic may be found liable for genocide, war crimes, and crimes against humanity in his private capacity and for other violations in his capacity as a state actor, and that he is not immune from service of process. We therefore reverse and remand.

Background

The plaintiffs-appellants are Croat and Muslim citizens of the internationally recognized nation of Bosnia-Herzegovina, formerly a republic of Yugoslavia. Their complaints, which we accept as true for purposes of this appeal, allege that they are victims, and representatives of victims, of various atrocities, including brutal acts of rape, forced prostitution, forced impregnation, torture, and summary execution, carried out by Bosnian-Serb military forces as part of a genocidal campaign conducted in the course of the Bosnian civil war. Karadzic, formerly a citizen of Yugoslavia and now a citizen of Bosnia-Herzegovina, is the President of a three-man presidency of the self-proclaimed Bosnian-Serb republic within Bosnia-Herzegovina, sometimes referred to as "Srpska," which claims to exercise lawful authority, and does in fact exercise actual control, over large parts of the territory of Bosnia-Herzegovina.

In his capacity as President, Karadzic possesses ultimate command authority over the Bosnian-Serb military forces, and the injuries perpetrated upon plaintiffs were committed as part of a pattern of systematic human rights violations that was directed by Karadzic and carried out by the military forces under his command. The complaints allege that Karadzic acted in an official capacity either as the titular head of Srpska or in collaboration with the government of the recognized nation of the former Yugoslavia and its dominant constituent republic, Serbia.

The two groups of plaintiffs asserted causes of action for genocide, rape, forced prostitution and impregnation, torture and other cruel, inhuman, and degrading treatment, assault and battery, sex and ethnic inequality, summary execution, and wrongful death. They sought compensatory and punitive damages, attorney's fees, and, in one of the cases, injunctive relief. Plaintiffs grounded subject-matter jurisdiction in the Alien Tort Act, the Torture Victim Protection Act of 1991 ("Torture Victim Act"), Pub. L. No. 102–256, 106 Stat. 73 (1992), codified at 28 U.S.C. sec. 1350 note (Supp. V 1993), the general federal-question jurisdictional statute, 28 U.S.C. sec. 1331 (1988), and principles of supplemental jurisdiction, 28 U.S.C. sec. 1367 (Supp. V 1993).

In early 1993, Karadzic was admitted to the U.S. on three separate occasions as an invitee of the United Nations. According to affidavits submitted by the plaintiffs, Karadzic was personally served with the summons and complaint in each action during two of these visits while he was physically present in Manhattan.

Karadzic admits that he received the summons and complaint in the Kadic action, but disputes whether the attempt to serve him personally in the Doe action was effective. In the District Court, Karadzic moved for dismissal of both actions on the grounds of insufficient service of process, lack of personal jurisdiction, lack of subject-matter jurisdiction, and non justiciability of plaintiffs' claims. However, Karadzic submitted a memorandum of law and supporting papers only on the issues of service of process and personal jurisdiction, while reserving the issues of subject-matter jurisdiction and non justiciability for further briefing, if necessary. The plaintiffs submitted papers responding only to the issues raised by the defendant.

Without notice or a hearing, the District Court by-passed the issues briefed by the parties and dismissed both actions for lack of subject-matter jurisdiction. In an Opinion and Order, reported at 866 F. Supp. 734, the District Judge preliminarily noted that the Court might be deprived of jurisdiction if the Executive Branch were to recognize Karadzic as the head of state of a friendly nation, see Lafontant v Aristide, 844 F. Supp. 128 (E.D.N.Y. 1994) (head-of-state immunity), and that this possibility could render the plaintiffs' pending claims requests for an advisory opinion. The District Judge recognized that this consideration was not dispositive but believed that it "militates against this Court exercising jurisdiction." Doe, 866 F. Supp. at 738.

Turning to the issue of subject-matter jurisdiction under the Alien Tort Act, the Court concluded that "acts committed by non-state actors do not violate the law of nations," id. at 739. Finding that "the current Bosnian-Serb warring military faction does not constitute a recognized state," id. at 741 and that "the members of Karadzic's faction do not act under the color of any recognized state law," id., the Court concluded that "the acts alleged in the instant actions, while grossly repugnant, cannot be remedied through [the Alien Tort Act]," id. at 740–41. The Court did not consider the plaintiffs' alternative claim that Karadzic acted under color of law by acting in concert with the Serbian Republic of the former Yugoslavia, a recognized nation.

The District Judge also found that the apparent absence of state action barred plaintiffs' claim under the Torture Victim Act, which expressly requires that an individual defendant act "under actual or apparent authority, or color of law, of any foreign nation," Torture Victim Act sec. 2(a). With respect to plaintiffs' further claim that the law of nations, as incorporated into federal common law, gives rise to an implied cause of action over which the Court would have jurisdiction pursuant to section 1331, the Judge found that the law of nations does not give rise to implied rights of action absent specific Congressional authorization, and that, in any event, such an implied right of action would not lie in the absence of state action. Finally, having dismissed all of plaintiffs' federal claims, the Court declined to exercise supplemental jurisdiction over their state-law claims.

Discussion

Though the District Court dismissed for lack of subject matter jurisdiction, the parties have briefed not only that issue but also the threshold issues of personal jurisdiction and justiciability under the political question doctrine. Karadzic urges us to affirm on any one of these three grounds. We consider each in turn.

I. Subject-Matter Jurisdiction

Appellants allege three statutory bases for the subject matter jurisdiction of the District Court—the Alien Tort Act, the Torture Victim Act, and the general federal-question jurisdictional statute.

A. The Alien Tort Act

1. General Application to Appellants' Claims

The Alien Tort Act provides:

The district courts shall have original jurisdiction of any civil action by an alien for a tort only, committed in violation of the law of nations or a treaty of the U.S. 28 U.S.C. sec. 1350 (1988). Our decision in Filartiga established that this statute confers federal subject-matter jurisdiction when the following three conditions are satisfied: (1) an alien sues (2) for a tort (3) committed in violation of the law of nations (i.e., international law).[1] Id. at 887; see also Amerada Hess Shipping Corp. v Argentine Republic, 830 F.2d 421, 425 (2d Cir. 1987), rev'd on other grounds, 488 U.S. 428 (1989). The first two requirements are plainly satisfied here, and the only disputed issue is whether plaintiffs have pleaded violations of international law.

Because the Alien Tort Act requires that plaintiffs plead a "violation of the law of nations" at the jurisdictional threshold, this statute requires a more searching review of the merits to establish jurisdiction than is required under the more flexible "arising under" formula of section 1331. See Filartiga, 630 F.2d at 887–88. Thus, it is not a sufficient basis for jurisdiction to plead merely a colorable violation of the law of nations. There is no federal subject-matter jurisdiction under the Alien Tort Act unless the complaint adequately pleads a violation of the law of nations (or treaty of the U.S.).

Filartiga established that courts ascertaining the content of the law of nations "must interpret international law not as it was in 1789, but as it has evolved and exists among the nations of the world today." Id. at 881; see also Amerada Hess, 830 F.2d at 425. We find the norms of contemporary international law by "'consulting the works of jurists, writing professedly on public law; or by the general usage and practice of nations; or by judicial decisions recognizing and enforcing that law.'" Filartiga, 630 F.2d at 880 (quoting U.S. v Smith, 18 U.S. (5 Wheat.) 153, 160–61 (18)). If this inquiry discloses that the defendant's alleged conduct violates "well-established, universally recognized norms of international law," id. at 888, as opposed to "idiosyncratic legal rules," id. at 881, then federal jurisdiction exists under the Alien Tort Act.

Karadzic contends that appellants have not alleged violations of the norms of international law because such norms bind only states and persons acting under color of a state's law, not private individuals. In making this contention, Karadzic advances the contradictory positions that he is not a state actor, see Brief for Appellee at 19, even as he asserts that he is the President of the self-proclaimed Republic of Srpska, see statement of Radovan Karadzic, May 3, 1993, submitted with Defendant's Motion to Dismiss. For their part, the Kadic appellants also take somewhat inconsistent positions in pleading defendant's role as President of Srpska, Kadic Complaint P 13, and also contending that "Karadzic is not an official of any government," Kadic Plaintiffs' Memorandum in Opposition to Defendant's Motion to Dismiss at 21 n.25.

Judge Leisure accepted Karadzic's contention that "acts committed by non-state actors do not violate the law of nations," Doe, 866 F. Supp. at 739, and considered him to be a non-state actor.[2] The Judge appears to have deemed state action required primarily on the basis of cases determining the need for state action as to claims of official torture, see, e.g., Carmichael v United Technologies Corp., 835 F.2d 109 (5th Cir. 1988), without consideration of the substantial body of law, discussed below, that renders private individuals liable for some international law violations.

We do not agree that the law of nations, as understood in the modern era, confines its reach to state action. Instead, we hold that certain forms of conduct violate the law of nations whether undertaken by those acting under the auspices of a state or only as private individuals. An early example of the application of the law of nations to the acts of private individuals is the prohibition against piracy. See U.S. v Smith, 18 U.S. (5 Wheat.) 153, 161 (18); U.S. v Furlong, 18 U.S. (5 Wheat.) 184, 196–97 (18). In The Brig Malek Adhel, 43 U.S. (2 How.) 210, 232 (1844), the Supreme Court observed that pirates were "hostis humani generis" (an enemy of all mankind) in part because they acted "without . . . any pretense of public authority." See generally 4 William Blackstone, Commentaries on the Laws of England 68 (facsimile of 1st ed. 1765–1769, Univ. of Chi., ed. 1979). Later examples are prohibitions against the slave trade and certain war crimes. See M. Cherif Bassiouni, Crimes Against Humanity in International Criminal Law 193 (1992); Jordan Paust, The Other Side of Right: Private Duties Under Human Rights Law, 5 Harv. Hum. Rts. J. 51 (1992).

The liability of private persons for certain violations of customary international law and the availability of the Alien Tort Act to remedy such violations was early recognized by the Executive Branch in an opinion of Attorney General Bradford in reference to acts of American citizens aiding the French fleet to plunder British property off the coast of Sierra Leone in 1795. See Breach of Neutrality, 1 Op. Att'y Gen. 57, 59 (1795). The Executive Branch has emphatically restated in this litigation its position that private persons may be found liable under the Alien Tort Act for acts of genocide, war crimes, and other violations of international humanitarian law. See Statement of Interest of the U.S. at 5–13.

The Restatement (Third) of the Foreign Relations Law of the U.S. (1986) ("Restatement (Third)") proclaims: "Individuals may be held liable for offenses against international law, such as piracy, war crimes, and genocide." Restatement (Third) pt. II, introductory note. The Restatement is careful to identify those violations that are actionable when committed by a state, Restatement (Third) sec. 702,[3] and a more limited category of violations of "universal concern," id. sec. 404,[4] partially overlapping with those listed in section 702. Though the immediate focus of section 404 is to identify those offenses for which a state has jurisdiction to punish without regard to territoriality or the nationality of the offenders, cf. id. sec. 402(1)(a), (2), the inclusion of piracy and slave trade from an earlier era and aircraft hijacking from the modern era demonstrates that the offenses of "universal concern" include those capable of being committed by non-state actors. Although the jurisdiction authorized by section 404 is usually exercised by application of criminal law, international law also permits states to establish appropriate civil remedies, id. sec. 404 cmt. b, such as the tort actions authorized by the Alien Tort Act. Indeed, the two cases invoking the Alien Tort Act prior to Filartiga both applied the civil remedy to private action. See Adra v Clift, 195 F. Supp. 857 (D. Md. 1961); Bolchos v Darrel, 3 F. Cas. 810 (D.S.C. 1795) (No. 1,607).

Karadzic disputes the application of the law of nations to any violations committed by private individuals, relying on Filartiga and the concurring opinion of Judge Edwards in Tel-Oren v Libyan Arab Republic, 726 F.2d 774, 775 (D.C. Cir. 1984), cert. denied, 470 U.S. 1003 (1985).[5] Filartiga involved an allegation of torture committed by a state official. Relying on the United Nations' Declaration on the Protection of All Persons from Being Subjected to Torture, G.A. Res. 3452, U.N. GAOR, U.N. Doc. A/1034 (1975) (hereinafter "Declaration on Torture"), as a definitive statement of norms of customary international law prohibiting states from permitting torture, we ruled that "official torture is now prohibited by the law of nations." Filartiga, 630 F.2d at 884 (emphasis added). We had no occasion to consider whether international law violations other than torture are actionable against private individuals, and nothing in Filartiga purports to preclude such a result.

Karadzic also contends that Congress intended the state-action requirement of the Torture Victim Act to apply to actions under the Alien Tort Act. We disagree. Congress enacted the Torture Victim Act to codify the cause of action recognized by this Circuit in Filartiga, and to further extend that cause of action to plaintiffs who are U.S. citizens. See H.R. Rep. No. 367, 102d Cong., 2d Sess., at 4 (1991), reprinted in 1992 U.S.C.C.A.N. 84, 86 (explaining that codification of Filartiga was necessary in light of skepticism expressed by Judge Bork's concurring opinion in Tel-Oren). At the same time, Congress indicated that the Alien Tort Act "has other important uses and should not be replaced," because claims based on torture and summary executions do not exhaust the list of actions that may appropriately be covered [by the Alien Tort Act]. That statute should remain intact to permit suits based on other norms that already exist or may ripen in the future into rules of customary international law. Id. The scope of the Alien Tort Act remains undiminished by enactment of the Torture Victim Act.

2. Specific Application of Alien Tort Act to Appellants' Claims

In order to determine whether the offenses alleged by the appellants in this litigation are violations of the law of nations that may be the subject of Alien Tort Act claims against a private individual, we must make a particularized examination of these offenses, mindful of the important precept that "evolving standards of international law govern who is within the [Alien Tort Act's] jurisdictional grant." Amerada Hess, 830 F.2d at 425. In making that inquiry, it will be helpful to group the appellants' claims into three categories: (a) genocide, (b) war crimes, and (c) other instances of inflicting death, torture, and degrading treatment.

(a) Genocide. In the aftermath of the atrocities committed during the Second World War, the condemnation of genocide as contrary to international law quickly achieved broad acceptance by the community of nations. In 1946, the General Assembly of the United Nations declared that genocide is a crime under international law that is condemned by the civilized world, whether the perpetrators are "private individuals, public officials or statesmen." G.A. Res. 96(I), 1 U.N. GAOR, U.N. Doc. A/64/Add.1, at 188–89 (1946). The General Assembly also affirmed the principles of Article 6 of the Agreement and Charter Establishing the Nuremberg War Crimes Tribunal for punishing "'persecutions on political, racial, or religious grounds,'" regardless of whether the offenders acted "'as individuals or as members of organizations,'" In re Extradition of Demjanjuk, 612 F. Supp. 544, 555 n.11 (N.D. Ohio) (quoting Article 6). See G.A. Res. 95(I), 1 U.N. GAOR, U.N. Doc. A/64/Add.1, at 188 (1946).

The Convention on the Prevention and Punishment of the Crime of Genocide, 78 U.N.T.S. 277, entered into force Jan. 12, 1951, for the U.S. Feb. 23, 1989 (hereinafter "Convention on Genocide"), provides a more specific articulation of the prohibition of genocide in international law. The Convention, which has been ratified by more than 120 nations, including the U.S., see U.S. Dept. of State, Treaties in Force 345 (1994), defines "genocide" to mean any of the following acts committed with intent to destroy, in whole or in part, a national, ethnical, racial or religious group, as such: (a) Killing members of the group; (b) Causing serious bodily or mental harm to members of the group; (c) Deliberately inflicting on the group conditions of life calculated to bring about its physical destruction in whole or in part; (d) Imposing measures intended to prevent births with the group; (e) Forcibly transferring children of the group to another group.

Convention on Genocide art. II. Especially pertinent to the pending appeal, the Convention makes clear that "persons committing genocide . . . shall be punished, whether they are constitutionally responsible rulers, public officials or private individuals." Id. art. IV (emphasis added). These authorities unambiguously reflect that, from its incorporation into international law, the proscription of genocide has applied equally to state and non-state actors.

The applicability of this norm to private individuals is also confirmed by the Genocide Convention Implementation Act of 1987, 18 U.S.C. sec. 1091 (1988), which criminalizes acts of genocide without regard to whether the offender is acting under color of law, see id. sec. 1091(a) ("whoever" commits genocide shall be punished), if the crime is committed within the U.S. or by a U.S. national, id. sec. 1091(d). Though Congress provided that the Genocide Convention Implementation Act shall not "be construed as creating any substantive or procedural right enforceable by law by any party in any proceeding," id. sec. 1092, the legislative decision not to create a new private remedy does not imply that a private remedy is not already available under the Alien Tort Act. Nothing in the Genocide Convention Implementation Act or its legislative history reveals an intent by Congress to repeal the Alien Tort Act insofar as it applies to genocide,[6] and the two statutes are surely not repugnant to each other. Under these circumstances, it would be improper to construe the Genocide Convention Implementation Act as repealing the Alien Tort Act by implication. See Rodriguez v U.S., 480 U.S. 522, 524 (1987) ("Repeals by implication are not favored and will not be found unless an intent to repeal is clear and manifest") (citations and internal quotation marks omitted); U.S. v Cook, 922 F.2d 1026, 1034 (2d Cir.) ("mutual exclusivity" of statutes is required to demonstrate Congress's "clear, affirmative intent to repeal"), cert. denied, 500 U.S. 941 (1991).

Appellants' allegations that Karadzic personally planned and ordered a campaign of murder, rape, forced impregnation, and other forms of torture designed to destroy the religious and ethnic groups of Bosnian Muslims and Bosnian Croats clearly state a violation of the international law norm proscribing genocide, regardless of whether Karadzic acted under color of law or as a private individual. The District Court has subject-matter jurisdiction over these claims pursuant to the Alien Tort Act.

(b) War crimes. Plaintiffs also contend that the acts of murder, rape, torture, and arbitrary detention of civilians, committed in the course of hostilities, violate the law of war. Atrocities of the types alleged here have long been recognized in international law as violations of the law of war. See In re Yamashita, 327 U.S. 1, 14 (1946). Moreover, international law imposes an affirmative duty on military commanders to take appropriate measures within their power to control troops under their command for the prevention of such atrocities. Id. at 15–16.

After the Second World War, the law of war was codified in the four Geneva Conventions,[7] which have been ratified by more than 180 nations, including the U.S., see Treaties in Force, supra, 398–99. Common article 3, which is substantially identical in each of the four Conventions, applies to "armed conflicts not of an international character" and binds "each Party to the conflict . . . to apply, as a minimum, the following provisions": "Persons taking no active part in the hostilities . . . shall in all circumstances be treated humanely, without any adverse distinction founded on race, colour, religion or faith, sex, birth or wealth, or any other similar criteria. To this end, the following acts are and shall remain prohibited at any time and in any place whatsoever with respect to the above-mentioned persons:

(a) violence to life and person, in particular murder of all kinds, mutilation, cruel treatment and torture;

(b) taking of hostages;

(c) outrages upon personal dignity, in particular humiliating and degrading treatment;

(d) the passing of sentences and carrying out of executions without previous judgment pronounced by a regularly constituted court. . . . " Geneva Convention I art. 3(1).

Thus, under the law of war as codified in the Geneva Conventions, all "parties" to a conflict—which includes insurgent military groups—are obliged to adhere to these most fundamental requirements of the law of war.

The offenses alleged by the appellants, if proved, would violate the most fundamental norms of the law of war embodied in common article 3, which binds parties to internal conflicts regardless of whether they are recognized nations or roving hordes of insurgents. The liability of private individuals for committing war crimes has been recognized since World War I and was confirmed at Nuremberg after World War II, see Telford Taylor, Nuremberg Trials: War Crimes and International Law, 450 Int'l Conciliation 304 (April 1949) (collecting cases), and remains today an important aspect of international law, see Jordan Paust, After My Lai: The Case for War Crimes Jurisdiction Over Civilians in Federal District Courts, in The Vietnam War and International Law 447 (R. Falk ed. 1976). The District Court has jurisdiction pursuant to the Alien Tort Act over appellants' claims of war crimes and other violations of international humanitarian law.

(c) Torture and summary execution. In Filartiga, we held that official torture is prohibited by universally accepted norms of international law, see 630 F.2d at 885, and the Torture Victim Act confirms this holding and extends it to cover summary execution. Torture Victim Act secs. 2(a), 3(a). However, torture and summary execution—when not perpetrated in the course of genocide or war crimes—are proscribed by international law only when committed by state officials or under color of law. See Declaration on Torture art. 1 (defining torture as being "inflicted by or at the instigation of a public official"); Convention Against Torture and Other Cruel, Inhuman, or Degrading Treatment or Punishment pt. I, art. 1, 23 I.L.M. 1027 (1984), as modified, 24 I.L.M. 535 (1985), entered into force June 26, 1987, ratified by U.S. Oct. 21, 1994, 34 I.L.M. 590, 591 (1995) (defining torture as "inflicted by or at the instigation of or with the consent or acquiescence of a public official or other person acting in an official capacity"); Torture Victim Act sec. 2(a) (imposing liability on individuals acting "under actual or apparent authority, or color of law, of any foreign nation").

In the present case, appellants allege that acts of rape, torture, and summary execution were committed during hostilities by troops under Karadzic's command and with the specific intent of destroying appellants' ethnic-religious groups. Thus, many of the alleged atrocities are already encompassed within the appellants' claims of genocide and war crimes. Of course, at this threshold stage in the proceedings it cannot be known whether appellants will be able to prove the specific intent that is an element of genocide, or prove that each of the alleged torts were committed in the course of an armed conflict, as required to establish war crimes. It suffices to hold at this stage that the alleged atrocities are actionable under the Alien Tort Act, without regard to state action, to the extent that they were committed in pursuit of genocide or war crimes, and otherwise may be pursued against Karadzic to the extent that he is shown to be a state actor. Since the meaning of the state action requirement for purposes of international law violations will likely arise on remand and has already been considered by the District Court, we turn next to that requirement.

3. The State Action Requirement for International Law Violations

In dismissing plaintiffs' complaints for lack of subject-matter jurisdiction, the District Court concluded that the alleged violations required state action and that the "Bosnian-Serb entity" headed by Karadzic does not meet the definition of a state. Doe, 866 F. Supp. at 741 n.12. Appellants contend that they are entitled to prove that Srpska satisfies the definition of a state for purposes of international law violations and, alternatively, that Karadzic acted in concert with the recognized state of the former Yugoslavia and its constituent republic, Serbia.

(a) Definition of a state in international law. The definition of a state is well established in international law: Under international law, a state is an entity that has a defined territory and a permanent population, under the control of its own government, and that engages in, or has the capacity to engage in, formal relations with other such entities. Restatement (Third) sec. 1; accord Klinghoffer, 937 F.2d at 47; National Petrochemical, 860 F.2d at 553; see also Texas v White, 74 U.S. (7 Wall.) 700, 7 (1868). "Any government, however violent and wrongful in its origin, must be considered a de facto government if it was in the full and actual exercise of sovereignty over a territory and people large enough for a nation." Ford v Surget, 97 U.S. (7 Otto) 594, 6 (1878) (Clifford, J., concurring).

Although the Restatement's definition of statehood requires the capacity to engage in formal relations with other states, it does not require recognition by other states. See Restatement (Third) sec. 2 cmt. b ("An entity that satisfies the requirements of sec. 1 is a state whether or not its statehood is formally recognized by other states"). Recognized states enjoy certain privileges and immunities relevant to judicial proceedings, see, e.g., Pfizer Inc. v India, 434 U.S. 308, 318 (1978) (diversity jurisdiction); Sabbatino, 376 U.S. at 408–12 (access to U.S. courts); Lafontant, 844 F. Supp. at 131 (head-of-state immunity), but an unrecognized state is not a juridical nullity. Our courts have regularly given effect to the "state" action of unrecognized states. See, e.g., U.S. v Insurance Cos., 89 U.S. (22 Wall.) 99, 101–03 (1875) (seceding states in Civil War); Thorington v Smith, 75 U.S. (8 Wall.) 1, 9–12 (1869) (same); Carl Zeiss Stiftung v VEB Carl Zeiss Jena, 433 F.2d 686, 699 (2d Cir. 1970), cert. denied, 403 U.S. 905 (1971) (post–World War II 33] East Germany).

The customary international law of human rights, such as the proscription of official torture, applies to states without distinction between recognized and unrecognized states. See Restatement (Third) secs. 7, 702. It would be anomalous indeed if non-recognition by the U.S., which typically reflects disfavor with a foreign regime—sometimes due to human rights abuses—had the perverse effect of shielding officials of the unrecognized regime from liability for those violations of international law norms that apply only to state actors.

Appellants' allegations entitle them to prove that Karadzic's regime satisfies the criteria for a state, for purposes of those international law violations requiring state action. Srpska is alleged to control defined territory, control populations within its power, and to have entered into agreements with other governments. It has a president, a legislature, and its own currency. These circumstances readily appear to satisfy the criteria for a state in all aspects of international law. Moreover, it is likely that the state action concept, where applicable for some violations like "official" torture, requires merely the semblance of official authority. The inquiry, after all, is whether a person purporting to wield official power has exceeded internationally recognized standards of civilized conduct, not whether statehood in all its formal aspects exists.

(b) Acting in concert with a foreign state. Appellants also sufficiently alleged that Karadzic acted under color of law insofar as they claimed that he acted in concert with the former Yugoslavia, the statehood of which is not disputed. The "color of law" jurisprudence of 42 U.S.C. sec. 1983 is a relevant guide to whether a defendant has engaged in official action for purposes of jurisdiction under the Alien Tort Act. See Forti v Suarez-Mason, 672 F. Supp. 1531, 1546 (N.D. Cal. 1987), reconsideration granted in part on other grounds, 694 F. Supp. 707 (N.D. Cal. 1988). A private individual acts under color of law within the meaning of section 1983 when he acts together with state officials or with significant state aid. See Lugar v Edmonson Oil Co., 457 U.S. 922, 937 (1982). The appellants are entitled to prove their allegations that Karadzic acted under color of law of Yugoslavia by acting in concert with Yugoslav officials or with significant Yugoslavian aid.

B. The Torture Victim Protection Act The Torture Victim Act, enacted in 1992, provides a cause of action for official torture and extrajudicial killing: An individual who, under actual or apparent authority, or color of law, of any foreign nation—

(1) subjects an individual to torture shall, in a civil action, be liable for damages to that individual; or

(2) subjects an individual to extrajudicial killing shall, in a civil action, be liable for damages to the individual's legal representative, or to any person who may be a claimant in an action for wrongful death. Torture Victim Act sec. 2(a). The statute also requires that a plaintiff exhaust adequate and available local remedies, id. sec. 2(b), imposes a ten-year statute of limitations, id. sec. 2(c), and defines the terms "extrajudicial killing" and "torture," id. sec. 3. By its plain language, the Torture Victim Act renders liable only those individuals who have committed torture or extrajudicial killing "under actual or apparent authority, or color of law, of any foreign nation." Legislative history confirms that this language was intended to "make clear that the plaintiff must establish some governmental involvement in the torture or killing to prove a claim," and that the statute "does not attempt to deal with torture or killing by purely private groups." H.R. Rep. No. 367, 102d Cong., 2d Sess., at 5 (1991), reprinted in 1992 U.S.C.C.A.N. 84, 87. In construing the terms "actual or apparent authority" and "color of law," courts are instructed to look to principles of agency law and to jurisprudence under 28 U.S.C. sec. 1983, respectively. Id.

Though the Torture Victim Act creates a cause of action for official torture, this statute, unlike the Alien Tort Act, is not itself a jurisdictional statute. The Torture Victim Act permits the appellants to pursue their claims of official torture under the jurisdiction conferred by the Alien Tort Act and also under the general federal question jurisdiction of section 1331, see Xuncax v Gramajo, 886 F. Supp. 162, 178 (D. Mass. 1995), to which we now turn.

C. Section 1331

The appellants contend that section 1331 provides an independent basis for subject-matter jurisdiction over all claims alleging violations of international law. Relying on the settled proposition that federal common law incorporates international law, see The Paquete Habana, 175 U.S. 677, 700 (1900); In re Estate of Ferdinand E. Marcos Human Rights Litigation (Marcos I), 978 F.2d 493, 502 (9th Cir. 1992), cert. denied, 113 S. Ct. 2960 (1993); Filartiga, 630 F.2d at 886, they reason that causes of action for violations of international law "arise under" the laws of the U.S. for purposes of jurisdiction under section 1331. Whether that is so is an issue of some uncertainty that need not be decided in this case.

In Tel-Oren Judge Edwards expressed the view that section 1331 did not supply jurisdiction for claimed violations of international law unless the plaintiffs could point to a remedy granted by the law of nations or argue successfully that such a remedy is implied. Tel-Oren, 726 F.2d at 779–80 n.4. The law of nations generally does not create private causes of action to remedy its violations, but leaves to each nation the task of defining the remedies that are available for international law violations. Id. at 778 (Edwards, J., concurring). Some district courts, however, have upheld section 1331 jurisdiction for international law violations. See Abebe-Jiri v Negewo, No. 90-10 (N.D. Ga. Aug., 1993), appeal argued, No. 93–9133 (11th Cir. Jan. 10, 1995); Martinez-Baca v Suarez-Mason, No. 87-57, slip op. at 4–5 (N.D. Cal. Apr. 22, 1988); Forti v Suarez-Mason, 672 F. Supp. 1531, 1544 (N.D. Cal. 1987).

We recognized the possibility of section 1331 jurisdiction in Filartiga, 630 F.2d at 887 n.22, but rested jurisdiction solely on the applicable Alien Tort Act. Since that Act appears to provide a remedy for the appellants' allegations of violations related to genocide, war crimes, and official torture, and the Torture

Victim Act also appears to provide a remedy for their allegations of official torture, their causes of action are statutorily authorized, and, as in Filartiga, we need not rule definitively on whether any causes of action not specifically authorized by statute may be implied by international law standards as incorporated into U.S. law and grounded on section 1331 jurisdiction.

. . .

III. Justiciability

We recognize that cases of this nature might pose special questions concerning the judiciary's proper role when adjudication might have implications in the conduct of this nation's foreign relations. We do not read Filartiga to mean that the federal judiciary must always act in ways that risk significant interference with U.S. foreign relations. To the contrary, we recognize that suits of this nature can present difficulties that implicate sensitive matters of diplomacy historically reserved to the jurisdiction of the political branches. See First National Bank v Banco Nacional de Cuba, 406 U.S. 759, 767 (1972). We therefore proceed to consider whether, even though the jurisdictional threshold is satisfied in the pending cases, other considerations relevant to justiciability weigh against permitting the suits to proceed.

Two nonjurisdictional, prudential doctrines reflect the judiciary's concerns regarding separation of powers: the political question doctrine and the act of state doctrine. It is the "'constitutional' underpinnings" of these doctrines that influenced the concurring opinions of Judge Robb and Judge Bork in Tel-Oren. Although we too recognize the potentially detrimental effects of judicial action in cases of this nature, we do not embrace the rather categorical views as to the inappropriateness of judicial action urged by Judges Robb and Bork. Not every case "touching foreign relations" is non-justiciable, see Baker v Carr, 369 U.S. 186, 211 (1962); Lamont v Woods, 948 F.2d 825, 831–32 (2d Cir. 1991), and judges should not reflexively invoke these doctrines to avoid difficult and somewhat sensitive decisions in the context of human rights. We believe a preferable approach is to weigh carefully the relevant considerations on a case-by-case basis. This will permit the judiciary to act where appropriate in light of the express legislative mandate of the Congress in section 1350, without compromising the primacy of the political branches in foreign affairs.

Karadzic maintains that these suits were properly dismissed because they present nonjusticiable political questions. We disagree. Although these cases present issues that arise in a politically charged context, that does not transform them into cases involving nonjusticiable political questions. "The doctrine is one of 'political questions,' not one of 'political cases.'" Klinghoffer, 937 F.2d at 49 (quoting Baker, 369 U.S. at 217). A nonjusticiable political question would ordinarily involve one or more of the following factors:

[1] a textually demonstrable constitutional commitment of the issue to a coordinate political department; or [2] a lack of judicially discoverable and manageable standards for resolving it; or [3] the impossibility of deciding without an initial policy determination of a kind clearly for nonjudicial discretion; or [4] the impossibility of a court's undertaking independent resolution without expressing lack of the respect due coordinate branches of government; or [5] an unusual need for unquestioning adherence to a political decision already made; or [6] the potentiality of embarrassment from multifarious pronouncements by various departments on one question. Baker v Carr, 369 U.S. at 217; see also Can v U.S., 14 F.3d 160, 163 (2d Cir. 1994).

With respect to the first three factors, we have noted in a similar context involving a tort suit against the PLO that "the department to whom this issue has been 'constitutionally committed' is none other than our own—the Judiciary." Klinghoffer, 937 F.2d at 49. Although the present actions are not based on the common law of torts, as was Klinghoffer, our decision in Filartiga established that universally recognized norms of international law provide judicially discoverable and manageable standards for adjudicating suits brought under the Alien Tort Act, which obviates any need to make initial policy decisions of the kind normally reserved for nonjudicial discretion. Moreover, the existence of judicially discoverable and manageable standards further undermines the claim such suits relate to matters that are constitutionally committed to another branch. See Nixon v U.S., 113 S. Ct. 732, 735 (1993).

The fourth through sixth Baker factors appear to be relevant only if judicial resolution of a question would contradict prior decisions taken by a political branch in those limited contexts where such contradiction would seriously interfere with important governmental interests. Disputes implicating foreign policy concerns have the potential to raise political question issues, although, as the Supreme Court has wisely cautioned, "it is 'error to suppose that every case or controversy which touches foreign relations lies beyond judicial cognizance.'" Japan Whaling Ass'n v American Cetacean Society, 478 U.S. 221, 229–30 (1986) (quoting Baker, 369 U.S. at 211).

The act of state doctrine, under which courts generally refrain from judging the acts of a foreign state within its territory, see Banco Nacional de Cuba v Sabbatino, 376 U.S. 398, 428; Underhill v Hernandez, 168 U.S. 250, 252 (1897), might be implicated in some cases arising under section 1350. However, as in Filartiga, 630 F.2d at 889, we doubt that the acts of even a state official, taken in violation of a nation's fundamental law and wholly unratified by that nation's government, could properly be characterized as an act of state.

In the pending appeal, we need have no concern that interference with important governmental interests warrants rejection of appellants' claims. After commencing their action against Karadzic, attorneys for the plaintiffs in Doe wrote to the Secretary of State to oppose reported attempts by Karadzic to be granted immunity from suit in the U.S.; a copy of plaintiffs' complaint was attached to the letter. Far from intervening in the case to urge rejection of the suit on the ground that it presented political questions, the Department responded with a letter indicating that Karadzic was not immune from suit as an invitee of the United Nations. See Habib Letter, supra.[10] After oral argument in the pending appeals, this Court wrote to the Attorney General to inquire whether the U.S. wished to offer any further views concerning any of the issues raised. In a "Statement of Interest," signed by the Solicitor General and the State Department's Legal Adviser, the U.S. has expressly disclaimed any concern that the political question doctrine should be invoked to prevent the litigation of these lawsuits: "Although there might be instances in which federal courts are asked to issue rulings under the Alien Tort Statute or the Torture Victim Protection Act that might raise a political question, this is not one of them." Statement of Interest of the U.S. at 3. Though even an assertion of the political question doctrine by the Executive Branch, entitled to respectful consideration, would not necessarily preclude adjudication, the Government's reply to our inquiry reinforces our view that adjudication may properly proceed.

As to the act of state doctrine, the doctrine was not asserted in the District Court and is not before us on this appeal. See Filartiga, 630 F.2d at 889. Moreover, the appellee has not had the temerity to assert in this Court that the acts he allegedly committed are the officially approved policy of a state. Finally, as noted, we think it would be a rare case in which the act of state doctrine precluded suit under section 1350. Banco Nacional was careful to recognize the doctrine "in the absence of . . . unambiguous agreement regarding controlling legal principles," 376 U.S. at 428, such as exist in the pending litigation, and applied the doctrine only in a context—expropriation of an alien's property—in which world opinion was sharply divided, see id. at 428–30.

Finally, we note that at this stage of the litigation no party has identified a more suitable forum, and we are aware of none. Though the Statement of the U.S. suggests the general importance of considering the doctrine of forum non conveniens, it seems evident that the courts of the former Yugoslavia, either in Serbia or war-torn Bosnia, are not now available to entertain plaintiffs' claims, even if circumstances concerning the location of witnesses and documents were presented that were sufficient to overcome the plaintiffs' preference for a U.S. forum.

Conclusion

The judgment of the District Court dismissing appellants' complaints for lack of subject-matter jurisdiction is reversed, and the cases are remanded for further proceedings in accordance with this opinion.

Notes

1. Filartiga did not consider the alternative prong of the Alien Tort Act: suits by aliens for a tort committed in violation of "a treaty of the U.S." See id. at 880. As in Filartiga, plaintiffs in the instant cases "primarily rely upon treaties and other international instruments as evidence of an emerging norm of customary international law, rather than independent sources of law," id. at 880 n.7.

2. Two passages of the District Court's opinion arguably indicate that Judge Leisure found the pleading of a violation of the law of nations inadequate because Srpska, even if a state, is not a state "recognized" by other nations. "The current Bosnian-Serb warring military faction does not constitute a recognized state. . . . " Doe, 866 F. Supp. at 741; "the Bosnian-Serbs have achieved neither the level of organization nor the recognition that was attained by the PLO [in Tel-Oren v Libyan Arab Republic, 726 F.2d 774 (D.C. Cir. 1984)]," id. However, the opinion, read as a whole, makes clear that the Judge believed that Srpska is not a state and was not relying on lack of recognition by other states. See, e.g., id. at 741 n.12 ("The Second Circuit has limited the definition of 'state' to 'entities that have a defined [territory] and a permanent population, that are under the control of their own government, and that engage in or have the capacity to engage in, formal relations with other entities.' Klinghoffer v S.N.C. Achille Lauro, 937 F.2d 44, 47 (2d Cir. 1991) (quotation,

brackets and citation omitted). The current Bosnian-Serb entity fails to meet this definition." We quote Judge Leisure's quotation from Klinghoffer with the word "territory," which was inadvertently omitted.

3. Section 702 provides:

A state violates international law if, as a matter of state policy, it practices, encourages, or condones

(a) genocide,

(b) slavery or slave trade,

(c) the murder or causing the disappearance of individuals,

(d) torture or other cruel, inhuman, or degrading treatment or punishment,

(e) prolonged arbitrary detention,

(f) systematic racial discrimination, or

(g) a consistent pattern of gross violations of internationally recognized human rights.

4. Section 404 provides:

A state has jurisdiction to define and prescribe punishment for certain offenses recognized by the community of nations as of universal concern, such as piracy, slave trade, attacks on or hijacking of aircraft, genocide, war crimes, and perhaps certain acts of terrorism, even where [no other basis of jurisdiction] is present.

5. Judge Edwards was the only member of the Tel-Oren panel to confront the issue whether the law of nations applies to non-state actors. Then-Judge Bork, relying on separation of powers principles, concluded, in disagreement with Filartiga, that the Alien Tort Act did not apply to most violations of the law of nations. Tel-Oren, 726 F.2d at 798. Judge Robb concluded that the controversy was non-justiciable. Id. at 823. Nor did Judge Edwards in his scholarly opinion in Tel-Oren reject the application of international law to any private action. On the contrary, citing piracy and slave-trading as early examples, he observed that there exists a "handful of crimes to which the law of nations attributes individual responsibility," id. at 795. Reviewing authorities similar to those consulted in Filartiga, he merely concluded that torture—the specific violation alleged in Tel-Oren—was not within the limited category of violations that do not require state action.

6. The Senate Report merely repeats the language of section 1092 and does not provide any explanation of its purpose. See S. Rep. 333, 100th Cong., 2d Sess., at 5 (1988), reprinted at 1988 U.S.C.C.A.N. 4156, 4160. The House Report explains that section 1092 "clarifies that the bill creates no new federal cause of action in civil proceedings." H.R. Rep. 566, 100th Cong., 2d Sess., at 8 (1988) (emphasis added). This explanation confirms our view that the Genocide Convention Implementation Act was not intended to abrogate civil causes of action that might be available under existing laws, such as the Alien Tort Act.

7. Convention for the Amelioration of the Condition of the Wounded and Sick in Armed Forces in the Field, entered into force Oct. 21, 1950, for the U.S. Feb. 2, 1956, 6 U.S.T. 3114, T.I.A.S. 3362, 75 U.N.T.S. 31 (hereinafter "Geneva Convention I"); Convention for the Amelioration of the Condition of the Wounded, Sick, and Shipwrecked Members of Armed Forces at Sea, entered into force Oct. 21, 1950, for the U.S. Feb. 2, 1956, 6 U.S.T. 3217, T.I.A.S. 3363, 75 U.N.T.S. 85; Convention Relative to the Treatment of Prisoners of War, entered into force Oct. 21, 1950, for the U.S. Feb. 2, 1956, 6 U.S.T. 3316, T.I.A.S. 3364, 75 U.N.T.S. 135; Convention Relative to the Protection of Civilian Persons in Time of War, entered into force Oct. 21, 1950, for the U.S. Feb. 2, 1956, 6 U.S.T. 3516, T.I.A.S. 3365, 75 U.N.T.S. 287.

. . .

10. The Habib letter on behalf of the US State Department added: We share your repulsion at the sexual assaults and other war crimes that have been reported as part of the policy of ethnic cleansing in Bosnia-Herzegovina. The U.S. has reported rape and other grave breaches of the Geneva Conventions to the United Nations. This information is being investigated by a United Nations Commission of Experts, which was established at U.S. initiative.

1. *U.S. v Roy M. Belfast*, U.S. Court of Appeals for the 11th Circuit (Excerpted)
   Cite as 611 F.3d 783 (2010)

U.S. v ROY M. BELFAST (the "Chuckie Taylor" Case)

Roy M. Belfast, Jr., a/k/a Charles McArthur Emmanuel, a/k/a Charles Taylor, Jr., a/k/a Chuckie Taylor, II ("Emmanuel"), appeals his convictions and 97-year sentence for committing numerous acts of torture and other atrocities in Liberia between 1999 and 2003, during the presidency of his father, Charles Taylor.

Emmanuel, who is the first individual to be prosecuted under the Torture Act, 18 U.S.C. § 2340-2340A ("the Torture Act"), seeks reversal of his convictions on the ground that the Torture Act is unconstitutional. Primarily, Emmanuel contends that congressional authority to pass the Torture Act derives solely from the U.S.'s obligations as a signatory to the Convention Against Torture and Other Cruel, Inhuman or Degrading Treatment or Punishment, Dec. 10, 1984, 1465 U.N.T.S. 85 (the "CAT"); he says the Torture Act impermissibly exceeds the bounds of that authority, both in its definition of torture and its proscription against conspiracies to commit torture . . .

. . . the facts of this case are riddled with extraordinary cruelty and evil. The defendant, Charles McArthur Emmanuel, was born in Massachusetts in 1977, the son of Bernice Yolanda Emmanuel and Charles Taylor. Taylor returned to his native Liberia sometime thereafter . . . In 1997, Taylor was elected to the presidency. President Taylor soon charged the twenty-year-old Emmanuel with overseeing the state's creation of an Anti-Terrorism Unit ("ATU")-also known in Liberia as the "Demon Forces"-which was responsible for protecting Taylor and his family . . . Between 1999 and 2002, the defendant wielded his power in a terrifying and violent manner, torturing numerous individuals in his custody who were never charged with any crime or given any legal process . . .

. . . In 2003, Liberia's civil war ended. President Taylor resigned, left the country, and was ultimately extradited to the Hague, where he is currently on trial for crimes against humanity in the Special Court for Sierra Leone. Emmanuel left Liberia in July 2003. Between 2004 and 2005, he called the U.S. Defense Attaché in Liberia from Trinidad several times, seeking information about the United Nations travel ban on certain persons, inquiring about joining the U.S. Marines, and claiming that he was an American who could go home whenever he wanted.

On March 30, 2006, when Emmanuel arrived at Miami International Airport on a flight from Trinidad, officials executed a warrant for his arrest for attempting to enter the U.S. using a false passport . . .

Analysis

. . . Congress passed the Torture Act to implement the U.S.'s obligations under the Convention Against Torture, which itself was the product of a long-evolving international consensus against torture committed by official actors. The CAT was adopted by the United Nations General Assembly on December 10, 1984. The preamble to the CAT recognizes the obligation of nations, under the U.N. Charter, to "promote universal respect for, and observance of, human rights and fundamental freedoms." See CAT, pmbl. The preamble thus announced the treaty's broad purpose of "mak[ing] more effective the struggle against torture and other cruel, inhuman or degrading treatment or punishment throughout the world." Id . . .

. . . The Torture Act provides that "[w]hoever outside the U.S. commits or attempts to commit torture shall be fined . . . or imprisoned not more than 20 years, or both, and if death results . . . shall be punished by death or imprisoned for any term of years or for life." 18 U.S.C. § 2340A(a). The federal courts have jurisdiction if "the alleged offender is a national of the U.S.[,] or [if] the alleged offender is present in the U.S., irrespective of the nationality of the victim or alleged offender." Id. § 2340A(b). A person who conspires to commit an offense under the Torture Act is subject to the same penalties prescribed for the offense itself. Id. § 2340A(c) . . .

. . . The heart of Emmanuel's argument is that the Torture Act is invalid because its definition of torture sweeps more broadly than that provided by the CAT . . .

. . . [W]e are satisfied that the Torture Act is a valid exercise of congressional power under the Necessary and Proper Clause, because the Torture Act tracks the provisions of the CAT in all material respects. The plain language of the CAT controls the analysis of its scope, Sale v Haitian Ctrs. Council, Inc., 509 U.S. 155, 194, 113 S.Ct. 2549, 125 L.Ed.2d 128 (1993), and the CAT declares broadly that its provisions are "without prejudice to any international instrument or national legislation which does or may contain provisions of wider application," CAT, art. 1(2). Put simply, the CAT created a floor, not a ceiling, for its signatories in their efforts to combat torture. Moreover, settled rules of treaty interpretation require that we construe the CAT generously:

In choosing between conflicting interpretations of a treaty obligation, a narrow and restricted construction is to be avoided as not consonant with the principles deemed controlling in the interpretation of international agreements. Considerations which should govern the diplomatic relations between nations, and the good faith of treaties, as well, require that their obligations should be liberally construed so as to effect the apparent intention of the parties to secure equality and reciprocity between them. For that reason if a treaty fairly admits of two constructions, one restricting the rights which may be claimed under it, and the other enlarging it, the more liberal construction is to be preferred.

Factor v Laubenheimer, 290 U.S. 276, 293-94, 54 S.Ct. 191, 78 L.Ed. 315 (1933) . . .

. . . Emmanuel also claims that the Torture Act is unconstitutional because it applies during armed conflicts, but that claim is easily rejected. The CAT itself says that "[n]o exceptional circumstances whatsoever, whether a state of war or a threat of war, internal political instability or any other public emergency, may be invoked as a justification of torture." CAT, art. 2(2). Referring to that provision, the Senate Executive Report explained that:

> [t]he use of torture in wartime is already prohibited within the scope of the Geneva Conventions, to which the U.S. and virtually all other countries are Parties, and which in any event generally reflect customary international law. The exclusion of public emergency as an excuse for torture is necessary if the Convention is to have significant effect, as public emergencies are commonly invoked as a source of extraordinary powers or as a justification for limiting fundamental rights and freedoms.

S. Exec. Rep. 101-30, at 15; see also Nuru v Gonzales, 404 F.3d 1207, 1222 (9th Cir.2005) ("Even in war, torture is not authorized."). Accordingly, there is no merit to Emmanuel's contention that the CAT, or legislation authorized by the CAT, cannot apply during armed conflicts . . .

. . . Emmanuel also fails to persuade us that he cannot be prosecuted for torture committed before Liberia became a signatory to the Convention Against Torture in 2004. Nothing in the CAT limits its application to torture committed within the territorial borders of its signatories. Indeed, such a limitation would be at odds with the treaty's core purpose of "mak[ing] more effective the struggle against torture . . . throughout the world," CAT, pmbl., inasmuch as any nation that wished to practice torture, even on a huge scale, could avoid all responsibility by not signing the CAT in the first place, or by withdrawing from the CAT before engaging in torture. To avoid precisely those possibilities, the CAT requires each state party to "ensure that all acts of torture are offences under its criminal law." Id. art. 4(1). Congress faithfully implemented the CAT's directive to prosecute torture wherever it may occur, applying the proscriptions of the Torture Act to "[w]hoever outside the U.S. commits . . . torture." 18 U.S.C. § 2340A(a) (emphasis added) . . .

. . . Next, Emmanuel argues that his convictions are invalid because the Torture Act allows federal courts to take jurisdiction over an act of torture based solely on the presence of the alleged torturer in the U.S., something he claims is not authorized by the CAT or any other provision of law. Notably, there was no need to invoke this so-called "present-in" jurisdiction in this case because Emmanuel is a U.S. citizen. See 18 U.S.C. § 2340A(b)(1) (conferring jurisdiction over acts of torture where "the alleged offender is a national of the U.S."). Thus, we address Emmanuel's objection to "present-in" jurisdiction only in the context of his facial challenge to the Torture Act.

Article 5(2) of the CAT obligates a signatory nation to assert jurisdiction over an "alleged offender" who is "present in any territory under its jurisdiction" and whom it does not extradite. It is difficult to see what clearer authorization of "present-in" jurisdiction the CAT might have contained . . .

. . . Emmanuel also challenges his Torture Act convictions on the ground that the Torture Act does not apply to the extraterritorial conduct of a U.S. citizen. He is, once again, incorrect, because Congress has the power to regulate extraterritorial conduct, and the requisite expression of congressional intent to do so is found in the Torture Act.

. . . It has long been established that Congress has the power to regulate the extraterritorial acts of U.S. citizens. U.S. v Plummer, 221 F.3d 1298, 1304 (11th Cir.2000); see also U.S. v Baker, 609 F.2d 134, 136 (5th Cir.1980) (noting that "[s]ince an early date, it has been recognized that Congress may attach extraterritorial effect to its penal enactments," and that "a nation's 'power to secure itself from injury may certainly be exercised beyond the limits of its territory.'") (quoting Church v Hubbart, 6 U.S. (2 Cranch) 187, 234, 2 L.Ed. 249 (1804) (Marshall, C.J.)). As we have explained, however, whether Congress has chosen to exercise that authority . . . is an issue of statutory construction . . .

. . . The language of the Torture Act itself evinces an unmistakable congressional intent to apply the statute extraterritorially. It punishes "[w]hoever outside the U.S. commits . . . torture." 18 U.S.C. § 2340A(a) (emphasis added). Further, even if the language of the Torture Act were not so remarkably clear, the intent to apply the statute to acts occurring outside U.S. territory could be inferred along the lines set forth in Plummer, 221 F.3d at 1310. First, the nature of the harm to which the CAT and the Torture Act are directed- "torture and other cruel, inhuman or degrading treatment or punishment throughout the world," see CAT, prmbl.-is quintessentially international in scope. Second, and relatedly, the international focus of the statute is "self-evident": Congress's concern was not to prevent official torture within the borders of the U.S., but in nations where the rule of law has broken down and the ruling government has become the enemy, rather than the protector, of its citizens. Finally, limiting the prohibitions of the Torture Act to conduct occurring in the U.S. would dramatically, if not entirely, reduce their efficacy.

In short, all of Emmanuel's substantive convictions under the Torture Act are fully consonant with the U.S. Constitution.

Emmanuel also argues that by criminalizing conspiracy to commit torture, the Torture Act exceeded Congress's constitutional authority, because conspiracy, Emmanuel says, is recognized in neither the CAT nor international law. We remain un-persuaded.

Article 4(1) of the CAT explicitly requires that "[e]ach State Party . . . ensure that all acts of torture are offenses under its criminal law," and it provides that "[t]he same shall apply . . . to an act by any person which constitutes complicity or participation in torture." CAT, art. 4(1) (emphasis added). In other words, the CAT specifically instructs its signatories to criminalize not only the act of torture itself, but also conduct that encourages and furthers the commission of torture by others. Conspiracy plainly amounts to such conduct. Indeed, the ordinary meaning of the term "complicity" is "association or participation in," Webster's New Int'l Dictionary 465 (3d ed.2002); see also Black's Law Dictionary 324 (9th ed.2004) (defining complicity as "[a]ssociation or participation in a criminal act"), and those notions squarely encompass the acts of conspirators in furtherance of a conspiracy. Thus, the plain language of the CAT, which controls our analysis, supports Congress's decision to criminalize conspiracies to commit torture in the Torture Act. 18 U.S.C. § 2340A(c).

The only case Emmanuel cites in support of his contrary position is Hamdan v Rumsfeld, 548 U.S. 557, 126 S.Ct. 2749, 165 L.Ed.2d 723 (2006). The Supreme Court did conclude in Hamdan that a conspiracy to violate the customary international law of war was not an offense punishable under that body of law in a military commission. Id. at 601-12, 126 S.Ct. 2749. That conclusion, however, has no bearing on this case. For one, this case does not concern the law of war. Even more importantly, this case does not require us to seek justification for the prohibition on conspiracies to commit torture in customary international law, because an express international treaty obligation-the CAT-requires its signatories to punish such conduct. Congress did so in the Torture Act.

Emmanuel also suggests that his prosecution for conspiracy went beyond the terms of the Torture Act itself, because all of his alleged acts in furtherance of the conspiracy to commit torture were "governmental self-preservation tactics." That suggestion, however, lacks any merit. The Torture Act prohibits an individual from conspiring to torture and torturing others while acting under the color of law. The indictment against Emmanuel alleged that the object of the conspiracy was to maintain, preserve, protect and strengthen the power and authority of Charles McArthur Taylor's presidency, and to intimidate, neutralize, punish, weaken and eliminate actual and perceived opponents of and threats to his administration, by means of torture, in violation of Title 18, U.S. Code, Sections 2340A and 2340(1) . . .

. . . More fundamentally, the entire premise of Emmanuel's argument-that a conspiracy to commit torture is permissible whenever its object is to preserve governmental power-is unacceptable under the CAT. Official torture is most likely to occur precisely when an illegitimate regime perceives a threat to its dominance from dissenters. In recognition of this reality, the CAT itself unambiguously provides that "[n]o exceptional circumstances whatsoever, whether a state of war or a threat of war, internal political instability or any other public emergency, may be invoked as a justification of torture." CAT, art. 2(2). The CAT thus anticipated prosecutions such as this one, where torture is committed by a regime in order to maintain its brutal control over an unhappy populace. The conspiracy prosecution here was fully consistent with the mandate that such acts may be prosecuted.

Finally, Emmanuel says that the Torture Act's prohibition on conspiracy cannot apply extraterritorially. However, extraterritorial jurisdiction over a conspiracy charge exists whenever the underlying substantive crime applies to extraterritorial conduct. See U.S. v Yousef, 327 F.3d 56, 87-88 (2d Cir.2003) (citing U.S. v Bowman, 260 U.S. 94, 98, 43 S.Ct. 39, 67 L.Ed. 149 (1922), for the proposition that "if Congress intended U.S. courts to have jurisdiction over [a] substantive crime, it is reasonable to conclude that Congress also intended to vest in U.S. courts the requisite jurisdiction over an extraterritorial conspiracy to commit that crime."). Because, as we have explained, there is extraterritorial jurisdiction to prohibit torture under the Torture Act, it follows that there is extraterritorial jurisdiction to prohibit conspiracy to commit violations of the Torture Act as well.

Emmanuel's conviction for conspiracy to commit torture is constitutional, and his acts fell within the proscriptions of the Torture Act .

4. *Hill v Rincon Band of Luiseno Indians* (Excerpted)
   Cite as: Not Reported in F.Supp.2d, 2007 WL 2429327, 2007

HILL v RINCON BAND OF LUISENO INDIANS
U.S District Court for the Southern District of California
August 22, 2007, Not Reported in F.Supp.2d, 2007 WL 2429327

Plaintiff filed her complaint against Defendants Rincon Band of Luiseno Indians ("Rincon"), Tuukut Sass and Rob Shafer (collectively "Defendants") on November 17, 2006. Rincon's first motion to dismiss was granted on March 16, 2007. Doc. No. 5. This Court's order provided that if the amended complaint fails to establish subject matter jurisdiction, it will be dismissed with prejudice.

Plaintiff filed her first amended complaint against Defendants on May 9, 2007 seeking damages for intentional infliction of emotional distress, negligent infliction of emotional distress, and human rights violation under international law. Doc. No. 15. Plaintiff alleges that Rincon hired her as a water technician in August 2003, and that during the course of her employment, she "was the target of offensive, threatening and dangerous conduct by male co-workers." Amended Complaint. at ¶ 14. The harassing conduct allegedly included making sexual gestures and advances, urinating on her car tire, spitting and touching Plaintiff, directing derogatory and lewd comments to Plaintiff, aiming and firing a shotgun at Plaintiff, and harassing and threatening Plaintiff with phone messages. Id. Plaintiff contends that the harassing conduct spanned over a period of eighteen months, and included acts on Rincon's property, as well as in the county of San Diego. Id. at ¶ 15.

Plaintiff further alleges that Rincon created and forced Plaintiff to work in a dangerous environment by requiring her to transport concentrated chlorine in her personal vehicle. Amended Complaint at ¶ 20. Plaintiff claims that this behavior and environment caused her to suffer an emotional breakdown, where she could no longer work with Rincon and was forced to stop working in July 2005, and eventually resigned in October 2005. Id. at ¶ 19. Plaintiff further asserts that complaints made to her supervisors were ignored, and that Defendant Shafer, Rincon's Tribal Administrator, never brought her complaints to the attention of the tribal council. Id. at ¶ 18.

The relevant new and revised allegations in the first amended complaint are as follows:

9. This action is based upon violations of basic human rights under international law committed by Rincon and/or its agents, including each defendant, and directed toward MS. HILL.

10. This Court has jurisdiction pursuant to 28 U.S.C. § 1331, which provides federal question jurisdiction in cases arising under the Constitution and laws of the U.S. International human rights law constitutes the law of the U.S., under the established doctrine that customary international law is a part of the federal common law.

12. RINCON expressly waived its tribal sovereign immunity with respect to claims resulting from gaming-related activities. MS. HILL'S claims arise from gaming-related activities. RINCON also has no immunity from claims for violation of basic human rights under international law.

Further, Plaintiff deleted Count I for "civil rights violation" under the unconstitutional provision of the Violence Against Women Act, 42 U.S.C. § 13981. Plaintiff added Count III for "Violation of Human Rights Under International Law." The relevant paragraph states:

35. The conduct of Defendants toward MS. HILL as alleged above violated MS. HILL'S basic human rights pursuant to fundamental norms of international law, as established in the United Nations Charter, the Universal Declaration of Human Rights, and other international human rights law sources, and which also arise under Federal common law . . .

Analysis

. . . The allegations in the amended complaint do not invoke international law or refer to international relations. Plaintiff added a claim that the Rincon violated Plaintiff's basic human rights under fundamental norms of customary international law which arise under Federal common law. Doc. No. 18, at 3-4. These allegations do not provide an independent basis for jurisdiction by this Court. Plaintiff provides no authority for her claim that an Indian tribe is a foreign state for purposes of invoking international law.

For purposes of foreign relations law, Rincon is not a "state." See Restatement (Third) of the Foreign Relations Law of the U.S. § 201, comment (e) "Capacity to conduct international relations." Indian tribes cannot engage in foreign relations; they lack authority to make treaties and are subject to federal legislative power. See Felix S. Cohen, Handbook of Federal Indian Law § 4.02(1) (2005 ed.). Plaintiff's claim of basic human rights violations under fundamental norms of international law is vague and provides no specific international law allegedly violated. See e.g. Bruns v Nat'l Credit Union Admin., 122 F.3d 1251, 1257 (9th Cir.1997).

The fundamental norms of international law that Plaintiff's alleges have been violated are those "established in the United Nations Charter, the Universal Declaration of Human Rights, and other international human rights law sources." Amended Complaint at ¶ 35. These claims lack legal authority. In Sosa v Alvarez-Machain, 542 U.S. 692, 124 S.Ct. 2739, 159 L.Ed.2d 718 (2004), the Supreme court held that the Universal Declaration of Human Rights does not impose obligations as a matter of international law, does not impose legal obligations as would a treaty or international agreement, and does not itself "establish the relevant and applicable rule of international law," but rather sets forth a "common standard of achievement for all peoples and all nations".. Id. at 734-735. The Supreme court found that the allegations under the Declaration did not violate customary international law "so well defined as to support creation of a federal remedy." Id.

Similarly, much of the United Nations Charter is aspirational. See Tel-Oren v Libyan Arab Republic, 726 F.2d 774, 809 (D.C.Cir.1984). The Charter does not speak in terms of individual rights but rather speaks about obligations on nations. None of the purposes and principles are intended to be judicially enforceable by individuals. Id.

This Court reviewed all the cases cited by Plaintiff in support of her arguments relating to the applicability of fundamental norms of customary international law to this case, and position that this Court should find the conduct of Rincon violates well-defined norms of customary international law and justifies a federal remedy. The fatal flaw in Plaintiff's claims under "international law" is that Rincon is not a foreign state.

Each case cited by Plaintiff involves the interests or laws of a foreign sovereign. Since at least 1831, the Supreme Court has held that Indian tribes are not "foreign nations" or "foreign states", but rather "domestic depend nations." Cherokee Nation, 30 U.S. at 17, 19-20; Montoya v U.S., 180 U.S. 261, 265, 36 Ct.Cl. 577, 21 S.Ct. 358, 45 L.Ed. 521 (U.S.1901). The Ninth Circuit has followed suit and held that Indian tribes are not "foreign states." See Allen v Gold Country Casino, 464 F.3d 1044, 1048 (9th Cir.2006); Krystal Energy Co. v Navajo Nation, 357 F.3d 1055, 1058 (9th Cir.2004).

Rincon is not a "state" for purposes of international law. There is no authority cited by Plaintiff, and this court is not aware of any, that suggests or dictates that Indian tribes should be treated as foreign nations or foreign states for purposes of applying international human rights law. This Court therefore finds that international law principles do not apply in this case involving an employment claim against an Indian tribe. . . .

> 5. Kiobel v Royal Dutch Petroleum. U.S. Court Of Appeals for the
> Second Circuit (Excerpted)
> Cite as: Docket Nos. 06-4800-cv, 06-4876-cv

KIOBEL V ROYAL DUTCH PETROLEUM
September 17, 2010

ESTHER KIOBEL, individually and on behalf of her late husband, DR. BARINEM KIOBEL, [et al.] *Plaintiffs-Appellants-Cross-Appellees,*

v

ROYAL DUTCH PETROLEUM CO., SHELL TRANSPORT AND TRADING COMPANY PLC, *Defendants-Appellees-Cross-Appellants,*
SHELL PETROLEUM DEVELOPMENT COMPANY OF NIGERIA, LTD.,
Defendant.
Before: JACOBS, *Chief Judge,* LEVAL, and CABRANES, *Circuit Judges.*
Plaintiffs assert claims for aiding and abetting violations of the law of nations against defendants—all of which are corporations—under the Alien Tort Statute ("ATS"), 28 U.S.C. § 1350, a statute enacted by the first Congress as part of the Judiciary Act of 1789. We hold, under the precedents of the Supreme Court

and our own Court over the past three decades, that in ATS suits alleging violations of customary international law, the scope of liability—who is liable for what—is determined by customary international law itself. Because customary international law consists of only those norms that are specific, universal, and obligatory in the relations of States *inter se*, and because no corporation has ever been subject to *any* form of liability (whether civil or criminal) under the customary international law of human rights, we hold that corporate liability is not a discernable—much less universally recognized—norm of customary international law that we may apply pursuant to the ATS. Accordingly, plaintiffs' ATS claims must be dismissed for lack of subject matter jurisdiction. The order of the U.S. District Court for the Southern District of New York (Kimba M. Wood, *Judge*) is **AFFIRMED** insofar as it dismissed plaintiffs' claims against the corporate defendants and **REVERSED** insofar as it declined to dismiss plaintiffs' claims against the corporate defendants.

. . .

JOSÉ A. CABRANES, *Circuit Judge*:

Once again we consider a case brought under the Alien Tort Statute ("ATS"), 28 U.S.C. § 1350, a jurisdictional provision unlike any other in American law and of a kind apparently unknown to any other legal system in the world. Passed by the first Congress in 1789, the ATS laid largely dormant for over 170 years. Judge Friendly called it a "legal Lohengrin"—"no one seems to know whence it came." Then, in 1980, the statute was given new life, when our Court first recognized in *Filartiga v Pena-Irala* that the ATS provides jurisdiction over (1) tort actions, (2) brought by aliens (only), (3) for violations of the law of nations (also called "customary international law") including, as a general matter, war crimes and crimes against humanity—crimes in which the perpetrator can be called "*hostis humani generis*, an enemy of all mankind." Since that time, the ATS has given rise to an abundance of litigation in U.S. district courts. For the first fifteen years after *Filartiga*—that is, from 1980 to the mid-1990s—aliens brought ATS suits in our courts onl y against notorious foreign *individuals*; the first ATS case alleging, in effect, that a corporation (or "juridical" person) was an "enemy of all mankind" apparently was brought as recently as 1997. Such civil lawsuits, alleging heinous crimes condemned by customary international law, often involve a variety of issues unique to ATS litigation, not least the fact that the events took place abroad and in troubled or chaotic circumstances. The resulting complexity and uncertainty—combined with the fact that juries hearing ATS claims are capable of awarding multibillion-dollar verdicts—has led many defendants to settle ATS claims prior to trial. Thus, our Court has published only nine significant decisions on the ATS since 1980 (seven of the nine coming in the last decade), and the Supreme Court in its entire history has decided only one ATS case.

Because appellate review of ATS suits has been so uncommon, there remain a number of unresolved issues lurking in our ATS jurisprudence—issues that we have simply had no occasion to address in the handful of cases we have decided in the thirty years since the revival of the ATS. This case involves one such unresolved issue: Does the jurisdiction granted by the ATS extend to civil actions brought against corporations under the law of nations?

Plaintiffs are residents of Nigeria who claim that Dutch, British, and Nigerian corporations engaged in oil exploration and production aided and abetted the Nigerian government in committing violations of the law of nations. They seek damages under the ATS, and thus their suit may proceed only if the ATS provides jurisdiction over tort actions brought against corporations under customary international law.

A legal culture long accustomed to imposing liability on corporations may, at first blush, assume that corporations must be subject to tort liability under the ATS, just as corporations are generally liable in tort under our domestic law (what international law calls "municipal law"). But the substantive law that determines our jurisdiction under the ATS is neither the domestic law of the U.S. nor the domestic law of any other country. By conferring subject matter jurisdiction over a limited number of offenses defined by *international law*, the ATS requires federal courts to look beyond rules of domestic law—however well-established they may be—to examine the specific and universally accepted rules that the nations of the world treat as binding *in their dealings with one another*. As Judge Friendly carefully explained, customary international law includes only "those standards, rules or customs (a) affecting the relationship between states or between an individual and a foreign state, and (b) used by those states for their common good and/or in dealings *inter se*."

Our recognition of a norm of liability as a matter of *domestic law*, therefore, cannot create a norm of customary international law. In other words, the fact that corporations are liable as juridical persons under domestic law does not mean that they are liable under international law (and, therefore, under the ATS). Moreover, the fact that a legal norm is found in most or even all "civilized nations" does not make that norm a part of customary interna- tional law. As we explained in *Filartiga*:

[T]he mere fact that every nation's municipal [*i.e.*, domestic] law may prohibit theft does not incorporate "the Eighth Commandment, 'Thou Shalt not steal' . . . into the law of nations." It is only where the nations of the world have demonstrated that the wrong is of mutual, and not merely several, concern, by means of express international accords, that a wrong generally recognized becomes an international law violation within the meaning of the [ATS].

Accordingly, absent a relevant treaty of the U.S.—and none is relied on here—we must ask whether a plaintiff bringing an ATS suit against a corporation has alleged a violation of customary international law.

The singular achievement of international law since the Second World War has come in the area of human rights, where the subjects of customary international law—*i.e.*, those with international rights, duties, and liabilities—now include not merely *states*, but also *individuals*. This principle was most famously applied by the International Military Tribunal at Nuremberg. As Justice Robert H. Jackson, chief prosecutor for the U.S. at Nurem- berg, explained:

[The Nurnberg trials] for the first time made explicit and unambiguous what was theretofore, as the Tribunal has declared, implicit in International Law, namely, that to prepare, incite, or wage a war of aggression . . . and that to persecute, oppress, or do violence to individuals or minorities on political, racial, or religious grounds in connection with such a war, or to exterminate, enslave, or deport civilian populations, is an international crime, *and that for the commission of such crimes individuals are responsible*. Robert H. Jackson, *Final Report to the President Concerning the Nurnberg War Crimes Trial* (1946) (emphasis added), *reprinted in* 20 Temp. L.Q. 338, 342 (1946).

From the beginning, however, the principle of individual liability for violations of international law has been limited to natural persons—not "juridical" persons such as corporations—because the moral responsibility for a crime so heinous and unbounded as to rise to the level of an "international crime" has rested solely with the individual men and *The Nurnberg Trial* (*U.S. v Goering*), 6 F.R.D. 69, 110 women who have perpetrated it. As the Nuremberg tribunal unmistakably set forth in explaining the rationale for individual liability for violations of international law: "Crimes against international law are committed by men, not by abstract entities, and only by punishing individuals who commit such crimes can the provisions of international law be enforced."

(Int'l Military Trib. at Nuremberg 1946) (rejecting the argument that only states could be liable under international law).

After Nuremberg, as new international tribunals have been created, the customary international law of human rights has remained focused not on abstract entities but on the individual men and women who have committed international crimes universally recognized by the nations of the world. This principle has taken its most vivid form in the recent design of the International Criminal Court ("ICC"). Although there was a proposal at the Rome Conference to grant the ICC jurisdiction over corporations and other "juridical" persons, that proposal was soundly rejected, and the Rome Statute, the ICC's constitutive document, hews to the tenet set forth in Nuremberg that international norms should be enforced by the punishment of the individual men and women who violate them.

In short, because customary international law imposes individual liability for a limited number of international crimes—including war crimes, crimes against humanity (such as genocide), and torture—we have held that the ATS provides jurisdiction over claims in tort against individuals who are alleged to have committed such crimes. As we explain in detail below, however, customary international law has steadfastly rejected the notion of corporate liability for international crimes, and no international tribunal has ever held a corporation liable for a violation of the law of nations.

We must conclude, therefore, that insofar as plaintiffs bring claims under the ATS against corporations, plaintiffs fail to allege violations of the law of nations, and plaintiffs' claims fall outside the limited jurisdiction provided by the ATS.

We emphasize that the question before us is not whether corporations are "immune" from suit under the ATS: That formulation improperly assumes that there is a norm imposing liability in the first place. Rather, the question before us, as the Supreme Court has explained, "is whether international law extends the scope of liability for a violation of a given norm to the perpetrator being sued, if the defendant is a private actor such as a corporation or individual." Looking to international law, we find a jurisprudence, first set forth in Nuremberg and repeated by every international tribunal of which we are aware, that offenses against the law of nations (*i.e.*, customary international law) for violations of human rights can be charged against States and against individual men and women but not against juridical persons such as corporations. As a result, although international law has sometimes extended the scope of liability for a violation of a given norm to individuals, it has *never* extended the scope of liability to a corporation.

We pause briefly to acknowledge and reply to the separate opinion of our colleague, Judge Leval. As an initial matter, we are perplexed by Judge Leval's repeated insistence that there is no "basis" for our holding because "[n]o precedent of international law endorses" it. *See, e.g.*, Concurring Op. 3. In an ATS suit, we may apply only those international norms that are "specific, universal, and obligatory."20 As a result, the responsibility of establishing a norm of customary international law lies with those wishing to invoke it, and in the absence of sources of international law endorsing (or refuting) a norm, the norm simply cannot be applied in a suit grounded on customary international law under the ATS.

. . . .

We agree with Judge Leval that whether to enact a civil remedy for violations of international law is a matter to be determined by each State; the U.S. has done so in enacting the ATS. But the ATS does not specify who is liable; it imposes liability only for a "violation of the law of nations," 28 U.S.C. § 1350, and thus it leaves the question of the nature and scope of liability—who is liable for what—to customary international law. As we explain in detail below, therefore, whether a defendant is liable under the ATS depends entirely upon whether that defendant is subject to liability under international law. It is inconceivable that a defendant who is *not liable* under customary international law could be *liable* under the ATS.

. . . .

BACKGROUND

These cross-appeals come to us from the U.S. District Court for the Southern District of New York (Kimba M. Wood, *Judge*). At this stage of the proceedings, we accept as true all non conclusory factual allegations relevant to this decision. *See Ashcroft v Iqbal*, 129 S. Ct. 1937, 1949-50 (2009).

I. Factual Background

Plaintiffs, who are, or were, residents of the Ogoni Region of Nigeria, allege that defendants Royal Dutch Petroleum Company ("Royal Dutch") and Shell Transport and Trading Company PLC ("Shell"), through a subsidiary named Shell Petroleum Development Company of Nigeria, Ltd. ("SPDC"), aided and abetted the Nigerian government in committing human rights abuses directed at plaintiffs. Royal Dutch and Shell are holding companies incorporated respectively in the Netherlands and the United Kingdom.25 SPDC is incorporated in Nigeria. All defendants are corporate entities—that is, "juridical" persons, rather than "natural" persons.

SPDC has been engaged in oil exploration and production in the Ogoni region of Nigeria since 1958. In response to SPDC's activities residents of the Ogoni region organized a group named the "Movement for Survival of Ogoni People" to protest the environmental effects of oil exploration in the region. According to plaintiffs, in 1993 defendants responded by enlisting the aid of the Nigerian government to suppress the Ogoni resistance. Throughout 1993 and 1994, Nigerian military forces are alleged to have shot and killed Ogoni residents and attacked Ogoni villages—beating, raping, and arresting residents and destroying or looting property—all with the assistance of defendants. Specifically, plaintiffs allege that defendants, *inter alia*, (1) provided transportation to Nigerian forces, (2) allowed their property to be utilized as a staging ground for attacks, (3) provided food for soldiers involved in the attacks, and (4) provided compensation to those soldiers.

Plaintiffs brought claims against defendants under the ATS for aiding and abetting the Nigerian government in alleged violations of the law of nations. Specifically plaintiffs brought claims of aiding and abetting (1) extra- judicial killing; (2) crimes against humanity; (3) torture or cruel, inhuman, and degrading treatment; (4) arbitrary arrest and detention; (5) violation of the rights to life, liberty, security, and association; (6) forced exile; and (7) property destruction.

II. Procedural History

Plaintiffs commenced this lawsuit by filing a putative class action complaint in September 2002, which was amended in May 2004. They alleged that defendants aided and abetted, or were otherwise complicit in, violations of the law of nations by the Nigerian government. Relying on the Supreme Court's June 2004 decision in *Sosa v Alvarez-Machain*, 542 U.S. 692 (2004), defendants moved to dismiss.

In September 2006, the District Court dismissed plaintiffs' claims for aiding and abetting property destruction; forced exile; extrajudicial killing; and violations of the rights to life, liberty, security, and association. . . .

DISCUSSION

. . . . As we have explained above, this appeal presents a question that has been lurking for some time in our ATS jurisprudence. Since our first case upholding claims brought under the ATS in 1980, *see Filartiga v Pena-Irala*, 630 F.2d 876 (2d Cir. 1980), our Court has never directly addressed whether our jurisdiction under the ATS extends to civil actions against corporations, . . .

In answering the question presented we proceed in two steps. First, we consider which body of law governs the question—international law or domestic law—and conclude that international law governs. Second, we consider what the sources of international law reveal with respect to whether corporations can be subject to liability for violations of customary international law. We conclude that those sources lead inescapably to the conclusion that the customary international law of human rights has not to date recognized liability for corporations that violate its norms.

I. Customary International Law Governs Our Inquiry

The ATS grants federal district courts jurisdiction over claims "by an alien for a tort only, committed in violation of the law of nations or a treaty of the U.S." 28 U.S.C. § 1350.27 In 2004, the Supreme Court held in *Sosa* that the ATS is a jurisdictional statute only; it creates no cause of action, Justice Souter explained, because its drafters understood that "the common law would provide a cause of action for the modest number of international law violations with a potential for personal liability at the time." 542 U.S. at 724. Indeed, at the time of its adoption, the ATS "enabled federal courts to hear claims in a very limited category defined by the law of nations and recognized at common law." *Id.* at 712. These included "three specific offenses against the law of nations addressed by the criminal law of England [and identified by Blackstone]: violation of safe conducts, infringement of the rights of ambassadors, and piracy"— . . .

The Supreme Court did not, however, limit the jurisdiction of the federal courts under the ATS to those three offenses recognized by the law of nations in 1789. Instead, the Court in *Sosa* held that federal courts may recognize claims "based on the present-day law of nations" provided that the claims rest on "norm[s] of international character accepted by the civilized world and defined with a specificity comparable to the features of the 18th-century paradigms [the Court had] recognized." *Id.* at 725. The Supreme Court cautioned that "the determination whether a norm is sufficiently definite to support a cause of action should (and, indeed, inevitably must) involve an element of judgment about the practical consequences of making that cause available to litigants in the federal courts." *Id.* at 732-33 (footnote omitted). The Court also observed that "a related consideration is whether *international law* extends the scope of liability for a violation of a given norm to the perpetrator being sued, if the defendant is a private actor such as a corporation or an individual." *Id.* at 732 n.20 (emphasis added). We conclude—based on international law, *Sosa*, and our own precedents—that international law, and not domestic law, governs the scope of liability for violations of customary international law under the ATS.

A. International Law Defines the Scope of Liability for Violations of Its Norms

International law is not silent on the question of the *subjects* of international law—that is, "those that, to varying extents, have legal status, personality, rights, and *duties* under international law and whose acts and relationships are the principal concerns of international law." Restatement (Third) of the Foreign Relations Law of the U.S. ("Restatement (Third)"), pt. II, at 70 introductory note (emphasis added); *see* 1 *Oppenheim's International Law* § 33, at 119 (Sir Robert Jennings & Sir Arthur Watts eds., 9th ed. 1996) ("An international person is one who possesses legal personality in international law, meaning one who is a *subject* of international law so as itself to enjoy rights, duties or powers established in international law, and, generally, the capacity to act on the international plane . . . ." (emphasis added) (footnotes omitted)). Nor does international law leave to individual States the responsibility of defining those subjects. Rather, "[t]he concept of international person is . . . derived from international law." 1 *Oppenheim's International Law* § 33, at 120; *see also* Restatement (Third), pt. II, at 70 introductory note ("[I]ndividuals and private juridical entities can have any status, capacity, rights, or duties *given them by international law or agreement* . . . ." (emphasis added)).

That the subjects of international law are determined by international law, and not individual States, is evident from the International Military Tribunal at Nuremberg ("Tribunal") in the aftermath of the Second World War. The significance of the judgment of the Tribunal—and of the judgments of the tribunals established pursuant to Allied Control Council Law No. 10—was not simply that it recognized genocide and aggressive war as violations of international law. The defining legal achievement of the Nuremberg trials is that they explicitly recognized *individual liability* for the violation of specific, universal, and obligatory norms of international human rights. In its judgment the Tribunal noted that the defendants had argued that "international law is concerned with the actions of sovereign states, and provides no punishment for individuals." *The Nurnberg Trial (U.S. v Goering)*, 6 F.R.D. 69, 110 (Int'l Military Trib. at Nuremberg 1946).

The Tribunal rejected that view, however, declaring that "*international law* imposes duties and liabilities upon individuals as well as upon states" and that "individuals can be punished for violations of international law." *Id.* (emphasis added).

The significance of that aspect of the Tribunal's judgment was not lost on observers at the time. Justice Jackson, who served as chief prosecutor for the U.S. for the trial before the Tribunal, explained in his final report to President Truman that "[the Nurnberg trials] for the first time made explicit and unambiguous what was theretofore, as the Tribunal has declared, implicit in International Law," namely, that the conduct of the leaders of Nazi Germany violated international law, "*and that for the commission of such crimes individuals are respon- sible.*" Robert H. Jackson, *Final Report tothe President Concerning the Nurnberg War Crimes Trial* (1946) (emphasis added), *reprinted in* 20 Temp. L.Q. 338, 342 (1946) (emphasis added). . .

B. *Sosa* and Our Precedents Require Us to Look to International Law to Determine the Scope of Liability

In *Sosa* the Supreme Court instructed the lower federal courts to consider "whether *international law* extends the scope of liability for a violation of a given norm to the perpetrator being sued, if the defendant is a private actor such as a corporation or individual." *Sosa*, 542 U.S. at 732 n.20 (emphasis added). That language requires that we look to *international law* to determine our jurisdiction over ATS claims against a particular class of defendant, such as corporations. That conclusion is reinforced by Justice Breyer's reformulation of the issue in his concurring opinion: "The norm [of international law] must extend liability to the *type of perpetrator* (*e.g.*, a private actor) the plaintiff seeks to sue." *See id.* at 760 (Breyer, J., concurring) (emphasis added) (citing *id.* at 732 n.20 (majority opinion)).

The Supreme Court's instruction to look to international law to determine the scope of liability under the ATS did not involve a revolutionary interpretation of the statute—in fact, it had long been the law of this Circuit. In *Filartiga*, we had looked to international law to determine our jurisdiction and to delineate the type of defendant who could be sued. *See* 630 F.2d at 889 ("[T]he question of federal jurisdiction under the Alien Tort Statute . . . requires consideration of the law of nations."); *id.* at 880 ("In light of the universal condemnation of torture in numerous international agreements, and the renunciation of torture as an instrument of official policy by virtually all of the nations of the world (in principle if not in practice), we find that an act of torture *committed by a state official* against one held in detention violates established norms of the international law of human rights, and hence the law of nations." (emphasis added)); *see also Khulumani*, 504 F.3d at 269 (Katzmann, J., concurring) ("We have repeatedly emphasized that the scope of the [ATS's] jurisdictional grant should be determined by reference to international law.").

Likewise, in *Kadic v Karadžiæ*, 70 F.3d 232 (2d Cir. 1995) (Newman, J.), and in Judge Harry T. Edwards's notable concurring opinion in *Tel-Oren v Libyan Arab Republic*, 726 F.2d 774, 775 (D.C. Cir. 1984) (Edwards, J., concurring)—both cited with approval by the Supreme Court in *Sosa*—international law provided the rules by which the court decided whether certain conduct violated the law of nations *when committed by non-state actors*. In *Kadic*, we held that a private actor could be liable under the law of nations for genocide, war crimes, and crimes against humanity, 70 F.3d at 239-241, but in *Tel-Oren*, Judge Edwards expressed the view that a private actor could not be liable for torture under the ATS, 726 F.2d at 791-95 (Edwards, J., concurring); *see also, e.g., Flores*, 414 F.3d at 254-66 (looking to customary international law for the applicable norms).

Since *Sosa*, we have continued to adhere to the method prescribed in *Sosa* footnote 20 by looking to customary international law to determine *both* whether certain conduct leads to ATS liability *and* whether the scope of liability under the ATS extends to the defendant being sued. As recently as our decision of 2009 in *Presbyterian Church*, this same panel (including Judge Leval) declared that "footnote 20 of *Sosa*, while nominally concerned with the liability of non-state actors, supports the broader principle that the scope of liability for ATS violations should be derived from international law." 582 F.3d at 258 (footnote omitted); *see also id.* at 261 n.12 (noting that the court "need not reach . . . the question of 'whether international law extends the scope of liability' to corporations" (quoting *Sosa*, 542 U.S. at 732 n.20)). In *Presbyterian Church*, we looked to *international law* to determine the circumstances in which aiders and abettors could be liable for violations of the customary international law of human rights. *Id.* at 258-59. We did so because "[r]ecognition of secondary liability is no less significant a decision than whether to recognize a whole new tort in the first place." *Id.* at 259. Thus, our holding today is consistent with *Presbyterian Church,* where we looked to international law to determine not only what conduct is cognizable under the ATS, but also the identity of the persons to whom that conduct is attributable (in that case, aiders and abettors).

. . . .

504 F.3d at 280 (Katzmann, J., concurring) (quoting *U.S. v Smith,* 198 F.3d 377, 383 (2d Cir. 1999) (some internal quotation marks omitted)). Judge Katzmann further explained that "[w]hile [footnote 20 of *Sosa*] specifically concerns the liability of non-state actors, its general principle is equally applicable to the question of where to look to determine whether the scope of liability for a violation of international law should extend to aiders and abettors." *Id.* at 269. He therefore concluded that "to assure itself that it has jurisdiction to hear a claim under the [ATS], [a court] should first determine whether the alleged tort was in fact 'committed in violation of the law of nations,' 28 U.S.C. § 1350, and whether *this law would recognize the defendants' responsibility for that violation.*" *Id.* at 270 (emphasis added); *see also id.* at 281 ("Because aiding and abetting is a generally applicable means of identifying *who should be held responsible* for a particular act, . . . it is . . . reasonable to consider whether the theory is accepted as a *general principle of customary international law* . . . ." (emphases added)).

Significantly, it was only because we looked to international law that we were able to recognize a norm of aiding and abetting liability under the ATS.

. . . .

In sum, we have little difficulty holding that, under international law, *Sosa,* and our three decades of precedent, we are required to look to international law to determine whether corporate liability for a "violation of the law of nations," 28 U.S.C. § 1350, is a norm "accepted by the civilized world and defined with a specificity" sufficient to provide a basis for jurisdiction under the ATS, *Sosa,* 542 U.S. at 725. We have looked to international law to determine whether state officials, *see Filartiga,* 630 F.2d at 880, private individuals, *see Kadic,* 70 F.3d at 239-41, and aiders and abettors, *see Presbyterian Church,* 582 F.3d at 258-59, can be held liable under the ATS. There is no principled basis for treating the question of corporate liability differently. Like the issue of aiding and abetting liability, whether corporations can be liable for alleged violations of the law of nations "is no less significant a decision than whether to recognize a whole new tort in the first place." *Presbyterian Church,* 582 F.3d at 259. It is, therefore, a decision properly made only by reference to customary international law.

Having concluded that international law controls our inquiry, we next consider what the sources of international law reveal with respect to the existence of a norm of corporate liability under customary international law.

II. Corporate Liability Is Not a Norm of Customary International Law

To attain the status of a rule of customary international law, a norm must be "specific, universal, and obligatory." *Sosa,* 542 U.S. at 732 (quoting with approval the statement of a lower court) (internal quotation marks omitted); *see also Flores,* 414 F.3d at 248 ("[C]ustomary international law is composed only of those rules that States universally abide by, or accede to, out of a sense of legal obligation and mutual concern."); Restatement (Third) § 102(2) ("Customary international law results from a general and consistent practice of states followed by them from a sense of legal obligation."). Defining such norms "is no simple task," as "[c]ustomary international law is discerned from myriad decisions made in numerous and varied international and domestic arenas." *Flores,* 414 F.3d at 247. The sources consulted are therefore of the utmost importance. As the Supreme Court re-emphasized in *Sosa,* we look to "those sources we have long, albeit cautiously, recognized":

"[W]here there is no treaty, and no controlling executive or legislative act or judicial decision, resort must be had to the *customs and usages of civilized nations*; and, as evidence of these, to the works of jurists and commentators, who by years of labor, research and experience, have made themselves peculiarly well acquainted with the subjects of which they treat. Such works are resorted to by judicial tribunals, not for the speculations of their authors concerning what the law ought to be, but for trustworthy evidence of what the law really is." 542 U.S. at 733-34 (emphasis added) (quoting *The Paquete Habana,* 175 U.S. at 700); *see also U.S. v Smith,* 18 U.S. (5 Wheat.) 153, 160-61 (1820) (Story, J.) (identifying "the general usage and practice of nations[;] . . . judicial decisions recognising and enforcing that law[;]" and "the works of jurists, writing professedly on public law" as proper sources of customary international law); *cf. U.S. v Yousef,* 327 F.3d 56,

100 n.33 (2d Cir. 2003) (explaining that, "in the parlance of international law," "jurists" and "publicists" are used as synonyms for "scholars"). Agreements or declarations that are merely aspirational, and that "do[ ] not of [their] own force impose obligations as a matter of international law," are of "little utility" in discerning norms of customary international law. *Sosa*, 542 U.S. at 734 (discussing the limited utility of the Universal Declaration of Human Rights, G.A. Res. 217A (III), U.N. Doc. A/810 (1948)).

In this Circuit we have long recognized as authoritative the sources of international law identified in Article 38 of the Statute of the International Court of Justice ("ICJ Statute"). *See Filartiga*, 630 F.2d at 880-81 & n.8 (describing Article 38 as consistent with the Supreme Court's historical approach to sources of international law); *see also* J.L. Brierly, *The Law of Nations* 56 (Sir Humphrey Waldock ed., 6th ed. 1963) (referring to Article 38 as "a text of the highest authority"); Restatement (Third) § 103 (describing similar sources as evidence of international law). Article 38 provides in relevant part:

1. The Court, whose function is to decide in accordance with international law such disputes as are submitted to it, shall apply:

a. international conventions, whether general or particular, establishing rules expressly recognized by the contesting states;

b. international custom, as evidence of a general practice accepted as law;

c. the general principles of law recognized by civilized nations;

d. subject to the provisions of Article 59, judicial decisions and the teachings of the most highly qualified publicists [*i.e.*, scholars or "jurists"] of the various nations, as *subsidiary means for the determination of rules of law*.ICJ Statute, art. 38, June 26, 1945, 59 Stat. 1055, 1060, 33 U.N.T.S. 993 (emphasis added). With those principles in mind, we consider whether the sources of international law reveal that corporate liability has attained universal acceptance as a rule of customary international law.

A. International Tribunals

Insofar as international tribunals are established for the specific purpose of imposing liability on those who violate the law of nations, the history and conduct of those tribunals is instructive. We find it particularly significant, therefore, that no international tribunal of which we are aware has *ever* held a corporation liable for a violation of the law of nations.

1. The Nuremberg Tribunals

The Charter of the International Military Tribunal, commonly known as the "London Charter," authorized the punishment of the major war criminals of the European Axis following the Second World War. *See* Agreement for the Prosecution and Punishment of the Major War Criminals of the European Axis (the "London Charter"), Aug. 8, 1945, 59 Stat. 1544, 82 U.N.T.S.

279. The London Charter and the trials at Nuremberg that followed are collectively the single most important source of modern customary international law concerning liability for violations of fundamental human rights.36 As Justice Jackson explained, the London Charter "is a basic charter in the International Law of the future," and the Nuremberg trials took great strides in "ma[king] explicit and unambiguous" the human rights norms that had "theretofore . . . [been] implicit in International Law." . . .

The London Charter also granted the International Military Tribunal the authority to declare organizations "criminal"—and several German government and military organizations, such as the SS and the Gestapo, were, in fact, indicted. London Charter, *ante*, art. 9, 59 Stat. at 1548 ("At the trial of any individual member of any group or organization the Tribunal may declare . . . that the group or organization of which the individual was a member was a criminal organization."); AnnTusa & John Tusa, *The Nuremberg Trial* 425 (1983) (describing the indict-ment of six organizations).

See generally The Nurnberg Trial, 6 F.R.D. at 136-43 (describing the structure of the SS and the Gestapo and the criminal activities of their members). Such a declaration following indictment, however, did not result in the organization being punished or having liability assessed against it. Rather, the effect of declaring an organization criminal was merely to facilitate the prosecution of *individuals* who were members of the organization. *See* London Charter, *ante*, art. 10, 59 Stat. at 1548 ("In cases where a group or organization is declared criminal by the Tribunal, the competent national authority of any Signatory shall have the right to bring individuals to trial for membership therein before national, military or occupation courts. *In any such case the criminal nature of the group or organization is considered proved and shall not be questioned.*" (emphasis added)).

Echoing the London Charter's imposition of liability on natural persons only, the subsequent U.S. Military Tribunals, established under Control Council Law No. 10, prosecuted *corporate executives* for their role in violating customary international law during the Second World War, but not the corporate entities themselves.

The depth of the partnership [between the Nazi state and I.G. Farben] was reached at Auschwitz, the extermination center [in Poland], where four million human beings were destroyed in accordance with the "Final Solution of the Jewish Question," Hitler's plan to destroy an entire people. Drawn by the almost limitless reservoir of death camp labor, I.G. [Farben] chose to build a great industrial complex at Auschwitz for the production of synthetic rubber and oil.

. . . .

Those statements parallel the oft-cited passage of the Nuremberg judgment, made in response to the argument that international law is concerned only with the actions of sovereign states: "Crimes against international law are committed by men, not by abstract entities, and only by punishing individuals who commit such crimes can the provisions of international law be enforced." *The Nurnberg Trial*, 6 F.R.D. at 110.

In declining to impose corporate liability under international law in the case of the most nefarious corporate enterprise known to the civilized world, while prosecuting the men who led I.G. Farben, the military tribunals established under Control Council Law No. 10 expressly defined liability under the law of nations as liability that could not be divorced from *individual* moral responsibility. It is thus clear that, at the time of the Nuremberg trials, corporate liability was not recognized as a "specific, universal, and obligatory" norm of customary international law. *See Sosa*, 542 U.S. at 732 (internal quotation marks omitted).

We turn now to international tribunals convened since Nuremberg to determine whether there is any evidence that the concept corporate liability has coalesced into a "specific, universal, and obligatory" norm.

2. International Tribunals Since Nuremberg

Since Nuremberg, international tribunals have continually declined to hold corporations liable for violations of customary international law. For example, the charters establishing both the International Criminal Tribunal for the former Yugoslavia, or "ICTY," and the International Criminal Tribunal for Rwanda, or "ICTR," expressly confined the tribunals' jurisdiction to "natural persons." . . . . The commentary contained in the Report of the Secretary-General of the United Nations on the ICTY reveals that jurisdiction over corporations was considered but expressly rejected: "[T]he ordinary meaning of the term 'persons responsible for serious violations of international humanitarian law' would be *natural persons to the exclusion of juridical persons.*" . . .

The Secretary-General believes that this concept should not be retained in regard to the International Tribunal. The criminal acts set out in this statute are carried out by natural persons . . . ."); *cf.* London Charter, *ante*, art. 9, 59 Stat. at 1548. Thus, to the extent that the International Military Tribunal at Nuremberg possessed some limited authority to declare corporations criminal—which, as explained above, operated merely as an evidentiary rule for later trials imposing liability on *individuals*—subsequent tribunals have not retained that procedure.

More recently, the Rome Statute of the ICC also limits that tribunal's jurisdiction to "natural persons." *See* The Rome Statute of the International Criminal Court ("Rome Statute") art. 25(1), *opened for signature* July 17, 1998, 37 I.L.M. 1002, 1016; *see also* Albin Eser, *Individual Criminal Responsibility*, in 1 *The Rome Statute of the International Criminal Court* 767, 778 (Antonio Cassese et al. eds., 2002) ("[W]hen reading paragraphs (1), (2), and (3) of Article 25 of the ICC Statute together, there can be no doubt that by limiting criminal responsibility to individual natural persons, the Rome Statute implicitly negates—at least for its own jurisdiction—the punishability of corporations and other legal entities.").

. . . .

In sum, modern international tribunals make it abundantly clear that, since Nuremberg, the concept of corporate liability for violations of customary international law has not even begun to "ripen[ ]" into a universally accepted norm of international law. *Cf. The Paquete Habana*, 175 U.S. at 686 (explaining that a practice can "gradually ripen[ ] into a rule of international law" through "usage among civilized nations").

B. International Treaties

Treaties "are proper evidence of customary international law because, and insofar as, they create *legal obligations* akin to contractual obligations on the States parties to them." *Flores*, 414 F.3d at 256. Although all treaties ratified by more than one State provide *some* evidence of the custom and practice of nations, "a treaty will only constitute *sufficient proof* of a norm of *customary international law* if an overwhelming majority of States have ratified the treaty, *and* those States uniformly and consistently act in accordance with its principles." . . .

One district court in our Circuit erroneously overvalued the importance of a number of international treaties in finding that corporate liability has attained the status of customary international law. *See Presbyterian Church of Sudan v Talisman Energy, Inc.*, 244 F. Supp. 2d 289, 316-17 (S.D.N.Y. 2003) (denying defendants' motion to dismiss). *But see Presbyterian Church of Sudan v Talisman Energy, Inc.*, 453 F. Supp. 2d

633 (S.D.N.Y. 2006) (granting summary judgment to defendants on different grounds), *affirmed by* 582 F.3d 244 (2d Cir. 2009). None of the treaties relied upon in the district court's 2003 *Presbyterian Church* opinion has been ratified by the U.S., and most of them have not been ratified by other States whose interests would be most profoundly affected by the treaties' terms. *Cf. Flores*, 414 F.3d at 256-57 (explaining that a treaty's evidentiary value is dependent, in part, on the number and "relative influence . . . in international affairs" of the States that have ratified it). Those treaties are therefore insufficient—considered either individually or collectively—to demonstrate that corporate liability is universally recognized as a norm of customary international law.

Even if those specialized treaties had been ratified by an "overwhelming majority" of states, *id.* at 256—as some recent treaties providing for corporate liability have been, *see, e.g.*, Convention Against Transnational Organized Crime, art. 10(1), *adopted* Nov. 15, 2000, S. Treaty Doc. 108-16; Convention on Combating Bribery of Foreign Public Officials in International Business Transactions, art. 2, *done* Dec. 17, 1997, S. Treaty Doc. No. 105-43—the fact that those treaties impose obligations on corporations in the context of the treaties' particular subject matter tells us nothing about whether corporate liability for, say, violations of *human rights*, which are not a subject of those treaties, is universally recognized as a norm of *customary international law*. Significantly, to find that a treaty embodies or creates a rule of customary international law would mean that the rule applies beyond the limited subject matter of the treaty and *to nations that have not ratified it*. *See* 1 *Oppenheim's International Law* § 626, at 1261. To construe those treaties as so-called "law-making" treaties— that is, treaties that codify existing norms of customary international law or crystalize an emerging rule of customary international law—would be wholly inappropriate and without precedent. *See id.* § 583, at 1203-04 (discussing "law-making" treaties).

As noted above, there is no historical evidence of an existing or even nascent norm of customary international law imposing liability on corporations for violations of human rights. It cannot be said, therefore, that those treaties on specialized questions codify an existing, general rule of customary international law. Nor can those recent treaties, in light of their limited number and specialized subject matter, be viewed as crystalizing an emerging norm of customary international law. *See id.* § 583, at 1204 (explaining that "relatively extensive participation in a treaty, coupled with a *subject matter of general significance* and stipulations which accord with the general sense of the international community, do establish for some treaties an influence far beyond the limits of formal participation in them" (footnote omitted)) . . . .

For a treaty provision to attain the status of a norm of customary international law, the ICJ explained, "[i]t would in the first place be necessary that the provision concerned should, at all events potentially, be of a *fundamentally norm-creating character* such as could be regarded as forming the basis of a general rule of law." *Id.* at 374 (emphasis added).

Provisions on corporate liability in a handful of specialized treaties cannot be said to have a "fundamentally norm-creating character." . . . Accordingly, provisions imposing corporate liability in some recent specialized treaties have not established corporate liability as a norm of customary international law.

In reaching the contrary conclusion in *Presbyterian Church*, the judge to whom the case was originally assigned in the district court acknowledged that "most treaties *do not* bind corporations" but reasoned that "[i]f corporations can be liable for unintentional torts such as oil spills or nuclear accidents, *logic would suggest* that they can be held liable for intentional torts such as complicity in genocide, slave trading, or torture." . . . . Rather, as the Supreme Court has explained, it develops, if at all, through the custom and practice "among civilized nations . . . gradually ripening into a rule of international law." *Sosa*, 542 U.S. at 715 (quoting *The Paquete Habana*, 175 U.S. at 686).

It bears underscoring that the purpose of the ATS was not to encourage U.S. courts to create new norms of customary international law unilaterally. *Sosa*, 542 U.S. at 728 (explaining that federal courts have "no congressional mandate to seek out and define new and debatable violations of the law of nations"). Instead, the statute was rooted in the ancient concept of comity among nations and was intended to provide a remedy for violations of customary international law that "threaten[ ] serious consequences in international affairs." *Id.* at 715 (noting that this concern "was probably on the minds of the men who drafted the ATS"). Unilaterally recognizing new norms of customary international law—that is, norms that have not been universally accepted by the rest of the civilized world—would potentially create friction in our relations with foreign nations and, therefore, would contravene the international comity the statute was enacted to promote.

We conclude, therefore, that the relatively few international treaties that impose particular obligations on corporations do not establish corporate liability as a "specific, universal, and obligatory" norm of customary international law. . . .

C. Works of Publicists

Although the works of publicists (*i.e.*, scholars or "jurists") can be a relevant source of customary international law, "[s]uch works are resorted to by judicial tribunals, not for the speculations of their authors concerning what the law ought to be, but for trustworthy evidence of what the law really is." *Sosa*, 542 U.S. at 734 (quoting *The Paquete Habana*, 175 U.S. at 700); *see also* ICJ Statute, *ante*, art. 38(1)(d), 59 Stat. at 1060 (directing the ICJ to apply "judicial decisions and the teachings of the most highly qualified publicists of the various nations, as *subsidiary means for the determination of rules of law*." (emphasis added)); *see* note 47, *post*.

In light of the evidence discussed above, it is not surprising that two renowned professors of international law, Professor James Crawford and Professor (now Judge) Christopher Greenwood, forcefully declared in litigation argued before this panel on the same day as this case, that customary international law does not recognize liability for corporations that violate its norms. According to Professor Crawford, "no national court [outside of the U.S.] and no international judicial tribunal has so far recognized corporate liability, as opposed to individual liability, *in a civil or criminal context* on the basis of a violation of the law of nations or customary international law." *See* Declaration of James Crawford . . . .

Even those who favor using the ATS as a means of holding corporations accountable for human rights violations reluctantly acknowledge that "the universe of international criminal law does not reveal any prosecutions of corporations per se." Ratner, note 43, *ante*, at 477.

Together, those authorities demonstrate that imposing liability on corporations for violations of customary international law has not attained a discernible, much less universal, acceptance among nations of the world in their relations *inter se*. Because corporate liability is not recognized as a "specific, universal, and obligatory" norm, *see Sosa*, 542 U.S. at 732 (internal quotation marks omitted), it is not a rule of customary international law that we may apply under the ATS.

Accordingly, insofar as plaintiffs in this action seek to hold only corporations liable for their conduct in Nigeria (as opposed to individuals within those corporations), and only under the ATS, their claims must be dismissed for lack of subject matter jurisdiction.

III. The Concurring Opinion

Judge Leval concedes that "international law, of its own force, imposes no liabilities on corporations or other private juridical entities." Concurring Op. 67. In other words, despite his perplexing but forceful contentions otherwise, Judge Leval does not disagree with Part II of our opinion. What he disputes is our conclusion in Part I that customary international law supplies the rule of decision.

. . . .

Judge Leval's criticisms distort our holding and betray several fundamental misunderstandings of customary international law. First, Judge Leval attempts to shift to us the burden of identifying a norm of customary international law that supports our "rule." But it is entirely inappropriate to begin, as Judge Leval apparently begins, with a presumption that a violation of customary international law can be attributed to *any defendant* unless, and until, a norm of customary international law declares otherwise. This reasoning turns customary international law on its head. Customary international law arises from the customs and practices "among civilized nations . . . gradually ripening into a rule of international law." *Sosa*, 542 U.S. at 715 (quoting *The Paquete Habana*, 175 U.S. at 686). Accordingly, the responsibility lies with those who seek to demonstrate that "international law extends the scope of liability for a violation of a given norm to the perpetrator being sued." *Id.* at 732 n.20. Judge Leval produces no evidence that international law extends the scope of liability to corporations, and, in fact, he concedes that it does not.

. . . .

We hold that corporate liability is not a norm that we can recognize and apply in actions *under the ATS* because the customary international law of human rights does not impose *any* form of liability on corporations (civil, criminal, or otherwise).

Finally, and most importantly, Judge Leval incorrectly categorizes the scope of liability under customary international law—that is, who can be liable for violations of international law—as merely a question of remedy to be determined independently by each state. *Id.* at 48. As we explained above, *see* Part I.A, *ante*, the *subjects* of international law have always been defined by reference to international law itself. Judge Leval is therefore wrong to suggest that "international law takes no position" on the question of who can be liable for violations of international law. *Id.* at 5.49

. . . .

The potential for civil damages under the ATS arises only if *customary international law* recognizes that a particular class of defendant is a subject of international law in the first place. *See* 28 U.S.C. § 1350 (providing jurisdiction over "torts . . . committed *in violation of the law of nations*" (emphasis added)). Contrary to Judge Leval's suggestion, therefore, *individual liability* under the ATS is wholly consistent with our holding today. Congress chose in the ATS to grant jurisdiction over torts committed "in violation of the law of nations," *id.*, and since the Nuremberg trials, customary international law has recognized *individual liability* for the violation of international human rights.

Thus, the ATS merely permits courts to recognize a remedy (civil liability) for heinous crimes universally condemned by the family of nations against individuals already recognized as subjects of international law. To permit courts to recognize *corporate liability* under the ATS, however, would require, at the very least, a different statute—one that goes beyond providing jurisdiction over tort committed "in violation of the law of nations" to authorize suits against entities that *are not* subjects of customary international law.

CONCLUSION

The ATS provides federal district courts jurisdiction over a tort, brought by an alien only, alleging a "violation of the law of nations or a treaty of the U.S." 28 U.S.C. § 1350. When an ATS suit is brought under the "law of nations," also known as "customary international law," jurisdiction is limited to those cases alleging a violation of an international norm that is "specific, universal, and obligatory." *Sosa v Alvarez-Machain*, 542 U.S. 692, 732 (2004) (quoting with approval the statement of a lower court); *see also Flores v S. Peru Copper Corp.*, 414 F.3d 233, 238 (2d Cir. 2003) ("[C]ustomary international law is composed only of those rules that States universally abide by, or accede to, out of a sense of legal obligation and mutual concern.").

No corporation has ever been subject to *any* form of liability (whether civil, criminal, or otherwise) under the customary international law of human rights. Rather, sources of customary international law have, on several occasions, explicitly rejected the idea of corporate liability. Thus, corporate liability has not attained a discernable, much less universal, acceptance among nations of the world in their relations *inter se*, and it cannot not, as a result, form the basis of a suit under the ATS.

Acknowledging the absence of corporate liability under customary international law is not a matter of conferring "immunity" on corporations. It is, instead, a recognition that the States of the world, in their relations with one another, *see IIT v Vencap, Ltd.*, 519 F.2d 1001, 1015 (2d Cir. 1975) (Friendly, J.), *abrogated on other grounds by Morrison v Nat'l Austl. Bank Ltd.*, 130 S. Ct. 2869 (2010),have determined that moral and legal responsibility for heinous crimes should rest on the individual whose conduct makes him or her "'*hostis humani generis*, an enemy of all mankind.'" *Sosa* 542 U.S. at 732 (quoting *Filartiga v Pena-Irala*, 630 F.2d 876, 890 (2d Cir. 1980)). Nothing in this opinion limit or forecloses suits under the ATS against a corporation's employees, managers, officers, directors, or any other person who commits, or purposefully aids and abets, violations of international law.

Moreover, nothing in this opinion limits or forecloses corporate liability under any body of law *other than the ATS*—including the domestic statutes of other States—and nothing in this opinion limits or forecloses Congress from amending the ATS to bring corporate defendants within our jurisdiction.

Corporate liability, however, is simply not "accepted by the civilized world and defined with a specificity comparable to the features of the 18th-century paradigms" recognized as providing a basis for suit under the law prescribed by the ATS, customary international law. *Sosa*, 542 U.S. at 725.

We do not know whether the concept of *corporate* liability will "gradually ripen[ ] into a rule of international law." *Id.* at 715 (quoting *The Paquete Habana*, 175 U.S. 677, 700 (1900)). It can do so, however, only by achieving universal recognition and acceptance as a norm in the relations of States *inter se*. For now, and for the foreseeable future, the Alien Tort Statute does not provide subject matter jurisdiction over claims against corporations.

To summarize, we hold as follows:

(1) Since *Filartiga*, which in 1980 marked the advent of the modern era of litigation for violations of human rights under the Alien Tort Statute, all of our precedents—and the Supreme Court's decision in *Sosa*, 542 U.S. at 732 n.20—require us to look to international law to determine whether a particular class of defendant, such as corporations, can be liable under the Alien Tort Statute for alleged violations of the law of nations.

(2) The concept of corporate liability for violations of customary international law has not achieved universal recognition or acceptance as a norm in the relations of States with each other. *See Vencap*, 519 F.2d at 1015. Inasmuch as plaintiffs assert claims against corporations only, their complaint must be dismissed for lack of subject matter jurisdiction.

Accordingly, the September 29, 2006 order of the District Court is **AFFIRMED** insofar as it dismissed some of plaintiffs' claims against the corporate defendants and **REVERSED** insofar as it declined to dismiss plaintiffs' remaining claims against the corporate defendants.

6. *Graham v Florida*, Supreme Court of the U.S. (Excerpted)
   Cite as: 130 S. Ct. 2011 (2010),

TERRANCE JAMAR GRAHAM, PETITIONER v FLORIDA
May 17, 2010

ON WRIT OF CERTIORARI TO THE DISTRICT COURT OF APPEAL OF FLORIDA, FIRST DISTRICT

JUSTICE KENNEDY delivered the opinion of the Court.

The issue before the Court is whether the Constitution permits a juvenile offender to be sentenced to life in prison without parole for a non-homicide crime. The sentence was imposed by the State of Florida. Petitioner challenges the sentence under the Eighth Amendment's Cruel and Unusual Punishments Clause, made applicable to the States by the Due Process Clause of the Fourteenth Amendment. Robinson v California, 370 U. S. 660 (1962).

I

Petitioner is Terrance Jamar Graham. He was born on January 6, 1987. . . . Graham was diagnosed with attention deficit hyperactivity disorder in elementary school. He began drinking alcohol and using tobacco at age 9 and smoked marijuana at age 13.

In July 2003, when Graham was age 16, he and three other school-age youths attempted to rob a barbeque restaurant in Jacksonville, Florida. One youth, who worked at the restaurant, left the back door unlocked just before closing time. Graham and another youth, wearing masks, entered through the unlocked door. Graham's masked accomplice twice struck the restaurant manager in the back of the head with a metal bar. . . . Under Florida law, it is within a prosecutor's discretion whether to charge 16- and 17-year-olds as adults or juveniles for most felony crimes. . . . Graham's prosecutor elected to charge Graham as an adult. The charges against Graham were armed burglary with assault or battery, a first-degree felony carrying a maximum penalty of life imprisonment without the possibility of parole . . . and attempted armed-robbery, a second-degree felony carrying a maximum penalty of 15 years' imprisonment . . . .

On December 18, 2003, Graham pleaded guilty to both charges under a plea agreement. Graham wrote a letter to the trial court. After reciting "this is my first and last time getting in trouble," he continued "I've decided to turn my life around."

. . .

The trial court accepted the plea agreement. The court withheld adjudication of guilt as to both charges and sentenced Graham to concurrent 3-year terms of probation. Graham was required to spend the first 12 months of his probation in the county jail, but he received credit for the time he had served awaiting trial, and was released on June 25, 2004.

Less than 6 months later . . . Graham again was arrested. . . . Graham participated in a home invasion robbery. His two accomplices were Meigo Bailey and Kirkland Lawrence, both 20-year-old men. According to the State, at 7 p.m. that night, Graham, Bailey, and Lawrence knocked on the door of the home where Carlos Rodriguez lived. Graham, followed by Bailey and Lawrence, forcibly entered the home and held a pistol to Rodriguez's chest. For the next 30 minutes, the three held Rodriguez and another man, a friend of Rodriguez, at gunpoint while they ransacked the home searching for money. Before leaving, Graham and his accomplices barricaded Rodriguez and his friend inside a closet.

The State further alleged that Graham, Bailey, and Lawrence, later the same evening, attempted a second robbery, during which Bailey was shot. Graham, who had borrowed his father's car, drove Bailey and Lawrence to the hospital and left them there. As Graham drove away, a police sergeant signaled him to stop. Graham continued at a high speed but crashed into a telephone pole. He tried to flee on foot but was apprehended. Three handguns were found in his car.

. . . The night that Graham allegedly committed the robbery, he was 34 days short of his 18th birthday

. . .

The trial court held hearings on Graham's violations about a year later, in December 2005 and January 2006. . . .

The court . . . found that Graham had violated his probation by committing a home invasion robbery, by possessing a firearm, and by associating with persons engaged in criminal activity.

The trial court held a sentencing hearing. Under Florida law the minimum sentence Graham could receive absent a downward departure by the judge was 5 years' imprisonment. The maximum was life imprisonment. Graham's attorney requested the minimum non-departure sentence of 5 years. . . . The State recommended that Graham receive 30 years on the armed burglary count and 15 years on the attempted armed robbery count.

After hearing Graham's testimony, the trial court explained the sentence it was about to pronounce:

"Mr. Graham, as I look back on your case, yours is really candidly a sad situation. . . . You had a lot of people who wanted to try and help you get your life turned around including the court system, and you had a judge who took the step to try and give you direction through his probation order to give you a chance to get back onto track.

. . .

"And I don't understand why you would be given such a great opportunity to do something with your life and why you would throw it away. The only thing that I can rationalize is that you decided that this is how you were going to lead your life and that there is nothing that we can do for you.

. . .

"I have reviewed the statute. I don't see where any further juvenile sanctions would be appropriate. I don't see where any youthful offender sanctions would be appropriate. Given your escalating pattern of criminal conduct, it is apparent to the Court that you have decided that this is the way you are going to live your life and that the only thing I can do now is to try and protect the community from your actions."

. . .

The trial court found Graham guilty of the earlier armed burglary and attempted armed robbery charges. It sentenced him to the maximum sentence authorized by law on each charge: life imprisonment for the armed burglary and 15 years for the attempted armed robbery. Because Florida has abolished its parole system . . . a life sentence gives a defendant no possibility of release unless he is granted executive clemency.

Graham filed a motion in the trial court challenging his sentence under the Eighth Amendment. The motion was deemed denied after the trial court failed to rule on it within 60 days. The First District Court of Appeal of Florida affirmed, concluding that Graham's sentence was not grossly disproportionate to his crimes. 982 So. 2d 43 (2008). . . . The court concluded . . . that Graham was incapable of rehabilitation. . . . The Florida Supreme Court denied review. 990 So. 2d 1058 (2008) (table).

We granted certiorari.

II

The Eighth Amendment states: "Excessive bail shall not be required, nor excessive fines imposed, nor cruel and unusual punishments inflicted." To determine whether a punishment is cruel and unusual, courts must look beyond historical conceptions to "'the evolving standards of decency that mark the progress of a maturing society.'" Estelle v Gamble, 429 U. S. 97, 102 (1976) (quoting Trop v Dulles, 356 U. S. 86, 101 (1958) (plurality opinion)). "This is because '[t]he standard of extreme cruelty is not merely descriptive, but necessarily embodies a moral judgment. The standard itself remains the same, but its applicability must change as the basic mores of society change.'" Kennedy v Louisiana, 554 U. S. . . . (2008) (quoting Furman v Georgia, 408 U. S. 238, 382 (1972) (Burger, C. J., dissenting)).

The Cruel and Unusual Punishments Clause prohibits the imposition of inherently barbaric punishments under all circumstances. See, e.g., Hope v Pelzer, 536 U. S. 730 (2002). . . . These cases underscore the essential principle that, under the Eighth Amendment, the State must respect the human attributes even of those who have committed serious crimes.

For the most part, however, the Court's precedents consider punishments challenged not as inherently barbaric but as disproportionate to the crime.

. . .

The second classification of cases has used categorical rules to define Eighth Amendment standards. The previous cases in this classification involved the death penalty. The classification in turn consists of two subsets, one considering the nature of the offense, the other considering the characteristics of the offender.

. . . In cases turning on the characteristics of the offender, the Court has adopted categorical rules prohibiting the death penalty for defendants who committed their crimes before the age of 18, Roper v Simmons, 543 U. S. 551 (2005), or whose intellectual functioning is in a low range, Atkins v Virginia, 536 U. S. 304 (2002). See also Thompson v Oklahoma, 487 U. S. 815 (1988).

In the cases adopting categorical rules the Court has taken the following approach. The Court first considers "objective indicia of society's standards, as expressed in legislative enactments and state practice" to determine whether there is a national consensus against the sentencing practice at issue. Roper, supra, at 563. . . .

The present case involves an issue the Court has not considered previously: a categorical challenge to a term-of-years sentence. . . . This case implicates a particular type of sentence as it applies to an entire class of offenders who have committed a range of crimes. As a result, a threshold comparison between the severity of the penalty and the gravity of the crime does not advance the analysis. Here, in addressing the question presented, the appropriate analysis is the one used in cases that involved the categorical approach, specifically Atkins, Roper, and Kennedy.

III
A

The analysis begins with objective indicia of national consensus. "[T]he 'clearest and most reliable objective evidence of contemporary values is the legislation enacted by the country's legislatures.'" Atkins, supra, at 312 . . . Six jurisdictions do not allow life without parole sentences for any juvenile offenders. . . . Seven jurisdictions permit life without parole for juvenile offenders, but only for homicide crimes. Id., Part II. Thirty-seven States as well as the District of Columbia permit sentences of life without parole for a juvenile non-homicide offender in some circumstances. Id., Part I. . . . Relying on this metric, the State and its amici argue that there is no national consensus against the sentencing practice at issue.

This argument is incomplete and unavailing. "There are measures of consensus other than legislation." Kennedy, supra . . . . Although these statutory schemes contain no explicit prohibition on sentences of life without parole for juvenile non-homicide offenders, those sentences are most infrequent. According to a recent study, nationwide there are only 109 juvenile offenders serving sentences of life without parole for non-homicide offenses.

. . .

The evidence of consensus is not undermined by the fact that many jurisdictions do not prohibit life without parole for juvenile non-homicide offenders. The Court confronted a similar situation in Thompson, where a plurality concluded that the death penalty for offenders younger than 16 was unconstitutional.

. . .

B

. . . In accordance with the constitutional design, "the task of interpreting the Eighth Amendment remains our responsibility." Roper, 543 U. S., at 575. The judicial exercise of independent judgment requires consideration of the culpability of the offenders at issue in light of their crimes and characteristics, along with the severity of the punishment in question. Id., at 568 . . . . Roper established that because juveniles have lessened culpability they are less deserving of the most severe punishments. 543 U. S., at 569.

. . .

Life without parole is an especially harsh punishment for a juvenile. Under this sentence a juvenile offender will on average serve more years and a greater percentage of his life in prison than an adult offender. A 16-year-old and a 75-year-old each sentenced to life without parole receive the same punishment in name only. See Roper, supra, at 572. . . .

. . .

A sentence of life imprisonment without parole, however, cannot be justified by the goal of rehabilitation. The penalty forswears altogether the rehabilitative ideal.

. . .

This clear line is necessary to prevent the possibility that life without parole sentences will be imposed on juvenile non-homicide offenders who are not sufficiently culpable to merit that punishment. Because "[t]he age of 18 is the point where society draws the line for many purposes between childhood and adulthood," those who were below that age when the offense was committed may not be sentenced to life with- out parole for a non-homicide crime. Roper, 543 U. S., at 574.

A State is not required to guarantee eventual freedom to a juvenile offender convicted of a non-homicide crime. What the State must do, however, is give defendants like Graham some meaningful opportunity to obtain release based on demonstrated maturity and rehabilitation.

C

. . .

Another possible approach would be to hold that the Eighth Amendment requires courts to take the offender's age into consideration as part of a case-specific gross disproportionality inquiry, weighing it against the seriousness of the crime. This approach would allow courts to account for factual differences between cases and to impose life without parole sentences for particularly heinous crimes. . . .

The case-by-case approach to sentencing must, however, be confined by some boundaries. The dilemma of juvenile sentencing demonstrates this. For even if we were to assume that some juvenile non homicide offenders might have "sufficient psychological maturity, and at the same time demonstrat[e] sufficient depravity," Roper, 543 U. S., at 572, to merit a life without parole sentence, it does not follow that courts taking a case-by-case proportionality approach could with sufficient accuracy distinguish the few incorrigible juvenile offenders from the many that have the capacity for change.

. . .

A categorical rule against life without parole for juvenile non homicide offenders avoids the perverse consequence in which the lack of maturity that led to an offender's crime is reinforced by the prison term. . . . The State has denied him any chance to later demonstrate that he is fit to rejoin society based solely on a nonhomicide crime that he committed while he was a child in the eyes of the law. This the Eighth Amendment does not permit.

D

There is support for our conclusion in the fact that, in continuing to impose life without parole sentences on juveniles who did not commit homicide, the U.S. adheres to a sentencing practice rejected the world over. This observation does not control our decision. The judgments of other nations and the international community are not dispositive as to the meaning of the Eighth Amendment. But "'[t]he climate of international opinion concerning the acceptability of a particular punishment'" is also "'not irrelevant.'" Enmund, 458 U. S., at 796, n. 22. The Court has looked beyond our Nation's borders for support for its independent conclusion that a particular punishment is cruel and unusual. See, e.g., Roper, 543 U. S., at 575–578; Atkins, supra, at 317–318, n. 21; Thompson, 487 U. S., at 830 (plurality opinion); Enmund, supra, at 796–797, n. 22; Coker, 433 U. S., at 596, n. 10 (plurality opinion); Trop, 356 U. S., at 102–103 (plurality opinion).

Today we continue that longstanding practice in noting the global consensus against the sentencing practice in question. A recent study concluded that only 11 nations authorize life without parole for juvenile offenders under any circumstances; and only 2 of them, the U.S. and Israel, ever impose the punishment in practice. See M. Leighton & C. de la Vega, Sentencing Our Children to Die in Prison: Global Law and Practice 4 (2007). An up-dated version of the study concluded that Israel's "laws allow for parole review of juvenile offenders serving life terms," but expressed reservations about how that parole review is implemented. De la Vega & Leighton, Sentencing Our Children to Die in Prison: Global Law and Practice, 42 U. S. F. L. Rev. 983, 1002–1003 (2008). But even if Israel is counted as allowing life without parole for juvenile offenders, that nation does not appear to impose that sentence for non-homicide crimes; all of the seven Israeli prisoners whom commentators have identified as serving life sentences for juvenile crimes were convicted of homicide or attempted homicide. See Amnesty International, Human Rights Watch, The Rest of Their Lives: Life with- out Parole for Child Offenders in the U.S. 106, n. 322 (2005); Memorandum and Attachment from Ruth Levush, Law Library of Congress, to Supreme Court Library (Feb. 16, 2010) (available in Clerk of Court's case file).

Thus, as petitioner contends and respondent does not contest, the U.S. is the only Nation that imposes life without parole sentences on juvenile non-homicide offenders. We also note, as petitioner and his amici emphasize, that Article 37(a) of the United Nations Convention on the Rights of the Child, Nov. 20, 1989, 1577 U. N. T. S. 3 (entered into force Sept. 2, 1990), ratified by every nation except the U.S. and Somalia, prohibits the imposition of "life imprisonment without possibility of release . . . for offences committed by persons below eighteen years of age." Brief for Petitioner 66; Brief for Amnesty International et al. as Amici Curiae 15–17. As we concluded in Roper with respect to the juvenile death penalty, "the U.S. now stands alone in a world that has turned its face against" life without parole for juvenile non-homicide offenders. 543 U. S., at 577.

The State's amici stress that no international legal agreement that is binding on the U.S. prohibits life without parole for juvenile offenders and thus urge us to ignore the international consensus. See Brief for Solidarity Center for Law and Justice et al. as Amici Curiae 14–16; Brief for Sixteen Members of U.S. House of Representatives as Amici Curiae 40–43. These arguments miss the mark. The question before us is not whether international law prohibits the U.S. from imposing the sentence at issue in this case. The question is whether that punishment is cruel and unusual. In that inquiry, "the overwhelming weight of international opinion against" life without parole for non-homicide offenses committed by juveniles "provide[s] respected and significant confirmation for our own conclusions." Roper, supra, at 578.

The debate between petitioner's and respondent's amici over whether there is a binding jus cogens norm against this sentencing practice is likewise of no import. See Brief for Amnesty International 10–23; Brief for Sixteen Members of U.S. House of Representatives 4–40. The Court has treated the laws and practices of other nations and international agreements as relevant to the Eighth Amendment not because those norms are binding or controlling but because the judgment of the world's nations that a particular sentencing practice is inconsistent with basic principles of decency demonstrates that the Court's rationale has respected reasoning to support it.

***

The Constitution prohibits the imposition of a life with- out parole sentence on a juvenile offender who did not commit homicide. A State need not guarantee the offender eventual release, but if it imposes a sentence of life it must provide him or her with some realistic opportunity to obtain release before the end of that term. The judgment of the First District Court of Appeal of Florida affirming Graham's conviction is reversed, and the case is remanded for further proceedings not inconsistent with this opinion.
It is so ordered.

7. *Roper v Simmons*, Supreme Court of the U.S. (Excerpted)
   Cite as 543 U.S. 551 (2005)

ROPER v SIMMONS
March 1, 2005

ON WRIT OF CERTIORARI TO THE SUPREME COURT OF MISSOURI

At the age of 17, when he was still a junior in high school, Christopher Simmons, the respondent here, committed murder. About nine months later, after he had turned 18, he was tried and sentenced to death. There is little doubt that Simmons was the instigator of the crime. Before its commission Simmons said he wanted to murder someone. In chilling, callous terms he talked about his plan, discussing it for the most part with two friends, Charles Benjamin and John Tessmer, then aged 15 and 16 respectively. Simmons proposed to commit burglary and murder by breaking and entering, tying up a victim, and throwing the victim off a bridge. Simmons assured his friends they could "get away with it" because they were minors . . .

. . . The State charged Simmons with burglary, kidnaping, stealing, and murder in the first degree. As Simmons was 17 at the time of the crime, he was outside the criminal jurisdiction of Missouri's juvenile court system. See Mo.Rev.Stat. §§ 211.021 (2000) and 211.031 (Supp.2003). He was tried as an adult. At trial the State introduced Simmons' confession and the videotaped reenactment of the crime, along with testimony that Simmons discussed the crime in advance and bragged about it later. The defense called no witnesses in the guilt phase. The jury having returned a verdict of murder, the trial proceeded to the penalty phase.

The State sought the death penalty. As aggravating factors, the State submitted that the murder was committed for the purpose of receiving money; was committed for the purpose of avoiding, interfering with, or preventing lawful arrest of the defendant; and involved depravity of mind and was outrageously and wantonly vile, horrible, and inhuman. The State called Shirley Crook's husband, daughter, and two sisters, who presented moving evidence of the devastation her death had brought to their lives . . .

. . . After these proceedings in Simmons' case had run their course, this Court held that the Eighth and Fourteenth Amendments prohibit the execution of a mentally retarded person. Atkins v Virginia, 536 U.S.

304, 122 S.Ct. 2242, 153 L.Ed.2d 335 (2002). Simmons filed a new petition for state post conviction relief, arguing that the reasoning of Atkins established that the Constitution prohibits the execution of a juvenile who was under 18 when the crime was committed . . .

Analysis

. . . Petitioner cannot show national consensus in favor of capital punishment for juveniles but still resists the conclusion that any consensus exists against it. Petitioner supports this position with, in particular, the observation that when the Senate ratified the International Covenant on Civil and Political Rights (ICCPR), Dec. 19, 1966, 999 U.N.T.S. 171 (entered into force Mar. 23, 1976), it did so subject to the President's proposed reservation regarding Article 6(5) of that treaty, which prohibits capital punishment for juveniles. Brief for Petitioner 27. This reservation at best provides only faint support for petitioner's argument. First, the reservation was passed in 1992; since then, five States have abandoned capital punishment for juveniles. Second, Congress considered the issue when enacting the Federal Death Penalty Act in 1994, and determined that the death penalty should not extend to juveniles. See 18 U.S.C. § 3591. The reservation to Article 6(5) of the ICCPR provides minimal evidence that there is not now a national consensus against juvenile executions . . .

. . . Our determination that the death penalty is disproportionate punishment for offenders under 18 finds confirmation in the stark reality that the U.S. is the only country in the world that continues to give official sanction to the juvenile death penalty. This reality does not become controlling, for the task of interpreting the Eighth Amendment remains our responsibility. Yet at least from the time of the Court's decision in Trop, the Court has referred to the laws of other countries and to international authorities as instructive for its interpretation of the Eighth Amendment's prohibition of "cruel and unusual punishments." 356 U.S., at 102-103, 78 S.Ct. 590 (plurality opinion) ("The civilized nations of the world are in virtual unanimity that statelessness is not to be imposed as punishment for crime"); see also Atkins, supra, at 317, n. 21, 122 S.Ct. 2242 (recognizing that "within the world community, the imposition of the death penalty for crimes committed by mentally retarded offenders is overwhelmingly disapproved"); Thompson, supra, at 830-831, and n. 31, 108 S.Ct. 2687 (plurality opinion) (noting the abolition of the juvenile death penalty "by other nations that share our Anglo-American heritage, and by the leading members of the Western European community," and observing that "[w]e have previously recognized the relevance of the views of the international community in determining whether a punishment is cruel and unusual"); Enmund, supra, at 796-797, n. 22, 102 S.Ct. 3368 (observing that "the doctrine of felony murder has been abolished in England and India, severely restricted in Canada and a number of other Commonwealth countries, and is unknown in continental Europe"); Coker, supra, at 596, n. 10, 97 S.Ct. 2861 (plurality opinion) ("It is . . . not irrelevant here that out of 60 major nations in the world surveyed in 1965, only 3 retained the death penalty for rape where death did not ensue").

As respondent and a number of amici emphasize, Article 37 of the United Nations Convention on the Rights of the Child, which every country in the world has ratified save for the U.S. and Somalia, contains an express prohibition on capital punishment for crimes committed by juveniles under 18. United Nations Convention on the Rights of the Child, Art. 37, Nov. 20, 1989, 1577 U.N.T.S. 3, 28 I.L.M. 1448, 1468-1470 (entered into force Sept. 2, 1990); Brief for Respondent 48; Brief for European Union et al. as Amici Curiae 12-13; Brief for President James Earl Carter, Jr., et al. as Amici Curiae 9; Brief for Former U.S. Diplomats Morton Abramowitz et al. as Amici Curiae 7; Brief for Human Rights Committee of the Bar of England and Wales et al. as Amici Curiae 13-14. No ratifying country has entered a reservation to the provision prohibiting the execution of juvenile offenders. Parallel prohibitions are contained in other significant international covenants. See ICCPR, Art. 6(5), 999 U.N.T.S., at 175 (prohibiting capital punishment for anyone under 18 at the time of offense) (signed and ratified by the U.S. subject to a reservation regarding Article 6(5), as noted, supra, at 1194); American Convention on Human Rights: Pact of San Jose, Costa Rica, Art. 4(5), Nov. 22, 1969, 1144 U.N.T.S. 146 (entered into force July 19, 1978) (same); African Charter on the Rights and Welfare of the Child, Art. 5(3), OAU Doc. CAB/LEG/ 24.9/49 (1990) (entered into force Nov. 29, 1999) (same).

Respondent and his amici have submitted, and petitioner does not contest, that only seven countries other than the U.S. have executed juvenile offenders since 1990: Iran, Pakistan, Saudi Arabia, Yemen,

Nigeria, the Democratic Republic of Congo, and China. Since then each of these countries has either abolished capital punishment for juveniles or made public disavowal of the practice. Brief for Respondent 49-50. In sum, it is fair to say that the U.S. now stands alone in a world that has turned its face against the juvenile death penalty.

Though the international covenants prohibiting the juvenile death penalty are of more recent date, it is instructive to note that the United Kingdom abolished the juvenile death penalty before these covenants came into being. The United Kingdom's experience bears particular relevance here in light of the historic ties between our countries and in light of the Eighth Amendment's own origins. The Amendment was modeled on a parallel provision in the English Declaration of Rights of 1689, which provided: "[E]xcessive Bail ought not to be required nor excessive Fines imposed; nor cruel and unusual Punishments inflicted." 1 W. & M., ch. 2, § 10, in 3 Eng. Stat. at Large 441 (1770); see also Trop, supra, at 100, 78 S.Ct. 590 (plurality opinion). As of now, the United Kingdom has abolished the death penalty in its entirety; but, decades before it took this step, it recognized the disproportionate nature of the juvenile death penalty; and it abolished that penalty as a separate matter. In 1930 an official committee recommended that the minimum age for execution be raised to 21. House of Commons Report from the Select Committee on Capital Punishment (1930), 193, p. 44. Parliament then enacted the Children and Young Person's Act of 1933, 23 Geo. 5, ch. 12, which prevented execution of those aged 18 at the date of the sentence. And in 1948, Parliament enacted the Criminal Justice Act, 11 & 12 Geo. 6, ch. 58, prohibiting the execution of any person under 18 at the time of the offense. In the 56 years that have passed since the United Kingdom abolished the juvenile death penalty, the weight of authority against it there, and in the international community, has become well established.

It is proper that we acknowledge the overwhelming weight of international opinion against the juvenile death penalty, resting in large part on the understanding that the instability and emotional imbalance of young people may often be a factor in the crime. See Brief for Human Rights Committee of the Bar of England and Wales et al. as Amici Curiae 10-11. The opinion of the world community, while not controlling our outcome, does provide respected and significant confirmation for our own conclusions . . .
* * *

The Eighth and Fourteenth Amendments forbid imposition of the death penalty on offenders who were under the age of 18 when their crimes were committed. The judgment of the Missouri Supreme Court setting aside the sentence of death imposed upon Christopher Simmons is affirmed.

It is so ordered.

8. *Rasul v Bush*, Supreme Court of the U.S. (Excerpted)
   Cite as 542 U.S. 466; 124 S. Ct. 2686; 159 L. Ed. 2d 548; (2004)

RASUL et al. *v* GEORGE W. BUSH, PRESIDENT OF THE U.S., et al.
No. 03—334. Argued April 20, 2004–Decided June 28, 2004

CERTIORARI TO THE U.S. COURT OF APPEALS FOR THE DISTRICT
OF COLUMIBA CIRCUIT

Justice Stevens delivered the opinion of the Court.

These two cases present the narrow but important question whether U.S. courts lack jurisdiction to consider challenges to the legality of the detention of foreign nationals captured abroad in connection with hostilities and incarcerated at the Guantánamo Bay Naval Base, Cuba.

I

On September 11, 2001, agents of the al Qaeda terrorist network hijacked four commercial airliners and used them as missiles to attack American targets. While one of the four attacks was foiled by the heroism of the plane's passengers, the other three killed approximately 3,000 innocent civilians, destroyed hundreds of millions of dollars of property, and severely damaged the U.S. economy. In response to the attacks, Congress passed a joint resolution authorizing the President to use "all necessary and appropriate force against those nations, organizations, or persons he determines planned, authorized, committed, or aided the terrorist attacks . . . or harbored such organizations or persons." Authorization for Use of Military Force, Pub. L. 107—40,

§§1—2, 115 Stat. 224. Acting pursuant to that authorization, the President sent U.S. Armed Forces into Afghanistan to wage a military campaign against al Qaeda and the Taliban regime that had supported it.

Petitioners in these cases are 2 Australian citizens and 12 Kuwaiti citizens who were captured abroad during hostilities between the U.S. and the Taliban. [T]he U.S. military has held them . . . at the Naval Base at Guantánamo Bay. The U.S. occupies the Base . . . pursuant to a 1903 Lease Agreement executed with the newly independent Republic of Cuba . . . . Under the Agreement, "the U.S. recognizes the continuance of the ultimate sovereignty of the Republic of Cuba over the [leased areas]," while "the Republic of Cuba consents that during the period of the occupation by the U.S. . . . the U.S. shall exercise complete jurisdiction and control over and within said areas." . . . . In 2002, petitioners . . . filed various actions in the U.S. District Court for the District of Columbia challenging the legality of their detention at the Base. All alleged that none of the petitioners has ever been a combatant against the U.S. or has ever engaged in any terrorist acts. They also alleged that none has been charged with any wrongdoing, permitted to consult with counsel, or provided access to the courts or any other tribunal.

[T]wo Australians each filed a petition for writ of habeas corpus, seeking release from custody, access to counsel, freedom from interrogations . . . . [O]ther . . . detainees filed a complaint seeking to be informed of the charges against them, to be allowed to meet with their families and with counsel, and to have access to the courts or some other impartial tribunal. *Id.*, at 34. They claimed that denial of these rights violates the Constitution, international law, and treaties of the U.S.

Construing all three actions as petitions for writs of habeas corpus, the District Court dismissed them for want of jurisdiction. The court held, in reliance on our opinion in *Johnson v Eisentrager*, 339 U.S. 763 (1950), that "aliens detained outside the sovereign territory of the U.S. [may not] invok[e] a petition for a writ of habeas corpus." 215 F. Supp. 2d 55, 68 (DC 2002). The Court of Appeals affirmed. Reading *Eisentrager* to hold that " 'the privilege of litigation' does not extend to aliens in military custody who have no presence in 'any territory over which the U.S. is sovereign,'" 321 F.3d 1134, 1144 (CADC 2003) (quoting *Eisentrager*, 339 U.S., at 777—778), it held that the District Court lacked jurisdiction over petitioners' habeas actions . . . . . We granted certiorari, 540 U.S. 1003 (2003), and now reverse.

II

Congress has granted federal district courts, "within their respective jurisdictions," the authority to hear applications for habeas corpus by any person who claims to be held "in custody in violation of the Constitution or laws or treaties of the U.S." 28 U.S.C. § 2241(a), (c)(3). . . . .

Habeas corpus is, however, "a writ antecedent to statute, . . . throwing its root deep into the genius of our common law." *Williams v Kaiser*, 323 U.S. 471, 484, n. 2 (1945) (internal quotation marks omitted). The writ . . . received explicit recognition in the Constitution, which forbids suspension of "[t]he Privilege of the Writ of Habeas Corpus . . . unless when in Cases of Rebellion or Invasion the public Safety may require it," Art. I, §9, cl. 2.

As it has evolved over the past two centuries, the habeas statute clearly has expanded habeas corpus "beyond the limits that obtained during the 17th and 18th centuries." *Swain v Pressley*, 430 U.S. 372, 380, n. 13 (1977). But "[a]t its historical core, the writ of habeas corpus has served as a means of reviewing the legality of Executive detention, and it is in that context that its protections have been strongest." *INS v St. Cyr*, 533 U.S. 289, 301 (2001). See also *Brown v Allen*, 344 U.S. 443, 533 (1953) (Jackson, J., concurring in result) ("The historic purpose of the writ has been to relieve detention by executive authorities without judicial trial"). As Justice Jackson wrote in an opinion respecting the availability of habeas corpus to aliens held in U.S. custody:

"Executive imprisonment has been considered oppressive and lawless since John, at Runnymede, pledged that no free man should be imprisoned, dispossessed, outlawed, or exiled save by the judgment of his peers or by the law of the land. The judges of England developed the writ of habeas corpus largely to preserve these immunities from executive restraint." *Shaughnessy v U.S. ex rel. Mezei*, 345 U.S. 206, 218—219 (1953) (dissenting opinion).

Consistent with the historic purpose of the writ, this Court has recognized the federal courts' power to review applications for habeas relief in a wide variety of cases involving Executive detention, in wartime as well as in times of peace. . . . . The question now before us is whether the habeas statute confers a right to judicial review of the legality of Executive detention of aliens in a territory over which the U.S. exercises plenary and exclusive jurisdiction, but not "ultimate sovereignty."

III

Respondents' primary submission is that the answer to the jurisdictional question is controlled by our decision in *Eisentrager*. In that case, we held that a Federal District Court lacked authority to issue a writ of habeas corpus to 21 German citizens who had been captured by U.S. forces in China, tried and convicted of war crimes by an American military commission headquartered in Nanking, and incarcerated in the Landsberg Prison in occupied Germany. . . . . [T]his Court summarized the six critical facts in the case: ". . . these prisoners are entitled . . . *habeas corpus*. To support that assumption we must hold that a prisoner of our military authorities is constitutionally entitled to the writ, even though he (a) is an enemy alien; (b) has never been or resided in the U.S.; (c) was captured outside of our territory and there held in military custody as a prisoner of war; (d) was tried and convicted by a Military Commission sitting outside the U.S.; (e) for offenses against laws of war committed outside the U.S.; (f) and is at all times imprisoned outside the U.S." 339 U.S., at 777.

On this set of facts, the Court concluded, "no right to the writ of *habeas corpus* appears." *Id.*, at 781.

Petitioners in these cases differ from the *Eisentrager* detainees in important respects: They are not nationals of countries at war with the U.S., and they deny that they have engaged in or plotted acts of aggression against the U.S.; they have never been afforded access to any tribunal, much less charged with and convicted of wrongdoing; and for more than two years they have been imprisoned in territory over which the U.S. exercises exclusive jurisdiction and control.

. . . .

In *Braden* v *30th Judicial Circuit Court of Ky.*, 410 U.S. 484, 495 (1973), this Court held . . . that the prisoner's presence within the territorial jurisdiction of the district court is not "an invariable prerequisite" to the exercise of district court jurisdiction under the federal habeas statute. Rather, because "the writ of habeas corpus does not act upon the prisoner who seeks relief, but upon the person who holds him in what is alleged to be unlawful custody," a district court acts "within [its] respective jurisdiction" within the meaning of §2241 as long as "the custodian can be reached by service of process." 410 U.S., at 494—495.

. . . .

Because *Braden* overruled the statutory predicate to *Eisentrager*'s holding, *Eisentrager* plainly does not preclude the exercise of §2241 jurisdiction over petitioners' claims.

IV

[R]espondents contend that we can discern a limit on §2241 through application of the "longstanding principle of American law" that congressional legislation is presumed not to have extraterritorial application unless such intent is clearly manifested. *EEOC* v *Arabian American Oil Co.*, 499 U.S. 244, 248 (1991). Whatever traction the presumption against extraterritoriality might have in other contexts, it certainly has no application to the operation of the habeas statute with respect to persons detained within "the territorial jurisdiction" of the U.S. *Foley Bros., Inc.* v *Filardo*, 336 U.S. 281, 285 (1949). By the express terms of its agreements with Cuba, the U.S. exercises "complete jurisdiction and control" over the Guantánamo Bay Naval Base, and may continue to exercise such control permanently if it so chooses. 1903 Lease Agreement, Art. III; 1934 Treaty, Art. III. . . . . Considering that the statute draws no distinction between Americans and aliens held in federal custody, there is little reason to think that Congress intended the geographical coverage of the statute to vary depending on the detainee's citizenship. Application of the habeas statute to persons detained at the base is consistent with the historical reach of the writ of habeas corpus. At common law, courts exercised habeas jurisdiction over the claims of aliens detained within sovereign territory of the realm, as well as the claims of persons detained in the so-called "exempt jurisdictions," where ordinary writs did not run, and all other dominions under the sovereign's control. As Lord Mansfield wrote in 1759, even if a territory was "no part of the realm," there was "no doubt" as to the court's power to issue writs of habeas corpus if the territory was "under the subjection of the Crown." *King* v *Cowle*, 2 Burr. 834, 854—855, 97 Eng. Rep. 587, 598—599 (K. B.). Later cases confirmed that the reach of the writ depended not on formal notions of territorial sovereignty, but rather on the practical question of "the exact extent and nature of the jurisdiction or dominion exercised in fact by the Crown." *Ex parte Mwenya*, [1960] 1 Q. B. 241, 303 (C. A.) (Lord Evershed, M. R.).

In the end, the answer to the question presented is clear. Petitioners contend that they are being held in federal custody in violation of the laws of the U.S. No party questions the District Court's jurisdiction over petitioners' custodians. Cf. *Braden*, 410 U.S., at 495. Section 2241, by its terms, requires nothing more. We therefore hold that §2241 confers on the District Court jurisdiction to hear petitioners' habeas corpus challenges to the legality of their detention at the Guantánamo Bay Naval Base.

V

In addition to invoking the District Court's jurisdiction under §2241, the *Al Odah* petitioners' complaint invoked the court's jurisdiction under 28 U.S.C. § 1331 the federal question statute, as well as §1350, the Alien Tort Statute. The Court of Appeals, again relying on *Eisentrager*, held that the District Court correctly dismissed the claims founded on §1331 and §1350 for lack of jurisdiction . . . . *Eisentrager* itself erects no bar to the exercise of federal court jurisdiction over the petitioners' habeas corpus claims. It therefore certainly does not bar the exercise of federal-court jurisdiction over claims that merely implicate the "same category of laws listed in the habeas corpus statute." But in any event, nothing in *Eisentrager* or in any of our other cases categorically excludes aliens detained in military custody outside the U.S. from the "'privilege of litigation'" in U.S. courts. 321 F.3d, at 1139. The courts of the U.S. have traditionally been open to nonresident aliens. Cf. *Disconto Gesellschaft v Umbreit*, 208 U.S. 570, 578 (1908) ("Alien citizens, by the policy and practice of the courts of this country, are ordinarily permitted to resort to the courts for the redress of wrongs and the protection of their rights"). And indeed, 28 U.S.C. § 1350 explicitly confers the privilege of suing for an actionable "tort . . . committed in violation of the law of nations or a treaty of the U.S." on aliens alone. The fact that petitioners in these cases are being held in military custody is immaterial to the question of the District Court's jurisdiction over their non habeas statutory claims.

VI

Whether and what further proceedings may become necessary after respondents make their response to the merits of petitioners' claims are matters that we need not address now. What is presently at stake is only whether the federal courts have jurisdiction to determine the legality of the Executive's potentially indefinite detention of individuals who claim to be wholly innocent of wrongdoing. Answering that question in the affirmative, we reverse the judgment of the Court of Appeals and remand for the District Court to consider in the first instance the merits of petitioners' claims.

It is so ordered.

9. *Hamdi v Rumsfeld*, Supreme Court of the U.S. (Excerpted)
   Cite as: 542 U.S. 507 (2004)

HAMDI ET AL.

v

DONALD RUMSFELD, SECRETARY OF DEFENSE, ET AL.

June 28, 2004.

CERTIORARI TO THE U.S. COURT OF APPEALS FOR THE FOURTH CIRCUIT

. . . .

At this difficult time in our Nation's history, we are called upon to consider the legality of the Government's detention of a U.S. citizen on U.S. soil as an "enemy combatant" and to address the process that is constitutionally owed to one who seeks to challenge his classification as such. The U.S. Court of Appeals for the Fourth Circuit held that petitioner Yaser Hamdi's detention was legally authorized and that he was entitled to no further opportunity to challenge his enemy-combatant label. We now vacate and remand. We hold that although Congress authorized the detention of combatants in the narrow circumstances alleged here, due process demands that a citizen held in the U.S. as an enemy combatant be given a meaningful opportunity to contest the factual basis for that detention before a neutral decision maker.

On September 11, 2001, the al Qaeda terrorist network used hijacked commercial airliners to attack prominent targets in the U.S. Approximately 3,000 people were killed in those attacks. One week later, in response to these "acts of treacherous violence," Congress passed a resolution authorizing the President to "use all necessary and appropriate force against those nations, organizations, or persons he determines planned, authorized, committed, or aided the terrorist attacks" or "harbored such organizations or persons, in order to prevent any future acts of international terrorism against the U.S. by such nations, organizations or persons." Authorization for Use of Military Force (AUMF), 115 Stat. 224. Soon thereafter, the President ordered U.S. Armed Forces to Afghanistan, with a mission to subdue al Qaeda and quell the Taliban regime that was known to support it.

This case arises out of the detention of a man whom the Government alleges took up arms with the Taliban during this conflict. His name is Yaser Esam Hamdi. Born in Louisiana in 1980, Hamdi moved with his family to Saudi Arabia as a child. By 2001, the parties agree, he resided in Afghanistan. At some point that year, he was seized by members of the Northern Alliance, a coalition of military groups opposed to the Taliban government, and eventually was turned over to the U.S. military. The Government asserts that it initially detained and interrogated Hamdi in Afghanistan before transferring him to the U.S. Naval Base in Guantánamo Bay in January 2002. In April 2002, upon learning that Hamdi is an American citizen, authorities transferred him to a naval brig in Norfolk, Virginia, where he remained until a recent transfer to a brig in Charleston, South Carolina. The Government contends that Hamdi is an "enemy combatant," and that this status justifies holding him in the U.S. indefinitely — without formal charges or proceedings — unless and until it makes the determination that access to counsel or further process is warranted.

In June 2002, Hamdi's father, Esam Fouad Hamdi, filed the present petition for a writ of habeas corpus under 28 U. S. C. § 2241 in the Eastern District of Virginia, naming as petitioners his son and himself as next friend. The elder Hamdi alleges in the petition that he has had no contact with his son since the Government took custody of him in 2001, and that the Government has held his son "without access to legal counsel or notice of any charges pending against him." App. 103, 104. The petition contends that Hamdi's detention was not legally authorized. Id., at 105. It argues that, "[a]s an American citizen, . . . Hamdi enjoys the full protections of the Constitution," and that Hamdi's detention in the U.S. without charges, access to an impartial tribunal, or assistance of counsel "violated and continue[s] to violate the Fifth and Fourteenth Amendments to the U.S. Constitution." Id., at 107.

The District Court found that Hamdi's father was a proper next friend, appointed the federal public defender as counsel for the petitioners, and ordered that counsel be given access to Hamdi. Id., at 113-116. The U.S. Court of Appeals for the Fourth Circuit reversed that order, holding that the District Court had failed to extend appropriate deference to the Government's security and intelligence interests. 296 F. 3d 278, 279, 283 (2002).

On remand, the Government filed a response and a motion to dismiss the petition. It attached to its response a declaration from one Michael Mobbs (hereinafter Mobbs Declaration), who identified himself as Special Advisor to the Under Secretary of Defense for Policy. . . . .

Mobbs then set forth what remains the sole evidentiary support that the Government has provided to the courts for Hamdi's detention. The declaration states that Hamdi "traveled to Afghanistan" in July or August 2001, and that he thereafter "affiliated with a Taliban military unit and received weapons training." Ibid. It asserts that Hamdi "remained with his Taliban unit following the attacks of September 11" and that, during the time when Northern Alliance forces were "engaged in battle with the Taliban," "Hamdi's Taliban unit surrendered" to those forces, after which he "surrender[ed] his Kalishnikov assault rifle" to them. Id., at 148-149 . . . . .

After the Government submitted this declaration, the Fourth Circuit directed the District Court to proceed in accordance with its earlier ruling and, specifically, to "'consider the sufficiency of the Mobbs declaration as an independent matter before proceeding further.'" 316 F. 3d 450, 462 (2003). The District Court found that the Mobbs Declaration fell "far short" of supporting Hamdi's detention. App. 292. It criticized the generic and hearsay nature of the affidavit, calling it "little more than the government's 'say-so.'" Id., at 298.

Finally, the Fourth Circuit rejected Hamdi's contention that its legal analyses with regard to the authorization for the detention scheme and the process to which he was constitutionally entitled should be altered by the fact that he is an American citizen detained on American soil. Relying on Ex parte Quirin, 317 U. S. 1 (1942), the court emphasized that "[o]ne who takes up arms against the U.S. in a foreign theater of war, regardless of his citizenship, may properly be designated an enemy combatant and treated as such." 316 F. 3d, at 475. ". . . .

The Fourth Circuit denied rehearing en banc, 337 F. 3d 335 (2003), and we granted certiorari. 540 U. S. 1099 (2004). We now vacate the judgment below and remand.

II

The threshold question before us is whether the Executive has the authority to detain citizens who qualify as "enemy combatants." There is some debate as to the proper scope of this term, and the Government has never provided any court with the full criteria that it uses in classifying individuals as such. It has made clear, however, that, for purposes of this case, the "enemy combatant" that it is seeking to detain is an individual who, it alleges, was "'part of or supporting forces hostile to the U.S. or coalition partners'" in Afghanistan and who "'engaged in an armed conflict against the U.S.'" there. Brief for Respondents 3. We therefore answer only the narrow question before us: whether the detention of citizens falling within that definition is authorized.

The Government maintains that no explicit congressional authorization is required, because the Executive possesses plenary authority to detain pursuant to Article II of the Constitution. We do not reach the question whether Article II provides such authority, however, because we agree with the Government's alternative position, that Congress has in fact authorized Hamdi's detention, through the AUMF.

Our analysis on that point, set forth below, substantially overlaps with our analysis of Hamdi's principal argument for the illegality of his detention. He posits that his detention is forbidden by 18 U. S. C. § 4001(a). Section 4001(a) states that "[n]o citizen shall be imprisoned or otherwise detained by the U.S. except pursuant to an Act of Congress." Congress passed § 4001(a) in 1971 as part of a bill to repeal the Emergency Detention Act of 1950, 50 U. S. C. § 811 et seq., which provided procedures for executive detention, during times of emergency, of individuals deemed likely to engage in espionage or sabotage. Congress was particularly concerned about the possibility that the Act could be used to reprise the Japanese-American internment camps of World War II. H. R. Rep. No. 92-116 (1971); id., at 4 ("The concentration camp implications of the legislation render it abhorrent"). being detained "pursuant to an Act of Congress"—the AUMF. Id., at 21-22. Again, because we conclude that the Government's second assertion is correct, we do not address the first. In other words, . . . for the reasons that follow, we conclude that the AUMF is explicit congressional authorization for the detention of individuals in the narrow category we describe (assuming, without deciding, that such authorization is required), and that the AUMF satisfied § 4001(a)'s requirement that a detention be "pursuant to an Act of Congress" (assuming, without deciding, that § 4001(a) applies to military detentions).

The AUMF authorizes the President to use "all necessary and appropriate force" against "nations, organizations, or persons" associated with the September 11, 2001, terrorist attacks. 115 Stat. 224. There can be no doubt that individuals who fought against the U.S. in Afghanistan as part of the Taliban, an organization known to have supported the al Qaeda terrorist network responsible for those attacks, are individuals Congress sought to target in passing the AUMF. We conclude that detention of individuals falling into the limited category we are considering, for the duration of the particular conflict in which they were captured, is so fundamental and accepted an incident to war as to be an exercise of the "necessary and appropriate force" Congress has authorized the President to use.

The capture and detention of lawful combatants and the capture, detention, and trial of unlawful combatants, by "universal agreement and practice," are "important incident[s] of war." Ex parte Quirin, supra, at 28, 30. The purpose of detention is to prevent captured individuals from returning to the field of battle and taking up arms once again. . . .

There is no bar to this Nation's holding one of its own citizens as an enemy combatant. In Quirin, one of the detainees, Haupt, alleged that he was a naturalized U.S. citizen. 317 U. S., at 20. We held that "[c]itizens who associate themselves with the military arm of the enemy government, and with its aid, guidance and direction enter this country bent on hostile acts, are enemy belligerents within the meaning of . . . the law of war." Id., at 37-38. . . .

In light of these principles, it is of no moment that the AUMF does not use specific language of detention. Because detention to prevent a combatant's return to the battlefield is a fundamental incident of waging war, in permitting the use of "necessary and appropriate force," Congress has clearly and unmistakably authorized detention in the narrow circumstances considered here.

Hamdi objects, nevertheless, that Congress has not authorized the indefinite detention to which he is now subject. The Government responds that "the detention of enemy combatants during World War II was just as 'indefinite' while that war was being fought." Id., at 16. We take Hamdi's objection to be not to the lack of certainty regarding the date on which the conflict will end, but to the substantial prospect of perpetual detention. We recognize that the national security underpinnings of the "war on terror," although crucially important, are broad and malleable. As the Government concedes, "given its unconventional nature, the current conflict is unlikely to end with a formal cease-fire agreement." Ibid. The prospect Hamdi raises is therefore not farfetched. If the Government does not consider this unconventional war won for two generations, and if it maintains during that time that Hamdi might, if released, rejoin forces fighting against the U.S., then the position it has taken throughout the litigation of this case suggests that Hamdi's detention could last for the rest of his life.

It is a clearly established principle of the law of war that detention may last no longer than active hostilities. See Article 118 of the Geneva Convention (III) Relative to the Treatment of Prisoners of War, Aug. 12, 1949, [1955] 6 U. S. T. 3316, 3406, T. I. A. S. No. 3364 ("Prisoners of war shall be released and repatriated without delay after the cessation of active hostilities"). . . .

Hamdi contends that the AUMF does not authorize indefinite or perpetual detention. Certainly, we agree that indefinite detention for the purpose of interrogation is not authorized. Further, we understand Congress' grant of authority for the use of "necessary and appropriate force" to include the authority to detain for the duration of the relevant conflict, and our understanding is based on longstanding law-of-war principles. If the practical circumstances of a given conflict are entirely unlike those of the conflicts that informed the development of the law of war, that understanding may unravel. But that is not the situation we face as of this date. Active combat operations against Taliban fighters apparently are ongoing in Afghanistan. . . . The U.S. may detain, for the duration of these hostilities, individuals legitimately determined to be Taliban combatants who "engaged in an armed conflict against the U.S." If the record establishes that U.S. troops are still involved in active combat in Afghanistan, those detentions are part of the exercise of "necessary and appropriate force," and therefore are authorized by the AUMF.

. . .

Quirin was a unanimous opinion. It both postdates and clarifies *Milligan,* providing us with the most apposite precedent that we have on the question of whether citizens may be detained in such circumstances. Brushing aside such precedent—particularly when doing so gives rise to a host of new questions never dealt with by this Court—is unjustified and unwise.

. . .

III

Even in cases in which the detention of enemy combatants is legally authorized, there remains the question of what process is constitutionally due to a citizen who disputes his enemy-combatant status. Hamdi argues that he is owed a meaningful and timely hearing and that "extra-judicial detention [that] begins and ends with the submission of an affidavit based on third-hand hearsay" does not comport with the Fifth and Fourteenth Amendments. Brief for Petitioners 16. The Government counters that any more process than was provided below would be both unworkable and "constitutionally intolerable." Brief for Respondents 46. Our resolution of this dispute requires a careful examination both of the writ of habeas corpus, which Hamdi now seeks to employ as a mechanism of judicial review, and of the Due Process Clause, which informs the procedural contours of that mechanism in this instance.

A

Though they reach radically different conclusions on the process that ought to attend the present proceeding, the parties begin on common ground. All agree that, absent suspension, the writ of habeas corpus remains available to every individual detained within the U.S. U. S. Const., Art. I, § 9, cl. 2 ("The Privilege of the Writ of Habeas Corpus shall not be suspended, unless when in Cases of Rebellion or Invasion the public Safety may require it"). Only in the rarest of circumstances has Congress seen fit to suspend the writ. See, *e. g.*; Act of Mar. 3, 1863, ch. 81, § 1, 12 Stat. 755; Act of Apr. 20, 1871, ch. 22, § 4, 17 Stat. 14. At all other times, it has remained a critical check on the Executive, ensuring that it does not detain individuals except in accordance with law. See INS v St. Cyr, 533 U. S. 289, 301 (2001). All agree suspension of the writ has not occurred here. Thus, it is undisputed that Hamdi was properly before an Article III court to challenge his detention under 28 U. S. C. § 2241. Brief for Respondents 12. Further, all agree that § 2241 and its companion provisions provide at least a skeletal outline of the procedures to be afforded a petitioner in federal habeas review. Most notably, § 2243 provides that "the person detained may, under oath, deny any of the facts set forth in the return or allege any other material facts," and § 2246 allows the taking of evidence in habeas proceedings by deposition, affidavit, or interrogatories.

The simple outline of § 2241 makes clear both that Congress envisioned that habeas petitioners would have some opportunity to present and rebut facts and that courts in cases like this retain some ability to vary the ways in which they do so as mandated by due process. The Government recognizes the basic procedural protections required by the habeas statute, *id.*, at 37-38, but asks us to hold that, given both the flexibility of the habeas mechanism and the circumstances presented in this case, the presentation of the Mobbs Declaration to the habeas court completed the required factual development. It suggests two separate reasons for its position that no further process is due.

B

First, the Government urges the adoption of the Fourth Circuit's holding below—that because it is "undisputed" that Hamdi's seizure took place in a combat zone, the habeas determination can be made purely as a matter of law, with no further hearing or factfinding necessary. This argument is easily rejected. As the dissenters from the denial of rehearing en banc noted, the circumstances surrounding Hamdi's seizure cannot in any way be characterized as "undisputed," as "those circumstances are neither conceded in fact, nor susceptible to concession in law, because Hamdi has not been permitted to speak for himself or even through counsel as to those circumstances." 337 F. 3d, at 357 (opinion of Luttig, J.); see also *id.*, at 371-372 (opinion of Motz, J.). Further, the "facts" that constitute the alleged concession are insufficient to support Hamdi's detention. Under the definition of enemy combatant that we accept today as falling within the scope of Congress' authorization, Hamdi would need to be "part of or supporting forces hostile to the U.S. or coalition partners" and "engaged in an armed conflict against the U.S." to justify his detention in the U.S. for the duration of the relevant conflict. . . .

C

The Government's second argument requires closer consideration. This is the argument that further factual exploration is unwarranted and inappropriate in light of the extraordinary constitutional interests at stake. Under the Government's most extreme rendition of this argument, "[r]espect for separation of powers and the limited institutional capabilities of courts in matters of military decision-making in connection with an ongoing conflict" ought to eliminate entirely any individual process, restricting the courts to investigating only whether legal authorization exists for the broader detention scheme. . . .

In response, Hamdi emphasizes that this Court consistently has recognized that an individual challenging his detention may not be held at the will of the Executive without recourse to some proceeding before a neutral tribunal to determine whether the Executive's asserted justifications for that detention have basis in fact and warrant in law. See, *e.g.*, *Zadvydas v Davis*, 533 U. S. 678, 690 (2001); *Addington v Texas*, 441 U. S. 418, 425-427 (1979). He argues that the Fourth Circuit inappropriately "ceded power to the Executive during wartime to define the conduct for which a citizen may be detained, judge whether that citizen has engaged in the proscribed conduct, and imprison that citizen indefinitely," . . .

Both of these positions highlight legitimate concerns. And both emphasize the tension that often exists between the autonomy that the Government asserts is necessary in order to pursue effectively a particular goal and the process that a citizen contends he is due before he is deprived of a constitutional right. The ordinary mechanism that we use for balancing such serious competing interests, and for determining the procedures that are necessary to ensure that a citizen is not "deprived of life, liberty, or property, without due process of law," U. S. Const., Amdt. 5, is the test that we articulated in *Mathews v Eldridge*, 424 U. S. 319 (1976). See, *e.g.*, *Heller v Doe, 509 U. S. 312, 330-331 (1993)*; *Zinermon v Burch*, 494 U. S. 113, 127-128 (1990); *U.S. v Salerno*, 481 U. S. 739, 746 (1987); *Schall v Martin*, 467 U. S. 253, 274-275 (1984); *Addington v Texas, supra,* at 425. *Mathews* dictates that the process due in any given instance is determined by weighing "the private interest that will be affected by the official action" against the Government's asserted interest, "including the function involved" and the burdens the Government would face in providing greater process. 424 U. S., at 335. The *Mathews* calculus then contemplates a judicious balancing of these concerns, through an analysis of "the risk of an erroneous deprivation" of the private interest if the process were reduced and the "probable value, if any, of additional or substitute procedural safeguards." *Ibid.* We take each of these steps in turn.

1

It is beyond question that substantial interests lie on both sides of the scale in this case. Hamdi's "private interest . . . affected by the official action," *ibid.*, is the most elemental of liberty interests—the interest in being free from physical detention by one's own government. *Foucha v Louisiana, 504 U. S. 71, 80 (1992)* ("Freedom from bodily restraint has always been at the core of the liberty protected by the Due Process Clause from arbitrary governmental action"); see also *Parham v J. R. , 442 U. S. 584, 600 (1979)* (noting the "substantial liberty interest in not being confined unnecessarily"). "In our society liberty is the norm," and detention without trial "is the carefully limited exception." *Salerno, supra,* at 755. "We have always been careful not to `minimize the importance and fundamental nature' of the individual's right to liberty," *Foucha, supra,* at 80 (quoting Salerno, supra, at 750), and we will not do so today.

Nor is the weight on this side of the *Mathews* scale offset by the circumstances of war or the accusation of treasonous behavior, for "[i]t is clear that commitment for *any* purpose constitutes a significant deprivation of liberty that requires due process protection," <u>Jones v U.S., 463 U. S. 354, 361 (1983)</u> (emphasis added; internal quotation marks omitted), and at this stage in the *Mathews* calculus, we consider the interest of the *erroneously* detained individual. <u>Carey v Piphus, 435 U. S. 247, 259 (1978)</u> ("Procedural due process rules are meant to protect persons not from the deprivation, but from the mistaken or unjustified deprivation of life, liberty, or property"); see also *id.*, at 266 (noting "the importance to organized society that procedural due process be observed," and emphasizing that "the right to procedural due process is `absolute' in the sense that it does not depend upon the merits of a claimant's substantive assertions"). . . . ("[The Founders] knew—the history of the world told them—the nation they were founding, be its existence short or long, would be involved in war; how often or how long continued, human foresight could not tell; and that unlimited power, wherever lodged at such a time, was especially hazardous to freemen"). Because we live in a society in which "[m]ere public intolerance or animosity cannot constitutionally justify the deprivation of a person's physical liberty," <u>O'Connor v Donaldson, 422 U. S. 563, 575 (1975),</u> our starting point for the *Mathews v Eldridge* analysis is unaltered by the allegations surrounding the particular detainee or the organizations with which he is alleged to have associated. We reaffirm today the fundamental nature of a citizen's right to be free from involuntary confinement by his own government without due process of law, and we weigh the opposing governmental interests against the curtailment of liberty that such confinement entails.

2. On the other side of the scale are the weighty and sensitive governmental interests in ensuring that those who have in fact fought with the enemy during a war do not return to battle against the U.S. As discussed above, supra, at 518, the law of war and the realities of combat may render such detentions both necessary and appropriate, and our due process analysis need not blink at those realities. Without doubt, our Constitution recognizes that core strategic matters of warmaking belong in the hands of those who are best positioned and most politically accountable for making them. <u>Department of Navy v Egan, 484 U. S. 518, 530 (1988)</u> (noting the reluctance of the courts "to intrude upon the authority of the Executive in military and national security affairs"); <u>Youngstown Sheet & Tube Co. v Sawyer, 343 U.S. 579, 587 (1952)</u> (acknowledging "broad powers in military commanders engaged in day-to-day fighting in a theater of war").

. . .

3. Striking the proper constitutional balance here is of great importance to the Nation during this period of ongoing combat. But it is equally vital that our calculus not give short shrift to the values that this country holds dear or to the privilege that is American citizenship. It is during our most challenging and uncertain moments that our Nation's commitment to due process is most severely tested; and it is in those times that we must preserve our commitment at home to the principles for which we fight abroad. See <u>Kennedy v Mendoza-Martinez, 372 U. S. 144, 164-165 (1963)</u> ("The imperative necessity for safeguarding these rights to procedural due process under the gravest of emergencies has existed throughout our constitutional history, for it is then, under the pressing exigencies of crisis, that there is the greatest temptation to dispense with fundamental constitutional guarantees which, it is feared, will inhibit governmental action"); see also <u>U.S. v Robel, 389 U. S. 258, 264 (1967)</u> ("It would indeed be ironic if, in the name of national defense, we would sanction the subversion of one of those liberties . . . which makes the defense of the Nation worthwhile").

With due recognition of these competing concerns, we believe that neither the process proposed by the Government nor the process apparently envisioned by the District Court below strikes the proper constitutional balance when a U.S. citizen is detained in the U.S. as an enemy combatant. That is, "the risk of an erroneous deprivation" of a detainee's liberty interest is unacceptably high under the Government's proposed rule, while some of the "additional or substitute procedural safeguards" suggested by the District Court are unwarranted in light of their limited "probable value" and the burdens they may impose on the military in such cases. <u>Mathews, 424 U. S., at 335.</u>

We therefore hold that a citizen-detainee seeking to challenge his classification as an enemy combatant must receive notice of the factual basis for his classification, and a fair opportunity to rebut the Government's factual assertions before a neutral decisionmaker. See <u>Cleveland Bd. of Ed. v Loudermill, 470 U. S. 532, 542</u> (1985) ("An essential principle of due process is that a deprivation of life, liberty, or property `be preceded by notice and opportunity for hearing appropriate to the nature of the case'" (quoting <u>Mullane v Central Hanover Bank & Trust Co., 339 U.S. 306, 313 (1950)</u>); <u>Concrete Pipe & Products of Cal., Inc. v Construction Laborers Pension Trust for Southern Cal., 508 U. S. 602, 617 (1993)</u> ("due process requires a `neutral and detached judge in the first instance'" (quoting _Ward v Monroeville_, 409 U. S. 57, 61-62 (1972))). "For more than a century the central meaning of procedural due process has been clear: `Parties whose rights are to be affected are entitled to be heard; and in order that they may enjoy that right they must first be notified.' It is equally fundamental that the right to notice and an opportunity to be heard `must be granted at a meaningful time and in a meaningful manner.'" _Fuentes v Shevin_, 407 U. S. 67, 80 (1972) (quoting _Baldwin v Hale_, 1 Wall. 223, 233 (1864); _Armstrong v Manzo_, 380 U. S. 545, 552 (1965) (other citations omitted)). These essential constitutional promises may not be eroded.

At the same time, the exigencies of the circumstances may demand that, aside from these core elements, enemy-combatant proceedings may be tailored to alleviate their uncommon potential to burden the Executive at a time of ongoing military conflict. Hearsay, for example, may need to be accepted as the most reliable available evidence from the Government in such a proceeding. Likewise, the Constitution would not be offended by a presumption in favor of the Government's evidence, so long as that presumption remained a rebuttable one and fair opportunity for rebuttal were provided. Thus, once the Government puts forth credible evidence that the habeas petitioner meets the enemy-combatant criteria, the onus could shift to the petitioner to rebut that evidence with more persuasive evidence that he falls outside the criteria. A burden-shifting scheme of this sort would meet the goal of ensuring that the errant tourist, embedded journalist, or local aid worker has a chance to prove military error while giving due regard to the Executive once it has put forth meaningful support for its conclusion that the detainee is in fact an enemy combatant. In the words of _Mathews_, process of this sort would sufficiently address the "risk of an erroneous deprivation" of a detainee's liberty interest while eliminating certain procedures that have questionable additional value in light of the burden on the Government. 424 U. S., at 335.

We think it unlikely that this basic process will have the dire impact on the central functions of war making that the Government forecasts. The parties agree that initial captures on the battlefield need not receive the process we have discussed here; that process is due only when the determination is made to _continue_ to hold those who have been seized. The Government has made clear in its briefing that documentation regarding battlefield detainees already is kept in the ordinary course of military affairs. Brief for Respondents 3-4. . . . While we accord the greatest respect and consideration to the judgments of military authorities in matters relating to the actual prosecution of a war, and recognize that the scope of that discretion necessarily is wide, it does not infringe on the core role of the military for the courts to exercise their own time-honored and constitutionally mandated roles of reviewing and resolving claims like those presented here. Cf. _Korematsu v U.S._, 323 U. S. 214, 233-234 (1944) (Murphy, J., dissenting) ("[L]ike other claims conflicting with the asserted constitutional rights of the individual, the military claim must subject itself to the judicial process of having its reasonableness determined and its conflicts with other interests reconciled"); _Sterling v Constantin_, 287 U. S. 378, 401 (1932) ("What are the allowable limits of military discretion, and whether or not they have been overstepped in a particular case, are judicial questions").

In sum, while the full protections that accompany challenges to detentions in other settings may prove unworkable and inappropriate in the enemy-combatant setting, the threats to military operations posed by a basic system of independent review are not so weighty as to trump a citizen's core rights to challenge meaningfully the Government's case and to be heard by an impartial adjudicator.

D

In so holding, we necessarily reject the Government's assertion that separation of powers principles mandate a heavily circumscribed role for the courts in such circumstances. Indeed, the position that the courts must forgo any examination of the individual case and focus exclusively on the legality of the broader detention scheme cannot be mandated by any reasonable view of separation of powers, as this approach serves only to _condense_ power into a single branch of government. We have long since made clear that a state of war is not a blank check for the President when it comes to the rights of the Nation's citizens. _Youngstown Sheet & Tube_, 343 U. S., at 587. Whatever power the U.S. Constitution envisions for the Executive in its exchanges with other nations or with enemy organizations in times of conflict, it most assuredly envisions a role for all three branches when individual liberties are at stake. _Mistretta v U.S._, 488 U. S. 361, 380 (1989) (it was "the central judgment of the Framers of the Constitution that, within our political scheme, the separation of governmental powers into three coordinate Branches is essential to the preservation of liberty"); _Home Building & Loan Assn. v Blaisdell_, 290 U. S. 398, 426 (1934) (The war power "is a power to wage war successfully, and thus it permits the harnessing of the entire energies of the people in a supreme cooperative effort to preserve the nation. But even the war power does not remove constitutional limitations safeguarding essential liberties"). Likewise, we have made clear that, unless Congress acts to suspend it, the Great Writ of habeas corpus allows the Judicial Branch to play a necessary role in maintaining this delicate balance of governance, serving as an important judicial check on the Executive's discretion in the realm of detentions. See St. Cyr, 533 U. S., at 301 ("At its historical core, the writ of habeas corpus has served as a means of reviewing the legality of Executive detention, and it is in that context that its protections have been strongest"). Thus, while we do not question that our due process assessment must pay keen attention to the particular burdens faced by the Executive in the context of military action, it would turn our system of checks and balances on its head to suggest that a citizen could not make his way to court with a challenge to the factual basis for his detention by his government, simply because the Executive opposes making available such a challenge. Absent suspension of the writ by Congress, a citizen detained as an enemy combatant is entitled to this process.

Because we conclude that due process demands some system for a citizen detainee to refute his classification, the proposed "some evidence" standard is inadequate. Any process in which the Executive's factual assertions go wholly unchallenged or are simply presumed correct without any opportunity for the alleged combatant to demonstrate otherwise falls constitutionally short. . . . This standard therefore is ill suited to the situation in which a habeas petitioner has received no prior proceedings before any tribunal and had no prior opportunity to rebut the Executive's factual assertions before a neutral decision maker.

Today we are faced only with such a case. Aside from unspecified "screening" processes, Brief for Respondents 3-4, and military interrogations in which the Government suggests Hamdi could have contested his classification, Tr. of Oral Arg. 40, 42, Hamdi has received no process. An interrogation by one's captor, however effective an intelligence-gathering tool, hardly constitutes a constitutionally adequate fact finding before a neutral decisionmaker. Compare Brief for Respondents 42-43 (discussing the "secure interrogation environment," and noting that military interrogations require a controlled "interrogation dynamic" and "a relationship of trust and dependency" and are "a critical source" of "timely and effective intelligence") with Concrete Pipe, 508 U. S., at 617-618 ("[O]ne is entitled as a matter of due process of law to an adjudicator who is not in a situation which would offer a possible temptation to the average man as a judge . . . which might lead him not to hold the balance nice, clear and true" (internal quotation marks omitted)). That even purportedly fair adjudicators "are disqualified by their interest in the controversy to be decided is, of course, the general rule." Tumey v Ohio, 273 U. S. 510, 522 (1927). Plainly, the "process" Hamdi has received is not that to which he is entitled under the Due Process Clause.

There remains the possibility that the standards we have articulated could be met by an appropriately authorized and properly constituted military tribunal . . . We have no reason to doubt that courts faced with these sensitive matters will pay proper heed both to the matters of national security that might arise in an individual case and to the constitutional limitations safeguarding essential liberties that remain vibrant even in times of security concerns.

IV

Hamdi asks us to hold that the Fourth Circuit also erred by denying him immediate access to counsel upon his detention and by disposing of the case without permitting him to meet with an attorney. Brief for Petitioners 19. Since our grant of certiorari in this case, Hamdi has been appointed counsel, with whom he has met for consultation purposes on several occasions, and with whom he is now being granted unmonitored meetings. He unquestionably has the right to access to counsel in connection with the proceedings on remand. No further consideration of this issue is necessary at this stage of the case.

The judgment of the U.S. Court of Appeals for the Fourth Circuit is vacated, and the case is remanded for further proceedings.

It is so ordered.

[Footnotes omitted]

10. *Hamdan v Rumsfeld*, Supreme Court of the U.S. (Excerpted)
    Cite As 548 U.S. 557 (2006), 415 F.3d 33, reversed and remanded.

HAMDAN
v
DONALD RUMSFELD, SECRETARY OF DEFENSE, ET AL.
ON WRIT OF CERTIORARI TO THE U.S. COURT OF APPEALS FOR THE DISTRICT OF
COLUMBIA CIRCUIT
[June 29, 2006]

Petitioner Salim Ahmed Hamdan, a Yemeni national, is in custody at an American prison in Guantánamo Bay, Cuba. In November 2001, during hostilities between the U.S. and the Taliban (which then governed Afghanistan), Hamdan was captured by militia forces and turned over to the U.S. military. In June 2002, he was transported to Guantánamo Bay. Over a year later, the President deemed him eligible for trial by military commission for then-unspecified crimes. After another year had passed, Hamdan was charged with one count of conspiracy "to commit . . . offenses triable by military commission."

Hamdan filed petitions for writs of habeas corpus and mandamus to challenge the Executive Branch's intended means of prosecuting this charge. He concedes that a court-martial constituted in accordance with the Uniform Code of Military Justice (UCMJ), 10 U.S.C. §801 et seq. (2000 ed. and Supp. III), would have authority to try him. His objection is that the military commission the President has convened lacks such authority, for two principal reasons: First, neither congressional Act nor the common law of war supports trial by this commission for the crime of conspiracy—an offense that, Hamdan says, is not a violation of the law of war. Second, Hamdan contends, the procedures that the President has adopted to try him violate the most basic tenets of military and international law, including the principle that a defendant must be permitted to see and hear the evidence against him.

For the reasons that follow, we conclude that the military commission convened to try Hamdan lacks power to proceed because its structure and procedures violate both the UCMJ and the Geneva Conventions. Four of us also conclude, see Part V, infra, that the offense with which Hamdan has been charged is not an "offens[e] that by . . . the law of war may be tried by military commissions." 10 U.S.C. §821.

I

On September 11, 2001, agents of the al Qaeda terrorist organization hijacked commercial airplanes and attacked the World Trade Center in New York City and the national headquarters of the Department of Defense in Arlington, Virginia. Americans will never forget the devastation wrought by these acts. Nearly 3,000 civilians were killed.

Congress responded by adopting a Joint Resolution authorizing the President to "use all necessary and appropriate force against those nations, organizations, or persons he determines planned, authorized, committed, or aided the terrorist attacks . . . in order to prevent any future acts of international terrorism against the U.S. by such nations, organizations or persons." Authorization for Use of Military Force (AUMF), 115 Stat. 224, note following 50 U.S.C. §1541 (2000 ed., Supp. III). Acting pursuant to the AUMF, and having determined that the Taliban regime had supported al Qaeda, the President ordered the Armed Forces of the U.S. to invade Afghanistan. In the ensuing hostilities, hundreds of individuals, Hamdan among them, were captured and eventually detained at Guantánamo Bay.

On November 13, 2001, while the U.S. was still engaged in active combat with the Taliban, the President issued a comprehensive military order intended to govern the "Detention, Treatment, and Trial of Certain Non-Citizens in the War Against Terrorism," 66 Fed. Reg. 57833 (hereinafter November 13 Order or Order). Those subject to the November 13 Order include any noncitizen for whom the President determines "there is reason to believe" that he or she (1) "is or was" a member of al Qaeda or (2) has engaged or participated in terrorist activities aimed at or harmful to the U.S. Id., at 57834. Any such individual "shall, when tried, be tried by military commission for any and all offenses triable by military commission that such individual is alleged to have committed, and may be punished in accordance with the penalties provided under applicable law, including imprisonment or death." Ibid. The November 13 Order vested in the Secretary of Defense the power to appoint military commissions to try individuals subject to the Order, but that power has since been delegated to John D. Altenberg, Jr., a retired Army major general and longtime military lawyer who has been designated "Appointing Authority for Military Commissions."

On July 3, 2003, the President announced his determination that Hamdan and five other detainees at Guantánamo Bay were subject to the November 13 Order and thus triable by military commission. In December 2003, military counsel was appointed to represent Hamdan. Two months later, counsel filed demands for charges and for a speedy trial pursuant to Article 10 of the UCMJ, 10 U.S.C. §810. On February 23, 2004, the legal adviser to the Appointing Authority denied the applications, ruling that Hamdan was not entitled to any of the protections of the UCMJ. Not until July 13, 2004, after Hamdan had commenced this action in the U.S. District Court for the Western District of Washington, did the Government finally charge him with the offense for which, a year earlier, he had been deemed eligible for trial by military commission.

The charging document, which is unsigned, contains 13 numbered paragraphs. The first two paragraphs recite the asserted bases for the military commission's jurisdiction—namely, the November 13 Order and the

President's July 3, 2003, declaration that Hamdan is eligible for trial by military commission. The next nine paragraphs, collectively entitled "General Allegations," describe al Qaeda's activities from its inception in 1989 through 2001 and identify Osama bin Laden as the group's leader. Hamdan is not mentioned in these paragraphs.

Only the final two paragraphs, entitled "Charge: Conspiracy," contain allegations against Hamdan. Paragraph 12 charges that "from on or about February 1996 to on or about November 24, 2001," Hamdan "willfully and knowingly joined an enterprise of persons who shared a common criminal purpose and conspired and agreed with [named members of al Qaeda] to commit the following offenses triable by military commission: attacking civilians; attacking civilian objects; murder by an unprivileged belligerent; and terrorism." App. to Pet. for Cert. 65a. There is no allegation that Hamdan had any command responsibilities, played a leadership role, or participated in the planning of any activity.

On November 7, 2005, we granted certiorari to decide whether the military commission convened to try Hamdan has authority to do so, and whether Hamdan may rely on the Geneva Conventions in these proceedings.

II

On February 13, 2006, the Government filed a motion to dismiss the writ of certiorari. The ground cited for dismissal was the recently enacted Detainee Treatment Act of 2005 (DTA), Pub. L. 109–148, 119 Stat. 2739. We postponed our ruling on that motion pending argument on the merits, 546 U.S. ___ (2006), and now deny it. . . . .

For these reasons, we deny the Government's motion to dismiss.

III

Finally, the Government has identified no other "important countervailing interest" that would permit federal courts to depart from their general "duty to exercise the jurisdiction that is conferred upon them by Congress." *Id.*, at 716 (majority opinion). To the contrary, Hamdan and the Government both have a compelling interest in knowing in advance whether Hamdan may be tried by a military commission that arguably is without any basis in law and operates free from many of the procedural rules prescribed by Congress for courts-martial—rules intended to safeguard the accused and ensure the reliability of any conviction. While we certainly do not foreclose the possibility that abstention may be appropriate in some cases seeking review of ongoing military commission proceedings (such as military commissions convened on the battlefield), the foregoing discussion makes clear that, under our precedent, abstention is not justified here. We therefore proceed to consider the merits of Hamdan's challenge.

IV

The military commission, a tribunal neither mentioned in the Constitution nor created by statute, was born of military necessity. See W. Winthrop, Military Law and Precedents 831 (rev. 2d ed. 1920) (hereinafter Winthrop). Though foreshadowed in some respects by earlier tribunals like the Board of General Officers that General Washington convened to try British Major John André for spying during the Revolutionary War, the commission "as such" was inaugurated in 1847. *Id.*, at 832; G. Davis, A Treatise on the Military Law of the U.S. 308 (2d ed. 1909) (hereinafter Davis). As commander of occupied Mexican territory, and having available to him no other tribunal, General Winfield Scott that year ordered the establishment of both " '*military commissions*' " to try ordinary crimes committed in the occupied territory and a "*council of war*" to try offenses against the law of war. Winthrop 832 (emphases in original).

The Constitution makes the President the "Commander in Chief" of the Armed Forces, Art. II, §2, cl. 1, but vests in Congress the powers to "declare War . . . and make Rules concerning Captures on Land and Water," Art. I, §8, cl. 11, to "raise and support Armies," *id.*, cl. 12, to "define and punish . . . Offences against the Law of Nations," *id.*, cl. 10, and "To make Rules for the Government and Regulation of the land and naval Forces," *id.*, cl. 14. The interplay between these powers was described by Chief Justice Chase in the seminal case of Ex parte Milligan:

"The power to make the necessary laws is in Congress; the power to execute in the President. Both powers imply many subordinate and auxiliary powers. Each includes all authorities essential to its due exercise. But neither can the President, in war more than in peace, intrude upon the proper authority of Congress, nor Congress upon the proper authority of the President . . . . Congress cannot direct the conduct of campaigns, nor can the President, or any commander under him, without the sanction of Congress, institute tribunals for the trial and punishment of offences, either of soldiers or civilians, unless in cases of a controlling necessity, which justifies what it compels, or at least insures acts of indemnity from the justice of the legislature." 4 Wall., at 139–140.

Together, the UCMJ, the AUMF, and the DTA at most acknowledge a general Presidential authority to convene military commissions in circumstances where justified under the "Constitution and laws," including the law of war. Absent a more specific congressional authorization, the task of this Court is, as it was in Quirin, to decide whether Hamdan's military commission is so justified. It is to that inquiry we now turn.

V

The common law governing military commissions may be gleaned from past practice and what sparse legal precedent exists. Commissions historically have been used in three situations. See Bradley & Goldsmith, Congressional Authorization and the War on Terrorism, 118 Harv. L. Rev. 2048, 2132–2133 (2005); Winthrop 831–846; Hearings on H. R. 2498 before the Subcommittee of the House Committee on Armed Services, 81st Cong., 1st Sess., 975 (1949). First, they have substituted for civilian courts at times and in places where martial law has been declared. Their use in these circumstances has raised constitutional questions, see *Duncan* v *Kahanamoku*, 327 U.S. 304 (1946) ; *Milligan*, 4 Wall., at 121–122, but is well recognized. See Winthrop 822, 836–839. Second, commissions have been established to try civilians "as part of a temporary military government over occupied enemy territory or territory regained from an enemy where civilian government cannot and does not function." *Duncan*, 327 U.S., at 314; see *Milligan*, 4 Wall., at 141–142 (Chase, C.J., concurring in judgment) (distinguishing "MARTIAL LAW PROPER" from "MILITARY GOVERNMENT" in occupied territory). Illustrative of this second kind of commission is the one that was established, with jurisdiction to apply the German Criminal Code, in occupied Germany following the end of World War II. See *Madsen* v *Kinsella*, 343 U.S. 341, 356 (1952).

The third type of commission, convened as an "incident to the conduct of war" when there is a need "to seize and subject to disciplinary measures those enemies who in their attempt to thwart or impede our military effort have violated the law of war," *Quirin*, 317 U.S., at 28–29, has been described as "utterly different" from the other two.

The charge against Hamdan, described in detail in Part I, *supra*, alleges a conspiracy extending over a number of years, from 1996 to November 2001. All but two months of that more than 5-year-long period preceded the attacks of September 11, 2001, and the enactment of the AUMF—the Act of Congress on which the Government relies for exercise of its war powers and thus for its authority to convene military commissions. Neither the purported agreement with Osama bin Laden and others to commit war crimes, nor a single overt act, is alleged to have occurred in a theater of war or on any specified date after September 11, 2001. None of the overt acts that Hamdan is alleged to have committed violates the law of war.

These facts alone cast doubt on the legality of the charge and, hence, the commission; as Winthrop makes plain, the offense alleged must have been committed both in a theater of war and *during*, not before, the relevant conflict. But the deficiencies in the time and place allegations also underscore—indeed are symptomatic of—the most serious defect of this charge: The offense it alleges is not triable by law-of-war military commission. See *Yamashita*, 327 U.S., at 13 ("Neither congressional action nor the military orders constituting the commission authorized it to place petitioner on trial unless the charge proffered against him is of a violation of the law of war").

At a minimum, the Government must make a substantial showing that the crime for which it seeks to try a defendant by military commission is acknowledged to be an offense against the law of war. That burden is far from satisfied here. The crime of "conspiracy" has rarely if ever been tried as such in this country by any law-of-war military commission not exercising some other form of jurisdiction, and does not appear in either the Geneva Conventions or the Hague Conventions—the major treaties on the law of war. Winthrop explains that under the common law governing military commissions, it is not enough to intend to violate the law of war and commit overt acts in furtherance of that intention unless the overt acts either are themselves offenses against the law of war or constitute steps sufficiently substantial to qualify as an attempt.

Finally, international sources confirm that the crime charged here is not a recognized violation of the law of war.

In sum, the sources that the Government and JUSTICE THOMAS rely upon to show that conspiracy to violate the law of war is itself a violation of the law of war in fact demonstrate quite the opposite. Far from making the requisite substantial showing, the Government has failed even to offer a "merely colorable" case for inclusion of conspiracy among those offenses cognizable by law-of-war military commission. Cf. *Quirin*, 317 U.S., at 36. Because the charge does not support the commission's jurisdiction, the commission lacks authority to try Hamdan.

The charge's shortcomings are not merely formal, but are indicative of a broader inability on the Executive's part here to satisfy the most basic precondition—at least in the absence of specific congressional authorization—for establishment of military commissions: military necessity. Hamdan's tribunal was appointed not by a military commander in the field of battle, but by a retired major general stationed away from any active hostilities. Cf. *Rasul v Bush*, 542 U.S., at 487 (KENNEDY, J., concurring in judgment) (observing that "Guantánamo Bay is . . . far removed from any hostilities"). Hamdan is charged not with an overt act for which he was caught redhanded in a theater of war and which military efficiency demands be tried expeditiously, but with an *agreement* the inception of which long predated the attacks of September 11, 2001 and the AUMF. That may well be a crime, but it is not an offense that "by the law of war may be tried by military commissio[n]." 10 U.S.C. §821. None of the overt acts alleged to have been committed in furtherance of the agreement is itself a war crime, or even necessarily occurred during time of, or in a theater of, war.

VI

Whether or not the Government has charged Hamdan with an offense against the law of war cognizable by military commission, the commission lacks power to proceed. The UCMJ conditions the President's use of military commissions on compliance not only with the American common law of war, but also with the rest of the UCMJ itself, insofar as applicable, and with the "rules and precepts of the law of nations," *Quirin*, 317 U.S., at 28—including, *inter alia*, the four Geneva Conventions signed in 1949. See *Yamashita*, 327 U.S., at 20–21, 23–24. The procedures that the Government has decreed will govern Hamdan's trial by commission violate these laws.

A

The commission's procedures are set forth in Commission Order No. 1, which was amended most recently on August 31, 2005—after Hamdan's trial had already begun. Every commission established pursuant to Commission Order No. 1 must have a presiding officer and at least three other members, all of whom must be commissioned officers. §4(A)(1). The presiding officer's job is to rule on questions of law and other evidentiary and interlocutory issues; the other members make findings and, if applicable, sentencing decisions. §4(A)(5). The accused is entitled to appointed military counsel and may hire civilian counsel at his own expense so long as such counsel is a U.S. citizen with security clearance "at the level SECRET or higher." §§4(C)(2)–(3).

The accused also is entitled to a copy of the charge(s) against him, both in English and his own language (if different), to a presumption of innocence, and to certain other rights typically afforded criminal defendants in civilian courts and courts-martial. See §§5(A)–(P). These rights are subject, however, to one glaring condition: The accused and his civilian counsel may be excluded from, and precluded from ever learning what evidence was presented during, any part of the proceeding that either the Appointing Authority or the presiding officer decides to "close." Grounds for such closure "include the protection of information classified or classifiable . . . ; information protected by law or rule from unauthorized disclosure; the physical safety of participants in Commission proceedings, including prospective witnesses; intelligence and law enforcement sources, methods, or activities; and other national security interests." §6(B)(3). Appointed military defense counsel must be privy to these closed sessions, but may, at the presiding officer's discretion, be forbidden to reveal to his or her client what took place therein. Ibid.

Another striking feature of the rules governing Hamdan's commission is that they permit the admission of any evidence that, in the opinion of the presiding officer, "would have probative value to a reasonable person." §6(D)(1). Under this test, not only is testimonial hearsay and evidence obtained through coercion fully admissible, but neither live testimony nor witnesses' written statements need be sworn. See §§6(D)(2)(b), (3). Moreover, the accused and his civilian counsel may be denied access to evidence in the form of "protected information" (which includes classified information as well as "information protected by law or rule from unauthorized disclosure" and "information concerning other national security interests," §§6(B)(3), 6(D)(5)(a)(v)), so long as the presiding officer concludes that the evidence is "probative" under §6(D)(1) and that its admission without the accused's knowledge would not "result in the denial of a full and fair trial." §6(D)(5)(b). Finally, a presiding officer's determination that evidence "would not have probative value to a reasonable person" may be overridden by a majority of the other commission members. §6(D)(1).

B

Hamdan raises both general and particular objections to the procedures set forth in Commission Order No. 1. His general objection is that the procedures' admitted deviation from those governing courts-martial itself renders the commission illegal. Chief among his particular objections are that he may, under the Commission Order, be convicted based on evidence he has not seen or heard, and that any evidence admitted against him need not comply with the admissibility or relevance rules typically applicable in criminal trials and court-martial proceedings.

C

In part because the difference between military commissions and courts-martial originally was a difference of jurisdiction alone, and in part to protect against abuse and ensure evenhandedness under the pressures of war, the procedures governing trials by military commission historically have been the same as those governing courts-martial.

. . . .There is a glaring historical exception to this general rule. The procedures and evidentiary rules used to try General Yamashita near the end of World War II deviated in significant respects from those then governing courts-martial. See 327 U.S. 1 . The force of that precedent, however, has been seriously undermined by post-World War II developments.

At least partially in response to subsequent criticism of General Yamashita's trial, the UCMJ's codification of the Articles of War after World War II expanded the category of persons subject thereto to include defendants in Yamashita's (and Hamdan's) position, and the Third Geneva Convention of 1949 extended prisoner-of-war protections to individuals tried for crimes committed before their capture. See 3 Int'l Comm. of Red Cross, Commentary: Geneva Convention Relative to the Treatment of Prisoners of War 413 (1960) (hereinafter GCIII Commentary) (explaining that Article 85, which extends the Convention's protections to "[p]risoners of war prosecuted under the laws of the Detaining Power for acts committed prior to capture," was adopted in response to judicial interpretations of the 1929 Convention, including this Court's decision in *Yamashita*). The most notorious exception to the principle of uniformity, then, has been stripped of its precedential value.

The uniformity principle is not an inflexible one; it does not preclude all departures from the procedures dictated for use by courts-martial. But any departure must be tailored to the exigency that necessitates it. See Winthrop 835, n. 81. That understanding is reflected in Article 36 of the UCMJ, which provides:

"(a) The procedure, including modes of proof, in cases before courts-martial, courts of inquiry, military commissions, and other military tribunals may be prescribed by the President by regulations which shall, so far as he considers practicable, apply the principles of law and the rules of evidence generally recognized in the trial of criminal cases in the U.S. district courts, but which may not be contrary to or inconsistent with this chapter.

"(b) All rules and regulations made under this article shall be uniform insofar as practicable and shall be reported to Congress." 70A Stat. 50.

Article 36 places two restrictions on the President's power to promulgate rules of procedure for courts-martial and military commissions alike. First, no procedural rule he adopts may be "contrary to or inconsistent with" the UCMJ—however practical it may seem. Second, the rules adopted must be "uniform insofar as practicable." That is, the rules applied to military commissions must be the same as those applied to courts-martial unless such uniformity proves impracticable.

Hamdan argues that Commission Order No. 1 violates both of these restrictions; he maintains that the procedures described in the Commission Order are inconsistent with the UCMJ and that the Government has offered no explanation for their deviation from the procedures governing courts-martial, which are set forth in the Manual for Courts-Martial, U.S. (2005 ed.) (Manual for Courts-Martial) . . . . .

The Government has three responses. First, it argues, only 9 of the UCMJ's 158 Articles—the ones that expressly mention "military commissions"—actually apply to commissions, and Commission Order No. 1 sets forth no procedure that is "contrary to or inconsistent with" those 9 provisions. Second, the Government contends, military commissions would be of no use if the President were hamstrung by those provisions of the UCMJ that govern courts-martial. Finally, the President's determination that "the danger to the safety of the U.S. and the nature of international terrorism" renders it impracticable "to apply in military commissions . . . the principles of law and rules of evidence generally recognized in the trial of criminal cases in the U.S. district courts," November 13 Order §1(f), is, in the Government's view, explanation enough for any deviation from court-martial procedures. See Brief for Respondents 43–47, and n. 22.

Hamdan has the better of this argument. Without reaching the question whether any provision of Commission Order No. 1 is strictly "contrary to or inconsistent with" other provisions of the UCMJ, we conclude that the "practicability" determination the President has made is insufficient to justify variances from the procedures governing courts-martial. Subsection (b) of Article 36 was added after World War II, and requires a different showing of impracticability from the one required by subsection (a). Subsection (a) requires that the rules the President promulgates for courts-martial, provost courts, and military commissions alike conform to those that govern procedures in *Article III courts*, "so far as *he considers* practicable." 10 U.S.C. §836(a) (emphasis added). Subsection (b), by contrast, demands that the rules applied in courts-martial, provost courts, and military commissions—whether or not they conform with the Federal Rules of Evidence—be "uniform *insofar as practicable*." §836(b) (emphasis added). Under the latter provision, then, the rules set forth in the Manual for Courts-Martial must apply to military commissions unless impracticable.

The President here has determined, pursuant to subsection (a), that it is impracticable to apply the rules and principles of law that govern "the trial of criminal cases in the U.S. district courts," §836(a), to Hamdan's commission. We assume that complete deference is owed that determination. The President has not, however, made a similar official determination that it is impracticable to apply the rules for courts-martial. And even if subsection (b)'s requirements may be satisfied without such an official determination, the requirements of that subsection are not satisfied here.

Nothing in the record before us demonstrates that it would be impracticable to apply court-martial rules in this case. Under the circumstances, then, the rules applicable in courts-martial must apply. Since it is undisputed that Commission Order No. 1 deviates in many significant respects from those rules, it necessarily violates Article 36(b).

D

The procedures adopted to try Hamdan also violate the Geneva Conventions. The Court of Appeals dismissed Hamdan's Geneva Convention challenge on three independent grounds: (1) the Geneva Conventions are not judicially enforceable; (2) Hamdan in any event is not entitled to their protections; and (3) even if he is entitled to their protections, *Councilman* abstention is appropriate. Judge Williams, concurring, rejected the second ground but agreed with the majority respecting the first and the last. As we explained in Part III, *supra*, the abstention rule applied in *Councilman*, 420 U.S. 738 , is not applicable here. And for the reasons that follow, we hold that neither of the other grounds the Court of Appeals gave for its decision is persuasive.

I

. . . .

ii

The conflict with al Qaeda is not, according to the Government, a conflict to which the full protections afforded detainees under the 1949 Geneva Conventions apply because Article 2 of those Conventions (which appears in all four Conventions) renders the full protections applicable only to "all cases of declared war or of any other armed conflict which may arise between two or more of the High Contracting Parties." 6 U. S. T., at 3318. Since Hamdan was captured and detained incident to the conflict with al Qaeda and not the conflict with the Taliban, and since al Qaeda, unlike Afghanistan, is not a "High Contracting Party"—*i.e.*, a signatory of the Conventions, the protections of those Conventions are not, it is argued, applicable to Hamdan.

We need not decide the merits of this argument because there is at least one provision of the Geneva Conventions that applies here even if the relevant conflict is not one between signatories. Article 3, often referred to as Common Article 3 because, like Article 2, it appears in all four Geneva Conventions, provides that in a "conflict not of an international character occurring in the territory of one of the High Contracting Parties, each Party to the conflict shall be bound to apply, as a minimum," certain provisions protecting "[p]ersons taking no active part in the hostilities, including members of armed forces who have laid down their arms and those placed *hors de combat* by . . . detention." *Id.*, at 3318. One such provision prohibits "the passing of sentences and the carrying out of executions without previous judgment pronounced by a regularly constituted court affording all the judicial guarantees which are recognized as indispensable by civilized peoples." *Ibid.*

The Court of Appeals thought, and the Government asserts, that Common Article 3 does not apply to Hamdan because the conflict with al Qaeda, being "'international in scope,'" does not qualify as a "'conflict not of an international character.'" 415 F. 3d, at 41. That reasoning is erroneous. The term "conflict not of an international character" is used here in contradistinction to a conflict between nations. So much is demonstrated by the "fundamental logic [of] the Convention's provisions on its application." *Id.*, at 44 (Williams, J., concurring). Common Article 2 provides that "the present Convention shall apply to all cases of declared war or of any other armed conflict which may arise between two or more of the High Contracting

Parties." 6 U. S. T., at 3318 (Art. 2, ¶1). High Contracting Parties (signatories) also must abide by all terms of the Conventions vis-À-vis one another even if one party to the conflict is a nonsignatory "Power," and must so abide vis-À-vis the nonsignatory if "the latter accepts and applies" those terms. *Ibid.* (Art. 2, ¶3). Common Article 3, by contrast, affords some minimal protection, falling short of full protection under the Conventions, to individuals associated with neither a signatory nor even a nonsignatory "Power" who are involved in a conflict "in the territory of" a signatory. The latter kind of conflict is distinguishable from the conflict described in Common Article 2 chiefly because it does not involve a clash between nations (whether signatories or not). In context, then, the phrase "not of an international character" bears its literal meaning.

. . .

Although the official commentaries accompanying Common Article 3 indicate that an important purpose of the provision was to furnish minimal protection to rebels involved in one kind of "conflict not of an international character," *i.e.*, a civil war, see GCIII Commentary 36–37, the commentaries also make clear "that the scope of the Article must be as wide as possible," *id.*, at 36. In fact, limiting language that would have rendered Common Article 3 applicable "especially [to] cases of civil war, colonial conflicts, or wars of religion," was omitted from the final version of the Article, which coupled broader scope of application with a narrower range of rights than did earlier proposed iterations. See GCIII Commentary 42–43.

iii

Common article 3, then, is applicable here and, as indicated above, requires that Hamdan be tried by a "regularly constituted court affording all the judicial guarantees which are recognized as indispensable by civilized peoples." 6 U.S.T., at 3320 (art. 3, ¶1(d)). While the term "regularly constituted court" is not specifically defined in either common article 3 or its accompanying commentary, other sources disclose its core meaning. The commentary accompanying a provision of the Fourth Geneva Convention, for example, defines " 'regularly constituted' " tribunals to include "ordinary military courts" and "definitely exclud[e] all special tribunals." GCIV commentary 340 (defining the term "properly constituted" in article 66, which the commentary treats as identical to "regularly constituted"); 64 see also Yamashita, 327 u.s., at 44 (Rutledge, j., dissenting) (describing military commission as a court "specially constituted for a particular trial"). and one of the Red Cross' own treatises defines "regularly constituted court" as used in common article 3 to mean "established and organized in accordance with the laws and procedures already in force in a country." Int'l Comm. of Red Cross, 1 Customary International Humanitarian Law 355 (2005); see also GCIV commentary 340 (observing that "ordinary military courts" will "be set up in accordance with the recognized principles governing the administration of justice").

The Government offers only a cursory defense of Hamdan's military commission in light of Common Article 3. See Brief for Respondents 49–50. As JUSTICE KENNEDY explains, that defense fails because "[t]he regular military courts in our system are the courts-martial established by congressional statutes." *Post*, at 8 (opinion concurring in part). At a minimum, a military commission "can be 'regularly constituted' by the standards of our military justice system only if some practical need explains deviations from court-martial practice." *Post*, at 10. As we have explained, see Part VI–C, *supra*, no such need has been demonstrated here.

iv

Inextricably intertwined with the question of regular constitution is the evaluation of the procedures governing the tribunal and whether they afford "all the judicial guarantees which are recognized as indispensable by civilized peoples." 6 U. S. T., at 3320 (Art. 3, ¶1(d)). Like the phrase "regularly constituted court," this phrase is not defined in the text of the Geneva Conventions. But it must be understood to incorporate at least the barest of those trial protections that have been recognized by customary international law. Many of these are described in Article 75 of Protocol I to the Geneva Conventions of 1949, adopted in 1977 (Protocol I). Although the U.S. declined to ratify Protocol I, its objections were not to Article 75 thereof. Indeed, it appears that the Government "regard[s] the provisions of Article 75 as an articulation of safeguards to which all persons in the hands of an enemy are entitled." Taft, The Law of Armed Conflict After 9/11: Some Salient Features, 28 Yale J. Int'l L. 319, 322 (2003). Among the rights set forth in Article 75 is the "right to be tried in [one's] presence." Protocol I, Art. 75(4)(e).

We agree with JUSTICE KENNEDY that the procedures adopted to try Hamdan deviate from those governing courts-martial in ways not justified by any "evident practical need," *post*, at 11, and for that reason, at least, fail to afford the requisite guarantees. See *post*, at 8, 11–17. We add only that, as noted in Part VI–A, *supra*, various provisions of Commission Order No. 1 dispense with the principles, articulated in Article 75 and indisputably part of the customary international law, that an accused must, absent disruptive conduct or consent, be present for his trial and must be privy to the evidence against him. See §§6(B)(3), (D). That the Government has a compelling interest in denying Hamdan access to certain sensitive information is not doubted. Cf. *post*, at 47–48 (THOMAS, J., dissenting). But, at least absent express statutory provision to the contrary, information used to convict a person of a crime must be disclosed to him.

v

Common Article 3 obviously tolerates a great degree of flexibility in trying individuals captured during armed conflict; its requirements are general ones, crafted to accommodate a wide variety of legal systems. But *requirements* they are nonetheless. The commission that the President has convened to try Hamdan does not meet those requirements.

VII

We have assumed, as we must, that the allegations made in the Government's charge against Hamdan are true. We have assumed, moreover, the truth of the message implicit in that charge—viz., that Hamdan is a dangerous individual whose beliefs, if acted upon, would cause great harm and even death to innocent civilians, and who would act upon those beliefs if given the opportunity. It bears emphasizing that Hamdan does not challenge, and we do not today address, the Government's power to detain him for the duration of active hostilities in order to prevent such harm. But in undertaking to try Hamdan and subject him to criminal punishment, the Executive is bound to comply with the Rule of Law that prevails in this jurisdiction.

The judgment of the Court of Appeals is reversed, and the case is remanded for further proceedings.

It is so ordered.

[Footnotes omitted]

11. *Boumediene v Bush*, Supreme Court of the U.S. (Excerpted)
    Cite as: 553 U. S. 723; 128 S. Ct. 2229 (2008)

BOUMEDIENE, ET AL., v GEORGE W. BUSH, PRESIDENT OF THE U.S., ET AL.
June 12, 2008

JUSTICE KENNEDY delivered the opinion of the Court.

Petitioners are aliens designated as enemy combatants and detained at the U.S. Naval Station at Guantánamo Bay, Cuba. . . . .

Petitioners present a question not resolved by our earlier cases relating to the detention of aliens at Guantánamo: whether they have the constitutional privilege of habeas corpus, a privilege not to be withdrawn except in conformance with the Suspension Clause, Art. I, §9, cl. 2. We hold these petitioners do have the habeas corpus privilege. Congress has enacted a statute, the Detainee Treatment Act of 2005 (DTA), 119 Stat. 2739, that provides certain procedures for review of the detainees' status. We hold that those procedures are not an adequate and effective substitute for habeas corpus. Therefore §7 of the Military Commissions Act of 2006 (MCA), 28 U. S. C. A. §2241(e) (Supp. 2007), operates as an unconstitutional suspension of the writ. We do not address whether the President has authority to detain these petitioners nor do we hold that the writ must issue. These and other questions regarding the legality of the detention are to be resolved in the first instance by the District Court.

I

Under the Authorization for Use of Military Force (AUMF) . . . the President is authorized "to use all necessary and appropriate force against those nations, organizations, or persons he determines planned, authorized, committed, or aided the terrorist attacks that occurred on September 11, 2001, or harbored such organizations or persons, in order to prevent any future acts of international terrorism against the U.S. by such nations, organizations or persons."

. . .

[T]he Department of Defense ordered the detention of these petitioners, and they were transferred to Guantánamo. Some of these individuals were apprehended on the battlefield in Afghanistan . . . . All are foreign nationals, but none is a citizen of a nation now at war with the U.S. Each denies he is a member of the al Qaeda terrorist network that carried out the September 11 attacks or of the Taliban regime that provided sanctuary for al Qaeda. Each petitioner appeared before a separate CSRT; was determined to be an enemy combatant; and has sought a writ of habeas corpus in the U.S. District Court for the District of Columbia.

The first actions commenced in February 2002. The District Court ordered the cases dismissed for lack of jurisdiction because the naval station is outside the sovereign territory of the U.S. See Rasul v Bush, 215 F. Supp. 2d 55 (2002). The Court of Appeals for the District of Columbia Circuit affirmed. See Al Odah v U.S., 321 F. 3d 1134, 1145 (2003). We granted certiorari and reversed, holding that 28 U. S. C. §2241 extended statutory habeas corpus jurisdiction to Guantánamo. See Rasul v Bush, 542 U. S. 466, 473 (2004). The constitutional issue presented in the instant cases was not reached in Rasul. Id., at 476.

After Rasul, petitioners' cases were consolidated and entertained in two separate proceedings.

. . .

While appeals were pending from the District Court decisions, Congress passed the DTA . . . . to provide that "no court, justice, or judge shall have jurisdiction to hear or consider . . . an application for a writ of habeas corpus filed by or on behalf of an alien detained by the Department of Defense at Guantánamo Bay, Cuba." 119 Stat. 2742. . . . . In Hamdan v Rumsfeld, 548 U. S. 557, 576–577 (2006), the Court held this provision did not apply to cases (like petitioners') pending when the DTA was enacted. Congress responded by passing the MCA, 10 U. S. C. A. §948a et seq. (Supp. 2007), which again amended §2241.

. . .

The Court of Appeals' ruling, 476 F. 3d 981 (CADC 2007), is the subject of our present review and today's decision. The Court of Appeals concluded that MCA §7 must be read to strip from it, and all federal courts, jurisdiction to consider petitioners' habeas corpus applications, id., at 987; that petitioners are not entitled to the privilege of the writ or the protections of the Suspension Clause, id., at 990–991; and, as a result, that it was unnecessary to consider whether Congress provided an adequate and effective substitute for habeas corpus in the DTA. We granted certiorari.

II

As a threshold matter, we must decide whether MCA §7 denies the federal courts jurisdiction to hear habeas corpus actions pending at the time of its enactment. We hold the statute does deny that jurisdiction, so that, if the statute is valid, petitioners' cases must be dismissed.

. . .

Petitioners argue, nevertheless, that MCA §7(b) is not a sufficiently clear statement of congressional intent to strip the federal courts of jurisdiction in pending cases. See Ex parte Yerger, 8 Wall. 85, 102–103 (1869). We disagree.

. . .

The Court of Appeals . . . we agree with its conclusion that the MCA deprives the federal courts of jurisdiction to entertain the habeas corpus actions now before us.

III

In deciding the constitutional questions now presented we must determine whether petitioners are barred from seeking the writ or invoking the protections of the Suspension Clause either because of their status, i.e., petitioners' designation by the Executive Branch as enemy combatants, or their physical location, i.e., their presence at Guantánamo Bay. . . . Petitioners contend they do have cognizable constitutional rights and that Congress, in seeking to eliminate recourse to habeas corpus as a means to assert those rights, acted in violation of the Suspension Clause.

We begin with a brief account of the history and origins of the writ. . . . . [T]o the extent there were settled precedents or legal commentaries in 1789 regarding the extra-territorial scope of the writ or its application to enemy aliens, those authorities can be instructive for the present cases.

A

. . . Magna Carta decreed that no man would be imprisoned contrary to the law of the land. Art. 39, in Sources of Our Liberties 17 (R. Perry & J. Cooper eds. 1959) . . . . Holdsworth tells us, however, that gradually the writ of habeas corpus became the means by which the promise of Magna Carta was fulfilled. 9 W. Holdsworth, A History of English Law 112 (1926) (hereinafter Holdsworth).

The development was painstaking . . . . Yet at the outset it was used to protect not the rights of citizens but those of the King and his courts. The early courts were considered agents of the Crown, designed to assist the King in the exercise of his power. . . . Thus the writ . . . was in its earliest use a mechanism for securing compliance with the King's laws.

. . .

Even so, from an early date it was understood that the King, too, was subject to the law. As the writers said of Magna Carta, "it means this, that the king is and shall be below the law." 1 F. Pollock & F. Maitland, History of English Law 173 (2d ed. 1909); see also 2 Bracton On the Laws and Customs of England 33 (S. Thorne transl. 1968). . . . And, by the 1600's, the writ was deemed less an instrument of the King's power and more a restraint upon it.

. . .

Still, the writ proved to be an imperfect check.

. . .

A notable example from this period was Darnel's Case, 3 How. St. Tr. 1 (K. B. 1627). . . . Charles I demanded that Darnel and at least four others lend him money. Upon their refusal, they were imprisoned. The prisoners sought a writ of habeas corpus; and the King filed a return in the form of a warrant signed by the Attorney General. Ibid. The court held this was a sufficient answer and justified the subjects' continued imprisonment. Id., at 59. There was an immediate outcry of protest. The House of Commons promptly passed the Petition of Right, 3 Car. 1, ch. 1 (1627), 5 Statutes of the Realm 23, 24 (reprint 1963), which condemned executive "imprison[ment] without any cause" shown, and declared that "no freeman in any such manner as is before mencioned [shall] be imprisoned or detained."

. . .

[N]ot until 1679 did Parliament try once more to secure the writ, this time through the Habeas Corpus Act of 1679, 31 Car. 2, ch. 2, id., at 935. The Act, which later would be described by Blackstone as the "stable bulwark of our liberties," 1 W. Blackstone, Commentaries *137 (hereinafter Blackstone), established procedures for issuing the writ; and it was the model upon which the habeas statutes of the 13 American Colonies were based, see Collings, supra, at 338–339.

This history was known to the Framers. It no doubt confirmed their view that pendular swings to and away from individual liberty were endemic to undivided, uncontrolled power. The Framers' inherent distrust of govern- mental power was the driving force behind the constitutional plan that allocated powers among three independent branches. This design serves not only to make Government accountable but also to secure individual liberty. See Loving v U.S., 517 U. S. 748, 756 (1996) . . . Because the Constitution's separation-of-powers structure, like the substantive guarantees of the Fifth and Fourteenth Amendments, see Yick Wo v Hopkins, 118 U. S. 356, 374 (1886), protects persons as well as citizens, foreign nationals who have the privilege of litigating in our courts can seek to enforce separation-of-powers principles, see, e.g., INS v Chadha, 462 U. S. 919, 958–959 (1983).

. . .

Alexander Hamilton likewise explained that by providing the detainee a judicial forum to challenge detention, the writ preserves limited government. As he explained in The Federalist No. 84:

> "[T]he practice of arbitrary imprisonments, have been, in all ages, the favorite and most formidable instruments of tyranny. . . . . And as a remedy for this fatal evil he is everywhere peculiarly emphatical in his encomiums on the habeas corpus act, which in one place he calls 'the BULWARK of the British Constitution.'" C. Rossiter ed., p. 512 (1961) (quoting 1 Blackstone *136, 4 id., at *438).

Post-1789 habeas developments in England, though not bearing upon the Framers' intent, do verify their foresight. Those later events would underscore the need for structural barriers against arbitrary suspensions of the writ. . . . . Parliament suspended the writ for much of the period from 1792 to 1801, resulting in rampant arbitrary imprisonment. See Hall & Albion 550. Even as late as World War I, at least one prominent English jurist complained that the Defence of the Realm Act, 1914, 4 & 5 Geo. 5, ch. 29(1)(a), effectively had suspended the privilege of habeas corpus for any person suspected of "communicating with the enemy." See King v Halliday, [1917] A. C. 260, 299; see generally A. Simpson, In the Highest Degree Odious: Detention Without Trial in War- time Britain 6–7, 24–25 (1992).

. . . The separation-of-powers doctrine, and the history that influenced its design, therefore must inform the reach and purpose of the Suspension Clause.

B

The broad historical narrative of the writ and its function is central to our analysis, but we seek guidance as well from founding-era authorities addressing the specific question before us: whether foreign nationals, apprehended and detained in distant countries during a time of serious threats to our Nation's security, may assert the privilege of the writ and seek its protection. The Court has been careful not to foreclose the possibility that the protections of the Suspension Clause have expanded along with post-1789 developments that define the present scope of the writ. See INS v St. Cyr, 533 U. S. 289, 300–301 (2001). But the analysis may begin with precedents as of 1789, for the Court has said that "at the absolute minimum" the Clause protects the writ as it existed when the Constitution was drafted and ratified. Id., at 301.

To support their arguments, the parties in these cases have examined historical sources to construct a view of the common-law writ as it existed in 1789—as have amici whose expertise in legal history the Court has relied upon in the past. . . . . The Government argues the common-law writ ran only to those territories over which the Crown was sovereign. Petitioners argue that jurisdiction followed the King's officers . . . . Diligent search by all parties reveals no certain conclusions. In none of the cases cited do we find that a common-law court would or would not have granted, or refused to hear for lack of jurisdiction, a petition for a writ of habeas corpus brought by a prisoner deemed an enemy combatant, under a standard like the one the Department of Defense has used in these cases, and when held in a territory, like Guantánamo, over which the Government has total military and civil control. . . .

The Government argues, in turn, that Guantánamo is more closely analogous to Scotland and Hanover, territories that were not part of England but nonetheless con- trolled by the English monarch (in his separate capacities as King of Scotland and Elector of Hanover). See Cowle, 2 Burr., at 856, 97 Eng. Rep., at 600. Lord Mansfield can be cited for the proposition that, at the time of the founding, English courts lacked the "power" to issue the writ to Scotland and Hanover, territories Lord Mansfield referred to as "foreign." Ibid. But what matters for our purposes is why common-law courts lacked this power. Given the English Crown's delicate and complicated relationships with Scotland and Hanover in the 1700's, we cannot disregard the possibility that the common-law courts' refusal to issue the writ to these places was motivated not by formal legal constructs but by what we would think of as prudential concerns. . . .

By the mid-19th century, British courts could issue the writ to Canada, notwithstanding the fact that Canadian courts also had the power to do so. See 9 Holdsworth 124 (citing Ex parte Anderson, 3 El. and El. 487 (1861)). This might be seen as evidence that the existence of a separate court system was no barrier to the running of the common- law writ. . . .

. . .

Each side in the present matter argues that the very lack of a precedent on point supports its position.

. . .

Recent scholarship points to the inherent shortcomings in the historical record. . . . . We decline, therefore, to infer too much, one way or the other, from the lack of historical evidence on point.

. . .

IV

Drawing from its position that at common law the writ ran only to territories over which the Crown was sovereign, the Government says the Suspension Clause affords petitioners no rights because the U.S. does not claim sovereignty over the place of detention.

Guantánamo Bay is not formally part of the U.S. See DTA §1005(g), 119 Stat. 2743. And under the terms of the lease between the U.S. and Cuba, Cuba retains "ultimate sovereignty" over the territory while the U.S. exercises "complete jurisdiction and control."

. . .

The U.S. contends, nevertheless, that Guantánamo is not within its sovereign control. This was the Government's position well before the events of September 11, 2001. . . . We . . . do not question the Government's position that Cuba, not the U.S., maintains sovereignty, in the legal and technical sense of the term, over Guantánamo Bay. But this does not end the analysis. . . . See, e.g., Fleming v Page, 9 How. 603, 614 (1850) (noting that the port of Tampico, conquered by the U.S. during the war with Mexico, was "undoubtedly . . . subject to the sovereignty and dominion of the U.S.," but that it "does not follow that it was a part of the U.S., or that it ceased to be a foreign country"); King v Earl of Crewe ex parte Sekgome, [1910] 2 K. B. 576, 603– 604 (C. A.) (opinion of Williams, L. J.) (arguing that the Bechuanaland Protectorate in South Africa was "under His Majesty's dominion in the sense of power and jurisdiction, but is not under his dominion in the sense of territorial domin- ion"). . . . . [T]he U.S., by virtue of its complete jurisdiction and control over the base, maintains de facto sovereignty over this territory. See 542 U. S., at 480; id., at 487 (KENNEDY, J., concurring in judgment).

A

. . . .

In a series of opinions later known as the Insular Cases, the Court addressed whether the Constitution, by its own force, applies in any territory that is not a State. See De Lima v Bidwell, 182 U. S. 1 (1901); Dooley v U.S., 182 U. S. 222 (1901); Armstrong v U.S., 182 U. S. 243 (1901); Downes v Bidwell, 182 U. S. 244 (1901); Hawaii v Mankichi, 190 U. S. 197 (1903); Dorr v U.S., 195 U. S. 138 (1904). The Court held that the Constitution has independent force in these territories, a force not contingent upon acts of legislative grace. Yet it took note of the difficulties inherent in that position.

. . .

These [Co]nsiderations resulted in the doctrine of territorial incorporation, under which the Constitution applies in full in incorporated Territories surely destined for statehood but only in part in unincorporated Territories. See Dorr, supra, at 143. . . . [A]s early as Balzac in 1922, the Court took for granted that even in unincorporated Territories the Government of the U.S. was bound to provide to noncitizen inhabitants "guaranties of certain fundamental personal rights declared in the Constitution." 258 U. S., at 312 . . .

. . .

B

The Government's formal sovereignty-based test raises troubling separation-of-powers concerns as well. The political history of Guantánamo illustrates the deficiencies of this approach. The U.S. has maintained complete and uninterrupted control of the bay for over 100 years. At the close of the Spanish-American War, Spain ceded control over the entire island of Cuba to the U.S. and specifically "relinquishe[d] all claim [s] of sovereignty . . . and title." See Treaty of Paris, Dec. 10, 1898, U. S.-Spain, Art. I, 30 Stat. 1755, T. S. No. 343. From the date the treaty with Spain was signed until the Cuban Republic was established on May 20, 1902, the U.S. governed the territory "in trust" for the benefit of the Cuban people. Neely v Henkel, 180 U. S. 109, 120 (1901); H. Thomas, Cuba or The Pursuit of Freedom 436, 460 (1998). And although it recognized, by entering into the 1903 Lease Agreement, that Cuba retained "ultimate sovereignty" over Guantánamo, the U.S. continued to maintain the same plenary control it had enjoyed since 1898. Yet the Government's view is that the Constitution had no effect there, at least as to noncitizens, be- cause the U.S. disclaimed sovereignty in the formal sense of the term. The necessary implication of the argument is that by surrendering formal sovereignty over any unincorporated territory to a third party, while at the same time entering into a lease that grants total control over the territory back to the U.S., it would be possible for the political branches to govern without legal constraint.

Our basic charter cannot be contracted away like this. The Constitution grants Congress and the President the power to acquire, dispose of, and govern territory, not the power to decide when and where its terms apply. Even when the U.S. acts outside its borders, its powers are not "absolute and unlimited" but are subject "to such restrictions as are expressed in the Constitution." Murphy v Ramsey, 114 U. S. 15, 44 (1885).

. . .

C

As we recognized in Rasul, 542 U. S., at 476; id., at 487 (KENNEDY, J., concurring in judgment), the outlines of a framework for determining the reach of the Suspension Clause are suggested by the factors the Court relied upon in Eisentrager.

. . .

Based on . . . language from Eisentrager, and the reasoning in our other extraterritoriality opinions, we conclude that at least three factors are relevant in determining the reach of the Suspension Clause: (1) the citizenship and status of the detainee and the adequacy of the process through which that status determination was made; (2) the nature of the sites where apprehension and then detention took place; and (3) the practical obstacles inher- ent in resolving the prisoner's entitlement to the writ.

. . . The Eisentrager petitioners were charged by a bill of particulars that made detailed factual allegations against them. See 14 United Nations War Crimes Commission, Law Reports of Trials of War Criminals 8–10 (1949) (reprint 1997). To rebut the accu- sations, they were entitled to representation by counsel, allowed to introduce evidence on their own behalf, and permitted to cross-examine the prosecution's witnesses. See Memorandum by Command of Lt. Gen. Wedemeyer, Jan. 21, 1946 (establishing "Regulations Governing the

Trial of War Criminals" in the China Theater), in Tr. of Record in Johnson v Eisentrager, O. T. 1949, No. 306, pp. 34–40.

In comparison the procedural protections afforded to the detainees in the CSRT hearings are far more limited, and, we conclude, fall well short of the procedures and adversarial mechanisms that would eliminate the need for habeas corpus review.

. . .

As to the second factor relevant to this analysis, the detainees here are similarly situated to the Eisentrager petitioners in that the sites of their apprehension and detention are technically outside the sovereign territory of the U.S. As noted earlier, this is a factor that weighs against finding they have rights under the Suspension Clause. But there are critical differences between Landsberg Prison, circa 1950, and the U.S. Naval Station at Guantánamo Bay in 2008. Unlike its present control over the naval station, the U.S.' control over the prison in Germany was neither absolute nor indefinite. Like all parts of occupied Germany, the prison was under the jurisdiction of the combined Allied Forces. See Declaration Regarding the Defeat of Germany and the Assumption of Supreme Authority with Respect to Germany, June 5, 1945, U. S.-U. S. S. R.-U. K.-Fr.,60 Stat. 1649, T. I. A. S. No. 1520. The U.S. was therefore answerable to its Allies for all activities occurring there. Cf. Hirota v MacArthur, 338 U. S. 197, 198 (1948) (per curiam) (military tribunal set up by Gen. Douglas MacArthur, acting as "the agent of the Allied Powers," was not a "tribunal of the U.S."). The Allies had not planned a long-term occupation of Germany, nor did they intend to displace all German institutions even during the period of occupation. See Agreements Respecting Basic Principles for Merger of the Three Western German Zones of Occupation, and Other Matters, Apr. 8, 1949, U. S.-U. K.-Fr., Art. 1, 63 Stat. 2819, T. I. A. S. No. 2066 . . . .

The Court's holding in Eisentrager was thus consistent with the Insular Cases, where it had held there was no need to extend full constitutional protections to territories the U.S. did not intend to govern indefinitely. Guantánamo Bay, on the other hand, is no transient possession. In every practical sense Guantánamo is not abroad; it is within the constant jurisdiction of the U.S. See Rasul, 542 U. S., at 480; id., at 487 (KENNEDY, J., concurring in judgment).

. . .

The detainees, moreover, are held in a territory that, while technically not part of the U.S., is under the complete and total control of our Government. Under these circumstances the lack of a precedent on point is no barrier to our holding.

We hold that Art. I, §9, cl. 2, of the Constitution has full effect at Guantánamo Bay. . . . The MCA does not purport to be a formal suspension of the writ; and the Government, in its submissions to us, has not argued that it is. Petitioners, therefore, are entitled to the privilege of habeas corpus to challenge the legality of their detention.

V

In light of this holding the question becomes whether the statute stripping jurisdiction to issue the writ avoids the Suspension Clause mandate because Congress has provided adequate substitute procedures for habeas corpus.

. . .

Our case law does not contain extensive discussion of standards defining suspension of the writ or of circumstances under which suspension has occurred. This simply confirms the care Congress has taken throughout our Nation's history to preserve the writ and its function. Indeed, most of the major legislative enactments pertaining to habeas corpus have acted not to contract the writ's protection but to expand it or to hasten resolution of prisoners' claims.

. . . When Congress has intended to replace traditional habeas corpus with habeas-like substitutes . . . it has granted to the courts broad remedial powers to secure the historic office of the writ.

. . .

Indeed, common-law habeas corpus was, above all, an adaptable remedy. Its precise application and scope changed depending upon the circumstances. See 3 Blackstone *131 (describing habeas as "the great and efficacious writ, in all manner of illegal confinement") . . . .

. . .

Habeas corpus is a collateral process that exists, in Justice Holmes' words, to "cu[t] through all forms and g[o] to the very tissue of the structure. It comes in from the outside, not in subordination to the proceedings, and although every form may have been preserved opens the inquiry whether they have been more than an empty shell." Frank v Mangum, 237 U. S. 309, 346 (1915) (dissenting opinion). Even when the procedures authorizing detention are structurally sound, the Suspension Clause remains applicable and the writ relevant. See 2 Chambers, Course of Lectures on English Law 1767–1773, at 6 ("Liberty may be violated either by arbitrary imprisonment without law or the appearance of law, or by a lawful magistrate for an unlawful reason").

. . .

Practical considerations and exigent circumstances inform the definition and reach of the law's writs, including habeas corpus. The cases and our tradition reflect this precept.

In cases involving foreign citizens detained abroad by the Executive, it likely would be both an impractical and unprecedented extension of judicial power to assume that habeas corpus would be available at the moment the prisoner is taken into custody.

. . .

Our decision today holds only that the petitioners before us are entitled to seek the writ; that the DTA review procedures are an inadequate substitute for habeas corpus; and that the petitioners in these cases need not exhaust the review procedures in the Court of Appeals before proceeding with their habeas actions in the District Court. The only law we identify as unconstitutional is MCA §7, 28 U. S. C. A. §2241(e) (Supp. 2007). Accordingly, both the DTA and the CSRT process remain intact. Our holding with regard to exhaustion should not be read to imply that a habeas court should intervene the moment an enemy combatant steps foot in a territory where the writ runs. The Executive is entitled to a reasonable period of time to determine a detainee's status before a court entertains that detainee's habeas corpus petition.

. . .

Officials charged with daily operational responsibility for our security may consider a judicial discourse on the history of the Habeas Corpus Act of 1679 and like matters to be far removed from the Nation's present, urgent concerns. Established legal doctrine, however, must be consulted for its teaching. Remote in time it may be; irrelevant to the present it is not. . . . Chief among these are freedom from arbitrary and unlawful restraint and the personal liberty that is secured by adherence to the separation of powers. It is from these principles that the judicial authority to consider petitions for habeas corpus relief derives.

. . .

It bears repeating that our opinion does not address the content of the law that governs petitioners' detention. That is a matter yet to be determined. We hold that petitioners may invoke the fundamental procedural protections of habeas corpus. . . .

The determination by the Court of Appeals that the Suspension Clause and its protections are inapplicable to petitioners was in error. The judgment of the Court of Appeals is reversed. The cases are remanded to the Court of Appeals with instructions that it remand the cases to the District Court for proceedings consistent with this opinion.

It is so ordered.

12. *Sosa v Alvarez-Machain* , Supreme Court of the U.S. (Excerpted)
    Cites as 542 U.S. 692; 124 S. Ct 2739 (2004)

SOSA V ALVAREZ-MACHAIN
June 29, 2004
ON WRIT OF CERTIORARI TO THE U.S. COURT
OF APPEALS FOR THE NINTH CIRCUIT

. . . We have considered the underlying facts before, U.S. v Alvarez-Machain, 504 U.S. 655, 112 S.Ct. 2188, 119 L.Ed.2d 441 (1992). In 1985, an agent of the Drug Enforcement Administration (DEA), Enrique Camarena-Salazar, was captured on assignment in Mexico and taken to a house in Guadalajara, where he was tortured over the course of a 2-day interrogation, then murdered. Based in part on eyewitness testimony, DEA officials in the U.S. came to believe that respondent Humberto Alvarez-Machain (Alvarez), a Mexican physician, was present at the house and acted to prolong the agent's life in order to extend the interrogation and torture. Id., at 657, 112 S.Ct. 2188.

In 1990, a federal grand jury indicted Alvarez for the torture and murder of Camarena-Salazar, and the U.S. District Court for the Central District of California issued a warrant for his arrest. 331 F.3d

604, 609 (C.A.9 2003) (en banc). The DEA asked the Mexican Government for help in getting Alvarez into the U.S., but when the requests and negotiations proved fruitless, the DEA approved a plan to hire Mexican nationals to seize Alvarez and bring him to the U.S. for trial. As so planned, a group of Mexicans, including petitioner Jose Francisco Sosa, abducted Alvarez from his house, held him overnight in a motel, and brought him by private plane to El Paso, Texas, where he was arrested by federal officers. Ibid.

Once in American custody, Alvarez moved to dismiss the indictment on the ground that his seizure was "outrageous governmental conduct," Alvarez-Machain, 504 U.S., at 658, 112 S.Ct. 2188, and violated the extradition treaty between the U.S. and Mexico. The District Court agreed, the Ninth Circuit affirmed, and we reversed, id., at 670, 112 S.Ct. 2188, holding that the fact of Alvarez's forcible seizure did not affect the jurisdiction of a federal court. The case was tried in 1992, and ended at the close of the Government's case, when the District Court granted Alvarez's motion for a judgment of acquittal.

In 1993, after returning to Mexico, Alvarez began the civil action before us here. He sued Sosa, Mexican citizen and DEA operative Antonio Garate-Bustamante, five unnamed Mexican civilians, the U.S., and four DEA agents. 331 F.3d, at 610. So far as it matters here, Alvarez sought damages from the U.S. under the FTCA, alleging false arrest, and from Sosa under the ATS, for a violation of the law of nations. The former statute authorizes suit "for . . . personal injury . . . caused by the negligent or wrongful act or omission of any employee of the Government while acting within the scope of his office or employment." 28 U.S.C. § 1346(b)(1). The latter provides in its entirety that "[t]he district courts shall have original jurisdiction of any civil action by an alien for a tort only, committed in violation of the law of nations or a treaty of the U.S." § 1350 . . .

Analysis

. . . The Government seeks reversal of the judgment of liability under the FTCA on two principal grounds. It argues that the arrest could not have been tortious, because it was authorized by 21 U.S.C. § 878, setting out the arrest authority of the DEA, and it says that in any event the liability asserted here falls within the FTCA exception to waiver of sovereign immunity for claims "arising in a foreign country," 28 U.S.C. § 2680(k). We think the exception applies and decide on that ground . . .

. . . Here the significant limitation on the waiver of immunity is the Act's exception for "[a]ny claim arising in a foreign country," § 2680(k), a provision that on its face seems plainly applicable to the facts of this action. In the Ninth Circuit's view, once Alvarez was within the borders of the U.S., his detention was not tortious, see 331 F.3d, at 636-637; the appellate court suggested that the Government's liability to Alvarez rested solely upon a false arrest claim. Id., at 640-641. Alvarez's arrest, however, was said to be "false," and thus tortious, only because, and only to the extent that, it took place and endured in Mexico. The actions in Mexico are thus most naturally understood as the kernel of a "claim arising in a foreign country," and barred from suit under the exception to the waiver of immunity . . .

. . . Notwithstanding the straightforward language of the foreign country exception, the Ninth Circuit allowed the action to proceed under what has come to be known as the "headquarters doctrine" . . . Headquarters claims "typically involve allegations of negligent guidance in an office within the U.S. of employees who cause damage while in a foreign country, or of activities which take place within a foreign country." Cominotto v U.S., 802 F.2d 1127, 1130 (C.A.9 1986). In such instances, these courts have concluded that § 2680(k) does not bar suit . . .

. . . The potential effect of this sort of headquarters analysis flashes the yellow caution light. "[I]t will virtually always be possible to assert that the negligent activity that injured the plaintiff [abroad] was the consequence of faulty training, selection or supervision-or even less than that, lack of careful training, selection or supervision-in the U.S." Beattie v U.S., 756 F.2d 91, 119 (C.A.D.C.1984) (Scalia, J., dissenting). Legal malpractice claims, Knisley v U.S., 817 F.Supp. 680, 691-693 (S.D.Ohio 1993), allegations of negligent medical care, Newborn v U.S., 238 F.Supp.2d 145, 148-149 (D.D.C.2002), and even slip-and-fall cases, Eaglin v U.S., Dept. of Army, 794 F.2d 981, 983-984 (C.A.5 1986), can all be repackaged as headquarters claims based on a failure to train, a failure to warn, the offering of bad advice, or the adoption of a negligent policy. If we were to approve the headquarters exception to the foreign country exception, the "'headquarters claim' [would] become a standard part of FTCA litigation" in cases potentially implicating the foreign country exception.

Beattie, supra, at 119 (Scalia, J., dissenting). The headquarters doctrine threatens to swallow the foreign country exception whole, certainly at the pleadings stage . . .

. . . Alvarez has also brought an action under the ATS against petitioner Sosa, who argues (as does the U.S. supporting him) that there is no relief under the ATS because the statute does no more than vest federal courts with jurisdiction, neither creating nor authorizing the courts to recognize any particular right of action without further congressional action. Although we agree the statute is in terms only jurisdictional, we think that at the time of enactment the jurisdiction enabled federal courts to hear claims in a very limited category defined by the law of nations and recognized at common law . . .

. . . Alvarez's detention claim must be gauged against the current state of international law, looking to those sources we have long, albeit cautiously, recognized.

"[W]here there is no treaty, and no controlling executive or legislative act or judicial decision, resort must be had to the customs and usages of civilized nations; and, as evidence of these, to the works of jurists and commentators, who by years of labor, research and experience, have made themselves peculiarly well acquainted with the subjects of which they treat. Such works are resorted to by judicial tribunals, not for the speculations of their authors concerning what the law ought to be, but for trustworthy evidence of what the law really is." The Paquete Habana, 175 U.S., at 700, 20 S.Ct. 290.

To begin with, Alvarez cites two well-known international agreements that, despite their moral authority, have little utility under the standard set out in this opinion. He says that his abduction by Sosa was an "arbitrary arrest" within the meaning of the Universal Declaration of Human Rights (Declaration), G.A. Res. 217A (III), U.N. Doc. A/810 (1948). And he traces the rule against arbitrary arrest not only to the Declaration, but also to article nine of the International Covenant on Civil and Political Rights (Covenant), Dec. 16, 1966, 999 U.N.T.S. 171, to which the U.S. is a party, and to various other conventions to which it is not. But the Declaration does not of its own force impose obligations as a matter of international law. See Humphrey, The UN Charter and the Universal Declaration of Human Rights, in The International Protection of Human Rights 39, 50 (E. Luard ed.1967) (quoting Eleanor Roosevelt calling the Declaration "'a statement of principles . . . setting up a common standard of achievement for all peoples and all nations'" and "'not a treaty or international agreement . . . impos[ing] legal obligations'"). And, although the Covenant does bind the U.S. as a matter of international law, the U.S. ratified the Covenant on the express understanding that it was not self-executing and so did not itself create obligations enforceable in the federal courts. See supra, at 2763. Accordingly, Alvarez cannot say that the Declaration and Covenant themselves establish the relevant and applicable rule of international law. He instead attempts to show that prohibition of arbitrary arrest has attained the status of binding customary international law . . .

. . . Alvarez thus invokes a general prohibition of "arbitrary" detention defined as officially sanctioned action exceeding positive authorization to detain under the domestic law of some government, regardless of the circumstances. Whether or not this is an accurate reading of the Covenant, Alvarez cites little authority that a rule so broad has the status of a binding customary norm today. He certainly cites nothing to justify the federal courts in taking his broad rule as the predicate for a federal lawsuit, for its implications would be breathtaking. His rule would support a cause of action in federal court for any arrest, anywhere in the world, unauthorized by the law of the jurisdiction in which it took place, and would create a cause of action for any seizure of an alien in violation of the Fourth Amendment, supplanting the actions under Rev. Stat. § 1979, 42 U.S.C. § 1983, and Bivens v Six Unknown Fed. Narcotics Agents, 403 U.S. 388, 91 S.Ct. 1999, 29 L.Ed.2d 619 (1971), that now provide damages remedies for such violations. It would create an action in federal court for arrests by state officers who simply exceed their authority; and for the violation of any limit that the law of any country might place on the authority of its own officers to arrest. And all of this assumes that Alvarez could establish that Sosa was acting on behalf of a government when he made the arrest, for otherwise he would need a rule broader still . . .

. . . Whatever may be said for the broad principle Alvarez advances, in the present, imperfect world, it expresses an aspiration that exceeds any binding customary rule having the specificity we require. Creating a private cause of action to further that aspiration would go beyond any residual common law discretion we think it appropriate to exercise. It is enough to hold that a single illegal detention of less than a day, followed by the transfer of custody to lawful authorities and a prompt arraignment, violates no norm of customary international law so well defined as to support the creation of a federal remedy . . .

331 F 3d 604 Reversed and Remanded.

13. *Samantar v Yousuf*, Supreme Court of the U.S. (Excerpted)
Cite as: 130 S. Ct. 2278; 560 U.S. ____(2010)

MOHAMED ALI SAMANTAR, PETITIONER v BASHE ABDI YOUSUF ET AL.
[June 1, 2010]

ON WRIT OF CERTIORARI TO THE U.S. COURT
OF APPEALS FOR THE FOURTH CIRCUIT

JUSTICE STEVENS delivered the opinion of the Court.

From 1980 to 1986 petitioner Mohamed Ali Samantar was the First Vice President and Minister of Defense of Somalia, and from 1987 to 1990 he served as its Prime Minister. Respondents are natives of Somalia who allege that they, or members of their families, were the victims of torture and extrajudicial killings during those years. They seek damages from petitioner based on his alleged authorization of those acts. The narrow question we must decide is whether the Foreign Sovereign Immunities Act of 1976 (FSIA or Act), 28 U. S. C. §§1330, 1602 et seq., provides petitioner with immunity from suit based on actions taken in his official capacity. We hold that the FSIA does not govern the determination of petitioner's immunity from suit.

. . .

Analysis

. . . Prior to 1952, the State Department followed a general practice of requesting immunity in all actions against friendly sovereigns, but in that year the Department announced its adoption of the "restrictive" theory of sovereign immunity. Verlinden, 461 U.S., at 486-487, 103 S.Ct. 1962; see also Letter from Jack B. Tate, Acting Legal Adviser, Department of State, to Acting Attorney General Philip B. Perlman (May 19, 1952), reprinted in 26 Dept. State Bull. 984-985 (1952). Under this theory, "immunity is confined to suits involving the foreign sovereign's public acts, and does not extend to cases arising out of a foreign state's strictly commercial acts." Verlinden, 461 U.S., at 487, 103 S.Ct. 1962. This change threw "immunity determinations into some disarray," because "political considerations sometimes led the Department to file 'suggestions of immunity in cases where immunity would not have been available under the restrictive theory.'" Republic of Austria v Altmann, 541 U.S. 677, 690, 124 S.Ct. 2240, 159 L.Ed.2d 1 (2004) (quoting Verlinden, 461 U.S., at 487, 103 S.Ct. 1962).

Congress responded to the inconsistent application of sovereign immunity by enacting the FSIA in 1976. Altmann, 541 U.S., at 690-691, 124 S.Ct. 2240; see also Verlinden, 461 U.S., at 487-488, 103 S.Ct. 1962. Section 1602 describes the Act's two primary purposes: (1) to endorse and codify the restrictive theory of sovereign immunity, and (2) to transfer primary responsibility for deciding "claims of foreign states to immunity" from the State Department to the courts. After the enactment of the FSIA, the Act-and not the pre-existing common law-indisputably governs the determination of whether a foreign state is entitled to sovereign immunity . . . What we must now decide is whether the Act also covers the immunity claims of foreign officials . . .

. . . The FSIA provides that "a foreign state shall be immune from the jurisdiction of the courts of the U.S. and of the States" except as provided in the Act. § 1604. Thus, if a defendant is a "foreign state" within the meaning of the Act, then the defendant is immune from jurisdiction unless one of the exceptions in the Act applies. See §§ 1605-1607 (enumerating exceptions). The Act, if it applies, is the "sole basis for obtaining jurisdiction over a foreign state in federal court." Argentine Republic v Amerada Hess Shipping Corp., 488 U.S. 428, 439, 109 S.Ct. 683, 102 L.Ed.2d 818 (1989). The question we face in this case is whether an individual sued for conduct undertaken in his official capacity is a "foreign state" within the meaning of the Act.

The Act defines "foreign state" in § 1603 as follows:

"(a) A 'foreign state' . . . includes a political subdivision of a foreign state or an agency or instrumentality of a foreign state as defined in subsection (b).

"(b) An 'agency or instrumentality of a foreign state' means any entity-

"(1) which is a separate legal person, corporate or otherwise, and

"(2) which is an organ of a foreign state or political subdivision thereof, or a majority of whose shares or other ownership interest is owned by a foreign state or political subdivision thereof, and

"(3) which is neither a citizen of a State of the U.S. as defined in section 1332(c) and (e) of this title, nor created under the laws of any third country."

The term "foreign state" on its face indicates a body politic that governs a particular territory. See, e.g., Restatement § 4 (defining "state" as "an entity that has a defined territory and population under the control of a government and that engages in foreign relations"). In § 1603(a), however, the Act establishes that "foreign state" has a broader meaning, by mandating the inclusion of the state's political subdivisions, agencies, and instrumentalities. Then, in § 1603(b), the Act specifically delimits what counts as an agency or instrumentality. Petitioner argues that either "foreign state," § 1603(a), or "agency or instrumentality," § 1603(b), could be read to include a foreign official. Although we agree that petitioner's interpretation is literally possible, our analysis of the entire statutory text persuades us that petitioner's reading is not the meaning that Congress enacted.

We turn first to the term "agency or instrumentality of a foreign state," § 1603(b). It is true that an individual official could be an "agency or instrumentality," if that term is given the meaning of "any thing or person through which action is accomplished," In re Terrorist Attacks on Sept. 11, 2001, 538 F.3d 71, 83 (C.A.2 2008). But Congress has specifically defined "agency or instrumentality" in the FSIA, and all of the textual clues in that definition cut against such a broad construction.

First, the statute specifies that "'agency or instrumentality . . . ' means any entity" matching three specified characteristics, § 1603(b) (emphasis added), and "entity" typically refers to an organization, rather than an individual. See, e.g., Black's Law Dictionary 612 (9th ed.2009). Furthermore, several of the required characteristics apply awkwardly, if at all, to individuals. The phrase "separate legal person, corporate or otherwise," § 1603(b)(1), could conceivably refer to a natural person, solely by virtue of the word "person." But the phrase "separate legal person" typically refers to the legal fiction that allows an entity to hold personhood separate from the natural persons who are its shareholders or officers. Cf. First Nat. City Bank v Banco Para El Comercio Exterior de Cuba, 462 U.S. 611, 625, 103 S.Ct. 2591, 77 L.Ed.2d 46 (1983) ("Separate legal personality has been described as 'an almost indispensable aspect of the public corporation'"). It is similarly awkward to refer to a person as an "organ" of the foreign state. See § 1603(b)(2). And the third part of the definition could not be applied at all to a natural person. A natural person cannot be a citizen of a State "as defined in section 1332(c) and (e)," § 1603(b)(3), because those subsections refer to the citizenship of corporations and estates. Nor can a natural person be "created under the laws of any third country." Ibid. Thus, the terms Congress chose simply do not evidence the intent to include individual officials within the meaning of "agency or instrumentality." Cf. Dole Food Co. v Patrickson, 538 U.S. 468, 474, 123 S.Ct. 1655, 155 L.Ed.2d 643 (2003) (describing § 1603(b) as containing "indicia that Congress had corporate formalities in mind") . . .

Petitioner proposes a second textual route to including an official within the meaning of "foreign state." He argues that the definition of "foreign state" in § 1603(a) sets out a nonexhaustive list that "includes" political subdivisions and agencies or instrumentalities but is not so limited. See Brief for Petitioner 22-23. It is true that use of the word "include" can signal that the list that follows is meant to be illustrative rather than exhaustive. And, to be sure, there are fewer textual clues within § 1603(a) than within § 1603(b) from which to interpret Congress' silence regarding foreign officials. But even if the list in § 1603(a) is merely illustrative, it still suggests that "foreign state" does not encompass officials, because the types of defendants listed are all entities. See Russell Motor Car Co. v U.S., 261 U.S. 514, 519, 58 Ct.Cl. 708, 43 S.Ct. 428, 67 L.Ed. 778 (1923) ("[A] word may be known by the company it keeps").

. . . Moreover, elsewhere in the FSIA Congress expressly mentioned officials when it wished to count their acts as equivalent to those of the foreign state, which suggests that officials are not included within the unadorned term "foreign state." Cf. Kimbrough v U.S., 552 U.S. 85, 103, 128 S.Ct. 558, 169 L.Ed.2d 481 (2007) ("Drawing meaning from silence is particularly inappropriate . . . [when] Congress has shown that it knows how to [address an issue] in express terms") . . . For example, Congress provided an exception from the general grant of immunity for cases in which "money damages are sought against a foreign state" for an injury in the U.S. "caused by the tortious act or omission of that foreign state or of any official or employee of that foreign state while acting within the scope of his office." § 1605(a)(5) (emphasis added) . . . If the term "foreign state" by definition includes an individual acting within the scope of his office, the phrase "or of any official or employee . . . " in 28 U.S.C. § 1605(a)(5) would be unnecessary. See Dole Food Co., 538 U.S., at 476-477, 123 S.Ct. 1655 ("[W]e should not construe the statute in a manner that is strained and, at the same time, would render a statutory term superfluous") . . .

. . . In sum, "[w]e do not . . . construe statutory phrases in isolation; we read statutes as a whole." U.S. v Morton, 467 U.S. 822, 828, 104 S.Ct. 2769, 81 L.Ed.2d 680 (1984). Reading the FSIA as a whole, there is nothing to suggest we should read "foreign state" in § 1603(a) to include an official acting on behalf of the foreign state, and much to indicate that this meaning was not what Congress enacted. The text does not expressly foreclose petitioner's reading, but it supports the view of respondents and the U.S. that the Act does not address an official's claim to immunity.

. . . Petitioner argues that the FSIA is best read to cover his claim to immunity because of its history and purpose. As discussed at the outset, one of the primary purposes of the FSIA was to codify the restrictive theory of sovereign immunity, which Congress recognized as consistent with extant international law. See § 1602. We have observed that a related purpose was "codification of international law at the time of the FSIA's enactment," Permanent Mission of India to United Nations v City of New York, 551 U.S. 193, 199, 127 S.Ct. 2352, 168 L.Ed.2d 85 (2007), and have examined the relevant common law and international practice when interpreting the Act, id., at 200-201, 127 S.Ct. 2352. Because of this relationship between the Act and the common law that it codified, petitioner argues that we should construe the FSIA consistently with the common law regarding individual immunity, which-in petitioner's view-was coextensive with the law of state immunity and always immunized a foreign official for acts taken on behalf of the foreign state. Even reading the Act in light of Congress' purpose of codifying state sovereign immunity, however, we do not think that the Act codified the common law with respect to the immunity of individual officials . . .

. . . Petitioner urges that a suit against an official must always be equivalent to a suit against the state because acts taken by a state official on behalf of a state are acts of the state. See Brief for Petitioner 26. We have recognized, in the context of the act of state doctrine, that an official's acts can be considered the acts of the foreign state, and that "the courts of one country will not sit in judgment" of those acts when done within the territory of the foreign state. See Underhill v Hernandez, 168 U.S. 250, 252, 254, 18 S.Ct. 83, 42 L.Ed. 456 (1897). Although the act of state doctrine is distinct from immunity, and instead "provides foreign states with a substantive defense on the merits," Altmann, 541 U.S., at 700, 124 S.Ct. 2240, we do not doubt that in some circumstances the immunity of the foreign state extends to an individual for acts taken in his official capacity. But it does not follow from this premise that Congress intended to codify that immunity in the FSIA. It hardly furthers Congress' purpose of "clarifying the rules that judges should apply in resolving sovereign immunity claims," id., at 699, 124 S.Ct. 2240, to lump individual officials in with foreign states without so much as a word spelling out how and when individual officials are covered . . .

. . . Petitioner would have a stronger case if there were any indication that Congress' intent to enact a comprehensive solution for suits against states extended to suits against individual officials . . . [A]lthough questions of official immunity did arise in the pre-FSIA period, they were few and far between. The immunity of officials simply was not the particular problem to which Congress was responding when it enacted the FSIA. The FSIA was adopted, rather, to address "a modern world where foreign state enterprises are every day participants in commercial activities," and to assure litigants that decisions regarding claims against states and their enterprises "are made on purely legal grounds." H.R. Rep., at 7, U.S.Code Cong. & Admin. News 1976, at p. 6606. We have been given no reason to believe that Congress saw as a problem, or wanted to eliminate, the State Department's role in determinations regarding individual official immunity . . .

. . . Our review of the text, purpose, and history of the FSIA leads us to the conclusion that the Court of Appeals correctly held the FSIA does not govern petitioner's claim of immunity. The Act therefore did not deprive the District Court of subject-matter jurisdiction. We emphasize, however, the narrowness of our holding. Whether petitioner may be entitled to immunity under the common law, and whether he may have other valid defenses to the grave charges against him, are matters to be addressed in the first instance by the District Court on remand.

The judgment of the Court of Appeals is affirmed, and the case is remanded for further proceedings consistent with this opinion.

Non U.S. Forum Human Rights Decisions etc.

14. *Djamel Ameziane v U.S.*, Case pending in the Inter-American Commission of Human Rights
(Excerpted)
Pleadings and Correspondence between Petitioner-Victim-Client and the Inter- American Commission
on Human Rights
a. Petition and Request for Precautionary Measures. Following is the pleading ("Petition") prepared and
submitted by the lawyers for Dzamel Ameziane, Petitioner, who was a Guanatanmo Detainee at the time.
Also included is a request for Precautionary Measures, a sort of temporary injunction, which the Petitioner's
lawyers ask the Inter-American Commission to request from the U.S.

IN THE

INTER-AMERICAN COMMISSION ON HUMAN RIGHTS

DJAMEL AMEZIANE,

Prisoner, U.S. Naval Station, Guantánamo Bay, Cuba

Petitioner,

v

U.S.,

Defendant.

PETITION AND REQUEST FOR PRECAUTIONARY MEASURES (EXCERPTS)

Dated:　　　　August 6, 2008

*Respectfully submitted on behalf of
Djamel Ameziane:*
Pardiss Kebriaei Shayana Kadidal
CENTER FOR CONSTITUTIONAL RIGHTS
666 Broadway, 7th Floor
New York, NY 10012
(Tel) 212-614-6452
(Fax) 212-614-6499
Viviana Krsticevic
Ariela Peralta
Francisco Quintana
Michael Camilleri
CENTER FOR JUSTICE AND INTERNATIONAL LAW
(CEJIL)
1630 Connecticut Ave., NW Suite 401
Washington, D.C. 20009-1053
(Tel) 202-319-3000
(Fax) 202-319-3019

[Table of Contents omitted]

I. PRELIMINARY STATEMENT

1. Djamel Ameziane is a prisoner at the U.S. Naval Base at Guantánamo Bay, Cuba, where he has been held virtually *incommunicado*, without charge or judicial review of his detention, for six and a half years. While arbitrarily and indefinitely detained by the U.S. at Guantánamo, Mr. Ameziane has been physically and psychologically tortured, denied medical care for health conditions resulting from his confinement, prevented from practicing his religion without interference and insult, and deprived of developing his private and family life. The stigma of Guantánamo will continue to impact his life long after he is released from the prison. These harms, as well as the denial of any effective legal recourse to seek accountability and reparations for the violations he has suffered, constitute violations of fundamental rights under the American Declaration of the Rights and Duties of Man ("American Declaration"). The U.S. government, as a signatory to the Declaration, is obliged to respect these rights vis-à-vis Mr. Ameziane by virtue of holding him as its prisoner.

2. A citizen of Algeria. Mr. Ameziane left his home country in the 1990s to escape escalating violence and insecurity and in search of a better life. He went first to Austria, where he worked as a high-paid chef, and then to Canada, where he sought political asylum and lived for five years but was ultimately denied refuge. Fearful of being deported to Algeria and faced with few options, Mr. Ameziane went to Afghanistan. He fled that country as soon as the fighting began in October 2001, but was captured by the local police and turned over to U.S. forces, presumably for a bounty.

3. From the point of his capture, Mr. Ameziane was shipped to a detention facility at the U.S.-occupied Air Base in Kandahar. Afghanistan, where his torture began. Military prison guards beat, punched and kicked Mr. Ameziane and other prisoners without provocation, menaced them with working dogs, subjected them to brutal searches and desecrated their Qur'ans.

4. In February 2002, Mr. Ameziane was transferred from Kandahar to Guantánamo Bay, just weeks after the prison opened. As one of the first prisoners to arrive, Mr. Ameziane was held in Camp X-Ray – the infamous camp of the early regime at Guantánamo – in a small wire-mesh cage, exposed to the sun and the elements. In March 2007, he was transferred to Camp VI – the newest maximum security facility at Guantánamo – where, according to unclassified information to date, he sits in isolation all day, every day, in a small concrete and steel cell with no windows to the outside or natural light or air, and where he is slowly going blind.

5. During his imprisonment at Guantánamo, Mr. Ameziane has been interrogated hundreds of times. In connection with these interrogations, he has been beaten, subjected to simulated drowning, denied sleep for extended periods of time, held in solitary confinement, and subjected to blaring music designed to torture. His abuse and conditions of confinement have resulted in injuries and long-term health conditions for which he has never received proper treatment, despite repeated requests. Medical treatment has furthermore been withheld to coerce his cooperation in interrogations.

6. Mr. Ameziane's imprisonment at Guantánamo has also deprived him of precious years during the prime of his life, during which he would have wished to marry, start a family and pursue a career. It also denied him the chance to say goodbye to his father, who passed away while Mr. Ameziane has been imprisoned.

7. For more than six years, the U.S. has denied Mr. Ameziane the right not only to challenge his detention, but also to seek accountability and effective relief for the other harms he has suffered. At no time has the U.S. charged him with any crime, nor accused him of participating in any hostile action at any time, of possessing or using any weapons, of participating in any military training activity or of being a member of any alleged terrorist organization.

8. As this petition is filed, Mr. Ameziane continues to be indefinitely and inhumanely detained, and he faces an uncertain future. While the U.S. Supreme Court's ruling in *Boumediene v Bush* in June 2008 restores Guantánamo detainees' right to habeas corpus, a remedy that Mr. Ameziane will pursue, the fact remains that he is still sitting in his cell at Guantánamo Bay without charge and that he has been deprived of any semblance of meaningful review of his detention for over six years.

9. Were Mr. Ameziane to be released from Guantánamo, he would need a third country in which to resettle safely. He is currently applying for resettlement in Canada, where he legally resided for five years prior to his detention. Mr. Ameziane confronts an ongoing risk of persecution in Algeria, the country he fled

16 years ago as a young man in hope of finding peace and security, only to end up at Guantánamo because of circumstances beyond his making or control.

I. BACKGROUND AND CONTEXT
A. The U.S.' Response to September 11

10. Days after the attacks on the World Trade Center and the Pentagon on September 11, 2001, the U.S. Congress passed a joint resolution that broadly authorized the President to "use all necessary and appropriate force against those nations, organizations, or persons he determines planned, authorized, committed, or aided the terrorist attacks . . . in order to prevent any future acts of international terrorism against the U.S. by such nations, organizations or persons." This resolution, the Authorization for the Use of Military Force ("AUMF"), provided the legal basis for the U.S.' military campaign against the Taliban regime in Afghanistan and the al Qaeda elements that supported it.

11. Two months later, on November 13, 2001, the President signed an executive order that defined a sweeping category of non-U.S. citizens whom the Department of Defense was authorized to detain in its "war against terrorism." The order provided that the President alone would determine which individuals fit within the purview of that definition and could be detained. It also explicitly denied all such detainees being held in U.S. custody anywhere the right to challenge any aspect of their detention in any U.S. or foreign court or international tribunal, and authorized trial by military commissions for individuals who would be charged.

12. Pursuant to the AUMF and this order, hundreds of individuals were captured in the weeks and months following September 11, not only in Afghanistan, but in areas of the world where there was no armed conflict involving the U.S. They were detained and interrogated in U.S. custody in various locations, including in U.S. military bases in Afghanistan and Guantánamo Bay, in foreign prisons and in secret sites operated by the CIA.

13. Confidential government memos written in the days, weeks and months after September 11 reveal that the U.S. did not intend to be bound by its constitutional or international legal obligations in responding to the attacks. A memo from the Director of the CIA from September 16, 2001 declared, "All the rules have changed," while a subsequent memo from the Office of the Legal Counsel at the Department of Justice counseled the President that there were essentially no limits to his authority "as to any terrorist threat, the amount of military force to be used in response, or the method, timing, and nature of the response." In January 2002, as the first prisoners began to arrive at Guantánamo, additional memos from the Office of the Legal Counsel and from the President's White House Counsel advised the President that captured members of al Qaeda and the Taliban were not protected by the Third Geneva Convention, reasoning that this "new kind of war . . . renders obsolete Geneva's strict limitations on questioning of enemy prisoners" and that not applying "Geneva" would "substantially reduce" the risk that U.S. officials would later be prosecuted for war crimes under the War Crimes Act. The President issued an order one month later declaring that Taliban and al Qaeda detainees were not entitled to prisoner of war status under the Geneva Conventions.

14. The manner in which the U.S. has conducted its "war on terror" has given rise to abuses that have been widely decried by the international community. While the United Nations Security Council adopted a strong anti-terrorism resolution only two weeks after September 11 condemning the attacks and calling upon States to take legislative, procedural and economic measures to prevent, prohibit and criminalize terrorist acts, subsequent resolutions also called upon "[s]tates [to] ensure that any measure[s] taken to combat terrorism comply with all their obligations under international law, in particular international human rights, refugee and humanitarian law." The U.S. has failed to respect these obligations. In the report of his mission to the U.S., the UN Special Rapporteur on Human Rights and Counter-Terrorism criticized the "serious situations of incompatibility between international human rights obligations and the counter-terrorism law and practice of the U.S." and the fact that "a number of important mechanisms [in U.S. law] for the protection of rights have been removed or obfuscated under law and practice since the events of 11 September." For years, this Commission and other international bodies, as well as U.S. officials themselves, have called for the U.S. to close the prison at Guantánamo without further delay.

B. International Network of Detention Facilities, Including in Kandahar and at Bagram Air Force Base, Afghanistan; in Iraq; and in Guantánamo Bay, Cuba

15. As part of its response to September 11, the U.S. seized and detained hundreds, if not thousands, of individuals in sites and facilities away from public scrutiny, including U.S. military bases around the world,

foreign prisons and secret CIA sites. As an indication that the U.S. is scaling up, not down, its global detention operations, recent news reports state that the Pentagon has planned to build a new, larger detention facility on the U.S. Air Base at Bagram, Afghanistan to replace the existing dilapidated one. Currently, in known sites alone, the U.S. holds some 270 persons in Guantánamo, some 700 persons in Afghanistan, including over 600 in Bagram, and over 20,000 persons in Iraq. As was the path for Mr. Ameziane, many of those held in Afghanistan were subsequently transferred to Guantánamo.

1. Kandahar Detention Facility

16. During the first week of December 2001, in the later stages of the U.S. invasion of Afghanistan, U.S. Marines took control of the international airport in Kandahar and established a temporary U.S. base, including a prison reportedly capable of holding 100 detainees. The U.S. military occupied and controlled the base over the following months, including the five-week period of Mr. Ameziane's detention there. The prison at Kandahar subsequently became what the U.S. military calls an "intermediate" site, a holding facility where detainees await transportation to other permanent facilities. News reports from February 2002, around the period of Mr. Ameziane's detention at Kandahar, described the facility as one of two main jails in Afghanistan for more than 200 terrorism suspects, many of whom were awaiting transfer to Guantánamo. Detention conditions at Kandahar have been described by international monitors as below human rights standards.

2. Guantánamo Bay Detention Facility

17. The territory of the Guantánamo Bay Naval Base has been under U.S. control since the end of the Spanish-American War. The U.S. occupies the territory pursuant to a 1903 Lease Agreement executed with Cuba in the aftermath of the war, which expressly provides for the U.S.' "complete jurisdiction and control" over the area – control it may exercise permanently if it so chooses. In *Rasul v Bush*, the U.S. Supreme Court rejected the government's argument that the right to habeas corpus does not extend to the prisoners at Guantánamo Bay because they are outside of U.S. territory. As one Justice wrote, "Guantánamo Bay is in every practical respect a U.S. territory" over which the U.S. has long exercised "unchallenged and indefinite control."

18. The first prisoners were transferred to Guantánamo on January 11, 2002. At its peak, the prison held more than 750 men from over 40 countries, ranging in age from 10 to 80, most of whom U.S. officials have admitted should never have been held there in the first place. As of August 2008, there were approximately 260 prisoners from about 30 countries being held at Guantánamo. These include approximately 50 men, like Mr. Ameziane, who cannot return to their home country for fear of torture or persecution and need a safe third country for resettlement.

19. The conditions of detention at Guantánamo have been described by international monitors as inhumane. The first prisoners at Guantánamo, including Mr. Ameziane – who arrived blindfolded and goggled, wearing earmuffs and face masks, handcuffed and shackled – were held for the first few months of their imprisonment in open air wire-mesh cages in the infamous Camp X-Ray. For more than two years, the prisoners were virtually cut off from the outside world, until *Rasul* opened Guantánamo to lawyers in 2004, but communication with lawyers, family members and other prisoners continues to be severely restricted. Today, about 70% of all prisoners are held in solitary confinement or isolation in one of three camps - Camps 5 and 6, and Camp Echo. International NGOs have described Camp VI, where Mr. Ameziane is detained, as more severe in some respects than the most restrictive "super-maximum" facilities

. . .

II. STATEMENT OF FACTS

A. Background

36. Mr. Ameziane was bom on April 14, 1967 in Algiers, the sixth in a close-knit family of eight brothers and sisters. Mr. Ameziane's brother remembers that as a child, Mr. Ameziane was quiet and loved to read, and was content to sit in his room for hours surrounded by stacks of books. Mr. Ameziane attended primary school, secondary school and university in Algeria, and worked as a hydraulics technician after obtaining his university diploma.

37. Mr. Ameziane's hometown is in Kabylie, an unstable region in the north of Algeria known for frequent, violent clashes between the Algerian army and Islamic resistance groups. Practicing Muslims living in that region, such as Mr. Ameziane and his family, are automatically suspected of being supporters of such groups and are frequently harassed and targeted by the government solely by virtue of being observant Muslims. Mr. Ameziane left his family home in 1992 to escape this discrimination and insecurity and to seek

greater stability and peace abroad. He obtained a visa to travel to Italy, through which he transited to Vienna, Austria, where he lived for three years.

38. In Austria, Mr. Ameziane began working as a dishwasher, but his skill and talent led him to rise quickly to become the highest-paid chef at *Al Caminetto Trattoria*, a well-known Italian restaurant. In 1995, following the election of a conservative anti-immigrant government, new immigration policies prevented Mr. Ameziane from extending or renewing his visa, and his work permit was denied without explanation. Mr. Ameziane was forced to leave the country. He traveled directly to Canada, hoping that country's French-speaking population and progressive immigration policies would allow him to settle down and make a permanent home. Immediately upon his arrival, he told immigration officials at the airport that he wanted to apply for asylum because he was afraid of being deported to Algeria. As he awaited a decision, he obtained a temporary work pemit and worked diligently for an office supply company and various restaurants in Montreal. His application was ultimately denied in 2000, and he was forced once again to uproot his life and leave the country he had made his home for five years.

39. Displaced, fearful of being forcibly returned to Algeria and – after eight years of searching for refuge only to be denied time and again – perceiving that he had few options, he went to Afghanistan, where he felt he could live without discrimination as a Muslim man, and where he would not fear deportation to Algeria. As soon as the war started, he fled to escape the fighting. He was captured by local police while trying to cross the border into Pakistan, and turned over by Pakistani authorities to U.S. forces, presumably for a bounty.

. . .

III. ADMISSIBILITY
A. Mr. Ameziane's Petition is Admissible Under the Commission's Rules of Procedure.

74. Mr. Ameziane's petition is admissible in its entirety under the IACHR Rules. In particular, the Commission has jurisdiction *ratione personae*, *ratione materiae*, *ratione temporis* and *ratione loci* to examine the petition, and Mr. Ameziane is exempt from the exhaustion of domestic remedies requirement under the terms of 31.2 of the IACHR Rules. The Commission should therefore reach a favorable admissibility finding and proceed in earnest to examine the merits of this grave case of human rights abuse.

1. The Commission has Jurisdiction *Ratione Personae, Ratione Materiae, Ratione Temporis,* and *Ratione Loci* to Consider Mr. Ameziane's Petition.

75. The Commission is competent *ratione personae*, *ratione materiae*, *ratione temporis* and *ratione loci* to examine the complaints presented by Mr. Ameziane.

76. The Commission is competent *ratione personae* to consider Mr. Ameziane's complaint because Mr. Ameziane is a natural person who was subject to the jurisdiction of the U.S. and whose rights were protected under the American Declaration when the violations detailed in this petition occurred. Although the violations took place outside the formal territory of the U.S., the Commission has long established that it may exercise jurisdiction over conduct with an extra-territorial locus where the person concerned is present in the territory of one State, but subject to the authority and control of another OAS Member State.

77. The Commission's authority to hear such extra-territorial claims was directly addressed and upheld in two 1999 decisions, *Coard et al.* v *U.S.* and *Alejandre v Cuba*. In *Coard*, the Commission, considering allegations of U.S. violations during its 1983 invasion of Grenada, held that the Commission's jurisdictional analysis focuses on the state control over the individual whose rights have been violated. The Commission found that the phrase "subject to [the OAS country's] jurisdiction," the jurisdictional language commonly used in international human rights instruments, "may, under given circumstances, refer to conduct with an extraterritorial locus where the person concerned is present in the territory of one state, but subject to the control of another state . . . ."

78. In *Alejandre*, the Commission found that Cuba, an OAS member state, exercised "authority and control" over the unarmed civilian aircraft the Cuban military shot down, sufficient for the Commission to hear the petitioners' complaint. In *Alejandre*, there was no territorial nexus between the victims of the alleged violations and the state of Cuba, or between the actions themselves and Cuban territory. Two of the victims had been born in the U.S.; none of the activities relevant to the petition took place on Cuban soil; and none of the victims were in a Cuban airplane. Nevertheless, in taking aim upon the civilian passenger plane, the Commission found, "the agents of the Cuban state, although outside their territory", placed the civilian pilots . . . under their authority." This placed the victims within the jurisdiction of Cuba for purposes of triggering

Cuba's human rights obligations: "In principle, the [jurisdictional] investigation refers not to the nationality of the alleged victim or his presence in a particular geographic area, but to whether, in those specific circumstances, the state observed the rights of a person subject to its authority or control." In other words, the jurisdictional analysis is not predicated on the nature and characteristics of the alleged victim of the claim. Rather, whether the Commission has the authority to contemplate an OAS Member State's actions turns on whether the state has lived up to its responsibilities regarding the human rights of persons over whom the state exercised control.

79. Under the "authority and control" theory, the Commission has already established that Guantánamo detainees are subject to the jurisdiction of the U.S. and therefore benefit from the protection of the American Declaration. On this basis, the Commission has exercised its own jurisdiction to enforce the American Declaration to the benefit of such persons. In the present case, there is no doubt that Mr. Ameziane has been subject to the jurisdiction of the U.S. since being transferred to Guantánamo Bay – he has been detained by the U.S. on a U.S. military base governed by an indefinite lease establishing U.S. control since 1903. The U.S. Supreme Court itself has referred to the "obvious and uncontested fact that the U.S., by virtue of its complete jurisdiction and control over the [Guantánamo Bay Naval] base, maintains de facto sovereignty over this territory." The Commission is therefore competent ratione personae to hear claims based on Mr. Ameziane's detention at Guantánamo.

80. Furthermore, Mr. Ameziane was under the authority and control of the U.S. while detained by the U.S. military at the airbase in Kandahar, Afghanistan. The airbase was occupied by U.S. Marines in December 2001 and, during the five-week period when Mr. Ameziane was detained there from January to February 2001 the facility was clearly under U.S. control. The Commission may therefore exercise its ratione personae jurisdiction with respect to all the facts described in this petition, whether they occurred in Kandahar, Afghanistan or Guantánamo Bay, Cuba.

81. As Mr. Ameziane's petition alleges the violation of several articles of the American Declaration, the Commission is also competent ratione materiae to consider the complaint. Although the U.S. has repeatedly contested the authority of the Commission to declare violations of rights enshrined in the American Declaration, the Commission has long held that the Declaration constitutes a source of binding international obligations for the U.S.

82. Furthermore, the Commission is competent ratione temporis to consider the petition, as the violations of Mr. Ameziane's rights occurred subsequent to the adoption of the American Declaration in 1948, to the U.S.' ratification of the OAS Charter on June 19, 1951, and to the creation of the IACHR in 1959.

83. Finally, the Commission is competent ratione loci to consider the violations alleged by Mr. Ameziane, as the petition alleges facts which occurred while he was under the jurisdiction of the U.S. as described above.

2. Mr. Ameziane Has Met the Exhaustion of Domestic Remedies Requirement.

84. Pursuant to Article 31 of the IACHR Rules of Procedure, individual petitions are admissible only where domestic remedies have been exhausted or where such remedies are unavailable as a matter of law or fact. . . .

   . . .

5. Conclusion: Mr. Ameziane's Petition is Admissible under the Commission's Rules of Procedure.

112. Mr. Ameziane's petition plainly complies with the admissibility requirements established in the Commission's Rules of Procedure. The Commission has jurisdiction ratione personae because Mr. Ameziane is a natural person who is subject to the complete jurisdiction and control of the U.S. and whose rights have been protected under the American Declaration, since the ongoing violations alleged in the petition commenced. The Commission has ratione materiae, ratione temporis and ration loci jurisdiction because the petition alleges violations of rights protected under the American Declaration; the violations occurred subsequent to the adoption of the American Declaration, the U.S.' ratification of the OAS Charter and the creation of the Commission; and they occurred while Mr. Ameziane was under the jurisdiction of the U.S. Furthermore, one or more exceptions to the exhaustion to the domestic remedies rule applies to each of the violations alleged in the petition because judicial remedies are either unavailable by law or have been rendered ineffective by excessive delay. Finally, this petition complies with the formal requirements outlined in Article 28 of the Rules of Procedure, with the timeliness requirement, and with the prohibition on duplicate proceedings. The Commission should therefore determine Mr. Ameziane's petition to be admissible.

IV. VIOLATIONS OF THE AMERICAN DECLARATION ON THE RIGHTS AND DUTIES OF MAN

A. The U.S. has Arbitrarily Deprived Mr. Ameziane of his Liberty and Denied his Right to Prompt Judicial Review in Violation of Article XXV of the American Declaration.

113. The ongoing detention of Mr. Ameziane as an "enemy combatant" – until recently without the prospect of court review – constitutes an arbitrary deprivation of his liberty and a denial of his right to prompt judicial review of the legality of his detention in violation of Article XXV of the American Declaration. While the U.S. Supreme Court recently ruled in *Boumediene* that Guantánamo detainees have the right to habeas, as it did in 2004, the fact is that Mr. Ameziane remains imprisoned after more than six years, and a court has yet to examine the lawfulness of his detention, despite his best efforts to seek review. The violation of his right not to be arbitrarily detained and to have a court ascertain the legality of Iris detention without delay occurred years ago, and it will continue until the day that a U.S. federal court rules on his habeas petition.

Article XXV of the American Declaration provides:

No person may be deprived of his liberty except . . . according to the procedures established by pre-existing law.

. . .

Every individual who has been deprived of his liberty has the right to have the legality of his detention ascertained without delay by a court.

114. These protections, like international human rights law in general, apply in all situations, including those of armed conflict. In the latter context, however, international humanitarian law may serve as the *lex specialis* in interpreting international human rights instruments, such as the American Declaration. Under international humanitarian law, certain deprivations of liberty, which would otherwise constitute violations of international human rights law, may be justified.

115. Properly determining the legal status of Mr. Ameziane, and whether international humanitarian law is indeed the *lex specialis* in interpreting his rights or whether his rights are governed strictly by international human rights law, is of critical importance in assessing the legality of his detention, and is an obligation of the U.S. as the detaining state. This determination has been rendered impossible by the U.S. government's definition of "enemy combatant," pursuant to which Mr. Ameziane is being held at Guantánamo, and furthermore by the inadequacy of the CSRT review process. The failure of the U.S. to determine Mr. Ameziane's status and define the law pursuant to which his detention is governed has deprived him and other Guantánamo detainees of the ability to know and exercise their rights.

116. The sections that follow begin by establishing the U.S.' failure to properly determine Mr. Ameziane's status under international law, the result of which is that the exact legal framework applicable to Mr. Ameziane's deprivation of liberty remains unclear. As the subsequent sections demonstrate, however, regardless of whether Mr. Ameziane's right to personal liberty would be properly analyzed under international human rights or humanitarian law, his detention at Guantánamo Bay for more than six years without charge or a fair judicial process to challenge his detention constitutes a clear violation of his Article XXV right not to be arbitrarily detained.

1. The U.S.' Failure to Adequately Determine Mr. Ameziane's Legal Status has Frustrated the Appropriate Application of Article XXV to his Case.

117. The U.S. has an obligation to determine Guantánamo detainees' legal status. It has failed to satisfy this obligation in two ways: by applying an ambiguous definition of "enemy combatant" as the basis for holding detainees at Guantánamo, and by creating the flawed CSRTs as the only mechanism to review detainees' status.

118. Since it first adopted precautionary measures in March 2002, the Commission has insisted that the U.S. take the "urgent measures necessary to have the legal status of the detainees at Guantánamo Bay determined by a competent tribunal," expressing concern that "it remains entirely unclear from their treatment by the U.S. what minimum rights under international human rights and humanitarian law the detainees are entitled to." The Commission reiterated this request in 2003, 2004 and 2005, before calling on the U.S. to close Guantánamo in 2006. As the Commission has explained, determining detainees' status is indispensable to identifying the scope of their rights and assessing whether their rights have been respected.

119. Notwithstanding the Commission's repeated admonitions, the U.S. has failed in its obligation to determine detainees' legal status in two critical ways.

120. First, the definition of "enemy combatant" eludes a determinate status for detainees. The class of individuals whose detention the U.S. has authorized pursuant to its "war on terror" has been variously defined since 2001, but at the time of Mr. Ameziane's CSRT in 2004, Guantánamo detainees were determined to be properly held if they met the following definition:

> An "enemy combatant" . . . shall mean an individual who was part of or supporting Taliban or al Qaida forces, or associated forces that are engaged in hostilities against the U.S. or its coalition partners. This includes any person who has committed a belligerent act or has directly supported hostilities in aid of enemy armed forces.

Currently, the MCA authorizes the detention of "unlawful enemy combatants" at Guantánamo and under U.S. custody elsewhere, which are defined as:

> (i) a person who has engaged in hostilities or who has purposefully and materially supported hostilities against the U.S. or its co-belligerents who is not a lawful enemy combatant (including a person who is part of the Taliban, al Qaeda, or associated forces); or

> (ii) a person who. before, on, or after the date of the enactment of the Military Commissions Act of 2006, has been determined to be an unlawful enemy combatant by a Combatant Status Review Tribunal or another competent tribunal established under the authority of the President or the Secretary of Defense.

121. The breadth and vagueness of these definitions, which conflate different categories of individuals whose detention and rights would be governed by different regimes of international law, render it impossible to determine the specific rights of Guantánamo detainees and the obligations of the U.S. In the context of armed conflict, international humanitarian law distinguishes between, and provides different protections for, "combatants," who take direct part in the hostilities and whose rights are governed by tire Third Geneva Convention, and "non-combatants" (or civilians), who are present in die zone of conflict but do not directly participate in the hostilities and whose rights are governed by the Fourth Geneva Convention. The Geneva Conventions further distinguish between lawful (or privileged) and unlawful (or unprivileged) combatants, the former of which are entitled to prisoner-of-war (POW) status.

. . .

2. Ensure that Mr. Ameziane's conditions of confinement comply with international standards for the treatment of prisoners for the remainder of his detention at Guantánamo, namely: prohibit his detention in conditions of isolation; ensure that his cell meets minimum requirements for floor space, lighting, ventilation and temperature, and has windows affording natural light and air, and ensure that he is permitted adequate daily exercise in open air;

3. Prohibit all corporal punishment and punishment that may be prejudicial to Mr. Ameziane's physical or mental health, and prohibit the use of chains and irons as restraints;

4. Take immediate measures to provide Mr. Ameziane with prompt and effective treatment for his physical and psychological health, and ensure that such care is not made contingent on his cooperation with interrogators or any other condition;

5. Ensure that Mr. Ameziane is able to satisfy the needs of his religious life without interference, including group prayer with other prisoners;

6. Enable Mr. Ameziane to communicate regularly with his family through correspondence and visits.

II. CONCLUSION AND PRAYER FOR RELIEF

232. For the aforementioned reasons, Petitioners respectfully request that the Honorable Commission:

1. With regard to Mr. Ameziane's request for precautionary measures:

    a. Urgently issue the necessary and appropriate precautionary measures to prevent further irreparable harm to Mr. Ameziane's fundamental rights, in accordance with Sections VI.B.3 and VI.C.2:

2. With regard to Mr. Ameziane's individual petition against the U.S.:

a. Consider the admissibility and merits of this petition simultaneously, in accordance with Article 37(4) of the Commission's Rules of Procedure, given the serious and urgent nature of the case and the ongoing violations of Mr. Ameziane's fundamental rights;

b. Declare the petition admissible and find that the U.S. has violated Mr. Ameziane's rights enshrined in Articles I, III, V, VI, XI, XVIII, XXV, and XXVI of the American Declaration of the Rights and Duties of Man; and

c. Order the U.S. to provide prompt and adequate reparations for the violations suffered by Mr. Ameziane.

The Petitioners thank the Commission for its careful attention to this pressing matter.

Dated: August 6, 2008 Respectfully submitted,

Pardiss Kebriaei
Shayana Kadidal
CENTER FOR CONSTITUTIONAL RIGHTS
666 Broadway, 7th Floor
New York, NY 10012
(Tel) 212-614-6452
(Fax) 212-614-6499

Viviana Krsticevic
Ariela Peralta
Francisco Quintana
Michael Camileri
CENTER FOR JUSTICE AND
INTERNATIONAL LAW (CEJIL)
1630 Connecticut Ave, NW, Suite 401
Washington, D.C. 20009
(Tel) 202-319-3000
(Fax) 202-319-3019

15. *Cherokee Nation v U.S.* Inter-American Commission on Human Rights, Organization of American States (Excerpted)

Cite as: Case 11.071 Report no. 6/97 U.S.* March 12, 1997

Cherokee Nation v U.S.

Decision On Admissibility

I. Allegations in Petition

1. The following allegations of facts which form the basis of the petition, are referred to in several communications submitted to the Inter-American Commission on Human Rights ("the Commission"), June 18, 1992, August 24, 1992, and October 30, 1992. On June 18, 1992, the Commission received a communication from the Petitioner alleging violations of the human rights of the Cherokee Nation by the U.S. These allegations were later reiterated in a petition, which was received by the Commission, on August 24, 1992, and which was filed on behalf of the Cherokee Nation west of the Mississippi River. On October 30, 1992, the Commission received additional information from the petitioner which is included in the allegations found in the petition.

2. The Petitioner alleged that a claim was filed on behalf of the entire Cherokee Nation, west of the Mississippi River against the U.S. for its attempt to deny their rights as Indians in their ancestors' homelands. The claim arose out of a lawsuit in which the government sued the Cherokee Nation in the Indian Claims Commission, to quiet the Cherokee Nation's title in their former homelands. It is alleged that the government told the Cherokee Nation that their homelands consisted of one million acres, and that it would pay them $1.00 per acre for a one million acre claim when, in fact, the area was in excess of a million acres, and most of the land had a value of over $100.00 an acre. In the lawsuit settlement, the government said that their agreement would be withdrawn if any other Indians objected. The date of the letter containing the lawsuit settlement agreement between the U.S. and the Eastern Band of Cherokees, was "June 15, 1972." This letter was composed by Kent Frizzell and addressed to Paul M. Niebell. This letter can be found in the Indian Claims Commission Decisions, which is available at the Library of Congress, Volume 28, page 391.

3. The Petitioner also alleged, that this agreement was with the Eastern Band, however, it constituted an acknowledgement of liability to the Cherokee Nation, for half of the Western Band. It is also alleged that according to the Bureau of Indian Affairs, the Eastern Band was that portion of the Cherokee Nation that refused to forfeit their lands in the eastern half of the U.S., and the Western Band, complied with the demands of the U.S. Government, which were often made at gunpoint. Furthermore, it is alleged that all of the Indian Nations recognized that the exclusive negotiating authority rested within the Federal Government, and not with the States because of this published rule of law in the U.S. It is also alleged that "when and if the Western Band reaches a settlement with the U.S. Government, it will be treated as if it had been with each state wherein they currently reside, the major state being Oklahoma."

4. The Petitioner further alleged, that the western Cherokees attempted to object with no effect, and the petitioner was compelled to file a lawsuit against the U.S. over their objection, in Creek County in northeast Oklahoma. The Government chose not to appear in the case nor to defend it. It is also alleged that the petitioner sought and was granted a Default Judgment on September 11, 1991, by Judge Thompson, to protect the Cherokee Nation from the wrongs which had been committed against them. The petitioner further alleged that the judgment was a valid judgment which set aside the Indian claims case which was brought by the U.S. It further alleged that there is a global due process rule which requires a state judge to relinquish jurisdiction over a case after thirty days, and this rule was published in the case of McNac. v Kinch.[1]

5. Moreover, the Petitioner alleged, that the U.S. Government conspired with the Bank of Oklahoma's attorney, Christopher L. Coyle, to deny the petitioner due process of law, and that on the 15th day of May, 1992, Judge Thompson of the District Court continued to deny the petitioner due process of law when he vacated the previous valid Default Judgment and stated that his justification for doing so, was defective service. It is also alleged that the requirement of service of process on the U.S. was waived when it made a General Appearance in the Court in Oklahoma to set aside the Default Judgment. This rule of law which

cured any defect in service was published by Mr. Justice Brandeis in Richardson Machinery Co. v Scott.[2] It is alleged that the rule stated that "failure to follow this rule by Oklahoma would constitute a denial of the Cherokee Nation's right to due process of law."

6. Furthermore, the Petitioner alleged, that the Cherokee Nation west of the Mississippi River was denied due process in the State Court of Oklahoma, in Creek County, and was discriminated against by the Court because of their Indian Nationality. The petitioner alleged violations of Article II (discrimination against the Indians), Article XXVI, paragraph 1, and Article XVIII, of the American Declaration of the Rights and Duties of Man. The petitioner claimed that for five years it has provided legal services and financial resources in the amount of $50,000 in pursuing this claim on behalf of the Cherokee Nation, while the Government has paid the attorney for the eastern Cherokees $100,000.00 to obtain this fraudulent settlement. The petitioner claimed that it is unable to exhaust further remedies in the U.S. courts, because it has exhausted its resources to the extent that it has lost home, cars, and its spouse, and cannot give any more, and nothing more should be expected of it. Moreover, the petitioner alleged that, in the interim, the Government has filed several dilatory pleadings in the Creek County Court in pursuing its tactics. During this period, two-tenths of the organizers of the Thrift Coop have died.

II. Articles of the American Declaration Allegedly Violated

7. The Petitioner alleged violations of Article II (right to equality before the law), XXVI, paragraph 1 (right to due process of law), and Article XVIII (right to a fair trial).

III. Petitioner Requests That:

8. The Commission uses its office to obtain a friendly settlement in this matter. The Petitioner offers to accept $100,000,000, which it alleged is substantially less than the amount dictated by the U.S. Government in the Court of Claims suit which attempted to settle this matter.

IV. Proceedings Before the Commission

A. Receipt of Documentary Materials

9. Upon receipt of the petition dated August 24, 1992, additional information, and up to the presentment of the petition, the Commission has complied with the procedural requirements of its Regulations. It has studied, examined, and considered all information submitted by the parties.

10. During this period it communicated with the Petitioner and the U.S. Government by notes. It sent the pertinent parts of the petition on October 19, 1992, and additional information to the U.S. Government with requests that it supply information which it deemed appropriate to the allegations referred to in the petition, and additional information, and which addressed the issue of exhaustion of domestic legal remedies. The Commission qualified these requests by stating that "the request for information did not constitute a decision as to the admissibility of the communication."

. . . .

20. The U.S. also argued that, the policies and practices of the U.S. Government which form the basis of the Petitioner's complaint before the Commission were initially the subject of litigation in domestic courts in the U.S. in the case of First American Thrift Coop. Assn. v Commissioner of Indian Affairs. The Default Judgment in this case, which was in favor of the Petitioner was vacated, without prejudice, in later judicial proceedings. First American Thrift could have filed a timely appeal of the order vacating the earlier default judgment, but failed to do so. The Petitioner should be barred from alleging that such a remedy has been exhausted when the Petitioner has failed to invoke his right to pursue a domestic remedy at the time when it was available. Most importantly, the Petitioner continues to have the right to pursue his initial claim in the Oklahoma District Court. First American Thrift Cooperative Association has not been deprived of a forum to examine the merits of its claims. It simply is required to follow the rules of service and notice of the forum which it has selected.

21. Moreover, the U.S. argued that the Petitioner should not be allowed to avoid the exhaustion of domestic remedies required by Article 37(2) of this Commission's Regulations. First, domestic law in the U.S. clearly provided due process of law for protection of the rights claimed by the petitioner. A mechanism through which to seek compensation for a wrongful taking of the kind alleged by the Petitioner, is available. The availability of this remedy is vividly illustrated by the earlier Default Judgment in favor of the Petitioner. Second the Petitioner has not been denied access to domestic remedies or prevented from exhausting them. The Petitioner could have filed a timely appeal of the decision to vacate the Default Judgment, but failed to do so. In addition, the order vacating the Default Judgment has not prejudiced the petitioner from once again filing suit in either state or federal court. Finally, there has been no unwarranted delay in rendering final

judgment under the aforementioned remedies. The only delay in the adjudication of the Petitioner's claims is the result of the Petitioner's failure to pursue available remedies.

22. Finally, the U.S. argued that, since the Petitioner's claim has not been fully adjudicated in the domestic courts of the U.S., and because the Petitioner continues to possess a judicial remedy in the wake of the District Court's decision to vacate the earlier default judgment, clearly the Petitioner has failed to exhaust judicial remedies available in this country. Therefore, the Petitioner fails to satisfy the exhaustion requirement of Article 37, and the U.S. respectfully requests the Commission to declare the petition inadmissible, in accordance with Article 41(a). The U.S. stated that, because it believes that the complaint is inadmissible, it did not address in detail the interpretations of law and factual assertions presented in the petition.

C. The Petitioner's Response to the Government's Reply to Petition

23. The Petitioner responded to the Government's Reply to the petition in three communications dated April 14, April 21, and May 10, 1993, and argued that the U.S. Government has claimed lack of service as an excuse for denying the Cherokee Nation a day in court. The Default Judgment reflected a finding that the defendant (U.S.) had been properly served, the Motion to Vacate the Judgment was filed by the U.S. on March 16, 1992, which was 187 days after the Judgment. In every legal system in America, judgment becomes final and non-attackable in 30 days. Furthermore, the enclosed court minute reveals, that the appearance was general, and both of these general appearances obviated service or cured any service defects. Therefore, the U.S. cannot be heard on the quest of whether a sheriff of Creek County, Oklahoma, appeared and personally served the U.S. Government.

24. The Petitioner also argued that, on the question of exhausting judicial remedies, the U.S. will have to be more specific as to which remedies it refers to, and whether it will guarantee the rights to pursue said remedies and cease its harassment of the American Indians in the pursuit of their remedies. The U.S. has for the first time interposed a supposed substantive defense to the claims of the Western Cherokees, that they have been paid by the offer of the Oklahoma Territories. The U.S. has admitted that the Western Cherokees never accepted this offer for removal, and it further admitted that these agreements were broken. The said admissions can be found in the excellent Government document entitled "Federal Indian Law."[5]

25. Furthermore, the Petitioner argued that the U.S. has stated that it has paid the Eastern Cherokees, and the Western Cherokees and has not denied the possibility that, the Eastern Cherokees have been paid for the residual. All of the foregoing representations were resolved in a judgment of the Court of Creek County, Oklahoma, which the U.S. Government submitted to, by the General Appearance of Mr. Pinnell, U.S. Assistant District Attorney. It is interesting to note that the U.S. Government stated that it has never revealed a delay of several terms of Court before it appeared and destroyed the human rights vested in the Indians, of their right to a day in Court, when it enforced the said final judgment.

26. The Petitioner further argued that, if the U.S. Government was giving additional remedies in the judicial process, and, which it specifically enumerated the said rights, it would be necessary for the U.S. Government to provide immediate funds for the Petitioner to exercise these rights, because all of its resources have been depleted. The compensation requested would be one-half of the funds which the U.S. gave Mr. Nibell for his expenses in representing the Eastern Cherokees. The Petitioner further stated that "it offers to accept, $100,000,000 as a friendly settlement in this matter." The Petitioner also stated that it hoped that the U.S. Government would see that this amount was substantially less than the amount dictated by the U.S. Government in the Court of Claims suit which attempted to settle this matter. The Petitioner stated that the said amount of $1.00 per acre for land which was worth $10.00 per acre, of which the aggregate amount of acres were well in excess of 1,000,000,000 acres.

27. Moreover, the Petitioner stated that, insofar as the question of its authority to represent the Cherokees, the Government has cited 25 USCS Section 81. The Petitioner argued that the said Statute provided an exception which constituted sufficient compliance with the section. Petitioner also argued that, it agreed to comply with the compensation stated, and that it was not necessary to show that a contract was required because it would show by separate cover that it was an heir of an enrolled Cherokee named L.B. Butler with roll No. 13690.

. . .

V. Commission's Decision on Admissibility
A. Issues Raised as to Admissibility of Petition

33. The contested issues raised by the parties on admissibility of the petition are the following:

(a) Has the Petitioner invoked and exhausted domestic remedies?

(b) Does the claim of indigence by the Petitioner excuse it from invoking and exhausting available domestic remedies?

B. Analysis

34. The Commission has reviewed, studied, and considered the record, including arguments, and exhibits submitted by the parties in this case in accordance with its regulations. It has determined that this petition "is not pending settlement in another procedure under an international governmental organization of which the State concerned is a member, and it does not essentially duplicate a pending petition or already examined and settled by the Commission or by another international governmental organization of which the state concerned is a member."[6] The Commission now examines below whether the Petitioner has invoked and exhausted domestic remedies pursuant to Article 37 of the Commission's Regulations, and/or is excused from so doing because of a claim of indigence.

(a) Have Domestic Remedies been Invoked and Exhausted

35. Article 37 of the Commission's Regulations provides:

1. For a petition to be admitted by the Commission, the remedies under domestic jurisdiction must have been invoked and exhausted in accordance with the general principles of international law.

1. The provisions of the preceding paragraph shall not be applicable when:

a. the domestic legislation of the State concerned does not afford due process of law for protection of the right or rights that have allegedly been violated;

b. the party alleging violation of his rights has been denied access to the remedies under domestic law or has been prevented from exhausting them;

c. there has been unwarranted delay in rendering a final judgment under the aforementioned remedies.

. . .

3. When the petitioner contends that he is unable to prove exhaustion as indicated in this Article, it shall be up to the government against which this petition has been lodged to demonstrate to the Commission that the remedies under domestic law have not previously been exhausted, unless it is clearly evident from the background information contained in the petition.

36. Upon reviewing the record, the Commission notes that the Petitioner has alleged that a valid Default Judgment was obtained on behalf of the Cherokee Nation west of the Mississippi River on September 11, 1991, in the State Court of Oklahoma, against the U.S. who failed to appear at the hearing. The Petitioner also alleged that the U.S. was properly served in accordance with the State laws. Petitioner submitted several exhibits to the Commission, including a copy of a Court Order dated August 21, 1991, signed by the District Judge of the District Court of Creek County, in the State of Oklahoma, entitled "Order—Setting Hearing Date on Application For Preliminary (Temporary) Restraining Order—Directing Clerk To Issue Notice." The Order stated that "the verified petition and motions were set down for hearing at the Courthouse at Sapulpa, Oklahoma, Creek County, State of Oklahoma, in accordance with this order, on September 11, 1991, at 9.30 a.m., and the Clerk shall also mail or cause to be mailed to the Defendant a Certified copy of this order by U.S. Mail (registered or certified) with return receipt requested. Address to be supplied by Plaintiff."

37. The Court Order stated that "Copies of this Order to be sent to Mr. James Fisk, Attorney, and the Commissioner of Indian Affairs." The record before the Commission also included a document entitled "Certificate of Service," dated September 3rd, 1991, which stated the following: "I, Pat Hobbs, Court Clerk of Creek County, Oklahoma, certify that a true, correct and exact copy of the foregoing Order Setting Hearing was by me duly enclosed in an envelope addressed to the above named defendant__, with postage thereon prepaid, and the same mailed to said defendant__, or service agent of said defendant, by certified mail with a request for a return receipt from addressee only on the 21 day of August, 1991, (and that attached hereto is the certified mail receipt), and the return receipt card with the date of receipt of said return card by the Court Clerk endorsed hereon." The exhibit was signed by the Deputy. The exhibit also had attached to it a copy of a document entitled "Attached Return Receipt Card Received This 3rd day of Sept. 1991." The Article No. is P778–588–964. In the Address section of the Return Receipt, stated that "Article Addressed to David Matheson, Department of Interior, Washington, D.C., 240," and was delivered on 8/27/91.

38. The record before the Commission reflects that the U.S. appeared before the Oklahoma Court and had the Default Judgment set aside on May 11, 1992, and a "Motion To Reconsider" the Court's decision was filed by the plaintiff before the Court on April 9, 1992, in which it was argued that the Court should apply the 30 day Rule, and that the U.S. had made a "general appearance" before the court when it appeared, which waived and cured any jurisdictional defects, and that failure to apply the 30 day rule was a denial of due process. The Court did not reinstate its Default Judgment of September 1991.

39. The Commission also notes the U.S.' argument which has merit, that the Petitioner has not invoked and exhausted the available domestic remedies in the U.S., that these remedies were still available to the Petitioner, and therefore, the Commission should find the petition inadmissible pursuant to Article 37 of the Commission's Regulations. In the case of Velásquez Rodriguez, the Inter-American Court of Human Rights, in construing the exceptions to the exhaustion of domestic remedies as provided by Article 46 of the American Convention, stated that: "the State claiming non-exhaustion has an obligation to prove that domestic remedies remain to be exhausted and that they are effective."[7]

40. In the Inter-American Court's later decision, it stated that: "The Court now affirms that if a State which alleges non-exhaustion proves the existence of specific domestic remedies that should have been utilized, the opposing party has the burden of showing that those remedies were exhausted or that the case comes within the exceptions of Article 46(2). It must not be rashly presumed that a State party to the Convention has failed to comply with its obligation to provide effective domestic remedies."[8] The Inter-American Court of Human Rights further stated that: "The rule of prior exhaustion of domestic remedies allows the state to resolve the problem under its internal law before being confronted with an international proceeding. This is particularly true in the international jurisdiction of human rights, because the latter reinforces or complements the domestic jurisdiction."[9]

41. The Commission finds that Article 37 of its Regulations is the controlling instrument in deciding the issue of admissibility and its provisions are applicable. The Petitioner has not met its burden of sufficiently demonstrating that the Courts of the U.S. do not afford due process of law for protection of its rights. There are still available, domestic remedies in the U.S. to be invoked and exhausted. The decision of a single judge granting a Default Judgment on a procedural issue in the Petitioner's favor, and who later vacated the Default Judgment at the request of the U.S. based on legal rules, does not in itself negate the fact that these remedies are still available to be pursued and exhausted. The Petitioner has not demonstrated that he has been denied access to the remedies under domestic law, or he has been prevented by the U.S. from exhausting them. Furthermore, he has not demonstrated that there has been unwarranted delay in rendering a final judgment under the domestic remedies. According to the record before the Commission, the U.S. courts have not rendered a final decision on the merits, and the U.S. has argued that the Petitioner still has this option.

42. The Commission notes that the Petitioner has also argued that it was unable to pursue, and exhaust the available domestic remedies because it is indigent. Furthermore, it has pursued this claim for the past five years, its legal and financial resources are depleted, and have expended $50,000 in pursuing the said claim, and in the interim the Government has filed several dilatory pleadings in the Creek County Court in Oklahoma in pursuing its tactics.

43. The question therefore, is, should the Petitioner be excused from invoking and exhausting the available domestic remedies because of indigence. The Inter-American Court of Human Rights considered the question of "indigence" in an Advisory Opinion requested by the Commission.[10] The Court construed Article 46 of the American Convention which applies to States Parties, which is similar to Article 37 of the Commission's Regulations. The Court stated that:

"The Commission states that it has received certain petitions in which the victim alleges that he has not been able to comply with the requirement of the exhaustion of remedies set forth in the domestic legislation because he cannot afford legal representation or, in some cases, the obligatory filing fees. Upon applying the foregoing analysis to the examples set forth by the Commission, it must be concluded that if legal services are required either as a matter of law or fact in order for a right guaranteed by the Convention to be recognized and a person is unable to obtain such services because of his indigence, that person would be exempted from the requirement to exhaust domestic remedies. The same would be true of cases requiring the payment of a filing fee. That is to say, if it is impossible for an indigent to deposit such a fee, he cannot be required to exhaust domestic remedies unless the state provides some alternative mechanism."

44. The Court finally concluded by stating that "Once a State Party has shown the existence of domestic remedies for the enforcement of a particular right guaranteed by the Convention, the burden of proof shifts to the complainant, who must then demonstrate that the exceptions provided for in Article 46(2) are applicable, whether as a result of indigence. . . . "[11]

45. The Commission notes that the Petitioner has alleged that it is indigent and has expended $50,000 in pursuing the claim on behalf of the Cherokee Nation; however, the record before the Commission is insufficient to establish that "indigence" prevented the Petitioner from invoking and exhausting domestic remedies in the U.S. Courts pursuant to Article 37 of the Commission's Regulations. Allegations of indigence are insufficient without other evidence produced by the Petitioner to prove that he was prevented from invoking and exhausting the domestic remedies of the U.S.

46. Conclusion: The Commission concludes that this petition is inadmissible for failure to invoke and exhaust domestic remedies in the U.S.

Based on the Foregoing Reasons, the Inter-American Commission on Human Rights Concludes That:

47. This petition is inadmissible pursuant to Article 37 of the Commission's Regulations.

48. This case be closed.

49. This Report will be transmitted to the parties.

50. This Report will be published in the Commission's Annual Report to the General Assembly.

Notes

*Commissioners Dean Claudio Grossman and Prof. Robert Goldman took no part in the proceedings, in accordance to Article 19.2 of the Commission's Regulations. Dean Grossman is a U.S. resident, and Professor Goldman is a U.S. national.

. . . .

16. *Haitian Centre for Human Rights et al. v U.S.*, Inter-American Commission on Human Rights (Excerpted)
Cite as: Case 10.675, Report No. 51/96, Decision of the Commission as to the Merits of Case 10.675, March 13, 1997

Inter-Am.C.H.R., OEA/Ser.L/V/II.95 Doc. 7 rev. at 550 (1997). U.S.
10.675, Report No. 51/96,
Inter-Am.C.H.R., OEA/Ser.L/V/II.95 Doc. 7 rev. at 550 (1997). Report N Ba 51/96

Decision of the Commission as to the Merits of Case 10.675
U.S.
March 13, 1997
I. Summary of Allegations:

1. On October 1, 1990, the Commission received a petition submitted on behalf of the following petitioners:

a. The Haitian Centre for Human Rights, Port-au-Prince, Haiti.

b. Centre Karl Leveque, Port-au-Prince, Haiti.

(and others)

2. The petition alleged that Haitian boat people have been and continue to be interdicted and returned to Haiti pursuant to:

(a) the Haitian Migrant Interdiction Program established by Proclamation 4865 and Executive Order 12324 issued by then President Ronald Reagan on September 29, 1981, and (b) a cooperative agreement between the U.S. Administration and the Duvalier regime entered on September 23, 1981, through an exchange of diplomatic notes.

3. The petition further alleged that many of these boat people had a reasonable fear that they would be persecuted if returned to Haiti, but were denied a proper forum and processing procedures for resolution of their claims. This denial was in violation of the U.S. Government's obligation not to return a refugee in any manner whatsoever to the frontiers of a territory where his or her life or freedom would be threatened on account of race, religion, nationality, membership in a particular social group, or political opinion.

Despite promises made by the Haitian Government (in diplomatic exchange of letters) that returnees would not be punished for leaving Haiti, boat people involuntarily interdicted and returned by the U.S. Government have been routinely detained upon their return to Haiti.

4. On May 7, 8, and 13, 1990, forty-three (43) returnees, including some Haitians who had been detained in Immigration and Naturalization Service's (INS) Krome Detention Center in Miami, Florida, were immediately arrested by Haitian military authorities upon their arrival in Port-au-Prince. They were held in the National Penitentiary, some for longer than one week, before being released. On June 5th, 1990, another group of thirty-one (31) Haitians deported from Krome were arrested upon arrival in Haiti and they alleged, that they were told that their whereabouts would thereafter be closely monitored by the Government. Military authorities stated that at least 16 of the group were boat people. The petitioners alleged that they were informed and believed that boat people who departed in whole or in part because their lives or freedom were threatened almost always faced an even greater threat following their interdiction and forcible return to the military authorities in Haiti.

5. An affidavit of a dissident involved in organizing demonstrations against the military regime in Haiti stated that in 1987, after he decided it was too dangerous to remain in Haiti, he fled but was interdicted and returned to Haiti by the Coast Guard. He declares that: "The immigration inspector who interviewed me declared that since there was a new government, they will return me to Haiti. They refused to admit that I had good reasons to leave Haiti and that death threats were still hanging on my head . . . Since my return to Haiti I have been forced to move from house to house, never sleeping in the same place in order to ensure that the Army never learns of my whereabouts and arrests me." Since the inception of the program over 361 boats carrying 21,461 Haitians have been intercepted, and only six Haitians have been allowed to come to the U.S. to file asylum claims.

. . . .

8. According to information provided to the petitioners' counsel in a telephone conversation with an Immigration and Naturalization Service (INS) Press Officer on February 5th, 1992, the INS estimated that "since November of 1991, 15,081 Haitians had been interdicted." Historically only 1.8% of those Haitians permitted to present asylum claims, would actually be given asylum. (See Refugee Reports, Vol. XII, No. 12, Dec. 30, 1991 at 12.) Given the ongoing violence in Haiti, the inability of the interdiction program to fairly identify those with legitimate claims of asylum, and the inability of the U.S. Government to meaningfully ensure that the Haitians returned would not be harmed, the Haitian Interdiction Program represented a serious violation of several provisions of international law. (Articles allegedly violated are listed in part II of this report.)

. . . .

10. Later many of the repatriated interdictees were arrested at home. Some never made it home and were arrested at pre-established roadblocks. Several of those arrested were later found shot to death. Some were beaten in public by the military, which forced people, at gunpoint, to identify the repatriated Haitians. Others were taken to the National Penitentiary where they were beaten daily and not fed, and some were tortured to death in prison. Detainees were told by at least one prison guard that they were being tortured for having fled Haiti, and that others would suffer the same fate. Others were informed that a local judge had issued arrest warrants for repatriated interdictees because they had left Haiti and criticized the military Government.

II. In This Connection the Petitioners Allege Violations of:

a. Articles I, II, XVII, XVIII, XXIV, XXVII, of the American Declaration of the Rights and Duties of Man (American Declaration).

b. Articles 22(2)(7)(8), 24 and 25 of the American Convention on Human Rights (American Convention) as supplemented by Article 18 of the Vienna Convention on the Law of Treaties.

c. Articles 55 and 56 of the United Nations Charter (U.N. Charter).

d. Articles 3, 16(1) and 33 of the United Nations Convention Relating to the Status of Refugees, July 28, 1951, 189 U.N.T.S. 150 (U.N. Refugee Convention).

e. The United Nations Protocol Relating to the Status of Refugees (U.N. Refugee Protocol), opened for signature January 31, 1967, entered into force for the U.S. November 1, 1968, 19 U.N.T.S. 6224, T.A.I.S. No. 6577.

f. Articles 8, 13(2) and 14 of the United Nations' Universal Declaration of Human Rights (Universal Declaration).

g. Customary international law which enjoins the U.S. from preventing the departure of people from their countries, or returning refugees to persecution or danger to life or freedom, and guaranteeing the right to an effective remedy.

III. The Petitioners Request:

11. During the pendency of this petition the petitioners made several requests to the Commission. Included in these requests were inter alia, that the Commission should resolve:

a. To seek immediate, interim relief from the U.S. Government in the form of temporary suspension of the Haitian Migrant Interdiction program, and the deportation of interdicted Haitians to Haiti until the restoration of lawful order in Haiti, and the subsiding of the grave personal danger that now faces Haitians from random and state-sponsored violence ("Migrant Program").

b. To declare that the Migrant Program constitutes a serious violation of internationally protected human rights, including Articles XXVII (the right to asylum), XXIV (the right to petition), and XVIII (the right to effective remedy) of the American Declaration of the Rights and Duties of Man.

c. In the alternative, if such relief is denied, to insist that the U.S. Government implement policies and procedures which ensure that the program will provide access and equal protection of the laws in the presentation and consideration of their claim to persecution and requests for asylum, and to have such claims reviewed and decided in a competent, objective and non-discriminatory manner, and to receive explanations of the basis for the decisions in their case.

d. To conduct, as soon as possible, a fact-finding visit to Haiti to evaluate the level of political violence taking place there and the ability of third-party countries to ensure the safety of Haitians forcibly repatriated.

e. To permit legal counsel to consult with the interdictees in the preparation of their requests for political asylum.

f. To reach a final decision on the merits of this case at its 87th period of Sessions in September of this year.

IV. Proceedings Before the Commission

12. Upon receipt of the petition of October 3rd, 1990, the Commission complied with all the procedural requirements of its Regulations. It communicated with the petitioners and the U.S. Government; it sent several notes to them; it studied, considered and examined all information submitted by the parties.

13. Included in the notes sent to the U.S. Government was a telex dated October 4th, 1991, addressed to then U.S. Secretary of State James A. Baker III, during its 80th period of Sessions, which stated that: "It has decided pursuant to paragraph 4 of Resolution 1/91 of the Ad Hoc Meeting of Ministers of Foreign Affairs, entitled 'Support to the Democratic Government of Haiti,' to request that the U.S. Government suspend its policy of interdiction of Haitian nationals who are attempting to seek asylum in the U.S. and are being sent back to Haiti, because of the danger to their lives, until the situation in Haiti has been normalized."

14. On February 6th, 1992, the Commission sent a note (included in the several notes mentioned above) signed by the Chairman of the Commission to then Secretary of State James A. Baker III stating that: "The Inter-American Commission on Human Rights notes that the return of the Haitians from the U.S. recommended on February 3, 1992 and that the implementation of the present policy will result in the transfer of some 12,000 Haitians. Given the uncertain situation in Haiti, the Members of the Commission unanimously and respectfully request the U.S. Government to suspend, for humanitarian reasons, the return of Haitians."

15. On February 26th, 1993, at a hearing held before the Commission, the petitioners argued that the petition was admissible; they requested precautionary measures; presented documentary evidence as to the health conditions of those interdictees held at Guantánamo Bay and presented three witnesses who testified before the Commission. The first witness testified as to the violence and persecution he faced before leaving Haiti to emigrate to the U.S. He also gave detailed testimony as to brutality he was subjected to by the Haitian police/military after he was interdicted and returned to Haiti. He further testified that after leaving Haiti for the second time, upon arrival in the U.S. and upon being given a reasonable opportunity to present his claim to Immigration Authorities, he acquired refugee status in the U.S. The second witness testified as to why "in country processing" was not working in Haiti. The third witness leader of a recent Congressional Delegation mission to Haiti testified briefly of his most recent visit to Haiti and strongly requested that the Commission apply the human rights principles enunciated in the American Declaration of Human Rights in the resolution of this petition.

16. On March 5th, 1993, attorneys for the U.S. Government appeared before the Commission and submitted arguments requesting that the Commission find the petitioners' claim inadmissible. They submitted

various documents and exhibits which supported the Government's policy with regard to the Interdiction Program; press releases containing the efforts made by the Government to expedite the processing of "in country refugee claims" in Haiti, the restoration of constitutional government and the return of President Aristide to Haiti, and two declarations. One declaration was made by Bernard W. Aronson, the former Assistant Secretary of State for Inter-American Affairs which supported the Interdiction Program, and the other declaration was made by Dudley G. Sipprelle, Consul General at the U.S. Embassy in Port-au-Prince, Haiti, who declared that it was determined after investigation that an interdictee who was returned to Haiti had not been persecuted upon her return.

. . . .

29. In each of the most recent repatriations, people had been arrested and imprisoned for up to two weeks. On December 7, ten out of 28 repatriates were arrested. They were only released at the end of the month. On December 10, six out of every 84 repatriates were arrested. Most recently, seven out of 53 were arrested on February 4, and they were still in prison.

. . .

35. With regard to the U.S. in-country processing of refugees (ICP), the refugees who wished to apply to the program had to go through the same channels as everyone else. Returnees were given questionnaires on the boat. Most people did not know the destination of the questionnaires, and who might read them. Therefore, they were reluctant to put information on the questionnaires which might endanger them. People who wanted to apply to ICP had to go to specific addresses that were well known to all. They waited in line outside the building. Everyone knew the reason why they were there. Therefore, soldiers were able to easily identify them.

. . .

39. On April 12, 1994, the petitioners sent a letter to the Commission in which, inter alia, they referred the Commission to two recent articles, both of which they stated established the urgency of the need for a final resolution in this case. That on Saturday, April 2, 1994, the New York Times published an article entitled, "A Rising Tide of Political Terror Leaves Hundreds Dead in Haiti," by Howard W. French. The Article stated in part "PORT-AU-PRINCE, Haiti, March 31, Hundreds of supporters of the Rev. Jean Bertrand Aristide and other civilians have been killed in Haiti in recent months in the bloodiest wave of political terror since the army overthrew Father Aristide as President two and a half years ago. The violence accelerated this year, with 50 or more bodies turning up in the streets of this town each month. Many were badly mutilated or bore clear signs of torture. Diplomats there said the campaign, aimed at wiping out resistance to army rule, has relied on other techniques novel to Haiti, like burning down entire neighborhoods to flush out suspects and raping and kidnapping the wives and children of political organizers who are sought by the authorities."

40. The article further stated that, "In recent months, each time the U.S. Coast Guard has returned fleeing boat people to Haiti, plainclothes agents have pulled returnees out of Red Cross processing lines and have taken them away to be arrested. The disfigured body of one returnee, Yvon Desanges, was recently found near the airport, his eyes plucked out, a rope around his neck, his hands tied and a red handkerchief crudely marked 'President of the Red Army'."

. . .

46. On May 4, 1994, the U.S. Government replied to the merits of the petition. In summary it stated that: "It is of the view that the petition fails to establish any violation of the American Declaration. Furthermore, the U.S. believes that the interdiction program is a sound approach to the illegal migration of Haitians by sea. The policy of the U.S. is a lawful and humane response to illegal migration and the potential tragedy of Haitians risking their lives at sea. The U.S. believes that the policy of in-country refugee processing of individuals claiming refugee status coupled with direct repatriation of those Haitians who risk their lives at sea constitutes the best balance between enforcing U.S. immigration law, providing refuge to those who qualify for it under international standards and preventing loss of life on the high seas. Consequently, it respectfully requests the Commission to declare that this petition fails to establish any violation of the American Declaration."

. . .

V. Submissions of the Parties

50. The U.S. Government submitted several responses to the petitioners' arguments, including arguments as to the inadmissibility of the petition.

In addition it submitted a detailed Response on the merits of the petition and argued the following points:

Response of the U.S. to the Merits of the Petition

51. The U.S. submits that this program is consistent with the human rights standards of the American Declaration of the Rights and Duties of Man and is a proper exercise of the U.S.' sovereign right to prevent illegal immigration to the U.S.

Since no other country in the region has been willing to accept significant numbers of Haitians departing by sea, the only relevant options are return or admission to the U.S. There is no legal duty, however, on the U.S. or any other nation to accept fleeing Haitians, including those with legitimate refugee claims. In light of the firm belief that bringing all interdicted Haitians to the U.S. would likely precipitate a massive and danger-ous outflow, the U.S. has chosen to return Haitians to Haiti. Nonetheless, the U.S. has undertaken extensive efforts to afford Haitian nationals the opportunity to pursue refugee claims in a safe alternative to boat depar-tures, through the in-country refugee processing program.

52. The issue for consideration here is not whether there are human rights abuses occurring in Haiti. By all accounts, Haiti is suffering serious human rights violations under the military dictatorship, which began with the coup d'etat of September 30, 1991, overthrowing the democratically-elected government of Jean-Bertrand Aristide.

Rather, the issue for consideration here is whether the action of the U.S. in interdicting Haitian nation-als on the high seas and repatriating them to Haiti violates Articles I (the right to life, liberty and personal security), II (the right to equality before the law), XVII (the right to recognition of juridical personality and civil rights), XVIII (the right to an effective remedy), XXIV (the right to petition), or XXVII (the right to asylum) of the American Declaration of the Rights and Duties of Man.

53. The action of the U.S. is both consistent with these provisions of the American Declaration and constitutes a sound approach to the illegal migration of Haitians by sea. The policy of the U.S. is a lawful and humane means of controlling illegal immigration by sea, a phenomenon which is exacerbated by the fact that the voyage is undertaken at great risk to life.

54. The U.S. objects, in the strongest possible terms, to the petitioners' suggestion that the interdiction of Haitians by the U.S. has put their lives in additional jeopardy. But for the efforts of the U.S. Coast Guard, countless more Haitians would have lost their lives at sea. . . . .

55. The specific gravamen of petitioners' complaint is that many of the interdicted Haitians had a reasonable fear that they would be persecuted if returned to Haiti but were denied a proper forum and pro-cessing procedures for resolution of these claims, in violation of the Government's obligations with respect to refugees. Initially, the petitioners' claims asserted an inadequacy of the screening procedures employed by the Government of the U.S. Now, presumably, petitioners' claims rest on the lack of any such procedure for determining which interdicted Haitians should not be returned to their country of origin.

56. The Government of the U.S. does not dispute that petitioners meet the requirements of Article 26 of the Commission's Regulations, concerning the presentation of petitions. A number of the allegations raised in the various submissions of the petitioners since the original petition was filed in 1990, relate to factual situations which no longer subsist. The Government of the U.S. expects that the Commission will find, pur-suant to paragraph c of Article 35 of the Regulations of the Commission concerning preliminary questions, that these particular grounds for the petition no longer subsist and therefore these elements of the file are effectively closed.

. . .

62. As of April 22, 1994, a total of 55,694 preliminary refugee questionnaires have been received by the U.S. at the three processing facilities for consideration. Of these, 13,129 cases representing 15,293 per-sons have been interviewed by the immigration and Naturalization Service for possible refugee admission. Of these, 2,937 persons have been approved for refugee admission into the U.S. and over 2, 0 have already departed Haiti for the U.S. This number is in addition to the approximately 10,500 Haitians paroled into the U.S. to pursue their asylum claims based on the asylum pre-screening process that was conducted aboard the Coast Guard cutters and at the Guantánamo Bay Naval Base. Of course, it is also in addition to the substan-tial number of Haitians who immigrate legally each year to the U.S.

. . .

66. Petitioners have alleged violations of the American Declaration of the Rights and Duties of Man, the American Convention on Human Rights as well as other human rights instruments and principles. As the

U.S. is not a party to the American Convention, the Commission must look to the American Declaration for the relevant standards, as is reflected in Articles 1(2)(b) and (a) of its statute and Articles 26 and 51 of its Regulations. In this connection, the U.S. rejects the petitioners' contention that the American Declaration has acquired legally binding force by virtue of U.S. membership in the OAS and ratification of the Charter of the OAS. Because the U.S. has previously noted, the Declaration is not a treaty and has not acquired binding legal force.

67. This remains the view of the U.S. notwithstanding the Commission's decision in Case No. 2141 (U.S.), Res. 23/81, OEA/Ser.L/V/II.51, Doc. 48, Mar. 6, 1981, its decision in Case No. 9647 (U.S.), Res. 3/87, OEA/Ser. L/V/II.71, Doc. 9, rev. 1, Mar. 27, 1987, and the Advisory Opinion of the Inter-American Court of Human Rights OC-10/89 (Colombia) of July 14, 1989. Under the Charter of the OAS, the Commission has the competence and responsibility to promote observance of and respect for the standards and principles set forth in the Declaration. The U.S. has consistently displayed its respect for and support of the Commission in this regard, inter alia, by responding to petitions presented against it on the basis of the Declaration. But as the U.S. stated for the record in the OAS General Assembly following issuance of the Court's Advisory opinion:

"The U.S. accepts and promotes the importance of the American Declaration. It is a solemn moral and political statement of the OAS MEMBER STATES, against which each member state's respect for human rights is to be evaluated and monitored, including the policies and practices of the U.S. . . . The U.S. does not believe, however, that the American Declaration has binding legal force as would an international treaty."

. . .

68. The U.S. considers that the binding statutory and treaty standards in U.S. law upon which interdicted Haitians, advocacy groups representing them and parties in interest in this case, presented and had their claims considered in the U.S. courts, including the Supreme Court, are fully consonant with the principles set forth in the American Declaration. The U.S. denies that the interdiction and repatriation program deprives the Haitians of their right to life, right to equality before the law, to recognition of juridical personality and civil rights, to a fair trial, to petition, and to seek and receive asylum, as set forth in Articles I, II, XVII, XVIII, XXIV, and XXVII of the American Declaration.

69. Petitioners allege that the interdiction program violates Articles I (protecting the right to life, liberty and personal security), II (the right to equality before the law), XVII (the right to recognition of juridical personality and civil rights), XVIII (the right to a fair trial), XXIV (the right to petition), and XXVII (the right to asylum) because the claims of boat people cannot be effectively made or evaluated while they are exhausted, hungry, ill, malnourished, afraid, uninformed and without legal counsel on the high seas. As noted above, screening is no longer conducted on Coast Guard cutters on the high seas. Screening through the in-country refugee processing program does not even arguably involve the same potential deficiencies. Haitians may approach the in-country processing facilities at their convenience.

70. The U.S. notes that it is widely recognized that the right to seek asylum imposes no obligation on states to grant asylum to any particular individual or to permit the entry of an alien to pursue any asylum claim. See, e.g., A. Grahl-Madsen, The Status of Refugees in International Law, 79–107 (1972). Indeed, in regard to Haitian nationals, no other state in the hemisphere has been prepared to provide refuge to significant numbers of Haitian asylum-seekers, even on a temporary basis.

Consequently, there is no obligation on the Government of the U.S. to allow Haitians to enter the U.S. to pursue asylum claims. The "right of asylum" articulated here is deliberately limited by the qualifying language "in accordance with the laws of each country and international arrangements."

. . .

75. Nonetheless, the U.S.' actions are entirely consistent with the object and purpose of the American Convention. Contrary to petitioners' assertions, the U.S. is not only preventing Haitians from leaving Haiti (Article 22 (2)), for example, by crossing the land border with the Dominican Republic, but is also providing Haitian nationals a safe and effective means of leaving their own country as well as of both seeking (Article 22(7)) and receiving asylum in the U.S. While not applicable to the current situation, far from unequal treatment (Article 24), the Haitians are receiving a benefit that is not generally afforded to nationals of other countries in the possibility for in-country refugee processing. As noted above, this program is in addition, of course, to opportunities for Haitians to come to the U.S. through legal immigration channels.

77. Petitioners' claim that the U.S. has violated customary international law is equally unfounded. Evidence of a customary norm requires indication of "extensive and virtually uniform" state practice, North Continental Shelf Cases (W. Ger. v Den; W. Ger. v Neth.), 196 I.C.J. 3, 43, and not merely hortatory declarations of what principles should be adopted as ideals. Jean v Nelson, 727 F.2d at 964 n. 4; 7 Encyclopedia of Pub. Int'l 62, 63 (1984). It is not enough that certain international declarations espouse a general rule, for custom must derive from the repetition of acts by the community of states as a whole taken out of a sense of legal obligation. Other than their unsubstantiated assertion, petitioners have pointed to no evidence suggesting the existence of such widespread and concordant practice regarding the obligation of states to refugees outside their borders.

. . .

79. Petitioners' reliance on the Universal Declaration of Human Rights and the United Nations Charter also is misplaced. The Declaration, which was adopted by the General Assembly of the United Nations in 1948 (G.A. Res. 217, 3 U.N. GAOR, U.N. Doc. 1/777 (1948)), is a non-binding resolution. "It is not a Treaty; it is not and does not purport to be a statement of law or of legal obligation." XIX Bulletin, Department of State, No. 494, Dec. 1948, p. 751 (quoted in 5 Whiteman, Digest of International Law 243 (1965)). The Universal Declaration is authoritative only in so far as it reflects customary international law; as noted above, there is no relevant customary international law. While the United Nations Charter is a treaty, the provisions cited by petitioners (Articles 55 & 56) are far too general to create binding legal obligations with respect to the specific rights asserted in this case.

. . .

Petitioners' Reply to the U.S. Government's Response to Petition

. . .

82. There is no other evidence before the Commission in this case that other countries have violated their obligations under international law when processing Haitian asylum and refugee claims. No other country has joined the USG's interdiction program, nor has any other country initiated its own interdiction program. The very fact that it is well known that Haitians are "suffering serious human rights violations under the military dictatorship" adds urgency to this petition and the need for the USG to provide full, fair and non-discriminatory asylum processing for Haitians fleeing their country.

. . .

83. A government cannot avoid Commission review of an illegal policy by simply changing the policy every few months. While it stopped providing any interviews to interdicted Haitians in April 1992, a change in policy is also challenged by petitioners in several submissions and hearings before the Commission, as repeatedly stated by President Clinton and other high U.S. Government officials, its policy is constantly under review and changing.

. . .

85. While the U.S. Government now claims that only the boat owners and smugglers are detained upon return, a 1993 U.S. Department of State cable we submitted to the Commission on April 26, 1994, clearly states Haitian authorities "questioned all returnees as usual. . . . The interrogation . . . appeared to be a fishing expedition for persons considered troublemakers by the police and probably designed to intimidate returnees."

. . .

87. The U.S. Government argues that there is no legal duty on the U.S. to accept fleeing Haitians, including those with legitimate refugee claims. For the reasons expressed in our previous submissions and stated in the Interim Measure resolution issued by the Commission in February 1993, we respectfully disagree. The interdiction of Haitian nationals and their forced return to Haiti without a full and fair opportunity to have their refugee claims considered violates the various Articles of the Declaration, American Convention, the other international human rights instruments and customary international law. Contrary to the position of the U.S. Government, the American Declaration has acquired legally binding force by virtue of U.S. membership in the OAS and ratification of the Charter of the OAS. See. e.g., Case No. 2141 (U.S. Res. 23/81, OEA/Ser.L/V/II.52, Doc. 48, Mar. 6, 1981, and the Advisory Opinion of the Inter-American Court of Human Rights OC-10/89 (Colombia) of July 14, 1989.

88. Customary international law in this case has been violated because there has been extensive and virtually uniform adoption of the policy of non-refoulement throughout the world. The policy of interdict-

ing Haitians based on their national origin (while, coincidentally, liberally admitting others, such as Cuban nationals), and forcibly returning them to Haiti without asylum interviews of any sort, clearly violated the principle of non-refoulement.

89. While the U.S. Government urged the military de facto government in Haiti to comply with OAS and the United Nations resolutions, it has not complied with the communications from this Commission regarding the conduct of its interdiction program. While the U.S. Government condemned "in principle and in practice" the former British policy of interdicting and repatriating Vietnamese boat people fleeing to Hong Kong, New York Times, Jan. 25, 1990, p. A6, it has initiated its own interdiction and forced repatriation program aimed at only one group of people: poor, black Haitians. It cannot be doubted that the majority of these Haitians are fleeing political violence, bloodshed, death and disappearances. Since this petition was filed, the U.S. Government has had four years to modify its policies and make them consistent with international law and norms of legal and moral conduct.

. . .

The Government's Reply to the Commission's Inquiry 9/26/94

91. The U.S. Government submitted its reply to the Commission's inquiry concerning the meaning and applicability of the articles of the American Declaration allegedly violated in relation to the facts of the case and stated the following:

92. Since the filing of the U.S.' merits brief on May 4, 1994, there have been a number of significant developments both in the U.S.' Haiti migrants policy and in Haiti itself, most notably the restoration of democracy to Haiti. These developments have alternatively rendered this petition moot or inadmissible for failure to exhaust domestic remedies, as is articulated more fully in the attached memorandum. Moreover, the U.S. Government is of the view that the petition fails to establish any violation of the American Declaration. The majority of the provisions of the American Declaration cited by petitioners simply are not relevant to the facts of this case.

93. The article that is relevant to the Haitian interdiction program (Article XXVII concerning the right to asylum) does not require that the U.S. admit fleeing Haitians into the U.S. or preclude the U.S. from repatriating Haitians to Haiti, even those who may have a legitimate fear of persecution. The U.S. believes that the interdiction program is a sound approach to the illegal migration of Haitians by sea. The policy of the U.S. has been and continues to be a lawful and humane response to illegal migration and the potential tragedy of Haitians risking their lives at sea. The U.S. Government respectfully requests the Commission, in the alternative, to declare that this petition is moot, inadmissible or that it fails to establish any violation of the American Declaration.

. . .

96. Meaning of "Security" in Article I—Article I of the Declaration underwent a number of substantial changes prior to its final articulation. The negotiating record on this article strongly suggests that the right to security as petitioners apparently perceive it is not what the formulators of the American Declaration had in mind. The original Juridical Committee draft contained separate articles on the right to life (inspired by the American Declaration of Independence) and the right to personal liberty, and contained no article on security of the person. The Juridical Committee's self-explanatory annex noted the value of affirming this fundamental right in a general form, leaving for subsequent disposition the definition of the special aspects of the right and restrictions of which it is necessarily the subject. The changes made by the Juridical Committee's revised project to these two articles are not material to the present discussion.

97. Application to the facts of this case—The U.S. maintains that the protection of life, liberty and security of the person is a solemn principle which should guide the actions of all states. In keeping with this principle, we continue to strive towards the full realization of personal security for individuals everywhere. Nonetheless, the right to security of the person as understood in the American Declaration simply is not relevant to the factual situation of the Haitian Interdiction program. The right to security of the person does not create an obligation on states to provide admission to persons fleeing their country by sea or preclude their repatriation, even in the case of a bona fide refugee. Nor does it require that safe haven be provided. As discussed in our May 4 submission, the U.S. has no evidence to indicate that repatriated Haitians were subjected to abuse or harassment as a result of their status as repatriated interdictees. In its monitoring of repatriates, the U.S. found no evidence of systemic persecution of returned boat people. The physical integrity of interdicted Haitians simply is not negatively affected by U.S. actions.

. . .

99. Meaning of Article II—The right to equality before the law was viewed by the drafters of the American Declaration as perhaps the most important as it "qualified" all the other rights (Explanatory Annex to the Preliminary Draft of the Declaration, p. 72), is "implicit" in all the others (ibid, p. 103), and constitutes the theoretical underpinning on which all the other rights rest. The right to equality is in essence, a derivative right since first there must be a substantive right—for example embodied in a law—and then it must be applied so that all persons are equal before that law. This right does not necessarily prohibit different treatment, for example of foreigners as compared to nationals. In sum, the right to equality before the law is a right to equality with respect to the application of the substantive rights articulated in the Declaration as fundamental rights. Consequently, the Commission must first consider what rights articulated in the American Declaration apply to the situation of the Haitian interdiction program, the meaning of those rights as applied to this context, and then assess whether those substantive rights are being applied consistent with the prescription of Article II. As was stated in the introduction to this submission, the U.S. believes that the only right articulated in the American Declaration that is relevant to the Haitian interdiction program is the right to asylum of Article XXVII. Consequently, in the view of the U.S., the Commission's inquiry should focus on what is called for by Article XXVII and then whether the right to asylum articulated there is being applied consistently with Article II's right to equality before the law.

100. Moreover, even with respect to particular rights, Article II, like comparable articles in other human rights instruments, does not forbid every difference in treatment in the exercise of rights and freedoms recognized . . . " in the Declaration, provided that the difference is objective and reasonable. Case Relating to Aspects of Laws on the Use of Languages in Education in Belgium, 1EHRR 252.

101. Application to the facts of this case—The U.S. reaffirms the goals established in Article II of the Declaration. Equality before the law remains deeply embedded in our national jurisprudence as one of the fundamental tenets of the U.S. legal system. U.S. jurisprudence on this point is succinctly summarized by the American Law Institute in its Restatement (Third) of the Foreign Relations Law of the U.S. (1987). Section 722 of the Restatement follows:

(a) An alien in the U.S. is entitled to the guarantees of the Constitution other than those expressly reserved for citizens.

(b) Under subsection (1), an alien in the U.S. may not be denied the equal protection of the laws, but equal protection does not preclude reasonable distinctions between aliens and citizens, or between different categories of aliens.

102. The legal rights of aliens as described in the Restatement is further articulated in several opinions of the U.S. Supreme Court. Through these decisions, the U.S. recognized a commitment under the Fifth and Fourteenth Amendments of our Constitution which hold that the Government must extend equal protection of the laws to all persons "within the jurisdiction" of the U.S. Plyler v Doe, 457 U.S. 2 (1982). The law is also clear that the U.S. Government does not have a legal obligation under the Constitution to afford equal protection of the laws to persons outside the jurisdiction of the U.S. U.S. ex. rel. Turner v Williams, 194 U.S. 279, 292 (1904); Matthews v Diaz, 426 U.S. 67, 79 (1976). In Diaz, the U.S. Supreme Court noted that: "A host of constitutional and statutory provisions rest on the premise that a legitimate distinction between citizens and aliens may justify the attributes and benefits for one class not accorded to the other . . . The whole of Title 8 of the U.S. Code, regulating aliens and nationality, is founded on the legitimacy of distinguishing between citizens and aliens. A variety of other federal statutes provide for disparate treatment of aliens and citizens." 426 U.S. 67, 78.

103. The policy of the U.S. in this regard is consistent with the Restatement and with the principles set forth in Article II of the Declaration. The U.S. believes that its immigration and refugee laws treat aliens in a fair, consistent and judicious fashion. Indeed, as a country of immigrants, the U.S. values aliens and has some of the broadest protections for aliens of any country in the world. The U.S. must consider political and economic factors unique in Haiti in determining the best way to honor the commitments created by the Refugee Convention and all other applicable laws.

. . . .

109. Meaning of Article XVIII—Article XVIII is based on Articles XI (right to protection against arbitrary imprisonment) and XII (right to a fair trial) of the Juridical Committee's Preliminary Draft Text. Article XI of the original draft stated, among other things, that every person accused of a crime shall have the right to a prompt trial and to adequate ("humane" in the Juridical Committee's final draft) treatment during the

time of detention. Article XII stated that every person accused of a crime shall have the right to have his case ventilated before an impartial and public audience ("to a legal, impartial and public hearing of the case" in the Juridical Committee's final draft), to be confronted with witnesses, and to be judged by tribunals established in accordance with law in force at the time the act was committed ("and to be judged by the law in force at the time the act was committed and by previously established tribunals" in the Juridical Committee's final draft). Both of these Articles were addressed to the situation of a person accused of a crime and, in that sense, are not relevant to the present discussion. The revised draft of the Sixth Commission's Working Group became the approved text. This Article does not require the courts to reach a certain outcome with respect to the alleged denial of legal rights. Instead, Article XVIII is addressed to ensuring that there is a procedure available to ensure respect for legal rights.

110. Application to the facts of this case—The U.S. has, and is firmly committed to maintaining, a fair and efficient judicial system capable of determining an individual's legal rights. Judicial protection of individual rights represents one of the most important and respected functions of the U.S. legal system. First, however, there must be an underlying right. As repeatedly demonstrated by the courts of the U.S. in their consideration of the various claims raised by the petitioners over the years related to the Haitian interdiction program, aliens outside the U.S. have no general rights under U.S. law to be admitted to the U.S. except as provided in U.S. Immigration law. More specifically, aliens outside the U.S. have no rights to alleged procedural protections in the consideration of their claims to asylum, or to avoid repatriation to their homes, even in the face of persecution at the hands of their governments. This proposition was firmly and conclusively established by the U.S. Supreme Court in Sale. The Court made clear that neither U.S. Immigration law Sec. 243(h) (of the Immigration and Nationality Act) nor Article 33 of the Refugee Convention require admission to the U.S. or preclude repatriation to Haiti of Haitian nationals encountered by U.S. officials outside the U.S. Since these legal rights do not exist under U.S. law, there is no right for the courts to secure.

111. Nor, to our knowledge, do other OAS member states interpret Article XVIII as requiring their authorities to admit non-nationals for the purpose of pursuing asylum claims or to provide extraterritorial procedures.

. . . .

116. The phrase "in accordance . . . with international agreements," while not clear from the negotiating record, suggests an unwillingness in the context of the American Declaration to take on any international legal obligation beyond what had already been, or would be, assumed in the context of binding international negotiations. While the 1951 Refugee Convention post-dates the American Convention, there was already a long tradition of international agreements concerning asylum in the Latin American region, beginning with Title II of the Treaty on International Penal Law, Montevideo, 23 January 1889 and including the Havana Convention fixing the Rules to be observed for the Granting of Asylum of February 1928 [132 LNTS 323], the Montevideo Convention on Political Asylum of 26 December, 1933 and the Montevideo Treaty on Political Asylum of 4 August 1939. These agreements reflect the uniquely Latin approach to asylum, focused on the notions of diplomatic and territorial asylum, and have not been adopted by the U.S. The U.S. adheres to the approach enshrined in the 1951 Refugee Convention. While it is not at all clear that the Latin asylum tradition would require anything other than what U.S. practice reflects, the U.S. is not a party to and therefore is not bound by the Latin asylum conventions. They therefore provide no guidance for the current case.

. . . .

119. Application to the facts of this case—The Haitian interdiction program of the U.S., in each of its forms since the initiation of this proceeding, has been and continues to be consistent with the right to seek and receive asylum in other countries in Article XXVII of the American Declaration. As was made clear in the preceding discussion of the meaning of Article XXVII, the right to seek and receive asylum under the Declaration is to be implemented in accordance with national law. As fully articulated in the merits brief submitted by the U.S. on May 4, 1994, U.S. law on the question of the "right to asylum" of Haitians interdicted at sea pursuant to the Haitian interdiction program is perfectly clear; Haitians interdicted by the U.S. at sea are not entitled to enter the U.S. or to avoid repatriation to Haiti, even if they are refugees under the standards of the 1951 Refugee Convention or the standards of U.S. law.

. . . .

121. The U.S. policy regarding interdiction and repatriation of Haitian nationals has been and continues to be consistent with human rights standards articulated in the American Declaration of the Rights

and Duties of Man. It has protected the lives of Haitians at sea, afforded both temporary protection outside the U.S. and permanent resettlement in the U.S. to countless Haitians in need of such protection, and provided a humane approach to addressing attempts to enter the U.S. in violation of U.S. immigration law. This policy further allows the U.S. to retain within the political branches the power to implement the foreign policy which eventually restored democracy and human rights in Haiti. The U.S. maintains that the Commission should affirm that the interdiction and repatriation policy is acceptable under and consistent with the humanitarian principles expressed in the Declaration.

Petitioners' Reply to Commission's Inquiry

122. Meaning of Article I—The right to "security" is also found in the American Convention on Human Rights at Article 7(1). "Every person has the right to personal liberty and security." The Universal Declaration on Human Rights at Article 3, Article 9(1) of the International Covenant on Civil and Political Rights and the European Convention on Human Rights. The Inter-American Commission found a violation of Article I's security guarantee "where a Minister of the Interior sends a message to a man for whose arrest a warrant has been issued saying, on behalf of the National Guard, that if he surrenders to the warrant, they were not guaranteeing his life." International Law of Human Rights, 142, citing Case 2509 (Panama) AR 1979/80,63. Article I protects the right to "life, liberty and the security" of all persons. The right to "life" appears to mean the right not to have one's life arbitrarily ended. The right to "liberty" appears to apply to the right to freedom from arbitrary detention. The right to "security" appears to mean the right to be free from arbitrary arrest and danger or risk of personal harm or injury.

. . .

127. Despite promises made by the Haitian Government (in diplomatic exchange of letters) that returnees would not be punished for leaving Haiti, boat people involuntarily interdicted and returned by the U.S. Government have been routinely detained upon their return to Haiti. On May 7, 8, and 13, 1990, forty-three (43) returnees, including some Haitians who had been detained in INS's Krome detention Center in Miami, Florida, were immediately arrested and detained in the National Penitentiary by Haitian military authorities upon their arrival in Port-au-Prince. On June 5, 1990, another group of thirty one (31) Haitians deported from Krome were arrested upon arrival in Haiti and alleged that they were told that their whereabouts would thereafter be closely monitored by the Government.

. . . .

140. Meaning and application of Article XXVII, the Right to Seek and Receive Asylum—International Agreements—The Commission specifically requests argument on the significance of the phrase "in accordance with the laws of each country and with international agreements." In summary this language means that Haitians interdicted and detained by the USG have the right to "seek" and to "receive" asylum in a manner consistent with international agreements" and "the laws" of the U.S. In its Preamble, the 1951 Convention Relating to the Status of Refugees assured refugees the widest possible exercise of their fundamental rights and freedoms, and non-refoulement constitutes the most fundamental of these rights. Lowenstein International Human Rights Clinic, Aliens and the Duty of Non refoulement: Haitian Centers Council v McNary, 6 Harv. Human Rts.J. 1, 14 (1993). Non-refoulement "is one of the few rights considered may enter any reservation . . ." Id. Article 33.1 of the Convention Relating to the Status of Refugees proclaims: "No Contracting State shall expel or return ('refouler') a refugee in any manner whatsoever to the frontiers or territories where his life or freedom would be threatened on account of race, religion, nationality, membership of a particular social group or political opinion."

141. International law prohibits State action beyond a State's borders that violates other rights regarded as fundamental. The United Nations Human Rights Committee has held, that a State party may be accountable under Article 2(1) of the 1966 International Covenant on Civil and Political Rights for violations of the rights recognized in the ICCPR committed by its agents in the territory of another State, whether with or without the acquiescence of the government of that State. The Committee determined that the qualification "subject to its jurisdiction," contained in article 29(1) of the Covenant, does not refer to the place where the violation occurs but to the relationship between the individual and the State concerned. The European Commission on Human Rights has concluded that States' obligations under the European Convention on Human Rights extend to "all persons under their actual authority and responsibility, whether that authority is exercised within their own territory or abroad." P. Sieghart, The International Law of Human Rights 58 (1983).

. . . .

147. Petitioners have already submitted a copy of the Sale v Haitian Centers Council in which the U.S. Supreme Court upheld the USG's position thereby failing to uphold the principle of non-refoulement and conferring "domestic authority" on the decision to violate international law. In the absence of any domestic remedy, the responsibility of the U.S. is beyond dispute. As Guy S. Goodwin-Gill writes: "[I]it is not the U.S. Supreme Court which alone is responsible for the violation of international law. Rather, it is the system of administration as a whole, beginning with the executive acts of the President, that has produced the result contrary to the principle of non-refoulement. The guarantee of non-refoulement for refugees is a specific and fundamental protection, independent from the question of admission or the grant of asylum." Guy S. Goodwin-Gill, The Haitian Refoulement Case: A Comment, 6 Int. J. Refugee L. 103, 109 (1994).

VI. The Issue

148. The issue which this case presents is whether the Government of the U.S. has violated the articles of the American Declaration of the Rights and Duties of Man as alleged by the petitioners.

VII. Commission's Analysis

149. The petitioners allege violations by the U.S. Government of several international human rights instruments. The controlling instrument is the American Declaration of the Rights and Duties of Man. The U.S. is a signatory to the American Convention on Human Rights, but has not ratified the same.

150. The Articles of the American Declaration of the Rights and Duties of Man allegedly violated are the following:

a. Article I, which provides: "Every human being has the right to life, liberty and the security of his person."

b. Article II provides: "All persons are equal before the law and have the rights and duties established in this Declaration, without distinction as to race, sex, language, creed or any other factor."

c. Article XVII provides: "Every person has the right to be recognized everywhere as a person having rights and obligations, and to enjoy the basic civil rights."

d. Article XVIII provides: "Every person may resort to the courts to ensure respect for his legal rights. There should likewise be available to him a simple, brief procedure whereby the courts will protect him from acts of authority, that to his prejudice, violate any fundamental constitutional rights."

e. Article XXIV provides: "Every person has the right to submit respectful petitions to any competent authority, for reasons of either general or private interest, and the right to obtain a prompt decision thereon."

f. Article XXVII provides: "Every person has the right, in case of pursuit not resulting from ordinary crimes, to seek and receive asylum in foreign territory, in accordance with the laws of each country and with international agreements."

151. It is convenient to begin with an analysis of Article XXVII of the American Declaration. Article XXVII of the American Declaration is entitled "Right of Asylum." This Article outlines two criteria which are cumulative and both of which must be satisfied in order for the right to exist. The first criterion is that the right to seek and receive asylum on foreign territory must be in "accordance with the laws of each country," that is the country in which asylum is sought. The second criterion is that the right to seek asylum in foreign territory must be "in accordance with international agreements."

152. The travaux preparatoires show that the first draft in the Article did not have the phrase "in accordance with the laws of each country." That phrase was added in the Sixth Session of the Sixth Commission's of the Inter-American Juridical Committee at the Ninth International Conference of American States in Bogota in 1948, and discussed in the Seventh session of the Sixth Commission, to preserve the states' sovereignty in questions of asylum.

153. The effect of the dual cumulative criteria in Article XXVII is that if the right is established in international but not in domestic law, it is not a right which is recognized by Article XXVII of the Declaration.

154. The Commission observes that Article 22(7) of the American Convention on Human Rights, which was adopted twenty one years after the American Declaration, has a formulation similar to Article XXVII of the American Declaration. Article 22(7) provides: "Every person has the right to

seek and be granted asylum in a foreign territory, in accordance with the legislation of the state and international conventions, in the event he is being pursued for political offenses or related common crimes."

155. The Commission will now address the question of the application of the two criteria and will deal first with the criterion of conformity with "international agreements." The relevant international agreement is the Convention Relating to the Status of Refugees 1951 and the 1967 Protocol Relating to the Status of Refugees to which the U.S. is a party. The Convention establishes certain criteria for the qualification of a person as a "refugee." The Commission believes that international law has developed to a level at which there is recognition of a right of a person seeking refuge to a hearing in order to determine whether that person meets the criteria in the Convention.

156. An important provision of the 1951 Convention is Article 33(1) which provides that: "No Contracting State shall expel or return ('refouler') a refugee in any manner whatsoever to the frontiers of territories where his life or freedom would be threatened on account of his race, religion, nationality, membership of a particular social group or political opinion." The Supreme Court of the U.S., in the case of Sale, Acting Commissioner, Immigration and Naturalization Service, et. al. v Haitian Centers Council, Inc., et. al., No. 92–344, decided June 21, 1993, construed this provision as not being applicable in a situation where a person is returned from the high seas to the territory from which he or she fled. Specifically, the Supreme Court held that the principle of non-refoulement in Article 33 did not apply to the Haitians interdicted on the high seas and not in the U.S.' territory.

157. The Commission does not agree with this finding. The Commission shares the view advanced by the United Nations High Commissioner for Refugees in its Amicus Curiae brief in its argument before the Supreme Court, that Article 33 had no geographical limitations.

158. However, the finding by the Commission that the U.S. Government has breached its treaty obligations in respect of Article 33 does not resolve the issue as to whether the U.S. Government is in breach of Article XXVII of the American Declaration because the cumulative effect of the dual criteria in that Article is that, for the right to seek and receive asylum in foreign territory to exist, it must not only be in accordance with international agreements, but in accordance with the domestic laws of the country in which refuge is sought.

159. After several judicial hearings in respect of the Haitian boat people the U.S.' domestic law in this matter was finally settled by the Supreme Court in the case of Sale, Acting Commissioner, Immigration and Naturalization Service, et. al. v Haitian Centers Council, Inc., et. al., No. 92–344, decided June 21, 1993. In its reply of January 19, 1995, to the Commission's specific question on the meaning of the phrase "in accordance with the laws of each country," the U.S. Government stated that: "As fully articulated in the merits brief submitted by the U.S. on May 4, 1994, U.S. law on the question of the 'right to asylum' of Haitians is perfectly clear: Haitians interdicted by the U.S. at sea are not entitled to enter the U.S. or to avoid repatriation to Haiti, even if they are refugees under the standards of the 1951 Refugee Convention or the standards of U.S. law." This statement derives from the Supreme Court's decision in the Sale case. However, under the U.S. domestic law Haitians and other refugees who have made it to the U.S. shores are entitled to "seek" asylum in accordance with U.S. law. But there is no mandatory grant of "asylum." Asylum is only granted to refugees who meet the criteria of a "refugee" under U.S. domestic law and its international obligations.

160. The Commission has noted that both prior to and subsequent to the Supreme Court's decision the U.S. recognized and acknowledged the right of Haitian refugees to seek and receive asylum in the U.S. This is found in the U.S. Government's argument on page 2 of its submission of January 19, 1995, in which it states that:

"On May 8, 1994, President Clinton announced his decision to end the policy of directly repatriating, without an opportunity to present a refugee claim, Haitians interdicted at sea by the U.S. Coast Guard, in light of the deteriorating human rights conditions in Haiti. The U.S. entered into agreements with some nations in the Latin America region to permit the processing for refugee status within their territory or territorial waters of Haitians interdicted at sea. With the assistance of the United Nations High Commissioner for Refugees, in June of this year, the U.S. began processing interdicted Haitians aboard the U.S. Naval Ship Comfort within Jamaican territorial waters for refugee status and resettlement in the U.S. The numbers of Haitians fleeing Haiti by sea soon overwhelmed the capacity of the U.S. to process their claims on board the Comfort and in the beginning of July, President Clinton announced the decision to provide safe haven for all interdicted Haitians desiring protection at either the U.S. Naval Station at Guantánamo Bay, Cuba or at other safe haven facilities in the region. To this end the U.S. entered safe haven agreements with a number of countries in the region."

. . .

162. It is noted that Article XXVII provides for a right to seek and receive asylum in "foreign territory." A question however arises, whether the action of the U.S. in interdicting Haitians on the high seas is not in breach of their right under Article XXVII of the American Declaration to seek and receive asylum in some foreign territory other than the U.S. This statement from the petitioners has not been contested or contradicted by the U.S. The Commission has noted that subsequent to the coup ousting President Aristide from office on September 30, 1991, during the interdiction period, Hatian refugees exercised their right to seek and receive asylum in other foreign territories, such as the Dominican Republic, Jamaica, Bahamas, Cuba (provided asylum to 3,851 Haitians during 1992), Venezuela, Suriname, Honduras, the Turks and Caico Islands and other Latin American countries.

163. The Commission finds that the U.S. summarily interdicted and repatriated Haitian refugees to Haiti without making an adequate determination of their status, and without granting them a hearing to ascertain whether they qualified as "refugees." The Commission also finds that the dual criteria test of the right to "seek" and "receive" asylum as provided by Articles XXVII in "foreign territory" (in accordance with the laws of each country and with international agreements) of the American Declaration has been satisfied. Therefore, the Commission finds that the U.S. breached Article XXVII of the American Declaration when it summarily interdicted, and repatriated Jeanette Gedeon, Dukens Luma, Fito Jean, and unnamed Haitians to Haiti, and prevented them from exercising their right to seek and receive asylum in foreign territory as provided by the American Declaration.

164. Article I of the American Declaration provides that: "Every human being has the right to life, liberty, and the security of the person." In construing this Article with regard to the "right to life," the petitioners cite numerous instances of violence directed toward the Haitians who were repatriated to Haiti and in particular the statements contained in four interviews conducted by the United Nations officers with Haitians at the U.S. Naval Base, in Guantánamo and referred to in Part I, page 4, paragraphs 9 and 10 of this report. Petitioners alleged (paragraph 10) that "the interviews allegedly removed all doubt that the Haitian interdictees forcibly repatriated by the U.S. Government have been, and will be brutalized by the military government upon their return to Haiti."

. . .

167. The Commission has noted the petitioners' argument that by exposing the Haitian refugees to the genuine and foreseeable risk of death, the U.S. Government's policy of interdiction and repatriation clearly violated their right to life protected by Article I. The Commission has also noted the international case law which provides that if a State party extradites a person within its jurisdiction in circumstances, and if, as a result, there is a real risk that his or her rights under the Covenant will be violated in another jurisdiction, the State party itself may be in violation of the Covenant. The U.S. in its submissions has argued that the interdiction of the boats carrying Haitian refugees rescued and saved lives, because the boats were un-seaworthy and since December of 1982 approximately 435 Haitians have drowned en route to U.S. shores.

. . .

169. With regard to the "right to liberty" as provided by Article I of the American Declaration of the Rights and Duties of Man, the Commission finds that the act of interdicting the Haitians in vessels on the high seas constituted a breach of the Haitians' right to liberty within the terms of Article I of the American Declaration. The Commission therefore finds that the right to liberty of Jeannette Gedeon, Dukens Luma, Fito Jean, the four Haitians who were interviewed at the U.S. Naval Base at Guantánamo, and other unnamed Haitians was breached by the U.S. Government.

170. The petitioners also alleged violation of Article I of the American Declaration of the Rights and Duties of Man which refers to the "right to security of the person." Article I provides: "Every human being has the right to life, liberty and the security of his person." This right is defined as "a person's legal and uninterrupted enjoyment of his life, his limbs, his body, his health, and his reputation." The petitioners' evidence is compelling and establishes that the security of the persons of both named and unnamed Haitians who were repatriated to Haiti against their will were violated upon their return to Haiti. This is clearly illustrated by the evidence before the Commission of the four Haitians who were interviewed at the U.S. Naval Station at Guantánamo and the testimony of Dukens Luma, Fito Jean, and Pierre Esperance.

171. The Commission therefore finds that the U.S. Government's act of interdicting Haitians on the high seas, placing them in vessels under their jurisdiction, returning them to Haiti, and leaving them exposed to acts of brutality by the Haitian military and its supporters constitutes a breach of the right to security of the Haitian refugees. Based on the testimony and evidence presented to the Commission by Dukens Luma, Fito Jean, Pierre Esperance, and the four interviewees who were interviewed by the Office of the United Nations High Commission for Refugees, some of these repatriates were arrested, detained, imprisoned and suffered violence at the hands of the Haitian military upon their return to Haiti. The Commission however, limits this breach of the "right to security of the person" to Dukens Luma, the four interviewees at Guantánamo, and some unnamed Haitians. The petitioners have not proved that the right to "security of the person" of Jeannette Gedeon has been violated.

. . . .

177. The Commission finds that the U.S. Government has violated the right to equality before the law with respect to the following matters:

(a) The interdiction of Haitians on the high seas in contradistinction to the position of Cubans and nationals of other countries who so far from being interdicted are favorably treated by being brought into the U.S. by the U.S. Coast Guard.

(b) The failure to grant Haitians interdicted on the high seas any hearing, or any adequate hearing as to their claim for refugee status; in contradistinction to Cuban asylum seekers and nationals of other countries who are intercepted on the high seas and brought to the U.S. for their claims to be processed by the U.S. Immigration and Naturalization Service.

178. The Commission wishes to point out that a breach of Article II arises not only in the application of a substantive right but also in respect of any unreasonable differentiation in respect of the actual treatment of persons belonging to the same class or category. Thus, the finding that the Haitians have a substantive right to asylum under Article XXVII does not preclude a finding of a breach of Article II in respect of unreasonable differentiation in the treatment of Haitians and nationals of other countries seeking refuge in the U.S. The Commission finds that the "right to equality before the law" as provided by Article II of the American Declaration was breached by the U.S. with regard to Jeannette Gedeon, Dukens Luma, Fito Jean, the four interviewees at Guantánamo and unnamed Haitians.

179. With regard to the right allegedly violated in Article XVII of the American Declaration, the Commission does not find any violation of Article XVII of the American Declaration.

180. With regard to Article XVIII of the American Declaration, the Commission does not agree with the U.S. that this right is confined to persons accused of crimes. The Commission finds that some of the petitioners (Haitian refugees) who landed on the shores of the U.S. were able to resort to the courts of the U.S., in an effort to vindicate their rights, as is evidenced by the several cases instituted in the U.S. The Commission finds however, that Jeannette Gedeon, Dukens Luma, Fito Jean and the unnamed Haitian Nationals were unable to resort to the courts in the U.S. to vindicate their rights because they were summarily interdicted and repatriated to Haiti without being given an opportunity to exercise their rights. Therefore, the Commission finds that the U.S. breached Article XVIII of the American Declaration in respect of Jeannette Gedeon, Dukens Luma, Fito Jean and the unnamed Haitian Nationals who were interdicted and summarily repatriated to Haiti.

181. With regard to Article XXIV of the American Declaration, the Commission feels that this Article is wider in scope than Article XVIII which is confined to the courts in respect of legal rights. On the basis of the evidence, the Commission finds no breach of this Article.

182. On November 6, 1996, the Commission transmitted a copy of its decision on the merits of the case to the U.S. Government. On January 3, 1997, the U.S. responded by letter and stated the following:

"The U.S. Government has long been one of the strongest supporters of the Commission. We are also a strong supporter of democracy and human rights in Haiti, and a leading contributor to UN and OAS operations in Haiti designed to foster peace, stability and the protection of human rights."

We must respectfully disagree with the conclusions reached by the Commission in this case. I will not here repeat the response of the U.S. to each allegation made in this case. Our views were set forth in detail in our lengthy submissions to the Commission, and, we believe, demonstrated why the actions of the U.S. did not contravene any human rights standards contained in the American Declaration of the Rights and Duties of Man. In particular, our submissions demonstrated that there is no basis for interpreting those human rights standards to require the U.S. to admit fleeing Haitians into the U.S. Nor do those standards preclude the U.S. from repatriating the migrants to Haiti.

My government also believes that the Commission's analysis is legally flawed. For example, it was error to hold that the 1967 Protocol to the UN Convention on the Status of Refugees applies to Haitian migrants interdicted on the high seas. It was also error to interpret the non-refoulement obligation to require high seas interdictees to receive the same hearing on their asylum claims as they would receive if they were present within the territory of the interdicting state and to hold that one group of intending immigrants is entitled to receive the more preferential treatment given another group. Moreover, there is no basis in law to hold the U.S. liable for acts and omissions of another government with respect to that government's own citizens.

The U.S. Government has been and remains deeply committed to restoring democracy in Haiti, to saving human lives and to the fair treatment of genuine refugees. We believe that our actions were consistent with those goals and violated no human rights obligations. However, for the reasons explained here and detailed in our previous submissions to the Commission, we can find no basis on which to agree with the Commission's decision and thus will not comply with its demand to pay compensation.

Therefore:

The Inter-American Commission on Human Rights Finds That,

183. The U.S. has breached the "right to life" pursuant to Article I of the American Declaration, of unnamed Haitian refugees identified by the petitioners who were interdicted and repatriated to Haiti by the U.S.

184. The U.S. has breached the "right to liberty" contained in Article I of the American Declaration with regard to the Jeannette Gedeon, Dukens Luma, Fito Jean, the four interviewees at Guantánamo, and Unnamed Haitian Interdictees.

185. The U.S. has breached the "right to security of the person" referred to in Article I of the American Declaration with regard to Dukens Luma, the four interviewees at Guantánamo, and Unnamed Haitian Interdictees.

186. The U.S. has breached the "right to equality before the law" as provided by Article II of the American Declaration with regard to Jeannette Gedeon, Dukens Luma, Fito Jean, the four interviewees at Guantánamo, and Unnamed Haitian Interdictees.

187. The U.S. has breached the "right to resort to the courts" to ensure respect for the legal rights of Jeannette Gedeon, Dukens Luma, Fito Jean, the four interviewees at Guantánamo, and Unnamed Haitian Interdictees pursuant to Article XVIII of the American Declaration.

188. The U.S. has breached the right to "seek and receive asylum" as provided by Article XXVII of the American Declaration with regard to Jeannette Gedeon, Dukens Luma, Fito Jean, the four interviewees at Guantánamo, and Unnamed Haitian Interdictees.

The Commission Recommends That:

189. The U.S. must provide adequate compensation to the victims for the breaches mentioned in paragraphs 183–188, above, and inform the appropriate authorities of its decision.

190. In conformity with the requirement established in Article 54(5) of its Regulations, the Commission has decided that this Report be published in its Annual Report to the General Assembly. Approved by the Commission during its 93rd Session on October 17, 1996. Revised and adopted as a final Report at its 95th Session on March 13, 1997.

[Footnote omitted]

17. *Ng v Canada* Human Rights Committee, United Nations (Excerpted)

CCPR/C/49/D/469/1991
7 January 1994
Communication No. 469/1991: Canada.
07/01/94. CCPR/C/49/D/469/1991. (Jurisprudence)
United Nations Human Rights Committee
ANNEX
Views of the Human Rights Committee under article 5, paragraph 4, of the Optional Protocol to the International Covenant on Civil and Political Rights
   Submitted by: Charles Chitat Ng (a U.S resident, represented by counsel)
   Victim: The author
   State party: Canada
   . . .

The facts as submitted by the author

1. The author of the communication is Charles Chitat Ng, a British subject, born on 24 December 1960 in Hong Kong, and a resident of the United States of America, at the time of his submission detained in a penitentiary in Alberta, Canada, and on 26 September 1991 extradited to the U.S. He claims to be a victim of a violation of his human rights by Canada because of his extradition. He is represented by counsel.

2.1 The author was arrested, charged and convicted in 1985 in Calgary, Alberta, following an attempted store theft and shooting of a security guard. In February 1987, the U.S. formally requested the author's extradition to stand trial in California on 19 criminal counts, including kidnapping and 12 murders, committed in 1984 and 1985. If convicted, the author could face the death penalty.

2.2 In November 1988, a judge of the Alberta Court of Queen's Bench ordered the author's extradition. In February 1989, the author's habeas corpus application was denied, and on 31 August 1989 the Supreme Court of Canada refused the author leave to appeal.

2.3 Article 6 of the Extradition Treaty between Canada and the U.S. provides:

"When the offence for which extradition is requested is punishable by death under the laws of the requesting State and the laws of the requested State do not permit such punishment for that offence, extradition may be refused, unless the requesting State provides such assurances as the requested State considers sufficient that the death penalty shall not be imposed or, if imposed, shall not be executed."

Canada abolished the death penalty in 1976, except for certain military offences.

2.4 The power to seek assurances that the death penalty will not be imposed is discretionary and is conferred on the Minister of Justice pursuant to section 25 of the Extradition Act. In October 1989, the Minister of Justice decided not to seek these assurances.

2.5 The author subsequently filed an application for review of the Minister's decision with the Federal Court. On 8 June 1990, the issues in the case were referred to the Supreme Court of Canada, which rendered judgement on 26 September 1991. It found that the author's extradition without assurances as to the imposition of the death penalty did not contravene Canada's constitutional protection for human rights nor the standards of the international community. The author was extradited on the same day.

The complaint

3. The author claims that the decision to extradite him violates articles 6, 7, 9, 10, 14 and 26 of the [ICCPR] Covenant. He submits that the execution of the death sentence by gas asphyxiation, as provided for under California statutes, constitutes cruel and inhuman treatment or punishment per se, and that the conditions on death row are cruel, inhuman and degrading. He further alleges that the judicial procedures in California, inasmuch as they relate specifically to capital punishment, do not meet basic requirements of justice. In this context, the author alleges that in the U.S., racial bias influences the imposition of the death penalty.

The State party's initial observations and the author's comments thereon:

4.1 The State party submits that the communication is inadmissible ratione personae, loci and materiae.

4.2 It is argued that the author cannot be considered a victim within the meaning of the Optional Protocol, since his allegations are derived from assumptions about possible future events, which may not materialize and which are dependent on the law and actions of the authorities of the U.S. The State party refers in this connection to the Committee's views in communication No. 61/1979, where it was found that the Committee "has only been entrusted with the mandate of examining whether an individual has suffered an actual violation of his rights. It cannot review in the abstract whether national legislation contravenes the Covenant."

4.3 The State party indicates that the author's allegations concern the penal law and judicial system of a country other than Canada. It refers to the Committee's inadmissibility decision in communication No. 217/1986,[b] where the Committee observed that "it can only receive and consider communications in respect of claims that come under the jurisdiction of a State party to the Covenant." The State party submits that the Covenant does not impose responsibility upon a State for eventualities over which it has no jurisdiction.

4.4 Moreover, it is submitted that the communication should be declared inadmissible as incompatible with the provisions of the Covenant, since the Covenant does not provide for a right not to be extradited. In this connection, the State party quotes from the Committee's inadmissibility decision in communication No. 117/1981:[c] "There is no provision of the Covenant making it unlawful for a State party to seek extradition of a person from another country." It further argues that even if extradition could be found to fall within the scope of protection of the Covenant in exceptional circumstances, these circumstances are not present in the instant case.

4.5 The State party further refers to the United Nations Model Treaty on Extradition,[d] which clearly contemplates the possibility of extradition without conditions by providing for discretion in obtaining assurances regarding the death penalty in the same fashion as is found in article 6 of the Extradition Treaty between Canada and the U.S. It concludes that interference with the surrender of a fugitive pursuant to legitimate requests from a treaty partner would defeat the principles and objects of extradition treaties and would entail undesirable consequences for States refusing these legitimate requests. In this context, the State party points out that its long, unprotected border with the U.S. would make it an attractive haven for fugitives from U.S. justice. If these fugitives could not be extradited because of the theoretical possibility of the death penalty, they would be effectively irremovable and would have to be allowed to remain in the country, unpunished and posing a threat to the safety and security of the inhabitants.

4.6 The State party finally submits that the author has failed to substantiate his allegations that the treatment he may face in the U.S. will violate his rights under the Covenant. In this connection, the State party points out that the imposition of the death penalty is not per se unlawful under the Covenant. As regards the delay between the imposition and the execution of the death sentence, the State party submits that it is difficult to see how a period of detention during which a convicted prisoner would pursue all avenues of appeal, can be held to constitute a violation of the Covenant.

5.1 In his comments on the State party's submission, counsel submits that the author is and was himself actually and personally affected by the decision of the State party to extradite him and that the communication is therefore admissible ratione personae. In this context, he refers to the Committee's views in communication No. 35/1978,[e] and argues that an individual can claim to be a victim within the meaning of the Optional Protocol if the laws, practices, actions or decisions of a State party raise a real risk of violation of rights set forth in the Covenant.

5.2 Counsel further argues that, since the decision complained of is one made by Canadian authorities while the author was subject to Canadian jurisdiction, the communication is admissible ratione loci. In this connection, he refers to the Committee's views in communication No. 110/1981,[f] where it was held that article 1 of the Covenant was "clearly intended to apply to individuals subject to the jurisdiction of the State party concerned at the time of the alleged violation of the Covenant."

5.3 Counsel finally stresses that the author does not claim a right not to be extradited; he only claims that he should not have been surrendered without assurances that the death penalty would not be imposed. He submits that the communication is therefore compatible with the provisions of the Covenant. He refers in this context to the Committee's views on communication No. 107/1981,[g] where the Committee found that anguish and stress can give rise to a breach of the Covenant; he submits that this finding is also applicable in the instant case.

The Committee's consideration of and decision on admissibility:

6.1 During its forty-sixth session, in October 1992, the Committee considered the admissibility of the communication. It observed that extradition as such is outside the scope of application of the Covenant,[h] but that a State party's obligations in relation to a matter itself outside the scope of the Covenant may still be engaged by reference to other provisions of the Covenant.[i] The Committee noted that the author does not claim that extradition as such violates the Covenant, but rather that the particular circumstances related to the effects of his extradition would raise issues under specific provisions of the Covenant. Accordingly, the Committee found that the communication was thus not excluded ratione materiae.

6.2 The Committee considered the contention of the State party that the claim is inadmissible ratione loci. Article 2 of the Covenant requires States parties to guarantee the rights of persons within their jurisdiction. If a person is lawfully expelled or extradited, the State party concerned will not generally have responsibility under the Covenant for any violations of that person's rights that may later occur in the other jurisdiction. In that sense, a State party clearly is not required to guarantee the rights of persons within another jurisdiction. However, if a State party takes a decision relating to a person within its jurisdiction, and the necessary and foreseeable consequence is that this person's rights under the Covenant will be violated in another jurisdiction, the State party itself may be in violation of the Covenant. That follows from the fact that a State party's duty under article 2 of the Covenant would be negated by the handing over of a person to another State (whether a State party to the Covenant or not) where treatment contrary to the Covenant is certain or is the very purpose of the handing over. For example, a State party would itself be in violation of the Covenant if it handed over a person to another State in circumstances in which it was foreseeable that torture would take place. The foreseeability of the consequence would mean that there was a present violation by the State party, even though the consequence would not occur until later on.

6.3 The Committee therefore considered itself, in principle, competent to examine whether the State party is in violation of the Covenant by virtue of its decision to extradite the author under the Extradition Treaty of 1976 between Canada and the U.S., and the Extradition Act of 1985.

6.4 The Committee observed that pursuant to article 1 of the Optional Protocol, the Committee may only receive and consider communications from individuals subject to the jurisdiction of a State party to the Covenant and to the Optional Protocol "who claim to be victims of a violation by that State party of any of their rights set forth in the Covenant." It considered that in the instant case, only the consideration of the merits of the circumstances under which the extradition procedure and all its effects occurred, would enable the Committee to determine whether the author is a victim within the meaning of article 1 of the Optional Protocol. Accordingly, the Committee found it appropriate to consider this issue, which concerned the admissibility of the Communication, together with the examination of the merits of the case.

7. On 28 October 1992, the Human Rights Committee therefore decided to join the question of whether the author was a victim within the meaning of article 1 of the Optional Protocol to the consideration of the merits. The Committee expressed its regret that the State party had not acceded to the Committee's request, under rule 86, to stay extradition of the author.

The State party's further submission on the admissibility and the merits of the communication.

8.1 In its submission dated 14 May 1993, the State party elaborates on the extradition process in general, on the Canada–U.S. extradition relationship and on the specifics of the present case. It also submits comments with respect to the admissibility of the communication, in particular with respect to article 1 of the Optional Protocol.

8.2 The State party recalls that:

". . . extradition exists to contribute to the safety of the citizens and residents of States. Dangerous criminal offenders seeking a safe haven from prosecution or punishment are removed to face justice in the State in which their crimes were committed. Extradition furthers international cooperation in criminal justice matters and strengthens domestic law enforcement. It is meant to be a straightforward and expeditious process. Extradition seeks to balance the rights of fugitives with the need for the protection of the residents of the two States parties to any given extradition treaty. The extradition relationship between Canada and the U.S. dates back to 1794 . . . In 1842, the U.S. and Great Britain entered into the Ashburton-Webster Treaty, which contained articles governing the mutual surrender of criminals . . . This treaty remained in force until the present Canada–U.S. Extradition Treaty of 1976."

8.3 With regard to the principle aut dedere aut judicare, the State party explains that while some States can prosecute persons for crimes committed in other jurisdictions in which their own nationals are either the offender or the victim, other States, such as Canada and certain other States in the common law tradition, cannot.

8.4 Extradition in Canada is governed by the Extradition Act and the terms of the applicable treaty. The Canadian Charter of Rights and Freedoms, which forms part of the constitution of Canada and embodies many of the rights protected by the Covenant, applies. Under Canadian law, extradition is a two-step process. The first involves a hearing at which a judge considers whether a factual and legal basis for extradition exists. The person sought for extradition may submit evidence at the judicial hearing. If the judge is satisfied with the evidence that a legal basis for extradition exists, the fugitive is ordered committed to await surrender to the requesting State. Judicial review of a warrant of committal to await surrender can be sought by means of an application for a writ of habeas corpus in a provincial court. A decision of the judge on the habeas corpus application can be appealed to the provincial court of appeal and then, with leave, to the Supreme Court of Canada. The second step in the extradition process begins following the exhaustion of the appeals in the judicial phase. The Minister of Justice is charged with the responsibility of deciding whether to surrender the person sought for extradition. The fugitive may make written submissions to the Minister, and counsel for the fugitive, with leave, may appear before the Minister to present oral argument. In coming to a decision on surrender, the Minister considers a complete record of the case from the judicial phase, together with any written and oral submissions from the fugitive, and while the Minister's decision is discretionary, the discretion is circumscribed by law. The decision is based upon a consideration of many factors, including Canada's obligations under the applicable treaty of extradition, facts particular to the person and the nature of the crime for which extradition is sought. In addition, the Minister must consider the terms of the Canadian Charter of Rights and Freedoms and the various instruments, including the Covenant, which outline Canada's international human rights obligations. Finally, a fugitive may seek judicial review of the Minister's decision by a provincial court and appeal a warrant of surrender, with leave, up to the Supreme Court of Canada. In interpreting Canada's human rights obligations under the Canadian Charter, the Supreme Court of Canada is guided by international instruments to which Canada is a party, including the Covenant.

8.5 With regard to surrender in capital cases, the Minister of Justice decides whether or not to request assurances to the effect that the death penalty should not be imposed or carried out on the basis of an examination of the particular facts of each case. The Extradition Treaty between Canada and the U.S. was not intended to make the seeking of assurances a routine occurrence; rather, assurances had to be sought only in circumstances where the particular facts of the case warrant a special exercise of discretion.

8.6 With regard to the abolition of the death penalty in Canada, the State party notes that:

". . . certain States within the international community, including the U.S., continue to impose the death penalty. The Government of Canada does not use extradition as a vehicle for imposing its concepts of criminal law policy on other States. By seeking assurances on a routine basis, in the absence of exceptional circumstances, Canada would be dictating to the requesting State, in this case the U.S., how it should punish its criminal law offenders. The Government of Canada contends that this would be an unwarranted interference with the internal affairs of another State. The Government of Canada reserves the right . . . to refuse to extradite without assurances. This right is held in reserve for use only where exceptional circumstances exist. In the view of the Government of Canada, it may be that evidence showing that a fugitive would face certain or foreseeable violations of the Covenant would be one example of exceptional circumstances which would warrant the special measure of seeking assurances under article 6. However, the evidence presented by Ng during the extradition process in Canada (which evidence has been submitted by counsel for Ng in this communication) does not support the allegations that the use of the death penalty in the U.S. generally, or in the State of California in particular, violates the Covenant."

8.7 The State party also refers to article 4 of the United Nations Model Treaty on Extradition, which lists optional, but not mandatory, grounds for refusing extradition:

"(d) If the offence for which extradition is requested carries the death penalty under the law of the Requesting State, unless the State gives such assurance as the Requested State considers sufficient that the death penalty will not be imposed or, if imposed, will not be carried out."

Similarly, article 6 of the Extradition Treaty between Canada and the U.S. provides that the decision with respect to obtaining assurances regarding the death penalty is discretionary.

8.8 With regard to the link between extradition and the protection of society, the State party submits that Canada and the U.S. share a 4,800 kilometre unguarded border, that many fugitives from U.S. justice cross that border into Canada and that in the last 12 years there has been a steadily increasing number of extradition requests from the U.S. In 1980, there were 29 such requests; by 1992, the number had increased to 88.

"Requests involving death penalty cases are a new and growing problem for Canada . . . a policy of routinely seeking assurances under article 6 of the Canada–U.S. Extradition Treaty will encourage even more criminal law offenders, especially those guilty of the most serious crimes, to flee the U.S. for Canada. Canada does not wish to become a haven for the most wanted and dangerous criminals from the U.S. If the Covenant fetters Canada's discretion not to seek assurances, increasing numbers of criminals may come to Canada for the purpose of securing immunity from capital punishment."

9.1 With regard to Mr. Ng's case, the State party recalls that he challenged the warrant of committal to await surrender in accordance with the extradition process outlined above, and that his counsel made written and oral submissions to the Minister to seek assurances that the death penalty would not be imposed. He argued that extradition to face the death penalty would offend his rights under section 7 (comparable to articles 6 and 9 of the Covenant) and section 12 (comparable to article 7 of the Covenant) of the Canadian Charter of Rights and Freedoms. The Supreme Court heard Mr. Ng's case at the same time as the appeal by Mr. Kindler, an American citizen who also faced extradition to the U.S. on a capital charge,ʲ and decided that their extradition without assurances would not violate Canada's human rights obligations.

9.2 With regard to the admissibility of the communication, the State party once more reaffirms that the communication should be declared inadmissible ratione materiae because extradition per se is beyond the scope of the Covenant. A review of the travaux preparatoires reveals that the drafters of the Covenant specifically considered and rejected a proposal to deal with extradition in the Covenant. In the light of the negotiating history of the Covenant, the State party submits that:

". . . a decision to extend the Covenant to extradition treaties or to individual decisions pursuant thereto would stretch the principles governing the interpretation of human rights instruments in unreasonable and unacceptable ways. It would be unreasonable because the principles of interpretation which recognize that human rights instruments are living documents and that human rights evolve over time cannot be employed in the face of express limits to the application of a given document. The absence of extradition from the articles of the Covenant when read with the intention of the drafters must be taken as an express limitation."

. . .

10.1 On the merits, the State party stresses that Mr. Ng enjoyed a full hearing on all matters concerning his extradition to face the death penalty.

"If it can be said that the Covenant applies to extradition at all . . . an extraditing State could be said to be in violation of the Covenant only where it returned a fugitive to certain or foreseeable treatment or punishment, or to judicial procedures which in themselves would be a violation of the Covenant."

In the present case, the State party submits that since Mr. Ng's trial has not yet begun, it was not reasonably foreseeable that he would be held in conditions of incarceration that would violate rights under the Covenant or that he would in fact be put to death. The State party points out that if convicted and sentenced to death, Mr. Ng is entitled to many avenues of appeal in the U.S. and that he can petition for clemency. Furthermore, he is entitled to challenge in the courts of the U.S. the conditions under which he is held while his appeals with respect to the death penalty are outstanding.

. . .

10.3 Finally, the State party observes that it is "in a difficult position attempting to defend the criminal justice system of the U.S. before the Committee. It contends that the Optional Protocol process was never intended to place a State in the position of having to defend the laws or practices of another State before the Committee."

10.4 With respect to the issue of whether the death penalty violates article 7 of the Covenant, the State party submits that:

". . . article 7 cannot be read or interpreted without reference to article 6. The Covenant must be read as a whole and its articles as being in harmony . . . It may be that certain forms of execution are contrary to article 7. Torturing a person to death would seem to fall into this category, as torture is a violation of article 7. Other forms of execution may be in violation of the Covenant because they are cruel, inhuman or degrading. However, as the death penalty is permitted within the narrow parameters set by article 6, it must be that some methods of execution exist which would not violate article 7."

10.5 As to the method of execution, the State party submits that there is no indication that execution by cyanide gas asphyxiation, the chosen method in California, is contrary to the Covenant or to international law. It further submits that no specific circumstances exist in Mr. Ng's case which would lead to a different conclusion concerning the application of this method of execution to him; nor would execution by gas asphyxiation be in violation of the Safeguards guaranteeing protection of the rights of those facing the death penalty, adopted by the Economic and Social Council in its resolution 1984/50 of 25 May 1984.

. . .

10.7 With respect to the question of the foreseeable length of time Mr. Ng would spend on death row if sentenced to death, the State party stated that:

". . . [t]here was no evidence before the Minister or the Canadian courts regarding any intentions of Ng to make full use of all avenues for judicial review in the U.S. of any potential sentence of death. There was no evidence that either the judicial system in the State of California or the Supreme Court of the U.S. had serious problems of backlogs or other forms of institutional delay which would likely be a continuing problem when and if Ng is held to await execution."

In this connection, the State party refers to the Committee's jurisprudence that prolonged judicial proceedings do not per se constitute cruel, inhuman or degrading treatment even if they can be a source of mental strain for the convicted prisoners.[k] The State party contends that it was not reasonably foreseeable on the basis of the facts presented by Mr. Ng during the extradition process in Canada that any possible period of prolonged detention upon his return to the U.S. would result in a violation of the Covenant, but that it was more likely that any prolonged detention on death row would be attributable to Mr. Ng pursuing the many avenues for judicial review in the U.S.

. . .

11.2 As regards article 6 of the Extradition Treaty, counsel recalls that when the Treaty was signed in December 1971, the Canadian Criminal Code still provided for capital punishment in cases of murder, so that article 6 could have been invoked by either contracting State. Counsel submits that article 6 does not require assurances to be sought only in particularly "special" death penalty cases. He argues that the provision of the possibility to ask for assurances under article 6 of the Treaty implicitly acknowledges that offences punishable by death are to be dealt with differently, that different values and traditions with regard to the death penalty may be taken into account when deciding upon an extradition request and that an actual demand for assurances will not be perceived by the other party as unwarranted interference with the internal affairs of the requesting State. In particular, article 6 of the Treaty is said to ". . . allow the requested State . . . to maintain a consistent position: if the death penalty is rejected within its own borders . . . it could negate any responsibility for exposing a fugitive through surrender, to the risk of imposition of that penalty or associated practices and procedures in the other State." It is further submitted that "it is very significant that the existence of the discretion embodied in article 6, in relation to the death penalty, enables the contracting parties to honour both their own domestic constitutions and their international obligations without violating their obligations under the bilateral Extradition Treaty."

. . .

11.4 As regards the extradition proceedings against Mr. Ng, counsel notes that his Federal Court action against the Minister's decision to extradite the author without seeking assurances never was decided upon by the Federal Court, but was referred to the Supreme Court to be decided together with Mr. Kindler's appeal. In this context, counsel notes that the Supreme Court, when deciding that the author's extradition would not violate the Canadian constitution, failed to discuss criminal procedure in California or evidence adduced in relation to the death row phenomenon in California.

11.5 As to the State party's argument that extradition is beyond the scope of the Covenant, counsel argues that the travaux préparatoires do not show that the fundamental human rights set forth in the Covenant should never apply to extradition situations:

"Reluctance to include an express provision on extradition because the Covenant should 'lay down general principles' or because it should lay down 'fundamental human rights and not rights which are corollaries thereof' or because extradition was 'too complicated to be included in a single article' simply does not bespeak an intention to narrow or stultify those 'general principles' or 'fundamental human rights' or evidence a consensus that these general principles should never apply to extradition situations."

. . .

11.7 The author refers to the Committee's decision of 28 October 1992 and submits that in the circumstances of his case, the very purpose of his extradition without seeking assurances was to foreseeably expose him to the imposition of the death penalty and consequently to the death row phenomenon. In this connection, counsel submits that the author's extradition was sought upon charges which carry the death penalty, and that the prosecution in California never left any doubt that it would indeed seek the death penalty. He quotes the Assistant District Attorney in San Francisco as saying that: "there is sufficient evidence to convict and send Ng to the gas chamber if he is extradited . . . ."

11.8 In this context, counsel quotes from the judgment of the European Court of Human Rights in the Soering case:

"In the independent exercise of his discretion, the Commonwealth's attorney has himself decided to seek and persist in seeking the death penalty because the evidence, in his determination, supports such action. If the national authority with responsibility for prosecuting the offence takes such a firm stance, it is hardly open to the court to hold that there are no substantial grounds for believing that the applicant faces a real risk of being sentenced to death and hence experiencing the 'death row phenomenon'."

Counsel submits that, at the time of extradition, it was foreseeable that the author would be sentenced to death in California and therefore be exposed to violations of the Covenant.

11.9 Counsel refers to several resolutions adopted by the General Assembly in which the abolition of the death penalty was considered desirable.[1] He further refers to Protocol 6 of the European Convention for the Protection of Human Rights and Fundamental Freedoms and to the Second Optional Protocol to the International Covenant on Civil and Political Rights: "[O]ver the last fifty years there has been a progressive and increasingly rapid evolution away from the death penalty. That evolution has led almost all Western democracies to abandon it." He argues that this development should be taken into account when interpreting the Covenant.

11.10 As to the method of execution in California, cyanide gas asphyxiation, counsel argues that it constitutes inhuman and degrading punishment within the meaning of article 7 of the Covenant. He notes that asphyxiation may take up to 12 minutes, during which condemned persons remain conscious, experience obvious pain and agony, drool and convulse and often soil themselves (reference is made to the execution of Robert F. Harris at San Quentin Prison in April 1992). Counsel further argues that, given the cruel character of this method of execution, a decision of Canada not to extradite without assurances would not constitute a breach of its Treaty obligations with the U.S. or undue interference with the latter's internal law and practices. Furthermore, counsel notes that cyanide gas execution is the sole method of execution in only three States in the U.S. (Arizona, Maryland and California), and that there is no evidence to suggest that it is an approved means of carrying out judicially mandated executions elsewhere in the international community.

. . .

Further submission from the author and the State party's reaction thereto.

12.1 In an affidavit dated 5 June 1993, signed by Mr. Ng and submitted by his counsel, the author provides detailed information about the conditions of his confinement in Canada between 1985 and his extradition in September 1991. He notes that following his arrest on 6 July 1985, he was kept at the Calgary Remand Center in solitary confinement under a so-called "suicide watch," which meant 24-hour camera supervision and the placement of a guard outside the bars of the cell. He was only allowed one hour of exercise each day in the Center's "mini-yard," on "walk-alone status" and accompanied by two guards. As the extradition process unfolded in Canada, the author was transferred to a prison in Edmonton; he complains about "drastically more severe custodial restrictions" from February 1987 to September 1991, which he links to the constant and escalating media coverage of the case. Prison guards allegedly began to tout him, he was kept in total isolation, and contact with visitors was restricted.

. . .

Review of admissibility and consideration of merits:

13.1 In his initial submission, author's counsel alleged that Mr. Ng was a victim of violations of articles 6, 7, 9, 10, 14 and 26 of the Covenant.

13.2 When the Committee considered the admissibility of the communication during its forty-sixth session and adopted a decision relating thereto (decision of 28 October 1992), it noted that the communication raised complex issues with regard to the compatibility with the Covenant, ratione materiae, of extradition to face capital punishment, in particular with regard to the scope of articles 6 and 7 of the Covenant to such situations and their application in the author's case. It noted, however, that questions about the issue of whether the author could be deemed a "victim" within the meaning of article 1 of the Optional Protocol remained, but held that only consideration of the merits of all the circumstances under which the extradition procedure and all its effects occurred, would enable the Committee to determine whether Mr. Ng was indeed a victim within the meaning of article 1. The State party has made extensive new submissions on both admissibility and merits and reaffirmed that the communication is inadmissible because "the evidence shows that Ng is not the victim of any violation in Canada of rights set out in the Covenant." Counsel, in turn, has filed detailed objections to the State party's affirmations.

13.3 In reviewing the question of admissibility, the Committee takes note of the contentions of the State party and of counsel's arguments. It notes that counsel, in submissions made after the decision of 28 October 1992, has introduced entirely new issues which were not raised in the original communication, and which relate to Mr. Ng's conditions of detention in Canadian penitentiaries, the stress to which he was exposed as the extradition process proceeded, and alleged deceptive manoeuvres by Canadian prison authorities.

13.4 These fresh allegations, if corroborated, would raise issues under articles 7 and 10 of the Covenant, and would bring the author within the gambit of article 1 of the Optional Protocol. While the wording of the decision of 28 October 1992 would not have precluded counsel from introducing them at this stage of the procedure, the Committee, in the circumstances of the case, finds that it need not address the new claims, as domestic remedies before the Canadian courts were not exhausted in respect of them. It transpires from the material before the Committee that complaints about the conditions of the author's detention in Canada or about alleged irregularities committed by Canadian prison authorities were not raised either during the committal or the surrender phase of the extradition proceedings. Had it been argued that an effective remedy for the determination of these claims is no longer available, the Committee finds that it was incumbent upon counsel to raise them before the competent courts, provincial or federal, at the material time. This part of the author's allegations is therefore declared inadmissible under article 5, paragraph 2 (b), of the Optional Protocol.

13.5 It remains for the Committee to examine the author's claim that he is a "victim" within the meaning of the Optional Protocol because he was extradited to California on capital charges pending trial, without the assurances provided for in article 6 of the Extradition Treaty between Canada and the U.S. In this connection, it is to be recalled that: (a) California had sought the author's extradition on charges which, if proven, carry the death penalty; (b) the U.S. requested Mr. Ng's extradition on those capital charges; (c) the extradition warrant documents the existence of a prima facie case against the author; (d) U.S. prosecutors involved in the case have stated that they would ask for the death penalty to be imposed; and (e) the State of California, when intervening before the Supreme Court of Canada, did not disavow the prosecutors' position. The Committee considers that these facts raise questions with regard to the scope of articles 6 and 7, in relation to which, on issues of admissibility alone, the Committee's jurisprudence is not dispositive. As indicated in the case of Kindler v Canada,[m] only an examination on the merits of the claims will enable the Committee to pronounce itself on the scope of these articles and to clarify the applicability of the Covenant and Optional Protocol to cases concerning extradition to face the death penalty.

14.1 Before addressing the merits of the communication, the Committee observes that what is at issue is not whether Mr. Ng's rights have been or are likely to be violated by the U.S., which is not a State party to the Optional Protocol, but whether by extraditing Mr. Ng to the U.S., Canada exposed him to a real risk of a violation of his rights under the Covenant. States parties to the Covenant will also frequently be parties to bilateral treaty obligations, including those under extradition treaties. A State party to the Covenant must ensure that it carries out all its other legal commitments in a manner consistent with the Covenant. The starting-point for consideration of this issue must be the State party's obligation, under article 2, paragraph 1, of the Covenant, namely, to ensure to all individuals within its territory and subject to its jurisdiction the rights recognized in the Covenant. The right to life is the most essential of these rights.

14.2 If a State party extradites a person within its jurisdiction in such circumstances, and if, as a result, there is a real risk that his or her rights under the Covenant will be violated in another jurisdiction, the State party itself may be in violation of the Covenant.

15.1 With regard to a possible violation by Canada of article 6 of the Covenant by its decision to extradite Mr. Ng, two related questions arise:

(a) Did the requirement under article 6, paragraph 1, to protect the right to life prohibit Canada from exposing a person within its jurisdiction to the real risk (i.e., a necessary and foreseeable consequence) of being sentenced to death and losing his life in circumstances incompatible with article 6 of the Covenant as a consequence of extradition to the U.S.?

(b) Did the fact that Canada had abolished capital punishment except for certain military offences require Canada to refuse extradition or request assurances from the U.S., as it was entitled to do under article 6 of the Extradition Treaty, that the death penalty would not be imposed against Mr. Ng?

15.2 Counsel claims that capital punishment must be viewed as a violation of article 6 of the Covenant "in all but the most horrendous cases of heinous crime; it can no longer be accepted as the standard penalty for murder." Counsel, however, does not substantiate this statement or link it to the specific circumstances of the present case. In reviewing the facts submitted by author's counsel and by the State party, the Committee notes that Mr. Ng was convicted of committing murder under aggravating circumstances; this would appear to bring the case within the scope of article 6, paragraph 2, of the Covenant. In this connection the Committee recalls that it is not a "fourth instance" and that it is not within its competence under the Optional Protocol to review sentences of the courts of States. This limitation of competence applies a fortiori where the proceedings take place in a State that is not party to the Optional Protocol.

15.3 The Committee notes that article 6, paragraph 1, must be read together with article 6, paragraph 2, which does not prohibit the imposition of the death penalty for the most serious crimes. Canada did not itself charge Mr. Ng with capital offences, but extradited him to the U.S., where he faces capital charges and the possible (and foreseeable) imposition of the death penalty. If Mr. Ng had been exposed, through extradition from Canada, to a real risk of a violation of article 6, paragraph 2, in the U.S., this would have entailed a violation by Canada of its obligations under article 6, paragraph 1. Among the requirements of article 6, paragraph 2, is that capital punishment be imposed only for the most serious crimes, under circumstances not contrary to the Covenant and other instruments, and that it be carried out pursuant to a final judgement rendered by a competent court. The Committee notes that Mr. Ng was extradited to stand trial on 19 criminal charges, including 12 counts of murder. If sentenced to death, that sentence, based on the information which the Committee has before it, would be based on a conviction of guilt in respect of very serious crimes. He was over 18 years old when the crimes of which he stands accused were committed. Finally, while the author has claimed before the Supreme Court of Canada and before the Committee that his right to a fair trial would not be guaranteed in the judicial process in California, because of racial bias in the jury selection process and in the imposition of the death penalty, these claims have been advanced in respect of purely hypothetical events. Nothing in the file supports the contention that the author's trial in the Calaveras County Court would not meet the requirements of article 14 of the Covenant.

15.4 Moreover, the Committee observes that Mr. Ng was extradited to the U.S. after extensive proceedings in the Canadian courts, which reviewed all the charges and the evidence available against the author. In the circumstances, the Committee concludes that Canada's obligations under article 6, paragraph 1, did not require it to refuse Mr. Ng's extradition.

15.5 The Committee notes that Canada has itself, except for certain categories of military offences, abolished capital punishment; it is not, however, a party to the Second Optional Protocol to the Covenant. As to issue (b) in paragraph 15.1 above, namely, whether the fact that Canada has generally abolished capital punishment, taken together with its obligations under the Covenant, required it to refuse extradition or to seek the assurances it was entitled to seek under the Extradition Treaty, the Committee observes that abolition of capital punishment does not release Canada of its obligations under extradition treaties.

However, it should be expected that, when exercising a permitted discretion under an extradition treaty (namely, whether or not to seek assurances that the death penalty would not be imposed), a State party, which itself abandoned capital punishment, will give serious consideration to its own chosen policy. The Committee notes, however, that Canada has indicated that the possibility of seeking assurances would normally be exercised where special circumstances existed; in the present case, this possibility was considered and rejected.

15.6 While States must be mindful of their obligation to protect the right to life when exercising their discretion in the application of extradition treaties, the Committee does not find that the terms of article 6 of the Covenant necessarily require Canada to refuse to extradite or to seek assurances. The Committee notes that the extradition of Mr. Ng would have violated Canada's obligations under article 6 of the Covenant if the decision to extradite without assurances had been taken summarily or arbitrarily. The evidence before the Committee reveals, however, that the Minister of Justice reached his decision after hearing extensive arguments in favour of seeking assurances. The Committee further takes note of the reasons advanced by the Minister of Justice in his letter dated 26 October 1989 addressed to Mr. Ng's counsel, in particular, the absence of exceptional circumstances, the availability of due process and of appeal against conviction and the importance of not providing a safe haven for those accused of murder.

15.7 In the light of the above, the Committee concludes that Mr. Ng is not a victim of a violation by Canada of article 6 of the Covenant.

16.1 In determining whether, in a particular case, the imposition of capital punishment constitutes a violation of article 7, the Committee will have regard to the relevant personal factors regarding the author, the specific conditions of detention on death row and whether the proposed method of execution is particularly abhorrent. In the instant case, it is contended that execution by gas asphyxiation is contrary to internationally accepted standards of humane treatment, and that it amounts to treatment in violation of article 7 of the Covenant. The Committee begins by noting that whereas article 6, paragraph 2, allows for the imposition of the death penalty under certain limited circumstances, any method of execution provided for by law must be designed in such a way as to avoid conflict with article 7.

16.2 The Committee is aware that, by definition, every execution of a sentence of death may be considered to constitute cruel and inhuman treatment within the meaning of article 7 of the Covenant; on the other hand, article 6, paragraph 2, permits the imposition of capital punishment for the most serious crimes. None the less, the Committee reaffirms, as it did in its general comment (44) on article 7 of the Covenant that, when imposing capital punishment, the execution of the sentence "must be carried out in such a way as to cause the least possible physical and mental suffering." n/

16.3 In the present case, the author has provided detailed information that execution by gas asphyxiation may cause prolonged suffering and agony and does not result in death as swiftly as possible, as asphyxiation by cyanide gas may take over 10 minutes. The State party had the opportunity to refute these allegations on the facts; it has failed to do so. Rather, the State party has confined itself to arguing that in the absence of a norm of international law which expressly prohibits asphyxiation by cyanide gas, "it would be interfering to an unwarranted degree with the internal laws and practices of the U.S. to refuse to extradite a fugitive to face the possible imposition of the death penalty by cyanide gas asphyxiation."

16.4 In the instant case and on the basis of the information before it, the Committee concludes that execution by gas asphyxiation, should the death penalty be imposed on the author, would not meet the test of "least possible physical and mental suffering," and constitutes cruel and inhuman treatment, in violation of article 7 of the Covenant. Accordingly, Canada, which could reasonably foresee that Mr. Ng, if sentenced to death, would be executed in a way that amounts to a violation of article 7, failed to comply with its obligations under the Covenant, by extraditing Mr. Ng without having sought and received assurances that he would not be executed.

16.5 The Committee need not pronounce itself on the compatibility with article 7 of methods of execution other than that which is at issue in this case.

17. The Human Rights Committee, acting under article 5, paragraph 4, of the International Covenant on Civil and Political Rights, is of the view that the facts as found by the Committee reveal a violation by Canada of article 7 of the Covenant.

18. The Human Rights Committee requests the State party to make such representations as might still be possible to avoid the imposition of the death penalty and appeals to the State party to ensure that a similar situation does not arise in the future.

. . .

[Other Opinions Omitted]

18. *Soering v United Kingdom* European Court of Human Rights, Council of Europe (Excerpted) Cite as: Case No. 1/1989/161/217.

In the Soering case,
Judgment of the European Court of Human Rights, taking its decision in plenary session in pursuance of Rule 50 of the Rules of Court and composed of the following judges: (Names of 18 Judges and Registrar)
Having deliberated in private on 27 April and 26 June 1989,
Delivers the following judgment, which was adopted on the last-mentioned date:
Procedure
1. The case was brought before the Court on 25 January 1989 by the European Commission of Human Rights ("the Commission"), on 30 January 1989 by the Government of the United Kingdom of Great Britain and Northern Ireland and on 3 February 1989 by the Government of the Federal Republic of Germany, within the three-month period laid down by Article 32 A7 1 and Article 47 (art. 32–1, art. 47) of the Convention for the Protection of Human Rights and Fundamental Freedoms ("the Convention"). It originated in an application (no. 14038/88) against the United Kingdom lodged with the Commission under Article 25 (art. 25) by a German national, Mr. Jens Soering, on 8 July 1988.

The Commission's request referred to Articles 44 and 48 (art. 44, art. 48) and to the declaration whereby the United Kingdom recognised the compulsory jurisdiction of the Court (Article 46) (art. 46). The object of the request and of the two governmental applications was to obtain a decision from the Court as to whether or not the facts of the case disclosed a breach by the respondent State of its obligations under Articles 3, 6 and 13 (art. 3, art. 6, art. 13) of the Convention.

. . .

I. Particular circumstances of the case

. . .

11. The applicant, Mr. Jens Soering, was born on 1 August 1966 and is a German national. He is currently detained in prison in England pending extradition to the United States of America to face charges of murder in the Commonwealth of Virginia.

12. The homicides in question were committed in Bedford County, Virginia, in March 1985. The victims, William Reginald Haysom (aged 72) and Nancy Astor Haysom (aged 53), were the parents of the appli-

cant's girlfriend, Elizabeth Haysom, who is a Canadian national. Death in each case was the result of multiple and massive stab and slash wounds to the neck, throat and body.

. . .

13. On 13 June 1986 a grand jury of the Circuit Court of Bedford County indicted him on charges of murdering the Haysom parents. The charges alleged capital murder of both of them and the separate non-capital murders of each.

14. On 11 August 1986 the Government of the United States of America requested the applicant's and Miss Haysom's extradition under the terms of the Extradition Treaty of 1972 between the U.S. and the United Kingdom.

15. On 29 October 1986 the British Embassy in Washington addressed a request to the U.S. authorities in the following terms:

"Because the death penalty has been abolished in Great Britain, the Embassy has been instructed to seek an assurance, in accordance with the terms of . . . the Extradition Treaty, that, in the event of Mr. Soering being surrendered and being convicted of the crimes for which he has been indicted. . . ., the death penalty, if imposed, will not be carried out.

Should it not be possible on constitutional grounds for the U.S. Government to give such an assurance, the United Kingdom authorities ask that the U.S. Government undertake to recommend to the appropriate authorities that the death penalty should not be imposed or, if imposed, should not be executed."

. . .

16. On 11 February 1987 the local court in Bonn issued a warrant for the applicant's arrest in respect of the alleged murders. On 11 March the Government of the Federal Republic of Germany requested his extradition to the Federal Republic under the Extradition Treaty of 1872 between the Federal Republic and the United Kingdom (see paragraph 31 below). The Secretary of State was then advised by the Director of Public Prosecutions that, although the German request contained proof that German courts had jurisdiction to try the applicant, the evidence submitted, since it consisted solely of the admissions made by the applicant to the Bonn prosecutor in the absence of a caution, did not amount to a prima facie case against him and that a magistrate would not be able under the Extradition Act 1870 to commit him to await extradition to Germany on the strength of admissions obtained in such circumstances.

. . .

17. On 23 April the U.S., by diplomatic note, requested the applicant's extradition to the U.S. in preference to the Federal Republic of Germany.

18. On 8 May 1987 Elizabeth Haysom was surrendered for extradition to the U.S. After pleading guilty on 22 August as an accessory to the murder of her parents, she was sentenced on 6 October to 90 years' imprisonment (45 years on each count of murder).

19. On May 1987 the United Kingdom Government informed the Federal Republic of Germany that the U.S. had earlier "submitted a request, supported by prima facie evidence, for the extradition of Mr Soering." The United Kingdom Government notified the Federal Republic that they had "concluded that, having regard to all the circumstances of the case, the court should continue to consider in the normal way the U.S. request." They further indicated that they had sought an assurance from the U.S. authorities on the question of the death penalty and that "in the event that the court commits Mr. Soering, his surrender to the U.S. authorities would be subject to the receipt of satisfactory assurances on this matter."

20. On 1 June 1987 Mr. Updike swore an affidavit in his capacity as Attorney for Bedford County, in which he certified as follows:

"I hereby certify that should Jens Soering be convicted of the offence of capital murder as charged in Bedford County, Virginia . . . a representation will be made in the name of the United Kingdom to the judge at the time of sentencing that it is the wish of the United Kingdom that the death penalty should not be imposed or carried out."

This assurance was transmitted to the United Kingdom Government under cover of a diplomatic note on 8 June. It was repeated in the same terms in a further affidavit from Mr. Updike sworn on 16 February 1988 and forwarded to the United Kingdom by diplomatic note on 17 May 1988. In the same note the Federal Government of the U.S. undertook to ensure that the commitment of the appropriate authorities of the Commonwealth of Virginia to make representations on behalf of the United Kingdom would be honoured.

During the course of the present proceedings the Virginia authorities informed the United Kingdom Government that Mr. Updike was not planning to provide any further assurances and intended to seek the death penalty in Mr. Soering's case because the evidence, in his determination, supported such action.

21. On 16 June 1987 at the Bow Street Magistrates' Court committal proceedings took place before the Chief Stipendiary Magistrate.

. . .

On behalf of the applicant psychiatric evidence was adduced from a consultant forensic psychiatrist that he was immature and inexperienced and had lost his personal identity in a symbiotic relationship with his girlfriend—a powerful, persuasive and disturbed young woman. The psychiatric report concluded:

"There existed between Miss Haysom and Soering a 'folie a deux', in which the most disturbed partner was Miss Haysom.

. . .

In conclusion, it is my opinion that, at the time of the offences, Soering was suffering from an abnormality of mind which, in this country, would constitute a defence of 'not guilty to murder but guilty of manslaughter'."

. . .

22. On 29 June 1987 Mr. Soering applied to the Divisional Court for a writ of habeas corpus in respect of his committal and for leave to apply for judicial review. On 11 December both applications were refused by the Divisional Court (Lord Justice Lloyd and Mr. Justice Macpherson).

In support of his application for leave to apply for judicial review, Mr. Soering had submitted that the assurance received from the U.S. authorities was so worthless that no reasonable Secretary of State could regard it as satisfactory under Article IV of the Extradition Treaty between the United Kingdom and the U.S. (see paragraph 36 below). In his judgment Lord Justice Lloyd agreed that "the assurance leaves something to be desired."

. . .

23. On 30 June 1988 the House of Lords rejected the applicant's petition for leave to appeal against the decision of the Divisional Court.

24. On 14 July 1988 the applicant petitioned the Secretary of State, requesting him to exercise his discretion not to make an order for the applicant's surrender under section 11 of the Extradition Act 1870 (see paragraph 34 below).

This request was rejected, and on 3 August 1988 the Secretary of State signed a warrant ordering the applicant's surrender to the U.S. authorities. However, the applicant has not been transferred to the U.S. by virtue of the interim measures indicated in the present proceedings firstly by the European Commission and then by the European Court (see paragraphs 4 above and 77 below).

. . .

26. By a declaration dated March 1989 submitted to this Court, the applicant stated that should the United Kingdom Government require that he be deported to the Federal Republic of Germany he would consent to such requirement and would present no factual or legal opposition against the making or execution of an order to that effect.

. . .

A. Criminal law

. . .

28. English courts do not exercise criminal jurisdiction in respect of acts of foreigners abroad except in certain cases immaterial to the present proceedings. Consequently, neither the applicant, as a German citizen, nor Elizabeth Haysom, a Canadian citizen, was or is amenable to criminal trial in the United Kingdom.

B. Extradition

29. The relevant general law on extradition is contained in the Extradition Acts 1870–1935.

30. The extradition arrangements between the United Kingdom and the United States of America are governed by the Extradition Treaty signed by the two Governments on 8 June 1972, a Supplementary Treaty signed on 25 June 1982, and an Exchange of Notes dated 19 and August 1986 amending the Supplementary Treaty. These arrangements have been incorporated into the law of the United Kingdom by Orders in Council (the United States of America (Extradition) Order 1976, S.I. 1976/2144 and the United States of America (Extradition) (Amendment) Order 1986, S.I. 1986).

By virtue of Article I of the Extradition Treaty, "each Contracting Party undertakes to extradite to the other, in the circumstances and subject to the conditions specified in this Treaty, any person found in its territory who has been accused or convicted of any offence [specified in the Treaty and including murder], committed within the jurisdiction of the other Party."

. . .

However, the courts will not review any decision of the Secretary of State by reason of the fact only that he failed to consider whether or not there was a breach of the European Convention on Human Rights (R v Secretary of State, ex parte Kirkwood [1984] 1 Weekly Law Reports 913). "The written undertakings about the death penalty that the Secretary of State obtains from the Federal authorities amount to an undertaking that the views of the United Kingdom will be represented to the judge. At the time of sentencing he will be informed that the United Kingdom does not wish the death penalty to be imposed or carried out. That means that the United Kingdom authorities render up a fugitive or are prepared to send a citizen to face an American court on the clear understanding that the death penalty will not be carried out—it has never been carried out in such cases. It would be a fundamental blow to the extradition arrangements between our two countries if the death penalty were carried out on an individual who had been returned under those circumstances." (Hansard, 10 March 1987, col. 955)

There has, however, never been a case in which the effectiveness of such an undertaking has been tested.

III. Relevant domestic law in the Commonwealth of Virginia

A. The law relating to murder

. . .

40. Section 18.2–31 of the Virginia Code provides that eight types of homicide constitute capital murder, punishable as a Class 1 felony, including "the wilful, deliberate and premeditated killing of more than one person as a part of the same act or transaction" (sub-section (g)). The punishment for a Class 1 felony is "death or imprisonment for life" [Virginia Code, section 18.2–10(a)]. Murder other than capital murder is classified as murder in the first.

42. The sentencing procedure in a capital murder case in Virginia is a separate proceeding from the determination of guilt. Following a determination of guilt of capital murder, the same jury, or judge sitting without a jury, will forthwith proceed to hear evidence regarding punishment. All relevant evidence concerning the offence and the defendant is admissible. Evidence in mitigation is subject to almost no limitation, while evidence of aggravation is restricted by statute (Virginia Code, section 19.2–264.4).

43. Unless the prosecution proves beyond a reasonable doubt the existence of at least one of two statutory aggravating circumstances—future dangerousness or vileness—the sentencer may not return a death sentence.

. . .

51. In a capital murder trial, the defendant's mental condition at the time of the offence, including any level of mental illness, may be pleaded as a mitigating factor at the sentencing stage. Evidence on this may include, but is not limited to, showing that the defendant was under the influence of extreme mental or emotional disturbance.

52. The Supreme Court of Virginia reviews automatically every case in which a capital sentence has been passed, regardless of the plea entered by the defendant at his trial.

. . .

After this appeal process is completed, the sentence of death will be executed unless a stay of execution is entered. As a practical matter, a stay will be entered when the prisoner initiates further proceedings. There has apparently been only one case since 1977 where the Virginia Supreme Court has itself reduced a death sentence to life imprisonment.

53. The prisoner may apply to the U.S. certiorari review of the decision of the Supreme Court of Virginia. If unsuccessful, he may begin collateral attacks upon the conviction and sentence in habeas corpus proceedings in both State and Federal courts.

. . .

54. The Virginia and Federal statutes and rules of court set time-limits for the presentation of appeals following conviction or appeals against the decisions in habeas corpus proceedings. There are, however, no time-limits for filing the initial State and Federal habeas corpus petitions.

. . .

56. The average time between trial and execution in Virginia, calculated on the basis of the seven executions which have taken place since 1977, is six to eight years. The delays are primarily due to a strategy by con-

victed prisoners to prolong the appeal proceedings as much as possible. The U.S. Supreme Court has not as yet considered or ruled on the "death row phenomenon" and in particular whether it falls foul of the prohibition of "cruel and unusual punishment" under the Eighth Amendment to the Constitution of the U.S.

E. Legal assistance for appeals

57. All prisoners who have been sentenced to death have individual lawyers to represent them, whether privately recruited or court-appointed. On the other hand, there is no statutory provision expressly mandating legal assistance to be made available to the indigent prisoner to file habeas corpus petitions. However, it has recently been affirmed by a U.S. Court of Appeal that the Commonwealth of Virginia is required to provide indigent prisoners who have been sentenced to death with the assistance of lawyers to pursue challenges to their death sentences in State habeas corpus actions (Giarratano v Murray, 847 F.2d 1118 (4th Circuit 1988) (en banc)—case currently pending before the U.S. Supreme Court). In Federal habeas corpus and certiorari proceedings case-law does not impose the same obligation (ibid., p. 1122, column 1), for the reason that the Federal courts would have available the appellate briefs, a transcript and State court opinion (in certiorari proceedings) and the briefs of counsel, a transcript and opinion (in habeas corpus proceedings).

. . .

G. Prison conditions in Mecklenburg Correctional Center

61. There are currently 40 people under sentence of death in Virginia. The majority are detained in Mecklenburg Correctional Center, which is a modern maximum-security institution with a total capacity of 335 inmates. Institutional Operating Procedures (IOP 821.1) establish uniform operating procedures for the administration, security, control and delivery of necessary services to death row inmates in Mecklenburg. In addition conditions of confinement are governed by a comprehensive consent decree handed down by the U.S. District Court in Richmond in the case of Alan Brown et al. v Allyn R. Sielaff et al. (5 April 1985). Both the Virginia Department of Corrections and the American Civil Liberties Union monitor compliance with the terms of the consent decree. The U.S. District Court also retains jurisdiction to enforce compliance with the decree.

. . .

64. The applicant adduced much evidence of extreme stress, psychological deterioration and risk of homosexual abuse and physical attack undergone by prisoners on death row, including Mecklenburg Correctional Center. This evidence was strongly contested by the United Kingdom Government on the basis of affidavits sworn by administrators from the Virginia Department of Corrections.

. . .

H. The giving and effect of assurances in relation to the death penalty

69. Relations between the United Kingdom and the United States of America on matters concerning extradition are conducted by and with the Federal and not the State authorities. However, in respect of offences against State laws the Federal authorities have no legally binding power to provide, in an appropriate extradition case, an assurance that the death penalty will not be imposed or carried out. In such cases the power rests with the State. If a State does decide to give a promise in relation to the death penalty, the U.S. government has the power to give an assurance to the extraditing Government that the State's promise will be honoured.

. . .

I. Mutual assistance in criminal matters

. . .

Proceedings Before the Commission

76. Mr. Soering's application (no. 14038/88) was lodged with the European Commission on Human Rights on 8 July 1988. In his application Mr. Soering stated his belief that, notwithstanding the assurance given to the United Kingdom Government, there was a serious likelihood that he would be sentenced to death if extradited to the United States of America. He maintained that in the circumstances and, in particular, having regard to the "death row phenomenon" he would thereby be subjected to inhuman and degrading treatment and punishment contrary to Article 3 (art. 3) of the Convention. In his further submission his extradition to the U.S. would constitute a violation of Article 6 A7 3 (c) (art.6-3-c) because of the absence of legal aid in the State of Virginia to pursue various appeals. Finally, he claimed that, in breach of Article 13 (art. 13), he had no effective remedy under United Kingdom law in respect of his complaint under Article 3 (art. 3).

. . .

Final Submissions to the Court by the United Kingdom Government

79. At the public hearing on 24 April 1989 the United Kingdom Government maintained the concluding submissions set out in their memorial, whereby they requested the Court to hold:

1. that neither the extradition of the applicant nor any act or decision of the United Kingdom Government in relation thereto constitutes a breach of Article 3 (art. 3) of the Convention;

2. that neither the extradition of the applicant nor any act or decision of the United Kingdom Government in relation thereto constitutes a breach of Article 6.3 (c) (art. 6–3-c) of the Convention;

3. that there has been no violation of Article 13 (art. 13) of the Convention;

4. that no issues arise under Article 50 (art. 50) of the Convention which call for consideration by the Court.

They also submitted that further complaints under Article 6 (art. 6) made by the applicant before the Court were not within the scope of the case as declared admissible by the Commission.

As to the Law

I. Alleged Breach of Article 3 (art. 3)

80. The applicant alleged that the decision by the Secretary of State for the Home Department to surrender him to the authorities of the United States of America would, if implemented, give rise to a breach by the United Kingdom of Article 3 (art. 3) of the Convention, which provides:

"No one shall be subjected to torture or to inhuman or degrading treatment or punishment."

A. Applicability of Article 3 (art. 3) in cases of extradition

81. The alleged breach derives from the applicant's exposure to the so-called "death row phenomenon." This phenomenon may be described as consisting in a combination of circumstances to which the applicant would be exposed if, after having been extradited to Virginia to face a capital murder charge, he were sentenced to death.

82. In its report (at paragraph 94) the Commission reaffirmed "its case-law that a person's deportation or extradition may give rise to an issue under Article 3 (art. 3) of the Convention where there are serious reasons to believe that the individual will be subjected, in the receiving State, to treatment contrary to that Article (art. 3)."

The Government of the Federal Republic of Germany supported the approach of the Commission, pointing to a similar approach in the case-law of the German courts.

The applicant likewise submitted that Article 3 (art. 3) not only prohibits the Contracting States from causing inhuman or degrading treatment or punishment to occur within their jurisdiction but also embodies an associated obligation not to put a person in a position where he will or may suffer such treatment or punishment at the hands of other States. For the applicant, at least as far as Article 3 (art. 3) is concerned, an individual may not be surrendered out of the protective zone of the Convention without the certainty that the safeguards which he would enjoy are as effective as the Convention standard.

83. The United Kingdom Government, on the other hand, contended that Article 3 (art. 3) should not be interpreted so as to impose responsibility on a Contracting State for acts which occur outside its jurisdiction. In particular, in their submission, extradition does not involve the responsibility of the extraditing State for inhuman or degrading treatment or punishment which the extradited person may suffer outside the State's jurisdiction. To begin with, they maintained, it would be straining the language of Article 3 (art. 3) intolerably to hold that by surrendering a fugitive criminal the extraditing State has "subjected" him to any treatment or punishment that he will receive following conviction and sentence in the receiving State. Further arguments advanced against the approach of the Commission were that it interferes with international treaty rights; it leads to a conflict with the norms of international judicial process, in that it in effect involves adjudication on the internal affairs of foreign States not Parties to the Convention or to the proceedings before the Convention institutions; it entails grave difficulties of evaluation and proof in requiring the examination of alien systems of law and of conditions in foreign States; the practice of national courts and the international community cannot reasonably be invoked to support it; it causes a serious risk of harm in the Contracting State which is obliged to harbour the protected person, and leaves criminals untried, at large and unpunished.

In the alternative, the United Kingdom Government submitted that the application of Article 3 (art. 3) in extradition cases should be limited to those occasions in which the treatment or punishment abroad is certain, imminent and serious. In their view, the fact that by definition the matters complained of are only anticipated, together with the common and legitimate interest of all States in bringing fugitive criminals to justice, requires a very high degree of risk, proved beyond reasonable doubt, that ill-treatment will actually occur.

84. The Court will approach the matter on the basis of the following considerations.

85. As results from Article 5.1 (f) (art. 5–1-f), which permits "the lawful . . . detention of a person against whom action is being taken with a view t . . . extradition," no right not to be extradited is as such protected by the Convention. Nevertheless, in so far as a measure of extradition has consequences adversely affecting the enjoyment of a Convention right, it may, assuming that the consequences are not too remote, attract the obligations of a Contracting State under the relevant Convention guarantee (see, mutatis mutandis, the Abdulaziz, Cabales and Balkandali judgment of 25 May 1985, Series A no. 94, pp. 31–32, 59–60—in relation to rights in the field of immigration). What is at issue in the present case is whether Article 3 (art. 3) can be applicable when the adverse consequences of extradition are, or may be, suffered outside the jurisdiction of the extraditing State as a result of treatment or punishment administered in the receiving State.

86. Article 1 (art. 1) of the Convention, which provides that "the High Contracting Parties shall secure to everyone within their jurisdiction the rights and freedoms defined in Section I," sets a limit, notably territorial, on the reach of the Convention. In particular, the engagement undertaken by a Contracting State is confined to "securing" ("reconna" tre" in the French text) the listed rights and freedoms to persons within its own "jurisdiction." Further, the Convention does not govern the actions of States not Parties to it, nor does it purport to be a means of requiring the Contracting States to impose Convention standards on other States. Article 1 (art. 1) cannot be read as justifying a general principle to the effect that, notwithstanding its extradition obligations, a Contracting State may not surrender an individual unless satisfied that the conditions awaiting him in the country of destination are in full accord with each of the safeguards of the Convention. Indeed, as the United Kingdom Government stressed, the beneficial purpose of extradition in preventing fugitive offenders from evading justice cannot be ignored in determining the scope of application of the Convention and of Article 3 (art. 3) in particular.

In the instant case it is common ground that the United Kingdom has no power over the practices and arrangements of the Virginia authorities which are the subject of the applicant's complaints. It is also true that in other international instruments cited by the United Kingdom Government—for example the 1951 United Nations Convention relating to the Status of Refugees (Article 33), the 1957 European Convention on Extradition (Article 11) and the 1984 United Nations Convention against Torture and Other Cruel, Inhuman and Degrading Treatment or Punishment (Article 3)—the problems of removing a person to another jurisdiction where unwanted consequences may follow are addressed expressly and specifically. These considerations cannot, however, absolve the Contracting Parties from responsibility under Article 3 (art. 3) for all and any foreseeable consequences of extradition suffered outside their jurisdiction.

87. In interpreting the Convention regard must be had to its special character as a treaty for the collective enforcement of human rights and fundamental freedoms (see the Ireland v the United Kingdom judgment of 18 January 1978, Series A no. 25, p. 90, A7 239). Thus, the object and purpose of the Convention as an instrument for the protection of individual human beings require that its provisions be interpreted and applied so as to make its safeguards practical and effective (see, inter alia, the Artico judgment of 13 May 1980, Series A no. 37, p. 16, A7 33). In addition, any interpretation of the rights and freedoms guaranteed has to be consistent with "the general spirit of the Convention, an instrument designed to maintain and promote the ideals and values of a democratic society" (see the Kjeldsen, Busk Madsen and Pedersen judgment of 7 December 1976, Series A no. 23, p. 27, 53).

88. Article 3 (art. 3) makes no provision for exceptions and no derogation from it is permissible under Article 15 (art. 15) in time of war or other national emergency. This absolute prohibition of torture and of inhuman or degrading treatment or punishment under the terms of the Convention shows that Article 3 (art. 3) enshrines one of the fundamental values of the democratic societies making up the Council of Europe. It is also to be found in similar terms in other international instruments such as the 1966 International Covenant on Civil and Political Rights and the 1969 American Convention on Human Rights and is generally recognised as an internationally accepted standard.

The question remains whether the extradition of a fugitive to another State where he would be subjected or be likely to be subjected to torture or to inhuman or degrading treatment or punishment would itself engage the responsibility of a Contracting State under Article 3 (art. 3). That the abhorrence of torture has such implications is recognised in Article 3 of the United Nations Convention Against Torture and Other Cruel, Inhuman or Degrading Treatment or Punishment, which provides that "no State Party shall . . . extradite a person where there are substantial grounds for believing that he would be in danger of being subjected to torture." The fact that a specialised treaty should spell out in detail a specific obligation attaching to the prohibition of torture does not mean that an essentially similar obligation is not already inherent in the general terms of Article 3 (art. 3) of the European Convention. It would hardly be compatible with the underlying values of the Convention, that "common heritage of political traditions, ideals, freedom and the rule of law" to which the Preamble refers, were a Contracting State knowingly to surrender a fugitive to another State where there were substantial grounds for believing that he would be in danger of being subjected to torture, however heinous the crime allegedly committed. Extradition in such circumstances, while not explicitly referred to in the brief and general wording of Article 3 (art. 3), would plainly be contrary to the spirit and intendment of the Article, and in the Court's view this inherent obligation not to extradite also extends to cases in which the fugitive would be faced in the receiving State by a real risk of exposure to inhuman or degrading treatment or punishment proscribed by that Article (art. 3).

. . .

91. In sum, the decision by a Contracting State to extradite a fugitive may give rise to an issue under Article 3 (art. 3), and hence engage the responsibility of that State under the Convention, where substantial grounds have been shown for believing that the person concerned, if extradited, faces a real risk of being subjected to torture or to inhuman or degrading treatment or punishment in the requesting country. The establishment of such responsibility inevitably involves an assessment of conditions in the requesting country against the standards of Article 3 (art. 3) of the Convention. Nonetheless, there is no question of adjudicating on or establishing the responsibility of the receiving country, whether under general international law, under the Convention or otherwise. In so far as any liability under the Convention is or may be incurred, it is liability incurred by the extraditing Contracting State by reason of its having taken action which has as a direct consequence the exposure of an individual to proscribed ill-treatment.

B. Application of Article 3 (art. 3) in the particular circumstances of the present case

92. The extradition procedure against the applicant in the United Kingdom has been completed, the Secretary of State having signed a warrant ordering his surrender to the U.S. authorities (see paragraph 24 above); this decision, albeit as yet not implemented, directly affects him. It therefore has to be determined on the above principles whether the foreseeable consequences of Mr. Soering's return to the U.S. are such as to attract the application of Article 3 (art. 3). This inquiry must concentrate firstly on whether Mr. Soering runs a real risk of being sentenced to death in Virginia, since the source of the alleged inhuman and degrading treatment or punishment, namely the "death row phenomenon," lies in the imposition of the death penalty. Only in the event of an affirmative answer to this question need the Court examine whether exposure to the "death row phenomenon" in the circumstances of the applicant's case would involve treatment or punishment incompatible with Article 3 (art. 3).

1. Whether the applicant runs a real risk of a death sentence and hence of exposure to the "death row phenomenon."

93. The United Kingdom Government, contrary to the Government of the Federal Republic of Germany, the Commission and the applicant, did not accept that the risk of a death sentence attains a sufficient level of likelihood to bring Article 3 (art. 3) into play. Their reasons were fourfold.

Firstly, as illustrated by his interview with the German prosecutor here he appeared to deny any intention to kill (see paragraph 16 above), the applicant has not acknowledged his guilt of capital murder as such.

Secondly, only a prima facie case has so far been made out against him. In particular, in the United Kingdom Government's view the psychiatric evidence (see paragraph 21 above) is equivocal as to whether Mr. Soering was suffering from a disease of the mind sufficient to amount to a defence of insanity under Virginia law (as to which, see paragraph 50 above).

Thirdly, even if Mr. Soering is convicted of capital murder, it cannot be assumed that in the general exercise of their discretion the jury will recommend, the judge will confirm and the Supreme Court of Virginia will uphold the imposition of the death penalty (see paragraphs 42–47 and 52 above). The United Kingdom Government referred to the presence of important mitigating factors, such as the applicant's age and mental condition at the time of commission of the offence and his lack of previous criminal activity, which would have to be taken into account by the jury and then by the judge in the separate sentencing proceedings (see paragraphs 44–47 and 51 above).

Fourthly, the assurance received from the U.S. must at the very least significantly reduce the risk of a capital sentence either being imposed or carried out (see paragraphs 27, 37 and 69 above). At the public hearing the Attorney General nevertheless made clear his Government's understanding that if Mr. Soering were extradited to the U.S. there was "some risk," which was "more than merely negligible," that the death penalty would be imposed.

94. As the applicant himself pointed out, he has made to American and British police officers and to two psychiatrists admissions of his participation in the killings of the Haysom parents, although he appeared to retract those admissions somewhat when questioned by the German prosecutor (see paragraphs 13, 16 and 21 above). It is not for the European Court to usurp the function of the Virginia courts by ruling that a defence of insanity would or would not be available on the psychiatric evidence as it stands. The United Kingdom Government are justified in their assertion that no assumption can be made that Mr. Soering would certainly or even probably be convicted of capital murder as charged (see paragraphs 13 in fine and 40 above). Nevertheless, as the Attorney General conceded on their behalf at the public hearing, there is "a significant risk" that the applicant would be so convicted.

. . .

97. The Commonwealth's Attorney for Bedford County, Mr. Updike, who is responsible for conducting the prosecution against the applicant, has certified that "should Jens Soering be convicted of the offence of capital murder as charged . . . a representation will be made in the name of the United Kingdom to the judge at the time of sentencing that it is the wish of the United Kingdom that the death penalty should not be imposed or carried out" (see paragraph above). The Court notes, like Lord Justice Lloyd in the Divisional Court (see paragraph 22 above), that this undertaking is far from reflecting the wording of Article IV of the 1972 Extradition Treaty between the United Kingdom and the U.S., which speaks of "assurances satisfactory to the requested Party that the death penalty will not be carried out" (see paragraph 36 above). However, the offence charged, being a State and not a Federal offence, comes within the jurisdiction of the Commonwealth of Virginia; it appears as a consequence that no direction could or can be given to the Commonwealth's Attorney by any State or Federal authority to promise more; the Virginia courts as judicial bodies cannot bind themselves in advance as to what decisions they may arrive at on the evidence; and the Governor of Virginia does not, as a matter of policy, promise that he will later exercise his executive power to commute a death penalty (see paragraphs 58–60 above).

This being so, Mr. Updike's undertaking may well have been the best "assurance" that the United Kingdom could have obtained from the U.S. Federal Government in the particular circumstances. According to the statement made to Parliament in 1987 by a Home Office Minister, acceptance of undertakings in such terms "means that the United Kingdom authorities render up a fugitive or are prepared to send a citizen to face an American court on the clear understanding that the death penalty will not be carried out . . . It would be a fundamental blow to the extradition arrangements between our two countries if the death penalty were carried out on an individual who had been returned under those circumstances" (see paragraph 37 above). Nonetheless, the effectiveness of such an undertaking has not yet been put to the test.

98. The applicant contended that representations concerning the wishes of a foreign government would not be admissible as a matter of law under the Virginia Code or, if admissible, of any influence on the sentencing judge.

. . .

99. The Court's conclusion is therefore that the likelihood of the feared exposure of the applicant to the "death row phenomenon" has been shown to be such as to bring Article 3 (art. 3) into play.

. . .

2. Whether in the circumstances the risk of exposure to the "death row phenomenon" would make extradition a breach of Article 3 (art. 3)

(a) General considerations

100. As is established in the Court's case-law, ill-treatment, including punishment, must attain a minimum level of severity if it is to fall within the scope of Article 3 (art. 3). The assessment of this minimum is, in the nature of things, relative; it depends on all the circumstances of the case, such as the nature and context of the treatment or punishment, the manner and method of its execution, its duration, its physical or mental effects and, in some instances, the sex, age and state of health of the victim (see the above-mentioned Ireland v the United Kingdom judgment, Series A no. 25, p. 65, A7 162; and the Tyrer judgment of 25 April 1978, Series A no. 26, pp. 14–15, 29 and 30).

. . .

101. Capital punishment is permitted under certain conditions by Article 2. 1 (art. 2–1) of the Convention, which reads:

"Everyone's right to life shall be protected by law. No one shall be deprived of his life intentionally save in the execution of a sentence of a court following his conviction of a crime for which this penalty is provided by law."

In view of this wording, the applicant did not suggest that the death penalty per se violated Article 3 (art. 3). He, like the two Government Parties, agreed with the Commission that the extradition of a person to a country where he risks the death penalty does not in itself raise an issue under either Article 2 (art. 2) or Article 3 (art. 3). On the other hand, Amnesty International in their written comments (see paragraph 8 above) argued that the evolving standards in Western Europe regarding the existence and use of the death penalty required that the death penalty should now be considered as an inhuman and degrading punishment within the meaning of Article 3 (art. 3).

102. Certainly, "the Convention is a living instrument which . . . must be interpreted in the light of present-day conditions"; and, in assessing whether a given treatment or punishment is to be regarded as inhuman or degrading for the purposes of Article 3 (art. 3), "the Court cannot but be influenced by the developments and commonly accepted standards in the penal policy of the member States of the Council of Europe in this field" (see the above-mentioned Tyrer judgment, Series A no. 26, pp. 15–16, A7 31). De facto the death penalty no longer exists in time of peace in the Contracting States to the Convention. In the few Contracting States which retain the death penalty in law for some peacetime offences, death sentences, if ever imposed, are nowadays not carried out. This "virtual consensus in Western European legal systems that the death penalty is, under current circumstances, no longer consistent with regional standards of justice," to use the words of Amnesty International, is reflected in Protocol No. 6 (P6) to the Convention, which provides for the abolition of the death penalty in time of peace.

Protocol No. 6 (P6) was opened for signature in April 1983, which in the practice of the Council of Europe indicates the absence of objection on the part of any of the Member States of the Organisation; it came into force in March 1985 and to date has been ratified by thirteen Contracting States to the Convention, not however including the United Kingdom. Whether these marked changes have the effect of bringing the death penalty per se within the prohibition of ill-treatment under Article 3 (art. 3) must be determined on the principles governing the interpretation of the Convention.

103. The Convention is to be read as a whole and Article 3 (art. 3) should therefore be construed in harmony with the provisions of Article 2 (art. 2) (see, mutatis mutandis, the Klass and Others judgment of 6 September 1978, Series A no. 28, p. 31, A7 68). On this basis Article 3 (art. 3) evidently cannot have been intended by the drafters of the Convention to include a general prohibition of the death penalty since that would nullify the clear wording of Article 2.1 (art. 2–1).

Subsequent practice in national penal policy, in the form of a generalised abolition of capital punishment, could be taken as establishing the agreement of the Contracting States to abrogate the exception provided for under Article 2.1 (art. 2–1) and hence to remove a textual limit on the scope for evolutive interpretation of Article 3 (art. 3). However, Protocol No. 6 (P6), as a subsequent written agreement, shows that the intention of the Contracting Parties as recently as 1983 was to adopt the normal method of amendment of the text in order to introduce a new obligation to abolish capital punishment in time of peace and, what is more, to do so by an optional instrument allowing each State to choose the moment when to undertake such an engagement. In these conditions, notwithstanding the special character of the Convention (see paragraph 87 above), Article 3 (art. 3) cannot be interpreted as generally prohibiting the death penalty.

104. That does not mean however that circumstances relating to a death sentence can never give rise to an issue under Article 3 (art. 3). The manner in which it is imposed or executed, the personal circumstances of the condemned person and a disproportionality to the gravity of the crime committed, as well as the conditions of detention awaiting execution, are examples of factors capable of bringing the treatment or punishment received by the condemned person within the proscription under Article 3 (art. 3). Present-day attitudes in the Contracting States to capital punishment are relevant for the assessment whether the acceptable threshold of suffering or degradation has been exceeded.

(b) The particular circumstances

105. The applicant submitted that the circumstances to which he would be exposed as a consequence of the implementation of the Secretary of State's decision to return him to the U.S., namely the "death row phenomenon," cumulatively constituted such serious treatment that his extradition would be contrary to

Article 3 (art. 3). He cited in particular the delays in the appeal and review procedures following a death sentence, during which time he would be subject to increasing tension and psychological trauma; the fact, so he said, that the judge or jury in determining sentence is not obliged to take into account the defendant's age and mental state at the time of the offence; the extreme conditions of his future detention on "death row" in Mecklenburg Correctional Center, where he expects to be the victim of violence and sexual abuse because of his age, colour and nationality; and the constant spectre of the execution itself, including the ritual of execution. He also relied on the possibility of extradition or deportation, which he would not oppose, to the Federal Republic of Germany as accentuating the disproportionality of the Secretary of State's decision.

The Government of the Federal Republic of Germany took the view that, taking all the circumstances together, the treatment awaiting the applicant in Virginia would go so far beyond treatment inevitably connected with the imposition and execution of a death penalty as to be "inhuman" within the meaning of Article 3 (art. 3).

On the other hand, the conclusion expressed by the Commission was that the degree of severity contemplated by Article 3 (art. 3) would not be attained. The United Kingdom Government shared this opinion. In particular, they disputed many of the applicant's factual allegations as to the conditions on death row in Mecklenburg and his expected fate there.

. . .

ii. Conditions on death row

107. As to conditions in Mecklenburg Correctional Center, where the applicant could expect to be held if sentenced to death, the Court bases itself on the facts which were uncontested by the United Kingdom Government, without finding it necessary to determine the reliability of the additional evidence adduced by the applicant, notably as to the risk of homosexual abuse and physical attack undergone by prisoners on death row (see paragraph 64 above).

. . .

iii. The applicant's age and mental state

108. At the time of the killings, the applicant was only 18 years old and there is some psychiatric evidence, which was not contested as such, that he "was suffering from [such] an abnormality of mind . . . as substantially impaired his mental responsibility for his acts" (see paragraphs 11, 12 and 21 above).

Unlike Article 2 (art. 2) of the Convention, Article 6 of the 1966 International Covenant on Civil and Political Rights and Article 4 of the 1969 American Convention on Human Rights expressly prohibit the death penalty from being imposed on persons aged less than 18 at the time of commission of the offence. Whether or not such a prohibition be inherent in the brief and general language of Article 2 (art. 2) of the European Convention, its explicit enunciation in other, later international instruments, the former of which has been ratified by a large number of States Parties to the European Convention, at the very least indicates that as a general principle the youth of the person concerned is a circumstance which is liable, with others, to put in question the compatibility with Article 3 (art. 3) of measures connected with a death sentence. It is in line with the Court's case-law (as summarised above at paragraph 100) to treat disturbed mental health as having the same effect for the application of Article 3 (art. 3).

109. Virginia law, as the United Kingdom Government and the Commission emphasized, certainly does not ignore these two factors. Under the Virginia Code account has to be taken of mental disturbance in a defendant, either as an absolute bar to conviction if it is judged to be sufficient to amount to insanity or, like age, as a fact in mitigation at the sentencing stage (see paragraphs 44–47 and 50–51 above). Additionally, indigent capital murder defendants are entitled to the appointment of a qualified mental health expert to assist in the preparation of their submissions at the separate sentencing proceedings (see paragraph 51 above). These provisions in the Virginia Code undoubtedly serve, as the American courts have stated, to prevent the arbitrary or capricious imposition of the death penalty and narrowly to channel the sentencer's discretion (see paragraph 48 above). They do not however remove the relevance of age and mental condition in relation to the acceptability, under Article 3, art. 3), of the "death row phenomenon" for a given individual once condemned to death.

Although it is not for this Court to prejudge issues of criminal responsibility and appropriate sentence, the applicant's youth at the time of the offence and his then mental state, on the psychiatric evidence as it stands, are therefore to be taken into consideration as contributory factors tending, in his case, to bring the treatment on death row within the terms of Article 3 (art. 3).

iv. Possibility of extradition to the Federal Republic of Germany

110. For the United Kingdom Government and the majority of the Commission, the possibility of extraditing or deporting the applicant to face trial in the Federal Republic of Germany (see paragraphs 16, 19, 26, 38 and 71–74 above), where the death penalty has been abolished under the Constitution (see paragraph 72 above), is not material for the present purposes. Any other approach, the United Kingdom Government submitted, would lead to a "dual standard" affording the protection of the Convention to extraditable persons fortunate enough to have such an alternative destination available but refusing it to others not so fortunate.

This argument is not without weight. Furthermore, the Court cannot overlook either the horrible nature of the murders with which Mr. Soering is charged or the legitimate and beneficial role of extradition arrangements in combating crime. The purpose for which his removal to the U.S. was sought, in accordance with the Extradition Treaty between the United Kingdom and the U.S., is undoubtedly a legitimate one. However, sending Mr. Soering to be tried in his own country would remove the danger of a fugitive criminal going unpunished as well as the risk of intense and protracted suffering on death row. It is therefore a circumstance of relevance for the overall assessment under Article 3 (art. 3) in that it goes to the search for the requisite fair balance of interests and to the proportionality of the contested extradition decision in the particular case (see paragraphs 89 and 104 above).

(c) Conclusion

111. For any prisoner condemned to death, some element of delay between imposition and execution of the sentence and the experience of severe stress in conditions necessary for strict incarceration are inevitable. The democratic character of the Virginia legal system in general and the positive features of Virginia trial, sentencing and appeal procedures in particular are beyond doubt. The Court agrees with the Commission that the machinery of justice to which the applicant would be subject in the U.S. is in itself neither arbitrary nor unreasonable, but, rather, respects the rule of law and affords not inconsiderable procedural safeguards to the defendant in a capital trial. Facilities are available on death row for the assistance of inmates, notably through provision of psychological and psychiatric services (see paragraph 65 above).

However, in the Court's view, having regard to the very long period of time spent on death row in such extreme conditions, with the ever present and mounting anguish of awaiting execution of the death penalty, and to the personal circumstances of the applicant, especially his age and mental state at the time of the offence, the applicant's extradition to the U.S. would expose him to a real risk of treatment going beyond the threshold set by Article 3 (art. 3). A further consideration of relevance is that in the particular instance the legitimate purpose of extradition could be achieved by another means which would not involve suffering of such exceptional intensity or duration.

Accordingly, the Secretary of State's decision to extradite the applicant to the U.S. would, if implemented, give rise to a breach of Article 3 (art. 3).

This finding in no way puts in question the good faith of the United Kingdom Government, who have from the outset of the present proceedings demonstrated their desire to abide by their Convention obligations, firstly by staying the applicant's surrender to the U.S. authorities in accord with the interim measures indicated by the Convention institutions and secondly by themselves referring the case to the Court for a judicial ruling (see paragraphs 1, 4, 24 and 77 above).

. . .

IV. Application of Article 50 (art. 50)

125. Under the terms of Article 50 (art. 50),

"If the Court finds that a decision or a measure taken by a legal authority or any other authority of a High Contracting Party is completely or partially in conflict with the obligations arising from the . . . Convention, and if the internal law of the said Party allows only partial reparation to be made for the consequences of this decision or measure, the decision of the Court shall, if necessary, afford just satisfaction to the injured party."

Mr. Soering stated that, since the object of his application was to secure the enjoyment of his rights guaranteed by the Convention, just satisfaction of his claims would be achieved by effective enforcement of the Court's ruling. He invited the Court to assist the States Parties to the case and himself by giving directions in relation to the operation of its judgment.

. . .

126. No breach of Article 3 (art. 3) has as yet occurred. Nevertheless, the Court having found that the Secretary of State's decision to extradite to the United States of America would, if implemented, give rise to a breach of Article 3 (art. 3), Article 50 (art. 50) must be taken as applying to the facts of the present case.

127. The Court considers that its finding regarding Article 3 (art. 3) of itself amounts to adequate just satisfaction for the purposes of Article 50 (art. 50). The Court is not empowered under the Convention to make accessory directions of the kind requested by the applicant (see, mutatis mutandis, the Dudgeon judgment of 24 February 1983, Series A no. 59, p. 8, 15). By virtue of Article 54 (art. 54), the responsibility for supervising execution of the Court's judgment rests with the Committee of Ministers of the Council of Europe.

The applicant's essential concern, and the bulk of the argument on all sides, focused on the complaint under Article 3 (art. 3), and on that issue the applicant has been successful. The Court therefore considers that in equity the applicant should recover his costs and expenses in full.

For These Reasons, the Court Unanimously

1. Holds that, in the event of the Secretary of State's decision to extradite the applicant to the United States of America being implemented, there would be a violation of Article 3 (art. 3);

2. Holds that, in the same event, there would be no violation of Article 6.3 (c) (art. 6-3-c);

3. Holds that it has no jurisdiction to entertain the complaint under Article 6.1 and 3 (d) (art. 6-1, art. 6-3-d);

4. Holds that there is no violation of Article 13 (art. 13);

5. Holds that the United Kingdom is to pay to the applicant, in respect of legal costs and expenses, the sum of A326,752.80 (twenty-six thousand seven hundred and fifty-two pounds sterling and eighty pence) and 5,030.60 FF (five thousand and thirty French francs and sixty centimes), together with any value-added tax that may be chargeable;

6. Rejects the remainder of the claim for just satisfaction.

Done in English and in French, and delivered at a public hearing in the Human Rights Building, Strasbourg, on 7 July 1989.

Signed: Rolv RYSSDAL
President
For the Registrar
Signed: Herbert PETZOLD
Deputy Registrar
{\Rear}

19. *Mexico v United States of America (Avena)*, International Court of Justice, The Hague, Netherlands Cite as: Summary of the Judgment of 31 March 2004. Summary 2004/1 (Summary Not an offical document.)

**Case concerning Avena and other Mexican Nationals (MEXICO v UNITED STATES OF AMERICA) (Excerpted)
Summary of the Judgment of 31 March 2004**

History of the proceedings and submissions of the Parties (paras. 1-14)

The Court begins by recalling that on 9 January 2003 the United Mexican States (hereinafter referred to as "Mexico") instituted proceedings against the United States of America (hereinafter referred to as the "U.S.") for "violations of the Vienna Convention on Consular Relations" of 24 April 1963 (hereinafter referred to as the "Vienna Convention") allegedly committed by the U.S.

In its Application, Mexico based the jurisdiction of the Court on Article 36, paragraph 1, of the Statute of the Court and on Article I of the Optional Protocol concerning the Compulsory Settlement of Disputes, which accompanies the Vienna Convention (hereinafter referred to as the "Optional Protocol"). On the same day, Mexico also filed a request for the indication of provisional measures. By an Order of 5 February 2003, the Court indicated the following provisional measures:

"(a) The United States of America shall take all measures necessary to ensure that Mr. César Roberto Fierro Reyna, Mr. Roberto Moreno Ramos and Mr. Osvaldo Torres Aguilera are not executed pending final judgment in these proceedings;

(b) The Government of the United States of America shall inform the Court of all measures taken in implementation of this Order."

It further decided that, "until the Court has rendered its final judgment, it shall remain seised of the matters" which formed the subject of that Order.

In a letter of 2 November 2003, the Agent of the U.S. advised the Court that the U.S. had "informed the relevant state authorities of Mexico's application"; that, since the Order of 5 February 2003, the U.S. had "obtained from them information about the status of the fifty-four cases, including the three cases identified in paragraph 59 (I) (a) of that Order"; and that the U.S. could "confirm that none of the named individuals [had] been executed". A Memorial by Mexico and a Counter-Memorial by the U.S. were filed within the time-limits extended by the Court.

The Court further recalled that, in order to ensure the procedural equality of the Parties, it had decided not to authorize a requested amendment by Mexico of its submissions so as to include two additional Mexican nationals, while taking note that the U.S. had made no objection to the withdrawal by Mexico of its request for relief in two other cases. Since the Court included upon the Bench no judge of Mexican nationality, Mexico chose Mr. Bernardo Sepúlveda to sit as judge ad hoc in the case.

Public sittings were held between 15 and 19 December 2003. At the oral proceedings, the following final submissions were presented by the Parties: On behalf of the Government of Mexico,"The Government of Mexico respectfully requests the Court to adjudge and declare

(1) That the United States of America, in arresting, detaining, trying, convicting, and sentencing the 52 Mexican nationals on death row described in Mexico's Memorial, violated its international legal obligations to Mexico, in its own right and in the exercise of its right to diplomatic protection of its nationals, by failing to inform, without delay, the 52 Mexican nationals after their arrest of their right to consular notification and access under Article 36 (1) (b) of the Vienna Convention on Consular Relations, and by depriving Mexico of its right to provide consular protection and the 52 nationals' right to receive such protection as Mexico would provide under Article 36 (1) (a) and (c) of the Convention;

(2) That the obligation in Article 36 (1) of the Vienna Convention requires notification of consular rights and a reasonable opportunity for consular access before the competent authorities of the receiving State take any action potentially detrimental to the foreign national's rights;

(3) That the United States of America violated its obligations under Article 36 (2) of the Vienna Convention by failing to provide meaningful and effective review and reconsideration of convictions and sentences impaired by a violation of Article 36 (1); by substituting for such review and reconsideration clemency proceedings; and by applying the "procedural default" doctrine and other municipal law doctrines that fail to attach legal significance to an Article 36 (1) violation on its own terms;

(4) That pursuant to the injuries suffered by Mexico in its own right and in the exercise of diplomatic protection of its nationals, Mexico is entitled to full reparation for those injuries in the form of *restitutio in integrum*;

(5) That this restitution consists of the obligation to restore the status quo ante by annulling or otherwise depriving of full force or effect the convictions and sentences of all 52 Mexican nationals;

(6) That this restitution also includes the obligation to take all measures necessary to ensure that a prior violation of Article 36 shall not affect the subsequent proceedings;

(7) That to the extent that any of the 52 convictions or sentences are not annulled, the U.S. shall provide, by means of its own choosing, meaningful and effective review and reconsideration of the convictions and sentences of the 52 nationals, and that this obligation cannot be satisfied by means of clemency proceedings or if any municipal law rule or doctrine inconsistent with paragraph (3) above is applied; and

(8) That the United States of America shall cease its violations of Article 36 of the Vienna Convention with regard to Mexico and its 52 nationals and shall provide appropriate guarantees and assurances that it shall take measures sufficient to achieve increased compliance with Article 36 (1) and to ensure compliance with Article 36 (2)."

On behalf of the Government of the U.S., "On the basis of the facts and arguments made by the U.S. in its Counter-Memorial and in these proceedings, the Government of the United States of America requests that the Court, taking into account that the U.S. has conformed its conduct to this Court's Judgment in the LaGrand Case (Germany v United States of America), not only with respect to German nationals but, consistent with the Declaration of the President of the Court in that case, to all detained foreign nationals, adjudge and declare that the claims of the United Mexican States are dismissed."

The Court finally gives a short description of the dispute and of the facts underlying the case, and in paragraph 16 it lists by name the 52 Mexican nationals involved.

Mexican objection to the U.S. objections to jurisdiction and admissibility (paras. 22-25)

The Court notes at the outset that the U.S. has presented a number of objections to the jurisdiction of the Court, as well as to the admissibility of the claims advanced by Mexico; that it is however the contention of Mexico that all the objections raised by the U.S. are inadmissible as having been raised after the expiration of the time-limit laid down by Article 79, paragraph 1, of the Rules of Court as amended in 2000.

The Court notes, however, that Article 79 of the Rules applies only to preliminary objections. It observes that an objection that is not presented as a preliminary objection in accordance with paragraph 1 of Article 79 does not thereby become inadmissible; that there are of course circumstances in which the party failing to put forward an objection to jurisdiction might be held to have acquiesced in jurisdiction; that, however, apart from such circumstances, a party failing to avail itself of the Article 79 procedure may forfeit the right to bring about a suspension of the proceedings on the merits, but can still argue the objection along with the merits. The Court finds that that is indeed what the U.S. has done in this case; and that, for reasons to be indicated below, many of its objections are of such a nature that they would in any event probably have had to be heard along with the merits. The Court concludes that it should not exclude from consideration the objections of the U.S. to jurisdiction and admissibility by reason of the fact that they were not presented within three months from the date of filing of the Memorial.

U.S. objections to jurisdiction (paras. 26-35)

By its first jurisdictional objection, the U.S. suggested that the Mexican Memorial is fundamentally addressed to the treatment of Mexican nationals in the federal and state criminal justice systems of the U.S., and to the operation of the U.S. criminal justice system as a whole; for the Court to address such issues would be an abuse of its jurisdiction. The Court recalls that its jurisdiction in the present case has been invoked under the Vienna Convention and Optional Protocol to determine the nature and extent of the obligations undertaken by the U.S. towards Mexico by becoming party to that Convention. If and so far as the Court may find that the obligations accepted by the parties to the Vienna Convention included commitments as to the conduct of their municipal courts in relation to the nationals of other parties, then in order to ascertain whether there have been breaches of the Convention, the Court must be able to examine the actions of those courts in the light of international law. How far it may do so in the present case is a matter for the merits; the first objection of the U.S. to jurisdiction cannot therefore be upheld.

The second jurisdictional objection presented by the U.S. was addressed to Mexico's submission "that the U.S. in arresting, detaining, trying, convicting, and sentencing [to death] Mexican nationals, violated its international legal obligations to Mexico, in its own right and in the exercise of its right of diplomatic protection of its nationals, as provided by Article 36 of the Vienna Convention. The U.S. pointed out that Article 36 of the Vienna Convention "creates no obligations constraining the rights of the U.S. to arrest a foreign national"; and that, similarly, the "detaining, trying, convicting and sentencing" of Mexican nationals could not constitute breaches of Article 36, which merely lays down obligations of notification. The Court observes, however, that Mexico argues that depriving a foreign national facing criminal proceedings of the right to consular notification and assistance renders those proceedings fundamentally unfair. In the Court's view that is to argue in favour of a particular interpretation of the Vienna Convention. Such an interpretation may or may not be confirmed on the merits, but is not excluded from the jurisdiction conferred on the Court by the Optional Protocol to the Vienna Convention. The second objection of the U.S. to jurisdiction cannot therefore be upheld.

The third objection by the U.S. to the jurisdiction of the Court refers to the first submission concerning remedies in the Mexican Memorial, namely that Mexico is entitled to *restitutio in integrum*, and that the U.S. therefore is under an obligation to restore the status quo ante. The U.S. objects that this would intrude deeply into the independence of its courts; and that for the Court to declare that the U.S. is under a specific obligation to vacate convictions and sentences would be beyond its jurisdiction. The Court recalls in this regard, as it did in the LaGrand case, that, where jurisdiction exists over a dispute on a particular matter, no separate basis for jurisdiction is required by the Court in order to consider the remedies a party has requested for the breach of the obligation (I.C.J. Reports 2001, p. 485, para. 48). Whether or how far the Court may order the remedy requested by Mexico are matters to be determined as part of the merits of the dispute; the third objection of the U.S. to jurisdiction cannot therefore be upheld.

The fourth and last jurisdictional objection of the U.S. is that, contrary to the contentions of Mexico, "the Court lacks jurisdiction to determine whether or not consular notification is a 'human right', or to declare fundamental requirements of substantive or procedural due process". The Court observes that Mexico has presented this argument as being a matter of interpretation of Article 36, paragraph 1 (b), and therefore belonging to the merits. The Court considers that this is indeed a question of interpretation of the Vienna Convention, for which it has jurisdiction; the fourth objection of the U.S. to jurisdiction cannot therefore be upheld.

U.S. objections to admissibility (paras. 36-48)

The Court notes that the first objection of the U.S. under this head is that "Mexico's submissions should be found inadmissible because they seek to have this Court function as a court of criminal appeal"; that there is, in the view of the U.S., "no other apt characterization of Mexico's two submissions in respect of remedies". The Court observes that this contention is addressed solely to the question of remedies. The U.S. does not contend on this ground that the Court should decline jurisdiction to enquire into the question of breaches of the Vienna Convention at all, but simply that, if such breaches are shown, the Court should do no more than decide that the U.S. must provide "review and reconsideration" along the lines indicated in the Judgment in the LaGrand case (I.C.J. Reports 2001, pp. 513-514, para. 125). The Court notes that this is a matter of merits; the first objection of the U.S. to admissibility cannot therefore be upheld.

The Court then turns to the objection of the U.S. based on the rule of exhaustion of local remedies. The U.S. contends that the Court "should find inadmissible Mexico's claim to exercise its right of diplomatic protection on behalf of any Mexican national who has failed to meet the customary legal requirement of exhaustion of municipal remedies". The Court recalls that in its final submissions Mexico asks the Court to adjudge and declare that the U.S., in failing to comply with Article 36, paragraph 1, of the Vienna Convention, has "violated its international legal obligations to Mexico, in its own right and in the exercise of its right of diplomatic protection of its nationals". The Court observes that the individual rights of Mexican nationals under subparagraph 1 (b) of Article 36 of the Vienna Convention are rights which are to be asserted, at any rate in the first place, within the domestic legal system of the U.S. Only when that process is completed and local remedies are exhausted would Mexico be entitled to espouse the individual claims of its nationals through the procedure of diplomatic protection. In the present case Mexico does not, however, claim to be acting solely on that basis. It also asserts its own claims, basing them on the injury which it contends that it has itself suffered, directly and through its nationals, as a result of the violation by the U.S. of the obligations incumbent upon it under Article 36, paragraph 1 (a), (b) and (c). The Court finds that, in these special circumstances of interdependence of the rights of the State and of individual rights, Mexico may, in submitting a claim in its own name, request the Court to rule on the violation of rights which it claims to have suffered both directly and through the violation of individual rights conferred on Mexican nationals under Article 36, paragraph 1 (b). The duty to exhaust local remedies does not apply to such a request. The Court accordingly finds that the second objection by the U.S. to admissibility cannot be upheld.

The Court then turns to the question of the alleged dual nationality of certain of the Mexican nationals the subject of Mexico's claims. The U.S. contends that in its Memorial Mexico had failed to establish that it may exercise diplomatic protection based on breaches of Mexico's rights under the Vienna Convention with respect to those of its nationals who are also nationals of the U.S. The Court recalls, however, that Mexico, in addition to seeking to exercise diplomatic protection of its nationals, is making a claim in its own right on the basis of the alleged breaches by the U.S. of Article 36 of the Vienna Convention. Seen from this standpoint, the question of dual nationality is not one of admissibility, but of merits. Without prejudice to the outcome of such examination, the third objection of the U.S. to admissibility cannot therefore be upheld.

The Court then turns to the fourth objection advanced by the U.S. to the admissibility of Mexico's claims: the contention that "The Court should not permit Mexico to pursue a claim against the U.S. with respect to any individual case where Mexico had actual knowledge of a breach of the [Vienna Convention] but failed to bring such breach to the attention of the U.S. or did so only after considerable delay." The Court recalls that in the case of Certain Phosphate Lands in Nauru (Nauru v Australia), it observed that "delay on the part of a claimant State may render an application inadmissible", but that "international law does not lay down any specific time-limit in that regard" (I.C.J. Reports 1992, pp. 253-254, para. 32). It notes that in that case it had recognized that delay might prejudice the Respondent State, but fines that there has been no suggestion of any such risk of prejudice in the present case. So far as inadmissibility might be based on an implied waiver of rights, the Court considers that only a much more prolonged and consistent inaction on the part of Mexico than any that the U.S. has alleged might be interpreted as implying such a waiver. The Court notes, furthermore, that Mexico indicated a number of ways in which it brought to the attention of the U.S. the breaches which it perceived of the Vienna Convention; the fourth objection of the U.S. to admissibility cannot therefore be upheld.

The Court finally examines the objection of the U.S. that the claim of Mexico is inadmissible in that Mexico should not be allowed to invoke against the U.S. standards that Mexico does not follow in its own practice. The Court recalls in this respect that it is essential to have in mind the nature of the Vienna Convention. That Convention lays down certain standards to be observed by all States parties, with a view to the "unimpeded conduct of consular relations". Even if it were shown, therefore, that Mexico's practice as regards the application of Article 36 was not beyond reproach, this would not constitute a ground of objection to the admissibility of Mexico's claim; the fifth objection of the U.S. to admissibility cannot therefore be upheld.

The Court then turns to the merits of Mexico's claims. Article 36, paragraph 1, of the Vienna Convention (paras. 49-106)

The Court notes that in the first of its final submissions, Mexico asks the Court to adjudge and declare that, "the United States of America, in arresting, detaining, trying, convicting, and sentencing the 52 Mexican nationals on death row described in Mexico's Memorial, violated its international legal obligations to Mexico, in its own right and in the exercise of its right to diplomatic protection of its nationals, by failing to inform, without delay, the 52 Mexican nationals after their arrest of their right to consular notification and access under Article 36 (1) (b) of the Vienna Convention on Consular Relations, and by depriving Mexico of its right to provide consular protection and the 52 nationals' right to receive such protection as Mexico would provide under Article 36 (1) (a) and (c) of the Convention".

It recalls that it has already in its Judgment in the LaGrand case described Article 36, paragraph 1, as "an interrelated régime designed to facilitate the implementation of the system of consular protection" (I.C.J. Reports 2001, p. 492, para. 74). After citing the full text of the paragraph, the Court observes that the U.S. as the receiving State does not deny its duty to perform the obligations indicated therein. However, it claims that those obligations apply only to individuals shown to be of Mexican nationality alone, and not to those of dual Mexican/U.S. nationality. The U.S. further contends inter alia that it has not committed any breach of Article 36, paragraph 1 (b), upon the proper interpretation of "without delay" as used in that subparagraph.

Article 36, paragraph 1 (b) (paras. 52-90)

The Court finds that thus two major issues under Article 36, paragraph 1 (b) are in dispute between the Parties: first, the question of the nationality of the individuals concerned; and second, the question of the meaning to be given to the expression "without delay".

Nationality of the individuals concerned (paras. 53-57)

The Court begins by noting that the Parties disagree as to what each of them must show as regards nationality in connection with the applicability of the terms of Article 36, paragraph 1, and as to how the principles of evidence have been met on the facts of the cases.

The Court finds that it is for Mexico to show that the 52 persons listed in paragraph 16 of the Judgment held Mexican nationality at the time of their arrest. It notes that to this end Mexico has produced birth certificates and declarations of nationality, whose contents have not been challenged by the U.S. The Court observes further that the U.S. has questioned whether some of these individuals were not also U.S. nationals. The Court takes the view that it was for the U.S. to demonstrate that this was so and to furnish the Court with all information on the matter in its possession. In so far as relevant data on that matter are said by the U.S. to lie within the knowledge of Mexico, it was for the U.S. to have sought that information from the Mexican authorities. The Court finds that, at no stage, however, has the U.S. shown the Court that it made specific enquiries of those authorities about particular cases and that responses were not forthcoming. The Court accordingly concludes that the U.S. has not met its burden of proof in its attempt to show that persons of Mexican nationality were also U.S. nationals. The Court therefore finds that, as regards the 52 persons listed in paragraph 16 of the Judgment, the U.S. had obligations under Article 36, paragraph 1 (b).

Requirement to inform "without delay" (paras. 58-90).

APPENDIX J

The Court continues by noting that Mexico, in its second final submission, asks the Court to find that "the obligation in Article 36, paragraph 1, of the Vienna Convention requires notification of consular rights and a reasonable opportunity for consular access before the competent authorities of the receiving State take any action potentially detrimental to the foreign national's rights".

The Court notes that Mexico contends that, in each of the 52 cases before the Court, the U.S. failed to provide the arrested persons with information as to their rights under Article 36, paragraph 1 (b), "without delay". It further notes that the U.S. disputes both the facts as presented by Mexico and the legal analysis of Article 36, paragraph 1 (b), of the Vienna Convention offered by Mexico.

The Court first turns to the interpretation of Article 36, paragraph 1 (b), having found that it is applicable to the 52 persons listed in paragraph 16 of the Judgment. It begins by noting that Article 36, paragraph 1 (b), contains three separate but interrelated elements: the right of the individual concerned to be informed without delay of his rights under Article 36, paragraph 1 (b); the right of the consular post to be notified without delay of the individual's detention, if he so requests; and the obligation of the receiving State to forward without delay any communication addressed to the consular post by the detained person (this last element not having been raised in the case).

Beginning with the right of an arrested individual to information, the Court finds that the duty upon the arresting authorities to give the Article 36, paragraph 1 (b), information to the individual arises once it is realized that the person is a foreign national, or once there are grounds to think that the person is probably a foreign national. Precisely when this may occur will vary with circumstances.

Bearing in mind the complexities of establishing such a fact as explained by the U.S., the Court begins by examining the application of Article 36, paragraph 1 (b), of the Vienna Convention to the 52 cases. In 45 of these cases, it finds that it has no evidence that the arrested persons claimed U.S. nationality, or were reasonably thought to be U.S. nationals, with specific enquiries being made in timely fashion to verify such dual nationality. It notes, however, that seven persons are asserted by the U.S. to have stated at the time of arrest that they were U.S. citizens.

After examination of those seven cases the Court concludes that Mexico has failed to prove the violation by the U.S. of its obligations under Article 36, paragraph 1 (b), in only one of these. As regards the other individuals who are alleged to have claimed U.S. nationality on arrest, the Court finds that the argument of the U.S. cannot be upheld.

The Court points out that the question nonetheless remains as to whether, in each of these 51 cases, the U.S. did provide the required information to the arrested persons "without delay". It is to that question that the Court then turns. The Court notes that in 47 cases the U.S. nowhere challenges the fact that the Mexican nationals were never informed of their rights under Article 36, paragraph 1 (b), but that in four cases some doubt remains whether the information that was given was provided "without delay"; for these, some examination of the term is thus necessary.

The Court notes that the Parties have very different views on this. According to Mexico, the timing of the notice to the detained person "is critical to the exercise of the rights provided by Article 36" and the phrase "without delay" in paragraph 1 (b) requires "unqualified immediacy". Mexico further contends that, in view of the object and purpose of Article 36, which is to enable "meaningful consular assistance" and the safeguarding of the vulnerability of foreign nationals in custody, "consular notification . . . must occur immediately upon detention and prior to any interrogation of the foreign detainee, so that the consul may offer useful advice about the foreign legal system and provide assistance in obtaining counsel before the foreign national makes any ill-informed decisions or the State takes any action potentially prejudicial to his rights".

The U.S. disputed this interpretation of the phrase "without delay". In its view it did not mean "immediately, and before interrogation" and such an understanding was supported neither by the terminology, nor by the object and purpose of the Vienna Convention, nor by its travaux préparatoires. According to the U.S., the purpose of Article 36 was to facilitate the exercise of consular functions by a consular officer: "The significance of giving consular information to a national is thus limited . . . It is a procedural device that allows the foreign national to trigger the related process of notification . . . [It] cannot possibly be fundamental to the criminal justice process."

The Court begins by noting that the precise meaning of "without delay", as it is to be understood in Article 36, paragraph 1 (b), is not defined in the Convention. This phrase therefore requires interpretation according to the customary rules of treaty interpretation reflected in Articles 31 and 32 of the Vienna

Convention on the Law of Treaties. After examination of the text of the Vienna Convention on Consular Relations, its object and purpose, as well as its travaux préparatoires, the Court finds that "without delay" is not necessarily to be interpreted as "immediately" upon arrest, nor can it be interpreted to signify that the provision of the information must necessarily precede any interrogation, so that the commencement of interrogation before the information is given would be a breach of Article 36. The Court observes, however, that there is nonetheless a duty upon the arresting authorities to give the information to an arrested person as soon as it is realized that the person is a foreign national, or once there are grounds to think that the person is probably a foreign national.

Applying this interpretation of "without delay" to the facts of the four outstanding cases, the Court finds that the U.S. was in breach of its obligations under Article 36, paragraph 1 (b), in respect of these individuals also. The Court accordingly concludes that, with respect to all save one of the 52 individuals listed in paragraph 16 of the Judgment, the U.S. has violated its obligation under Article 36, paragraph 1 (b), of the Vienna Convention to provide information to the arrested person.

Article 36, paragraph 1 (a) and (c) (paras. 91-107)

The Court begins by recalling its observation above that Article 36, paragraph 1 (b), contains three elements. Thus far, it observes, it has been dealing with the right of an arrested person to be informed that he may ask for his consular post to be notified. The Court then turns to another aspect of Article 36, paragraph 1 (b). It finds the U.S. is correct in observing that the fact that a Mexican consular post was not notified under Article 36, paragraph 1 (b), does not of necessity show that the arrested person was not informed of his rights under that provision. He may have been informed and declined to have his consular post notified. The Court finds in one of the two cases mentioned by the U.S. in this respect, that that was the case. In two of three further cases in which the U.S. alleges that the consular post was formally notified without prior information to the individual, the Court finds that the U.S. did violate its obligations under Article 36, paragraph 1 (b).

The Court notes that, in the first of its final submissions, Mexico also asks the Court to find that the violations it ascribes to the U.S. in respect of Article 36, paragraph 1 (b), have also deprived "Mexico of its right to provide consular protection and the 52 nationals' right to receive such protection as Mexico would provide under Article 36 (1) (a) and (c) of the Convention".

The Court recalls that the relationship between the three subparagraphs of Article 36, paragraph 1, has been described by it in its Judgment in the LaGrand case (I.C.J. Reports 2001, p. 492, para. 74) as "an interrelated régime". The legal conclusions to be drawn from that interrelationship necessarily depend upon the facts of each case. In the LaGrand case, the Court found that the failure for 16 years to inform the brothers of their right to have their consul notified effectively prevented the exercise of other rights that Germany might have chosen to exercise under subparagraphs (a) and (c). The Court is of the view that it is necessary to revisit the interrelationship of the three subparagraphs of Article 36, paragraph 1, in the light of the particular facts and circumstances of the present case.

It first recalls that, in one case, when the defendant was informed of his rights, he declined to have his consular post notified. Thus in this case there was no violation of either subparagraph (a) or subparagraph (c) of Article 36, paragraph 1.

In the remaining cases, because of the failure of the U.S. to act in conformity with Article 36, paragraph 1 (b), Mexico was in effect precluded (in some cases totally, and in some cases for prolonged periods of time) from exercising its right under paragraph 1 (a) to communicate with its nationals and have access to them. As the Court has already had occasion to explain, it is immaterial whether Mexico would have offered consular assistance, "or whether a different verdict would have been rendered. It is sufficient that the Convention conferred these rights" (I.C.J. Reports 2001, p. 492, para. 74), which might have been acted upon.

The Court observes that the same is true, pari passu, of certain rights identified in subparagraph (c): "consular officers shall have the right to visit a national of the sending State who is in prison, custody or detention, and to converse and correspond with him . . . ". Mexico, it notes, laid much emphasis in this litigation upon the importance of consular officers being able to arrange for such representation before and during trial, and especially at sentencing, in cases in which a severe penalty may be imposed. Mexico has further indicated the importance of any financial or other assistance that consular officers may provide to defence counsel, inter alia for investigation of the defendant's family background and mental condition, when such information is relevant to the case. The Court observes that the exercise of the rights of the sending State under Article 36, paragraph 1 (c), depends upon notification by the authorities of the receiving State. It may be, however, that information drawn to the attention of the sending State by other means may still enable its consular officers to assist in arranging legal representation for its national. The Court finds that has been so in 13 cases.

The Court concludes on this aspect of the case in paragraph 106 of the Judgment, where it summarizes its findings as to the violation of the different obligations incumbent upon the U.S. under Article 36, paragraph 1, in the cases before it.

Article 36, paragraph 2 of the Vienna Convention (paras. 107-114)

The Court then recalls that in its third final submission Mexico asks the Court to adjudge and declare that "the U.S. violated its obligations under Article 36(2) of the Vienna Convention by failing to provide meaningful and effective review and reconsideration of convictions and sentences impaired by a violation of Article 36 (1)". More specifically, Mexico contends that:

"The U.S. uses several municipal legal doctrines to prevent finding any legal effect from the violations of Article 36. First, despite this Court's clear analysis in LaGrand, U.S. courts, at both the state and federal level, continue to invoke default doctrines to bar any review of Article 36 violations — even when the national had been unaware of his rights to consular notification and communication and thus his ability to raise their violation as an issue at trial, due to the competent authorities' failure to comply with Article 36."

Against this contention by Mexico, the U.S. argues that:

"the criminal justice systems of the U.S. address all errors in process through both judicial and executive clemency proceedings, relying upon the latter when rules of default have closed out the possibility of the former. That is, the 'laws and regulations' of the U.S. provide for the correction of mistakes that may be relevant to a criminal defendant to occur through a combination of judicial review and clemency. These processes together, working with other competent authorities, give full effect to the purposes for which Article 36 (1) is intended, in conformity with Article 36 (2). And, insofar as a breach of Article 36 (1) has occurred, these procedures satisfy the remedial function of Article 36 (2) by allowing the U.S. to provide review and reconsideration of convictions and sentences consistent with LaGrand."

The Court observes that it has already considered the application of the so called "procedural default" rule in the LaGrand case, when the Court addressed the issue of its implications for the application of Article 36, paragraph 2, of the Vienna Convention. The Court emphasized that "a distinction must be drawn between that rule as such and its specific application in the present case" stating:

"In itself, the rule does not violate Article 36 of the Vienna Convention. The problem arises when the procedural default rule does not allow the detained individual to challenge a conviction and sentence by claiming, in reliance on Article 36, paragraph 1, of the Convention, that the competent national authorities failed to comply with their obligation to provide the requisite consular information 'without delay', thus preventing the person from seeking and obtaining consular assistance from the sending State." (I.C.J. Reports 2001, p. 497, para. 90.)

On this basis, the Court concluded that "the procedural default rule prevented counsel for the LaGrands to effectively challenge their convictions and sentences other than on U.S. constitutional grounds" (ibid., para. 91). The Court deems this statement to be equally valid in relation to the present case, where a number of Mexican nationals have been placed exactly in such a situation.

The Court further observes that the procedural default rule has not been revised, nor has any provision been made to prevent its application in cases where it has been the failure of the U.S. itself to inform that may have precluded counsel from being in a position to have raised the question of a violation of the Vienna Convention in the initial trial. The Court notes moreover that in several of the cases cited in Mexico's final submissions the procedural default rule has already been applied, and that in others it could be applied at subsequent stages in the proceedings. It also points out, however, that in none of the cases, save for the three mentioned below, have the criminal proceedings against the Mexican nationals concerned already reached a stage at which there is no further possibility of judicial re-examination of those cases; that is to say, all possibility is not yet excluded of "review and reconsideration" of conviction and sentence, as called for in the LaGrand case, and as explained in subsequent paragraphs of the Judgment. The Court finds that it would therefore be premature for the Court to conclude at this stage that, in those cases, there is already a violation of the obligations under Article 36, paragraph 2, of the Vienna Convention.

By contrast, the Court notes that in the case of three named Mexican nationals, conviction and sentence have become final. Moreover, in one of these cases, the Oklahoma Court of Criminal Appeals has set an execution date. The Court finds therefore that it must conclude that, subject to its observations below in regard to clemency proceedings, in relation to these three individuals, the U.S. is in breach of its obligations under Article 36, paragraph 2, of the Vienna Convention.

Legal consequences of the breach (paras. 115-150)

Having concluded that in most of the cases brought before the Court by Mexico in the 52 instances, there has been a failure to observe the obligations prescribed by Article 36, paragraph 1 (b), of the Vienna Convention, the Court proceeds to the examination of the legal consequences of such a breach and of the legal remedies therefor.

It recalls that Mexico in its fourth, fifth and sixth submissions asks the Court to adjudge and declare:

"(4) that pursuant to the injuries suffered by Mexico in its own right and in the exercise of diplomatic protection of its nationals, Mexico is entitled to full reparation for these injuries in the form of restitutio in integrum;

(5) that this restitution consists of the obligation to restore the status quo ante by annulling or otherwise depriving of full force or effect the conviction and sentences of all 52 Mexican nationals; [and]

(6) that this restitution also includes the obligation to take all measures necessary to ensure that a prior violation of Article 36 shall not affect the subsequent proceedings."

The U.S. on the other hand argues:

"LaGrand's holding calls for the U.S. to provide, in each case, 'review and reconsideration' that 'takes account of' the violation, not 'review and reversal', not across-the-board exclusions of evidence or nullification of convictions simply because a breach of Article 36 (1) occurred and without regard to its effect upon the conviction and sentence and, not . . . 'a precise, concrete, stated result: to re-establish the status quo ante' ".

The Court points out that its task in the present case is to determine what would be adequate reparation for the violations of Article 36. The Court finds it to be clear from what has been observed above that the internationally wrongful acts committed by the U.S. were the failure of its competent authorities to inform the Mexican nationals concerned, to notify Mexican consular posts and to enable Mexico to provide consular assistance. It is of the view that it follows that the remedy to make good these violations should consist in an obligation on the U.S. to permit review and reconsideration of these nationals' cases by the U.S. courts, with a view to ascertaining whether in each case the violation of Article 36 committed by the competent authorities caused actual prejudice to the defendant in the process of administration of criminal justice.

The Court considers that it is not to be presumed, as Mexico asserts, that partial or total annulment of conviction or sentence provides the necessary and sole remedy. In the present case it is not the convictions and sentences of the Mexican nationals which are to be regarded as a violation of international law, but solely certain breaches of treaty obligations which preceded them. Mexico, the Court notes, has further contended that the right to consular notification and consular communication under the Vienna Convention is a human right of such a fundamental nature that its infringement will ipso facto produce the effect of vitiating the entire process of the criminal proceedings conducted in violation of this fundamental right. The Court observes that the question of whether or not the Vienna Convention rights are human rights is not a matter that it need decide. It points out, however, that neither the text nor the object and purpose of the Convention, nor any indication in the travaux préparatoires, support the conclusion that Mexico draws from its contention in that regard. The Court finds that for these reasons, Mexico's fourth and fifth submissions cannot be upheld.

In elaboration of its sixth submission, Mexico contends that "As an aspect of restitutio in integrum, Mexico is also entitled to an order that in any subsequent criminal proceedings against the nationals, statements and confessions obtained prior to notification to the national of his right to consular assistance be excluded". The Court is of the view that this question is one which has to be examined under the concrete circumstances of each case by the U.S. courts concerned in the process of their review and reconsideration. For this reason, the sixth submission of Mexico cannot be upheld.

Although rejecting the fourth, fifth and sixth submissions of Mexico relating to the remedies for the breaches by the U.S. of its international obligations under Article 36 of the Vienna Convention, the Court points out that the fact remains that such breaches have been committed, and that it is thus incumbent upon the Court to specify what remedies are required in order to redress the injury done to Mexico and to its nationals by the U.S. through non-compliance with those international obligations.

In this regard, the Court recalls that Mexico's seventh submission also asks the Court to adjudge and declare:

"That to the extent that any of the 52 convictions or sentences are not annulled, the U.S. shall provide, by means of its own choosing, meaningful and effective review and reconsideration of the convictions and sentences of the 52 nationals, and that this obligation cannot be satisfied by means of clemency proceedings or if any municipal law rule or doctrine [that fails to attach legal significance to an Article 36 (1) violation] is applied."

On this question of "review and reconsideration", the U.S. takes the position that it has conformed its conduct to the LaGrand Judgment. In a further elaboration of this point, the U.S. argues that "[t]he Court said in LaGrand that the choice of means for allowing the review and reconsideration it called for 'must be left' to the U.S.".

The Court points out that, in stating in its Judgment in the LaGrand case that "the United States of America, by means of its own choosing, shall allow the review and reconsideration of the conviction and sentence" (I.C.J. Reports 2001, p. 516, para. 128; emphasis added), the Court acknowledged that the concrete modalities for such review and reconsideration should be left primarily to the U.S. It should be underlined, however, that this freedom in the choice of means for such review and reconsideration is not without qualification: as the passage of the Judgment quoted above makes abundantly clear, such review and reconsideration has to be carried out "by taking account of the violation of the rights set forth in the Convention" (I.C.J. Reports 2001, p. 514, para. 125), including, in particular, the question of the legal consequences of the violation upon the criminal proceedings that have followed the violation.

The Court observes that the current situation in the U.S. criminal procedure, as explained by the Agent at the hearings, is such that a claim based on the violation of Article 36, paragraph 1, of the Vienna Convention, however meritorious in itself, could be barred in the courts of the U.S. by the operation of the procedural default rule. The Court is of the view that the crucial point in this situation is that, by the operation of the procedural default rule as it is applied at present, the defendant is effectively limited to seeking the vindication of his rights under the U.S. Constitution.

The Court takes note in this regard that Mexico, in the latter part of its seventh submission, has stated that "this obligation [of providing review and reconsideration] cannot be satisfied by means of clemency proceedings". Furthermore, Mexico argues that the clemency process is in itself an ineffective remedy to satisfy the international obligations of the U.S. It concludes: "clemency review is standardless, secretive, and immune from judicial oversight".

Against this contention of Mexico, the U.S. claims that it "gives 'full effect' to the 'purposes for which the rights accorded under [Article 36, paragraph 1,] are intended' through executive clemency". It argues that "[t]he clemency process is well suited to the task of providing review and reconsideration". The U.S. explains that, "Clemency . . . is more than a matter of grace; it is part of the overall scheme for ensuring justice and fairness in the legal process" and that "Clemency procedures are an integral part of the existing 'laws and regulations' of the U.S. through which errors are addressed".

The Court emphasizes that the "review and reconsideration" prescribed by it in the LaGrand case should be effective. Thus it should "tak[e] account of the violation of the rights set forth in [the] Convention" (I.C.J. Reports 2001, p. 516, para. 128 (7)) and guarantee that the violation and the possible prejudice caused by that violation will be fully examined and taken into account in the review and reconsideration process. Lastly, review and reconsideration should be both of the sentence and of the conviction.

Accordingly, in a situation of the violation of rights under Article 36, paragraph 1, of the Vienna Convention, the defendant raises his claim in this respect not as a case of "harm to a particular right essential to a fair trial" — a concept relevant to the enjoyment of due process rights under the U.S. Constitution — but as a case involving the infringement of his rights under Article 36, paragraph 1. The rights guaranteed under the Vienna Convention are treaty rights which the U.S. has undertaken to comply with in relation to the individual concerned, irrespective of the due process rights under U.S. constitutional law. The Court is of the view that, in cases where the breach of the individual rights of Mexican nationals under Article 36, paragraph 1 (b), of the Convention has resulted, in the sequence of judicial proceedings that has followed, in the individuals concerned being subjected to prolonged detention or convicted and sentenced to severe penalties, the legal consequences of this breach have to be examined and taken into account in the course of review and reconsideration. The Court considers that it is the judicial process that is suited to this task.

As regards the clemency procedure, the Court points out what is at issue in the present case is whether the clemency process as practised within the criminal justice systems of different states in the U.S. can, in and of itself, qualify as an appropriate means for undertaking the effective "review and reconsideration of the conviction and sentence by taking account of the violation of the rights set forth in the Convention", as the Court prescribed in the LaGrand Judgment (I.C.J. Reports 2001, p. 514, para. 125). The Court notes that the clemency process, as currently practised within the U.S. criminal justice system, does not appear to meet the above-mentioned requirements and that it is therefore not sufficient in itself to serve as an appropriate means of "review and reconsideration" as envisaged by the Court in the LaGrand case.

Finally, the Court considers the eighth submission of Mexico, in which it asks the Court to adjudge and declare:

"That the [U.S.] shall cease its violations of Article 36 of the Vienna Convention with regard to Mexico and its 52 nationals and shall provide appropriate guarantees and assurances that it shall take measures sufficient to achieve increased compliance with Article 36 (1) and to ensure compliance with Article 36 (2)."

The Court recalls that Mexico, although recognizing the efforts by the U.S. to raise awareness of consular assistance rights, notes with regret that "the U.S. program, whatever its components, has proven ineffective to prevent the regular and continuing violation by its competent authorities of consular notification and assistance rights guaranteed by Article 36". It also recalls that the U.S. contradicts this contention of Mexico by claiming that "its efforts to improve the conveyance of information about consular notification are continuing unabated and are achieving tangible results". It contends that Mexico "fails to establish a 'regular and continuing' pattern of breaches of Article 36 in the wake of LaGrand".

Referring to the fact that the Mexican request for guarantees of non-repetition is based on its contention that beyond 52 cases there is a "regular and continuing pattern of breaches by the U.S. of Article 36, the Court observes that, in this respect, there is no evidence properly before it that would establish a general pattern. While it is a matter of concern that, even in the wake of the LaGrand Judgment, there remain a substantial number of cases of failure to carry out the obligation to furnish consular information to Mexican nationals. The Court notes that the U.S. has been making considerable efforts to ensure that its law enforcement authorities provide consular information to every arrested person they know or have reason to believe is a foreign national. The Court further notes in this regard that in the LaGrand case Germany sought, inter alia, "a straightforward assurance that the U.S. will not repeat its unlawful acts" (I.C.J. Reports 2001, p. 511, para. 120). With regard to this general demand for an assurance of non-repetition, the Court stated:

"If a State, in proceedings before this Court, repeatedly refers to substantial activities which it is carrying out in order to achieve compliance with certain obligations under a treaty, then this expresses a commitment to follow through with the efforts in this regard. The programme in question certainly cannot provide an assurance that there will never again be a failure by the U.S. to observe the obligations of notification under Article 36 of the Vienna Convention. But no State could give such a guarantee and Germany does not seek it. The Court considers that the commitment expressed by the U.S. to ensure implementation of the specific measures adopted in performance of its obligations under Article 36, paragraph 1(b), must be regarded as meeting Germany's request for a general assurance of non-repetition." (I.C.J. Reports 2001, pp. 512-513, para. 124.)

The Court believes that as far as the request of Mexico for guarantees and assurances of non-repetition is concerned, what the Court stated in this passage of the LaGrand Judgment remains applicable, and therefore meets that request.*

The Court then re-emphasizes a point of importance. It points out that in the present case it has been addressing the issues of principle raised in the course of the present proceedings from the viewpoint of the general application of the Vienna Convention, and there can be no question of making an a contrario argument in respect of any of the Court's findings in the present Judgment. In other words, the fact that in this case the Court's ruling has concerned only Mexican nationals cannot be taken to imply that the conclusions reached by it in the present Judgment do not apply to other foreign nationals finding themselves in similar situations in the U.S.

The Court finally points out that its Order of 5 February 2003 indicating provisional measures mentioned above, according to its terms and to Article 41 of the Statute, was effective pending final judgment, and that the obligations of the U.S. in that respect are, with effect from the date of the Judgment, replaced by those declared in this Judgment. The Court observes that it has found in relation to the three persons concerned in the Order (among others), that the U.S. has committed breaches of its obligations under Article 36, paragraph 1, of the Vienna Convention; and that moreover, in respect of those three persons alone, the U.S. has also committed breaches of Article 36, paragraph 2. The review and reconsideration of conviction and sentence required by Article 36, paragraph 2, which is the appropriate remedy for breaches of Article 36, paragraph 1, has not been carried out.

The Court considers that in these three cases it is for the U.S. to find an appropriate remedy having the nature of review and reconsideration according to the criteria indicated in the Judgment.

* In subparagraphs 4 to 11 (on the merits) of operative paragraph 153 of its Judgment, the Court

- "finds, by fourteen votes to one, that, by not informing, without delay upon their detention, the 51 Mexican nationals referred to in paragraph 106 (1) above of their rights under Article 36, paragraph 1 (b), of the Vienna Convention on Consular Relations of 24 April 1963, the United States of America breached the obligations incumbent upon it under that subparagraph;
- finds, by fourteen votes to one, that, by not notifying the appropriate Mexican consular post without delay of the detention of the 49 Mexican nationals referred to in paragraph 106 (2) above and thereby depriving the United Mexican States of the right, in a timely fashion, to render the assistance provided for by the Vienna Convention to the individuals concerned, the United States of America breached the obligations incumbent upon it under Article 36, paragraph 1 (b);
- finds, by fourteen votes to one, that, in relation to the 49 Mexican nationals referred to in paragraph 106 (3) above, the United States of America deprived the United Mexican States of the right, in a timely fashion, to communicate with and have access to those nationals and to visit them in detention, and thereby breached the obligations incumbent upon it under Article 36, paragraph 1 (a) and (c), of the Convention;
- finds, by fourteen votes to one, that, in relation to the 34 Mexican nationals referred to in paragraph 106 (4) above, the United States of America deprived the United Mexican States of the right, in a timely fashion, to arrange for legal representation of those nationals, and thereby breached the obligations incumbent upon it under Article 36, paragraph 1 (c), of the Convention;
- finds, by fourteen votes to one, that, by not permitting the review and reconsideration, in the light of the rights set forth in the Convention, of the conviction and sentences of Mr. César Roberto Fierro Reyna, Mr. Roberto Moreno Ramos and Mr. Osvaldo Torres Aguilera, after the violations referred to in subparagraph (4) above had been established in respect of those individuals, the United States of America breached the obligations incumbent upon it under Article 36, paragraph 2, of the Convention;
- finds, by fourteen votes to one, that the appropriate reparation in this case consists in the obligation of the United States of America to provide, by means of its own choosing, review and reconsideration of the convictions and sentences of the Mexican nationals referred to in subparagraphs (4), (5), (6) and (7) above, by taking account both of the violation of the rights set forth in Article 36 of the Convention and of paragraphs 138 to 141 of this Judgment;
- unanimously takes note of the commitment undertaken by the United States of America to ensure implementation of the specific measures adopted in performance of its obligations under Article 36, paragraph 1 (b), of the Vienna Convention; and finds that this commitment must be regarded as meeting the request by the United Mexican States for guarantees and assurances of non-repetition;
- unanimously finds that, should Mexican nationals nonetheless be sentenced to severe penalties, without their rights under Article 36, paragraph 1 (b), of the Convention having been respected, the United States of America shall provide, by means of its own choosing, review and reconsideration of the conviction and sentence, so as to allow full weight to be given to the violation of the rights set forth in the Convention, taking account of paragraphs 138 to 141 of this Judgment."

20. Advisory Opinion of the International Court of Justice on the Legality of the Threat or Use of Nuclear Weapons (Summary)(Excerpted)
8 July 1996, The Hague

Advisory Opinion on the Legality of the Threat or Use of Nuclear Weapons

The Court handed down its Advisory Opinion on the request made by the General Assembly of the United Nations on the question concerning the legality of the threat or use of nuclear weapons. The final paragraph of the opinion reads as follows:
"For these reasons,
The Court
(2) Replies in the following manner to the question put by the General Assembly:
A. Unanimously,

There is in neither customary nor conventional international law any specific authorization of the threat or use of nuclear weapons;

B. By eleven votes to three,

There is in neither customary nor conventional international law any comprehensive and universal prohibition of the threat or use of nuclear weapons as such;

C. Unanimously,

A threat or use of force by means of nuclear weapons that is contrary to Article 2, paragraph 4, of the United Nations Charter and that fails to meet all the requirements of Article 51, is unlawful;

D. Unanimously,

A threat or use of nuclear weapons should also be compatible with the requirements of the international law applicable in armed conflict particularly those of the principles and rules of international humanitarian law, as well as with specific obligations under treaties and other undertakings which expressly deal with nuclear weapons;

E. By seven votes to seven, by the President's casting vote,

It follows from the above-mentioned requirements that the threat or use of nuclear weapons would generally be contrary to the rules of international law applicable in armed conflict, and in particular the principles and rules of humanitarian law;

However, in view of the current state of international law, and of the elements of fact at its disposal, the Court cannot conclude definitively whether the threat or use of nuclear weapons would be lawful or unlawful in an extreme circumstance of self-defence, in which the very survival of a State would be at stake;

F. Unanimously,

There exists an obligation to pursue in good faith and bring to a conclusion negotiations leading to nuclear disarmament in all its aspects under strict and effective international control."

The Court was composed as follows: President Bedjaoui, Vice-President Schwebel; Judges Oda, Guillaume, Shahabuddeen, Weeramantry, Ranjeva, Herczegh, Shi, Fleischhauer, Koroma, Vereshchetin, Ferrari Bravo, Higgins; Registrar Valencia-Ospina.

Submission of the request and subsequent procedure (paras. 1–9)

The Court begins by recalling that by a letter dated 19 December 1994, filed in the Registry on 6 January 1995, the Secretary-General of the United Nations officially communicated to the Registrar the decision taken by the General Assembly to submit a question to the Court for an advisory opinion.

"Legal Question" (para. 13)

. . .

It finds that the question put to the Court by the General Assembly is indeed a legal one, since the Court is asked to rule on the compatibility of the threat or use of nuclear weapons with the relevant principles and rules of international law. To do this, the Court must identify the existing principles and rules, interpret them and apply them to the threat or use of nuclear weapons, thus offering a reply to the question posed based on law.

. . .

The Applicable Law (paras. 23–34)

In seeking to answer the question put to it by the General Assembly, the Court must decide, after consideration of the great corpus of international law norms available to it, what might be the relevant applicable law.

The Court considers that the question whether a particular loss of life, through the use of a certain weapon in warfare, is to be considered an arbitrary deprivation of life contrary to Article 6 of the International Covenant on Civil and Political Rights, as argued by some of the proponents of the illegality of the use of nuclear weapons, can only be decided by reference to the law applicable in armed conflict and not deduced from the terms of the Covenant itself. The Court also points out that the prohibition of genocide would be pertinent in this case if the recourse to nuclear weapons did indeed entail the element of intent, towards a group as such, required by Article II of the Convention on the Prevention and Punishment of the Crime of Genocide. In the view of the Court, it would only be possible to arrive at such a conclusion after having taken due account of the circumstances specific to each case. And the Court further finds that while the existing international law relating to the protection and safeguarding of the environment does not specifically prohibit the use of nuclear weapons, it indicates important environmental factors that are properly to be taken into account in the context of the implementation of the principles and rules of the law applicable in armed conflict.

In the light of the foregoing the Court concludes that the most directly relevant applicable law governing the question of which it was seized, is that relating to the use of force enshrined in the United Nations Charter and the law applicable in armed conflict which regulates the conduct of hostilities, together with any specific treaties on nuclear weapons that the Court might determine to be relevant.

Unique characteristics of nuclear weapons (paras. 35 and 36)

The Court notes that in order correctly to apply to the present case the Charter law on the use of force and the law applicable in armed conflict, in particular humanitarian law, it is imperative for it to take account of the unique characteristics of nuclear weapons, and in particular their destructive capacity, their capacity to cause untold human suffering, and their ability to cause damage to generations to come.

Provisions of the Charter relating to the threat or use of force (paras. 37–50)

The Court then addresses the question of the legality or illegality of recourse to nuclear weapons in the light of the provisions of the Charter relating to the threat or use of force.

In Article 2, paragraph 4, of the Charter the use of force against the territorial integrity or political independence of another State or in any other manner inconsistent with the purposes of the United Nations is prohibited.

This prohibition of the use of force is to be considered in the light of other relevant provisions of the Charter. In Article 51, the Charter recognizes the inherent right of individual or collective self-defence if an armed attack occurs. A further lawful use of force is envisaged in Article 42, whereby the Security Council may take military enforcement measures in conformity with Chapter VII of the Charter.

These provisions do not refer to specific weapons. They apply to any use of force, regardless of the weapons employed. The Charter neither expressly prohibits, nor permits, the use of any specific weapon, including nuclear weapons.

The entitlement to resort to self-defence under Article 51 is subject to the conditions of necessity and proportionality. As the Court stated in the case concerning Military and Paramilitary Activities in and against Nicaragua (Nicaragua v United States of America) (I.C.J. Reports 1986, p. 94, para. 176): "there is a specific rule whereby self-defence would warrant only measures which are proportional to the armed attack and necessary to respond to it, a rule well established in customary international law."

The proportionality principle may thus not in itself exclude the use of nuclear weapons in self-defence in all circumstances. But at the same time, a use of force that is proportionate under the law of self-defence, must, in order to be lawful, also meet the requirements of the law applicable in armed conflict which comprise in particular the principles and rules of humanitarian law. And the Court notes that the very nature of all nuclear weapons and the profound risks associated therewith are further considerations to be borne in mind by States believing they can exercise a nuclear response in self-defence in accordance with the requirements of proportionality.

In order to lessen or eliminate the risk of unlawful attack, States sometimes signal that they possess certain weapons to use in self-defence against any State violating their territorial integrity or political independence. Whether a signalled intention to use force if certain events occur is or is not a "threat" within Article 2, paragraph 4, of the Charter depends upon various factors. The notions of "threat" and "use" of force under Article 2, paragraph 4, of the Charter stand together in the sense that if the use of force itself in a given case is illegal—for whatever reason—the threat to use such force will likewise be illegal. In short, if it is to be lawful, the declared readiness of a State to use force must be a use of force that is in conformity with the Charter. For the rest, no State—whether or not it defended the policy of deterrence—suggested to the Court that it would be lawful to threaten to use force if the use of force contemplated would be illegal.

Rules on the lawfulness or unlawfulness of nuclear weapons as such (paras. 49–73)

Having dealt with the Charter provisions relating to the threat or use of force, the Court turns to the law applicable in situations of armed conflict. It first addresses the question whether there are specific rules in international law regulating the legality or illegality of recourse to nuclear weapons per se; it then examines the question put to it in the light of the law applicable in armed conflict proper, i.e., the principles and rules of humanitarian law applicable in armed conflict, and the law of neutrality.

The Court notes by way of introduction that international customary and treaty law does not contain any specific prescription authorizing the threat or use of nuclear weapons or any other weapon in general or in certain circumstances, in particular those of the exercise of legitimate self-defence. Nor, however, is there any principle or rule of international law which would make the legality of the threat or use of nuclear weapons or of any other weapons dependent on a specific authorization. State practice shows that the illegality of the use of certain weapons as such does not result from an absence of authorization but, on the contrary, is formulated in terms of prohibition.

It does not seem to the Court that the use of nuclear weapons can be regarded as specifically prohibited on the basis of certain provisions of the Second Hague Declaration of 1899, the Regulations annexed to the Hague Convention IV of 1907 or the 1925 Geneva Protocol. The pattern until now has been for weapons of mass destruction to be declared illegal by specific instruments. But the Court does not find any specific prohibition of recourse to nuclear weapons in treaties expressly prohibiting the use of certain weapons of mass destruction; and observes that, although, in the last two decades, a great many negotiations have been conducted regarding nuclear weapons, they have not resulted in a treaty of general prohibition of the same kind as for bacteriological and chemical weapons.

The Court notes that the treaties dealing exclusively with acquisition, manufacture, possession, deployment and testing of nuclear weapons, without specifically addressing their threat or use, certainly point to an increasing concern in the international community with these weapons; it concludes from this that these treaties could therefore be seen as foreshadowing a future general prohibition of the use of such weapons, but that they do not constitute such a prohibition by themselves. As to the treaties of Tlatelolco and Rarotonga and their Protocols, and also the declarations made in connection with the indefinite extension of the Treaty on the Non-Proliferation of Nuclear Weapons, it emerges from these instruments that:

(a) a number of States have undertaken not to use nuclear weapons in specific zones (Latin America; the South Pacific) or against certain other States (non-nuclear-weapon States which are parties to the Treaty on the Non-Proliferation of Nuclear Weapons);

(b) nevertheless, even within this framework, the nuclear-weapon States have reserved the right to use nuclear weapons in certain circumstances; and

(c) these reservations met with no objection from the parties to the Tlatelolco or Rarotonga Treaties or from the Security Council.

The Court then turns to an examination of customary international law to determine whether a prohibition of the threat or use of nuclear weapons as such flows from that source of law.

It notes that the Members of the international community are profoundly divided on the matter of whether non-recourse to nuclear weapons over the past fifty years constitutes the expression of an opinio juris. Under these circumstances the Court does not consider itself able to find that there is such an opinio juris. It points out that the adoption each year by the General Assembly, by a large majority, of resolutions recalling the content of resolution 1653 (XVI), and requesting the member States to conclude a convention prohibiting the use of nuclear weapons in any circumstance, reveals the desire of a very large section of the international community to take, by a specific and express prohibition of the use of nuclear weapons, a significant step forward along the road to complete nuclear disarmament. The emergence, as lex lata, of a customary rule specifically prohibiting the use of nuclear weapons as such is hampered by the continuing tensions between the nascent opinio juris on the one hand, and the still strong adherence to the doctrine of deterrence (in which the right to use those weapons in the exercise of the right to self-defence against an armed attack threatening the vital security interests of the State is reserved) on the other.

International humanitarian law (paras. 74–87)

Not having found a conventional rule of general scope, nor a customary rule specifically proscribing the threat or use of nuclear weapons per se, the Court then deals with the question whether recourse to nuclear weapons must be considered as illegal in the light of the principles and rules of international humanitarian law applicable in armed conflict and of the law of neutrality.

After sketching the historical development of the body of rules which originally were called "laws and customs of war" and later came to be termed "international humanitarian law," the Court observes that the cardinal principles contained in the texts constituting the fabric of humanitarian law are the following. The first is aimed at the protection of the civilian population and civilian objects and establishes the distinction between combatants and non-combatants; States must never make civilians the object of attack and must consequently never use weapons that are incapable of distinguishing between civilian and military targets. According to the second principle, it is prohibited to cause unnecessary suffering to combatants: it is accordingly prohibited to use weapons causing them such harm or uselessly aggravating their suffering. In application of that second principle, States do not have unlimited freedom of choice of means in the weapons they use.

The Court also refers to the Martens Clause, which was first included in the Hague Convention II with Respect to the Laws and Customs of War on Land of 1899 and which has proved to be an effective means of addressing the rapid evolution of military technology. A modern version of that clause is to be found in Article 1, paragraph 2, of Additional Protocol I of 1977, which reads as follows:

"In cases not covered by this Protocol or by other international agreements, civilians and combatants remain under the protection and authority of the principles of international law derived from established custom, from the principles of humanity and from the dictates of public conscience."

The extensive codification of humanitarian law and the extent of the accession to the resultant treaties, as well as the fact that the denunciation clauses that existed in the codification instruments have never been used, have provided the international community with a corpus of treaty rules the great majority of which had already become customary and which reflected the most universally recognized humanitarian principles. These rules indicate the normal conduct and behaviour expected of States.

Turning to the applicability of the principles and rules of humanitarian law to a possible threat or use of nuclear weapons, the Court notes that nuclear weapons were invented after most of the principles and rules of humanitarian law applicable in armed conflict had already come into existence; the Conferences of 1949 and 1974–1977 left these weapons aside, and there is a qualitative as well as quantitative difference between nuclear weapons and all conventional arms. However, in the Court's view, it cannot be concluded from this that the established principles and rules of humanitarian law applicable in armed conflict did not apply to nuclear weapons. Such a conclusion would be incompatible with the intrinsically humanitarian character of the legal principles in question which permeates the entire law of armed conflict and applies to all forms of warfare and to all kinds of weapons, those of the past, those of the present and those of the future. In this respect it seems significant that the thesis that the rules of humanitarian law do not apply to the new weaponry, because of the newness of the latter, has not been advocated in the present proceedings.

The principle of neutrality (paras. 88 and 89)

The Court finds that as in the case of the principles of humanitarian law applicable in armed conflict, international law leaves no doubt that the principle of neutrality, whatever its content, which is of a fundamental character similar to that of the humanitarian principles and rules, is applicable (subject to the relevant provisions of the United Nations Charter), to all international armed conflict, whatever type of weapons might be used.

Conclusions to be drawn from the applicability of international humanitarian law and the principle of neutrality (paras. 90–97) According to one point of view, the fact that recourse to nuclear weapons is subject to and regulated by the law of armed conflict, does not necessarily mean that such recourse is as such prohibited. Another view holds that recourse to nuclear weapons, in view of the necessarily indiscriminate consequences of their use, could never be compatible with the principles and rules of humanitarian law and is therefore prohibited. A similar view has been expressed with respect to the effects of the principle of neutrality. Like the principles and rules of humanitarian law, that principle has therefore been considered by some to rule out the use of a weapon the effects of which simply cannot be contained within the territories of the contending States.

The Court observes that, in view of the unique characteristics of nuclear weapons, to which the Court has referred above, the use of such weapons in fact seems scarcely reconcilable with respect for the requirements of the law applicable in armed conflict. It considers nevertheless, that it does not have sufficient elements to enable it to conclude with certainty that the use of nuclear weapons would necessarily be at variance with the principles and rules of law applicable in armed conflict in any circumstance. Furthermore, the Court cannot lose sight of the fundamental right of every State to survival, and thus its right to resort to self-defence, in accordance with Article 51 of the Charter, when its survival is at stake. Nor can it ignore the practice referred to as "policy of deterrence," to which an appreciable section of the international community adhered for many years.

Accordingly, in view of the present state of international law viewed as a whole, as examined by the Court, and of the elements of fact at its disposal, the Court is led to observe that it cannot reach a definitive conclusion as to the legality or illegality of the use of nuclear weapons by a State in an extreme circumstance of self-defence, in which its very survival would be at stake.

Obligation to negotiate nuclear disarmament (paras. 98–103)

Given the eminently difficult issues that arise in applying the law on the use of force and above all the law applicable in armed conflict to nuclear weapons, the Court considers that it needs to examine one further aspect of the question before it, seen in a broader context.

In the long run, international law, and with it the stability of the international order which it is intended to govern, are bound to suffer from the continuing difference of views with regard to the legal status of weapons as deadly as nuclear weapons. It is consequently important to put an end to this state of affairs: the long-promised complete nuclear disarmament appears to be the most appropriate means of achieving that result.

In these circumstances, the Court appreciates the full importance of the recognition by Article VI of the Treaty on the Non-Proliferation of Nuclear Weapons of an obligation to negotiate in good faith a nuclear disarmament. The legal import of that obligation goes beyond that of a mere obligation of conduct; the obligation involved here is an obligation to achieve a precise result—nuclear disarmament in all its aspects—by adopting a particular course of conduct, namely, the pursuit of negotiations on the matter in good faith. This twofold obligation to pursue and to conclude negotiations formally concerns the 182 States parties to the Treaty on the Non-Proliferation of Nuclear Weapons, or, in other words, the vast majority of the international community. Indeed, any realistic search for general and complete disarmament, especially nuclear disarmament, necessitates the co-operation of all States.

The Court finally emphasizes that its reply to the question put to it by the General Assembly rests on the totality of the legal grounds set forth by the Court above (paragraphs 20 to 103), each of which is to be read in the light of the others. Some of these grounds are not such as to form the object of formal conclusions in the final paragraph of the Opinion; they nevertheless retain, in the view of the Court, all their importance.

Appendix K: Universal Periodic Review

The following documents are from the U.S. participation in the Universal Periodic Review process of the United Nations Human Rights Council, as of press time. Several days prior to completion of this book the HRC voted to adopt the final Outcome Report putting an end to the first UPR process for the US. The documents in this Appendix should be read in conjunction with Primary Documents 86 and 87.

On November 5, 2010, U.S. government representatives appeared before the U.N. Human Rights Council to present and defend its national human rights report (Primary Document 86). Following the November 9, 2010 Draft Report, the Outcome Report came out on January 9, 2011. The final Outcome Report is found in Primary Document 87. The March 10, 2011, U.S. State Department Response to the Recommendations of the Human Rights Council contained in this Outcome Report follows as Document 4 in this Appendix. It is an official response. The Final Outcome Report was adopted by vote of the Council on March 18, 2011. The reader may check the UN web report on the summary and debate before the vote to adopt the final Outcome Report: *E:\US UPR March 18 2011 vote debate summaryDisplayNews.mhte*.

The U.N. UPR website is: http://www.ohchr.org/EN/HRbodies/UPR. The Dept. of State website is: http://www.state.gov/g/drl/upr/

Documents:

Document 1.
UNITED NATIONS   A/HRC/WG.6/9/USA/2
General Assembly   Distr.:
HUMAN RIGHTS COUNCIL   GENERAL
Working Group on the Universal Periodic Review   12 August 2010
Ninth session   Original: ENGLISH
Geneva, 1–12 November 2010   A/HRC/WG.6/9/USA/2

**Compilation prepared by the Office of the High
Commissioner for Human Rights in accordance
with paragraph 15 (b) of the annex to
Human Rights Council resolution 5/1
United States of America**

The present report is a compilation of the information contained in the reports of treaty bodies, special procedures, including observations and comments by the State concerned, and other relevant official United Nations documents. It does not contain any opinions, views or suggestions on the part of the Office of the United Nations High Commissioner for Human Rights (OHCHR), other than those contained in public reports issued by OHCHR. It follows the structure of the general guidelines adopted by the Human Rights Council. Information included herein has been systematically referenced in endnotes. The report has been prepared taking into consideration the four-year periodicity of the first cycle of the review. In the absence of recent information, the latest available reports and documents have been taken into consideration, unless they are outdated. Since this report only compiles information contained in official United Nations documents, lack of information or focus on specific issues may be due to non-ratification of a treaty and/or to a low level of interaction or cooperation with international human rights mechanisms.

I. Background and framework
A. Scope of international obligations[1]

Universal human rights treaties[2]	Date of ratification, accession or succession	Declarations/reservations	Recognition of specific competences of treaty bodies
ICERD	21 October 1994	Yes (arts. 2, para. 1 (c) and (d), 3, 4, 5, 7 22)[3]	Individual Complaints (art. 14) : No
ICCPR	8 June 1992	Yes (arts. 1–27 not self-executing) 5, para. 2; 6; 7; 10, paras. 2 (B) and 3: 14, para. 4; 15, para. 1; 19, para. 3; 20; 47)[4]	Inter-State (arts. complaints (art. 41): Yes Yes
CAT	21 October 1994	Yes (arts. 16 and 30, para. 1)[5]	Inter-State complaints (art. 21): Yes
			Individual Complaints (art. 22): No
			Inquiry procedure (art. 20): Yes

(continued)

| OP-CRC-AC | 23 December 2002 | Binding declaration under art. 3, para. 2: 17 years[6] | - |
| OP-CRC-SC | 23 December 2002 | Yes (arts. 3, para. 1, and 4, para. 1)[7] | - |

Treaties to which United States of America is not a party:
ICESCR (signature only, 1977), OP-ICESCR[8], ICCPR-OP 1, ICCPR-OP 2, CEDAW (signature only, 1980), OP-CEDAW,
OP-CAT, CRC (signature only, 1995), ICRMW, CRPD (signature only, 2009), OP-CRPD and CED.

Other main relevant international instruments[9] Ratification, accession or succession	
Convention on the Prevention and Punishment of the Crime of Genocide	Yes
Rome Statute of the International Criminal Court	No (signature only)
Palermo Protocol[10]	Yes
Refugees and stateless persons[11]	No, except 1967 Protocol
Geneva Conventions of 12 August 1949 and Additional Protocols thereto[12]	Yes (signatory to Addit. Protocols I and II)
ILO fundamental conventions[13]	No, except C.105 and C.182
UNESCO Convention against Discrimination in Education	No

1. In 2008, the Committee on the Rights of the Child (CRC) recommended that the United States of America proceed to become party to the Convention on the Rights of the Child. The Working Group of experts on people of African descent noted that the U.S. has not ratified the Convention or the ILO Convention No. 111 concerning Discrimination in Respect of Employment and Occupation.

2. In 2008, the Special Rapporteur on the human rights of migrants recommended that the U.S. consider ratifying the International Convention on the Protection of the Rights of All Migrant Workers and Members of Their Families.

3. CRC recommended that the State consider ratifying Additional Protocols I and II to the Geneva Conventions of 12 August 1949.

4. The Committee against Torture (CAT) invited the State to reconsider its intention not to become party to the Rome Statute of the International Criminal Court. CRC made a similar recommendation.

5. In 2006, CAT recommended that the State ensure that the Convention applies at all times, whether in peace, war or armed conflict and that the provisions of the Convention expressed as applicable to "territory under the State party's jurisdiction" apply to all persons under the effective control of its authorities.

6. In 2006, the Human Rights Committee (HR Committee) encouraged the State to withdraw its reservation to article 6, paragraph 5, of ICCPR, which forbids imposition of the death penalty on offenders who were under the age of 18 when their crimes were committed. Other committees recommended that reservations and understandings to relevant human rights treaties be withdrawn.

B. Constitutional and legislative framework

7. The Working Group of experts on people of African descent noted that the abolition of slavery is not absolute. The Thirteenth amendment allows slavery "as a punishment for crime whereof the party shall have been duly convicted... within the U.S., or any place subject to their jurisdiction".

8. The Committee on the Elimination of Racial Discrimination (CERD) recommended that the State review the definition of racial discrimination used in the federal and state legislation and in court practice, so as to ensure it is consistent with that of the Convention.

9. CRC recommended that the State define and prohibit child prostitution both at federal and state levels.

10. CRC encouraged the State to raise the minimum age for recruitment into the armed forces to 18 years, and recommended that the State ensure that violations of OP-CRC-AC regarding the recruitment

and involvement of children in hostilities be explicitly criminalized in its legislation; and that it consider establishing extraterritorial jurisdiction for these crimes.

C. Institutional and human rights infrastructure

11. As of 12 July 2010, the U.S. does not have a national human rights institution accredited by the International Coordinating Committee of National Institutions for the Promotion and Protection of Human Rights. CERD recommended that the State consider the establishment of a national human rights institution in accordance with the Paris Principles. CRC and the Working Group of experts on people of African descent made similar recommendations.

12. CERD recommended that the State ensure a coordinated approach towards the implementation of the Convention at the federal, state and local levels. CAT noted that the State had a federal structure, but recalled that it had the obligation to implement the Convention against Torture in full at the domestic level. Likewise, CRC recommended strengthening coordination in the areas covered by OP-CRC-SC, both at federal and state levels.

D. Policy measures

13. CAT recommended that training on all provisions of the Convention be conducted on a regular basis, in particular for personnel involved in the interrogation of suspects.

14. UN-Habitat stated that the Helping Families Save Their Homes Act of 2009 aims to prevent mortgage foreclosures and enhance mortgage credit availability and contains provisions protecting tenants living in foreclosed buildings.Complaints on illegal discrimination on housing rights may be filed through a process administered by the Department of Housing and Urban Development.

II. Promotion and protection of human rights on the ground

A. Cooperation with human rights mechanisms

1. Cooperation with treaty bodies

Treaty body	Latest report submitted and considered	latest concluding observations	Follow-up response	Reporting status
CERD	2007	March 2008	Submitted in January 2009.	Seventh, eighth and ninth Reports due in 2011
HR Committee	2005	July 2006	Submitted in November 2007 and July 2009.	Fourth report due in 2010
CAT	2005	May 2006	Submitted in July 2007.	Fifth report due in 2011
OP-CRC-AC	2007	June 2008 –	Second report submitted in 2010	
OP-CRC-SC	2007	June 2008 –	Second report submitted in 2010	

15. CAT noted with satisfaction the contributions of the U.S. to the United Nations Voluntary Fund for the Victims of Torture.

2. Cooperation with special procedures

16. CAT encouraged the State to invite the Special Rapporteur on torture and other cruel, inhuman or degrading treatment or punishment to visit Guantánamo and any other detention facility under its de facto control. In June 2004, the Chairperson-Rapporteur of the Working Group on Arbitrary Detention, the Special Rapporteur on the independence of judges and lawyers, the Special Rapporteur on the question of torture, the Special Rapporteur on freedom of religion or belief, and the Special Rapporteur on the right of everyone to the enjoyment of the highest attainable standard of physical and mental health (hereinafter referred to as the five mandate holders) requested the U.S. to allow them to visit Guantánamo, but in the absence of assurances from the Government that it would comply with the terms of reference, the five mandate holders decided to cancel the visit in November 2005.

Standing invitation issued No

Latest visits or mission reports

Special Rapporteur on the human rights of migrants (30 April-18 May 2007); Special Rapporteur on the promotion and protection of human rights and fundamental freedoms while countering terrorism (16–25 May 2007); Special Rapporteur on contemporary forms of racism, racial discrimination, xenophobia and related intolerance (19 May–6 June 2008); Special Rapporteur on extrajudicial, summary or arbitrary executions (16–30 June 2008); Working Group on the use of mercenaries as a means of violating human rights and impeding the exercise of the right of peoples to self-determination (20 July–3 August 2009); Special Rapporteur on adequate housing as a component of the right to an adequate standard of living (22 October–8 November 2009); Working Group of experts on people of African descent (25–29 January 2010).

Visits agreed upon in principle

Working Group on Arbitrary Detention; Special Rapporteur on the sale of children, child prostitution and child pornography (October 2010).

Visits requested and not yet agreed upon

Independent expert on the issue of human rights obligations related to access to safe drinking water and sanitation (2009); Special Rapporteur on violence against women, its causes and consequences (2009).

Facilitation/cooperation during missions

Several mandate holders expressed their gratitude to the Government.

Follow-up to visits—Responses to letters of allegations and urgent appeals

During the period under review, 70 communications were sent. The Government replied to 31 communications.

Responses to questionnaires on thematic issues

The U.S. responded to 5 of the 23 questionnaires sent by special procedures mandate holders.

3. Cooperation with the Office of the High Commissioner for Human Rights

17. The U.S. contributed financially to OHCHR in the period under consideration.

B. Implementation of international human rights obligations, taking into account applicable international humanitarian law

1. Equality and non-discrimination

18. The HR Committee observed that the State should take all steps necessary to ensure the equality of women before the law and effective protection against discrimination on the ground of sex, particularly in employment.

19. CERD remained concerned about the persistent racial disparities regarding the imposition of the death penalty. The Special Rapporteur on contemporary forms of racism, racial discrimination, xenophobia and related intolerance recommended mandatory minimum sentences be reviewed to assess disproportionate impact on racial and ethnic minorities. The Working Group of experts on people of African descent was concerned by the ongoing structural discrimination that cannot be effectively addressed with the existing legal mechanisms and legislation.

20. The same Special Rapporteur said the Government should establish a bipartisan Commission to evaluate the progress and failures in the fight against racism and the ongoing process of re-segregation, particularly in housing and education, with broad participation from civil society. CERD reiterated that the adoption of special measures "when circumstances so warrant" is an obligation arising from article 2, paragraph 2, of the Convention.

21. The Working Group of experts on people of African descent found that the challenges faced by people of African descent related, inter alia, mainly to disproportionately high levels of unemployment, lower income levels, access to education and to quality health-care services. The Working Group recommended, inter alia, the adoption of an anti-discrimination act.

22. CERD recommended that the State guarantee the right of everyone to equal treatment before tribunals and all other organs administering justice. It urged the State to put an end to the National Entry and Exit Registration System for nationals of 25 countries, all located in the Middle East, South Asia or North Africa, and to eliminate other forms of racial profiling against Arabs, Muslims and South Asians. In its follow-up report to CERD, the U.S. provided information on measures to combat racial profiling.

23. The Special Rapporteur recommended that the Government clarify to law enforcement officials the obligation of equal treatment and, in particular, the prohibition of racial profiling, and recommended that

adequate consultation mechanisms be put in place for a coordinated approach at the federal, state and local levels of government.

24. CRC recommended that the State ensure that recruitment in the armed forces does not occur in a manner which specifically targets minorities and children of low-income families, and that any reported irregularity or misconduct by recruiters be investigated.

2. Right to life, liberty and security of the person

25. CERD recommended that the State adopt all necessary measures, including a moratorium, to ensure that the death penalty is not imposed as a result of racial bias. The HR Committee, while welcoming the 2002 Supreme Court decision that executions of mentally retarded criminals are cruel and unusual punishments, made a similar recommendation, adding that the U.S. should review federal and state legislation with a view to restricting the number of offences carrying the death penalty. CAT recommended that the State should carefully review its execution methods, in particular lethal injection, in order to prevent severe pain and suffering. The U.S. voted against the draft resolution on a moratorium on the use of the death penalty in 2007.

26. OHCHR expressed concerns, in August 2008, about the decision of the authorities in Texas to proceed with the execution of a national of a third country, despite an order to the contrary by the International Court of Justice. OHCHR recalled that the U.S. has an international legal obligation to comply with decisions of the International Court of Justice.

27. The Special Rapporteur on extrajudicial, summary or arbitrary executions and the Special Rapporteur on the promotion and protection of human rights and fundamental freedoms while countering terrorism sent, in March 2006, a joint allegation letter regarding incidents of air strikes by U.S. unmanned aircrafts that had resulted in the death of 31 civilians near the Afghan border. The former also sent an allegation letter regarding a raid conducted by the multinational force in Iraq, in which American troops allegedly executed 10 civilians, including 6 children.

28. The Special Rapporteur on extrajudicial, summary or arbitrary executions stated that for too long, there has been de facto impunity for killings by private contractors and civilian intelligence agents operating in Iraq, Afghanistan and elsewhere, and recommended that the Government explicate the rules of international law it considers to cover targeted killings. The Secretary-General stated that there were continued reports implicating private security companies in the killing of civilians or bystanders. Such incidents attracted wide media attention and official complaints by Iraqi authorities. He also stated that the result was a tightening of control over those companies by the U.S. and the extension of court-martial proceedings to some contractors for serious offences.

29. On 25 September 2007, the Working Group on mercenaries sent an allegation letter to the Government on the events of 16 September 2007 in Nisoor Square in Baghdad, in which employees of a private security company opened fire, killing 17 and injuring more than 20 civilians. The U.S. replied to the Working Group's letter.

30. CERD remained concerned about allegations of brutality and use of excessive or deadly force by law enforcement officials against, inter alia, Latino and African American persons and undocumented migrants. It recommended increasing the State's efforts to eliminate police brutality and to ensure that incidents of excessive use of force are investigated and that perpetrators are prosecuted. In 2006, the HR Committee and CAT expressed similar concerns. The Special Rapporteur on extrajudicial, summary or arbitrary executions recommended that all deaths in immigration detention should be promptly and publicly reported and investigated.

31. CAT noted with concern that the State did not always register persons detained in territories under its jurisdiction, depriving them of an effective safeguard against acts of torture. The U.S. provided the Committee with a follow-up reply. CAT recommended that the State adopt all necessary measures to prohibit and prevent enforced disappearance in any territory under the U.S.' jurisdiction, and prosecute perpetrators.

32. CAT recommended that the State enact a federal crime of torture consistent with the Convention, and investigate, prosecute and punish perpetrators under the federal extraterritorial criminal torture statute The Committee also recommended that the State adopt clear legal provisions to implement the principle of absolute prohibition of torture without any possible derogation.

33. In 2006, the HR Committee and CAT expressed concerns over the use of enhanced interrogation techniques. The HR Committee was concerned, inter alia, that the State refused to acknowledge that such techniques

violate the prohibition of torture. CAT called upon the State to rescind any interrogation technique that constitutes torture or punishment, in all places of detention under its de facto effective control. The five mandate holders made a similar recommendation. The U.S. provided CAT and the HR Committee with a follow-up reply. The U.S. also sent a letter to OHCHR concerning the report of the five mandate holders.

34. CAT was concerned about acts of torture or ill-treatment committed by certain members of the State's military or civilian personnel in Afghanistan and Iraq, and recommended that the State take immediate measures to eradicate all forms of torture and ill-treatment of detainees by military or civilian personnel, in any territory under its jurisdiction, and thoroughly investigate such acts. The Special Rapporteur on the promotion and protection of human rights and fundamental freedoms while countering terrorism urged the U.S. to ensure that all its officials and agencies comply with international standards, including article 7 of ICCPR, the Convention against Torture and, in the context of an armed conflict, common article 3 of the Geneva Conventions.

35. In March 2010, the United Nations High Commissioner for Human Rights indicated that the U.S. should conduct thorough investigations into allegations of torture and the detention in Guantánamo and Bagram.

36. CAT was concerned by allegations that the State had established secret detention facilities, and that those detained in such facilities could be held for prolonged periods and face torture. The HR Committee raised similar concerns. CAT recommended investigating and disclosing the existence of any such facilities and the authority under which they had been established. The HR Committee recommended that the State immediately cease this practice, grant the International Committee of the Red Cross access to detainees, and ensure that, regardless of their place of detention, they benefit from the full protection of the law. The U.S. replied to the HR Committee. The Special Rapporteur on the promotion and protection of human rights and fundamental freedoms while countering terrorism made similar recommendations.

37. CAT was concerned that the State considered that the non-refoulement obligation did not extend to a person detained outside its territory, and also by the State's rendition of suspects to States where they face a real risk of torture. It recommended, inter alia, that suspects have the possibility to challenge decisions of refoulement. The HR Committee and CERD raised similar concerns. The U.S. provided CAT and the HR Committee with responses.

38. The HR Committee recommended that the State scrutinize conditions of detention in prisons, in particular in maximum security prisons, with a view to guaranteeing that persons deprived of their liberty be treated in accordance with article 10 of the Covenant and the United Nations Standard Minimum Rules for the Treatment of Prisoners. CAT recommended that the State should implement appropriate measures to prevent all sexual violence in all its detention centres.

39. The Working Group on Arbitrary Detention issued the following opinion: the deprivation of liberty of Mr. Antonio Herreros Rodríguez, Mr. Fernando González Llort, Mr. Gerardo Hernández Nordelo, Mr. Ramón Labañino Salazar and Mr. René González Schweret is arbitrary, being in contravention of article 14 of the International Covenant on Civil and Political Rights. The Working Group requested the Government to adopt the necessary steps to remedy this situation.

40. CERD remained concerned about the incidence of rape and sexual violence experienced by women belonging to minority groups, particularly regarding American Indian and Alaska Native women and female migrant workers, especially domestic workers, and recommended that the State increase its efforts to prevent and punish violence against them.

41. The HR Committee noted with concern allegations of violent crimes perpetrated against persons of minority sexual orientation, including by law enforcement officials.

42. CRC was concerned at the number of children in U.S.-administered detention facilities in Iraq and Afghanistan, detained over extended periods of time and who may have been subject to cruel, inhuman or degrading treatment, without access to legal advisory services or recovery measures. CRC recommended, inter alia, that the State ensure that children be detained only as a measure of last resort and that a periodic review of their detention be guaranteed.

43. CRC was concerned, inter alia, that efforts to prevent child abuse and neglect did not cover sufficiently large groups of vulnerable children and recommended adopting measures to prevent exploitation of children, and assisting victims.

44. In 2010, the ILO Committee of Experts urged the U.S. to take immediate and effective measures to comply with article 1 of the Worst Forms of Child Labour Convention (No. 182), read with article 3 (d), to prohibit children under 18 years of age from engaging in dangerous work in agriculture.

3. Administration of justice, including impunity, and the rule of law

45. On 22 January 2009, the High Commissioner for Human Rights welcomed the decision by the U.S. Administration to close the detention facility in Guantánamo, as well as the decision to ban methods of interrogation that contravene international law. She also called for a review of the U.S.' approach to detaining individuals abroad, in third countries, as well as the practice of "rendition".

46. On 12 June 2008, the High Commissioner for Human Rights welcomed the decision by the U.S. Supreme Court in *Boumediene v Bush* that foreign detainees held in Guantánamo have the right to challenge their detention by habeas corpus in the civilian courts. She expressed the hope that the civilian courts will be able to move promptly to assess the situation of individual detainees.

47. CAT recommended that the State cease to detain any person at Guantánamo and close this detention facility, and permit access by the detainees to judicial process or release them as soon as possible. The five mandate holders made similar recommendations. In July 2010, the Special Rapporteur on the question of torture and the Special Rapporteur on the promotion and protection of human rights and fundamental freedoms while countering terrorism called on the Government to ensure that it does not forcibly transfer anyone to another State where a person could be subject to torture. The U.S. provided CAT with a follow-up reply, and sent a letter to OHCHR concerning the report of the five mandate holders.

48. The HR Committee recommended that the State conduct prompt and independent investigations into allegations concerning suspicious deaths in custody and torture and ill treatment inflicted by U.S. military and non-military personnel or contract employees, in detention facilities in Guantánamo, Afghanistan, Iraq and other overseas locations, and recommended ensuring that those responsible be prosecuted and punished. The Special Rapporteur on extrajudicial, summary or arbitrary executions made similar recommendations. The U.S. provided the HR Committee with a follow-up reply.

49. Regarding the 2005 Detainee Treatment Act, CAT recommended that independent procedures of review be available to all detainees. It also recommended ensuring that mechanisms to obtain full redress, compensation and rehabilitation are accessible to all victims of acts of torture or abuse. The five mandate holders stated that the U.S. should ensure that all victims of torture are provided with fair and adequate compensation, in accordance with article 14 of the Convention against Torture, including the means for a full rehabilitation. The U.S. sent a letter to OHCHR concerning the report of the five mandate holders.

50. The Special Rapporteur on extrajudicial, summary or arbitrary executions stated that the U.S. has an obligation under international law to provide detainees with fair trials, regardless of whether persons are to be tried for crimes allegedly committed during peace or armed conflict.

51. Regarding persons detained in Guantánamo, the HR Committee was concerned that proceedings before Combatant Status Review Tribunals and Administrative Review Boards may not offer adequate safeguards of due process. The Committee was further concerned that detention in other locations, such as Afghanistan and Iraq, is reviewed by mechanisms providing even fewer guarantees. CAT expressed similar concerns.

52. The Special Rapporteur on the promotion and protection of human rights and fundamental freedoms while countering terrorism recommended that the categorization of persons as "unlawful enemy combatants" be abandoned. He called upon the U.S. to release or to put on trial those persons detained under that categorization. CERD made a similar recommendation.

53. The ILO Committee of Experts asked the Government to supply information on any measures to ensure that there is no discrimination in the imposition of prison sentences involving an obligation to perform labour. The Working Group of experts on people of African descent was concerned with aspects of the administration of justice that adversely affect the African American population, particularly the disproportionate incarceration rates compared to the general population.

4. Right to privacy

54. The HR Committee was concerned that the State had monitored and still monitors private communications of individuals both within and outside the country, without any judicial or other independent oversight. The Committee recommended ensuring that any infringement on an individual's rights to privacy is strictly necessary and duly authorized by law, and that the rights of individuals in this regard are respected.

5. Freedom of expression

55. On 25 September 2006, the Special Rapporteur on the promotion and protection of the right to freedom of opinion and expression sent an urgent appeal concerning the imprisonment of a freelance journalist for refusing to provide to a Grand Jury his unedited video footage of a protest in San Francisco. The Government replied to that communication.

56. On 24 August 2007, the same Special Rapporteur, jointly with the Special Rapporteurs on health and on the question of torture, sent an urgent appeal concerning a cameraman who had been detained in Guantánamo since June 2002. The Government replied to that communication.

6. Right to work and to just and favourable conditions of work

57. The Working Group of experts on people of African descent stated that African Americans are still underrepresented in employment. While people of African descent made up 11 per cent of the labour force in 2009, they represented 18 per cent of the unemployed and 25 per cent of the long-term unemployed (persons unemployed for 27 weeks or longer).

58. CERD regretted that workers belonging to minorities, in particular women and undocumented migrant workers, continue to face discriminatory treatment and abuse in the workplace.

7. Right to social security and to an adequate standard of living

59. CERD made reference to the high incidence of unintended pregnancies and greater abortion rates affecting African American women, and the growing disparities in HIV infection rates for minority women and recommended that efforts be continued to address wide racial disparities, which still exist in the field of sexual and reproductive health.

60. The UN-Habitat Advisory Group on Forced Evictions found allegations of instances of forced evictions caused by, inter alia, the demolition of public housing and the unequal distribution of hurricane recovery funds.

61. The Special Rapporteur on adequate housing considered that, given the crisis in affordable housing, an immediate moratorium is required on the demolition and disposition of public housing until the right to return is guaranteed to all residents. The Special Rapporteur recommended that residents of public housing should have effective participation in decision-making process affecting their access to housing.

62. CERD urged the State to intensify its efforts aimed at reducing the phenomenon of residential segregation based on racial, ethnic and national origins. The HR Committee was concerned that some 50 per cent of homeless people are African American although they constitute only 12 per cent of the population.

8. Right to education

63. CERD remained concerned about the persistence of de facto racial segregation in public schools, and recommended that the State elaborate effective strategies aimed at promoting school desegregation and providing equal educational opportunity. In 2006, the HR Committee raised similar concerns.

9. Minorities and indigenous peoples

64. CERD recommended, inter alia, that the State recognize the right of Native Americans to participate in decisions affecting them, and consult in good faith with them before adopting and implementing any activity in their lands, and that the United Nations Declaration on the Rights of Indigenous Peoples be used as a guide to interpret the State obligations under the Convention relating to indigenous peoples.

10. Migrants, refugees and asylum-seekers

65. The Office of the United Nations High Commissioner for Refugees (UNHCR) was concerned over the U.S. immigration and asylum laws that have been amended in a variety of ways that are inconsistent with international standards. It urged the State to ensure that new asylum regulations to be issued in 2010 would not require overly restrictive conditions for meeting the refugee definition.

66. UNHCR noted that the State is currently detaining over 380,000 non-citizens in the U.S. for removal proceedings, using over 300 different facilities, the majority of which are in remote locations. It urged the U.S. to provide legal representation to all such children who are seeking asylum or in immigration court removal proceedings.

67. The Special Rapporteur on the human rights of migrants recommended that immigration detainees placed in removal proceedings have the right to appointed counsel.

Migrant women who are suffering the effects of persecution or abuse, or who are pregnant, should not be detained. Children should be placed in home-like facilities.

68. UNHCR urged the U.S. to provide a pathway to permanent legal status for stateless persons within the country. For those who may not qualify for legal status, it recommended adopting suggested administrative reforms to ease restrictions placed on stateless persons.

11. Internally displaced persons

69. The Representative of the Secretary-General on the human rights of internally displaced persons, in the aftermath of Hurricane Katrina, stated that the main challenges for persons still displaced, belonging to ethnic minorities or living in poverty, were decent housing at affordable prices, access to jobs, low-level incomes and poor prospects in the medium and long term.

70. CERD remained concerned about many low-income African American residents who continued to be displaced after Hurricane Katrina, and recommended that the State increase its efforts to facilitate their return to their homes or to guarantee access to adequate and affordable housing. The HR Committee shared similar concerns and made a similar recommendation. In its follow-up response to CERD and to the HR Committee the U.S. reported on measures taken to assist victims.

12. Human rights and counter-terrorism

71. The Special Rapporteur on the promotion and protection of human rights and fundamental freedoms while countering terrorism urged the Government to restrict definitions of "international terrorism", "domestic terrorism" and "material support to terrorist organizations" in a way that is precise and restricted to the type of conduct identified by the Security Council as conduct to be suppressed in the fight against terrorism.

72. The HR Committee expressed concerns about the potentially overbroad reach of the definitions of terrorism under domestic law and recommended that the legislation adopted be limited to crimes that would justify being assimilated to terrorism. UNHCR made a similar recommendation.

73. The HR Committee was also concerned that, following the 9/11 attacks, many non- U.S. citizens suspected to have committed terrorism-related offences have been detained for long periods pursuant to immigration laws with fewer guarantees than in the context of criminal procedures.

74. The HR Committee noted that the decision of the Supreme Court in *Hamdan v Rumsfeld*, according to which Guantánamo detainees accused of terrorism offences are to be judged by a regularly constituted court, remains to be implemented. The U.S. provided the Committee with a follow-up response.

III. Achievements, best practices, challenges and constraints

75. CERD notes with satisfaction the work carried out by various executive departments and agencies which have responsibilities in the field of the elimination of racial discrimination, including the Civil Rights Division of the Department of Justice and the Department of Housing and Urban Development.

76. The HR Committee welcomes the Supreme Court's decision in *Lawrence et al. v Texas* (2003), which declared unconstitutional legislation criminalizing homosexual relations between consenting adults.

77. The Special Rapporteur on the promotion and protection of human rights and fundamental freedoms while countering terrorism identified elements of best practice in the U.S.' fight against terrorism, including compensation for victims of terrorism. He also, in contrast, identified serious situations of incompatibility between international human rights obligations and the counter-terrorism law and practice.

78. UN-Habitat stated that the Home Affordable Modification Program provides over 1.2 million borrowers offers for modification trials. The Fair Housing Act prohibits discrimination in housing on the basis of race, colour, national origin, religion, sex, familial status and disability.

IV. Key national priorities, initiatives and commitments

A. Pledges by the State

79. As a party to ICERD, the U.S. is committed to seeing the goals of this Covenant fully realized. Particular emphasis should be placed on eliminating any remaining legal barriers to equality and confronting the reality of continuing discrimination and inequality within institutions and societies. The U.S. is committed to working to consider the possible ratification of human rights treaties, including but not limited to CEDAW and ILO Convention No. 111 concerning Discrimination in Respect of Employment and Occupation. It is committed to cooperating with the human rights mechanisms of the United Nations, as well as the Inter-American Commission on Human Rights and other regional human rights bodies, by responding to inquiries, engaging in dialogues and hosting visits.

B. Specific recommendations for follow-up

80. Information on follow-up measures requested by CAT, CERD and the HR Committee was provided by the U.S. in July 2007, January 2009, and November 2007 and July 2009, respectively.

V. Capacity-building and technical assistance

N/A

Notes

[1] Unless indicated otherwise, the status of ratifications of instruments listed in the table may be found in *Multilateral Treaties Deposited with the Secretary-General: Status as at 31 December 2006* (ST/LEG/SER.E.25), supplemented by the official website of the United Nations Treaty Collection database, Office of Legal Affairs of the United Nations Secretariat, http://treaties.un.org/.

[2] The following abbreviations have been used for this document:

ICERD International Convention on the Elimination of All Forms of Racial Discrimination

ICESCR International Covenant on Economic, Social and Cultural Rights

OP-ICESCR Optional Protocol to ICESCR

ICCPR International Covenant on Civil and Political Rights

ICCPR-OP 1 Optional Protocol to ICCPR

ICCPR-OP 2 Second Optional Protocol to ICCPR, aiming at the abolition of the death penalty

CEDAW Convention on the Elimination of All Forms of Discrimination against Women

OP-CEDAW Optional Protocol to CEDAW

CAT Convention against Torture and Other Cruel, Inhuman or Degrading Treatment or Punishment

OP-CAT Optional Protocol to CAT

CRC Convention on the Rights of the Child

OP-CRC-AC Optional Protocol to CRC on the involvement of children in armed conflict

OP-CRC-SC Optional Protocol to CRC on the sale of children, child prostitution and child pornography

ICRMW International Convention on the Protection of the Rights of All Migrant Workers and Members of their Families

CRPD Convention on the Rights of Persons with Disabilities

OP-CRPD Optional Protocol to the Convention on the Rights of Persons with Disabilities

CED International Convention for the Protection of All Persons from Enforced Disappearance

[3] The U.S. also made an understanding and a declaration upon ratification.

[4] The U.S. made understandings and declarations upon ratification. Understandings: arts. 2, para. 1; 26; 4, para. 1; 9, para. 5; 14, para. 6; 10, paras. 2 (a) and 3; 14, para. 3 (b) and (d); 3 (e); 14, para. 7; and 50; declarations: arts. 27, para. 1; 5, para. 2; 19, para. 3; and 47.

[5] The U.S. also made understandings of arts. 1, 3, 10 to 14, and 16, as well as a declaration.

[6] The U.S. also made understandings of arts. 1, 3 and 4.

[7] The U.S. also made understandings of art. 2 (c) and art. 3, para. 1 (a) (i) and (ii) and para. 5.

[8] Adopted by the General Assembly in its resolution 63/117 of 10 December 2008. Article 17, paragraph 1, of OP-ICESCR states that "The present Protocol is open for signature by any State that has signed, ratified or acceded to the Covenant".

[9] Information relating to other relevant international human rights instruments, including regional instruments, may be found in the pledges and commitments undertaken by the U.S. before the Human Rights Council, as contained in the letter dated 22 April 2009 sent by the Permanent Mission of the United States of America to the United Nations addressed to the President of the General Assembly (A/63/831).

[10] Protocol to Prevent, Suppress and Punish Trafficking in Persons, Especially Women and Children, supplementing the United Nations Convention against Transnational Organized Crime.

[11] 1951 Convention relating to the Status of Refugees and its 1967 Protocol, 1954 Convention relating to the status of Stateless Persons and 1961 Convention on the Reduction of Statelessness.

[12] Geneva Convention for the Amelioration of the Condition of the Wounded and Sick in Armed Forces in the Field (First Convention); Geneva Convention for the Amelioration of the Condition of Wounded, Sick and Shipwrecked Members of Armed Forces at Sea (Second Convention); Convention relative to the Treatment of Prisoners of War (Third Convention); Convention relative to the Protection of Civilian Persons in Time of War (Fourth Convention); Protocol Additional to the Geneva Conventions of 12 August 1949, and relating to the Protection of Victims of International Armed Conflicts (Protocol I); Protocol Additional to the Geneva Conventions of 12 August 1949, and relating to the Protection of Victims of Non-International Armed Conflicts (Protocol II); Protocol Additional to the Geneva Conventions of 12 August 1949, and relating to the Adoption of an Additional Distinctive Emblem (Protocol III). For the official status of ratifications, see the Federal Department of Foreign Affairs of Switzerland, at www.eda.admin.ch/eda/fr/home/topics/intla/intrea/chdep/warvic.html.

[13] International Labour Organization Convention No. 29 concerning Forced or Compulsory Labour; Convention No. 105 concerning the Abolition of Forced Labour, Convention No. 87 concerning Freedom of Association and Protection of the Right to Organize; Convention No. 98 concerning the Application of the Principles of the Right to Organize and to Bargain Collectively; Convention No. 100 concerning Equal Remuneration for Men and Women Workers for Work of Equal Value; Convention No. 111 concerning Discrimination in Respect of Employment and Occupation; Convention No. 138 concerning the Minimum Age for Admission to Employment; Convention No. 182 concerning the Prohibition and Immediate Action for the Elimination of the Worst Forms of Child Labour.

. . . .

(Rest of Footnotes omitted; see websites for complete list.)

Document 2.

UNITED NATIONS   A/HRC/WG.6/9/USA/3

General Assembly   Distr.:
HUMAN RIGHTS COUNCIL   GENERAL
Working Group on the Universal Periodic Review   20 August 2010
Ninth session   Original: ENGLISH
Geneva, 1–12 November 2010

Summary prepared by the Office of the High Commissioner for Human Rights in accordance with paragraph 15 (c) of the annex to Human Rights Council resolution 5/1

The present report is a summary of 103 stakeholders' submissions1 to the universal periodic review. It follows the structure of the general guidelines adopted by the Human Rights Council. It does not contain any opinions, views or suggestions on the part of the Office of the United Nations High Commissioner for Human Rights (OHCHR), nor any judgment or determination in relation to specific claims. The information included herein has been systematically referenced in endnotes and, to the extent possible, the original texts have not been altered. Lack of information or focus on specific issues may be due to the absence of submissions by stakeholders regarding these particular issues. The full texts of all submissions received are available on the OHCHR website. The report has been prepared taking into consideration the four-year periodicity of the first cycle of the review.

United States of America*

I. Background and framework

A. Scope of international obligations

1. Amnesty International (AI) recommended embarking upon a programme of ratification, and ensure implementation into domestic law, of human rights and other instruments, including CEDAW, CRC, ICESCR, OPCAT, the International Convention for the Protection of All Persons from Enforced Disappearance, the Rome Statute of the International court, the American Convention on Human Rights, and the Vienna Convention on the Law of Treaties. The Inter-American Commission of Human Rights (IACHR) informed that the U.S. (US) has not yet ratified any of the regional human rights instruments.

2. Four Freedoms Forum (FFF) recommended accepting the optional protocols and articles that allow for individual communications.

3. First Peoples Human Rights Coalition (FPHRC), US Human Rights Network (USHRN) and Episcopal Diocese of Maine (EDM) recommended endorsing the UN Declaration on the Rights of Indigenous Peoples without qualification and, in partnership with Indigenous peoples, fully implement it. USHRN called on the US to use the Declaration as a guide for interpretation of legally binding obligations vis-à-vis Indigenous Peoples.

4. USHRN and AI recommended withdrawing all reservations, understandings and declarations that serve to undermine compliance with the treaties or undermine their object and purpose.

5. AI and International Commission of Jurists (ICJ) recommended recognizing and giving effect to the extra-territorial application of international human rights law to actions by US personnel vis-à-vis territories and individuals over which they exercise effective control, at all times, and; the dual applicability of human rights and international humanitarian law in case of armed conflicts.

6. Conservation Centre of Environmental & Reserves in Iraq (CCERF) and other organizations stressed the responsibility of the US as an occupying power to fulfill its obligations deriving from human rights and humanitarian law, and to be held accountable for violations.

7. Center for Economic and Social Rights (CESR) noted that in signing the ICESCR, CRC and CEDAW, the US has already indicated an intention to be bound by their provisions and not to violate their objective and purpose.

8. USHRN noted the failure of the US to signal intent to ratify the CRC and CEDAW. While commending the signature of the Convention on the Rights of Persons with Disabilities, USHRN noted that it lingers without ratification.

B. Constitutional and legislative framework

9. AI indicated that in the domestic arena, the US has many laws, mechanisms and institutions to protect human rights and provide remedy for violations of the US Constitution. However, laws and practices fall short of international human rights standards, as noted by the treaty monitoring bodies. USHRN indicated that while the Constitution incorporates ratified international treaties, treaties are non-self-executing. The US issued a declaration that the federal government will only implement the treaties to the extent that it "exercises jurisdiction" over the treaty provision, raising federalism as a barrier to mplementation.

10. Institute for Human Rights and Business (IHRB) recommended passing legislation for individuals to seek redress under US law for human rights abuses involving US registered companies at home and abroad.

11. Disability Rights Education and Defense Fund indicated that legal and structural problems result in gaps in the enjoyment of their human rights by persons with disabilities.

C. Institutional and human rights infrastructure

12. USHRN noted that hampering the advancement of human rights in the US is the lack of an independent human rights commission to monitor compliance with human rights standards or an effective mechanism designed to ensure a coordinated approach towards the implementation of human rights at the federal, state and, local level.

13. FFF indicated that there must be a national human rights institution in accordance with the Paris Principles and that the commission on civil rights could facilitate the national dialogue following the UPR review.

14. AI recommended issuing an Executive Order to ensure that the administration's Inter-Agency Working Group on Human Rights serves as a coordinating body among federal agencies and departments to enforce and implement the US human rights obligations; to make mandatory human rights impact assessments and studies to ensure government policies, pending legislation and regulations are consistent with US human rights obligations; to require that Inspectors General incorporate human rights obligations and analysis into their reviews and investigations of government agencies, policies and programmes; and to ensure collaboration between federal, state and local governments.

15. CESR recommended establishing an effective and inclusive process to follow-up on the recommendations from the universal periodic review.

D. Policy measures

16. USHRN recommended adopting a National Action Plan on Racial Discrimination , and a process by which policies and practices are reviewed for discriminatory impact.

17. USHRN recommended adopting a human rights centered macro-economic and financial policy in the US.

18. Accountability Counsel recommended improving the human rights corporate accountability mechanism. IHRB recommended the development of a Business and Human Rights Policy.

19. Center for Human Rights and Global Justice (CHRGJ) recommended adopting a human rights-based approach to international assistance.

20. Global Justice Center (GJC) raised concerns on the Helms Amendment to the Foreign Assistance Act on the prohibition from supporting abortion as a method of family planning using U.S. funds.

21. PIJIP-GAP reported on the US use of trade agreements and foreign aid to promote intellectual property and pharmaceutical regulations that restrict access to affordable medications in developing countries.

22. LA Asociación Nacional de Economistas y Contadores (ANEC) citó el incumplimiento del compromiso de los Estados Unidos de América (EUA) con la ayuda al desarrollo, el cual es sólo 0.16% de su Producto Interno Bruto.

23. La Asociación Cubana de las Naciones Unidas (ACNU) y ANEC se refirieron al impacto del bloqueo económico, financiero y comercial contra Cuba, el cual perjudica también al pueblo norteamericano.

II. Promotion and protection of human rights on the ground

A. Cooperation with human rights mechanisms

Cooperation with treaty bodies

24. Meiklejohn Civil Liberties Institute noted the failure to report to treaty bodies on local conditions. FFF recommended engaging civil society in the reporting process.

B. Implementation of international human rights obligations, taking into account applicable international humanitarian law

1. Equality and non-discrimination

25. USHRN noted the failure to address de facto and de jure discrimination and the definition of discrimination is not in accordance with the ICERD.

26. AI indicated that fully enjoyment of the treaty rights of those under US jurisdiction is affected by factors such as race, nationality, ethnicity, indigenous status, income and gender. US law falls short of international standards by generally protecting only against intentional discrimination, not policies or practices that have a discriminatory effect, as required under ICERD and other international human rights treaties.

27. Despite extensive anti-discrimination and civil rights legislation, there remain wide inequalities in areas such as housing, employment, education, healthcare and the criminal justice system. Racial disparities continue to exist at every stage of the criminal justice system. AI called on the US to address racial disparities in the criminal justice system and to pass legislation to bar racial profiling in law enforcement, with effective complaints and compliance procedures.

28. Joint Submission-11 (JS-11) indicated that Indigenous Peoples continue to be subjected to widespread discrimination.

29. Joint Submission-10 (JS-10) reported that discrimination on the basis of sexual orientation and/or gender identity prevents LGBT people from accessing health care, education, relationship recognition and other benefits.

2. Right to life, liberty and security of the person

30. USHRN referred to the discriminatory imposition of the *death penalty*; the lack of compliance with the International Court of Justice's judgment in *Avena and Other Mexican Nationals*; the execution of persons with mental disabilities; and the inhumane and degrading conditions of death row facilities. ABA reported that some jurisdictions in the US continue to impose the death penalty in a manner that reflects racial disparities and fails to meet fundamental standards of competency of defense counsel and judicial review of constitutional claims following conviction. ABA indicated that post-conviction collateral review continues to be curtailed by the Antiterrorism and Effective Death Penalty Reform Act of 1996. AI indicated the US capital justice punishment is marked by arbitrariness, discrimination and error. AI noted that people with serious mental illness continue to be subjected to the death penalty, despite the 2002 US Supreme Court ruling that people with "mental retardation" be exempt from the death penalty. AI also referred to the harsh conditions on death rows in many states. USHRN recommended adopting a moratorium on executions and on the imposition of new death sentences. Advocates for Human Rights (AHR) recommended abolishing the death penalty and commuting all sentences to a life imprisonment term.

31. Catholic Family & Human Rights Institute (C-FAM), referred to a Supreme Court decision, ruling that the mother's right to privacy was superior to any right to life of the unborn child.[46]

32. AI indicated that there are frequent reports of ill-treatment and excessive force by police or custody officials. Officials are rarely prosecuted for abuses and some law enforcement agencies, as well as many prisons and jails, lack effective, independent oversight bodies.

33. American Bar Association (ABA) noted that current US prohibitions of torture lack sufficient status in law, are unclear, and their implementation lacks transparency. In ratifying CAT and the ICCPR, the US attached reservations stating that it "*considers itself bound by the obligation . . . to prevent 'cruel, inhuman or degrading treatment or punishment,' only insofar as [that] term . . . means the cruel, unusual and inhumane treatment or punishment prohibited by the Fifth, Eighth, and/or Fourteenth Amendments*" to the US Constitution. In the past these reservations were sometimes interpreted broadly to permit such harsh interrogation techniques as "water boarding," considered by most experts to be a form of torture. In an effort to correct such abuses, the President has issued an Executive Order banning all torture, and mandating that all interrogations of persons in US custody or physical control be carried out only by techniques specified in the Army Field Manual. ABA indicated that it is unclear as to whether or not this policy restricts torture or CID outside the context of armed conflict.

34. AI indicated that there are no binding national guidelines governing use of restraints or "less lethal" weapons such as electroshock weapons. More than 12,000 US law enforcement agencies deploy electroshock weapons. Over 400 people have died in the USA since 2001 after being struck by police electroshock weapons, raising serious concern about the safety of such devices. Coroners have found the electroshock weapons

played a role in more than 50 deaths, and there are other cases where the cause of death was unclear. electroshock weapons are widely used against individuals who do not pose a serious threat, including children, the elderly and people under the influence of drink or drugs.

35. AI noted that more than 30 states and the federal government have introduced "super maximum security" facilities for the control of prisoners who are considered disruptive or a security threat. Prisoners in the most restrictive units are typically confined for 23 to 24 hours a day in small, sometimes windowless, solitary cells, with no work or rehabilitation programs, or daily exercise. Although courts have ordered improvements to some super maximum prisons, conditions remain extremely harsh in many states and often the review procedures for assignment to such facilities are inadequate.

36. AI also noted that most US states have no laws to restrict the use of restraints on pregnant women inmates, including during labour, a practice which can endanger the health of the woman and her baby. AI indicated that the US has not implemented the Human Rights Committee recommendation in July 2006 to prohibit the shackling of detained women during childbirth.

37. Human Rights First (HRF) reported that people of African descent, LGBT, migrants, Jews, Muslims and Christians continue to be subjected to violent acts motivated by racism, bigotry and intolerance. Council for Global Equality (CGE) noted that State and local jurisdictions must pass laws to protect victims, as well as report hate crimes to federal authorities.

38. National Organization for Women referred to gun related violence and noted the inadequate gun control and firearms regulations.

39. Human Rights Watch (HRW) recommended ensuring access protective and rehabilitative services by victims of domestic violence. AHR recommended passing laws and developing guidelines for child custody determinations taking domestic violence concerns into account.

40. EPOCH reported that parents are legally permitted to use physical punishment on children in all states, and that 223,190 children were subjected to corporal punishment in schools in 2006–2007, with many requiring medical treatment. Thirty states have banned corporal punishment in schools.

41. Joint Submission-3 (JS-3) recommended revising the Trafficking Victims Protection Act to bring the definition of human trafficking in line with the Palermo Protocol. JS 3recommended increasing efforts to prosecute those responsible for trafficking and to assist victims, particularly victims of sexual exploitation. JS5 recommended to provide comprehensive services and legal support for migrant sex workers.

42. JDI recommended adopting national standards for addressing sexual violence and other abuses in prisons, jails and other detention facilities.

43. HRW referred to the treatment of child farm workers and recommended passing the Children's Act for Responsible Employment.

44. JS-14 indicated that there is no integrated system for the protection of human rights defenders and recommended establishing an independent federal office to prevent, investigate and prosecute violations against human rights defenders.

3. Administration of justice, including impunity and the rule of law

45. USHRN indicated that the US falls short of its human rights obligations in the administration of justice, particularly relating racially sentencing and sentencing of juveniles to life without parole, conditions of confinement violating women's reproductive rights, and rights of pisoners with disabilities; treatment of individuals in high security facilities and of political prisoners. Dui Hua Foundation (Dui Hua) recommended that US states with indeterminate parole systems establish independent parole boards with judiciary oversight. HRAlert referred to corruption in the courts and the legal profession, and discrimination of US law enforcement in California.

46. USHRN made reference to prisoners who endure solitary confinement, poor medical health care and perfunctory parole hearings resulting in denial of release.

47. Earth Rights International recommended ensuring that the interpretation of US law is consistent with the obligation to provide a remedy to victims of human rights abuses, and to hold those responsible for abuses accountable. National Whistleblowers Center noted that the US has failed to protect whistleblowers.

48. International Human Rights Law Society (IHRLS) noted that there is no uniform minimum age for criminal prosecution in state criminal codes and the sentence is set by each states' own laws. Two states prohibit sentencing juveniles to life without the possibility of parole (JLWOP) and five permit such sentences but make offenders eligible for parole. The remaining 43 states have some form of mandatory or discretionary JLWOP. AI recommended to end the use of life imprisonment without parole for offenders under 18 years

old at the time of the crime, and to review all existing sentences in order to ensure that any such convicted offender has the possibility of parole.

49. ACNU, MOVPAZ y FMC hicieron referencia al caso de 5 cubanos presos en cárceles norteamericanas, a las medidas carcelarias a las que son sometidos y la negativa de visado para ingresar al país a las esposas de dos de ellos para visitarlos.

50. RCF voiced concern over the failure to initiate independent investigations into violations of the rights of US citizens abroad.

4. Right to privacy, marriage and family life

51. PEN recommended restoring full privacy protections; end dragnet and warrantless surveillance.

52. JS-10 noted that in state and federal law, the terms "family," "parent," and "spouse" commonly exclude LGBT families. JS-10 recommended prohibiting discrimination against LGBT parents in adoption.

5. Freedom of religion or belief, expression, association and peaceful assembly and right to participate in public and political life

53. JS-11 reported that the US courts provide little protection to Indigenous People's traditional religious practices.

54. Conscience and Peace Tax International reported on compulsory registration for military services, recruitment of persons under 18, difficulties encountered by serving members who develop a conscientious objection and the use of taxes of persons with a conscientious objection for military expenditures.

55. USHRN noted that US security laws and policies create unnecessary and unreasonable barriers to the activities of civil society organizations.

6. Right to work and to just and favourable conditions of work

56. USHRN noted that the National Labor Relations Act intended to encourage collective bargaining, however its provisions only apply to the private sector, offer inadequate protection for workers and are poorly enforced. USHRN noted that there are five states that completely prohibit collective bargaining in the public sector. CESRreferred to disparities in wage levels among ethnic groups and between men and women.

57. USHRN indicated that the Pregnancy Discrimination and the Family and Medical Leave Acts offer incomplete protection for pregnant women in the workplace. Furthermore, the US is the only industrialized country with no mandated maternity leave policy.

58. USHRN indicated that domestic and agricultural workers, and independent contractors, are exempt from the full protection of labour laws, in particular regarding minimum wages, the payment of overtime and safe and healthy work environment.

7. Right to social security and to an adequate standard of living

59. USHRN noted that around 30% of the population lacks an adequate income to meet basic needs, with 24.7% of African Americans and 14.5% of women living below the federal poverty level. CESR noted that one in five children live in poverty. JS-11 indicated that most Indigenous communities suffer grave economic and social deprivation. AI indicated that there is an unequal access in the US to basic amenities such as adequate food, shelter, work, healthcare, and education. There is also a lack of affordable housing, job shortages and income insecurity, particularly among minorities and women.

60. USHRN reported that 101,000 people are estimated to die each year because of the way the health system is organized, and 45,000 deaths per year are attributed to the lack of health insurance. CESR referred to maternal mortality rates, highlighting ethnic disparities. Unfortunately, the health reform law of 2010 continues to rely on the market based system. AI indicated that although legislation has recently been passed that will extend healthcare, millions will remain without coverage. AI noted that healthcare, along with housing and employment, is still not recognized in the US as a universal right.

61. USHRN and National Advocates for Pregnant Women reported on laws and policies that create barriers to abortion and other reproductive health care. AI indicated that hundreds of women die each year from preventable pregnancy-related complications, with wide disparities in access to health care based on race, ethnicity, immigration or indigenous status and income. AI called on the US to ensure that all women have access to maternal health care services.

62. JS-10 recommended to prioritize/adequately fund HIV prevention efforts.

63. EMF Sensitivity.org reported on the widespread use of electromagnetic fields and their harmful effects on health.

64. Centre on Housing Rights and Evictions indicated that the lack of adequate housing is exacerbated by an increase in evictions, particularly in the context of the financial crisis and the privatization of public housing.

65. JS-3 referred to the effect of genetic engineering technology on the right to food and recommended to use a sustainable rights-based approach to agriculture, making sure that food requiring the labelling of genetically engineered food, is nutritionally adequate and free from any adverse substance.

66. Joint Submission-13 referred to the obligation of the US to reduce national greenhouse gas emissions and to cooperate with the international community to mitigate threats to human rights due to climate change.

8. Right to education and to participate in the cultural life of the community

67. USHRN indicated that the education system is highly segregated. Lack of adequate funding and zero-tolerance discipline policies push young people out of school. USHRN called on the US to implement the recommendations of CERD regarding school segregation and discrimination in educational opportunities. CESR referred to gaps in educational achievements among ethnic groups.

68. FFF encouraged the creation of a national human rights education curriculum.

9. Minorities and indigenous peoples

69. Nation of Hawai'i recommended securing the rights of all indigenous peoples under ICCPR. FPHRC noted that, as a Member of the Human Rights Council, the US should set a positive example in upholding Indigenous people's human rights.

70. According to the Navajo Nation, and the Navajo Nation Human Rights Commission (NNHRC) the US continues to deprive indigenous peoples of their right to equal protection under law.

71. International Indian Treaty Council (IITC) recommended questioning the US about: the failure to comply with the CERD and the IACHR decision regarding the Western Shoshone; the destruction, desecration of, and denial of access to Indigenous Sacred Areas; the failure to consult with Indigenous Peoples and to acquire their free, prior and informed consent regarding matters that directly affect their interests; the unilateral termination of Treaties with Indigenous Peoples; and the failure to implement a process to address violations of these Treaties.

72. Southeast Indigenous Peoples' Center (SIPC) noted that though the Constitution says that it will deal with 'Indian Tribes' as nations, the US does not negotiate with indigenous peoples.

73. The Society for Threatened Peoples (STP) noted that the Havasupai and Hualapai tribes have struggled for decades for the protection of their land from mining and expressed concern at the risk of radioactive pollution.

74. American Indians Rights and Resources Organization made reference to the impact of the disenrollment and banishment of Indians from their tribes.

75. Akiak Native Community indicated that the indigenous people are still devastated by the culture and traditions forcibly induced to the indigenous people.

10. Migrants, refugees and asylum-seekers

76. USHRN called on the US to reform its immigration system, to ensure due process and to protect family unity. HRW referred to the detention of large number of noncitizens. Lutheran Immigration and Refugee Service (LIRS), reported on conditions of immigration detention, where freedom of movement is restricted; detainees wear prison uniforms and are kept in a punitive setting.

77. Dui Hua called for increased monitoring and accountability in Immigration and Customs Enforcement and noted that detainees should have access to legal representation. Edmund Rice International raised concerns on the lack of access to medical benefits and family visas for workers under the Guestworker Programmes.

78. Seton Hall University reported on restrictive immigrant eligibility for publicly supported health care, which has resulted in hospitals deporting immigrant patients without due process. Atlanta Public Sector Alliance reported on racial disparities in access to health care services with respect to undocumented immigrants in Georgia.

79. Joint Submission-15 recommended restoring judicial discretion in cases involving the deportation of lawful permanent residents who have US citizen children.

80. USHRN recommended reforming the US refugee and asylum system, to ensure that it meets obligations under the 1951 Convention, and in particular, elimination of the one year filing deadline for asylum claims, and of the Tier 3 "terrorism" category; reform the immigrant detention system to end arbitrary detention and ensure that those who are detained are afforded humane treatment.

81. RI recommended identifying the scope of statelessness on US territories and to refrain from detention of persons who pose no risk to the community. RI recommended that the US become a party to the 1954 Convention relating to the Status of Stateless Persons and the 1961 Convention on the Reduction of Statelessness.

11. Internally displaced persons

82. AI indicated that nearly five years after Hurricane Katrina, there is a continued lack of access to housing and health care in the region, as well as resource problems within parts of the criminal justice system, preventing many displaced persons from returning home and compromising the rights of those who have returned. Not enough has been done at the federal, state or local level to replace affordable rental units and demolished public housing, as well as schools and hospitals, failings which have disproportionately impacted on the poor and communities of colour. AI called on the US to abide by the UN Guiding Principles on Internal Displacement and recognize that all internally displaced persons have the right to return to their homes or places of origin; and to ensure that the principles of equality and non-discrimination are applied to resettlement and return.

83. Diné Homeowners & Communities Association recommended prohibiting forced relocation of indigenous people in the Americas.

12. Human rights and counter-terrorism

84. CHRGJ indicated that since September 11, 2001, the US has institutionalized discriminatory profiling against members of Muslim, Arab, South Asian, and Middle-Eastern communities. CHRGJ called for *inter alia* federal legislation that prohibits profiling on *all* grounds, with no exceptions for national security and an in-depth audit of government databases/watchlists.

85. While welcoming developments since 2009, the International Commission of Jurists (ICJ) referred to the persistent impunity and lack of accountability for serious human rights violations and crimes under international law. International Centre for Transitional Justice (ICTJ) noted that accountability measures should include full disclosure, analysis of the facts pertaining to the nature and extent of counterterrorism detainee abuses; meaningful access to redress for victims and institutional reforms ensuring restoration of due process.

86. HRF, as well as ICJ and other organizations, expressed concern about detainees in military facilities at Guantánamo Bay and in Afghanistan without charge or trial and in US facilities in Iraq. ICJ recommended closing the facility at Guantánamo Bay; try those that may be charged with a recognizable offence under international law in accordance with international standard of fair trial; end the system of administrative detention without charge or trial; provide independent and impartial judicial review to challenge detention in Afghanistan and Iraq; allow for the right to legal representation and; review all definitions of ëunprivileged enemy belligerent' to bring them into full compliance with the requirements of international humanitarian law.

87. HRF also reported on the failure to provide adequate information about detainees reportedly in a "black site" in Afghanistan. The Organization for Defending Victims of Violence expressed concern that the ICRC does not have access to secret detention facilities.

88. ICJ referred to US counter-terrorism laws, policies and practices since the new administration took office in 2009. ICJ indicated that the Executive Order on Ensuring Lawful Interrogations recommitted the US to respecting the absolute prohibition on torture as regards all persons within US custody. In the Executive Order the CIA was mandated that no individual detained by the US in an armed conflict may be subjected to any interrogation technique not listed in the Army Field Manual. ICJ noted that although the Manual prohibits a range of abusive interrogation methods, it permits several physically and psychologically coercive techniques. These techniques—especially when used in combination—violate the prohibition of torture and cruel, inhuman and degradingtreatment. ICJ also remained concerned about narrow definitions of torture and cruel or inhuman treatment under US law and referred to provisions in the Torture Act and the War Crimes Act. ICJ recommended revising the Army Field Manual; to bring the definitions of torture and cruel or inhuman treatment in all legislative acts in compliance with the CAT requirements, and to withdraw relevant reservations to CAT. Joint Submission-7 (JS-7) reported on the failure to supervise military prisons and recommended giving access to the ICRC and the UN. Physicians for Human Rights (PHR) indicated that during the period 2002 through 2008 the Bush Administration authorized so-called "enhanced" interrogation techniques, resulting in physical and psychological torture of detainees in US military and CIA custody. PHP indicated the US has a responsibility to prosecute alleged perpetrators, as well as to ensure that victims receive reparations and assistance.

89. ICJ urged the Human Rights Council to request to the US information on: transfers/renditions that may still be practiced, and to call for the full respect of the principle of *non-refoulement*.

90. ICJ recommended repealing the system of military commissions; granting exclusive jurisdiction to civilian courts, prohibiting the extentions of military jurisdiction to civilians and ensuring that the right to be tried in full compliance with ICCPR article 14 is respected. ABA referred to doubts whether persons allegedly responsible for the terrorist attacks on the US on 11 September may now be tried before military commissions.

91. CHRGJ recommended incorporating gender considerations into counter-terrorism programs and policies.

92. Joint Submission-2 recommended that the US re-assess its national security and counter-terrorism laws as applied to civil society organizations.

III. Achievements, best practices, challenges and constraints

93. ABA commended the US for recent steps to improve compliance with international human rights commitments. Among other measures, the President has banned torture and cruel, inhuman or degrading treatment or punishment by all agencies of the U.S. government; closed secret interrogation centers formerly operated by the Central Intelligence Agency; announced his intention to close the detention center at the U.S. Naval Base at Guantánamo Bay, Cuba; and signed a law enhancing procedural safeguards for persons accused of war crimes in trials before military commissions. ABA believes and indicated that more should be done to enhance US respect for human rights.

94. Heritage Foundation noted that while admittedly not perfect, the US system of government and its judicial system are on the whole exemplary in observing and protecting human rights and serve as a model of best practice.

IV. Key national priorities, initiatives and commitments
A. Pledges by the State

95. CGE referred to the US commitment to the United Nations General Assembly Statement on human rights sexual orientation and gender identity, but noted that it must ensure that those same protections are afforded to LGBT Americans in the country.

B. Specific recommendations for follow-up

96. AI recommended reviewing all outstanding recommendations from treaty bodies and experts with a view to implementing them.

97. JS-11 noted that the US has ignored the recommendations of human rights bodies with regard to the rights of Indigenous Peoples.

98. USHRN noted that the US has not taken measures to address CERD recommendations vis-à-vis Indigenous, or those made by the Human Rights Committee.

V. Capacity-building and technical assistance

99. JS 14 indicated that the US should work with the UN Commission on Narcotic Drugs and Office on Drugs and Crime, and the International Narcotics Control Board to create a *care model* for drug abuse treatment based on human rights principles.

Notes

[1] The stakeholders listed below have contributed information for this summary; the full texts of all original submissions are available at: www.ohchr.org. (One asterisk denotes a non-governmental organization in consultative status with the Economic and Social Council.)

Civil society

ABA American Bar Association*, USA;
AC Accountability Counsel, USA
ACNU Asociación Cubana de las Naciones Unidas*, Cuba;
AFRE All For Reparations and Emancipation*, USA;
AHR Advocates for Human Rights*, Minnesota, USA;
AI Amnesty International*, UK;
AIJ The Association of Iraqi Jurists, Iraq;
AIRRO American Indians Rights and Resources Organization, USA;
AMSI-ABMA Joint submission No. 22—Human Rights Division of the Association of Muslims Scholars in Iraq—Al-Basaer Media Association, Iraq;
ANC Tribal Council of the Akiak Native Community, USA;
ANEC Asociación Nacional de Economistas y Contadores, Cuba;
APSA Atlanta Public Sector Alliance, USA;

Becket Fund The Beckett Fund for Religious Liberty*, USA;
CCERF Conservation Centre of Environmental and Reserves in Iraq, Iraq;
CEA Centro de Estudios sobre América, Cuba;
CESR Center for Economic and Social Rights*, USA;
C-FAM Catholic Family & Human Rights Institute, USA;
CGE Joint Submission No. 1—The Council for Global Equality, USA;
CHRGJ Center for Human Rights and Global Justice, USA;
CISV Charitable Institute for Social Victims*, Iran;
COHRE Centre on Housing Rights and Evictions*, Geneva (Switzerland);
CONFEDERACY Haudenosaunee Confederacy Grand Council, USA;
CPTI Conscience and Peace Tax International*, Leuven (Belgium);
CSN Joint Submission No. 2—Charity and Security Network, USA;
CURE Citizens United for Rehabilitation of Errants*, USA;
DHCA The Diné Homeowners & Communities Association, USA;
DREDF Disability Rights Education and Defense Fund, USA;
Dui Hua The Dui Hua Foundation*, USA;
Earth Rights Earth Rights International*, USA;
EDM Episcopal Diocese of Maine, USA;
EMF EMF Sensitivity.org, USA;
EPOCH EPOCH-USA, USA;
ERI Edmund Rice International, Geneva (Switzerland);
FFF Four Freedoms Forum, USA;
FLOC-OXFAM Joint Submission No. 21—Farm Labor Organizing Committee (FLOC) and OXFAM, USA;
FMC Federación de Mujeres Cubanas, Cuba;
FPHRC First Peoples Human Rights Coalition, USA;
GFIW- GWAF Joint submission No. 23- General Federation of Iraqi Women and General Arab Women Federation, Iraq;
GJC Global Justice Center, USA;
HAWAII Nation of Hawaii, USA;
Heritage The Heritage Foundation, USA;
HRA Human Rights Advocates*, USA;
HRAlert Human Rights Alert, USA;
HRF Human Rights First*, USA;
HRW Human Rights Watch*, New York (USA);
ICHR Iraqi Commission for Human Rights, Baghdad (Iraq);
ICJ International Commission of Jurists*, Geneva (Switzerland);
ICTJ International Center for Transitional Justice, New York (USA);
IHRB Institute for Human Rights and Business, Geneva (Switzerland);
IHRLS International Human Rights Law Society, Indiana (USA);
IITC International Indian Treaty Council*, USA;
ITHACA Ithaca rights, USA;
JDI Just Detention International, USA;
JS-3 Joint Submission No. 3—Franciscans International*; the International Presentation Association of the Sisters of the Presentation of the Blessed Virgin Mary and UNANIMA International*, USA;
JS-4 Joint Submission No. 4—Black Communities Process (Proceso de Comunidades Negras –PCN), Colombia and AFRODES USA;
JS-5 Joint Submission No. 5—Best Practices Policy Project, Desiree Alliance, and the Sexual Rights Initiative;
JS-6 Joint Submission No. 6—Indigenous Peoples and Nations Coalition and the Koani Foundation;
JS-7 Joint Submission No. 7—Institute for Redress & Recovery, The Institute for Study of Psychosocial Trauma and the Heartland Alliance Marjorie Kovler Center , USA;
JS-9 Joint Submission No. 9—Minnesota Tenants Union , Minnesota Chapter of the National Lawyers Guild, Minnesota Coalition for a Peoples' Bailout, St. Paul Branch of the NAACP, USA;

JS-10 Joint Submission No. 10—National Coalition for LGBT Health and the Sexuality Information and Education Council of the U.S., USA;

JS-12 Joint Submission No. 12—International Association against Torture* and the December 12th Movement International Secretariat*, USA;

JS-13 Joint Submission No. 13—Earthjustice*, Greenpeace USA; Human Rights Advocates*; and Many Strong Voices USA;

JS-14 Joint Submission No. 14—Medical Whistleblower Stakeholder Advocacy Network, USA;

JS-19 Joint Submission No. 19—Heartland Alliance's National Immigrant Justice Center (NIJC); American Friends Service Committee (AFSC) The Center for Victims of Torture (CVT); Chad Doobay (attorney doing pro-bono representation to asylum seekers at National Immigrant Justice Center); Florida Immigrant Advocacy Center (FIAC); Denise Gilman (professor at the University of Texas School of Immigration Clinic); Immigration Equality; Jewish Council on Urban Affairs (JCUA); King Hall Immigrant Detention Project at University of California Davis School of Law; Legal Aid Justice Center's Immigrant Advocacy Program; Michigan Immigrant Rights Center (MIRC); Midwest Coalition for Human Rights Physicians for Human Rights (PHR); Dr. Mary White (volunteer with Physicians for Human Rights); World Relief, USA;

JS-24 Joint submission No. 24—Organization for Justice and Democracy in Iraq (OJDI) and The International Organization for the Elimination of All Forms of Racial Discrimination (EAFORD), Iraq;

JS-25 Joint submission No. 25—The Iraqi Association Against War (IAAW) and The Indian Movement (TUPAJ AMARU)*;

LIRS Lutheran Immigration and Refugee Service, USA;

LPDOC Leonard Peltier Defense Offense Committee, USA;

MCLI Meiklejohn Civil Liberties Institute, USA;

MICJ Maria Iñamagua Campaign for Justice, USA;

MITA- CMP Joint Submission No. 20—Indian Movement Tupaj Amaru*, Geneva (Switzerland) and Consejo Mundial por la Paz,

MOVPAZ Movimiento Cubano por la Paz y la Solidaridad, * La Habana, Cuba;

NACG Native American Church of the Ghost Dancers, USA;

NAPW National Advocates for Pregnant Women, USA;

NAVAJO The Navajo Nation Department of Justice, USA;

NCBL National Conference of Black Lawyers, USA;

NIYC The National Indian Youth Council,* USA;

NNHRC Navajo Nation Human Rights Commission, USA;

NOW West Virginia National Organization for Women,* USA;

NWC National Whistleblowers Center, USA;

OAK Joint Submission No. 16—Organizations Associating for the Kind of Change America Really Needs, USA;

ODVV Organization for Defending Victims of Violence,* Iran;

OSPAAAL Organización de Solidaridad de los Pueblos de ¡frica, Asia y América Latina, Cuba;

PEN International Pen*, London (United Kingdom) and PEN American Center, USA;

PHR Physicians for Human Rights,* USA;

RCF The Rachel Corrie Foundation for Peace and Justice, USA;

RI Refugees International,* USA;

SCHRD Studies Center of Human Rights and Democracy, Iraq;

SIPC Southeast Indigenous Peoples' Center, USA;

STP Society for Threatened Peoples*, Göttingen (Deutschland);

The 5-11 Campaign The 5-11 Campaign, USA;

USHRN Joint Submission No. 17—US Human Rights Network (23 annexes), USA;

WILD The Women's Institute for Leadership Development for Human Rights, USA;

WR Worldrights, USA;

WWA-OWO Joint submission No. 26—Women's Will Association and the Organization for Widows and Orphans, Iraq;

YAMASI Yamasi People, USA;

YAMASSEE At-sik-hata Nation of Yamassee Moors, USA;

Academic

JS-8 Joint Submission No. 8—International Human Rights Law Clinic, University of California, Berkeley, School of Law; Chief Justice Earl Warren Institute on Race, Ethnicity and Diversity, University of California, Berkeley, School of Law; Immigration Law Clinic, University of California, Davis, School of Law, USA;

JS-11 Joint Submission No. 11—University of Arizona, Indigenous Peoples Law & Policy Program; Western Shoshone Defense Project; Human Rights Research Fund; First Peoples Human Rights Coalition, USA;

JS-15 Joint Submission No. 15—International Human Rights Law Clinic, University of California, Berkeley, School of Law; Chief Justice Earl Warren Institute on Race, Ethnicity and Diversity, University of California, Berkeley, School of Law; Immigration Law Clinic, University of California, Davis, School of Law, USA;

PIJIP-GAP Joint submission No. 18—American University Washington College of Law's Program on Information Justice and Intellectual Property (PIJIP) and Health Global Access Project (Health GAP), USA; SHUSL Center for Social Justice of the Seton Hall University School of Law, USA;

Regional organizations

IACHR Inter-American Commission of Human Rights, USA

Annexe 1—Report No. 63/08, Case 12.534, Admissibility and Merits (Publication), Andrea Mortlock, U.S., July 25, 2008.

Annexe 2—Report No. 90/09, Case 12.644, Admissibility and Merits (Publication), Medellín, Ramirez and Leal García, U.S., August 7, 2009.

Annexe 3—Report No. 26/06, Petition 434-03, Isamu Carlos Shibayama et al., U.S., March 16, 2006.

Annexe 5—Report No. 57/06, petition 526-03, Hugo Armendariz, U.S., July 20, 2006.

Annexe 4—Report No. 56/06, Petition 8-03, Wayne Smith, U.S., July 20, 2006.

Annexe 6—Report No. 52/07, petition 1490-05, Jessica González and Others, U.S., July 24, 2007.

Annexe 7—Report No. 60/09, Case 12.706, Frank Enwonwu, U.S., July 20, 2009.

Annexe 8—Report No. 77/09, petition 1349-07, Orlando Cordia Hall, U.S., August 5, 2009.

Annexe 9—Report No. 78/08, Petition 478-05, undocumented migrant, Legal Resident, and the US Citizen Victims of Anti-Immigrant vigilantes, U.S., August 5, 2009.

Annexe 10—Report No. 100/09, Petition 1177-04, Warren Wesley Summerline et al., U.S., October 29, 2009.

Annexe 11—Access to justice for women victims of violence in the Americas

Annexe 12—Precautionary Measures granted by the IACHR in 2009 PM 385-09—31 Undocumented Immigrants Residing in Atlanta, Georgia, U.S.

Annexe 13—IACHR Table of ratifications: USA

....

(Rest of Footnotes omitted. See websites for rest of footnotes)

Document 3.
INTERACTIVE DIALOGUE ON THE U.S. UNIVERSAL PERIODIC REVIEW: OPENING STATEMENT BY THE U.S. DELEGATION

Esther Brimmer—Assistant Secretary, Bureau of International Organization Affairs

Michael H. Posner—Assistant Secretary, Bureau of Democracy, Human Rights, and Labor Geneva, Switzerland November 5, 2010

Thank you, Mr. President.

The U.S. is honored to present our first Universal Periodic Review report to the United Nations Human Rights Council. It is my pleasure to introduce our delegation, which is comprised of senior officials from eleven U.S. departments and agencies, a representative of our local authorities, and two advisers from civil society groups. Their participation reflects the depth of our commitment to human rights at home, which spans the federal government as well as state, local, and tribal governments across our country, and which is complemented by the deep commitment from President Obama and Secretary Clinton to multilateral engagement, human rights, and the rule of law.

As President Obama has said, our country's "Declaration of Independence, the Constitution, the Bill of Rights are not simply words written into aging parchment. They are the foundation of liberty and justice in [our] country, and a light that shines for all who seek freedom, fairness, equality and dignity in the world." We take our place in the UPR process with pride in our accomplishments, honesty in facing continued challenges, and a commitment to using the international system to elevate and advance the protection of human rights at home and abroad.

The Universal Periodic Review is comprised of three important ideas. The first, *Universality*, reflects the norm of full participation at the heart of the Universal Declaration of Human Rights: in short, these rights must be for all. The UPR has examined countries that exemplify human rights leadership; those that uphold human rights in the face of devastating obstacles; and those that defy their international obligations and silence and punish any who would expose their abuses.

Equally important is the Review's *Periodic* character, premised on the idea that advancement and enforcement of human rights must be pursued persistently over time, with accountability, follow through, continuing effort, and constant improvement. For the U.S., our early years witnessed profound gaps between our ideals and practice, including slavery, the treatment of Native Americans, and limited franchise. Yet our own history has been one of progress, built on a strong foundation of fundamental freedoms of speech, association, and religion, this is the foundation for building a "more perfect Union."

The third UPR premise is *Review*, the idea that governments' records should be scrutinized, discussed, and debated by other governments, civil society, human rights defenders, a free press, and their own citizenry. In America, such dialogue is heard every day. Each morning we awake to a cacophony of opinions, from editorial boards, columnists, politicians, bloggers, and other commentators. Some are respectful and constructive; some less so. Some carry moral authority; some do not. But we protect it all. We bring that willingness to listen and engage to today's discussion.

For the U.S., the UPR is a conversation in Geneva, but also one at home with our own people, to whom we are ultimately accountable. We have made the participation of citizens and civil society a centerpiece of our UPR process. We held eleven consultations hosted by nongovernmental organizations across the U.S.—in New Orleans, San Francisco, Chicago, New York City, El Paso, the Navajo Nation reservation, and elsewhere. We heard from men and women of all races, ethnicities, religions, ages, and affiliations. These rich exchanges have informed our UPR report, shaped our thinking, and served as a potent impetus for progress. This morning's presentation only continues a conversation that will resume this afternoon at a Town Hall meeting, here in Geneva and in Washington, with more than 100 civil society organizations. We commend to all governments a similar depth of engagement with civil society in the UPR process, to expand citizens' voices in advancing human rights, here in Geneva and around the world. This morning's presentation therefore is not the end, but only a milestone in our long-term engagement to promote our human rights aspirations. We have approached this process with a seriousness of purpose and a commitment to engage genuinely with comments and questions raised in good faith. While we cannot respond to every idea raised in hundreds of conversations or debated in the blogosphere, we welcome the opportunity today to talk with thoughtful interlocutors in a constructive dialogue.

I would now like to turn to Assistant Secretary of State for Democracy, Human Rights and Labor Michael Posner to introduce our interactive dialogue.

Assistant Secretary Michael Posner

Thank you, very much, Assistant Secretary Brimmer. It is an honor to be here today. Last fall, I became Assistant Secretary of State for Democracy, Human Rights, and Labor after working for 30 years with Human Rights First, a non-governmental advocacy organization.

The U.S. is a country founded on the moral truths reflected in the Universal Declaration of Human Rights, and our Constitution has provided the legal framework and foundation for our progress toward a more perfect union over the last 221 years. Our Declaration of Independence reaffirmed the "inalienable rights" of all people. In the wake of our Civil War, its glaring original flaw of tolerating slavery was removed. Decades later, in1920, it was amended to provide women the right to vote. And in 1924, Federal law granted full citizenship for Native Americans.

Throughout our history as a nation, the Constitution has been our firm foundation: the sacred principles of equality and liberty for all persons have guided us and have been the measure of our earthly progress, beckoning us ever-closer to an ideal. And although our progress has not been linear, it has been undeniable. In the story of the U.S., the arc of history has bent toward justice.

The story of our nation has been a struggle for a more perfect union. Our system of government reflects an apparent paradox: that the most perfect system of government is one that assumes its own imperfection. For any government or system of laws that pretends to be perfect cannot be so; it is only by admitting the possibility of imperfection that the creation of mechanisms for improvement can be justified, and that progress toward a more perfect union can occur. Our laws have never fully reflected the principles that underlie our Constitution: changes in the world around us and in our understanding of it always reveal new opportunities to improve. We acknowledge imperfection; we discuss and debate it; we welcome and encourage the involvement of our civil society; and we work through democratic legislatures and independent courts to remedy it—the ability to do this has been and continues to be a source of strength.

Our UPR report provides an account of laws created, and of measures established to ensure their fair implementation, in order to protect the rights of individuals in the U.S. We respect freedom; we challenge obstacles to freedom, and we seek to ensure the pathways to freedom. The freedoms of speech and assembly, and of thought, conscience and religion remain vigorously protected. We have expansive legal protections against unfair discrimination and in the last half century have made significant progress in ensuring that the law protects equal opportunity for all Americans in areas such as education, employment, health, housing, and voting. And we have made changes in the laws and policies that govern our criminal justice system to see that it accords all people with due process of law and equal protection under the law.

In addition to protections of individuals' fundamental freedoms and rights against discrimination and abuse, other laws and programs have helped lay the foundation for the enjoyment of rights. Recent legislation will improve access to quality healthcare, particularly for the vulnerable. And investments currently underway in our education system and our economy are paving the way for stronger schools that can provide a high quality education to all students and a strong economy that is ready to harness the skills students learn in school.

As our report acknowledges, though we are proud of our achievements, we are not satisfied with the status quo. We will continue to work to ensure that our laws are fair and justly implemented, and to foster a society in which people are empowered to enjoy their rights.

From their first moments in office, President Obama and Secretary of State Clinton have made their own deep commitments to the rule of law, to multilateral engagement, and to bringing international human rights home. As you know, along with many allies, the U.S. is currently in armed conflicts in Afghanistan, Iraq, and with Al Qaeda and associated forces, and we have reported on the human rights obligations of the U.S. in the context of our international actions. The U.S. is committed to complying with the Constitution and all applicable domestic and international law, and to the idea that there are no "law-free zones." On his second day in office, President Obama signed three Executive Orders—on detention, interrogation, and transfer policies—and these reflect our broader commitment to ensuring security consistent with our Constitution and with the international rule of law. We conduct our armed conflicts pursuant to, and limited by, the laws of war as they apply to this 21st century situation. Although the realities of the world we live in mean that the security of our people, and that of others around the world, will sometimes demand and justify the use of force, we recognize that, as the theologian Paul Ramsey put it, "that which justifies, also limits."

A few weeks ago, the U.S. and the world lost a giant in the field of human rights. Louis Henkin, born in present-day Belarus, came to our country as an immigrant and went on to an historic legal and academic career as a gentle, wise, steadfast intellectual beacon for human rights. In 1990, Professor Henkin wrote that: "[T]here is now a working consensus that every man and woman, between birth and death, counts, and has a claim to an irreducible core of integrity and dignity. In that consensus, in the world we have and are shaping, the idea of human rights is the essential idea." The U.S. is committed to human rights at home and abroad. We are committed to deepening the consensus that every man and woman, every girl and boy, counts, and to promoting its promise by doing our part to help shape a world that better reflects the essential idea of human rights.

We look forward to a productive and constructive conversation.
Thank you.

Document 4.
U.S. RESPONSE TO U.N. HUMAN RIGHTS COUNCIL WORKING GROUP REPORT
(Response of the U.S. to Recommendations of the (UPR) Final Outcome Report) (See Primary Document 87 for the Final Outcome Report of the HRC Working group on the Universal Periodic Review [U.S.] containing the Recommendations.)

March 10, 2011

Report of the United States of America Submitted to the U.N. High Commissioner for Human Rights In Conjunction with the Universal Periodic Review
Response to the U.N. Human Rights Council Working Group Report

1. The Government of the U.S. has carefully reviewed the 228 recommendations received during its Universal Periodic Review ("UPR"). This response reflects our continuing endeavor, in consultation with civil society, to create, in the words of our Constitution, a more perfect union.

2. Given the number and complexity of the recommendations, we responded generally in November 2010, discussing the recommendations in categories. This Addendum similarly addresses the recommendations by categories, and will be supplemented by our oral presentation.

3. What it means for a recommendation to enjoy our support needs explanation. Some recommendations ask us to achieve an ideal, e.g., end discrimination or police brutality, and others request action not entirely under the control of our Federal Executive Branch, e.g., adopt legislation, ratify particular treaties, or take action at the state level. Such recommendations enjoy our support, or enjoy our support in part, when we share the ideal that the recommendations express, are making serious efforts toward achieving their goals, and intend to continue to do so. Nonetheless, we recognize, realistically, that the U.S. may never completely accomplish what is described in the literal terms of the recommendation. We are also comfortable supporting a recommendation to do something that we already do, and intend to continue doing, without in any way implying that we agree with a recommendation that understates the success of our ongoing efforts.

4. Some countries added to their recommendations inaccurate assumptions, assertions, or factual predicates, some of which are contrary to the spirit of the UPR. In such cases, we have decided whether we support a recommendation by looking past the rhetoric to the specific action or objective being proposed. When we say we "support in part" such recommendations, we mean that we support the proposed action or objective but reject the often provocative assumption or assertion embedded in the recommendation.

Civil rights and discrimination

5. The following recommendations enjoy our support:

114, 116, 167, 191, and 198.

86. We agree that no one should face violence or discrimination in access to public services based on sexual orientation or their status as a person in prostitution, as this recommendation suggests.

107 and 111. We have comprehensive Federal and State legislation and strategies to combat racial discrimination. We are working diligently toward better enforcement and implementation of these laws and programs.

68, 101, and 219, in that profiling — the invidious use of race, ethnicity, national origin or religion — is prohibited under the U.S. Constitution and numerous pieces of national legislation.

112. We have recently taken concrete steps to address discrimination on the basis of sexual orientation and gender identity, and are engaged in further efforts.

The following enjoy our support, in part:

62, as explained in paragraphs 3 and 4, i.e., we disagree with some of the premises embedded in this recommendation, but we are committed to the objectives it states, in this case combating discrimination and promoting tolerance. While we recognize there is always room for improvement, we believe that our law is consistent with our CERD obligations. Also see the explanations of 65, and of 107 and 111.

64, 67, 94, 98, 100, and 189, as explained in paragraphs 3 and 4. The explanation above for 107 and 111 also applies here.

99, as explained in paragraphs 3 and 4, while noting that a migrant's eligibility for full benefits under certain programs may depend on his/her lawful status.

103, as explained in paragraphs 3 and 4, and as it regards investigating and, where appropriate, prosecuting persons who violate criminal laws. We cannot support the part of the recommendation asking that we "guarantee … fair compensation." Although mechanisms for remedies are available through our courts, we cannot make commitments regarding outcomes.

190. We take effective measures to counter intolerance, violence and discrimination against all members of all minority groups, including Muslims. We cannot support this recommendation, however, to the extent that it asks us to take legislative measures countering insults. Insults (unlike discrimination, threats, or violence) are speech protected by our Constitution.

Criminal justice issues

7. The following enjoy our support:

70, 95, 96, 97, 151, 162, 163, 177, and 179.

145, as U.S. law prohibits torture in all prisons and detention facilities under its control.

208 and 209, noting that law enforcement and immigration officers are lawfully permitted to use deadly force under certain exceptional circumstances, e.g., self-defense or defense of another person.

152, as U.S. law prohibits mistreatment of detainees in U.S. custody, requires investigations of credible mistreatment allegations, and prescribes accountability measures for violations.

The following enjoy our support, in part:

118, in that we will continue to ensure that implementation of the death penalty complies with our international obligations; the portion asking that we end capital punishment does not enjoy our support.

134 and 135. We cannot support recommendation 134 with respect to prosecution. We support both recommendations with respect to executions regarding minors and persons with certain intellectual disabilities, but not regarding all persons with any mental illness.

150, as explained in paragraphs 3 and 4. The explanations above for 145, and for 208 and 209, also apply.

173. The first part of this recommendation enjoys our support; we cannot support the recommendation's second part ("proceed to extradite former Bolivian authorities ..."). See notes on extradition in paragraph 31.

174 and 175, as explained in paragraph 4. We are committed to holding accountable persons responsible for human rights violations and war crimes. We cannot, however, support the portion of 174 regarding compensation and remedies, because those are not always applicable. Nor can we support the part of 175 that we accede to the Rome Statute, although we are engaging with State Parties to the Rome Statute on issues of concern.

178. We support this recommendation to the extent that some State laws conform with it. Most inmates do not have the right to vote, however, and former felons do not have the right to vote in some States.

186. We support this recommendation to the extent provided for under the U.S. Constitution and U.S. laws, and consistent with our international obligations.

The following do not enjoy our support:

56, 180, and 181.

119 through 133 (capital punishment).

Indigenous issues

The following enjoy our support:

85.

83, 200, 202, 203, 205, and 206, consistent with the "Announcement of U.S. Support for the United Nations Declaration on the Rights of Indigenous Peoples – Initiatives to Promote the Government-to-Government Relationship & Improve the Lives of Indigenous Peoples" (Announcement).

The following enjoy our support, in part:

199, as explained in paragraph 4.

201. We cannot accept its first part ("recognize ... without conditions"), but its second part ("implement ...") enjoys our support, consistent with the Announcement.

The following does not enjoy our support:

204.

National security

The following enjoy our support:

89, 90, 139, and 161.

58 and 176, insofar as they recommend compliance with our international law obligations.

66 and 146, because existing Federal criminal laws comply with our obligations under the Convention against Torture.

149, although noting that some of the referenced points may not be fully applicable in every context.

159 and 160. We have made clear our desire to close the Guantánamo Bay detention facility and will continue to work with Congress, the courts, and other countries to do so in a responsible manner that is consistent with our international obligations. Until it is closed, this Administration will continue to ensure that operations there are consistent with our international legal obligations.

188, because our Constitution's Fourth Amendment and existing U.S. law prohibit the use of modern technology for excessive and unjustified interference in individuals' private lives.

218. Persons who are charged with terrorist-related crimes are tried under legally established processes in either civilian courts or military commissions, depending on the nature of the crime and the individual. They are afforded all applicable protections under domestic and international law.

The following enjoy our support, in part:

59, as explained in paragraph 4. Our Constitution and laws contain appropriate rules to protect the privacy of communications, consistent with our international human rights obligations.

88, as explained in paragraph 4. The U.S. has consistently invited United Nations Special Rapporteurs to tour the detention facility at Guantánamo, to observe detention conditions, and to observe military commission proceedings. That invitation remains.

60, 137, 138, 140, 155, 166, and 217, as explained in paragraph 4. The U.S. supports recommendations calling for prohibition and vigorous investigation and prosecution of any serious violations of international law, as consistent with existing U.S. law, policy and practice. We reject those parts of these recommendations that amount to unsubstantiated accusations of ongoing serious violations by the U.S.

136, 147, 148, 156, and 157. We intend to close the Guantánamo Bay detention facility. The President has closed all CIA detention facilities and has prohibited CIA operation of such facilities. We allow the International Committee of the Red Cross access to individuals detained by the U.S. pursuant to armed conflict. We investigate allegations of torture, and prosecute where appropriate. We cannot accept portions of these recommendations concerning reparation, redress, remedies, or compensation. Although mechanisms for remedies are available through U.S. courts, we cannot make commitments regarding their outcome. We cannot accept the part of 136 that we close *all* detention centers; the U.S. maintains certain internment facilities abroad, consistent with applicable U.S. and international law. We cannot agree to the part of 156 that we release all individuals detained pursuant to an armed conflict who are not promptly brought to trial. Regarding recommendation 157, transfers of detainees to their home countries will only be conducted in accordance with our humane treatment policies.

142, as explained in paragraph 4. Our contractors are not authorized to engage in direct hostilities or offensive operations or to commit assassinations. Like U.S. Government personnel, contractors may only use force consistent with our international and domestic legal obligations. We have expressed support for the International Code of Conduct for Private Security Service Providers.

143, as explained in paragraph 4. In U.S. military operations, great care is taken to ensure that only legitimate objectives are targeted and that collateral damage is kept to a minimum.

187, as explained in paragraph 4, and noting that we collect information about our citizens only in accordance with U.S. law and international obligations.

The following do not enjoy our support:

141, 158, and 170.

Immigration

The following enjoy our support:

80, 104, 108, 165, 183, 212, and 220.

106, insofar as it involves enforcing our laws, e.g., hate crimes legislation, and taking appropriate administrative actions.

144, insofar as it allows for the exercise of prosecutorial discretion.

164, 184, and 210, insofar as they recommend compliance with our obligations under international human rights law.

185, insofar as "entitled" to counsel means that a migrant in removal proceedings in immigration court enjoys the right to counsel at his/her own expense, and "fully understand their rights" means to have been provided information in a language they understand.

213, understanding "consular assistance" to mean access consistent with Article 36 of the Vienna Convention on Consular Relations and similar provisions in bilateral consular agreements.

214, understanding that "basic services" refers to services such as primary education and emergency health services that are provided to migrants regardless of status.

223, because this recommendation comports with the U.S.' general practice of widely disseminating information on its consular notification and access outreach and training efforts, including to foreign missions in the U.S.

The following enjoy our support, in part:

79 and 105, as explained in paragraph 4. We will continue to both conduct human rights training and awareness campaigns and, where appropriate, bring civil or criminal actions regarding racial profiling, police brutality, and excessive use of force, and other actionable civil rights violations against immigrants. While unlawful presence in the U.S. is not a crime, and the federal government does not support state initiatives that aim to criminalize mere status, we cannot support the parts related to the "criminalization" of migrants, as certain immigration offenses are subject to criminal sanction, e.g., illegal entry.

82, as explained in paragraph 4. It is consistent with our continuing efforts to improve our immigration policies and to eliminate xenophobia, racism, and intolerance in our society.

102, as explained in paragraph 4, and as our Constitution and numerous statutes prohibit the invidious use of race or ethnicity. The registration requirements of the National Security Entry-Exit Registration System are under review at this time.

207, as explained in paragraphs 3 and 4.

The following do not enjoy our support:

110, as the Federal Executive Branch lacks the authority to repeal or refuse to enforce laws enacted at the State level.

182, as we endeavor not to detain irregular immigrants unnecessarily, but our statutes, policies, and practices result in detention other than in "exceptional circumstances."

211. Nevertheless, we note that undocumented migrants in the U.S. already have access to publicly supported healthcare through an extensive network of Migrant Health Centers.

Economic, social, and cultural rights and measures, and the environment

The following enjoy our support:

109, 113, 197, and 226.

195, while noting that we are a non-party to the International Covenant on Economic, Social and Cultural Rights, and accordingly we understand the references to rights to food and health as references to rights in other human rights instruments that we have accepted. We also understand that these rights are to be realized progressively.

196, because the U.S. Government seeks to improve the safety net that our country provides for the less fortunate.

The following enjoy our support, in part:

51, 221, and 222, as explained in paragraph 4, i.e., disagreeing with premises embedded in these recommendations, but agreeing with their essential objectives (reduce greenhouse gas emissions and cooperate internationally).

The following does not enjoy our support:

216.

Labor and trafficking

The following enjoy our support:

168, 169, and 193.

115, as we have comprehensive laws aimed at ensuring gender equality at work, and we are taking further action through the President's Equal Pay Taskforce.

192, as we support the 1998 ILO Declaration on Fundamental Principles and Rights at Work, which reaffirms the commitment of all ILO member States to respect, promote, and realize principles concerning fundamental rights in four categories including freedom of association and collective bargaining. Although not a party to ILO conventions 87 and 98 on those topics, we have robust laws addressing their fundamental principles.

The following enjoys our support, in part:

81. Members of minority groups enjoy important anti-discrimination and labor protections. While labor laws apply to undocumented migrant workers, such individuals may not be entitled to certain types of remedies.

The following does not enjoy our support:

194, as maternity leave is not "mandatory" for either mothers or employers, although employers of a certain size are required to allow certain leave that may be used in connection with the birth or adoption of a child.

Domestic implementation of human rights

The following enjoy our support:

225.

65. We regularly engage in such reviews of our laws in light of our human rights obligations, including through the enforcement of our Federal civil rights laws and implementation of our domestic civil rights programs, litigation and judicial review, our reports to U.N. human rights treaty bodies, engagement with U.N. Special Procedures, and active discussions with civil society. Although the Federal government does not consistently or systematically review State laws, our civil rights mechanisms allow for review of State laws, as appropriate.

74. There are Federal and State institutions to monitor human rights; we are considering whether this network of protection is in need of improvement.

87. Programs at the Federal and State levels provide training on human rights, particularly on issues related to civil rights and non-discrimination; we are continuing to explore ways to strengthen such programs.

The following enjoys our support, in part.

227. This recommendation enjoys our support except for the last part regarding making our decision-making publicly available. We apply the Leahy laws (which impose human rights-related restrictions on assistance to foreign security forces) to all countries receiving U.S. security assistance, and we respond appropriately in

cases of abuse. However, to do so, we consider information from all sources, including classified sources, and cannot make our decision-making public.

The following do not enjoy our support:

224, although we will continue to support fully the UPR and its strengthening.

72 and 73. Although we are reviewing whether domestic institutions that monitor human rights need improvement, we cannot now commit to a particular plan.

84. The State Department's annual human rights reports do not rank the human rights situations of countries. We do, however, engage in robust assessment of our own record of respecting human rights, as described in paragraph 25.

228, due to currently applicable restrictions.

Treaties and international human rights mechanisms

The following enjoy our support:

10, 11, 13, 14, 20, 21, 22, 26, 28, 30, 33, 34, 35, 39, 43, 47, 48, 49, and 93. We support the recommendations asking us to ratify the Convention on the Elimination of All Forms of Discrimination against Women, the *Convention* on the Rights of Persons with *Disabilities*, and ILO Convention 111. We also support the recommendations that we ratify the Convention on the Rights of the Child, as we support its goals and intend to review how we could move toward its ratification. We also support recommendations urging deliberative treaty actions, such as that we "consider ratifying" them.

54. This recommendation is consistent with the longstanding U.S. policy of supporting the International Court of Justice and taking appropriate action to comply with judgments of the Court. The U.S. intends to continue to make best efforts to ensure compliance with the Avena judgment.

The following enjoy our support, in part:

1 through 9, 15 through19, 23, 24, 25, 27, 37, 38, 40, 41, and 42. We support the parts of these recommendations asking us to ratify those treaties, identified above, of which the Administration is most committed to pursuing ratification. We cannot support the other portions. Nor can we support "without reservations" in 1.

29. We support the second part ("observe international standards …"), understanding such standards to mean applicable international human rights law.

44 and 45, as explained in paragraph 4. We do not believe that any reservations, understandings, and declarations accompanying our ratification of international instruments undermine our obligations, or the treaty's object or purpose. We cannot support the part of 45 regarding individual procedures.

52, as explained in paragraph 4. The US Government complies with its international humanitarian law obligations, but we note that international humanitarian law governs conduct in the context of armed conflict, and cannot accept this recommendation's implication that we are in an armed conflict with the Palestinian people.

The following do not enjoy our support:

12, 31, 32, 36, 46, 50, 91, and 92.

53. Following discussions between the two governments, the Government of Nicaragua decided not to pursue any further action based on this case, and the International Court of Justice accordingly removed the case from its list on September 26, 1991.

63. We believe that our law is consistent with our CERD obligations.

71, while noting that the U.S. takes all reasonable measures, consistent with the Optional Protocol, to prevent servicemembers under 18 years of age from engaging directly in hostilities

Other recommendations

We received a few recommendations that do not fit neatly into specific categories. Some call on the U.S. Government to extradite particular individuals. Decisions on extradition cases are made on a case-by-case basis, consistent with our international legal obligations, and the U.S. cannot prejudge the outcome of any particular case.

The following do not enjoy our support:

55, 57, 61, 69, 75, 76, 77, 78, 117, 153, 154, 171, 172, and 215.

Found at : http://www.state.gov/g/drl/upr/157986.htm

Document 5.
HUMAN RIGHTS PROJECT AT THE URBAN JUSTICE CENTER, OPPOSITE

Human Rights Project
at the Urban Justice Center

A PRACTICAL GUIDE TO THE UNITED NATIONS' UNIVERSAL PERIODIC REVIEW (UPR)

January 2010

Table of Contents

Glossary

HRP	Human Rights Project at the Urban Justice Center
UN	United Nations
OHCHR	Office of the High Commissioner for Human Rights
HRC	UN Human Rights Council
UPR	Universal Periodic Review
CAT	Convention against Torture and Other Cruel, Inhuman or Degrading Treatment or Punishment
CEDAW	Convention on the Elimination of All Forms of Discrimination against Women
ICERD	International Convention on the Elimination of All Forms of Racial Discrimination
NGO	Non-governmental organization
ICCPR	International Covenant on Civil and Political Rights

Civil Society   The term civil society is used to include groups that are not part of the government like grassroots organizations, NGOs, religious groups, students, labor unions, professionals, businesses, etc.

Member States   The term member States is used to describe countries that are part of the UN (192 countries), or any other UN bodies.

Observer Countries   In this context, observer countries are all the members of the UN that have not been elected to the Human Rights Council but can still participate in the UPR sessions.

Introduction

The Universal Periodic Review (UPR) provides a new and exciting opportunity for advocates to hold the United States government accountable to all its human rights obligations and commitments. Similar to other human rights mechanisms, the UPR encourages advocates to engage in dialogue and challenge their governments to respect, protect and fulfill the broad range of human rights under the umbrella of international law and agreements.

The UPR is also a unique instrument available to United States advocates to advance economic and social rights such as the right to work, to housing, to health, etc; rights that are recognized by the Universal Declaration of Human Rights (UDHR)—one of the documents used in the UPR— as well as several other human rights treaties.

Participation by advocates in the UPR is a key part of the process and can be effective at different levels. The Human Rights Project (HRP) at the Urban Justice Center employed its extensive experience and knowledge from engaging advocates in other human rights mechanisms to develop this UPR toolkit. We hope advocates will use it to strategically engage in the UPR process.

Acknowledgements

The content of this toolkit is based on information from several meetings with UN human rights staff and advocates. We thank them for their generosity and willingness to share their knowledge and experience in the UPR process. We also borrowed liberally from the UN Office of the High Commissioner on Human Rights (OHCHR) handbook, *Working with the United Nations Human Rights Programme*. Finally, we thank the staff of UPR-info for their helpful contributions and responsiveness to our inquiries.

This manual was written by Tatiana Bejar and edited by Ejim Dike. Mai Schwartz provided research assistance.

The report was generously supported by the U.S. Human Rights Fund.

© Human Rights Project (HRP) at the Urban Justice Center

January 2010

About the Human Rights Project

The Human Rights Project (HRP) at the Urban Justice Center works to hold the government to a higher standard of accountability in addressing poverty and discrimination by advocating for the local implementation of universally accepted human rights standards and law, particularly as they relate to economic and social rights. HRP accomplishes its mission through a combination of education and training; documentation and policy analysis; legislative and policy advocacy; and organizing and movement building. With a particular focus on New York City, we share our lessons with other social justice groups around the country through educational workshops and materials.

2001: HRP coordinated and submitted a shadow report on the United States government's compliance with the International Convention on the Elimination of All Forms of Racial Discrimination (ICERD) to the UN. Shadow reports are submitted to treaty bodies by stakeholders as alternative information to the government's report.

2002. HRP established the New York City Human Rights Initiative (NYCHRI) to tackle problems of inequality at the city level. NYCHRI has more than 100 coalition members and is working to pass a bill to locally implement the human rights treaties ICERD and CEDAW.

2007: HRP coordinated more than 30 NYC groups to submit a shadow report on the United States government's compliance with ICERD. HRP released the ICERD shadow report "Race Realities in New York City" and it has become a tool for advocates to advance human rights for all New Yorkers.

2008: HRP coordinated the official visit of the Special Rapporteur on contemporary forms of racism, racial discrimination, xenophobia, and related intolerance, Dr. Doudou Diene, in New York City, including meetings with local organizations.

Human Rights Project at the Urban Justice Center
123 William Street, 16th Floor, New York, NY 10038
www.hrpujc.org

BASIC ASPECTS OF THE UNIVERSAL PERIODIC REVIEW (UPR)

What is the UPR The Universal Periodic Review (UPR) is a new human rights mechanism of the Human Rights Council (HRC) created on March 15, 2006 by the UN General Assembly resolution 60/251.[1] The UPR reviews the fulfillment by all 192 UN member States (or countries) on their human rights obligations and commitments, as well as their progress, challenges, and needs for improvement. Countries are reviewed every four years.

The UPR was created in response to criticism that previous UN mechanisms focused too much on certain regions. The UPR is designed to be applied more universally and uniformly.

How does the UPR work Unlike the review process of the treaty bodies such as the Committee on the Elimination of Racial Discrimination (CERD), which is conducted by independent experts, the UPR is a peer review – based on the model used by the African Union[2]. This is an innovative and cooperative mechanism based on an interactive dialogue between the country that is reviewed and any other UN country[3]. During this interactive dialogue, the country under review presents its report, answers questions, and receives recommendations from other countries. The interactive dialogue is followed by the informal adoption of an "outcome document" that includes all the recommendations made to the country under review. The outcome document is officially adopted at the next Human Rights Council regular session.

UPR Working Group The UPR Working Group hosts the sessions of the UPR and is essentially the same body as the Human Rights Council. It consists of all 47 countries[4] of the Human Rights Council and is chaired by the President[5] of the Human Rights Council. The UPR Working Group generally meets three times a year from February to March, April to May, and November to December. Each session meets for approximately ten days. Around 16 UN countries are reviewed during each session, and 48 are reviewed per year. The UPR Working Group met for the first time in April 2008. Please see list of troikas and timetable for 2009 and 2010 UPR sessions: http://www.ohchr.org/EN/HRbodies/UPR/Pages/UPRSessions.aspx

Goals of the UPR The main goals of the UPR are:

1. Addressing inequalities and all forms of discrimination.
2. Advancing the human rights situation for all.

3. Pushing governments to fulfill their human rights obligations and commitments.
4. Reviewing positive developments and challenges faced by countries.
5. Sharing best practices between the countries and stakeholders.

UPR cycle Based on a four-year cycle, the UPR mechanism allows the Human Rights Council to review all the 192 countries that belong to the UN. There are five steps to the UPR.

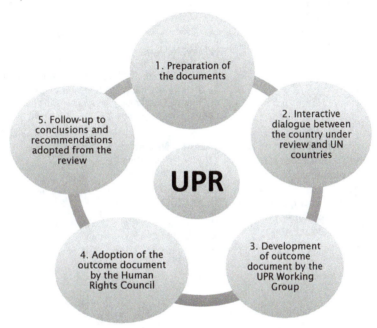

Universality of the UPR
1. Countries are selected randomly ("by lot") for the review.
2. All countries that are part of the UN will be reviewed.
3. The initial members of the Human Rights Council, especially those elected for one or two terms, will be reviewed first.
4. Countries that are part of the Human Rights Council, as well as observer countries will be also reviewed.
5. A fair geographic distribution is considered in the selection of countries for review.

Box 1: Key dates for the United States participation in the UPR	
Deadline for U.S. NGO submissions	**April 19, 2010**
Deadline for U.S. government report submission	**August 23, 2010**
U.S. Review (Interactive dialogue)	**Friday, November 5, 2010** The United States will be reviewed for the first time on November 5, 2010 during the ninth UPR session of the Human Rights Council in Geneva. The time of the review will be from 9:00am to 12:00pm Central European Time (CET), 3:00am to 6:00am EST.
Informal adoption of U.S. outcome document	**Tuesday, November 9, 2010** 12:00pm to 12:30pm CET 9:00am to 9:30am EST
Formal adoption of the U.S. outcome document	**March 2011** The next Human Rights Council regular session will take place in March 2011.

THE REVIEW PROCESS

Basis of review During the UPR process, each country is reviewed on the basis of the following human rights agreements:

1. The Charter of the United Nations (UN Charter)
2. Universal Declaration of Human Rights (UDHR)
3. The human rights instruments to which the country is a party (treaties or conventions)
4. The country's voluntary pledges and commitments, including those undertaken when presenting its candidature for election to the Human Rights Council
5. Applicable international humanitarian law

> **The United States is tentatively scheduled for its first periodic review on Friday, November 5, 2010 from 9:00am to 12:00pm CET (3:00am to 6:00am EST) during the ninth UPR session of the Human Rights Council in Geneva.** Please visit this link to see the UPR Working Group 9th session timetable: http://www.upr-info.org/IMG/pdf/Timetable_9th_Session.pdf

The Troika The ***Troika*** is the name given to the three rapporteurs that are assigned to facilitate the review process. Troika members are selected randomly and represent countries that are part of the Human Rights Council; however they are also regionally balanced. Countries under review have the right to veto one of the troika members, and to request that one member of the troika is from its region. A country can be excused from participating as a troika member for a specific review.

B1 Steps of the UPR process

Table 1. Steps of the UPR Process		
Before the review	**1.**	Submission of documentation including the country's report, compilation of the UN information, and the summary of stakeholders' submissions
At the review	**2.**	3-hour interactive dialogue between the country under review and other UN countries
	3.	Informal adoption of the outcome document in the UPR Working Group that includes a list of recommendations made during the review
After the review	**4.**	Official adoption of the outcome document by the Human Rights Council
	5.	Follow-up and implementation of recommendations

B1.1   Before the review

Documentation

Written reports   This is a preliminary step of the process. In preparation for each country's review, member States are provided with three different documents:

The government report for the UPR is generally due 3 to 4 months prior to the review. The U.S. government report is due on August 23, 2010.

1. **Information prepared by the country under review:** The country under review provides a 20-page report with detailed information on how it has fulfilled its human rights obligations and commitments including information on achievements, best practices, challenges, and limitations. Countries are encouraged to meet with civil society to gather information for the report. In the United States, the State Department is responsible for the government's involvement in the UPR process. For a sample, see the United Kingdom's national report at http://www.upr-info.org/IMG/pdf/A_HRC_WG6_1_GBR_1_E.pdf.

Box 2. Why countries need to dialogue with stakeholders
The country under review is encouraged to prepare its report in accordance with the Human Rights Council guidelines for the UPR. Under these guidelines, the government should open broad consultations with civil society, including stakeholders, NGOs, and National Human Rights Institutions (NHRIs) before drafting its report. **Link of General Guidelines:** http://ap.ohchr.org/documents/E/HRC/decisions/A_HRC_DEC_6_102.pdf

2. **A compilation of information from UN mechanisms prepared by the OHCHR:** This is a 10-page report with relevant information from treaty bodies, independent experts or special rapporteurs, UN agencies, and other relevant documents from the UN, compiled by the OHCHR. Read the OHCHR compilation of the UN documents for the Germany's review: http://lib.ohchr.org/HRBodies/UPR/Documents/Session4/DE/A_HRC_WG6_4_DE U_2_E.PDF

> The U.S. NGO reports for the UPR are due on April 19, 2010.

3. **Summary of Stakeholder/NGO submissions prepared by the OHCHR:** This is a 10-page summary of "credible and reliable information" provided by national stakeholders, NGOs, grassroots organizations, and other relevant groups. NGOs submissions are crucial to the UPR because they provide a direct and grassroots assessment of the human rights situation. Read a summary of United Kingdom's stakeholders: http://www.upr-info.org/IMG/pdf/A_HRC_WG6_1_GBR_3_E.pdf.

> All submissions are published on the OHCHR website 6 weeks before the interactive dialogue.
>
> Click here to read all UPR reports:
>
> http://www.ohchr.org /EN/HRBodies/UPR/P ages/UPRMain.aspx

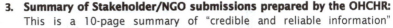

Box 3: General Guidelines for preparation of documents⁶

The Human Rights Council has developed these General Guidelines for the preparation of the documents for countries, stakeholders, and for the OHCHR in the preparation of documents under its responsibility. All documentation should include:

Sections:

A. Description of the methodology and broad consultation process.
B. Background and framework for promotion and protection of human rights, (constitution, legislation, policy measures, national jurisprudence, human rights infrastructure, and the international obligations identified in the basis of review).
C. Promotion and protection of human rights on the ground, including the progress on implementation of the international human rights obligations.
D. Identification of achievements, best practices, challenges, and limitations.
E. Key national priorities, initiatives, and commitments.
F. Expectations for the country in terms of capacity building, and if requested technical assistance.
G. Presentation by the country concerned of the follow-up to the previous review.

See full document at:
http://ap.ohchr.org/documents/E/HRC/decisions/A_HRC_DEC_6_102.pdf

B1.2   At the review

Interactive dialogue between the country under review and other UN countries

How does the actual review take place?   The actual review consists of three hours of interactive dialogue between the country under review and UN member States. During this session, the country under review has one hour to introduce its report, respond to questions or recommendations, and to make concluding comments at the end of the review. Countries are allowed to ask questions and suggest recommendations to the country under review for about 2 hours.
Watch the webcast video of any UPR Working Group session at http://www.un.org/webcast/unhrc/index.asp.

Table 2: Three-hour interactive dialogue at the UPR Working Group session

Country under review (1 hour)	**Introduction of the country's report** **20-40 mins**	Estimated* time that the country under review uses to introduce its national report. Usually a high level representative of the country under review presents the report. For example, Colombia's government sent the Vice President to introduce the government's report[7].
	Time to respond to questions and recommendations **30-25 mins**	Estimated time that the country under review takes to respond to questions and recommendations raised during the interactive dialogue by other countries. The country under review responds after approximately 15 to 30 comments made by countries. Usually the country under review responds three times during its review.
	Final remarks **5-10 mins**	At the end of the review, the country under review has only few minutes to make final comments. Estimated time is 5 to 10 minutes.
UN countries (2 hours)	**Countries ask questions and make recommendations** **120 mins**	A total of two hours is allotted for countries to ask questions and make comments or recommendations to the country under review. **Countries that are part of the Human Rights Council can speak for 3 minutes and observer countries 2 minutes.** However, some countries use 1 minute of their allotted time to make comments or recommendations. Approximately 20 to 40 oral recommendations are made per review. The number of recommendations generally depends on the level of interest, preparation, and engagement of other UN countries and NGOs with respect to the country under review.

Estimates come from HRP research on past reviews.

Informal adoption of outcome document

Preparation of the
outcome document

NGOs should observe the process closely, and push their governments to accept recommendations.

After the dialogue, the UPR Working Group writes a report – generally within 48 hours of the conclusion of the session – summarizing the list of questions and recommendations raised during the review, as well as any voluntary commitments made by the country under review. The troika is responsible for preparing the report with the involvement of the country under review and assistance from the OHCHR.

Two business days after the review, the report is presented to the Human Rights Council to be informally adopted. **Thirty minutes are allocated for the informal adoption of the report or outcome document.** The outcome document presented at this point may include recommendations that the country under review accepted, rejected, or those pending a response. However, since many countries reserve judgment on which recommendations to accept or reject until the final adoption, their outcome documents may list all recommendations with no indication of which have been accepted or rejected. Both refused and accepted recommendations are included in the final outcome document that will be officially adopted in the next Human Rights Council session. Modifications, which may include accepting pending recommendations, or making other voluntary commitments, can be made to the report by the country under review within the following two weeks.[8]

During these 2 weeks, NGOs should lobby countries under review to accept recommendations on key human rights issues that they previously rejected.

For a sample, read the outcome document on the review of Canada go to the UPR info website or to this link: http://lib.ohchr.org/HRBodies/UPR/Documents/Session4/CA/A_HRC_11_17_CAN_E.pdf.

Box 4: Content of the informal outcome document

1. Assessment of the situation of human rights in the reviewed country, including positive developments and challenges.
2. Identification of best practices.
3. Proposals for cooperation in the promotion and protection of human rights.
4. Provision of technical assistance.
5. Summary of comments, questions, and recommendations made by countries.
6. Accepted and rejected recommendations by the country under review.
7. Recommendations that the country under review wants to defer decision on.

B1.3   After the review

Official adoption of outcome document

Adoption of the outcome document

The outcome document is officially adopted by the Human Rights Council at its next regular session (around four months after the review).

During the plenary session of the Human Rights Council, the country under review can answer questions and issues that still need to be addressed and respond to recommendations that were raised by other countries during the review. Countries may express their comments on the outcome of the review, and **NGOs and other stakeholders from civil society are permitted to make general comments.**

One hour of the plenary session is allocated to the adoption.

Table 3: Official adoption of the outcome document

	20 minutes	Country under review makes a formal statement and replies to questions and recommendations.
60 Minutes	20 minutes	Countries express their opinion on the outcome document. Human Rights Council member States have 4 minutes for each intervention and observer countries 3 minutes.
	20 minutes	NGOs can make "general comments". Each speaker has only 2 minutes for intervention. NGOs should coordinate before speaking at the session. *(See Page 23)*

All comments made during this session by countries and stakeholders are compiled in a separate document (not included on the outcome), called Summary of Views and General Comments[9].

Follow-up and implementation of recommendations

Implementation of the UPR outcomes This is the final step in the UPR process. NGOs and grassroots organizations should play a key role in ensuring that governments will implement recommendations they accepted in the outcome document, as well as adopt and implement recommendations they previously rejected. During a country's second or follow-up review, it must provide information on steps it has taken to implement the recommendations accepted during the first review or previous review (four years earlier).[10]

Table 4: Mechanisms to monitor and ensure implementation

1. At the international level	**Monitoring implementation according to the Human Rights Council resolution 5/1** a. Outcome documents should be implemented by governments, with the involvement of stakeholders. b. The next review should focus on implementation of previous outcomes. c. Capacity building and technical assistance are available for countries to use during the implementation part of the UPR process. d. The Human Rights Council can also view cases in which countries are not cooperating. If a country does not show cooperation with the UPR, the Human Rights Council may decide what measures it will take in response to that country.
2. At the domestic level	**UPR outcome document as a human right tool** a. UPR outcome document provides new paths for local organizations to be involved in the implementation process[11] and work with the government. b. NGOs can monitor the government's implementation of recommendations in the outcome document. c. Outcome documents can be a useful tool to push policies that address key human rights issues. d. Outcome documents can also be part of shadow report to treaty bodies.

ENTRY POINTS FOR NGOs C

How to engage in the UPR process

There are many ways to think about engaging the UPR process to make it useful in the context of the ongoing work of advocacy groups. Although the review process provides limited space for NGO participation, the work before and after the review is key to implementing concrete recommendations of the outcome document.

Ways to participate

Listed below are some ways that NGOs can participate in the UPR process:

NGOs do not need to have ECOSOC status in order to participate in most parts of the UPR process.

1. Engage in consultations with the government
2. Submit a stakeholder report
3. Lobby countries
4. Attend the UPR Working Group session
5. Attend and participate in the Human Rights Council session
6. Follow-up and push for implementation of recommendations

C1 Engage in consultations with the government

Get involved in the government report

The OHCHR strongly encourages countries to consult with civil society in the preparation of the country's national report. In the United States, the State Department is responsible for the preparation of this report, therefore NGOs should insist on substantive, inclusive, and ongoing consultation. This will help NGOs inform what topics the government's report will address, identify the strengths and weaknesses of their coverage, and prepare to fill the gaps in the national report with additional information.

Contact the State Department

The State Department has a new section on United States participation in the UPR on its website: http://www.state.gov/g/drl/upr/index.htm. The government is asking organizations to send feedback on issues that affect their communities to this email: upr_info@state.gov by April, 2010.

C2 Submit a stakeholder report

NGO submissions Similar to the treaty system, NGOs can also submit a report on human rights issues and their country's compliance with human rights obligations. For the UPR, stakeholders' reports are considered for inclusion in the summary of reports prepared by the OHCHR. NGOs do not have to be accredited to submit a report.

Content and Format According to the technical guidelines for the submissions of stakeholders' *for NGO reports* information to the OHCHR[12], reports should include:

U.S. stakeholders' submissions must be sent in by April 19, 2010 at 6:00am New York time (EST) - 12:00pm Geneva time (CET). Reports have to be sent to UPRsubmissions@ohchr.org.

1. **An introductory paragraph:** Written submissions should include an introductory executive summary, capturing the main points contained in the report.

2. **Information on the NGO:** The report should also provide a short paragraph on the objectives and work of the NGO/coalition that is submitting the report.

3. **Language:** The OHCHR prefers that reports be written in English, French or Spanish, or any other official UN language.

4. **Page Limit:** Reports should be short and they must not exceed 5 pages if submitted by an individual organization or 10 pages if submitted by a coalition of groups. Annexes and supporting information may be attached only for reference. There is no limit to the size of annexes; however they should not include pictures, maps, organizations' annual reports or reports from other organizations. It is preferred that reports not include an extensive number of footnotes.

5. **Format:** Reports should be saved as a Word document only, i.e. not as PDF file, in Times New Roman, font size 12. Paragraphs and pages of each submission should be numbered.

6. **Time Period:** The UPR is scheduled to occur every four years for each country. All actors submitting information to be reviewed (countries, OHCHR, NGOs) should limit the scope of their submissions to four years.

7. **Deadline:** Information on report deadlines can be found at http://www.ohchr.org/EN/HRBodies/UPR/Pages/NewDeadlines.aspx. In general, NGO reports must be submitted around seven months before the review.

Box 5: Reports will not be considered:
1. If exceeding more than 5-page report (individual organization) or 10-page report (coalition)
2. If written in a non official UN language
3. If submitted after the deadlines
4. If containing abusive or incendiary language

For a sample of a NGO report, please go to Appendix A (page 28).

OHCHR Summary outline of NGOs submissions

NGOs submissions will be summarized by the OHCHR in a 10-page document. It is important for NGOs to study the following outline (Box 6) to think about where the issues and recommendations highlighted in their reports might fit it. Some of the sections may vary depending on the human rights situation in the country under review. The OHCHR can omit some of the sections or include new ones.

To see a summary of stakeholders by the OHCHR on the review of Canada go to the following link:
http://lib.ohchr.org/HRBodies/UPR/Documents/Session4/CA/A_HRC_WORKING GROUP6_4_CAN_2_E.PDF

Box 6: Outline of the OHCHR summary of NGO submissions

I.   Background and Framework
     A.   Scope of international obligations
     B.   Constitutional and legislative framework
     C.   Institutional and human rights infrastructure
     D.   Policy measures

II.   Promotion and Protection of human rights on the ground
     A.   Cooperation with human rights mechanisms
         1.   Cooperation with treaty bodies
         2.   Cooperation with special procedures
         3.   Cooperation with the Office of the High Commissioner of Human Rights
     B.   Implementation of international human rights obligations
         1.   Equality and non-discrimination
         2.   Right to life, liberty, and security of the person
         3.   Administration of justice and the rule of law
         4.   Freedom of religion or belief, association, and peaceful assembly and the right to participate in public and political life
         5.   Right to work and to just and favorable conditions of work
         6.   Right to social security and to an adequate standard of living
         7.   Right to education and to participate in the cultural life of the community
         8.   Minorities and indigenous peoples
         9.   Migrants, refugees, and asylum-seekers
         10. Human rights and counter-terrorism

III.   Achievements, best practices, challenges, and constraints

IV.   Key national priorities, initiatives, and commitments
     A.   Pledges by the State
     B.   Specific recommendations for follow-up

V.   Capacity-building and technical assistance

Table 5: Tips for a successful NGO report

Bridging the local and national divide	The UPR is conducted at the national level, however, it is also important to highlight local problems when writing the report. Reports should strike a good balance in highlighting national and local issues. If the report focuses solely on local issues, it is possible that recommendations may not get raised in the OHCHR summary. On the other hand, if the report is able to show that local examples of a problem are also occurring nationwide and emblematic of a country-wide issue, then it is more likely to be highlighted in the OHCHR summary of NGO reports.
Highlighting recommendations	The UPR report should focus on solutions and not problems. NGO reports that summarize the problem and then focus on making concrete recommendations for improvement will be stronger and more effective. This makes it easier for other countries to suggest specific issues and recommendations for adoption. When addressing the problem, NGO reports should give concrete and real examples that can help to facilitate the discussion during the review.
Be aware of U.S. obligations and commitments	Before drafting a report, it is important to take into consideration the human rights obligations and commitments that the United States has made. *(Please see Page 20)*
Opportunity to work as a coalition	There are benefits to submitting a coalition report or coordinating multiple individual reports to emphasize key issues in terms of getting them into the summary report and raised in the UPR session itself. Coalition work also has obvious benefits unrelated to the outcome of the UPR. This is an opportunity to engage with other groups doing work in a specific area, share challenges, successes, and best practices, learn from each other, and identify possible avenues for continued coalition or allied work. NGOs should: 1. Contact NGOs, and grassroots organizations that work on related issues, and educate them on the UPR process. 2. Discuss the issues that should be included in the report. 3. Decide whether it would be best for NGOs to bring up the same issues, or whether it would be better to divide the list of issues between groups of NGOs. Issues should be covered in depth, and connections on the interdependence of rights made.
What not to do	Please do not reproduce concluding observations and recommendations of human rights treaty bodies or special procedures of the Human Rights Council. The OHCHR will already be doing this in its own compilation report.

NGOs can submit an individual report, be part of a joint report (coalition work), and endorse a national NGO report. Because the United States has an active civil society, NGOs may be able to work on multiple reports, however please verify this possibility with the OHCHR (see contact information on Page 28).

Table 6: United States human rights obligations and commitments for review

1. Charter of the United Nations (UN Charter) – 1945*

The UN Charter established the organization called the United Nations with the mission to maintain peace and stability. The United States played an active role in its creation and the name "United Nations" was suggested by President Franklin D. Roosevelt[13]. The UN Charter was signed in 1945 and has been ratified by most countries, including the United States. All member States or countries are bound by the articles of the UN Charter. The UN Charter reaffirms "faith in fundamental human rights, and dignity and worth of the human person" and commits all member States or countries to promote "universal respect for, and observance of, human rights and fundamental freedoms for all without distinction as to race, sex, language or religion." Read the full document at http://www.un.org/en/documents/charter/index.shtml.

2. Universal Declaration of Human Rights (UDHR) – 1948*

The UDHR was adopted by the UN General Assembly on December 10, 1948. The UDHR is the founding document of international human rights law that embraces universally accepted principles that all human beings are entitled to human rights without any distinction. The United States also played an active role in the preparation and adoption of the UDHR. The UDHR is composed of 30 articles that include economic, social, cultural, political, and civil rights as indivisible and interconnected. The UDHR has been translated to more than 370 languages[14], and is the most translated document in the world.
The UDHR is available at http://www.un.org/en/documents/udhr/.

3. Human rights treaties ratified by the United States*

The UN human rights treaties are an important part of international human rights law. There are eight human rights treaties, and every UN country has ratified one or more treaties. When a country ratifies a treaty it becomes a "state party". This means the country is legally bound to the mandates of the treaty/treaties it ratifies. There are other instruments with different legal status: declarations, principles, guidelines, standard rules and recommendations that may not have a legal effect, however they provide of a moral force to countries. Link: http://www2.ohchr.org/english/law/.

Please visit the OHCHR website to view complete information on the use of human rights instruments http://www2.ohchr.org/english/law/.

√ International Covenant on Civil and Political Rights (ICCPR) – 1992*

√ International Convention on the Elimination of All Forms of Racial Discrimination (ICERD) -1994*

√ Convention against Torture and Other Cruel, Inhuman or Degrading Treatment or Punishment (CAT) – 1994 *

√ Optional protocol to the Convention on the Rights of the Child on the involvement of children in armed conflict – 2002*

√ Optional protocol to the Convention on the Rights of the Child on the sale of children, child prostitution and child pornography – 2002*

4. Voluntary Pledges and Commitments

As part of its candidacy to a seat at the Human Rights Council, the U.S. government pledged to work "with principled determination for a balanced, credible, and effective Human Rights Council to advance the purpose of the Universal Declaration of Human Rights." The United States also committed to "promote universality, transparency, and objectivity in all of the Council's endeavors" and to participate actively in its first review. Finally, the United States committed to work with "international partners in the spirit of openness, consultation, and respect" and reaffirmed that expressions of concern about the human rights situation in any country, including the United States, are appropriate matters for international discussion.
See whole document on pledges and commitments at the U.S. Mission to the UN or at http://geneva.usmission.gov/2009/04/27/human-rights-pledges/.

5. International Humanitarian Law

√   Geneva Convention relative to the Treatment of Prisoners of War – 1949*
√   Geneva Convention relative to the Protection of Civilian Persons in Time of War – 1949*

Year of adoption or ratification.

C3 Lobby other countries

Why lobby countries Because NGOs may attend but not speak at the review session itself, lobbying countries about important human rights issues is the only way to make sure recommendations will be raised during the review.

Who and where to lobby NGOs should identify countries that might be sympathetic to their issues and schedule meetings with representatives from embassies, consulates, and missions in the home country and/or Geneva. The best place for NGOs to lobby in the United States is Washington DC and New York City where the embassies and important diplomats are assigned. Another opportunity for United States NGOs to lobby is in Geneva during the Human Rights Council session.

Table 7. Possible countries to lobby.[15] *Examples of countries that have:*

Submitted questions in advance	Asked about Indigenous peoples	Asked about migrants	Asked about racial discrimination	Asked about the death Penalty	Asked about LGBT rights
Netherlands	Mexico	Mexico	Algeria	Italy	Czech Republic
Sweden	Bolivia	Algeria	Mexico	Mexico	Netherlands
Denmark	United Kingdom	Canada	Egypt	Brazil	Slovenia
United Kingdom	Denmark	Egypt	Canada	United Kingdom	Canada
Germany	Algeria	Phillipines	Brazil	Chile	Sweden

A majority of the recommendations tend to be on civil and political rights. We will update this chart on economic and social rights as we get more information.

Table 8: Tips for successful lobbying		
Before the review	Lobby country under review	1. The open consultation with government representatives of the country under review is an opportunity to lobby the government to reflect and address critical issues in its report.
For the interactive dialogue	List of issues and recommendations	2. Prepare a list of the issues and recommendations that your organization wants to see raised during the interactive dialogue. Please see sample of suggested questions and recommendations submitted in advance by NGOs for the review of Brazil at http://www.upr-info.org/IMG/pdf/UPR_Brasil_ConectasandGajop.pdf. 3. Distribute the list to delegations of countries that you have identified to lobby in Geneva. For advocates in the United States, we also recommend that you provide the list to as many embassies, consulates, and missions as possible. Sometimes, delegates—who are interested in a particular review but not adequately prepared—will contact their embassies and consulates for more information on the country under review. 4. Because the information provided by the country under review might not reflect the real human rights conditions, NGOs should meet with delegates in Geneva to educate them on the problems and suggest specific recommendations before the review.
	Identify countries to lobby	5. Lobby countries that are members of the Human Rights Council and observer countries to raise key human rights questions/issues during the interactive dialogue. NGOs are encouraged to focus lobbying efforts on countries that are more likely to make recommendations, and cannot be easily dismissed by the country under review.[16] Please see example of Canada dismissing recommendations at http://www.canada.com/news/Canada+rejects+human+rights+recommendations/1678153/story.html. 6. Countries usually ask the same kinds of questions during reviews. For example Norway, Denmark, and Slovenia generally ask questions on women's rights. Also, Mexico, Bolivia, and Algeria ask questions on indigenous and migrants' rights. Please see list of recommendations and responses per session and per country under review at http://www.upr-info.org/-Recommendations-.html.
Before formal adoption of outcome document		7. Lobby the country under review to make voluntary commitments and to accept specific recommendations to advance human rights. 8. Some countries can make recommendations against human rights, like the right to sexual orientation, or against abortion, so NGOs should make sure the country under review does not accept those recommendations.

Although NGOs can lobby troikas to update them on human rights concerns, troikas do not have the power to influence the outcome document. The role of the troika is basically to facilitate the process.

C4 Attend the UPR Working Group session – Interactive Dialogue

Organize a side event One way to ensure that NGO voices are heard during the review is holding a side event in which human rights issues that concern the country under review are highlighted. The side event should serve as an informative session to countries that are sympathetic to human rights. We recommend that the side event be held a day before the review.

Attend review NGOs with ECOSOC status and that have been accredited may attend sessions of the UPR Working Group, but they cannot make any oral statements at the session meetings. Please see Box 7 (Page 24) for complete information on accreditation.

Meet with government NGOs should push for a meeting with delegates of the country under review both before the interactive dialogue session, as well as in the 48 hours afterwards, to try and influence the government's decision on accepting or rejecting key recommendations.

C5 Participate in the Human Rights Council

Participation in the UPR plenary The plenary session of the Human Rights Council - which takes place three to four months after the review - allows NGOs to make oral or written statements, and to make comments or ask questions to the country under review before the adoption of the outcome document. Only accredited organizations in consultative status with ECOSOC may attend the session.

Prepare NGO statement Twenty minutes of the session are allocated for oral statements from NGOs. Each speaker has 2 minutes to make its comment. It is important that organizations prepare joint statements during the session as coalition statements will be prioritized. NGOs should be prepared to attend the session early in order to be one of the first names on the list of speakers. NGOs can also submit written statements; however, they will have less impact than oral ones. Please see sample of a joint statement at http://www.upr-info.org/IMG/pdf/IMADR_India_Plenary.pdf.

Guidelines and forms for submission of written statements can be found at http://www2.ohchr.org/english/bodies/hrcouncil/guidelines.htm. (UPR is item 6).

> 1. During sessions, some NGOs were interrupted because their interventions did not refer to a specific paragraph in the outcome document.
> 2. Countries under review sometimes respond to a few recommendations. NGOs should be aware of information gaps in the oral statements made by the country under review during the initial part of the session, and should be ready to raise recommendations that are being ignored.

Box 7: Information for NGO accreditation to the UPR sessions[17]

NGOs in consultative status with ECOSOC wishing to accredit representatives to UPR Working Group sessions are invited to send their letter of accreditation request to the Secretariat of the Council at the following address:

upraccreditation@ohchr.org
Fax number: 011 41 (0) 22 917 90 11

During the session:
Fax number: 011 41 (0) 22 917 04 94

The letter requesting accreditation should contain the following elements:

√ It should be submitted on the official letterhead of the organization.
√ It should clearly state the title and duration of the session the organization wishes to attend, e.g. "[Name of NGO], in consultative status with ECOSOC, wishes to send the following members to attend the [x th] session of the UPR Working Group [from .... to....].
√ The letter needs to be signed by the President or the Main Representative of the organization in Geneva.
√ It should also indicate the name/s (first name and family name) of the person/s who will represent the organization at the UPR Working Group session.
√ Names of persons must appear exactly as they appear in the ID document.
√ Family names have to be capitalized.

Please take note that:

It is important to ensure that the name(s) of those members already in possession of a valid identity badge issued by UNOG Security and Safety Section, and who plan to attend a particular UPR Working Group session, is/are included in the accreditation letter, with an indication that the person(s) hold(s) an annual badge.

Annual or temporary representatives of NGOs in possession of an identity badge issued by UNOG Security and Safety Section and valid for the duration of the session will have access to conference rooms.

Any other participants without a UNOG identity badge should apply in person to the security entrance at Pregny Gate, 8-14 Avenue de la Paix; on presentation of an identity document and a copy of the letter of accreditation, a photo-badge valid for the duration of the Council session will be issued.

The accreditation office for the UPR Working Group will be located at the security entrance "Pregny Gate" and will be open from Monday to Friday from 9:00 am and 5:00 pm throughout the session.

NGO Liaison Office contact details

During the session of the working group, an NGO Liaison Office will be located behind the plenary room in Room E-3062.

C6 Follow-up work to ensure implementation of outcome document

Countries are responsible for implementing the conclusions, recommendations, voluntary pledges and commitments that are part of the outcome documents. However, NGOs play a key role during the implementation of the outcome document and should have a clear advocacy plan to do so.

Some ways to get involved and influence the implementation of outcomes include:

1. **Organize a press conference.** Publicize the results of the outcome document that has been approved by the country under review, which means it has accepted recommendations and made voluntary commitments for improvement. Also highlight recommendations that were rejected and/or put on hold.
2. **Use the media.** There are many media tools like the use of Facebook, Twitter, blogs and other avenues that can be used to spread the word, educate the public, and put pressure on the government to fulfill its UPR obligations. Each subsequent review will be based largely on implementation efforts and improvement in key areas identified in the previous review.
3. **Organize meetings.** Discuss the relevance of the outcome document with your community, and how community members can engage in the implementation process.
4. **Develop a strategy to monitor implementation**. Organizations should monitor government progress as well as problems or limitations during the 4 years between reviews.
5. **Participate in implementation.** NGOs should engage in dialogue with the government to share expertise in the human rights field of concern, and to make the process and methods of implementation as effective and targeted as possible.
6. **Organize a web casting.** Organizations in other countries have successfully organized events to inform civil society on the results of the review. Groups can host a webcasting event showing the interactive dialogue for their communities. Depending on the time, people may be able to watch live webcast of reviews. Please check this link to follow live webcast reviews: http://www.un.org/webcast/unhrc/.

Table 9: Entry Points for U.S. NGOs

UPR	TIMELINE	What to do
Before the Review	January to August 2010	▪ Participate in consultations with the U.S. government for the preparation of the country report.
	December 2009 to April 2010	▪ Submit a report (5 pages for an individual organization, 10 pages for joint report) on human rights concerns to be used by OHCHR for the summary of stakeholders report.
	January to December 2010	▪ Lobby countries to educate their representatives on issues and concerns to be raised during the review. Embassies, consulates, and missions can be contacted in Washington DC, New York City, and Geneva.
During the Review	November 2010	▪ Attend the review. ▪ Organize a side event. ▪ Meet with other NGOs to collectively assess the U.S. review. ▪ Hold a press conference or write a press release to give your assessment on the U.S. review. Please see samples of press statements at http://www.upr-info.org/-NGOs-Press-statements-.html.
After the Review	March 2010	▪ Make an oral statement providing general comments before the adoption of the outcomes by the plenary (20 minutes are allocated to NGOs, coalition of NGOs are given priority). Please see samples of NGO oral statements at http://www.upr-info.org/NGO-plenary-statements.html. ▪ Release a written statement.
Between reviews	2010-2014	▪ Make public accepted recommendations and voluntary commitments of the U.S. government. Recommendations that were rejected should also be publicized. ▪ Monitor their implementation. ▪ Engage in consultation with the U.S. government to participate in the implementation.

Table 10: Key contacts on the UPR

At the United Nations Level	**OHCHR Human Rights Council Branch** Office of the United Nations High Commissioner for Human Rights Palais des Nations 8-14, avenue de la Paix CH-1211 Geneva 10 – Switzerland Phone: 011 41 (0)22 917 92 69 Fax: 011 41 (0)22 917 90 11 **OHCHR Civil Society Unity** Office of the United Nations High Commissioner for Human Rights Palais des Nations 8-14, avenue de la Paix CH-1211 Geneva 10 – Switzerland Phone: 011 41(0)22 917 90 00 Email: civilsocietyunit@ohchr.org
At the United States Level	**U.S. State Department** upr_info@state.gov http://www.state.gov/g/drl/upr/index.htm **U.S. Human Rights Network** 250 Georgia Avenue SW suite 330 Atlanta, GA 30312 Telephone: 404-588-9761 Fax: 404-588-9763 Email: info@ushrnetwork.org **Human Rights Project at the Urban Justice Center** 123 William Street, 16th Floor New York, NY 10038 Telephone: 646-602-5629 Fax: 212-533-4598 Email: info@hrpujc.org
General websites for UPR information	http://www.upr-info.org/ www.ushrnetwork.org http://www.ohchr.org/EN/Pages/WelcomePage.aspx

Appendix A

DRAFT
United States of America

Submission to the United Nations
Universal Periodic Review

Ninth Session of the Working Group on the UPR
Human Rights Council
1-12 November 2010

EXECUTIVE SUMMARY
This should be an introduction that captures the main points of the submission. Organizations may wish to include:
- Highlights and major recommendations of submission;
- Key words ("domestic violence" is the example from the Technical Guidelines);
- Short description of methodology to establish information is objective and reliable;
- A paragraph describing the main activities of the submitting organization/coalition, as well as date of establishment;
- Should the submission be prepared jointly, the names of all submitting stakeholders should appear at the beginning of the submission text

BACKGROUND AND FRAMEWORK
Information about the methodology and the broad consultation process followed nationally for the preparation of information provided to the UPR by the country under review.[1]

Current Normative and Institutional Framework for the Promotion And Protection Of Human Rights[2]

Areas to address:

- Scope of international obligations
- Constitutional and legislative framework
- Institutional and human rights infrastructure
- Policy measures such as national action plans
- National jurisprudence
- Human rights infrastructure including national human rights institutions

---

[1] Section I.a. of General Guidelines/ Technical Guidelines Section IV.B.8.a
[2] Section I.b. of General Guidelines/ Technical Guidelines Section IV.B.8.b

650 Third Avenue South • Suite 550 • Minneapolis, MN 55402-1940 • USA
Tel: 612.341.3302 • Fax: 612.341.2971 • Email: hrights@advrights.org • www.theadvocatesforhumanrights.org

PROMOTION AND PROTECTION OF HUMAN RIGHTS ON THE GROUND[3]

(implementation and efficiency of the normative and institutional framework for the promotion and protection of human rights)

Information on the implementation of international human rights obligations

- Equality and non-discrimination
- Right to life, liberty and security of the person
- Administration of justice, including impunity, and the rule of law
- Freedom of movement
- Right to privacy, marriage and family life
- Freedom of expression, association and peaceful assembly, and the right to participate in public and political life
- Right to work and to just and favourable conditions of work
- Right to social security and adequate standard of living
- Right to education and to participate in the cultural life of the community
- Minorities and indigenous peoples
- Migrants, refugees and asylum-seekers
- Human rights and counter-terrorism

Information on commitments at the national and the international levels

- Information on the implementation of commitments made at international conferences and other United Nations for a;
- of constitutional and legal reforms aimed at protecting human rights
- national action plans
- mechanisms and remedies aimed at improving human rights
- activities of national human rights institutions
- human rights education and public awareness

Cooperation with human rights mechanisms[4]

Information about cooperation with:

- with human rights mechanisms
- national human rights institutions
- NGOs
- rights holders
- human rights defenders
- other relevant national human rights stakeholders
- at the national, regional and international levels

[3] Section I.c of General Guidelines/ Technical Guidelines Section IV.B.8.c
[4] Section I.d of General Guidelines/ Technical Guidelines Section IV.B.8.d

650 Third Avenue South • Suite 550 • Minneapolis, MN 55402-1940 • USA
Tel: 612.341.3302 • Fax: 612.341.2971 • Email: hrights@advrights.org • www.theadvocatesforhumanrights.org

ACHIEVEMENTS, BEST PRACTICES, CHALLENGES AND CONSTRAINTS[5]

Information about:

- Achievements made in the past 4 years
- Best practices which have emerged
- Challenges and constraints faced by the country under review;

Key National Priorities[6]

- Initiatives and commitments that the State concerned should undertake to overcome challenges and constraints and improve human rights situations on the ground.

  - national strategies
  - areas where further progress is required
  - steps regarding implementation and follow-up to recommendations made by human rights mechanisms
  - commitments for future cooperation with OHCHR and human rights mechanisms and agencies;

CAPACITY-BUILDING AND TECHNICAL ASSISTANCE[7]

- Expectations
- Recommendations for bilateral, regional and international cooperation.

RECOMMENDATIONS

The following are recommendations based on the human rights concerns described in this submission.

APPENDIX: Documents for further reference

- Annexes to the submissions should NOT include pictures, maps, organizations' annual reports or reports from other organizations
- Include detailed citation information and web links for all documents suggested for further reference.
- Identify those references included as attachments/exhibits to the submission.
- If possible, include a short description of the information contained in the document.
- If numerous documents/suggested resources are listed, organize documents by sub-issue and list under separate headings

---

[5] Section I.e. of General Guidelines/ Technical Guidelines Section IV.B.8.e
[6] Section I.f of General Guidelines/ Technical Guidelines Section IV.B.8.f
[7] Section I.g of General Guidelines/ Technical Guidelines Section IV.B.8.g

650 Third Avenue South • Suite 550 • Minneapolis, MN 55402-1940 • USA
Tel: 612.341.3302 • Fax: 612.341.2971 • Email: hrights@advrights.org • www.theadvocatesforhumanrights.org

APPENDIX K

Appendix **B**   Sample of NGO submission

United Kingdom

Submission to the UN Universal Periodic Review

First session of the HRC UPR Working Group, 7-18 April 2008

In this submission, Amnesty International provides information under sections B, C and D (as stipulated in the General Guidelines for the Preparation of Information under the Universal Periodic Review):

- Under B, Amnesty International raises concern over shortcomings of the ratification of international human rights standards, the extraterritorial applicability of human rights protection and the failure to initiate independent investigations.
- In section C, we describe concerns related to human rights violations in the context of counter-terrorism, failures to accountability, violence against women, asylum and refugee protection.
- In each section Amnesty International makes a number of recommendations in the areas of concerns listed.

B. Normative and institutional framework of State Ratification of international human rights standards
- Amnesty International recommends that the UK should ratify the Optional Protocol to the Convention on the Rights of the Child, on the sale of children, child prostitution and child pornography, and the Convention on the Rights of Persons with Disabilities; and that the UK should sign and ratify the Optional Protocol to the International Covenant on Civil and Political Rights, the International Convention on the Protection of the Rights of All Migrant Workers and Members of their Families and the International Convention for Protection of All Persons from Enforced Disappearance.

- Amnesty International recommends that the UK should set a deadline for the ratification of the Council of Europe Convention on Action against Trafficking in Human Beings, which it signed in March 2007; and should sign and ratify Protocol No. 12 to the European Convention for the Protection of Human Rights and Fundamental Freedoms (ECHR).

Extraterritorial applicability of human rights protection: accountability for UK armed forces serving overseas
Amnesty International is concerned at attempts by the UK authorities to deny, or limit, the applicability of their obligations under international human rights treaties and domestic human rights law to the conduct of the UK's armed forces overseas.

Both the Committee against Torture (CAT)1 and the UK parliamentary Joint Committee on Human Rights (JCHR)2 have expressed concern at the narrow view taken by the UK of the extraterritorial application of the UN Convention against Torture. The UK has contended, including in appearances before the CAT, that the acts of UK service personnel overseas "comply with the prohibitions set out in the Convention", but that the UK is not required to ensure compliance with the "broader obligations under the Convention, such as those in Articles 2 and 16 to prevent torture or other acts of cruel, inhumane or degrading treatment or punishment"3, even in overseas territory over which its forces are exercising *de facto* control.

- Amnesty International considers that there should be no limitation on the extraterritorial applicability of the Convention against Torture.

Amnesty International is similarly concerned at attempts by the UK to deny or limit the applicability of the ECHR, and of the domestic Human Rights Act (HRA), which is supposed to provide a remedy before the UK courts for violations of rights protected by the ECHR, to individuals who suffer violations of ECHR rights through the conduct of UK service personnel overseas. In this context Amnesty International draws the attention of the Council to the cases of Baha Mousa and Hilal Al Jedda (below).

- Amnesty International calls on the UK to make clear that any individual arrested or detained by UK service personnel abroad should be considered to be within the jurisdiction of the UK from the moment of arrest, wherever that arrest or detention takes place, and should therefore be afforded all the protection of human rights envisaged both by the HRA and by the UK's international obligations.

. . .

1 See *Conclusions and recommendations : UK. 10/12/2004, CAT/C/CR/33/3*, para. 4(b).
2 See *The UN Convention against Torture (UNCAT): Nineteenth Report of Session 2005–06*, HC 701-I, para. 73.
3 *UK – Opening Address to the Committee against Torture*, 17-18 November 2004, para. 92.
AI Index: EUR 45/020/2007

Amnesty International

1508

. . .

Document 6.
INFORMATION AND GUIDELINES FOR RELEVANT STAKEHOLDERS[1] ON THE UNIVERSAL PERIODIC REVIEW MECHANISM [as of July 2008], by the United Nations Human Rights Council.

I. BACKGROUND

1. The Universal Periodic Review (UPR), established by General Assembly resolution 60/251 of 15 March 2006, is a new human rights mechanism. Through the UPR, the Human Rights Council (HRC) reviews, on a periodic basis, the fulfillment by each of the United Nations' 192 Member States of their human rights obligations and commitments. Resolution 60/251 provides that the UPR shall:[2]

- Be based on objective and reliable information of the fulfillment by each State of its human rights obligations and commitments;
- Be conducted in a manner which ensures universality of coverage and equal treatment with respect to all States;
- Be a cooperative mechanism, based on an interactive dialogue, with the full involvement of the country concerned and with consideration given to its capacity-building needs; and
- Complement and not duplicate the work of treaty bodies.

2. HRC resolution 5/1 of 18 June 2007 provides that the UPR should *ensure the participation of all relevant stakeholders, including non-governmental organizations and national human rights institutions, in accordance with General Assembly resolution 60/251 of 15 March 2006 and Economic and Social Council resolution 1996/31 of 25 July 1996, as well as any decisions that the Council may take in this regard"*[3]

II. BASIS OF THE REVIEW

3. States are reviewed on the basis of:

The Charter of the UN;

The Universal Declaration of Human Rights;

Human rights instruments to which the State is party;

Voluntary pledges and commitments, including (where relevant) those undertaken when presenting candidature for election to the HRC; and

Applicable international humanitarian law.

III. UNIVERSAL PERIODIC REVIEW AS A PROCESS

4. Reviewing all 192 UN Member States over a four-year cycle, the UPR is to be seen as a process consisting of several steps:

- Preparation of the information upon which reviews are based, including: (i) information prepared by the State under review (national report); (ii) a compilation of UN information on the State under review prepared by the OHCHR, and (iii) a summary of information submitted by other relevant stakeholders, also prepared by OHCHR. The UPR review is based on these three documents, all of which are public;
- The review itself takes place in Geneva in the Working Group on the UPR, composed of the 47 Member States of the HRC, and takes the form of an interactive dialogue held between the State under review and the Member and Observer States of the HRC. The Working Group meets in three two-week sessions each year and reviews 16 States at each session—a total of 48 States each year;
- The Working Group's adoption of an outcome document at the end of each review;

- The HRC's consideration and adoption of the UPR outcome, normally at the next regular HRC session; and
- Follow-up by reviewed States on the implementation of the conclusions and recommendations contained within outcome documents.

5. The participation of all relevant stakeholders is encouraged throughout all relevant steps of the process. According to Human Rights Council resolution 5/1 of 18 June 2007: (a) States are encouraged to prepare the information they submit "through a broad consultation process at the national level with all relevant stakeholders" (paragraph 15 (a)); (b) Other relevant stakeholders may submit additional, credible and reliable information to the universal periodic review. Input received from stakeholders will be summarized by the Office of the High Commissioner for Human Rights in a Summary of Stakeholders' information which shall not exceed 10 pages (paragraph 15 (c));

(c) Other relevant stakeholders may attend the review in the working group (paragraph. 18 (c)), while not taking active part in the interactive dialogue; -3- 3

(d) Before the adoption of the outcome by the plenary of the Council, the State concerned is offered the opportunity to present replies to questions or issues; Other relevant stakeholders will have the opportunity to make general comments before the adoption of the outcome by the plenary (paragraphs 29 and 31); (e) The outcome of the universal periodic review, as a cooperative mechanism, should be implemented primarily by the State concerned and, as appropriate, by other relevant stakeholders (paragraph 33).

IV.
CONTRIBUTING WRITTEN SUBMISSIONS TOWARDS THE UPR PROCESS
A. Documentation upon which reviews are based

6. The documents on which reviews are based are:[5]

(a) Information prepared by the State concerned, which can take the form of a national report, on the basis of General Guidelines adopted by the HRC at its sixth session, and any other information considered relevant by the State concerned, which could be presented either orally or in writing, provided that the written presentation summarizing the information will not exceed 20 pages.

(b) A compilation prepared by OHCHR of the information contained in the reports of treaty bodies, special procedures, including observations and comments by the State concerned, and other relevant official UN documents, which shall not exceed 10 pages.

(c) Additional, credible and reliable information provided by other relevant stakeholders to the UPR which should also be taken into consideration by the HRC in the review. OHCHR will prepare a summary of such information which shall not exceed 10 pages.
B. Content and format of written submissions by relevant stakeholders to the OHCHR

7. HRC decision 6/102[6] sets out General Guidelines for the preparation of information under the UPR. These Guidelines (available at http://ap.ohchr.org/documents/sdpage_e.aspx?b=10&se=69&t=3) apply to States and other stakeholders, as well as to OHCHR for the preparation of the documents under its responsibility.[7]

8. Drawing from the above-mentioned general guidelines, stakeholders may wish to include in their submissions: (a) The methodology and the broad consultation process followed nationally for the preparation of information provided to the UPR by the country under review; (b) The current normative and institutional framework of the country under review for the promotion and protection of human rights: constitution, legislation, policy measures such as national action plans, national jurisprudence, human rights infrastructure including national human rights institutions ...; (c) The implementation and efficiency of the normative and institutional framework for the promotion and protection of human rights as described at subparagraph (b) above. This includes information on the implementation of the country's human rights obligations and commitments at the national and the international levels (for example information on the implementation of commitments made by the country under review at international conferences and other United Nations fora; of constitutional and legal reforms aimed at protecting human rights, of national action plans, of mechanisms and remedies aimed at improving human rights); on the activities of national human rights institutions; on human rights education and public awareness ....; (d) Cooperation of the country under review with human rights mechanisms, and with national human rights institutions, NGOs, rights holders, human rights defenders, and other relevant national human rights stakeholders, both at the national, regional and international levels; (e) Achievements made by the country under review, best practices which have emerged, and challenges and constraints faced by the country under review;

(f) Key national priorities as identified by stakeholders, initiatives and commitments that the State concerned should undertake, in the view of stakeholders, to overcome these challenges and constraints and improve human rights situations on the ground. This includes, for example, national strategies, areas where further progress is required, steps regarding implementation and follow-up to recommendations made by human rights mechanisms, commitments for future cooperation with OHCHR and human rights mechanisms and agencies, etc.;

(g) Expectations in terms of capacity-building and technical assistance provided and/or recommended by stakeholders through bilateral, regional and international cooperation.

9. Stakeholders are strongly encouraged to provide written submissions that:
- Are specifically tailored for the UPR;
- Contain credible and reliable information on the State under review;
- Highlight the main issues of concern and identify possible recommendations and/or best practices;
- Cover a maximum four-year time period;
- Do not contain language manifestly abusive;
- Are no longer than five pages in the case of individual submissions, to which additional documentation can be annexed for reference. Submissions by large coalitions of stakeholders can be up to ten pages.

10. Stakeholders are encouraged, while drafting their contribution, in accordance with Human Rights Council resolution 5/1 (paragraph 1), to take into consideration all human rights obligations and commitments, including those set out in the United Nations Charter, the Universal Declaration of Human Rights, Human Rights instruments to which the country under review is a party, voluntary pledges and commitments made by that country, as well as applicable international humanitarian law.

11. Stakeholders may also, if they so wish, draw attention to specific conclusions and recommendations made by international and regional human rights mechanisms, and refer to the extent of implementation. However, stakeholders should refrain from listing all treaties ratification, concluding observations and recommendations of the human rights treaty bodies and/or the special procedures of the HRC, as the latter are reflected in the UN compilation prepared by OHCHR.

12. The UPR mechanism does not provide for confidentiality and is conducted on the basis of public documents. Submissions, as originally received, will be made available on-line on OHCHR's website, including the name of the submitting party (provided they do not contain language manifestly abusive).

13. Stakeholders are encouraged to consult with one another at the national level for the preparation of the UPR submissions. Joint submissions by a large number of stakeholders are encouraged.

For detailed technical guidance on modalities for stakeholders' submissions please refer to the information box annexed to these guidelines.

C. How and when should relevant stakeholders submit information?

14. Stakeholders' submissions should be sent to **uprsubmissions@ohchr.org.**

15. Deadlines for stakeholders' submissions can be found here.

17. For future country reviews under the UPR, stakeholders should note that written submissions to OHCHR should be sent indicatively at least five months before the relevant session of the Working Group on UPR, to take into account UN Conference Services' requirements. The exact deadlines will be posted in due course on the website.

V. PARTICIPATION IN THE UNIVERSAL PERIODIC REVIEW

18. NGOs in consultative relationship with ECOSOC may attend sessions of the Working Group on the UPR.[8] At these sessions there is no provision for such NGOs to take the floor or submit written information;

19. NGOs in consultative relationship with ECOSOC may participate in regular sessions of the HRC, at which UPR outcomes are considered and adopted, and make brief general comments before the adoption of outcome documents by the HRC.[9] For information on how to be accredited to HRC sessions please visit **http://www2.ohchr.org/english/bodies/hrcouncil/.**

VI. FOLLOW-UP TO THE UNIVERSAL PERIODIC REVIEW

20. Relevant stakeholders may wish to contribute to the follow-up to the outcome of the UPR process, to the extent that this is appropriate: (a) Follow-up action could be undertaken in cooperation with the State entities, to whom the recommendations are addressed; and (b) Stakeholders may disseminate the outcome of the UPR at the national level.

21. Stakeholders are encouraged to further disseminate these guidelines and raise awareness on the UPR. -7- 7

VII. CONTACT INFORMATION

22. For further information, please contact: **OHCHR Civil Society Unit Tel: +41 22 917 96 56 Fax: +41 22 917 90 11**

Technical guidelines for the submission of stakeholders' information to OHCHR

Where to submit?

Written information for the UPR review should be sent to the following address: uprsubmissions@ohchr. org. Please avoid sending information to other OHCHR electronic addresses. Please note (a) the OHCHR secretariat will confirm electronically receipt of your message and submission; and (b) while stakeholders are discouraged to fax or mail a hardcopy of their submission to the OHCHR secretariat, they may do so in the case of repeated technical difficulties with electronic mail to: +41 22 917 90 11. Format of the written submission:

- Each electronic submission and relevant e-mail message should refer to one country only. In the e-mail message accompanying the submitted documents kindly include:
  - In the title of the e-mail message: the name of the (main) stakeholder/NGO submitting the contribution, the kind of contribution (individual and/or joint), the name of the reviewed country and indicate the month and year of relevant UPR session, e.g., "Women's coalition—joint UPR submission—Brazil—April 2008";
  - In the text of the e-mail message accompanying the submission, stakeholders should indicate the details of the relevant contact person;
  - A paragraph describing the main activities of the submitting organization/coalition, as well as date of establishment, especially for those organizations which interrelate for the first time with the UN, would be also welcomed;
- Should the submission be prepared jointly, the names of all submitting stakeholders should appear at the beginning of the submission text (not in the relevant e-mail message).
- Stakeholders' submissions should not be longer than five pages, to which a more detailed and factual report maybe attached; submissions by large coalitions of stakeholders can be up to ten pages;
- Written submissions should be saved as a Word document only, i.e. not as PDF file, in Times New Roman, font 12;
- Written contributions should be submitted in UN official languages only, preferably in English, French or Spanish;
- Written submissions should be final; in principle, it will not be possible to accommodate revisions;
- Paragraphs and pages of each submission should be numbered;
- Stakeholders are encouraged to include in their written submissions an introductory executive summary, capturing the main points contained therein; as a way of introduction, key words may also be indicated (e.g., domestic violence);
- Written submissions should not include second-hand information (except when it clearly supports original information). Facts and details to support the identified priority issues and recommendations may be annexed for reference to the submission;
- Annexes to the submissions should NOT include pictures, maps, organizations' annual reports or reports from other organizations;
- OHCHR's summary will not refer to names of individuals mentioned in the written submission, except if they refer to emblematic cases;
- The extensive use of footnotes is discouraged;
- Please note also:
- Submissions in excess of the five/ten page maximum will not be considered;
- Submissions received in a language other than the six official UN languages will not be considered;
- Submissions received after specified deadlines will not be considered; and
- Submissions containing language manifestly abusive (i.e. incitement to violence, inherently racist language, etc.) will not be considered.

Notes

1 Stakeholders, which are referred to in resolution 5/1, include, *inter alia*, NGOs, national human rights institutions, human rights defenders, academic institutions and research institutes, regional organizations, as well as civil society representatives.

2 See operative paragraph (op.) 5(e).

3 See para 3(m) of the Annex to resolution 5/1.

4 See para 1 of the Annex to resolution 5/1.

5 See para 15 of the Annex to resolution 5/1

6 Of 27 September 2007.

7 See section I. "General guidelines for the preparation of information under the Universal Periodic Review" of HRC decision 6/102.

8 See para. 18(c) of the Annex to resolution 5/1.

9 See para. 31 of the Annex to resolution 5/1.

APPENDIX L: SELECTED HUMAN RIGHTS REPORT RELATED DOCUMENTS

The purpose of this Appendix is to show how international human rights norms are being implemented at the national level in the U.S., or used by the U.S. to judge other countries. Monitoring human rights compliance by states is done through various mechanisms. One of them is the drafting and submission of human rights reports, sometimes about a particular country, sometimes about a particular issue and sometimes about a particular issue in a particular country, for example, housing and human rights in the U.S. Sometimes reports are created by international inter-governmental institutions like the U.N. or the Organization of American States. Sometimes they are done by non-governmental organizations such as Freedom House or Human Rights Watch. Sometimes they are done by state governments, such as the annual U.S. Country Reports on Human Rights about human rights in other countries. Sometimes they are reports by a state about itself in its own periodic self-assessment under a human rights treaty such as the ICCPR.

Following are several reports either by or about the U.S. and human rights. These are part of the text of international human rights discourse about human rights in light of human rights legal norms.

No claim is made about the correctness or accuracy of any these reports or their conclusions or recommendations. They are not being presented to criticize the U.S., and are presented only for informing the reader about international issues and discourse of human rights as they relate to the U.S.

Due to their size these reports are highly excerpted. The reader is advised to view the entire original document at the web site indicated.

Document (Excerpted): Report of the Special Rapporteur on extrajudicial, summary or arbitrary executions

A/HRC/13/20/Add.4

General Assembly	Distr.:
HUMAN RIGHTS COUNCIL	GENERAL
Thirteenth session	12 February 2010
Agenda item 3	Original: ENGLISH

PROMOTION AND PROTECTION OF ALL HUMAN RIGHTS, CIVIL, POLITICAL, ECONOMIC, SOCIAL AND CULTURAL RIGHTS, INCLUDING THE RIGHT TO DEVELOPMENT

Report of the Special Rapporteur on adequate housing as a component of the right to an adequate standard of living, and on the right to non-discrimination in this context, Raquel Rolnik*
Addendum
MISSION TO THE UNITED STATES OF AMERICA**

Summary

The Special Rapporteur on adequate housing as a component of the right to an adequate standard of living, and on the right to non-discrimination in this context, undertook an official visit to the United States of America from 22 October to 8 November 2009 to examine the realization of the right to adequate housing, in particular in relation to subsidized housing programmes, the homeless situation and the foreclosure crisis. The first part of the report provides a brief overview of the evolution of housing policies, focusing on public subsidized housing programmes. It refers to the context of the current affordable housing crisis—with a growing proportion of people living in the U.S. facing serious challenges in accessing affordable housing. The second part of the report discusses the realization of the right to adequate housing, particularly affordability, discrimination and participation. The report highlights the implications of significant cuts in federal funding for low-income housing, the persistent impact of discrimination in housing, substandard conditions such as overcrowding and health risks, as well as the consequences of the foreclosure crisis. It also focuses on participation and underlines the importance of adequately informing the public of housing opportunities and involving them in the planning, decision-making, and implementation of programmes and policies that directly affect their lives.

The Special Rapporteur discusses and welcomes new measures adopted to address the current housing crisis, and concludes her report with a number of recommendations to contribute to these efforts.

Annex
REPORT OF THE SPECIAL RAPPORTEUR ON ADEQUATE HOUSING AS A COMPONENT OF THE RIGHT TO AN ADEQUATE STANDARD OF LIVING, AND ON THE RIGHT TO NON-DISCRIMINATION IN THIS CONTEXT, RAQUEL ROLNIK, ON HER MISSION TO THE UNITED STATES OF AMERICA
(22 October–8 November 2009)

[Contents omitted]

I. Introduction

1. At the invitation of the Government, the Special Rapporteur on adequate housing as a component of the right to an adequate standard of living, and on the right to nondiscrimination in this context, undertook an official visit to the United States of America from 22 October to 8 November 2009. The main purpose of the mission was to examine the realization of the right to adequate housing in the country and the achievements and difficulties encountered in its fulfilment, in particular in relation to the existing subsidized housing programmes, the homeless situation and the foreclosure crisis. Given the size of the country, the nature of the federal system and the limited duration of the mission, the Special Rapporteur focused on specific themes and concentrated particularly on federal policies and programmes, and their impact at the local level.

2. The Special Rapporteur visited Washington D.C., New York, Chicago, New Orleans, Pine Ridge Reservation, Los Angeles and Pacoima (California). During her visit, the Special Rapporteur met with high-ranking officials and representatives of the federal, state and local governments. The Special Rapporteur

also held meetings with members of Congress, people affected by housing issues, members of civil society and nongovernmental organizations.

3. She warmly expresses her gratitude to the Government of the United States of America for the invitation, the constructive dialogue and openness, and support throughout and after the visit, and welcomes the engagement of the present administration to progress the implementation of the right to adequate housing as a policy goal for all.

II. Institutional and legal framework

4. Modern housing policy in the U.S. began during the Depression, with the National Housing Act of 1934, which created the Federal Housing Administration (FHA) to underwrite and insure mortgages and provide security to lenders in case of default. The Government also created the Federal National Mortgage Association (Fannie Mae) to buy mortgages from lenders, enabling them to increase their liquidity and thus offer more loans to buyers.

. . .

7. The face of public housing changed rapidly. Initially racial minorities represented 26 to 39 percent of all tenants in public housing but had reached over 60 per cent by 1978. Concurrently, the median income of tenants fell from 64 per cent to 37 per cent of the national median from 1950 to 1970. From the 1950s through the 1970s, large tracts of predominantly high-density public housing were built, whose residents were mainly African American.

8. Simultaneously, homeownership for the (predominantly white) middle class was greatly facilitated through federal financing of more than half of all suburban homes during the 1950s and 1960s. This led to an increase in the home-ownership rate from 30 per cent in 1930 to over 60 per cent by 1960. Due to a variety of discriminatory laws and practices, the vast majority of loans were not accessible to African Americans, and whites received 98 percent of federally approved loans between 1934 and 1968.

9. Public housing was established by the Federal Government with the aim of providing decent and safe rental housing for eligible low-income families, older persons, and persons with disabilities. However, over the years, the model of high-density public housing "projects" was increasingly questioned as they became more and more stigmatized as centres of extreme poverty, crime and segregation. Reasons for the perceived decline in the quality of public housing include physical deterioration related to the ageing of the public housing stock and poor maintenance, while little was done to deal with the larger systemic issue of racial and economic segregation in some cities.

10. In 1974 the Housing and Community Development Act effectively ended most new construction of public housing. It also initiated the Housing Choice Voucher Program (commonly referred to as Section 8), consisting of both project-based and tenant-based rent subsidies. In the former instance, its use is limited to a specific housing development; in the latter case beneficiaries are free to choose a housing unit on the private market from a landlord who accepts the vouchers. Tenants pay a proportion of the rent (based on income, and generally not more than 30 percent of total household income), while the rest is paid from federal funds. The Section 8 programme marked an important change in public housing policy as it shifted funds from public housing authorities to the private sector. It was created to avoid concentrations of low-income people, as public housing developments tended to do. However, it faced resistance from tenants and buildings in middle-income neighbourhoods and in some cities "the concentration of [Section 8] buildings and tenants has been blamed, just like public housing, for community decline".

. . .

14. Federal housing policy has resulted, on the one hand, in the achievement of a high rate of homeownership—about 69 percent. On the other hand, it has also resulted in the decreasing supply of public housing—currently 1.2 million units. This loss has been accompanied by the progressive withdrawal of Government from the housing sector. The policy has included the promotion of private homeownership for lower-income households, and the privatization of subsidized housing complexes, allowing private developers to promote mixed-income developments. The subprime mortgage crisis has widened an already large gap between the supply homes and demand for affordable housing. The economic crisis which followed has led to increased unemployment and an even greater need for affordable housing.

. . .

III. Affordability

17. The Department of Housing and Urban Development (HUD) definition of affordable housing is that a household spend no more than 30 per cent of its income on housing. In 2007, about 22 per cent of the 36.9 million rental households in the U.S. were spending more than half their income on rental

costs.12 At the same time, about 8.8 million renter households with low incomes were spending more than half of their income for housing. The number of households facing serious affordability constraints increased by 33 per cent between 2000 and 2007, and the poorest and most vulnerable people face the heaviest burdens in terms of housing costs. Nearly two thirds of the low-income households that face severe housing-cost burdens have family members who are children, elderly, or persons with disabilities.13 About 12.7 million children—more than one in six—in the U.S. live in households spending more than half their incomes on housing.

A. Subsidized housing programmes

1. Federal housing assistance programmes for low-income households

18. Federal housing assistance programmes play a very important role in covering the difference between the rents that low-income families are able to afford and the cost of rental housing. The main federal assistance programmes to help households access affordable housing are the Housing Choice Voucher Program (Section 8), project-based Section 8 rental assistance, and public housing. All these programmes provide rental assistance to households, which reduces their housing costs to about 30 per cent of their income.

19. Today there are approximately 1.2 million households living in public housing units, managed by approximately 3,300 housing authorities, which include a variety of options from single-family houses to high-rise apartments. Almost two thirds of all public housing households include an older person or a person with disabilities.

. . .

2. Cuts in low-income housing assistance programmes

21. In past years there were significant cuts in low-income housing assistance programmes. Budget cuts in the 1980s resulted in the gradual erosion and poor maintenance of the public housing system. Further subsequent funding cuts have also significantly affected the preservation of public housing. By the early 1990s, hundreds of thousands of public housing units had become dilapidated. Over the past decade there has been a net loss of approximately 170,000 public housing units due to deterioration and decay, and much of the current public housing stock needs substantial repairs and rehabilitation. However, annual funding for public housing fell by 25 per cent between 1999 and 2006.

22. When federal funding is inadequate, housing agencies reduce their own expenses. Measures have included shifting units to tenants with higher incomes (who can be charged higher rents than lower-income households but typically have less need for assistance), or cutting back in areas such as security or maintenance.

23. The Special Rapporteur wishes to emphasize that low-income housing assistance programmes should receive additional funding. The Federal Government provides much higher levels of subsidies to high-income homeowners via tax exemptions as compared to subsidies for low-income housing assistance. "Each year, the federal government spends more than three times as much on tax breaks for homeowners—with a large share of the resulting tax benefits going to upper-income households—as it spends on low-income housing assistance."

. . .

3. Mixed-income developments and demolition of public housing

25. The cuts in federal funding for low-income housing have led to a decrease in the quality of subsidized housing. At the same time, a new housing policy based on mixed income developments on public housing sites has been promoted, especially on those sites in prime locations within cities. HOPE VI gave local agencies funds to demolish distressed or obsolete public housing and replace it with mixed-income communities, usually with the collaboration of private developers. Over the past 15 years, the programme has invested $6.1 billion of federal funding in 235 projects to demolish 96,200 public housing units and produce 107,800 new or renovated housing units, 56,800 of which will be affordable. In addition, 78,000 housing vouchers have been issued. Besides the fact that some demolished units are replaced by market-rate housing, many "affordable" units are too costly for many public housing tenants.

. . .

27. The policy goal of creating diverse and inclusive mixed neighbourhoods is a positive one. While this policy has benefited residents in different locations, its implementation has also drawn criticism. Units were demolished without sufficient mechanisms in place for tenants to find comparable housing in the interim. Displaced residents often had to move to other subsidized housing in neighbourhoods as distressed as their original one, or were discriminated against in their new neighbourhoods. The interim period of redevelopment

has been much longer than forecast and insufficient efforts were made to keep track of tenants in order to offer them housing once redevelopments were complete. In fact, less than 12 per cent of former public housing residents make it back to live in the redeveloped communities. The number of units rebuilt has often not matched the number of units demolished, in fact far from it, and the number of new units of public housing has usually been far fewer than formerly.

28. An example is Cabrini Green in Chicago. Cabrini Green originally had 3,114 highrise public housing units, of which 2,700 were demolished. Since the demolition, only 305 public housing units have been built in mixed-income developments. As a result many residents were displaced and are unable to return to the area.[22] The Housing Authority plans to demolish the remaining 414 high-rise units in September 2010.

29. On 15 June 2009 Massachusetts Congressman Barney Frank and California Congresswoman Maxine Waters sent a letter to HUD Secretary Shaun Donovan urging him to "impose a one-year moratorium on the approval of applications for the demolition or disposition of public housing units". Mr. Frank and Ms. Waters had sent a similar letter in August 2008 expressing their concern about the loss of public housing units which had reached "epic proportions". No moratorium has been imposed.

. . .

31. Rental housing assistance was offered by HUD to more than 33,000 New Orleans households, many of them living in other cities and states. This programme assisted residents for more than four years and continues to assist about 12,000 families in New Orleans.

32. The Special Rapporteur wishes to emphasize that many public housing units are in good physical condition and provide adequate homes; however, in some cases, even these units are under threat. During her visit to Los Angeles, the Special Rapporteur visited several public housing complexes which were in very good condition, such as Mar Vista Gardens. Located in a relatively wealthy community, Mar Vista Gardens achieves HUD's stated goal of mixing households with different levels of income and provides housing in a neighbourhood which offers opportunities to residents. However, the Los Angeles Housing Authority (HACLA) has announced a plan to remove it from the public housing stock.

When public housing is disposed of, ownership is often transferred from the housing authority to a private entity—most often for-profit developers, although sometimes nonprofit owners—putting its future as affordable housing at great risk. Tenants thus live in fear that the long-term affordability and stability of their housing is threatened and that they might be displaced in the future.

. . .

4. Expiring long-term rental assistance contracts and Section 8 vouchers

34. Options for low-income families and individuals are further reduced due to other pressures on the stock of affordable housing including "expiring use". In the 1960s, the Federal Government partnered with private developers to provide affordable housing. In exchange for subsidies in the form of tax benefits or subsidized mortgages, developers providing affordable units signed contracts with the Federal Government for leases of 20 to 40 years. Depending on the type of subsidy, landlords had the option of repaying their mortgage after 20 years, converting the units to market rate and/or opting out of renewing contracts once they expired. Many of these contracts are now ending, with landlords opting out of renewal. Thousands of units have already been lost, and a report estimates that an additional 300,000 units will see contracts expire within the next five years. Incentives are needed to encourage owners to remain in the Section 8 programmes, thus preserving housing for low-income families.

. . .

5. Habitability, availability and location

37. The link between housing and health was stressed to the Special Rapporteur throughout her visit. Poor housing conditions expose residents—especially children—to a number of diseases. Most residents of public housing with whom the Special Rapporteur spoke complained of asthma, attributed to mould from poor maintenance of units. A resident in Los Angeles described living in slum housing conditions with rats, cockroaches, bedbugs, deteriorated piping and lead-based paint, and as a result developing chronic asthma.

38. In several cities, many of the subsidized residents with whom the Special Rapporteur spoke complained of bedbugs. In Section 8 housing, the insect infestation problem is compounded by the fact that some residents do not complain about poor maintenance because they fear that they will be forced to move if their unit does not meet Section 8 standards, while alternative low-income options are extremely scarce.

39. During the mission, the Special Rapporteur observed many families living in subsidized housing units in conditions of severe overcrowding. This was particularly the case amongst immigrant families in

Los Angeles, and most strikingly on Pine Ridge Native American Reservation, where it was described as commonplace to have three to four families living in a three-bedroom house. The conditions in the houses on the Reservation were the worst seen by the Special Rapporteur during her mission, evidence of the urgent and severe need for additional subsidized housing units there.

. . .

42. The Special Rapporteur is also concerned about the effects of gentrification on the poorest. As middle- and upper-income families choose to move to or to stay in the cities, inner-city subsidized housing developments face increasing pressure as developers vie for prime land. Gentrification pushes out the poorest to areas with reduced services and employment opportunities. Legislation is needed to safeguard affordable housing in prime locations.

. . .

6. Predatory equity

44. One tool utilized by certain districts in the U.S. to provide affordable housing is through the use of rent regulation legislation. This legislation was introduced at the federal level during the Second World War, when President Franklin D. Roosevelt signed into law the Emergency Price Control Act (EPCA) in 1942. Subsequently various states and local jurisdictions instituted rent control measures and many still exist today.32This rental stock is facing growing pressure from real estate markets, and more recently from the threat of "predatory equity".

45. Predatory equity appeared during the recent real estate bubble, described as an investor purchasing a rent-stabilized building, with a mortgage which is securitized and sold repeatedly over a short period of time for ever-increasing sums. The resulting mortgage payments increase with each sale, with existing rent rolls insufficient to cover the cost. As a result, new owners engage in aggressive tactics to evict residents in order to raise rents to subsequent residents, and eventually remove the building from the rent stabilization scheme. Given the downturn in the real estate market, there exists a high risk that such mortgages will default, and the Special Rapporteur heard reports of investors simply walking away, leaving the building to the bank, and tenants with uncertain futures. The Special Rapporteur also noticed that while the impacts of predatory equity are being felt across the country, they have been most acute in New York, where the full effect of foreclosures has yet to be felt. In New York alone, one civil society organization has identified over 90,000 rent-stabilized units subject to predatory equity.

46. In addition to the long-standing challenges of affordability, more and more households are losing their homes to foreclosure, putting even more pressure on already stressed housing markets.

B. Foreclosure

47. As stated by HUD, "the extent of the housing and economic crisis is now painfully apparent. (. . .) approximately 3.7 million borrowers began the foreclosure process in 2007 and 2008".34 RealtyTrac reported a 32 per cent increase in foreclosure filings from April 2008 to April 2009.35 A growing number of owners are losing their properties due to foreclosure and are displaced into the rental housing market. Families who were previously owners are now seeking to rent. Although housing markets vary widely in the U.S., in some areas this increased demand for rental units has contributed to a rise in rents while real estate prices are falling.

. . .

49. In spring 2009, the Federal Government also announced the Making Home Affordable programme. It seeks, inter alia, to prevent foreclosures by working with private industry to offer affordable loan refinancing and loan modifications. From the inception of this programme there have been questions as to whether it could diminish the wave of foreclosures.

C. Homelessness

50. The economic crisis and significantly increasing numbers of foreclosures are increasing the risk of homelessness in communities across the country. Many families—renters and homeowners—have been caught in the foreclosure crisis and become homeless, moving in with relatives or friends, going to emergency shelters or living on the streets. According to the 2008 study conducted by the U.S. Conference of Mayors, of the 25 cities with data available, 12 reported an increase in homelessness because of the foreclosure crisis.

51. It is estimated that over 800,000 people are homeless on any given night in the U.S., and as many as 3.5 million people experience homelessness annually, living in shelters, transitional housing, or public places. Including those who have lost their own homes and live with family or friends, the number reaches 4.5 million.

52. The exact number of homeless people is difficult to determine, both due to the nature of homelessness and the definition used. The model used by HUD to record the homeless includes two surveys: one records the number of individuals and families that accessed emergency shelter or stayed in transitional housing during a one-year period while the other is a point-in-time analysis, which attempts to count the number of homeless, whether in a shelter or not, on a given night in January.

. . .

54. More than 1.5 million children in the U.S. experience homelessness each year. In many cases, there are no adequate shelter facilities where parents and children can stay together and children are often removed from their parents and placed in foster care.

. . .

56. Homeless people need access to affordable housing; the lack of it is the main cause of homelessness. Many cities that do not provide enough affordable housing and shelters are resorting to the criminal justice system to punish people living on the streets. Some of the measures adopted include prohibition of sleeping, camping, eating, sitting, and/or begging in public spaces and include criminal penalties for violation of these laws. The Helping Families Save Their Home Act of 2009, recently signed into law, requires the federal Interagency Council on Homelessness to create constructive alternatives to criminalization measures.

. . .

IV. Discrimination

59. The U.S. has strong legislation against discrimination in housing on the basis of race, colour, religion, national origin or disability. On a federal level the most fundamental and overarching legislation is Title VIII of the Civil Rights Act of 1968 (also known as the Fair Housing Act), which gives HUD the responsibility to enforce the Act. It also requires HUD to act in an affirmative way to further fair housing. The Fair Housing Act is generally thought to provide a robust legal framework, however there have been significant problems in its enforcement, and further strengthening is required. The Act governs both private and public housing stock. States and cities have additional legislative codes which bar discrimination on other grounds, for example source of income.

. . .

61. HUD's authority to investigate housing discrimination complaints is shared with state and local government agencies that participate in the Fair Housing Assistance Program (FHAP). These agencies received 80 per cent of the housing discrimination complaints filed in HUD's jurisdiction in fiscal year 2008. The total number of housing discrimination complaints filed in 2008 was 10,552, the highest number on record.

A. Persons with disabilities

62. Adequate housing must be accessible to all. Thus, such disadvantaged groups as older persons, children, persons with disabilities, the terminally ill, HIV-positive individuals, persons with persistent medical problems, victims of natural disasters, people living in disaster-prone areas and other groups should be assured some degree of priority in housing law and policy.

. . .

B. Racial and related discrimination

64. Evidence shows that subprime loans were five times more likely to be made in neighbourhoods of African American people as compared to neighbourhoods of whites. Such loans were found to have been particularly marketed to minorities, even in cases where individuals qualified for traditional loan products. Minority women were particularly targeted. A report submitted to the Committee on the Elimination of Racial Discrimination recommended that the Department of Justice investigate and prosecute cases of lending discrimination, and that the U.S. Congress enact robust anti bpredatory lending legislation.

65. The 2008 concluding observations of the Committee on the Elimination of Racial Discrimination on the report of the U.S. expressed deep concern that minority groups are disproportionately concentrated in poor areas characterized by substandard housing conditions. The Committee's recommendations on this issue are firmly supported by the Special Rapporteur. The Committee also stated its concern regarding the de facto racial segregation in U.S. public schools. In many communities this issue is directly linked to housing, as some public school districts are funded by the property taxes of the local community, thus providing more resources to schools in wealthier neighbourhoods.

. . .

C. Indigenous peoples

67. Article 27 of the International Covenant on Civil and Political Rights prohibits States from denying the right of minorities to enjoy their own culture. Housing construction including building materials used and the relevant policies must appropriately enable the expression of cultural identity and diversity of housing. In its general comment No. 4 (1991) on the right to adequate housing, the Committee on Economic, Social and Cultural Rights found that development or modernization activities should not sacrifice such cultural dimensions of housing.

68. The issues facing Native Americans both off and on reservations are complex, and housing is but one aspect. The subsidized housing visited by the Special Rapporteur was built as "cluster housing", in a traditional suburban model of a cluster of several homes in close proximity.

. . .

D. Discrimination based on economic and other status
"One strike and you're out" zero tolerance policies

70. Subsidized housing applicants are subject to denial based on their criminal or drug record, and tenants are subject to eviction based on such records. Such policies were introduced with the 1988 Anti-Drug Abuse Act, part of the country's "war on drugs". The Anti-Drug Abuse Act required public housing authorities to adopt leases which required eviction of public housing tenants who engaged in criminal activity on or near public housing premises. It was later reinforced in 1990 by the Cranston-Gonzalez National Affordable Housing Act.

71. In March 1996 President Clinton signed into law the Housing Opportunity Program Extension Act of 1996 creating a new HUD policy which gave additional authority to public housing authorities to screen tenants, enforce leases, and evict tenants. This Act authorized public housing authorities to evict tenants for criminal or drug-related activity which took place both "on or off" housing authority premises, whereas previous laws allowed for such evictions only if such activity occurred "on or near" housing authority premises. The Act also states that the "National Crime Information Center, police departments, and other law enforcement agencies shall upon request, provide information to public housing agencies regarding the criminal conviction records of adult applicants for, or tenants of, public housing for purposes of applicant screening, lease enforcement, and eviction". The Act stipulates that public housing agencies must provide the tenant with a copy of his/her criminal record, as well as an opportunity to dispute its accuracy and relevance. Thus, public housing authorities were given the mandate to establish their own standards to achieve these federal mandates. . . .

Housing discrimination based on source of income

76. Housing discrimination based on the source of income is prohibited only in certain districts. Such laws prevent anyone from refusing to sell, rent, or otherwise transfer housing based on the source of a person's income. The Special Rapporteur repeatedly heard reports that tenants with Section 8 vouchers had great difficulty finding landlords willing to accept these vouchers. This puts voucher holders at risk of losing their benefit, as they can lose the voucher if they do not obtain housing within 90 days and do not obtain an extension. Once a voucher is lost, beneficiaries may have to go back on a long waiting list, or lose their chance to benefit at all if the waiting list is closed. In addition, properties that do accept such vouchers tend to be in poorer neighbourhoods and in buildings with poor maintenance.

V. Participation

77. The realization of the right to adequate housing requires that individuals and communities are consulted and able actively to participate in the decisions that affect their right to housing. In its general comment No. 25 (1996) on participation in public affairs and the right to vote, the Human Rights Committee recognizes the right of every citizen to take part in the conduct of public affairs. Unfortunately, government agencies too often make decisions without the necessary information on how they will affect the lives of the people involved. In adopting measures to achieve the full realization of the right to adequate housing, a genuine consultation with, and participation by, all those affected, including the homeless, the inadequately housed and their representatives, should be guaranteed. Efforts should be made to ensure that residents are involved from the beginning of any redevelopment or other projects, and continue to be engaged during the entire process.

. . .

VI. Conclusions and recommendations

79. The Special Rapporteur acknowledges the high quality of the majority of housing in the U.S., as well as the availability and quality of utilities and services. However, she expresses her deep concern

about the millions of people living in the U.S. today who face serious challenges in accessing affordable and adequate housing, issues long faced by the poorest people and today affecting a greater proportion of society. A new face of homelessness is appearing, with increasing numbers of working families and individuals finding themselves on the streets, or living in shelters or in transitional housing arrangements with friends and family. Federal funding for low-income housing has been cut over the past decades, leading to a reduced stock and quality of subsidized housing. In addition, several cities have experienced a real estate boom which has led to increased housing prices. The subprime mortgage crisis has increased an already large gap between the supply and demand of affordable housing, and the economic crisis which followed has led to increased unemployment and an even greater need for affordable housing.

80. The Special Rapporteur noted throughout the visit that there is a long-standing commitment to provide adequate housing within their means for all Americans and an acknowledgement that the history of housing policy in the U.S. has been problematic. HUD Secretary Shaun Donovan has stated that in many cases neighbourhoods of concentrated poverty were the result of government policy.

81. Housing is not simply about bricks and mortar, nor is it simply a financial asset. Housing includes a sense of community, trust and bonds built between neighbours over time; the schools which educate the children; and the businesses which support the local economy and provide needed goods and services. Government policy has sometimes resulted in tearing apart this important sense of community, removing a source of stability for subsidized housing residents, and engendering a sense of mistrust of Government regard for their interests.

82. The present Government is actively pursuing policy change to better meet the housing needs of its population. The Special Rapporteur strongly urges the Government to increase opportunities for dialogue with civil society and tenant organizations. The town hall format which was used during her visit was met with broad support from civil society organizations, and she recommends that it be explored for interaction between local public housing authorities and residents. Real participation of those affected by the housing crisis is essential for a successful outcome to current efforts to change and reform.

83. The Special Rapporteur welcomes the measures adopted by the new Administration to improve access to adequate housing, including committing significant resources to housing, addressing mortgage modification programmes, and neighbourhood enhancement and emergency recovery initiatives through the American Recovery and Reinvestment Act.

84. In a spirit of cooperation and dialogue, the Special Rapporteur makes several recommendations which echo the voices of the hundreds of individuals with whom she spoke during her visit. She hopes this report will serve as a tool for further dialogue between civil society organizations and residents, and the Government.

Federal housing assistance programmes

85. The Special Rapporteur welcomes the existing federal housing assistance programmes that play a very important role in providing affordable housing to low income residents. Given their importance, the Special Rapporteur believes that they should receive more funding.

Public housing

86. Funding cuts in the past years have severely affected the maintenance of public housing. Some units have become dilapidated; many have been lost due to deterioration and decay. Additional funding is needed to properly maintain and restore the remaining public housing stock. The Government should also strengthen legislation on health standards for subsidized buildings, and ensure proper maintenance and pest control.

87. The Special Rapporteur considers that, given the crisis in affordable housing, an immediate moratorium is required on the demolition and disposition of public housing until such time as one-for-one replacement housing is secured, and the right to return is guaranteed to all residents. Housing should be made available for displaced residents before any unit is demolished.

88. The Special Rapporteur urges the Government to ensure that, in the context of the Choice Neighborhoods Initiative, poor communities will be able to stay in their neighbourhoods once development takes place.

89. In some cases the geographic area used to define the area median income should be re-examined, so that income threshold criteria actually lead to access to affordable housing.

Section 8

90. The Special Rapporteur calls on the Government to assign more resources to Section 8 vouchers. Legislative mechanisms should be established in order to encourage the extension of expiring Section 8 unit contracts, as well as other expiring affordable housing programmes involving private landlords.

91. The Special Rapporteur urges Congress to reinsert the provision on the right to first purchase in the draft preservation bill.

Foreclosure crisis

92. Tenant protection legislation should be further strengthened for renters of foreclosed properties. The Helping Families Save Their Home Act (P.L. 111-22): Protecting Tenants at Foreclosure Act (Title VII) should be extended beyond 2012 and become permanent protection.

93. Empty foreclosed properties should be made available using incentives for the sale of the property to non-profit organizations or community land trusts, in order to increase the stock of affordable housing.

94. The Making Home Affordable Program is a positive initiative addressing foreclosure prevention. Further measures are necessary to ensure that an increased number of homeowners are benefited by the programme. The Special Rapporteur encourages the Senate to continue its discussion on the adoption of new legislation on the creation of a national foreclosure prevention programme, and encourages the Government to develop a study on the impact of this programme and alternative measures to address the foreclosure crisis in the medium and long term.

Homelessness

95. The Interagency Council on Homelessness should develop constructive alternatives to the criminalization of homelessness in full consultation with members of civil society. When shelter is not available in the locality, homeless persons should be allowed to shelter themselves in public areas.

96. The Administration and Congress should encourage the expansion of the definition of homelessness to include those living with family or friends due to economic hardship. The Department of Housing and Urban Development (HUD) should ensure that households living with others due to economic hardship are eligible for rental and other assistance, including from the Emergency Shelter Grant programme.

. . .

Discrimination

99. The Special Rapporteur supports the housing-related recommendations of the Committee on the Elimination of Racial Discrimination in its concluding observations in paragraph 16 on subsidized housing, paragraph 17 on segregation in schools, and paragraph 22 on indigent persons.

Discrimination against persons with disabilities

100. The Special Rapporteur urges the U.S. Government to strengthen its enforcement and implementation of the Fair Housing Act and to promote accessible universal design in its contracts for subsidized housing, and to promote equal opportunity and access to affordable housing for persons with disabilities. The Special Rapporteur welcomes HUD's plans to strengthen its enforcement of the Fair Housing Act.

Discrimination and zero tolerance policies

101. The Special Rapporteur acknowledges the Government's efforts to maintain a safe environment within subsidized housing developments. However, she suggests that zero tolerance policies are not an answer for achieving this aim, and suggests the Government commit resources to determine the real effects of such policies on families, particularly minority families, and reform these policies.

Indigenous peoples

102. The Special Rapporteur was dismayed to observe the dire housing situation faced by some Native American tribes. She encourages the Government to devote greater resources and attention to this urgent question and would welcome further information on any plans and developments in this respect. She also encourages tribal housing authorities to institutionalize mechanisms for real community participation and transparency.

Housing discrimination based on source of income

103. The Special Rapporteur commends those districts that prohibit housing discrimination on the basis of source of income, and recommends that the U.S. enact legislation to extend this to the national level.

Such a policy would address a grave form of discrimination, as well as assist in the full utilization of the voucher programme, thus alleviating some of the difficulties in finding landlords who will accept vouchers.

Discriminatory criteria for access to subsidized housing

104. The Special Rapporteur recommends that the U.S. federally prohibit the use of criteria such as drug tests and criminal records, for gaining access to subsidized housing.

Participation

105. Residents of public housing should have direct, active and effective participation in the planning and decision-making process affecting their access to housing. Residents should be seen as essential partners working alongside the Government in transforming public housing.

106. The Government should create mechanisms to improve the participation of affected tenants in planning and decision-making processes. Residents' councils should be directly elected by residents and not appointed by housing agencies.

107. Public-private partnerships undertaking housing developments should include residents at all stages of planning, implementation, and decision-making.

Ratification of international treaties

108. The Special Rapporteur strongly encourages the U.S. Government to ratify the International Covenant on Economic, Social and Cultural Rights.

[Footnotes omitted]

Document (Excerpted):

UNITED NATIONS	A/HRC/11/36/Add.3
General Assembly	Distr.
HUMAN RIGHTS COUNCIL	GENERAL
Eleventh session	28 April 2009
Agenda item 9	Original: ENGLISH

RACISM, RACIAL DISCRIMINATION, XENOPHOBIA AND RELATED FORMS OF INTOLERANCE, FOLLOW-UP TO AND IMPLEMENTATION OF THE DURBAN DECLARATION AND PROGRAMME OF ACTION

Report of the Special Rapporteur on contemporary forms of racism, racial discrimination, xenophobia and related intolerance, Doudou Diène*

Addendum

MISSION TO THE UNITED STATES OF AMERICA**

Summary

At the invitation of the Government, the Special Rapporteur visited the United States of America from 19 May to 6 June 2008. During the mission, the Special Rapporteur visited Washington, D.C., New York, Chicago, Omaha, Los Angeles, New Orleans and the Louisiana and Mississippi Gulf Coast, Miami and San Juan (Puerto Rico).

The Special Rapporteur had extensive meetings with state institutions, including the Supreme Court, civil society organizations active in the field of racism, minority communities and victims of racism.

The Special Rapporteur formulates several recommendations, including that:

(a) Congress establish a bipartisan commission to evaluate the progress and failures in the fight against racism and the ongoing process of resegregation, particularly in housing and education, and to find responses to check these trends;

(b) The Government reassess existing legislation on racism, racial discrimination, xenophobia and related intolerance in view of two main guidelines: addressing the overlapping nature of poverty and race or ethnicity; and linking the fight against racism to the construction of a democratic, egalitarian and inter-active multiculturalism, in order to strengthen inter-community relations;

(c) The Government should intensify its efforts to enforce federal civil rights laws;

(d) The Government clarify to law enforcement officials the obligation of equal treatment and, in particular, the prohibition of racial profiling.

Annex
REPORT SUBMITTED BY THE SPECIAL RAPPORTEUR ON CONTEMPORARY FORMS OF RACISM, RACIAL DISCRIMINATION, XENOPHOBIA AND RELATED INTOLERANCE, DOUDOU DIÈNE, ON HIS MISSION TO THE UNITED STATES OF AMERICA
(19 May–6 June 2008)

[Contents omitted]

Introduction

1. At the invitation of the Government, the Special Rapporteur visited the United States of America from 19 May to 6 June 2008 ((Washington, D.C., New York, Chicago, Omaha, Los Angeles, New Orleans and the Louisiana and Mississippi Gulf Coast, Miami and San Juan, Puerto Rico). He held extensive meetings with federal authorities at the executive, legislative and judicial branches as well as with local authorities (see appendix).

2. Apart from the agenda with state institutions, including the Supreme Court, the Special Rapporteur also had extensive meetings with civil society organizations active in the area of racism and xenophobia, minority communities as well as victims of racism and racial discrimination.

3. The Special Rapporteur wishes to express his gratitude to the Government of the U.S. for its full cooperation and openness throughout the visit as well as a particular appreciation to Justice Stephen Breyer at the Supreme Court. He also wishes to express his sincere thanks to all civil society organizations that actively participated and contributed to the success of his mission. In particular, he wishes to thank Global Rights for its support throughout the mission.

I. GENERAL BACKGROUND

A. Historical and political context

4. The first inhabitants of North America are believed to have arrived crossing from the Bering Strait towards the end of the last Ice Age. Before the advent of European explorers in the late 15th century, a population of one to two million people is believed to have populated North America. Epidemic diseases brought by the Europeans and violence obliterated many Native American peoples.

5. The United States of America became an independent State after the American Revolutionary War (1775–1783). The three documents that emerged from independence—the Declaration of Independence (1776), the U.S. Constitution (1787) and the Bill of Rights (1791)—are among the first formal legally-binding documents recognizing inalienable individual rights such as freedom of religion, freedom of expression and freedom of assembly.

6. The contradictions between the agrarian and slave-based South and the manufacturing, liberalizing and generally anti-slavery North exploded when the Republican candidate, Abraham Lincoln, won the 1860 presidential election. By that time, 4 million slaves and 488,000 free blacks lived in the U.S. alongside 27 million whites. While the American Civil War (1861–1865) brought about the legal end of slavery and the adoption of the fourteenth amendment to the Constitution, including the equal protection clause, differential treatment to blacks living in the South would continue well into the twentieth century. Jim Crow laws were enacted in many States, legitimated by the "separate but equal" doctrine legitimated by the Supreme Court in *Plessy v Ferguson*.

7. The "separate but equal" doctrine remained until the emergence of the civil rights movement in the mid-twentieth century. Though the starting point of the movement is difficult to trace, the landmark decision by the Supreme Court on *Brown v Board of Education* in 1954, striking down racial segregation in schools, certainly had a fundamental impact in unleashing the changes that took place in subsequent years. The movement culminated in the adoption of the Civil Rights Act of 1964, a milestone document that set the institutional framework for the protection of human rights in contemporary United States of America.

B. Demographic, ethnic and religious composition

8. According to the U.S. Census Bureau, in 2006 the U.S. had a population of around 299 million, composed as follows: 73.9 percent white, 12.4 percent black or African American, 4.4 percent Asian, 0.8 percent American Indian and Alaska Native, 0.1 percent Native Hawaiian and other Pacific Islander, 6.3 percent of other races and 2 percent of people with two or more races. The U.S. Census Bureau correctly does not define Hispanic or Latinos as a race, as individuals of South and Central American origin may be of any race. In 2006 Hispanics or Latinos composed 14.8 percent of the population.

9. In 2007, the foreign-born population in the U.S. (those not U.S. citizens or U.S. nationals at birth) amounted to approximately 38 million people, or 12.6 percent of the total population. 42.5 percent of those foreign born residents were naturalized citizens. Out of the foreign born population, 47.5 percent are Hispanics, 23.4 percent are Asians, 20.3 percent are non-Hispanic whites and 7.8 percent are blacks.

C. International human rights instruments

10. The U.S. is party to the International Covenant on Civil and Political Rights(ICCPR), the International Convention on the Elimination of All Forms of Racial Discrimination (ICERD) and other international human rights instruments. With respect to both the ICCPR and the ICERD, the U.S. has adopted a number of formal reservations, understandings and declarations. In the case of ICERD, with respect to Articles 4 and 7, and in the case of ICCPR, with respect to Article 20, the U.S. has taken treaty reservations to these provisions, explaining that their scope is at odds with the extensive protections contained in the U.S. Constitution and U.S. laws in the areas of individual freedom of speech, expression and association.

D. Methodology

11. The Special Rapporteur carried out extensive meetings with authorities at the executive, legislative and judiciary branches to collect their views and opinions as well as information concerning government programmes, legislation and judicial decisions. Additionally, an agenda with civil society organizations, communities and associations representing minority groups, victims of discrimination, journalists and student leaders was organized.

12. The Special Rapporteur structured his meetings around three questions: (i) Is there still racism, racial discrimination, xenophobia and related intolerance in the U.S.? (ii) If so, who are their main victims and what are their main manifestations and expressions? (iii) What are or should be the govern- mental policies and programmes to fight these phenomena at the political, legal and cultural levels?

II. LEGAL FRAMEWORK

13. The fourteenth amendment of the Constitution, adopted on the aftermath of the Civil War, contains an Equal Protection Clause that formally recognizes the principle of equality before the law. It provides that "[No State shall] *deny to any person within its jurisdiction the equal protection of the laws*". The fifteenth amendment, ratified on 3 February 1870, further extends the right to vote to all races.

14. The civil rights movement in the 1960s led to the signature by President Lyndon B. Johnson of the Civil Rights Act in 1964. The Act constitutes a historic landmark in the elimination of *de jure* racial discrimination in the country and to set up the institutional and legal structure to combat discrimination. The Act also set up the Commission on Civil Rights, which was mandated to inter alia investigate denials of the right to vote, study and collect information concerning legal developments constituting a denial of equal protection of the laws under the Constitution and appraise the laws and policies of the Federal Government in thisregard. The Act was further complemented by the Civil Rights Act of 1968, which prohibited discrimination in the sale, rental, and financing of housing.

15. The enforcement of non-discrimination provisions of the Constitution and federal legislation is primarily carried out by the Civil Rights Division at the Department of Justice, which is composed of over 700 staff. The Civil Rights Division carries out enforcement actions in areas that include criminal cases, disability rights, education, employment, housing and voting. Other Federal agencies are also involved in the enforcement of equal protection legislation, such as the Equal Employment Opportunity Commission and the Office of Fai Housing and Equal Opportunity at the Department of Housing and Urban Development.

III. PUBLIC POLICIES AND MEASURES TO FIGHT RACISM, RACIAL DISCRIMINATION, XENOPHOBIA AND RELATED INTOLERANCE

A. Law enforcement

16. Law enforcement in the U.S. involves agencies at the federal, state and local levels. While the Special Rapporteur met with several officials at the local level, his analysis is based primarily on agencies, and policies developed, at the Federal level.

17. Racial discrimination by law enforcement agencies is prohibited by the Constitution and federal statutes. These include the Violent Crime Control and Law Enforcement Act of 1994and the Omnibus Crime Control and Safe Streets Act of 1968. Officials at the Civil Rights Division of the Department of Justice underscored the fundamental importance that it attaches to combating police misconduct, including racial discrimination by police officers, which amounts to approximately half of its Criminal Section's caseload.

18. Officials at the Civil Rights Division as well as at the Department of Homeland Security highlighted the importance of training of law enforcement officials. A Federal Law Enforcement Training Center exists since 1970 and currently provides law enforcement training to over80 Federal agencies. Particular trainings focusing on cultural awareness and relations with minority communities have also been developed.

19. In what concerns overrepresentation of minorities in the criminal justice system, it was recognized that disparities in incarceration rates exist between minorities, particularly African Americans, and whites. However, as the U.S. affirmed in its latest periodic report to the Committee on the Elimination of Racial Discrimination (CERD), the reasons for such disparities are complex and do not necessarily indicate differential treatment of persons in the criminal justice system.

Racial profiling

20. The Supreme Court has produced solid jurisprudence prohibiting racial profiling. For example, in *Wren v U.S.* (1996), the Court stated that "the Constitution prohibits selective enforcement of the law based on considerations such as race", making explicit reference to the Equal Protection Clause. In *U.S. v Armstrong* (1996), repeating *Oyler v Boles* (1962), the Court further affirmed that "the decision whether to prosecute may not be based on an unjustifiable standard such as race, religion, or other arbitrary classification".

The ruling in *U.S. v Montero-Camargo* (1996) further cautioned against the use off actors that are facially race-neutral but in effect can be discriminatorily used against minorities(e.g. searches against individuals living in "high-crime" areas that are also predominantly inhabited by minorities).

21. In June 2003, responding to a call made by President Bush in his State of the Union address in 2001, the Department of Justice issued a *Guidance Regarding the Use of Race by Federal Law Enforcement Agencies* prohibiting the use of race or ethnicity in law enforcement practices, the first time such guidelines have been issued. The guidance was formally adopted by the Department of Homeland Security in June 2004. Officials at the Civil Rights Division highlighted that the guidelines were also incorporated in the training modules that all law enforcement officials have to undergo. While officials recognized that the guidelines do not create rights that can be affirmed in court, they highlighted that racial profiling violates the equal protection clause of the Constitution, which therefore offers overarching protection against this practice.

B. Hate crimes

22. According to the U.S. Criminal Code, crimes motivated by race, color, religion or national origin can be investigated and prosecuted by federal authorities only when the crime occurs because of the victim's participation in a federally protected activity (e.g. public education, employment, etc). In cases that do not meet the latter requirement, the jurisdiction lies at the state level. Apart from federal regulations, 47 states have laws on hate crimes.

23. The number of hate crimes reported in the U.S. has decreased from 8,063 reported incidents in 2000 to 7,624 reported incidents in 2007, a fact that was highlighted by officials at the Civil Rights Division. The trend in the past two years is however the opposite, with a 6 percent increase from 2005 to 2007. In 2001, a peak of 9,730 such incidents was reached (a 20 percent increase in comparison to 2000), which the FBI Hate Crimes Statistics relates to the aftermath of 9/11. The number of yearly reported incidents fell back to its normal trend from 2002.

. . .

C. Education

26. Educational policy at the federal level is carried out by the Department of Education. An Office for Civil Rights within the Department is mandated "to ensure equal access to education and to promote educational excellence throughout the nation through vigorous enforcement of civil rights". This Office enforces several federal laws that prohibit discrimination, including Titles VI of the Civil Rights Act of 1964 (discrimination on the basis of race, color and national origin). The Office for Civil Rights enforces this law in all institutions, including elementary and secondary schools, colleges and universities that receive funds from the Department of Education.

. . .

D. Housing

28. Extensive legislation to prevent discrimination on housing and lending has been set up over the past decades. This includes the Fair Housing Act (Title VIII of the Civil Rights Act of1968), which prohibits discrimination in the sale, rental or financing of housing on the basis of race, color, religion, sex, familial status or national origin. The Act expanded the protections offered by the Civil Rights Act of 1964 (Title VI),

which prohibited discrimination in programs and activities receiving federal financial assistance but refrained from regulating private conduct in the domain of housing.

. . .

E. Employment

32. Discrimination related to employment on the basis of race, color, religion, sex, or national origin is prohibited under the Civil Rights Act of 1964 (Title VII). The enforcement of these provisions, along with other legislation prohibiting employment discrimination is conducted by the Equal Employment Opportunity Commission (EEOC). The EEOC has a total staff of some 2200 employees in 52 offices throughout the country and a budget of around US$ 330 million, which allows it to file around 80,000 charges per year. In 2007, charges related to employment discrimination based on race were 37 percent of the total whereas national origin represented 11.4 percent of all charges.

. . .

F. Measures to prevent discrimination in the aftermath of the events of 11 September 2001

36. Many officials have noted symbolic and concrete actions taken to prevent discrimination against people of Arab and Muslim descent in the aftermath of 9/11, starting with the remarks made by President Bush during a visit to the Islamic Center on 17 September 2001. These community outreach efforts were described as a best practice in the fight against terrorism by the Special Rapporteur on the promotion and protection of human rights and fundamental freedoms while countering terrorism in his report on the U.S.

37. The Special Rapporteur was briefed on the *Initiative to Combat Post 9/11 Discriminatory Backlash*, designed by the Department of Justice to combat violations of civil rights against Arab, Muslim, Sikh and South-Asian Americans. Key strategies within this programme include measures to ensure that cases of discrimination are reported and handled promptly, identifying policies that might involve bias crimes and discrimination and reaching out to affected communities to inform them of existing mechanisms. Two special positions were created at the Civil Rights Division: a Special Counsel for Post 9/11 National Origin Discrimination and a Special Counsel for Religious Discrimination.

38. Experts from the Department of Homeland Security also highlighted some initiatives developed after 9/11 to prevent discrimination against people of Arab and Muslim descent. Reference was made to the *Guidance Regarding the Use of Race by Federal Law Enforcement Agencies*, in particular its provision that "in investigating or preventing threats to national security or other catastrophic events [. . .] Federal law enforcement officers may not consider race or ethnicity except to the extent permitted by the Constitution and laws of the U.S.". The Special Rapporteur was also informed of the Traveller Redress Inquiry Program, which allows the public to clarify problems of misidentifications with individuals placed on watchlists.

G. Measures taken in the aftermath of Hurricane Katrina

39. Since the Special Rapporteur received allegations concerning possible racial bias in reconstruction efforts in the aftermath of Hurricane Katrina, he raised the issue with several Government authorities in order to collect additional information from some of the federal agencies and visited affected areas.

40. The Civil Rights Division of the Department of Justice highlighted its proactive role in the aftermath of Katrina, reflected in the launching of Operation Home Sweet Home in February 2006. While the initiative had a nationwide focus, it initially concentrated on the areas where Katrina victims were relocated, increasing the reach of its testing programme to identify cases of housing discrimination. Emphasis was also place in areas where a surge of hate crimes had occurred, as these crimes are often correlated with housing discrimination.

. . .

42. The Special Rapporteur also makes reference to the U.S. latest periodic report to CERD, which analyzed concerns about the disparate effects of Katrina on racial or ethnic minorities. In the report, the U.S. stated that "recognizing the overlap between race and poverty in the U.S., many commentators conclude nonetheless that the post-Katrina issues were the result of poverty (i.e., the inability of many of the poor to evacuate) rather than racial discrimination *per se*".

H. Immigration

43. The Special Rapporteur met with the Office of Citizenship at the U.S. Citizenship and Immigration Service (CIS), and was briefed concerning CIS's policy to reinvigorate assimilation efforts, particularly in what concerns English proficiency of migrants. Officials pointed out that they viewed assimilation of migrants

into the U.S. as a key element for integration into the labor market, the educational system and social life more broadly, but this did not imply the abandonment of cultural or religious diversity, upon which the U.S. was founded. The Special Rapporteur was informed that CIS had intensified its efforts to diminish the backlog in citizenship applications and thus respond more rapidly to applicants.

. . .

45. Immigrants are entitled to some constitutionally-protected rights regardless of their immigration status. In *Plyler v Doe*, the Supreme Court established that denying free public education to children on the basis of immigration status is unlawful. Furthermore, although the Immigration and Nationality Act protects only documented migrants from employment discrimination, unfair documentary practices and retaliation, EEOC noted several judicial decisions that prevent courts from disclosing the immigration status of plaintiffs in employment discrimination cases.

IV. VIEWS OF CIVIL SOCIETY AND COMMUNITIES CONCERNED
A. Law enforcement

46. One of the key issues mentioned by civil society was the weak record of civil rights enforcement by the Federal Government. In particular, reference was made to the limited number of cases filed by the Civil Rights Division of the Department of Justice, especially when compared to previous administrations. This has led to a growing perception of discredit by civil society organizations in the Division's commitment to enforce civil rights laws.

Racial disparities in the criminal justice system

47. The most critical issue of concern raised by civil society organizations, minority communities and victims themselves was related to racial disparities in the criminal justice system. Interlocutors pointed to an overrepresentation of individuals belonging to racial and ethnic minorities in the criminal justice system. While in mid-2007 black males constituted around 12.5 percent of the population, they comprised 38.9 percent of the number of people in U.S. prisons and jails. Black males are therefore 6.5 more likely to be incarcerated than white, non-Hispanic males. While many civil society organizations agreed that part of the explanation to these disparities is related to social factors, particularly the overlap of poverty and race, it was pointed out that racial discrimination also plays a key role in explaining this phenomenon.

48. Studies have identified racial disparities at several stages of law enforcement activities. A key example is traffic stops. A report by the Department of Justice recently found that whereas white, black and Hispanic drivers were stopped by the police at similar rates, black and Hispanic drivers were approximately 2.5 times more likely to be searched; the rate of arrests was two times higher for blacks and 50 percent higher for Hispanics; blacks were 3.5 times more and Hispanics were almost 2 times more likely to experience use of police force.[22] Another example concerns sentencing outcomes. A majority of studies show evidence of racially discriminatory sentencing; in particular, that individuals belonging to minorities tend to be disadvantaged in terms of the decision to incarcerate or not and in receiving harsher sentences than white individuals with comparable social and economic status.

49. Mandatory minimum penalties have been pointed out as an important factor that promotes racial bias. A striking example refers to mandatory minimum sentences for possession of crack and powder cocaine. These sentences establish more severe penalties for persons arrested for possessing or selling crack cocaine, 81 percent of whom are African American, than for those in possession of or selling powder cocaine, 71.8 percent of whom are white or Hispanic.

50. Civil society also pointed to evidences of racial bias in the application of the death penalty. In 2005, African Americans comprised nearly 42 percent of the number of death row inmates but only around 12 percent of the general population. The key factor that shows evidence of racial bias in the death penalty, according to many organizations, is the race of the victim. Nationwide, even though the absolute number of murders of blacks and whites is similar, some 80 percent of people on death row have been convicted of crimes against white victims. Interlocutors pointed to the critical situation in some states. In Alabama, for example, whereas 65 percent of all murders involve black victims, 80 percent of people currently awaiting execution in the state were convicted of crimes in which the victims were white.

. . .

Racial profiling

52. Civil society generally refers to two main forms of racial profiling. First, a particular form of the practice targets predominantly African-American or Hispanic minorities, generally but not exclusively in stops and searches by local and state police. Second, in the context of counterterrorism policies, racial profiling

practices have reportedly targeted primarily people of Arab, Muslim, South Asian or Middle-Eastern descent, particularly in air travel and border control.

53. Some civil society accounts point to widespread existence of racial profiling. It has been suggested that approximately 32 million people in the U.S. report having been victims of this practice. While exact numbers may be difficult to assert, it was a common recognition among virtually all interlocutors that the practice of racial profiling continues to exist. Numerous anecdotal accounts of victims of racial profiling in stop and search operations by the police were heard, including a testimony by an African American Member of Congress victim of such an incident.

. . .

55. Civil society organizations expressed criticisms regarding recent attempts to address the issue. The *Guidance Regarding the Use of Race by Federal Law Enforcement Agencies* issued by the Department of Justice was criticized, particular because it "does not cover profiling based on religion, religious appearance or national origin; does not apply to local law enforcement agencies; does not include any enforcement mechanism; does not require data collection; does not specify any punishment for federal officers who disregard it; contains a blanket exception for cases of 'threat to national security and other catastrophic events' and 'in enforcing laws and protecting the integrity of the Nations' borders'".

B. Hate crimes

56. Interlocutors highlighted that the main weakness of federal hate crimes legislation is the dual requirement that needs to be met for the Federal Government to be able to investigate and prosecute a case: bias-motivated violence and relation to a federally protected activity. In cases that do not meet these requirements, the jurisdiction lies at the state level. However, many states lack the capacity and resources to thoroughly investigate and prosecute such crimes. In this regard, a Local Law Enforcement Hate Crimes Prevention Act designed to strengthen the role of the Federal Government in the investigation and prosecution of such crimes and to expand the grounds for protection was approved in the House of Representatives and the Senate in 2007.

However, it was withdrawn after an expression by the White House that the President would veto the bill, which was seen as "unnecessary and constitutionally questionable".

57. While many interlocutors expressed concern regarding the number of hate crimes in the U.S., some NGOs highlighted that the government response has in general been morevigorous than in other countries.

C. Education

De facto school segregation

58. One of the most important decisions by the U.S. Supreme Court in the fight for racial equality was *Brown v Board of Education* prohibiting school segregation. However, interlocutors pointed out that despite the end of *de jure* segregation and positive changes, particularly in the 1960–1980 period, the trend has since been reversed. The percentage of black students in predominantly minority schools, which was 77 percent in 1968 and decreased to63 percent in 1988, had surged to 73 percent in 2005. Civil society organizations expressed concern at recent U.S. Supreme Court decisions—*Parents Involved in Community Schools v Seattle School District* and *Meredith v Jefferson County Board of Directors*—that ruled that race-conscious integration measures are unconstitutional. In the view of many NGOs, these race-conscious measures are a necessary measure to ensure racial integration and made an essential contribution to de-segregation of schools, particularly in the South.

Achievement gaps

59. Civil society representatives highlighted that while the achievement gap between students belonging to minorities and white students has narrowed in the past years, it is still in a similar level to 1990. The introduction of the No Child Left Behind Act placed high emphasis on educational performance; however, interlocutors highlighted the negative incentives created by the Act and its disproportionate effects on minority children. In particular, it was argued that the focus on standardized performance tests that penalize schools that underperform creates an incentive for schools to push out low-performing, at-risk students—a group that is composed disproportionately of minorities—in order to improve the overall school performance.

Schools as an entry point to the criminal justice system

60. Many NGOs used the metaphor of the "school to prison pipeline" to refer to the failure of the school system to educate pupils adequately, serving rather as a conduit to juvenile and criminal justice. Among the chief causes of this phenomenon, interlocutors referred to the widespread application of Zero Tolerance

Policies, which call for severe punishment for minor infractions. These measures are considered to have gone beyond reasonable policies to prevent violence in school, leading to what is considered to be an overreliance on disciplinary methods(e.g. suspensions and expulsions) and the criminalization of school misbehaviour (i.e. by referring students with non-violent behaviour to juvenile courts).

D. Housing

61. Concerns about fair housing expressed by civil society generally focus on two major issues: direct discriminatory practices and structural factors that have an impact, even if unintended, on the housing situation of minorities.

62. According to interlocutors, direct discriminatory practices in housing continue to exist. Data produced in paired testing, which allows for a comparison of treatment between whites and persons of color when they have similar qualifications, identified subtle forms of direct discrimination. This includes the practice of "steering" members of racial or ethnic groups towards neighbourhoods primarily occupied by those same groups, prohibited under the Fair Housing Act. Steering practices have generally contributed to a persistence of residential segregation. Direct discrimination has also been detected in rental and sale of houses as well as in mortgage lending, with people of colour being more likely to receive higher cost or sub prime loans than white borrowers with similar income and other characteristics.

. . .

64. A particular dimension of the housing problem highlighted by civil society lies in homelessness. The Special Rapporteur visited the Skid Row area in Los Angeles, interacting with a number of homeless persons and civil society support groups. Interlocutors highlighted the disproportionate impact of homelessness among minorities, particular African Americans, as also highlighted by the Human Rights Committee in its 2006 of the U.S. periodicreport. This problem is often reinforced by the reduction of funds for the construction of public housing. In addition, relations between law enforcement and homeless persons were also highlighted as an important problem, particularly with regard to the enforcement of minor law enforcement violations which often take a disproportionately high number of African American homeless persons to the criminal justice system.

65. The issue of residential segregation was directly observed by the Special Rapporteur, who examined the issue in-depth in his visits outside the capital. Despite some progresses in the1980–2000 period, they contributed little to change the overall static patterns of residential segregation in the country. Furthermore, civil society noted that residential segregation has a direct impact on school segregation and that the two problems should be tackled together.

E. Employment

66. Interlocutors stated that ethnic disparities in employment and, more generally, poverty levels have fundamental consequences for the overall situation of racial and ethnic minorities in the U.S. Whereas the unemployment rate for non-Hispanic whites in 2007 was 5.2 percent, it was 12.6 percent for American Indians or Alaskan Natives, 12 percent for African-Americans and 7.3 percent for Hispanics.

67. While many interlocutors pointed these disparities in unemployment level as an indication of the interplay of race and socio-economic status, concerns over forms of direct and indirect discrimination in employment were also raised. One of the issues that was raised concerns the legal remedies available to undocumented migrants (see subsection III. h). Another issue of concern regards the lack of protection for certain occupations, particularly domestic and agricultural workers, which disproportionately affect Africa-Americans and Hispanics. In some cases, these occupations may be excluded from the legal protections offered by a number of statutes, such as minimum wages, overtime pay and job safety.

. . .

F. Discrimination in the aftermath of the events of 11 September 2001

69. The Special Rapporteur met with several representatives of the Arab, Sikh, Middle Eastern and South Asian communities in the U.S. to hear their views concerning the situation after 9/11. Their common view was that their situation had deteriorated quickly in the aftermath of 9/11, particularly due to the extension of national security measures that in their view discriminate against these communities. One of the major concerns regards instances of racial profiling, particularly in airports, as well as programs such as NSEERS (see section III.A above).

70. An increase in cases of discrimination and harassment in the workplace was also reported, not only towards people of Arab or Muslim descent, but also against Sikhs. Serious concern was expressed regarding

the long delay in the processing of citizenship applications, which had been disproportionately high for individuals of Arab, Middle Eastern or South Asian descent.

71. More broadly, these organizations referred to overall negative perceptions of the American public towards Muslims. Reference was made to a recent USA Today/Gallup poll that showed that 39 percent of Americans felt at least some prejudice against Muslims and that 22 percent would not want Muslims as neighbors. While a number of organizations welcomed out reach initiatives developed by the Government in the aftermath of 9/11, they expressed the need for comprehensive actions to address issues of stereotyping and concrete policy changes in areas that have a discriminatory impact on individuals of Arab, Sikh, Middle Eastern and South Asian descent.

G. Measures taken in the aftermath of Hurricane Katrina

72. The Special Rapporteur travelled to New Orleans, as well as the Louisiana and Mississippi Gulf coast, in order to hear local civil society, community leaders and residents about their concerns in the aftermath of Katrina. In addition, he visited different neighborhoods that were severely affected by the storm, including the 9th Ward of New Orleans. He also met with the Mayor of New Orleans, with whom he discussed the reconstruction efforts and implications for minorities.

. . .

74. Interlocutors in the Gulf coast, including displaced families, argued that the Federal Government is not fulfilling its obligation to create adequate conditions for the return of the displaced, particularly in terms of housing. Serious concerns were voiced regarding the demolition of public housing and substitution by private development projects. The demolition of public housing in New Orleans was deemed to have a particularly grave impact for the African-American population, which constitutes the vast majority of public housing residents.

. . .

H. Immigration

77. The Special Rapporteur held a number of meetings with migrant workers across the country as well as civil society organizations working with migrant workers. In all of the meetings, migrant workers, particularly those who are undocumented, expressed serious concerns about their vulnerability and dire conditions.

. . .

V. ANALYSIS AND ASSESSMENT

80. Racism and racial discrimination have profoundly and lastingly marked and structured American society. The U.S. has made decisive progress in the political and legal combat against racism, through the resistance of communities of victims, the exemplary and powerful struggle of civil rights movements and the growing political confrontation of racism. However, the historical, cultural and human depth of racism still permeates all dimensions of life of American society.

81. The Special Rapporteur noted a strong awareness at all levels of government and society regarding the challenges in the fight against racism. He interprets this finding as a direct legacy of the continuous and determined struggle of the civil rights movement. In particular, he noted the recognition by authorities of the persistence of different manifestations of racism in the country and willingness to tackle this phenomenon. The Special Rapporteur considers awareness and open recognition of manifestations of racism as a precondition of any efforts to adequately tackle the problem. In particular, he commends the U.S. for the quantity and quality of information on issues related to his mandate, produced both by State institutions and civil society, and including racially- and ethnically-disaggregated data on demographic, social and cultural indicators. This information is essential for identifying trends and designing effective public policies.

82. The legacy of the civil rights movement is also reflected in the solid and comprehensive legal framework put in place in the country, particularly after the adoption of the Civil Rights Act of 1964 and extended in a variety of federal and local statutes and institutions. The Special Rapporteur would also like to note the central role played historically by the U.S. Supreme Court in the fight against racial discrimination, starting in *Brown v Board of Education* and expanded thereafter. The legal and institutional frameworks are in any State the first lines of defence against racism, not only enforcing the obligation to equal treatment, but also giving victims access to remedies and, ultimately, to justice.

83. The vitality of civil society is a third decisive element that contributes to the fight against racism. The Special Rapporteur was impressed with the quality of the work conducted by NGOs across the country, playing a key role in holding governments accountable to its obligation to enforce civil rights laws.

84. The Special Rapporteur identified a number of challenges in the fight against racism that should be addressed, both at the Federal and local levels.

85. Throughout his mission and in the analysis of documents, the Special Rapporteur was exposed to three broad types of issues: instances of direct racial discrimination; laws and policies that are *prima facie* non-discriminatory, but that have disparate effects for certain racial or ethnic groups; and problems that arise from the overlap of class, specifically poverty, and race or ethnicity.

86. Instances of direct discrimination and concrete racial bias still exist and are most pronounced with regards to law enforcement agencies. Despite the clear illegality of racial profiling under the fourteenth amendment, recent evidence shows practices that still prevail in law enforcement, such the disparity in the rate of arrests of minority and white drivers stopped by the police (see para. 52). In the educational system, evidence also shows racial bias in the type of disciplinary action given to white or minority students (see para. 64). In the justice system, evidence of racial bias in conviction rates and length of sentences of both juvenile and criminal courts exist (see paras. 50–55). In addition, programs such as NSEERS have clear ethnic or religious connotations (see para. 58). Direct discrimination was also found in many studies that used paired testing techniques, particularly in the areas of housing and employment. While these cases do not directly involve discrimination by state agents, strong enforcement of human rights is required. The Special Rapporteur notes that the right institutions are already in place to enforce existing laws, however, more robust efforts are required to increase the number of cases taken up every year, creating an important deterrent against future discrimination.

87. The Special Rapporteur also noted some laws and policies that are *prima facie* non-discriminatory but they have disparate effects for certain racial or ethnic groups. The key example of such practices is mandatory minimum sentences (see para. 53 above). While the Special Rapporteur welcomes the decision of the U.S. Sentencing Commission to revise the sentencing guidelines for crack cocaine offences, additional work needs to be done to review mandatory minimum sentences for crack cocaine, which disproportionately affect African-Americans.

88. Socio-economic indicators show that poverty and race or ethnicity continue to overlap in the U.S. In 2007, whereas 9 percent of non-Hispanic whites were below the poverty level, 24.7 percent of African-Americans, 25.3 percent of American Indian and Alaskan Native and 20.7 percent of Hispanics were in that situation. This reality is a direct legacy of the past, in particular slavery, segregation, the forcible resettlement of Native Americans, which was confronted by the U.S. during the civil rights movement. However, whereas the country managed to establish equal treatment and non-discrimination in its laws, it has yet to redress the socio-economic consequences of the historical legacy of racism. While noting some progress in this area, particularly in what concerns the representation and participation of racial and ethnic minorities in the high echelons of the political, economic and cultural arenas and the emergence of a middle class within minority groups, the Special Rapporteur underlines that much still needs to be done in this area.

89. The overlap between poverty and race in the U.S. creates structural problems that go far beyond patterns of income. Rather, it interacts with a number of mutually reinforcing factors, such as poor educational attainment, low-paying wages and inadequate housing, which create a vicious cycle of marginalization and exclusion of minorities. The over representation of minorities in inferior schools, more vulnerable neighbourhoods, the juvenile justice system and the criminal justice system are to a large extent linked to their overall socio-economic situation. At the same time, these trends also contribute to reinforce prejudices and stereotypes, such as an association of minorities to criminality or to poor educational performance.

90. The consequences of the overlap of poverty and race were clearly seen in the aftermath of Hurricane Katrina. Minorities, as the poorest segments of the population, lived in more vulnerable neighbourhoods and were more exposed to the effects of the storm. It is thus not unexpected that these groups suffered from disproportional displacement or loss of their homes. Katrina therefore illustrates the pernicious effects of socio-economic marginalization and shows the need for a robust and targeted governmental response to ensure that racial disparities are addressed.

91. The Special Rapporteur also noted that the socio-economic marginalization of racial or ethnic minorities has become more acute due to what he perceived as a slow process of *de facto* re-segregation in many areas of the American society. In particular, in his visits to metropolitan areas, he noted the striking pattern of ethnic and racial cleavages that persist and which are being reinforced by processes such as gentrification

in neighbourhoods historically inhabited by minorities. A related aspect is the process of re-segregation in public schools. Several studies have shown that the present level of segregation is similar to that of the late 1960s. These processes not only contribute to keep racial groups physically separated, but also affect the marginalization of public services in areas that are predominantly attended by minorities.

Ultimately, this creates an obstacle in the most important means of promoting equality of opportunity, which is to offer quality education for all students. In this regard, the Special Rapporteur is particularly concerned about the retraction of affirmative action policies, which make a tangible contribution to enhancing diversity and integration in schools.

92. The Special Rapporteur would like to make specific reference to the situation of Native Americans, which have been the first people to be historically discriminated in the continent. He was particularly sensitive to the statements made by the Principal Chief of the Cherokee Nation, Mr. Chad Smith, whom the Special Rapporteur met in Miami, as well as other indigenous leaders met in Omaha and Los Angeles, who highlighted the dire socio-economic conditions faced by many Native Americans and the difficulties in preserving their cultural heritage. Here calls the need for constant vigilance for the situation of Native Americans, which should be the subject of particular attention in view of the historical legacy of discrimination against them.

. . .

94. The Special Rapporteur recalls the idea that he has put forward in many of his reports concerning the need to go beyond a legal strategy that guarantees non-discrimination. While essential, the legal strategy is only the first stage in the fight against racism. A long-term strategy needs to address the root causes of the phenomenon, particularly in terms of intellectual constructs, prejudices and perceptions. To fight these manifestations, the only effective solution is to link the fight against racism to the deliberate politically conscious construction of a democratic, egalitarian and interactive multiculturalism. In his views, this is the most important problem the U.S. needs to face. A key notion in this regard is the need to promote interaction among different communities as an important means to create tolerance and mutual understanding, strengthening the social networks that hold a society together. Racial or ethnic communities in the U.S. still experience very little interaction with each other: racially- delimited neighbourhoods, schools and churches prevail. The promotion of more interaction among racial minorities is an essential step that needs to be taken to address the root causes of racism in the U.S.

95. This notion of interactions among communities is also central to understand that the problem of racism in the U.S. is not solely that between a white majority and minorities, but also occurs among minorities themselves. In particular, many minority groups have been isolated, competing for jobs and social services. Apart from enforcing civil rights laws robustly, promoting more interaction among minorities themselves is an essential step in the fight against racism in the U.S.

96. During the drafting of this report the U.S. elected President Barack Obama as its next Head of State. The Special Rapporteur would like to underscore the importance of this event in giving new visibility to minorities in the country. It further corroborates the view expressed in this report that the U.S. has made fundamental progress in the past decades in giving visibility to members of minorities in the political, economic and cultural arena. More significantly, this election is the outer reflection of the slow but profound transformation process in the deeper layers of consciousness of every citizen of the U.S. from all racial and ethnic communities, in the individual confrontation to racism in all dimensions and instances of every day life.

VI. RECOMMENDATIONS

97. Congress should establish a bipartisan Commission to evaluate the progress and failures in the fight against racism and the ongoing process of re-segregation, particularly in housing and education, and to find responses to check these trends. In this process, broad participation from civil society should be ensured.

98. The Government should reassess existing legislation on racism, racial discrimination, xenophobia and related intolerance in view of two main guidelines: addressing the overlapping nature of poverty and race or ethnicity; and linking the fight against racism to the construction of a democratic, egalitarian and interactive multiculturalism, in order to strengthen inter-community relations.

99. The Federal Government, in particular the Civil Rights Division of the Department of Justice, the Equal Employment Opportunities Commission and the Office of Fair Housing and Equal Opportunity of the Department of Housing and Urban Development should intensify their efforts to enforce federal civil rights laws in their respective domains.

100. Since the fight against racism needs to take place at the federal, state and local levels of government, the Special Rapporteur recommends that adequate consultation mechanisms be put in place for a coordinated approach at all levels of Government.

101. As a matter of urgency, the Government should clarify to law enforcement officials the obligation of equal treatment and, in particular, the prohibition of racial profiling. This process would benefit from the adoption by Congress of the End Racial Profiling Act. State Governments should also adopt comprehensive legislation prohibiting racial profiling.

102. To monitor trends regarding racial profiling and treatment of minorities by law enforcement, federal, state and local governments should collect and publicize data about police stops and searches as well as instances of police abuse. Independent oversight bodies should be established within police agencies, with real authority to investigate complaints of human rights violations in general and racism in particular. Adequate resources should also be provided to train police and other law enforcement officials.

103. Mandatory minimum sentences should be reviewed to assess disproportionate impact on racial or ethnic minorities. In particular, the different minimum sentences for crack and powder cocaine should be reassessed.

104. In order to diminish the impact of socio-economic marginalization of minorities in what concerns their access to justice, the Government should improve, including with adequate funding, the state of public defenders.

105. The Special Rapporteur recommends that complementary legislation be considered to further clarify the responsibility of law enforcement and criminal justice officials not only to protect human rights, but as key agents in the fight against racism.

106. In view of the recent recommendations by the Human Rights Committee, the Committee Against Torture and the Committee on the Elimination of RacialDiscrimination, 60 and considering that the use of life imprisonment without parole against young offenders, including children, has had a disproportionate impact for racial minorities, federal and state governments should discontinue this practice against persons under the age of eighteen at the time the offence was committed.

107. The Government should intensify funding for testing programs and "pattern and practice" investigations to assess discrimination, particularly in the areas of housing and employment. Robust enforcement actions should be taken whenever civil rights violations are found.

108. The Department of Education, in partnership with state and local agencies, should conduct an impact assessment of disciplinary measures in public schools, including the criminalization of school misbehaviour, and revisit those measures that are disproportionately affecting racial or ethnic minorities.

109. Special measures to promote the integration of students in public schools as well as to reduce the achievement gap between white and minority students should be developed, in accordance with article 2, paragraph 2, of ICERD.

110. The Federal Government and the States of Louisiana, Alabama and Mississippi should increase its assistance to the persons displaced by Hurricane Katrina, particularly in the realm of housing. The principle that "competent authorities have the primary duty and responsibility to establish conditions, as well as provide the means, which allow internally displaced persons to return voluntarily, in safety and with dignity, to their homes or places of habitual residence" should be respected.
[Footnotes omitted]

Appendix
LIST OF OFFICIAL MEETINGS
Federal level
Executive Branch
Department of State
Department of Justice (Civil Rights Division and Federal Bureau of Prisons)
Department of Homeland Security (Office of Civil Rights and Civil Liberties and U.S.
Citizenship and Immigration Services)
Department of Interior (Assistant Secretary for Indian Affairs)
Department of Labor
Department of Education
Department of Housing and Urban Development
Equal Employment Opportunity Commission

Legislative Branch
Chairman of the Committee on the Judiciary, U.S. House of Representatives
Congressional Black Caucus
Staff of the Committees on the Judiciary and on Foreign Affairs, U.S. House of
Representatives
Judiciary Branch
Justice Stephen Breyer, U.S. Supreme Court
Local level
Mr. Chad Smith, Principal Chief, Cherokee Nation
New York, NY: New York City Commission on Human Rights
Chicago, IL: Chicago Commission on Human Relations and members of the Mayor's office
Los Angeles, CA: Office of the Mayor of Los Angeles County, Commission on Human
Relations, Men's Central Jail
New Orleans, LA: Mayor C. Ray Nagin
Miami, FL: officials working in the Miami-Date County government
Puerto Rico: Ombudsman, Civil Rights Commission, Guerrero Prison

Document: Report of the Special Rapporteur on extrajudicial, summary or arbitrary executions,

UNITED NATIONS	A/HRC/11/2/Add.5
General Assembly	Distr.
HUMAN RIGHTS COUNCIL	GENERAL
Eleventh session	28 May 2009
Agenda item 3	Original: ENGLISH

PROMOTION AND PROTECTION OF ALL HUMAN RIGHTS, CIVIL, POLITICAL, ECONOMIC, SOCIAL AND CULTURAL RIGHTS, INCLUDING THE RIGHT TO DEVELOPMENT
Report of the Special Rapporteur on extrajudicial, summary or arbitrary executions, Philip Alston*
Addendum
MISSION TO THE UNITED STATES OF AMERICA**

Summary

There is a good deal to commend about the record of the United States of America on extra judicial killings: in most instances, there is no lack of laws or procedures for addressing potentially unlawful killings and, at least domestically, data are generally gathered systematically and responsibly. I found, however, three areas in which significant improvement is necessary if the Government of the U.S. is to bring its actions into line with its stated commitment to human rights and the rule of law. First, the Government must ensure that the imposition of the death penalty complies with fundamental due process requirements; the current system's flaws increase the likelihood that innocent people will be executed. Second, the Government must provide greater transparency in law enforcement, military and intelligence operations that result in potentially unlawful deaths.

Third, it must overcome the current failure of political will and ensure greater accountability for potentially unlawful deaths in its international operations; political expediency is never a permissible basis for any State to deviate from its obligation to investigate and punish violations of the right to life. It is widely acknowledged that innocent people have likely been sentenced to death and executed. Yet, in Alabama and Texas, I found a shocking lack of urgency with regard to the need to reform glaring criminal justice system flaws. Each State should undertake a systematic inquiry into its criminal justice system and ensure that the death penalty is applied fairly, justly and only for the most serious crimes. Deficiencies that should be remedied include the lack of adequate counsel for indigent defendants and racial disparities in sentencing. The system of electing judges in both States should be reconsidered, because it politicizes the death penalty and unfairly increases the likelihood of a capital sentence. Given the inadequacies of state criminal justices systems, Congress should enact legislation permitting federal court habeas review of state and federal death penalty cases on the merits.

I am also concerned that the death penalty could be imposed under the Military Commissions Act of 2006, the provisions of which violate the due process requirements of international human rights and humanitarian law. I welcome the Government's stay of commission proceedings. It should not resort to prosecutions under the Act again. Significant attention needs to be given to promoting transparency in the case of potentially unlawful killings. Domestically, although the Government does a strong job of collecting data generally, it fails to provide timely and meaningful information about deaths in immigration detention or arising out of law-enforcement activities.

Transparency failures are far more acute in the Government's international military and intelligence operations. First, the Government has failed to track and make public the number of civilian casualties or the conditions under which deaths occurred. Second, the military justice system fails to provide ordinary people, including U.S. citizens and the families of Iraqi or Afghan victims, basic information on the status of investigations into civilian casualties or prosecutions resulting therefrom. Third, the Government has refused to disclose the legal basis for targeted killings conducted through drone attacks on the territory of other States or to identify any safeguards in place to reduce collateral civilian casualties and ensure that the Government has targeted the correct person.

These transparency failures contribute to the lack of accountability for wrongful deaths. They represent a lost opportunity to learn from mistakes and apply policies and practices that reduce casualties. Unsurprisingly, they have undermined support for operations by the U.S. Such failures are remedied relatively easily, and the measures I recommend should be implemented expeditiously. All States have an obligation to effectively investigate, prosecute and punish violations of the right to life, including in situations of armed conflict. It is important, of course, to acknowledge the unique characteristics and challenges of armed conflict, including that intentional killing may be permitted. The obligation to enforce the law, however, does not change: the rule of law must be upheld in war as in peace.

Some aspects of the rule of law have been taken seriously during U.S. military operations. Thus, after visiting Afghanistan in May 2008, I noted no evidence that international forces in Afghanistan, including those of the U.S., were committing widespread intentional killings in violation of human rights or humanitarian law. In addition, the Government has implemented compensation programmes for civilian victims of U.S. military operations. While these programmes should be improved, the U.S. has shown admirable leadership in relation to compensation payments.

However, there have been chronic and deplorable accountability failures with respect to policies, practices and conduct that resulted in alleged unlawful killings, including possible war crimes, in the international operations conducted by the U.S. The Government has failed to effectively investigate and punish lower-ranking soldiers for such deaths, and has not held senior officers responsible under the doctrine of command responsibility. Worse, it has effectively created a zone of impunity for private contractors and civilian intelligence agents by failing to investigate and prosecute them.

These accountability failures arise in part from a lack of political and prosecutorial will that is utterly inconsistent with the Government's stated commitment to upholding the rule of law. The new administration's expressed desire to "move forward" from past unlawful policies and practices is understandable, but cannot be accomplished without accountability. It would set a dangerous precedent, domestically and internationally, if the Government were to bow to political pressure and fail to enforce its own laws against wrongful deaths and illegal abuse.

Although there is no substitute for prosecution of violations of the right to life, in the short term there are other steps that the Government can take towards transparency and accountability. One is the creation of a national commission of inquiry to conduct an independent, systematic and sustained investigation of policies and practices that lead to deaths and other abuses. Another is the appointment of a special prosecutor independent of the pressures on the political branches of Government. Adoption of both mechanisms would send a strong message that the U.S. is truly "moving forward".

Annex
REPORT OF THE SPECIAL RAPPORTEUR ON EXTRAJUDICIAL, SUMMARY OR ARBITRARY EXECUTIONS, PHILIP ALSTON, ON HIS MISSION TO THE UNITED STATES OF AMERICA
(16 –30 June 2008)

[Contents omitted]

I. BACKGROUND AND INTERNATIONAL LEGAL FRAMEWORK

1. I spent two weeks (16–30 June 2008) visiting the United States of America at the invitation of the Government and met with federal and state officials, judges, civil society groups, and victims and witnesses in Washington DC, New York City, Montgomery (Alabama), and Austin(Texas).

2. I am grateful to the Government of the U.S. for its cooperation and for facilitating meetings with officials from the Departments of State, Justice, Defense and Homeland Security, as well as officials in Alabama and Texas. The Government's willingness to invite me and to engage in a constructive dialogue sends an important message. I am also grateful to the representatives of civil society organizations who met with me.

3. Although the title of my mandate may seem complex, it should be simply understood as including any killing that violates international human rights or humanitarian law. This may include unlawful killings by the police, deaths in military or civilian custody, killings of civilians in armed conflict in violation of humanitarian law, and patterns of killings by private individuals which are not adequately investigated and prosecuted by the authorities. My mandate is not abolitionist, but the death penalty falls within it with regard to due process guarantees, the death penalty's limitation to the most serious crimes and its prohibition for juvenile offenders and the mentally ill.

4. The U.S. is party to the International Covenant on Civil and Political Rights, the Convention against Torture and the Geneva Conventions of 1949. Like all parties to armed conflicts, the U.S. is also bound by customary and conventional international humanitarian law.

II. DOMESTIC ISSUES

A. The death penalty: the risk of executing the innocent

5. In the U.S., 35 states, the federal Government and the U.S. military provide for the death penalty. Some 3,300 people are on death row across the country, and, since 1976,1,145 people have been executed. My mission focused on the federal death penalty and the application of the death penalty in Alabama and Texas. Alabama has the highest per capita rate of executions in the U.S., while Texas has the largest total number of executions and one of the largest death row populations.

6. Since 1973, 130 death row inmates have been exonerated across the U.S. This number continues to grow. While I was in Texas, the conviction of yet another person on death row was overturned by the Court of Criminal Appeals. Although in that case DNA testing ultimately prevented the execution of an innocent man, other possible innocents have been less fortunate. In many cases, either because of inadequate laws or practices governing the preservation of evidence or because of the passage of time, there is no longer any physical evidence that can be DNA tested and potentially exonerate the inmate. In some states, legal barriers—such as a lack of a post-conviction DNA access laws—make DNA testing difficult for death row inmates to obtain. In yet other cases, biological evidence is immaterial and other evidentiary or procedural issues preclude a just or reliable basis for imposing the death penalty.

7. I met a range of officials and others who acknowledged that innocent people might have been executed. Serious flaws in the system are of obvious significance to the innocent convicted person, but also of serious concern for victims' families and the wider community, because wrongful convictions mean that true criminals remain at large.

8. At present, a great deal of time and energy is spent trying to expedite executions. A better priority would be to analyze where the criminal justice system is failing in capital cases and why innocent people are being sentenced to death. In Texas, there is at least official recognition that reforms are needed and that innocent people may have been executed. In Alabama, the situation remains highly problematic. Government officials seem strikingly indifferent to the risk of executing innocent people and have a range of standard responses to due process concerns(which are sometimes seen as "technicalities"), most of which are characterized by a refusal to engage with the facts. When I confronted them with cases in which death row inmates have been retried and acquitted, officials explained that a "not guilty" verdict does not mean the defendant was actually innocent and that most defendants "played the system" and probably were guilty. But the truth is that Alabama's capital system is simply not designed to uncover cases of innocence, however compelling they might be. Alabama may already have executed innocent people, but its officials would rather deny than confront criminal justice system flaws.

9. Given the rising number of innocent people being exonerated nationwide, both state and federal Governments need to investigate and fix the problems in their criminal justice systems. As a start, I recommend that:

(1) problems already recognized as such, including lack of judicial independence and the absence of an adequate right to counsel, should be addressed immediately;

(2) systematic review of criminal justice system flaws, including racial disparities in capital cases, should be undertaken to identify needed reforms; and

(3) federal courts should be authorized to review all substantive claims of injustice in capital cases. In light of the U.S.' international law obligations with respect to the death penalty, I also recommend that:

(4) state and federal legislatures ensure that the death penalty only be applied for the "most serious crimes"; and (5) review and reconsideration be provided to foreign nationals on death row who were denied the right to consular notification.

1. Judicial independence

10. Alabama and Texas both have partisan elections for judges. My mandate does not extend to an evaluation of how a system of multi-million dollar campaigns for judicial office comports with judicial independence requirements. But if—as research and practice show—the outcome of such a system is to jeopardize the right of capital defendants to a fair trial and appeal, there is clearly a need to consider changes. Studies reveal that in states where judges are elected there is a direct correlation between the level of public support for the death penalty and judges' willingness to impose or uphold death sentences. There is no such correlation in non-elective states. In particular, research shows that, in order to attract votes or campaign funds, judges are more likely to impose or refuse to reverse death sentences when: elections are nearing; elections are tightly contested; pro-capital punishment interest organizations are active within a district or state; and judges have electoral experience.

11. The goal of an independent judiciary is to ensure that justice is done in individual cases according to law. Too often, though, under judicial electoral systems, the death penalty is treated as a political rather than a legal matter. The significant impact of judicial electoral systems on capital punishment cases was recognized by many with whom I spoke. They strongly suggested that judges in both Texas and Alabama consider themselves to be under popular pressure to impose and uphold death sentences and that decisions to the contrary would lead to electoral defeat. Numerous government officials in both states openly stated that it was not possible to speak out against the death penalty and hope to get re-elected.

12. In Alabama, the problem of politicizing death sentences is heightened because state law permits judges to "override" the jury's opinion in sentencing. Thus, even if a jury unanimously decides to sentence a defendant to life in prison, the judge can instead impose a death sentence. When judges override jury decisions, it is nearly always to increase the sentence to death rather than to decrease it to life—90% of overrides imposed the death penalty. And a significant proportion of those on death row would not be there if jury verdicts had been respected. Over 20% of those currently on death row were given the death sentence by a judge overruling a jury decision for life without parole. According to one study, judicial overrides are twice as common in the year before a judge seeks re-election than in other years. In light of concerns about possible innocence and the irreversible nature of the death penalty, Alabama should relieve judges of the invidious influence of politics by repealing the law permitting judicial override.

2. Right to counsel

13. One of the most fundamental rights Governments must provide criminal defendants is the right to counsel, which helps ensure defendants receive fair trials. But the right is empty, and reliable and just trial outcomes are threatened, if the quality of counsel is poor. In both Alabama and Texas, a surprisingly broad range of people in and out of government acknowledged that existing programs for providing criminal defense counsel to indigent defendants are inadequate.

14. Neither state has a statewide public defender system. Instead, individual counties in each state determine how counsel for the indigent will be appointed, with most opting for court-appointed counsel. One effect of such a system is that defense counsel are less likely to be independent. Counsel must appear before the same judges for their appointed death penalty cases as for the rest of their legal practice. Not surprisingly, this can create structural disincentives for vigorous capital defense. Such structural problems are compounded by inadequate compensation for counsel. Until 1998, court-appointed counsel in Alabama could only be compensated up to $1,000 per phase of the case. A significant proportion of current death row inmates were convicted during the time that cap was in place. Although hourly caps were subsequently enacted, they bear similarly little relation to the true costs of effectively defending a death penalty case.

15. Failure to provide an adequately-funded state-wide public defender has the predictable result of poor legal representation for defendants in capital cases. In Texas, one well-informed Government official referred

to the overall quality of appointed defense counsel as "abysmal." In Alabama, I read appellate legal briefs, submitted on behalf of defendants on death row, that barely reached ten pages, did not request oral argument, or were largely a bare restatement of the facts. Cost concerns also limit the extent to which qualified experts can or will be retained for thedefense.

16. For there to be a meaningful right to counsel, major reforms are required. A positive first step is the system recently established in West Texas—a pilot multi-county public defender to provide capital defense in 85 counties. This project is an exception, however, and in both and Alabama, state officials are considering half-measures they perceive to be money-saving, instead of the necessary establishment of state-wide, well-funded, independent public defender services.

3. Racial disparities

17. Studies from across the country show racial disparities in the application of the deathpenalty. The weight of the scholarship suggests that the death penalty is more likely to be imposed when the victim is white, and/or the defendant is African American.

18. When I raised racial disparity concerns with federal and state Government officials, I was met with indifference or flat denial. Some officials had not read any specific reports or studies on race disparity and showed little concern for the issue. Others conceded racial disparity exists, but invoked a handful of studies suggesting the cause was not racial bias. Thus, I was told that the overrepresentation of African Americans among those sentenced to death as opposed to life without parole was related to racial disparities in criminality, or to the overrepresentation of African Americans in the prison population generally. Many officials dismissed the results of studies showing racial disparity as biased, claiming they were written by researchers with anti-death penalty views. Some dismissed the results of studies but then admitted that they had not carefully looked at them.

These responses are highly disappointing. They suggest a damaging unwillingness to confront the role that race can play in the criminal justice system generally, and in the imposition of the death penalty specifically. Given the stakes, both state and federal Governments need to systematically review and respond to concerns about continuing racial disparities.

4. Systematic evaluation of the criminal justice system

19. There is a clear onus on states to systematically evaluate the workings of their criminal justice systems to ensure that the death penalty is not imposed unjustly. In Texas, the Court of Criminal Appeals recently set up a Criminal Justice Integrity Unit to examine wrongful conviction issues. This is a positive development, but much more is needed. An appropriate approach would be for the Texas legislature to establish, as some have proposed, an Innocence Commission designed to assess systematically why people have been wrongly convicted and then to apply those lessons with recommendations for criminal justice system reform.

20. Alabama could draw on the in-depth analysis of its system produced by the American Bar Association (ABA). While various state officials dismissed the ABA as biased, they generally acknowledged that those who conducted the study were serious lawyers. In any event, none of the officials with whom I spoke had undertaken a thorough analysis of the report. Given the seriousness of the problems identified, and officials' reluctance to undertake any alternative in-depth study, it is incumbent upon the authorities to formally respond to the ABA's findings and recommendations. Alabama officials could indicate the seriousness of their concern about alleged injustices if they gave reasons for accepting or rejecting the ABA's specific recommendations.

5. Federal habeas corpus review

21. A capital defendant convicted by a state court can (after exhausting state habeas corpus review) bring a habeas corpus suit in federal court to challenge the conviction. But federal courts' role in reviewing state-imposed death sentences has been curtailed by legislation designed to "expedite" such cases. The Antiterrorism and Effective Death Penalty Act of 1996 (AEDPA) prevents federal habeas review of many issues, imposes a six-month statute of limitation for inmates seeking to file federal habeas claims, and restricts access to an evidentiary hearing at the federal level. As initially enacted, AEDPA permitted states to opt in to federal review of death penalty cases if the state provided counsel for indigent death row inmates in post-conviction cases. But federal courts, which were originally responsible for determining whether states qualified for expedited review, found that few states met statutory requirements for proper provision of counsel. (Texas was among those states denied qualification.) The appropriate response to the federal courts' findings would have been to improve state indigent defense systems. Instead, Congress amended the law to permit the Department of Justice (DOJ) to issue regulations under which DOJ, rather than the courts,

would certify state indigent defensesystems. The regulations that came into effect on 12 January 2009 are grossly inadequate. They do not specify: the level of competency that must be exhibited by state appointed counsel; the amount of litigation expenses that counsel must be provided with; or that counsel must receive reasonable or adequate compensation. Such matters are left to the discretion of the states, thus effectively eviscerating both the federal oversight function and incentives for states to improve indigent defense. These regulations should be amended or repealed.

22. When I asked one official with responsibility for handling federal habeas cases about the impact of AEDPA, I was told that although the restrictive legislation may prevent some meritorious claims from being raised, rules were necessary to enforce finality. I agree that finality is important in criminal cases, and that it serves important purposes both for victims and the system as a whole. But presently, too much weight is given to finality and too little to the due process rights of the accused and to the Government's obligation to ensure that innocent people are not executed. Given the serious concerns about the fairness of state-level trials and appeals, the federal writ of habeas corpus plays a critical role in capital cases. Congress should investigate whether state criminal justice systems fail to protect constitutional rights in capital cases, and also enact legislation permitting federal courts to review *de novo* all merits issues in death penalty cases, with appropriate exceptions, such as where a defendant attempts deliberately to bypass state court procedures.

6. Most serious crimes

23. States that retain the death penalty may only permit capital punishment for the "most serious crimes." Under international law, this means crimes requiring an intention to kill that results in the loss of life. However, several U.S. jurisdictions allow the death penalty for lesser crimes. For example, the Federal Death Penalty Act of 1994 permits the death penalty for crimes such as the running of large-scale drug enterprises. During my mission, there was an encouraging development when the U.S. Supreme Court decided in *Kennedy v Louisiana* that the death penalty could not be imposed for the crime of rape of a child where death did not result. The Court's decision brings U.S. law further in line with international human rights law. Federal and state Governments should amend the remaining laws permitting capital punishment to conform to international law.

7. Consular notification

24. Of particular importance in Texas are the cases in which foreign nationals have been sentenced to death without the opportunity to contact their national consulates for assistance as required by the Vienna Convention on Consular Relations (VCCR), to which the U.S. has been a party since 1969. In 2008, Texas executed two Mexican nationals who had not been notified of their consular rights. Of the remaining 25 foreign nationals on Texas's death row, 14 (twelve Mexicans, one Honduran and one Argentinean) were not informed of their consular rights at the appropriate time.

25. The federal Government has acknowledged that it has a legal obligation to provide review and reconsideration of the cases of Mexican nationals on death row who were not notified of their consular rights. Review is necessary to determine whether any of these individuals was prejudiced by the lack of consular notification. But the Texas Legislature has failed to authorize state courts to provide this review, and the U.S. Congress has similarly failed to authorize federal courts to do so. The very simplicity of the available solutions makes it all the more disturbing that nothing has been done.

26. Texas officials told me their refusal to provide review was supported by the U.S. Supreme Court's decision, in *Medellin v Texas*, that the federal Government could not force Texas to abide by the U.S.' international legal obligations. As one senior Texas official noted, it is not a popular notion in Texas to be seen to be "submitting" to the International Court of Justice. But it is a bedrock principle of international law that when a country takes on international legal obligations, those obligations bind the entire state apparatus, whether or not it is organized as a federal system. There are many federal systems around the world, and they have all devised means to ensure that treaties, whether dealing with trade, investment, diplomatic immunities, or human rights, bind the entire state, including its constituent parts. Nor is it "submission" to respect the treaty rights and obligations by which the U.S. voluntarily agreed to abide—and from which American citizens have benefitted for nearly 40 years.

Consular rights protection not only affects foreign nationals currently on death row in Texas, it applies equally to any American who travels to another country.

27. Texas's refusal to provide review of the foreign nationals' cases undermines the U.S.' role in the international system, and threatens nation States' reciprocity with respect to the rights of each others' nationals. If Texas opts to put the U.S. in breach of its international legal obligations, Congress must act to ensure compliance at the federal level.

B. Deaths in immigration detention

28. In June 2008, the Government acknowledged there had been at least 74 deaths in immigration deten-tion facilities since 2003. Subsequent newspaper reports indicate a significantly higher number. I received credible reports from various sources that deaths were due to: denial of necessary medical care; inadequate or delayed care; and provision of inappropriate medication.

29. Immigration detention facilities, managed by Immigration and Customs Enforcement (ICE), an arm of the Department of Homeland Security (DHS), hold immigrants with ongoing immigration legal proceed-ings, or awaiting removal from the U.S. ICE's Office of Detention and Removal Operations (DRO) carries out the detention function. The standards of detention at each of these facilities are set by ICE's National Detention Standards, which include general medical care provisions. The details of the medical care to be provided to detainees are in ICE's Division of Immigration Health Services (DIHS) Medical Dental Detainee Covered Services Package. The package states that it primarily covers emergency care, and other care is generally excluded unless it is judged necessary for the detainee to remain healthy enough for deportation. Specialty care and testing believed necessary by the detainee's on-site doctor must be pre-approved by DIHS in Washington, DC. Reliable reports indicate that DIHS often applies an unduly restrictive interpretation in determining the provision of medical care. Officials at various detention centers have themselves reported difficulties in getting approval for medical care. In defense, DIHS and DRO explained that truly urgent care is provided at the discretion of medical personnel at each detention center without the need for prior autho-rization. However, the care provider will not be reimbursed unless subsequent DIHS authorization is given. Denials of such requests have a chilling effect on medical personnel's subsequent decisions about proceeding without authorization.

30. The ICE standards are merely internal guidelines rather than legally-enforceable regulations. This has insulated ICE policies from the external oversight provided by the normal regulatory process and limits the legal remedies available to detainees when the medical care provided is deficient. DHS should promul-gate legally enforceable administrative regulations and these should be consistent with international stan-dards on the provision of medical care in detention facilities.

31. With respect to detention center conditions, I met with the DHS IG, whose office has prepared some valuable reports. A report on deaths in immigration detention was released shortly after my visit, and made important recommendations, but it reviewed only two deaths in detail. And the accountability system is incomplete by virtue of the fact that internal and external accountability functions are more or less com-bined. The law enforcement officers who investigate abuses by DHS personnel themselves report to the IG. Existing IG peer review arrangements appear to be an unlikely check on the performance of the IG in rela-tion to sensitive and problematic cases.

32. ICE has no legal reporting requirements when a death occurs in ICE custody. The result has been a clear failure of transparency. Both civil society groups and Congressional staff members told me that for years they were unable to obtain any information at all on the numbers of deaths in ICE custody. ICE's recent public reporting of numbers, and its voluntary undertaking to report future deaths, are encouraging, but insuf-ficient. ICE should be required to promptly and publicly report all deaths in custody, and each of these deaths should be fully investigated.

C. Killings by law-enforcement officials

33. Data on deaths in custody in federal and state prisons and jails are compiled by the Bureau of Justice Statistics (BJS) of the Department of Justice (DOJ).

34. Generally, police killings are investigated by a police department's internal affairs unit and prosecuted by the local district attorney. However, in cases involving the "willful" violation of constitutional rights, the Federal Bureau of Investigations (FBI) may investigate, and the Civil Rights Division of the federal Department of Justice may prosecute. Statistics on the total number of prosecutions and convictions in such cases are not avail-able, but it is clear that the number of prosecutions is small and the number of convictions smaller still. Because there are no statistics on killings that involved the use of excessive force, it is difficult to evaluate whether the low conviction rate reflects impunity for abuse or whether the use of lethal force is limited and disciplined.

35. Two measures that would improve transparency and analysis are: (1) enhanced use of technology to record police conduct, and (2) adapting existing data collection efforts to be more comprehensive and to play an "early warning" and "hot spot identification" role for unlawful killings by law enforcement officers.

36. Both prosecutors and plaintiffs' counsel emphasized the importance of increased use of video and audio recording equipment in police cars, jails, and prisons. These recordings have helped build cases that

would otherwise be impossible to prove. At the same time, the presence of recording equipment deters many law enforcement officers from using excessive force. The primary limits to the effectiveness of recording are that it is not sufficiently widespread and that tapes too often "disappear." Additional federal funding and incentives would address the first problem. Measures to safeguard tapes include: increasing the penalties for tape destruction; establishing a presumption in civil litigation that the destruction of a tape indicates liability; and, making it technically impossible for individual officers to access the tapes.

37. Data collection by the Government on deaths related to law enforcement activities serves to create an historical record that is useful, *inter alia*, in assessing long-term trends. It is quite unhelpful, however, in providing "early warning" of emerging problems, whether at the national level or in particular jurisdictions. Indeed, most of the available statistics are three years out of date. Officials explained that one cause of delay is the need to obtain local medical examiners certificates on the cause of death in each case. While such efforts are commendable, and the resulting impulse to delay the release of data understandable, BJS should consider adopting "justifiable homicides" as compiled by the FBI. These data are likely to be undercounts because three states and the federal Government did not report to BJS, and the law enforcement agencies concerned were often the principal sources of information.

III. INTERNATIONAL OPERATIONS

A. Death penalty under the Military Commissions Act

38. Five men detained at the U.S. Naval Station at Guantánamo Bay, Cuba, have been charged with capital offences under the Military Commissions Act (MCA) and a number of other Guantánamo detainees face charges that may carry the death penalty. I welcome the President's decision to seek a stay of all commission proceedings and to order a review of whether, and in what forum, individual detainees may be prosecuted. Such steps send a strong signal that the U.S. is restoring its commitment to the rule of law in its treatment, detention and prosecution of Guantánamo detainees. However, the President's order appears to leave open the possibility that detainees may still be prosecuted—and subjected to the death penalty—under the MCA. Any such prosecution would be a violation of the U.S.' obligations under international human rights and humanitarian law because the MCA does not comport with fundamental fair trial principles.

39. The U.S. has an obligation under international law to provide detainees with fair trials that afford all essential judicial guarantees. No State may derogate from this obligation, regardless of whether persons are to be tried for crimes allegedly committed during peace or armed conflict . . .

. . .

41. The MCA's provisions constitute a gross infringement on the right to a fair trial and it would violate international law to execute someone under this statute.

B. Detainee deaths at Guantánamo

42. Of the five reported deaths of detainees in U.S. custody at Guantánamo, four were classified by Government officials as suicides, and one was attributed to cancer. In the custodial environment, a state has a heightened duty to ensure and respect the right to life. Thus, there is a rebuttable presumption of state responsibility—whether through acts of commission or omission - for custodial deaths. The state must affirmatively show that it lacks responsibility to avoid this inference, and has an obligation to investigate and publicly report its findings and the evidence supporting them. But until forced to do so through Freedom of Information Act lawsuits, the Department of Defense (DOD) provided little public information MCA, section 3, amending Subtitle A of Title 10 U.S.C. §949d(f) and Title 10 U.S.C. §949d(b)(2)(B). Classified information can be privileged from disclosure. Also see §949j(c). Such secrecy impedes the defense's ability to answer accusations, and particularly inhibits the accused's ability to investigate whether specific evidence was acquired through torture or other coercion.

C. Lack of transparency regarding civilian casualties

1. Military

43. DOD officials confirmed to me that the military does not systematically compile statistics on civilian casualties in its operations in Afghanistan or Iraq. The purported reason is that "body counts" are not relevant to evaluating the effectiveness or legality of military operations. It is true that a simple "body count" may not on its own be useful. However, systematically tracking how different kinds of operations result in different levels of civilian casualties is critical if the U.S. is serious about minimizing casualties. Indeed, the Government's own experience shows why this is so. Despite the general policy against tracking civilian casualties, in Iraq the military reportedly tracked checkpoint deaths when soldiers fire at civilians they believe, sometimes mistakenly, to be suicide bombers or other attackers. I understand these monitoring efforts resulted in procedural changes that saved lives. This kind of effort to track, analyze, and learn from the consequences

of military operations should be routine, not exceptional. The numbers and trends should be reported publicly to strengthen external accountability.

44. The challenges of compiling statistics on civilian casualties during military operations are undeniable. The lack of secure access to incident sites, especially those of aerial bombardments, can make it difficult to determine the number of persons killed, much less the proportion that were civilians. Thus, the DOD has noted that, while information on civilian casualties is included in significant activity (SIGACT) reports, this information is not necessarily accurate. But the solution is not to avoid compiling civilian casualty statistics altogether but to eschew simple counts in favor of releasing information that continually and systematically presents ranges and estimates with the necessary qualifications.

45. In relation to deaths in military custody, operational difficulties cannot be used to justify a failure to compile statistics. Making the numbers and causes of such deaths public is part of the U.S.' obligation to exercise diligence, to prevent deaths of prisoners in its custody, and to investigate and prosecute any illegal conduct.

2. Private contractors

46. There have been numerous and credible accounts of private security and other contractors(PCs) engaging in a pattern of indiscriminate or otherwise questionable use of force against civilians. At least in Iraq, that use of force has resulted in a significant number of casualties, conservatively estimated to be in the hundreds, perhaps thousands. Yet the failures of reporting and transparency by PCs employed by various Government military and civilian agencies are even more dramatic than those for the military. For example, in Iraq, the DOD established Reconstruction Operating Councils (ROCs), administered by a private security contractor, to provide coordination between the military and security contractors. While in theory DOD contractors report casualties and use of force in serious incident reports (SIRs) to the ROCs, doing so has not been compulsory for all contractors. The most comprehensive study to date found that few firms ever report shooting incidents, that such incidents are often misreported, and that SIRs that are filed are almost uniformly cursory and uninformative.

3. Civilian intelligence agencies

47. There are credible reports of at least five custodial deaths caused by torture or other coercion in which the Central Intelligence Agency (CIA) has been implicated.[73] Although the page 24role of the CIA in these wrongful deaths has reportedly been investigated (and in one instance, a CIA contractor prosecuted), no investigation has ever been released and alleged CIA involvement has never been publicly confirmed or denied. The CIA Inspector General told me that the number of cases involving possibly unlawful killings referred by the CIA to the DOJ is classified.

D. Transparency and accountability for unlawful killings and custodial deaths

48. As discussed above, the Government's failure to track civilian casualties in Iraq and Afghanistan means a lost opportunity to analyze causes and the lost possibility of reducing those deaths. Similarly, a failure to undertake transparent and effective investigations into, and meaningful prosecution of, wrongful deaths means the Government cannot fulfill its obligation to ensure accountability for violations of the right to life.

1. Military justice system failures

(a) Lack of transparency

49. During my visit to Afghanistan, I saw first hand how the opacity of the military justice system reduces confidence in the Government's commitment to public accountability for illegalconduct. It is remarkably difficult for the U.S. public, victims' families, or even commanders to obtain up-to-date information on the status of cases, the schedule of upcoming hearings, or even judgments and pleadings. This lack of transparency is, in part, a side-effect of the decentralized character of the system, in which commanders around the world are given the authority to conduct preliminary investigations and act as "convening authorities" to initiate courts-martial.

50. This problem can be solved relatively quickly and easily. Each service, for example, is required by law to maintain a Court-Martial Management Information System for records of general and special courts-martial. A centralized system for reporting and providing public information about all courts-martial and non-judicial proceedings relating to civilian casualties could be added to the existing system, and this would markedly improve accountability and reduce the sense among Afghan and Iraqi civilians, and others around the world, that U.S. forces operate with impunity.

(b) Lack of effective investigation and prosecution

51. While the U.S. military justice system has achieved a number of convictions for unlawful killings in Afghanistan and Iraq, numerous other cases have either been inadequately investigated or senior officers have

used administrative (non-judicial) proceedings instead of criminal prosecutions. In cases in which criminal convictions were obtained, some sentences appear too light for the crime committed, and senior officers have not been held to account for the wrongful conduct of their subordinates.

52. The legal obligation to effectively punish violations is as vital to the rule of law in war as in peace. It is thus alarming when States either fail to investigate or permit lenient punishment of crimes committed against civilians and combatants. The legal duty to investigate and punish violations of the right to life is not a formality. Effective investigation and prosecution vindicates the rights of the victims and prevents impunity for the perpetrators. Yet, based on the military's own documents, one study of almost 100 detainee deaths in U.S. custody between August 2002 and February 2006 found that investigations were fundamentally flawed, often violated the military's own regulations for investigations, and resulted in impunity and a lack of transparency into the policies and practices that may have contributed to the deaths.

53. States must punish individuals responsible for violations of law in a manner commensurate with the gravity of their crimes. I raised this issue with the Government in relation to the January 2006 sentencing of Chief Warrant Officer Lewis E. Welshofer Jr. to two months confinement to his base, a fine of $6,000, and a letter of reprimand after being found guilty of negligent homicide and negligent dereliction of duty for the death of Major General Abed Hamed Mowhoush, an Iraqi general who had turned himself in to military authorities. I have received no response.

54. I also received no response to my request for data on sentences imposed for particular offences. But military records released in Freedom of Information Act litigation make clear that the Welshofer sentence is not an anomaly. Data compiled by journalists also reinforce the perception that sentences have not consistently been proportionate to the offence committed.

According to a review of cases in Iraq between June 2003 and February 2006 conducted by the Washington Post, 39 service members were formally accused in connection with the deaths of 20 Iraqis, but only 24 were charged with murder, negligent homicide or manslaughter, of whom only 12 ultimately served prison time (with sentences ranging from 45 days to 25 years), 3 were convicted with no confinement, 1 was acquitted, charges against two others were dropped, and 6 received administrative, non-judicial punishments.

55. It is noteworthy that "command responsibility," a basis for criminal liability recognized since the trials after World War II, is absent both from the Uniform Code of Military Justice (UCMJ) and the War Crimes Act. It appears that no U.S. officer above the rank of major has ever been prosecuted for the wrongful actions of the personnel under his or her command.

Instead, in some instances, commanders have exercised their discretion to lessen the punishment of subordinates for wrongful conduct that resulted in a custodial death. Such failures of accountability undermine the importance of hierarchy and discipline within the military as well as the essential role of the commander in preventing and punishing war crimes. The criminal liability of commanders for failure to prevent or punish the crimes committed by subordinates should be codified in the UCMJ and the War Crimes Act.

2. Civilian justice system failures

56. For far too long, there has been a zone of *de facto* impunity for killings by private contractors (PCs) and civilian intelligence agents operating in Iraq, Afghanistan, and elsewhere. There is some debate whether federal court jurisdiction extends to PCs of Government agencies other than DOD, a debate that Congress should resolve expeditiously by clarifying that it does. But the principal accountability problem today is not the inadequacy of the applicable legal framework. Rather, U.S. prosecutors have failed to use the laws on the books to investigate and prosecute PCs and civilian agents for wrongful deaths, including, in some cases, deaths credibly alleged to have resulted from torture and abuse. Prosecutors have also failed, even years after alleged wrongful deaths, to disclose the status of their investigations or the bases for decisions not to prosecute. One well-informed source succinctly described the situation: "The DOJ has been AWOL in response to these incidents." This must change.

57. The Department of Justice (DOJ) is responsible for prosecuting PCs and civilian Government employees, as well as former military personnel who commit war crimes. DOJ has failed miserably. Its efforts are coordinated by two bodies. The first is a task force based at the U.S. Attorney's Office for the Eastern District of Virginia, which handles detainee abuse cases.

This task force has admitted that 24 cases of alleged detainee abuse were referred to it and that it has declined to prosecute 22 of these cases. It is unclear why more cases have not been referred (or if they have, how many more), or how many of the 24 referred cases involved the detainee deaths credibly alleged to have occurred at the hands of PCs or the CIA.

58. The second entity, the Domestic Security Section (DSS) of DOJ's Criminal Division, coordinates the prosecution of other cases involving PCs, such as unlawful shootings committed while protecting convoys. Its track record has been somewhat better, although too often it appears investigations and prosecutions follow only the most notorious public cases, such as the shootings in Nissor Square.

59. DSS representatives acknowledged the lack of convictions to me, but refused to provide even ballpark statistics on the allegations received or the status of investigations. They emphasized that conducting investigations in a war zone is extremely difficult and that they ultimately rely on the military either to conduct the investigation or to provide the FBI with logistical and security support. While there are significant challenges to conducting investigations in the context of armed conflict, DSS representatives' responses suggested serious thought had not been given to how such investigations can be conducted. Investigations into PCs's conduct can be conducted successfully, and one interlocutor who has done so suggested that these cases are actually relatively easy to investigate because they tend to take place in daylight in front of numerous witnesses who can go to safe locations to be interviewed.

60. The lamentable bottom line is that DOJ has brought a scant few cases against PCs for civilian casualties, achieved a conviction only in one case involving a CIA contractor, and brought no cases against CIA employees. Government officials with whom I met acknowledged this lack of accountability, and it now seems clear that this vacuum is neither legally norethically defensible. Indeed, many PCs themselves accept the need for legal regulation andaccountability. Unfortunately, accountability for CIA officials appears more remote because of a lack of political will.

3. Ensuring transparency and accountability

61. The key to overcoming this record of failure, both in the civilian and military justice systems, is prosecutorial and political will to enforce the rule of law. However, the nearly universal sense I was given during my visit by those in Government is that systematic accounting of, and prosecutions for, wrongful deaths are unlikely. In short, war crimes prosecutions in particular are "politically radioactive." That sense continues to be reflected by Government statements which indicate more of a commitment to "moving forward" than to ensuring transparency and accountability for policies, practices and conduct that led to illegal killings by Government personnel and their agents. But a refusal to look back inevitably means moving forward in blindness. Political expediency is never a permissible justification for a State's failure to investigate and prosecute alleged crimes.

62. Although there is no substitute for prosecution of violations of the right to life, in the short term there are a number of steps the Government can take towards transparency and accountability. One such step is the creation of a national "commission of inquiry" tasked with carrying out an independent, systematic and sustained investigation of policies and practices that lead to deaths and other abuses. Over the 27 years of their mandate, successive Special Rapporteurs for extrajudicial execution have focused on the procedures and results that make such commissions effective and give them credibility. I described in a recent report to the Council the situations to which a commission is best suited, and the principles and standards necessary for it to be successful.

63. A commission is an especially attractive option in this context because it is likely that extrajudicial killings resulted from a set of policy failures on the part of a variety of Government actors and agents. In such complex circumstances, transparency may best be achieved through a commission rather than through prosecution alone. The commission could propose structural or long-term reforms that would better ensure the right to life and other fundamental humanrights. Another option is the appointment of a special prosecutor who would be independent of the kinds of institutional and political pressures that could—and have—hindered effective investigation and prosecution by DOJ. Some have made proposals about the particular form a commission could take, and the merits of a special or independent prosecutor. I do not endorse any specific proposal, although I do note that a commission and an independent prosecutor are not mutually exclusive.

64. Regardless of the specific form of the commission, it should meet certain fundamental requirements, including that it must: be independent, impartial and competent; have the powers necessary to obtain all the information it requires; have sufficient resources and personnel; and, report all of its findings and recommendations publicly and disseminate them widely. When the report is completed, the Government should reply publicly and indicate what it intends to do inresponse. Any commission designed to provide the appearance of accountability rather than to establish the truth, or one that undermines the possibility of eventual prosecution, would fall short of the same international standards to which the U.S. often seeks to hold other countries.

65. The most credible response to the military justice system's investigative failures and sentencing distortions would be the creation of a Director of Military Prosecutions (DMP) position. Such positions have recently been instituted in Australia, Canada, Ireland, New Zealand and the United Kingdom to ensure greater separation between the chain of command and the prosecution function. Rather than permitting commanding officers to decide whether to prosecute their own soldiers—a decision in which superior officers have a direct and potentially conflicting interest—a DMP makes independent decisions.

Somalia, but it also established a Commission of Inquiry to determine the institutional defects that allowed those abuses to occur. By identifying pervasive problems in how rules of engagement were drafted, were disseminated through the chain of command, and were taught to soldiers on the ground, Canada improved its institutional capacity to better ensure the right to life in the future.").

66. Regarding investigation and prosecution of PCs, a significant problem is that cases are handled by U.S. Attorneys offices around the country. Prosecutors do not have an incentive to prioritize such difficult and expensive cases, especially when expected to conduct investigations within their ordinary operating budget. An office should be established within DOJ dedicated solely to investigating and prosecuting cases involving PCs, civilian Government employees, and former military personnel, and to provide appropriate funding.

4. Reparations for civilian casualties

67. The Government has implemented a number of programs to provide compensation and restitution to civilian victims of U.S. military operations. While the motivation for these programs is often cited as "winning hearts and minds" they are also responsive to international law's requirement of reparations for violations of human rights and humanitarian law. In some respects, the Government has done less than the law requires by de-linking reparation from the question of whether illegal conduct occurred. In other respects, the Government has done more, by providing reparations to the families of those killed in lawful attacks. My overall assessment is that the Government's approach has, in practice, meant far more people have received reparations for the loss of their loved ones than has often been the case in previous conflicts, but that reparation programs need to be made more consistent and comprehensive.

68. The Foreign Claims Act authorizes payment of legal claims arising from a death negligently or wrongfully caused by military personnel outside of combat. Payment under this law can be higher than in other programs. Two other programs make death-related payments without any admission of fault or liability. In Afghanistan and Iraq, the military makes" condolence payments" using funds from the Commander's Emergency Response Program (CERP). In Afghanistan, the military also makes "solatia payments." The maximum payment amount provided under either program for a death is roughly $2,500.

. . .

70. The lack of systematic compensation for civilian casualties caused by private contractors is acute. While some have offered compensation on their own account, this does not appear to be an approach that could be systematized. One interlocutor suggested the best approach would before the Government to provide reparations for casualties caused by its contractors and then deduct the amount of this compensation from payments made under the contract.

E. Targeted killings: lack of transparency regarding the legal framework and targeting choices

71. The Government has credibly been alleged to have engaged in targeted killings on the territory of other States. Senior Government officials have confirmed the existence of a program through which drones are used to target particular individuals, but have also caused civilian casualties. On several occasions I have asked the Government to explain the legal basis on which a particular individual was targeted. While I have welcomed the Government's willingness to engage in dialogue on targeted killings, it has been evasive about its grounds for targeting, and I am disturbed by the broader implications of its positions. Briefly, those positions are that: (a) the Government's actions against al-Qaeda constitute a world-wide armed conflict to which international humanitarian law applies; (b) international humanitarian law operates to the exclusion of human rights law; (c) international humanitarian law falls outside the mandate of the Special Rapporteur and of the Human Rights Council; and (d) States may determine for themselves whether an individual incident is governed by humanitarian law or human rights law.

72. I responded to these positions in detail both directly to the Government and in my 2007 report to the Council. I have discussed the extent to which these positions constitute a radical departure from past practice, and the highly negative consequences that would flow from them. Under the Government's reinterpretation of the law and the Council's and my mandate, the U.S. would function in a public accountability void—as could other States—to the detriment of the advances made by the international human rights and humanitarian law regimes over the past sixty years.

73. The new administration should reconsider these positions and move to ensure the necessary transparency and accountability. Withholding such information replaces public accountability with unverifiable Government assertions of legality, inverting the very idea of due process.

IV. RECOMMENDATIONS

A. Domestic issues

74. Due process in death penalty cases

- The system of partisan elections for judges should be reformed to ensure that capital defendants receive a fair trial and appeals process.
- Alabama and Texas should establish well-funded, state-wide public defender services. Oversight of these should be independent of the executive and judicial branches.
- Texas should establish a commission to review cases in which convicted people have been subsequently exonerated, analyze the reasons, and make recommendations to enable the criminal justice system to prevent future mistakes.
- Alabama should evaluate and respond in detail to the findings and recommendations of the American Bar Association report on the implementation of its death penalty.
- Federal and state governments should systematically review and respond to concerns about continuing racial disparities in the criminal justice system generally, and in the imposition of the death penalty specifically.
- In light of uncorrected flaws in state criminal justice systems, and given the finality of executions, Congress should enact legislation permitting federal courts to review on the merits all issues in death penalty post-conviction cases.
- Regulations permitting the Department of Justice to certify the adequacy of state indigent defense systems based on factors left to states' discretion should be amended or repealed.
- Federal and state governments should ensure that capital punishment is imposed only for the most serious crimes, requiring an intent to kill resulting in a loss of life.
- Foreign nationals who were denied the right to consular notification should have their executions stayed and their cases fully reviewed and reconsidered.

75. Deaths in immigration detention

- All deaths in immigration detention should be promptly and publicly reported and investigated.
- The Department of Homeland Security should promulgate regulations, through the normal administrative rulemaking process, for provision of medical care that are consistent with international standards.

76. Tracking and responding to killings by law enforcement officials Video and audio recording of interactions between law enforcement officers and members of the public should be increased. The destruction of tapes should be minimized through technical means and through the imposition of penalties.

- Existing data collection efforts regarding killings by law enforcement officers should be improved to increase their usefulness in an "early warning" and "hotspot identification" role.

77. Guantánamo Bay detainees

- The Military Commissions Act should not be used for capital prosecutions of any detainees, including those in Guantánamo. Any such prosecutions should meet due process requirements under international human rights and humanitarian law.
- Complete and unredacted investigations and autopsy results into the deaths of Guantánamo detainees should be released to family members.

B. International operations

78. Transparency into civilian casualties

- The Government should track and publicly disclose all civilian casualties caused by military or other operations or that occur in the custody of the Government or its agents.

79. Enhancing military justice transparency

- The Department of Defense should establish a central office or "registry" to maintain a docket and track cases from investigation through final disposition. The system should be capable of providing up-to-date statistical information. The registry should include information on upcoming hearings and copies of the findings of formal and informal investigations, rulings, pleadings, transcripts of testimony, and exhibits. Public internet access to the registry should be available, subject only to legal non-disclosure requirements related to national security and individual privacy.

80. Ensuring comprehensive criminal jurisdiction over offences in armed conflict

- The doctrine of "command responsibility" as a basis for criminal liability should be codified in the Uniform Code of Military Justice and the War Crimes Act.
- Congress should adopt legislation that comprehensively provides criminal jurisdiction over all private contractors and civilian employees, including those working for intelligence agencies.

81. Ensuring accountability

- A commission of inquiry should be established to conduct an independent, systematic and sustained investigation of policies and practices that led to deaths and other abuses in U.S. operations. The commission should have the mandate and resources to conduct a full investigation. Its results and recommendations should be publicly and widely disseminated, and the Government should publicly respond thereto. Given the importance of prosecutions, an independent special prosecutor should be considered and the commission should not undermine the possibility of eventual prosecution.
- Consideration should be given to establishing a Director of Military Prosecutions to ensure separation between the chain of command and the prosecution function.
- An office dedicated to investigation and prosecution of crimes by private contractors, civilian Government employees, and former military personnel should be established within the DOJ. The office should receive the resources and investigative support necessary to handle these cases. The DOJ should make public statistical information on the status of these cases, disaggregated by the kind, year, and country of alleged offence.

82. Enhancing reparations programs

- Existing reparation programs should be combined or replaced by a comprehensive and adequately-funded compensation program for the families of those killed in U.S. operations, including by military and intelligence personnel and private contractors. In missions involving a range of international forces, such as those in Afghanistan and Iraq, the Government should urge allies to implement similar programs and should promote coordination to ensure that all casualties are compensated.

83. Enhancing transparency in targeted killings

- The Government should explicate the rules of international law it considers to cover targeted killings. It should specify the bases for decisions to kill rather than capture particular individuals, and whether the State in which the killing takes place has given consent. It should specify the procedural safeguards in place, if any, to ensure in advance of drone killings that they comply with international law, and the measures the Government takes after any such killing to ensure that its legal and factual analysis was accurate and, if not, the remedial measures it would take.
- The Government should make public the number of civilians collaterally killed as a result of drone attacks, and the measures in place to prevent such casualties.

[Footnotes omitted]

Appendix I
PROGRAMME OF THE MISSION

1. I visited the U.S. from 16–30 June 2008. I met with Government officials, judges, civil society groups, and victims and witnesses in Washington DC, New York City, Montgomery (Alabama), and Austin (Texas).

2. At the federal level, I met with officials from a range of Departments. In the State Department, I met with officials from the Office of the Legal Advisor, the Bureau of International Organizational Affairs, the Bureau of Democracy, Human Rights and Labor, and Diplomatic Security. At the Justice Department, I met with a range of officials. At the Department of Defence, I met with officials from the General Counsel's Office and the Air Force's Military Justice Division.

3. In the Department of Homeland Security, I met with the Office of Detention and Removal Operations and the Division of Health Services. I met with Inspectors-General or their staff from the State Department, the Department of Homeland Security, and the Central Intelligence Agency. In Washington DC, I also met with a range of Congressional staff members, including those working for Senators on the Armed Services Committee and the Judiciary Committee, and for House Representatives on the Committee on Oversight and Government Reform.

4. In both Alabama and Texas, I met with the Governor's office, the Attorney-General's office, the Board of Pardons and Paroles, judges from the highest state courts, and state Senators. In Alabama, I also met with the Federal Defender's office. In Texas, I met with the Consul General of Mexico.

5. On all issues, I met with a range of civil society advocates. In New York, Washington DC, Alabama and Texas, I met with lawyers and advocates for immigration detainees. In Texas and Alabama, I met with lawyers for death row inmates. In Washington DC and New York, I met with lawyers working on military commission cases and representatives from human rights and civil liberties organizations.

Appendix II

CASE STUDY: LACK OF TRANSPARENCY IN THE MILITARY JUSTICE SYSTEM

1. The troublingly opaque character both of investigation and of prosecution in the U.S. military justice system is well illustrated by a case described to me by witnesses and investigators when I visited Afghanistan. **a** On 4 March 2007, U.S. Marines responded to a suicide attack on their convoy, in which one soldier was wounded, by killing some 19 Afghans and wounding many others in the space of a ten mile retreat. I asked the regional commander in Afghanistan what follow-up had occurred. He could not tell me and explained that his unit had just arrived in Afghanistan, that accountability for incidents involving the previous unit was that unit's responsibility, and that the prior unit had taken all the relevant files when it left the country. In fact, at that time, a Court of Inquiry into the incident was proceeding in North Carolina.

2. Shortly after I returned from Afghanistan, the U.S. military released a short statement on this incident, indicating that the commander of U.S. Marine Corps Forces Central Command had conducted a "thorough review of the report of a Court of Inquiry" and had determined that the soldiers had "acted appropriately and in accordance with the rules of engagement and tactics, techniques and procedures in place at the time in response to a complex attack." **b** Unsurprisingly, this conclusory and unsubstantiated response to such a serious incident was met with dismay in Afghanistan. Afghans—and Americans—have a right to ask on what basis this conclusion was reached. But all of the documents produced by the Court of Inquiry have remained classified. The record of proceedings has not been released. The 12,000-page report of the Court of Inquiry, including recommendations and factual findings, has not been released. The Government has even disregarded its own regulation requiring the convening authority to ensure that an executive summary of the report be made public. The use of Courts of Inquiry is provided for in Article 135 of the Uniform Code of Military Justice (UCMJ). While the UCMJ authorizes the President to prescribe regulations to implement UCMJ provisions, with respect to Courts of Inquiry, the President has delegated most of this authority to the Secretaries of the Army, Navy, and Air Force. For the Navy, which includes the Marine Corps, the key regulation is JAGINST 5830.1A, "Procedures Applicable to Courts and Boards of Inquiry" (31 October 2005). This regulation distinguishes between three products of a Court of Inquiry: the "record of proceedings", the "report", and the "executive summary". On this last, the regulation states that: Given the nature of the major incidents investigated, officials of the DON, the DOD, other executive agencies, the legislative branch, and the media, often desire copies of the investigation. Where the incident results in death, the next of kin also will normally request a copy of the investigation. The report of the investigation, transcript of the proceedings, and enclosures can often be thousands of pages in length. For persons unfamiliar with military organizations, terminology, and operations, the task of deciphering an investigation can be difficult. Accordingly, convening authorities should ensure that an executive summary in plain English, which accurately reflects the findings, opinions, and recommendations of the investigation, is prepared prior to forwarding the investigation. The summary may be a part of the convening authority's endorsement or an enclosure thereto. There is nothing improper with requiring counsel to the investigation or the president of a Court or Board of Inquiry to prepare the summary. Participation by public affairs personnel in the preparation of the executive summary may also be advisable." (JAGINST 5830.1A, para. 9.)

Appendix III

LEGAL FRAMEWORK APPLICABLE TO PROSECUTIONS OF PRIVATE CONTRACTORS AND CIVILIAN GOVERNMENT EMPLOYEES

1. Congress has adopted a series of statutes expanding and clarifying jurisdiction over offences committed by contractors and civilian Government employees operating in areas of armed conflict and in peacetime. To date, however, these legislative initiatives have been largely reactive to specific incidents such as the abuses at Abu Ghraib and the shooting incident at Nisoor Square. The result is legislation that closes particular jurisdictional gaps but leaves others.

Nevertheless, these statutes together should permit the justice system to punish all or virtually all killings prohibited by human rights or humanitarian law.

2. The USA Patriot Act of 2001 expanded the scope of "special maritime and territorial jurisdiction" over crimes committed overseas to include offenses committed "by or against a national of the U.S." on U.S. bases, facilities and diplomatic missions. a This expanded jurisdiction applies to about 30 criminal statutes and is most likely to be of use in cases involving deaths in custody. b Indeed, the only private security contractor ever successfully prosecuted in the civilian justice system was convicted under this statute after beating a detainee to death during an interrogation in Afghanistan.

3. When the Military Extraterritorial Jurisdiction Act (MEJA) was enacted in 2000, it covered Department of Defense employees, former military personnel, contractors, and sub-contractors accompanying the military outside the U.S. c After it came to light that contractors to other Government agencies were implicated in the torture and abuse of prisoners at Abu Ghraib, Congress amended MEJA in 2004 to cover any federal employee or Government contractor whose "employment relates to supporting the mission of the Department of Defense overseas" (except contractors who are nationals or residents of the country in which the missions takes place). d The intent was to cover the range of civilian employees and contractors operating in Afghanistan and Iraq, but there is some debate whether a court would agree that all such persons are "supporting the mission of the Department of Defense." I was briefed by a number of Congressional staffers on ongoing efforts to adopt new legislation that would definitively clarify MEJA in this regard. e This is most encouraging. There was, however, also talk of including a so-called "intelligence carve-out" that would provide impunity for contractors and employees working for U.S. intelligence agencies. This would be wholly inappropriate, and Congress should adopt legislation that comprehensively provides criminal jurisdiction over contractors and civilian employees.

4. The War Crimes Act was adopted in 1996 and amended in 1997 and 2006. f In contrast to MEJA and the Patriot Act, which define the scope of federal jurisdiction but do not codify new criminal offences, the War Crimes Act provides jurisdiction over a number of violations of international humanitarian law, including, *inter alia*, the "willful killing" of "protected persons" within the meaning of the Geneva Conventions (in international armed conflicts) and "murder" (in a non-international armed conflict). g In accordance with the U.S. 'humanitarian law obligations, the War Crimes Act originally made all violations of the Common Article 3 of the Geneva Conventions a war crime under U.S. domestic law. The 2006 amendments to the War Crimes Act—made as part of the Military Commissions Act of 2006—however, exempted certain violations of Common Article 3 from prosecution as war crimes, including "humiliating and degrading treatment," and sentencing or execution by courts that fail to provide "all the judicial guarantees . . . recognized as indispensable by civilized peoples." Such provisions narrow the U.S.' obligations under international humanitarian law and, together with the MCA's provisions that violate fair trial principles, should be repealed.

5. Finally, pursuant to a 2006 amendment, the Uniform Code of Military Justice (UCMJ) also provides jurisdiction over "persons serving with or accompanying an armed force in the field" f The War Crimes Act was originally adopted in Public Law 104-192 (enacted 21 August 1996) and was significantly amended in Public Law 105-118 (enacted 26 November 1997) and Public Law 109-366 (enacted 17 October 2006).

Note that jurisdiction is also provided over several other offences that involve killing. The provision most relevant killings in the current conflicts in Afghanistan and Iraq is, however, that of "murder". This is defined as:

"The act of a person who intentionally kills, or conspires or attempts to kill, or kills whether intentionally or unintentionally in the course of committing any other offense under this subsection, one or more persons taking no active part in the hostilities, including those placed out of combat by sickness, wounds, detention, or any other cause. "This definition is qualified by another provision, which declares that the "intent specified . . . precludes the applicability of [the murder provision] to an offense under [Common Article 3] with respect to—(A) collateral damage; or (B) death, damage, or injury incident to a lawful attack." (18 U.S.C. § 2441(d)(3).) whether "[i]n time of declared war or a contingency operation." h This first conviction of a private security contractor under this provision occurred in June 2008 in response to one contractor stabbing another in Iraq.

6. There may be incidents over which both the military justice system and the civilian justice system have jurisdiction. With respect to killings by contractors or civilian Government officials in the context of armed conflicts, the military justice system may have jurisdiction under the UCMJ, and the civilian justice system may also have jurisdiction under a variety of statutes. With respect to unlawful killings by soldiers, both the UCMJ and the War Crimes Act could apply.

7. The current arrangement in cases implicating contractors or civilian Government employees is that the DOJ will generally prosecute the case in the federal courts, and the military justice system will only act if the DOJ declines to do so. i While the DOJ's performance in these cases has thus far been abysmal, as I discuss in the body of this report, this is the right arrangement in principle.

Document (Excerpted): 2009 Human Rights Country Report: China (includes Tibet, Hong Kong, and Macau) U.S. Department of State Bureau of Democracy, Human Rights, and Labor

U.S. Department of State 2009 Country Reports on Human Rights Practices
March 11, 2010
(The section for Tibet, the report for Hong Kong, and the report for Macau are appended below.)

The People's Republic of China (PRC), with a population of approximately 1.3 billion, is an authoritarian state in which the Chinese Communist Party (CCP) constitutionally is the paramount source of power. Party members hold almost all top government, police, and military positions. Ultimate authority rests with the 25-member political bureau (Politburo) of the CCP and its nine-member standing committee. Hu Jintao holds the three most powerful positions as CCP general secretary, president, and chairman of the Central Military Commission. Civilian authorities generally maintained effective control of the security forces.

The government's human rights record remained poor and worsened in some areas. During the year the government increased the severe cultural and religious repression of ethnic minorities in the Xinjiang Uighur Autonomous Region (XUAR). Tibetan areas remained under tight government controls. The detention and harassment of human rights activists increased, and public interest lawyers and law firms that took on cases deemed sensitive by the government faced harassment, disbarment and closure. The government limited freedom of speech and controlled the Internet and Internet access. Abuses peaked around high-profile events, such as the 20th anniversary of the Tiananmen Square uprising, the 50th anniversary of the Tibetan uprising, and the 60th anniversary of the founding of the People's Republic of China.

As in previous years, citizens did not have the right to change their government. Other serious human rights abuses included extrajudicial killings, executions without due process, torture and coerced confessions of prisoners, and the use of forced labor, including prison labor. The government continued to monitor, harass, detain, arrest, and imprison journalists, writers, dissidents, activists, petitioners, and defense lawyers and their families, many of whom sought to exercise their rights under the law. A lack of due process and restrictions on lawyers, particularly human rights and public interest lawyers, had serious consequences for defendants who were imprisoned or executed following proceedings that fell short of international standards. The party and state exercised strict political control of courts and judges, conducted closed trials, and continued the use of administrative detention. Prolonged illegal detentions at unofficial holding facilities, known as black jails, were widespread.

Individuals and groups, especially those deemed politically sensitive by the government, continued to face tight restrictions on their freedom to assemble, practice religion, and travel. The government failed to protect refugees and asylum-seekers adequately, and the detention and forced repatriation of North Koreans continued. The government increased pressure on other countries to repatriate citizens back to China, including citizens who were being processed by UNHCR as political refugees. Nongovernmental organizations (NGOs), both local and international, continued to face intense scrutiny and restrictions. The government failed to address serious social conditions that affected human rights, including endemic corruption, trafficking in persons, and discrimination against women, minorities, and persons with disabilities. The government continued its coercive birth limitation policy, in some cases resulting in forced abortion or forced sterilization. Workers cannot choose an independent union to represent them in the workplace, and the law does not protect workers' right to strike.

In April the government unveiled its first National Human Rights Action Plan. The 54-page document outlined human rights goals to be achieved over the next two years and addressed issues such as prisoners' rights and the role of religion in society. However, the plan has not yet been implemented.

RESPECT FOR HUMAN RIGHTS

Section 1 Respect for the Integrity of the Person, Including Freedom From:

a. Arbitrary or Unlawful Deprivation of Life

During the year security forces reportedly committed arbitrary or unlawful killings. No official statistics on deaths in custody were available.

In January Lin Guoqiang died suddenly while in custody at the Fuqing Detention Center in Fujian Province. His family claimed that his body was swollen and covered with bruises. At year's end there was no official investigation into the case.

On February 8, Li Qiaoming was reportedly beaten to death in a detention center in Jinning County, Yunnan Province. Prison officials initially claimed he died after accidentally running into a wall during a game of "hide and seek." However, Li's father, who viewed the corpse, reported Li's head was swollen and his body covered with purple abrasions. Following Li's death, public security officials launched a campaign to eliminate "unnatural deaths" in prisons. An investigation determined three inmates were responsible for the death. The inmates, along with two prison guards, were sentenced to prison.

Defendants in criminal proceedings were executed following convictions that sometimes took place under circumstances involving severe lack of due process and inadequate channels for appeal.

b. Disappearance

On February 4, authorities detained human rights lawyer Gao Zhisheng, who had represented Chinese Christians and Falun Gong practitioners. At year's end his whereabouts remained unconfirmed, although according to NGO reports, in August he reportedly was seen in his hometown under heavy police escort. Before his arrest Gao published a letter detailing his torture during a previous period of detention.

On March 30, underground Catholic bishop Julius Jia Zhiguo of Zhengding, Hebei Province, was arrested; at year's end his whereabouts were unknown. The whereabouts of underground Catholic priests Zhang Li and Zhang Jianlin, from near Zhangjiakou city in Hebei Province, whom authorities detained in May 2008, and Wu Qinjing, the bishop of Zhouzhi, Shaanxi Province, who was detained in 2007, also remained unknown.

In an October report, the NGO Human Rights Watch documented the disappearances of hundreds of Uighur men and boys following the July protests in Urumqi.

c. Torture and Other Cruel, Inhuman, or Degrading Treatment or Punishment

The law prohibits the physical abuse of detainees and forbids prison guards from extracting confessions by torture, insulting prisoners' dignity, and beating or encouraging others to beat prisoners. However, during the year there were reports that officials used electric shocks, beatings, shackles, and other forms of abuse.

According to a November Human Rights Watch report, on March 6, An Weifeng was released on bail from Bancheng prison in Chengde City, Henan Province, for medical treatment. His father claimed that An Weifeng's body was swollen and scarred as a result of beatings and the administration of electric shocks.

In 2007, 30 farmers from Chengdu, Sichuan Province, who traveled to Beijing seeking resolution of a land dispute were abducted and taken to a military base, where they were tortured, threatened, and starved. One of them allegedly attempted suicide, "because (the guards) didn't allow me to sleep or eat in order to force me to write self-criticisms." According to the same report, a 15-year-old girl who traveled to Beijing to get help for her disabled father was kidnapped and taken back to Gansu Province, where she was beaten and held incommunicado for nearly two months. There were no new developments in this case during the year.

In November 2008 the UN Committee Against Torture (UNCAT) stated its deep concern about the routine and widespread use of torture and mistreatment of suspects in police custody, especially to extract confessions or information used in criminal proceedings. However, UNCAT acknowledged government efforts to address the practice of torture and related problems in the criminal justice system. Many alleged acts of torture occurred in pretrial criminal detention centers or Reeducation Through Labor (RTL) centers. Sexual and physical abuse and extortion occurred in some detention centers.

According to China News Weekly, the country had 22 "ankang" institutions (high-security psychiatric hospitals for the criminally insane) directly administered by the Ministry of Public Security (MPS). Political activists, underground religious believers, persons who repeatedly petitioned the government, members of the banned Chinese Democracy Party (CDP), and Falun Gong adherents were among those housed with mentally ill patients in these institutions. The regulations for committing a person to an ankang facility were not clear, and detainees had no mechanism for objecting to public security officials' determinations of mental illness. Patients in these hospitals reportedly were given medicine against their will and forcibly subjected to electric shock treatment. Activists sentenced to administrative detention also reported they were strapped to beds or other devices for days at a time, beaten, forcibly injected or fed medications, and denied food and use of toilet facilities.

Prison and Detention Center Conditions

Conditions in penal institutions for both political prisoners and common criminals generally were harsh and often degrading. Prisoners and detainees often were kept in overcrowded conditions with poor sanitation.

Inadequate prison capacity remained a problem in some areas. Food often was inadequate and of poor quality, and many detainees relied on supplemental food and medicines provided by relatives; some prominent dissidents were not allowed to receive such goods.

On March 2, an inmate at the Danzhou First Detention Center in Hainan was beaten to death by inmates while guards looked on.

Forced labor remained a serious problem in penal institutions. Many prisoners and detainees in penal and RTL facilities were required to work, often with no remuneration. Information about prisons, including associated labor camps and factories, was considered a state secret and was tightly controlled.

Conditions in administrative detention facilities, such as RTL camps, were similar to those in prisons. Beating deaths occurred in administrative detention and RTL facilities. According to NGO reports, conditions in these facilities were similar to those in prisons, with detainees reporting beatings, sexual assaults, lack of proper food, and no access to medical care.

The government generally did not permit independent monitoring of prisons or RTL camps, and prisoners remained inaccessible to local and international human rights organizations, media groups, and the International Committee of the Red Cross (ICRC).

d. Arbitrary Arrest or Detention

Arbitrary arrest and detention remained serious problems. The law permits police and security authorities to detain persons without arresting or charging them. Because the government tightly controlled information, it was impossible to determine accurately the total number of persons subjected to arbitrary arrest or detention.

Role of the Police and Security Apparatus

The security apparatus is made up of the Ministries of State Security and Public Security, the People's Armed Police, the People's Liberation Army (PLA), and the state judicial, procuratorial, and penal systems. The Ministries of State Security and Public Security and the People's Armed Police were responsible for internal security. SPP and Supreme People's Court (SPC) officials admitted that courts and prosecutors often deferred to the security ministries on policy matters and individual cases. The SPP was responsible for the investigation of corruption and duty crimes (crimes committed by public officials or state functionaries, including corruption, crimes of dereliction of duty, and crimes involving violations of a citizen's personal rights). The PLA was responsible for external security but also had some domestic security responsibilities.

Arrest Procedures and Treatment While in Detention

Public security organs do not require court-approved warrants to detain suspects under their administrative detention powers. After detention the procuracy can approve formal arrest without court approval. According to the law, in routine criminal cases police can unilaterally detain persons for up to 37 days before releasing them or formally placing them under arrest. After a suspect is arrested, the law allows police and prosecutors to detain a person for up to seven months while public security organs further investigate the case. Another 45 days of detention are allowed where public security organs refer a case to the procuratorate to decide whether to file charges. If charges are filed, authorities can detain a suspect for an additional 45 days between filing and trial. In practice the police sometimes detained persons beyond the time limits stipulated by law. In some cases investigating security agents or prosecutors sought repeated extensions, resulting in pretrial detention of a year or longer. The criminal procedure law allows detainees access to lawyers before formal charges are filed, although police often limited such access.

The criminal procedure law requires a court to provide a lawyer to a defendant who has not already retained a lawyer; who is blind, deaf, mute, a minor; or who may be sentenced to death. This law applies whether or not the defendant is indigent. Courts may also provide lawyers to other criminal defendants who cannot afford them, although courts often did not appoint counsel in such circumstances.

Detained criminal suspects, defendants, their legal representatives, and close relatives are entitled to apply for bail; however, in practice few suspects were released on bail pending trial.

The government used incommunicado detention. The law requires notification of family members within 24 hours of detention, but individuals often were held without notification for significantly longer periods, especially in politically sensitive cases. Under a sweeping exception, officials were not required to provide notification if doing so would "hinder the investigation" of a case. In some cases police treated those with no immediate family more severely.

The law permits nonjudicial panels, called labor reeducation panels, to sentence persons without trial to three years in RTL camps or other administrative detention programs. The labor reeducation committee is authorized to extend a sentence up to one year. Defendants could challenge RTL sentences under the administrative litigation law and appeal for a reduction in, or suspension of, their sentences. However, appeals rarely succeeded. Many other persons were detained in similar forms of administrative detention, known as "custody and education" (for women engaged in prostitution and those soliciting prostitution) and "custody and training" (for minors who committed crimes). Administrative detention was used to intimidate political activists and prevent public demonstrations.

On February 1, Zhu Lijin was arrested for distributing Falun Gong pamphlets. She was sentenced to 15 months in RTL without a trial. Authorities used special reeducation centers to prolong detention of Falun Gong practitioners who had completed terms in RTL.

Authorities arrested persons on allegations of revealing state secrets, subversion, and other crimes as a means to suppress political dissent and social advocacy. Citizens also were also detained under broad and ambiguous state secrets laws for, among other actions, disclosing information on criminal trials, meetings, and government activity.

Human rights activists, journalists, unregistered religious figures, and former political prisoners and their family members were among those targeted for arbitrary detention or arrest.

The government continued to use house arrest as a nonjudicial punishment and control measure against dissidents, former political prisoners, family members of political prisoners, petitioners, underground religious figures, and others it deemed politically sensitive. Numerous dissidents, activists, and petitioners were placed under house arrest during the October 1 National Day holiday period. House arrest encompassed varying degrees of stringency but sometimes included complete isolation in one's home or another location under lock and guard.

Police continued the practice of placing under surveillance, harassing, and detaining citizens around politically sensitive events, including the plenary sessions of the National People's Congress (NPC) and the Chinese People's Political Consultative Conference (CPPCC), the 60th anniversary of the founding of the PRC and the 20th anniversary of the Tiananmen Square student uprising. In early June authorities in Hangzhou placed several dissidents, including Charter 08 signatories Wen Kejian and Zou Wei and CDP activist Zhu Yufu, under house arrest for several days. Published in December 2008, Charter 08 calls for free elections and greater freedom of speech. Coauthored by Liu Xiaobo, who was later imprisoned, the document, originally signed by more than 300 Chinese activists and intellectuals, received more than 7,000 signatories online. Many dissidents in Beijing reported that police prevented them from leaving their houses on June 4, the anniversary of the Tiananmen Square Massacre. Authorities in the XUAR used house arrest and other forms of arbitrary detention against those accused of subscribing to the "three evils" of religious extremism, "splittism," and terrorism. Raids, detentions, arrests, and judicial punishments indiscriminately affected not only those suspected of supporting terrorism but also those who peacefully sought to pursue political goals or worship.

e. Denial of Fair Public Trial

The law states that the courts shall exercise judicial power independently, without interference from administrative organs, social organizations, and individuals. However, in practice the judiciary was not independent. It received policy guidance from both the government and the CCP, whose leaders used a variety of means to direct courts on verdicts and sentences, particularly in politically sensitive cases. At both the central and local levels, the government and CCP frequently interfered in the judicial system and dictated court decisions. Trial judges decided individual cases under the direction of the adjudication committee in each court. In addition, the CCP's law and politics committee, which includes representatives of the police, security services, procuratorate, and courts, had the authority to review and influence court operations at all levels of the judiciary. People's congresses also had authority to alter court decisions, but this happened rarely.

Corruption often influenced judicial decision making, and safeguards against corruption were vague and poorly enforced. Local governments appointed judges at the corresponding level of the judicial structure. Judges received their court finances and salaries from these government bodies and could be replaced by them. Local authorities often exerted undue influence over the judges they appointed and financed. Several high-profile corruption cases involved procuracy officials.

Courts lacked the independence and authority to rule on the constitutionality of laws. The law permits organizations or individuals to question laws and regulations they believe contradict the constitution, but a constitutional challenge first requires consultation with the body drafting the questioned regulation and can be appealed only to the NPC. Accordingly, lawyers had little or no opportunity to use the constitution in litigation.

Trial Procedures

Trials took place before a judge, who often was accompanied by "people's assessors," laypersons hired by the court to assist in decision making. According to law, people's assessors had authority similar to judges, but in practice they often deferred to judges and did not exercise an independent jury-like function.

There was no presumption of innocence, and the criminal justice system was biased toward a presumption of guilt, especially in high-profile or politically sensitive cases. The combined conviction rate for first- and second-instance criminal trials was more than 99 percent in 2008; 1,008,677 defendants were tried, and 1,373 were found not guilty. In many politically sensitive trials, which rarely lasted more than several hours, the courts handed down guilty verdicts immediately following proceedings. Courts often punished defendants who refused to acknowledge guilt with harsher sentences than those who confessed. There was an appeals process, but appeals rarely resulted in reversed verdicts. Appeals processes failed to provide sufficient avenues for review, and there were inadequate remedies for violations of defendants' rights.

SPC regulations require all trials to be open to the public, with certain exceptions, such as cases involving state secrets, privacy, and minors. Authorities used the legal exception for cases involving state secrets to keep politically sensitive proceedings closed to the public and sometimes even to family members, and to withhold access to defense counsel. Under the regulations, foreigners with valid identification are allowed the same access to trials as citizens, but in practice foreigners were permitted to attend court proceedings by invitation only. As in past years, foreign diplomats and journalists sought permission to attend a number of trials only to have court officials reclassify them as "state secret" cases, fill all available seats with security officials, or otherwise close them to the public. For example, foreign diplomats requested but were denied permission to attend human rights advocate Huang Qi's February trial on charges of illegally possessing state secrets. Huang's trial was adjourned without a verdict. Some trials were broadcast, and court proceedings were a regular television feature. A few courts published their verdicts on the Internet.

The law gives most suspects the right to seek legal counsel shortly after their initial detention and interrogation, although police frequently interfered with this right. Individuals who face administrative detention do not have the right to seek legal counsel. Human rights lawyers reported that they were denied the ability to defend certain clients or threatened with punishment if they did.

Lawyers often refused to represent defendants in politically sensitive cases, and defendants frequently found it difficult to find an attorney. The government took steps to discourage lawyers from taking sensitive cases. For example, following the July unrest in the XUAR, the Beijing Municipal Judicial Bureau posted a note on its Web site urging justice bureaus, the Beijing Municipal Lawyers Association, and law firms in Beijing to "exercise caution" in representing cases related to the riots. Similar measures were taken with respect to Tibetan defendants. In some cases Beijing-based rights lawyers were told they could not represent jailed Tibetans. Local governments in the XUAR and Tibetan areas imposed arbitrary rules that defendants could be represented only by locally registered attorneys.

When defendants were able to retain counsel in politically sensitive cases, government officials sometimes prevented effective representation of counsel. Officials deployed a wide range of tactics to obstruct the work of lawyers representing sensitive clients, including unlawful detentions, disbarment, intimidation, refusal to allow a case to be tried before a court, and physical abuse. For example, in April Beijing lawyer Cheng Hai was attacked and beaten while on his way to meet with a Falun Gong client in Chengdu. According to Cheng, those responsible for the attack were officials from the Jinyang General Management Office, Wuhou District, Chengdu. In May police officers in Chongqing arrested and beat lawyers Zhang Kai and Li Chunfu when they interviewed the family of a Falun Gong practitioner who allegedly died in police custody.

According to the law, defense attorneys can be held responsible if their client commits perjury, and prosecutors and judges have wide discretion to decide what constitutes perjury. In some sensitive cases, lawyers had no pretrial access to their clients, and defendants and lawyers were not allowed to speak during trials. In practice criminal defendants often were not assigned an attorney until a case was brought to court. Even in nonsensitive criminal trials, only one in seven defendants reportedly had legal representation.

The mechanism that allows defendants to confront their accusers was inadequate; the percentage of witnesses who came to court in criminal cases was less than 10 percent and as low as 1 percent in some courts. According to one expert, only 1 to 5 percent of trials involved witnesses. In most criminal trials, prosecutors read witness statements, which neither the defendants nor their lawyers had an opportunity to question. Approximately 95 percent of witnesses in criminal cases did not appear in court to testify, sometimes due to hardship or fear of reprisals. Although the criminal procedure law states that pretrial witness statements cannot serve as the sole basis for conviction, officials relied heavily on such statements to support their cases. Defense attorneys had no authority to compel witnesses to testify or to mandate discovery, although they could apply for access to government-held evidence relevant to their case. In practice pretrial access to information was minimal, and the defense often lacked adequate opportunity to prepare for trial.

Police and prosecutorial officials often ignored the due process provisions of the law, which led to particularly egregious consequences in death penalty cases. By law there are at least 68 capital offenses, including nonviolent financial crimes such as counterfeiting currency, embezzlement, and corruption.

Political Prisoners and Detainees

Government officials continued to deny holding any political prisoners, asserting that authorities detained persons not for their political or religious views but because they violated the law; however, the authorities continued to confine citizens for reasons related to politics and religion. Tens of thousands of political prisoners remained incarcerated, some in prisons and others in RTL camps or administrative detention. The government did not grant international humanitarian organizations access to political prisoners.

Foreign NGOs estimated that several hundred persons remained in prison for the crime of "counterrevolution," repealed in 1997, and thousands of others were serving sentences under the state security law, which authorities stated covers crimes similar to counterrevolution. Foreign governments urged the government to review the cases of those charged before 1997 with counterrevolution and to release those who had been jailed for nonviolent offenses under provisions of the criminal law, which were eliminated when the law was revised. At year's end no systematic review had occurred. The government maintained that prisoners serving sentences for counterrevolution and endangering state security were eligible on an equal basis for sentence reduction and parole, but political prisoners benefited from early release at lower rates than those enjoyed by other prisoners.

Activist Huang Qi, a long-time campaigner for public recognition of Tiananmen victims, was arrested in June 2008 for possessing state secrets. On August 5, Huang was tried in Sichuan Province on charges of "illegal possession of state secrets," and on November 24, he was sentenced to three years' imprisonment. Also in August activist Tan Zuoren went on trial for defaming the CCP, a charge allegedly linked to his work on social issues perceived by the government as sensitive. At year's end no verdict had been issued in his case.

Many political prisoners remained in prison or under other forms of detention at year's end, including rights activists Hu Jia and Wang Bingzhang; Alim and Ablikim Abdureyim, sons of Uighur activist Rebiya Kadeer; journalist Shi Tao; dissident Wang Xiaoning; lawyer and activist Yang Maodong (also known as Guo Feixiong); land-rights activist Yang Chunlin; Internet writer Xu Wei; labor activists Hu Mingjun, Huang Xiangwei, Kong Youping, Ning Xianhua, Li Jianfeng, Li Xintao, Lin Shun'an, Li Wangyang, and She Wanbao; CDP cofounder Qin Yongmin; family-planning whistleblower Chen Guangcheng; Catholic bishop Su Zhimin; Christian activist Zhang Rongliang; Inner Mongolian activist Hada; Uighur activist Dilkex Tilivaldi; and Tibetan Tenzin Deleg.

Political prisoners obtained parole and sentence reduction much less frequently than ordinary prisoners. In Civil Judicial Procedures and Remedies Courts deciding civil matters suffered from internal and external limitations on judicial independence. The State Compensation Law provides administrative and judicial remedies for deprivations of criminal rights, such as wrongful arrest or conviction, extortion of confession by torture, or unlawful use of force resulting in bodily injury. In civil matters prevailing parties often found it difficult to enforce court orders, and resistance to the enforcement sometimes extended to forcible resistance to court police.

f. Arbitrary Interference with Privacy, Family, Home, or Correspondence

The law states that the "freedom and privacy of correspondence of citizens are protected by law"; however, in practice authorities often did not respect the privacy of citizens. Although the law requires warrants before law enforcement officials can search premises, this provision frequently was ignored; moreover, the Public Security Bureau (PSB) and prosecutors can issue search warrants on their own authority without judicial consent, review, or consideration. Cases of forced entry by police officers continued to be reported.

Authorities monitored telephone conversations, fax transmissions, e-mail, text messaging, and Internet communications. Authorities also opened and censored domestic and international mail. Security services routinely monitored and entered residences and offices to gain access to computers, telephones, and fax machines. All major hotels had a sizable internal security presence, and hotel guestrooms sometimes had concealed listening devices and were searched for sensitive or proprietary materials.

Some citizens were under heavy surveillance and routinely had their telephone calls monitored or telephone service disrupted, particularly in the XUAR and Tibetan areas. The authorities frequently warned dissidents and activists, underground religious figures, former political prisoners, and others whom the government considered to be troublemakers not to meet with foreign journalists or diplomats, especially before sensitive anniversaries, at the time of important government or party meetings, and during the visits of high-level foreign officials. Security personnel also harassed and detained the family members of political prisoners, including following them to meetings with foreign reporters and diplomats and urging them to remain silent about the cases of their relatives.

In the case of families that already had two children, one parent was often pressured to undergo sterilization. The penalties sometimes left women with little practical choice but to undergo abortion or sterilization.

Laws and regulations forbid the termination of pregnancies based on the sex of the fetus, but because of the intersection of birth limitations with the traditional preference for male children, particularly in rural areas, many families used ultrasound technology to identify female fetuses and terminate these pregnancies. National Population and Family-planning Commission regulations ban nonmedically necessary determinations of the sex of the fetus and sex-selective abortions, but some experts believed that the penalties for violating the regulations were not severe enough to deter unlawful behavior. According to government estimates released in February 2008, the male-female sex ratio at birth was 120 to 100 at the end of 2007 (compared with norms elsewhere of between 103 and 107 to 100).

Section 2 Respect for Civil Liberties, Including:

a. Freedom of Speech and Press

The law provides for freedom of speech and of the press, although the government generally did not respect these rights in practice. The government interpreted the CCP's "leading role," as mandated in the constitution, as superseding and circumscribing these rights. The government continued to control print, broadcast, and electronic media tightly and used them to propagate government views and CCP ideology. During the year the government increased censorship and manipulation of the press and the Internet during sensitive anniversaries.

Foreign journalists were largely prevented from obtaining permits to travel to Tibet except for highly controlled press visits. While foreign journalists were allowed access to Urumqi during and after the July riots, authorities forced foreign journalists to leave other cities in the XUAR.

Media outlets received regular guidance from the Central Propaganda Department (CPC), which listed topics that should not be covered, including politically sensitive topics. After events such as the July riots or the Sichuan earthquake, media outlets were told to cover the stories using content carried by government-controlled Xinhua and China Central Television. In the period preceding the October celebration of the 60th anniversary of the founding of the PRC, authorities mandated that newspapers, magazines, and other news outlets minimize the reporting of negative stories.

The General Administration of Press and Publication; the State Administration of Radio, Film, and Television, and the CPC remained active in issuing restrictive regulations and decisions constraining the content of broadcast media.

The government also frequently monitored gatherings of intellectuals, scholars, and dissidents where political or sensitive issues were discussed. Those who aired views that disagreed with the government's position on controversial topics or disseminated such views to domestic and overseas audiences risked punishment ranging from disciplinary action at government work units to police interrogation and detention. In December 2008, to commemorate human rights day, a group of 303 intellectuals and activists released a petition entitled Charter 08, calling for human rights and democracy. Within one month more than 7,300 persons signed the petition, of whom police questioned at least 100. Many Charter 08 signers reported experiencing harassment during the year, especially around the time of sensitive anniversaries, trials, or official visits.

International media were not allowed to operate freely and faced heavy restrictions. In February two New York Times reporters were detained for 20 hours after police stopped their car in a Tibetan area of Gansu Province. Authorities made the two spend the night in Lanzhou, the provincial capital, and eventually forced them to return to Beijing. In April reporters with the Voice of America (VOA) were detained for two hours in Sichuan Province before being told that they could not proceed farther. Local authorities first told them that it was illegal for tourists to visit the area and later told them they could not proceed because of "hazardous road conditions."

Authorities barred foreign journalists from filming in, or entering, Tiananmen Square during the 20th anniversary of the crackdown on prodemocracy demonstrations. On July 10, police detained and deported an Associated Press photographer for taking pictures in Kashgar. In September police broke into the hotel room of three journalists from Kyodo News covering a National Day parade rehearsal, beat them, and destroyed their computers. On September 4, antiriot police beat three Hong Kong reporters in Urumqi. Five other Hong Kong reporters were briefly detained the same day in Urumqi to prevent them from filming protests.

The law permits only government-approved publishing houses to print books. The State Press and Publications Administration (PPA) controlled all licenses to publish. No newspaper, periodical, book, audio, video, or electronic publication may be printed or distributed without the PPA and relevant provincial publishing authorities' approval of both the printer and distributor. Individuals who attempted to publish without government approval faced imprisonment, fines, confiscation of their books, and other sanctions. The CCP exerted control over the publishing industry by preemptively classifying certain topics as off limits.

Many intellectuals and scholars exercised self-censorship, anticipating that books or papers on political topics would be deemed too sensitive to be published. The censorship process for private and government media also increasingly relied on self-censorship and, in a few cases, post publication sanctions.

b. Internet Freedom

During the year the China Internet Network Information Center reported that the number of Internet users increased to 338 million, 94 percent of whom had broadband access. The government increased its efforts to monitor Internet use, control content, restrict information, block access to foreign and domestic Web sites, encourage self-censorship, and punish those who violated regulations, but these measures were not universally effective.

The government consistently blocked access to Web sites it deemed controversial, especially those discussing Taiwan and Tibetan independence, underground religious and spiritual organizations, democracy activists, and the 1989 Tiananmen crackdown. The government also at times blocked access to selected sites operated by major foreign news outlets, health organizations, foreign governments, educational institutions, and social networking sites, as well as search engines, that allow rapid communication or organization of users.

Regulations prohibit a broad range of activities that authorities interpret as subversive or slanderous to the state. Internet service providers were instructed to use only domestic media-news postings, to record information useful for tracking users and their viewing habits, to install software capable of copying e-mails, and to end immediately transmission of "subversive material."

c. Freedom of Religion

The constitution and laws provide for freedom of religious belief and the freedom not to believe. The constitution limits protection of religious activities to those the government defined as "normal." The constitution states that religious bodies and affairs are not to be "subject to any foreign domination" and that the individual exercise of rights "may not infringe upon the interests of the state."

The government continued to strictly control religious practice and repress religious activity outside government-sanctioned organizations and registered places of worship. The government controlled the growth and scope of the activity of both registered and unregistered religious groups, including house churches. Government authorities limited proselytizing, particularly by foreigners and unregistered religious groups, but permitted proselytizing in state-approved religious venues and private settings. Throughout the country foreign citizens' participation in religious activities was viewed by the government as highly suspect and, in some cases, led to repercussions against both Chinese citizens and foreign citizens.

Several large house churches reported increased government interference with their activities in periods preceding sensitive anniversaries. In Beijing the government reportedly pressured landlords to stop renting space to house church groups. During an outdoor worship service, authorities reportedly conducted surveillance, used loudspeakers to warn against unauthorized public gatherings, detained church leaders to prevent them from attending services, and closed public parks to dissuade the groups from gathering.

TIBET

The government's human rights record in Tibetan areas of China remained poor, and the severe repression of freedoms of speech, religion, association, and movement that increased dramatically following the March 2008 Lhasa riots and subsequent unrest that occurred across the Tibetan Plateau continued during the year. Authorities continued to commit serious human rights abuses, including extrajudicial killings, torture, arbitrary arrests, extrajudicial detention, and house arrest. The preservation and development of Tibet's unique religious, cultural, and linguistic heritage remained a concern.

In March 2008 monks and nuns from a number of monasteries in Lhasa and other Tibetan communities mounted peaceful protests to commemorate the anniversary of the 1959 Tibetan uprising. After four days the protests and security response devolved into rioting by Tibetans and a violent police crackdown in Lhasa.

Some protesters resorted to violence, in some cases deadly, against Han and Hui residents. The ensuing police resulted in actions an unknown number of deaths, injuries, arrests, and human rights abuses.

Document (Excerpted): The Human Rights Record of the U.S. in 2009, by China.

China's Information Office of the State Council published a report titled "*The Human Rights Record of the U.S. in 2009*" yesterday. The full text of China's State Council assessment of U.S. human rights violations as published in Xinhuanews follows:

The State Department of the U.S. released its Country Reports on Human Rights Practices for 2009 on March 11, 2010, posing as "the world judge of human rights" again. As in previous years, the reports are full of accusations of the human rights situation in more than 190 countries and regions including China, but turn a blind eye to, or dodge and even cover up rampant human rights abuses on its own territory. The Human Rights Record of the U.S. in 2009 is prepared to help people around the world understand the real situation of human rights in the U.S.

I. On Life, Property and Personal Security

Widespread violent crimes in the U.S. posed threats to the lives, properties and personal security of its people.

In 2008, U.S. residents experienced 4.9 million violent crimes, 16.3 million property crimes and 137,000 personal thefts, and the violent crime rate was 19.3 victimizations per 1,000 persons aged 12 or over, according to a report published by the U.S. Department of Justice in September 2009 (Criminal Victimization 2008, U.S. Department of Justice, http://www.ojp.usdoj.gov). In 2008, over 14 million arrests occurred for all offenses (except traffic violations) in the country, and the arrest rate for violent crime was 198.2 per 100,000 inhabitants (Crime in the U.S., 2008, http://www.fbi.gov). In 2009, a total of 35 domestic homicides occurred in Philadelphia, a 67 percent increase from 2008 (The New York Times, December 30, 2009). In New York City, 461 murders were reported in 2009, and the crime rate was 1,151 cases per 100,000 people.

The U.S. ranks first in the world in terms of the number of privately-owned guns. According to the data from the FBI and the Bureau of Alcohol, Tobacco, Firearms and Explosives (ATF), American gun owners, out of 309 million in total population, have more than 250 million guns, while a substantial proportion of U.S. gun owners had more than one weapon.

In the U.S., about 30,000 people die from gun-related incidents each year (The China Press, April 6, 2009). According to a FBI report, there had been 14,180 murder victims in 2008 (USA Today, September 15, 2009). Firearms were used in 66.9 percent of murders, 43.5 percent of robberies and 21.4 percent of aggravated assaults (http://www.thefreelibrary.com). USA Today reported that a man named Michael McLendon killed 10 people in two rural towns of Alabama before turning a gun on himself on March 11, 2009.

Campuses became an area worst hit by violent crimes as shootings spread there and kept escalating. The U.S. Heritage Foundation reported that 11.3 percent of high school students in Washington D.C. reported being "threatened or injured" with a weapon while on school property during the 2007–2008 school year.

II. On Civil and Political Rights

In the U.S., civil and political rights of citizens are severely restricted and violated by the government.

The country's police frequently impose violence on the people. Chicago Defender reported on July 8, 2009 that a total of 315 police officers in New York were subject to internal supervision due to unrestrained use of violence during law enforcement. The figure was only 210 in 2007. Over the past two years, the number of New York police officers under review for garnering too many complaints was up 50 percent (http://www.chicagodefender.com). According to a New York Police Department firearms discharge report released on Nov. 17, 2009, the city' s police fired 588 bullets in 2007, killing 10 people, and 354 bullets in 2008, killing 13 people (http://gothamist.com, November 17, 2009). On September 3, 2009, a student of the San Jose State University was hit repeatedly by four San Jose police officers with batons and a Taser gun for more than ten times (http://www.mercurynews.com, October 27, 2009). On September 22, 2009, a Chinese student in Eugene, Oregon was beaten by a local police officer for no reason (The Oregonian, October 23, 2009, http://blog.oregonlive.com). According to the Amnesty International, in the first ten months of 2009, police officers in the U.S. killed 45 people due to unrestrained use of Taser guns. The youngest of the victims was only 15. From 2001 to October, 2009, 389 people died of Taser guns used by police officers (http://theduckshoot.com).

Abuse of power is common among U.S. law enforcers. In July 2009, the Federal Bureau of Investigation put four police officers in the Washington area under investigation for taking money to protect a gambling ring frequented by some of the region's most powerful drug dealers over the past two years (The Washington Post, July, 19, 2009). In September 2009, an off-duty police officer in Chicago attacked a bus driver for "cutting him off in traffic" as he rode a bicycle (Chicago Tribune, September 2009, http://www.chicagobreakingnews.com). In the same month, four former police officers in Chicago were charged with extorting close to 500,000 U.S. dollars from a Hispanic driving an expensive car with out-of-state plates and suspected drug dealers in the name of law enforcement, and offering bribes to their superiors (Chicago Tribune, September 19, 2009).

Prisons in the United State are packed with inmates. According to a report released by the U.S. Justice Department on Dec. 8, 2009, more than 7.3 million people were under the authority of the U.S. corrections system at the end of 2008. The correctional system population increased by 0.5 percent in 2008 compared with the previous year (http://www.wsws.org). About 2.3 million were held in custody of prisons and jails, the equivalent of about one in every 198 persons in the country. From 2000 to 2008, the U.S. prison population increased an average of 1.8 percent annually (http://mensnewsdaily.com, January 18, 2010). The California government even suggested sending tens of thousands of illegal immigrants held in the state to Mexico, in order to ease its overcrowded prison system (http://news.yahoo.com, January 26, 2010).

The basic rights of prisoners in the U.S. are not well-protected. Raping cases of inmates by prison staff members are widely reported. According to the U.S. Justice Department, reports of sexual misconduct by prison staff members with inmates in the country's 93 federal prison sites doubled over the past eight years. Of the 90 staff members prosecuted for sexual abuse of inmates, nearly 40 percent were also convicted of other crimes (The Washington Post, September 11, 2009).

Chaotic management of prisons in the United State also led to wide spread of diseases among the inmates. According to a report from the U.S. Justice Department, a total of 20,231 male inmates and 1,913 female inmates had been confirmed as HIV carriers in the U.S. federal and state prisons at yearend 2008. The percentage of male and female inmates with HIV/AIDS amounted to 1.5 and 1.9 percent respectively (http://www.news-medical.net, December 2, 2009). From 2007 to 2008, the number of HIV/AIDS cases in prisons in California, Missouri and Florida increased by 246, 169, and 166 respectively. More than 130 federal and state inmates in the U.S. died of AIDS-related causes in 2007 (http://thecrimereport.org, December 2, 2009). A report by the Human Rights Watch released in March 2009 said although the New York State prison registered the highest number of prisoners living with HIV in the country, it did not provide the inmates with adequate access to treatment, and even locked the inmates up separately, refusing to provide them with treatment of any kind. (www.hrw.org, March 24, 2009).

While advocating "freedom of speech," "freedom of the press" and "Internet freedom," the U.S. government unscrupulously monitors and restricts the citizens' rights to freedom when it comes to its own interests and needs.

The U.S. citizens' freedom to access and distribute information is under strict supervision. According to media reports, the U.S. National Security Agency (NSA) started installing specialized eavesdropping equipment around the country to wiretap calls, faxes, and emails and collect domestic communications as early as 2001. The wiretapping programs was originally targeted at Arab-Americans, but soon grew to include other Americans. The NSA installed over 25 eavesdropping facilities in San Jose, San Diego, Seattle, Los Angeles, and Chicago among other cities. The NSA also announced recently it was building a huge one million square feet data warehouse at a cost of 1.5 billion U.S. dollars at Camp Williams in Utah, as well as another massive data warehouse in San Antonio, as part of the NSA's new Cyber Command responsibilities.

After the September 11 attack, the U.S. government, in the name of anti-terrorism, authorized its intelligence authorities to hack into its citizens' mail communications, and to monitor and erase any information that might threaten the U.S. national interests on the Internet through technical means. The country's Patriot Act allowed law enforcement agencies to search telephone, email communications, medical, financial and other records, and broadened the discretion of law enforcement and immigration authorities in detaining and deporting foreign persons suspected of terrorism-related acts. The Act expanded the definition of terrorism, thus enlarging the number of activities to which law enforcement powers could be applied. On July 9, 2008, the U.S. Senate passed the Foreign Intelligence Surveillance Act Amendments Act of 2008, granting legal immunity to telecommunication companies that take part in wiretapping programs and authorizing the government to wiretap international communications between the U.S. and people overseas for anti-terrorism purposes without court approval (The New York Times, July 10, 2008). Statistic showed that from 2002 to 2006, the FBI collected thousands of phones records of U.S. citizens through mails, notes and phone calls. In September 2009, the country set up an Internet security supervision body, further worrying U.S. citizens that the U.S. government might use Internet security as an excuse to monitor and interfere with personal systems.

The so-called "freedom of the press" of the U.S. was in fact completely subordinate to its national interests, and was manipulated by the U.S. government. According to media reports, the U.S. government and the Pentagon had recruited a number of former military officers to become TV and radio news commentators to give "positive comments" and analysis as "military experts" for the U.S. war in Iraq and Afghanistan, in order to guide public opinions, glorify the wars, and gain public support of its anti-terrorism ideology (The New York Times, April 20, 2009). At yearend 2009, the U.S. Congress passed a bill which imposed sanctions on several Arab satellite channels for broadcasting contents hostile to the U.S. and instigating violence (http://blogs.rnw.nl).

III. On Economic, Social and Cultural Rights

Poverty, unemployment and the homeless are serious problems in the U.S., where workers' economic, social and cultural rights cannot be guaranteed.

Unemployment rate in the U.S. in 2009 was the highest in 26 years. The number of bankrupt businesses and individuals kept rising due to the financial crisis. The Associated Press reported in April 2009 that nearly 1.2 million businesses and individuals filed for bankruptcy in the previous 12 months—about four in every 1,000 people, a rate twice as high as that in 2006 (http://www.floridabankruptcyblog.com). By December 4, 2009, a total of 130 U.S. banks had been forced to close in the year due to the financial crisis (Chicago Tribune, December 4, 2009). Statistics released by the U.S. Labor Department on Nov. 6, 2009 showed unemployment rate in October 2009 reached 10.2 percent, the highest since 1983 (The New York Times, November 7, 2009).

The population in poverty was the largest in 11 years. The Washington Post reported on September 10, 2009, that altogether 39.8 million Americans were living in poverty by the end of 2008, an increase of 2.6 million from that in 2007. The poverty rate in 2008 was 13.2 percent, the highest since 1998. The number of people aged between 18 to 64 living in poverty in 2008 had risen to 22.1 million, 170,000 more than in 2007. Up to 8.1 million families were under poverty, accounting for 10.3 percent of the total families (The Washington Post, September 11, 2009). According to a report of the New York Times on Sept. 29, 2009, the poverty rate in New York City in 2008 was 18.2 percent and nearly 28 percent of the Bronx borough's residents were living in poverty (The New York Times, September 29, 2009). From August 2008 to August 2009, more than 90,000 poor households in California suffered power and gas cuts. A 93-year-old man was frozen to death at his home (http://www.msnbc.msn.com). Poverty led to a sharp rise in the number of suicides in the U.S.

The population in hunger was the highest in 14 years. The U.S. Department of Agriculture reported on Nov. 16, 2009, that 49.1 million Americans living in 17 million households, or 14.6 percent of all American families, lacked consistent access to adequate food in 2008, up 31 percent from the 13 million households, or 11.1 percent of all American families, that lacked stable and adequate supply of food in 2007, which was the highest since the government began tracking "food insecurity" in 1995 (The New York Times, November 17, 2009; 14.6% of Americans Could Not Afford Enough Food in 2008, http://business.theatlantic.com). The number of people who lacked "food security," rose from 4.7 million in 2007 to 6.7 million in 2008 (http://www.livescience.com, November 26, 2009). About 15 percent of families were still working for adequate food and clothing (The Associated Press, November 27, 2009). Statistics showed 36.5 million Americans, or about one eighth of the U.S. total population, took part in the food stamp program in August 2009, up 7.1 million from that of 2008. However, only two thirds of those eligible for food stamps actually received them (http://www.associatedcontent.com).

Workers' rights were seriously violated. The New York Times reported on Sept. 2, 2009 that 68 percent of the 4,387 low-wage workers in a survey said they had experienced reduction of wages. And 76 percent of those who had worked overtime were not paid accordingly, and 57 percent of those interviewed had not received pay documents to make sure pay was legal and accurate. Only eight percent of those who suffered serious injuries on the job filed for compensation. Up to 26 percent of those surveyed were paid less than the national minimum wage.

The number of people without medical insurance has kept rising for eight consecutive years. Data released by the U.S. Census Bureau on Sept. 10, 2009, showed 46.3 million people were without medical insurance in 2008, accounting for 15.4 percent of the total population, comparing 45.7 million people who were without medical insurance in 2007, which was a rise for the eighth year in a row. About 20.3 percent of Americans between 18 to 64 years old were not covered by medical insurance in 2008, higher than the 19.6 percent in 2007 (http://www.census.gov). A study released by the Commonwealth Fund showed health insurance coverage of adults aged 18 to 64 declined in 31 U.S. states from 2007 to 2009 (Reuters, October 8, 2009). The number of states with extremely high number of adults who were not covered by medical insurance increased from two in 1999 to nine in 2009. More than one in every four people in Texas were uninsured, the highest percentage among all states (http://www.ncpa.org). Houston had 40.1 percent of its residents uninsured (http://www.msnbc.msn.com). The number of homeless has been on the rise. Statistics show that by September 2008, an upward of 1.6 million homeless people in the U.S. had been receiving shelter, and the number of those in families rose from 473,000 in 2007 to 517,000 in 2008 (USA Today, July 9, 2009). Since 2009, homeless enrollments in the six counties of Chicago area had climbed, with McHenry County seeing the biggest hike—an increase of 125 percent over the previous year (Chicago Tribune, November 28, 2009). These families could only live in shabby places such as wagons. In March 2009, a sprawling tent city was seen in Sacramento of California where hundreds of homeless gathered.

IV. On Racial Discrimination

Racial discrimination is still a chronic problem of the U.S.

Black people and other minorities are the most impoverished groups in the U.S. According to a report issued by the U.S. Bureau of Census, the real median income for American households in 2008 was 50,303 U.S. dollars. That of the non-Hispanic white households was 55,530 U.S. dollars, Hispanic households 37,913 U.S. dollars, black households only 34,218 U.S. dollars. The median incomes of Hispanic and black households were roughly 68 percent and 61.6 percent of that of the non-Hispanic white households. Median income of minority groups was about 60 to 80 percent of that of majority groups under the same conditions of education and skill background (The Wall Street Journal, September 11, 2009; USA Today, September 11, 2009). According to the U.S. Bureau of Census, the poverty proportion of the non-Hispanic white was 8.6 percent in 2008, those of African-Americans and Hispanic were 24.7 percent and 23.2 percent respectively, almost three times of that of the white (The New York Times, September 29, 2009).

Employment and occupational discrimination against minority groups is very serious. Minority groups bear the brunt of the U.S. unemployment. According to news reports, the U.S. unemployment rate in October 2009 was 10.2 percent. The jobless rate of the U.S. African-Americans jumped to 15.7 percent, that of the Hispanic rose to 13.1 percent and that of the white was 9.5 percent (USA Today, November 6, 2009). Unemployment rate of the black aged between 16 and 24 saw a record high of 34.5 percent, more than three times the average rate. Unemployment rates for the black in cities such as Detroit and Milwaukee had reached 20 percent (The Washington Post, December 10, 2009). Racial discrimination in law enforcement and judicial system is very distinct. According to the U.S. Department of Justice, by the end of 2008, 3,161 men and 149 women per 100,000 persons in the U.S. black population were under imprisonment (www.ojp.usdoj.gov). The number of life imprisonment without parole given to African-American young people was ten times of that given to white young people in 25 states. The figure in California was 18 times. In major U.S. cities, there are more than one million people who were stopped and questioned by police in streets, nearly 90 percent of them were minority males. Among those questioned, 50 percent were African-Americans and 30 percent were Hispanics. Since the Sept. 11 event, discrimination against Muslims is increasing. Nearly 58 percent of Americans think Muslims are subject to "a lot" of discrimination, according to two combined surveys released by the Pew Research Center. About 73 percent of young people aged 18 to 29 are more likely to say Muslims are the most discriminated against (http://www.washingtontimes.com, September 10, 2009).

Immigrants live in misery. According to a report by the U.S. branch of Amnesty International, more than 300,000 illegal immigrants were detained by U.S. immigration authorities each year, and the illegal immigrants under custody exceeded 30,000 for each single day (World Journal, March 26, 2009). At the same time, hundreds of legal immigrants were put under arrest, denied entry or even sent back under escort every year (Sing Tao Daily, April 13, 2009). A report released by the Constitution Project and Human Rights Watch revealed that from 1999 to 2008, about 1.4 million detained immigrants were transferred. Tens of thousands of longtime residents of cities like Los Angeles and Philadelphia were sent, by force, to remote immigrant jails in Texas or Louisiana (The New York Times, November 2, 2009).

Ethnic hatred crimes are frequent. According to statistics released by the U.S. Federal Investigation Bureau on November 23, 2009, a total of 7,783 hate crimes occurred in 2008 in the U.S., 51.3 percent of which were originated by racial discrimination and 19.5 percent were for religious bias and 11.5 percent were for national origins (www.fbi.gov). Among those hate crimes, more than 70 percent were against black people. In 2008, anti-black offenses accounted for 26 persons per 1,000 people, and anti-white crimes accounted for 18 persons per 1,000 people (victim characteristics, October 21, 2009, www.fbi.gov).

V. On the Rights of Women and Children

The living conditions of women and children in the U.S. are deteriorating and their rights are not properly guaranteed.

Women do not enjoy equal social and political status as men. Women account for 51 percent of the U.S. population, but only 92 women, or 17 percent of the seats, serve in the current 111th U.S. Congress. Seventeen women serve in the Senate and 75 women serve in the House (Members of the 111th U.S. Congress, http://en.wikipedia.org). A study shows minorities and women are unlikely to hold top positions at big U.S. charities and nonprofits.

Women have difficulties in finding a job and suffer from low income and poor financial situations. According to statistics from the U.S. Equal Employment Opportunity Commission (EEOC), workplace discrimination charge filings with the federal agency nationwide rose to 95,402 during Fiscal Year 2008, a 15 percent increase from the previous fiscal year. Charge of workplace discrimination because of a job applicant's sex maintained a high proportion (www.eeoc.gov, November 3, 2009). According to statistics released by the U.S. Census Bureau in September 2009, the median incomes of full-time female workers in 2008 were 35,745 U.S. dollars, 77 percent of those of corresponding men whose median earnings were 46,367 U.S. dollars, which is lower than the 78 percent in 2007 (The Wall Street Journal, September 11, 2009; www.census.gov, September 10, 2009).

Women are frequent victims of violence and sexual assault. It is reported that the U.S. has the highest rape rate among countries which report such statistics. It is 13 times higher than that of England and 20 times higher than that of Japan (Occurrence of rape, http://www.sa.rochester.edu). In San Diego, a string of similar attacks happened to five women who have been sexually assaulted by a home invader in March 2009 (Sing Tao Daily, March 14, 2009). According to a report released by the Pentagon, more than 2,900 sexual assaults in the military were reported in 2008, up nearly 9 percent from the year before. And of those, only 292 cases resulted in a military trial.

American children suffer from hunger and cold. A report from the U.S. Department of Agriculture showed that 16.7 million children, or one fourth of the U.S. total, had not enough food in 2008 (The Washington Post, USA Today, November 17, 2009). The food relief institution Feeding America said in a report that more than 3.5 million children under the age of five face hunger or malnutrition. This figure accounts for 17 percent of American children aged five and under. In 11 states, more than 20 percent of young children were at risk for hunger.

VI. On U.S. Violations of Human Rights against Other Nations

The U.S. with its strong military power has pursued hegemony in the world, trampling upon the sovereignty of other countries and trespassing their human rights.

As the world's biggest arms seller, its deals have greatly fueled instability across the world. The U.S. also expanded its military spending, already the largest in the world, by 10 percent in 2008 to 607 billion U.S. dollars, accounting for 42 percent of the world total (The AP, June 9, 2009).

According to a report by the U.S. Congress, the U.S. foreign arms sales in 2008 soared to 37.8 billion U.S. dollars from 25.4 billion a year earlier, up by nearly 50 percent, accounting for 68.4 percent of the global arms sales that were at its four-year low (Reuters, September 6, 2009). At the beginning of 2010, the U.S. government announced a 6.4-billion-U.S. dollar arms sales package to Taiwan despite strong protest from the Chinese government and people, which seriously damaged China's national security interests and aroused strong indignation among the Chinese people.

The wars of Iraq and Afghanistan have placed heavy burden on American people and brought tremendous casualties and property losses to the people of Iraq and Afghanistan. The war in Iraq has led to the death of more than 1million Iraqi civilians, rendered an equal number of people homeless and incurred huge economic losses. In Afghanistan, incidents of the U.S. army killing innocent people still keep occurring. Five Afghan farmers were killed in a U.S. air strike when they were loading cucumbers into a van on August 5, 2009 (http://www.rawa.org). On June 8, the U.S. Department of Defense admitted that the U.S. raid on Taliban on May 5 caused death of Afghan civilians as the military failed to abide by due procedures. The Afghan authorities have identified 147 civilian victims, including women and children, while a U.S. officer put the death toll under 30 (The Philadelphia Inquirer, June 9, 2009).

Prisoner abuse is one of the biggest human rights scandals of the U.S. A report presented to the 10th meeting of Human Rights Council of the United Nations in 2009 by its Special Rapporteur on the promotion and protection of human rights and fundamental freedoms while countering terrorism showed that the U.S. has pursued a comprehensive set of practices including special deportation, long-term and secret detentions and acts violating the United Nations Convention against Torture. The rapporteur also said, in a report submitted to the 64th General Assembly of the United Nations, that the U.S. and its private contractors tortured male Muslims detained in Iraq and other places by stacking the naked prisoners in pyramid formation, coercing the homosexual sexual behaviors and stripping them in stark nakedness (The Washington Post, April 7, 2009). The U.S. Central Intelligence Agency (CIA) has begun interrogation by torture since 2002. The U.S. government lawyers disclosed that since 2001, CIA has destroyed 92 videotapes relating to the interrogation to suspected terrorists, 12 of them including the use of torture (The Washington Post, March 3, 2009). The CIA interrogators used a handgun and an electric drill to frighten a captured al-Qaeda commander into giving up information (The Washington Post, August 22, 2009). The U.S. Justice Department memos revealed the CIA kept prisoners shackled in a standing position for as long as 180 hours, more than a dozen of them deprived of sleep for at least 48 hours, three for more than 96 hours, and one for the nearly eight-day maximum. Another seemed to endorse sleep deprivation for 11 days, stated on one memo (http://www.chron.com). The CIA interrogators used waterboarding 183 times against the accused 9/11 major plotter Khalid Sheikh Mohammed, and 83 times against suspected Al-Qaeda leader Abu Zubaydah (The New York Times, April 20, 2009).

The U.S. has been building its military bases around the world, and cases of violation of local people's human rights are often seen. The U.S. is now maintaining 900 bases worldwide, with more than 190,000 military personnel and 115,000 relevant staff stationed. These bases are bringing serious damage and environmental contamination to the localities. Toxic substances caused by bomb explosions are taking their tolls on the local children. It has been reported that toward the end of the U.S. military bases' presence in Subic and Clark, as many as 3,000 cases of raping the local women had been filed against the U.S. servicemen, but all were dismissed (http://www.lexisnexis.com, May 17, 2009).

The U.S. has been maintaining its economic, commercial and financial embargo against Cuba for almost 50 years. The blockade has caused an accumulated direct economic loss of more than 93 billion U.S. dollars to Cuba. On October 28, 2009, the 64th session of the United Nations General Assembly adopted a resolution on the "Necessity of ending the economic, commercial and financial embargo imposed by the United States of America against Cuba," with a recorded vote of 187 in favor to three against, and two abstentions. This marked the 18th consecutive year the assembly had overwhelmingly called on the U.S. to lift the blockade without delay (Overwhelming International Rejection of US Blockade of Cuba at UN, www.cubanews.ain.cu).

The U.S. is pushing its hegemony under the pretence of "Internet freedom." The U.S. monopolizes the strategic resources of the global Internet, and has been retaining a tight grip over the Internet ever since its first appearance. There are currently 13 root servers of Internet worldwide, and the U.S. is the place where the only main root server and nine out of the rest 12 root servers are located. All the root servers are managed by the ICANN (Internet Corporation for Assigned Names and Numbers), which is, by the authority of the U.S. government, responsible for the management of the global root server system, the domain name system and the Internet Protocol address. The U.S. has declined all the requests from other countries as well as international organizations including the United Nations to break the U.S. monopoly over the root servers and to decentralize its management power over the Internet. The U.S. has been intervening in other countries' domestic affairs in various ways taking advantage of its control over Internet resources. The U.S. has a special troop of hackers, which is made up of hacker proficients recruited from all over the world.

The U.S. is using a global interception system named "ECHELON" to eavesdrop on communications worldwide. A report of the European Parliament pointed out that the "ECHELON" system is a network controlled by the U.S. for intelligence gathering and analyzing. The system is able to intercept and monitor the content of telephone calls, fax, e-mail and other digital information transmitted via public telephone networks, satellites and microwave links. The European Parliament has criticized the U.S. for using its "ECHELON" system to commit crimes such as civilian's privacy infringement or state-conducted industrial espionage, among which was the most striking case of Saudi Arabia's 6-billion-dollar aircraft contract (see Wikipedia). Telephone calls of British Princess Diana had been intercepted and eavesdropped because her global campaign against land-mines was in conflict with the U.S. policies. The Washington Post once reported that such spying activities conducted by the U.S. authorities were reminiscent of the Vietnam War when the U.S. imposed wiretapping and surveillance upon domestic anti-war activists.

The U.S. ignores international human rights conventions, and takes a passive attitude toward international human rights obligations. It signed the International Covenant on Economic, Social and Cultural Rights 32 years ago and the Convention on the Elimination of All Forms of Discrimination Against Women 29 years ago, but has ratified neither of them yet. It has not ratified the Convention on the Rights of Persons with Disabilities either. On Sept. 13, 2007, the 61st UN General Assembly voted to adopt the Declaration on the Rights of Indigenous Peoples, which has been the UN's most authoritative and comprehensive document to protect the rights of indigenous peoples. The U.S. also refused to recognize the declaration.

The above-mentioned facts show that the U.S. not only has a bad domestic human rights record, but also is a major source of many human rights disasters around the world. For a long time, it has placed itself above other countries, considered itself "world human rights police" and ignored its own serious human rights problems. It releases Country Reports on Human Rights Practices year after year to accuse other countries and takes human rights as a political instrument to interfere in other countries' internal affairs, defame other nations' image and seek its own strategic interests. This fully exposes its double standards on the human rights issue, and has inevitably drawn resolute opposition and strong denouncement from world people. At a time when the world is suffering a serious human rights disaster caused by the U.S. subprime crisis-induced global financial crisis, the U.S. government still ignores its own serious human rights problems but revels in accusing other countries. It is really a pity.

We hereby advise the U.S. government to draw lessons from the history, put itself in a correct position, strive to improve its own human rights conditions and rectify its acts in the human rights field.
Source: Xinhuanews

Document (Excerpts): Annual Report of the U.S. Commission on International Religious Freedom May 2010 (Covering April 1, 2009–March 31, 2010)

Commissioners

Leonard A. Leo, *Chair (July 2009–June 2010)*; Felice D. Gaer, *Chair (July 2008–June 2009)*; Michael Cromartie; Dr. Elizabeth H. Prodromou *Vice Chairs, (July 2008–June 2010)*;
Dr. Don Argue, Imam Talal Y. Eid, Felice D. Gaer, Dr. Richard D. Land, Nina Shea
Ambassador Jackie Wolcott *Executive Director*
[Table of Contents omitted]

April 29, 2010
The President
The White House
Washington, D.C. 20500

Dear Mr. President:

I am pleased to transmit the 2010 Annual Report of the U.S. Commission on International Religious Freedom (USCIRF). This report covers the period of April 2009 through March 2010, and was prepared in compliance with section 202(a)(2) of the International Religious Freedom Act of 1998 (IRFA), 22 U.S.C. 6401 et seq., P.L. 105-292, as amended by P.L. 106-55 and P.L. 107-228.

The Annual Report documents religious freedom abuses and limitations in 28 countries around the world, as well as concerns at the United Nations and the Organization for Security and Cooperation in Europe. The Annual Report:

• Recommends that the State Department designate five additional "countries of particular concern," or CPCs, under IRFA for egregious violations of religious freedom—Iraq, Nigeria, Pakistan, Turkmenistan, and Vietnam;
• Recommends eight countries be re-designated as CPCs—Burma, China, Eritrea, Iran, North Korea, Saudi Arabia, Sudan, and Uzbekistan—and that additional actions are taken;
• Documents violations of religious freedom in countries placed on the USCIRF Watch List and urges increased U.S. government response;

• Highlights efforts of some member states at the United Nations to undermine religious freedom standards through the flawed "defamation of religions" concept; and

• Discusses measures still required to address flaws in U.S. policy regarding expedited removal of asylum seekers. USCIRF concludes that the adoption of these and other recommendations found in the Annual Report would considerably advance U.S. efforts to protect and promote the universal right to freedom of religion or belief worldwide.

We would welcome the opportunity to discuss these policy recommendations with you.
Sincerely,
Leonard Leo
Chair

INTRODUCTION

The term religious persecution brings to mind images of a foreign government preventing people from worshiping or otherwise mistreating them for their beliefs. A second and equally egregious threat to religious freedom, however, commonly occurs but receives far less attention. Many governments fail to punish religiously motivated violence perpetrated by private actors. This breakdown in justice—known as impunity—has been repeatedly confronted as a harsh reality in many places by the U.S. Commission on International Religious Freedom (USCIRF).

USCIRF has seen the effects of impunity firsthand—particularly on vulnerable minority religious groups—during fact-finding trips to Egypt, Nigeria, and Sudan. USCIRF also has monitored the state's failure to punish private, religiously-motivated violence in Afghanistan, Eritrea, India, Iran, Iraq, and Pakistan. The absence of accountability breeds lawlessness, which encourages individuals to attack, and even kill, others who dissent from or fail to embrace their own religious views, including members of minority religious communities. This often leads to endless cycles of sectarian violence. Countering impunity is among the greatest challenges the U.S. government faces as it develops policies to effectively promote and protect freedom of religion or belief around the world.

Nigeria is a tragic case in point. Having visited Nigeria three times over the past year, USCIRF has observed how unchecked waves of sectarian violence—for which no perpetrator has yet been brought to justice—have engulfed this key nation in a conflagration of impunity. Since 1999, as many as 12,000 Nigerians have been killed in a dozen incidents. One religious community is pitted against another in repeated acts of retributive violence. Victims and perpetrators have included both Muslims and Christians. Most recently, in early 2010, 500 persons in a Christian village near the northern city of Jos were killed in such sectarian clashes. In this incident, men, women, and children were hacked to death with machetes and then dumped into wells. Not a single criminal, Muslim or Christian, has been convicted and sentenced in Nigeria's ten years of religious violence. Therein lies the problem. The Nigerian government and judicial system have so far been unwilling or unable to protect either side. Until this changes, we can only expect more violence. Already we are seeing the creation of conditions for the proliferation of extremist ideology and terrorism.

Of course, there are other disturbing trends that threaten freedom of religion across the globe. There is the exportation of extremist ideology, which USCIRF has observed in Saudi Arabia's dissemination of educational materials that instill hate and incite violence throughout the world. In Iran, the government persecutes many of its political opponents in the name of religion under blasphemy and apostasy laws, and denies all rights to one disfavored religious group, the Baha'is. There are also countless instances of state-sponsored repression of religion: Vietnam imprisons individuals for reasons related to their exercise or advocacy of freedom of religion or belief; the Egyptian government fails to provide Baha'is, Coptic Christians and other religious minorities the very basic benefits and privileges that others enjoy; North Korea bans virtually all worship and imprisons in its infamous labor camps even the grandchildren of those caught praying; and China seriously restricts religious activities, church governance, and places of worship.

Even in the most demoralizing of conditions, where repression seems to have all but smothered the human spirit, USCIRF has drawn inspiration and determination from people of faith who stand up for their freedom and human rights. In December 2009, USCIRF witnessed firsthand a group of irrepressible Sudanese political reformers in Khartoum who, only hours before, had been beaten and arrested for calling for faithful implementation of the Comprehensive Peace Agreement—implementation that is essential to preventing another bloody civil war that could result in the deaths of additional millions of people from the predominantly Christian and traditional-believing South. In Egypt, USCIRF visited Baha'is and Koranists whose co-religionists, because they refuse to compromise their religious principles, have been imprisoned for apostasy and blasphemy, and, in some cases, dismissed from jobs, expelled from universities, prevented from receiving inheritance, and denied rights, among others, to open bank accounts, buy cars, or obtain marriage certificates, birth certificates, or driver's licenses, all as a consequence of religious discrimination.

The photo on the cover of this report captures this spirit well: a lone Uighur Muslim woman facing down a column of armed Chinese security forces, defiant with her fist raised, declaring that her hope and courage will prevail over repressive state policies that seek to crush Uighur rights to religious education and to appoint their own religious leaders. With these and other profiles in courage, can there be any doubt that it is right and just for the preservation of freedom of religion to be among the fundamental principles of our nation's foreign policy, national security, and economic development agendas? Created by the International Religious Freedom Act of 1998 (IRFA), USCIRF is an independent U.S. government commission that monitors religious freedom worldwide and makes policy recommendations to the President, Secretary of State, and Congress. Separate from the State Department, USCIRF is the only government commission in the world with the sole mission of reviewing and making policy recommendations on the facts and circumstances of violations of religious freedom globally. The creation of USCIRF is one tangible example of the historic commitment of the U.S. to religious freedom for all. This 2010 Annual Report represents the culmination of a year's work to expose, counter and correct religious freedom abuses.

The Annual Report covers 28 countries from the period of April 2009 through March 2010. Country chapters provide a one-page overview of USCIRF's findings, the justification for the country's designation by USCIRF, and priority recommendations for action. Each chapter then more fully reports on events that took place over the reporting period, emphasizes important elements of the bilateral relationship, and details recommendations that would promote freedom of religion or belief as a more integral part of U.S. policy. The report is divided into five sections: the first section highlights countries which USCIRF has recommended that the State Department designate as "countries of particular concern" (CPCs) for severe violations of religious freedom; the second focuses on countries USCIRF has placed on a Watch List for violations of religious freedom not meeting the CPC threshold but requiring very close attention; the third on other countries USCIRF is closely monitoring; the fourth on multilateral organizations; and the fifth on U.S. policy on expedited removal of asylum seekers.

Over the past year, USCIRF has placed particular emphasis on eight priority countries—China, Egypt, Iran, Nigeria, Pakistan, Saudi Arabia, Sudan, and Vietnam—while continuing to monitor violations of religious freedom in other countries and recommending actions to address and to end these violations. To carry out its work on priority countries, USCIRF has undertaken delegations to Nigeria, Sudan, Egypt, and Vietnam, in addition to consultations at the European Union, the Holy See, the OSCE, and the Philippines. USCIRF has also convened civil society roundtables to monitor progress in Sudan; held press events focused on religious freedom and the rule of law in China and made detailed recommendations to the State Department on ways to improve human rights diplomacy with China; highlighted to President Obama needed U.S. engagement with Saudi Arabia; organized Congressional and NGO action before Vietnam's May 2009 Universal Periodic Review session at the UN; met with Secretary of State Hillary Clinton and Deputy Secretary James Steinberg on separate occasions to raise concerns about severe religious freedom abuses in Iran and Pakistan, among other countries; and testified on the status of human rights and religious freedom in China, Iran, and Vietnam, stressing the need to improve U.S. engagement on religious freedom. USCIRF also has advocated on behalf of a diverse array of religious communities: Uighur Muslims in China; Shi'a and Ismaili Muslims in Saudi Arabia; Ahmadi Muslims in Pakistan and Indonesia; Baha'is, Christians and dissident Muslims in Iran; Buddhists in Vietnam and China; and a range of indigenous faiths and spiritual movements in China, Egypt, Iraq, and Vietnam.

Additionally, USCIRF played a leading role in mobilizing Congress to engage key countries on the problematic "defamation of religions" resolutions when they came before the UN Human Rights Council and General Assembly. These are just some of the Commission's activities over the past 12 months, but they fairly represent the nature and breadth of its work.

In fulfilling its mandate and in response to the many abuses of religious freedom around the world, USCIRF repeatedly engaged the Obama administration on ways to promote religious freedom on issues critical to U.S. foreign policy. There have been a number of meetings with high-ranking officials from the State Department and National Security Council, as well as U.S. ambassadors to key countries. To create an "echo chamber" for having the U.S. government more fully address freedom of religion issues, Commissioners and staff met with representatives of religious communities and institutions, human rights groups, and academics, as well as other non-governmental organizations and policy experts. USCIRF advised members of Congress and their staffs, met with high-ranking officials from foreign governments and international organizations, participated with U.S. delegations to international meetings and conferences, and helped provide training to Foreign Service officers and other U.S. officials. USCIRF also held hearings and published op-eds in the *Wall Street Journal*, the *Miami Herald*, the *Atlanta Journal-Constitution*, the *Washington Times*, and the *Huffington Post*.

USCIRF's work is accomplished through the leadership of its Commissioners and engagement of its professional staff. Three Commissioners are appointed by the President, while six are appointed by the leadership of both parties in the House and Senate. This formula provides that four Commissioners are appointed by the Congressional leaders of the party that is not the President's party, and the party in the White House appoints five. (One Commissioner seat was vacant during the reporting period.) The Ambassador-at-Large for International Religious Freedom, a position at the State Department also created by IRFA, serves as a non-voting *ex officio* member. (To date, the position has not been filled by the Obama administration.)

In the end, USCIRF's mandate is to delve into the human rights "hot spots" of the world where freedom of religion is being obstructed and trampled, and to offer policy solutions to improve conditions in that small but critically important point of intersection of foreign policy, national security, and international religious freedom standards. Regrettably, that small point seems to shrink year-after-year for the White House and the State Department. This is a deepening problem despite the fact that religious freedom should be increasingly more important as one of the core considerations in foreign policy and national security. Neither prior Democratic and Republican administrations, nor the current administration, have been sufficiently engaged in promoting the freedom of religion or belief abroad. The U.S. must redouble its efforts to raise these concerns at the highest levels of the world community. Anything less betrays our history and values, and fails to leverage the extraordinary capacity we have as a nation to promote religious freedom and related human rights for all.

REPORT OVERVIEW AND IRFA IMPLEMENTATION
Countries of Particular Concern and the Watch List

In May 2009, for the first time, the U.S. Commission on International Religious Freedom(USCIRF or the Commission) recommended that Nigeria be designated a "country of particular concern" (CPC). This determination was based on the fact that after years of Muslim-Christian clashes resulting in over 12,000 deaths and many more displaced, not a single perpetrator had been brought to justice. The Commission warned that this climate of impunity could fuel further violent extremism. Just two months later, the radical Islamic sect Boko Haram ignited a wave of violence resulting in about 900 deaths in the name of having a stricter version of sharia law imposed in northern Nigeria. In December 2009, Nigerian Umar Farouk Abdulmutallab attempted to destroy a Northwest Airline flight on approach to Detroit. USCIRF visited Nigeria again in March 2010 and found federal government officials, who previously did not meet with USCIRF, attentive and even grateful for its concerns and willing to work closely with the U.S. government in finding a solution to the breakdown in justice. Indeed, during this visit, the Ministry of Justice filed 41 prosecutions in the courts of Jos in response to the latest Christian-Muslim clashes. The State Department is now redoubling its efforts to work with Christian and Muslim leaders alike in northern Nigeria. Much more needs to be done, but it seems a process toward reform has at least started.

USCIRF's work relating to Nigeria over the past 12 months, Vietnam's release of religious prisoner Father Ly, and the elimination by Saudi Arabia of some schoolbook passages that promote intolerance and incite violence, along with other developments described in this 2010 Annual Report, illustrate why the Commission is uniquely positioned to provide advice to the President, the Secretary of State, and the Congress as to which countries should be designated as "countries of particular concern," or CPCs. USCIRF provides for each country detailed policy recommendations for improving religious freedom conditions. USCIRF missions abroad give a focus to USCIRF's mandate: to identify "hot spots" where freedom of religion is obstructed and related human rights are trampled, and develop and recommend U.S. policy solutions at the critical convergence of foreign policy, national security, and international human rights. Advice and recommendations are based on USCIRF's ongoing review of the facts and circumstances of violations of religious freedom through its contacts with non-governmental organizations (NGOs), religious groups, U.S. government agencies, and foreign governments, and its missions.

1. A note on sources: In addition to information gathered from USCIRF's trips and meetings, this report is based on information from a variety of news sources; reports by the U.S. government and international organizations; written communications from foreign governments and embassies; communications from individuals abroad who are victims of religious freedom abuses; and reports by numerous U.S. and international non-governmental organizations. Non-governmental sources include, but are not limited to, the following: African Centre for Justice and Peace Studies, Ahmadiyya Movement in Islam USA, the Almaty Helsinki Committee, American Enterprise Institute, the American Islamic Congress, American Jewish Committee, Amnesty International, the Anti-Defamation League, Baha'i International Community, the Bangladesh Hindu, Buddhist and Christian Unity Council USA, Boat People SOS, Brookings Institution, Cardinal Kung Foundation, Carnegie Endowment for International Peace, Center "Demos," Center for the Study of Islam and Democracy, Center for Strategic and International Studies, Chatham House, Christian Solidarity International, Christian Solidarity Worldwide, Citizen's Alliance for Human Rights in North Korea, Committee for Religious Freedom in Vietnam, Compass Direct, Coptic Assembly of America, Council on Foreign Relations, CubaNet, Democracy Network Against NK Gulag, the Enough Project, Falun Dafa Information Center, Farsi Christian News Network, Forum 18, Religious News Service, Free North Korea Radio, Freedom House, the Friends of St. Elizabeth's Church, the Hindu American Foundation, Holy Spirit Study Center, the Hudson Institute Center for Religious Freedom, Human Rights First, Human Rights Watch, the Initiative Group USCIRF is one of several mechanisms established by the International Religious Freedom Act of 1998 (IRFA), along with the Office of International Religious Freedom at the Department of State, headed by an Ambassador-at-Large for International Religious Freedom. IRFA also mandated that the State Department review religious freedom conditions worldwide, by collecting information through its embassies and consulates abroad, and issue annually a global report on religious freedom (the *Annual Report on International Religious Freedom*). Based on that review, IRFA's provisions require the President, who has delegated this authority to the Secretary of State, to designate "countries of particular concern" (CPCs) whose governments have engaged in or tolerated "particularly severe" violations of religious freedom. IRFA defines "particularly severe" violations as ones that are "systematic, ongoing, and egregious," including acts such as torture, prolonged detention without charges, disappearances, or "other flagrant denial[s] of the right to life, liberty, or the security of persons." After a country is designated a CPC, the President is required by law to take one or more of the actions specified in IRFA, or to invoke a waiver if circumstances warrant. In this reporting period, USCIRF recommends that the Secretary of State designate the following 13 countries as CPCs: Burma, the Democratic People's Republic of Korea (North Korea), Eritrea, Iran, Iraq, Nigeria, Pakistan, the People's Republic of China, Saudi Arabia, Sudan, Turkmenistan, Uzbekistan, and Vietnam.

The State Department's January 2009 CPC designations repeated the 2006 designations of eight countries: Burma, the Democratic People's Republic of Korea (North Korea), Eritrea, Iran, the People's Republic of China, Saudi Arabia, Sudan, and Uzbekistan. The State Department issued a 180-day waiver on taking any action against Uzbekistan and an indefinite waiver for Saudi Arabia, in both cases to "further the purposes of the [International Religious Freedom] Act." As a result of these waivers, the U.S. will not implement any policy response to the particularly severe violations of religious freedom in either country. USCIRF continues to express concern and disappointment that the Secretary of State, in this as well as previous administrations, has declined to designate as CPCs the additional countries USCIRF has recommended.

USCIRF also names countries to a Watch List, based on the need to closely monitor serious violations of religious freedom engaged in or tolerated by the governments of countries that do not meet the CPC threshold. The Watch List provides advance warning of negative trends that could develop into severe violations of religious freedom, thereby providing policymakers with the opportunity to engage early and of Independent Human Rights Defenders of Uzbekistan, the Institute for Gulf Affairs, Institute for Security Studies, Inter American Dialogue, Internal Displacement Monitoring Centre, International Campaign for Tibet, International Christian Concern, the International Crisis Group, the International Rescue Committee, Iran Human Rights Documentation Center, the Jehovah's Witnesses USA, Jubilee Campaign USA, Justice Africa, the Kazakhstan International Bureau on Human Rights and the Rule of Law, the Mandaean Human Rights Group, the Middle East Institute, Minority Rights Group International, the Moscow Helsinki Group, the Najot Human Rights Group, the National Conference on Soviet Jewry, National Democratic Institute for International Affairs, the National Endowment for Democracy, the National Spiritual Assembly of the Baha'is of the U.S., North Korea Freedom Coalition, Open Doors USA, the Open Society Institute, Project on Middle East Democracy, Public International Law and Policy Group, Que Me, Redress, Reporters Without

Borders, the Russian-Chechen Friendship Society, SETARA Institute for Democracy and Peace, the Slavic Center for Law and Justice, the SOVA Center, the Turkish Economic and Social Studies Foundation, the Turkmen Initiative for Human Rights, the Union of Councils for Jews in the Former Soviet Union, United Sikhs, U.S. Campaign for Burma, U.S. Committee for Human Rights in North Korea, the U.S. Conference of Catholic Bishops, the U.S. Institute of Peace, Uyghur-American Conference, Vietnam Committee for Human Rights, Voices for a Democratic Egypt, Voices for Sudan, Wahid Institute, the Washington Institute for Near East Policy.

2. While joining the Commission's report on Iraq, Commissioners Cromartie, Eid, and Land dissented from the CPC recommendation, concluding that Iraq should be placed on the Commission's Watch List. *Overview and IRFA Implementation* increasing the likelihood of preventing or diminishing the violations. USCIRF's Watch List in this reporting period consists of Afghanistan, Belarus, Cuba, Egypt, India[3], Indonesia, Laos, Russia, Somalia, Tajikistan, Turkey, and Venezuela.

Countries Designated as CPCs by the Department of State: Burma, China, Eritrea Iran, North Korea, Saudi Arabia, Sudan, Uzbekistan

USCIRF Recommendations for CPC Designation: Burma, China, Eritrea, Iran, North Korea, Saudi Arabia, Sudan, Uzbekistan, Iraq, Nigeria, Pakistan, Turkmenistan, Vietnam.

USCIRF Watch List Countries: Afghanistan, Belarus, Cuba, Egypt, India, Indonesia, Laos, Russia, Somalia, Tajikistan, Turkey, Venezuela

Current CPC and Watch List Countries

Designating a country as a CPC provides the Secretary of State with a range of flexible and specific policy options to address serious violations of religious freedom. Sanctions (referred to as Presidential actions in IRFA) are not automatically imposed. Rather, the Secretary of State is empowered to enter into direct consultations with a government to find ways to bring about improvements in religious freedom. While sanctions are a possible policy outcome, IRFA provides the Secretary with other options. For instance, IRFA permits the development of a binding agreement with the CPC-designated government on specific actions that it will take to end the violations that gave rise to the designation or the taking of a "commensurate action." Also, the Secretary may determine that pre-existing sanctions are adequate or waive the requirement of taking action in furtherance of the Act.

However, in practice the flexibility provided in IRFA has been underutilized and, as a result, the statute has not been employed to bring about real progress. The U.S. government generally has not implemented new Presidential actions pursuant to CPC designations, but rather has relied on pre-existing sanctions. Of the eight countries designated as CPCs by the State Department, only one—Eritrea—faces sanctions specifically imposed under IRFA for religious freedom violations. While relying on pre-existing sanctions is technically correct under the statute, the practice of "double-hatting" has provided little incentive for the other CPC-designated governments to reduce or end egregious violations of religious freedom. For these mechanisms to have any real impact on promoting religious freedom, the designation of an egregious religious freedom violator as a CPC must be followed by the implementation of a clear, direct, and specific Presidential action. [Footnotes omitted]

Document (Excerpted): Report of the United Nations High Commissioner for Human Rights on the implementation of Human Rights Council resolution 10/22 entitled "Combating defamation of religions"

UNITED NATIONS	A/HRC/13/57_
General Assembly	Distr.:
HUMAN RIGHTS COUNCIL	GENERAL
Thirteenth session	11 January 2010
Agenda item 9	Original: ENGLISH

RACISM, RACIAL DISCRIMINATION, XENOPHOBIA AND RELATED FORMS OF INTOLERANCE, FOLLOW-UP AND IMPLEMENTATION OF THE DURBAN DECLARATION AND PROGRAMME OF ACTION

Report of the United Nations High Commissioner for Human Rights on the implementation of Human Rights Council resolution 10/22 entitled "Combating defamation of religions"

Summary

By resolution 10/22, the Human Rights Council requested the High Commissioner for Human Rights to report to the Council on the implementation of the same resolution, including on the possible correlation between defamation of religions and the upsurge in incitement, intolerance and hatred in many parts of the world.

The present report is submitted pursuant to this request of the Council. Information is provided about measures taken to address acts of violence, discriminatory practices, profiling, stigmatization, derogatory stereotyping based on religion or belief, the desecration of places of worship or spirituality, the targeting of religious symbols, incitement to religious hatred and instances of religious intolerance, including Islamophobia and anti-Semitism.

The report contains information from Member States and regional organizations. In addition, the report updates the Secretary-General's report of 31 July 2009 to the General Assembly at its sixty-fourth session on combating defamation of religions 1 by giving information on the latest developments at the level of human rights treaty bodies, special procedures and the United Nations.

[Contents omitted]

I. Introduction

1. In its resolution 10/22 on combating defamation of religions of 26 March 2009, the Human Rights Council (hereafter "the Council") expressed deep concern over the negative stereotyping of religions and manifestations of discrimination in matters of religion or belief. The Council strongly deplored all acts of violence, and incitement thereto, against persons on the basis of their religion or belief, and against their businesses, properties, cultural centres and places of worship, as well as the targeting of holy sites, religious symbols and venerated personalities of all religions. Deep concern was also expressed over the frequent and wrong association of Islam with terrorism, the ethnic and religious profiling of Muslim minorities in the aftermath of the tragic events of 11 September 2001, and the stigmatization of Muslim minorities.

2. In paragraph 19 of resolution 10/22, the Council requested the High Commissioner for Human Rights to report to the Council at its twelfth session on the implementation of the resolution, including on the possible correlation between defamation of religions and the upsurge in incitement, intolerance and hatred in many parts of the world. In implementation of this request, notes verbales were sent by the Office of the High Commissioner for Human Rights to Member States, United Nations entities and regional organizations to solicit information on measures and activities undertaken to combat defamation of religions. To be able to include the broadest number of contributions in her report, the High Commissioner, in a note by the Secretariat on 9 July 2009, requested that the submission of her report to the Council be delayed to its thirteenth session. Hence, the present report is submitted accordingly to the thirteenth session of the Council pursuant to the request contained in resolution 10/22.

. . .

6. Specific reference is also made to the study of the High Commissioner for Human Rights compiling existing legislation and jurisprudence concerning defamation of and contempt for religions and the report by the High Commissioner for Human Rights pursuant to resolution 7/19 on combating defamation of religions, both submitted to the Council at its ninth session. Compiling contributions from States, regional and nongovernmental organizations (NGOs), the latter report concluded that most replies reflected concern that there was a growing trend towards the negative portrayal of religion in the media and in political discourse, and policies and practices that seemed targeted at persons because of their religion.

7. The present report contains information from States, regional organizations and the United Nations on various elements described in Council resolution 10/22 on combating defamation of religions. In addition, the report updates the Secretary-General's report of 31 July 2009 to the General Assembly at its sixty-fourth session on combating defamation of religions 16 by giving information on the latest developments at the level of human rights treaty bodies and special procedures.

II. Member States

Algeria

8. Algeria gave information on relevant constitutional provisions and international human rights instruments that it had ratified which were directly applicable and could be invoked by citizens and migrant workers. In the area of national legislation, it was noted that Ordinance 06-03 established the conditions for practising religions other than Islam. The Ordinance guaranteed freedom of religion, as well as tolerance and respect among different religions and the protection by the State of non-Muslim religious organizations.

. . .

Guatemala

[Original: Spanish]

11. Guatemala reported that the spiritual practices of the indigenous people of Guatemala had historically been prohibited or disdained, but that, at the present time, freedom of religion was an integral element of the country's vision of a culture of peace and the creation of a multicultural, multi-ethnic and multilingual State. In the period from 2004–2008, the national human rights institution of Guatemala had received 17 complaints invoking negative stereotyping of indigenous spirituality, accusations of witchcraft, and disrespect for places and symbols of worship.

. . .

Kazakhstan

15. Kazakhstan reported that it was historically at the crossroads of religions, cultures and civilizations. It reported that 40 confessions and denominations, as well as 130 nationalities and ethnic groups, coexisted peacefully and that Kazakhstan ensured religious freedom for Muslims, Christians and Jews.

. . .

Pakistan

18. Pakistan, in its submission, gave an overview of global events affecting Muslims in the world, Islamophobia as a rapidly increasing phenomenon, the basic principles governing the relation of Islam with Christianity and Judaism, and the centrality of peace and dialogue in Islam.

19. It further reported that article 33 of the Constitution of Pakistan stipulated the discouragement by the State of parochial, racial, tribal, sectarian and provincial prejudices among its citizens. Sections 295–298 of the Pakistani Criminal Code addressed defamation of religions, providing sanctions of imprisonment, fines, or both, for the following: acts of vandalism in a place of worship with the intent of insulting a religion, deliberate and malicious acts intended to outrage religious feelings or beliefs, disturbance of religious ceremonies or assembly, trespassing of places of worship or burial, and speech or gestures deliberately intended to hurt religious feelings.

. . .

Qatar

21. Qatar reported that it had undertaken legislative, institutional and awareness-raising activities to promote and protect religious freedoms and combat defamation of religions as part of its efforts to promote and protect human rights. Articles 18, 19, 34 and 35 of the Constitution of Qatar prohibited discrimination on the grounds of sex, origin, language or religion. Article 50 of the Constitution further guaranteed freedom of worship for all.

. . .

Serbia

25. Serbia reported on its legal guarantees against discrimination on the grounds of religion or belief, in particular articles 21, 43 and 49 of the Constitution. Serbia noted that while according to article 50, paragraph 3, of the Constitution censorship was not allowed, a competent court could prevent the dissemination of information when this was necessary to prevent advocacy of racial, ethnic or religious hatred inciting discrimination, hostility or violence.

. . .

Singapore

30. Singapore reported on its approach to fostering harmonious interreligious relations and combating defamation of religions in Singapore. The principle of meritocracy was enshrined in the Constitution and prohibited discrimination or disadvantage on the basis of religion. Within the context of a secular State, religion was generally considered as having a positive influence on society. Multiracialism, it was noted, was a key feature of the national identity of Singapore. Therefore, each community could practise its own beliefs as long as the rights and sensitivities of other groups were not infringed.

. . .

United States of America

[Original: English]

41. The United States of America, in its contribution, affirmed that the concept of defamation of religions was inconsistent with international human rights law and risked being abused by Governments to restrict the human rights of religious minorities or dissidents. While sharing the concerns underlying Human Rights Council resolution 10/22, such as the negative stereotyping of religious groups, particularly minority groups, and the contribution of such stereotypes to disrespect and discrimination, the U.S. considered that

placing limitations on freedom of speech was unacceptable and, moreover, inadequately addressed genuine concerns.

42. After 11 September 2001, the Justice Department had implemented the Backlash Initiative to combat violence and threats against Arabs, Muslims, Sikhs and South Asians, or individuals perceived as such. More than 700 incidents had been investigated and 34 federal convictions obtained. The initiative had also assisted local law enforcement agencies in bringing over 160 criminal cases to justice. Since 2001, the Department of Justice Community Relations Service had held over 250 community meetings around the country to address backlash issues and deployed conflict resolution specialists to over 50 communities. Likewise, based on feedback and input from the Arab, Muslim, Sikh, South Asian and Middle Eastern American communities, cultural competency training had been developed for personnel of the Department of Homeland Security. The U.S. also actively encouraged civil society actors, including religious groups, to participate in interfaith dialogue, education efforts and alliance-building with domestic and international religious groups and leaders to foster understanding within and among communities and promote conflict prevention.

43. The U.S. also reported on its strong belief in and vigorous defence of the freedoms of religion, belief and expression. As a result of its protection of freedom of religion, the Department of Justice had won the right for a Muslim school bus driver to have his schedule adjusted so that he could attend Friday prayers. As a result of its protection of freedom of speech, U.S. courts had upheld the rights of neo-Nazis, Holocaust deniers and white supremacist groups to march in public and distribute literature. The U.S. expressed the view that Government censorship or prohibition of speech based on stereotypical or intolerant content only forced hateful ideology to find new and alternative outlets. Instead, the U.S. advocated concrete action in support of tolerance and individual rights as the best way to combat hateful ideologies.

Bolivarian Republic of Venezuela

44. The Bolivarian Republic of Venezuela reported its attachment to ethnic, cultural and religious diversity at the domestic and international levels. Article 59 of the Constitution guaranteed freedom of religion and religious practice. Articles 169–171 of the Venezuelan Criminal Code established offences for infringement on freedom of worship, vandalism of places of worship and burial, and other violations of freedom of religion.

. . .

III. Regional organizations
European Commission against Racism and Intolerance of the Council of Europe

46. The European Commission against Racism and Intolerance ("the Commission") is an independent human rights monitoring body of the Council of Europe specialized in questions relating to racism and intolerance. It is composed of independent experts, appointed on the basis of their moral authority and recognized expertise in dealing with racism, xenophobia, anti-Semitism and intolerance. In its annual report covering the period from 1 January through 31 December 2008, the Commission provided information with respect to contemporary forms of racism and racial discrimination in the geographic area covered by the Council of Europe. It pointed to a negative climate in public opinion which, it noted, played a key role in the appearance of manifestations of racism or intolerance. Such a climate, according to the Commission, was fuelled by some media and also by the increasing use of racist and xenophobic arguments in political discourse. Faced with this situation, ECRI advocated strengthening legal protection against racist acts and discrimination on the grounds of race, colour, language, religion, nationality or national or ethnic origin. The Commission welcomed the fact that member States of the Council of Europe were continuing to adopt and fine-tune criminal law provisions against racist acts and anti-discrimination legislation. However, it noted that many States were yet to fill remaining gaps in their legislation.

47. The Commission also reported that, in 2008, the negative portrayal of Muslims in the media continued to be one of the main obstacles to their integration in member States of the Council of Europe. Islamophobia manifested itself through prejudice and stereotypes against Muslims, which in turn led to acts of discrimination and intolerance against them in everyday life. While some European Governments had taken initiatives to encourage greater tolerance of religious diversity, such as the establishment of forums for intercultural dialogue, the Commission noted that greater efforts were necessary to remove legal and psychological barriers which still existed in some countries with respect to Muslims practising their religion. Particular reference was made to the construction of mosques.

. . .

European Union

50. On 28 May 2009, the Fundamental Rights Agency of the European Union released, as part of its European Union Minorities and Discrimination Survey series, a report examining discrimination against Muslims in the European Union under the title, "Data in Focus—Report 2: Muslims". The report reflected the views of Muslim respondents of diverse ethnic origins.

. . .

Organization of the Islamic Conference (OIC)

54. The Organization of the Islamic Conference (OIC) did not provide information on defamation of religions or measures adopted to address this problem in the geographical region covered by the organization. However, in its Second OIC Observatory Report on Islamophobia, issued at the thirty-sixth Council of Foreign Ministers in May 2009 submitted to the Secretariat, the OIC provides an account of manifestations and incidents of Islamophobia in Western societies, as monitored by the Observatory from June 2008 to April 2009, including incidents related to mosques, desecration of Muslim graves, incidents related to the *Hijab* (headscarf), political and social campaigns against Islam and Muslims, intolerance against sacred symbols of Islam, and discrimination against Muslims in education, the workplace and airports. In addition, the report cites good practices to combat Islamophobia.

. . .

IV. The United Nations

Economic and Social Commission for Western Asia

58. In its report on the implementation of Human Rights Council resolution 10/22, the Economic and Social Commission for Western Asia ("the Commission") focused on a pilot study undertaken between December 2008 and January 2009 to shed light on ethnosectarian coexistence, ethno-sectarian tensions and manifestations of incitement, intolerance and hatred among religious communities. The pilot study, conducted in the Lebanon, involved 15 focus group discussions with 113 youths aged 18–25 years.

. . .

Department of Public Information

60. On 17 June 2009, the United Nations appealed to parents, the Internet industry and policymakers to join hands to eradicate hate speech from cyberspace. Addressing a daylong seminar titled "Unlearning Intolerance" on the danger of cyberhate, the Secretary-General lauded the benefits of the Internet but regretted that some used information technology to reinforce stereotypes, spread misinformation and propagate hate. He warned that some of the newest technologies were being used to peddle some of the oldest fears, decrying what he called "digital demonization" which targeted innocents because of their faith, their race or their ethnicity. The Secretary-General said that the Internet industry could help ensure that hate speech did not proliferate online and he urged policymakers to safeguard people while balancing basic freedoms and human rights. The United Nations began its "Unlearning Intolerance" series in 2004 with a forum on anti-Semitism and Islamophobia and has since continued the programme with lectures and seminars.

Office of the High Commissioner for Human Rights

61. Reference is made to the chapter on the Office of the High Commissioner for Human Rights ("the Office") in the report of the Secretary-General to the General Assembly at its sixty-fourth session on combating defamation of religions.21 On 2 and 3 October 2008, the Office organized an expert consultation on the links between articles 19 and 20 of the International Covenant on Civil and Political Rights entitled, "Freedom of expression and advocacy of religious hatred that constitutes incitement to discrimination, hostility or violence". Participants included 12 experts and over 200 observers, including from Governments, United Nations agencies, regional organizations, the media and NGOs.

62. In 2008–2009, the Office served as the Secretariat for the Durban Review process which culminated in the adoption of the outcome document by the Durban Review Conference.22 Although the document did not refer to the notion of defamation of religions, it made a number of provisions to address the scourges described in resolution Human Rights Council 10/22, including paragraphs 12, 68, 69 and 134.

63. The outcome document also emphasizes the critical importance of intercultural and interreligious dialogue as a means to prevent, combat and eradicate racism, racial discrimination, xenophobia and related intolerance. Intercultural and interreligious issues are considered in various forums and bodies of the United Nations system, as reflected in the report on the subject by the Secretary-General to the sixty-fourth session of the General Assembly, to which the Office contributed. A major initiative, relevant for the implementation of

the Council's resolution 10/22, is the declaration of 2010 as the International Year on the Rapprochement of Cultures.

. . .

67. The High Commissioner for Human Rights took up the profiling of Muslim minorities in the aftermath of the tragic events of 11 September 2001 with the Counter-Terrorism Committee of the Security Council. In her address to the Committee on 29 October 2009, she expressed concern over profiling based on national or ethnic origin or religion with respect to the right to privacy and the principles of equality and nondiscrimination. She emphasized that the latter were central to human rights law and allowed no derogation. She warned that discriminatory and stigmatizing measures affected the rights of entire communities and might lead to further marginalization.

. . .

V. Human rights treaty bodies

69. Reference is made to the study of the High Commissioner for Human Rights, submitted to the Human Rights Council at its ninth session and compiling jurisprudence concerning defamation and contempt for religions, as well as the chapter on treaty bodies in the report of the Secretary-General to the General Assembly at its sixty-fourth session on combating defamation of religions.

70. At its ninety-fourth session from 13 to 31 October 2008, the Human Rights Committee decided to revise its general comment on article 19 (freedom of expression) of the International Covenant on Civil and Political Rights. A first reading of the draft general comment was initiated by the Human Rights Committee at its ninety-seventh session, held from 12 to 30 October 2009.

. . .

VI. Human rights special procedures

77. Reference is made to the chapter on special procedures in the report of the Secretary-General to the General Assembly at its sixty-fourth session on combating defamation of religions which gives an overview of the positions of the Special Rapporteur on contemporary forms of racism, racial discrimination, xenophobia and related intolerance, the Special Rapporteur on freedom of religion or belief, the independent expert on minority issues and the Special Rapporteur on the promotion and protection of the right to freedom of opinion and expression. Specific reference is made to a joint statement by three mandate holders stating that "difficulties in providing an objective definition of the term 'defamation of religions' at the international level make the whole concept open to abuse".

78. During his presentation of his interim report before the General Assembly, the Special Rapporteur on contemporary forms of racism, racial discrimination, xenophobia and related intolerance, Mr. Githu Muigai, noted that the terminology controversy around the concepts of "defamation of religions" and "incitement to racial or religious hatred" had unfortunately detracted the attention from real problems affecting the persons to be protected. He therefore recommended focusing on the rights of individuals affected by racial and religious intolerance, discrimination or violence, as well as on the best ways to prevent and combat such deplorable acts. In doing so, he took the view that it was necessary to rely on existing human rights norms in order to find a way out of the terminology controversy. The debate obviously needed to be continued and he expressed his sincere hope that its outcome would provide effective and concrete responses to individuals who are victims of discrimination or violence on the grounds of ethnicity, religion or belief.

79. During a seminar on the strengthening of cooperation between the European Union and the United Nations in the struggle against all forms of discrimination held in Brussels on 14 October 2009, the Special Rapporteur on contemporary forms of racism, racial discrimination, xenophobia and related intolerance was invited to speak about intolerance and discrimination against Arabs and Muslims. In his statement,[32] he noted that discrimination targeting Muslims fell within the remit of his mandate when linked to discrimination on the ground of ethnic origin. While he focused his presentation mainly on intolerance and discrimination against Arabs and Muslims in Europe, he stressed that other regions were also affected by instances of racial and religious discrimination and incitement to hatred. Moreover, he underlined that discrimination and incitement to hatred affected members of other religious and ethnic groups and should also be addressed.

80. The Special Rapporteur on freedom of religion or belief, Ms. Asma Jahangir, in her report to the General Assembly at its sixty-fourth session, identified the dissemination of religious intolerance and stereotypes via new information technologies as a new challenge of the twenty-first century. The Special Rapporteur stressed that religious or belief communities had been the object of critical analysis ranging from merely

theological points of view to the most extreme forms of incitement to violence or hatred against members of a religious group. The Special Rapporteur emphasized that impunity in cases of incitement to religious hatred emboldened forces of bigotry.

81. Another general pattern identified by the Special Rapporteur on freedom of religion or belief was the targeting of places of worship and other religious buildings and properties. The Special Rapporteur expressed concern about reports of frequent attacks on places of worship, the desecration of cemeteries and the exhumation of dead bodies. Attacks or other forms of restriction of places of worship in many cases violated the rights not only of a single believer, but also of the community attached to the place in question.

82. Finally, the Special Rapporteur on freedom of religion or belief regretted that, eight years after the World Conference against Racism, Racial Discrimination, Xenophobia and Related Intolerance, she continued to receive frequent and worrisome reports of religious intolerance and acts of violence against members of virtually all religious or belief communities. The Special Rapporteur also criticized counter-terrorism measures based on discriminatory profiling, implemented according to perceived religious affiliation.

83. On 30 November 2009, the Special Rapporteur on freedom of religion or belief issued a press release regretting the outcome of the vote to ban the construction of minarets in Switzerland and expressing her concern over its negative consequences for members of the Muslim community in Switzerland. She called for education and awareness-raising measures to help eliminate the grounds for irrational fears towards Muslims.

VII. Conclusions

84. The information from States, regional organizations, United Nations entities, human rights treaty bodies and special procedures raises concern about acts of violence, protracted discrimination and stigmatization on the basis of religion or belief. Some contributions also suggest a negative portrayal of religion, as well as incitement to ethnic and religious hatred by some political parties and some media. Indeed, religious minorities seem to be frequent targets of abusive, violent and repetitive criticism against their group, often as a result of entrenched negative stereotypes.

85. Initiatives to combat the human rights violations described in Human Rights Council resolution 10/22 include measures in the constitutional and legislative areas, in the areas of law enforcement and the administration of justice (including access hereto), policy measures, prejudice-reduction programmes for key professionals (including the media), intercultural dialogue and awareness-raising initiatives, as well as the creation of specialized bodies at the national level or the establishment of focal points within existing national human rights institutions to monitor trends and/or assist victims.

Document (Excerpts): U.S. Government response to [U.N.] Office of the High Commissioner for Human Rights regarding the Defamation of Religions resolution—Tabs 1 and 2.
U.S. Government Response to the United Nations Office of the High Commissioner for Human Rights concerning Combating Defamation of Religions, Tab 1.
General Introduction

We are writing in response to your letter dated April 25, 2008 referring to General Assembly resolution 62/154, entitled "Combating Defamation of Religions," which requests the Secretary General to submit a report on the implementation of the resolution. Resolution 62/154 was adopted by a splintered vote of 108 (in favor), 51 (against), and 25 abstentions.

The divisions in the international community about the concept of "defamation of religions" are more than an academic or theoretical debate. There have been numerous reports that this concept is being used in some member states to justify torture, imprisonment, and other forms of abuse. There are also examples of governments issuing execution orders against individuals and religious groups who do not subscribe to a particular "State" religion, who wish to convert to another religion according to their conscience, or who are merely exercising their right to freedom of expression and opinion or assembly.

The U.S. therefore believes that the concept of "defamation of religions" is not supported by international law and that efforts to combat "defamation of religions" typically result in restrictions on the freedoms of thought, conscience, religion, and expression. While appearing in name to promote tolerance, implementation of this concept actually fosters intolerance and has served to justify restrictions on human rights and fundamental freedoms such as the freedoms of religion and expression for all persons, including those who may or may not belong to a particular faith. Accordingly, the U.S. considers this concept to be inherently flawed.

At the same time, the Unites States reiterates that it does not support statements intended to insult religious traditions and works to promote a climate of tolerance, respect, and understanding. The Unites States condemns discrimination based on such grounds as race, ethnicity, religion or gender and supports international efforts to combat such discrimination. The U.S. understands that religion is a central organizing principle for many societies. We sympathize with those who seek to promote tolerance and take a strong stand against offensive speech. Restricting the rights of individuals, however, is not the way to achieve this goal.

Legal Problems with the Concept of Defamation of Religions

From a legal perspective, the "defamation of religions" concept is deeply problematic. Under existing human rights law, individuals—not religions, ideologies, or beliefs—are the holders of human rights and are protected by the law. However, the concept of "defamation of religions" seeks to convey the idea that a religion itself can be a subject of protection under human rights law, thereby potentially undermining protections for individuals.

In addition, "defamation" carries a particular legal meaning and application in domestic systems that makes the term wholly unsuitable in the context of "religions." A defamatory statement (or other communication) is more than just an offensive one. It is also a statement that is false. Because one defense to a charge of defamation is that the statement is in fact true, the concept does not properly apply to that which cannot be verified as either true or false, such as statements of belief or opinion. Even offensive opinions and beliefs are not defamatory.

It is also unclear how "defamation" could be defined considering that one individual's sincere belief that his or her creed alone is the truth inevitably conflicts with another's sincerely held view of the truth. Even between adherents of the same religion there are divergent views that some might find offensive or "defamatory." How could an international framework or entity properly adjudicate such deeply held individual beliefs as "defamatory" to another belief?

Even if a defamation standard were to be legally enforceable, and even if it could be enforced in an equitable manner, it would lead to numerous legal claims and counterclaims between majority and minority religious communities or dissenting members of a faith. Instead of fostering tolerance, such a standard would almost certainly lead to greater conflict and intolerance. What is considered to be a sacred statement by one may be viewed as sacrilegious to another, and could therefore be legally actionable as a "defamation of religion".

Examples of Abuse of Defamation Laws

When the "defamation of religions" concept has been promulgated or invoked in national legal systems, the resulting anti-defamation provisions have often been abused and used against minority religious communities or dissident members of the majority faith. These legal provisions have also been used to deter and/or punish public comment or dissent against political figures.

Here are a few examples of when defamation-related laws have been abused by governments and used to restrict human rights:

• In January 2008, a provincial court sentenced a student to death for distributing "blasphemous" material regarding the role of women in Islamic societies. The student was arrested in October 2007 for downloading the material from the internet and passing it to students at the university he attended. The case is on appeal.

• In December 2007, a court reportedly sentenced two foreigners to six months in prison for allegedly marketing a book deemed offensive to Aisha, one of Prophet Mohammed's wives.

• In November 2007, a court sentenced a British teacher to 15 days in jail for "insulting religion," after she named a class teddy bear Mohammed. A 7-year-old student named Mohammed had reportedly requested that the bear be named after him. The teacher was pardoned and deported the following month.

The U.S. has also observed that some Member States promoting the "defamation of religions" concept do not appear to be speaking out against and condemning intolerant statements made in their own countries about minority faiths or seeking to change policies and laws that favor or promote one religion over another. Domestic political leadership is critical to promoting a culture of religious tolerance and respect. Governmental representatives and elected leaders must be willing to object openly to instances of religious intolerance against any faith, whether majority or minority, and to promote laws and policies that respect freedom of religion, expression, and assembly.

The U.S. Domestic Approach

The U.S. is home to individuals from a vast array of religious and cultural traditions—from those practiced by the over 560 federally recognized indigenous tribes to those traditions that immigrants have brought from around the world. We believe that promoting freedom of expression, religion, and assembly are the cornerstones that have allowed such diversity—as well as respect for such diversity—to flourish in the U.S.

The First Amendment to the U.S. Constitution guarantees the right to freedom of religion. It prohibits the federal government from making any law that establishes a national religion (Establishment Clause) or prohibits free exercise of religion (Free Exercise Clause). The Free Exercise Clause as interpreted includes the right to freedom of belief and worship and the freedom to not believe in any faith. The First Amendment also prohibits the federal legislature from making laws that infringe on freedom of speech, freedom of the press, the right to assemble peacefully, and the right to petition the government.

Democracy depends upon a knowledgeable citizenry whose access to uncensored ideas, opinions, and information enables it to participate as fully as possible in public life. For this reason, although freedom of expression that threatens the public good is not absolute, prohibitions are restricted to forms of expression that threaten the public good by, for example, inciting imminent violence or other unlawful activity; expression is not restricted merely for being offensive. This view was summarized well by Thomas Jefferson, third U.S. President and eminent political philosopher, who stated, "(w)e have nothing to fear from the demoralizing reasonings of some, if others are left free to demonstrate their errors and especially when the law stands ready to punish the first criminal acts produced by the false reasonings. . . ."

We believe it is not a useful function for governments to judge the offensiveness of speech and imprison or punish their citizens for such offensive speech. We adhere to the philosophy that freedom of expression helps to protect "a marketplace of ideas." Government should not prohibit or punish speech, even offensive or hateful speech, because of an underlying confidence that in a free society such hateful ideas will fail on account of their own intrinsic lack of merit.

The U.S. agrees that more must be done to promote inter-religious understanding and believes concrete action supporting tolerance and individual rights is the best way to combat abusive actions and hateful ideologies. The U.S. takes many actions aimed at promoting a global dialogue based on respect for human rights and religious diversity. The Fifth, Thirteenth, Fourteenth, and Fifteenth Amendments to the U.S. Constitution guarantee that no public authority may engage in any act or practice of racial discrimination against persons, groups of persons, or institutions. These prohibitions apply with equal force at the federal, state, and local levels, and all public authorities and institutions must comply.

The U.S. International Approach

At the international level, the U.S. Department of State focuses on promoting the rights to freedom of religion, expression, and assembly through its Bureau of Democracy, Human Rights and Labor. In addition to the annual Country Reports on Human Rights, which also addresses these rights, the Bureau's Office of International Religious Freedom is devoted entirely to promoting religious freedom around the world for all faiths, including Islam. The Office monitors religious discrimination and persecution worldwide, and recommends and implements policies to promote religious freedom. The Office also meets with religious leaders and engages them in promoting religious diversity and tolerance. Finally, the Office writes annual religious freedom reports which document the status of religious freedom across the globe.

As part of our diplomacy and assistance efforts around the world, the U.S. advocates and seeks to create the conditions for religious freedom, freedom of expression, and political participation because we believe those are the rights of all people. The U.S. Government will continue to sponsor educational programs at all levels in partnership with countries across the world.

Alongside our own international efforts, the U.S. participates in the UN's efforts to promote a culture of peace, tolerance and religious diversity through dialogue and global frameworks such as the "Global Agenda for Dialogue among Civilizations" and its Programme of Action adopted by the UN General Assembly and initiated by UNESCO, and the UN Global Counterterrorism Strategy. The U.S. participated in a high-level ministerial meeting in early October 2007 in New York on Inter-Religious and Inter-Cultural Cooperation.

The U.S. also supports these goals bilaterally, in regional and multilateral fora such as the OSCE, the AU, and the OAS. The President of the U.S. recently appointed Ambassador Sada Cumber as the Special Envoy to the Organization of the Islamic Conference, in order to promote mutual understanding between the U.S. and Muslim communities around the world and to build forward-looking partnerships to advance common purposes.

[Footnotes omitted]

USG response to OHCHR regarding the Defamation of Religions resolution—Tab2

General Introduction: Please refer to previous OHCHR Reports from the United States of America for augmentation of the following issues.

The most obvious and important purpose of U.S. Constitutional protections on free speech is to prevent the government from restricting expression "because of its message, its ideas, its subject matter, or its content." In other words, to be permissible, any regulation on speech and other forms of expression must generally be content neutral. Thus, the right to engage in propaganda of war is as protected as the right to advocate pacifism. The advocacy of hatred is as protected as the advocacy of fellowship.

Of course, the U.S. abhors all forms of hateful expression. But in our view, because such forms of expression tend to lack merit, they tend to collapse under their own weight. In other words, they are unlikely to survive or thrive in a marketplace of ideas. In the words of Justice Oliver Wendell Holmes, "The best test of truth is the power of the thought to get it accepted in the competition of the market."—not, in other words, by criminalizing the expression of ideas, however offensive they may be.

We believe an approach such as "defamation of religions" entails a slippery slope, and endangers the very freedom of expression that international human rights treaties are designed to protect and that is essential in a democratic society.

Query 1: Actions at local and national level, undertaken by the State to prohibit discrimination based on religion and faith.

Query 2: Legal and Constitutional guarantees, national policies, aimed at protecting against discrimination based on religion and faith, acts of hatred and violence, xenophobia and related intolerance, intimidation and coercion resulting from defamation of religions.

Response to Queries 1 and 2:

a. The First Amendment of the U.S. Constitution guarantees the right to freedom of religion. It prohibits the federal government from making any law that establishes a national religion (Establishment Clause) or prohibits free exercise of religion (Free Exercise Clause). The Free Exercise Clause as interpreted includes the right to freedom of belief and worship, and the freedom to not believe in any faith.

b. The First Amendment also prohibits the federal legislature from making laws that infringe on freedom of speech, freedom of the press, the right to assemble peacefully, and to petition the government.

c. The 14th Amendment extends these protections against encroachment by state as well as federal officers.

d. Additionally, many state constitutions have Bills of Rights which guarantee freedom of religion at the state level.

e. The Religious Freedom Restoration Act, passed by Congress in 1993, aims to prevent laws which substantially burden a person's free exercise of religion.

f. The freedom of speech clause protects individual expression relating to views on religion, even if these views may be perceived by some as negative, insulting, or offensive. Freedom of speech is one of the fundamental freedoms in the country, and the U.S. rejects the concept of "defamation of religion."

1. Human rights law vests rights in individuals, not in groups, ideologies, or beliefs, including religions.

2. "Defamation" carries a particular legal meaning and application in the U.S. and indeed elsewhere which makes the term wholly unsuitable in the context of "religions" as a term of use in multilateral fora. Because one defense to a charge of defamation is the truth, and merely issuing an opinion about something cannot be verified one way or another as true, this term is simply not appropriate.

3. The U.S. has voted against every United Nations resolution on Defamation of Religion since the inception of this notion in Pakistan's 1999 "Defamation of Islam" resolution, which was altered to a "Defamation of Religions" resolution. The U.S. does not believe it should be illegal to express an opinion on a particular religion, including those which are highly critical. These resolutions carve out a special status for Islam, above concerns for other religions, and infringe on basic freedom of speech rights, such as the right to state opinions, publish books and articles, and freely express views in other ways which may be critical of religions. The U.S. Constitution would not permit any international agreement or treaty purporting to prohibit unpopular opinions and viewpoints to have legal effect in the U.S.

4. The U.S. does not outlaw statements or expressions such as Holocaust denial, and allows groups that are considered racist, xenophobic or otherwise intolerant to congregate peacefully. Of course any acts of violence are not protected under the U.S. Constitution and may be criminally punished. It is peaceful worship, belief, and speech that are afforded the widest protections under the U.S. Constitution.

5. The U.S. believes that the issues of concern for Muslims described in the UN Defamation of Religions resolutions in toto are better dealt with under the auspices of the International Covenant for Civil and Political Rights (ICCPR) and the International Convention on the Elimination of All Forms of Discrimination Based on Race (ICERD), rather than in this new sui generis and deeply-flawed concept of "defamation of religions."

6. The U.S. is deeply concerned with the use of the concept of "defamation of religions" to justify torture, imprisonment, abuse, and even issue execution orders against individuals and religious groups who do not subscribe to a particular "state" religion, or who wish to convert to another religion according to their conscience. The defamation of religions concept has also been promulgated into national legal systems in order to halt any public comment or dissent against political figures, and is now being promoted at the international level to promote and justify blasphemy laws in some countries. The U.S. believes that the employment of this concept jeopardizes freedom of religion, expression, assembly, association, and press.

g. The U.S. has significant legislation in place which prohibits discrimination based on religion in several contexts. The Civil Rights Act of 1964 has many protections against discrimination. Title II outlaws discrimination in places of public accommodation and amusement, including hotels, motels, restaurants, and theaters. Title III prohibits state and municipal governments from denying access to public facilities on the grounds of race, religion or ethnicity. Title IV prohibits discrimination on the basis of race, religion, or ethnicity by public schools, colleges, and universities. Title VII prohibits discrimination in the employment context based on race, color, religion, sex or national origin. Public and private employers, with certain exceptions including the federal government and small private businesses, may not discriminate based on the above categories. Executive Order 11246, as amended, prohibits most federal contractors and subcontractors and federally assisted contractors and subcontractors from discriminating in employment decisions on the basis of "race, color, sex, religion or national origin." The Fair Housing Act, 42 U.S.C. §3601, prohibits discrimination based on "race, color, religion, sex, national origin, handicap, and familial status" in activities relating to the sale, rental, financing, and advertising of housing. These laws are vigorously enforced. The Religious Land Use and Institutionalized Persons Act of 2000 protects the religious rights of persons in institutions such as prisons or mental institutions, and protects houses of worship and religious schools from abuses by local zoning authorities.

h. Additionally, hate crime laws establish prohibitions on actions which are motivated by hatred towards individuals of a particular social group. Crimes against individuals because they are of a particular religion are outlawed as hate crimes as well as common crimes.

i. The U.S. Supreme Court has ruled on numerous cases upholding the free exercise of religion. As just one example, the Court ruled that unemployment compensation may not be denied to a beneficiary who is unwilling to accept employment that would require working on his or her Sabbath (*Sherbert v Verner*). The beneficiary's beliefs need not be based on the tenets of an established religious sect, if his or her belief is a sincere religious one (Frazee v Illinois Department of Employment).

j. The separation of church and state has, in part, been preserved by the judicial doctrine that when there is a dispute within a religious order or organization, courts will not inquire into religious doctrine, but will defer to the decision-making body recognized by the church and give effect to whatever decision is officially and properly made.

k. These broad statutory and constitutional protections are implemented in practice. Criminal investigations and prosecutions can be initiated against any person exercising the authority of any local, state or federal government who violates the civil rights of individuals, including freedom of religion. Investigations and prosecutions can be undertaken at the federal level, state level, or sometimes both.

l. The Civil Rights Division (CRD) of the U.S. Department of Justice has primary authority over prosecutions for violations of federal criminal civil rights laws. The CRD welcomes complaints from members of the public, which are reviewed to determine whether the facts warrant a criminal investigation. If an investigation develops sufficient evidence to prove a case beyond a reasonable doubt, a federal prosecution can be brought.

m. In February 2007, the U.S. Attorney General launched an initiative to increase enforcement of federal laws protecting against religious discrimination and religious hate crimes. He also released a report detailing the Department of Justice's successes in these areas in the past six years. The report is available at the initiative's website, www.FirstFreedom.gov, which also describes the various facets of the initiative.

n. Where there are allegations of constitutional violations pervading an institution or department, private citizens can file a class action lawsuit using federal civil rights statutes, including 42 U.S.C. §1983.

Query 3: Measures adopted to prohibit the dissemination of racist and xenophobic ideas and material aimed at any religion or its followers that constitute incitement to discrimination, hostility, or violence.

Query 4: Measures adopted to ensure that physical attacks and assaults on businesses, cultural centres and places of worship of all religions as well as targeting of religious symbols are offences punishable by law.

Responses to Queries 3 and 4:

a. In accordance with the 1st and 14th Amendments to the U.S. Constitution which protect freedom of speech, the U.S. may not criminalize racist and xenophobic ideas, expressed either in conversation or in published materials. The concept of free speech is very important in the U.S. and protects individuals with diverse ideas, including prejudicial ones. The Constitution provides broad protection for speech that may be considered objectionable by most of society. Courts have carved out narrow categories, such as libel, obscenity, fighting words and threats of injury, in which an individual's statements may not be protected by the First Amendment. See Chaplinsky v New Hampshire, 315 U.S. 569, 572 (1942); New York Times v Sullivan, 376 U.S. 254, 270 (1964).

b. Accordingly, the U.S. has made reservations, understandings, and declarations to certain provisions in international treaties that prohibit the dissemination of racist ideas or otherwise restrict freedom of expression. For example, when the U.S. ratified the ICCPR and ICERD, it attached reservations, understandings, and declarations concerning provisions insofar as they are inconsistent with the U.S. Constitution. These cover, inter alia, ICCPR Article 20(2), which requires Parties to "prohibit advocacy of national, racial or religious hatred that constitutes incitement to discrimination, hostility or violence," and ICERD Article 4, which condemns propaganda and organizations which promote racial hatred or discrimination, and requires parties to punish dissemination of "ideas based on racial superiority."

c. U.S. law does allow for suppression of or legal sanctions against harmful conduct motivated by racism and other forms of social intolerance. Racist conduct that incites violence or itself inflicts injury has been characterized as outside of First Amendment protections, and is therefore punishable. Under the U.S. Constitution, hateful speech can be criminalized only if it is intended to incite "imminent lawless action" (Brandenburg v Ohio). Some courts/states require for a conviction of incitement to violence, that the person must not only have made speech which advocates unlawful action, but that the circumstances must indicate that there was some likelihood that the unlawful action would actually occur.

d. Hate crimes in the U.S. exist at both the federal and state levels. Laws vary from state to state, but 45 states and the District of Columbia have statutes criminalizing various types of hate crimes—examples include laws prohibiting assault, murder or other violent crimes perpetrated against a person because of one's race, color, religion, sex and other categories. Thirty-one (31) states allow a civil cause of action for hate crimes, in addition to a criminal penalty.

e. Many states' laws allow hate crimes—crimes motivated by hate due to religion and other factors—to have more severe punishments than the comparable crime not stirred by such motivations, and this is constitutionally permissible. The U.S. Supreme Court considers punishing prejudice as a motive for conduct that is already criminal to be different than punishment for abstract beliefs, which would not be constitutional.

f. The federal law goes even further. The Hate Crime Sentencing Enhancement Act of 1994 requires the U.S. Sentencing Commission to increase penalties for crimes committed on the basis of actual or perceived race, color, religion, national origin, ethnicity, and other factors. This act only applies to federal crimes.

g. 18 U.S.C. Sec. 245, also known as the 1969 law (federal) permits federal prosecution of an individual who "by force or threat of force willfully injures, intimidates or interferes with . . . any person because of his race, color, religion or national origin and because he is or has been" attempting to engage in one of six types of federally protected activities, including voting or going to school. To date, this law has been upheld in the courts.

h. Laws which prohibit racist conduct which stops short of clearly inciting violence or inflicting injury are fairly likely to be held unconstitutional. In a seminal Supreme Court case, (R.A.V. v City of St. Paul, Minnesota, 505 U.S. 377 (1992)), the Court held that a city hate speech ordinance (which made it a misdemeanor [minor crime] to place on public or private property a symbol, graffiti, object or other expression which reasonably arouses anger or resentment in others on the basis of religion and other factors) was unconstitutional.

i. Laws are in place to ensure that any destruction of another's property is an offense punishable by law. These laws will generally suffice to punish those who physically attack and assault businesses, cultural center and places of worship.

j. Under the Hate Crimes Sentencing Enhancement Act, if the destruction of a building was motivated by religious hatred, the sentence for the crime would increase.

k. Targeting of religious symbols accompanied by violence or destruction of property is similarly punishable.

Query 5: Action undertaken to ensure that counter-terrorism measures do not incite acts of violence, xenophobia or related intolerance and discrimination against Islam or any other religion.

Response to Query 5:

a. The U.S. takes action to ensure that counter-terrorism measures do not incite acts of violence, xenophobia or related intolerance and discrimination against Islam or any other religion.

b. Terrorism cannot and should not be associated or identified with any specific religion, nationality, civilization or ethnic group. That said, the U.S. goes to great lengths to respect the religious freedom of accused and convicted terrorists. One example of this is the Joint Task Force, the military personnel responsible for providing security for detainees at Guantánamo Bay, Cuba. It is both the policy and conduct of the Task Force to respect detainees' religious practices and beliefs. Officials maintain a program which educates service members about Muslim beliefs, provides cultural competency training, and ensures that they incorporate religious practices into on-site life. The Joint Task Force makes every effort to provide detainees with religious articles, accommodate prayers, and provide special meals, subject to any dietary requirements. A loudspeaker at the camp signals a Muslim call to prayer five times a day—after each signal, detainees get 20 minutes of uninterrupted time to practice their faith. Strict measures are in place to ensure appropriate treatment of the Koran, and every detainee is issued a personal copy.

Query 6: Action undertaken to ensue that the print, audio-visual and electronic media, including the Internet, and any other means do not incite acts of violence, xenophobia or related intolerance and discrimination against Islam or any other religion.

Response to Query 6:

a. The free speech guarantee of the First Amendment has been interpreted by the U.S. Supreme Court to extend to speech advocating illegal conduct, and regulation of such speech is permissible only in narrow circumstances: "the constitutional guarantees of free speech and free press do not permit a State to forbid or proscribe advocacy of the use of force or of law violation, except where such advocacy is directed to inciting or producing imminent lawless actions and is likely to incite or produce that action" (Brandenburg v Ohio). Notwithstanding the First Amendment limitations on the regulation of speech, speech that is tantamount to conduct—or that is simply the means of effecting conduct—may itself be legitimately proscribed, punished, or regulated incidentally to the constitutional enforcement of generally applicable statutes.

b. A number of U.S. statutes criminalize speech-related conduct in certain circumstances, including general laws criminalizing the solicitation to commit acts of violence, conspiracy, and aiding and abetting. More specific laws forbid such acts as seditious conspiracy; advocating the overthrow of the government; conspiring within the jurisdiction of the U.S. to kill, kidnap, or maim any individual outside the U.S. or in a foreign country with which the U.S. is at peace; mailing material that incites murder, assassination, or arson; and providing material support to designated terrorist organizations or in support of terrorist acts.

c. The U.S. material support laws are broad-based charging statutes that provide an important vehicle for prosecuting terrorists' recruitment, training, and fundraising efforts, which is sometimes conducted by terrorists online. Material support may include actions such as providing funding, training, expert advice or assistance, personnel, or providing communications equipment (which could include ISPs and other web services, among other things). The material support provisions, however, either require proof that the defendant knew or intended that the support was to be used in the preparing or carrying out of a terrorist activity, or proof that the defendant knowingly provided material support to a designated foreign terrorist organization, regardless of whether the defendant knew that the support would be used for a terrorist activity. Additionally, U.S. law also prohibits certain financial transactions with certain designated foreign states or individuals.

d. Depending on the specific facts and circumstances, these criminal laws and other civil (non-criminal) tools may be applicable to unlawful conduct that occurs on a U.S. website, and could be used to close U.S. terrorist used or related websites. However, prosecution for speech-related conduct on the Internet would face significant First Amendment, due process, and other statutory challenges.

Query 7: Measures undertaken, including appropriate education and training, to ensure that all public officials, including members of law enforcement bodies, the military, civil servants and educators, in the course of their official duties, respect different religions and beliefs and do not discriminate against persons on the grounds of their religion or belief.

Response to Query 7:

a. All public officials are subject to the US laws concerning freedom of religion and belief and discrimination laid out in the aforementioned discussion above.

b. Freedom of religion and proscription of discrimination based on religion form the foundation of U.S. society. The Pilgrims came to the U.S. in order to set up a society based on this "first freedom" of the human soul. The U.S. education system teaches freedom of religion and all other freedoms guaranteed in the Constitution, and all public officials take an oath to uphold the Constitution.

c. Mandating "respect" for any particular religion or belief, outside of prohibitions on violence, destruction of property, intimidations or threats, etc., would violate the First Amendment of the U.S. Constitution.

d. The Department of Justice has investigated a number of cases involving discrimination against or harassment of Muslim children in public schools. For example, the Department brought an action against a school district that barred a Muslim girl from wearing a hijab to school, resulting in a consent decree that will protect the rights of students to wear religious garb. Similarly, the Department obtained a settlement in a case in which another girl was harassed by a teacher and students because she was Muslim.

Query 8: Measures adopted to ensure equal access to education for all, in law and in practice, including access to free primary education for all children, both girls and boys, and access for adults to lifelong learning and education based on respect for human rights, diversity and tolerance, without discrimination of any kind.

Response to Query 8:

a. Under the U.S. federal system, education is primarily a state and local function, subject to constitutional and statutory constraints. All children in primary and secondary grades residing in the U.S. are required by law to attend school, and states are required to offer schooling in the language that the child can understand until the child can learn English.

b. The Equal Protection Clause, contained in the Fourteenth Amendment of the Constitution, provides that '[n]o State shall deny to any person within its jurisdiction the equal protection of the laws." The Equal Protection Clause has been interpreted to bar public schools and universities from discrimination on the grounds of race, sex, religion, or national origin.

c. Under Title IV of the Civil Rights Act of 1964, the U.S. Department of Justice may bring suit against a school board that deprives children of equal protection of the laws, or against a public university that denies admission to any person on the grounds of "race, color, religion, sex or national origin." The Department of Justice continues to enforce court-issued consent decrees against local school boards that had engaged in racial segregation in the past in cases that may date back 40 years. The Department of Justice also investigates and brings new cases of education discrimination.

d. The U.S. Department of Education administers a number of programs to help ensure that all students, including minorities and women, have access to elementary and secondary education programs, and opportunities to pursue higher education.

Query 9: Measures undertaken to promote tolerance and respect for all religions and their value systems.

Response to Query 9:

a. The U.S. government in its dialogue broadly promotes religious tolerance and respect for all religions.

b. As indicated above, the U.S. generally does not criminalize private citizens' intolerance of other religions. However, several laws are in place to prevent religious discrimination in institutional settings such as schools, public accommodations and employment.

Query 10: Actions aimed at supporting and promoting a global dialogue for a culture of peace and tolerance based on respect for human rights and religious diversity.

Response to Query 10:

a. The U.S. takes many actions aimed at promoting a global dialogue based on respect for human rights and religious diversity. The President of the U.S. meets with various religious leaders to promote religious freedom and diversity. Recently, he attended the opening of a new mosque, and noted how in the U.S. a mosque will be on the same street as a synagogue, a Catholic church, a Presbyterian parish and a Buddhist temple. He frequently makes comments noting the importance of religious freedom, diversity and tolerance.

b. The U.S. supports the United Nations' efforts to promote a culture of peace, tolerance and religious diversity through dialogue and global frameworks such as the "Global Agenda for Dialogue among Civilizations" and its Programme of Action adopted by the UN General Assembly and initiated by the UNESCO; the UN Global Counterterrorism Strategy; and the "Alliance of Civilizations" established by the UN Secretary General.

c. The U.S. also supports these goals bilaterally, in regional and multilateral fora, such as the OSCE and OAS.

d. The U.S. President recently established the position of Special Envoy to the Organization of the Islamic Conference, in order to foster better relationships with the Muslim world.

e. The U.S. Department of State has an office, the Office of International Religious Freedom (DRL/IRF), devoted entirely to promoting religious freedom around the world. The office monitors religious discrimination and persecution worldwide, and recommends and implements policies to promote religious freedom. The office also meets with world religious leaders and engages them in promoting religious diversity and tolerance. Finally, DRL/IRF writes annual religious freedom reports which document the status of religious freedom across the globe. The State Department of course also has offices which promote human rights more generally.

f. The U.S. has been invited to participate in a high-level ministerial meeting in early October 2007 in New York on Inter-Religious and Inter-Cultural Cooperation.

g. The U.S. regularly contributes to discussions on resolutions under the agenda item "Culture of Peace" in the UN General Assembly.

h. The Human Rights Democracy Fund, part of the Democracy, Human Rights and Labor (DRL) Bureau at the Department of State, creates and organizes programs which seek to promote human rights and democracy around the world. For example, HRDF plans to start a project which is designed to promote a balanced and moderate media to counteract biased reporting which exacerbates hatred and conflict. The project will train journalists across the Middle East/Gulf region to conduct accurate reporting that will encourage peace, enhance tolerance, defuse conflict and aid reconciliation. Starting in 2002, HRDF particularly directed its efforts toward the Muslim world, Central Asia and China.

APPENDIX M: HUMAN RIGHTS AND SECURITY/ THE WAR ON TERRORISM

The purpose of this Appendix is to expose the reader to a portion of what has been written and reported or enacted in the U.S. and in the international legal/political realm concerning the U.S. and human rights in relation to the war on terrorism. This concerns our national struggle for human and national security in relation to international human rights standards. There are many differing political and legal viewpoints on the U.S. and the war on terrorism, both within the U.S. and between the U.S. and the international community. These documents look more closely at the international legal realm and whether the U.S. is fulfilling its international legal obligations under those legal instruments and customary norms binding upon it, as it wages the so-called war on terrorism.

Because of its importance in the war on terrorism and the U.S. treatment of its detainees, also included here is the Military Commissions Act of 2009. This Act was enacted in light of the changes in Administration in 2009, the Obama campaign promises, and the Supreme Court cases which arose from previous attempts to create law to establish a military tribunal, particularly the Military Commission Act of 2006 (Document 96).

The purpose of using these following documents is not to criticize the U.S., but to show what the international legal discourse is in the fields of human rights and humanitarian law in relation to the actions of the U.S. in countering terrorism. In the U.S. we continue to debate how far the government can go in counter terrorism and protection of national security and how it treats and prosecutes arrested and detained alleged terrorists.

These documents reflect a snapshot of a specific time, and that the debate and discourse and documentation will continue to change and develop over the year to come. The reader must update this information and seek the latest documents pertinent to specific issues to keep abreast of the discourse. This appendix merely opens the door to an area of law and politics about which most Americans have probably never heard or read. To some degree, it is about how the rest of the world looks at the U.S. legally in light of the norms with which we nations have agreed and promised and covenanted to comply.

The reader is advised to review Primary Document 6, 8, and 19 on the applicable international legal norms, and Primary Document 15A on articles 4, 7, 9, 13, 17, and especially Primary Documents 21A, 21B, 21C, 21D and 22, as they relate to U.S. counter terrorism measures. These give a fuller view of the international human rights and humanitarian law standards binding on the U.S., and the interplay between the U.S. and the international community in an inter governmental institutional context, as to its compliance with such standards.

Documents:

Document 1: Report of the Special Rapporteur on the promotion and protection of human rights and fundamental freedoms while countering terrorism, Martin Scheinin Addendum, Mission To The United States of America*(Excerpted)

UNITED NATIONS	A
General Assembly	Distr.
HUMAN RIGHTS COUNCIL	GENERAL
Sixth session	A/HRC/6/17/Add.3
Agenda item 3	22 November 2007
	Original: ENGLISH

PROMOTION AND PROTECTION OF ALL HUMAN RIGHTS,
CIVIL, POLITICAL, ECONOMIC, SOCIAL AND CULTURAL
RIGHTS, INCLUDING THE RIGHT TO DEVELOPMENT
Report of the Special Rapporteur on the promotion and protection of
human rights and fundamental freedoms while countering terrorism,
Martin Scheinin
Addendum
MISSION TO THE UNITED STATES OF AMERICA*

*The summary of this mission report is being circulated in all official languages. The report itself contained in the annex to the summary is being circulated in the language of submission only. The footnotes to the report are circulated as received in the language of submission only.

Summary

The Special Rapporteur on the promotion and protection of human rights and fundamental freedoms while countering terrorism, Martin Scheinin, visited the United States of America from 16 to 25 May 2007, during which he met with senior officials of the Government, members of Congress and their staff, academics and non-governmental organizations, as well as with the Inter-American Commission on Human Rights. The objective of the visit was to undertake a fact-finding exercise and a legal assessment of U.S. law and practice in the fight against terrorism, measured against international law. His visit also aimed at identifying and disseminating best practice in the countering of terrorism.

Chapter I of this report considers the role of the U.S. in countering terrorism, concluding that it has a special responsibility in the protection of human rights while countering terrorism. The Special Rapporteur identifies his visit to the U.S. as one step in the process of restoring its role as a positive example for respecting human rights, even in the context of the fight against terrorism. He also strongly encourages the U.S. to take a strong role in and give support for the United Nations led effort in countering terrorism and implementing the United Nations Global Counter-Terrorism Strategy. The Special Rapporteur concludes that the international fight against terrorism is not a "war" in the true sense of the word, and reminds the U.S. that even during an armed conflict triggering the application of international humanitarian law, international human rights law continues to apply. He reiterates that international human rights law is also binding upon a State in respect of any person subject to its jurisdiction, even when it acts outside its territory. Military detention facilities are considered in Chapter II. In the context of detainees at Guantánamo Bay, the Special Rapporteur concludes that the categorization of detainees as "unlawful enemy combatants" is a term of convenience without legal effect. He expresses grave concern about the inability of detainees to seek full judicial review of determinations as to their combatant status, which amounts to non-compliance with the International Covenant on Civil and Political Rights' prohibitions against arbitrary detention, the right to judicial review capable of ordering release, and the right to a fair trial within a reasonable time. Noted also is the purported exclusion of habeas corpus rights under the Military Commissions Act of 2006. He urges continued and determined action towards the expressed wish of the U.S. to move towards closure of Guantánamo Bay. The Special Rapporteur also reminds the U.S. and other States responsible for the detention of persons in Afghanistan and Iraq that these detainees also have the right to a fair trial within a reasonable time if suspected of a crime or, failing this, to release.

The Special Rapporteur considers, in chapter III, the use of military commissions to try terrorist suspects. He identifies jurisdictional problems regarding certain offences (terrorism, providing material support for terrorism, wrongfully aiding the enemy, spying, and conspiracy) which do not form part of the laws of war and, to the extent that applicable offence provisions were not in force at the time of the commission of conduct in respect of which detainees might be charged, involve the retrospective application of criminal law. He further notes that the Government's justification for military commissions is incorrect as a matter of fact because ordinary courts martial have had the jurisdiction to try violations of the laws of armed conflict since 1916 under the Uniform Code of Military Justice, and that the nexus between the events of 11 September and U.S. citizens would allow ordinary courts to try other offences such as conspiracy and terrorism. As to the composition and operation of military commissions, the Special Rapporteur next considers issues surrounding the independence of the commissions, their potential use to try civilians, and their lack of appearance of impartiality. He also addresses various matters concerning the use and availability of evidence in proceedings before military commissions, their ability to impose the death penalty, and the consequences of acquittal or completion of sentence following conviction.

Chapter IV first turns to the question of the interrogation of terrorist suspects, considering both the Central Intelligence Agency (CIA) programme of "enhanced interrogation techniques" and interrogation methods outlined in the revised U.S. Army Field Manual. The Special Rapporteur addresses the "extraordinary rendition" of terrorist suspects, and their detention in "classified locations", and the accountability of those responsible for conducting interrogation by techniques amounting to torture or cruel, inhuman or degrading treatment.

The Special Rapporteur considers, in chapters V and VI, issues relating to the definitions of terrorism under U.S. law, the alleged targeted killings of terrorist suspects by U.S. agents, the provision of compensation to victims of terrorism, profiling, community outreach, and immigration and refugee status. Privacy and surveillance are matters examined in chapter VII, including consideration of a programme of secret surveillance by the National Security Agency, authorized by an Executive Order of the President of the U.S., and the use by the Federal Bureau of Investigation and other intelligence services of National Security Letters to expedite access to private records. Finally, the Special Rapporteur reiterates his conclusions and formulates recommendations for consideration by the Government.

Annex
REPORT OF THE SPECIAL RAPPORTEUR ON THE PROMOTION AND PROTECTION OF HUMAN RIGHTS AND FUNDAMENTAL FREEDOMS WHILE COUNTERING TERRORISM ON HIS VISIT TO THE UNITED STATES OF AMERICA (16-25 MAY 2007)

CONTENTS

I. INTRODUCTION

1. Pursuant to Commission on Human Rights resolution 2005/80, the Special Rapporteur on the promotion and protection of human rights and fundamental freedoms while countering terrorism, Mr. Martin Scheinin, conducted an official visit to the United States of America from 16 to 25 May 2007, at the invitation of the Government.

2. The Special Rapporteur had meaningful meetings on a specialist level with the Department of State, Department of Homeland Security, Department of Defense, and Department of Justice. He also met with members of Congress and their staff, academics and non-governmental organizations, as well as with the Inter-American Commission on Human Rights. He travelled to Miami to observe a day of the trial against Jose Padilla and others. It was disappointing that the Special Rapporteur was not provided access to places of detention, including at Guantánamo Bay, with guarantees permitting private interviews of detainees. It is a part of the Standard Terms of Reference of all United Nations Special Rapporteurs that any visits to detention centres involve unmonitored interviews with detained persons. This is a universally applied term of reference, which in many parts of the world is essential for the protection of individuals against abuse. It would give a wrong message to the world if the Special Rapporteur were to deviate from this standard condition in respect of the U.S. The Special Rapporteur therefore hopes that he is able to visit the U.S. again for the purpose of visiting places of detention, including Guantánamo Bay, prior to the consideration of this report by the Human Rights Council. Such a visit should also include observing military commission hearings at Guantánamo Bay.

A. Role of the U.S. in countering terrorism

3. In a world community which has adopted global measures to counter terrorism, the U.S. is a leader. This position carries with it a special responsibility to also take leadership in the protection of human rights while countering terrorism. The example of the U.S. will have its followers, in good and in bad. The Special Rapporteur has a deep respect for the long traditions in the U.S. of respect for individual rights, the rule of law, and a strong level of judicial protection. Despite the existence of a tradition in the U.S. of respect for the rule of law, and the presence of self-correcting mechanisms under the U.S. Constitution, it is most regretful that a number of important mechanisms for the protection of rights have been removed or obfuscated under law and practice since the events of 11 September, including under the USA PATRIOT Act of 2001, the Detainee Treatment Act of 2005, the Military Commissions Act of 2006, and under Executive Orders and classified programmes.

A draft mission report was sent to the Government on 28 June and extensive comments received on 2 August 2007.

4. The Special Rapporteur saw his visit as one step in the process of restoring the role of the U.S. as a positive example for respecting human rights, including in the context of the fight against terrorism. He dismisses the perception that the U.S. has become an enemy of human rights. It is a country which still has a great deal to be proud of.

5. In September 2006, the General Assembly adopted the first-ever Global Counter-Terrorism Strategy. The Strategy treats human rights as a central part of all aspects of effective global action to counter international terrorism and seeks, in part, to enhance cooperation between the growing number of international and regional bodies, with often overlapping mandates, pertaining to counter-terrorism. The U.S. has been strategic in the establishment of an international counter-terrorism machinery, including the Counter-Terrorism Committee and the Al-Qaida and Taliban Sanctions Committee of the Security Council. An effective and well coordinated United Nations led effort in countering terrorism will be one of the keys to the successful implementation of the Global Counter-Terrorism Strategy, and the Special Rapporteur strongly encourages continued involvement in and support for this by the U.S.

B. The framework of public international law

6. During high-level meetings with Government officials, it was repeated that the U.S. sees itself as being engaged in an armed conflict with Al-Qaida and the Taliban, commencing prior to the events of 11 September. This position has been reaffirmed by the President of the U.S. in his Executive Order of 20 July 2007. The Department of Defense described this "war" as continuing until the capabilities of Al-Qaida are so degraded that their conduct can be dealt with through regular law enforcement mechanisms. The U.S. consequently identifies humanitarian law as the applicable international law to the apprehension, detention and trial of persons detained at Guantánamo Bay. However, these statements do not suggest that any form of terrorism would amount to armed conflict or that the international fight against terrorism would as a whole be governed by the law of armed conflict.

7. The Special Rapporteur reminds the U.S. of the well-established principle that regard less of issues of classification, international human rights law continues to apply in armed conflict. This is a point made clear, for example, by the Human Rights Committee in its general comment No. 31, and confirmed by the International Court of Justice. As further explained in its advisory opinion on the *Legal Consequences of the Construction of a Wall in the Occupied Palestinian Territories*, the International Court stated that "… the protection offered by human rights conventions does not cease in case of armed conflict, save through the effect of provisions for derogation of the kind to be found in Article 4 of the International Covenant on Civil and Political Rights". The conduct of the U.S. must therefore comply not only with international humanitarian law, but also with applicable international human rights law.

8. The Human Rights Committee and the International Court of Justice have confirmed as well that human rights, including those enshrined in the International Covenant on Civil and Political Rights (ICCPR), are legally binding upon a State when it acts outside its internationally recognized territory. This means that the U.S. is obliged to respect and ensure the rights guaranteed by the Covenant binding upon it, such as the Convention against Torture and Other Cruel, Inhuman or Degrading Treatment and customary international law—including the absolute prohibition of torture or any other form of cruel, inhuman or degrading treatment—to anyone within its power or effective control, even if not situated within the territory of the U.S. The fact that the U.S. more than 50 years ago, when the ICCPR was being drafted, expressed that it could not be expected to "legislate" for occupied countries was not meant as a justification to engage extraterritorially in outright human rights violations such as arbitrary detention, torture, or other cruel, inhuman or degrading treatment.

9. The Special Rapporteur accepts that the U.S. was engaged in an international armed conflict from the commencement of "Operation Enduring Freedom", proclaimed as an exercise of self-defence under Article 51 of the Charter of the United Nations, and until the fall of the Taliban regime as the de facto government of Afghanistan. He further accepts in principle that a non-State armed group, including one called a "terrorist organization", if organized as an armed force, is capable of being engaged in a trans border armed conflict, albeit technically a non-international one (one which is not between two States). Furthermore, although some acts of terrorism may constitute a threat to international peace and security, this does not mean that any act of terrorism would amount to a threat to peace and security, or would create an armed conflict. These matters must be determined separately and upon the particular circumstances of each case.

10. The Special Rapporteur is aware of the reservations and declarations entered by the U.S. upon its ratification of the ICCPR and the Convention against Torture. Under international law, reservations that are contrary to the object and purpose of a treaty are impermissible. The relevant treaty bodies—the Human Rights Committee and the Committee against Torture—have in this context requested that the U.S. withdraw its reservations and declarations. While supporting the competence of the respective treaty bodies to address the permissibility and legal effect of the reservations in question, the Special Rapporteur sees his own mandate as requiring him to address the law and practice of the U.S. with reference to international treaty standards, without making an assessment of whether its reservations and declarations are permissible. Further, many human rights norms are binding as customary law and even as peremptory norms of international law (juscogens).

II. MILITARY DETENTION FACILITIES
A. Guantánamo Bay detainees as "unlawful enemy combatants"

11. The persons detained at the military facility at Guantánamo Bay have been categorized by the U.S. as alien "unlawful enemy combatants", regardless of the circumstances of their capture. The adjective "unlawful" was used together with the noun "combatant" by Allan Rosas, in his treatise *The Legal Status of Prisoners of War* to describe persons who commit hostile acts in international conflicts without authorization to do so under the law of war. "Unprivileged belligerent" would be a synonymous expression. While such persons may not be entitled to prisoner of war status, they nevertheless enjoy certain minimum protections in respect of detention and trial. The Special Rapporteur wishes to make clear that the term "unlawful enemy combatant" is a description of convenience, meaningful only in international armed conflicts, and even then only denoting persons taking a direct part in hostilities while not being members of the regular armed forces or of assimilated units.

12. Privileged combatants apprehended during the course of an international armed conflict may be detained as prisoners of war and shall be released at the end of hostilities. This will however not be the case for persons who are held as persons suspected of war crimes.

Furthermore, combatants in a non-international armed conflict may be held as security detainees for the duration of the hostilities, but also treated as criminal suspects for their use of violence. While acknowledging the need to ensure that there is no impunity for those who commit war crimes, the Special Rapporteur emphasizes that the chance of ensuring a fair trial diminishes over time. At the end of hostilities, persons captured during international or non-international armed conflict should be released, or tried if suspected of war crimes or other crimes. The Special Rapporteur considers that the detention of persons for a period of several years without charge fundamentally undermines the right of fair trial. The same conclusion applies, of course, to those detainees that never were engaged in an armed conflict. The right of persons to be tried without undue delay, as guaranteed by article 14, paragraph 3 (c), of the ICCPR is particularly relevant to this point, as the prolonged period of detention has placed the U.S., by its own inaction, in a position of having to release many of these persons without charge.

13. There are serious concerns about the ability of detainees at Guantánamo Bay to seek a judicial determination of their status, and of their continuing detention. Upon the arrival of a detainee at Guantánamo Bay, a Combatant Status Review Tribunal (CSRT) is convened to determine whether the detainee is an "enemy combatant" and whether that person should continue to be detained. This occurs once only, unless new evidence about the person's status becomes available. Added to this, an administrative Review Board (ARB) undertakes annual reviews of each detainee's status to confirm whether continued detention is required. If a detainee declines to participate in proceedings before the ARB, he will be provided with the opportunity to be heard and to present information to the Review Board. When classified information is presented at such hearings, the detainee is excluded from proceedings.

14. As confirmed by the Department of Defense, these are administrative processes rather than judicial ones. Detainees are not provided with a lawyer during the course of hearings. Even more problematic is the fact that the decisions of the CSRT and ARB are subject to limited judicial review only. The most that a reviewing court may do is to order reconsideration of a decision, not release. These restrictions result in non-compliance with the ICCPR, which prohibits arbitrary detention (art. 9 (1)), requires court review of any form of detention and entailing a possibility of release (art. 9 (4)), and provides a right to a fair trial within reasonable time for anyone held as a criminal suspect (arts. 9 (3) and 14 (3)). Article 9, paragraph 4, is also relevant to the removal of habeas corpus rights under section 7 of the Military Commissions Act of 2006, which purports to expressly deny the jurisdiction of ordinary courts to hear an application for habeas corpus. The Special Rapporteur reminds that according to the Human Rights Committee, article 9 (4) cannot be derogated from even during a state of emergency. Hence, the right to judicial review of any form of detention does not depend on whether humanitarian law is also applicable. All Guantánamo Bay detainees are entitled to this right, irrespective of whether they were involved in armed conflict or the status of proceedings against them.

15. Noting that persons brought to Guantánamo Bay under the age of 15 have since been repatriated, the Special Rapporteur is concerned that this does not apply to all persons who were children at the material time of their alleged conduct. It is a matter of concern to the Special Rapporteur whether juvenile Guantánamo Bay detainees have been segregated from adults and accorded treatment appropriate to their age and legal status in accordance with article 10, paragraphs 2 (b) and 3 of the Covenant, and that the Military Commissions Act does not, as it stands, make room for procedural adjustments that will take account of the age of juvenile defendants and the desirability of promoting their rehabilitation. Further, the Special Rapporteur received alarming reports that the young age of some of the detainees was only taken into account by applying interrogation methods that utilized their age-specific phobias and fears.

B. Closure of Guantánamo Bay

16. The Special Rapporteur is encouraged by the announcement of the President of the U.S. that he wishes to move towards the closure of Guantánamo Bay, and urges continued and determined action to that end. The Special Rapporteur has been advised that between 40 and 80 Guantánamo Bay detainees are expected to be tried by military commissions, and that the U.S. wishes to return the remaining detainees to their countries of origin or, where necessary, to a surrogate country. He was advised that the Government is conducting negotiations with countries for this purpose.

17. The Special Rapporteur supports initiatives to return detainees to their countries of origin, but also concludes that although the U.S. has advised that it will not do so in breach of the principle of non-refoulement, the current U.S. standard applied under this principle fails to comply with international law. While international law (primarily ICCPR, article 7) requires that a person not be returned to a country where there is a "real risk" of torture, or any form of cruel, inhuman or degrading treatment, the U.S.

applies a lower threshold of non-return only where it is "more likely than not" that a person will be subject to torture as narrowly defined by the U.S. itself. The Special Rapporteur further underlines that diplomatic assurances sought from a receiving State to the effect that a person will not be subjected to torture or cruel, inhuman or degrading treatment do not absolve the duty of the sending State to assess individually the existence of a "real risk". Despite the fact that the U.S. has not yet abolished the death penalty, he emphasizes that the principle of non-refoulement is also applicable where a person is liable to the imposition of the death penalty in a jurisdiction where the standards of trial fall short of rigorous compliance with article 14 of the ICCPR on the right to a fair trial. The Special Rapporteur emphasizes that the U.S. has the primary responsibility to resettle any individuals among those detained in Guantánamo Bay who are in need of international protection.

C. Detainees in Afghanistan and Iraq

18. The Special Rapporteur is mindful of the fact that there are in Afghanistan some 700 and in Iraq around 18,000 persons detained under the control of the U.S. Some of these detainees appear to be held for reasons related to the fight against terrorism, under a legal status analogous to that at Guantánamo Bay. He reminds the U.S. and other States responsible for the detention of persons in Afghanistan and Iraq that these detainees also have a right to court review of the lawfulness of their detention.

III. THE USE OF MILITARY COMMISSIONS TO TRY TERRORIST SUSPECTS

19. By Military Order in 2001, the President of the U.S. established military commissions for the purpose of trying enemy combatants. The Supreme Court ruled in 2006 that military commissions established under the Military Order were unlawful, since they were not established under the express authority of Congress, and that the structure and procedures of the commissions violated both the U.S. Uniform Code of Military Justice (UCMJ) and the four Geneva Conventions. Congress subsequently enacted the Military Commissions Act of 2006 (MCA), which largely reflects the military commission structure under the 2001 Military Order. The establishment of military commissions is not restricted geographically, permitting any non-U.S. citizen, including those holding permanent resident status, to be subject to trial by military commission if designated as an enemy combatant. Various aspects relating to the jurisdiction and operation of military commissions raise significant human rights concerns.

A. Jurisdiction of military commissions

20. One of the principal reasons given by the Government for the establishment of military omissions rather than the use of ordinary courts has been that those courts would not have jurisdiction over certain crimes which some detainees are suspected to have committed. Three matters of concern are raised by this position. First, the MCA purports to be a piece of legislation which codifies the laws of war and establishes the jurisdiction of military commissions over war crimes. However, the offences listed in Section 950v (24)-(28) of the Act (terrorism, providing material support for terrorism, wrongfully aiding the enemy, spying, and conspiracy) go beyond offences under the laws of war. The establishment of these offences, and the way in which they are described, therefore means that the military commissions have been given jurisdiction over offences which do not in fact form part of the laws of war and thus, taken the indistinctive application of the notion of "unlawful enemy combatant", may result in civilians being tried by military tribunals.

21. The second problem, concerning these same offences, is that to the extent they were not covered by the law applicable at the time of the commission of the actual acts, the military commissions will be applying criminal law retroactively, in breach of ICCPR, article 15, and universally acknowledged general principles of law. Finally, it appears that the Government's justification for military commissions is incorrect as a matter of fact because the nexus between the events of 11 September and U.S. citizens would allow ordinary courts to try offences such as conspiracy and terrorism. This is borne out by the fact that the bombings of the U.S. Embassies in Kenya and Tanzania in 1998 were prosecuted by ordinary U.S. courts, and that Osama bin Laden was indicted for his action in the attacks on the USS Cole by a Grand Jury in 2000. The ability of ordinary courts to hear charges of conspiracy and material support for terrorism is further borne out by the fact that those being prosecuted in *U.S. v Padilla and others* in the District Court at Miami were charged with such offences. In contrast, a suspected co-conspirator, who is an alien and currently detained at Guantánamo Bay, is likely to face these charges before a military commission.

22. A separate matter concerning the jurisdiction of military commissions concerns determinations of the CSRT that a person is an "alien unlawful enemy combatant". Section 948 (b) of the MCA specifically precludes military commissions from exercising jurisdiction over lawful enemy combatants, thus restricting the jurisdiction of these tribunals over unlawful enemy combatants. In a decision of the military commission,

charges against Omar Khadr were dismissed without prejudice on the basis that determinations of the CSRT were separate to and insufficient for the purposes of proceedings before military commissions. This, combined with the fact that the MCA does not confer upon military commissions the ability to determine an accused person's status, led the commission to conclude that it could not be satisfied that it had initial jurisdiction to try Mr. Khadr.

B. Composition of military commissions

23. As to the composition of military commissions, the Special Rapporteur has serious concerns about their independence and impartiality, their potential use to try civilians, and the lack of appearance of impartiality. As stated by the Human Rights Committee, the right to trial by an independent and impartial tribunal is so central to the due process of law that it is an absolute right that may suffer no exception. In a long line of helpful jurisprudence on the subject, the European Court of Human Rights has spoken of the need for a tribunal to be subjectively free of prejudice or personal bias, as well as having an appearance of impartiality from an objective viewpoint.

24. Whereas, in this regard, military judges in courts martial are appointed from a panel of judges by lottery, judges and members in a military commission are selected for each trial. Furthermore, although the current convening authority is a civilian and former judge, she is employed by the Department of Defense, so that, as a result, the appearance of impartial selection by the convening authority of members of individual commissions is undermined. Moreover, there is no prohibition against the selection of members of a commission who fall within the same chain of command; more junior members of a military commission, despite any advice to the contrary, may be directly or indirectly influenced in their consideration of the facts.

25. The ability of the convening authority to intervene in the conduct of trials before a military commission is also troubling. The plea agreement in the trial of David Hicks, for example, was negotiated between the convening authority and his counsel, without any reference to the prosecuting trial counsel. The involvement of the executive in such matters further adds to an appearance that military commissions are not independent.

C. Use and availability of evidence

26. The use and availability of evidence in proceedings before military commissions is also of concern to the Special Rapporteur. Certain evidence, due to its classified status, may not be disclosed to trial or defence counsel. This is problematic since such evidence may be exculpatory or otherwise beneficial to the defence case. Although this does not create an inequality of arms, since such evidence would not be provided to the prosecution, it has the potential to undermine the presumption of innocence. The protection given to classified information, while understand able, is of particular concern in the context of the security classification of interrogation techniques, as discussed below.

27. The Special Rapporteur is concerned that although evidence which has been obtained by torture is categorically inadmissible, evidence obtained by other forms of coercion may, by determination of the military judge, be admitted into evidence. Three problems arise in this context. The first is that an accused may not be aware of the fact that evidence has been obtained by torture or coercion since the interrogation techniques used to obtain evidence subsequently presented at trial may themselves be classified and thereby outside the knowledge of the accused.

A further problem is that the definition of torture for the purpose of proceedings before a military commission is restricted, not catching all forms of coercion that amount to torture or cruel, inhuman or degrading treatment, equally prohibited in non-derogable terms by ICCPR article 7. The final issue of considerable concern is that the prohibition of admission of evidence obtained by torture is limited. Testimony obtained through abusive interrogation techniques that were used prior to the Detainee Act of 2005 may in fact be used if such evidence is found to be "reliable" and its use "in the interests of justice". There may, however, be no circumstances in which the use of evidence obtained by torture or cruel, inhuman or degrading treatment may be used for the purpose of trying and punishing a person. This is a clear and established principle of international law.

28. This concern is further exacerbated by the preclusion of classified information and the fact that hearsay evidence may be admitted in proceedings before a military commission, in the form of a written summary of the evidence, if it is determined by the military judges to be "reliable" and "probative". The admissibility of such evidence presents problems with the right to fair trial since it does not permit an accused to cross-examine the witness, and thereby undermines the guarantee to examine witnesses under ICCPR article 14, paragraph 3 (f). More importantly, if hearsay evidence was obtained through torture or coercion, and the interrogation techniques applied were themselves classified, an accused will never know whether the

evidence was obtained by such methods and should therefore be challenged. It also means that if a military judge determines that hearsay evidence was obtained by coercion (rather than torture) but that the evidence should nevertheless be admitted, a federal judge would be unable to assess whether such a determination is valid, since the defence counsel would, owing to lack of knowledge of the circumstances by which the evidence was obtained, not be able to challenge such a decision.

This means that a federal court judge would be unable to review a military judge's determination of whether the hearsay evidence was obtained by torture or coercion and if the evidence is determined to have been obtained by coercion, whether it should have been admitted under the rules established under the Military Commissions Act.

D. Equality of arms

29. The Special Rapporteur is concerned at reports that the distribution of resources is such that military defence counsel are significantly under-resourced as compared to military trial counsel, i.e. the prosecuting party. The disproportionate aggregation of resources is a matter that strikes at the heart of the principle of the equality of arms required in the safeguarding of a fair trial.

E. Trial of civilians

30. In the case of persons who might be categorized by the U.S. as unlawful enemy combatants but who in fact were not involved as combatants in an armed conflict, the possibility arises that civilians be tried by a military commission. In its general comment No. 13, the Human Rights Committee emphasized that the trying of civilians by military courts should be very exceptional and should only take place under conditions which genuinely afford the full guarantees of a fair hearing stipulated in article 14.

F. Death penalty

31. The Special Rapporteur is furthermore concerned at the ability of a military commission to determine charges in respect of which the death penalty may be imposed. It is well established that article 6 of the ICCPR requires that where a State seeks to impose the death penalty, it is obliged to ensure that fair trial rights under article 14 of the ICCPR are rigorously guaranteed. Given that any appeal rights subsequent to conviction are limited to matters of law, coupled with the concerns pertaining to the lack of fair trial guarantees in proceedings before military commissions, the Special Rapporteur concludes that any imposition of the death penalty as a result of a conviction by a military commission is likely to be in violation of article 6.

G. Consequences of acquittal

32. Finally, the Special Rapporteur notes with concern that the acquittal of a person by a military commission or the completion of a term of imprisonment following conviction does not result in a right of release. This further undermines the principles of fair trial and would, if immediate release was not provided in an individual case, involve arbitrary detention in contravention of article 9 (1) of the ICCPR.

IV. INTERROGATION, RENDITION, AND DETENTION IN SECRET LOCATIONS OF TERRORIST SUSPECTS

A. CIA programme of "enhanced interrogation techniques"

33. As a result of an apparent internal leak from the CIA, the media in the U.S. learned and published information about "enhanced interrogation techniques" used by the CIA in its interrogation of terrorist suspects and possibly other persons held because of their links with such suspects. Various sources have spoken of techniques involving physical and psychological means of coercion, including stress positions, extreme temperature changes, sleep deprivation, and "waterboarding" (means by which an interrogated person is made to feel as if drowning).

With reference to the well-established practice of bodies such as the Human Rights Committee and the Committee against Torture, the Special Rapporteur concludes that these techniques involve conduct that amounts to a breach of the prohibition against torture and any form of cruel, inhuman or degrading treatment. The Special Rapporteur notes that the U.S. understanding of cruel, inhuman or degrading treatment is what the U.S. Constitution prohibits as cruel and unusual punishment, not the relevant international standards as such. It is encouraging to see that the July 2007 Executive Order of the President now requires the Director of the CIA to ensure that interrogation practices are "safe for use", based upon professional advice, and that there is effective monitoring of the CIA interrogation programmes. Nevertheless, the Executive Order retains the restrictive interpretations of "torture" and "cruel, inhuman, or degrading treatment". The Special Rapporteur again reminds the U.S. that torture and cruel, inhuman or degrading treatment are equally prohibited in non-derogable terms by ICCPR article 7.

34. In a meeting with the Special Rapporteur, the Acting General Counsel for the CIA refused to engage in any meaningful interaction aimed at clarifying the means of compliance with international standards of methods of interrogation and accountability in respect of possible abuses. Despite repeated requests on the part of the Special Rapporteur, the CIA did not make themselves available to meet again with him. In the light of this lack of cooperation and corroborating evidence from multiple sources, the Special Rapporteur can only conclude that the conduct of his country visit gives further support to the suspicion that the CIA had indeed been involved, and continued to be involved, in the use of enhanced interrogation techniques that violate international law.

B. U.S. Army Field Manual

35. The Special Rapporteur welcomes the revision of the U.S. Army Field Manual in September 2006. Although this Manual clearly states that acts of violence or intimidation against detainees is prohibited, and that interrogation techniques must not expose a person to inhumane treatment, there are nevertheless aspects of the revised Manual (when compared to the earlier version) that cause concern. On the positive side, the revised Manual explicitly prohibits the use of water boarding, something not expressly prohibited before. Nevertheless, a comparison of the two recent versions of the Army Field Manual could leave the impression that the present Manual neither authorizes nor prohibits, during the conduct of an interrogation, to slap a person being questioned, subject a person to extreme changes in temperature falling short of the medical state of hypothermia, isolate a detainee for prolonged periods, make use of stress positions, or subject a person to questioning for periods of up to 40 hours without sleep. The Special Rapporteur concludes that these techniques involve conduct that would amount to a breach of the prohibition against torture and any form of cruel, inhuman or degrading treatment. In order to remove any ambiguity, he expects the Government to make it clear that the enumeration of permitted interrogation techniques in the Manual is exhaustive.

C. Rendition and detention in "classified locations"

36. The Special Rapporteur acknowledges that there are various forms of rendition. The transfer of a person from one jurisdiction to another (or from the custody and control of one State to another) can occur by various means, including: rendition under established extradition rules; removal under immigration law; resettlement under refugee law; or "rendition to justice", where Page 18 a person is outside formal extradition arrangements but is nevertheless handed to another State for the purpose of standing trial in that State. As long as there is full compliance with the obligation of non-refoulement, these mechanisms may be lawful, although it should be noted that the particular circumstances in which a person is "rendered to justice" may involve an unlawful detention. Impermissible under international law is the "extraordinary rendition" of a person to another State for the purpose of interrogation or detention without charge. Rendition in these circumstances also runs the risk of the detained person being made subject to torture or cruel, inhuman or degrading treatment. Detention without charge or for prolonged periods even when charged, also amounts to a violation of articles 9 and 14 of the ICCPR and may constitute enforced disappearance. Furthermore, the removal of a person outside legally prescribed procedures amounts to an unlawful detention in violation of article 9 (1) of the ICCPR, and raises other human rights concerns if a detainee is not given a chance to challenge the transfer.

37. The Special Rapporteur is aware of various sources pointing to the rendition by the CIA of terrorist suspects or other persons to "classified locations" (also known as places of secret detention) and/or to a territory in which the detained person may be subjected to indefinite detention and/or interrogation techniques that amount to a violation of the prohibition against torture or cruel, inhuman or degrading treatment. These reports suggest that such interrogation techniques may have been used, either directly by CIA agents or by others while in CIA presence. The existence of classified locations was confirmed by the President of the U.S. on 6 September 2006, when he announced the transfer of 14 "high-value detainees" from these locations to Guantánamo Bay. Although the President announced that at that time the CIA no longer held any persons in classified locations, he reserved the possibility of resuming this programme. Since then, one more "high-value detainee" has been transferred to Guantánamo Bay, and the whereabouts of many others are unknown.

38. In addition, the use by the CIA of civil aircraft for the transportation of persons subjected to extraordinary rendition, whether by contract or by the establishment of airlines controlled by it, is in violation of the Convention on International Civil Aviation. Again due to the refusal of the Acting General Counsel for the CIA to engage in any meaningful interaction, and in the light of corroborating evidence, the Special Rapporteur concludes that his visit supports the suspicion that the CIA has been involved and continues to

be involved in the extraordinary rendition of terrorism suspects and possibly other persons. This conclusion is corroborated by the recent findings of the Committee against Torture in the case of *Agiza v Sweden* and by the Human Rights Committee in *Alzery v Sweden*, in both of which Sweden was found to have violated its human rights treaty obligations by handing over Mr. Agiza and Mr. Alzery to CIA agents in the course of their rendition to Egypt. The Special Rapporteur also concludes that it is unlikely that the CIA would be able to run a global programme of rendition and detention of terrorist suspects without at least logistical support by the U.S. military authorities.

D. Accountability of those responsible for conducting interrogation by techniques amounting to torture or cruel, inhuman or degrading treatment

39. The Convention against Torture requires States parties to prevent, within their territory, any acts of torture, or cruel, inhuman or degrading treatment. By virtue of the extraterritorial application of the prohibition of such acts, considered earlier in this report, and the obligations under customary international law and Articles 55 and 56 of the Charter of the United Nations, States must also ensure that their officials do not undertake such practices overseas and that they are not complicit in such conduct by other persons. It is thus essential that accountability is borne by those responsible (either directly, or by command responsibility) for conducting or colluding in interrogation techniques amounting to torture or cruel, inhuman or degrading treatment. The Special Rapporteur is troubled by reports indicating that while a number of military persons have been investigated or prosecuted for abuses, this has not happened in the case of CIA agents or persons higher up in the chain of command, and that the Department of Justice has not taken action to initiate prosecution in cases reported to it.

V. DEFINITIONS OF TERRORISM, TARGETED KILLINGS, AND VICTIMS OF TERRORISM

A. Definitions of terrorism

40. Terrorism is referred to within various items of U.S. legislation. Two particular aspects of this legislation are of concern to the Special Rapporteur. Title 18 of the US Code, in section 2331 (1), defines international terrorism as involving "violent acts or acts dangerous to human life" without making a link to the consequences intended by such acts. Security Council resolution 1566 (2004) describes conduct that is to be suppressed in the fight against terrorism and requires, as one of three cumulative elements, that such conduct is restricted to that which is committed with the intent to cause death or serious bodily injury. The definition of domestic terrorism, under section 2331 (5), equally lacks this link.

41. The USA PATRIOT Act of 2001 is also of concern to the Special Rapporteur, which in its amendment of the Immigration and Nationality Act (INA) concerning persons "engaged in terrorist activities" includes the provision of material support to proscribed entities. While new section 212 (a) (3) (B) (iv) (VI) of the INA provides a list of forms of conduct that can amount to material support, the provision is expressed in terms that are not exclusive and thereby renders the expression "material support" too vague. This lack of precision is particularly problematic for communities, including Muslim ones, which are unable to determine whether the provision of funds by them to what they may believe are charities or humanitarian organizations abroad will be treated as material support to a terrorist entity. The Special Rapporteur observes that any determination of proscribed status of organizations, including purported charities, should be public, transparent, non-retroactive and reasoned.

B. Targeted killings

42. The Special Rapporteur on extrajudicial, summary or arbitrary executions, Philip Alston, has reported on communications between himself and the U.S. concerning allegations of extrajudicial executions of various persons, including those suspected of having committed terrorist acts. Such acts have occurred outside the territory of the U.S. and outside the context of actual hostilities related to an armed conflict. The Special Rapporteur reiterates that international human rights, including the rights to life and fair trial under articles 6 and 14 of ICCPR, apply extraterritorially to the conduct of State agents. He further emphasizes that while the targeting of a combatant directly participating in hostilities is permitted under the laws of war, there are no circumstances in which the targeting of any other person can be justified.

C. Victims of terrorism

43. The Special Rapporteur is deeply mindful of the tragic events of 11 September 2001, as well as preceding acts of international terrorism against the U.S., including the bombing of its Embassies in Kenya and Tanzania. He is also mindful of domestic acts of terrorism, including the Oklahoma City bombing. Addressing the situation of victims of terrorism with appropriate compensation and access to health care and

rehabilitation is an important aspect of a comprehensive strategy against terrorism, and should be seen as a matter of best practice. The Special Rapporteur notes with encouragement the establishment, by the U.S. Government, of a process by which the victims of the terrorist attacks of 11 September have been able to seek compensation.

44. The Special Rapporteur notes with encouragement that following the catastrophic events in New Orleans in 2005, the Department of Homeland Security has taken steps to evaluate and consider the position of persons with disabilities and their care providers during relief efforts, which may also include events following a terrorist attack.

VI. PROFILING, COMMUNITY OUTREACH, AND IMMIGRATION AND REFUGEE STATUS

A. Profiling

45. The Special Rapporteur notes with encouragement, and as an element of best practice, that the Secretary of Homeland Security has clearly stated that his department is not, in law or practice, involved in racial or religious profiling. The Special Rapporteur nevertheless notes that the country of origin has been, or may be, used as a proxy for such profiling. It is a significant problem in certain regions of the world that the religious affiliation of persons is wrongly confused with the identification of such persons as potential terrorists.

B. Community outreach

46. The Special Rapporteur is very much encouraged by the initiation of community outreach programmes by various governmental agencies, including the Department of Homeland Security. Both at its own initiative, as well as in conjunction with civil society, the Department of Homeland Security has initiated a number of programmes aimed at creating a constructive dialogue with communities, including Muslims, and at explaining the Islamic faith and practice to members of the public and State employees. The alienation of segments of society, and the discriminatory treatment of groups in violation of their human rights, has been recognized by the international community as constituting conditions conducive to the emergence of terrorism or recruitment into terrorist organizations. The Special Rapporteur therefore identifies the efforts to reach out to the community as a best practice in the fight against terrorism.

C. Immigration and refugee status

47. There are a number of troubling developments in the law and practice of the U.S. concerning the treatment of immigrants, those applying for visas, and those claiming refugee status. The USA PATRIOT Act of 2001 amended provisions of the Immigration and Nationality Act, expanding the definition of terrorist activity beyond the bounds of conduct which is truly terrorist in nature, in particular in respect of the provision of "material support to terrorist organizations". The definition captures, for example, the payment of a ransom to have a family member released by a terrorist organization, or the providing of funds to a charity organization which at the time was not classified as a terrorist organization. The PATRIOT Act provides for the mandatory detention of those suspected of such conduct and the refusal of refugee status for such persons. However, the Secretary of Homeland Security has announced a policy of "duress waiver". The Special Rapporteur is troubled by the lack of transparency and judicial remedies in the application of such a waiver to persons, some of whom may themselves be victims of terrorist conduct.

VII. PRIVACY AND SURVEILLANCE, AND FREEDOM OF EXPRESSION

A. Privacy and surveillance generally

49. The Fourth Amendment to the U.S. Constitution guarantees the right of US citizens to privacy. International human rights law accommodates interference with privacy where necessary for legitimate purposes and implemented in a proportionate manner. In its 1972 decision in *U.S. v U.S. District Court*, the Supreme Court held that the Fourth Amendment prohibits the surveillance of "US persons" without a warrant, even if this surveillance is carried out for national security reasons. Under U.S. law, the surveillance of "US persons" (citizens or permanent residents of the U.S.) can only occur when authorized by the Wiretap Act of 1968 or the Foreign Intelligence Surveillance Act of 1978 (FISA). The PATRIOT Act of 2001 expanded the provisions of FISA so that applications for a surveillance warrant need only establish that foreign intelligence gathering is a significant purpose of the proposed surveillance rather than "the purpose" of surveillance, as previously required under FISA. This regime raises a number of concerns. Firstly, the low threshold in the availability of surveillance warrants leaves open the possibility for interference with privacy where this is not necessary for legitimate purposes. Next is the fact that the Attorney General's guidelines on the availability of surveillance warrants for the investigation of terrorist and related offences, or the gathering of related intelligence, is classified, as are the "minimization

procedures" required under Title 50 of the US Code to ensure that the surveillance of US persons is undertaken by the least intrusive means possible. Although the Special Rapporteur has been advised by the Department of Justice that these guidelines and procedures comply with international human rights law, there is no way of assessing the accuracy of this position, nor is there any transparency to guarantee compliance with the dual requirements of article 17 of the ICCPR to not interfere with privacy and to protect against the arbitrary interference with privacy. It is also relevant that the ICCPR obliges States parties to comply with these requirements not only in respect of citizens and permanent residents, but also in respect of all persons within the jurisdiction of the State. It is furthermore troubling that the use of FISA warrants, which have traditionally been treated as an exception to surveillance conducted under the Wiretap Act of 1968, has increased substantially since 11 September.

Added to this is the almost universal granting of surveillance warrants by the Foreign Intelligence Security Court, which brings into question whether the Court acts as a genuine judicial check of executive power in this area.

B. NSA programme of secret surveillance

50. The National Security Agency (NSA) operated a programme of secret surveillance without warrant outside the scope of FISA, authorized by an Executive Order of the President. The existence of this programme apparently came to light as a result of an internal leak. Whereas it is a crime under U.S. law to undertake surveillance without a court order, the NSA surveillance programme was said to have been established under an inherent right of the President to authorize warrantless surveillance under Article II of the U.S. Constitution.

Whether or not this is correct, the use of surveillance techniques without a warrant amounts to an interference with privacy not authorized by a "prescription by law" within the meaning of ICCPR article 17, thus rendering such surveillance unlawful within the terms of that article.

Following media reports in 2005 exposing the existence of the NSA programme, the President acknowledged the existence of such a programme and stated that NSA surveillance would in the future be carried out under FISA.

C. National Security Letters

51. A further development impacting upon privacy rights was the extended use of National Security Letters, a form of administrative subpoena facilitating expedited access by the Federal Bureau of Investigation and other intelligence agencies to private records. Prior to the PATRIOT Act of 2001, the availability of National Security Letters was restricted to financial records, customer call records and consumer reports, with the requirement that a certifying officer be satisfied that the subject of investigation was acting on behalf of a foreign power. The Act broadened the type of records accessible under National Security Letters and extended the authority to counter-terrorism investigations. The Special Rapporteur is concerned at the weakness of checks and balances in this authority, failing to properly ensure that there is no arbitrary interference with privacy, as required by ICCPR article 17.

D. Freedom of expression

52. The exercise of freedom of expression is a cornerstone of democratic society and of ensuring accountable governance. It is evident that the freedom of the press, and its ability to bring executive action to light, has been a significant factor in raising public awareness and creating a debate on issues central to the promotion and protection of human rights and fundamental freedoms in the U.S.. The Special Rapporteur is encouraged, in that regard, by the fact that the Government of the U.S. has not acted to restrain media interest or publication. The free media of the U.S. itself has in the years following 11 September operated as a device for ensuring transparency and account- ability in respect of the adverse consequences upon human rights of counter-terrorism measures undertaken by the Government. This is a feature of best practice which all countries should aspire to.

VIII. CONCLUSIONS AND RECOMMENDATIONS

A. Conclusions

53. The Special Rapporteur has identified elements of best practice in the U.S.' fight against terrorism and the compliance of this with human rights and fundamental freedoms, including compensation for victims of terrorism, community outreach, and non-interference with the freedom of the press. He has, in contrast, also identified serious situations of incompatibility between international human rights obligations and the counter-terrorism law and practice of the U.S. Such situations include the prohibition against torture, or cruel, inhuman or degrading treatment; the right to life; and the right to a fair trial. He has also identified

deficiencies in U.S. law and practice pertaining to the principle of non-refoulement; the rendition of persons to places of secret detention; the definition of terrorism; non-discrimination; checks in the application of immigration laws; and the obtaining of private records of persons and the unlawful surveillance of persons, including a lack of sufficient balances in that context.

B. Recommendations

54. The Special Rapporteur has described his visit to the U.S. as a step in the process of restoring the role of the U.S. as a positive example for respecting human rights, including in the context of the fight against terrorism, and he hopes that these steps continue to progress. He likewise recommends that the U.S. take a strong role in the implementation of the United Nations Global Counter-Terrorism Strategy.

55. The Special Rapporteur recommends that the categorization of persons as "unlawful enemy combatants" be abandoned. He calls upon the U.S. to release or to put on trial those persons detained under that categorization. In the case of those suspected of war crimes, the international community has recognized the need to ensure that there is no impunity for such offending, but the Special Rapporteur is gravely concerned about the increasing risks of an unfair trial as time continues to pass, and he therefore urges a determined effort to proceed with and conclude such prosecutions.

56. The Special Rapporteur further recommends that legislative amendments be made to remove the denial of habeas corpus rights under the Military Commissions Act 2006 and the restrictions upon the ability of Guantánamo Bay detainees to seek full judicial review of their combatant status, with the authority of the reviewing court to order release.

57. Notwithstanding the primary responsibility of the U.S. to resettle any individuals among those detained in Guantánamo Bay who are in need of international protection, the Special Rapporteur recommends that other States be willing to receive persons currently detained at Guantánamo Bay. The U.S. and the United Nations High Commissioner for Refugees should work together to establish a joint process by which detainees can be resettled in accordance with international law, including refugee law and the principle of non-refoulement.

58. In particular, the Special Rapporteur urges the U.S. to invite the United Nations High Commissioner for Refugees to conduct confidential individual interviews with the detainees, in order to determine their qualification as refugees and to recommend their resettlement to other countries. He also urges the U.S. not to require from receiving countries the detention or monitoring of those returned in cases where such measures would not have basis in international and domestic law, and equally urges receiving States not to accept such conditions.

59. Due to the various concerns identified in this report pertaining to the composition and operation of military tribunals under the Military Commissions Act of 2006, involving multiple incompatibilities with the ICCPR, the Special Rapporteur recommends that these commissions be disestablished. Wherever possible, ordinary civilian courts should be used to try terrorist suspects.

60. In the case of persons charged with war crimes, being those crimes identified in the Rome Statute of the International Criminal Court, such persons may be tried by military courts martial provided that safeguards are in place to check against the exercise of bias or executive interference, including rights of appeal to civilian courts. In any such proceedings, the security classification of information should not interfere with the presumption of innocence or the equality of arms, nor should evidence obtained by any form of torture or cruel, inhuman or degrading treatment be admitted in proceedings. The U.S. should take steps to ensure that any person acquitted of charges is released upon acquittal, or in the case of a person convicted of an offence, that release occurs upon completion of the sentence imposed. The Special Rapporteur further recommends that the imposition of the death penalty be excluded for military tribunals or courts martial.

61. Gravely concerned at the enhanced interrogation techniques reportedly used by the CIA, the Special Rapporteur urges the U.S. to ensure that all its officials and agencies comply with international standards, including article 7 of ICCPR, the Convention against Torture and, in the context of an armed conflict, common article 3 of the Geneva Conventions. Noting the U.S. understanding of cruel, inhuman or degrading punishment, he reminds the Government that there are no circumstances in which cruel, inhuman or degrading treatment may be justified, and recommends that steps be taken to reflect this in its domestic law.

62. The Special Rapporteur has concluded that the interrogation techniques identified in this report, which are not explicitly prohibited in the U.S. Army Field Manual, involve conduct that may amount to a breach of the prohibition against torture and any form of cruel, inhuman or degrading treatment. He recommends that the Manual be revised to expressly state that only enumerated techniques are permissible. As a practice which is not permissible in international law, and one that creates the real risk of torture or other ill-treatment of persons, the Special Rapporteur urges the Government to take transparent steps to ensure that the CIA practice of "extraordinary rendition" is completely discontinued and is not conducted in the future, and that CIA interrogation techniques are regulated in line with the position expressed above in respect of the Army Field Manual.

63. The Special Rapporteur also calls on the U.S. to ensure that all detainees are held in accordance with international human rights standards, including the requirement that all detainees be held in regularized facilities, that they be registered, that they be allowed contact with the outside world (lawyers, International Committee of the Red Cross, where applicable, family), and that any form of detention is subject to accessible and effective court review, which entails the possibility of release.

64. The Special Rapporteur urges the Government to restrict definitions of "international terrorism", "domestic terrorism" and "material support to terrorist organizations" in a way that is precise and restricted to the type of conduct identified by the Security Council as conduct to be suppressed in the fight against terrorism. He strongly urges the U.S. to ensure that it does not participate in the extrajudicial execution of any person, including terrorist suspects.

65. The Special Rapporteur recommends that all States, including the U.S., do not use the country of origin of a person as a proxy for racial or religious profiling. He further urges all States not to act in a manner which might be seen as advocating the use of race and religion for the identification of persons as terrorists.

66. In the context of the compulsory detention of persons suspected of providing material support to terrorist organizations, the Special Rapporteur recommends that a transparent system be established for the application of the "duress waiver" established by the Department of Homeland Security, including the provision of judicial oversight.

67. Due to the fact that the U.S. Attorney General's guidelines on the availability of surveillance warrants under FISA, and the minimization procedures applicable to the surveillance of US persons are classified, the Special Rapporteur recommends that the Government introduce independent mechanisms, preferably involving the judiciary, to ensure that these guidelines and procedures are compliant with both the Constitution and the international obligations of the U.S.. The Special Rapporteur further urges the Government to extend these, and existing safeguards, to all persons within the jurisdiction and control of the U.S., not simply those falling within the definition of "US persons".

68. The Special Rapporteur urges the Government to take steps to introduce independent checks and balances upon the authority of the FBI and other intelligence agencies to use National Security Letters.

Document 2: Report of the United Nations High Commissioner for Human Rights on the protection of human rights and fundamental freedoms while countering terrorism, A/HRC/13/36. (Excerpted)

UNITED NATIONS	A/HRC/13/36
General Assembly	Distr:
HUMAN RIGHTS COUNCIL	GENERAL
Thirteenth session	22 January 2010
Agenda item 3	Original: ENGLISH

PROMOTION AND PROTECTION OF ALL HUMAN RIGHTS, CIVIL, POLITICAL, ECONOMIC, SOCIAL AND CULTURAL RIGHTS, INCLUDING THE RIGHT TO DEVELOPMENT
Report of the United Nations High Commissioner for Human
Rights on the protection of human rights and fundamental
freedoms while countering terrorism*

Summary

The present report is submitted in accordance with Human Rights Council resolution 10/15 of 26 March 2009 on the protection and promotion of human rights while countering terrorism, in which the Council requested the United Nations High Commissioner for Human Rights "to present [her report], bearing in mind the content of the present resolution, to the Council at its thirteenth session under agenda item 3, inconformity with its annual programme of work". In that resolution, the Human Rights Council called upon States to ensure access to an effective remedy in cases where human rights have been violated as a result of counterterrorism measures, and provide adequate, prompt and effective reparations for victims. The Council recalled the absolute prohibition of torture and the right to be equal before courts and tribunals, and urged States to guarantee due process. It also reaffirmed resolution7/7, in which the Council, among other things, urged States to respect their non refoulement obligations as well as the safeguards concerning the liberty, security and dignity of the person.1

*The present report is submitted late so as to include as much up-to-date information as possible.

1 In resolutions 7/7 and 10/15 the Human Rights Council reaffirmed the non-derogability of certain rights in all circumstances, as well as the exceptional and temporary nature of derogations.

The present report highlights the need to protect and promote all human rights and to maintain effective counter-terrorism measures. These are mutually reinforcing objectives that must be pursued together as part of the duty of States to protect human rights. It outlines the High Commissioner's activities regarding counter-terrorism measures and her role in the implementation of the United Nations Global Counter-Terrorism Strategy and its Plan of Action. It concludes with the identification of challenges related to complying with human rights obligations, in particular the issues of accountability, ending impunity and effective remedies in the context of countering terrorism.

GE.10-10442

Contents

I. Introduction

1. The present report is submitted in accordance with Council resolution 10/15. In its resolution 7/7, the Human Rights Council requested the United Nations High Commissioner for Human Rights to continue her efforts to implement the mandate given to her by the Commission on Human Rights in its resolution 2005/80 and the General Assembly in its resolution 60/158, and report to the Council. These two resolutions request the High Commissioner for Human Rights, making use of existing mechanisms, to continue:

(a) To examine the question of the protection of human rights and fundamental freedoms countering terrorism, taking into account reliable information from all sources;

(b) To make general recommendations concerning the obligation of States to promote and protect human rights and fundamental freedoms while taking actions to counter terrorism;

(c) To provide assistance and advice to States, upon their request, on the protection of human rights and fundamental freedoms while countering terrorism, as well as to relevant United Nations bodies.

2. In its resolution 10/15, the Human Rights Council called upon States to ensure access to an effective remedy where human rights are violated as a result of counterterrorism measures, and provide adequate, prompt and effective reparations for victims.

The present report addresses developments in respect of the protection of human rights while countering terrorism over the past year. In the same resolution, the Human Rights Council requested the High Commissioner for Human Rights "to present [her report], bearing in mind the content of the present resolution, to the Council at its thirteenth session under its agenda item 3, in conformity with its annual programme of work".

II. Recent developments

A. Implementation of the United Nations Global Counter-Terrorism Strategy and the Counter-Terrorism Implementation Task Force

3. Through the United Nations Global Counter-Terrorism Strategy and Plan of Action, adopted by the General Assembly in its resolution 60/288, Member States reaffirmed that acts, methods and practices of terrorism in all its forms and manifestations are activities aimed at the destruction of human rights, fundamental freedoms and democracy. They committed to adopting measures to ensure respect for human rights for all and to use the rule of law as the fundamental basis of the fight against terrorism. Member States also resolved to ensure that measures taken to counter terrorism comply with their obligations under international human rights law.

4. In the Plan of Action, it was reaffirmed that the Office of the United Nations High Commissioner for Human Rights (OHCHR) should play a lead role in examining the protection of human rights while countering terrorism. OHCHR continued to lead the Working Group on Protecting Human Rights While Countering Terrorism of the Counter-Terrorism Implementation Task Force established by the Secretary-General in 2005, in an effort to ensure a coordinated and coherent approach across the United Nations system to counter-terrorism. In 2008, the Monitoring Team of the Security Council Committee established pursuant to resolution 1267 (1999) (Counter-Terrorism Committee) joined the Working Group and the Office for the Coordination of Humanitarian Affairs and the Office of the United Nations High Commissioner for Refugees as observers. The aim of the Working Group is to support efforts by Member States to ensure the promotion and protection of human rights in the context of counter-terrorism through, among other things, the development and implementation of legislation and policies that are compliant with human rights.

5. To assist Member States in strengthening the protection of human rights in 10 specific areas, my Office, in consultation with Member States, started to develop a series of basic technical reference guides on countering terrorism with the endeavour of providing full respect for human rights. Following consultations with Member States, the first four guides being developed are on (a) proscription of organizations, (b) stopping and searching of persons, (c) designing security infrastructure, and (d) the principle of legality in national counter-terrorism legislation.

6. On 14 and 15 October 2009, my Office participated in the Counter-Terrorism Implementation Task Force retreat in Vienna. This yearly meeting was focused on taking stock of the work that the Task Force and its working groups accomplished in the past year.

It also set forth the plans for the future. Key issues discussed included, among others, the institutionalization of the Task Force in accordance with General Assembly resolution 62/272 and the communications strategy of the Task Force.

...

B. The work of the Security Council

8. On 29 October 2009, I addressed the Counter-Terrorism Committee. Guided by Security Council resolutions 1373 (2001) and 1624 (2005), the Committee has been working to enhance the ability of States Members of the United Nations to prevent terrorist acts both within their borders and across regions. The Committee is assisted in its efforts by the Counter-Terrorism Committee Executive Directorate, which carries out the policy decisions of the Committee, conducts expert assessments of each Member State and facilitates counter-terrorism technical assistance to countries. This was the third time that a High Commissioner for Human Rights addressed this important body.

9. During this briefing, I reiterated that upholding human rights while countering terrorism is an inescapable imperative, because human rights law offers a framework that can both meet public security concerns and protect human dignity and the rule of law.

Some measures taken to counter terrorism, such as resorting to the use of excessive force and indiscriminate repression by the police, security and army personnel, can strengthen terrorists' support bases, undermining the goals that States set out to achieve. Upholding human rights creates trust between the State and those under its jurisdiction, and such trust can serve as the foundation of an effective response to terrorism. I highlighted that meaningful protection also includes tackling the underlying causes of terrorism, such as the obstacles to the enjoyment of economic, social and cultural rights.

10. I sought to underscore that the time had come for the Security Council's counterterrorism bodies to consider a broader approach in their vital work in this area, such as that of the General Assembly in the United Nations Global Counter-Terrorism Strategy and Plan of Action, which stressed not only the need for counter-terrorism measures, but also the impact of such measures on human rights. I noted that because the Counter-Terrorism Committee and the United Nations human rights machinery review counter-terrorism laws and measures in parallel, better cooperation between them could provide additional legitimacy and coherence to the United Nations system as a whole.

11. I shared with the Counter-Terrorism Committee my views that it could play a key role in placing the rule of law and human rights at the core of the fight against terrorism. I mentioned six areas in particular:

(a) The question of legality, including vague definitions of acts of terrorism that have led to the prosecution of individuals for the legitimate, non-violent exercise of their rights to freedom of expression, association and assembly, and which represent a violation of the principle of legality;

(b) The need to respect and protect non-derogable rights. I noted in this respect that national, ethnic, racial or religious profiling raises concerns with regard to the nonderogable principles of equality and non-discrimination. I also raised the question of torture and ill-treatment. These discriminatory and stigmatizing measures affect the rights of communities and may lead to further marginalization and possibly radicalization within those communities;

(c) The expansion of surveillance powers and capacities of law enforcement agencies and the need to adequately protect the right to privacy, which may severely undermine international cooperation; as well as the use of torture and ill-treatment for intelligence gathering, which taints evidence and makes it inadmissible at trial;

(d) Accountability for human rights violations, which is especially crucial to effective counter-terrorism strategies. True security can only be achieved where all members of society cooperate with State authorities and are confident that the measures adopted by these authorities to counter-terrorism are effective, proportionate, and respectful of their human rights and dignity;

(e) The issue of targeted sanctions. I noted that while I welcomed the recent improvements in procedures related to the United Nations targeted sanctions regime, further improvements were necessary to ensure a transparent listing process based on clear criteria, and with a uniformly applied standard of evidence. Accessible and independent mechanisms for review are also necessary;

(f) Issues regarding the proper integration of a human rights approach to the technical work of the Counter-Terrorism Committee. I suggested that consideration should be given to include a human rights expert on all Committee visits to Member States and to devote additional resources to this area of the Committee's work.

I also reaffirmed the OHCHR commitment to supporting the Committee and its Executive Directorate on all issues related to States' compliance with human rights.

12. From 8 to 10 November 2009, the Counter-Terrorism Committee Executive Directorate and the Government of Bangladesh held a regional workshop in Dhaka on effective counter-terrorism practices for senior police officers and prosecutors from Afghanistan, Bangladesh, Bhutan, India, Maldives, Nepal, Pakistan and Sri Lanka; a representative of the South Asian Association for Regional Cooperation (SAARC) also attended. OHCHR participated in this workshop offering views on how human rights can be upheld at the operational level in the context of international legal cooperation.

13. On 17 December 2009 the Security Council adopted resolution 1904 (2009) to meet the challenges faced by Member States in implementing the sanctions regime against Al-Qaida and the Taliban. The resolution was aimed at improving the procedures to ensure that they are fair and the procedures are clear. In it, the Security Council decided, among other things, to create an office of the ombudsperson, which would assist in analysing available information concerning the delisting requests of those seeking removal from the Council's sanctions list.

C. The work of the General Assembly

14. In December 2009, the General Assembly adopted resolution 64/168 on the protection of human rights and fundamental freedoms while countering terrorism. In the resolution, the General Assembly, among other things:

(a) Expresses serious concern at the occurrence of violations of human rights and fundamental freedoms;

(b) Urges States countering terrorism to comply with their obligations in a number of areas, such as the prohibition of torture and other cruel, inhuman or degrading treatment or punishment, the guarantee for liberty and security, the treatment of prisoners, non-refoulement, the legality in the criminalization of acts of terrorism, non-discrimination, the right to an effective remedy, due process and the right to a fair trial;

(c) Highlights the need to protect economic, social and cultural rights;

(d) Notes the need to continue ensuring that fair and clear procedures under the United Nations terrorism-related sanctions regime are strengthened to enhance their efficiency and transparency;

(e) Urges States to ensure the rule of law and to include adequate human rights guarantees in their national listing procedures;

(f) Requests OHCHR to continue to contribute to the work of the Counter-Terrorism Implementation Task Force, including by raising awareness on the need to protect human rights and the rule of law while countering terrorism;

(g) Encourages the Security Council and its Counter-Terrorism Committee to strengthen dialogue with relevant human rights bodies, in particular with OHCHR, the Special Rapporteur on the promotion and protection of human rights and fundamental freedoms while countering terrorism, other relevant special procedures and mechanisms of the Human Rights Council and relevant treaty bodies.

D. Other relevant activities

15. The annual report of the Special Representative of the Secretary-General for Children and Armed Conflict (A/HRC/12/49) presented to the Human Rights Council at its twelfth session addresses terrorism and counter-terrorism and their impact on children. The Special Rapporteur noted that anti-terrorism measures often target children; in some cases, children are arrested or detained for reasons of alleged association with terrorist groups, and legal and practical safeguards are disregarded. The Special Representative also focused on "collateral damage", in which children are often the victims, resulting from precision aerial bombardment and other types of military operation.

16. The United Nations human rights treaty bodies have continued to take up issues related to terrorism in their examination of State party reports and individual complaints. In their concluding observations, different committees have urged States parties to recognize and ensure that the human rights treaties apply at all times, in any territory under their jurisdiction. The Secretary-General has recently reported on key developments in this field to the General Assembly (see A/64/186); I would like to focus on the most recent developments.

. . .

III. Issues of concern: accountability and reparations

19. A major challenge facing States today is accountability for serious violations of human rights that have taken place in the context of counter-terrorism measures and the rights of victims to remedy and reparations. In recent years, serious violations have taken place affecting fundamental rights, including wilful killings, summary executions, disappearances, torture and arbitrary detention. These practices have rarely been investigated thoroughly, perpetrators have often not been punished, and reparations to victims have not been forthcoming.

20. In article 2, paragraph 3, of the International Covenant on Civil and Political Rights, it is spelled out that in addition to effective protection of Covenant rights, States parties must ensure that individuals have accessible and effective remedies to vindicate those rights, which was restated by the Human Rights Committee in its general comment No. 31(2004). The Committee stated that it attaches importance to States parties establishing appropriate judicial and administrative mechanisms for addressing claims of rights violations under domestic law. The Committee noted that the enjoyment of the rights recognized under the Covenant can be effectively assured by the judiciary in many different ways, including direct applicability of the Covenant, application of comparable constitutional or other provisions of law, or the interpretive effect of the Covenant in the application of national law. Administrative mechanisms are particularly required to give effect to the general obligation to investigate allegations of violations promptly, thoroughly and effectively through independent and impartial bodies. National human rights institutions, endowed with appropriate powers, can contribute to this end.

. . .

A. Accountability

22. Where serious violations of human rights occur, States have the duty to ensure that such violations are properly investigated and, wherever possible, investigation should lead to a judicial or other appropriate response. The failure to conduct an independent investigation of serious human rights violations not only reinforces the violations that have already been committed but can lead to the serious deterioration of larger countrywide human rights situations. On the other hand, a timely and efficient inquiry can have a preventive effect and improve the overall national human rights situation. Failure to investigate also violates the human rights of the victims. Also, a failure by a State party to investigate allegations of violations could give rise to a separate breach of the Covenant. Cessation of an ongoing violation is an essential element of the right to an effective remedy.

23. States are under the obligation to investigate all human rights violations. Under extreme circumstances, where a state of emergency is declared, derogations from some rights and freedoms are permissible under article 4 of the International Covenant on Civil and Political Rights, but they should not exceed the exigencies of the situation. Article 4(2) of the Covenant lists various rights which are non-derogable at all times, such as: the right to life; the prohibition of torture and other inhuman or degrading treatment; the prohibition of retroactive criminal laws; freedom of thought, conscience and religion; and the prohibition of the death penalty (article 6 of the Second Optional Protocol to the International Covenant on Civil and Political Rights).

24. Under article 2 (1) of the International Covenant on Civil and Political Rights, State parties are obliged to respect and ensure the Covenant rights to all persons who may be within their territory and to all persons subject to their jurisdiction. General comment No. 15 of the Human Rights Committee indicates that this obligation is not limited to a State's citizens, but must be guaranteed to all individuals, regardless of nationality or statelessness, such as asylum-seekers, refugees, migrant workers and others who may find themselves subject to the jurisdictional regulations of the territory in which they are found.

25. Procedurally, States commit themselves to establishing suitable institutions (i.e. primarily judicial institutions, such as criminal, civil, constitutional and special human rights courts, or also national human rights institutions and torture rehabilitation bodies) to enable victims of torture to obtain redress. National mechanisms are required to give prompt, thorough, and effective attention to the obligations to investigate allegations of violations through independent and impartial bodies. National human rights institutions, endowed with appropriate powers, can contribute to this end by referring all those responsible for committing gross human rights violations to the criminal justice system for investigation.

26. The Special Rapporteur on torture and other cruel, inhuman or degrading treatment or punishment indicated that in the light of the consistent international jurisprudence suggesting that the prohibition of amnesties leading to impunity for serious human rights has become a rule of customary international law, he expresses his opposition to the passing, application and non-revocation of amnesty laws which prevent torturers from being brought to justice and hence contribute to a culture of impunity. He called on States to refrain from granting or acquiescing in impunity at the national level, inter alia, by the granting of amnesties, such impunity itself constituting a violation of international law. 12 Article 4 of the Convention against Torture and Other Cruel, Inhuman or Degrading Treatment or Punishment states that each State party must ensure that all acts of torture are offences under its criminal law; this also applies to an attempt to commit torture and to an act by any person which constitutes complicity or participation in torture. It also states that each State party must make these offences punishable by appropriate penalties which take into account their grave nature. The Convention against Torture contains obligations aimed at punishing perpetrators, preventing torture and assisting victims of torture.

27. With regards to the right to life, in general comment No. 6 (1982) the Human Rights Committee specifies that not only do States have a negative obligation not to arbitrarily interfere with the individual right to life, but also, States have a positive obligation to adopt all measures that are appropriate to protect and preserve the right to life and to prevent and punish deprivations of life by criminal acts as well as arbitrary killings by their own security forces. The police have the duty to prepare and plan counter-terrorism operations so as to avoid any loss of life. Public investigations of any death in which State agents may be implicated are necessary.

28. Covert actions raise particular challenges for accountability. Since they are secretive types of action, where information is classified, it is difficult for the legislator and the judiciary to be aware of them. It should be recalled that all measures taken by law enforcement agencies must be lawful under national and

international law, and compatible with States' human rights obligations. This means that all activities undertaken by intelligence agencies, including intelligence-gathering covert surveillance, activities, searches and data collection must be regulated by law, monitored by independent agencies, and subject to judicial review. The lack of transparency that prevails in a number of the investigations and trials related to terrorism is a cause for concern. Through the adoption or revival of State secrecy or immunity doctrines or the adoption of other measures to shield intelligence, military or diplomatic sources and information, in the name of national security interests, States have limited the access to the necessary information for an effective investigation and prosecution of cases relating to acts of terrorism. States are required to ensure that confined powers, review of accountability and oversight mechanisms are established against the misuse of exceptional powers granted to intelligence, military agencies or special police to counter terrorism. Such controls might encompass the process or authorizing special powers and the remedies for people claiming abuse of these powers. Controls can occur either before or after the use of powers.

29. The Convention against Torture requires States parties to prevent, within their territory, any acts of torture, or cruel, inhuman or degrading treatment. By virtue of the extraterritorial application of the prohibition of such acts, and the obligations under customary international law and Articles 55 and 56 of the Charter of the United Nations, States must also ensure that their officials do not undertake such practices overseas and that they are not complicit in such conduct by other persons. It is thus essential that those responsible for conducting or colluding in interrogation techniques amounting to torture or cruel, inhuman or degrading treatment are held accountable.

30. The practice of holding terrorist suspects in secret detention has led to the denial of several rights of detainees, not only with respect to their rights associated with liberty, but also for example their right to a fair trial. In such circumstances, where confessions are extracted by torture and evidence gathered illegally through secret agents, the possibility of bringing to justice people who are responsible for committing the above-mentioned violations is unlikely. In its general comment No. 21 on article 10 of the International Covenant on Civil and Political Rights, the Human Rights Committee imposes on States an obligation to individuals who are vulnerable, such as juveniles, due to their status of persons deprived of liberty to be treated with humanity and with respect for the inherent dignity of the human person.

31. Accountability and the right to effective remedies are connected to the right to a fair trial as guaranteed by article 14 of the Covenant, clarified by general comment No. 32 of the Human Rights Committee. Protecting the right of terrorist suspects to a fair trial is critical not only for ensuring that anti-terrorism measures respect the rule of law, but also for ensuring that perpetrators of human rights violations are held accountable. Indeed, violations carried out in the execution of "extraordinary renditions" and collecting evidence by illegal means are very unlikely to be adequately brought to light, and perpetrators brought to justice, if suspects of terrorism are tried in special courts with special procedures or sealed evidence which do not fully guarantee the right to a fair trial. Therefore, the guarantees of a fair trial are essential to ensure accountability and to combat impunity, as well as to provide effective remedies.

32. Article 10 of the International Covenant on Civil and Political Rights has a clear relationship with the protection from torture, inhuman and degrading treatment and punishment. Human Rights Committee general comment No. 21 clarifies that article 10 imposes on States parties a positive obligation towards persons who are particularly vulnerable because of their status as persons deprived of liberty, and complements for them the ban on torture or other cruel, inhuman or degrading treatment or punishment contained in article 7 of the Covenant. The Committee also recalls that the principle set forth in article 10, paragraph 1, constitutes the basis for the more specific obligations of States parties in respect of criminal justice, which are set forth in article 10, paragraphs 2 and 3.

33. In the endeavour to protect intelligence sources, some States have amended the regulations governing legal or administrative procedures to allow the non-disclosure of materials to suspects. Secrecy and immunity doctrines should not be applied where serious human rights violations are being investigated, such as the absolute prohibition of torture and cases of killings or disappearances. Independent, impartial, transparent and credible investigations are required by law to ensure accountability. Individual responsibility cannot be avoided through amnesties or immunities, and other limitations to the recognition of legal responsibility.

34. States must refrain from granting or acquiescing in impunity at the national level through amnesties. Amnesties for gross and serious violations of human rights and humanitarian law may also violate customary international law, and the continued passing, application and non-revocation of amnesty laws contributes to a culture of impunity.

35. Since September 2001, there has been a trend towards outsourcing the collection of intelligence to private contractors. While the involvement of private actors can be necessary as a technical matter in order to have access to information (for instance for electronic surveillance), there are reasons to be wary of using contractors to interrogate persons who are deprived of their liberty. The responsibility to protect the right to life, physical integrity or liberty of individuals should remain within the exclusive domain of the State. The combination of a lack of proper training, the introduction of a profit motive into situations which are prone to human rights violations, and the often questionable prospect that such contractors will be subject to judicial and parliamentary accountability mechanisms are all elements that should be considered by Member States to ensure that those actors are accountable.

36. A particular concern is that of rendition and extraordinary rendition that arises from increased intelligence cooperation. Extraordinary rendition is almost certain to constitute or facilitate a violation of a variety of human rights, especially the rights that protect individuals against arbitrary arrest, forcible transfer, enforced disappearance or the subjection of torture and other cruel, inhuman or degrading treatment. States must fulfill their obligations under the different treaties and standards, and ensure that their territory is not used to transfer persons to places where they are likely to be subjected to torture.

37. In the absence of procedural safeguards that protect legal rights such as due process, persons who are subject to such transfers have no means of challenging their transfer.

Hence, States should take all practical steps to determine whether foreign movements through their territories involve practices that can lead to irreparable harm. States have an obligation to investigate the role of their agents (both military and intelligence) who may have been involved in facilitating these renditions, to sanction those responsible, and to provide reparation for victims. States also have a responsibility to put in place procedures to address these issues, whether in reference to their own agents or to foreign agents, and to regulate the use of their airspace. States are further required to ensure accountability for past practices.

38. There should be controls against the misuse of exceptional powers by institutions that are not subject to sufficient democratic and civilian control, in particular intelligence or military agencies or special police. States need to ensure confined powers, the review of accountability and oversight mechanisms. Such controls might encompass the process of authorizing special powers and the remedies for people claiming abuse of these powers. Controls can occur either before or after the use of powers.

39. Intelligence-gathering activities must be regulated by law, monitored as much as possible by independent agencies, and subject to judicial review. Under international human rights law, any act that impacts human rights must be lawful; it must be prescribed and regulated by law. This means that any search, seizure, surveillance activity, apprehension or data collection about a person must be clearly authorized by law. States amending regulations governing legal or administrative procedures to prevent the non-disclosure of materials to suspects must ensure they do so in conformity with their human rights obligations, in particular, with due process.

40. Counter-terrorism measures that have an impact on the enjoyment of economic and social rights should also respect the principles of proportionality, effectiveness and legitimacy. Access to justice and the existence of remedies, including adequate reparation for the victims, are key to upholding the accountability of States and to reducing impunity for violations of economic, social and cultural rights. In the context of countering terrorism, evictions and house demolitions are sometimes used as forms of targeted punishment for residents who are suspected of supporting terrorist groups. Where this constitutes a form of collective punishment it is considered a gross violation of human rights. It is often suffered by vulnerable communities, such as women, ethnic, religious and other minorities and indigenous peoples, who are suspected of supporting terrorist groups.

B. Remedies and reparation

41. In addition to States' duties to bring perpetrators of gross human rights violations before the criminal justice system, States' obligations have been described as requiring them to respect the right to truth, to justice and to reparation. The right to truth puts an obligation on the State to investigate human rights violations and to present the facts to the public. The right to reparation comprises not only the right to compensation and restitution, but also the right to rehabilitation, satisfaction and guarantees of non repetition, as described by the United Nations set of principles for the protection and promotion of human rights through action to combat impunity.

...

44. According to the Declaration of Basic Principles of Justice for Victims of Crime and Abuse of Power, victims include "persons who, individually or collectively, have suffered harm, including physical or mental injury, emotional suffering, economic loss or substantial impairment of their fundamental rights, through

acts or omissions that are in violation of criminal laws operative within Member States, including those laws proscribing criminal abuse of power". In the Declaration, it is noted that an individual may be considered a victim "regardless of whether the perpetrator is identified, apprehended, prosecuted or convicted and regardless of the familial relationship between the perpetrator and the victim".

...

47. The Basic Principles and Guidelines provide for different categories of reparation. Since torture constitutes a particularly serious violation of human rights, criminal prosecution and appropriate punishment is perceived by the victim as the most effective means of satisfaction and justice. Criminal investigations serve the purpose of establishing truth and pave the way for other forms of reparation. Guarantees of non-repetition, such as amending relevant laws, fighting impunity and taking effective preventive or deterrent measures, constitute a form of reparation if torture is practiced in a widespread or systematic manner. Monetary compensation for the immaterial damage (pain and suffering) or material damage (rehabilitation costs, etc.) may provide satisfaction as an additional form of reparation.

48. In its general comment No. 15, the Human Rights Committee indicates that under article 2 (1) of the International Covenant on Civil and Political Rights, the obligation is not limited to a State's citizens, but must be guaranteed to all individuals, regardless of nationality or statelessness, such as asylum-seekers, refugees, migrant workers and others who may find themselves subject to the jurisdictional regulations of the territory in which they are found. Such remedies should be appropriately adapted to take account of the special vulnerability of certain categories of person, including in particular children. As was confirmed by general comment No. 31, this principle also applies to those within the power or effective control of the forces of a State acting outside its territory, regardless of the circumstances in which such power or effective control was obtained. States must ensure that individuals have accessible and effective remedies to vindicate the aforementioned rights, which should be appropriately adapted to the special vulnerability of certain categories of persons, particularly children.

IV. Conclusions and recommendations

49. States are urged to ensure that measures taken to combat crimes of terrorism comply with their obligations under international human rights law, in particular the right to an effective remedy for victims of human rights violations.

50. States are urged to respect all rights, in particular non-derogable rights. It is extremely important that the Member States reconfirm their commitment to the absolute prohibition of torture and cruel, inhuman and degrading treatment, which are not to be permitted under any circumstances.

51. States are urged to cooperate with the special procedures of the Human Rights Council in enforcing accountability mechanisms and measures and means of providing remedies to victims.

52. States are urged to issue a standing invitation to all special procedures of the Human Rights Council, and in particular to the Special Rapporteur on the promotion and protection of human rights and fundamental freedoms while countering terrorism, the Special Rapporteur on torture and other cruel, inhuman or degrading treatment or punishment, the Special Rapporteur on extrajudicial, summary or arbitrary executions and the Working Groups on Arbitrary Detention and on Enforced or Involuntary Disappearances.

53. States are urged to strengthen legislation to protect the rights of arrested and detained individuals from torture and physical mistreatment and ensure they are afforded the full complement of due process rights in accordance with their obligations under international human rights.

54. States should ensure that national human rights institutions have the necessary capacity to contribute meaningfully to the protection of human rights and in particular to the provision of effective remedies in cases of substantive violations.

55. States should provide their law enforcement authorities, including intelligence agencies and prison staff, with training on international human rights laws and standards, including on the obligation to ensure effective remedies and accountability in the case of violations of human rights when committed by State agents or public officials.

56. To ensure accountability, torture or cruel, inhuman and degrading treatment committed by public officials and State agents should give rise to criminal liability and/or disciplinary measures. All allegations of torture or ill-treatment by any of the above-mentioned officers should be investigated and those found responsible punished. National laws and relevant regulating documents for public officials and State agents, including the police, intelligence officials and the military must comply with international human rights obligations to ensure that appropriate investigation and, where necessary, prosecution of alleged violations occur.

Document 3: Report of the Special Rapporteur on extrajudicial, summary or arbitrary executions, Philip Alston, Study on targeted killings, Addendum, A/HRC/14/24/Add.6. (Excerpted)

UNITED NATIONS	A/HRC/14/24/Add.6
General Assembly	Distr.:
HUMAN RIGHTS COUNCIL	GENERAL
Fourteenth session	28 May 2010
Agenda item 3	ENGLISH only

PROMOTION AND PROTECTION OF ALL HUMAN RIGHTS, CIVIL, POLITICAL, ECONOMIC, SOCIAL AND CULTURAL RIGHTS, INCLUDING THE RIGHT TO DEVELOPMENT
Report of the Special Rapporteur on extrajudicial, summary or arbitrary executions, Philip Alston*
Addendum
STUDY ON TARGETED KILLINGS**

Summary

In recent years, a few States have adopted policies that permit the use of targeted killings, including in the territories of other States. Such policies are often justified as a necessary and legitimate response to "terrorism" and "asymmetric warfare", but have had the very problematic effect of blurring and expanding the boundaries of the applicable legal frameworks. This report describes the new targeted killing policies and addresses the main legal issues that have arisen.

*Late submission.

**Owing to time constraints, the present report is circulated as received, in the language of submission only.

Contents

I. Introduction

1. A targeted killing is the intentional, premeditated and deliberate use of lethal force, by States or their agents acting under colour of law, or by an organized armed group in armed conflict, against a specific individual who is not in the physical custody of the perpetrator. In recent years, a few States have adopted policies, either openly or implicitly, of using targeted killings, including in the territories of other States.

2. Such policies have been justified both as a legitimate response to "terrorist" threats and as a necessary response to the challenges of "asymmetric warfare." In the legitimate struggle against terrorism, too

many criminal acts have been re-characterized so as to justify addressing them within the framework of the law of armed conflict. New technologies, and especially unarmed combat aerial vehicles or "drones", have been added into this mix, by making it easier to kill targets, with fewer risks to the targeting State.

3. The result of this mix has been a highly problematic blurring and expansion of the boundaries of the applicable legal frameworks—human rights law, the laws of war, and the law applicable to the use of inter-state force. Even where the laws of war are clearly applicable, there has been a tendency to expand who may permissibly be targeted and under what conditions. Moreover, the States concerned have often failed to specify the legal justification for their policies, to disclose the safeguards in place to ensure that targeted killings are in fact legal and accurate, or to provide accountability mechanisms for violations. Most troublingly, they have refused to disclose who has been killed, for what reason, and with what collateral consequences. The result has been the displacement of clear legal standards with a vaguely defined licence to kill, and the creation of a major accountability vacuum.

4. In terms of the legal framework, many of these practices violate straightforward applicable legal rules. To the extent that customary law is invoked to justify a particular interpretation of an international norm, the starting point must be the policies and practice of the vast majority of States and not those of the handful which have conveniently sought to create their own personalized normative frameworks. It should be added that many of the justifications for targeted killings offered by one or other of the relevant States in particular current contexts would in all likelihood not gain their endorsement if they were to be asserted by other States in the future.

5. This report describes the publicly available information about new targeted killing policies and addresses the main legal issues that have arisen. It identifies areas in which legal frameworks have been clearly violated or expanded beyond their permissible limits; where legal issues are unclear, it suggests approaches which would enable the international community to return to a normative framework that is consistent with its deep commitment to protection of the right to life, and the minimization of exceptions to that constitutive principle.

. . .

II. Background
A. Definition of "targeted killing"

7. Despite the frequency with which it is invoked, "targeted killing" is not a term defined under international law. Nor does it fit neatly into any particular legal framework. It came into common usage in 2000, after Israel made public a policy of "targeted killings" of alleged terrorists in the

Occupied Palestinian Territories.[1] The term has also been used in other situations, such as:

- The April 2002 killing, allegedly by Russian armed forces, of "rebel warlord" Omar Ibnal Khattab in Chechnya.
- The November 2002 killing of alleged al Qaeda leader Ali Qaed Senyan al-Harithi and five other men in Yemen, reportedly by a CIA-operated Predator drone using a Hellfire missile.
- Killings in 2005—2008 by both Sri Lankan government forces and the opposition LTTE group of individuals identified by each side as collaborating with the other.
- The January 2010 killing, in an operation allegedly carried out by 18 Israeli Mossad intelligence agents, of Mahmoud al-Mahbouh, a Hamas leader, at a Dubai hotel. According to Dubai officials, al-Mahbouh was suffocated with a pillow; officials released videotapes of those responsible, whom they alleged to be Mossad agents.

8. Targeted killings thus take place in a variety of contexts and may be committed by governments and their agents in times of peace as well as armed conflict, or by organized armed groups in armed conflict. The means and methods of killing vary, and include sniperfire, shooting at close range, missiles from helicopters, gunships, drones, the use of car bombs, and poison. A Legal Analysis of the Israeli Policy of Targeted Killings, 36 Cornell Int'l L.J. 233, 234 (2003). Although this report uses the common terms "terrorism" and "terrorist", I agree with the Special Rapporteur on the promotion and protection of human rights while countering terrorism that the continuing lack of a "universal, comprehensive and precise" definition of these terms hampers the protection of human rights, E/CN.4/2006/98, para. 50, and in particular, the right to life. The work of the Ad Hoc Committee established under GA Res. 51/210 to work on a draft convention on international terrorism is critical and urgent.

9. The common element in all these contexts is that lethal force is intentionally and deliberately used, with a degree of pre-meditation, against an individual or individuals specifically identified in advance by the perpetrator. In a targeted killing, the specific goal of the operation is to use lethal force. This distinguishes targeted killings from unintentional, accidental, or reckless killings, or killings made without conscious choice. It also distinguishes them from law enforcement operations, e.g., against a suspected suicide bomber. Under such circumstances, it may be legal for law enforcement personnel to shoot to kill based on the imminence of the threat, but the goal of the operation, from its inception, should not be to kill.

10. Although in most circumstances targeted killings violate the right to life, in the exceptional circumstance of armed conflict, they may be legal. This is in contrast to other terms with which "targeted killing" has sometimes been interchangeably used, such as "extrajudicial execution", "summary execution", and "assassination", all of which are, by, definition, illegal.

B. New targeted killing policies

11. The phenomenon of targeted killing has been present throughout history. In modern times, targeted killings by States have been very restricted or, to the extent that they are not, any *de facto* policy has been unofficial and usually denied, and both the justification and the killings themselves have been cloaked in secrecy. When responsibility for illegal targeted killings could be credibly assigned, such killings have been condemned by the international community—including by other States alleged to practice them.

12. More recently, however, a few States have either openly adopted policies that permit targeted killings, or have formally adopted such a policy while refusing to acknowledge its existence.

...

The USA

18. The U.S. has used drones and airstrikes for targeted killings in the armed conflicts in Afghanistan and Iraq, where the operations are conducted (to the extent publicly known) by the armed forces. The US also reportedly adopted a secret policy of targeted killings soon after the attacks of 11 September 2001, pursuant to which the Government has credibly been alleged to have engaged in targeted killings in the territory of other States. The secret targeted killing program is reportedly conducted by the Central Intelligence Agency (CIA) using "Predator" or "Reaper" drones, although there have been reports of involvement by special operations forces, and of the assistance of civilian contractors with the implementation of the program.

19. The first credibly reported CIA drone killing occurred on 3 November 2002, when a Predator drone fired a missile at a car in Yemen, killing Qaed Senyan al-Harithi, an al-Qaeda leader allegedly responsible for the *USS Cole* bombing. Since then, there have reportedly been over 120 drone strikes, although it is not possible to verify this number.

The accuracy of drone strikes is heavily contested and also impossible for outsiders to verify. Reports of civilian casualties in Pakistan range from approximately 20 (according to anonymous US Government officials quoted in the media) to many hundreds.

20. The CIA reportedly controls its fleet of drones from its headquarters in Langley, Virginia, in coordination with pilots near hidden airfields in Afghanistan and Pakistan who handle takeoffs and landings. The CIA's fleet is reportedly flown by civilians, including both intelligence officers and private contractors (often retired military personnel).

According to media accounts, the head of the CIA's clandestine services, or his deputy, generally gives the final approval for a strike. There is reportedly a list of targets approved by senior Government personnel, although the criteria for inclusion and all other aspects of the program are unknown. The CIA is not required to identify its target by name; rather, targeting decisions may be based on surveillance and "pattern of life" assessments.

21. The military also has a target list for Afghanistan. A Senate Foreign Relations Committee Report released on 10 August 2009 disclosed that the military's list included drug lords suspected of giving money to help finance the Taliban. According to the report,"[t]he military places no restrictions on

---

[1] Infra, section II.B. Orna Ben-Naftali & Keren Michaeli, We Must Not Make a Scarecrow of the Law:

the use of force with these selected targets, which means they can be killed or captured on the battle-field ... standards for getting on the list require two verifiable human sources and substantial additional evidence."

22. The Legal Adviser to the Department of State recently outlined the Government's legal justifications for targeted killings. They were said to be based on its asserted right to self-defence, as well as on IHL, on the basis that the US is "in an armed conflict with Al Qaeda, as well as the Taliban and associated forces." While this statement is an important starting point, it does not address some of the most central legal issues including: the scope of the armed conflict in which the US asserts it is engaged, the criteria for individuals who may be targeted and killed, the existence of any substantive or procedural safeguards to ensure the legality and accuracy of killings, and the existence of accountability mechanisms.

...

C. New technology

27. Drones were originally developed to gather intelligence and conduct surveillance and reconnaissance. More than 40 countries now have such technology. Some, including Israel, Russia, Turkey, China, India, Iran, the United Kingdom and France either have or are seeking drones that also have the capability to shoot laser-guided missiles ranging in weight from 35 pounds to more than 100 pounds. The appeal of armed drones is clear: especially in hostile terrain, they permit targeted killings at little to no risk to the State personnel carrying them out, and they can be operated remotely from the home State. It is also conceivable that non-state armed groups could obtain this technology.

III. Legal issues

A. The applicable legal frameworks and basic rules

28. Whether or not a specific targeted killing is legal depends on the context in which it is conducted: whether in armed conflict, outside armed conflict, or in relation to the interstate use of force. The basic legal rules applicable to targeted killings in each of these contexts are laid out briefly below.

In the context of armed conflict

29. **The legal framework:** Both IHL and human rights law apply in the context of armed conflict; whether a particular killing is legal is determined by the applicable *lex specialis*. To the extent that IHL does not provide a rule, or the rule is unclear and its meaning cannot be ascertained from the guidance offered by IHL principles, it is appropriate to draw guidance from human rights law.

30. **Under the rules of IHL:** Targeted killing is only lawful when the target is a "combatant" or "fighter" or, in the case of a civilian, only for such time as the person" directly participates in hostilities." In addition, the killing must be militarily necessary, the use of force must be proportionate so that any anticipated military advantage is considered in light of the expected harm to civilians in the vicinity, and everything feasible must be done to prevent mistakes and minimize harm to civilians. These standards apply regardless of whether the armed conflict is between States (an international armed conflict) or between a State and a non-state armed group (non-international armed conflict), including alleged terrorists. Reprisal or punitive attacks on civilians are prohibited.

Outside the context of armed conflict

31. **The legal framework:** The legality of a killing outside the context of armed conflict is governed by human rights standards, especially those concerning the use of lethal force. Although these standards are sometimes referred to as the "law enforcement" model, they do not in fact apply only to police forces or in times of peace. The "law enforcement officials" who may use lethal force include all government officials who exercise police powers, including a State's military and security forces, operating in contexts where violence exists, but falls short of the threshold for armed conflict.

32. **Under human rights law:** A State killing is legal only if it is required to protect life (making lethal force *proportionate*) and there is no other means, such as capture or nonlethal incapacitation, of preventing that threat to life (making lethal force *necessary*). The proportionality requirement limits the permissible level of force based on the threat posed by the suspect to others. The necessity requirement imposes an obligation to minimize the level of force used, regardless of the amount that would be proportionate, through, for example, the use of warnings, restraint and capture.

33. This means that under human rights law, a targeted killing in the sense of an intentional, premeditated and deliberate killing by law enforcement officials cannot be legal because, unlike in armed conflict, it is never permissible for killing to be the *sole objective* of an operation. Thus, for example, a

"shoot-to-kill" policy violates human rights law. This is not to imply, as some erroneously do, that law enforcement is incapable of meeting the threats posed by terrorists and, in particular, suicide bombers. Such an argument is predicated on a misconception of human rights law, which does not require States to choose between letting people be killed and letting their law enforcement officials use lethal force to prevent such killings. In fact, under human rights law, States' duty to respect and to ensure the right to life entails an obligation to exercise "due diligence" to protect the lives of individuals from attacks by criminals, including terrorists. Lethal force under human rights law is legal if it is strictly and directly necessary to save life.

The use of inter-state force

34. *The legal framework:* Targeted killings conducted in the territory of other States raise sovereignty concerns. Under Article 2(4) of the UN Charter, States are forbidden from using force in the territory of another State. When a State conducts a targeted killing in the territory of another State with which it is not in armed conflict, whether the first State violates the sovereignty of the second is determined by the law applicable to the use of inter-state force, while the question of whether the specific killing of the particular individual(s) is legal is governed by IHL and/or human rights law.

35. *Under the law of inter-state force:* A targeted killing conducted by one State in the territory of a second State does not violate the second State's sovereignty if either (a) the second State consents, or (b) the first, targeting, State has a right under international law to use force in self-defence under Article 51 of the UN Charter, because (i) the second State is responsible for an armed attack against the first State, or (ii) the second State is unwilling or unable to stop armed attacks against the first State launched from its territory. International law permits the use of lethal force in self-defence in response to an "armed attack" as long as that force is necessary and proportionate.

36. While the basic rules are not controversial, the question of which framework applies, and the interpretation of aspects of the rules, have been the subject of significant debate. Both issues are addressed in greater detail below.

B. Sovereignty issues and States' invocation of the right to self-defence Consent

37. The proposition that a State may consent to the use of force on its territory by another State is not legally controversial. But while consent may permit the use of force, it does not absolve either of the concerned States from their obligations to abide by human rights law and IHL with respect to the use of lethal force against a specific person. The consenting State's responsibility to protect those on its territory from arbitrary deprivation of the right to life applies at all times. A consenting State may only lawfully authorize a killing by the targeting State to the extent that the killing is carried out in accordance with applicable IHL or human rights law.

38. To meet its legal obligations, therefore, the consenting State should, at a minimum, require the targeting State to demonstrate verifiably that the person against whom lethal force is to be used can be lawfully targeted and that the targeting State will comply with the applicable law. After any targeted killing, the consenting State should ensure that it was legal. In case of doubt, the consenting State must investigate the killing and, upon a finding of wrongdoing, seek prosecution of the offenders and compensation for the victims.

The right to self-defence

39. In the absence of consent, or in addition to it, States may invoke the right to self defence as justification for the extraterritorial use of force involving targeted killings.74 As noted above, international law permits the use of lethal force in self-defence in response to an "armed attack" as long as that force is necessary and proportionate.75 Controversy has arisen, however, in three main areas: whether the self-defence justification applies to the use of force against non-state actors and what constitutes an armed attack by such actors; the extent to which self-defence alone is a justification for targeted killings; and, the extent to which States have a right to "anticipatory" or "pre-emptive" self-defence.

Self-defence and non-state actors

40. It has been a matter of debate whether Article 51 permits States to use force against non-state actors. The argument that it does not finds support in judgments of the International Court of Justice (ICJ) holding that States cannot invoke Article 51 against armed attacks by non-state actors that are not imputable to another State. On the other hand, some States, including the US, argue that Article 51 does not displace the customary international law right to act in self-defence, including against non-state actors,

and that' state practice supports that position. Commentators find support for that argument in Security Council Resolutions 1368 and 1373 issued in the wake of the September 11 attacks, as well as NATO's invocation of the North Atlantic Treaty's Article 5 collective self-defence provision. But even if it were to be accepted that Article 51 has not displaced customary law, the reality is that it will only be in very rare circumstances that a non-state actor whose activities do not engage the responsibility of any State will be able to conduct the kind of armed attack that would give rise to the right to use extraterritorial force. In such exceptional circumstances, the UN Charter would require that Security Council approval should be sought.

41. A more difficult question concerns the extent to which persistent but discrete attacks, including by a non-state actor, would constitute an "armed attack" under Article 51. In a series of decisions, the ICJ has established a high threshold for the kinds of attacks that would justify the extraterritorial use of force in self-defence. In its view, sporadic, low intensity attacks do not rise to the level of armed attack that would permit the right to use extra territorial force in self-defence, and the legality of a defensive response must be judged in light of each armed attack, rather than by considering occasional, although perhaps successive, armed attacks in the aggregate. While this approach has been criticized, few commentators have supported an approach that would accommodate the invocation of the right to self-defence in response to most of the types of attack that have been at issue in relation to the extraterritorial targeted killings discussed here. Any such approach would diminish hugely the value of the foundational prohibition contained in Article 51.

The relationship between self-defence and IHL and human rights law

42. The second area of controversy arises particularly in the context of the use of force by the US against alleged terrorists in other countries, especially Pakistan. Some US scholars and commentators advocate a "robust" form of self-defence in which, once the doctrine is invoked, no other legal frameworks or limiting principles—such as IHL—would apply to targeted killings.

Under this view, once it is justified to use force in self-defence, IHL and human rights law would not be applicable to that use of force. This approach reflects an unlawful and disturbing tendency in recent times to permit violations of IHL based on whether the broader cause in which the right to use force is invoked is "just," and impermissibly conflates jus ad bellum and jus ad bello. Proponents of a "robust" right to self-defence cite to the ICJ's Nuclear Weapons Advisory Opinion, in which the court found that "the threat or use of nuclear weapons would generally" violate IHL, but held that it could not conclude that such threat or use "would be lawful or unlawful in an extreme circumstance of self-defence, in which the very survival of a State would be at stake." While this aspect of the opinion has been criticized as being vague and confusing, it seeks to address only the most extreme situation involving a State's very survival. Invoking such an extreme exception to permit the violation of IHL on self-defence grounds in the type of situations under consideration here would be tantamount to abandoning IHL.

43. The "robust" self-defence approach also ignores the very real differences between the law of inter-state force and the law applicable to the conduct of hostilities. Whether the use of force is legal is a question that usually arises at the start of an armed conflict, while the law applicable to the conduct of that armed conflict applies throughout it. The limitations on each are distinct. Proportionality under self-defence requires States to use force only defensively and to the extent necessary to meet defensive objectives, whereas the test for proportionality under IHL requires States to balance the incidental harm or death of civilians caused by an operation to the military advantage that would result.

Necessity in under self-defence requires a State to assess whether it has means to defend itself other than through armed force, while necessity in IHL requires it to evaluate whether an operation will achieve the goals of the military operation and is consistent with the other rules of IHL. Finally, the "robust" self-defence approach fails to take into account the existence of two levels of responsibility in the event that a targeted killing for which self defence is invoked is found to be unlawful. Violation of the limitations on the right to self defence results in State and individual criminal responsibility for aggression. There is also liability for the unlawful killing itself—if it violates IHL, it may be a war crime. The Articles on State Responsibility make abundantly clear that States may not invoke self defence as justification for their violations of IHL.

44. In sum, even if the use of inter-state force is offered as justification for a targeted killing, it does not dispose of the further question of whether the killing of the particular targeted individual or individuals is

lawful. The legality of a specific killing depends on whether it meets the requirements of IHL and human rights law (in the context of armed conflict) or human rights law alone (in all other contexts).

Anticipatory and pre-emptive self-defence

45. The third key area of controversy is the extent to which States seek to invoke the right to self-defence not just in response to an armed attack, but in anticipatory self defence, or alternatively, as a pre-emptive measure in response to a threat that is persistent and may take place in the future, but is not likely to take place imminently. Under a restrictive view of Article 51, the right to self-defence may only be invoked after an attack has taken place. In contrast, under a more permissive view that more accurately reflects State practice and the weight of scholarship, self-defence also includes the right to use force against a real and imminent threat when "the necessity of that self-defence is instant, overwhelming, and leaving no choice of means, and no moment of deliberation." A third view, invoked exceptionally by the US Bush administration, but which apparently may still reflect US policy, would permit "pre-emptive self-defence", the use of force even when a threat is not imminent and "uncertainty remains as to the time and place of the enemy's attack." This view is deeply contested and lacks support under international law.

C. The existence and scope of armed conflict

46. Whether an armed conflict exists is a question that must be answered with reference to objective criteria, which depend on the facts on the ground, and not only on the subjective declarations either of States (which can often be influenced by political considerations rather than legal ones) or, if applicable, of non-state actors, including alleged terrorists (which may also have political reasons for seeking recognition as a belligerent party). Traditionally, States have refused to acknowledge the existence of an armed conflict with non-state groups. The reasons include not wanting to accord such groups recognition as "belligerents" or "warriors", and instead being able to insist that they remain common criminals subject to domestic law. States also do not want to appear "weak" by acknowledging that they are unable to stop large scale violence, and/or that rebels or insurgent groups have control over State territory. In recent times, for example, the United Kingdom (with respect to Northern Ireland) and Russia (with respect to Chechnya) have refused to acknowledge the existence of internal armed conflicts.

47. On the other hand, both the US and Israel have invoked the existence of an armed conflict against alleged terrorists ("non-state armed groups"). The appeal is obvious: the IHL applicable in armed conflict arguably has more permissive rules for killing than does human rights law or a State's domestic law, and generally provides immunity to State armed forces.96 Because the law of armed conflict has fewer due process safeguards, States also see a benefit to avoiding compliance with the more onerous requirements for capture, arrest, detention or extradition of an alleged terrorist in another State. IHL is not, in fact, more permissive than human rights law because of the strict IHL requirement that lethal force be necessary. But labeling a situation as an armed conflict might also serve to expand executive power both as a matter of domestic law and in terms of public support.

48. Although the appeal of an armed conflict paradigm to address terrorism is obvious, so too is the significant potential for abuse. Internal unrest as a result of insurgency or other violence by non-state armed groups, and even terrorism, are common in many parts of the world. If States unilaterally extend the law of armed conflict to situations that are essentially matters of law enforcement that must, under international law, be dealt with under the framework of human rights, they are not only effectively declaring war against a particular group, but eviscerating key and necessary distinctions between international law frameworks that restricts States' ability to kill arbitrarily.

49. The IHL applicable to non-international armed conflict is not as well-developed as that applicable to international armed conflict. Since 11 September 2001, this fact has often been cited either to criticize IHL in general or as a justification for innovative interpretations which go well beyond generally accepted approaches. It is true that non international armed conflict rules would benefit from development, but the rules as they currently exist offer more than sufficient guidance to the existence and scope of an armed conflict. The key is for States to approach them with good faith intent to apply the rules as they exist and have been interpreted by international bodies, rather than to seek ever expanding flexibility.

50. There are essentially four possibilities under international law for the existence of an armed conflict:

(i) The conflict is an international armed conflict.

(ii) The conflict is a non-international armed conflict meeting the threshold of Common Article 3 to the Geneva Conventions.

(iii) The conflict is a non-international armed conflict meeting the threshold of both Common Article 3 to the Geneva Conventions and Additional Protocol II to the Geneva Conventions

(iv) The level of violence does not rise to the level of an armed conflict, but is instead isolated and sporadic and human rights law determines the legality of the use of lethal force.

51. The test for the existence of an *international* armed conflict is clear under IHL: "Any difference arising between two States and leading to the intervention of armed forces" qualifies as armed conflict, regardless of its intensity, duration or scale. The IHL of international armed conflict applies also to "all cases of total or partial occupation of the territory of a High Contracting Party" to the Geneva Conventions. Following these criteria, an international armed conflict cannot exist between a State and a non-state group.

52. The tests for the existence of a *non-international* armed conflict are not as categorical as those for international armed conflict. This recognizes the fact that there may be various types of non-international armed conflicts. The applicable test may also depend on whether a State is party to Additional Protocol II to the Geneva Conventions. Under treaty and customary international law, the elements which would point to the existence of a non-international armed conflict against a non-state armed group are:

(i) The non-state armed group must be identifiable as such, based on criteria that are objective and verifiable. This is necessary for IHL to apply meaningfully, and so that States may comply with their obligation to distinguish between lawful targets and civilians. The criteria include:

- Minimal level of organization of the group such that armed forces are able to identify an adversary (GC Art. 3; AP II).
- Capability of the group to apply the Geneva Conventions (i.e., adequate command structure, and separation of military and political command) (GC Art. 3; AP II).
- Engagement of the group in collective, armed, anti-government action (GC Art. 3).
- For a conflict involving a State, the State uses its regular military forces against the group (GC Art. 3).
- Admission of the conflict against the group to the agenda of the UN Security Council or the General Assembly (GC Art. 3).
- (ii) There must be a minimal threshold of intensity and duration. The threshold of violence is higher than required for the existence of an international armed conflict.
- To meet the minimum threshold, violence must be:
- "Beyond the level of intensity of internal disturbances and tensions, such as riots, isolated and sporadic acts of violence and other acts of a similar nature"(AP II).
- "[P]rotracted armed violence" among non-state armed groups or between a non-state armed group and a State;
- If an isolated incident, the incident itself should be of a high degree of intensity, with a high level of organization on the part of the non-state armed group;
- (iii) The territorial confines can be:
- Restricted to the territory of a State and between the State's own armed forces and the non-state group (AP II); or
- A transnational conflict, i.e., one that crosses State borders (GC Art. 3). This does not mean, however, that there is no territorial nexus requirement.

53. Taken cumulatively, these factors make it problematic for the US to show that —outside the context of the armed conflicts in Afghanistan or Iraq—it is in a transnational non-international armed conflict against "al Qaeda, the Taliban, and other associatedforces" without further explanation of how those entities constitute a "party" under the IHL of non-international armed conflict, and whether and how any violence by any such group rises to the level necessary for an armed conflict to exist.

54. The focus, instead, appears to be on the "transnational" nature of the terrorist threat. Al-Qaeda and entities with various degrees of "association" with it are indeed known to have operated in numerous countries around the world including in Saudi Arabia, Indonesia, Pakistan, Germany, the United Kingdom and Spain, among others, where they have conducted terrorist attacks. Yet none of these States, with the possible exception of Pakistan, recognize themselves as being part of an armed conflict against al-Qaeda or its" associates" in their territory. Indeed, in each of those States, even when there have been terrorist attacks by al-Qaeda or other groups claiming affiliation with it, the duration and intensity of such attacks has not risen to the level of an armed conflict. Thus, while it is true that non-international armed conflict can exist across State borders, and indeed often does, that is only one of a number of cumulative factors that must be considered for the objective existence of an armed conflict.

55. With respect to the existence of a non-state group as a "party", al-Qaeda and other alleged "associated" groups are often only loosely linked, if at all. Sometimes they appear to be not even groups, but a few

individuals who take "inspiration" from al Qaeda. The idea that, instead, they are part of continuing hostilities that spread to new territories as new alliances form or are claimed may be superficially appealing but such "associates' cannot constitute a "party" as required by IHL—although they can be criminals, if their conduct violates US law, or the law of the State in which they are located.

56. To ignore these minimum requirements, as well as the object and purpose of IHL, would be to undermine IHL safeguards against the use of violence against groups that are not the equivalent of an organized armed group capable of being a party to a conflict—whether because it lacks organization, the ability to engage in armed attacks, or because it does not have a connection or belligerent nexus to actual hostilities. It is also salutary to recognize that whatever rules the US seeks to invoke or apply to al Qaeda and any" affiliates" could be invoked by other States to apply to other non-state armed groups. To expand the notion of non-international armed conflict to groups that are essentially drug cartels, criminal gangs or other groups that should be dealt with under the law enforcement framework would be to do deep damage to the IHL and human rights frameworks.

D. Who may lawfully be targeted, when, and on what basis

57. The greatest source of the lack of clarity with respected to targeted killings in the context of armed conflict is who qualifies as a lawful target, and where and when the person may be targeted.

58. In international armed conflict, combatants may be targeted at any time and any place (subject to the other requirements of IHL). Under the IHL applicable to non international armed conflict, the rules are less clear. In non-international armed conflict, there is no such thing as a "combatant." Instead—as in international armed conflict—States are permitted to directly attack only civilians who "directly participate in hostilities"(DPH). Because there is no commonly accepted definition of DPH, it has been left open to States' own interpretation—which States have preferred not to make public—to determine what constitutes DPH.

59. There are three key controversies over DPH. First, there is dispute over the kind of conduct that constitutes "direct participation" and makes an individual subject to attack. Second, there is disagreement over the extent to which "membership" in an organized armed group may be used as a factor in determining whether a person is directly participating in hostilities. Third, there is controversy over how long direct participation lasts.

60. It is not easy to arrive at a definition of direct participation that protects civilians and at the same time does not "reward" an enemy that may fail to distinguish between civilians and lawful military targets, that may deliberately hide among civilian populations and put them at risk, or that may force civilians to engage in hostilities. The key, however, is to recognize that regardless of the enemy's tactics, in order to protect the vast majority of civilians, direct participation may only include conduct close to that of a fighter, or conduct that directly supports combat. More attenuated acts, such as providing financial support, advocacy, or other non-combat aid, does not constitute direct participation.

61. Some types of conduct have long been understood to constitute direct participation, such as civilians who shoot at State forces or commit acts of violence in the context of hostilities that would cause death or injury to civilians. Other conduct has traditionally been excluded from direct participation, even if it supports the general war effort; such conduct includes political advocacy, supplying food or shelter, or economic support and propaganda (all also protected under other human rights standards). Even if these activities ultimately impact hostilities, they are not considered "direct participation." But there is a middle ground, such as for the proverbial "farmer by day, fighter by night", that has remained unclear and subject to uncertainty.

62. In 2009, the ICRC issued its Interpretive Guidance on DPH, which provides a useful starting point for discussion. In non-international armed conflict, according to the ICRC Guidance, civilians who participate directly in hostilities and are members of an armed group who have a "continuous combat function" may be targeted at all times and in all places. With respect to the temporal duration of DPH for all other civilians, the ICRC Guidance takes the view that direct participation for civilians is limited to each single act: the earliest point of direct participation would be the concrete preparatory measures for that specific act (e.g., loading bombs onto a plane), and participation terminates when the activity ends.

63. Under the ICRC's Guidance, each specific act by the civilian must meet three cumulative requirements to constitute DPH: (i) There must be a "threshold of harm" that is objectively likely to result from the act, either by adversely impacting the military operations or capacity of the opposing party, or by causing the loss of life or property of protected civilian persons or objects; and (ii) The act must cause the expected harm directly, in one step, for example, as an integral part of a specific and coordinated combat operation (as opposed

to harm caused in unspecified future operations); and (iii) The act must have a "belligerent nexus"—i.e., it must be specifically designed to support the military operations of one party to the detriment of another.

64. These criteria generally exclude conduct that is clearly indirect, including general support for the war effort through preparation or capacity building (such as the production of weapons and military equipment). They also exclude conduct that is protected by other human rights standards, including political support for a belligerent party or an organized armed group. Importantly, the ICRC's Guidance makes clear that the lawfulness of an act under domestic or international law is not at issue, rather, the sole concern of the direct participation inquiry is whether the conduct "constitute[s] an integral part of armed confrontations occurring between belligerents." Thus, although illegal activities, e.g., terrorism, may cause harm, if they do not meet the criteria for direct participation *inhostilities*, then States' response must conform to the lethal force standards applicable to self-defence and law enforcement. In general, the ICRC's approach is correct, and comports both with human rights law and IHL.

65. Nevertheless, the ICRC's Guidance raises concern from a human rights perspective because of the "continuous combat function" (CCF) category of armed group members who may be targeted anywhere, at any time.118 In its general approach to DPH, the ICRC is correct to focus on function (the kind of act) rather than status (combatant v unprivileged belligerent), but the creation of CCF category is, *de facto*, a status determination that is questionable given the specific treaty language that limits direct participation to "for such time" as opposed to "all the time."

66. Creation of the CCF category also raises the risk of erroneous targeting of someone who, for example, may have disengaged from their function. If States are to accept this category, the onus will be on them to show that the evidentiary basis is strong. In addition, States must adhere to the careful distinction the ICRC draws between continuous combatants who may always be subject to direct attack and civilians who (i) engage in sporadic or episodic direct participation (and may only be attacked during their participation), or (ii) have a general war support function ("recruiters, trainers, financiers and propagandists") or form the political wing of an organized armed group (neither of which is a basis for attack).

67. Especially given the ICRC's membership approach to CCF, it is imperative that the other constituent parts of the Guidance (threshold of harm, causation and belligerent nexus) not be diluted. It is also critical that DPH not include combat service support functions (selling food, providing supplies). While this may, in the view of some, create inequity between State forces and non-state actors, that inequity is built into IHL in order to protect civilians.

68. The failure of States to disclose their criteria for DPH is deeply problematic because it gives no transparency or clarity about what conduct could subject a civilian to killing. It also leaves open the likelihood that States will unilaterally expand their concept of direct participation beyond permissible boundaries. Thus, although the US has not made public its definition of DPH, it is clear that it is more expansive than that set out by the ICRC; in Afghanistan, the US has said that drug traffickers on the "battlefield" who have links to the insurgency may be targeted and killed. This is not consistent with the traditionally understood concepts under IHL—drug trafficking is understood as criminal conduct, not an activity that would subject someone to a targeted killing. And generating profits that might be used to fund hostile actions does not constitute DPH.

69. Given the ICRC's promulgation of its Guidance, and the hesitant or uncertain response of some States to date, in order for the issues to be addressed comprehensively, it would be very timely for there to be a convening of State representatives, including particularly those from key military powers, together with the ICRC and experts in human rights and IHL. Such a convening would perhaps be most useful if held under the auspices of a neutral body, such as the High Commissioner for Human Rights. The group could discuss and revise (if necessary) the ICRC's Guidance after a careful review of best practices.

E. Who may conduct a targeted killing

70. Reported targeted killings by the CIA have given rise to a debate over whether it is a violation of IHL for such killings to be committed by State agents who are not members of its armed forces. Some commentators have argued that CIA personnel who conduct targeted drone killings are committing war crimes because they, unlike the military, are "unlawful combatants", and unable to participate in hostilities. This argument is not supported by IHL. As a threshold matter, the argument assumes that targeted killings by the CIA are committed in the context of armed conflict, which may not be the case. Outside of armed conflict, killings by the CIA would constitute extrajudicial executions assuming that they do not comply with human rights law. If so, they must be investigated and prosecuted both by the US and the State in which the wrongful killing occurred.

The following discussion assumes, without accepting, that CIA killings are being conducted in the context of armed conflict.

71. Under IHL, civilians, including intelligence agents, are not prohibited from participating in hostilities. Rather, the consequence of participation is two-fold. First, because they are "directly participating in hostilities" by conducting targeted killings, intelligence personnel may themselves be targeted and killed. Second, intelligence personnel do not have immunity from prosecution under domestic law for their conduct. They are thus unlike State armed forces which would generally be immune from prosecution for the same conduct (assuming they complied with IHL requirements). Thus, CIA personnel could be prosecuted for murder under the domestic law of any country in which they conduct targeted drone killings, and could also be prosecuted for violations of applicable US law.

72. It is important to note that if a targeted killing violates IHL (by, for example, targeting civilians who were not "directly participating in hostilities"), then regardless of who conducts it—intelligence personnel or State armed forces—the author, as well as those who authorized it, can be prosecuted for war crimes.

73. Additionally, unlike a State's armed forces, its intelligence agents do not generally operate within a framework which places appropriate emphasis upon ensuring compliance with IHL, rendering violations more likely and causing a higher risk of prosecution both for war crimes and for violations of the laws of the State in which any killing occurs. To the extent a State uses intelligence agents for targeted killing to shield its operations from IHL and human rights law transparency and accountability requirements, it could also incur State responsibility for violating those requirements.

F. The use of less-than-lethal measures

74. As discussed above, the intentional use of lethal force in the context of law enforcement is only permitted in defence of life. Thus, outside the context of armed conflict, law enforcement officials are required to be trained in, to plan for, and to take less-than-lethal measures—including restraint, capture, and the graduated use of force—and it is only if these measures are not possible that a law enforcement killing will be legal. States should ensure public disclosure of the measures taken to "strictly control and limit the circumstances" in which law enforcement officers may resort to lethal force, including the level of force used at each stage. The legal framework must take into account the possibility that the threat is so imminent that graduated use of force is not possible, and ensure appropriate safeguards are in place so that the assessment of imminence is reliably made.

75. Although IHL does not expressly regulate the kind and degree of force that may be used against legitimate targets, it does envisage the use of less-than-lethal measures: in armed conflict, the "right of belligerents to adopt means of injuring the enemy is notunlimited" and States must not inflict "harm greater that that unavoidable to achieve legitimate military objectives." The limiting principles are not controversial—States may only exercise force that is militarily necessary and consistent with the principle of humanity. As the ICRC Guidance recognizes "it would defy basic notions of humanity to kill an adversary or to refrain from giving him or her an opportunity to surrender where there manifestly is no necessity for the use of lethal force."

76. The position taken by the ICRC in its Guidance has been the subject of controversy. The Guidance states that, "the kind and degree of force which is permissible against persons not entitled to protection against direct attack must not exceed what is actually necessary to accomplish a legitimate military purpose in the prevailing circumstances."

Some critics interpret this statement as requiring the use of a law enforcement paradigm in the context of armed conflict. However, as the Guidance makes clear, it states only the uncontroversial IHL requirement that the kind and amount of force used in a military operation be limited to what is "actually necessary to accomplish a legitimate military purpose in the prevailing circumstances." Especially in the context of targeted killings of civilians who directly participate in hostilities, and given that IHL does not create an unrestrained right to kill, the better approach is for State forces to minimize the use of lethal force to the extent feasible in the circumstances.

77. Less-than-lethal measures are especially appropriate when a State has control over the area in which a military operation is taking place, when "armed forces operate against selected individuals in situations comparable to peacetime policing," and in the context of non-international armed conflict, in which rules are less clear. In these situations, States should use graduated force and, where possible, capture rather than kill. Thus, rather than using drone strikes, US forces should, wherever and whenever possible, conduct arrests, or use less-than-lethal force to restrain. As the ICRC's Guidance intended to make clear, "the international lawfulness of a particular operation involving the use of force may not always depend exclusively on IHL but, depending on the circumstances, may potentially be influenced by other applicable legal frameworks, such as human rights law and the *jus ad bellum*."

78. In addition, precautionary measures that States should take in armed conflict to reduce casualties include:

- Provide effective advance warning to the civilian population, through leaflets, broadcast warnings, etc. in the areas in which targeted killings may take place. The warnings must be as specific as possible.
- Any such warning does not, however, discharge the obligation to distinguish between lawful targets and civilians. "Warnings are required for the benefit of civilians, but civilians are not obligated to comply with them. A decision to stay put—freely taken or due to limited options—in no way diminishes a civilian's legal protections."
- The use of civilians as "shields" is strictly prohibited. But one side's unlawful use of civilian shields does not affect the other side's obligation to ensure that attacks do not kill civilians in excess of the military advantage of killing the targeted fighter.

G. The use of drones for targeted killing

79. The use of drones for targeted killings has generated significant controversy. Some have suggested that drones as such are prohibited weapons under IHL because they cause, or have the effect of causing, necessarily indiscriminate killings of civilians, such as those in the vicinity of a targeted person. It is true that IHL places limits on the weapons States may use, and weapons that are, for example, inherently indiscriminate (such as biological weapons) are prohibited. However, a missile fired from a drone is no different from any other commonly used weapon, including a gun fired by a soldier or a helicopter or gunship that fires missiles. The critical legal question is the same for each weapon: whether its specific use complies with IHL.

80. The greater concern with drones is that because they make it easier to kill without risk to a State's forces, policy makers and commanders will be tempted to interpret the legal limitations on who can be killed, and under what circumstances, too expansively. States must ensure that the criteria they apply to determine who can be targeted and killed –i.e., who is a lawful combatant, or what constitutes "direct participation in hostilities" that would subject civilians to direct attack—do not differ based on the choice of weapon.

81. Drones' proponents argue that since drones have greater surveillance capability and afford greater precision than other weapons, they can better prevent collateral civilian casualties and injuries. This may well be true to an extent, but it presents an incomplete picture. The precision, accuracy and legality of a drone strike depend on the human intelligence upon which the targeting decision is based.

...

83. It was clear during my mission to Afghanistan how hard it is even for forces on the ground to obtain accurate information. Testimony from witnesses and victims' family members, showed that international forces were often too uninformed of local practices, or too credulous in interpreting information, to be able to arrive at a reliable understanding of a situation. International forces all too often based manned airstrikes and raids that resulted in killings on faulty intelligence. Multiple other examples show that the legality of a targeted killing operation is heavily dependent upon the reliability of the intelligence on which it is based. States must, therefore, ensure that they have in place the procedural safeguards necessary to ensure that intelligence on which targeting decisions are made is accurate and verifiable.

84. Furthermore, because operators are based thousands of miles away from the battlefield, and undertake operations entirely through computer screens and remote audio feed, there is a risk of developing a "Playstation" mentality to killing. States must ensure that training programs for drone operators who have never been subjected to the risks and rigors of battle instill respect for IHL and adequate safeguards for compliance with it.

85. Outside the context of armed conflict, the use of drones for targeted killing is almost never likely to be legal. A targeted drone killing in a State's own territory, over which the State has control, would be very unlikely to meet human rights law limitations on the use of lethal force.

86. Outside its own territory (or in territory over which it lacked control) and where the situation on the ground did not rise to the level of armed conflict in which IHL would apply, a State could theoretically seek to justify the use of drones by invoking the right to anticipatory self-defence against a non-state actor. It could also theoretically claim that human rights law's requirement of first employing less-than-lethal means would not be possible if the State has no means of capturing or causing the other State to capture the target. As a practical matter, there are very few situations outside the context of active hostilities in which the test for anticipatory self-defence—necessity that is "instant, overwhelming, and leaving no choice of means, and no moment of deliberation"—would be met. This hypothetical presents the same danger as the "ticking-time bomb" scenario does in the context of the use of torture and coercion during interrogations: a thought experiment that posits a rare emergency exception to an absolute prohibition can effectively institutionalize

that exception. Applying such a scenario to targeted killings threatens to eviscerate the human rights law prohibition against the arbitrary deprivation of life. In addition, drone killing of anyone other than the target (family members or others in the vicinity, for example) would be an arbitrary deprivation of life under human rights law and could result in State responsibility and individual criminal liability.

H. The requirements of transparency and accountability

87. The failure of States to comply with their human rights law and IHL obligations to provide transparency and accountability for targeted killings is a matter of deep concern. To date, no State has disclosed the full legal basis for targeted killings, including its interpretation of the legal issues discussed above. Nor has any State disclosed the procedural and other safeguards in place to ensure that killings are lawful and justified, and the accountability mechanisms that ensure wrongful killings are investigated, prosecuted and punished. The refusal by States who conduct targeted killings to provide transparency about their policies violates the international legal framework that limits the unlawful use of lethal force against individuals.

88. Transparency is required by both IHL and human rights law. A lack of disclosure gives States a virtual and impermissible license to kill.

89. Among the procedural safeguards States must take (and disclose) with respect to targeted killings in armed conflict are:

- Ensure that forces and agents have access to reliable information to support the targeting decision. These include an appropriate command and control structure, as well as safeguards against faulty or unverifiable evidence.
- Ensure adequate intelligence on "the effects of the weapons that are to be used … the number of civilians that are likely to be present in the target area at the particular time; and whether they have any possibility to take cover before the attack takes place."
- The proportionality of an attack must be assessed for each individual strike.
- Ensure that when an error is apparent, those conducting a targeted killing are able to abort or suspend the attack.

90. In order to ensure that accountability is meaningful, States must specifically disclose the measures in place to investigate alleged unlawful targeted killings and either to identify and prosecute perpetrators, or to extradite them to another State that has made out a prima facie case for the unlawfulness of a targeted killing.

91. States have also refused to provide factual information about who has been targeted under their policies and with what outcome, including whether innocent civilians have been collaterally killed or injured. In one instance, targeted killings take place in easily accessible urban areas, and human rights monitors and civil society are able to document the outcome. In others, because of remoteness or security concerns, it as been impossible for independent observers and the international community to judge whether killings ere lawful or not.

92. Transparency and accountability in the context of armed conflict or other situations that raise security concerns may not be easy. States may have tactical or security reasons not to disclose criteria for selecting specific targets (e.g. public release of intelligence source information could cause harm to the source). But without disclosure of the legal rationale as well as the bases for the selection of specific targets (consistent with genuine security needs), States are operating in an accountability vacuum. It is not possible for the international community to verify the legality of a killing, to confirm the authenticity or otherwise of intelligence relied upon, or to ensure that unlawful targeted killings do not result in impunity. The fact that there is no one-size-fits-all formula for such disclosure does not absolve States of the need to adopt explicit policies.

IV. Conclusions and recommendations

General

93. States should publicly identify the rules of international law they consider to provide a basis for any targeted killings they undertake. They should specify the bases for decisions to kill rather than capture. They should specify the procedural safeguards in place to ensure in advance of targeted killings that they comply with international law, and the measures taken after any such killing to ensure that its legal and factual analysis was accurate and, if not, the remedial measures they would take.

If a State commits a targeted killing in the territory of another State, the second State should publicly indicate whether it gave consent, and on what basis.

States should make public the number of civilians collaterally killed in a targeted killing operation, and the measures in place to prevent such casualties.

- The High Commissioner for Human Rights should convene a meeting of States, including representatives of key military powers, the ICRC and human rights and IHL experts to arrive at a broadly accepted definition of "direct participation in hostilities."

- Specific requirements under human rights law, applicable in and outside armed conflict, include:
- States should disclose the measures taken to control and limit the circumstances in which law enforcement officers may resort to lethal force.
- These include:
- permissible objectives (which may not include retaliation or punishment but must be strictly to prevent the imminent loss of life);
- the non-lethal tactics for capture or incapacitation that must be attempted if feasible;
- the efforts that must be made to minimize lethal force, including specifying the level of force that must be used at each stage;
- the legal framework should take into account the possibility that a threat may be so imminent that a warning and the graduated use of force are too risky or futile (e.g., the suspect is about to use a weapon or blow himself up). At the same time, it must put in place safeguards to ensure that the evidence of imminence is reliable, based on a high degree of certainty, and does not circumvent the requirements of necessity and proportionality.
- Disclosure of the measures in place to provide prompt, thorough, effective, independent and public investigations of alleged violations of law.
- The appropriate measures have been endorsed in the Principles on the Effective Prevention and Investigation of Extra-legal, Arbitrary and Summary Executions. These should guide States whenever they carry out law enforcement operations, including during armed conflicts and occupations. The State's duty to investigate and prosecute human rights abuses also applies in the context of armed conflict and occupation.
- Specific requirements under IHL, applicable in armed conflict, include:
  - Disclosure of the measures in place to investigate alleged unlawful targeted killings and either to identify and prosecute perpetrators, or to extradite them to another State that has made a prima facie case for the unlawfulness of a killing.
  - Ensure that State armed forces and agents use all reasonably available sources (including technological ones such as intelligence and surveillance) to obtain reliable information to verify that the target is lawful. These measures, which should be publicly disclosed to the extent consistent with genuine security needs, include:
  - State armed forces should have a command and control system that collects, analyzes and disseminates information necessary for armed forces or operators to make legal and accurate targeting decisions.
  - Targeted killings should never be based solely on "suspicious" conduct or unverified—or unverifiable—information. Intelligence gathering and sharing arrangements must include procedures for reliably vetting targets, and adequately verifying information.
  - State forces should ensure adequate intelligence on the effects of weapons to be used, the presence of civilians in the targeted area, and whether civilians have the ability to protect themselves from attack. It bears emphasis that State forces violate the IHL requirements of proportionality and precaution if they do not do everything feasible to determine who else is, or will be, in the vicinity of a target—and thus how many other lives will be lost or people injured—before conducting a targeted killing.
  - In the context of drone attacks and airstrikes, commanders on the ground and remote pilots may have access to different information (e.g.based on human intelligence, or visuals from satellites); it is incumbent on pilots, whether remote or not, to ensure that a commander's assessment of the legality of a proposed strike is borne out by visual confirmation that the target is in fact lawful, and that the requirements of necessity, proportionality and discrimination are met. If the facts on the ground change in substantive respects, those responsible must do everything feasible to abort or suspend the attack.
  - Ensure that compliance with the IHL proportionality principle is assessed for each attack individually, and not for an overall military operation.
  - Ensure that even after a targeting operation is under way, if it appears that the target is not lawful, or that the collateral loss of life or property damage is in excess of the original determination, targeting forces have the ability and discretion to cancel or postpone an attack.
  - Ensure procedures are in place to verify that no targeted killing is taken in revenge, or primarily to cause terror or to intimidate, or to gain political advantage.

- Especially in heavily populated urban areas, if it appears that a targeted killing will risk harm to civilians, State forces must provide effective advance warning, as specifically as possible, to the population.
- Warning does not, however, discharge the obligation to distinguish between lawful targets and civilians.
- Although the use of civilians as "shields" is prohibited, one side's unlawful use of civilian shields does not affect the other side's obligation to ensure that attacks do not kill civilians in excess of the military advantage of killing the targeted fighter.

[Footnotes Omitted]

Document 4: Report of the Special Rapporteur on the promotion and protection of human rights and fundamental freedoms while countering terrorism, Martin Scheinin, A/HRC/13/37. (Excerpted)

UNITED NATIONS	A/HRC/13/37

General Assembly	Distr.:
HUMAN RIGHTS COUNCIL	GENERAL
Thirteenth session	28 December 2009
Agenda item 3	Original: ENGLISH

PROMOTION AND PROTECTION OF ALL HUMAN RIGHTS, CIVIL, POLITICAL, ECONOMIC, SOCIAL AND CULTURAL RIGHTS, INCLUDING THE RIGHT TO DEVELOPMENT

Report of the Special Rapporteur on the promotion and protection of human rights and fundamental freedoms while countering terrorism, Martin Scheinin

Summary

The Special Rapporteur, in chapter I of the present report, lists his key activities from 1 August to 15 December 2009. The main report, contained in chapter II, highlights several concerns of the Special Rapporteur regarding the protection of the right to privacy in the fight against terrorism. The importance of the right to privacy and data protection is

Highlighted in section A. Article 17 of the International Covenant on Civil and Political Rights is flexible enough to enable necessary, legitimate and proportionate restrictions to the right to privacy.

The Special Rapporteur argues, in section B, that article 17 should be interpreted as containing elements of a permissible limitations test. In this context, he calls upon States to justify why a particular aim is legitimate justification for restrictions upon article 17, and upon the Human Rights Committee to adopt a new general comment on article 17.

The Special Rapporteur highlights the erosion of the right to privacy in the fight against terrorism in section C. This erosion takes place through the use of surveillance powers and new technologies, which are used without adequate legal safeguards. States have endangered the protection of the right to privacy by not extending pre-existing safeguards in their cooperation with third countries and private actors. These measures have not only led to violations of the right to privacy, but also have an impact on due process rights and the freedom of movement—especially at borders—and can have a chilling effect on the freedom of association and the freedom of expression.

Without a rigorous set of legal safeguards and a means to measure the necessity, proportionality and reasonableness of the interference, States have no guidance on minimizing the risks to privacy generated by their new policies. The Special Rapporteur has identified, in section D, some of the legal safeguards that have emerged through policymaking, jurisprudence, policy reviews and good practice from around the world.

The concluding section makes recommendations to various key actors (domestic legislative assemblies, domestic executive powers and the United Nations) in order to improve the protection of the right to privacy in the fight against terrorism.

Contents

I. Introduction

1. This report is submitted to the Human Rights Council by the Special Rapporteur on the promotion and protection of human rights and fundamental freedoms while countering terrorism, pursuant to General Assembly resolution 63/185 and Human Rights Council resolution 10/15. The main report lists the activities of the Special Rapporteur from 1August to 15 December 2009 and focuses thematically on the right to privacy as a human right in the counter-terrorism context. The addenda contain a communications report (A/HRC/13/37/Add.1) and a report on the fact-finding mission to Egypt from 17 to 21 April 2009 (A/HRC/13/37/Add.2).

II. Activities of the Special Rapporteur

3. On 18 and 19 September 2009, the Special Rapporteur convened an expert group meeting at the European University Institute in Florence to discuss thematic issues related to his mandate. The meeting partly coincided with a public event on the "Fight against Terrorism: Challenges for the Judiciary", jointly organized with the Venice Commission and the Sub-Committee on Crime Problems of the Council of Europe. The event was cofounded by the Åbo Akademi University Institute for Human Rights, through its project to support the mandate of the Special Rapporteur.

...

10. On 29 October 2009, the Special Rapporteur met with the Assistant Secretary for Democracy, Human Rights and Labor and other officials of the U.S. State Department in Washington D.C., to discuss current and future legal developments with the new Administration, in follow-up to his visit to the U.S. of America in 2007, and more general issues concerning international humanitarian and human rights law in the counter-terrorism context.

III. The right to privacy

A. The right to privacy as enshrined in constitutions and international human rights treaties

11. Privacy is a fundamental human right that has been defined as the presumption that individuals should have an area of autonomous development, interaction and liberty, a "private sphere" with or without interaction with others and free from State intervention and free from excessive unsolicited intervention by other uninvited individuals. The right to privacy has evolved along two different paths. Universal human rights instruments have focused on the negative dimension of the right to privacy, prohibiting any arbitrary interference with a person's privacy, family, home or correspondence, while some regional and domestic instruments have also included a positive dimension: everyone has the right to respect for his/her private and family life, his/her home and correspondence, or the right to have his/her dignity, personal integrity or good reputation recognized and respected. While privacy is not always directly mentioned as a separate right in constitutions, nearly all States recognize its value as a matter of constitutional significance. In some countries, the right to privacy emerges by extension of the common law of breach of confidence, the right to liberty, freedom of expression or due process. In other countries, the right to privacy emerges as a religious value. The right to privacy is therefore not only a fundamental human right, but also a human right that supports other human rights and forms the basis of any democratic society.

12. The State's ability to develop record-keeping facilities was enhanced with the development of information technology. Enhanced computing power enabled previously unimaginable forms of collecting, storing and sharing of personal data. International core data protection principles were developed, including the obligation to: obtain personal information fairly and lawfully; limit the scope of its use to the originally specified purpose; ensure that the processing is adequate, relevant and not excessive; ensure its accuracy; keep it secure; delete it when it is no longer required; and grant individuals the right to access their information and request corrections. The Human Rights Committee provided clear indications in its general comment No. 16 that these principles were encapsulated by the right to privacy, but data protection is also emerging as a distinct human or fundamental right. Some countries have recognized data protection even as a constitutional right, thereby highlighting its importance as an element of democratic societies. The detailed article 35 of the 1976 Constitution of Portugal can be seen as an example of best practice here.

13. The right to privacy is not an absolute right. Once an individual is being formally investigated or screened by a security agency, personal information is shared among security agencies for reasons of countering terrorism and the right to privacy is almost automatically affected. These are situations where States have a legitimate power to limit the right to privacy under international human rights law. However, countering terrorism is not a trump card which automatically legitimates any interference with the right to privacy. Every instance of interference needs to be subject to critical assessment.

B. Permissible limitations to the right to privacy

14. Article 17 of the International Covenant on Civil and Political Rights is the most important legally binding treaty provision on the human right to privacy at the universal level. The Covenant has been ratified by 165 States and signed by another 6 States.11 7 See the European Convention for the Protection of Human Rights and Fundamental Freedoms (art. 8) and the Cairo Declaration on Human Rights in Islam (A/45/421-S/21797, art. 18), 5 August 1990.

Article 4 of the Covenant allows States parties to derogate from some provisions of the Covenant, including article 17. Derogations can be made only during a state of emergency threatening the life of the nation and they are subject to several conditions. During the more than 30 years since the entry into force of the Covenant in 1976, fewer than 10 States parties have introduced a state of emergency with reference to acts, or the threat of, terrorism. Four of them have in that context sought to derogate also from article 17 of the Covenant. Another eight States have announced derogation from article 17 without an explicit reference to terrorism as the cause for a state of emergency. However, the notifications in question have remained rather generic, instead of specifying, in line with the requirements under article 4, what concrete measures derogating from article 17 are necessary within the exigencies of the situation. Overall, there is not a single case of a State seeking to derogate from article 17 with reference to terrorism that would demonstrate compliance with all requirements of article 4. Further, only one State has announced derogation from the Covenant with reference to the current (related to the events of 11 September 2001) threat of international terrorism. The situation is similar in respect of reservations to article 17. Although international law generally allows for reservations by States to human rights treaties, provided such reservations are not incompatible with the object and purpose of the treaty, only one State party has submitted a reservation to article17.

15. Consequently, it appears that States have only rarely resorted to the acknowledged mechanisms available under international law in general, and the Covenant in particular, for unilateral exceptions to the right to privacy. Even when notifications of derogation from article 17 have been submitted, those notifications have remained generic, instead of referring to practical measures and specific forms of derogation. To the Special Rapporteur, the State practice reported above demonstrates that, generally, States appear to be content that the framework of article 17 is flexible enough to enable necessary, legitimate and proportionate restrictions to the right to privacy by means of permissible limitations, including when responding to terrorism. The Special Rapporteur supports this view. Article 17 is written in a manner that allows States parties the possibility to introduce restrictions or limitations in respect of the rights enshrined in that provision, including the right to privacy.

Such restrictions and limitations will therefore be subject to the monitoring functions of the Human Rights Committee as the treaty body entrusted with the task of interpreting the provisions of the Covenant and addressing the conduct of States parties in respect of their treaty obligations. The main mechanisms for the exercise of those functions are the mandatory reporting procedure under article 40 of the Covenant and, for those 113 States that have ratified the First Optional Protocol to the Covenant, the procedure for individual complaints.

16. The wording of article 17 of the Covenant prohibits "arbitrary or unlawful" interference with privacy, family or correspondence, as well as "unlawful attacks" on a person's honour and reputation. This can be contrasted with the formulation of such provisions as article 12, paragraph 3; article 18, paragraph 3; article 19, paragraph 3; article 21 and article 22, paragraph 2, which all spell out the elements of a test for permissible limitations. In its most elaborate form, this test is expressed in article 21 and article 22, paragraph 3, as consisting of the following three elements: (a) restrictions must be prescribed by national law; (b) they must be necessary in a democratic society; and (c) they must serve one of the legitimate aims enumerated in each of the provisions that contain a limitations clause.

17. The Special Rapporteur takes the view that, despite the differences in wording, article 17 of the Covenant should also be interpreted as containing the said elements of a permissible limitations test. Restrictions that are not prescribed by law are "unlawful" in the meaning of article 17, and restrictions that fall short of being necessary or do not serve a legitimate aim constitute "arbitrary" interference with the rights provided under article 17.

Consequently, limitations to the right to privacy or other dimensions of article 17 are subject to a permissible limitations test, as set forth by the Human Rights Committee in its general comment No. 27 (1999). That general comment addresses freedom of movement (art. 12), one of the provisions that contains a limitations clause. At the same time, it codifies the position of the Human Rights Committee in the matter of permissible limitations to the rights provided under the Covenant. The permissible limitations test, as expressed in the general comment, includes, inter alia, the following elements: (a) Any restrictions must be provided by the law (paras. 11–12); (b) The essence of a human right is not subject to restrictions (para. 13); (c) Restrictions must be necessary in a democratic society (para. 11); (d) Any discretion exercised when implementing the restrictions must not be unfettered (para. 13); (e) For a restriction to be permissible, it is not enough that it serves one of the enumerated legitimate aims; it must be necessary for reaching the legitimate aim (para. 14); (f) Restrictive measures must conform to the principle of proportionality; they must be appropriate to achieve their protective function; they must be the least intrusive instrument amongst those which might achieve the desired result; and they must be proportionate to the interest to be protected (paras. 14–15); (g) Any restrictions must be consistent with the other rights guaranteed in the Covenant (para. 18).

18. The Special Rapporteur takes the view that these considerations apply also in respect of article 17 of the Covenant, as elaborations of the notions of "unlawful" and "arbitrary". Where the textual difference between article 17 and the Covenant provisions that explicitly introduce a limitations test nevertheless matters is in the absence of an exhaustive list of legitimate aims in article 17. Here, the Special Rapporteur calls upon States to justify why a particular aim is legitimate as justification for restrictions upon article 17, and upon the Human Rights Committee to continue monitoring measures undertaken by States parties, including through the consideration of periodic reports and of individual complaints.

19. In the view of the Special Rapporteur, the Human Rights Committee should draw up and adopt a new general comment on article 17, replacing current general comment No. 16 (1988). The existing general comment is very brief and does not reflect the bulk of the Committee's practice that has emerged during the more than 20 years since its adoption.

Nevertheless, many of the elements for a proper limitations clause, presented above in the light of the subsequent general comment No. 27, were already present in 1988. In its subsequent case law under the Optional Protocol, the Committee has emphasized that interference with the rights guaranteed in article 17 must cumulatively meet several conditions, i.e., it must be provided for by law, be in accordance with the provisions, aims and objectives of the Covenant, and be reasonable in the particular circumstances of the case.22 Further, in finding violations of article 17, the Committee has applied the requirements of legitimate aim, necessity and proportionality.

C. Erosion of the right to privacy by counter-terrorism policies

20. When considering current counter-terrorism policies, States often contend that there are two new dynamics that must be considered alongside privacy protection. First, States claim that their ability to prevent and investigate terrorist acts is linked intimately with increased surveillance powers. The majority of counter-terrorism legislation activities since the events of 11 September 2001 have therefore focused on expanding Governments' powers to conduct surveillance. Second, States claim that since terrorism is a global activity, the search for terrorists must also take place beyond national borders, with the help of third parties which potentially hold extensive amounts of information on individuals, generating a rich resource for identifying and monitoring terrorist suspects. States that previously lacked constitutional or statutory safeguards

have been able to radically transform their surveillance powers with few restrictions. In countries that have constitutional and legal safeguards, Governments have endangered the protection of the right to privacy by not extending these safeguards to their cooperation with third countries and private actors, or by placing surveillance systems beyond the jurisdiction of their constitutions.

1. Increasing surveillance measures

21. The range of surveillance operations runs from the specific to the general. At the specific level, legal systems are capable of authorizing and overseeing: undercover operations and covert surveillance to identify illegal conduct; the accumulation of intelligence on specific individuals to identify breaches of law; and targeted surveillance of individuals to build a legal case. The Special Rapporteur had earlier specified that States may make use of targeted surveillance measures, provided that it is case-specific interference, on the basis of a warrant issued by a judge on showing of probable cause or reasonable grounds. There must be some factual basis, related to the behaviour of an individual, which justifies the suspicion that he or she may be engaged in preparing a terrorist attack. Worldwide, there has been a rise in communications surveillance through the interception of communications by intelligence and law enforcement agencies. There is a remarkable convergence in the types of policies pursued to enhance surveillance powers to respond to terrorism threats.

Most of these policies rely upon existing or new technologies, such as "bugs" and tracing technologies that can access the geographical position of mobile phones, technology that reports to Governments the contents of private text conversations of users of voice over Internet protocol, or that installs spyware on suspects' computers in order to enable remote computer access. In some countries, security services have even proposed banning communication technologies that are more difficult to intercept, such as smartphones. The Special Rapporteur is also concerned about the tracking of cross-border communications without judicial authorization.

22. In the name of countering terrorism, States have expanded initiatives to identify, scan and tag the general public through the use of multiple techniques which might violate an individual person's right to privacy. When surveillance occurs of places and larger groups of people, the surveillance is typically subject to weaker regimes for authorization and oversight. Human rights standards have been tested, stretched and breached through the use of stop-and-searches; the compilation of lists and databases; the increased surveillance of financial, communications and travel data; the use of profiling to identify potential suspects; and the accumulation of ever larger databases to calculate the probability of suspicious activities and identify individuals seen as worthy of further scrutiny. More advanced techniques are applied as well, such as the collection of biometrics or the use of body scanners that can see through clothing. Some intrusions into people's lives can be permanent as people's physical and biographical details are frequently centralized in databases.

(a) Stop and search powers

23. States have expanded their powers to stop, question, search and identify individuals, and have reduced their controls to prevent abuse of these powers. These powers have given rise to concerns regarding racial profiling and discrimination in Europe and the Russian Federation and concerns that these powers antagonize the relationship between citizens and the State. Equally, the proportionality requirement in the limitations test to the right to privacy raises questions whether blanket stop and search powers in designated security zones, such as in the Russian Federation or the United Kingdom, are really necessary in a democratic society.

(b) The use of biometrics and dangers of centralized identity systems

24. A key component to new identity policies is the use of biometric techniques, such as facial recognition, fingerprinting and iris-scanning. While these techniques can, in some circumstances, be a legitimate tool for the identification of terrorist suspects, the Special Rapporteur is particularly concerned about cases where biometrics are not stored in an identity document, but in a central database, thereby increasing the information security risks and leaving individuals vulnerable. As the collection of biometric information increases, error rates may rise significantly. This may result in the wrongful criminalization of individuals or social exclusion. Meanwhile, unlike other identifiers, biometrics cannot be revoked: once copied and/or fraudulently used by a malicious party, it is not possible to issue an individual with a new biometric signature. In this context, it has to be noted that, contrary to its scientific objectivity, DNA evidence can also be falsified.

25. Centralized collection of biometrics creates a risk of causing miscarriages of justice, which is illustrated by the following example. Following the Madrid bombings of 11 March 2004, the Spanish police managed to lift a fingerprint from an unexploded bomb.

Fingerprint experts from the U.S. Federal Bureau of Investigation (FBI) declared that a lawyer's fingerprint was a match to the crime-scene sample. The person's fingerprint was on the national fingerprint system because he was a former soldier of the U.S.. The individual was detained for two weeks in solitary confinement, even though the fingerprint was not his. Examiners failed to sufficiently reconsider the match, a situation that was made worse for him when it was discovered that he, as a lawyer, had defended a convicted terrorist, was married to an Egyptian immigrant, and had himself converted to Islam.

(c) The circulation of secret watch lists

26. Another available technique is watch-list monitoring. The most common type of watch-list monitoring is the "no-fly/selectee" list. Such lists are circulated to airlines and security officials with instructions to detain and question any passenger with a certain name. Little is known of the extent to which these lists are being used, but where these systems are publicly overseen, a number of errors and privacy concerns have arisen, particularly in the U.S. and Canada. Data integrity issues remain, as the lists have to be continually checked for errors and the identification processes must be performed with great care. These lists are frequently kept secret as they could tip off suspected terrorists, but at the same time this secrecy gives rise to problems of individuals being continually subject to scrutiny without knowing that they are on some form of list, and without effective independent oversight. Such secret surveillance could constitute a violation of the right to privacy under article 17 of the International Covenant on Civil and Political Rights.

27. Where terrorist lists have been made public, article 17 of the Covenant is triggered in another form. The Human Rights Committee has concluded that the unjustified inclusion of a person on the United Nations 1267 Committee's Consolidated List constituted a violation of article 17. It considered that the dissemination of personal information constituted an attack on the honour and reputation of the listed persons, in view of the negative association that would be made between the names and the title of the sanctions list.

28. Public and secret watch lists often also breach fundamental principles of data protection. Information generated for one purpose is reused for secondary purposes, and sometimes shared with other institutions, without the knowledge or consent of the individuals concerned. Erroneous information is used to make decisions about people, which result in restrictions on travel. These individuals may be refused a visa, turned away at a border or prevented from boarding a plane, without having been presented with evidence of any wrongdoing.

(d) Checkpoints and borders

29. Through the use of new technologies and in response to rising concerns regarding terrorism, States are increasing the monitoring, regulation, interference and control of the movement of people at borders. Now, with the use of more advanced technologies and data-sharing agreements, States are creating comprehensive profiles on foreign travellers to identify terrorists and criminals even in advance of their arrival at borders, by accessing passenger manifests and passenger reservation records from carriers. States analyse this information to identify patterns that correspond to those of terrorists or criminals. At the border, individuals are subjected to further—potentially invasive—information collection practices.

30. Many States now require carriers to submit passenger manifests prior to departure. States are also seeking access to passenger name records, which include identification information (name, telephone number), transactional information (dates of reservations, travel agent, itineraries), flight and seat information, financial data (credit card number, invoice address), choice of meals and information regarding place of residence, medical data, prior travel information, and frequent-flyer information. This information is used for profiling and risk-assessing passengers, usually by submitting queries to various multi-agency law enforcement and terrorist databases and watch lists. As a result, foreign carriers may be restricted from issuing an individual with a boarding pass solely on the basis of the results of a database query in the destination country, without due process.

31. The increased monitoring of immigrants and travellers for various purposes gives rise to a number of privacy challenges. States are gaining information on travellers from third parties who are compelled to comply lest they be refused landing rights or given punitive fines, even though privacy guarantees may not meet the requirements of domestic privacy laws. Moreover, foreigners might not be granted equal access to judicial remedies in these countries and rights at borders are usually significantly restricted. The U.S. Government policy on access to travellers' laptops is a useful example. Despite the need to meet constitutional due process requirements for searching a laptop within the U.S., the Department of Homeland Security has approved the accessing of travellers' computers without judicial authorization.

32. Lastly, States are establishing additional information requirements. Individuals can be prevented from entering States for refusing to disclose information, and States may insist upon disclosure without ensuring that there is lawful authority to require this information.

Additionally, information collected for one purpose is now being used for additional purposes; for example, the European Union's European Dactyloscopie system (EURODAC) for managing applications of asylum-seekers and illegal immigrants through the use of fingerprints is now proposed to be extended to aid the prevention, detection, and investigation of terrorist offences and other serious offences. The European Data Protection Supervisor has expressed doubts as to whether these proposals are legitimate under the right to privacy.

2. How surveillance has affected other rights

33. Surveillance regimes adopted as anti-terrorism measures have had a profound, chilling effect on other fundamental human rights. In addition to constituting a right in itself, privacy serves as a basis for other rights and without which the other rights would not be effectively enjoyed. Privacy is necessary to create zones to allow individuals and groups to be able to think and develop ideas and relationships. Other rights such as freedom of expression, association, and movement all require privacy to be able to develop effectively. Surveillance has also resulted in miscarriages of justice, leading to failures of due process and wrongful arrest.

34. In many nations around the world, users are being monitored to review what sites they are visiting and with whom they are communicating. In Germany, the Federal Intelligence Service was found in 2006 to have been illegally spying on journalists using communications surveillance and placing spies in newsrooms. In Colombia, the Administrative Department of Security was found, in 2009, to have been conducting illegal surveillance of members of the media, human rights workers, Government officials and judges, and their families for seven years. In numerous countries across the world, internet users must show identification and their sessions are recorded for future use by authorities. For instance, in Internet service providers in Bangladesh were required in 2007 to turn over records of their users' identities, passwords and usage to the authorities. Some users were then visited by the authorities, who searched though their computers and contact lists. In the U.S., the FBI counter-terrorism unit monitored the activities of peace activists at the time of the 2004 political conventions. These surveillance measures have a chilling effect on users, who are afraid to visit websites, express their opinions or communicate with other persons for fear that they will face sanctions. This is especially relevant for individuals wishing to dissent and might deter some of these persons from exercising their democratic right to protest against Government policy.

35. In addition to surveillance powers, many anti-terrorism laws require individuals to proactively disclose information and provide broad powers for officials to demand information for investigations. In this context, the Special Rapporteur has earlier expressed his concerns about the use of national security letters in the U.S.. Some countries have expanded this power to require the disclosure of information originally collected for journalistic purposes. In Uganda, the 2002 Anti-Terrorism Act allows for wiretapping and searches of the media if there are "special reasonable grounds" that the information has "substantial value" in an anti-terrorism investigation. The Special Rapporteur stresses that the legitimate interest in the disclosure of confidential materials of journalists outweighs the public interest in the non-disclosure only where an over-riding need for disclosure is proved, the circumstances are of a sufficiently vital and serious nature and the necessity of the disclosure is identified as responding to a pressing social need.

36. The rights to freedom of association and assembly are also threatened by the use of surveillance. These freedoms often require private meetings and communications to allow people to organize in the face of Governments or other powerful actors. Expanded surveillance powers have sometimes led to a "function creep", when police or intelligence agencies have labelled other groups as terrorists in order to allow the use of surveillance powers which were given only for the fight against terrorism. In the U.S., environmental and other peaceful protestors were placed on terrorist watch lists by the Maryland State Police before political conventions in New York and Denver. In the United Kingdom, surveillance cameras are commonly used for political protests and images kept in a database. A recent poll in the United Kingdom found that one third of individuals were disinclined to participate in protests because of concern about their privacy.

37. Freedom of movement can also be substantially affected by surveillance. The creation of secret watch lists, excessive data collection and sharing and imposition of intrusive scanning devices or biometrics, all create extra barriers to mobility. As described in previous sections, there has been a substantial increase in the collection of information about people travelling both nationally and internationally. Information is

routinely shared and used to develop watch lists that have led to new barriers to travel. When profiles and watch lists are developed using information from a variety of sources with varying reliability, individuals may have no knowledge of the source of the information, may not question the veracity of this information, and have no right to contest any conclusions drawn by foreign authorities. A mosaic of data assembled from multiple databases may cause data-mining algorithms to identify innocent people as threats. If persons are prohibited from leaving a country, the State must provide information on the reasons requiring the restriction on freedom of movement. Otherwise, the State is likely to violate article 12 of the International Covenant on Civil and Political Rights.

38. One of the most serious effects of surveillance measures is that they may lead to miscarriages of justice and violate due process guarantees. The challenge of gaining access to judicial review is that some legal regimes may prevent access to the courts unless individuals can show that interference has taken place, which is precluded by the secretive nature of the surveillance programmes. Individuals may not be able to prove or demonstrate that they are actually under surveillance. As a result, individuals may not be able to appeal to courts for remedy. In relevant cases, courts have ruled that individuals lack standing because they cannot demonstrate that they were under surveillance and any injuries have been considered speculative. In other cases, where interference can be proven, States have sometimes applied the "State secrets" privilege to avoid scrutiny of illegal surveillance projects. The Special Rapporteur commends the approach of the European Court of Human Rights (ECHR) where individuals do not need to prove that such measures necessarily had applied to them.

3. Extending legal boundaries

39. Mutual legal assistance treaties are established to permit countries to cooperate in investigations and to share information in specific cases. Agreements have also been established to permit the sharing of information on individuals engaged in activities, e.g., all passengers travelling to another country or all individuals conducting interbank financial transactions. More opaque are the agreements between intelligence agencies to share databases and intelligence data. These databases are often subject to wide-ranging exemptions from the domestic legal system. Even if domestic legislation applies, the data may refer to foreign nationals who may not be permitted to exercise any rights in domestic courts. Individuals may not be aware of the fact that they are subject to surveillance—e.g., that they are on a list of suspected terrorists—because intelligence-driven lists are not publicly available and therefore they may not appeal for review. When that list is shared internationally individuals may not be able to identify why they were first placed on it, or otherwise be able to remove themselves from the multiplicity of lists that have emerged since then.

40. States have increased not only their cooperation with each other in the fight against terrorism, but also with private third parties that have personal information of individuals in order to identify and monitor terrorist suspects. Some Governments have subsequently endangered the protection of the right to privacy by not extending domestic privacy safeguards to their cooperation with third countries and private actors.

41. Third parties, such as banks, telephone companies or even cybercafes, now hold extensive personal information about individuals. Access to this information therefore provides significant details about the private lives of individuals. At the same time, government agencies may gain access to this information with fewer restrictions than if the information was held by individuals themselves, in the home, or even by other government agencies. In the U.S., for instance the Supreme Court has ruled that, as data provided to third parties such as banks or telephone companies is shared "freely" with these parties, individuals may not reasonably expect privacy. Where there is a lack of constitutional protections that require a legal basis for the interference in the private lives of individuals, the burden then falls on the private organization to decide how to respond to a request from a government agency. Generally, the private sector prefers that Governments establish a legal basis for obliging organizations to produce personal information upon request, as it removes their obligation to consider the nature of the case.

42. Third parties are also increasingly being called upon to collect more information than is necessary, and to retain this information for extended periods of time. The United Kingdom, for instance, has proposed that telecommunications companies actively monitor and retain information on individuals' online activities including social-networking activities—information that these companies have no justified interest in collecting.

Similarly, the European Union's data retention directive has generated considerable criticism. When, in 2008, the German Federal Constitutional Court temporarily suspended the German law implementing that directive, it noted that "the retention of sensitive data, comprehensive and without occasion, on virtually everyone, for Government purposes that at the time of the storage of the data cannot be foreseen in detail, may have a considerable intimidating effect". Also in Germany, research showed a chilling effect of data retention policies: 52 per cent of persons interviewed said they probably would not use telecommunication for contact with drug counsellors, psychotherapists or marriage counsellors because of data retention laws.

43. In this context, the Special Rapporteur is concerned that, in many countries, data retention laws have been adopted without any legal safeguards over the access to this information being established or without the fact that new technological developments are blurring the difference between content and communications data being considered. While constitutional provisions tend to require safeguards on access to communications content, the protection of transaction logs is more limited. While this information may be integral to investigations, it may also be just as privacy-sensitive as the content of communications transactions.

44. With the goal of combating terrorism financing and money laundering, States have obliged the financial industry to analyse financial transactions in order to automatically distinguish those "normal" from those "suspicious". For instance, the European Union established a directive in 2005 on "the prevention of the use of the financial system for the purpose of money laundering and terrorist financing"65 requiring that financial institutions follow due diligence by reporting suspicious and "threshold" activities to financial intelligence units (FIUs). The additional processing of this information by the FIUs remains opaque, but States like Australia and Canada are processing millions of transactions each year through advanced data-mining tools.

45. Third parties may also be subject to foreign laws requiring disclosure. The U.S. Government, for instance, issued administrative subpoenas to the Society for Worldwide Interbank Financial Telecommunication (SWIFT), the Belgian cooperative responsible for enabling messaging between more than 7,800 financial institutions in over 200 countries. By gaining access to the SWIFT data centre in the U.S., the country's Treasury was then able to monitor foreign financial transactions across the SWIFT network, to find and identify terrorist suspects. Human rights groups filed legal complaints in over 20 courts arguing that, by handing this information over to U.S. authorities, SWIFT was in breach of local privacy laws.

46. The Special Rapporteur is also concerned that surveillance is being embedded in technological infrastructures, and that these will create risks for individuals and organizations. For example, the development of standards for lawful interception of communications requires telecommunications companies to design vulnerabilities into their technologies to ensure that States may intercept communications. These capabilities were abused in Greece where unknown third parties were able to listen to the communications of the Prime Minister of Greece, and dozens of other high-ranking dignitaries. More recently, these same capabilities were reported to have been used by the Government of the Islamic Republic of Iran to monitor protestors. To avoid abuse, surveillance technologies should log who accesses data, thereby leaving a trail that can itself be monitored for abuse.

47. In some States, constitutional safeguards continue to apply, however. In Canada, for example, the Charter of Rights and Freedoms protects privacy of information held by third parties when it reveals "intimate details of the lifestyle and personal choices of the individual". This requires balancing of the societal interests in protecting individual dignity, integrity and autonomy with effective law enforcement. The jurisprudence of the European Convention of Human Rights has similarly extended the right to privacy to information held by third parties. The Convention for the Protection of Individuals with regard to Automatic Processing of Personal Data requires both the public and private sectors to protect the information that they hold and regulates the sharing of information with government agencies. Exceptions apply when protecting State security, public safety or the monetary interests of the State, suppressing criminal offences or protecting individuals or the rights and freedoms of others.

D. Best practices

48. The Special Rapporteur is concerned that there is a trend towards extending such State surveillance powers beyond terrorism. Following the events of 11 September 2001, a number of legislatures introduced sunset clauses into and reviews of anti-terrorism legislation, as it was assumed that extraordinary powers may be required for a short period of time to respond to the then danger. These sunset clauses and reviews were not included in some areas of policymaking and, in later policies, were not considered at all. Many of the investigative powers given to law enforcement agencies under anti-terror laws are granted to these agencies to conduct investigations unrelated to terrorism. Meanwhile, States are following each other's lead on policy without considering the human rights implications. Many of the policies outlined above were

introduced first as extraordinary, but then soon became regional and international standards. Collectively, such interference is having significant negative impacts on the protection of the right to privacy, as there is limited access to legal safeguards. Without a rigorous set of legal safeguards and a means to measure the necessity, proportionality, or reasonableness of the interference, States have no guidance on minimizing the risks to privacy generated by their new policies. The Special Rapporteur has identified the legal safeguards that have emerged through policymaking, jurisprudence, policy reviews and good practice from around the world.

1. The principle of minimal intrusiveness

49. Some interference with the private lives of individuals is more intrusive than others. Constitutional protection of property and people has been extended over the past 50 years to include communica- tions, information that is related to a biographical core and a right to the confidentiality and integrity of infor-mation-technological systems. These protections require States to have exhausted less-intrusive techniques before resorting to others. The United Kingdom Parliament's Home Affairs Committee reviewed and adapted these ideas for modern data-centred surveillance systems into the principle of data minimization, which is closely linked to purpose-specification. In its review, the Parliamentary committee recommended that Governments "resist a tendency to collect more personal information and establish larger databases. Any decision to create a major new database, to share information on databases, or to implement proposals for increased surveillance, should be based on a proven need". The Special Rapporteur contends that States must incorporate this principle into existing and future policies as they present how their policies are necessary, and in turn proportionate.

2. The principle of purpose specification restricting secondary use

50. Whereas data protection law should protect information collected for one purpose being used for another, national security and law enforcement policies are generally exempted from these restrictions. This is done through secrecy provisions in lawful access notices, broad subpoenas and exemption certificates such as national security certificates, which exempt a specific database from adhering to privacy laws. The Special Rapporteur is concerned that this limits the effectiveness of necessary safeguards against abuse. States must be obliged to provide a legal basis for the reuse of information, in accordance with constitutional and human rights principles. This must be done within the human rights framework, rather than resorting to derogations and exemptions. This is particularly important when information is shared across borders; furthermore, when information is shared between States, protections and safeguards must continue to apply.

3. The principle of oversight and regulated authorization of lawful access

51. Surveillance systems require effective oversight to minimize harm and abuses. Where safeguards exist, this has traditionally taken the form of an independent authorization through a judicial warrant and/or a subpoena process with the opportunity of independent review. Many policies have attempted to restrict oversight and lower authorization levels, however: communications interception laws have mini-mized authorization requirements for some communications; secret subpoenas are issued to gain access to information held by third parties and have restricted the ability to seek judicial protections; and States are increasingly allowing intelligence and law enforcement agencies to self-authorize access to personal information where previously some form of independent authorization and effective reporting was necessary.

52. Some States have taken measures to address the erosion of safeguards. In the U.S., after a number of court cases and because of the reauthorization requirements under the USA Patriot Act, more opportuni-ties for judicial review have been reintroduced. Changes to the communications surveillance practices in Sweden and the U.S. have reintroduced some limited safeguards in the form of judicial warrants. Similarly, the European Court of Justice ruled that courts had to review the domestic lawfulness of international watch lists.

53. The Special Rapporteur is concerned that the lack of effective and independent scrutiny of surveillance practices and techniques calls into question whether interferences are lawful (and thus accountable) and necessary (and thus applied proportionately). He commends the hard work of oversight bodies within gov-ernment agencies, including internal privacy offices, audit departments and inspectorate-generals, as they too play a key role in identifying abuses. The Special Rapporteur therefore calls for increased internal oversight to complement the processes for independent authorization and external oversight. This internal and external accountability system will ensure that there are effective remedies for individuals, with meaningful access to redress mechanisms.

4. The principle of transparency and integrity

54. The application of secrecy privileges for surveillance systems inhibits the ability of legislatures, judicial bodies and the public to scrutinize State powers. Individuals may be subject to inappropriate surveillance, where profiles are developed through data mining, and erroneous judgements, without any prior notification of the practice. Furthermore, the lack of clear and appropriate limitations to surveillance policies makes it difficult to prove that these powers are not used in arbitrary and indiscriminate manners.

55. The principle of transparency and integrity requires openness and communication about surveillance practices. In some States, individuals must be notified when and how they are under surveillance, or as soon as possible after the fact. Under *habeas data* constitutional regimes in Latin America and European data protection laws, individuals must be able to gain access to and correct their personal information held within data stores and surveillance systems. These rights must be ensured across borders by ensuring that legal regimes protect citizens and non-citizens alike.

56. Open debate and scrutiny is essential to understanding the advantages and limitations of surveillance techniques, so that the public may develop an understanding of the necessity and lawfulness of surveillance. In many States, parliaments and independent bodies have been charged with conducting reviews of surveillance policies and procedures, and on occasion have been offered the opportunity for pre-legislative review. This has been aided by the use of sunset and review clauses in legislation.

5. The principle of effective modernization

57. Even as more invasive information is available with greater ease, States have not developed commensurate protection. In fact, in the name of modernizing their surveillance powers, States sometimes have intentionally sought to apply older and weaker safeguard regimes to ever more sensitive information. Conscious of the need to consider how technology and policy change may have a negative impact on individuals, some States have introduced privacy impact assessments that articulate privacy considerations in the design of new surveillance techniques, including how policy- makers considered many of the principles listed above, including data minimization and rights to redress. The Special Rapporteur believes that the use of such tools as privacy impact assessments may help inform the public about surveillance practices, while instilling a culture of privacy within government agencies as they develop new surveillance systems to combat terrorism. International standards must also be adopted to require States to enhance their safeguards to reflect technological change.

IV. Conclusions and recommendations

A. Conclusions

58. The Special Rapporteur is concerned that what was once exceptional is now customary. First, States no longer limit exceptional surveillance schemes to combating terrorism and instead make these surveillance powers available for all purposes.

Second, surveillance is now engrained in policymaking. Critics of unwarranted surveillance proposals must now argue why additional information must not be collected, rather than the burden of proof residing with the State to argue why the interference is necessary. Third, the quality and effectiveness of nearly all legal protections and safeguards are reduced. This is occurring even as technological change allows for greater and more pervasive surveillance powers. Most worrying, however, is that these technologies and policies are being exported to other countries and often lose even the most basic protections in the process.

59. International legal standards must be developed to ensure against these forms of abuse. This would be aided by adherence to principles outlined in this report, including ensuring that surveillance is as unintrusive as possible and that new powers are developed with appropriate safeguards and limitations, effective oversight and authorization and regular reporting and review and are accompanied by comprehensive statements regarding the impact on privacy. The general public and legislatures have rarely had the opportunity to debate whether anti-terrorism powers are necessary, proportionate or reasonable. The Special Rapporteur believes that following emergent good practices may prove beneficial to all.

B. Recommendations

For legislative assemblies

60. The Special Rapporteur recommends again that any interference with the right to privacy, family, home or correspondence should be authorized by provisions of law that are publicly accessible, particularly precise and proportionate to the security threat, and offer effective guarantees against abuse. States should ensure that the competent authorities apply less intrusive investigation methods if such methods enable a terrorist offence to be detected, prevented or prosecuted with adequate Effective- ness. Decision-making authority should be structured so that the greater the invasion of privacy, the higher the level of authorization needed.

61. Adherence to international standards for privacy and human rights protection must be a tenet national law. Accordingly, a comprehensive data protection and privacy law is necessary to ensure that there are clear legal protections for individuals to prevent the excessive collection of personal information, that ensures measures are in place to ensure the accuracy of information, that creates limits on the use, storage, and sharing of the information, and which mandates that individuals are notified of how their information is used and that they have a right to access and redress, regardless of nationality and jurisdiction.

62. Strong independent oversight mandates must be established to review policies and practices, in order to ensure that there is strong oversight of the use of intrusive surveillance techniques and the processing of personal information. Therefore, there must be no secret surveillance system that is not under the review of an effective oversight body and all interferences must be authorized through an independent body.

63. All current and proposed counter-terrorism policies must include privacy impact assessments to review and communicate how the policy and technologies ensure that privacy risks are mitigated and privacy is considered at the earliest stages of policymaking.

64. The Special Rapporteur recommends that stronger safeguards be developed to ensure that the sharing of information between governments continues to protect the privacy of individuals.

65. The Special Rapporteur also recommends that stronger regulations are developed to limit Government access to information held by third parties, including reporting schemes, and to minimize the burden placed on third parties to collect additional information, and that constitutional and legal safeguards apply when third parties are acting on behalf of the State.

66. The Special Rapporteur warns that legislative language should be reconsidered to prevent the use of anti-terrorism powers for other purposes. New systems must be designed with a limitation of scope in the specifications.

For Governments

67. The Special Rapporteur urges Governments to articulate in detail how their surveillance policies uphold the principles of proportionality and necessity, in accordance with international human rights standards, and what measures have been taken to ensure against abuse.

68. The Special Rapporteur recommends open discussion and regular reporting on information-based surveillance programmes. Reports to legislative and oversight bodies, as well as independent reviews of practices will help inform future policymaking and deliberation on anti-terrorism policy.

69. Any watch list- or profile-based surveillance programme must include due process safeguards for all individuals, including rights to redress. The principle of transparency must be upheld so that individuals can be informed as to why and how they were added to watch lists or how their profile was developed, and of the mechanisms for appeal without undue burdens.

70. Given the inherent dangers of data mining, the Special Rapporteur recommends that any information-based counter-terrorism programme should be subjected to robust and independent oversight. The Special Rapporteur also recommends against the development and use of data-mining techniques for counterterrorism purposes.

71. In light of the risk of abuse of surveillance technologies, the Special Rapporteur recommends that equal amounts of research and development resources be devoted to privacy-enhancing technologies.

For the Human Rights Council

72. The Special Rapporteur recommends the development of a programme for global capacity-building on privacy protection. The international replication of antiterrorism laws and the global standards on surveillance must be counterbalanced with greater awareness of the necessary safeguards for the protection of individuals' dignity.

73. The Special Rapporteur urges the Human Rights Council to establish a process that builds on existing principles of data protection to recommend measures for the creation of a global declaration on data protection and data privacy.

For the Human Rights Committee

74. The Special Rapporteur recommends that the Human Rights Committee begins drafting a new general comment on article 17 of the International Covenant on Civil and Political Rights, with the goal of elaborating a proper limitation test, thereby providing guidance to States on appropriate safeguards. The general comment should also give due attention to data protection as an attribute of the right to privacy, as enshrined in article 17 of the Covenant.

[Footnotes Omitted]

Document 5: Joint Study On Global Practices In Relation To Secret Detention In The Context Of Countering Terrorism (Sarkin, Scheinen, Ali, Nowak), A/HRC/13/42. (Excerpted)

UNITED NATIONS	A
General Assembly	Distr.
HUMAN RIGHTS COUNCIL	GENERAL
Thirteenth session	A/HRC/13/42
Agenda item 3	19 February 2010
	Original: ENGLISH

PROMOTION AND PROTECTION OF ALL HUMAN RIGHTS, CIVIL, POLITICAL, ECONOMIC, SOCIAL AND CULTURAL RIGHTS, INCLUDING THE RIGHT TO DEVELOPMENT

JOINT STUDY ON GLOBAL PRACTICES IN RELATION TO SECRET DETENTION IN THE CONTEXT OF COUNTERING TERRORISM OF THE SPECIAL RAPPORTEUR ON THE PROMOTION AND PROTECTION OF HUMAN RIGHTS AND FUNDAMENTAL FREEDOMS WHILE COUNTERING TERRORISM, MARTIN SCHEININ; THE SPECIAL RAPPORTEUR ON TORTURE AND OTHER CRUEL, INHUMAN OR DEGRADING TREATMENT OR PUNISHMENT, MANFRED NOWAK; THE WORKING GROUP ON ARBITRARY DETENTION REPRESENTED BY ITS VICE-CHAIR, SHAHEEN SARDAR ALI; AND THE WORKING GROUP ON ENFORCED OR INVOLUNTARY DISAPPEARANCES REPRESENTED BY ITS CHAIR, JEREMY SARKIN

Summary

The present joint study on global practices in relation to secret detention in the context of countering terrorism was prepared, in the context of their respective mandates, by the Special Rapporteur on the promotion and protection of human rights and fundamental freedoms while countering terrorism, the Special Rapporteur on torture and other cruel, inhuman or degrading treatment or punishment, the Working Group on Arbitrary Detention (represented by its Vice-Chair), and the Working Group on Enforced and Involuntary Disappearances (represented by its Chair). Given that the violation of rights associated with secret detention fell within their respective mandates, and in order to avoid duplication of efforts and ensure their complementary nature, the four mandate holders decided to undertake the study jointly.

In conducting the present study, the experts worked in an open, transparent manner. They sought inputs from all relevant stakeholders, including by sending a questionnaire to all States Members of the United Nations. Several consultations were held with States, and the experts shared their findings with all States concerned before the study was finalized. Relevant excerpts of the report were shared with the concerned States on 23 and 24 December 2009. In addition to United Nations sources and the responses to the questionnaire from 44 States, primary sources included interviews conducted with persons who had been held in secret detention, family members of those held captive, and legal representatives of detainees. Flight data were also used to corroborate information. In addition to the analysis of the policy and legal decisions taken by States, the aim of the study was also to illustrate, in concrete terms, what it means to be secretly detained, how secret detention can facilitate the practice of torture or inhuman and degrading treatment, and how the practice of secret detention has left an indelible mark on the victims, and on their families as well.

The study initially describes the international legal framework applicable to secret detention. At the outset, an explanation is given of the terminology used for the purpose of the study on what constitutes secret detention in the context of countering terrorism. The legal assessment concludes that secret detention is irreconcilably in violation of international human rights law, including during states of emergency and armed conflict. Likewise, it is in violation of international humanitarian law during any form of armed conflict.

Secret detention violates the right to personal liberty and the prohibition of arbitrary arrest or detention. No jurisdiction should allow for individuals to be deprived of their liberty in secret for potentially indefinite periods, held outside the reach of the law, without the possibility of resorting to legal procedures, including *habeas corpus*. Secret detainees are typically deprived of their right to a fair trial when State authorities do not intend to charge or try them. Even if detainees are criminally charged, the secrecy and insecurity caused by the denial of contact to the outside world and the fact that family members have no knowledge of their whereabouts and fate violate the presumption of innocence and are conducive to confessions obtained under torture or other forms of ill-treatment. At the same time, secret detention amounts to an enforced disappearance. If resorted to in a widespread or systematic manner, secret detention may even reach the threshold of a crime against humanity. Every instance of secret detention is by definition incommunicado detention. Prolonged incommunicado detention may facilitate the perpetration of torture and other cruel, inhuman or degrading treatment or punishment, and may in itself constitute such treatment. The suffering caused to family members of a secretly detained (namely, disappeared) person may also amount to torture or other form of ill-treatment, and at the same time violates the right to the protection of family life.

It is not only States whose authorities keep the detainee in secret custody that are internationally responsible for violations of international human rights law. The practice of "proxy detention", involving the transfer of a detainee from one State to another outside the realm of any international or national legal procedure ("rendition" or "extraordinary rendition"), often in disregard of the principle of non-refoulement, also involves the responsibility of the State at whose behest the detention takes place. The Geneva Conventions, applicable to all armed conflicts, also prohibit secret detention under any circumstances.

The study also provides an historical overview of the use of secret detention. Secret detention in the context of counter-terrorism is not a new phenomenon. From the Nazi regime, with its *Nacht und Nebel Erlaß* (the night and fog decree), to the former Soviet Union and its Gulag system of forced-labour camps, States have often resorted to secret detention to silence opposition. Striking similarities can be identified in the security measures of the 1970s and 1980s used in Latin American countries and, in the past century, in other regions, such as Africa, Asia, Europe and the Middle East.

The methods used then as now consist in, inter alia, broad emergency laws, the enhanced role of military and special courts, the practice of torture and/or ill-treatment, kidnappings (renditions), enforced disappearances and, notably, secret detention. The aim is always the same: to have a deterrent effect, to ensure that detainees would vanish without a trace, and that no information would be given with regard to their whereabouts or fate.

The study then addresses the use of secret detention in the context of the so-called "global war on terror" in the post-11 September 2001 period. In this chapter, the experts describe the progressive and determined elaboration of a comprehensive and coordinated system of secret detention of persons suspected of terrorism, involving not only the authorities of the United States of America, but also of other States in almost all regions of the world. Following a description of the legal and policy decisions taken by the U.S. authorities, the experts give an overview of the secret detention facilities held by them. The report then enumerates proxy detention sites and related practices of extraordinary rendition. Various United Nations bodies have in the past heavily criticized the policy of extraordinary rendition in a detailed way, dismissing it as a clear violation of international law. They have also expressed concern about the use of diplomatic assurances.

The experts also address the level of involvement and complicity of a number of countries. For purposes of the study, they provide that a State is complicit in the secret detention of a person when it (a) has asked another State to secretly detain a person; (b) knowingly takes advantage of the situation of secret detention by sending questions to the State detaining the person, or solicits or receives information from persons kept in secret detention; (c) has actively participated in the arrest and/or transfer of a person when it knew, or ought to have known, that the person would disappear in a secret detention facility, or otherwise be detained outside the legally regulated detention system; (d) holds a person for a short time in secret detention before handing them over to another State where that person will be put in secret detention for a longer period; and (e) has failed to take measures to identify persons or airplanes that were passing through its airports or airspace after information of the CIA programme involving secret detention has already been revealed.

The study subsequently highlights the fact that secret detention in connection with counter-terrorism policies remains a serious problem on a global scale, through the use of secret detention facilities similar to those described in the study; the declaration of a state of emergency, which allows prolonged secret detention; or forms of "administrative detention", also allowing prolonged secret detention. The cases and situations referred to, while not exhaustive, serve the purpose of substantiating the existence of secret detention in all regions of the world within the confines of the definition presented earlier.

In their conclusions, the experts reiterate that international law clearly prohibits secret detention, which violates a number of human rights and humanitarian law norms that may not be derogated from under any circumstances. If secret detention constitutes an enforced disappearance and is widely or systematically practiced, it may even amount to a crime against humanity. However, in spite of these unequivocal norms, the practice of secret detention in the context of countering terrorism is widespread and has been reinvigorated by the "global war on terror". The evidence gathered by the experts clearly shows that many States, referring to concerns relating to national security—often perceived or presented as unprecedented emergencies or threats—resort to secret detention.

Secret detention effectively takes detainees outside the legal framework and renders safeguards contained in international instruments meaningless, including, importantly, that of *habeas corpus*. The most disturbing consequence of secret detention is, as many of the experts' interlocutors pointed out, the complete arbitrariness of the situation, together with the uncertainty surrounding the duration of the secret detention, and the feeling that there is no way the individual can regain control of his or her life.

States of emergency, armed conflicts and the fight against terrorism—often framed in vaguely defined legal provisions—constitute an "enabling environment" for secret detention. As in the past, extraordinary powers are today conferred on authorities, including armed forces, law enforcement bodies and/or intelligence agencies, under states of emergency or global war paradigms without, or with very restricted, control mechanisms by parliaments or judicial bodies.

In many contexts, intelligence agencies operate in a legal vacuum with no law, or no publicly available law, governing their actions. Many times, although intelligence bodies are not authorized by legislation to detain persons, they do so, sometimes for prolonged periods. In such situations, oversight and accountability mechanisms are either absent or severely restricted, with limited powers and hence ineffective.

Secret detention has relied on systems of trans-border (regional or global) cooperation; in many instances, foreign security forces indeed operate freely in the territory of other States. It also leads to the mutual exchange of intelligence information between States. A crucial element in international cooperation has been the transfer of alleged terrorists to other countries, where they may face a substantial risk of being subjected to torture and other cruel, inhuman and degrading treatment, in contravention of the principle of non-refoulement. Practices such as "hosting" secret detention sites or providing proxy detention have been supplemented by numerous other facets of complicity, including authorizing the landing of airplanes for refuelling, short-term deprivation of liberty before handing over the "suspect", the covering up of kidnappings, and so on. With very few exceptions, too little has been done to investigate allegations of complicity.

Secret detention as such may constitute torture or ill-treatment for the direct victims as well as for their families. The very purpose of secret detention, however, is to facilitate and, ultimately, cover up torture and inhuman and degrading treatment used either to obtain information or to silence people. While in some cases elaborate rules are put in place authorizing "enhanced" techniques that violate international standards of human rights and humanitarian law, most of the time secret detention has been used as a kind of defence shield to avoid any scrutiny and control, making it impossible to learn about treatment and conditions during detention.

The generalized fear of secret detention, and its corollaries such as torture and ill-treatment, tends to effectively result in limiting the exercise of a large number of human rights and fundamental freedoms. These include the freedom of expression and the freedom of association, as they often go hand in hand with the intimidation of witnesses, victims and their families.

The experts are extremely concerned that many victims of secret detention from many countries around the world indicated their fear of reprisal, against themselves personally or against their families, if they cooperated with the study and/or allowed their names to be used.

The injustice done by secretly detaining somebody is prolonged and replicated all too frequently once the victims are released, because the concerned State may try to prevent any disclosure about the fact that secret detention is practiced on its territory.

In almost no recent cases have there been any judicial investigations into allegations of secret detention, and practically no one has been brought to justice. Although many victims feel that the secret detention has stolen years of their lives and left an indelible mark, often in terms of loss of their livelihood and frequently their health, they have almost never received any form of reparation, including rehabilitation or compensation.

Such a serious human rights violation therefore deserves appropriate action and condemnation. The experts conclude with concrete recommendations that are aimed at curbing the resort to secret detention and the unlawful treatment or punishment of detainees in the context of counter-terrorism:

(a) Secret detention should be explicitly prohibited, along with all other forms of unofficial detention. Detention records should be kept, including in times of armed conflict, as required by the Geneva Conventions, and should include the number of detainees, their nationality and the legal basis on which they are being held, whether as prisoners of war or civilian internees. Internal inspections and independent mechanisms should have timely access to all places where persons are deprived of their liberty for monitoring purposes, at all times. In times of armed conflict, the location of all detention facilities should be disclosed to the International Committee of the Red Cross;

(b) Safeguards for persons deprived of their liberty should be fully respected. No undue restrictions on these safeguards under counter-terrorism or emergency legislation are permissible. In particular, effective *habeas corpus* reviews by independent judicial bodies are central to ensuring respect for the right to personal liberty. Domestic legislative frameworks should therefore not allow for any exceptions from *habeas corpus*, operating independently of the detaining authority and from the place and form of deprivation of liberty. The study shows that judicial bodies can play a crucial role in protecting people against secret detention. The law should foresee penalties for officials who refuse to disclose relevant information during *habeas corpus* proceedings;

(c) All steps necessary to ensure that the immediate families of those detained are informed of their relatives' capture, location, legal status and condition of health should be taken in a timely manner;

(d) Any action by intelligence services should be governed by law, which in turn should be in conformity with international norms. To ensure accountability in intelligence cooperation, truly independent intelligence review and oversight mechanisms should be established and enhanced. Such mechanisms should have access to all information, including sensitive information. They should be mandated to undertake reviews and investigate upon their initiative, and to make public reports;

(e) Institutions strictly independent of those that have allegedly been involved in secret detention should promptly investigate any allegations of secret detention and extraordinary rendition. Those individuals found to have participated in secretly detaining persons and any unlawful acts perpetrated during such detention, including their superiors if they have ordered, encouraged or consented to secret detentions, should be prosecuted without delay and, where found guilty, given sentences commensurate to the gravity of the acts perpetrated;

(f) The status of all pending investigations into allegations of ill-treatment and torture of detainees and detainee deaths in custody should be made public. No evidence or information obtained by torture or cruel, inhuman and degrading treatment should be used in any proceedings;

(g) Transfers, or the facilitation of transfers, from one State to the custody of authorities of another State must be carried out under judicial supervision and in line with international standards. The principle of non-refoulement of persons to countries where they would be at risk of torture or other inhuman, cruel or degrading treatment should be honoured;

(h) Victims of secret detention should be provided with judicial remedies and reparation in accordance with relevant international norms, which recognize the right of victims to adequate, effective and prompt reparation proportionate to the gravity of the violations and the harm suffered. Given that families of disappeared persons have been recognized as victims under international law, they should also benefit from rehabilitation and compensation;

(i) States should ratify and implement the International Covenant on Civil and Political Rights and the Convention against Torture and Other Cruel, Inhuman or Degrading Treatment or Punishment. Given that the Optional Protocol to the Convention against Torture requires the setting up of monitoring systems covering all situations of deprivation of liberty, adhering to this international instrument adds a layer of protection. States should ratify the Optional Protocol and create independent national preventive mechanisms that are in compliance with the Paris Principles, and ratify the International Convention for the Protection of All Persons from Enforced Disappearance. Other regional systems may wish to replicate the system put in place through the Inter-American Convention on Forced Disappearance of Persons;

(j) Governments have an obligation to protect their citizens abroad and provide consular protection to ensure that foreign States comply with their obligations under international law, including international human rights law;

(k) Under international human rights law, States have the obligation to provide witness protection, which is also a precondition for combating secret detention effectively.

CONTENTS

I. INTRODUCTION

1. The present joint study on global practices in relation to secret detention in the context of countering terrorism was prepared by the Special Rapporteur on the promotion and protection of human rights and fundamental freedoms while countering terrorism, the Special Rapporteur on torture and other cruel, inhuman or degrading treatment or punishment, the Working Group on Arbitrary Detention (represented by its Vice Chair), and the Working Group on Enforced and Involuntary Disappearances (represented by its Chair).

2. The study was prepared within the mandates of the above-mentioned special procedures. In particular, the Human Rights Council, in its resolution 6/28, requested the Special Rapporteur on the promotion and

protection of human rights and fundamental freedoms while countering terrorism to make concrete recommendations on the promotion and protection of human rights and fundamental freedoms while countering terrorism, and to work in close coordination with other relevant bodies and mechanisms of the United Nations, in particular with other special procedures of the Council, in order to strengthen the work for the promotion and protection of human rights and fundamental freedoms while avoiding unnecessary duplication of efforts.

3. In its resolution 8/8, the Council requested the Special Rapporteur on torture and other cruel, inhuman or degrading treatment or punishment to study, in a comprehensive manner, trends, developments and challenges in relation to combating and preventing torture and other cruel, inhuman or degrading treatment or punishment, and to make recommendations and observations concerning appropriate measures to prevent and eradicate such practices.

4. In its resolution 6/4, the Council requested the Working Group on Arbitrary Detention to seek and receive information from Governments and intergovernmental and non-governmental organizations, and receive information from the individuals concerned, their families or their representatives relevant to its mandate, and to formulate deliberations on issues of a general nature in order to assist States to prevent and guard against the practice of arbitrary deprivation of liberty. Like other mandates, it was asked to work in coordination with other mechanisms of the Council.

5. In its resolution 7/12, the Council requested the Working Group on Enforced or Involuntary Disappearances to consider the question of impunity in the light of the relevant provisions of the Declaration on the Protection of All Persons from Enforced Disappearances, having in mind the set of principles for the protection and promotion of human rights through action to combat impunity (E/CN.4/Sub.2/1997/20/Rev.1, annex II, and E/CN.4/2005/102/Add.1), and to provide appropriate assistance in the implementation by States of the Declaration and existing international rules.

6. In the above context, the four mandates endeavoured to address global practices in relation to secret detention in counter-terrorism. In the joint study, they describe the international legal framework applicable to secret detention and provide a historical overview of the use of secret detention. The study addresses the use of secret detention in the context of the "global war on terror" in the post-11 September 2001 period. To the extent possible, in order to demonstrate that the practice of secret detention is regrettably not an uncommon one, it also highlights a number of cases where it has been utilized in and by States from various geographical regions. Owing to its global nature, the present study cannot be exhaustive but rather aims to highlight and illustrate by examples the wide spread practice of secret detention and related impunity. Finally, the study concludes with concrete recommendations regarding these practices, aimed at curbing the use of secret detention and the unlawful treatment or punishment of detainees in the context of counter-terrorism.

7. Owing to the secrecy of the practice of secret detention, it was often difficult to gather first-hand information; nevertheless, a wide array of national, regional and international sources was consulted. While United Nations sources were drawn upon, primary sources included responses to a questionnaire sent to all Member States (annex I) and interviews with current or former detainees (summaries of which are given in annex II). In some cases, secondary sources such as media and other sources were used. Such accounts, while not always verifiable are utilized when regarded by the mandate holders as credible. Responses to the questionnaire were received from 44 States. A number of interviews were held with people who had been held in secret detention, family members of those held captive, as well as legal representatives of individuals held. The mandate holders conducted face to face interviews in Germany and the United Kingdom of Great Britain and Northern Ireland. Other interviews were conducted by telephone. Formal meetings at the level of capitals were held with officials in Berlin, London and Washington, D.C. The mandate holders thank those States that cooperated with them and facilitated their joint work. They also wish to thank the Office of the United Nations High Commissioner for Human Rights (OHCHR) as well as others who provided valuable research and other assistance to the study.

II. SECRET DETENTION UNDER INTERNATIONAL LAW

A. Terminology

8. For the purpose of the present report, it is construed that a person is kept in secret detention if State authorities acting in their official capacity, or persons acting under the orders thereof, with the authorization, consent, support or acquiescence of the State, or in any other situation where the action or omission of the detaining person is attributable to the State, deprive persons of their liberty; where the person is not

permitted any contact with the outside world ("incommunicado detention"); and when the detaining or otherwise competent authority denies, refuses to confirm or deny or actively conceals the fact that the person is deprived of his/her liberty hidden from the outside world, including, for example family, independent lawyers or non-governmental organizations, or refuses to provide or actively conceals information about the fate or whereabouts of the detainee. In the present report, the term "detention" is used synonymously with "deprivation of liberty", "keeping in custody" or "holding in custody". The distinction drawn between "detention" and "imprisonment" in the preamble to the Body of Principles for the Protection of All Persons under Any Form of Detention or Imprisonment, adopted by the General Assembly in its resolution 43/173, in the section entitled "Use of Terms", does not purport to provide a general definition.

9. Secret detention does not require deprivation of liberty in a secret place of detention; in other words, secret detention within the scope of the present report may take place not only in a place that is not an officially recognized place of detention, or in an officially recognized place of detention, but in a hidden section or wing that is itself not officially recognized, but also in an officially recognized site. Whether detention is secret or not is determined by its incommunicado character and by the fact that State authorities, as described in paragraph 1 above, do not disclose the place of detention or information about the fate of the detainee.

10. Any detention facility may fall within the scope of the present study. It can be a prison, police station, governmental building, military base or camp, but also, for example, a private residence, hotel, car, ship or plane.

11. Incommunicado detention, where the detainees may only have contact with their captors, guards or co-inmates, would amount to secret detention also if the International Committee of the Red Cross (ICRC) is granted access by the authorities, but is not permitted to register the case, or, if it is allowed to register the case, is not permitted by the State to, or does not, for whatever reason, notify the next of kin of the detainee on his or her whereabouts. In other words, access by ICRC alone, without it being able to notify others of the persons' whereabouts, would not be sufficient to qualify the deprivation of liberty as not being secret. However, it is understood that ICRC, in principle, would not accept access to a detention facility without the possibility of exercising its mandate, which includes notification of the family about the whereabouts and fate of the detainee.3 If ICRC access is granted within a week, it has been deemed sufficient to leave the case outside the scope of the present study. ICRC access to certain detainees may only be exceptionally and temporarily restricted for reasons of imperative military necessity in an armed conflict.

12. A case falls within the scope of the present study on secret detention in the name of counter-terrorism only if State authorities or persons acting under the orders, or with the authorization, consent, support or acquiescence of the State, or in any other way attributable to the State, detain secretly persons: (a) Who have committed, or are suspected of planning, aiding or abetting, terrorist offences, irrespective of what classification of these offences is used by a Government; (b) In any situation where terrorism or related notions (such as extremism or separatism)6 are used to describe or justify the context in, or basis upon, which a person has been detained; (c) In any situation where extraordinary detention powers or procedures are triggered (under notions such as anti-terrorism acts, states of emergency or national security acts).

13. The qualification by States of certain acts as "terrorist acts" is often aimed at applying a special regime with limited legal and procedural safeguards in place. The Special Rapporteur on the promotion and protection of human rights and fundamental freedoms while countering terrorism has expressed concern that the absence of a universal and comprehensive definition of the term of "terrorism", leaving it to individual States to define it carries the potential for unintended human rights abuses and even deliberate misuse of the term. He added that "it was essential to ensure that the term "terrorism" is confined in its use to conduct that is of a genuinely terrorist nature." The Working Group on Arbitrary Detention also noted with concern the frequent attempts by Governments to use normal legislation or to have recourse to emergency or special laws and procedures to combat terrorism and thereby permit, or at least increase, the risk of arbitrary detention. It added that such laws, either per se or in their application, by using an extremely vague and broad definition of terrorism, bring within their fold the innocent and the suspect alike, and thereby increase the risk of arbitrary detention, disproportionately reducing the level of guarantees enjoyed by ordinary persons in normal circumstances. Legitimate democratic opposition, as distinct from violent opposition, becomes a victim in the application of such laws." Examples of such a type of criminal offence couched in broad terms relate to the subversion of State powers or simply anti-subversion laws". Such attempts to circumvent the guarantees of applicable international human rights law inform a broad approach as to the scope of the

present study of what constitutes secret detention in the context of countering terrorism. See, for instance, the Shanghai Convention on Combating Terrorism, Separatism and Extremism, agreed upon in 2001 by Kazakhstan, China, Kyrgyzstan, the Russian Federation, Tajikistan and Uzbekistan. The parties agree to "reciprocally recognize acts of terrorism, separatism and extremism irrespective of whether their own national legislations include the corresponding acts in the same category of crimes or whether they use the same terms to describe them".

14. Organized crimes, such as drug or human trafficking, are not covered by the present study, unless anti-terrorism legislation is invoked. Whether the State has conferred on the case a link to terrorism may have to be inferred from elements uttered by State officials or if the person is later prosecuted on terrorism-related charges.

15. Detention by non-State actors, when not attributable to the State, is not addressed in the present study. Hence, hostage-taking, kidnapping or comparable conduct by terrorists, criminals, rebels, insurgents, paramilitary forces or other non-State actors do not fall within the ambit of the report, which focuses on secret detention by or attributable to States and is addressed to the Human Rights Council as an intergovernmental body.

16. Victims of the human rights violation of secret detention are not only the detainees themselves, but also their families, who are not informed of the fate of their loved ones deprived of their rights and held solely at the mercy of their captors.

B. Secret detention and international human rights law and international humanitarian law

17. Secret detention is irreconcilable with international human rights law and international Humanitarian law. It amounts to a manifold human rights violation that cannot be justified under any circumstances, including during states of emergency.

1. Secret detention and the right to liberty of the person

18. Secret detention violates the right to liberty and security of the person and the prohibition of arbitrary arrest or detention. Article 9, paragraph 1, of the International Covenant on Civil and Political Rights affirms that everyone has the right to liberty and security of person, that no one should be subjected to arbitrary arrest or detention nor be deprived of his or her liberty except on such grounds and in accordance with such procedure as are established by law. Furthermore, article 9, paragraph 4, of the Covenant stipulates that anyone deprived of their liberty by arrest or detention should be entitled to take proceedings before a court, in order that that court may decide, without delay, on the lawfulness of their detention and order their release if the detention is not lawful. The Human Rights Committee, in its general comment No. 8, highlighted that article 9, paragraphs 1 and 4, and paragraph 3, of the International Covenant on Civil and Political Rights as far as the right to be informed at the time of the arrest about the reasons therefore, is applicable to all deprivations of liberty, "whether in criminal cases or in other cases such as, for example, mental illness, vagrancy, drug addiction, educational purposes, immigration control, etc." 19. The practice of secret detention in itself violates the above-mentioned guarantees, or in most cases, automatically or inherently entails such consequences that amount to a violation. As secret detainees are held outside the reach of the law, no procedure established by law is being applied to them as required by article 9 of the International Covenant on Civil and Political Rights. Even if a State authorized in its domestic laws the practice of secret detention, such laws would in themselves be in violation of the right to liberty and security and would therefore not stand. Secret detention without contact with the outside world entails de facto that the detainees do not enjoy the right enshrined in article 9, paragraph 4 of the Covenant, namely the possibility to institute habeas corpus, *amparo*, or similar proceedings, personally or on their behalf, challenging the lawfulness of detention before a court of law that is competent to order their release in the event that the detention is found to be unlawful.

20. The Working Group on Arbitrary Detention has classified secret detention as being per se arbitrary, falling within category I of the categories of arbitrary detention that it has developed. The Working Group qualifies deprivation of liberty as arbitrary in terms of category I when it is clearly impossible to invoke any legal basis justifying the deprivation of liberty. In its opinion No. 14/2009 concerning a case of detention unacknowledged by the Government at an undisclosed place of custody, the Working Group held that no jurisdiction could allow for incommunicado detention where no access to counsel or relatives was granted and no judicial control over the deprivation of liberty was exercised; in short, where no legal procedure established by law whatsoever was followed.

21. In its opinion No. 12/2006, the Working Group on Arbitrary Detention considered the deprivation of liberty of two individuals, one of whom was held at a secret place of detention, to be arbitrary under

category I, as both had not been formally charged with any offence, informed of the duration of their custodial orders, brought before a judicial officer, allowed to name a lawyer to act on their behalf, nor otherwise been provided the possibility to challenge the legality of their detention.

22. Opinion No. 29/2006 of the Working Group on Arbitrary Detention concerned 26 individuals who were alleged to have been captured in various countries, partly handed over into the custody of the United States of America under its secret Central Intelligence Agency (CIA) rendition programme in the context of the so called "global war on terror". They were held incommunicado at various "black sites" under the jurisdiction of the U.S. for prolonged periods of time, without charge or trial, access to courts of law, and without their families being informed or aware of their fate or whereabouts. In spite of the absence of a response by the Government of the U.S. to these allegations, the Working Group considered itself in a position to render an opinion on the cases of these 26 individuals, many of whom were suspected of having been involved in serious crimes, and held that their detention clearly fell within category I of arbitrary detention.

23. In most cases, secret detention, as it is outside any international or national legal regime, also implies that the duration of detention is not known to the detainee; it rests at the sole discretion of the authorities ordering the detention. Hence, the very nature of secret detention may result in potentially, or actually, indefinite periods of detention, which render this type of detention arbitrary on this additional ground.

2. Secret detention and the right to a fair trial

24. Secret detention outside the protection of the law is often resorted to with the purpose of depriving the detainee of the rights that he or she would otherwise enjoy as a person charged with a criminal offence, namely the right to a fair trial, as enunciated in article 14 of the International Covenant on Civil and Political Rights and the complementary guarantees contained in article 9, paragraphs 2 and 3. Article 9, paragraph 2 of the Covenant stipulates that anyone who is arrested should be promptly informed of any charges against him. Paragraph 3 of the same article requires that anyone arrested or detained on a criminal charge be brought promptly before a judge or other officer authorized by law to exercise judicial power.

25. The above-mentioned provisions presuppose that anyone suspected of having committed a recognizeable criminal offence and arrested on these grounds must be informed of the underlying charges if the interest of justice requires the prosecution of such a crime; otherwise, the State could circumvent the additional rights extended to suspects of a crime spelled out in articles 9 and 14 of the Covenant. Equally, if someone suspected of a crime and detained on the basis of article 9 of the Covenant is charged with an offence but not brought to trial, the prohibitions of unduly delaying trials as provided for by article 9, paragraph 3, and article14, paragraph 3 (c) of the Covenant may be violated at the same time.

26. As the present study shows, in the majority of cases, State authorities who arrest and detain people incommunicado in a secret location often do not intend to charge the detainee with any crime, or even to inform him or her about any charges or to put the person on trial without undue delay before a competent, independent and impartial tribunal established by law where the guilt or innocence of the accused could be established, in violation of article 14, paragraphs 1 (clause 2), 2, 3 (a) and (c) of the International Covenant on Civil and Political Rights. Such detainees do not have adequate time and facilities for the preparation of their defence, and cannot communicate freely with counsel of their own choosing as required by article 14, paragraph 3 (c) of the Covenant.

27. The Working Group on Arbitrary Detention has considered secret detention a violation of the right to fair trial. Certain practices inherent in secret detention, such as the use of secrecy and insecurity caused by denial of contact to the outside world and the family's lack of knowledge of the whereabouts and fate of the detainee to exert pressure to confess to a crime, also infringe the right not to be compel- ed to testify against oneself or to confess guilt derived from the principle of presumption of innocence. Secret detention is furthermore conducive to confessions obtained under torture and other forms of ill-treatment.

3. Secret detention and enforced disappearance

28. Every instance of secret detention also amounts to a case of enforced disappearance. Article 2 of the International Convention for the Protection of All Persons from Enforced Disappearance defines enforced disappearance as: The arrest, detention, abduction or any other form of deprivation of liberty by agents of the State or by persons or groups of persons acting with the authorization, support or acquiescence of the State, followed by a refusal to acknowledge the deprivation of liberty or by concealment of the fate or whereabouts of the disappeared person, which place such a person outside the protection of the law. This definition does not require intent to put the person concerned outside the protection of the law as a defining element, but

rather refers to it as an objective consequence of the denial, refusal or concealment of the whereabouts and fate of the person. The International Convention, in its article 17, paragraph 1, explicitly prohibits secret detention.

The Working Group on Enforced or Involuntary Disappearances confirmed in its general comment on article 10 of the Declaration on the Protection of All Persons from Enforced Disappearance that under no circumstances, including states of war or public emergency, can any State interest be invoked to justify or legitimize secret centres or places of detention which, by definition, would violate the Declaration, without exception."

29. Article 24, paragraph 1, of the International Convention explicitly includes in the definition of "victim" of enforced disappearances not only the disappeared person, but also any individual who has suffered harm as the direct result of an enforced disappearance." When exercising its mandate to monitor the implementation by Member States to the Declaration on the Protection of All Persons from Enforced Disappearance, the Working Group on Enforced or Involuntary Disappearances has always adopted the perspective that families of the disappeared are to be considered victims themselves. According to article 1.2 of the Declaration, any act of enforced disappearance places the persons subjected thereto outside the protection of the law and inflicts severe suffering on them and their families."

30. Since secret detention amounts to an enforced disappearance, if resorted to in a widespread or systematic manner, such aggravated form of enforced disappearance can reach the threshold of a crime against humanity. In its article 7, the Rome Statute of the International Criminal Court labels the "enforced disappearance of persons" as a crime against humanity if it is committed as part of a widespread or systematic attack directed against any civilian population, with knowledge of the attack. 23 Article 5 of the International Convention for the Protection of All Persons from Enforced Disappearance states that the widespread or systematic practice of enforced disappearance constitutes a crime against humanity as defined in applicable international law, and should attract the consequences provided for under such applicable international law, thus confirming this approach.

4. Secret detention and the absolute prohibition of torture and other forms of ill-treatment

31. Every instance of secret detention is by definition incommunicado detention. According the Human Rights Committee, even comparably short periods of incommunicado detention may violate the obligation of States, as contained in article 10, paragraph 1, of the International Covenant on Civil and Political Rights, to treat all persons deprived of their liberty with humanity and with respect for the inherent dignity of the human person. The Committee confirmed that "prisoners should be allowed under necessary supervision to communicate with their family and reputable friends at regular intervals, by correspondence as well as by receiving mail." Although shorter time periods may also be prohibited, incommunicado detention of 15 days constitutes a violation of article 10 of the Covenant.25 Incommunicado detention includes situations where a detainee's family is informed that the person is "safe", without disclosure of the location or nature of the person's detention.

32. The ill-treatment threshold may be reached when the period of incommunicado detention is prolonged and additional circumstances prevail. For example, in the case of *Polay Campos v Peru*, the Human Rights Committee found a violation of both articles 7 and 10 of the Covenant as the detained submitter of the complaint had not been allowed to speak or to write to anyone, including legal representatives, for nine months, and had been kept in an unlit cell for 23 and a half hours a day in freezing temperatures. It held that the incommunicado detention to which the author was subjected for longer than eight months constituted inhuman and degrading treatment. Similarly, the Inter-American Court of Human Rights has stated that prolonged isolation and deprivation of communications are in themselves cruel and inhuman treatment, even if it is not known what has actually happened during the prolonged isolation of the particular individual. In *El-Megreisi v Libyan Arab Jamahiriya*, the Human Rights Committee found that the Government of the Libyan Arab Jamahiriya had violated articles 10, paragraphs 1 and 7 of the Covenant by detaining an individual for six years, the last three of which incommunicado and in an unknown location, which in the view of the Committee reached the torture threshold.

33. The practice of secret detention, as reflected by the cases covered in the present study, also confirms that incommunicado detention, including secret detention, facilitates the commission of acts of torture.

34. The General Assembly, in its resolution 60/148, and the Human Rights Council, in its resolution 8/8, both state that prolonged incommunicado detention or detention in secret places may facilitate the perpetration of torture and other cruel, inhuman or degrading treatment or punishment, and could in

itself constitute a form of such treatment. The link between secret detention and torture and other forms of ill-treatment is hence twofold: secret detention as such may constitute torture or cruel, inhuman and degrading treatment; and secret detention may be used to facilitate torture or cruel, inhuman and degrading treatment.

35. In addition, secret detention not only violates the prohibition against torture and other forms of ill-treatment as defined above with regard to the victim of secret detention; but the suffering caused to family members of a disappeared person may also amount to torture or other forms of ill-treatment, and also violates the right to family in terms of article 17, paragraph 1, and article 23, paragraph 1, of the International Covenant on Civil and Political Rights.

5. State responsibility in cases of secret detention by proxy

36. Secret detention, involving the denial or concealment of a person's detention, whereabouts or fate has the inherent consequence of placing the person outside the protection of the law. The practice of "proxy detention", where persons are transferred from one State to another outside the realm of any international or national legal procedure ("rendition" or "extraordinary rendition") for the specific purpose of secretly detaining them, or to exclude the possibility of review by the domestic courts of the State having custody of the detainee, or otherwise in violation of the well-entrenched principle of non-refoulement, entails exactly the same consequence. The practice of "proxy detention" involves the responsibility of both the State that is detaining the victim and the State on whose behalf or at whose behest the detention takes place.

37. According to article 2, clause 1, of the International Covenant on Civil and Political Rights, each State party undertakes to respect and to ensure to all individuals within its territory and subject to its jurisdiction the rights recognized in the Covenant, without distinction of any kind, such as race, colour, sex, language, religion, political or other opinion, national or social origin, property, birth or other status. The Human Rights Committee clarified, in its general comment No. 31, that a State party must respect and ensure the rights laid down in the Covenant to anyone within the power or effective control of that State party, even if not situated within the territory of the State party. Similarly, the International Court of Justice, in its advisory opinion on the *Legal Consequences of the Construction of a Wall in the Occupied Palestinian Territories*, recognized that the jurisdiction of States is primarily territorial, but concluded that the Covenant extends to "acts done by a State in the exercise of its jurisdiction outside of its own territory". An excessively literal reading of article 2, paragraph 1 of the Covenant would defeat the very purpose of the Covenant. As far as the Convention against Torture is concerned, article 2, paragraph 1, and article 16, paragraph 1, refer to each State party's obligation to prevent acts of torture "in any territory under its jurisdiction".

38. The removal of a person to a State for the purpose of holding that person in secret detention, or the exclusion of the possibility of review by domestic courts of the sending State, can never be considered compatible with the obligation laid down in article 2, paragraph 2, of the International Covenant on Civil and Political Rights. The Working Group on Arbitrary Detention has dismissed this practice of "reverse diplomatic assurances", in which the sending Government seeks assurances that the person handed over will be deprived of liberty, even though there are no criminal charges against him and no other recognizable legal basis for detention, as being at variance with international law. In its opinion No. 11/2007, the Working Group, concurring with the view of the Human Rights Committee expressed in its general comment No. 31, declared the Government of Afghanistan responsible for the arbitrary detention of an individual who was being detained at Bagram Airbase, under the control of the United States of America, but on Afghan soil with the knowledge of Afghan authorities.

39. Similarly, the Convention against Torture and other cruel, inhuman or degrading treatment or punishment not only expressly bans torture, but in its article 4, paragraph 1, it also implicitly prohibits complicity in acts of torture, as it requires each State party to ensure that all acts of torture, including those acts by any person that constitute complicity or participation in torture, are criminal offences under its criminal law. This approach has been supported by the Committee against Torture in its jurisprudence. In particular, the Committee considered complicity to include acts that amount to instigation, incitement, superior order and instruction, consent, acquiescence and concealment.

40. A State would thus also be responsible when it was aware of the risk of torture and ill-treatment, or ought to have been aware of the risk, inherently associated with the establishment or operation of such a facility or a given transfer to the facility, and did not take reasonable steps to prevent it; or when the State has received claims that someone had been subjected to torture or other ill-treatment, or an enforced

disappearance, or otherwise received information suggesting that such acts may have taken place but failed to have the claims impartially investigated.

41. A transferring State could also be internationally responsible under general rules of attribution of State responsibility for internationally wrongful acts. Recognizing that internationally wrongful conduct is often the result of the collaboration of more than one State, rather than one State acting alone—particularly found to be the case in the phenomenon of secret detention practices of the so called "global war on terror"— the general principles of State responsibility under international law establish the unlawfulness of the complicity of States in wrongful acts. In particular, a State that aids or assists another State in the commission of an internationally wrongful act is internationally responsible if it does so knowing the circumstances and if the act would have been wrongful if it had been committed by the assisting State. The real or probable conduct by another State may be decisive in assessing whether the first State has breached its own international obligations. Article 16 of the Articles on Responsibility of the Status for Internationally Wrongful Acts, reflecting a rule of customary international law, provides that: A State which aids or assists another State in the commission of an internationally wrongful act by the latter is internationally responsible for doing so if: (a) that State does so with knowledge of the circumstances of the internationally wrongful act; and (b) the act would be internationally wrongful if committed by that State.

42. Additionally, under the rules of State responsibility, where one State is in "serious breach" of its obligations under peremptory norms of international law—as would be the case if a State were to be torturing detainees—other States have a duty to cooperate to bring such a serious breach of the prohibition against torture to an end, and are required not to give any aid or assistance to its continuation.

43. Furthermore, the practice of "proxy detention" by a State in circumstances where there is a risk of torture in the hands of the receiving State could amount to a violation of the State's obligation under customary international law on non-refoulement—that is, not to transfer a person to another State where there are substantial grounds for believing that the person would be in danger of being subjected to torture. The Declaration on the Protection of All Persons from Enforced Disappearance and the International Convention for the Protection of All Persons from Enforced Disappearance states that the principle of non-refoulement applies to the risk of enforced disappearances. Article 17, paragraph 1, of the International Convention provides that "no State party shall expel, return ('refouler'), surrender or extradite a person to another State where there are substantial grounds for believing that he or she would be in danger of being subjected to enforced disappearance." The Working Group on Arbitrary Detention has argued that the risk of arbitrary detention in the country of destination, which includes secret detention, should prohibit the transfer of a person into the jurisdiction of the receiving State as well. Diplomatic assurances from the receiving State for the purpose of overcoming the obstacle of the non-refoulement principle do not release States from their obligations under international human rights, humanitarian and refugee law, in particular the principle of non-refoulement.

6. Secret detention and derogations from international human rights

44. Article 4, paragraph 1, of the International Covenant on Civil and Political Rights permits States to derogate from certain rights contained therein "in times of public emergency which threatens the life of the nation". However, this provision subjects such measures to a number of procedural and substantive safeguards regarding derogation measures: the State must have officially proclaimed a state of emergency; the derogation measures must be limited to those strictly required by the exigencies of the situation; they must not be inconsistent with other international obligations of the State; and they must not be discriminatory. In its general comment No. 29, the Human Rights Committee highlighted the exceptional and temporary character of derogations, stating that the Covenant required that, even during an armed conflict, measures derogating from the Covenant were allowed only if and to the extent that the situation constituted a threat to the life of the nation. Derogation measures must be lifted as soon as the public emergency or armed conflict ceases to exist. Most importantly, derogation measures must be "strictly required" by the emergency situation. This requirement of proportionality implies that derogations cannot be justified when the same aim could be achieved through less intrusive means.

45. Article 4, paragraph 2, of the Covenant lists certain rights that cannot be derogated from, including the prohibition of torture or cruel, inhuman or degrading treatment or punishment (art. 7).

46. Although articles 9 and 14 of the Covenant are not among the non-derogable rights enumerated in article 4, paragraph 2, the Human Rights Committee confirmed in its general comment No. 29 that the prohibitions against taking of hostages, abductions or unacknowledged detention were not subject to

derogation. It also considered that it was inherent in the protection of rights explicitly recognized as non-derogable in article 4, paragraph 2, that they must be secured by procedural guarantees, including, often, judicial guarantees. The provisions of the Covenant relating to procedural safeguards could never be made subject to measures that would circumvent the protection of non-derogable rights. Article 4 may not be resorted to in a way that would result in derogation from non-derogable rights. Safeguards related to deroga-tion, as embodied in article 4 of the Covenant, were based on the principles of legality and the rule of law inherent in the Covenant as a whole. As certain elements of the right to a fair trial are explicitly guaranteed under international humanitarian law during armed conflict, the Committee found no justification for dero-gation from these guarantees during other emergency situations, and was of the opinion that the principles of legality and the rule of law required that fundamental requirements of fair trial be respected during a state of emergency. Only a court of law could try and convict a person for a criminal offence. The presumption of innocence has to be respected. In order to protect non-derogable rights, the right to take proceedings before a court to enable the court to decide without delay on the lawfulness of detention should not be diminished by a State party's decision to derogate from the Covenant.

47. In short, the main elements of articles 9 and 14 of the Covenant, namely the right to *habeas corpus*, the presumption of innocence and minimum fair trial guarantees, as well as the prohibition of acknowledged detention, must be respected even in times of emergency, including armed conflict.

48. The Working Group on Arbitrary Detention, in its opinions No. 43/2006, 2/2009 and 3/2009, con-curred with the view of the Human Rights Committee that the right to *habeas corpus* must prevail even in states of emergency. The Working Group similarly stated that the right not to be detained incommunicado over prolonged periods of time could not be derogated from, even where a threat to the life of the nation existed.

49. The Working Group on Enforced or Involuntary Disappearances confirmed in its general comment on article 10 of the Declaration on the Protection of All Persons from Enforced Disappearance that under no circumstances, including states of war or public emergency, could any State interest be invoked to justify or legitimize secret centres or places of detention which, by definition, would violate the Declaration, without exception.

50. As the disappearance of persons is inseparably linked to treatment that amounts to a violation of article 7 of the Covenant, according to the jurisprudence of the Human Rights Committee,52 the prohibi-tion against enforced disappearance must not be derogated from, either. Similarly, article 1, paragraph 2, of the International Convention for the Protection of All Persons from Enforced Disappearance stipulates: No exceptional circumstances whatsoever, whether a state of war or a threat of war, internal political instability or any other public emergency, may be invoked as a justification for enforced disappearance.

51. Even if one were (wrongfully) to classify the global struggle against international terrorism in its entirety as a "war" for the purpose of applying the Third and Fourth Geneva Conventions, international human rights law continues to apply: the Covenant applies also in situations of armed conflict to which the rules of international humanitarian law are applicable.

While, in respect of certain Covenant rights, more specific rules of international humanitarian law may be especially relevant for the purposes of the interpretation of those rights, both spheres of law are comple-mentary, not mutually exclusive.

52. In its advisory opinion on the *Legality of the Threat or Use of Nuclear Weapons*, the International Court of Justice clearly affirmed the applicability of the Covenant during armed conflicts, stating that "the right not arbitrarily to be deprived of one's life applies also in hostilities. The test of what constitutes an arbitrary depri-vation of life, however, then must be determined by the applicable *lex specialis*, namely, the law applicable in armed conflict." The Court further developed its view in its advisory opinion on the *Legal Consequences of the Construction of a Wall in the Occupied Palestinian Territories*: The protection offered by human rights conven-tions does not cease in case of armed conflict, save through the effect of provisions for derogation of the kind to be found in article 4 of the [International Covenant on Civil and Political Rights]. As regards the relation-ship between international humanitarian law and human rights law, there are thus three possible situations: some rights may be exclusively matters of international humanitarian law; others may be exclusively matters of human rights law; yet others may be matters of both these branches of international law.

53. In its judgement in the Case concerning Armed Activities on the Territory of the Congo *Democratic Republic of the Congo v Uganda*), the Court already applied international humanitarian law and international human rights law in parallel, without as a first step identifying the *lex specialis* or the exclusive matter. In their report on the mission to Lebanon and Israel from 7 to 14 September 2006, the Special Rapporteur on

extrajudicial, summary or arbitrary executions, the Special Rapporteur on the right of everyone to the enjoyment of the highest attainable standard of physical and mental health, the Representative of the Secretary-General on the human rights of internally displaced persons and the Special Rapporteur on adequate housing as a component of the right to an adequate standard of living stated that human rights law and international humanitarian law were not mutually exclusive, but existed in a complementary relationship during armed conflict; a full legal analysis required consideration of both bodies of law. In respect of certain human rights, more specific rules of international humanitarian law might be relevant for the purposes of their interpretation. A complementary approach forming the basis of the present study is also supported by the principle of systemic integration contained in article 31, paragraph 3 (c), of the Vienna Convention on the Law of Treaties, which provides that, in interpreting an international treaty there shall be taken into account, together with the context … any relevant rules of international law applicable in the relations between the parties [of the treaty]." stated that in the case of a conflict between the provisions of the two legal regimes [international humanitarian law and international human rights law] with regard to a specific situation, the *lex specialis* will have to be identified and applied.

7. Secret detention and international humanitarian law

54. International humanitarian law prohibits secret detention as clearly as international human rights law does. Under the Geneva Conventions, which apply to all armed conflicts, there are situations in which persons falling into two categories may be detained: prisoners of war and civilians. Generally, prisoners of war are to be released at the end of active hostilities. Civilians may be detained by an occupying power under very strict conditions, namely (a) if such detention is "necessary for imperative reasons of security" and (b) for penal prosecutions. The use of novel status designations to avoid Geneva Convention protections, such as "unlawful enemy combatants", is irrelevant in this context from a legal point of view, as "it does not constitute a category recognized and defined under international law". This is true also for non-international armed conflicts, albeit the notion of prisoners of war is not directly applicable.

55. Notwithstanding the capacity to detain individuals, the entire system of detention provided for by the Geneva Conventions is founded on the notion that detainees must be registered and held in officially recognized places of detention. According to article 70 of the Third Geneva Convention, prisoners of war are to be documented, and their whereabouts and health conditions made available to family members and to the country of origin of the prisoner within one week.

Article 106 of the Fourth Geneva Convention governing the treatment of civilians establishes virtually identical procedures for the documentation and disclosure of information concerning civilian detainees. According to ICRC, these procedures are meant to ensure that internment is not a measure of punishment; interned persons must therefore not be held incommunicado. The prohibition of enforced disappearance is a rule of customary international humanitarian law applicable in all situations of armed conflict.

56. As incommunicado detention is also prohibited under international humanitarian law applicable to all armed conflicts65 and to all persons who no longer take direct part in hostilities, detainees must be registered, provided an effective opportunity to immediately inform their family and a centralized information bureau of their detention and any subsequent transfer, and must be permitted ongoing contact with family members and others outside the place of detention. Article 5 of the Fourth Geneva Convention permits the detaining power to deny to persons these rights and privileges "where absolute military security so requires" when an individual found physically in the State's own territory is "definitely suspected of or engaged in activities hostile to the security of the State", or when an individual in occupied territory is "detained as a spy or saboteur, or as a person under definite suspicion of activity hostile to the security of the Occupying Power". While the article states that these persons "shall also be granted the full rights and privileges of a protected person under the present Convention at the earliest date consistent with the security of the State or Occupying Power", ICRC stresses that article 5 may only be applied in individual cases of an exceptional nature, when the existence of specific charges makes it almost certain that penal proceedings will follow. Bare suspicion of hostile activities would not suffice; it would have to be a definite suspicion of such activities. The burden of definite suspicion is a high burden that must be individualized and must not be of a general nature.

III. SECRET DETENTION PRACTICES IN PAST CONTEXTS
A. The emergence of the recent practice of secret detention

57. The phenomenon of secret detention, closely intertwined with enforced disappearances, can be traced at least to the *Nacht und Nebel Erlafl* of the Nazi Germany, the "night and fog decree", according to which suspected resistance movement members could be arrested in occupied Europe and secretly transferred

to Germany "under cover of night". These measures were intended to have a deterrent effect, because detainees would vanish without leaving a trace and no information would be given as to their whereabouts or fate.

58. An incipient form of these practices was, however, already well known in the former Soviet Union, with its Gulag system of forced-labour camps, first established under Vladimir Lenin during the early Bolshevik years. The Gulag system ultimately resulted in a vast penal network, including hundreds of camp complexes, which functioned throughout the State, many in Siberia and the Soviet Far East. The system was enhanced after 1928 under Joseph Stalin.

59. Even though the above-mentioned practices were encompassed in a broader context of war or perpetuation of a state of terror, secret detention in the context of counter-terrorism is not a new phenomenon. Striking similarities can be identified between security measures in the 1970s and 1980s in the context of Latin America, but also other regions, such as northern Africa and South-East Asia, on the one hand, and the counter-terrorism measures adopted worldwide since 11 September 2001, on the other. The methods used then, as now, consisted of, inter alia, broad emergency laws, the enhanced role of military and special courts, the practice of torture and/or ill-treatment, kidnappings (renditions), enforced disappearances and notably secret detention.
B. The recent practice of secret detention
1. Secret detention in Latin America

60. Secret detention in Latin America was closely linked to the widespread pattern of enforced disappearances. On the basis of the reports produced by various national truth and reconciliation commissions, in the 1970s and 1980s, patterns of secret detention were identified in, inter alia, Argentina, Brazil, Chile, El Salvador, Paraguay, Peru and Uruguay. Thousands of Latin Americans were secretly kidnapped, tortured and killed by national security services. When these dictatorial regimes came to an end, some of the countries, on the basis of their archives, decided to prosecute former Government officials, as well as police and military officers. In other countries these attempts have long been hampered by impunity created as a result of, inter alia, amnesty laws or pardons.

C. The United Nations and regional responses towards the outlawing of the practice of secret detention . The United Nations has paid increasing attention to the issue of secret detention and its relation to enforced disappearances since 1978, in the context of denunciations by numerous non-governmental organizations and widespread concerns with human rights situations in Chile, Cyprus and Argentina. The Inter-American Commission on Human Rights was one of the first international human rights bodies to respond to the phenomenon of enforced disappearances and secret detentions during the 1970s, both in general terms and with regard to specific cases in Chile since the military coup d'état of 11 September 1973.

...

93. Following the 1988 session of the Working Group on Detention, a draft declaration on the protection of all persons from enforced or involuntary disappearances was proposed and, following amendments by the intersessional working group, was adopted first by the Commission on Human Rights in its resolution 1992/29, then in the same year by the General Assembly in its resolution 47/133.

94. Ever since, the Commission continuously called upon its special rapporteurs and working groups to give special attention to questions relating to the effective protection of human rights in the administration of justice, in particular with regard to unacknowledged detention of persons, and to provide, wherever appropriate, specific recommendation in this regard, including proposals for possible concrete measures under advisory services programmes.

95. In 1988, in its resolution 43/173, the General Assembly adopted the Body of Principles for the Protection of All Persons under Any Form of Detention or Imprisonment. This was the result of a long-standing process of ascertaining detainees' rights that had begun under the Subcommission on Prevention of Discrimination and Protection of Minorities. This instrument provides for the application of a set of safeguards while in detention, compliance with which in principle would avoid or substantially decrease the likelihood of threat to life and limb of detainees. The adoption of the document served as an incentive for the elaboration of complementary regional instruments, such as the Guidelines and Measures for the Prohibition and Prevention of Torture, Cruel, Inhuman or Degrading Treatment or Punishment in Africa, adopted by the African Commission on Human and Peoples' Rights in its resolution 61 (XXXII) 02 (2002), and the Principles and Best Practices on the Protection of Persons Deprived of Liberty in the Americas, of the Inter-American Commission on Human Rights.

...

97. A decisive moment in the long-standing process of outlawing practices of secret detention was the adoption of the International Convention on the Protection of All Persons from Forced Disappearance, which has been open for signature and ratification since 6 February 2007. This process started in 2001, when the Commission on Human Rights requested a study to identify any gaps in the existing international criminal and human rights framework with a view to drafting a legally-binding normative instrument for the protection of all persons from enforced disappearance. On the basis of the study prepared by an independent expert on the existing international criminal and human rights framework for the protection of persons from enforced or involuntary disappearances, and with his assistance, the Commission drafted the International Convention on the Protection of All Persons from Forced Disappearance, the final text of which was adopted by the Human Rights Council in its resolution 2006/1. The Convention contains elements necessary for filling the gaps in the framework of the current protection against enforced disappearances and secret detentions.

IV. SECRET DETENTION PRACTICES IN THE GLOBAL "WAR ON TERROR" SINCE 11 SEPTEMBER 2001

98. In spite of the prominent role played by the United States of America in the development of international human rights and humanitarian law, and its position as a global leader in the protection of human rights at home and abroad following the terrorist attacks on New York and Washington, D.C. on 11 September 2001, the U.S. embarked on a process of reducing and removing various human rights and other protection mechanisms through various laws and administrative acts, including the Authorization for Use of Military Force, the USA Patriot Act of 2001, the Detainee Treatment Act of 2005, the Military Commissions Act of 2006 (which sought to remove habeas corpus rights), as well as various executive orders and memoranda issued by the Office of Legal Counsel that interpreted the position of the U.S. on a number of issues, including torture. It also sanctioned the establishment of various classified programmes much more narrowly than before.

99. The Government of the U.S. declared a global "war on terror", in which individuals captured around the world were to be held neither as criminal suspects, put forward for federal court trials in the U.S., nor treated as prisoners of war protected by the Geneva Conventions, irrespective of whether they had been captured on the battlefield during what could be qualified as an armed conflict in terms of international humanitarian law. Rather, they were to be treated indiscriminately as "unlawful enemy combatants" who could be held indefinitely without charge or trial or the possibility to challenge the legality of their detention before a court or other judicial authority.

100. On 7 February 2002, the President of the U.S. issued a memorandum declaring that "common article 3 of Geneva does not apply to either Al-Qaida or Taliban detainees", that "Taliban detainees are unlawful combatants and, therefore, do not qualify as prisoners of war under article 4 of Geneva", and that "because Geneva does not apply to our conflict with Al-Qaida, Al-Qaida detainees also do not qualify as prisoners of war". This unprecedented departure from the Geneva Conventions was to be offset by a promise that, "as a matter of policy, the U.S. Armed Forces shall continue to treat detainees humanely and, to the extent appropriate and consistent with military necessity, in a manner consistent with the principles of Geneva". This detention policy was defended by the Government in various submissions to the United Nations, including on 10 October 2007, when the Government stated that the law of war, and not the International Covenant on Civil and Political Rights, was the applicable legal framework governing the detentions of "enemy combatants", and therefore such detentions did not fall within the mandate of the special procedures mandate holders.

101. By using this war paradigm, the U.S. purported to limit the applicable legal framework of the law of war (international humanitarian law) and exclude any application of human rights law. Even if and when human rights law were to apply, the Government was of the view that it was not bound by human rights law outside the territory of the U.S.. Therefore, by establishing detention centres in Guantánamo Bay and other places around the world, the U.S. was of the view that human rights law would not be applicable there. Guantánamo and other places of detention outside U.S. territory were intended to be outside the reach of domestic courts for habeas corpus applications by those held in custody in those places. One of the consequences of this policy was that many detainees were kept secretly and without access to the protection accorded to those in custody, namely the protection of the Geneva Conventions, international human rights law, the U.S. Constitution and various other domestic laws.

102. The secret detention policy took many forms. The Central Intelligence Agency (CIA) established its own secret detention facilities to interrogate so-called "high value detainees". It asked partners with poor human rights records to secretly detain and interrogate persons on its behalf. When the conflicts in Afghanistan and Iraq started, the U.S. secretly held persons in battlefield detention sites for prolonged periods of time. The present chapter therefore focuses on various secret detention sites and those held there, and also highlights examples of the complicity of other States.

A. The "high-value detainee" programme and CIA secret detention facilities

103. On 17 September 2001, President Bush sent a 12-page memorandum to the Director of the CIA through the National Security Council, which authorized the CIA to detain terrorists and set up detention facilities outside the U.S.. Until 2005, when the United Nations sent its first of many communications regarding this programme to the Government of the U.S., little was known about the extent and the details of the secret detention programme. Only in May 2009 could a definitive number of detainees in the programme be established. In a released, yet still redacted, memo, Principal Deputy Assistant Attorney General Stephen G. Bradbury stated that, to date, the CIA had taken custody of 94 detainees [redacted], and had employed enhanced techniques to varying degrees in the interrogations of 28 of those detainees.

104. In the report of 2007 on his country visit to the U.S. (A/HRC/6/17/Add.3), the Special Rapporteur on the promotion and protection of human rights and fundamental freedoms while countering terrorism described what was known at that time of these "enhanced techniques" and how they were regarded:

As a result of an apparent internal leak from the CIA, the media in the U.S. learned and published information about "enhanced interrogation techniques" used by the CIA in its interrogation of terrorist suspects and possibly other persons held because of page 46 their links with such suspects. Various sources have spoken of techniques involving physical and psychological means of coercion, including stress positions, extreme temperature changes, sleep deprivation, and "waterboarding" (means by which an interrogated person is made to feel as if drowning). With reference to the well-established practice of bodies such as the Human Rights Committee and the Committee against Torture, the Special Rapporteur concludes that these techniques involve conduct that amounts to a breach of the prohibition against torture and any form of cruel, inhuman or degrading treatment.

105. Several of the 28 detainees who, according to Mr. Bradbury, were subjected to "enhanced techniques to varying degrees" were also "high value detainees". Fourteen people were transferred from secret CIA custody in an undisclosed location to confinement at the Defense Department's detention facility in Guantánamo Bay, as announced by President Bush on 6 September 2006. They were: Abu Zubaydah (Palestinian), captured in Faisalabad, Pakistan, on 28 March 2002, Ramzi bin al-Shibh (Yemeni), captured in Karachi, Pakistan, on 11 September 2002, Abd al-Rahim al-Nashiri (Saudi), captured in the United Arab Emirates in October or November 2002, Khalid Sheikh Mohammed (Pakistani), captured in Rawalpindi, Pakistan, on 1 March 2003, Mustafa al-Hawsawi (Saudi), captured with Khalid Sheikh Mohammed in Rawalpindi, Pakistan, on 1 March 2003, Majid Khan (Pakistani), captured in Karachi, Pakistan, on 5 March 2003, Waleed Mohammed bin Attash (Yemeni), also known as Khallad, captured in Karachi, Pakistan, on 29 April 2003....

106. Beyond the transcripts of the Combatant Status Review Tribunals, held in 2007, and the facts reported in opinion No. 29/2006 (United States of America), adopted by the Working Group on Arbitrary Detention on 1 September 2006, the only available source on the conditions in the above-mentioned facilities is a report by ICRC leaked to the media by U.S. Government officials. In spite of the fact that the ICRC report was never officially published, the experts decided to refer to it since information on the 14 was scarce and the United States of America, in spite of requests to be allowed to speak to Guantánamo detainees, did not authorize them to do so. That report details the treatment that most of the 14 had described during individual interviews, and concluded that there had been cases of beatings, kicking, confinement in a box, forcible shaving, threats, sleep deprivation, deprivation/restriction on food provisions, stress positions, exposure to cold temperatures/cold water, suffocation by water and so on. It stressed that, for the entire detention periods, which ranged from 16 months to more than 3 and a half years, all 14 persons had been held in solitary confinement and incommunicado detention. According to the report, they had no knowledge of where they were being held, and no contact with persons other than their interrogators or guards." ICRC concluded that Twelve of the fourteen alleged that they were subjected to systematic physical and/or psychological ill-treatment. This was a consequence of both the treatment and the material conditions which formed part of the interrogation regime, as well as the overall detention regime. This regime was clearly designed to under-

mine human dignity and to create a sense of futility by inducing, in many cases, severe physical and mental pain and suffering, with the aim of obtaining compliance and extracting information, resulting in exhaustion, depersonalization and dehumanization. The allegations of ill-treatment of the detainees indicate that, in many cases, the ill-treatment to which they were subjected while held in the CIA program, either singly, or in combination, constituted torture. In addition, many other elements of the ill-treatment, either singly or in combination, constituted cruel inhuman or degrading treatment."

107. Despite the acknowledgement in September 2006 by President Bush of the existence of secret CIA detention facilities, the U.S. Government and the Governments of the States that hosted these facilities have generally refused to disclose their location or even existence. The specifics of the secret sites have, for the most part, been revealed through off-the-record disclosures.

108. In November 2005, for example, the Washington Post referred to "current and former intelligence officers and two other US Government officials" as sources for the contention that there had been a secret CIA black site or safe house in Thailand, "which included underground interrogation cells". 179 One month later, ABC news reported on the basis of testimonies from "current and former CIA officers" that Abu Zubaydah had been:

Whisked by the CIA to Thailand where he was housed in a small, disused warehouse on an active airbase. There, his cell was kept under 24-hour closed circuit TV surveillance and his life-threatening wounds were tended to by a CIA doctor specially sent from Langley headquarters to assure Abu Zubaydah was given proper care, sources said. Once healthy, he was slapped, grabbed, made to stand long hours in a cold cell, and finally handcuffed and strapped feet up to a water board until after 0.31 seconds he begged for mercy and began to cooperate. The details of Abu Zubaydah's treatment have been confirmed by his initial FBI interrogator, who has not confirmed or denied that the location where Abu Zubaydah was held was in Thailand. The Washington Post also reported that the officials had stated that Ramzi Binalshibh had been flown to Thailand after his capture.

The New York Times again stated in 2006 that Abu Zubaydah was held in Thailand "according to accounts from five former and current government officials who were briefed on the case."183 In January 2008, the Asia Times reported that political analysts and diplomats in Thailand suspected that the detention facility was "situated at a military base in the northeastern province of Udon Thani".

. . .

VI. CONCLUSIONS AND RECOMMENDATIONS
A. Conclusions

282. International law clearly prohibits secret detention, which violates a number of human rights and humanitarian law norms that may not be derogated from under any circumstances. If secret detention constitutes enforced disappearances and is widely or systematically practiced, it may even amount to a crime against humanity. However, inspite of these unequivocal norms, secret detention continues to be used in the name of countering terrorism around the world. The evidence gathered by the four experts for the present study clearly shows that many States, referring to concerns relating to national security—often perceived or presented as unprecedented emergencies or threats—resort to secret detention.

283. Resorting to secret detention effectively means taking detainees outside the legalframework and rendering the safeguards contained in international instruments, most importantly habeas corpus, meaningless. The most disturbing consequence of secret detention is, as many of the experts' interlocutors pointed out, the complete arbitrariness of the situation, together with the uncertainty about the duration of the secret detention and the feeling that there is no way the individual can regain control of his or her life.

284. A comparison of past and more recent practices of secret detention brings to the fore many common features, despite considerable variations in political and social contexts.

1. Emergency contexts

285. States of emergency, international wars and the fight against terrorism—often framed in vaguely defined legal provisions—constitute an "enabling environment" for secret detention. As in the past, extraordinary powers are today conferred on authorities, including armed forces, law enforcement bodies and/or intelligence agencies, under states of emergency or global war paradigms either without or with very restricted control mechanisms by parliaments or judicial bodies. This thus renders many, or even all, of the safeguards contained in criminal law and required by international human rights law ineffective. In some States, protracted states of emergency and broadly defined conflicts against vaguely conceived enemies have tended to turn exceptional, temporary rules into the norm.

2. Intelligence agencies

286. In many contexts, intelligence agencies operate in a legal vacuum with no law, or no publicly available law, governing their actions. Although intelligence bodies are not authorized by legislation to detain persons, they do so many times, sometimes for prolonged periods. In such situations, there are either no oversight and accountability mechanisms at all, or they are severely restricted, with limited powers, and hence ineffective.

3. International cooperation

287. From operation Condor in South America through to the global CIA network, secret detention has relied on systems of trans-border (regional or global) cooperation. This means that, in many instances, foreign security forces may operate freely in the territory of other States. It also leads to the mutual exchange of intelligence information between States, followed by its use for the purpose of detaining or trying the person before tribunals, the proceedings of which do not comply with international norms, often with reference to State secrets, making it impossible to verify how the information was obtained. 490 A crucial element in international cooperation, be it in the methods of operation Condor of the 1970s or the current policies of "extraordinary rendition", is the transfer of alleged terrorists to other countries, where they may face a substantial risk of being subjected to torture and other cruel, inhuman and degrading treatment in contravention of the principle of non-refoulement. Worse, in some cases, persons have been rendered to other countries precisely to circumvent the prohibition of torture and "rough" treatment. Practices such as "hosting" secret detention sites or providing proxy detention have, however, been supplemented by numerous other facets of complicity, including authorizing the landing of airplanes for refuelling, short-term deprivation of liberty before handing over the "suspect", the covering up of kidnappings, and so on. With very few exceptions, too little has been done to investigate allegations of complicity.

288. While the experts welcome the cooperation extended by a number of States, including through the responses submitted by 44 of them to the questionnaire, they express their regret that, although States have the obligation to investigate secret detention, many did not send responses, and a majority of those received did not contain sufficient information.

A lack of access to States' territories also meant that a number of interviews had to be conducted by telephone or Skype, with those interviewed fearing being monitored.

4. Torture and cruel, inhuman and degrading treatment.

289. Secret detention as such may constitute torture or ill-treatment for the direct victims as well as for their families. As many of the interviews and cases included in the present study illustrate, however, the very purpose of secret detention is to facilitate and, ultimately, cover up torture and inhuman and degrading treatment used either to obtain information or to silence people. While in some cases elaborate rules have been put in place to authorize "enhanced" techniques that violate international standards of human rights and humanitarian law, most of the time secret detention has been used as a kind of defence shield to avoid scrutiny and control, as well as to make it impossible to learn about treatment and conditions during detention.

5. Impact on other human rights and freedoms

290. The generalized fear of secret detention and its corollaries, such as torture and ill-treatment, tends to effectively result in limiting the exercise of a large number of human rights and fundamental freedoms, including freedom of expression and freedom of association. This fear often goes hand in hand with the intimidation of witnesses, victims and their families. Moreover, independent judiciaries and secret detention can hardly coexist; several examples identified by the experts indicated that the broader use of secret detention tends to lead to attempts to either influence or, worse, silence judges who take up cases of secret detention.

6. Witness protection and reparation

291. The experts are extremely concerned that many victims of secret detention from countries around the world indicated that they feared reprisals personally or against their families if they cooperated with the study and/or allowed their names to be used. The injustice done by secretly detaining somebody is prolonged and replicated all too frequently once the victims are released, because the State concerned may try to avoid any disclosure about the fact that secret detention is practiced on its territory. In almost no recent cases has there been any judicial investigation into allegations of secret detention, and practically no one has been brought to justice. Although many victims feel that secret detention has "stolen" years of their lives (the experts learned about one anonymous case of 30 years) and left an indelible mark, often in terms of loss of their jobs and frequently their health, they have almost never received any rehabilitation or compensation.

B. Recommendations

292. On the basis of the above conclusions, the experts put forward the recommendations set out below. In practice, concrete measures will need to be taken, depending on the specific context:

(a) Secret detention should be explicitly prohibited, along with all other forms of unofficial detention. Detention records should be kept, including in times of armed conflict as required by the Geneva Conventions, including with regard to the number of detainees, their nationality and the legal basis on which they are being held, whether as prisoners of war or civilian internees. Internal inspections and independent mechanisms should have timely access to all places where persons are deprived of their liberty for monitoring purposes at all times. In times of armed conflict, the location of all detention facilities should be disclosed to the International Committee of the Red Cross;

(b) Safeguards for persons deprived of their liberty should be fully respected. No undue restrictions on these safeguards under counter-terrorism or emergency legislation are permissible. In particular, effective habeas corpus reviews by independent judicial bodies are central to ensuring respect for the right to personal liberty. Therefore, domestic legislative frameworks should not allow for any exceptions from habeas corpus, operating independently from the detaining authority and from the place and form of deprivation of liberty. The study has shown that judicial bodies play a crucial role in protecting people against secret detention. The law should foresee penalties for officials who refuse to disclose relevant information during habeas corpus proceedings; (c) All steps necessary to ensure that the immediate families of those detained are informed of their relatives' capture, location, legal status and condition of health should be taken in a timely manner;

(d) Any action by intelligence services should be governed by law, which in turn should be in conformity with international norms. To ensure accountability in intelligence cooperation, truly independent intelligence review and oversight mechanisms should be established and enhanced. Such mechanisms should have access to any information, including sensitive information. They should be mandated to undertake reviews and investigate upon their initiative, and to make reports public:

(e) Institutions strictly independent of those that have been allegedly involved in secret detention should investigate promptly any allegations of secret detention and "extraordinary rendition". Those individuals who are found to have participated in secretly detaining persons and any unlawful acts perpetrated during such detention, including their superiors if they ordered, encouraged or consented to secret detentions, should be prosecuted without delay and, where found guilty, given sentences commensurate with the gravity of the acts perpetrated;

(f) The status of all pending investigations into allegations of ill-treatment and torture of detainees and detainee deaths in custody must be made public. No evidence or information that has been obtained by torture or cruel, inhuman and degrading treatment may be used in any proceedings;

(g) Transfers or the facilitation of transfers from one State to the custody of authorities of another State must be carried out under judicial supervision and in line with international standards. The principle of non-refoulement of persons to countries where they would be at risk of torture or other inhuman, cruel or degrading treatment must be honoured;

(h) Victims of secret detention should be provided with judicial remedies and reparation in accordance with relevant international norms. These international standards recognize the right of victims to adequate, effective and prompt reparation, which should be proportionate to the gravity of the violations and the harm suffered. As families of disappeared persons have been recognized as victims under international law, they should also benefit from rehabilitation and compensation;

(i) States should ratify and implement the International Covenant on Civil and Political Rights and the Convention against Torture and Other Cruel, Inhuman or Degrading Treatment or Punishment. Given that the Optional Protocol to the Convention against Torture requires the setting-up of monitoring systems covering all situations of deprivation of liberty, adhering to this international instrument adds a layer of protection. States should ratify the Optional Protocol and create independent national preventive mechanisms that are in compliance with the Paris Principles (Principles relating to the status of national institutions), and ratify the International Convention for the Protection of All Persons from Enforced Disappearance. Other regional systems may wish to replicate the system put in place by the Inter-American Convention on Forced Disappearance of Persons;

(j) Governments have an obligation to protect their citizens abroad and provide consular protection to ensure that foreign States comply with their obligations under international law, including international human rights law; (k) Under international human rights law, States have the obligation to provide witness protection. Doing so is indeed a precondition for effectively combating secret detention.

Document 6: Compilation of good practices on legal and institutional frameworks and measures that ensure respect for human rights by intelligence agencies while countering terrorism, including on their oversight . (Excerpted)

UNITED NATIONS	A/HRC/14/46
General Assembly	Distr.:
HUMAN RIGHTS COUNCIL	GENERAL
Fourteenth session	17 May 2010
Agenda item 3	Original: ENGLISH

PROMOTION AND PROTECTION OF ALL HUMAN RIGHTS, CIVIL, POLITICAL, ECONOMIC, SOCIAL AND CULTURAL RIGHTS, INCLUDING THE RIGHT TO DEVELOPMENT

Report of the Special Rapporteur on the promotion and
protection of human rights and fundamental freedoms while
countering terrorism, Martin Scheinin*
Compilation of good practices on legal and institutional frameworks
and measures that ensure respect for human rights by intelligence
agencies while countering terrorism, including on their oversight**

Summary

The present document is a compilation of good practices on legal and institutional frameworks and measures that ensure respect for human rights by intelligence agencies while countering terrorism, including on their oversight, as requested by the Human Rights Council and prepared by the Special Rapporteur on the protection and promotion of human rights and fundamental freedoms while countering terrorism. The compilation is the outcome of a consultation process where Governments, experts and practitioners in various ways provided their input. In particular, written submissions received from Governments by a deadline of 1 May 2010 have been taken into account. The submissions will be reproduced in the form of an addendum (A/HRC/14/46/Add.1).

The outcome of the process is the identification of 35 elements of good practice. The elements of good practice were distilled from existing and emerging practices in abroad range of States throughout the world. The compilation also draws upon international treaties, resolutions of international organizations and the jurisprudence of regional courts.

The substance of the elements of good practice is explained in the commentary, usually presented separately for each of the 35 elements. The sources of good practice are identified in the footnotes to the commentary, which include references to individual States. The notion of "good practice" refers to legal and institutional frameworks that serve to promote human rights and the respect for the rule of law in the work of intelligence services. Good practice not only refers to what is required by international law, including human rights law, but goes beyond these legally-binding obligations. The 35 areas of good practice included in the compilation are grouped into four "baskets", namely legal basis (practices 1–5), oversight and accountability (practices 6–10 and 14–18), substantive human rights compliance (practices 11–13 and 19–20) and issues related to specific functions of intelligence agencies (practices 21–35).

Contents

I. Introduction*

1. The present compilation of good practice on legal and institutional frameworks for intelligence services and their oversight is the outcome of a consultation process mandated by the Human Rights Council, which, in its resolution 10/15, called upon the Special Rapporteur to prepare, working in consultation with States and other relevant stakeholders, a compilation of good practices on legal and institutional frameworks and measures that ensure respect for human rights by intelligence agencies while countering terrorism, including on their oversight.

2. Intelligence services1 play a critical role in protecting the State and its population against threats to national security, including terrorism. They help to enable States to fulfill their positive obligation to safeguard the human rights of all individuals under their jurisdiction. Hence, effective performance and the protection of human rights can be mutually complementary goals for intelligence services.

3. The compilation is distilled from existing and emerging practice from a broad range of States throughout the world. These practices are primarily derived from national laws, institutional models, as well as the jurisprudence and recommendations of national oversight institutions and a number of civil society organizations. The compilation also draws upon international treaties, resolutions of international organizations and the jurisprudence of regional courts. In this context, the notion of "good practice" refers to legal and institutional frameworks which serve to promote human rights and the respect for the rule of law in the work of intelligence services. "Good practice" not only refers to what is required by international law, including human rights law, but goes beyond these legally binding obligations.

4. Very few States have included all of the practices outlined below in their legal and institutional frameworks for intelligence services and their oversight. Some States will be able to identify themselves as following the majority of the 35 elements of good practice.

Other States may start by committing themselves to a small number of these elements which they consider as essential to promoting human rights compliance by intelligence services and their oversight bodies.

5. It is not the purpose of this compilation to promulgate a set of normative standards that should apply at all times and in all parts of the world. Hence, the elements of good practice presented in this report are formulated in descriptive, rather than normative, language. It is nevertheless possible to identify common practices that contribute to the respect for the rule of law and human rights by intelligence services.

6. The Human Rights Council mandated the present compilation of good practices within the context of the role of intelligence services in counter-terrorism. However, it should be noted that the legal and institutional frameworks which apply to intelligence services' counter-terrorism activities cannot be separated from those which apply to their activities more generally.

While international terrorism has, since 2001, changed the landscape for the operation of intelligence agencies, the effects of that change go beyond the field of counter-terrorism.

7. The compilation highlights examples of good practice from numerous national laws and institutional models. It is, however, important to note that the citation of specific provisions from national laws or

institutional models does not imply a general endorsement of these laws and institutions as good practice in protecting human rights in the context of counter-terrorism. Additionally, the Special Rapporteur wishes to emphasize that the existence of legal and institutional frameworks which represent good practice is essential, but not sufficient for ensuring that intelligence services respect human rights in their counter-terrorism activities.

8. The 35 areas of good practice presented below are grouped into four different "baskets", namely legal basis (1–5), oversight and accountability (6–10 and 14–18), substantive human rights compliance (11–13 and 19–20) and issues relating to specific functions of intelligence agencies (21–35). For reasons of presentation, the elements are grouped under a somewhat higher number of subheadings.

. . .

II. Compilation of good practices on legal and institutional frameworks for intelligence services and their oversight
A. Mandate and legal basis

Practice 1. Intelligence services play an important role in protecting national security and upholding the rule of law. Their main purpose is to collect, analyse and disseminate information that assists policymakers and other public entities in taking measures to protect national security. This includes the protection of the population and their human rights.

Practice 2. The mandates of intelligence services are narrowly and precisely defined in a publicly available law. Mandates are strictly limited to protecting legitimate national security interests as outlined in publicly available legislation or national security policies, and identify the threats to national security that intelligence services are tasked to address. If terrorism is included among these threats, it is defined in narrow and precise terms.

Practice 3. The powers and competences of intelligence services are clearly and exhaustively defined in national law. They are required to use these powers exclusively for the purposes for which they were given. In particular, any powers given to intelligence services for the purposes of counter-terrorism must be used exclusively for these purposes.

11. It is a fundamental tenet of the rule of law that all powers and competences of intelligence services are outlined in law. An exhaustive enumeration of the powers and competences of intelligence services promotes transparency and enables people to foresee what powers may be used against them.

This is particularly important given that many of the powers held by intelligence services have the potential to infringe upon human rights and fundamental freedoms. This practice is closely connected to practice 2, because the mandates of intelligence services serve to define the framework within which they can use the powers given by the legislature.

Practice 4. All intelligence services are constituted through, and operate under, publicly available laws that comply with the Constitution and international human rights law. Intelligence services can only undertake or be instructed to undertake activities that are prescribed by and in accordance with national law. The use of subsidiary regulations that are not publicly available is strictly limited, and such regulations are both authorized by and remain within the parameters of publicly available laws. Regulations that are not made public do not serve as the basis for any activities that restrict human rights.

Practice 5. Intelligence services are explicitly prohibited from undertaking any action that contravenes the Constitution or international human rights law. These prohibitions extend not only to the conduct of intelligence services on their national territory but also to their activities abroad.

12. Intelligence services are organs of the State and thus, in common with other executive bodies, are bound by relevant provisions of national and international law, and in particular human rights law. This implies that they are based upon and operate in accordance with publicly available laws that comply with the Constitution of the State, as well as, inter alia, the State's international human rights obligations. States cannot rely upon domestic law to justify violations of international human rights law or indeed any other international legal obligations. The rule of law requires that the activities of intelligence services and any instructions issued to them by the political executive comply with these bodies of law in all of their work. Accordingly, intelligence services are prohibited from undertaking, or being asked to undertake, any action that would violate national statutory law, the Constitution or the State's human rights obligations. In many States, these requirements are implicit; however, it is notably good practice for national legislation to make

explicit reference to these broader legal obligations and, in particular, to the obligation to respect human rights. Subordinate regulations pertaining to the internal processes and activities of intelligence services are sometimes withheld from the public in order to protect their working methods. These types of regulations do not serve as the basis for activities that infringe human rights. It is good practice for any subordinate regulation to be based on and comply with applicable public legislation.

B. Oversight institutions

Practice 6. Intelligence services are overseen by a combination of internal, executive, parliamentary, judicial and specialized oversight institutions whose mandates and powers are based on publicly available law. An effective system of intelligence oversight includes at least one civilian institution that is independent of both the intelligence services and the executive. The combined remit of oversight institutions covers all aspects of the work of intelligence services, including their compliance with the law; the effectiveness and efficiency of their activities; their finances; and their administrative practices.

13. In common with intelligence services, the institutions that oversee their activities are based on law and, in some cases, founded on the Constitution.

Practice 7. Oversight institutions have the power, resources and expertise to initiate and conduct their own investigations, as well as full and unhindered access to the information, officials and installations necessary to fulfil their mandates. Oversight institutions receive the full cooperation of intelligence services and law enforcement authorities in hearing witnesses, as well as obtaining documentation and other evidence.

14. Oversight institutions enjoy specific powers to enable them to perform their functions. In particular, they have the power to initiate their own investigations into areas of the intelligence service's work that fall under their mandates, and are granted access to all information necessary to do so. These powers of access to information encompass the legal authority to view all relevant files and documents, inspect the premises of intelligence services, and to summon any member of the intelligence services to give evidence under oath. These powers help to ensure that overseers can effectively scrutinize the activities of intelligence services and fully investigate possible contraventions of the law. A number of States have taken steps to reinforce the investigative competences of oversight institutions by criminalizing any failure to cooperate with them.

This implies that oversight institutions have recourse to law enforcement authorities in order to secure the cooperation of relevant individuals.31 While strong legal powers are essential for effective oversight, it is good practice for these to be accompanied by the human and financial resources needed to make use of these powers, and, thus, to fulfil their mandates.

Practice 8. Oversight institutions take all necessary measures to protect classified information and personal data to which they have access during the course of their work. Penalties are provided for the breach of these requirements by members of oversight institutions.

15. Intelligence oversight institutions have access to classified and sensitive information during the course of their work. Therefore, a variety of mechanisms are put in place to ensure that oversight institutions and their members do not disclose such information either inadvertently or deliberately.

C. Complaints and effective remedy

Practice 9. Any individual who believes that her or his rights have been infringed by an intelligence service is able to bring a complaint to a court or oversight institution, such as an ombudsman, human rights commissioner or national human rights institution. Individuals affected by the illegal actions of an intelligence service have recourse to an institution that can provide an effective remedy, including full reparation for the harm suffered.

16. It is widely acknowledged that any measure restricting human rights must be accompanied by adequate safeguards, including independent institutions, through which individuals can seek redress in the event that their rights are violated.38 Intelligence services possess a range of powers—including powers of surveillance, arrest and detention, which, if misused, may violate human rights. Accordingly, institutions exist to handle complaints raised by individuals who believe their rights have been violated by intelligence services and, where necessary, to provide victims of human rights violations with an effective remedy. Two broad approaches can be distinguished in this regard. First, States have established a range of non-judicial institutions to handle complaints pertaining to intelligence services. These include the ombudsman, the national human rights commission, the national audit office, the parliamentary oversight body, the inspector general,

the specialized intelligence oversight body and the complaints commission for intelligence services. These institutions are empowered to receive and investigate complaints; however, since they cannot generally issue binding orders or provide remedies, victims of human rights violations have to seek remedies through the courts. Second, judicial institutions may receive complaints pertaining to intelligence services. These institutions may be judicial bodies set up exclusively for this purpose, or part of the general judicial system; they are usually empowered to order remedial action.

Practice 10. The institutions responsible for addressing complaints and claims for effective remedy arising from the activities of intelligence services are independent of the intelligence services and the political executive. Such institutions have full and unhindered access to all relevant information, the necessary resources and expertise to conduct investigations, and the capacity to issue binding orders.

17. In order for an institution to provide effective remedies for human rights violations, it must be independent of the institutions involved in the impugned activities, able to ensure procedural fairness, have sufficient investigative capacity and expertise, and the capacity to issue binding decisions. For this reason, States have endowed such institutions with the requisite legal powers to investigate complaints and provide remedies to victims of human rights violations perpetrated by intelligence services. These powers include full and unhindered access to all relevant information, investigative powers to summon witnesses and to receive testimony under oath, the power to determine their own procedures in relation to any proceedings, and the capacity to issue binding orders.

D. Impartiality and non-discrimination

Practice 11. Intelligence services carry out their work in a manner that contributes to the promotion and protection of the human rights and fundamental freedoms of all individuals under the jurisdiction of the State. Intelligence services do not discriminate against individuals or groups on the grounds of their sex, race, colour, language, religion, political or other opinion, national or social origin, or other status.

18. Intelligence services are an integral part of the State apparatus that contributes to safeguarding the human rights of all individuals under the jurisdiction of the State. They are bound by the well-established principle of international human rights law of nondiscrimination.

This principle requires States to respect the rights and freedoms of individuals without discrimination on any prohibited ground. Many States have enshrined the principle in national law, requiring their intelligence services to fulfill their mandates in a manner that serves the interests of the State and society as a whole. Intelligence services are explicitly prohibited from acting or being used to further the interests of any ethnic, religious, political or other group. In addition, States ensure that the activities of their intelligence services (in particular in the context of counter-terrorism) are undertaken on the basis of individuals' behaviour, and not on the basis of their ethnicity, religion or other such criteria. Some States have also explicitly proscribed their intelligence services from establishing files on individuals on this basis.

Practice 12. National law prohibits intelligence services from engaging in any political activities or from acting to promote or protect the interests of any particular political, religious, linguistic, ethnic, social or economic group.

19. Intelligence services are endowed with powers that have the potential to promote or damage the interest of particular political groups. In order to ensure that intelligence services remain politically neutral, national laws prohibit intelligence services from acting in the interest of any political group. This obligation is not only incumbent upon the intelligence services but also upon the political executives whom they serve.

Practice 13. Intelligence services are prohibited from using their powers to target lawful political activity or other lawful manifestations of the rights to freedom of association, peaceful assembly and expression.

20. Intelligence services have recourse to information-collection measures that may interfere with legitimate political activities and other manifestations of the freedoms of expression, association and assembly. These rights are fundamental to the functioning of a free society, including political parties, the media and civil society. Therefore, States have taken measures to reduce the scope for their intelligence services to target (or to be asked to target) these individuals and groups engaged in these activities.

E. State responsibility for intelligence services

Practice 14. States are internationally responsible for the activities of their intelligence services and agents, and any private contractors they engage, regardless of where these activities take place and who the victim of internationally wrongful conduct is. Therefore, the executive power takes measures to ensure and exercise overall control of and responsibility for their intelligence services.

21. States are responsible under international law for the activities of their intelligence services and agents wherever they operate in the world. This responsibility extends to any private contractors that States engage to undertake intelligence functions. States have a legal obligation to ensure that their intelligence services do not violate human rights and to provide remedies to the individuals concerned if such violations occur. Accordingly, they take steps to regulate and manage their intelligence services in a manner that promotes respect for the rule of law and in particular, compliance with international human rights law. Executive control of intelligence services is essential for these purposes and is therefore enshrined in many national laws.

F. Individual responsibility and accountability

Practice 15. Constitutional, statutory and international criminal law applies to members of intelligence services as much as it does to any other public official. Any exceptions allowing intelligence officials to take actions that would normally violate national law are strictly limited and clearly prescribed by law. These exceptions never allow the violation of peremptory norms of international law or of the human rights obligations of the State.

22. While great emphasis is placed on the institutional responsibilities of intelligence services, individual members of intelligence services are also responsible and held to account for their actions. As a general rule, constitutional, statutory and international criminal law applies to intelligence officers as much as it does to any other individual.

Many States have made it a cause for civil liability or a criminal offence for any member of an intelligence service to knowingly violate and/or order or request an action that would violate constitutional or statutory law.69 This practice promotes respect for the rule of law within intelligence services, and helps to prevent impunity.

Practice 16. National laws provide for criminal, civil or other sanctions against any member, or individual acting on behalf of an intelligence service, who violates or orders an action that would violate national law or international human rights law.

These laws also establish procedures to hold individuals to account for such violations.

23. States ensure that employees of intelligence services are held to account for any violations of the law by providing and enforcing sanctions for particular offences. This serves to promote respect for the rule of law and human rights within intelligence services.

Practice 17. Members of intelligence services are legally obliged to refuse superior orders that would violate national law or international human rights law. Appropriate protection is provided to members of intelligence services who refuse orders in such situations.

24. It is good practice for national laws to require members of intelligence services to refuse orders that they believe would violate national law or international human rights law. While this provision is more common in laws regulating armed forces, several States have included it in statutes regulating their intelligence services. A requirement for members of intelligence services to refuse illegal orders is an important safeguard against possible human rights abuses, as well as against incumbent Governments ordering intelligence services to take action to further or protect their own interests. It is a well established principle of international law that individuals are not absolved of criminal responsibility for serious human rights violations by virtue of having been requested to undertake an action by a superior. Hence, to avoid individual criminal liability, members of intelligence services are required to refuse to carry out any orders that they should understand to be manifestly unlawful. This underlines the importance of human rights training for intelligence officers because they need to be aware of their rights and duties under international law (see practice 19). In order to promote an environment in which human rights abuses are not tolerated, States provide legal protections against reprisals for members of intelligence services who refuse to carry out illegal orders. The obligation to refuse illegal orders is closely linked to the availability of internal and external mechanisms through which intelligence service employees can voice their concerns about illegal orders (see practice 18 below).

Practice 18. There are internal procedures in place for members of intelligence services to report wrongdoing. These are complemented by an independent body that has a mandate and access to the necessary information to fully investigate and take action to address wrongdoing when internal procedures have proved inadequate. Members of intelligence services who, acting in good faith, report wrongdoing are legally protected from any form of reprisal. These protections extend to disclosures made to the media or the public at large if they are made as a last resort and pertain to matters of significant public concern.

25. Employees of intelligence services are often first, and best, placed to identify wrongdoing within intelligence services, such as human rights violations, financial malpractice and other contraventions of statutory law. Accordingly, it is good practice for national law to outline specific procedures for members of intelligence services to disclose concerns about wrongdoing. These provisions aim to encourage members of intelligence services to report wrongdoing, while at the same time ensuring that disclosures of potentially sensitive information are made and investigated in a controlled manner. State practice demonstrates that there are several channels for such disclosures, including internal mechanisms to receive and investigate disclosures made by members of intelligence services, external institutions to receive and investigate disclosures, and members of intelligence services making disclosures directly to these institutions. In some systems, members of intelligence services may only approach the external institution if the internal body has failed to address adequately their concerns. In some States, members of intelligence services are permitted to make public disclosures as a last resort or when such disclosures concern particularly grave matters, such as a threat to life. Regardless of the precise nature of the channels for disclosure, it is good practice for national law to afford individuals who make disclosures authorized by law to protection against reprisals.

G. Professionalism

Practice 19. Intelligence services and their oversight institutions take steps to foster an institutional culture of professionalism based on respect for the rule of law and human rights. In particular, intelligence services are responsible for training their members on relevant provisions of national and international law, including international human rights law.

26. The institutional culture of an intelligence service refers to widely shared or dominant values, attitudes and practices of employees. It is one of the main factors defining the attitude of intelligence officials towards the rule of law and human rights. Indeed, legal and institutional frameworks alone cannot ensure that members of intelligence services comply with human rights and the rule of law. A number of States and their intelligence services have formulated codes of ethics or principles of professionalism in order to promote an institutional culture that values and fosters respect for human rights and the rule of law. Codes of conduct typically include provisions on appropriate behaviour, discipline and ethical standards that apply to all members of intelligence services.

H. Human rights safeguards

Practice 20. Any measures by intelligence services that restrict human rights and fundamental freedoms comply with the following criteria:

(a) They are prescribed by publicly available law that complies with international human rights standards;

(b) All such measures must be strictly necessary for an intelligence service to fulfil its legally prescribed mandate;

(c) Measures taken must be proportionate to the objective. This requires that intelligence services select the measure that least restricts human rights, and take special care to minimize the adverse impact of any measures on the rights of individuals, including, in particular, persons who are not suspected of any wrongdoing;

(d) No measure taken by intelligence services may violate peremptory norms of international law or the essence of any human right;

(e) There is a clear and comprehensive system for the authorization, monitoring and oversight of the use of any measure that restricts human rights;

(f) Individuals whose rights may have been restricted by intelligence services are able to address complaints to an independent institution and seek an effective remedy.

27. Under national law, most intelligence services are permitted to undertake activities that restrict human rights. These powers are primarily found in the area of intelligence collection but also include law enforcement measures, the use of personal data and the sharing of personal information. National laws contain human rights safeguards for two main reasons: to limit interference with the rights of individuals to what is permissible under international human rights law; and to prevent the arbitrary or unfettered use of these measures.

28. Any measure restricting human rights must be prescribed by a law that is compatible with international human rights standards and in force at the time the measure is taken. Such a law outlines these measures in narrow and precise terms, sets out strict conditions for their use and establishes that their use must be directly linked to the mandate of an intelligence service.

. . .

30. The principle of proportionality is enshrined in laws of many States and requires that any measures that restrict human rights must be proportionate to the specified (and legally permissible) aims.99 In order to ensure that measures taken by intelligence services are proportionate, many States require their intelligence services to use the least intrusive means possible for the achievement of a given objective.

31. Intelligence services are prohibited by national law from using any measures that would violate international human rights standards and/or peremptory norms of international law. Some States have included explicit prohibitions on serious human rights violations in their laws on intelligence services. While non-derogable human rights may be singled out as inviolable, every human right includes an essential core that is beyond the reach of permissible limitations.

33. It is a fundamental requirement of international human rights law that victims of human rights violations be able to seek redress and remedy. Many States have procedures in place to ensure that individuals have access to an independent institution that can adjudicate on such claims (see practices 9 and 10 above).

I. Intelligence collection

Practice 21. National law outlines the types of collection measures available to intelligence services; the permissible objectives of intelligence collection; the categories of persons and activities which may be subject to intelligence collection; the threshold of suspicion required to justify the use of collection measures; the limitations on the duration for which collection measures may be used; and the procedures for authorizing, overseeing and reviewing the use of intelligence collection measures.

34. In most States, intelligence services have recourse to intrusive measures, such as covert surveillance and the interception of communications, in order to collect information necessary to fulfil their mandates. It is a fundamental requirement of the rule of law that individuals must be aware of measures that public authorities may use to restrict their rights and be able to foresee which activities may give rise to their use.

Practice 22. Intelligence-collection measures that impose significant limitations on human rights are authorized and overseen by at least one institution that is external to and independent of the intelligence services. This institution has the power to order the revision, suspension or termination of such collection measures. Intelligence-collection measures that impose significant limitations on human rights are subject to a multilevel process of authorization that includes approval within intelligence services, by the political executive and by an institution that is independent of the intelligence services and the executive.

35. It is common practice for national laws to include detailed provisions on the process for authorizing all intelligence collection measures that restrict human rights. Authorization processes require intelligence services to justify the proposed use of intelligence-collection measures in accordance with a clearly defined legal framework (see practices 20 and 21 above). This is a key mechanism for ensuring that collection measures are used in accordance with the law. It is good practice for intrusive collection measures to be authorized by an institution that is independent of the intelligence services, i.e., a politically accountable member of the executive or a (quasi) judicial body. Judicial bodies are independent of the intelligence process and therefore best placed to conduct an independent and impartial assessment of an application to use intrusive collection powers. Furthermore, it is notably good practice for the authorization of the most intrusive intelligence collection methods (e.g. the interception of the content of communications, the interception of mail and surreptitious entry into property) to include senior managers in intelligence services, the politically accountable executive and a (quasi) judicial body.

36. States also ensure that intelligence collection is subject to ongoing oversight by an institution that is external to the intelligence services. It is good practice for intelligence services to be required to report on the use of collection measures on an ongoing basis and for the external oversight institution to have the power to order the termination of collection measures.114 In many States, external oversight bodies also conduct ex post oversight of the use of intelligence-collection measures to ascertain whether or not they are authorized and used in compliance with the law.115 This is particularly important in view of the fact that the individuals whose rights are affected by intelligence collection are unlikely to be aware of the fact and, thus, have limited opportunity to challenge its legality.

J. Management and use of personal data

Practice 23. Publicly available law outlines the types of personal data that intelligence services may hold, and which criteria apply to the use, retention, deletion and disclosure of these data. Intelligence services are permitted to retain personal data that are strictly necessary for the purposes of fulfilling their mandate.

37. There is a number of general principles that apply to the protection of personal data that are commonly included in national laws as well as in international instruments. These include the following requirements: that personal data be collected and processed in a lawful and fair manner; that the use of personal data be limited and confined to its original specified purpose; that steps be taken to ensure that records of personal data are accurate; that personal data files be deleted when no longer required; and that individuals have the right to have access to and correct their personal data file. In the context of personal data use by intelligence services, the opening, retention and disposal of personal data files can have serious human rights implications; therefore, guidelines for the management and use of personal data by intelligence services are set out in public statutory law. This is a legal safeguard against giving the executive or the intelligence services unchecked powers over these matters.

Practice 24. Intelligence services conduct regular assessments of the relevance and accuracy of the personal data that they hold. They are legally required to delete or update any information that is assessed to be inaccurate or no longer relevant to their mandate, the work of oversight institutions or possible legal proceedings.

38. States have taken steps to ensure that intelligence services regularly check whether personal data files are accurate and relevant to their mandate. Safeguards on the relevance and accuracy of personal data help to ensure that any ongoing infringement of the right to privacy is minimized.

Practice 25. An independent institution exists to oversee the use of personal data by intelligence services. This institution has access to all files held by the intelligence services and has the power to order the disclosure of information to individuals concerned, as well as the destruction of files or personal information contained therein.

39. In many States, the management of personal data files is subject to regular and continuous oversight by independent institutions. These institutions are mandated to conduct regular inspection visits and random checks of personal data files of current and past operations.

Practice 26. Individuals have the possibility to request access to their personal data held by intelligence services. Individuals may exercise this right by addressing a request to a relevant authority or through an independent data-protection or oversight institution. Individuals have the right to rectify inaccuracies in their personal data. Any exceptions to these general rules are prescribed by law and strictly limited, proportionate and necessary for the fulfilment of the mandate of the intelligence service. It is incumbent upon the intelligence service to justify, to an independent oversight institution, any decision not to release personal information.

40. Many States have given individuals the right to have access to their personal data held by intelligence services. This right may be exercised by addressing a request to the intelligence service, a relevant minister, or an independent oversight institution. The right of individuals to have access to their personal data files should be understood in the context of safeguards for privacy rights and the freedom of access to information. This safeguard is important not only because it allows individuals to check whether their personal data file is accurate and lawful, but also because it is a safeguard against abuse, mismanagement and corruption. Indeed, an individual's right to have access to personal data held by intelligence services serves to enhance transparency and accountability of the decision-making processes of the intelligence services and, therefore, assists in developing citizens' trust in Government actions.

K. The use of powers of arrest and detention

Practice 27. Intelligence services are not permitted to use powers of arrest and detention if they do not have a mandate to perform law enforcement functions. They are not given powers of arrest and detention if this duplicates powers held by law enforcement agencies that are mandated to address the same activities.

41. It is widely accepted as good practice for intelligence services to be prohibited explicitly from exercising powers of arrest and detention if their legal mandate does not require them to exercise law enforcement functions in relation to national security offences, such as terrorism. Strong arguments have been made against combining intelligence and law enforcement functions.

Practice 28. If intelligence services have powers of arrest and detention, they are based on publicly available law. The exercise of these powers is restricted to cases in which there is reasonable suspicion that an individual has committed or is about to commit a specific criminal offence. Intelligence services are not permitted to deprive persons of their liberty simply for the purpose of intelligence collection. The use of any powers and arrest and detention by intelligence services is subject to the same degree of oversight as applies to their use by law enforcement authorities, including judicial review of the lawfulness of any deprivation of liberty.

42. If intelligence services are given powers of arrest and detention, national law outlines the purposes of such powers and circumstances under which they may be used. It is good practice for the use of these powers to be strictly limited to cases where there is reasonable suspicion that a crime (falling under the mandate of the intelligence services) has been, or is about to be, committed detention, is not permissible under international human rights law. If national law permits intelligence services to apprehend and detain individuals, it is good practice for the exercise of these powers to be subject to the same degree of oversight applying to the use of these powers by law enforcement authorities. Most importantly, international human rights law requires that individuals have the right to challenge the lawfulness of their detention before a court.

Practice 29. If intelligence services possess powers of arrest and detention, they comply with international human rights standards on the rights to liberty and fair trial, as well as the prohibition of torture and inhuman and degrading treatment. When exercising these powers, intelligence services comply with international standards set out in, inter alia, the Body of Principles for the Protection of All Persons under Any Form of Detention or Imprisonment, the Code of Conduct for Law Enforcement Officials and the Basic Principles on the Use of Force and Firearms by Law Enforcement Officials.

...

Practice 30. Intelligence services are not permitted to operate their own detention facilities or to make use of any unacknowledged detention facilities operated by third parties.

44. It is good practice for intelligence services to be explicitly prohibited in national law from operating their own detention facilities. If intelligence services are permitted to exercise powers of arrest and detention, the individuals concerned are remanded in regular detention centres administered by law enforcement agencies. Equally, intelligence services are not permitted to make use of unacknowledged detention facilities run by third parties, such as private contractors.

L. Intelligence-sharing and cooperation

Practice 31. Intelligence-sharing between intelligence agencies of the same State or with the authorities of a foreign State is based on national law that outlines clear parameters for intelligence exchange, including the conditions that must be met for information to be shared, the entities with which intelligence may be shared, and the safeguards that apply to exchanges of intelligence.

45. A legal basis for intelligence-sharing is an important requirement of the rule of law, and is particularly important when personal data are exchanged, because this directly infringes the right to privacy and may affect a range of other rights and fundamental freedoms. In addition to ensuring that intelligence-sharing is based on national law, it is widely accepted as good practice that intelligence-sharing be based on written agreements or memoranda between the parties, which comply with guidelines laid down in national law.

Practice 32. National law outlines the process for authorizing both the agreements upon which intelligence-sharing is based and the ad hoc sharing of intelligence. Executive approval is needed for any intelligence-sharing agreements with foreign entities, as well as for the sharing of intelligence that may have significant implications for human rights.

46. It is good practice for national law to set out guidelines for the authorization of the sending of information on an ad hoc basis, as well as for the establishment of agreements for intelligence-sharing. This serves to ensure that there are established channels of responsibility for intelligence-sharing and that relevant individuals can be held to account for any decisions they make in this regard.

Practice 33. Before entering into an intelligence-sharing agreement or sharing intelligence on an ad hoc basis, intelligence services undertake an assessment of the counterpart's record on human rights and data protection, as well as the legal safeguards and institutional controls that govern the counterpart. Before handing over information, intelligence services make sure that any shared intelligence is relevant to the recipient's mandate, will be used in accordance with the conditions attached and will not be used for purposes that violate human rights.

47. Both the sending and receipt of intelligence can have important implications for human rights and fundamental freedoms. Information sent to a foreign Government or intelligence service may not only contribute to legal limitations on the rights of an individual, but could also serve as the basis for human rights violations. Similarly, intelligence received from a foreign entity may have been obtained in violation of international human rights law. Therefore, before entering into a sharing agreement or sharing any information, it is good practice for intelligence services to conduct a general assessment of a foreign counterpart's record

on human rights and the protection of personal data, as well as the legal and institutional safeguards (such as oversight) that apply to those services.

48. In view of the possible implications of intelligence-sharing for human rights, it is good practice for intelligence services to screen all outgoing information for accuracy and relevance before sending it to foreign entities.

Practice 34. Independent oversight institutions are able to examine intelligence sharing arrangements and any information sent by intelligence services to foreign entities.

49. It is good practice for oversight institutions to be mandated to review the agreements upon which intelligence-sharing is based, as well as any arrangements based on such agreements. Independent oversight institutions can scrutinize the legal framework and procedural dimensions of intelligence-sharing agreements to ensure that they comply with national laws and relevant international legal standards.

Practice 35. Intelligence services are explicitly prohibited from employing the assistance of foreign intelligence services in any way that results in the circumvention of national legal standards and institutional controls on their own activities. If States request foreign intelligence services to undertake activities on their behalf, they require these services to comply with the same legal standards that would apply if the activities were undertaken by their own intelligence services.

50. National laws regulating the activities of intelligence services provide legal and institutional safeguards to protect human rights and the constitutional legal order within the context of intelligence activities. In view of this, it would be contrary to the rule of law for States or their intelligence services to request a foreign entity to undertake activities in their jurisdiction that they could not lawfully undertake themselves

Annex

Good practices on legal and institutional frameworks for intelligence services and their oversight

Practice 1. Intelligence services play an important role in protecting national security and upholding the rule of law. Their main purpose is to collect, analyse and disseminate information that assists policymakers and other public entities in taking measures to protect national security. This includes the protection of the population and their human rights.

Practice 2. The mandates of intelligence services are narrowly and precisely defined in a publicly available law. Mandates are strictly limited to protecting legitimate national security interests as outlined in publicly available legislation or national security policies, and identify the threats to national security that intelligence services are tasked to address. If terrorism is included among these threats, it is defined in narrow and precise terms.

Practice 3. The powers and competences of intelligence services are clearly and exhaustively defined in national law. They are required to use these powers exclusively for the purposes for which they were given. In particular, any powers given to intelligence services for the purposes of counter-terrorism must be used exclusively for these purposes.

Practice 4. All intelligence services are constituted through, and operate under, publicly available laws that comply with the Constitution and international human rights law. Intelligence services can only undertake or be instructed to undertake activities that are prescribed by and in accordance with national law. The use of subsidiary regulations that are not publicly available is strictly limited, and such regulations are both authorized by and remain within the parameters of publicly available laws. Regulations that are not made public do not serve as the basis for any activities that restrict human rights.

Practice 5. Intelligence services are explicitly prohibited from undertaking any action that contravenes the Constitution or international human rights law. These prohibitions extend not only to the conduct of intelligence services on their national territory but also to their activities abroad.

Practice 6. Intelligence services are overseen by a combination of internal, executive, parliamentary, judicial and specialized oversight institutions whose mandates and powers are based on publicly available law. An effective system of intelligence oversight includes at least one civilian institution that is independent of both the intelligence services and the executive. The combined remit of oversight institutions covers all aspects of the work of intelligence services, including their compliance with the law; the effectiveness and efficiency of their activities; their finances; and their administrative practices.

Practice 7. Oversight institutions have the power, resources and expertise to initiate and conduct their own investigations, as well as full and unhindered access to the information, officials and installations necessary to fulfil their mandates. Oversight institutions receive the full cooperation of intelligence services and law enforcement authorities in hearing witnesses, as well as obtaining documentation and other evidence.

Practice 8. Oversight institutions take all necessary measures to protect classified information and personal data to which they have access during the course of their work. Penalties are provided for the breach of these requirements by members of oversight institutions.

Practice 9. Any individual who believes that her or his rights have been infringed by an intelligence service is able to bring a complaint to a court or oversight institution, such as an ombudsman, human rights commissioner or national human rights institution.

Individuals affected by the illegal actions of an intelligence service have recourse to an institution that can provide an effective remedy, including full reparation for the harm suffered.

Practice 10. The institutions responsible for addressing complaints and claims for effective remedy arising from the activities of intelligence services are independent of the intelligence services and the political executive. Such institutions have full and unhindered access to all relevant information, the necessary resources and expertise to conduct investigations, and the capacity to issue binding orders.

Practice 11. Intelligence services carry out their work in a manner that contributes to the promotion and protection of the human rights and fundamental freedoms of all individuals under the jurisdiction of the State. Intelligence services do not discriminate against individuals or groups on the grounds of their sex, race, colour, language, religion, political or other opinion, national or social origin, or other status.

Practice 12. National law prohibits intelligence services from engaging in any political activities or from acting to promote or protect the interests of any particular political, religious, linguistic, ethnic, social or economic group.

Practice 13. Intelligence services are prohibited from using their powers to target lawful political activity or other lawful manifestations of the rights to freedom of association, peaceful assembly and expression.

Practice 14. States are internationally responsible for the activities of their intelligence services and their agents, and any private contractors they engage, regardless of where these activities take place and who the victim of internationally wrongful conduct is. Therefore, the executive power takes measures to ensure and exercise overall control of and responsibility for their intelligence services.

Practice 15. Constitutional, statutory and international criminal law applies to members of intelligence services as much as it does to any other public official. Any exceptions allowing intelligence officials to take actions that would normally violate national law are strictly limited and clearly prescribed by law. These exceptions never allow the violation of peremptory norms of international law or of the human rights obligations of the State.

Practice 16. National laws provide for criminal, civil or other sanctions against any member, or individual acting on behalf of an intelligence service, who violates or orders an action that would violate national law or international human rights law. These laws also establish procedures to hold individuals to account for such violations.

Practice 17. Members of intelligence services are legally obliged to refuse superior orders that would violate national law or international human rights law. Appropriate protection is provided to members of intelligence services who refuse orders in such situations.

Practice 18. There are internal procedures in place for members of intelligence services to report wrongdoing. These are complemented by an independent body that has a mandate and access to the necessary information to fully investigate and take action to address wrongdoing when internal procedures have proved inadequate. Members of intelligence services who, acting in good faith, report wrongdoing are legally protected from any form of reprisal. These protections extend to disclosures made to the media or the public at large if they are made as a last resort and pertain to matters of significant public concern.

Practice 19. Intelligence services and their oversight institutions take steps to foster an institutional culture of professionalism based on respect for the rule of law and human rights. In particular, intelligence services are responsible for training their members on relevant provisions of national and international law, including international human rights law.

Practice 20: Any measures by intelligence services that restrict human rights and fundamental freedoms comply with the following criteria:

(a) They are prescribed by publicly available law that complies with international human rights standards;

(b) All such measures must be strictly necessary for an intelligence service to fulfil its legally prescribed mandate;

(c) Measures taken must be proportionate to the objective. This requires that intelligence services select the measure that least restricts human rights, and take special care to minimize the adverse impact of any measures on the rights of individuals, including, in particular, persons who are not suspected of any wrongdoing;

(d) No measure taken by intelligence services may violate peremptory norms of international law or the essence of any human right;

(e) There is a clear and comprehensive system for the authorization, monitoring and oversight of the use of any measure that restricts human rights;

(f) Individuals whose rights may have been restricted by intelligence services are able to address complaints to an independent institution and seek an effective remedy.

Practice 21. National law outlines the types of collection measures available to intelligence services; the permissible objectives of intelligence collection; the categories of persons and activities which may be subject to intelligence collection; the threshold of suspicion required to justify the use of collection measures; the limitations on the duration for which collection measures may be used; and the procedures for authorizing, overseeing and reviewing the use of intelligence-collection measures.

Practice 22. Intelligence-collection measures that impose significant limitations on human rights are authorized and overseen by at least one institution that is external to and independent of the intelligence services. This institution has the power to order the revision, suspension or termination of such collection measures. Intelligence collection measures that impose significant limitations on human rights are subject to a multilevel process of authorization that includes approval within intelligence services, by the political executive and by an institution that is independent of the intelligence services and the executive.

Practice 23. Publicly available law outlines the types of personal data that intelligence services may hold, and which criteria apply to the use, retention, deletion and disclosure of these data. Intelligence services are permitted to retain personal data that are strictly necessary for the purposes of fulfilling their mandate.

Practice 24. Intelligence services conduct regular assessments of the relevance and accuracy of the personal data that they hold. They are legally required to delete or update any information that is assessed to be inaccurate or no longer relevant to their mandate, the work of oversight institutions or possible legal proceedings.

Practice 25. An independent institution exists to oversee the use of personal data by intelligence services. This institution has access to all files held by the intelligence services and has the power to order the disclosure of information to individuals concerned, as well as the destruction of files or personal information contained therein.

Practice 26. Individuals have the possibility to request access to their personal data held by intelligence services. Individuals may exercise this right by addressing a request to a relevant authority or through an independent data-protection or oversight institution.

Individuals have the right to rectify inaccuracies in their personal data. Any exceptions to these general rules are prescribed by law and strictly limited, proportionate and necessary for the fulfillment of the mandate of the intelligence service. It is incumbent upon the intelligence service to justify, to an independent oversight institution, any decision not to release personal information.

Practice 27. Intelligence services are not permitted to use powers of arrest and detention if they do not have a mandate to perform law enforcement functions. They are not given powers of arrest and detention if this duplicates powers held by law enforcement agencies that are mandated to address the same activities.

Practice 28. If intelligence services have powers of arrest and detention, they are based on publicly available law. The exercise of these powers is restricted to cases in which there is reasonable suspicion that an individual has committed or is about to commit a specific criminal offence. Intelligence services are not permitted to deprive persons of their liberty simply for the purpose of intelligence collection. The use of any powers and arrest and detention by intelligence services is subject to the same degree of oversight as applies to their use by law enforcement authorities, including judicial review of the lawfulness of any deprivation of liberty.

Practice 29. If intelligence services possess powers of arrest and detention they comply with international human rights standards on the rights to liberty and fair trial, as well as the prohibition of torture and inhuman and degrading treatment. When exercising these powers, intelligence services comply with international standards set out in, inter alia, the Body of Principles for the Protection of All Persons under Any Form of Detention or Imprisonment, the Code of Conduct for Law Enforcement Officials and the Basic Principles on the Use of Force and Firearms by Law Enforcement Officials.

Practice 30. Intelligence services are not permitted to operate their own detention facilities or to make use of any unacknowledged detention facilities operated by third parties.

Practice 31. Intelligence-sharing between intelligence agencies of the same State or with the authorities of a foreign State is based on national law that outlines clear parameters for intelligence exchange, including the conditions that must be met for information to be shared, the entities with which intelligence may be shared, and the safeguards that apply to exchanges of intelligence.

Practice 32. National law outlines the process for authorizing both the agreements upon which intelligence-sharing is based and the ad hoc sharing of intelligence. Executive approval is needed for any intelligence-sharing agreements with foreign entities, as well as for the sharing of intelligence that may have significant implications for human rights.

Practice 33. Before entering into an intelligence-sharing agreement or sharing intelligence on an ad hoc basis, intelligence services undertake an assessment of the counterpart's record on human rights and data protection, as well as the legal safeguards and institutional controls that govern the counterpart. Before handing over information, intelligence services make sure that any shared intelligence is relevant to the recipient's mandate, will be used in accordance with the conditions attached and will not be used for purposes that violate human rights.

Practice 34. Independent oversight institutions are able to examine intelligence-sharing arrangements and any information sent by intelligence services to foreign entities.

Practice 35. Intelligence services are explicitly prohibited from employing the assistance of foreign intelligence services in any way that results in the circumvention of national legal standards and institutional controls on their own activities. If States request foreign intelligence services to undertake activities on their behalf, they require these services to comply with the same legal standards that would apply if the activities were undertaken by their own intelligence services.

Document 7: Interim report of the Special Rapporteur on torture and other cruel, inhuman or degrading treatment or punishment (Manfred Nowak), UN Secretary General Note, A/65/273. (Excerpted)

UNITED NATIONS	A/65/273
General Assembly	Distr.:
Sixty-fifth session	10 August 2010
Item 69 (b) of the provisional agenda*	Original: ENGLISH

PROMOTION AND PROTECTION OF HUMAN RIGHTS: HUMAN RIGHTS QUESTIONS, INCLUDING ALTERNATIVE APPROACHES FOR IMPROVING THE EFFECTIVE ENJOYMENT OF HUMAN RIGHTS AND FUNDAMENTAL FREEDOMS

Note by the Secretary-General

The Secretary-General has the honour to transmit the interim report of the Special Rapporteur of the Human Rights Council on torture and other cruel, inhuman or degrading treatment or punishment, Manfred Nowak, submitted in accordance with General Assembly resolution 64/153.

2 10-48049

Interim report of the Special Rapporteur on torture and other cruel, inhuman or degrading treatment or punishment

Summary

In the present report, submitted pursuant to General Assembly resolution 64/153, the Special Rapporteur addresses issues of special concern to him, in particular overall trends and developments with respect to questions falling within his mandate.

The Special Rapporteur draws the attention of the General Assembly to his assessment that torture continues to be widely practised in the majority of States, with impunity being one of its root causes. According to him, no further standard setting is required, as the Convention against Torture and Other Cruel, Inhuman or Degrading Treatment or Punishment contains a broad range of positive State obligations aimed at preventing and combating torture. In particular, the Convention requires its 147 States parties to criminalize torture, to establish broad jurisdictions, to investigate all allegations and suspicions of torture and to bring the perpetrators of torture to justice. Unfortunately, those specific positive obligations aimed at combating impunity have not been implemented by most States. If the commission of torture is established by a competent authority, the victims should enjoy the right to fair and adequate reparation, including the means for as full medical, psychological, social and other rehabilitation as possible. States, therefore, have a legal obligation to establish or at least support a sufficient number of rehabilitation centres for victims of torture and to ensure the safety of the staff and patients of such centres. In order to further prevent torture, the Special Rapporteur calls upon all States to promptly ratify the Optional Protocol to the Convention against Torture and to establish, in accordance with its provisions, independent and professional national preventive mechanisms tasked with conducting regular and unannounced visits to all places of detention. They should be granted unrestricted access to all places of detention and the opportunity to have private interviews with detainees, as well as the necessary financial and human resources to enable them to conduct their work effectively.

Contents

I. Introduction

1. The present report is the twelfth submitted to the General Assembly by the Special Rapporteur on torture and other cruel, inhuman or degrading treatment or punishment. It is submitted pursuant to paragraph 38 of General Assembly resolution 64/153 and is the sixth and final report submitted by the present mandate holder. His previous report to the General Assembly (A/64/215 and Corr.1) was devoted to the appalling conditions of detention found by the Special Rapporteur during his country missions. Various factors, including malfunctioning criminal justice systems throughout the world, corruption and a lack of empathy for persons deprived of liberty, have led to a global prison crisis, supported by statistics on the overcrowding of prisons, a high level of pretrial detainees and similar indicators.

The Special Rapporteur therefore continues to call upon the General Assembly to take action to improve the situation of the 10 million prisoners and many more detainees in police custody, psychiatric institutions and other places of detention worldwide. In particular, there is an urgent need to draft and adopt a special United Nations convention on the rights of detainees.

2. In the present report, the Special Rapporteur wishes to draw the attention of the General Assembly to the alarming situation concerning torture in the world.

During the past six years, he carried out fact-finding missions to 17 countries around the world and three joint studies together with other special procedures. In all but one country (Denmark, including Greenland), he found clear evidence of torture. In some countries there seemed to be only isolated cases of torture, but in the majority of countries he visited (which constitute a representative sample of all countries in the world), torture is practised in a routine, widespread and sometimes even systematic manner. Taking into account that torture constitutes one of the most serious human rights violations and a direct attack on the core of the personal integrity and dignity of human beings, this is an alarming conclusion.

3. When the United Nations was founded in the aftermath of the Second World War and the Nazi Holocaust, it was undisputed that the prohibition of torture should be included as one of the few absolute and non-derogable rights in the International Bill of Human Rights. Nevertheless, the practice of torture persisted in many regions of the world, most notably in the military dictatorships in Latin America established in the late 1960s. This prompted the United Nations to draft and adopt the Convention against Torture and Other Cruel, Inhuman or Degrading Treatment or Punishment in 1984. The Convention builds upon the absolute and non-derogable prohibition of torture and creates a number of specific obligations for States parties to prevent torture, to criminalize torture and bring the perpetrators of torture to justice on the basis of a wide range of jurisdictions, including universal jurisdiction, and to provide victims of torture with the right to an adequate remedy and reparations for the harm suffered. In 2002, the Convention against Torture was supplemented by an Optional Protocol with the aim of preventing torture and improving prison conditions through a system of unannounced and regular visits to all places where persons may be deprived of their liberty. Today, 147 of the 192 States Members of the United Nations, including 15 of the 17 States visited by the Special Rapporteur, are parties to the Convention and 54 are parties to the Optional Protocol. If States take their obligations under the Convention and the Optional Protocol seriously, torture could easily be eradicated in today's world. There is no need for further standard.

4. The fact that torture continues to be practised on such an alarming scale throughout the world shows that most States do not seem to take those obligations seriously. In the present report, the Special Rapporteur provides an analysis of the three main obligations under the Convention and the Optional Protocol (fighting impunity, providing victims with rehabilitation and establishing effective national preventive mechanisms to inspect places of detention) and how they have been implemented by States, above all those visited by him. Those 17 countries serve as a representative sample of all countries in the world and the Special Rapporteur wishes to express his sincere gratitude to the respective Governments for having extended an invitation to him and for their cooperation during his country missions.

. . .

III. Impunity as a root cause of the prevalence of torture
A. Prevalence of torture

35. The scale and scope of impunity found in many countries visited by the Special Rapporteur has been one of his most disappointing findings. During his time as mandate holder, the Special Rapporteur has been witness to the distressing reality that both torture and ill-treatment are widespread practices throughout the world.

The existing international legal framework provides a broad range of norms and standards to prohibit, prevent and eradicate torture. Their effective application, however, continues to be a challenge.

36. States bear the main responsibility for implementing international human rights standards, including the prohibition of torture. However, torture occurs because national legal frameworks are deficient and do not properly codify torture as a crime with appropriate sanctions. Torture persists because national criminal systems lack the essential procedural safeguards to prevent its occurrence, to effectively investigate allegations and to bring perpetrators to justice. Moreover, torture remains entrenched because of a climate of tolerance of excessive use of force by law enforcement officials in many countries.

B. Convention against Torture

37. Article 4 of the Convention against Torture sets out the obligation of States parties to ensure that all acts of torture are an offence under their criminal legislation and that appropriate penalties are foreseen. Article 4, paragraph 1, must be read in conjunction with article 1, paragraph 1, of the Convention, since it would be very difficult for a State party to criminalize an offence, establish the corresponding jurisdiction and institute prosecution, without formulating a proper definition of torture.

38. The alignment of national legislations with the Convention against Torture and Other Cruel, Inhuman or Degrading Treatment or Punishment is crucial for its effective implementation. Therefore, the definition of torture contained in article 1, paragraph 1, of the Convention, with all its elements (infliction of severe pain or suffering; intention and specific purpose; and involvement of a public official), must be taken into account by States when making torture an offence under domestic criminal law.

39. The Committee against Torture has been clear about the requirement to make "all acts of torture", including acts of attempt, complicity and participation, an offence under criminal law, with penalties commensurate to the gravity of the crimes. In addition, even if not explicitly stated in the Convention, the Committee considers instances that include "instigation, consent or acquiescence", to be covered by the terms "complicity or participation", giving rise to individual criminal responsibility under article 4 of all public officials sufficiently involved under article 1.

40. The Convention does not explicitly provide for a specific penalty and type or extent of sentence for the offence of torture, leaving it to the discretion of the State party to decide, taking into account the grave nature of the crime. The Committee against Torture has stated on several occasions that consideration of the appropriate penalty must take into account not only the gravity of the offence but the severity of penalties established for similar crimes in each State.

C. Factors contributing to impunity

41. During his fact-finding missions, the Special Rapporteur has been able to identify various factors that contribute to impunity and therefore to the persistence of torture. They include the lack of proper criminalization of torture; the absence of impartial investigations into allegations; and the lack of prosecution of perpetrators.

1. Criminalization of torture in domestic law

42. Of all the countries visited by the Special Rapporteur, only Jamaica and Papua New Guinea have not ratified the Convention against Torture and Other Cruel, Inhuman or Degrading Treatment or Punishment. The other 15 countries have ratified the Convention and accepted the obligations contained therein, including those of making torture an offence under criminal law and establishing appropriate penalties for perpetrators.

43. However, the reality is quite different. For the general prohibition of torture to become effective, national criminal legislation should incorporate such a prohibition and make torture a punishable offence. The Special Rapporteur found instances, including in Denmark, Nigeria and Jamaica, where torture is not explicitly defined in domestic criminal law. In Nepal, for example, torture is not a criminal offence and in Indonesia, although it is defined in its Human Rights Law, there are no provisions concerning torture in the criminal legislation.

44. In certain cases, the definition of torture in national criminal law is too narrow and/or leaves out important elements established in article 1 of the Convention against Torture and Other Cruel, Inhuman or Degrading Treatment or Punishment.

. . .

47. The criminal codes in many countries contain provisions outlawing certain acts which may fall within the scope of the Convention against Torture and Other Cruel, Inhuman or Degrading Treatment or Punishment, such as the infliction of bodily injuries or the use of duress. Nevertheless, while some of those acts may be part of an act of torture, the criminal codes fall short of providing comprehensive protection to the physical and psychological integrity of the victims. Some of the most sophisticated torture methods do not cause any physical injuries, but cause extreme pain and suffering.

. . .

2. Adequacy of penalties

49. The fact that torture is either not codified or not properly defined in national criminal laws facilitates too lenient penalties, not commensurate with the gravity of the crime. This is another factor that can contribute to a climate of impunity by sending a non-deterrent message to potential perpetrators and by nurturing a lack of awareness among judges and lawyers.

50. While the Convention does not indicate a specific penalty for torture, it is generally accepted that the punishment should be similar to the penalties established for the most serious offences in each national legal framework. This would ensure that sentences are commensurate with the gravity of the offence and that no statutes of limitations apply.

. . .

3. Impartial investigations

53. Throughout his fact-finding missions, the Special Rapporteur found that another factor contributing to impunity is the lack of investigation and prosecution following acts of torture and ill-treatment. Although prompt and impartial investigations should be carried out without delay whenever there is a suspicion of torture or an explicit allegation, this is too often not the case.

54. Despite the fact that, in many cases, detainees have visible signs of ill treatment, the authorities generally fail to initiate investigations. Medical examinations are often not conducted, nor are detainees provided with medical treatment. In Paraguay, the Special Rapporteur was concerned to see that officials completely disregarded their duty to initiate ex officio investigations. In Georgia, judges or procurators have an obligation to make inquiries or investigate allegations ex officio; however, no action is taken in the vast majority of cases. The same applies in the Republic of Moldova, where the legal provision calling for ex officio investigations is not applied in practice.

55. Ex officio investigations, as required by article 12 of the Convention against Torture and Other Cruel, Inhuman or Degrading Treatment or Punishment, are one of the strongest tools for preventing torture and combating impunity. As victims are often unaware of existing complaints mechanisms, they lack confidence that their complaints will be effectively addressed or they are afraid to file them. This problem is worse in countries where the obligation to initiate ex officio investigations is not enshrined in the law, as was observed by the Special Rapporteur in some of his missions, including those to Jamaica and Sri Lanka. Whenever there are reasonable grounds, including credible evidence, that an act of torture has been committed, States should conduct an investigation, irrespective of whether a complaint has been filed. In Jordan, the Special Rapporteur found that even though the Court of Cassation had overturned a number of convictions on the grounds that security officials had obtained confessions under torture, this did not trigger official criminal investigations against the perpetrators. The same holds true for Sri Lanka.

56. A further concern is the fact that the authorities entrusted with investigating allegations of torture and ill-treatment are frequently the same authorities who are accused of committing such acts (i.e. the police), as is the case in Denmark, Georgia, ...

4. Prosecutions

57. In terms of prosecutions, the Special Rapporteur was sadly surprised at the low number of people prosecuted for torture in the countries he visited. He came across cases of officials being subject to disciplinary or administrative procedures for offences such as abuse of power and, in some cases, convictions for offences such as causing physical injuries, as in Jordan and Paraguay. These types of convictions not only result from the lack of a specific criminal offence of torture, but are in some instances used to treat the act of torture as a minor offence.

...

75. The ultimate aim must be to prevent acts of torture and ill-treatment before they occur. There are numerous methods of prevention that have been developed in the past, which, if adequately implemented by States, could easily eradicate torture: abolition of secret and incommunicado detention; proper registration of every detainee from the moment of arrest or apprehension; prompt access to legal counsel within 24 hours; access to relatives; prompt access to an independent judge; presumption of innocence; prompt and independent medical examination of all detainees; video/audio recording of all interrogations; no detention under the control of the interrogators or investigators for more than 48 hours; prompt, impartial and effective investigation of all allegations or suspicions of torture; inadmissibility of evidence obtained under torture; and effective training of all officials involved in the custody, interrogation and medical care of detainees. As previously emphasized by the Special Rapporteur and his predecessors, the most effective preventive measure against torture and ill-treatment is the regular inspection of places of detention. Regular inspections can ensure the adequate implementation of the above-mentioned safeguards against torture, create a strong deterrent effect and provide a means to generate timely and adequate responses to allegations of torture and ill-treatment by law enforcement officials.

...

VI. Conclusions and recommendations

87. Although torture constitutes one of the most brutal human rights violations and a direct attack on the core of human dignity, it continues to be widely practiced in the majority of States in all parts of the world. This alarming conclusion of the Special Rapporteur on torture is based on his experience after carrying out the mandate for almost six years, and after conducting 17 fact finding missions to countries in all regions of the world and preparing three joint studies together with other special procedures mandate holders.

88. While the appalling conditions of detention in most countries of the world could be effectively addressed by adopting a special United Nations convention on the rights of detainees, no further standard

setting is required to combat torture. Its prohibition is one of the few absolute and non-derogable human rights and part of ius cogens, and the Convention against Torture and its Optional Protocol contain a broad range of very specific positive State obligations aimed at preventing and combating torture. If States parties to the Convention and the Optional Protocol would abide by their legally binding obligations, torture could easily be eradicated.

89. In order to combat increasing levels of crime, terrorism and other forms of organized crime effectively, Governments in too many countries seem willing to restrict certain human rights by granting their law enforcement, intelligence and security forces very extensive powers. This leads to an environment conducive to undermining the absolute prohibition of torture. The brutalization of many societies has reached a level where torture is simply regarded by Governments and the population at large as the "lesser evil". This trend is alarming. There is a need for a new global awareness-raising campaign to change this climate of tolerance towards excessive use of force by law enforcement officials. Governments need to be reminded that torture is not an effective means of combating crime. On the contrary, it contributes to the further brutalization of societies and the spiral of violence which many societies suffer from. Torture is nothing other than an act of barbarism.

90. Impunity is one of the root causes of the widespread practice of torture. This was recognized by the international community in the 1980s when adopting the Convention against Torture as the first human rights treaty with detailed obligations to criminalize torture, to establish broad jurisdictional competences, to investigate all allegations or suspicions of torture, and to arrest suspected perpetrators of torture and bring them to justice.

In most of the 147 States parties to the Convention against Torture, those legal obligations, deriving from articles 4 to 9, 12 and 13 of the Convention, have not been implemented. States should, first of all, ensure through legislative measures that torture, as defined in article 1 of the Convention, is made a crime with appropriate penalties, which must be applicable on the basis of the principles of territoriality, nationality and universal jurisdiction. Secondly, States shall establish professional authorities to promptly and impartially investigate all allegations and suspicions of torture, with the aim of identifying the perpetrators, including superior officers who ordered or condoned torture, and bringing them to justice.

91. Victims of torture have a right to complain to a professional authority which is independent from the authority accused of torture and which has the obligation to promptly and impartially examine all allegations or suspicions of torture. Victims and witnesses should be protected against all ill-treatment or intimidation as a consequence of their complaints or any evidence given. If torture is established by a competent authority, victims should enjoy the right to fair and adequate reparation, including the means for as full medical, psychological, social and other rehabilitation as possible. States, therefore, have a legal obligation to establish or at least support a sufficient number of rehabilitation centres for victims of torture and to ensure the safety of their staff and patients. The Special Rapporteur also urges States to ensure that survivors of torture who seek refuge in their countries have access to adequate medical and psychosocial treatment. Screening procedures allowing for the early identification of torture victims can be instrumental in that regard.

Asylum authorities should be required to consider seriously the medical expertise of domestic rehabilitation centres and take account of their assessments when deciding upon asylum requests. Health professionals should be provided with training on how to apply the Istanbul Protocol. The Special Rapporteur also calls upon Governments, not least those responsible for the practice of torture, to contribute generously to the United Nations Voluntary Fund for Victims of Torture.

92. Finally, all States have an international legal obligation to take effective legislative, administrative, judicial and other measures to prevent torture. In this respect, the Special Rapporteur calls upon all States to promptly ratify the Optional Protocol to the Convention against Torture and to establish, through legislative action on the basis of an inclusive and transparent process, independent and professional national preventive mechanisms tasked with conducting regular and unannounced visits to all places of detention. Such national preventive mechanisms should be granted unrestricted access to all places of detention and the opportunity to have private interviews with detainees. The Special Rapporteur urges all States parties to the Optional Protocol to the Convention against Torture to provide national preventive mechanisms with the necessary financial and human resources to enable them to regularly inspect all places of detention, to examine the treatment of detainees and to prevent acts of torture or ill-treatment in detention.

Document 8: U.N. Convention Against Torture (CAT): Overview and Application to Interrogation Techniques. Report to Congress. John Michael Garcia. Congressional Research Service 2009. (Excerpted)

Congressional Research Service
Prepared for Members and Committees of Congress
U.N. Convention Against Torture (CAT): Overview and Application to Interrogation Techniques

John Michael Garcia
Legislative Attorney
January 26, 2009

CRS Report for Congress
7-500
www.crs.gov
RL 32438

Summary

The United Nations Convention Against Torture and Other Cruel, Inhuman, or Degrading Treatment or Punishment (CAT) requires signatory parties to take measures to end torture within their territorial jurisdiction and to criminalize all acts of torture. Unlike many other international agreements and declarations prohibiting torture, CAT provides a general definition of the term.

CAT generally defines torture as the infliction of severe physical and/or mental suffering committed under the color of law. CAT allows for no circumstances or emergencies where torture could be permitted.

The U.S. ratified CAT, subject to certain declarations, reservations, and understandings, including that the treaty was not self-executing and required implementing legislation to be enforced by U.S. courts. In order to ensure U.S. compliance with CAT obligations to criminalize all acts of torture, the U.S. enacted chapter 113C of the U.S. Criminal Code, which prohibits torture occurring *outside* the U.S. (torture occurring inside the U.S. was already generally prohibited under several federal and state statutes criminalizing acts such as assault, battery, and murder). The applicability and scope of these statutes were the subject of widely-reported memorandums by the Department of Defense and Department of Justice in 2002. The memorandums were criticized by some for taking an overly restrictive view of treatment constituting torture. In late 2004, the Department of Justice released a memorandum superseding its earlier memo and modifying some of its conclusions. In January 2009, President Barack Obama issued an Executive Order providing that when conducting prospective interrogations, U.S. agents are generally forbidden from relying upon any interpretation of the law governing interrogations issued by the Department of Justice between September 11, 2001 and the final day of the Bush Administration, absent further guidance from the Attorney General.

Assuming for the purposes of discussion that a U.S. body had to review a harsh interrogation method to determine whether it constitutes torture under either CAT or applicable U.S. law, it might examine international jurisprudence analyzing whether certain interrogation methods constituted torture. Although these decisions are not binding precedent for the U.S., they may inform deliberations here.

Congress has approved additional, CAT-referencing guidelines concerning the treatment of detainees. The Detainee Treatment Act (DTA), which was enacted pursuant to both the Department of Defense, Emergency Supplemental Appropriations to Address Hurricanes in the Gulf of Mexico, and Pandemic Influenza Act, 2006 (P.L. 109-148), and the National Defense Authorization Act for FY2006 (P.L. 109-163), contained a provision prohibiting the cruel, inhuman and degrading treatment of persons under custody or control of the U.S. (this provision is commonly referred to as the McCain Amendment). The Military Commissions Act of 2006 (MCA, P.L. 109-366) contained an identical measure and also required the President to establish administrative rules and procedures implementing this standard. These Acts are discussed briefly in this report and in greater detail in CRS Report RL33655, *Interrogation of Detainees: Requirements of the Detainee Treatment Act*, by Michael John Garcia.

APPENDIX M

Contents

Over the past several decades, a number of international agreements and declarations has condemned and/or sought to prohibit the practice of torture by public officials, leading many to conclude that torture is now prohibited under customary international law. Perhaps the most notable international agreement prohibiting torture is the United Nations Convention against Torture and Other Cruel, Inhuman, or Degrading Treatment or Punishment (Convention or CAT), signed by the U.S. and more than 140 other countries.

Whereas a number of prior international agreements and declarations condemned and/or prohibited torture, CAT appears to be the first international agreement to actually attempt to define the term. CAT Article 1 specifies that, for purposes of the Convention, "torture" is understood to mean

> any act by which severe pain or suffering, whether physical or mental, is intentionally inflicted on a person for such purposes as obtaining from him or a third person information or a confession, punishing him for an act he or a third person has committed or is suspected of having committed, or intimidating or coercing him or a third person, or for any reason based on discrimination of any kind, when such pain or suffering is inflicted by or at the instigation of or with the consent or acquiescence of a public official or other person acting in an official capacity. It does not include pain or suffering arising only from, inherent in or incidental to lawful sanctions.

Importantly, this definition specifies that both physical and mental suffering can constitute torture, and that for such suffering to constitute torture, it must be purposefully inflicted. Further, acts of torture covered under the Convention must be committed by someone acting under the color of law. Thus, for example, if a private individual causes intense suffering to another, absent the instigation, consent, or acquiescence of a public official, such action does not constitute "torture" for purposes of CAT.

The Convention's definition of "torture" does not include all acts of mistreatment causing mental or physical suffering, but only those of a severe nature. According to the State Department's section-by-section analysis of CAT included in President Reagan's transmittal of the Convention to the Senate for its advice and consent, the Convention's definition of torture was intended to be interpreted in a "relatively limited fashion, corresponding to the common understanding of torture as an *extreme* practice which is universally condemned." For example, the State Department suggested that rough treatment falling into the category of police brutality, "while deplorable, does not amount to 'torture'" for purposes of the Convention, which is "usually reserved for extreme, deliberate, and unusually cruel practices ... [such as] sustained systematic beating, application of electric currents to sensitive parts of the body, and tying up or hanging in positions that cause extreme pain." This understanding of torture as a severe form of mistreatment is further made clear by CAT Article 16, which obligates Convention parties to "prevent in any territory under [their] jurisdiction other acts of cruel, inhuman, or degrading treatment or punishment which do not amount to acts of torture," thereby indicating that not all forms of inhumane treatment constitute torture.

In general, Convention parties are obligated to take "effective legislative, administrative, judicial or other measures to prevent acts of torture in any territory under [their] jurisdiction." They are also forbidden from expelling, returning, or extraditing a person to another State where there are "substantial grounds" for believing that he would be in danger of being subjected to torture.

A central objective of CAT is to criminalize all instances of torture. CAT Article 4 requires States to ensure that all acts of torture are criminal offenses, subject to appropriate penalties given their "grave nature." State parties are also required to apply similar criminal penalties to attempts to commit and complicity or participation in torture. Accordingly, it appears that even though CAT requires States to take "effective measures" to prevent torture only within their territorial jurisdiction, this does not mean that States are therefore permitted to engage in torture in territories not under their jurisdiction. Although a State might not be required to take proactive measures to prevent acts of torture beyond its territorial jurisdiction, it nevertheless has an obligation to criminalize such extraterritorial acts and impose appropriate penalties.

- CAT Article 5 establishes minimum jurisdictional measures that each State party must take with respect to offenses described in CAT Article 4. Pursuant to CAT Article 5, a State party must establish jurisdiction over CAT Article 4 offenses when The offenses are committed in any territory under its jurisdiction or on board a ship or aircraft registered in that State;
- The alleged offender is a national of that State;
- The victim was a national of that State if that State considers it appropriate; or
- The alleged offender is present in any territory under its jurisdiction and the State does not extradite him in accordance with CAT Article 8, which makes torture an extraditable offense.

CAT's prohibition of torture is absolute: "No exceptional circumstances whatsoever, whether a state of war or a threat or war, internal political instability or any other public emergency, may be invoked as a justification of torture." According to the State Department, this blanket prohibition was viewed by the drafters of CAT as "necessary if the Convention is to have significant effect, as public emergencies are commonly invoked as a source of extraordinary powers or as a justification for limiting fundamental rights and freedoms."

CAT Article 14 provides that signatory States must ensure that their legal systems provide victims of torture (or their dependents, in cases where the victim has died as a result of torture) with the ability to obtain civil redress in the form of "fair and adequate compensation including the means for as full rehabilitation as possible." According to the State Department, Article 14 was adopted with an express reference to this treaty obligation extending only to "the victim of an act of torture *committed in any territory under* [a signatory State's] *jurisdiction*," but this limiting clause was "deleted by mistake."

CAT Article 16 requires signatory States to take preventative measures to prevent "cruel, inhuman, or degrading treatment or punishment" within any territory under their jurisdiction when such acts are committed under the color of law. CAT does not define these terms, and the State Department suggested that the requirements of Article 16 concerning "degrading" treatment or punishment potentially include treatment "that would probably not be prohibited by the U.S. Constitution."13 Unlike in the case of torture, however, CAT does not expressly require States to criminalize acts of cruel, inhuman, or degrading treatment or punishment that occur within or outside their territorial jurisdiction.

CAT also established a Committee Against Torture (CAT Committee), composed of ten experts of recognized competence in the field of human rights who are elected to biannual terms by State parties. Each party is required to submit, within a year of the Convention entering into force for it, a report to the committee detailing the measures it has taken to give effect to the provisions of CAT, as well as supplementary reports every four years on any new measures taken, in addition to any other reports the committee may request. The committee monitors State compliance with Convention obligations, investigates allegations of systematic CAT violations by State parties and makes recommendations for improving compliance, and submits annual reports to CAT parties and the U.N. General Assembly.

CAT Article 30 provides that disputes between two or more signatory parties concerning the interpretation and application of the Convention can be submitted to arbitration upon request. If, within six months of the date of request for arbitration, the parties are unable to agree upon the organization of the arbitration, any of the parties may refer the dispute to the International Court of Justice. Article 30 contains an "opt-out" provision, however, that enables States (including the U.S.) to make a reservation at the time of CAT ratification declaring that they do not consider themselves to be bound by Article 30.

The U.S. signed CAT on April 18, 1988, and ratified the Convention on October 21, 1994, subject to certain declarations, reservations, and understandings. Perhaps most significantly, the U.S. included a declaration in its instruments of ratification that CAT Articles 1 through 16 were not self-executing. The following sections discuss relevant declarations, reservations, and understandings made by the U.S. to CAT, and U.S. laws implementing CAT Article 4 requirements to criminalize torture.

As previously mentioned, the Senate's advice and consent to CAT ratification was subject to the declaration that the Convention was not self-executing, meaning that implementing legislation was required to fulfill U.S. international obligations under CAT, and such implementing legislation was necessary for CAT to be given effect domestically. In providing its advice and consent to CAT, the Senate also provided a detailed list of understandings concerning the scope of the Convention's definition of torture. With respect to mental torture, a practice not specifically defined by CAT, the U.S. understands such actions to refer to prolonged mental harm caused or resulting from (1) the intentional infliction or threatened infliction of severe physical pain and suffering; (2) the administration of mind-altering substances or procedures to disrupt the victim's senses; (3) the threat of imminent death; or (4) the threat that another person will imminently be subjected to death, severe physical pain or suffering, or the administration or application of mind altering substances or other procedures calculated to disrupt profoundly the senses or personality.

The Convention's definition of torture includes not only acts committed by public officials, but also those acts to which they acquiesced. As expressed in a U.S. understanding on this point, for a public official to acquiesce to an act of torture, that official must, "prior to the activity constituting torture, have *awareness* of such activity and thereafter breach his or her legal responsibility to intervene to prevent such activity." U.S. implementing regulations barring the removal of aliens to countries where they would more likely than not face torture reflect this understanding. Subsequent jurisprudence and administrative decisions concerning the removal of aliens to countries where they may face torture have recognized that "willful blindness" by officials to torture may constitute "acquiescence," but acquiescence does not occur when a government or public official is aware of third-party torture but unable to stop it. In addition, mere noncompliance with applicable legal procedural standards does not *per se* constitute torture.

With regard to Article 14 of the Convention, obligating States to make civil redress available to victims of torture, the Senate's advice and consent was based on the understanding that a State was only obligated for provide a private right of action for acts of torture committed in territory under the State's jurisdiction.

With respect to Article 16 of the Convention, the Senate's advice and consent was based on the reservation that the U.S. considered itself bound to Article 16 to the extent that such cruel, unusual, and inhuman treatment or punishment was prohibited by the Fifth, Eighth, and/or Fourteenth Amendments to the U.S. Constitution. These Amendments apply in different contexts. The Eighth Amendment bars the use of "cruel and unusual punishment" as a form of criminal penalty. The constitutional restraint of persons in other areas, such as pre-trial interrogation, is found in the Due Process Clauses of the Fifth Amendment (concerning obligations owed by the U.S. Federal Government) and Fourteenth Amendment (concerning duties owed by U.S. state governments). These due process rights protect persons from executive abuses that "shock the conscience." The Fourteenth Amendment's Due Process Clause has also been interpreted to incorporate the Eighth Amendment's prohibition on "cruel and unusual punishment" at the state level.

The U.S. has also opted out of the dispute-settlement provisions of CAT Article 30, but it has reserved the right to specifically agree to follow its provisions or any other arbitration procedure to resolve particular disputes concerning CAT application.

To implement CAT Articles 4 and 5, Congress did not enact a new provision to criminalize acts of torture committed within the jurisdiction of the U.S.: It was presumed that such acts would "be covered by existing applicable federal and state statutes," such as those criminalizing assault, manslaughter, and murder. However, the U.S. did add chapter 113C to the U.S. Criminal Code (Federal Torture Statute, 18 U.S.C. §§ 2340-2340B), which criminalizes acts of torture that occur *outside* of the U.S.. "Torture" is defined as "an act committed by a person acting under the color of law specifically intended to inflict severe physical or mental pain or suffering (other than pain or suffering incidental to lawful sanctions) upon another person within his custody or physical control." 18 U.S.C. § 2340 further defines "severe mental pain and suffering" as prolonged mental harm caused by

- the intentional infliction or threatened infliction of severe physical pain or suffering;
- the administration or application, or threatened administration or application, of mind-altering substances or other procedures calculated to disrupt profoundly the senses or the personality;
- the threat of imminent death; or
- the threat that another person will imminently be subjected to death, severe physical pain or suffering, or the administration or application of mind-altering substances or other procedures calculated to disrupt profoundly the senses or personality.

Pursuant to § 2340A, any person who commits or attempts to commit an act of torture outside the U.S. is generally subject to a fine and/or imprisonment for up to 20 years. In cases where death results from the prohibited conduct, the offender may be subject to life imprison mentor the death penalty. A person who conspires to commit an act of torture committed or attempted outside the U.S. is generally subject to the same penalties faced by someone who commits or attempts to commit acts of torture outside the U.S., except that he cannot receive the death penalty for such an offense. Because § 2340A also criminalizes conspiracies to commit torture outside the U.S., it arguably could also apply in situations where a U.S. national conspired to transfer an individual "outside the U.S." so that the individual may be tortured.

Until 2004, for purposes of the Federal Torture Statute, the term "U.S." referred to all areas under the jurisdiction of the U.S., including those falling within its special maritime and territorial jurisdiction, such as military bases and buildings abroad when an offense was committed by or against a U.S. national. Accordingly, the Federal Torture Statute would not appear to have applied to cases of torture that might have occurred in such facilities, because they were not considered to be "outside the U.S.." However, pursuant to § 1089 of the Ronald W. Reagan National Defense Authorization Act for Fiscal Year 2005 (P.L. 108-375), the torture statute was amended so that, for purposes of the statute, "U.S." now refers to the several states of the U.S., the District of Columbia, and the commonwealths, territories, and possessions of the U.S.. Accordingly, the Federal Torture Statute now covers alleged acts of torture that might occur at U.S. facilities abroad. The U.S. claims jurisdiction over actions criminalized under the Federal Torture Statute when (1) the alleged offender is a national of the U.S. or (2) the alleged offender is present in the U.S., irrespective of the nationality of the victim or offender.

In addition, a number of federal criminal statutes explicitly cover actions that are committed outside of the territorial boundaries of the U.S., but nevertheless occur within the special maritime or territorial jurisdiction of the U.S., including statutes criminalizing assault, maiming with the intent to torture, manslaughter, and murder, as well as conspiracies to commit such crimes. Additionally, persons within the jurisdiction of the U.S. who conspire to kill, maim, or injure persons outside the U.S. are subject to criminal penalties. "Grave breaches" of the 1949 Geneva Conventions, including the torture or cruel treatment of detained combatants and civilians in armed conflicts, are criminalized under the War Crimes Act (18 U.S.C. § 2441), and persons convicted for an offense under the act may be sentenced to life imprisonment or, if death results from the breach, be executed. U.S. military law provides further restrictions on the treatment of individuals detained by the military.

Some of the criminal statutes described above, including § 2340A, provide that the specific intent of the actor is a necessary component of the criminal offense.57 Specific intent is "the intent to accomplish the precise criminal act that one is later charged with." This state of mind can be differentiated from that found in criminal offenses that only require an actor to possess a general intent with respect to the offense. General intent usually "takes the form of recklessness (involving actual awareness of a risk and the culpable taking of that risk) or negligence (involving blameworthy inadvertence)."

Two memorandums produced by the Department of Defense and the Department of Justice in 2002 discussed the distinction between general and specific intent with respect to § 2340A, and suggested that "knowledge alone that a particular result is certain to occur does not constitute specific intent." However, both memorandums made clear that this is "a theoretical matter," and note that juries may infer from factual circumstances that specific intent is present. Accordingly, "when a defendant knows that his actions will produce the prohibited result, a jury will in all likelihood conclude that the defendant acted with specific intent." In late 2004, the Department of Justice released a memorandum superseding its earlier memo and modifying some of its conclusions. The 2004 DOJ memo stated that "[i]n light of the President's directive that theU.S. not engage in torture, it would not be appropriate to rely on parsing the specific intent element of the statute to approve as lawful conduct that might otherwise amount to torture." Nevertheless, the 2004 DOJ memo alleged that it was unlikely that a person who "acted in good faith, and only after reasonable investigation establishing that his conduct would not inflict severe physical or mental pain or suffering," would possess the specific intent required to violate the Federal Torture Statute. The 2004 DOJ memo also distinguished intent to commit an offense from the motive behind committing an offense, stating that "a defendant's motive (to protect national security, for example) is not relevant to the question whether he has acted with the requisite specific intent under the statute." In January 2009, President Barack Obama issued an Executive Order providing that when conducting prospective interrogations, U.S. agents are generally forbidden from relying upon any interpretation of the law governing interrogations issued by the Department of Justice between September 11, 2001 and the final day of the Bush Administration, absent further guidance from the Attorney General.

Although § 2340A provides the U.S. with a wide jurisdictional grant to prosecute acts of torture, it has rarely been used. As of January 26, 2009, there appears to be only one instance in which a person has been charged and convicted for violating the Federal Torture Statute. Although the U.S. attached an understanding to its ratification of CAT expressing its view that CAT Article 14 did not require States to recognize a private right of action for victims of torture occurring outside their territorial jurisdiction, the U.S. nevertheless created in the Torture Victims Protection Act of 1991 (TVPA) a private right of action for victims of torture committed under actual or apparent authority, or color of law, of any *foreign* nation. For purposes of the TVPA, "torture" is defined in a similar manner to the definition found in the federal statute criminalizing torture. A claim under the TVPA must be commenced within 10 years after the cause of action arose, and a claimant must exhaust all adequate and available remedies in the country where the alleged torture occurred before a U.S. court can hear the claim.

If an act of torture occurs within the U.S., a tort claim could be brought by a person seeking redress under applicable state, federal statutory, or constitutional tort law.

Following ratification of CAT, Congress did not adopt implementing legislation with respect to CAT Article 16, which requires each CAT party to prohibit cruel, inhuman, and degrading treatment or punishment in "any territory under its jurisdiction." There has recently been debate over whether Congress's failure to pass legislation implementing CAT Article 16 was due to an oversight or whether Congress believed that the U.S. agreed to bind itself to CAT Article 16 only to the extent that it was already required to refrain from cruel, inhuman, and degrading treatment or punishment under the U.S. Constitution and any existing statutes covering such offenses.

As previously mentioned, the Senate made its advice and consent to CAT ratification contingent upon the reservation that the cruel, inhuman, and degrading treatment or punishment prohibited by CAT 16 covered only those forms of treatment or punishment prohibited under the U.S. Constitution. Given this understanding, U.S. obligations under Article 16 can be interpreted in one of two ways.

One way is to interpret the U.S. as having agreed to bind itself to CAT Article 16 only to the extent that cruel, inhuman, or degrading treatment is constitutionally prohibited. Although the U.S. Supreme Court has held that the Constitution applies to U.S. citizens abroad, thereby protecting them from the extraterritorial infliction by U.S. officials of treatment or punishment prohibited under the Constitution, non-citizens receive few, if any, constitutional protections until after they have effected entry into the U.S. (though non-citizens in foreign locations under the complete control of the U.S. may receive greater protections than non-citizens in other foreign locations). Under this interpretation, CAT Article 16, as agreed to by the U.S., would not necessarily prohibit the U.S. from subjecting certain non-U.S. citizens to "cruel, inhuman, and degrading treatment or punishment" at locations outside U.S. territorial boundaries where the U.S. nonetheless asserts territorial jurisdiction (e.g., on the premises of U.S. missions in foreign States). During the Bush Administration, the DOJ took the position that CAT Article 16, as agreed to by the U.S., does not cover aliens detained overseas. It is unclear whether this view shall be maintained by the Obama Administration.

On the other hand, others have argued that CAT Article 16, as agreed to by the U.S., requires the U.S. to prohibit cruel, inhuman, and degrading treatment or punishment in any territory under its jurisdiction if such treatment would be deemed unconstitutional if it occurred in the U.S. This view holds that the purpose of the U.S. reservation to CAT Article 16 was to more clearly define types of treatment that were "cruel, inhuman, and degrading," rather than to limit the geographic scope of U.S. obligations under CAT Article 16. At least one former State Department official involved in CAT's negotiation and ratification process has endorsed this interpretation as the correct one. The Committee Against Torture has also urged the U.S. to ensure that CAT Article 16 is applied to "all persons under the effective control of U.S. authorities, of whichever type, wherever located in the world."

Partially in light of this controversy, Congress passed additional guidelines concerning the treatment of detainees via the Detainee Treatment Act (DTA), which was enacted pursuant to both the Department of Defense, Emergency Supplemental Appropriations to Address Hurricanes in the Gulf of Mexico, and Pandemic Influenza Act, 2006 (P.L. 109-148), and the National Defense Authorization Act for FY2006 (P.L. 109-163), and prohibits the "cruel, inhuman and degrading treatment or punishment of persons under the detention, custody, or control of the U.S. Government." These provisions of the DTA, which were first introduced by Senator John McCain, have popularly been referred to as the "McCain Amendment." The Military Commissions Act of 2006 (MCA, P.L. 109-366) contained an identical measure and also required the President to establish administrative rules and procedures implementing this standard. These provisions are discussed in greater detail in CRS Report RL33655, *Interrogation of Detainees: Requirements of the Detainee Treatment Act*, by Michael John Garcia.

When signing the DTA into law, President Bush issued a signing statement claiming he would construe the McCain Amendment "in a manner consistent with the constitutional authority of the President to supervise the unitary executive branch and as Commander in Chief ... which will assist in achieving the shared objective of the Congress and the President ... of protecting the American people from further terrorist attacks." This statement has been interpreted as meaning that the President believes he may waive congressional restrictions on interrogation techniques in certain circumstances involving national security, pursuant to his constitutional authority as Commander in Chief. However, no similar signing statement was made when the President signed the MCA, even though it contained an identical provision barring "cruel, inhuman, and degrading treatment."

The McCain Amendment does not directly impose criminal or civil penalties on U.S. personnel who might engage in cruel, inhuman, or degrading treatment or punishment of detainees, though such persons could potentially be criminally liable for such conduct under other statutes.81 It does, however, provide an express legal defense to U.S. personnel in any civil or criminal action brought against them on account of their participation in the authorized interrogation of suspected foreign terrorists. The McCain Amendment specifies that a legal defense exists to civil action or criminal prosecution when the U.S. agent "did not know that the [interrogation] practices were unlawful and a person of ordinary sense and understanding would not know the practices were unlawful." A good faith reliance on the advice of counsel is specified to be "an important factor, among others, to consider in assessing whether a person of ordinary sense and understanding would have known the practices to be unlawful."

On September 6, 2006, the Department of Defense implemented the requirements of the McCain Amendment by amending the Army Field Manual to prohibit the "cruel, inhuman, or degrading treatment" of any person in the custody or control of the U.S. military. Eight techniques are expressly prohibited from being used in conjunction with intelligence interrogations:

- forcing the detainee to be naked, perform sexual acts, or pose in a sexual manner;
- placing hoods or sacks over the head of a detainee; using duct tape over the eyes;
- applying beatings, electric shock, burns, or other forms of physical pain;
- waterboarding;
- using military working dogs;
- inducing hypothermia or heat injury;
- conducting mock executions; and
- depriving the detainee of necessary food, water, or medical care.

In addition, the Manual restricts the use of certain other interrogation techniques, but these restrictions may be due to other legal obligations besides those imposed by the McCain Amendment. In October 2007, the *New York Times* reported that in early 2005, the DOJ issued a legal opinion, which remains classified, authorizing the use of certain harsh interrogation techniques by the CIA against terrorist suspects, including head-slapping, simulated drowning (waterboarding), and exposure to frigid temperatures. Later that year, as Congress considered enactment of the DTA, the DOJ reportedly issued another classified opinion declaring that these techniques would not be barred under the DTA, at least when employed against terrorist suspects with crucial information regarding a future terrorist attack. According to the *New York Times*, the memorandums "remain[ed] in effect, and their legal conclusions have been confirmed by several more recent memorandums" that are not publicly available. These opinions were the subject of controversy, with some Members of Congress disputing their legal conclusions and claiming that they had been unaware of the opinions' existence at the time the DTA was considered.

For its part, the Bush Administration claimed that appropriate congressional committees or Members were informed about interrogation techniques that had been approved by the Administration. According to CIA director Michael Hayden, the CIA waterboarded three high-level Al Qaeda suspects but had not used the technique since 2003. Gen. Hayden further stated in congressional testimony in 2008 that waterboarding was not a part of the current CIA interrogation program, and that "it is not certain that the technique would be considered to be lawful under current statute."

On July 20, 2007, President Bush signed an Executive Order concerning the detention and interrogation of certain alien detainees by the CIA, when those aliens (1) are determined to be members or supporters of Al Qaeda, the Taliban, or associated organizations; and (2) likely possess information that could assist in detecting or deterring a terrorist attack against the U.S. and its allies, or could provide help in locating senior leadership within Al Qaeda or the Taliban. The Executive Order did not specifically authorize the use of any particular interrogation techniques with respect to detainees, but instead barred any CIA detention and interrogation program from employing certain practices. Specifically, the Order prohibited the use of torture, as defined under the Federal Torture Statute (18 U.S.C. § 2340);

- cruel, inhuman, and degrading treatment, as defined under the DTA and the MCA;
- any activities subject to criminal penalties under the War Crimes Act (e.g., murder, rape, mutilation);
- other acts of violence serious enough to be considered comparable to the kind expressly prohibited under the War Crimes Act;
- willful and outrageous acts of personal abuse done for the purpose of humiliating or degrading the individual in a manner so serious that any reasonable person, considering the circumstances, would deem the acts to be beyond the bounds of human decency, such as sexual or sexually indecent acts undertaken for the purpose of humiliation, forcing the individual to perform sexual acts or to pose sexually, threatening the individual with sexual mutilation, or using the individual as a human shield; or
- acts intended to denigrate the religion, religious practices, or religious objects of the individual.

Although some types of conduct barred by the Order are easily recognizable (e.g., murder, rape, the performance of sexual acts), it is not readily apparent as to what interrogation techniques fell under the Order's prohibition against acts deemed to be "cruel, inhuman, and degrading" or "beyond the bounds of human decency." Certain interrogation techniques that have been the subject of controversy and are expressly prohibited from being used by the military under the most recent version of the Army Field Manual—waterboarding, hooding, sleep deprivation, or forced standing for prolonged periods, for example—were not specifically addressed by the Order. Whether or not such conduct was deemed by Bush Administration officials to be barred under the more general restrictive language of the Order is unclear.

On January 22, 2009, President Barack Obama issued an Executive Order rescinding President Bush's order of July 20, 2007, and instituting new requirements for interrogation by the CIA and other agencies. The new Order generally bars anyone in U.S. custody or control while in an armed conflict from being subjected to any interrogation technique or treatment other than that authorized under the Army Field Manual. The Order does not preclude federal law enforcement agencies from continuing to "use authorized, non-coercive techniques of interrogation that are designed to elicit voluntary statements and do not involve the use of force, threats, or promises."

The Executive Order also provides that when conducting interrogations, U.S. government officials, employees, and agents may not rely on any interpretation of the law governing interrogations issued by the Department of Justice between September 11, 2001 and January 20, 2009 (i.e., the final day of the Bush Administration), absent further guidance from the Attorney General. It further establishes a Special Interagency Task Force on Interrogation and Transfer Policies, chaired by the Attorney General, which is required

> to study and evaluate whether the interrogation practices and techniques in [the]Army Field Manual ... when employed by departments or agencies outside the military, provide an appropriate means of acquiring the intelligence necessary to protect the Nation, and, if warranted, to recommend any additional or different guidance for other departments or agencies...

The Task Force is required to issue a report to the President of its recommendations within 180 days of the Order's issuance.

In recent years, there has been some controversy regarding the application of CAT by the U.S. towards persons captured in Iraq, Afghanistan, and elsewhere in the context of the "war on terror" and how that application relates to the standards owed under the 1949 Geneva Conventions concerning the protections of civilians and prisoners of war during armed conflicts.

The rule of *lex specialis* provides that when two different legal standards may be applied to the same subject-matter, the more specific standard controls. Accordingly, the Geneva Conventions, which proscribe specific rules for the treatment of detainees during armed conflicts, establish the primary legal duties owed by the U.S. toward battlefield detainees rather than CAT, which is more general in scope.

There is some debate whether the rule of *lex specialis* means that the laws of war are the singular international standard governing the treatment of persons during armed conflict or whether human rights treaties such as CAT may impose complementary duties. The position of the Bush Administration appeared to be that CAT does not apply to armed conflicts. In a 2006 hearing before the Committee Against Torture, representatives of the U.S. State Department argued that CAT did not apply to detainee operations in Afghanistan, Iraq, and Guantánamo, which were controlled by the laws of armed conflict (though as a matter of policy the Bush Administration claimed that it acted consistently with CAT when deciding whether to transfer Guantánamo detainees to third countries). In support of this position, the U.S. argued that CAT's negotiating history revealed an understanding by the negotiating parties that the treaty was intended to cover domestic obligations owed by parties and was not meant to overlap with different treaties governing the standards owed in armed conflicts. The Committee Against Torture disagreed with this view and recommended that the U.S. "should recognize and ensure that the Convention applies at all times, whether in peace, war or armed conflict, in any territory under its jurisdiction." It is not known whether the Obama Administration will take the position that CAT does not legally govern the treatment of persons detained in armed conflict. However, President Obama has issued an Executive Order requiring that all detainees held by the U.S. during an armed conflict be treated consistently with several domestic statutes and international agreements, including CAT and the Federal Torture Statute.

Regardless of whether CAT itself applies during armed conflicts, certain legislation enacted by the U.S. to implement CAT requirements does. As mentioned previously, the Federal Torture Statute criminalizes torture anywhere outside the U.S., without regard to whether such conduct occurred in the context of an armed conflict. Both the DTA and MCA prohibit cruel, inhuman, and degrading treatment of persons in U.S. custody, regardless of where they are held or for what purpose. In the 110th Congress, several appropriation bills were enacted that barred funds made available from being used in contravention of CAT and its implementing legislation. Both the U.S. Troop Readiness, Veterans' Care, Katrina Recovery, and Iraq Accountability Appropriations Act, 2007 (P.L. 110-28), and the Department of Defense Appropriations Act, 2008 (P.L. 110-116), barred funds made available from being used in contravention of CAT and its implementing legislation and regulations, while the Consolidated Appropriations Act, 2008 (P.L. 110-161), more generally barred funds it made available from being used to support torture or cruel or inhumane treatment by any U.S. official or contract employee. It is possible that similar legislation will be considered in the 111th Congress.

Although U.S. courts and administrative bodies have found that severe beatings, maiming, sexual assault, rape, and (in certain circumstances) death threats may constitute "torture" for purposes of either CAT or the TVPA,105 there is little U.S. jurisprudence concerning whether harsh yet sophisticated interrogation techniques of lesser severity constitute "torture" under either CAT or U.S. implementing legislation. "Severe" pain or suffering constituting torture is not defined by either CAT or the Federal Torture Statute. In the 2004 DOJ Memo superseding the Department's earlier memorandum on torture, the DOJ rejected this earlier finding to the extent that it treated severe physical "suffering" as identical to severe physical pain, and concluded that "severe physical suffering" may constitute torture under the Federal Torture Statute even if such suffering does not involve "severe physical pain." The continuing relevance of this legal opinion to U.S. agents is unclear, given President Obama's Executive Order generally barring U.S. agents from relying on Bush-era DOJ opinions regarding the laws of interrogation.

Although few, if any, U.S. courts have had the opportunity to address this issue, decisions and opinions issued by foreign courts and international bodies might serve as indicators of an international consensus for the prohibition of certain interrogation techniques. Assuming for the purposes of discussion that a U.S. body reviewed certain interrogation methods to assess whether they constituted "torture" for purposes of CAT and domestic implementing legislation, it might consider looking at jurisprudence by non-U.S. bodies for guidance, though such jurisprudence would not be binding upon U.S. courts. It should also be noted that the U.S. military has also barred specified interrogation techniques it has deemed to rise to the level of torture, and a reviewing court may consider these prohibitions as well.

The next section briefly discusses two notable circumstances in which international or foreign State bodies have assessed whether a State's interrogation techniques constituted torture.

In 1978, the European Court of Human Rights (ECHR) heard a case brought by Ireland against the United Kingdom concerning British tactics used to counter secessionist movements and organizations in Northern Ireland during the early 1970s, and whether such tactics violated the European Convention for the Protection of Human Rights and Fundamental Freedoms (European Convention). One issue that the ECHR was asked to resolve was whether five interrogation techniques previously employed by British authorities and approved by "high level" British officials violated Article 3 of the European Convention, which provides that "no one shall be subjected to torture or to inhuman or degrading treatment or punishment." According to the ECHR, these five interrogation techniques, which were sometimes used in combination and other times individually, included

- wall-standing: forcing the detainees to remain for periods of some hours in a "stress position," described by those who underwent it as being "spread-eagled against the wall, with their fingers put high above the head against the wall, the legs spread apart and the feet back, causing them to stand on their toes with the weight of the body mainly on the fingers";
- hooding: putting a black or navy coloured bag over the detainees' heads and, at least initially, keeping it there all the time except during interrogation;
- subjection to noise: pending their interrogations, holding the detainees in a room where there was a continuous loud and hissing noise;
- deprivation of sleep: pending their interrogations, depriving the detainees of sleep; and
- deprivation of food and drink: subjecting the detainees to a reduced diet during their stay at the center and pending interrogations.

An investigation by the European Commission of Human Rights concluded that no physical injury resulted from the use of these techniques, though certain detainees suffered weight loss and adverse effects relating to their "acute psychiatric systems ... during interrogation." The ECHR concluded that the interrogation techniques employed by Britain violated the European Convention's prohibition upon "inhuman or degrading treatment," but found that the interrogation methods did not constitute "torture." The ECHR stated that a distinction exists between inhuman or degrading treatment and torture; a "distinction [that] derives principally from a difference in the intensity of the suffering inflicted." The ECHR concluded that while the five interrogation techniques, at least when used in combination, were inhuman or degrading treatment, "they did not occasion suffering of the particular intensity and cruelty implied by the word torture as so understood." The ECHR did not offer an in-depth analysis as to why these techniques did not cause sufficient suffering to constitute torture, although it should be noted that it appeared that few, if any, of the persons who were subject to the interrogation techniques sustained lasting, debilitating physical or mental injuries. It did note, however, that its inquiry required an evaluation of "all the circumstances of the case, such as the duration of the treatment, its physical or mental effects and, in some cases, the sex, age and state of health of the victim." Accordingly, it may be possible that in different circumstances these interrogation techniques might be judged by the ECHR to rise to the level of torture.

Beginning in the late 1980s and ending in the late 1990s, certain Israeli security forces were authorized to employ harsh interrogation techniques against Palestinian security detainees, including the use of "moderate physical pressure." In its initial report to the CAT Committee, Israel argued that the interrogation techniques it employed were in accordance with international law prohibiting torture. It specifically noted the ECHR decision declaring that the interrogation techniques employed by Britain in Northern Ireland during the early 1970s did not constitute torture. The committee concluded, however, that such tactics were "completely unacceptable" given Israel's obligations under CAT Articles 2 and 16.

In response to committee concerns about its interrogation techniques, Israel submitted additional information concerning the nature of the interrogation techniques it employed against Palestinian security detainees. According to the CAT Committee, these interrogation techniques included

- restraining in very painful conditions;
- hooding under special conditions;
- sounding of loud music for prolonged periods;
- sleep deprivation for prolonged periods;
- threats, including death threats;

- violent shaking; and
- using cold air to chill.

In 1997, after examining a special report by Israel discussing these tactics, the committee concluded that the tactics described violated Israel's obligations as a party to CAT, representing a breach of CAT Article 16 and constituting torture as defined by CAT Article 1. The committee opinion suggests that some of the interrogation techniques employed by Israel might constitute torture when employed singularly, although the committee did not specify how particular methods constituted torture. Despite acknowledging that Israel faced a "terrible dilemma ... in dealing with terrorist threats to its security," the committee noted that CAT provides that no exceptional circumstances permit State parties to engage in torture. Accordingly, the committee recommended that Israel immediately cease its use of the interrogation tactics described above.

The committee is an advisory body, and its rulings are not binding. However, in 1999, the Israeli Supreme Court sitting as the Israeli High Court of Justice concluded that the interrogation techniques evaluated by the committee were contrary to Israeli law, and prohibited their usage except in cases when "special permission" was granted for use against detainees believed to possess information about an imminent attack. In doing so, however, the High Court did not expressly determine whether such actions constituted "torture." According to the U.S. State Department, Israel is reported to have used such techniques at least 90 times since the Israeli High Court's ruling.

For its part, the State Department reported in 2000 that Israeli security forces "abused, and in some cases, tortured Palestinians suspected of security offenses." More recently, the State Department has noted that human rights groups claim that torture is being employed.

Michael John Garcia
Legislative Attorney
mgarcia@crs.loc.gov, 7-3873)

Document 9
Military Commission Act of 2009 (Excerpted)
SECTION 1. SHORT TITLE.
This Act may be cited as the "National Defense Authorization Act for Fiscal Year 2010".

....

TITLE XVIII—MILITARY COMMISSIONS
Sec. 1801. Short title.
Sec. 1802. Military commissions.
Sec. 1803. Conforming amendments.
Sec. 1804. Proceedings under prior statute.
Sec. 1805. Submittal to Congress of revised rules for military commissions.
Sec. 1806. Annual reports to Congress on trials by military commission.
Sec. 1807. Sense of Congress on military commission system.
SEC. 1801. SHORT TITLE.
This title may be cited as the "Military Commissions Act of 2009".
SEC. 1802. MILITARY COMMISSIONS.
Chapter 47A of title 10, U.S. Code, is amended to read as follows:
"CHAPTER 47A—MILITARY COMMISSIONS

SUBCHAPTER	Sec
I. General Provisions	948a.
II. Composition of Military Commissions	948h.
III. Pre-Trial Procedure	948q
IV. Trial Procedure	949a
V. Classified Information Procedures	949p–1
VI. Sentences	949s.
VII. Post-Trial Procedures and Review of Military Commissions	950a.
VIII. Punitive Matters	950p.

SUBCHAPTER I—GENERAL PROVISIONS

Sec.948a. Definitions.

948b. Military commissions generally.

948c. Persons subject to military commissions.

948d. Jurisdiction of military commissions.

§ 948a. Definitions

In this chapter:

(1) ALIEN.—The term 'alien' means an individual who is not a citizen of the U.S.

(2) CLASSIFIED INFORMATION.—The term 'classified information' means the following:

(A) Any information or material that has been determined by the U.S. Government pursuant to statute, Executive order, or regulation to require protection against unauthorized disclosure for reasons of national security.

(B) Any restricted data, as that term is defined in section 11 y. of the Atomic Energy Act of 1954 (42 U.S.C. 2014(y)).

(3) COALITION PARTNER.—The term 'coalition partner', with respect to hostilities engaged in by the U.S., means any State or armed force directly engaged along with the U.S. in such hostilities or providing direct operational support to the U.S. in connection with such hostilities.

(4) GENEVA CONVENTION RELATIVE TO THE TREATMENT OF PRISONERS OF WAR.—The term 'Geneva Convention Relative to the Treatment of Prisoners of War' means the Convention Relative to the Treatment of Prisoners of War, done at Geneva August 12, 1949 (6 UST 3316).

(5) GENEVA CONVENTIONS.—The term 'Geneva Conventions' means the international conventions signed at Geneva on August 12, 1949.

(6) PRIVILEGED BELLIGERENT.—The term 'privileged belligerent' means an individual belonging to one of the eight categories enumerated in Article 4 of the Geneva Convention Relative to the Treatment of Prisoners of War.

(7) UNPRIVILEGED ENEMY BELLIGERENT.—

The term 'unprivileged enemy belligerent' means an individual (other than a privileged belligerent) who—

(A) has engaged in hostilities against the U.S. or its coalition partners;

(B) has purposefully and materially supported hostilities against the U.S. or its coalition partners; or

(C) was a part of al Qaeda at the time of the alleged offense under this chapter.

(8) NATIONAL SECURITY.—The term 'national security' means the national defense and foreign relations of the U.S..

(9) HOSTILITIES.—The term 'hostilities' means any conflict subject to the laws of war.

§ 948b. Military commissions generally

(a) PURPOSE.—This chapter establishes procedures governing the use of military commissions to try alien unprivileged enemy belligerents for violations of the law of war and other offenses triable by military commission.

(b) AUTHORITY FOR MILITARY COMMISSIONS UNDER THIS CHAPTER.—The President is authorized to establish military commissions under this chapter for offenses triable by military commission as provided in this chapter.

(c) CONSTRUCTION OF PROVISIONS.—The procedures for military commissions set forth in this chapter are based upon the procedures for trial by general courts martial under chapter 47 of this title (the Uniform Code of Military Justice). Chapter 47 of this title does not, by its terms, apply to trial by military commission except as specifically provided therein or in this chapter, and many of the provisions of chapter 47 of this title are by their terms inapplicable to military commissions. The judicial construction and application of chapter 47 of this title, while instructive, is therefore not of its own force binding on military commissions established under this chapter.

(d) INAPPLICABILITY OF CERTAIN PROVISIONS.—

(1) The following provisions of this title shall not apply to trial by military commission under this chapter:

(A) Section 810 (article 10 of the Uniform Code of Military Justice), relating to speedy trial, including any rule of courts-martial relating to speedy trial.

(B) Sections 831(a), (b), and (d) (articles 31(a), (b), and (d) of the Uniform Code of Military Justice), relating to compulsory self-incrimination.

(C) Section 832 (article 32 of the Uniform Code of Military Justice), relating to pretrial investigation.

(2) Other provisions of chapter 47 of this title shall apply to trial by military commission under this chapter only to the extent provided by the terms of such provisions or by this chapter.

(e) GENEVA CONVENTIONS NOT ESTABLISHING PRIVATE RIGHT OF ACTION.—No alien unprivileged enemy belligerent subject to trial by military commission under this chapter may invoke the Geneva Conventions as a basis for a private right of action.

§ 948c. Persons subject to military commissions

Any alien unprivileged enemy belligerent is subject to trial by military commission as set forth in this chapter.

§ 948d. Jurisdiction of military commissions

A military commission under this chapter shall have jurisdiction to try persons subject to this chapter for any offense made punishable by this chapter, sections 904 and 906 of this title (articles 104 and 106 of the Uniform Code of Military Justice), or the law of war, whether such offense was committed before, on, or after September 11, 2001, and may, under such limitations as the President may prescribe, adjudge any punishment not forbidden by this chapter, including the penalty of death when specifically authorized under this chapter. A military commission is a competent tribunal to make a finding sufficient for jurisdiction.

SUBCHAPTER II—COMPOSITION OF MILITARY COMMISSIONS

Sec.

> 948h. Who may convene military commissions.
> 948i. Who may serve on military commissions.
> 948j. Military judge of a military commission.
> 948k. Detail of trial counsel and defense counsel.
> 948l. Detail or employment of reporters and interpreters.
> 948m. Number of members; excuse of members; absent and additional members.

§ 948h. Who may convene military commissions

Military commissions under this chapter may be convened by the Secretary of Defense or by any officer or official of the U.S. designated by the Secretary for that purpose.

§ 948i. Who may serve on military commissions

(a) IN GENERAL.—Any commissioned officer of the armed forces on active duty is eligible to serve on a military commission under this chapter, including commissioned officers of the reserve components of the armed forces on active duty, commissioned officers of the National Guard on active duty in Federal service, or retired commissioned officers recalled to active duty.

(b) DETAIL OF MEMBERS.—When convening a military commission under this chapter, the convening authority shall detail as members thereof such members of the armed forces eligible under subsection (a) who, in the opinion of the convening authority, are best qualified for the duty by reason of age, education, training, experience, length of service, and judicial temperament. No member of an armed force is eligible to serve as a member of a military commission when such member is the accuser or a witness for the prosecution or has acted as an investigator or counsel in the same case.

(c) EXCUSE OF MEMBERS.—Before a military commission under this chapter is assembled for the trial of a case, the convening authority may excuse a member from participating in the case.

§ 948j. Military judge of a military commission

(a) DETAIL OF MILITARY JUDGE.—A military judge shall be detailed to each military commission under this chapter. The Secretary of Defense shall prescribe regulations providing for the manner in which military judges are so detailed to military commissions. The military judge shall preside over each military commission to which such military judge has been detailed.

(b) ELIGIBILITY.—A military judge shall be a commissioned officer of the armed forces who is a member of the bar of a Federal court, or a member of the bar 6 of the highest court of a State, and who is certified to be qualified for duty under section 826 of this title (article 26 of the Uniform Code of Military Justice) as a military judge of general courts-martial by the Judge Advocate General of the armed force of which such military judge is a member.

(c) INELIGIBILITY OF CERTAIN INDIVIDUALS.—No person is eligible to act as military judge in a case of a military commission under this chapter if such person is the accuser or a witness or has acted as investigator or a counsel in the same case.

(d) CONSULTATION WITH MEMBERS; INELIGBILITY TO VOTE.—A military judge detailed to a military commission under this chapter may not consult with the members except in the presence of the accused (except as otherwise provided in section 949d of this title), trial counsel, and defense counsel, nor may such military judge vote with the members.

(e) OTHER DUTIES.—A commissioned officer who is certified to be qualified for duty as a military judge of a military commission under this chapter may perform such other duties as are assigned to such officer by or with the approval of the Judge Advocate General of the 4 armed force of which such officer is a member or the designee of such Judge Advocate General.

(f) PROHIBITION ON EVALUATION OF FITNESS BY CONVENING AUTHORITY.—The convening authority of a military commission under this chapter may not prepare or review any report concerning the effectiveness, fitness, or efficiency of a military judge detailed to the military commission which relates to such judge's performance of duty as a military judge on the military commission.

§ 948k. Detail of trial counsel and defense counsel

(a) DETAIL OF COUNSEL GENERALLY.—(1) Trial counsel and military defense counsel shall be detailed for each military commission under this chapter.

(2) Assistant trial counsel and assistant and associate defense counsel may be detailed for a military commission under this chapter.

(3) Military defense counsel for a military commission under this chapter shall be detailed as soon as practicable.

(4) The Secretary of Defense shall prescribe regulations providing for the manner in which trial counsel and military defense counsel are detailed for military commissions under this chapter and for the persons who are authorized to detail such counsel for such military commissions.

(b) TRIAL COUNSEL.—Subject to subsection (e), a trial counsel detailed for a military commission under this chapter shall be—"(1) a judge advocate (as that term is defined in section 801 of this title (article 1 of the Uniform Code of Military Justice)) who is—

(A) a graduate of an accredited law school or a member of the bar of a Federal court or of the highest court of a State; and (B) certified as competent to perform duties as trial counsel before general courts-martial by the Judge Advocate General of the armed force of which such judge advocate is a member; or "(2) a civilian who is—

(A) a member of the bar of a Federal court or of the highest court of a State; and

(B) otherwise qualified to practice before the military commission pursuant to regulations prescribed by the Secretary of Defense.

(c) DEFENSE COUNSEL.—(1) Subject to subsection (e), a military defense counsel detailed for a military commission under this chapter shall be a judge advocate (as so defined) who is—"(A) a graduate of an accredited law school or a member of the bar of a Federal court or of the highest court of a State; an (B) certified as competent to perform duties as defense counsel before general courts-martial by the Judge Advocate General of the armed force of which such judge advocate is a member.

(2) The Secretary of Defense shall prescribe regulations for the appointment and performance of defense counsel in capital cases under this chapter.

(d) CHIEF PROSECUTOR; CHIEF DEFENSE COUNSEL.—

(1) The Chief Prosecutor in a military commission under this chapter shall meet the requirements set forth in subsection (b)(1).

(2) The Chief Defense Counsel in a military commission under this chapter shall meet the requirements set forth in subsection (c)(1).

(e) INELIGIBILITY OF CERTAIN INDIVIDUALS.—No person who has acted as an investigator, military judge, or member of a military commission under this chapter in any case may act later as trial counsel or military defense counsel in the same case. No person who has acted for the prosecution before a military commission under this chapter may act later in the same case for the defense, nor may any person who has acted for the defense before a military commission under this chapter act later in the same case for the prosecution.

§ 948l. Detail or employment of reporters and interpreters

(a) COURT REPORTERS.—Under such regulations as the Secretary of Defense may prescribe, the convening authority of a military commission under this chapter shall detail to or employ for the military commission qualified court reporters, who shall prepare a verbatim record of the proceedings of and testimony taken before the military commission.

(b) INTERPRETERS.—Under such regulations as the Secretary of Defense may prescribe, the convening authority of a military commission under this chapter may detail to or employ for the military commission interpreters who shall interpret for the military commission, and, as necessary, for trial counsel and defense counsel for the military commission, and for the accused.

(c) TRANSCRIPT; RECORD.—The transcript of a military commission under this chapter shall be under the control of the convening authority of the military commission, who shall also be responsible for preparing the record of the proceedings of the military commission.

§ 948m. Number of members; excuse of members; absent and additional members

(a) NUMBER OF MEMBERS.—(1) Except as provided in paragraph (2), a military commission under this chapter shall have at least five members.

(2) In a case in which the accused before a military commission under this chapter may be sentenced to a penalty of death, the military commission shall have the number of members prescribed by section 949m(c) of this title.

(b) EXCUSE OF MEMBERS.—No member of a military commission under this chapter may be absent or excused after the military commission has been assembled for the trial of a case unless excused—

(1) as a result of challenge;

(2) by the military judge for physical disability or other good cause; or

(3) by order of the convening authority for good cause.

(c) ABSENT AND ADDITIONAL MEMBERS.—Whenever a military commission under this chapter is reduced below the number of members required by subsection (a), the trial may not proceed unless the convening authority details new members sufficient to provide not less than such number. The trial may proceed with the new members present after the recorded evidence previously introduced before the members has been read to the military commission in the presence of the military judge, the accused (except as provided in section 949d of this title), and counsel for both sides.

SUBCHAPTER III—PRE-TRIAL PROCEDURE

Sec.

948q. Charges and specifications.

948r. Exclusion of statements obtained by torture or cruel, inhuman, or degrading treatment; prohibition of self-incrimination; admission of other statements of the accused.

948s. Service of charges.

§ 948q. Charges and specifications

(a) CHARGES AND SPECIFICATIONS.—Charges and specifications against an accused in a military commission under this chapter shall be signed by a person subject to chapter 47 of this title under oath before a commissioned officer of the armed forces authorized to administer oaths and shall state—

(1) that the signer has personal knowledge of, or reason to believe, the matters set forth therein ;and best of the signer's knowledge and belief.

(b) NOTICE TO ACCUSED.—Upon the swearing of the charges and specifications in accordance with subsection (a), the accused shall be informed of the charges and specifications against the accused as soon as practicable.

§ 948r. Exclusion of statements obtained by torture or cruel, inhuman, or degrading treatment; prohibition of self-incrimination; admission of other statements of the accused.

(a) EXCLUSION OF STATEMENTS OBTAIN BY TORTURE OR CRUEL, INHUMAN, OR DEGRADING TREATMENT.—No statement obtained by the use of torture or by cruel, inhuman, or degrading treatment (as defined by section 1003 of the Detainee Treatment Act of 2005 (42 U.S.C. 2000dd)), whether or not under color of law, shall be admissible in a military commission under this chapter, except against a person accused of torture or such treatment as evidence that the statement was made.

"(b) SELF-INCRIMINATION PROHIBITED.—No person shall be required to testify against himself or herself at a proceeding of a military commission under this chapter.

(c) OTHER STATEMENTS OF THE ACCUSED.—A statement of the accused may be admitted in evidence in a military commission under this chapter only if the military judge finds—"(1) that the totality of the circumstances renders the statement reliable and possessing sufficient probative value; and

(2) that—(A) the statement was made incident to lawful conduct during military operations at the point of capture or during closely related active combat engagement, and the interests of justice would best be served by admission of the statement into evidence; or (B) the statement was voluntarily given.

(d) DETERMINATION OF VOLUNTARINESS.—In determining for purposes of subsection (c)(2)(B) whether a statement was voluntarily given, the military judge shall consider the totality of the circumstances, including, as appropriate, the following:

(1) The details of the taking of the statement, accounting for the circumstances of the conduct of military and intelligence operations during hostilities.

(2) The characteristics of the accused, such as military training, age, and education level.

(3) The lapse of time, change of place, or change in identity of the questioners between the statement sought to be admitted and any prior questioning of the accused.

§ 948s. Service of charges

The trial counsel assigned to a case before a military commission under this chapter shall cause to be served upon the accused and military defense counsel a copy of the charges upon which trial is to be had in English and, if appropriate, in another language that the accused understands, sufficiently in advance of trial to prepare a defense.

SUBCHAPTER IV—TRIAL PROCEDURE

Sec.949a. Rules.

949b. Unlawfully influencing action of military commission and U.S. Court of Military Commission Review.

949c. Duties of trial counsel and defense counsel.

949d. Sessions.

949e. Continuances.

949f. Challenges.

949g. Oaths.

949h. Former jeopardy.

949i. Pleas of the accused.

949j. Opportunity to obtain witnesses and other evidence.

949k. Defense of lack of mental responsibility.

949l. Voting and rulings.

949m. Number of votes required.

949n. Military commission to announce action.

949o. Record of trial.

§ 949a. Rules

(a) PROCEDURES AND RULES OF EVIDENCE.—Pretrial, trial, and post-trial procedures, including elements and modes of proof, for cases triable by military commission under this chapter may be prescribed by the Secretary of Defense. Such procedures may not be contrary to or inconsistent with this chapter. Except as otherwise provided in this chapter or chapter 47 of this title, the procedures and rules of evidence applicable in trials by general courts-martial of the U.S. shall apply in trials by military commission under this chapter.

(b) EXCEPTIONS.—(1) In trials by military commission under this chapter, the Secretary of Defense, in consultation with the Attorney General, may make such exceptions in the applicability of the procedures and rules of evidence otherwise applicable in general courts-martial as may be required by the unique circumstances of the conduct of military and intelligence operations during hostilities or by other practical need consistent with this chapter.

(2) Notwithstanding any exceptions authorized by paragraph (1), the procedures and rules of evidence in trials by military commission under this chapter shall include, at a minimum, the following rights of the accused:

(A) To present evidence in the accused's defense, to cross-examine the witnesses who testify against the accused, and to examine and respond to all evidence admitted against the accused on the issue of guilt or innocence and for sentencing, as provided for by this chapter.

(B) To be present at all sessions of the military commission (other than those for deliberations or voting), except when excluded under section 949d of this title.

(C)(i) When none of the charges preferred against the accused are capital, to be represented before a military commission by civilian counsel if provided at no expense to the Government, and by either the defense counsel detailed or the military counsel of the accused's own selection, if reasonably available.

(ii) When any of the charges preferred against the accused are capital, to be represented before a military commission in accordance with clause (i) and, to the greatest extent practicable, by at least one additional counsel who is learned in applicable law relating to capital cases and who, if necessary, may be a civilian and compensated in accordance with regulations prescribed by the Secretary of Defense.

(D) To self-representation, if the accused knowingly and competently waives the assistance of counsel, subject to the provisions of paragraph (4).

(E) To the suppression of evidence that is not reliable or probative.

(F) To the suppression of evidence the probative value of which is substantially outweighed by—

(i) the danger of unfair prejudice, confusion of the issues, or misleading the members; or

(ii) considerations of undue delay, waste of time, or needless presentation of cumulative evidence.

(3) In making exceptions in the applicability in trials by military commission under this chapter from the procedures and rules otherwise applicable in general courts-martial, the Secretary of Defense may provide the following:

(A) Evidence seized outside the U.S. shall not be excluded from trial by military commission on the grounds that the evidence was not seized pursuant to a search warrant or authorization.

(B) A statement of the accused that is otherwise admissible shall not be excluded from trial by military commission on grounds of alleged coercion or compulsory self-incrimination so long as the evidence complies with the provisions of section 948r of this title.

(C) Evidence shall be admitted as authentic so long as—

(i) the military judge of the military commission determines that there is sufficient evidence that the evidence is what it is claimed to be; and (ii) the military judge instructs the members that they may consider any issue as to authentication or identification of evidence in determining the weight, if any, to be given to the evidence.

(D) Hearsay evidence not otherwise admissible under the rules of evidence applicable in trial by general courts-martial may be admitted in a trial by military commission only if—

(i) the proponent of the evidence makes known to the adverse party, sufficiently in advance to provide the adverse party with a fair opportunity to meet the evidence, the proponent's intention to offer the evidence, and the particulars of the evidence (including information on the circumstances under which the evidence was obtained); and (ii) the military judge, after taking into account all of the circumstances surrounding the taking of the statement, including the degree to which the statement is corroborated, the indicia of reliability within the statement itself, and whether the will of the declarant was overborne, determines that—

(I) the statement is offered as evidence of a material fact;

(II) the statement is probative on the point for which it is offered;

(III) direct testimony from the witness is not available as a practical matter, taking into consideration the physical location of the witness, the unique circumstances of military and intelligence operations during hostilities, and the adverse impacts on military or intelligence operations that would likely result from the production of the witness; and

(IV) the general purposes of the rules of evidence and the interests of justice will best be served by admission of the statement into evidence.

(4)(A) The accused in a military commission under this chapter who exercises the right to self-representation under paragraph (2)(D) shall conform the accused's deportment and the conduct of the defense to the rules of evidence, procedure, and decorum applicable to trials by military commission.

(B) Failure of the accused to conform to the rules described in subparagraph (A) may result in a partial or total revocation by the military judge of the right of self-representation under paragraph (2)(D). In such case, the military counsel of the accused or an appropriately authorized civilian counsel shall perform the functions necessary for the defense.

(C) DELEGATION OF AUTHORITY TO PRESCRIBE REGULATIONS.—The Secretary of Defense may delegate the authority of the Secretary to prescribe regulations under this chapter.

(D) NOTICE TO CONGRESS OF MODIFICATION OF RULES.—Not later than 60 days before the date on which any proposed modification of the rules in effect for military commissions under this chapter goes into effect, the Secretary of Defense shall submit to the Committee on Armed Services of the Senate and the Committee on Armed Services of the House of Representatives a report describing the proposed modification.

§ 950t. Crimes triable by military commission

The following offenses shall be triable by military commission under this chapter at any time without limitation:

(1) MURDER OF PROTECTED PERSONS.—Any person subject to this chapter who intentionally kills one or more protected persons shall be punished by death or such other punishment as a military commission under this chapter may direct.

(2) ATTACKING CIVILIANS.—Any person subject to this chapter who intentionally engages in an attack upon a civilian population as such, or individual civilians not taking active part in hostilities, shall be punished, if death results to one or more of the victims, by death or such other punishment as a military commission under this chapter may direct, and, if death does not result to any of the victims, by such punishment, other than death, as a military commission under this chapter may direct.

(3) ATTACKING CIVILIAN OBJECTS.—Any person subject to this chapter who intentionally engages in an attack upon a civilian object that is not a military objective shall be punished as a military commission under this chapter may direct.

(4) ATTACKING PROTECTED PROPERTY.—Any person subject to this chapter who intentionally engages in an attack upon protected property shall be punished as a military commission under this chapter may direct.

(5) PILLAGING.—Any person subject to this chapter who intentionally and in the absence of military necessity appropriates or seizes property for private or personal use, without the consent of a person with authority to permit such appropriation or seizure, shall be punished as a military commission under this chapter may direct.

(6) DENYING QUARTER.—Any person subject to this chapter who, with effective command or control over subordinate groups, declares, orders, or otherwise indicates to those groups that there shall be no survivors or surrender accepted, with the intent to threaten an adversary or to conduct hostilities such that there would be no survivors or surrender accepted, shall be punished as a military commission under this chapter may direct.

(7) TAKING HOSTAGES.—Any person subject to this chapter who, having knowingly seized or detained one or more persons, threatens to kill, injure, or continue to detain such person or persons with the intent of compelling any nation, person other than the hostage, or group of persons to act or refrain from acting as an explicit or implicit condition for the safety or release of such person or persons, shall be punished, if death results to one or more of the victims, by death or such other punishment as a military commission under this chapter may direct, and, if death does not result to any of the victims, by such punishment, other than death, as a military commission under this chapter may direct.

(8) EMPLOYING POISON OR SIMILAR WEAPONS.—Any person subject to this chapter who intentionally, as a method of warfare, employs a substance or weapon that releases a substance that causes death or serious and lasting damage to health in the ordinary course of events, through its asphyxiating, bacteriological, or toxic properties, shall be punished, if death results to one or more of the victims, by death or such other punishment as a military commission under this chapter may direct, and, if death does not result to any of the victims, by such punishment, other than death, as a military commission under this chapter may direct.

(9) USING PROTECTED PERSONS AS A SHIELD.—Any person subject to this chapter who positions, or otherwise takes advantage of, a protected person with the intent to shield a military objective from attack. or to shield, favor, or impede military operations, shall be punished, if death results to one or more of the victims, by death or such other punishment as a military commission under this chapter may direct, and, if death does not result to any of the victims, by such punishment, other than death, as a military commission under this chapter may direct.

(10) USING PROTECTED PROPERTY AS A SHIELD.—Any person subject to this chapter who positions, or otherwise takes advantage of the location of, protected property with the intent to shield a military objective from attack, or to shield, favor, or impede military operations, shall be punished as a military commission under this chapter may direct.

(11) TORTURE.—

(A) OFFENSE.—Any person subject to this chapter who commits an act specifically intended to inflict severe physical or mental pain or suffering (other than pain or suffering incidental to lawful sanctions) upon another person within his custody or physical control for the purpose of obtaining information or a confession, punishment, intimidation, coercion, or any reason based on discrimination of any kind, shall be punished, if death results to one or more of the victims, by death or such other punishment as a military commission under this chapter may direct, and, if death does not result to any of the victims, by such punishment, other than death, as a military commission under this chapter may direct.

(B) SEVERE MENTAL PAIN OR SUFFERING DEFINED.—In this paragraph, the term 'severe mental pain or suffering' has the meaning given that term in section 2340(2) of title18.

(12) CRUEL OR INHUMAN TREATMENT.—Any person subject to this chapter who subjects another person in their custody or under their physical control, regardless of nationality or physical location, to cruel or inhuman treatment that constitutes a grave breach of common Article 3 of the Geneva Conventions shall be punished, if death results to the victim, by death or such other punishment as a military commission under this chapter may direct, and, if death does not result to the victim, by such punishment, other than death, as a military commission under this chapter may direct.

(13) INTENTIONALLY CAUSING SERIOUS BODILY INJURY.—

(A) OFFENSE.—Any person subject to this chapter who intentionally causes serious bodily injury to one or more persons, including privileged belligerents, in violation of the law of war shall be punished, if death results to one or more of the victims, by death or such other punishment as a military commission under this chapter may direct, and, if death does not result to any of the victims, by such punishment, other than death, as a military commission under this chapter may direct.

(B) SERIOUS BODILY INJURY DEFINED.—

In this paragraph, the term 'serious bodily injury' means bodily injury which involves—

(i) a substantial risk of death; (ii) extreme physical pain; (iii) protracted and obvious disfigurement; or (iv) protracted loss or impairment of the function of a bodily member, organ, or mental faculty.

(14) MUTILATING OR MAIMING.—Any person subject to this chapter who intentionally injures one or more protected persons by disfiguring the person or persons by any mutilation of the person or persons, or by permanently disabling any member, limb, or organ of the body of the person or persons, without any legitimate medical or dental purpose, shall be punished, if death results to one or more of the victims, by death or such other punishment as a military commission under this chapter may direct, and, if death does not result to any of the victims, by such punishment, other than death, as a military commission under this chapter may direct.

(15) MURDER IN VIOLATION OF THE LAW OF WAR.—Any person subject to this chapter who intentionally kills one or more persons, including privileged belligerents, in violation of the law of war shall be punished by death or such other punishment as a military commission under this chapter may direct.

(16) DESTRUCTION OF PROPERTY IN VIOLATION OF THE LAW OF WAR.—Any person subject to this chapter who intentionally destroys property belonging to another person in violation of the law of war shall punished as a military commission under this chapter may direct.

(17) USING TREACHERY OR PERFIDY.—Any person subject to this chapter who, after inviting the confidence or belief of one or more persons that they were entitled to, or obliged to accord, protection under the law of war, intentionally makes use of that confidence or belief in killing, injuring, or capturing such person or persons shall be punished, if death results to one or more of the victims, by death or such other punishment as a military commission under this chapter may direct, and, if death does not result to any of the victims, by such punishment, other than death, as a military commission under this chapter may direct.

(18) IMPROPERLY USING A FLAG OF TRUCE.—Any person subject to this chapter who uses a flag of truce to feign an intention to negotiate, surrender, or otherwise suspend hostilities when there is no such intention shall be punished as a military commission under this chapter may direct.

(19) IMPROPERLY USING A DISTINCTIVE EMBLEM.—Any person subject to this chapter who intentionally uses a distinctive emblem recognized by the law of war for combatant purposes in a manner prohibited by the law of war shall be punished as a military commission under this chapter may direct.

(20) INTENTIONALLY MISTREATING A DEAD BODY.—Any person subject to this chapter who in-tentionally mistreats the body of a dead person, without justification by legitimate military necessary, shall be punished as a military commission under this chapter may direct.

(21) RAPE.—Any person subject to this chapter who forcibly or with coercion or threat of force wrong-fully invades the body of a person by penetrating, however slightly, the anal or genital opening of the victim with any part of the body of the accused, or with any foreign object, shall be punished as a military commission under this chapter may direct.

(22) SEXUAL ASSAULT OR ABUSE.—Any person subject to this chapter who forcibly or with coercion or threat of force engages in sexual contact with one or more persons, or causes one or more persons to engage in sexual contact, shall be punished as a military commission under this chapter may direct.

(23) HIJACKING OR HAZARDING A VESSEL OR AIRCRAFT.—Any person subject to this chapter who intentionally seizes, exercises unauthorized control over, or endangers the safe navigation of a vessel or aircraft that is not a legitimate military objective shall be punished, if death results to one or more of the

victims, by death or such other punishment as a military commission under this chapter may direct, and, if death does not result to any of the victims, by such punishment, other than death, as a military commission under this chapter may direct.

(24) TERRORISM.—Any person subject to this chapter who intentionally kills or inflicts great bodily harm on one or more protected persons, or intentionally engages in an act that evinces a wanton disregard for human life, in a manner calculated to influence or affect the conduct of government or civilian population by intimidation or coercion, or to retaliate against government conduct, shall be punished, if death results to one or more of the victims, by death or such other punishment as a military commission under this chapter may direct, and, if death does not result to any of the victims, by such punishment, other than death, as a military commission under this chapter may direct.

(25) PROVIDING MATERIAL SUPPORT FOR TERRORISM.—

(A) OFFENSE.—Any person subject to this chapter who provides material support or resources, knowing or intending that they are to be used in preparation for, or in carrying out, an act of terrorism (as set forth in paragraph (24) of this section), or who intentionally provides material support or resources to an international terrorist organization engaged in hostilities against the U.S., knowing that such organization has engaged or engages in terrorism (as so set forth), shall be punished as a military commission under this chapter may direct.

(B) MATERIAL SUPPORT OR RESOURCES DEFINED.—In this paragraph, the term 'material support or resources' has the meaning given that term in section 2339A(b) of title 18.

26) WRONGFULLY AIDING THE ENEMY.—Any person subject to this chapter who, in breach of an allegiance or duty to the U.S., knowingly and intentionally aids an enemy of the U.S., or one of the co-belligerents of the enemy, shall be punished as a military commission under this chapter may direct.

(27) SPYING.—Any person subject to this chapter who, in violation of the law of war and with intent or reason to believe that it is to be used to the injury of the U.S. or to the advantage of a foreign power, collects or attempts to collect information by clandestine means or while acting under false pretenses, for the purpose of conveying such information to an enemy of the U.S., or one of the co-belligerents of the enemy, shall be punished by death or such other punishment as a military commission under this chapter may direct.

(28) ATTEMPTS.—(A) IN GENERAL.—Any person subject to this chapter who attempts to commit any of fense punishable by this chapter shall be punished as a military commission under this chapter may direct.

(B) SCOPE OF OFFENSE.—An act, done with specific intent to commit an offense under this chapter, amounting to more than mere preparation and tending, even though failing, to effect its commission, is an attempt to commit that offense.

(C) EFFECT OF CONSUMMATION.—Any person subject to this chapter may be convicted of an attempt to commit an offense although it appears on the trial that the offense was consummated.

(29) CONSPIRACY.—Any person subject to this chapter who conspires to commit one or more substantive offenses triable by military commission under this subchapter, and who knowingly does any overt act to effect the object of the conspiracy, shall be punished, if death results to one or more of the victims, by death or such other punishment as a military commission under this chapter may direct, and, if death does not result to any of the victims, by such punishment, other than death, as a military commission under this chapter may direct.

(30) SOLICITATION.—Any person subject to this chapter who solicits or advises another or others to commit one or more substantive offenses triable by military commission under this chapter shall, if the offense solicited or advised is attempted or committed, be punished with the punishment provided for the commission of the offense, but, if the offense solicited or advised is not committed or attempted, shall be punished as a military commission under this chapter may direct.

(31) CONTEMPT.—A military commission under this chapter may punish for contempt any person who uses any menacing word, sign, or gesture in its presence, or who disturbs its proceedings by any riot or disorder.

(32) PERJURY AND OBSTRUCTION OF JUSTICE.—A military commission under this chapter may try offenses and impose such punishment as the military commission may direct for perjury, false testimony, or obstruction of justice related to the military commission.

SEC. 1803. CONFORMING AMENDMENTS.

(a) UNIFORM CODE OF MILITARY JUSTICE.—

(1) PERSONS SUBJECT TO UCMJ.—Paragraph (13) of section 802(a) of title 10, U.S. Code (article 2(a) of the Uniform Code of Military Justice), is amended to read as follows:

(13) Individuals belonging to one of the eight categories enumerated in Article 4 of the Convention Relative to the Treatment of Prisoners of War, done at Geneva August 12, 1949 (6 UST 3316), who violate the law of war.

(2) CONSTRUCTION OF MILITARY COMMISSIONS WITH COURTS-MARTIAL.—Section 839 of such title (article 39 of the Uniform Code of Military Justice) is amended by adding at the end the following new subsection:

(d) The findings, holdings, interpretations, and other precedents of military commissions under chapter 47A of this title—

(1) may not be introduced or considered in any hearing, trial, or other proceeding of a court martial under this chapter; and

(2) may not form the basis of any holding, decision, or other determination of a court-martial.

(b) APPELLATE REVIEW UNDER DETAINEE TREATMENT ACT OF 2005.—Section 1005(e) of the Detainee Treatment Act of 2005 (title X of Public Law 109–359; 10 U.S.C. 801 note) is amended by striking paragraph (3).

SEC. 1804. PROCEEDINGS UNDER PRIOR STATUTE.

(a) PRIOR CONVICTIONS.—The amendment made by section 1802 shall have no effect on the validity of any conviction pursuant to chapter 47A of title 10, U.S. Code (as such chapter was in effect on the day before the date of the enactment of this Act).

(b) COMPOSITION OF MILITARY COMMISSIONS.—Notwithstanding the amendment made by section 1802—

(1) any commission convened pursuant to chapter 47A of title 10, U.S. Code (as such chapter was in effect on the day before the date of the enactment of this Act), shall be deemed to have been convened pursuant to chapter 47A of title 10, U.S. Code (as amended by section 1802);

(2) any member of the Armed Forces detailed to serve on a commission pursuant to chapter 47A of title 10, U.S. Code (as in effect on the day before the date of the enactment of this Act), shall be deemed to have been detailed pursuant to chapter 47A of title 10, U.S. Code (as so amended);

(3) any military judge detailed to a commission pursuant to chapter 47A of title 10, U.S. Code (as in effect on the day before the date of the enactment of this Act), shall be deemed to have been detailed pursuant to chapter 47A of title 10, U.S. Code (as so amended);

(4) any trial counsel or defense counsel detailed for a commission pursuant to chapter 47A of title 10, U.S. Code (as in effect on the day before the date of the enactment of this Act), shall be deemed to have been detailed pursuant to chapter 47A of title 10, U.S. Code (as so amended);

(5) any court reporters detailed to or employed by a commission pursuant to chapter 47A of title 10, U.S. Code (as in effect on the day before the date of the enactment of this Act), shall be deemed to have been detailed or employed pursuant to chapter 47A of title 10, U.S. Code (as so amended); and (6) any appellate military judge or other duly appointed appellate judge on the Court of Military Commission Review pursuant to chapter 47A of title 10, U.S. Code (as in effect on the day before the date of the enactment of this Act), shall be deemed to have been detailed or appointed to the U.S. Court of Military Commission Review pursuant to chapter 47A of title 10, U.S. Code (as so amended).(c) CHARGES AND SPECIFICATIONS.—Notwithstanding the amendment made by section 1802—

(1) any charges or specifications sworn or referred pursuant to chapter 47A of title 10, U.S. Code (as such chapter was in effect on the day before the date of the enactment of this Act), shall be deemed to have been sworn or referred pursuant to chapter 47A of title 10, U.S. Code (as amended by section 1802); and (2) any charges or specifications described in paragraph (1) may be amended, without prejudice, as needed to properly allege jurisdiction under chapter 47A of title 10, U.S. Code (as so amended), and crimes triable under such chapter.

(d) PROCEDURES AND REQUIREMENTS.—

(1) IN GENERAL.—Except as provided in subsections (a) through (c) and subject to paragraph (2), any commission convened pursuant to chapter 47A of title 10, U.S. Code (as such chapter was in effect on the day before the date of the enactment of this Act), shall be conducted after the date of the enactment of this

Act in accordance with the procedures and requirements of chapter 47A of title 10, U.S. Code (as amended by section 1802).

(2) TEMPORARY CONTINUATION OF PRIOR PROCEDURES AND REQUIREMENTS.—Any military commission described in paragraph (1) may be conducted in accordance with any procedures and requirements of chapter 47A of title 10, U.S. Code (as in effect on the day before the date of the enactment of this Act), that are not inconsistent with the provisions of chapter 47A of title 10, U.S. Code, (as so amended), until the earlier of—

(A) the date of the submittal to Congress under section 1805 of the revised rules for military commissions under chapter 47A of title 10, U.S. Code (as so amended); or (B) the date that is 90 days after the date of the enactment of this Act.

SEC. 1805. SUBMITTAL TO CONGRESS OF REVISED RULES FOR MILITARY COMMISSIONS.

(a) DEADLINE FOR SUBMITTAL.—Not later than 90 days after the date of the enactment of this Act, the Secretary of Defense shall submit to the Committees on Armed Services of the Senate and the House of Representatives the revised rules for military commissions prescribed by the Secretary for purposes of chapter 47A of title 10, U.S. Code (as amended by section 1802).

(b) TREATMENT OF REVISED RULES UNDER REQUIREMENT FOR NOTICE AND WAIT REGARDING MODIFICATION OF RULES.—The revised rules submitted to Congress under subsection (a) shall not be treated as a modification of the rules in effect for military commissions for purposes of section 949a(d) of title 10, U.S. Code (as so amended).

SEC. 1806. ANNUAL REPORTS TO CONGRESS ON TRIALS BY MILITARY COMMISSION.

(a) ANNUAL REPORTS REQUIRED.—Not later than January 31 of each year, the Secretary of Defense shall submit to the Committees on Armed Services of the Senate and the House of Representatives a report on any trials conducted by military commissions under chapter 47A of title 10, U.S. Code (as amended by section 1802), during the preceding year.

(b) FORM.—Each report under this section shall be submitted in unclassified form, but may include a classified annex.

SEC. 1807. SENSE OF CONGRESS ON MILITARY COMMISSION SYSTEM.

It is the sense of Congress that—

(1) the fairness and effectiveness of the military commissions system under chapter 47A of title 10, U.S. Code (as amended by section 1802), will depend to a significant degree on the adequacy of defense counsel and associated resources for individuals accused, particularly in the case of capital cases, under such chapter 47A; and (2) defense counsel in military commission cases, particularly in capital cases, under such chapter 47A of title 10, U.S. Code (as so amended), should be fully resourced as provided in such chapter 47A.

SEC. 1804. PROCEEDINGS UNDER PRIOR STATUTE.

(a) PRIOR CONVICTIONS.—The amendment made by section 1802 shall have no effect on the validity of any conviction pursuant to chapter 47A of title 10, U.S. Code (as such chapter was in effect on the day before the date of the enactment of this Act).

(b) COMPOSITION OF MILITARY COMMISSIONS.—Notwithstanding the amendment made by section 1802—(1) any commission convened pursuant to chapter 47A of title 10, U.S. Code (as such chapter was in effect on the day before the date of the enactment of this Act), shall be deemed to have been convened pursuant to chapter 47A of title 10, U.S. Code (as amended by section 1802);

(2) any member of the Armed Forces detailed to serve on a commission pursuant to chapter 47A of title 10, U.S. Code (as in effect on the day before the date of the enactment of this Act), shall be deemed to have been detailed pursuant to chapter 47A of title 10, U.S. Code (as so amended);

(3) any military judge detailed to a commission pursuant to chapter 47A of title 10, U.S. Code (as in effect on the day before the date of the enactment of this Act), shall be deemed to have been detailed pursuant to chapter 47A of title 10, U.S. Code (as so amended);

(4) any trial counsel or defense counsel detailed for a commission pursuant to chapter 47A of title10, U.S. Code (as in effect on the day before the date of the enactment of this Act), shall be deemed to have been detailed pursuant to chapter 47A of title 10, U.S. Code (as so amended);

(5) any court reporters detailed to or employed by a commission pursuant to chapter 47A of title 10, U.S. Code (as in effect on the day before the date of the enactment of this Act), shall be deemed to have been detailed or employed pursuant to chapter 47A of title 10, U.S. Code (as so amended); and (6) any appellate military judge or other duly appointed appellate judge on the Court of Military Commission Review pursuant to chapter 47A of title 10, U.S. Code (as in effect on the day before the date of the enactment of this Act), shall be deemed to have been detailed or appointed to the U.S. Court of Military Commission Review pursuant to chapter 47A of title 10, U.S. Code (as so amended).

(c) CHARGES AND SPECIFICATIONS.—Notwithstanding the amendment made by section 1802—

(1) any charges or specifications sworn or referred pursuant to chapter 47A of title 10, U.S. Code (as such chapter was in effect on the day before the date of the enactment of this Act), shall be deemed to have been sworn or referred pursuant to chapter 47A of title 10, U.S. Code (as amended by section 1802); and (2) any charges or specifications described in paragraph (1) may be amended, without prejudice, as needed to properly allege jurisdiction under chapter 47A of title 10, U.S. Code (as so amended), and crimes triable under such chapter.

(d) PROCEDURES AND REQUIREMENTS.—

(1) IN GENERAL.—Except as provided in subsections (a) through (c) and subject to paragraph (2), any commission convened pursuant to chapter 47A of title 10, U.S. Code (as such chapter was in effect on the day before the date of the enactment of this Act), shall be conducted after the date of the enactment of this Act in accordance with the procedures and requirements of chapter 47A of title

(2) TEMPORARY CONTINUATION OF PRIOR PROCEDURES AND REQUIREMENTS.—Any military commission described in paragraph (1) may be conducted in accordance with any procedures and requirements of chapter 47A of title 10, U.S. Code (as in effect on the day before the date of the enactment of this Act), that are not inconsistent with the provisions of chapter 47A of title 10, U.S. Code, (as so amended), until the earlier of—(A) the date of the submittal to Congress under section 1805 of the revised rules for military commissions under chapter 47A of title 10, U.S. Code (as so amended); or (B) the date that is 90 days after the date of the enactment of this Act.

SEC. 1805. SUBMITTAL TO CONGRESS OF REVISED RULES FOR MILITARY COMMISSIONS.

(a) DEADLINE FOR SUBMITTAL.—Not later than 90 days after the date of the enactment of this Act, the Secretary of Defense shall submit to the Committees on Armed Services of the Senate and the House of Representatives the revised rules for military commissions prescribed by the Secretary for purposes of chapter 47A of title 10, U.S. Code (as amended by section 1802).

(b) TREATMENT OF REVISED RULES UNDER REQUIREMENT FOR NOTICE AND WAIT REGARD- ING MODIFICATION OF RULES.—The revised rules submitted to Congress under subsection (a) shall not be treated as a modification of the rules in effect for military commissions for purposes of section 949a(d) of title 10, U.S. Code (as so amended).

SEC. 1806. ANNUAL REPORTS TO CONGRESS ON TRIALS BY MILITARY COMMISSION.

(a) ANNUAL REPORTS REQUIRED.—Not later than January 31 of each year, the Secretary of Defense shall submit to the Committees on Armed Services of the Senate and the House of Representatives a report on any trials conducted by military commissions under chapter 47A of title 10, U.S. Code (as amended by section 1802), during the preceding year.

(b) FORM.—Each report under this section shall be submitted in unclassified form, but may include a classified annex.

SEC. 1807. SENSE OF CONGRESS ON MILITARY COMMISSION SYSTEM.

It is the sense of Congress that—

(1) the fairness and effectiveness of the military commissions system under chapter 47A of title 10, U.S. Code (as amended by section 1802), will depend to a significant degree on the adequacy of defense counsel and associated resources for individuals accused, particularly in the case of capital cases, under such chapter 47A; and

(2) defense counsel in military commission cases, particularly in capital cases, under such chapter 47A of title 10, U.S. Code (as so amended), should be fully resourced as provided in such chapter 47A.

APPENDIX N: IMMIGRATION AND ALIENS

The purpose of this Appendix is to show how international human rights along with Refugee Law applies to immigration and the status of those who are not citizens of the country they are living. As applied to the U.S. this U.N. publication written primarily by an American Law Professor is about what human rights are held by every human being in the U.S. who are not U.S. citizens persons who are not national of the whatever be their legal status. This is not so much about who can enter and stay in the U.S. as it is about how the U.S. and state governments must treat non U.S. citizens just because they are human beings who possess inherent human dignity. States continue as a matter of sovereignty based on international law to determine who enters and who can stay in this country. How states such as the U.S. treat human beings in their territory is a matter of international human rights law such as permitted by the U.S. Constitution.

In addition to the following document on the human rights of non-citizens the following Primary Documents will be helpful: Document 42, Declaration on the Rights on the Human Rights of Individuals Who are not Nationals of the Country in which They Live; Document 15, Second and Third Reports to the Human Rights Committee, Articles 2, 9, 10, 13, 26 of the ICCPR; also Appendix E, Human Rights Committee General Comment No. 15 on the rights of aliens under the ICCPR.

Documents:

Office of the United Nations High Commissioner for Human Rights

The Rights of Non-citizens

Symbols of United Nations documents are composed of capital letters combined with figures. Mention of such a figure indicates a reference to a United Nations document.

The designations employed and the presentation of the material in this publication do not imply the expression of any opinion whatsoever on the part of the Secretariat of the United Nations concerning the legal status of any country, territory, city or area, or of its authorities, or concerning the delimitation of its frontiers or boundaries.

HR/PUB/06/11
UNITED NATIONS PUBLICATION *Sales No.* E.07.XIV.2
ISBN-13: 978-92-1-154175-5

. . . .

The Rights of Non-citizens

Contents
Introduction Page5

Committee on the Elimination of Racial Discrimination, general recommendation XXX (2004) on discrimination against non-citizens

Introduction

All persons should, by virtue of their essential humanity, enjoy all human rights. Exceptional distinctions, for example between citizens and non-citizens, can be made only if they serve a legitimate State objective and are proportional to the achievement of that objective.

Citizens are persons who have been recognized by a State as having an effective link with it. International law generally leaves to each State the authority to determine who qualifies as a citizen. Citizenship can ordinarily be acquired by being born in the country (known as *jus soli* or the law of the place), being born to a parent who is a citizen of the country (known as *jus sanguinis* or the law of blood), naturalization or a combination of these approaches.

A non-citizen is a person who has not been recognized as having these effective links to the country where he or she is located. There are different groups of non-citizens, including permanent residents, migrants, refugees, asylum-seekers, victims of trafficking, foreign students, temporary visitors, other kinds of non-immigrants and stateless people. While each of these groups may have rights based on separate legal regimes, the problems faced by most, if not all, non-citizens are very similar. These common concerns affect approximately 175 million individuals worldwide—or 3 per cent of the world's population.

Non-citizens should have freedom from arbitrary killing, inhuman treatment, slavery, arbitrary arrest, unfair trial, invasions of privacy, refoulement, forced labour, child labour and violations of humanitarian law. They also have the right to marry; protection as minors; peaceful association and assembly; equality; freedom of religion and belief; social, cultural and economic rights; labour rights (for example, as to collective bargaining, workers' compensation, healthy and safe working conditions); and consular protection. While all human beings are entitled to equality in dignity and rights, States may narrowly draw distinctions between citizens and non-citizens with respect to political rights explicitly guaranteed to citizens and freedom of movement.

For non-citizens, there is, nevertheless, a large gap between the rights that international human rights law guarantees to them and the realities that they face. In many countries, there are institutional and pervasive problems confronting non-citizens. Nearly all categories of non-citizens face official and non-official discrimination. While in some countries there may be legal guarantees of equal treatment and recognition of the importance of non-citizens in achieving economic prosperity, non-citizens face hostile social and practical realities. They experience xenophobia, racism and sexism; language barriers and unfamiliar customs; lack of political representation; difficulty realizing their economic, social and cultural rights—particularly the right to work, the right to education and the right to health care; difficulty obtaining identity documents; and lack of means to challenge violations of their human rights effectively or to have them remedied. Some non-citizens are subjected to arbitrary and often indefinite detention. They may have been traumatized by experiences of persecution or abuse in their countries of origin, but are detained side by side with criminals in prisons, which are frequently overcrowded, unhygienic and dangerous. In addition, detained non-citizens may be denied contact with their families, access to legal assistance and the opportunity to challenge their detention. Official hostility—often expressed in national legislation—has been especially flagrant during periods of war, racial animosity and high unemployment. For example, the situation has worsened since 11 September 2001, as some Governments have detained non-citizens in response to fears of terrorism. The narrow exceptions to the principle of non-discrimination that are permitted by international human rights law do not justify such pervasive violations of non-citizens' rights.

The principal objective of this publication is to highlight all the diverse sources of international law and emerging international standards protecting the rights of non-citizens, especially:

The relevant provisions of the International Convention on the Elimination of All Forms of Racial Discrimination and other human rights treaties;

The general comments, country conclusions and adjudications by the Committee on the Elimination of Racial Discrimination and other treaty bodies;

The reports of the United Nations Commission on Human Rights thematic procedures on the human rights of migrants and racism;

The relevant work of such other global institutions as the International Labour Organization and the Office of the United Nations High Commissioner for Refugees; and

The reports of regional institutions, such as the European Commission against Racism and Intolerance. Chapter I examines the general principle of equality for non-citizens. Chapter II explains in greater detail the sources and extent of specific non-citizen rights, including universal rights and freedoms; civil and political rights; and economic, social and cultural rights. Chapter III discusses the application of these rights to particular groups of non-citizens, such as stateless persons, refugees and asylum-seekers, non-citizen workers, and children.

I. THE GENERAL PRINCIPLE OF EQUALITY FOR NON-CITIZENS

International human rights law is founded on the premise that all persons, by virtue of their essential humanity, should enjoy all human rights without discrimination unless exceptional distinctions—for example between citizens and non-citizens—serve a legitimate State objective and are proportional to the achievement of that objective. Any approach to combating discrimination against non-citizens should take into account:

 (a) The interest of the State in specific rights (e.g., political rights, right to education, social security, other economic rights);

 (b) The different non-citizens and their relationship to that State (e.g., permanent residents, migrant workers, asylum-seekers, temporary residents, tourists, undocumented workers); and

 (c) Whether the State's interest or reason for distinguishing between citizens and non-citizens or among non-citizens (e.g., reciprocity, promoting development) is legitimate and proportionate.

> "All persons are equal before the law and are entitled without any discrimination to the equal protection of the law."
> (International Covenant on Civil and Political Rights, art. 26)

A. International Covenant on Civil and Political Rights

The International Covenant on Civil and Political Rights provides an example of the general principle of equality that underlies international human rights law as it relates to non-citizens, and the narrow nature of exceptions to that principle. According to its article 2 (1), each State party:

"undertakes to respect and to ensure to all individuals within its territory and subject to its jurisdiction the rights recognized in the present Covenant, without distinction of any kind, such as race, colour, sex, language, religion, political or other opinion, national or social origin, property, birth or other status."

Moreover, article 26 states that:

"All persons are equal before the law and are entitled without any discrimination to the equal protection of the law. In this respect, the law shall prohibit any discrimination and guarantee to all persons equal and effective protection against discrimination on any ground such as race, colour . . . national or social origin . . . or other status."

The Human Rights Committee has explained that:

"the rights set forth in the Covenant apply to everyone, irrespective of reciprocity, and irrespective of his or her nationality or statelessness. Thus, the general rule is that each one of the rights of the Covenant must be guaranteed without discrimination between citizens and aliens."

> Human Rights Committee: "the general rule is that each one of the rights of the Covenant must be guaranteed without discrimination between citizens and aliens."

The Human Rights Committee has also observed that the rights of non-citizens may be qualified only by such limitations as may be lawfully imposed under the International Covenant on Civil and Political Rights. Specifically, the Covenant permits States to draw distinctions between citizens and non-citizens with respect to two categories of rights: political rights explicitly guaranteed to citizens and freedom of movement. With regard to political rights, article 25 establishes that "every citizen" shall have the right to participate in public affairs, to vote and hold office, and to have access to public service.

Regarding freedom of movement, article 12 (1) grants "the right to liberty of movement and freedom to choose [one's] residence" only to persons who are "lawfully within the territory of a State"—that is, apparently permitting restrictions on undocumented migrants.

B. International Convention on the Elimination of All Forms of Racial Discrimination

The International Convention on the Elimination of All Forms of Racial Discrimination also illustrates the narrow nature of exceptions to the general principle of equality. It indicates that States may make distinctions between citizens and non-citizens, but—unlike the International Covenant on Civil and Political Rights—it requires all non-citizens to be treated similarly. It defines racial discrimination in article 1 (1):

"the term 'racial discrimination' shall mean any distinction, exclusion, restriction or preference based on race, colour, descent, or national or ethnic origin which has the purpose or effect of nullifying or impairing the recognition, enjoyment or exercise, on an equal footing, of human rights and fundamental freedoms in the political, economic, social, cultural or any other field of public life."

Article 1 (2) and (3) of the Convention, however, seems at first to limit its application with regard to discrimination against non-citizens. Article 1 (2) states: "This Convention shall not apply to distinctions, exclusions, restrictions or preferences made by a State Party to this Convention between citizens and non-citizens." Article 1 (3) refines article 1 (2) by stating that: "Nothing in this Convention may be interpreted as affecting in any way the legal provisions of States Parties concerning nationality, citizenship or naturalization, *provided that such provisions do not discriminate against any particular nationality*." (emphasis added)

The Committee on the Elimination of Racial Discrimination indicated in its general recommendation XI, however, that these provisions need to be read in the light of the totality of human rights law:

"Article 1, paragraph 2, must not be interpreted to detract in any way from the rights and freedoms recognized and enunciated in other instruments, especially the Universal Declaration of Human Rights, the International Covenant on Economic, Social and Cultural Rights and the International Covenant on Civil and Political Rights."

In its concluding observations regarding States' reports as well as its opinions on individual communications, the Committee has further underscored the need for States parties to:

Publicly condemn any acts of intolerance or hatred against persons belonging to particular racial, ethnic, national or religious groups, and promote a better understanding of the principle of non-discrimination and of the situation of non-citizens;

Make sure that non-citizens enjoy equal protection and recognition before the law;

Focus on the problems faced by non-citizens with regard to economic, social and cultural rights, notably in areas such as housing, education and employment;

Guarantee the equal enjoyment of the right to adequate housing for both citizens and non-citizens, as well as guarantee that non-citizens have equal access to social services that ensure a minimum standard of living;

Take measures to eliminate discrimination against non-citizens in relation to working conditions and language requirements, including rules and practices in employment that may be discriminatory in effect; and

Apply international and regional standards pertaining to refugees equally, regardless of the nationality of the asylum-seeker, and use all available means, including international cooperation, to address the situation of refugees and displaced persons, especially regarding their access to education, housing and employment.

In August 2004, the Committee adopted general recommendation XXX on discrimination against non-citizens. Some of its main principles are summarized here and the recommendation is reproduced in full in the annex below.

States are under an obligation to guarantee equality between citizens and non-citizens in the enjoyment of their civil, political, economic, social and cultural rights to the extent recognized under international law and enunciated especially in the Universal Declaration of Human Rights, the International

Covenant on Economic, Social and Cultural Rights, and the International Covenant on Civil and Political Rights;

Differential treatment based on citizenship or immigration status will constitute discrimination if the criteria for such differentiation are not applied pursuant to a legitimate aim and are not proportional to the achievement of this aim;

States must abstain from applying different standards of treatment to different categories of non-citizens, such as female non-citizen spouses of citizens and male non-citizen spouses of citizens;

Immigration policies and any measures taken in the struggle against terrorism must not discriminate, in purpose or effect, on grounds of race, colour, descent, or national or ethnic origin;

States have a duty to protect non-citizens from xenophobic attitudes and behaviour;

States are obliged to ensure that particular groups of non-citizens are not discriminated against with regard to access to citizenship or naturalization and that all non-citizens enjoy equal treatment in the administration of justice;

Deportation or other removal proceedings must not discriminate among non-citizens on the basis of race or national origin and should not result in disproportionate interference with the right to family life;

Non-citizens must not be returned or removed to a country or territory where they are at risk of being subject to serious human rights abuses;

Obstacles to non-citizens' enjoyment of economic, social and cultural rights, notably in education, housing, employment and health, must be removed.

Committee on the Elimination of Racial Discrimination: "States parties are under an obligation to guarantee equality between citizens and non-citizens in the enjoyment of [their civil, political, economic, social and cultural] rights. ..."

General recommendation XXX builds upon all the previous protections for non-citizens and their interpretations not only by the Committee on the Elimination of Racial Discrimination, but also by the Human Rights Committee and other human rights institutions. Accordingly, general recommendation XXX provides a comprehensive elaboration of the human rights of non-citizens as a guide to all countries and particularly those that have ratified the Convention. The more detailed implications of each paragraph of this recommendation are discussed in chapter II below.

The Committee on the Elimination of Racial Discrimination has indicated that States may draw distinctions between citizens and non-citizens only if such distinctions do not have the effect of limiting the enjoyment by non-citizens of the rights enshrined in other instruments. For example, in *A (FC) and Others* v *Secretary of State for the Home Department*, nine terrorism suspects successfully challenged their detention, alleging that the United Kingdom of Great Britain and Northern Ireland had violated article 5 (the right to liberty and security) of the European Convention on Human Rights. Differential treatment based on citizenship or immigration status will constitute forbidden discrimination if the criteria for such differentiation are inconsistent with the objectives and purposes of the International Convention on the Elimination of All Forms of Racial Discrimination; are not proportional to the achievement of those objectives and purposes; or do not fall within the scope of article 1 (4) of the Convention, which relates to special measures. For example, a Tunisian permanent resident married to a Danish citizen was denied a loan by a Danish bank because he was not a Danish citizen. The Committee noted that the Tunisian was denied the loan "on the sole ground of his non-Danish nationality and was told that the nationality requirement was motivated by the need to ensure that the loan was repaid. In the opinion of the Committee, however, nationality is not the most appropriate requisite when investigating a person's will or capacity to reimburse a loan. The applicant's permanent residence or the place where his employment, property or family ties are to be found may be more relevant in this context. A citizen may move abroad or have all his property in another country and thus evade all attempts to enforce a claim of repayment." Accordingly, the Committee found that the Tunisian had suffered discrimination.

C. International Covenant on Economic, Social and Cultural Rights

Like article 2 (1) of the International Covenant on Civil and Political Rights, article 2 (2) of the International Covenant on Economic, Social and Cultural Rights declares that States parties guarantee the rights enunciated in the Covenant "without discrimination of any kind as to race, colour ... national or social origin ... or other status." Article 2 (3), however, creates an exception to this rule of equality for developing countries: "Developing countries, with due regard to human rights and their national economy, may determine to what extent they would guarantee the economic rights recognized in the present Covenant to non-nationals." As an exception to the rule of equality, article 2 (3) must be narrowly construed, may be relied upon only by developing countries and only with respect to economic rights. States may not draw distinctions between citizens and non-citizens as to social and cultural rights.

D. Regional bodies

Regional human rights law is largely consistent with the protections provided by global standards, but reveals several important elaborations on those standards as well as particular exceptions to the general principle of equality. Article 5 (1) of the Convention for the Protection of Human Rights and Fundamental Freedoms (European Convention on Human Rights), for example, reiterates the global principle of the right to liberty and security of person, but elaborates upon that standard by providing that "[n]o one shall be deprived of his liberty" except in certain specified cases and only "in accordance with a procedure prescribed by law." The list of exceptions to the right to liberty in article 5 (1) is exhaustive and only a narrow interpretation of those exceptions is consistent with the aim of article 5, namely to protect the individual from arbitrary detention.

The European Court of Human Rights has found a distinction between European "citizens" and individuals of non-European nationality with regard to deportation permissible. In *C. v Belgium*, a Moroccan citizen who had lived in Belgium for 37 years was ordered to be deported owing to convictions for criminal damage, possession of drugs and conspiracy. He claimed discrimination on grounds of race and nationality in violation of article 14 of the European Convention because "his deportation amounted to less favourable treatment than was accorded to criminals who, as nationals of a member State of the European Union, were protected against such a measure in Belgium." The Court found no violation of article 14 of the European Convention because such preferential treatment was "based on an objective and reasonable justification, given that the member States of the European Union form a special legal order, which has ... established its own citizenship."

E. National constitutions

Some national constitutions guarantee rights to "citizens", whereas international human rights law would—with the exception of the rights of public participation and of movement and economic rights in developing countries—provide rights to all persons.

II. SPECIFIC RIGHTS OF NON-CITIZENS

A. FUNDAMENTAL RIGHTS AND FREEDOMS

1. *Right to life, liberty and security of the person*

Protection from arbitrary detention; freedom from torture and cruel, inhuman or degrading treatment or punishment; right of detained non-citizens to contact consular officials

Non-citizens have an inherent right to life, protected by law, and may not be arbitrarily deprived of life. They also have the right to liberty and security of the person. All individuals, including non-citizens, must be protected from arbitrary detention. If non-citizens are lawfully deprived of their liberty, they must be treated with humanity and with respect for the inherent dignity of their person. They must not be subjected to torture or to cruel, inhuman or degrading treatment or punishment, and may not be held in slavery or servitude. Detained non-citizens have the right to contact consular officials and the receiving State must notify them of this right.

States are obliged to respect the human rights of detainees, including legal protections, irrespective of whether they are in the territory of the State in question. Where persons find themselves within the authority and control of a State and where a circumstance of armed conflict may be involved, their fundamental rights may be determined in part by reference to international humanitarian law as well as international human rights law. States must allow a competent tribunal to determine the legal status of each detainee pursuant to international humanitarian law, in particular article 5 of the Geneva Convention relative to the Treatment of Prisoners of War. Where it may be considered that the protections of international humanitarian law do not apply, however, such persons remain the beneficiaries at least of the non-derogable protections under international human rights law. In short, no person under the authority and control of a State, regardless of his or her circumstances, is devoid of legal protection for his or her fundamental and non-derogable human rights. If the legal status of detainees is not clarified, the rights and protections to which they may be entitled under international or domestic law cannot be said to be the subject of effective legal protection by the State. So-called international zones administered by States to detain non-citizens, and where such non-citizens are denied legal or social assistance, are a legal fiction and a State cannot avoid its international human rights responsibilities by claiming that such areas have extraterritorial status.

States and international organizations must also ensure that measures taken in the struggle against terrorism do not discriminate in purpose or effect on grounds of race or national or ethnic origin.

States may nonetheless arrest or detain non-citizens against whom action is being taken with a view to deportation or extradition, regardless of whether such detention is reasonably considered necessary, for example, to prevent those non-citizens from committing offences or fleeing.

2. Protection from refoulement

Non-citizens enjoy the right to be protected from refoulement, or deportation to a country in which they may be subjected to persecution or abuse. This principle of non-refoulement exists in a number of international instruments with slightly varying coverage. Expulsions of non-citizens should not be carried out without taking into account possible risks to their lives and physical integrity in the countries of destination. With regard to non-refoulement, article 3 of the Convention against Torture and Other Cruel, Inhuman or Degrading Treatment or Punishment provides:

> "1. No State Party shall expel, return ('refouler') or extradite a person to another State where there are substantial grounds for believing that he would be in danger of being subjected to torture.
>
> "2. For the purpose of determining whether there are such grounds, the competent authorities shall take into account all relevant considerations including, where applicable, the existence in the State concerned of a consistent pattern of gross, flagrant or mass violations of human rights."

In assessing whether an expulsion order violates article 3, it must be determined whether the individual concerned would be exposed to a real and personal risk of being subjected to torture in the country to which he or she would be returned. All relevant considerations—including the existence of a consistent pattern of gross, flagrant or mass violations of human rights—must be taken into account pursuant to article 3 (2), but the lack of such a pattern does not mean that a person might not be subjected to torture in his or her specific circumstances. The risk of torture must be assessed on grounds that go beyond mere theory or suspicion. It does not, however, have to meet the test of being highly probable. A person subject to an expulsion order is required to establish that he or she would be in danger of being tortured and that the grounds for so believing are substantial in the way described above, and that such danger is personal and present. The following information, while not exhaustive, would also be pertinent to determining whether an expulsion order violates article 3 of the Convention:

(a) Is the State concerned one in which there is evidence of a consistent pattern of gross, flagrant or mass violations of human rights (see art. 3, para. 2)?

(b) Has the person claiming a violation of article 3 been tortured or maltreated by or at the instigation of or with the consent or acquiescence of a public official or other person acting in an official capacity in the past? If so, was this in the recent past?

(c) Is there medical or other independent evidence to support a claim by the person that he or she has been tortured or maltreated in the past? Has the torture had after-effects?

(d) Has the situation referred to in (a) above changed? Has the internal situation in respect of human rights altered?

(e) Has the person engaged in political or other activity within or outside the State concerned which would appear to make him or her particularly vulnerable to the risk of being placed in danger of torture were he or she to be expelled, returned or extradited to the State in question?

(f) Is there any evidence as to the credibility of the person?

This analysis was used by the European Court of Human Rights in *Chahal v The United Kingdom* in determining whether a Sikh leader of Indian nationality would be at risk of ill-treatment if he were deported from the United Kingdom to India.

The wording of article 3 (1) of the Convention against Torture is similar to, but not entirely congruent with, that of article 33 (1) of the Convention relating to the Status of Refugees. Whereas the former provides protection from refoulement only to persons who are in danger of becoming victims of torture, the latter provides protection against refoulement for persons in danger of falling victim to various kinds of persecution.

Torture victims cannot be expected to recall entirely consistent facts relating to events of extreme trauma, but they must be prepared to advance such evidence as there is in support of such a claim.

3. Liberty of movement and the right to enter one's own country

Persons do not have the right to enter or to reside in countries of which they are not citizens. However, non-citizens who are lawfully within the territory of a State have the right to liberty of movement and free choice of residence. Restrictions and other quotas on where such non-citizens can settle in a State—especially those restrictions and quotas that might involve an element of compulsion—may violate their right to liberty of movement. States are encouraged to ensure that the geographical distribution of non-citizens within their territory is made according to the principle of equity and does not lead to the violation of their rights as recognized under the International Convention on the Elimination of All Forms of Racial Discrimination. Asylum-seekers should be guaranteed freedom of movement wherever possible. All non-citizens shall be free to leave a State.

Article 12 (4) of the International Covenant on Civil and Political Rights provides that "[n]o one shall be arbitrarily deprived of the right to enter his own country." The Human Rights Committee has broadly interpreted this provision to give rights to stateless persons who are resident in a particular State and others with a long-term relationship with the country, but who are not citizens. States are urged to ensure that the residence permits of non-citizens who are long-term residents are withdrawn only under exceptional and clearly defined circumstances, and that adequate recourse to appeal against such decisions is made available. Requiring lawfully permanent residents of a State to obtain return visas to re-enter that State may not comply with article 12 (4). Any State with such a provision should review its legislation to ensure compliance with article 12 (4).

4. Protection from arbitrary expulsion

A non-citizen may be expelled only to a country that agrees to accept him or her and shall be allowed to leave for that country.

Instruments such as the United Nations Declaration on the Rights of Individuals who are not Nationals of the Country in which They Live, which is non-binding, and Protocol No. 4 to the European Convention on Human Rights prohibit the collective expulsion of non-citizens. Any measure that compels non-citizens, as a group, to leave a country is prohibited except where such a measure is taken on the basis of a reasonable and objective examination of the particular case of each individual non-citizen in the group. In other words, the procedure for the expulsion of a group of non-citizens must afford sufficient guarantees demonstrating that the personal circumstances of *each* of those non-citizens concerned has been genuinely and *individually* taken into account. Hence, for example, if one member of a group of non-citizens is found not to qualify for refugee status because there is a safe country of origin and is ordered to be deported, the other members of the group cannot be ordered to be deported unless they too are individually deemed not to qualify for refugee status.

There is, nonetheless, significant scope for States to enforce their immigration policies and to require departure of unlawfully present persons, such as those who remain in a State longer than the time allowed by limited-duration permits. Yet that discretion is not unlimited and may not be exercised arbitrarily. The case of *Winata and Lan Li v Australia*, for example, concerned a stateless married couple from Indonesia who had lost their Indonesian citizenship and had been residing in Australia for many years. After overstaying their visas, the couple faced deportation, but petitioned both on their own behalf and on behalf of their 13-year-old son, who was an Australian citizen. The Human Rights Committee found that deportation of the couple would amount to a violation of their rights under article 17 of the International Covenant on Civil and Political Rights in conjunction with article 23, and a violation of the rights of their son under article 24 (1). It also found that, while the mere fact that non-citizen parents have a child who is a citizen does not by itself make the proposed deportation of the parents arbitrary, the fact that the child in this case had grown up in Australia since his birth 13 years before, "attending Australian schools as an ordinary child would and developing the social relationships inherent in that," the State had the burden of showing additional factors justifying the deportation of both parents that went "beyond a simple enforcement of its immigration law in order to avoid a characterization of arbitrariness."

Non-citizens—even non-citizens suspected of terrorism—should not be expelled without allowing them a legal opportunity to challenge their expulsion. The International Covenant on Civil and Political Rights, however, provides the right to certain procedural protections in expulsion proceedings (art. 13) only to non-citizens "lawfully in the territory of a State party".

5. Freedom of thought and conscience

Right to hold and express opinions; right of peaceful assembly; freedom of association

Non-citizens have the right to freedom of thought and conscience, as well as the right to hold and express opinions. They also have the right to peaceful assembly and freedom of association. Membership in political parties, for example, should be open to non-citizens.

6. Protection from arbitrary interference with privacy, family, home or correspondence

Non-citizens may not be subjected to arbitrary or unlawful interference with their privacy, family, home or correspondence. Article 8 of the European Convention on Human Rights, for example, states:

> "1. Everyone has the right to respect for his private and family life, his home and his correspondence.

> "2. There shall be no interference by a public authority with the exercise of this right except such as is in accordance with the law and is necessary in a democratic society in the interests of national security, public safety or the economic well-being of the country, for the prevention of disorder or crime, for the protection of health or morals, or for the protection of the rights and freedoms of others."

Where a non-citizen has real family ties in the territory of a State from which he or she is ordered to be deported and the deportation would jeopardize those ties, the deportation is justified with regard to article 8 only if it is proportionate to the legitimate aim pursued. In other words, the deportation is justified only if the interference with family life is not excessive compared to the public interest to be protected.70 The public interest often balanced against the right to respect for family life is the State's interest in maintaining public order. It arises in the context of non-citizens convicted of criminal offences. There is no right of a migrant non-citizen to enter or to remain in a particular country after having committed a serious criminal offence, but to remove a person from a country where close members of his or her family are living may amount to an infringement of the right to respect for family life as guaranteed in article 8 (1) of the Convention, especially where the individual concerned poses little danger to public order or security.

A number of States, however, continue to discriminate with regard to the capacity of women to pass on their nationality to their children and several have made reservations to article 9 of the Convention. Such States may allow women to pass on their nationality to their children only if they are unmarried or their husbands are stateless.

Parents should be able to transmit their nationality to their children regardless of their sex and of whether they are married to the other parent. At the same time, the principle of *jus soli* (citizenship based on the place of birth) has become the international norm governing the nationality of children born to non-citizen parents, especially if they would otherwise be stateless. Children of non-citizens whose legal status has not yet been determined should be protected from any difficulties in acquiring citizenship.

B. Civil and political rights

1. Right to recognition and equal protection before the law

Equality before courts and tribunals; entitlement to a fair and public hearing; freedom from subjection to retrospective penal legislation

Non-citizens are entitled to equal protection and recognition before the law. They shall be equal before the courts and tribunals, and shall be entitled to a fair and public hearing by a competent, independent and impartial tribunal established by law in the determination of any criminal charge against them or of their rights and obligations in a suit at law. Non-citizens shall not be subjected to retrospective penal legislation and may not be imprisoned for failure to fulfil a contractual obligation.73

2. Right to acquire, maintain and transmit citizenship

States should take effective measures to ensure that all non-citizens enjoy the right to acquire citizenship without discrimination.74 Hence, States should not discriminate against particular groups of non-citizens on the basis of race or ethnic or national origin with regard to naturalization or the registration of births,75 and should eliminate from their legislation all discrimination between men and women with regard to the acquisition and transmission of nationality. Non-citizen spouses of citizens should be able to acquire citizenship in the same manner regardless of their sex. Article 9 of the Convention on the Elimination of All Forms of Discrimination against Women provides that:

> "1. States Parties shall grant women equal rights with men to acquire, change or retain their nationality. They shall ensure in particular that neither marriage to an alien nor change of nationality by the husband during marriage shall automatically change the nationality of the wife, render her stateless or force upon her the nationality of the husband.

> "2. States Parties shall grant women equal rights with men with respect to the nationality of their children."

Governments should pay greater attention to immigration policies that have a discriminatory effect on persons of a particular national or ethnic origin, and are encouraged to investigate possible barriers to naturalization, in terms of both the procedure and the lack of motivation to apply for citizenship.

3. Protection from discrimination on the basis of sex

States should eliminate from their legislation all discrimination between men and women with regard to the acquisition and transmission of nationality. The nationality and immigration laws of several countries discriminate between the capacity of male and female citizens to marry and live with their non-citizen spouses. For example, Mauritius adopted an immigration law which provided that, if a Mauritian woman married a man from another country, the husband must apply for residence in Mauritius and that permission may be refused. If, however, a Mauritian man married a foreign woman, the foreign woman was automatically entitled to residence in Mauritius. The Human Rights Committee held that Mauritius had violated the International Covenant on Civil and Political Rights by discriminating between men and women without adequate justification and by failing to respect the family's right to live together. Non-citizen spouses of citizens should be able to acquire citizenship in the same manner regardless of their sex, in keeping with article 5 (d) (iii) of the International Convention on the Elimination of All Forms of Racial Discrimination.

C. Economic, social and cultural rights

1. Rights of non-citizens as members of minorities

Right to enjoy one's culture, profess and practise one's religion, and use one's language

Since non-citizens are often of a different national or racial origin than citizens, States are encouraged to consider non-citizens as belonging to national minorities, and to ensure that they enjoy the rights that arise from such status.

Examples of the rights that non-citizens enjoy as members of minorities can be found in several legal instruments and in the jurisprudence of their monitoring bodies. For example, the Human Rights Committee has stated that "where aliens constitute a minority within the meaning of article 27 of the [International] Covenant on Civil and Political Rights, they shall not be denied the right, in community with other members of their group, to enjoy their own culture, to profess and practise their own religion and to use their own language." The rights of national and racial minorities to enjoy such rights, therefore, cannot be restricted to citizens.

In addition, the United Nations Declaration on the Rights of Persons Belonging to National or Ethnic, Religious and Linguistic Minorities, although not legally binding, elaborates upon the rights of national and ethnic minorities, which has been interpreted to include migrant communities.

Under the Rome Statute of the International Criminal Court, the Court apparently has jurisdiction to protect non-citizens from persecution and abuses committed with intent to cause annihilation of their national group. Article 5 of the Rome Statute lists the four crimes that fall within the Court's jurisdiction: the crime of genocide, crimes against humanity, war crimes and the crime of aggression. Article 6 defines genocide as certain acts "committed with intent to destroy, in whole or in part, a national, ethnical, racial or religious group, as such". These acts are, therefore, crimes within the jurisdiction of the Court. In addition, under article 7, "persecution against any identifiable group or collectivity on political, racial, national, ethnic, cultural, religious, gender ... or other grounds that are universally recognized as impermissible under international law" are also considered crimes against humanity.

Non-citizens enjoy the right to freedom of religion. Furthermore, States are urged to take measures necessary to prevent practices that deny non-citizens their cultural and ethnic identity, such as requirements that non-citizens change their name in order to be naturalized. Article 15 of the International Covenant on Economic, Social and Cultural Rights obliges States to take steps to ensure that everyone, regardless of citizenship, enjoys the right to take part in cultural life. Non-citizens have the right to marry when at marriageable age.

2. Right to health, education, housing, a minimum standard of living and social security

States must avoid different standards of treatment with regard to citizens and non-citizens that might lead to the unequal enjoyment of economic, social and cultural rights. Governments shall take progressive measures to the extent of their available resources to protect the rights of everyone—regardless of citizenship—to: social security; an adequate standard of living including adequate food, clothing, housing, and the continuous improvement of living conditions; the enjoyment of the highest attainable standard of physical and mental health; and education.

States should take effective measures to ensure that housing agencies and private landlords refrain from engaging in discriminatory practices.

Educational institutions must be accessible to everyone, without discrimination, within the jurisdiction of a State party. This "principle of non-discrimination extends to all persons of school age residing in the territory of a State party, including non-nationals, and irrespective of their legal status. "Furthermore, "the prohibition against discrimination enshrined in article 2 (2) of the [International] Covenant [on Economic, Social and Cultural Rights] is subject to neither progressive realization nor the availability of resources; it applies fully and immediately to all aspects of education and encompasses all internationally prohibited grounds of discrimination."

III. RIGHTS OF SELECTED NON-CITIZEN GROUPS

Different categories of undocumented non-citizens, such as stateless persons, refugees and asylum-seekers, undocumented economic migrants, women being trafficked into prostitution, and children, must each be dealt with in a manner appropriate to their particular situation.

A. Stateless persons

Some non-citizens are stateless. They either never acquired citizenship of the country of their birth or lost their citizenship, and have no claim to the citizenship of another State. Such persons include individuals native to the country of their residence who failed to register for citizenship during a specified period and have been denied it since then; and children born in States that recognize only the *jus sanguinis* principle of acquiring citizenship to non-citizen parents of States that recognize only the *jus soli* principle. The rights of stateless persons are enunciated in a number of international instruments, including the Convention relating to the Status of Stateless Persons and the Convention on the Reduction of Statelessness. The status of stateless persons—especially stateless persons who have been precluded from applying for residence permits or citizenship—should be regularized by, for example, simplifying procedures for applying for residence permits and through campaigns to make it clear that stateless persons would not risk expulsion when identifying themselves to the authorities. States should also seek to reduce the number of stateless persons, with priority for children, inter alia by encouraging parents to apply for citizenship on their behalf. Stateless persons should not be involuntarily repatriated to the countries of origin of their ancestors. Individuals who have taken the citizenship of a country other than their native country should be able to acquire citizenship of their native country.

Under article 12 (4) of the International Covenant on Civil and Political Rights, stateless persons should not be arbitrarily deprived of their right to enter their country of residence or a country with which they have a long-term relationship.

> The rights of stateless persons are enunciated in a number of international instruments, including the Convention relating to the Status of Stateless Persons and the Convention on the Reduction of Statelessness

B. Refugees and asylum-seekers

Five United Nations instruments form the basis of the rights of refugees in international human rights law: the 1951 Convention relating to the Status of Refugees and its 1967 Protocol; the Statute of the Office of the High Commissioner for Refugees; the Declaration on Territorial Asylum; and the Handbook on Procedures and Criteria for Determining Refugee Status.

International standards pertaining to refugees and asylum-seekers should be applied equally, regardless of the nationality of the asylum-seeker or refugee. Conditions in refugee shelters and conditions of detention faced by undocumented migrants and asylum-seekers should meet international standards. States should ensure that individuals caught in an illegal situation, such as asylum-seekers who are in a country unlawfully and whose claims are not considered valid by the authorities, are not treated as criminals.

The 2003 report of the Special Rapporteur on the human rights of migrants focused particularly on the detention of migrants and the conditions of their detention. Concerns included detention of asylum-seekers; prolonged detention periods; the arbitrary nature of detention decisions; detention on the basis of unspecified allegations related to terrorism or national security; detention of trafficking victims; detention of migrant children; absence of legal assistance and judicial review procedures; detention with ordinary criminals; solitary confinement; methods of restraint threatening physical integrity; detention in inappropriate facilities;

overcrowding and poor hygienic conditions; lack of medical care; lack of education for young detainees; and other problems.

1. Refugees

The 1951 Convention relating to the Status of Refugees and its 1967 Protocol provide that refugees should be entitled to treatment at least as favourable as that accorded to citizens with respect to: religion (art. 4); protection of intellectual property (art. 14); access to courts and legal assistance (art. 16); rationing measures (art. 20); elementary education (art. 22 (1)); public relief and assistance (art. 23); labour legislation and social security (art. 24); as well as fiscal charges (art. 29). The Convention and its Protocol also require that States parties accord to refugees treatment no less favourable than that accorded to non-citizens generally with respect to exemption from legislative reciprocity (art. 7 (1)); acquisition of property (art. 13); non-political and non-profit-making associations and trade unions (art. 15); wage-earning employment (art. 17); self-employment (art. 18); liberal professions (art. 19); housing (art. 21); post-elementary education (art. 22 (2)); and freedom of movement (art. 26). Employment, housing and social assistance should not be denied to recognized refugees, especially on grounds of their ethnicity.

States must ensure a more rigorous supervision of the application of measures aimed at facilitating the integration of refugees, particularly at the local level.

Some States have made positive efforts to create a comprehensive integration plan for new arrivals and offer them tools they will need for success in the society of the State.

2. Asylum-seekers

Certain rights apply particularly to asylum-seekers. Eligibility for asylum should not depend on the ethnic or national origin of applicants. Asylum-seekers should not be left in a destitute condition while awaiting examination of their asylum claims, since such poor conditions could reinforce prejudice, stereotypes and hostility towards asylum applicants. The procedure for determining eligibility for asylum should not be slow and States should ensure that applicants are given access to sufficient legal assistance. States should be encouraged to provide free legal advice to applicants. Time limits for registration to lodge asylum claims should not be so short as to deprive persons of the protection to which they are entitled under international law. International human rights law is also relevant in the context of defining adequate reception standards for asylum-seekers. Asylum-seekers should be granted the right to work. The human rights of asylum-seekers are also protected by regional human rights instruments in Africa, Europe and the Americas that apply to all persons residing within the jurisdiction of their respective States parties, regardless of their legal status in the country of asylum.

The holding of asylum-seekers in detention should be avoided to the greatest extent possible, particularly in the cases of persons arriving with families. Where detention does occur, it should not be for an indefinite period, and careful attention should be paid to the accommodation and facilities provided for the families—particularly the children—of asylum-seekers held in detention.

143 Asylum-seekers and refugees should not be detained alongside convicted criminals, nor should they be detained for lack of identity papers or their uncertainty about travel routes into the receiving State. Wherever possible, asylum-seekers should be guaranteed freedom of movement.

C. Non-citizen workers and their families

Everyone—regardless of citizenship—has the right to work and Governments are obliged to take progressive measures to safeguard this right. Non-citizens who are lawfully present in a State are entitled to treatment equal to that enjoyed by citizens in the realm of employment and work. Everyone, including non-citizens, has the right to just and favourable conditions of work, and international standards that provide protection in treatment and conditions at work in areas such as safety, health, hours of work and remuneration apply to all workers regardless of citizenship or status. States must ensure the right of everyone to establish and join trade unions. Non-citizen workers should not be barred from holding trade union office and their right to strike should not be restricted.

1. International Labour Organization (ILO)

International Labour Organization (ILO) conventions and recommendations (for example, on collective bargaining, discrimination, workers' compensation, social security, working conditions and environment, abolition of forced labour and child labour) generally protect the rights of all workers irrespective of citizenship. The eight fundamental ILO conventions and the recommendations that accompany them apply to all workers regardless of citizenship. Several ILO instruments specifically protect migrant workers and their families. The most significant are: Convention No. 97 concerning migration for employment; Convention No. 143 concerning working conditions and equal treatment of migrant workers; and Convention No. 118 concerning equality of treatment in social security. In many instances, the conventions guarantee certain rights—e.g., equal remuneration and minimum wage with respect to past employment and maintenance of social security benefits—to non-citizens regardless of the legality of the migrant's presence in the territory. Other rights are extended only to those persons lawfully within a territory, e.g., rights to equal opportunities and vocational training.

ILO Convention No. 143 provides specific guidance as to the treatment of irregular migrants and those migrants who are employed unlawfully. In laying out the minimum norms applicable to such persons, article 1, for example, establishes that States parties must "respect the basic human rights of all migrant workers" regardless of their migratory status or legal situation. The Committee of Experts on the Application of Conventions and Recommendations has interpreted these rights to be the fundamental human rights enshrined in the International Bill of Human Rights, the International Convention on the Protection of the Rights of All Migrant Workers and Members of Their Families, and the ILO Declaration on Fundamental Principles and Rights at Work.

2. International Convention on the Protection of the Rights of All Migrant Workers and Members of Their Families

The International Convention on the Protection of the Rights of All Migrant Workers and Members of Their Families, of which ILO Conventions Nos. 97 and 143 formed the basis, protects all migrant workers and their families, but does not generally include international organization employees, foreign development staff, refugees, stateless persons, students and trainees (arts. 1 and 3).

The Convention provides for: Non-discrimination (art. 7); Freedom for migrants to leave any country and to enter their country of origin (art. 8); The right to life (art. 9); Freedom from torture and ill-treatment (art. 10); Freedom from slavery or forced labour (art. 11); Freedom of thought, conscience and religion (art. 12); Freedom of opinion and expression (art. 13); Freedom from arbitrary or unlawful interference with privacy, family, home, correspondence or other communications (art. 14); Property rights (art. 15); Liberty and security of person (art. 16); The right of migrants deprived of their liberty to be treated with humanity (art. 17); A fair and public hearing by a competent, independent and impartial tribunal (art. 18); The prohibition of retroactive application of criminal laws (art. 19); The prohibition of imprisonment for failure to fulfill a contract (art. 20); The prohibition of the destruction of travel or identity documents (art. 21); The prohibition of expulsion on a collective basis or without fair procedures (art. 22); The right to consular or diplomatic assistance (art. 23); The right to recognition as a person before the law (art. 24); Equality of treatment between nationals and migrant workers as to work conditions and pay (art. 25); The right to participate in trade unions (art. 26); Equal access to social security (art. 27); The right to emergency medical care (art. 28); The right of a child to a name, birth registration and nationality (art. 29); and Equality of access to public education (art. 30).

In addition, States parties must ensure respect for migrants' cultural identity (art. 31); the right to repatriate earnings, savings and belongings (art. 32); and information about rights under the Convention (art. 33).

3. Inter-American Court of Human Rights

The Inter-American Court of Human Rights has confirmed the applicability of international labour standards to non-citizens, and particularly to non-citizens in irregular status. In an opinion issued in September 2003, the Court held that non-discrimination and the right to equality are *jus cogens* that are applicable to all residents regardless of immigration status. Hence, Governments cannot use immigration status as a justification for restricting the employment or labour rights of unauthorized workers, such as rights to social security. The Court found that Governments do have the right to deport individuals and refuse to offer jobs to people who do not possess employment documents, but held that, once an employment relationship has been initiated, unauthorized workers become entitled to all the employment and labour rights that are available to authorized workers.

The Court stated:

> "... the migratory status of a person cannot constitute a justification to deprive him of the enjoyment and exercise of human rights, including those of a labour-related nature. When assuming an employment relationship, the migrant acquires rights that must be recognized and ensured because he is an employee, irrespective of his regular or irregular status in the State where he is employed. These rights are a result of the employment relationship."

> Inter-American Court of Human Rights: "Non-discrimination and the right to equality are *jus cogens* that are applicable to all residents regardless of immigration status."

4. Committee on the Elimination of Racial Discrimination

The Committee on the Elimination of Racial Discrimination has frequently expressed concern that non-citizens who serve as domestic workers are subjected to debt bondage, other illegal employment practices, passport deprivation, illegal confinement, rape and physical assault.8 States are urged to put an end to the practice of employers retaining the passports of their foreign employees, in particular domestic workers. . .

Victims of trafficking

Non-citizens are often the target of trafficking. Persons who emigrate through irregular channels, such as smuggling and trafficking networks, risk suffocating in containers or drowning when an overloaded ship sinks. Adequate assistance and support, including formal protection, aid and education, should be provided to victims of trafficking.

E. Non-citizen children

Article 2 of the Convention on the Rights of the Child provides that "States Parties shall respect and ensure the rights set forth in the present Convention to each child within their jurisdiction without discrimination of any kind . . . " The Committee on the Rights of the Child encourages States to continue and strengthen their efforts to integrate the right to non-discrimination that is enshrined in article fully in all relevant legislation, and to ensure that this right is effectively applied in all political, judicial and administrative decisions and in projects, programmes and services which have an impact on all children, including non-citizen children and children belonging to minority groups. The Committee recommends that States should develop comprehensive and coordinated policies to address the developing phenomenon of immigration, including public information campaigns to promote tolerance; monitor and collect data on racially motivated acts; and study the situation of non-citizen children, especially in the school system, and the effectiveness of measures taken to facilitate their integration. States should also take effective measures to address discriminatory attitudes or prejudices, in particular towards non-citizen children, fully and effectively implement legal measures to prevent discrimination that are already adopted, and ensure that their legislation is in full compliance with article 2 of the Convention on the Rights of the Child.

> Citizenship based on the place of birth has emerged as the overriding international norm governing the nationality of children born to non-citizen parents, in particular if they would otherwise be stateless.

Children of non-citizens have the right to a name and the right to acquire a nationality. Under article 7 of the Convention on the Rights of the Child, a child "shall be registered immediately after birth and shall have the right from birth to a name, the right to acquire a nationality . . . States Parties shall ensure the implementation of these rights . . . in particular where the child would otherwise be stateless." In view of the nearly universal ratification of the Convention, the principle of *jus soli* (citizenship based on the place of birth) has emerged as the overriding international norm governing the nationality of children born to noncitizen parents, in particular if they would otherwise be stateless. The right of parents to transmit their citizenship to their children must be enforced without discrimination as to the sex of the parent. Article 7 of the Convention also requires transmittal of citizenship from a parent to his or her adopted child. Article 7 should be read in conjunction with article 8 (preservation of identity, including nationality, name and family relations), article 9 (avoiding separation from parents), article 10 (family reunification) and article 20 (continuity of upbringing of children deprived of their family environment). Within the holistic approach recommended by the Committee on the Rights of the Child for the interpretation of the Convention, those articles should be understood according to the general principles of the Convention as reflected in articles 2 (right to non-discrimination), 3 (principle of the best interests of the child), 6 (right to life and development) and 12 (right to respect for the child's views in all matters affecting the child and opportunity to be heard in any judicial or administrative proceedings affecting the child).

Children of non-citizens are entitled to those measures of protection required by their status as minors. Children of non-citizens without legal status should not be excluded from schools, and schools that allow children of non-citizens to be educated in programmes designed in their country of origin should be encouraged.

With specific regard to asylum-seekers who are children, the Convention on the Rights of the Child provides important guidance for designing and implementing reception policies under the "best interest" principle. States must guarantee: special protection and care to child asylum-seekers with respect to their special needs; avoidance of detention for asylum-seekers under 18 years of age; and access of children to legal and psychological assistance, including by enabling contact with non-governmental organizations offering such assistance. Asylum-seekers and refugees who are children should not be placed in institutions that are not equipped to provide the special care they require. Such children should not be the subject of discrimination in the enjoyment of economic, social and cultural rights such as access to education, health care and social services. States should ensure the full economic, social and cultural rights of all non-citizen children in detention without discrimination—especially the right to education—and ensure their right to integration into society.

Conclusions and recommendations

Almost all advocacy for non-citizens has focused on the rights of discrete groups, such as asylum-seekers, refugees, stateless persons, trafficked persons, etc. Unfortunately, however, little has been done to identify the common plights, needs and approaches for redress of the various non-citizen groups. Indeed, diverse groups of non-citizens—and their respective advocacy and interest groups—have traditionally seen themselves as separate and their problems as unique, despite similar goals and common circumstances. In addition, international law and mechanisms relating to non-citizens have, until recently, focused on non-citizen subgroups while neglecting broader protections for non-citizens as a whole. For example, various United Nations institutions have designated special rapporteurs on such themes as trafficking, migrants, indigenous people, refugees, and racial discrimination and xenophobia. Similarly, several treaties have been designed to protect trafficked persons, migrant workers, indigenous and tribal peoples, refugees, and stateless persons. While all of these measures are essential and do not overlap so much as to be rendered unnecessary, a unified effort for the protection of non-citizens is nonetheless needed.

A primary objective of any international effort to protect the rights of non-citizens begins by demonstrating, as indicated by this publication, that without clear, comprehensive standards governing the rights of non-citizens, their implementation by States and more effective monitoring of compliance, the discriminatory treatment of non-citizens in contravention of relevant international human rights instruments will continue.

Furthermore, since the seven principal human rights treaties deal with many of the problems encountered by non-citizens, States should pursue universal ratification and implementation of those treaties, particularly the International Convention on the Protection of the Rights of All Migrant Workers and Members of Their Families. States, as appropriate, should also ratify and implement such other relevant treaties as the Protocol relating to the Status of Refugees; ILO Conventions Nos. 97, 118, 143, etc.; the Conventions on the Reduction of Statelessness and relating to the Status of Stateless Persons; the Vienna Convention on Consular Relations and its Optional Protocols; Protocols Nos. 4 and 7 to the European Convention on Human Rights; and the European Framework Convention for the Protection of National Minorities. States should be encouraged to abide by the Declaration on the Human Rights of Individuals Who are not Nationals of the Country in which They Live.

Since problems relating to the treatment of non-citizens arise under each of the seven principal human rights treaties, it would be desirable for the treaty bodies to coordinate their work more effectively. One approach would be for the treaty bodies to prepare joint general comments/recommendations that would establish a consistent, structured approach to the protection of the rights of non-citizens. At a minimum, treaty bodies that have adopted specific standards should consider updating them and those bodies that have yet to issue interpretive guidance relating to non-citizens should do so. In addition, treaty bodies should intensify their dialogues with States parties with regard to the rights accorded to, and the actual situation faced by, non-citizens within their respective spheres of concern.

[Footnotes Omited]

Annex

Committee on the Elimination of Racial Discrimination, general recommendation XXX (2004) on discrimination against non-citizens

The Committee on the Elimination of Racial Discrimination,

Recalling the Charter of the United Nations and the Universal Declaration of Human Rights, according to which all human beings are born free and equal in dignity and rights and are entitled to the rights and freedoms enshrined therein without distinction of any kind, and the International Covenant on Economic, Social and Cultural Rights, the International Covenant on Civil and Political Rights and the International Convention on the Elimination of All Forms of Racial Discrimination,

Recalling the Durban Declaration in which the World Conference against Racism, Racial Discrimination, Xenophobia and Related Intolerance recognized that xenophobia against non-nationals, particularly migrants, refugees and asylum-seekers, constitutes one of the main sources of contemporary racism and that human rights violations against members of such groups occur widely in the context of discriminatory, xenophobic and racist practices,

Noting that, based on the International Convention on the Elimination of All Forms of Racial Discrimination and general recommendations XI and XX, it has become evident from the examination of the reports of States parties to the Convention that groups other than migrants, refugees and asylum-seekers are also of concern, including undocumented non-citizens and persons who cannot establish the nationality of the State on whose territory they live, even where such persons have lived all their lives on the same territory,

Having organized a thematic discussion on the issue of discrimination against non-citizens and received the contributions of members of the Committee and States parties, as well as contributions from experts of other United Nations organs and specialized agencies and from non-governmental organizations,

Recognizing the need to clarify the responsibilities of States parties to the International Convention on the Elimination of All Forms of Racial Discrimination with regard to non-citizens,

Basing its action on the provisions of the Convention, in particular article 5, which requires States parties to prohibit and eliminate discrimination based on race, colour, descent, and national or ethnic origin in the enjoyment by all persons of civil, political, economic, social and cultural rights and freedoms,

Affirms that:

1. RESPONSIBILITIES OF STATES PARTIES TO THE CONVENTION

1. Article 1, paragraph 1, of the Convention defines racial discrimination. Article 1, paragraph 2, provides for the possibility of differentiating between citizens and non-citizens. Article 1, paragraph 3, declares that, concerning nationality, citizenship or naturalization, the legal provisions of States parties must not discriminate against any particular nationality;

2. Article 1, paragraph 2, must be construed so as to avoid undermining the basic prohibition of discrimination; hence, it should not be interpreted to detract in any way from the rights and freedoms recognized and enunciated in particular in the Universal Declaration of Human Rights, the International Covenant on Economic, Social and Cultural Rights and the International Covenant on Civil and Political Rights;

3. Article 5 of the Convention incorporates the obligation of States parties to prohibit and eliminate racial discrimination in the enjoyment of civil, political, economic, social and cultural rights. Although some of these rights, such as the right to participate in elections, to vote and to stand for election, may be confined to citizens, human rights are, in principle, to be enjoyed by all persons. States parties are under an obligation to guarantee equality between citizens and non-citizens in the enjoyment of these rights to the extent recognized under international law;

4. Under the Convention, differential treatment based on citizenship or immigration status will constitute discrimination if the criteria for such differentiation, judged in the light of the objectives and purposes of the Convention, are not applied pursuant to a legitimate aim, and are not proportional to the achievement of this aim. Differentiation within the scope of article 1, paragraph 4, of the Convention relating to special measures is not considered discriminatory;

5. States parties are under an obligation to report fully upon legislation on non-citizens and its implementation. Furthermore, States parties should include in their periodic reports, in an appropriate form,

socio-economic data on the non-citizen population within their jurisdiction, including data disaggregated by gender and national or ethnic origin;

Recommends,

Based on these general principles, that the States parties to the Convention, as appropriate to their specific circumstances, adopt the following measures:

2. MEASURES OF A GENERAL NATURE

6. Review and revise legislation, as appropriate, in order to guarantee that such legislation is in full compliance with the Convention, in particular regarding the effective enjoyment of the rights mentioned in article 5, without discrimination;

7. Ensure that legislative guarantees against racial discrimination apply to non-citizens regardless of their immigration status, and that the implementation of legislation does not have a discriminatory effect on non-citizens;

8. Pay greater attention to the issue of multiple discrimination faced by non-citizens, in particular concerning the children and spouses of non-citizen workers, to refrain from applying different standards of treatment to female non-citizen spouses of citizens and male non-citizen spouses of citizens, to report on any such practices and to take all necessary steps to address them;

9. Ensure that immigration policies do not have the effect of discriminating against persons on the basis of race, colour, descent, or national or ethnic origin;

10. Ensure that any measures taken in the fight against terrorism do not discriminate, in purpose or effect, on the grounds of race, colour, descent, or national or ethnic origin and that non-citizens are not subjected to racial or ethnic profiling or stereotyping;

3. PROTECTION AGAINST HATE SPEECH AND RACIAL VIOLENCE

11. Take steps to address xenophobic attitudes and behaviour towards non-citizens, in particular hate speech and racial violence, and to promote a better understanding of the principle of non-discrimination in respect of the situation of non-citizens;

12. Take resolute action to counter any tendency to target, stigmatize, stereotype or profile, on the basis of race, colour, descent, and national or ethnic origin, members of "non-citizen" population groups, especially by politicians, officials, educators and the media, on the Internet and other electronic communications networks and in society at large;

4. ACCESS TO CITIZENSHIP

13. Ensure that particular groups of non-citizens are not discriminated against with regard to access to citizenship or naturalization, and to pay due attention to possible barriers to naturalization that may exist for long-term or permanent residents;

14. Recognize that deprivation of citizenship on the basis of race, colour, descent, or national or ethnic origin is a breach of States parties' obligations to ensure non-discriminatory enjoyment of the right to nationality;

15. Take into consideration that in some cases denial of citizenship for long-term or permanent residents could result in creating disadvantage for them in access to employment and social benefits, in violation of the Convention's anti-discrimination principles;

16. Reduce statelessness, in particular statelessness among children, by, for example, encouraging their parents to apply for citizenship on their behalf and allowing both parents to transmit their citizenship to their children;

17. Regularize the status of former citizens of predecessor States who now reside within the jurisdiction of the State party;

5. ADMINISTRATION OF JUSTICE

18. Ensure that non-citizens enjoy equal protection and recognition before the law and in this context, to take action against racially motivated violence and to ensure the access of victims to effective legal remedies and the right to seek just and adequate reparation for any damage suffered as a result of such violence;

19. Ensure the security of non-citizens, in particular with regard to arbitrary detention, as well as ensure that conditions in centres for refugees and asylum-seekers meet international standards;

20. Ensure that non-citizens detained or arrested in the fight against terrorism are properly protected by domestic law that complies with international human rights, refugee and humanitarian law;

21. Combat ill-treatment of and discrimination against non-citizens by police and other law enforcement agencies and civil servants by strictly applying relevant legislation and regulations providing for sanctions and by ensuring that all officials dealing with non-citizens receive special training, including training in human rights;

22. Introduce in criminal law the provision that committing an offence with racist motivation or aim constitutes an aggravating circumstance allowing for a more severe punishment;

23. Ensure that claims of racial discrimination brought by non-citizens are investigated thoroughly and that claims made against officials, notably those concerning discriminatory or racist behaviour, are subject to independent and effective scrutiny;

24. Regulate the burden of proof in civil proceedings involving discrimination based on race, colour, descent, and national or ethnic origin so that once a non-citizen has established a prima facie case that he or she has been a victim of such discrimination, it shall be for the respondent to provide evidence of an objective and reasonable justification for the differential treatment; **The Rights** of Non-citizens **51**

6. EXPULSION AND DEPORTATION OF NON-CITIZENS

25. Ensure that laws concerning deportation or other forms of removal of non-citizens from the jurisdiction of the State party do not discriminate in purpose or effect among non-citizens on the basis of race, colour or ethnic or national origin, and that non-citizens have equal access to effective remedies, including the right to challenge expulsion orders, and are allowed effectively to pursue such remedies;

26. Ensure that non-citizens are not subject to collective expulsion in particular in situations where there are insufficient guarantees that the personal circumstances of each of the persons concerned have been taken into account;

27. Ensure that non-citizens are not returned or removed to a country or territory where they are at risk of being subject to serious human rights abuses, including torture and cruel, inhuman or degrading treatment or punishment;

28. Avoid expulsions of non-citizens, especially of long-term residents, that would result in disproportionate interference with the right to family life;

7. ECONOMIC, SOCIAL AND CULTURAL RIGHTS

29. Remove obstacles that prevent the enjoyment of economic, social and cultural rights by non-citizens, notably in the areas of education, housing, employment and health;

30. Ensure that public educational institutions are open to non-citizens and children of undocumented immigrants residing in the territory of a State party;

31. Avoid segregated schooling and different standards of treatment being applied to non-citizens on grounds of race, colour, descent, and national or ethnic origin in elementary and secondary school and with respect to access to higher education;

32. Guarantee the equal enjoyment of the right to adequate housing for citizens and non-citizens, especially by avoiding segregation in housing and ensuring that housing agencies refrain from engaging in discriminatory practices;

33. Take measures to eliminate discrimination against non-citizens in relation to working conditions and work requirements, including employment rules and practices with discriminatory purposes or effects;

34. Take effective measures to prevent and redress the serious problems commonly faced by non-citizen workers, in particular by non-citizen domestic workers, including debt bondage, passport retention, illegal confinement, rape and physical assault;

35. Recognize that, while States parties may refuse to offer jobs to non-citizens without a work permit, all individuals are entitled to the enjoyment of labour and employment rights, including the freedom of assembly and association, once an employment relationship has been initiated until it is terminated;

36. Ensure that States parties respect the right of non-citizens to an adequate standard of physical and mental health by, inter alia, refraining from denying or limiting their access to preventive, curative and palliative health services;

37. Take the necessary measures to prevent practices that deny non-citizens their cultural identity, such as legal or de facto requirements that non-citizens change their name in order to obtain citizenship, and to take measures to enable non-citizens to preserve and develop their culture;

38. Ensure the right of non-citizens, without discrimination based on race, colour, descent, and national or ethnic origin, to have access to any place or service intended for use by the general public, such as transport, hotels, restaurants, cafés, theatres and parks;

39. The present general recommendation replaces general recommendation XI (1993).

ISBN-13: 978-92-1-154175-

Designed and printed at United Nations, Geneva
GE.06-45932–March 2007–4,015   **HR/PUB/2006/11**
United Nations publication Sales No E.07.XIV.2

Report of the Jorge Bustamante, Special Rapporteur to the U.N. Human Rights Council on the human rights of migrants, on his Mission To The United States of America, 2007

UNITED NATIONS	A
General Assembly	Distr.
HUMAN RIGHTS COUNCIL	GENERAL
Seventh session	A/HRC/7/12/Add.2
Agenda item 3	5 March 2008
	Original: ENGLISH

PROMOTION AND PROTECTION OF ALL HUMAN RIGHTS, CIVIL, POLITICAL, ECONOMIC, SOCIAL AND CULTURAL RIGHTS, INCLUDING THE RIGHT TO DEVELOPMENT

Report of the Special Rapporteur on the human rights of migrants,

Jorge Bustamante

Addendum

MISSION TO THE UNITED STATES OF AMERICA* **

* The summary of this document is being circulated in all official languages. The report, which is annexed to the summary, is being circulated in the language of submission only.

** The present document is submitted late to reflect the most recent information.

Summary

The present report is submitted in accordance with resolution 2001/52 of the Commission on Human Rights following the official visit of the Special Rapporteur on the human rights of migrants to the United States of America (the U.S.) between 30 April and 18 May 2007. The purpose of the mission was to examine and report on the status of the human rights of migrants living in the U.S. For the purposes of this report, "migrants" refers to all non-citizens living in the U.S., including, among others, undocumented non-citizens and non-citizens with legal permission to remain in the country, such as legal permanent residents, work visa holders, and persons with refugee status. The Special Rapporteur thanks the Government of the U.S. for extending an invitation for him to conduct such a mission. The Special Rapporteur was disappointed, however, that his scheduled and approved visits to the Hutto Detention Center in Texas and the Monmouth detention centre in New Jersey were subsequently cancelled without satisfactory explanation.

While noting the Government's interest in addressing some of the problems related to the human rights of migrants, the Special Rapporteur has serious concerns about the situation of migrants in the country, especially in the context of specific aspects of deportation and detention policies, and with regard to specific groups such as migrant workers in New Orleans and the Gulf Coast in the aftermath of Hurricane Katrina, migrant farm workers, and migrants in detention facilities. The Special Rapporteur wishes to highlight the fact that cases of indefinite detention – even of migrants fleeing adverse conditions in their home countries—were not uncommon according to testimonies he received. The Special Rapporteur learned from human rights advocates about the lack of due process for non-citizens in U.S. deportation proceedings and their ability to challenge the legality or length of their detention; as well as about the conditions of detained asylum-seekers, long-term permanent residents and parents of minors who are U.S. citizens. In some cases immigrant detainees spend days in solitary confinement, with overhead lights kept on 24 hours a day, and often in extreme heat and cold. According to official sources, the U.S. Government detains over 230,000 people a year—more than three times the number of people it held in detention nine years ago.

The Special Rapporteur notes with dismay that xenophobia and racism towards migrants in the U.S. has worsened since 9/11. The current xenophobic climate adversely affects many sections of the migrant population, and has a particularly discriminatory and devastating impact on many of the most vulnerable groups in the migrant population, including children, unaccompanied minors, Haitian and other Afro-Caribbean migrants, and migrants who are, or are perceived to be, Muslim or of South Asian or Middle Eastern descent.

The Special Rapporteur notes that the U.S. lacks a clear, consistent, long-term strategy to improve respect for the human rights of migrants. Although there are national laws prohibiting discrimination, there is no national legislative and policy framework implementing protection for the human rights of migrants against which the federal and local programmes and strategies can be evaluated to assess to what extent the authorities are respecting the human rights of migrants.

In light of numerous issues described in this report, the Special Rapporteur has come to the conclusion that the U.S. has failed to adhere to its international obligations to make the human rights of the 37.5 million migrants living in the country (according to Government census data from 2006) a national priority, using a comprehensive and coordinated national policy based on clear international obligations. The primary task of such a national policy should be to recognize that, with the exception of certain rights relating to political participation, migrants enjoy nearly all the same human rights protections as citizens, including an emphasis on meeting the needs of the most vulnerable groups.

The Special Rapporteur has provided a list of detailed recommendations and conclusions, stressing the need for an institution at the federal level with a mandate solely devoted to the human rights of migrants, a national body that truly represents the voices and concerns of the migrant population, and which could address underlying causes of migration and the human rights concerns of migrants within the U.S.

Annex

REPORT OF THE SPECIAL RAPPORTEUR ON THE HUMAN RIGHTS OF MIGRANTS, JORGE BUSTAMANTE, ON HIS MISSION TO THE UNITED STATES OF AMERICA
(30 April-18 May 2007)

CONTENTS

Introduction

1. Pursuant to his mandate the Special Rapporteur on the human rights of migrants visited the United States of America (the U.S.) from 30 April to 18 May at the invitation of the Government.

2. Inhabiting a large geographic area, the migrant population of the U.S. is complex. Hence, the Special Rapporteur did not have time to conduct a comprehensive investigation of all the issues related

to the various migrant populations residing in the U.S. The Special Rapporteur met with a great variety of organizations, State, national and local agencies, officials, and individuals. These included the following: the Indigenous Front of Binational Organizations and California Rural Legal Assistance; religious leaders and representatives; people whose homes were raided by the Department of Homeland Security's agency for Immigration and Customs Enforcement; the National Immigration Law Centre; members of the Youth Justice Coalition; Homies Unidos (which led tours of Pico Union, MacArthur Park and Koreatown in Los Angeles); the Florence detention centre in Arizona; officials at the U.S. Border Patrol; Nogales, Arizona; Dr. Bruce Parks, Pima County's Medical Examiner (who provided statistics and information about migrant deaths due to exposure); the Coalición de Derechos Humanos and other non-governmental organizations (NGOs) in the Phoenix area, including the Macehalli Day Labor Center and the Florence Immigrant and Refugee Rights Project; members of local Native American groups; advocates for migrant domestic workers in Maryland and elsewhere; the Farmworker Association of Florida in Immokalee; (while in Florida he also discussed detention and deportation procedures with the Haitian community); the US Human Rights Network and several of its member organizations; community members and advocates. Furthermore, numerous migrants provided testimonials about conditions directly experienced by themselves or by their migrant family members.

3. During his visit, the Special Rapporteur toured the U.S. border with Mexico and watched U.S. immigration officials at work. He met there with officials from the U.S. Customs and Border Protection (CBP), a division of the Department of Homeland Security (DHS), spending half a day with Border Patrol officers at the San Diego sector. In Los Angeles the Special Rapporteur conducted site visits, listened to presentations and witnessed community testimony on the system of immigration enforcement (including on raids and detention, workers' rights, deportation procedures, and the criminalization of immigrants).

4. In Tucson, Arizona, the Special Rapporteur met with advocates and lawyers who informed him of the practice of subjecting immigrants to disproportionate criminal charges in addition to civil charges for violation of the immigration laws of the U.S. In particular, the Special Rapporteur learned that immigration authorities and federal prosecutors are now charging some non-citizens with civil violations for being in the country illegally, as well as for the overly-broad charge of "self-smuggling" themselves into the country. This latter criminal charge is defined as a felony and therefore the migrant can be sentenced to prison upon conviction.

5. In Atlanta, Georgia, the Special Rapporteur attended a regional NGO briefing, "Directly Impacted Community Members Briefing and Press Conference", organized by the National Network of Immigrant and Refugee Rights and its member organizations the Georgia Latino Alliance for Human Rights (GLAHR), the Latin American and Caribbean Community Center (LACCC) and the American Civil Liberties Union (ACLU) of both Georgia and New York. He also attended a reception in Atlanta where he was able to meet with Georgia State Representatives and Senators. During the NGO briefings in Atlanta, the Special Rapporteur heard from migrants and migrant human rights advocates from different organizations and who travelled from across the southern U.S., including the Mississippi Immigrant Rights Alliance (MIRA), the New Orleans Workers' Center for Racial Justice, the Southern Poverty Law Center (SPLC), Queer Progressive Agenda (QPA), Raksha (South Asian community organization), the Mexican American Legal Defense and Education Fund (MALDEF), the Georgia Department of Education Program, and the Roman Catholic Archdiocese of Atlanta. Migrants and NGO advocates from these and other organization informed the Special Rapporteur of the plight of migrants in the south of the U.S., where the migrant population is booming.

6. The Special Rapporteur also attended a public hearing in New York on the rights of migrants organized by the ACLU of New York, regional NGOs and grass-roots organizations. In New York, the Special Rapporteur heard several individuals testify about the post-9/11 backlash, including the experiences of the some 750 migrants arrested and subjected to arbitrary and lengthy detention subsequent to the September 11, 2001 attacks on the U.S.

7. The visit concluded with meetings with senior officials of the Department of Homeland Security and the State Department in Washington, D.C. On the last day of his visit, the Special Rapporteur was informed that the cancellation of his visits to the detention facilities in Texas and New Jersey was due to a pending lawsuit filed against both facilities, in which the U.S. Government was not allowed to interfere. A statement was subsequently published in the press suggesting that the cancellation was because the

"Special Rapporteur declined the invitation"; the Special Rapporteur made clear that this latter allegation was false.

8. Migrant rights issues raised in these various meetings included, but were not limited to, the following: indefinite detention; arbitrary detention; mandatory detention; deportation without due process; family separation; anti-immigrant legislation; racial profiling; linguistic, racial, ethnic, gender and sexual-orientation discrimination; State violence; wage theft; forced labour; limited access to health and education; the growing anti-immigrant climate (including the post-9/11 backlash); and significant limitations on due process and judicial oversight. Most of these issues are addressed in this report.

I. INTERNATIONAL LAW AND STANDARDS

9. Since the early stages of the nation State, control over immigration has been understood as an essential power of government. In recent history, governments have allowed limits to be placed on their power regarding immigration policy, recognizing that it may only be exercised in ways that do not violate fundamental human rights. Therefore, while international law recognizes every State's right to set immigration criteria and procedures, it does not allow unfettered discretion to set policies for detention or deportation of non-citizens without regard to human rights standards.

A. Right to fair deportation procedures

10. The governmental power to deport should be governed by laws tailored to protect legitimate national interests. U.S. deportation policies violate the right to fair deportation procedures, including in cases in which the lawful presence of the migrant in question is in dispute, as established under article 13 of the International Covenant on Civil and Political Rights (ICCPR). These deportation policies, particularly those applied to migrants lawfully in the U.S. who have been convicted of crimes, also violate (a) international legal standards on proportionality; (b) the right to a private life, provided for in article 17 of the ICCPR; and (c) article 33 of the Convention relating to the Status of Refugees, which prohibits the return of refugees to places where they fear persecution, with very narrow exceptions.

11. The ICCPR, which the U.S. ratified in 1992, states in article 13 (to which the U.S. has entered no reservations, understandings or declarations): "An alien lawfully in the territory of a State Party to the present covenant may be expelled therefrom only in pursuance of a decision reached in accordance with law and shall, except where compelling reasons of national security otherwise require, be allowed to submit the reasons against his expulsion and to have his case reviewed by, and be represented for the purpose before, the competent authority or a person or persons especially designated by the competent authority."

12. The Human Rights Committee, which monitors State compliance with the ICCPR, has interpreted the phrase "lawfully in the territory" to include non-citizens who wish to challenge the validity of the deportation order against them. In addition, the Committee has made this clarifying statement: " ... if the legality of an alien's entry or stay is in dispute, any decision on this point leading to his expulsion or deportation ought to be taken in accordance with article 13." and further: "An alien must be given full facilities for pursuing his remedy against expulsion so that this right will in all the circumstances of his case be an effective one."

13. Similarly, article 8, paragraph 1 of the American Convention on Human Rights, which the U.S. signed in 1977, states that "Every person has the right to a hearing, with due guarantees and within a reasonable time, by a competent, independent, and impartial tribunal, previously established by law ... for the determination of his rights and obligations of a civil, labor, fiscal, or any other nature."

14. Applying this standard, the Inter-American Commission on Human Rights has stated that detention and deportation proceedings require "as broad as possible" an interpretation of due process requirements and include the right to a meaningful defence and to be represented by an attorney.

15. Because U.S. immigration laws impose mandatory deportation without a discretionary hearing where family and community ties can be considered, these laws fail to protect the right to private life, in violation of the applicable human rights standards.

16. Article 16, paragraph 3, of the Universal Declaration of Human Rights and article 23, paragraph 1, of the ICCPR state that "The family is the natural and fundamental group unit of society and is entitled to protection by society and the State." Furthermore, article 23, paragraph 3 states that the right of men and women to marry and found a family shall be recognized. This right includes the right to live together. Article 17, paragraph 1 of the International Covenant on Civil and Political Rights states that "No one shall be subjected to arbitrary or unlawful interference with his privacy, family or correspondence ... ".

17. As the international body entrusted with the power to interpret the ICCPR and decide cases brought under its Optional Protocol, the Human Rights Committee has explicitly stated that family unity imposes limits on the power of States to deport.

18. The American Declaration of the Rights and Duties of Man features several provisions relevant to the question of deportation of non-citizens with strong family ties. Article V states that "Every person has the right to the protection of the law against abusive attacks upon … his private and family life." Under article VI, "Every person has the right to establish a family, the basic element of society, and to receive protection therefor." The American Convention on Human Rights, to which the U.S. is a signatory, contains analogous provisions. The case of *Wayne Smith and Hugo Armendáriz v United States of America*, which came before the Inter-American Commission on Human Rights in 2006 relies on several of these provisions to challenge the U.S. policy of deporting non-citizens with criminal convictions without regard to family unity. In light of these international standards, the U.S. has fallen far behind the practice of providing protection for family unity in deportation proceedings.

19. Moreover, the rights of children to live together with their parents are violated by the lack of deportation procedures in which the State's interest in deportation is balanced against the rights of the children. U.S. mandatory deportation laws harm the human rights of children of non-citizen parents.

20. U.S. restrictions on relief for refugees convicted of crimes violate the Convention and the Protocol relating to the Status of Refugees.3 The U.S. provides two forms of relief for refugees fleeing persecution—withholding of removal, which provides bare protection against refoulement, and more robust asylum relief, which provides a pathway to permanent residence. Although petitioners' cases do not involve claims for refugee protection, a discussion of the effect of U.S. immigration laws on non-citizens with criminal convictions would be incomplete without an exploration of the effect of the laws on non-citizen refugees.

Even the weaker form of relief—withholding of removal—is per se unavailable to non-citizens with aggravated felonies sentenced to an aggregate term of at least five years' imprisonment and to those whom the Attorney General determines have been convicted of a particularly serious crime. U.S. law denies these refugees even a hearing for their refugee claims, instead denying relief on a categorical basis. U.S. laws therefore contravene the due process and substantive protections of the Declaration of the Rights and Duties of Man and the Convention and the Protocol relating to the Status of Refugees, which allow for exceptions to non-refoulement in only a narrow set of cases and after individualized hearings.

B. Right to liberty of person

21. Pursuant to the Immigration and Nationality Act, U.S. Immigration and Customs Enforcement (ICE) may detain non-citizens under final orders of removal only for the period necessary to bring about actual deportation. Additionally, two U.S. Supreme Court decisions, *Zadvydas v Davis*, and *Clark v Martinez*, placed further limits on the allowable duration of detention. As a result of those decisions, ICE may not detain an individual for longer than six months after the issuance of a final removal order if there is no significant likelihood of actual deportation (for example, because the home country refuses repatriation) in the reasonably foreseeable future.

22. Although these two court decisions limit the ability of ICE to detain non-citizens indefinitely, in practice, U.S. policy is a long way out of step with international obligations. Immigration enforcement authorities have failed to develop an appropriate appeals procedure, and for all practical purposes have absolute discretion to determine whether a non-citizen may be released from detention. Furthermore, those released from detention as a result of a post-order custody review are released under conditions of supervision, which in turn are monitored by ICE deportation officers. Again, ICE officers have absolute authority to determine whether an individual must return to custody. Given that these discretionary decisions are not subject to judicial review, current U.S. practices violate international law.

23. The Special Rapporteur wishes to stress that international conventions require that the decision to detain someone should be made on a case-by-case basis after an assessment of the functional need to detain a particular individual. He notes that the individual assessment of cases does not appear to be sufficient and that detention policies in the U.S. constitute serious violations of international due process standards. Based on individual testimonies, the Government's own admissions and reports he received, the Special Rapporteur notes that the violations include:
- Failing to promptly inform detainees of the charges against them
- Failing to promptly bring detainees before a judicial authority

- Denying broad categories of detainees release on bond without individualized assessments
- Subjecting detainees to investigative detention without judicial oversight
- Denying detainees access to legal counsel

24. In sum, in the current context the U.S. detention and deportation system for migrants lacks the kinds of safeguards that prevent certain deportation decisions and the detention of certain immigrants from being arbitrary within the meaning of the International Covenant on Civil and Political Rights (ICCPR), which the U.S. has signed and ratified.

C. Labour rights

25. The labour rights of migrants affected by conditions in certain portions of the labour market, including the tomato workers in Florida and migrants in regions of the country devastated by Hurricane Katrina, are also included in the Universal Declaration of Human Rights and ICCPR. The U.S. Government has committed itself to protecting these rights.

III. UNITED STATES OF AMERICA IMMIGRATION POLICY AND PRACTICE

A. Legal and political background

26. With regard to deportation policy, under current U.S. immigration law, individuals arriving in the U.S. without the necessary visas or other legal permission to enter, including asylum-seekers and refugees, are subject to mandatory detention. In addition, persons subject to deportation procedures after being lawfully present in the U.S., including legal permanent residents who have been convicted of crimes, are subject to detention.

All of these persons are detained in immigration detention centres, county jails or private prisons under contract with immigration enforcement agencies for months, and sometimes years.

According to testimonies heard by the Special Rapporteur, U.S. citizens erroneously identified as non-citizens, long-time lawful permanent residents, non-citizen veterans, and vulnerable populations with a regular legal status have also been detained for months without sufficient due process protections, including fair individualized assessments of the reasons for their detention.

27. In 2006, the Department of Homeland Security arrested over 1.6 million migrants, including both undocumented migrants and legal permanent residents, of which over 230,000 were subsequently held in detention.

28. On average, there are over 25,000 migrants detained by immigration officials on any given day. The conditions and terms of their detention are often prison-like: freedom of movement is restricted and detainees wear prison uniforms and are kept in a punitive setting. Many detainees are held in jails instead of detention centres, since the U.S. uses a combination of facilities owned and operated by ICE, prison facilities owned and operated by private prison contractors and over 300 local and county jails from which ICE rents beds on a reimbursable basis. As a result, the majority of non-criminal immigrants are held in jails where they are mixed in with the prison's criminal population. This is the case despite the fact that under U.S. law an immigration violation is a civil offence, not a crime. The mixture of criminal and immigrant detainees in these jails can result in the immigrants being treated in a manner that is inappropriate to their status as administrative, as opposed to criminal, pretrial or post-conviction inmates.

29. In 1996, the Immigration and Naturalization Service had a daily detention capacity of 8,279 beds. By 2006, that had increased to 27,500 with plans for future expansion. At an average cost of US$ 95 per person per day, immigration detention costs the U.S. Government US $ 1.2 billion per year.

30. ICE reported an average stay of 38 days for all migrant detainees in 2003. Asylum-seekers granted refugee status, spend an average of 10 months in detention, with the longest period in one case being three and a half years. There are instances of individuals with final orders of removal who languish in detention indefinitely, such as those from countries with whom the U.S. does not have diplomatic relations or that refuse to accept the return of their own nationals. Under U.S. law, migrant detainees about whom the U.S. has certain national security concerns are subject to the possibility of indefinite detention, in contravention of international standards.

31. Migrants in detention include asylum-seekers, torture survivors, victims of human trafficking, long-term permanent residents facing deportation for criminal convictions based on a long list of crimes (including minor ones), the sick, the elderly, pregnant women, transgender migrants detained according to their birth sex rather than their gender identity or expression, parents of children who are U.S. citizens, and families. Detention is emotionally and financially devastating, particularly when it divides families and leaves spouses and children to fend for themselves in the absence of the family's main financial provider.

32. Immigrants are also often transferred to remote detention facilities, which interferes substantially with access to counsel and to family members and often causes great financial and emotional hardship for family members who are not detained. Thousands of those held in immigration detention are individuals who, by law, could be released.

33. Detention has not always been the primary enforcement strategy relied upon by the U.S. immigration authorities, as it appears to be today. In 1954, the Immigration and Naturalization Service announced that it was abandoning the policy of detention except in rare cases when an individual was considered likely to be a security threat or flight risk. This reluctance to impose needless confinement was based on the concepts of individual liberty and due process, long recognized and protected in the American legal system, and also enshrined in international human rights standards.

34. Sweeping changes in immigration laws in 1996 drastically increased the number of people subject to mandatory, prolonged and indefinite detention. The increasing reliance of the U.S. authorities on detention as an enforcement strategy has meant that many individuals have been unnecessarily detained for prolonged periods without any finding that they are either a danger to society or a flight risk. These practices have continued despite attempts by the U.S. Supreme Court to limit the Government's discretion to indefinitely detain individuals.

35. Certain provisions of the Immigration and Nationality Act, as amended by two laws passed in 1996 (the Antiterrorism and Effective Death Penalty Act (AEDPA) and the Illegal Immigration Reform and Immigrant Responsibility Act (IIRAIRA)) require mandatory detention, pending removal proceedings, of virtually any non-citizen who is placed in proceedings on criminal grounds, as well as of persons who arrive at the country's borders in order to seek asylum from persecution without documentation providing for their legal entry into the country. These two laws have significantly increased the number of migrants subject to mandatory detention on a daily basis, since AEDPA requires the mandatory detention of non-citizens convicted of a wide range of offences, and IIRAIRA has further expanded the list of offences for which mandatory detention is required.

36. As a result of these legislative changes, minor drug offences—such as possession of paraphernalia—as well as minor theft or other property-related offences, can result in mandatory detention and in the past decade the use of detention as an immigration enforcement mechanism has become more the norm than the exception in U.S. immigration enforcement policy.

37. The policy of mandatory detention also strips immigration judges of the authority to determine during a full and fair hearing whether or not an individual presents a danger or a flight risk. Instead, certain previous convictions (and in some cases, merely the admission of having committed an offence) automatically trigger mandatory detention without affording non-citizens an opportunity to be heard as to whether or not they merit release from custody.

38. This policy also deprives immigration judges—and even the Department of Homeland Security—of the authority to order the release of an individual, even when it is clear that he or she poses no danger or flight risk that would warrant such detention.

39. In its landmark decision, *Zadvydas v Davis*,9 the Supreme Court held that indefinite immigration detention of non-citizens who have been ordered deported but whose removal is not reasonably foreseeable would raise serious constitutional problems.

40. Prior to *Zadvydas*, the Government had a policy of detaining individuals even when there was virtually no chance they would actually be removed (this has been especially common with migrants from countries such as Cuba, Iraq, the Islamic Republic of Iran, the Lao People's Democratic Republic, the former Soviet Union and Viet Nam). The Government often referred to these individuals as "lifers", in recognition of the fact that their detention was indefinite and potentially permanent. In the aftermath of *Zadvydas*, new regulations were promulgated in order to comply with the Supreme Court's decision. Under these regulations, if the Department of Homeland Security cannot remove a migrant within the 90-day removal period, the Government is required to provide a post-order custody review to determine if the individual can be released. If the individual remains in detention six months after the removal order has become final, another custody review is to be conducted. Once it is determined that removal is not reasonably foreseeable, the regulations require the individual to be released under conditions of supervision.

41. Unfortunately, many problems plague the post-order custody review process. For example, some detainees never receive notice of their 90-day or 6-month custody reviews, and therefore do not have the opportunity to submit documentation in support of their release. Others never receive timely custody reviews at either the 90-day or 6-month mark. In addition, decisions to continue detention are often based on faulty reasoning and erroneous facts, ignore the law outlined by the Supreme Court in *Zadvydas*, or are essentially rubber-stamp decisions that fail to cite any specific evidence in support of their conclusion.

42. Frequently, these decisions ignore documentation (including letters from the detained individual's consulate) that proves that there is no significant likelihood of removal in the reasonably foreseeable future. In other cases, the Department of Homeland Security has failed to present evidence of the likelihood of removal and instead blames detainees for failing to facilitate their own removal.

43. The Special Rapporteur notes that according to the law, individuals can be released on parole regardless of their immigration status. In practice, however, because migrants are not entitled to a review of their custody by an immigration judge, or are subjected to rubber-stamp administrative custody review decisions, their detention is essentially mandatory.

44. The Special Rapporteur acknowledges that the mission for the Department of Homeland Security is to "lead the unified national effort to secure America" through its Immigration and Customs Enforcement agency (ICE). ICE is the largest investigative branch of the Department of Homeland Security; and seeks to protect the U.S. against terrorist attacks by targeting undocumented immigrants, whom the agency considers to be "the people, money and materials that support terrorism and other criminal activities".

45. In that context, the ICE has recently shifted its approach to enforcement by bringing criminal charges against employers of irregular migrant workers, seizing their assets and charging them with money laundering violations.

B. Deportation policy

46. With regard to deportation policy, following changes to U.S. immigration law in 1996, non-citizens in the U.S. have been subjected to a policy of mandatory deportation upon conviction of a crime, including very minor ones. These persons are not afforded a hearing in which their ties to the U.S., including family relationships, are weighed against the Government's interest in deportation. According to Government sources, hundreds of thousands of persons have been deported since these laws went into effect in 1996.

47. One case that has been brought to the attention of the Special Rapporteur is that of a male migrant, originally from Haiti, who enlisted in the U.S. military in 1970. A lawful permanent resident, or green card holder, this individual served his adopted country for four years. Now a 52-year-old veteran with four U.S. citizen sons, two of whom are in the military themselves, he faces mandatory deportation because he was convicted of the possession and sale of small amounts of crack cocaine in the mid-1990s, for which he spent 16 months in prison.

48. Some 672,593 immigrants in the U.S.—many of whom, like the Haitian migrant described above, were legal residents—have been deported from the country under the 1996 legislation that requires mandatory deportation of non-citizens convicted of a crime after they have served their sentence. It does not matter whether the non-citizen has lived in the U.S. legally for decades, built a home and family, run a business, or paid taxes. And these laws do not apply only to serious crimes, but also to minor offences.

C. Local enforcement operations

57. While migration is a federal matter, ICE is actively seeking the assistance of State and local law enforcement in enforcing immigration law. Under a recent federal law, ICE has been permitted to enter into agreements with state and local law enforcement agencies through voluntary programmes which allow designated officers to carry out immigration law enforcement functions. These state and local law enforcement agencies enter into a memorandum of understanding (MOU) or a memorandum of agreement (MOA) that outlines the scope and limitation of their authority. According to ICE, over 21,485 officers nationwide are participating in this programme, and more than 40 municipal, county, and state agencies have applied. In 2006, this programme resulted in 6,043 arrests and so far in 2007, another 3,327.

58. Local law enforcement agencies that have signed MOUs so far are:
- Florida Department of Law Enforcement (the first to enter into the agreement)
- Alabama Department of Public Safety
- Arizona Department of Corrections

- Los Angeles, County Sheriff's Department
- San Bernardino County Sheriff-Coroner Department

D. Detention and removal system

59. On 2 November 2005 the Department of Homeland Security announced to the public a multi-year plan called the Secure Border Initiative (SBI) to increase enforcement along the U.S. borders and to reduce illegal migration. The SBI is divided into two phases.

60. The first phase includes a restructuring of the detention and removal system through the expansion of expedited removal and the creation of the "catch and return" initiative, in addition to greatly strengthening border security through additional personnel and technology.

61. The second phase, the interior enforcement strategy, was unveiled to the public on 20 April 2006. It is through this initiative that U.S. Immigration and Customs Enforcement (ICE) has expanded operations that target undocumented workers and individuals who are in violation of immigration law. The operations also target all non-citizens, including refugees, legal permanent residents, and others with permission to reside in the U.S., who have any of a long list of criminal offences on their records, including minor offences, which result in the mandatory detention and deportation of these individuals in accordance with the immigration laws passed in 1996.

62. The primary goal of the IES is to "Identify and remove criminal aliens, immigration fugitives and other immigration violators." According to the Office of Detention and Removal Operations:

66. The Special Rapporteur heard accounts from victims that ICE officials entered their homes without a warrant, denied them access to lawyers or a phone to call family members and coerced them to sign "voluntary departure "agreements.

67. Many who are subject to these raids and subsequent mandatory detention are long-time permanent residents who know far more about the country from which they are facing removal—the U.S.—than the country to which they may be removed. Although lawful permanent status is not terminated with detention, but only when a final order of removal is entered against an individual, lawful residents can be detained until there is a final resolution in their case.

E. Mandatory detention

68. Detention impairs an individual's ability to obtain counsel and present cases in removal proceedings. In 2005, 65 per cent of immigrants appeared at their deportation hearings without benefit of legal counsel. Despite the adversarial and legally complex nature of removal proceedings and the severe consequences at stake, detainees are not afforded appointed counsel.

69. Moreover, detention impacts an individual's ability to earn income, thereby also impeding the ability to retain counsel. To make matters worse, the Department of Homeland Security often transfers detainees hundreds or thousands of miles away from their home cities without any notice to their attorneys or family members, which violates the agency's own administrative regulations on detention and transfer of detainees. Non-citizens are often detained in particularly remote locations. Many private attorneys are put off from taking cases where clients are detained in such locations. Onerous distances, inflexible visitation schedules and advance notice scheduling requirements by facilities are all obstacles that impede the ability of detainees to secure and retain legal assistance.

70. Detention severely impairs the right of a respondent in removal proceedings to present evidence in her or his own defence. Extensive documentation is often required, including family ties, employment history, property or business ties, rehabilitation or good moral character. Obtaining admissible supporting documents from family members, administrative agencies, schools and hospitals, can be burdensome for anyone, but often practically impossible for detainees. Access to mail and property is often limited and can also create significant obstacles for detainees.

71. Faced with the prospect of mandatory and prolonged detention, detainees often abandon claims to legal relief from removal, contrary to international standards that require non-citizens to be able to submit reasons against their deportation to the competent authorities. Mandatory detention operates as a coercive mechanism, pressuring those detained to abandon meritorious claims for relief in order to avoid continued or prolonged detention and the onerous conditions and consequences it imposes.

72. U.S. immigration law allows for detention of migrants that is often neither brief nor determinate, and adjudication of defences against removal can be complicated and lengthy. An appeal to the Board of Immigration Appeals by either party extends the period of mandatory detention for many additional months. A petition for review to the Court of Appeals also extends mandatory detention, often for a period of years. A non-citizen is subject to mandatory detention even after being granted relief by the immigration judge, simply

upon the filing of a notice of intent to appeal by Government counsel. In fact, it is often the most meritorious cases that take the longest to adjudicate, and in which migrants spend the longest amount of time in detention. Often the cases subject to continuing appeals are cases where individuals may have the strongest ties to the U.S. and risk the severest consequences if removed.

78. Immigration laws are known for being particularly complex. It may take a non-citizen subject to mandatory detention months and sometimes years to ultimately prove that he or she was not deportable.

79. In one case a lawful permanent resident of the U.S. was detained for approximately three and a half years, subject to mandatory detention, for offences that the Court of Appeals for the Ninth Circuit ultimately found not to constitute deportable offences. Three and a half years after being placed in the custody of the Department of Homeland Security and charged as having been convicted of an aggravated felony, this person was released by the Department, as it was clear that nothing in his case made him removable and that removal proceedings would therefore be terminated.

80. The Security Through Regularized Immigration and a Vibrant Economy Act of 2007 (the STRIVE Act), introduced by Congress on 22 March 2007, is an example of recently proposed legislation that would further expand mandatory detention and indefinite immigration detention, and was an attempt to create comprehensive immigration reform through policy. It required that the Department of Homeland Security significantly increase the number of facilities for the detention of non-citizens, adding a minimum of 20 detention facilities with the capacity to detain an additional 20,000 non-citizens.

81. The STRIVE Act would have essentially overruled the limitations on indefinite detention outlined by the U.S. Supreme Court in *Zadvydas v Davis*12 by specifically authorizing the Department of Homeland Security to indefinitely detain certain non-citizens who have been ordered removed, even when their removal is not reasonably foreseeable. The STRIVE Act would also have increased the number of people subject to mandatory detention by further expanding the kinds of crimes that constitute an aggravated felony and providing the basis for such detention. During the Special Rapporteur's mission to the U.S. the bill died in the Congressional Subcommittee on 5 May 2007 as it did not come to a vote.

82. Despite efforts by activists, community members, lawyers, and other advocates to repair the significant damage resulting from the legislation introduced in 1996, the legislation and its effects have not been reversed nor mitigated. Moreover, at both state and federal levels, the anti-immigrant climate has resulted in legislation that leads to increased mandatory detention of non-citizens even before they are in Department of Homeland Security custody.

83. For example, in November 2006, Arizona voters approved Proposition 100, which became effective on 7 December 2006 upon its codification in Arizona Revised Statutes §13-3961. That section now provides that a person who is in criminal custody shall be denied bail "if the proof is evident or presumption great" that the person is guilty of a serious felony offence and the person "has entered or remained in the U.S. illegally". In addition to the serious due process and equal protection issues this provision raises, by mandating different treatment for non-citizens and citizens in criminal proceedings and requiring state officials with little understanding of the complexity of immigration laws to enforce those laws, it also virtually ensures the eventual transfer of these individuals to Department of Homeland Security custody (even if they are never convicted), further increasing the number of people potentially subject to mandatory, prolonged, and indefinite detention.

87. Without the ability to comply uniformly with the current regulations there can be no reasonable expectation that ICE has the capacity to handle its large caseload resulting in part from the efforts of the Department of Homeland Security to secure the border.

III. THE PLIGHT OF MIGRANT WORKERS: THE CASE OF HURRICANE KATRINA

A. Background

88. In the aftermath of Hurricane Katrina, which devastated New Orleans and other areas of the U.S. Gulf Coast in 2005, several hundred thousand workers, mostly African Americans, lost their jobs and their homes, and many became internally displaced persons (IDPs). Since the storm, these IDPs have faced tremendous structural barriers to returning home and to finding the employment necessary to rebuild their lives. Without housing, they cannot work; without work, they cannot afford housing. Since Hurricane Katrina, tens of thousands of migrant workers, most of them undocumented, have arrived in the Gulf Coast region to work in the reconstruction zones. They have made up much of the labour to rebuild the area, to keep businesses running and to boost tax revenue. To support their families, migrant workers often work longer hours for less pay than other labourers. For some migrant workers, wages continue to decrease.

Jobs are becoming scarcer because the most urgent work, gutting homes and removing debris, is mostly finished.

89. These migrant workers, like their original local counterparts, are finding barriers to safe employment, fair pay, and affordable housing, and in some cases, experience discrimination and exploitation amounting to inhuman and degrading treatment. In fact, many workers are homeless or living in crowded, unsafe and unsanitary conditions, harassed and intimidated by law enforcement, landlords and employers alike.

90. Migrant workers on the Gulf Coast are experiencing an unprecedented level of exploitation. They often live and work amid substandard conditions, homelessness, poverty, environmental toxicity, and the constant threat of police and immigration raids, without any guarantee of a fair day's pay. They also face structural barriers that make it impossible to hold public or private institutions accountable for their mistreatment; most have no political voice.

94. As noted above, the Universal Declaration of Human Rights, the International Covenant on Civil and Political Rights (ICCPR), the International Covenant on Economic, Social and Cultural Rights (ICESCR), and the International Convention on the Protection of the Rights of All Migrant Workers and Members of Their Families establish workers' rights to (a) a safe and healthful workplace, (b) compensation for workplace injuries and illnesses, (c) freedom of association and the right to form trade unions and bargain collectively, and (d) equality of conditions and rights for immigrant workers.

95. Immigrant workers, including those who migrated to work in the regions affected by Katrina, often experience violations of these rights. Lack of familiarity with U.S. law and language difficulties often prevent them from being aware of their rights as well as specific hazards in their work. Immigrant workers who are undocumented, as many are, risk deportation if they seek to organize to improve conditions. Fear of drawing attention to their immigration status also prevents them from seeking protection from Government authorities for their rights as workers. In 2002, the Supreme Court stripped undocumented workers of any remedies if they are illegally fired for union organizing activity. Under international law, however, undocumented workers are entitled to the same labour rights, including wages owed, protection from discrimination, protection for health and safety on the job and back pay, as are citizens and those working lawfully in a country.

96. Furthermore, pre- and post-Katrina policies and practices of local, state and federal government agencies have had a grossly disproportionate impact on migrants of colour, in violation of the U.S. Government's obligations under the Convention on the Elimination of All Forms of Racial Discrimination (CERD) and other human rights norms that the U.S. has ratified.

B. Institutional responsibility

97. Personal stories recounted to the Special Rapporteur illuminate the commonality of the struggles faced by migrant workers but also the institutional responsibility, and how both policies and practices perpetuate structural and institutional racism and xenophobia. Across the city of New Orleans, workers—both returning internally displaced persons and new migrant workers—list calamities that have become routine: homelessness, wage theft, toxic working conditions, joblessness, police brutality, and layers of bureaucracy. These shared experiences with structural racism unite low-wage workers across racial, ethnic, and industry lines.

Thousands of workers now live in the same conditions: they sleep in the homes they are gutting or in abandoned cars that survivors were forced to leave behind; they are packed in motels, sometimes 10 to a room; and they live on the streets. Most migrant workers were promised housing by their employers but quickly found upon arrival that no housing accommodation had been made available. Instead, they were left homeless.

98. By all accounts, state and local governments have turned a blind eye to this dismal housing situation. Although the city depends on migrant workers to act as a flexible, temporary workforce, it also made no arrangements to provide them with temporary housing. As a result, the workers who are rebuilding New Orleans often have nowhere to sleep.

99. The federal Government has sent mixed messages. On the one hand, it relaxed the immigration law requirements relating to hiring practices, thereby sending a message to contractors that hiring undocumented workers was permissible if not condoned. On the other hand, federal authorities failed to assure these workers and their family members that they would not be turned over to immigration authorities.

100. New migrant workers on the Gulf Coast have experienced a range of problems relating to wage theft which include:

- Non-payment of wages for work performed, including overtime
- Payment of wages with cheques that bounce due to insufficient funds
- Inability to identify the employer or contractor in order to pursue claims for unpaid wages
- Subcontractors—often migrants themselves—who want to but cannot pay wages because they have not been paid by the primary contractor (often a more financially stable white contractor)

101. These conditions are particularly salient for migrant workers, especially if they are undocumented as they are more easily exploitable. They may be hired for their hard manual labour and then robbed of their legally owed wages. The situation is exacerbated by the complexity of local employment structures. Because there are multiple tiers of subcontractors, often flowing from a handful of primary contractors with federal Government contracts, workers often do not know the identities of their employers. This is typical of the growing contingent of low-wage workers throughout the country. In New Orleans, workers explained that without knowing the identity of their employer, they cannot pursue wage claims against them.

IV. CONCLUSIONS

104. Contrary to popular belief, U.S. immigration policy did not become more severe after the terrorist attacks on September 11. Drastic changes made in 1996 have been at work for more than a decade, affecting communities across the nation and recent policy changes simply exacerbate what was put in motion then. Also, contrary to popular belief, these policies do not target only undocumented migrants—they apply to citizens born in the U.S. of undocumented parents and long-term lawful permanent residents (or green card holders) as well.

105. Not only have immigration laws become more punitive—increasing the types of crimes that can permanently sever a migrant's ties to the U.S.—but there are fewer ways for migrants to appeal for leniency. Hearings that used to happen in which a judge would consider a migrant's ties to the U.S., particularly their family relationships, were stopped in 1996. There are no exceptions available, no matter how long an individual has lived in the U.S. and no matter how much his spouse and children depend on him for their livelihood and emotional support.

106. Throughout the history of the U.S., many different kinds of non-citizens have been made subject to mandatory detention. People with lawful permanent resident status (or green card holders), including those who have lived lawfully in the U.S. for decades, are subject to deportation. So are other legal immigrants—refugees, students, business people, and those who have permission to remain because their country of nationality is in the midst of war or a humanitarian disaster. Undocumented non-citizens are also subject to mandatory detention and deportation regardless of whether they have committed a crime.

107. A primary principle of U.S. immigration law is that U.S. citizens can never be denied entry into the country; neither can they ever be forcibly deported from the U.S. By contrast, non-citizens, even those who have lived in the country legally for decades, are always vulnerable to mandatory detention and deportation.

108. In the wake of Hurricane Katrina, migrant workers from across the U.S. travelled to New Orleans. Ultimately, the voices of workers in post-Katrina New Orleans demonstrate that the actions and inactions of federal, state, and local governments and the actions of the private reconstruction industry have created deplorable working and living conditions for people striving to rebuild and return to the city. Because these workers are migrant, undocumented, and displaced they have little chance to hold officials and private industry accountable (e.g., many cannot vote, and displaced workers in New Orleans continue to experience barriers to voting) except through organized, collective action.

V. RECOMMENDATIONS

109. The Special Rapporteur would like to make the following recommendations to the [U.S.] Government.

On general detention matters

110. Mandatory detention should be eliminated; the Department of Homeland Security should be required to make individualized determinations of whether or not a non-citizen presents a danger to society or a flight risk sufficient to justify their detention.

111. The Department of Homeland Security must comply with the Supreme Court's decision in *Zadvydas v Davis* and *Clark v Martinez*. Individuals who cannot be returned to their home countries within the foreseeable future should be released as soon as that determination is made, and certainly no longer than six months after the issuance of a final order. Upon release, such

individuals should be released with employment authorization, so that they can immediately obtain employment.

112. The overuse of immigration detention in the U.S. violates the spirit of international laws and conventions and, in many cases, also violates the actual letter of those instruments. The availability of effective alternatives renders the increasing reliance on detention as an immigration enforcement mechanism unnecessary. Through these alternative programmes, there are many less restrictive forms of detention and many alternatives to detention that would serve the country's protection and enforcement needs more economically, while still complying with international human rights law and ensuring just and humane treatment of migrants.

Create detention standards and guidelines

113. At the eighty-seventh session of the Human Rights Committee in July 2006, the U.S. Government cited the issuance of the National Detention Standards in 2000 as evidence of compliance with international principles on the treatment of immigration detainees.13 While this is indeed a positive step, it is not sufficient. The U.S. Government should create legally binding human rights standards governing the treatment of immigration detainees in all facilities, regardless of whether they are operated by the federal Government, private companies, or county agencies.

114. Immigration detainees in the custody of the Department of Homeland Security and placed in removal proceedings, should have the right to appointed counsel. The right to counsel is a due process right that is fundamental to ensuring fairness and justice in proceedings. To ensure compliance with domestic and international law, court-appointed counsel should be available to detained immigrants.

115. Given that the difficulties in representing detained non-citizens are exacerbated when these individuals are held in remote and/or rural locations, U.S. Immigration and Customs Enforcement (ICE) should ensure that the facilities where non-citizens in removal proceedings are held, are located within easy reach of the detainees' counsel or near urban areas where the detainee will have access to legal service providers and pro bono counsel.

Deportation issues impacting due process and important human rights

116. U.S. immigration laws should be amended to ensure that all non-citizens have access to a hearing before an impartial adjudicator, who will weigh the non-citizen's interest in remaining in the U.S. (including their rights to found a family and to a private life) against the Government's interest in deporting him or her.

Detention/deportation issues impacting unaccompanied children

117. The Government should urge lawmakers to pass the Unaccompanied Alien Child Protection Act of 2007 reintroduced in March 2007.

118. Children should be removed from jail-like detention centres and placed in home-like facilities. Due care should be given to rights delineated for children in custody in the American Bar Association "Standards for the Custody, Placement, and Care; Legal Representation; and Adjudication of Unaccompanied Alien Children in the U.S.".

119. Temporary Protected Status (TPS) should be amended for unaccompanied children whose parents have TPS, so they can derive status through their parents.

Situation of migrant women detained in the U.S.

120. In collaboration with legal service providers and non-governmental organizations that work with detained migrant women, ICE should develop gender-specific detention standards that address the medical and mental health concerns of migrant women who have survived mental, physical, emotional or sexual violence.

121. Whenever possible, migrant women who are suffering the effects of persecution or abuse, or who are pregnant or nursing infants, should not be detained. If these vulnerable women cannot be released from ICE custody, the Department of Homeland Security should develop alternative programmes such as intense supervision or electronic monitoring, typically via ankle bracelets. These alternatives have proven effective during pilot programmes. They are not only more humane for migrants who are particularly vulnerable in the detention setting or who have family members who require their presence, but they also cost, on average, less than half the price of detention.

Judicial review

122. The U.S. should ensure that the decision to detain a non-citizen is promptly assessed by an independent court.

123. The Department of Homeland Security and the Department of Justice should work together to ensure that immigration detainees are given the chance to have their custody reviewed in a hearing before an immigration judge. Both departments should revise regulations to make clear that asylum-seekers can request these custody determinations from immigration judges.

124. Congress should enact legislation to ensure that immigration judges are independent of the Department of Justice, and instead part of a truly independent court system.

125. Families with children should not be held in prison-like facilities. All efforts should be made to release families with children from detention and place them in alternative accommodation suitable for families with children.

On migrant workers

126. The Government should ensure that state and federal labour policies are monitored, and their impact on migrant workers analysed. Policymakers and the public should be continually educated on the human needs and human rights of workers, including migrant workers. In this context, the Special Rapporteur strongly recommends that the U.S. consider ratifying the International Convention on the Protection of the Rights of All Migrant Workers and Members of Their Families.

127. A human services infrastructure should be built in disaster-affected communities to comprehensively meet the needs of workers facing substandard housing and homelessness, wage theft, unsafe working conditions and health issues.

128. Effective oversight of the enforcement of applicable labour laws by state and federal agencies should be ensured.

129. Existing health and safety laws should be assiduously enforced in order to curb exploitative hiring and employment practices by contractors.

130. Improved health and safety conditions should be ensured in places that are known to employ migrant workers, compensation for workers and health care for injured migrant workers should be provided, and the significant incidences of wage theft combated.

131. Local law enforcement and federal immigration authorities must cease harassing and racially profiling migrant workers. Law enforcement should instead focus on helping to promote the rights of workers, including the rights of migrant workers.

[Footnotes Omited]

APPENDIX O: LAW ENFORCEMENT, ARREST, DETENTION, AND DEATH PENALTY

The purpose of this Appendix is to give the reader a glimpse into how the matter of criminal law and procedure and related issues are regarded by the international community in light of international human rights standards. One must first look at the binding legal standards found in the Primary Documents such as the UDHR and ICCPR applicable to crimes, criminal procedure and detention, and then to the non-binding standards such as the Body of Principles for the Protection of All Persons under Any Form of Detention or Imprisonment, Document 47, and the Standard Minimum Rules for the Treatment of Prisoners, Document 48. Some of these non binding standards can be considered "soft law" in that although they are non-binding norms they provide states guidance on how to comply with the binding hard law standards.

Most of these binding and non-binding standards are meant to apply to domestic criminal law, procedure and detention. There also exists international criminal law and procedure. Many of the standards would apply to international criminal prosecutions, such as regarding treatment of prisoners. International criminal law norms are found in Primary Documents 68, 71, 76.

None of the following 15 documents are legally binding on the U.S. except number 14, the Vienna Convention on Consular Relations.

The U.S. was involved in the context of the U.N. in the articulation and drafting of these principles, guidelines and standard minimum rules, many of which have their origins in the U.S. criminal law and Constitutional norms such as procedural due process of law and the prohibition against cruel and unusual punishment, which is stated as cruel, inhuman or degrading treatment or punishment in the international human rights context.

Documents

Document 1: United Nations Declaration on Crime and Public Security* (Excerpted)

The General Assembly

Recalling the Declaration on the Occasion of the Fiftieth Anniversary of the United Nations,1 the Declaration on Measures to Eliminate International Terrorism2 and the Naples Political Declaration and Global Action Plan against Organized Transnational Crime,

Solemnly proclaims the following United Nations Declaration on Crime and Public Security:

Article 1

Member States shall seek to protect the security and well-being of their citizens and all persons within their jurisdiction by taking effective national measures to combat serious transnational crime, including organized crime, illicit drug and arms trafficking, smuggling of other illicit articles, organized trafficking in persons, terrorist crimes and the laundering of proceeds from serious crimes, and shall pledge their mutual cooperation in those efforts.

Article 2

Member States shall promote bilateral, regional, multilateral and global law enforcement cooperation and assistance, including, as appropriate, mutual legal assistance arrangements, to facilitate the detection, apprehension and prosecution of those who commit or are otherwise responsible for serious transnational crimes and to ensure that law enforcement and other competent authorities can cooperate effectively on an international basis.

Article 3

Member States shall take measures to prevent support for and operations of criminal organizations in their national territories. Member States shall, to the fullest possible extent, provide for effective extradition or prosecution of those who engage in serious transnational crimes in order that they find no safe haven.

Article 4

Mutual cooperation and assistance in matters concerning serious transnational crime shall also include, as appropriate, the strengthening of systems for the sharing of information among Member States and the provision of bilateral and multilateral technical assistance to Member States by utilizing training, exchange programmes and law enforcement training academies and criminal justice institutes at the international level.

Article 5

Member States that have not yet done so are urged to become parties as soon as possible to the principal existing international treaties relating to various aspects of the problem of international terrorism. States parties shall effectively implement their provisions in order to fight against terrorist crimes.

Member States shall also take measures to implement General Assembly resolution 49/60 of 9 December 1994, on measures to eliminate international terrorism, and the Declaration on Measures to Eliminate International Terrorism contained in the annex to that resolution.

Article 6

Member States that have not yet done so are urged to become parties to the international drug control conventions as soon as possible. States parties shall effectively implement the provisions of the Single Convention on Narcotic Drugs of 19614 as amended by the 1972 Protocol,5 the Convention on Psychotropic Substances of 1971,6 and the United Nations Convention against Illicit traffic in Narcotic Drugs and Psychotropic Substances of 1988.7 Member States specifically reaffirm that, on the basis of shared responsibility, they shall take all necessary preventive and enforcement measures to eliminate the illicit production of, trafficking in and distribution and consumption of narcotic drugs and psychotropic substances, including measures to facilitate the fight against those criminals involved in this type of transnational organized crime.

Article 7

Member States shall take measures within their national jurisdiction to improve their ability to detect and interdict the movement across borders of those who engage in serious transnational crime, as well as the instrumentalities of such crime, and shall take effective specific measures to protect their territorial boundaries, such as:

(a) Adopting effective controls on explosives and against illicit trafficking by criminals in certain materials and their components that are specifically designed for use in manufacturing nuclear, biological or chemical weapons and, in order to lessen risks arising from such trafficking, by becoming parties to and fully implementing all relevant international treaties relating to weapons of mass destruction;

(b) Strengthening supervision of passport issuance and enhancement of protection against tampering and counterfeiting;

(c) Strengthening enforcement of regulations on illicit transnational trafficking in firearms, with a view to both suppressing the use of firearms in criminal activities and reducing the likelihood of fuelling deadly conflict;

(d) Coordinating measures and exchanging information to combat the organized criminal smuggling of persons across national borders.

Article 8

To combat further the transnational flow of the proceeds of crime, Member States agree to adopt measures, as appropriate, to combat the concealment or disguise of the true origin of proceeds of serious transnational crime and the intentional conversion or transfer of such proceeds for that purpose. Member States agree to require adequate record-keeping by financial and related institutions and, as appropriate, the reporting of suspicious transactions and to ensure effective laws and procedures to permit the seizure and forfeiture of the proceeds of serious transnational crime. Member States recognize the need to limit the application of bank secrecy laws, if any, with respect to criminal operations and to obtain the cooperation of the financial institutions in detecting these and any other operations that may be used for the purpose of money-laundering.

Article 9

Member States agree to take steps to strengthen the overall professionalism of their criminal justice, law enforcement and victim assistance systems and relevant regulatory authorities through measures such as training, resource allocation and arrangements for technical assistance with other States and to promote the involvement of all elements of society in combating and preventing serious transnational crime.

Article 10

Member States agree to combat and prohibit corruption and bribery, which undermine the legal foundations of civil society, by enforcing applicable domestic laws against such activity. For this purpose, Member States also agree to consider developing concerted measures for international cooperation to curb corrupt practices, as well as developing technical expertise to prevent and control corruption.

Article 11

Actions taken in furtherance of the present Declaration shall fully respect the national sovereignty and territorial jurisdiction of Member States, as well as the rights and obligations of Member States under existing treaties and international law, and shall be consistent with human rights and fundamental freedoms as recognized by the United Nations.

[Commentary and Footnotes omitted]

DOCUMENT 2: PROCEDURES FOR THE EFFECTIVE IMPLEMENTATION OF THE STANDARD MINIMUM RULES FOR THE TREATMENT OF PRISONERS (EXCERPTED)

Procedure 1

All States whose standards for the protection of all persons subjected to any form of detention or imprisonment fall short of the Standard Minimum Rules for the Treatment of Prisoners shall adopt the Rules.

Procedure 2

Subject, as necessary, to their adaptation to the existing laws and culture but without deviation from the spirit and purpose of the Rules, the Standard Minimum Rules shall be embodied in national legislation and other regulations.

Procedure 3

The Standard Minimum Rules shall be made available to all persons concerned, particularly to law enforcement officials and correctional personnel, for purposes of enabling their application and execution in the criminal justice system.

Procedure 4

The Standard Minimum Rules, as embodied in national legislation and other regulations, shall also be made available and understandable to all prisoners and all persons under detention, on their admission and during their confinement.

Procedure 6

As part of the information mentioned in procedure 5 above, States should provide the Secretary-General with:

(*a*) Copies or abstracts of all laws, regulations and administrative measures concerning the application of the Standard Minimum Rules to persons under detention and to places and programmes of detention;

(*b*) Any data and descriptive material on treatment programmes, personnel and the number of persons under any form of detention, and statistics, if available;

(*c*) Any other relevant information on the implementation of the Rules, as well as information on the possible difficulties in their application.

Procedure 7

The Secretary-General shall disseminate the Standard Minimum Rules and the present implementing proce-dures, in as many languages as possible, and make them available to all States and intergovernmental and non-governmental organizations concerned, in order to ensure the widest circulation of the Rules and the present implementing procedures.

Procedure 8

The Secretary-General shall disseminate his reports on the implementation of the Rules, including analytical summaries of the periodic surveys, reports of the Committee on Crime Prevention and Control, reports prepared for the United Nations congresses on the prevention of crime and the treatment of offenders as well as the reports of the congresses, scientific publications and other relevant documentation as from time to time may be deemed necessary to further the implementation of the Standard Minimum Rules.

Procedure 9

The Secretary-General shall ensure the widest possible reference to and use of the text of the Standard Minimum Rules by the United Nations in all its relevant programmes, including technical cooperation activities.

Procedure 10

As part of its technical cooperation and development programmes the United Nations shall:

(*a*) Aid Governments, at their request, in setting up and strengthening comprehensive and humane correctional systems;

(*b*) Make available to Governments requesting them the services of experts and regional and interregional advisers on crime prevention and criminal justice;

(*c*) Promote national and regional seminars and other meetings at the professional and non-professional levels to further the dissemination of the Standard Minimum Rules and the present implementing procedures;

(*d*) Strengthen substantive support to regional research and training institutes in crime prevention and criminal justice that are associated with the United Nations.

The United Nations regional research and training institutes in crime prevention and criminal justice, in cooperation with national institutions, shall develop curricula and training materials, based on the Standard Minimum Rules and the present implementing procedures, suitable for use in criminal justice educational programmes at all levels, as well as in specialized courses on human rights and other related subjects.

Procedure 11

The United Nations Committee on Crime Prevention and Control shall:

(*a*) Keep under review, from time to time, the Standard Minimum Rules, with a view to the elaboration of new rules, standards and procedures applicable to the treatment of persons deprived of liberty;

(*b*) Follow up the present implementing procedures, including periodic reporting under procedure 5 above.

Procedure 12

The Committee on Crime Prevention and Control shall assist the General Assembly, the Economic and Social Council and any other United Nations human rights bodies, as appropriate, with recommendations relating to reports of ad hoc inquiry commissions, with respect to matters pertaining to the application and implementation of the Standard Minimum Rules.

Procedure 13

Nothing in the present implementing procedures should be construed as precluding resort to any other means or remedies available under international law or set forth by other United Nations bodies and agencies for the redress of violations of human rights, including the procedure on consistent patterns of gross violations of human rights under Economic and Social Council resolution 1503 (XLVIII) of 27 May 1970, the communication procedure under the Optional Protocol to the International Covenant on Civil and Political Rights2 and the communication procedure under the International Convention on the Elimination of All Forms of Racial Discrimination.

DOCUMENT 3: UNITED NATIONS STANDARD MINIMUM RULES FOR THE ADMINISTRATION OF JUVENILE JUSTICE (THE BEIJING RULES)* (EXCERPTED)

PART ONE

GENERAL PRINCIPLES

1. Fundamental perspectives

1.1 Member States shall seek, in conformity with their respective general interests, to further the well-being of the juvenile and her or his family.

1.2 Member States shall endeavour to develop conditions that will ensure for the juvenile a meaningful life in the community, which, during that period in life when she or he is most susceptible to deviant behaviour, will foster a process of personal development and education that is as free from crime and delinquency as possible.

1.3 Sufficient attention shall be given to positive measures that involve the full mobilization of all possible resources, including the family, volunteers and other community groups, as well as schools and other community institutions, for the purpose of promoting the well-being of the juvenile, with a view to reducing the need for intervention under the law, and of effectively, fairly and humanely dealing with the juvenile in conflict with the law.

1.4 Juvenile justice shall be conceived as an integral part of the national development process of each country, within a comprehensive framework of social justice for all juveniles, thus, at the same time, contributing to the protection of the young and the maintenance of a peaceful order in society.

1.5 These Rules shall be implemented in the context of economic, social and cultural conditions prevailing in each Member State.

1.6 Juvenile justice services shall be systematically developed and coordinated with a view to improving and sustaining the competence of personnel involved in the services, including their methods, approaches and attitudes.

2. Scope of the Rules and definitions used

2.1 The following Standard Minimum Rules shall be applied to juvenile offenders impartially, without distinction of any kind, for example as to race, colour, sex, language, religion, political or other opinions, national or social origin, property, birth or other status.

2.2 For purposes of these Rules, the following definitions shall be applied by Member States in a manner which is compatible with their respective legal systems and concepts:

(*a*) A juvenile is a child or young person who, under the respective legal systems, may be dealt with for an offence in a manner which is different from an adult;

(*b*) An offence is any behaviour (act or omission) that is punishable by law under the respective legal systems;

(*c*) A juvenile offender is a child or young person who is alleged to have committed or who has been found to have committed an offence.

2.3 Efforts shall be made to establish, in each national jurisdiction, a set of laws, rules and provisions specifically applicable to juvenile offenders and institutions and bodies entrusted with the functions of the administration of juvenile justice and designed:

(*a*) To meet the varying needs of juvenile offenders, while protecting their basic rights;

(*b*) To meet the needs of society;

(*c*) To implement the following rules thoroughly and fairly.

3. Extension of the Rules

3.1 The relevant provisions of the Rules shall be applied not only to juvenile offenders but also to juveniles who may be proceeded against for any specific behaviour that would not be punishable if committed by an adult.

3.2 Efforts shall be made to extend the principles embodied in the Rules to all juveniles who are dealt with in welfare and care proceedings.

3.3 Efforts shall also be made to extend the principles embodied in the Rules to young adult offenders.

4. *Age of criminal responsibility*

4.1 In those legal systems recognizing the concept of the age of criminal responsibility for juveniles, the beginning of that age shall not be fixed at too low an age level, bearing in mind the facts of emotional, mental and intellectual maturity.

5. *Aims of juvenile justice*

5.1 The juvenile justice system shall emphasize the well-being of the juvenile and shall ensure that any reaction to juvenile offenders shall always be in proportion to the circumstances of both the offenders and the offence.

6. *Scope of discretion*

6.1 In view of the varying special needs of juveniles as well as the variety of measures available, appropriate scope for discretion shall be allowed at all stages of proceedings and at the different levels of juvenile justice administration, including investigation, prosecution, adjudication and the follow-up of dispositions.

6.2 Efforts shall be made, however, to ensure sufficient accountability at all stages and levels in the exercise of any such discretion.

6.3 Those who exercise discretion shall be specially qualified or trained to exercise it judiciously and in accordance with their functions and mandates.

7. *Rights of juveniles*

7.1 Basic procedural safeguards such as the presumption of innocence, the right to be notified of the charges, the right to remain silent, the right to counsel, the right to the presence of a parent or guardian, the right to confront and cross-examine witnesses and the right to appeal to a higher authority shall be guaranteed at all stages of proceedings.

8. *Protection of privacy*

8.1 The juvenile's right to privacy shall be respected at all stages in order to avoid harm being caused to her or him by undue publicity or by the process of labeling.

8.2 In principle, no information that may lead to the identification of a juvenile offender shall be published.

9. *Saving clause*

9.1 Nothing in these Rules shall be interpreted as precluding the application of the Standard Minimum Rules for the Treatment of Prisoners4 adopted by the United Nations and other human rights instruments and standards recognized by the international community that relate to the care and protection of the young.

PART TWO

INVESTIGATION AND PROSECUTION

10. *Initial contact*

10.1 Upon the apprehension of a juvenile, her or his parents or guardian shall be immediately notified of such apprehension, and, where such immediate notification is not possible, the parents or guardian shall be notified within the shortest possible time thereafter.

10.2 A judge or other competent official or body shall, without delay, consider the issue of release.

10.3 Contacts between the law enforcement agencies and a juvenile offender shall be managed in such a way as to respect the legal status of the juvenile, promote the well-being of the juvenile and avoid harm to her or him, with due regard to the circumstances of the case.

11. *Diversion*

11.1 Consideration shall be given, wherever appropriate, to dealing with juvenile offenders without resorting to formal trial by the competent authority, referred to in rule 14.1 below.

11.2 The police, the prosecution or other agencies dealing with juvenile cases shall be empowered to dispose of such cases, at their discretion, without recourse to formal hearings, in accordance with the criteria laid down for that purpose in the respective legal system and also in accordance with the principles contained in these Rules.

11.3 Any diversion involving referral to appropriate community or other services shall require the consent of the juvenile, or her or his parents or guardian, provided that such decision to refer a case shall be subject to review by a competent authority, upon application.

11.4 In order to facilitate the discretionary disposition of juvenile cases, efforts shall be made to provide for community programmes, such as temporary supervision and guidance, restitution, and compensation of victims.

12. Specialization within the police

12.1 In order to best fulfill their functions, police officers who frequently or exclusively deal with juveniles or who are primarily engaged in the prevention of juvenile crime shall be specially instructed and trained. In large cities, special police units should be established for that purpose.

13. Detention pending trial

13.1 Detention pending trial shall be used only as a measure of last resort and for the shortest possible period of time.

13.2 Whenever possible, detention pending trial shall be replaced by alternative measures, such as close supervision, intensive care or placement with a family or in an educational setting or home.

13.3 Juveniles under detention pending trial shall be entitled to all rights and guarantees of the Standard Minimum Rules for the Treatment of Prisoners4 adopted by the United Nations.

13.4 Juveniles under detention pending trial shall be kept separate from adults and shall be detained in a separate institution or in a separate part of an institution also holding adults.

13.5 While in custody, juveniles shall receive care, protection and all necessary individual assistance—social, educational, vocational, psychological, medical and physical—that they may require in view of their age, sex and personality.

PART THREE
ADJUDICATION AND DISPOSITION

14. Competent authority to adjudicate

14.1 Where the case of a juvenile offender has not been diverted (under rule 11), she or he shall be dealt with by the competent authority (court, tribunal, board, council, etc.) according to the principles of a fair and just trial.

14.2 The proceedings shall be conducive to the best interests of the juvenile and shall be conducted in an atmosphere of understanding, which shall allow the juvenile to participate therein and to express herself or himself freely.

15. Legal counsel, parents and guardians

15.1 Throughout the proceedings the juvenile shall have the right to be represented by a legal adviser or to apply for free legal aid where there is provision for such aid in the country.

15.2 The parents or the guardian shall be entitled to participate in the proceedings and may be required by the competent authority to attend them in the interest of the juvenile. They may, however, be denied participation by the competent authority if there are reasons to assume that such exclusion is necessary in the interest of the juvenile.

Document 4: United Nations Guidelines for the Prevention of Juvenile Delinquency (the Riyadh Guidelines) (Excerpted)

I. FUNDAMENTAL PRINCIPLES

1. The prevention of juvenile delinquency is an essential part of crime prevention in society. By engaging in lawful, socially useful activities and adopting a humanistic orientation towards society and outlook on life, young persons can develop non-criminogenic attitudes.

2. The successful prevention of juvenile delinquency requires efforts on the part of the entire society to ensure the harmonious development of adolescents, with respect for and promotion of their personality from early childhood.

3. For the purposes of the interpretation of the present Guidelines, a child centered orientation should be pursued. Young persons should have an active role and partnership within society and should not be considered as mere objects of socialization or control.

4. In the implementation of the present Guidelines, in accordance with national legal systems, the well-being of young persons from their early childhood should be the focus of any preventive programme.

5. The need for and importance of progressive delinquency prevention policies and the systematic study and the elaboration of measures should be recognized. These should avoid criminalizing and penalizing a

child for behavior that does not cause serious damage to the development of the child or harm to others. Such policies and measures should involve:

(a) The provision of opportunities, in particular educational opportunities, to meet the varying needs of young persons and to serve as a supportive framework for safeguarding the personal development of all young persons, particularly those who are demonstrably endangered or at social risk and are in need of special care and protection;

(b) Specialized philosophies and approaches for delinquency prevention, on the basis of laws, processes, institutions, facilities and a service delivery network aimed at reducing the motivation, need and opportunity for, or conditions giving rise to, the commission of infractions;

(c) Official intervention to be pursued primarily in the overall interest of the young person and guided by fairness and equity;

(d) Safeguarding the well being, development, rights and interests of all young persons;

(e) Consideration that youthful behaviour or conduct that does not conform to overall social norms and values is often part of the maturation and growth process and tends to disappear spontaneously in most individuals with the transition to adulthood;

(f) Awareness that, in the predominant opinion of experts, labeling a young person as "deviant", "delinquent" or "pre-delinquent" often contributes to the development of a consistent pattern of undesirable behaviour by young persons.

6. Community-based services and programmes should be developed for the prevention of juvenile delinquency, particularly where no agencies have yet been established. Formal agencies of social control should only be utilized as a means of last resort.

II. SCOPE OF THE GUIDELINES

7. The present Guidelines should be interpreted and implemented within the broad framework of the Universal Declaration of Human Rights, the International Covenant on Economic, Social and Cultural Rights, the International Covenant on Civil and Political Rights, the Declaration of the Rights of the Child and the Convention on the Rights of the Child, and in the context of the United Nations Standard Minimum Rules for the Administration of Juvenile Justice (the Beijing Rules),5 as well as other instruments and norms relating to the rights, interests and well-being of all children and young persons.

8. The present Guidelines should also be implemented in the context of the economic, social and cultural conditions prevailing in each Member State.

III. GENERAL PREVENTION

9. Comprehensive prevention plans should be instituted at every level of government and include the following:

(a) In-depth analyses of the problem and inventories of programmes, services, facilities and resources available;

(b) Well-defined responsibilities for the qualified agencies, institutions and personnel involved in preventive efforts;

(c) Mechanisms for the appropriate coordination of prevention efforts between governmental and non-governmental agencies;

(d) Policies, programmes and strategies based on prognostic studies to be continuously monitored and carefully evaluated in the course of implementation;

(e) Methods for effectively reducing the opportunity to commit delinquent acts;

(f) Community involvement through a wide range of services and programmes;

(g) Close interdisciplinary cooperation between national, state, provincial and local governments, with the involvement of the private sector, representative citizens of the community to be served, and labour, childcare, health education, social, law enforcement and judicial agencies in taking concerted action to prevent juvenile delinquency and youth crime;

(h) Youth participation in delinquency prevention policies and processes, including recourse to community resources, youth self-help, and victim compensation and assistance programmes;

(i) Specialized personnel at all levels.

IV. SOCIALIZATION PROCESSES

10. Emphasis should be placed on preventive policies facilitating the successful socialization and integration of all children and young persons, in particular through the family, the community, peer groups, schools, vocational training and the world of work, as well as through voluntary organizations. Due respect should be

given to the proper personal development of children and young persons, and they should be accepted as full and equal partners in socialization and integration processes.

A. Family

11. Every society should place a high priority on the needs and well-being of the family and of all its members.

12. Since the family is the central unit responsible for the primary socialization of children, governmental and social efforts to preserve the integrity of the family, including the extended family, should be pursued. The society has a responsibility to assist the family in providing care and protection and in ensuring the physical and mental well-being of children. Adequate arrangements including day care should be provided.

13. Governments should establish policies that are conducive to the bringing up of children in stable and settled family environments. Families in need of assistance in the resolution of conditions of instability or conflict should be provided with requisite services.

14. Where a stable and settled family environment is lacking and when community efforts to assist parents in this regard have failed and the extended family cannot fulfill this role, alternative placements, including foster care and adoption, should be considered. Such placements should replicate, to the extent possible, a stable and settled family environment, while, at the same time, establishing a sense of permanency for children, thus avoiding problems associated with "foster drift".

15. Special attention should be given to children of families affected by problems brought about by rapid and uneven economic, social and cultural change, in particular the children of indigenous, migrant and refugee families. As such changes may disrupt the social capacity of the family to secure the traditional rearing and nurturing of children, often as a result of role and culture conflict, innovative and socially constructive modalities for the socialization of children have to be designed.

16. Measures should be taken and programmes developed to provide families with the opportunity to learn about parental roles and obligations as regards child development and child care, promoting positive parent-child relationships, sensitizing parents to the problems of children and young persons and encouraging their involvement in family and community-based activities.

17. Governments should take measures to promote family cohesion and harmony and to discourage the separation of children from their parents, unless circumstances affecting the welfare and future of the child leave no viable alternative.

18. It is important to emphasize the socialization function of the family and extended family; it is also equally important to recognize the future role, responsibilities, participation and partnership of young persons in society.

19. In ensuring the right of the child to proper socialization, Governments and other agencies should rely on existing social and legal agencies, but, whenever traditional institutions and customs are no longer effective, they should also provide and allow for innovative measures.

B. Education

20. Governments are under an obligation to make public education accessible to all young persons.

21. Education systems should, in addition to their academic and vocational training activities, devote particular attention to the following:

(a) Teaching of basic values and developing respect for the child's own cultural identity and patterns, for the social values of the country in which the child is living, for civilizations different from the child's own and for human rights and fundamental freedoms;

(b) Promotion and development of the personality, talents and mental and physical abilities of young people to their fullest potential;

(c) Involvement of young persons as active and effective participants in, rather than mere objects of, the educational process;

(d) Undertaking activities that foster a sense of identity with and of belonging to the school and the community;

(e) Encouragement of young persons to understand and respect diverse views and opinions, as well as cultural and other differences;

(f) Provision of information and guidance regarding vocational training, employment opportunities and career development;

(g) Provision of positive emotional support to young persons and the avoidance of psychological maltreatment;

(h) Avoidance of harsh disciplinary measures, particularly corporal punishment.

22. Educational systems should seek to work together with parents, community organizations and agencies concerned with the activities of young persons.

23. Young persons and their families should be informed about the law and their rights and responsibilities under the law, as well as the universal value system, including United Nations instruments.

24. Educational systems should extend particular care and attention to young persons who are at social risk. Specialized prevention programmes and educational materials, curricula, approaches and tools should be developed and fully utilized.

25. Special attention should be given to comprehensive policies and strategies for the prevention of alcohol, drug and other substance abuse by young persons. Teachers and other professionals should be equipped and trained to prevent and deal with these problems. Information on the use and abuse of drugs, including alcohol, should be made available to the student body.

26. Schools should serve as resource and referral centres for the provision of medical, counseling and other services to young persons, particularly those with special needs and suffering from abuse, neglect, victimization and exploitation.

27. Through a variety of educational programmes, teachers and other adults and the student body should be sensitized to the problems, needs and perceptions of young persons, particularly those belonging to under privileged, disadvantaged, ethnic or other minority and low-income groups.

28. School systems should attempt to meet and promote the highest professional and educational standards with respect to curricula, teaching and learning methods and approaches, and the recruitment and training of qualified teachers. Regular monitoring and assessment of performance by the appropriate professional organizations and authorities should be ensured.

29. School systems should plan, develop and implement extra-curricular activities of interest to young persons, in cooperation with community groups.

30. Special assistance should be given to children and young persons who find it difficult to comply with attendance codes, and to "dropouts".

31. Schools should promote policies and rules that are fair and just; students should be represented in bodies formulating school policy, including policy on discipline, and decision-making.

C. *Community*

32. Community-based services and programmes which respond to the special needs, problems, interests and concerns of young persons and which offer appropriate counseling and guidance to young persons and their families should be developed, or strengthened where they exist. 33. Communities should provide, or strengthen where they exist, a wide range of community-based support measures for young persons, including community development centres, recreational facilities and services to respond to the special problems of children who are at social risk. In providing these helping measures, respect for individual rights should be ensured.

34. Special facilities should be set up to provide adequate shelter for young persons who are no longer able to live at home or who do not have homes to live in.

35. A range of services and helping measures should be provided to deal with the difficulties experienced by young persons in the transition to adulthood. Such services should include special programmes for young drug abusers which emphasize care, counseling, assistance and therapy-oriented interventions.

36. Voluntary organizations providing services for young persons should be given financial and other support by Governments and other institutions.

37. Youth organizations should be created or strengthened at the local level and given full participatory status in the management of community affairs. These organizations should encourage youth to organize collective and voluntary projects, particularly projects aimed at helping young persons in need of assistance.

38. Government agencies should take special responsibility and provide necessary services for homeless or street children; information about local facilities, accommodation, employment and other forms and sources of help should be made readily available to young persons.

39. A wide range of recreational facilities and services of particular interest to young persons should be established and made easily accessible to them.

D. *Mass media*

40. The mass media should be encouraged to ensure that young persons have access to information and material from a diversity of national and international sources.

41. The mass media should be encouraged to portray the positive contribution of young persons to society.

42. The mass media should be encouraged to disseminate information on the existence of services, facilities and opportunities for young persons in society.

43. The mass media generally, and the television and film media in particular, should be encouraged to minimize the level of pornography, drugs and violence portrayed and to display violence and exploitation disfavourably, as well as to avoid demeaning and degrading presentations, especially of children, women and interpersonal relations, and to promote egalitarian principles and roles.

44. The mass media should be aware of its extensive social role and responsibility, as well as its influence, in communications relating to youthful drug and alcohol abuse. It should use its power for drug abuse prevention by relaying consistent messages through a balanced approach. Effective drug awareness campaigns at all levels should be promoted.

V. SOCIAL POLICY

45. Government agencies should give high priority to plans and programmes for young persons and should provide sufficient funds and other resources for the effective delivery of services, facilities and staff for adequate medical and mental health care, nutrition, housing and other relevant services, including drug and alcohol abuse prevention and treatment, ensuring that such resources reach and actually benefit young persons.

46. The institutionalization of young persons should be a measure of last resort and for the minimum necessary period, and the best interests of the young person should be of paramount importance. Criteria authorizing formal intervention of this type should be strictly defined and limited to the following situations:

(a) where the child or young person has suffered harm that has been inflicted by the parents or guardians;

(b) where the child or young person has been sexually, physically or emotionally abused by the parents or guardians;

(c) where the child or young person has been neglected, abandoned or exploited by the parents or guardians;

(d) where the child or young person is threatened by physical or moral danger due to the behaviour of the parents or guardians; and

(e) where a serious physical or psychological danger to the child or young person has manifested itself in his or her own behaviour and neither the parents, the guardians, the juvenile himself or herself nor non-residential community services can meet the danger by means other than institutionalization.

47. Government agencies should provide young persons with the opportunity of continuing in full-time education, funded by the State where parents or guardians are unable to support the young persons, and of receiving work experience.

48. Programmes to prevent delinquency should be planned and developed on the basis of reliable, scientific research findings, and periodically monitored, evaluated and adjusted accordingly.

49. Scientific information should be disseminated to the professional community and to the public at large about the sort of behaviour or situation which indicates or may result in physical and psychological victimization, harm and abuse, as well as exploitation, of young persons.

50. Generally, participation in plans and programmes should be voluntary. Young persons themselves should be involved in their formulation, development and implementation.

51. Government should begin or continue to explore, develop and implement policies, measures and strategies within and outside the criminal justice system to prevent domestic violence against and affecting young persons and to ensure fair treatment to these victims of domestic violence.

[Footnotes Omitted]

DOCUMENT 5: UNITED NATIONS RULES FOR THE PROTECTION OF JUVENILES DEPRIVED OF THEIR LIBERTY* (EXCERPTED)

I. FUNDAMENTAL PERSPECTIVES

1. The juvenile justice system should uphold the rights and safety and promote the physical and mental well-being of juveniles. Imprisonment should be used as a last resort.

2. Juveniles should only be deprived of their liberty in accordance with the principles and procedures set forth in these Rules and in the United Nations Standard Minimum Rules for the Administration of Juvenile

Justice (the Beijing Rules). Deprivation of the liberty of a juvenile should be a disposition of last resort and for the minimum necessary period and should be limited to exceptional cases. The length of the sanction should be determined by the judicial authority, without precluding the possibility of his or her early release.

3. The Rules are intended to establish minimum standards accepted by the United Nations for the protection of juveniles deprived of their liberty in all forms, consistent with human rights and fundamental freedoms, and with a view to counteracting the detrimental effects of all types of detention and to fostering integration in society.

4. The Rules should be applied impartially, without discrimination of any kind as to race, colour, sex, age, language, religion, nationality, political or other opinion, cultural beliefs or practices, property, birth or family status, ethnic or social origin, and disability. The religious and cultural beliefs, practices and moral concepts of the juvenile should be respected.

5. The Rules are designed to serve as convenient standards of reference and to provide encouragement and guidance to professionals involved in the management of the juvenile justice system.

6. The Rules should be made readily available to juvenile justice personnel in their national languages. Juveniles who are not fluent in the language spoken by the personnel of the detention facility should have the right to the services of an interpreter free of charge whenever necessary, in particular during medical examinations and disciplinary proceedings.

7. Where appropriate, States should incorporate the Rules into their legislation or amend it accordingly and provide effective remedies for their breach, including compensation when injuries are inflicted on juveniles. States should also monitor the application of the Rules.

8. The competent authorities should constantly seek to increase the awareness of the public that the care of detained juveniles and preparation for their return to society is a social service of great importance, and to this end active steps should be taken to foster open contacts between the juveniles and the local community.

9. Nothing in the Rules should be interpreted as precluding the application of the relevant United Nations and human rights instruments and standards, recognized by the international community, that are more conducive to ensuring the rights, care and protection of juveniles, children and all young persons.

10. In the event that the practical application of particular Rules contained in sections II to V, inclusive, presents any conflict with the Rules contained in the present section, compliance with the latter shall be regarded as the predominant requirement.

II. SCOPE AND APPLICATION OF THE RULES

11. For the purposes of the Rules, the following definitions should apply:

(a) A juvenile is every person under the age of 18. The age limit below which it should not be permitted to deprive a child of his or her liberty should be determined by law;

(b) The deprivation of liberty means any form of detention or imprisonment or the placement of a person in a public or private custodial setting, from which this person is not permitted to leave at will, by order of any judicial, administrative or other public authority.

12. The deprivation of liberty should be effected in conditions and circumstances which ensure respect for the human rights of juveniles. Juveniles detained in facilities should be guaranteed the benefit of meaningful activities and programmes which would serve to promote and sustain their health and self-respect, to foster their sense of responsibility and encourage those attitudes and skills that will assist them in developing their potential as members of society.

13. Juveniles deprived of their liberty shall not for any reason related to their status be denied the civil, economic, political, social or cultural rights to which they are entitled under national or international law, and which are compatible with the deprivation of liberty.

14. The protection of the individual rights of juveniles with special regard to the legality of the execution of the detention measures shall be ensured by the competent authority, while the objectives of social integration should be secured by regular inspections and other means of control carried out, according to international standards, national laws and regulations, by a duly constituted body authorized to visit the juveniles and not belonging to the detention facility.

15. The Rules apply to all types and forms of detention facilities in which juveniles are deprived of their liberty. Sections I, II, IV and V of the Rules apply to all detention facilities and institutional settings in which juveniles are detained, and section III applies specifically to juveniles under arrest or awaiting trial.

16. The Rules shall be implemented in the context of the economic, social and cultural conditions prevailing in each Member State.

III. JUVENILES UNDER ARREST OR AWAITING TRIAL

17. Juveniles who are detained under arrest or awaiting trial ("untried") are presumed innocent and shall be treated as such. Detention before trial shall be avoided to the extent possible and limited to exceptional circumstances.

Therefore, all efforts shall be made to apply alternative measures. When preventive detention is nevertheless used, juvenile courts and investigative bodies shall give the highest priority to the most expeditious processing of such cases to ensure the shortest possible duration of detention. Untried detainees should be separated from convicted juveniles.

18. The conditions under which an untried juvenile is detained should be consistent with the rules set out below, with additional specific provisions as are necessary and appropriate, given the requirements of the presumption of innocence, the duration of the detention and the legal status and circumstances of the juvenile. These provisions would include, but not necessarily be restricted to, the following:

(a) Juveniles should have the right of legal counsel and be enabled to apply for free legal aid, where such aid is available, and to communicate regularly with their legal advisers. Privacy and confidentiality shall be ensured for such communications;

(b) Juveniles should be provided, where possible, with opportunities to pursue work, with remuneration, and continue education or training, but should not be required to do so. Work, education or training should not cause the continuation of the detention;

(c) Juveniles should receive and retain materials for their leisure and recreation as are compatible with the interests of the administration of justice.

[Footnotes Omitted]

DOCUMENT 6: GUIDELINES FOR ACTION ON CHILDREN IN THE CRIMINAL JUSTICE SYSTEM* (EXCERPTED)

1. Pursuant to Economic and Social Council resolution 1996/13 of 23 July 1996, the present Guidelines for Action on Children in the Criminal Justice System were developed at the expert group meeting on the elaboration of a programme of action to promote the effective use and application of international standards and norms in juvenile justice, held at Vienna from 23 to 25 February 1997 with the financial support of the Government of Austria. In developing the Guidelines for Action, the experts took into account the views expressed and the information submitted by Governments.

2. Twenty-nine experts from eleven States in different regions, representatives of the Centre for Human Rights of the Secretariat, the United Nations Children's Fund and the Committee on the Rights of the Child, as well as observers for non-governmental organizations concerned with juvenile justice, participated in the meeting.

3. The Guidelines for Action are addressed to the Secretary-General and relevant United Nations agencies and programmes, States parties to the Convention on the Rights of the Child,1 as regards its implementation, as well as Member States as regards the use and application of the United Nations Standard Minimum Rules for the Administration of Juvenile Justice (the Beijing Rules), the United Nations Guidelines for the Prevention of Juvenile Delinquency (the Riyadh Guidelines) and the United Nations Rules for the Protection of Juveniles Deprived of their Liberty, hereinafter together referred to as "United Nations standards and norms in juvenile justice".

I. AIMS, OBJECTIVES AND BASIC CONSIDERATIONS

4. The aims of the Guidelines for Action are to provide a framework to achieve the following objectives:

(a) To implement the Convention on the Rights of the Child and to pursue the goals set forth in the Convention with regard to children in the context of the administration of juvenile justice, as well as to use and apply the United Nations standards and norms in juvenile justice and other related instruments, such as the Declaration of Basic Principles of Justice for Victims of Crime and Abuse of Power;

(b) To facilitate the provision of assistance to States parties for the effective implementation of the Convention and related instruments.

5. In order to ensure effective use of the Guidelines for Action, improved cooperation between Governments, relevant entities of the United Nations system, non-governmental organizations, professional groups, the media, academic institutions, children and other members of civil society is essential.

6. The Guidelines for Action should be based on the principle that the responsibility for implementing the Convention clearly rests with the States parties thereto.

7. The basis for the use of the Guidelines for Action should be the recommendations of the Committee on the Rights of the Child.

8. In the use of the Guidelines for Action at both the international and national levels, consideration should be given to the following:

(a) Respect for human dignity, compatible with the four general principles underlying the Convention, namely: non-discrimination, including gender sensitivity, upholding the best interests of the child, the right to life, survival and development and respect for the views of the child;

(b) A rights-based orientation;

(c) A holistic approach to implementation through maximization of resources and efforts;

(d) The integration of services on an interdisciplinary basis;

(e) The participation of children and concerned sectors of society;

(f) The empowerment of partners through a developmental process;

(g) Sustainability without continuing dependency on external bodies;

(h) Equitable application and accessibility to those in greatest need;

(i) Accountability and transparency of operations;

(j) Proactive responses based on effective preventive and remedial measures.

9. Adequate resources (human, organizational, technological, financial and information) should be allocated and utilized efficiently at all levels (international, regional, national, provincial and local) and in collaboration with relevant partners, including Governments, United Nations entities, non-governmental organizations, professional groups, the media, academic institutions, children and other members of civil society, as well as other partners.

I. PLANS FOR THE IMPLEMENTATION OF THE CONVENTION ON THE RIGHTS OF THE CHILD, THE PURSUIT OF ITS GOALS AND THE USE AND APPLICATION OF INTERNAT ION- AL STANDARDS AND NORMS IN JUVENILE JUSTICE

A. Measures of general application

10. The importance of a comprehensive and consistent national approach in the area of juvenile justice should be recognized, with respect for the interdependence and indivisibility of all rights of the child.

11. Measures relating to policy, decision-making, leadership and reform should be taken, with the goal of ensuring that:

(a) The principles and provisions of the Convention on the Rights of the Child and the United Nations standards and norms in juvenile justice are fully reflected in national and local legislation policy and practice, in particular by establishing a child-oriented juvenile justice system that guarantees the rights of children, prevents the violation of the rights of children, promotes children's sense of dignity and worth and fully respects their age, stage of development and their right to participate meaningfully in and contribute to society;

(b) The relevant contents of the above-mentioned instruments are made widely known to children in language accessible to children. In addition, if necessary, procedures should be established to ensure that each and every child is provided with the relevant information on his or her rights set out in those instruments, at least from his or her first contact with the criminal justice system, and is reminded of his or her obligation to obey the law;

(c) Understanding on the part of the public and the media of the spirit, aims and principles of justice centred on the child is promoted in accordance with the United Nations standards and norms in juvenile justice.

B. Specific targets

12. States should ensure the effectiveness of their birth registration programmes. In those instances where the age of the child involved in the justice system is unknown, measures should be taken to ensure that the true age of a child is ascertained by independent and objective assessment.

13. Notwithstanding the age of criminal responsibility, civil majority and the age of consent as defined by national legislation, States should ensure that children benefit from all their rights, as guaranteed to them by international law and, specifically in this context, those set forth in articles 3, 37 and 40 of the Convention.

14. Particular attention should be given to the following points:

(a) There should be a comprehensive child-centred juvenile justice process;

(b) Independent expert or other types of panels should review existing and proposed juvenile justice laws and their impact on children;

(c) No child who is under the legal age of criminal responsibility should be subject to criminal charges;

(d) States should establish juvenile courts with primary jurisdiction over juveniles who commit criminal acts and special procedures should be designed to take into account the specific needs of children. As an alternative, regular courts should incorporate such procedures, as appropriate. Wherever necessary, national legislative and other measures should be considered to accord all the rights of and protection for the child, where the child is brought before a court other than a juvenile court, in accordance with articles 3, 37 and 40 of the Convention.

15. A review of existing procedures should be undertaken and, where possible, diversion or other alternative initiatives to the classical criminal justice systems should be developed to avoid recourse to the criminal justice systems for young persons accused of an offence. Appropriate steps should be taken to make available throughout the State a broad range of alternative and educative measures at the pre-arrest, pre-trial, trial and post-trial stages, in order to prevent recidivism and promote the social rehabilitation of child offenders. Whenever appropriate, mechanisms for the informal resolution of disputes in cases involving a child offender should be utilized, including mediation and restorative justice practices, in particular processes involving victims. In the various measures to be adopted, the family should be involved, to the extent that it operates in favour of the good of the child offender. States should ensure that alternative measures comply with the Convention and the United Nations standards and norms in juvenile justice, as well as other existing standards and norms in crime prevention and criminal justice, such as the United Nations Standard Minimum Rules for Non-custodial Measures (the Tokyo Rules), with special regard to ensuring respect for due-process rules in applying such measures and for the principle of minimum intervention.

DOCUMENT 7: GUIDELINES FOR THE PREVENTION OF CRIME

I. INTRODUCTION

1. There is clear evidence that well-planned crime prevention strategies not only prevent crime and victimization, but also promote community safety and contribute to the sustainable development of countries. Effective, responsible crime prevention enhances the quality of life of all citizens. It has long-term benefits in terms of reducing the costs associated with the formal criminal justice system, as well as other social costs that result from crime. Crime prevention offers opportunities for a humane and more cost-effective approach to the problems of crime. The present Guidelines outline the necessary elements for effective crime prevention.

II. CONCEPTUAL FRAME OF REFERENCE

2. It is the responsibility of all levels of government to create, maintain and promote a context within which relevant governmental institutions and all segments of civil society, including the corporate sector, can better play their part in preventing crime.

3. For the purposes of the present Guidelines, "crime prevention" comprises strategies and measures that seek to reduce the risk of crimes occurring, and their potential harmful effects on individuals and society, including fear of crime, by intervening to influence their multiple causes. The enforcement of laws, sentences and corrections, while also performing preventive functions, falls outside the scope of the Guidelines, given the comprehensive coverage of the subject in other United Nations instruments.

4. The present Guidelines address crime and its effects on victims and society and take into account the growing internationalization of criminal activities.

5. Community involvement and cooperation/partnerships represent important elements of the concept of crime prevention set out herein. While the term "community" may be defined in different ways, its essence in this context is the involvement of civil society at the local level.

6. Crime prevention encompasses a wide range of approaches, including those which:

(a) Promote the well-being of people and encourage pro-social behavior through social, economic, health and educational measures, with a particular emphasis on children and youth, and focus on the risk and protective factors associated with crime and victimization (prevention through social development or social crime prevention);

(b) Change the conditions in neighbourhoods that influence offending, victimization and the insecurity that results from crime by building on the initiatives, expertise and commitment of community members (locally based crime prevention);

(c) Prevent the occurrence of crimes by reducing opportunities, increasing risks of being apprehended and minimizing benefits, including through environmental design, and by providing assistance and information to potential and actual victims (situational crime prevention);

(d) Prevent recidivism by assisting in the social reintegration of offenders and other preventive mechanisms (reintegration programmes).

III. BASIC PRINCIPLES

Government leadership

7. All levels of government should play a leadership role in developing effective and humane crime prevention strategies and in creating and maintaining institutional frameworks for their implementation and review.

Socio-economic development and inclusion

8. Crime prevention considerations should be integrated into all relevant social and economic policies and programmes, including those addressing employment, education, health, housing and urban planning, poverty, social marginalization and exclusion. Particular emphasis should be placed on communities, families, children and youth at risk.

Cooperation/partnerships

9. Cooperation/partnerships should be an integral part of effective crime prevention, given the wide-ranging nature of the causes of crime and the skills and responsibilities required to address them. This includes partnerships working across ministries and between authorities, community organizations, nongovernmental organizations, the business sector and private citizens.

Sustainability/accountability

10. Crime prevention requires adequate resources, including funding for structures and activities, in order to be sustained. There should be clear accountability for funding, implementation and evaluation and for the achievement of planned results.

Knowledge base

11. Crime prevention strategies, policies, programmes and actions should be based on a broad, multi-disciplinary foundation of knowledge about crime problems, their multiple causes and promising and proven practices.

Human rights/rule of law/culture of lawfulness

12. The rule of law and those human rights which are recognized in international instruments to which Member States are parties must be respected in all aspects of crime prevention. A culture of lawfulness should be actively promoted in crime prevention.

Interdependency

13. National crime prevention diagnoses and strategies should, where appropriate, take account of links between local criminal problems and international organized crime.

Differentiation

14. Crime prevention strategies should, when appropriate, pay due regard to the different needs of men and women and consider the special needs of vulnerable members of society.

IV. ORGANIZATION, METHODS AND APPROACHES

15. Recognizing that all States have unique governmental structures, this section sets out tools and methodologies that Governments and all segments of civil society should consider in developing strategies to prevent crime and reduce victimization. It draws on international good practice.

Community involvement

16. In some of the areas listed below, Governments bear the primary responsibility. However, the active participation of communities and other segments of civil society is an essential part of effective crime prevention. Communities, in particular, should play an important part in identifying crime prevention priorities, in implementation and evaluation, and in helping to identify a sustainable resource base.

A. Organization

Government structures

17. Governments should include prevention as a permanent part of their structures and programmes for controlling crime, ensuring that clear responsibilities and goals exist within government for the organization of crime prevention, by, inter alia:

(a) Establishing centres or focal points with expertise and resources;

(b) Establishing a crime prevention plan with clear priorities and targets;

(c) Establishing linkages and coordination between relevant government agencies or departments;

(*d*) Fostering partnerships with non-governmental organizations, the business, private and professional sectors and the community;

(*e*) Seeking the active participation of the public in crime prevention by informing it of the need for and means of action and its role.

Training and capacity-building

18. Governments should support the development of crime prevention skills by:

(*a*) Providing professional development for senior officials in relevant agencies;

(*b*) Encouraging universities, colleges and other relevant educational agencies to offer basic and advanced courses, including in collaboration with practitioners;

(*c*) Working with the educational and professional sectors to develop certification and professional qualifications;

(*d*) Promoting the capacity of communities to develop and respond to their needs.

Supporting partnerships

19. Governments and all segments of civil society should support the principle of partnership, where appropriate, including:

(*a*) Advancing knowledge of the importance of this principle and the components of successful partnerships, including the need for all of the partners to have clear and transparent roles;

(*b*) Fostering the formation of partnerships at different levels and across sectors;

(*c*) Facilitating the efficient operation of partnerships.

Sustainability

20. Governments and other funding bodies should strive to achieve sustainability of demonstrably effective crime prevention programmes and initiatives through, inter alia:

(*a*) Reviewing resource allocation to establish and maintain an appropriate balance between crime prevention and the criminal justice and other systems, to be more effective in preventing crime and victimization;

(*b*) Establishing clear accountability for funding, programming and coordinating crime prevention initiatives;

(*c*) Encouraging community involvement in sustainability.

B. Methods

Knowledge base

21. As appropriate, Governments and/or civil society should facilitate knowledge-based crime prevention by, inter alia:

(*a*) Providing the information necessary for communities to address crime problems;

(*b*) Supporting the generation of useful and practically applicable knowledge that is scientifically reliable and valid;

(*c*) Supporting the organization and synthesis of knowledge and identifying and addressing gaps in the knowledge base;

(*d*) Sharing that knowledge, as appropriate, among, inter alia, researchers, policymakers, educators, practitioners from other relevant sectors and the wider community;

(*e*) Applying this knowledge in replicating successful interventions, developing new initiatives and anticipating new crime problems and prevention opportunities;

(*f*) Establishing data systems to help manage crime prevention more cost-effectively, including by conducting regular surveys of victimization and offending;

(*g*) Promoting the application of those data in order to reduce repeat victimization, persistent offending and areas with a high level of crime.

Planning interventions

22. Those planning interventions should promote a process that includes:

(*a*) A systematic analysis of crime problems, their causes, risk factors and consequences, in particular at the local level;

(*b*) A plan that draws on the most appropriate approach and adapts interventions to the specific local problem and context;

(*c*) An implementation plan to deliver appropriate interventions that are efficient, effective and sustainable;

(*d*) Mobilizing entities that are able to tackle causes;

(*e*) Monitoring and evaluation.

Support evaluation

23. Governments, other funding bodies and those involved in programme development and delivery should:

(a) Undertake short- and longer-term evaluation to test rigorously what works, where and why;

(b) Undertake cost-benefit analyses;

(c) Assess the extent to which action results in a reduction in levels of crime and victimization, in the seriousness of crime and in fear of crime;

(d) Systematically assess the outcomes and unintended consequences, both positive and negative, of action, such as a decrease in crime rates or the stigmatization of individuals and/or communities.

C. Approaches

24. This section expands upon the social development and situational crime prevention approaches. It also outlines approaches that Governments and civil society should endeavour to follow in order to prevent organized crime.

Social development

25. Governments should address the risk factors of crime and victimization by:

(a) Promoting protective factors through comprehensive and non stigmatizing social and economic development programmes, including health, education, housing and employment;

(b) Promoting activities that redress marginalization and exclusion;

(c) Promoting positive conflict resolution;

(d) Using education and public awareness strategies to foster a culture of lawfulness and tolerance while respecting cultural identities.

Situational

26. Governments and civil society, including, where appropriate, the corporate sector, should support the development of situational crime prevention programmes by, inter alia:

(a) Improved environmental design;

(b) Appropriate methods of surveillance that are sensitive to the right to privacy;

(c) Encouraging the design of consumer goods to make them more resistant to crime;

(d) Target "hardening" without impinging upon the quality of the built environment or limiting free access to public space;

(e) Implementing strategies to prevent repeat victimization.

Prevention of organized crime

27. Governments and civil society should endeavour to analyze and address the links between transnational organized crime and national and local crime problems by, inter alia:

(a) Reducing existing and future opportunities for organized criminal groups to participate in lawful markets with the proceeds of crime, through appropriate legislative, administrative or other measures;

(b) Developing measures to prevent the misuse by organized criminal groups of tender procedures conducted by public authorities and of subsidies and licenses granted by public authorities for commercial activity;

(c) Designing crime prevention strategies, where appropriate, to protect socially marginalized groups, especially women and children, who are vulnerable to the action of organized criminal groups, including trafficking in persons and smuggling of migrants.

V. INTERNATIONAL COOPERATION

Standards and norms

28. In promoting international action in crime prevention, Member States are invited to take into account the main international instruments related to human rights and crime prevention to which they are parties, such as the Convention on the Rights of the Child (General Assembly resolution 44/25, annex), the Declaration on the Elimination of Violence against Women (General Assembly resolution 48/104), the United Nations Guidelines for the Prevention of Juvenile Delinquency (the Riyadh Guidelines) (General Assembly resolution 45/112, annex), the Declaration of Basic Principles of Justice for Victims of Crime and Abuse of Power (General Assembly resolution 40/34, annex), the guidelines for cooperation and technical assistance in the field of urban crime prevention (resolution 1995/9, annex), as well as the Vienna Declaration on Crime and Justice:

Meeting the Challenges of the Twenty-first Century (General Assembly resolution 55/59, annex) and the United Nations Convention against Transnational Organized Crime and the Protocols thereto (General Assembly resolution 55/25, annexes I-III, and resolution 55/255, annex).

Technical assistance

29. Member States and relevant international funding organizations should provide financial and technical assistance, including capacity-building and training, to developing countries and countries with economies in transition, communities and other relevant organizations for the implementation of effective crime prevention and community safety strategies at the regional, national and local levels. In that context, special attention should be given to research and action on crime prevention through social development.

Networking

30. Member States should strengthen or establish international, regional and national crime prevention networks with a view to exchanging proven and promising practices, identifying elements of their transferability and making such knowledge available to communities throughout the world.

Links between transnational and local crime

31. Member States should collaborate to analyse and address the links between transnational organized crime and national and local crime problems.

Prioritizing crime prevention

32. The Centre for International Crime Prevention of the Office for Drug Control and Crime Prevention of the Secretariat, the United Nations Crime Prevention and Criminal Justice Programme network of institutes and other relevant United Nations entities should include in their priorities crime prevention as set out in these Guidelines, set up a coordination mechanism and establish a roster of experts to undertake needs assessment and to provide technical advice.

Dissemination

33. Relevant United Nations bodies and other organizations should cooperate to produce crime prevention information in as many languages as possible, using both print and electronic media.

DOCUMENT 8: CODE OF CONDUCT FOR LAW ENFORCEMENT OFFICIALS (EXCERPTED)

Article 1

Law enforcement officials shall at all times fulfill the duty imposed upon them by law, by serving the community and by protecting all persons against illegal acts, consistent with the high degree of responsibility required by their profession.

Article 2

In the performance of their duty, law enforcement officials shall respect and protect human dignity and maintain and uphold the human rights of all persons.

Article 3

Law enforcement officials may use force only when strictly necessary and to the extent required for the performance of their duty.

Article 4

Matters of a confidential nature in the possession of law enforcement officials shall be kept confidential, unless the performance of duty or the needs of justice strictly require otherwise.

Article 5

No law enforcement official may inflict, instigate or tolerate any act of torture or other cruel, inhuman or degrading treatment or punishment, nor may any law enforcement official invoke superior orders or exceptional circumstances such as a state of war or a threat of war, a threat to national security, internal political instability or any other public emergency as a justification of torture or other cruel, inhuman or degrading treatment or punishment.

Article 6

Law enforcement officials shall ensure the full protection of the health of persons in their custody and, in particular, shall take immediate action to secure medical attention whenever required.

Article 7

Law enforcement officials shall not commit any act of corruption. They shall also rigorously oppose and combat all such acts.

Article 8

Law enforcement officials shall respect the law and the present Code. They shall also, to the best of their capability, prevent and rigorously oppose any violations of them. Law enforcement officials who have reason to believe that a violation of the present Code has occurred or is about to occur shall report the matter to their superior authorities and, where necessary, to other appropriate authorities or organs vested with reviewing or remedial power.

DOCUMENT 9: GUIDELINES FOR THE EFFECTIVE IMPLEMENTATION OF THE CODE OF CONDUCT FOR LAW ENFORCEMENT OFFICIALS (EXCERPTED)

I. APPLICATION OF THE CODE

A. *General principles*

1. The principles embodied in the Code shall be reflected in national legislation and practice.

2. In order to achieve the aims and objectives set out in article 1 of the Code and its Commentary, the definition of "law enforcement officials" shall be given the widest possible interpretation.

3. The Code shall be made applicable to all law enforcement officials, regardless of their jurisdiction.

4. Governments shall adopt the necessary measures to instruct, in basic training and all subsequent training and refresher courses, law enforcement officials in the provisions of national legislation connected with the Code as well as other basic texts on the issue of human rights.

B. *Specific issues*

1. *Selection, education and training.* The selection, education and training of law enforcement officials shall be given prime importance. Governments shall also promote education and training through a fruitful exchange of ideas at the regional and interregional levels.

2. *Salary and working conditions.* All law enforcement officials shall be adequately remunerated and shall be provided with appropriate working conditions.

3. *Discipline and supervision.* Effective mechanisms shall be established to ensure the internal discipline and external control as well as the supervision of law enforcement officials.

4. *Complaints by members of the public.* Particular provisions shall be made, within the mechanisms mentioned under paragraph 3 above, for the receipt and processing of complaints against law enforcement officials made by members of the public, and the existence of these provisions shall be made known to the public.

II. IMPLEMENTATION OF THE CODE

A. *At the national level*

1. The Code shall be made available to all law enforcement officials and competent authorities in their own language.

2. Governments shall disseminate the Code and all domestic laws giving effect to it so as to ensure that the principles and rights contained therein become known to the public in general.

3. In considering measures to promote the application of the Code, Governments shall organize symposiums on the role and functions of law enforcement officials in the protection of human rights and the prevention of crime.

B. *At the international level*

1. Governments shall inform the Secretary-General at appropriate intervals of at least five years on the extent of the implementation of the Code.

2. The Secretary-General shall prepare periodic reports on progress made with respect to the implementation of the Code, drawing also on observations and on the cooperation of specialized agencies and relevant inter-governmental organizations and non-governmental organizations in consultative status with the Economic and Social Council.

3. As part of the reports mentioned above, Governments shall provide to the Secretary-General copies of abstracts of laws, regulations and administrative measures concerning the application of the Code, any other relevant information on its implementation, as well as information on possible difficulties in its application.

4. The Secretary-General shall submit the above-mentioned reports to the Committee on Crime Prevention and Control for consideration and further action, as appropriate.

5. The Secretary-General shall make available the Code and the present guidelines to all States and inter-governmental and non-governmental organizations concerned, in all official languages of the United Nations.

6. The United Nations, as part of its advisory services and technical cooperation and development programmes, shall:

(a) Make available to Governments requesting them the services of experts and regional and interregional advisers to assist in implementing the provisions of the Code;

(b) Promote national and regional training seminars and other meetings on the Code and on the role and functions of law enforcement officials in the protection of human rights and the prevention of crime.

7. The United Nations regional institutes shall be encouraged to organize seminars and training courses on the Code and to carry out research on the extent to which the Code is implemented in the countries of the region as well as the difficulties encountered.

DOCUMENT 10: BASIC PRINCIPLES ON THE USE OF FORCE AND FIREARMS BY LAW ENFORCEMENT OFFICIALS (EXCERPTED)

Whereas the work of law enforcement officials is a social service of great importance and there is, therefore, a need to maintain and, whenever necessary, to improve the working conditions and status of these officials,

Whereas a threat to the life and safety of law enforcement officials must be seen as a threat to the stability of society as a whole,

Whereas law enforcement officials have a vital role in the protection of the right to life, liberty and security of the person, as guaranteed in the Universal Declaration of Human Rights and reaffirmed in the International Covenant on Civil and Political Rights,

Whereas the Standard Minimum Rules for the Treatment of Prisoners provide for the circumstances in which prison officials may use force in the course of their duties,

Whereas article 3 of the Code of Conduct for Law Enforcement Officials provides that law enforcement officials may use force only when strictly necessary and to the extent required for the performance of their duty,

Whereas the preparatory meeting for the Seventh United Nations Congress on the Prevention of Crime and the Treatment of Offenders, held at Varenna, Italy, agreed on elements to be considered in the course of further work on restraints on the use of force and firearms by law enforcement officials,

Whereas the Seventh Congress, in its resolution 14, inter alia, emphasizes that the use of force and firearms by law enforcement officials should be commensurate with due respect for human rights,

Whereas the Economic and Social Council, in its resolution 1986/10, section IX, of 21 May 1986, invited Member States to pay particular attention in the implementation of the Code to the use of force and firearms by law enforcement officials, and the General Assembly, in its resolution 41/149 of 4 December 1986, inter alia, welcomed this recommendation made by the Council,

Whereas it is appropriate that, with due regard to their personal safety, consideration be given to the role of law enforcement officials in relation to the administration of justice, to the protection of the right to life, liberty and security of the person, to their responsibility to maintain public safety and social peace and to the importance of their qualifications, training and conduct,

General provisions

1. Governments and law enforcement agencies shall adopt and implement rules and regulations on the use of force and firearms against persons by law enforcement officials. In developing such rules and regulations, Governments and law enforcement agencies shall keep the ethical issues associated with the use of force and firearms constantly under review.

2. Governments and law enforcement agencies should develop a range of means as broad as possible and equip law enforcement officials with various types of weapons and ammunition that would allow for a differentiated use of force and firearms. These should include the development of non-lethal incapacitating weapons for use in appropriate situations, with a view to increasingly restraining the application of means capable of causing death or injury to persons. For the same purpose, it should also be possible for law enforcement officials to be equipped with self-defensive equipment such as shields, helmets, bullet-proof vests and bullet-proof means of transportation, in order to decrease he need to use weapons of any kind.

3. The development and deployment of non-lethal incapacitating weapons should be carefully evaluated in order to minimize the risk of endangering uninvolved persons, and the use of such weapons should be carefully controlled.

4. Law enforcement officials, in carrying out their duty, shall, as far as possible, apply non-violent means before resorting to the use of force and firearms.
They may use force and firearms only if other means remain ineffective or without any promise of achieving the intended result.

5. Whenever the lawful use of force and firearms is unavoidable, law enforcement officials shall:

(a) Exercise restraint in such use and act in proportion to the seriousness of the offence and the legitimate objective to be achieved;

(b) Minimize damage and injury, and respect and preserve human life;

(c) Ensure that assistance and medical aid are rendered to any injured or affected persons at the earliest possible moment;

(d) Ensure that relatives or close friends of the injured or affected person are notified at the earliest possible moment.

6. Where injury or death is caused by the use of force and firearms by law enforcement officials, they shall report the incident promptly to their superiors, in accordance with principle 22.

7. Governments shall ensure that arbitrary or abusive use of force and firearms by law enforcement officials is punished as a criminal offence under their law.

8. Exceptional circumstances such as internal political instability or any other public emergency may not be invoked to justify any departure from these basic principles.

Special provisions

9. Law enforcement officials shall not use firearms against persons except in self-defence or defence of others against the imminent threat of death or serious injury, to prevent the perpetration of a particularly serious crime involving grave threat to life, to arrest a person presenting such a danger and resisting their authority, or to prevent his or her escape, and only when less extreme means are insufficient to achieve these objectives. In any event, intentional lethal use of firearms may only be made when strictly unavoidable in order to protect life.

10. In the circumstances provided for under principle 9, law enforcement officials shall identify themselves as such and give a clear warning of their intent to use firearms, with sufficient time for the warning to be observed, unless to do so would unduly place the law enforcement officials at risk or would create a risk of death or serious harm to other persons, or would be clearly inappropriate or pointless in the circumstances of the incident.

11. Rules and regulations on the use of firearms by law enforcement officials should include guidelines that:

(a) Specify the circumstances under which law enforcement officials are authorized to carry firearms and prescribe the types of firearms and ammunition permitted;

(b) Ensure that firearms are used only in appropriate circumstances and in a manner likely to decrease the risk of unnecessary harm;

(c) Prohibit the use of those firearms and ammunition that cause unwarranted injury or present an unwarranted risk;

(d) Regulate the control, storage and issuing of firearms, including procedures for ensuring that law enforcement officials are accountable for the firearms and ammunition issued to them;

(e) Provide for warnings to be given, if appropriate, when firearms are to be discharged;

(f) Provide for a system of reporting whenever law enforcement officials use firearms in the performance of their duty.

Policing unlawful assemblies

12. As everyone is allowed to participate in lawful and peaceful assemblies, in accordance with the principles embodied in the Universal Declaration of Human Rights and the International Covenant on Civil and Political Rights, Governments and law enforcement agencies and officials shall recognize that force and firearms may be used only in accordance with principles 13 and 14.

13. In the dispersal of assemblies that are unlawful but non-violent, law enforcement officials shall avoid the use of force or, where that is not practicable, shall restrict such force to the minimum extent necessary.

14. In the dispersal of violent assemblies, law enforcement officials may use firearms only when less dangerous means are not practicable and only to the minimum extent necessary. Law enforcement officials shall not use firearms in such cases, except under the conditions stipulated in principle 9.

Policing persons in custody or detention

15. Law enforcement officials, in their relations with persons in custody or detention, shall not use force, except when strictly necessary for the maintenance of security and order within the institution, or when personal safety is threatened.

16. Law enforcement officials, in their relations with persons in custody or detention, shall not use firearms, except in self-defence or in the defence of others against the immediate threat of death or serious injury, or when strictly necessary to prevent the escape of a person in custody or detention presenting the danger referred to in principle 9.

17. The preceding principles are without prejudice to the rights, duties and responsibilities of prison officials, as set out in the Standard Minimum Rules for the Treatment of Prisoners, particularly rules 33, 34 and 54.

Qualifications, training and counselling

18. Governments and law enforcement agencies shall ensure that all law enforcement officials are selected by proper screening procedures, have appropriate moral, psychological and physical qualities for the effective exercise of their functions and receive continuous and thorough professional training. Their continued fitness to perform these functions should be subject to periodic review.

19. Governments and law enforcement agencies shall ensure that all law enforcement officials are provided with training and are tested in accordance with appropriate proficiency standards in the use of force. Those law enforcement officials who are required to carry firearms should be authorized to do so only upon completion of special training in their use.

20. In the training of law enforcement officials, Governments and law enforcement agencies shall give special attention to issues of police ethics and human rights, especially in the investigative process, to alternatives to the use of force and firearms, including the peaceful settlement of conflicts, the understanding of crowd behaviour, and the methods of persuasion, negotiation and mediation, as well as to technical means, with a view to limiting the use of force and firearms. Law enforcement agencies should review their training programmes and operational procedures in the light of particular incidents.

21. Governments and law enforcement agencies shall make stress counseling available to law enforcement officials who are involved in situations where force and firearms are used.

Reporting and review procedures

22. Governments and law enforcement agencies shall establish effective reporting and review procedures for all incidents referred to in principles 6 and 11 (*f*).For incidents reported pursuant to these principles, Governments and law enforcement agencies shall ensure that an effective review process is available and that independent administrative or prosecutorial authorities are in a position to exercise jurisdiction in appropriate circumstances. In cases of death and serious injury or other grave consequences, a detailed report shall be sent promptly to the competent authorities responsible for administrative review and judicial control.

23. Persons affected by the use of force and firearms or their legal representatives shall have access to an independent process, including a judicial process.
In the event of the death of such persons, this provision shall apply to their dependants accordingly.

24. Governments and law enforcement agencies shall ensure that superior officers are held responsible if they know, or should have known, that law enforcement officials under their command are resorting, or have resorted, to the unlawful use of force and firearms, and they did not take all measures in their power to prevent, suppress or report such use.

25. Governments and law enforcement agencies shall ensure that no criminal or disciplinary sanction is imposed on law enforcement officials who, in compliance with the Code of Conduct for Law Enforcement Officials and these basic principles, refuse to carry out an order to use force and firearms, or who report such use by other officials.

26. Obedience to superior orders shall be no defence if law enforcement officials knew that an order to use force and firearms resulting in the death or serious injury of a person was manifestly unlawful and had a reasonable opportunity to refuse to follow it. In any case, responsibility also rests on the superiors who gave the unlawful orders.

DOCUMENT 11: BASIC PRINCIPLES ON THE ROLE OF LAWYERS (EXCERPTED)

Whereas in the Charter of the United Nations the peoples of the world affirm, inter alia, their determination to establish conditions under which justice can be maintained, and proclaim as one of their purposes the achievement of international cooperation in promoting and encouraging respect for human rights and fundamental freedoms without distinction as to race, sex, language, or religion,

Whereas the Universal Declaration of Human Rights1 enshrines the principles of equality before the law, the presumption of innocence, the right to a fair and public hearing by an independent and impartial tribunal, and all the guarantees necessary for the defence of everyone charged with a penal offence,

Whereas the International Covenant on Civil and Political Rights2 proclaims, in addition, the right to be tried without undue delay and the right to a fair and public hearing by a competent, independent and impartial tribunal established by law,

Whereas the International Covenant on Economic, Social and Cultural Rights2 recalls the obligation of States under the Charter to promote universal respect for, and observance of, human rights and freedoms,

Whereas the Body of Principles for the Protection of All Persons under Any Form of Detention or Imprisonment3 provides that a detained person shall be entitled to have the assistance of, and to communicate and consult with, legal counsel,

Whereas the Standard Minimum Rules for the Treatment of Prisoners recommend, in particular, that legal assistance and confidential communication with counsel should be ensured to untried prisoners,

Whereas the Safeguards guaranteeing protection of those facing the death penalty reaffirm the right of everyone suspected or charged with a crime for which capital punishment may be imposed to adequate legal assistance at all stages of the proceedings, in accordance with article 14 of the International Covenant on Civil and Political Rights,

Whereas the Declaration of Basic Principles of Justice for Victims of Crime and Abuse of Power4 recommends measures to be taken at the international and national levels to improve access to justice and fair treatment, restitution, compensation and assistance for victims of crime,

Whereas adequate protection of the human rights and fundamental freedoms to which all persons are entitled, be they economic, social and cultural, or civil and political, requires that all persons have effective access to legal services provided by an independent legal profession,

Whereas professional associations of lawyers have a vital role to play in upholding professional standards and ethics, protecting their members from persecution and improper restrictions and infringements, providing legal services to all in need of them, and cooperating with governmental and other institutions in furthering the ends of justice and public interest.

The Basic Principles on the Role of Lawyers, set forth below, which have been formulated to assist Member States in their task of promoting and ensuring the proper role of lawyers, should be respected and taken into account by Governments within the framework of their national legislation and practice and should be brought to the attention of lawyers as well as other persons, such as judges, prosecutors, members of the executive and the legislature, and the public in general. These principles shall also apply, as appropriate, to persons who exercise the functions of lawyers without having the formal status of lawyers.

Access to lawyers and legal services

1. All persons are entitled to call upon the assistance of a lawyer of their choice to protect and establish their rights and to defend them in all stages of criminal proceedings.

2. Governments shall ensure that efficient procedures and responsive mechanisms for effective and equal access to lawyers are provided for all persons within their territory and subject to their jurisdiction, without distinction of any kind, such as discrimination based on race, colour, ethnic origin, sex, language, religion, political or other opinion, national or social origin, property, birth, economic or other status.

3. Governments shall ensure the provision of sufficient funding and other resources for legal services to the poor and, as necessary, to other disadvantaged persons. Professional associations of lawyers shall cooperate in the organization and provision of services, facilities and other resources.

4. Governments and professional associations of lawyers shall promote programmes to inform the public about their rights and duties under the law and the important role of lawyers in protecting their fundamental

freedoms. Special attention should be given to assisting the poor and other disadvantaged persons so as to enable them to assert their rights and where necessary call upon the assistance of lawyers.

Special safeguards in criminal justice matters

5. Governments shall ensure that all persons are immediately informed by the competent authority of their right to be assisted by a lawyer of their own choice upon arrest or detention or when charged with a criminal offence.

6. Any such persons who do not have a lawyer shall, in all cases in which the interests of justice so require, be entitled to have a lawyer of experience and competence commensurate with the nature of the offence assigned to them in order to provide effective legal assistance, without payment by them if they lack sufficient means to pay for such services.

7. Governments shall further ensure that all persons arrested or detained, with or without criminal charge, shall have prompt access to a lawyer, and in any case not later than forty-eight hours from the time of arrest or detention.

366 *Compendium of United Nations standards and norms in crime prevention and criminal justice*

8. All arrested, detained or imprisoned persons shall be provided with adequate opportunities, time and facilities to be visited by and to communicate and consult with a lawyer, without delay, interception or censorship and in full confidentiality. Such consultations may be within sight, but not within the hearing, of law enforcement officials.

Qualifications and training

9. Governments, professional associations of lawyers and educational institutions shall ensure that lawyers have appropriate education and training and be made aware of the ideals and ethical duties of the lawyer and of human rights and fundamental freedoms recognized by national and international law.

10. Governments, professional associations of lawyers and educational institutions shall ensure that there is no discrimination against a person with respect to entry into or continued practice within the legal profession on the grounds of race, colour, sex, ethnic origin, religion, political or other opinion, national or social origin, property, birth, economic or other status, except that a requirement, that a lawyer must be a national of the country concerned, shall not be considered discriminatory.

11. In countries where there exist groups, communities or regions whose needs for legal services are not met, particularly where such groups have distinct cultures, traditions or languages or have been the victims of past discrimination, Governments, professional associations of lawyers and educational institutions should take special measures to provide opportunities for candidates from these groups to enter the legal profession and should ensure that they receive training appropriate to the needs of their groups.

Duties and responsibilities

12. Lawyers shall at all times maintain the honour and dignity of their profession as essential agents of the administration of justice.

13. The duties of lawyers towards their clients shall include:

(*a*) Advising clients as to their legal rights and obligations, and as to the working of the legal system in so far as it is relevant to the legal rights and obligations of the clients;

(*b*) Assisting clients in every appropriate way, and taking legal action to protect their interests;

Part four, chapter I. Good governance 367

(*c*) Assisting clients before courts, tribunals or administrative authorities, where appropriate.

14. Lawyers, in protecting the rights of their clients and in promoting the cause of justice, shall seek to uphold human rights and fundamental freedoms recognized by national and international law and shall at all times act freely and diligently in accordance with the law and recognized standards and ethics of the legal profession.

15. Lawyers shall always loyally respect the interests of their clients.

Guarantees for the functioning of lawyers

16. Governments shall ensure that lawyers (*a*) are able to perform all of their professional functions without intimidation, hindrance, harassment or improper interference; (*b*) are able to travel and to consult with their clients freely both within their own country and abroad; and (*c*) shall not suffer, or be threatened with, prosecution or administrative, economic or other sanctions for any action taken in accordance with recognized professional duties, standards and ethics.

17. Where the security of lawyers is threatened as a result of discharging their functions, they shall be adequately safeguarded by the authorities.

18. Lawyers shall not be identified with their clients or their clients' causes as a result of discharging their functions.

19. No court or administrative authority before whom the right to counsel is recognized shall refuse to recognize the right of a lawyer to appear before it for his or her client unless that lawyer has been disqualified in accordance with national law and practice and in conformity with these principles.

20. Lawyers shall enjoy civil and penal immunity for relevant statements made in good faith in written or oral pleadings or in their professional appearances before a court, tribunal or other legal or administrative authority.

21. It is the duty of the competent authorities to ensure lawyers access to appropriate information, files and documents in their possession or control in sufficient time to enable lawyers to provide effective legal assistance to their clients. Such access should be provided at the earliest appropriate time.

22. Governments shall recognize and respect that all communications and consultations between lawyers and their clients within their professional relationship are confidential.

Freedom of expression and association

23. Lawyers like other citizens are entitled to freedom of expression, belief, association and assembly. In particular, they shall have the right to take part in public discussion of matters concerning the law, the administration of justice and the promotion and protection of human rights and to join or form local, national or international organizations and attend their meetings, without suffering professional restrictions by reason of their lawful action or their membership in a lawful organization. In exercising these rights, lawyers shall always conduct themselves in accordance with the law and the recognized standards and ethics of the legal profession.

Professional associations of lawyers

24. Lawyers shall be entitled to form and join self-governing professional associations to represent their interests, promote their continuing education and training and protect their professional integrity. The executive body of the professional associations shall be elected by its members and shall exercise its functions without external interference.

25. Professional associations of lawyers shall cooperate with Governments to ensure that everyone has effective and equal access to legal services and that lawyers are able, without improper interference, to counsel and assist their clients in accordance with the law and recognized professional standards and ethics.

Disciplinary proceedings

26. Codes of professional conduct for lawyers shall be established by the legal profession through its appropriate organs, or by legislation, in accordance with national law and custom and recognized international standards and norms.

27. Charges or complaints made against lawyers in their professional capacity shall be processed expeditiously and fairly under appropriate procedures.
Lawyers shall have the right to a fair hearing, including the right to be assisted by a lawyer of their choice.

28. Disciplinary proceedings against lawyers shall be brought before an impartial disciplinary committee established by the legal profession, before an independent statutory authority, or before a court, and shall be subject to an independent judicial review.

Part four, chapter I. Good governance 369

29. All disciplinary proceedings shall be determined in accordance with the code of professional conduct and other recognized standards and ethics of the legal profession and in the light of these principles.

DOCUMENT 12: DECLARATION OF BASIC PRINCIPLES OF JUSTICE FOR VICTIMS OF CRIME AND ABUSE OF POWER (EXCERPTED)

A. *Victims of crime*

1. "Victims" means persons who, individually or collectively, have suffered harm, including physical or mental injury, emotional suffering, economic loss or substantial impairment of their fundamental rights, through acts or omissions that are in violation of criminal laws operative within Member States, including those laws proscribing criminal abuse of power.

2. A person may be considered a victim, under this Declaration, regardless of whether the perpetrator is identified, apprehended, prosecuted or convicted and regardless of the familial relationship between the perpetrator and the victim. The term "victim" also includes, where appropriate, the immediate family or dependants of the direct victim and persons who have suffered harm in intervening to assist victims in distress or to prevent victimization.

3. The provisions contained herein shall be applicable to all, without distinction of any kind, such as race, colour, sex, age, language, religion, nationality, political or other opinion, cultural beliefs or practices, property, birth or family status, ethnic or social origin, and disability.

Access to justice and fair treatment

4. Victims should be treated with compassion and respect for their dignity. They are entitled to access to the mechanisms of justice and to prompt redress, as provided for by national legislation, for the harm that they have suffered.

5. Judicial and administrative mechanisms should be established and strengthened where necessary to enable victims to obtain redress through formal or informal procedures that are expeditious, fair, inexpensive and accessible. Victims should be informed of their rights in seeking redress through such mechanisms.

6. The responsiveness of judicial and administrative processes to the needs of victims should be facilitated by:

(a) Informing victims of their role and the scope, timing and progress of the proceedings and of the disposition of their cases, especially where serious crimes are involved and where they have requested such information;

(b) Allowing the views and concerns of victims to be presented and considered at appropriate stages of the proceedings where their personal interests are affected, without prejudice to the accused and consistent with the relevant national criminal justice system;

(c) Providing proper assistance to victims throughout the legal process;

(d) Taking measures to minimize inconvenience to victims, protect their privacy, when necessary, and ensure their safety, as well as that of their families and witnesses on their behalf, from intimidation and retaliation;

(e) Avoiding unnecessary delay in the disposition of cases and the execution of orders or decrees granting awards to victims.

7. Informal mechanisms for the resolution of disputes, including mediation, arbitration and customary justice or indigenous practices, should be utilized where appropriate to facilitate conciliation and redress for victims.

Restitution

8. Offenders or third parties responsible for their behaviour should, where appropriate, make fair restitution to victims, their families or dependants. Such restitution should include the return of property or payment for the harm or loss suffered, reimbursement of expenses incurred as a result of the victimization, the provision of services and the restoration of rights.

9. Governments should review their practices, regulations and laws to consider restitution as an available sentencing option in criminal cases, in addition to other criminal sanctions.

10. In cases of substantial harm to the environment, restitution, if ordered, should include, as far as possible, restoration of the environment, reconstruction of the infrastructure, replacement of community facilities and reimbursement of the expenses of relocation, whenever such harm results in the dislocation of a community.

11. Where public officials or other agents acting in an official or quasi-official capacity have violated national criminal laws, the victims should receive restitution from the State whose officials or agents were responsible for the harm inflicted. In cases where the Government under whose authority the victimizing act or omission occurred is no longer in existence, the State or Government successor in title should provide restitution to the victims.

Compensation

12. When compensation is not fully available from the offender or other sources, States should endeavour to provide financial compensation to:

(a) Victims who have sustained significant bodily injury or impairment of physical or mental health as a result of serious crimes;

(b) The family, in particular dependents of persons who have died or become physically or mentally incapacitated as a result of such victimization.

13. The establishment, strengthening and expansion of national funds for compensation to victims should be encouraged. Where appropriate, other funds may also be established for this purpose, including in those cases where the State of which the victim is a national is not in a position to compensate the victim for the harm.

14. Victims should receive the necessary material, medical, psychological and social assistance through governmental, voluntary, community-based and indigenous means.

15. Victims should be informed of the availability of health and social services and other relevant assistance and be readily afforded access to them.

16. Police, justice, health, social service and other personnel concerned should receive training to sensitize them to the needs of victims, and guidelines to ensure proper and prompt aid.

17. In providing services and assistance to victims, attention should be given to those who have special needs because of the nature of the harm inflicted or because of factors such as those mentioned in paragraph 3 above.

B. Victims of abuse of power

18. "Victims" means persons who, individually or collectively, have suffered harm, including physical or mental injury, emotional suffering, economic loss or substantial impairment of their fundamental rights, through acts or omissions that do not yet constitute violations of national criminal laws but of internationally recognized norms relating to human rights.

19. States should consider incorporating into the national law norms proscribing abuses of power and providing remedies to victims of such abuses. In particular, such remedies should include restitution and/or compensation, and necessary material, medical, psychological and social assistance and support.

20. States should consider negotiating multilateral international treaties relating to victims, as defined in paragraph 18.

21. States should periodically review existing legislation and practices to ensure their responsiveness to changing circumstances, should enact and enforce, if necessary, legislation proscribing acts that constitute serious abuses of political or economic power, as well as promoting policies and mechanisms for the prevention of such acts, and should develop and make readily available appropriate rights and remedies for victims of such acts.

DOCUMENT 13: STATUS OF FOREIGN CITIZENS IN CRIMINAL PROCEEDINGS (EXCERPTED)

The Economic and Social Council,

Guided by the Universal Declaration of Human Rights, adopted and proclaimed by the General Assembly by its resolution 217 A (III) of 10 December 1948,

Bearing in mind the relevant international legal instruments in the field of human rights,

Bearing in mind also the Standard Minimum Rules for the Treatment of Prisoners, adopted by the First United Nations Congress on the Prevention of Crime and the Treatment of Offenders, held at Geneva from 22 August to 3 September 19551 and approved by the Economic and Social Council in its resolution 663 C (XXIV) of 31 July 1957, and the procedures for the effective implementation of the Standard Minimum Rules for the Treatment of Prisoners, approved by the Council in its resolution 1984/47 of 25 May 1984 and set out in the annex thereto,

Recalling General Assembly resolution 49/159 of 23 December 1994, in which the Assembly approved the Naples Political Declaration and Global Action Plan against Organized Transnational Crime adopted by the World Ministerial Conference on Organized Transnational Crime, held at Naples, Italy, from 21 to 23 November 1994,

Conscious of the need to respect human dignity and the recognized rights of persons undergoing criminal proceedings as set forth in the International Covenants on Human Rights,

Urges Member States that have not yet done so to consider adopting the following measures:

(a) Carefully examine whether foreign citizens under criminal prosecution are guaranteed universally recognized rights with regard to criminal prosecution at all stages of proceedings;

(b) Ensure that individuals are not subjected to more severe custodial penalties or inferior prison conditions in a State solely because they are not nationals of that State;

(c) Undertake the necessary arrangements to ensure that any foreign citizen subject to criminal proceedings whose native language is not that of the State conducting the proceedings against him or her and who, for that reason, is unable to understand the nature of such proceedings has access throughout his or her trial to the services of a suitable interpreter in his or her native language, to the extent possible;

(d) Whenever permitted by its internal law or practice, make available to foreign citizens as well as to nationals, provided that they fulfill the relevant legal requirements, alternative penal sentences or administrative penalties provided for under the legislation of the State conducting proceedings;

(e) Intensify efforts to implement applicable international instruments, such as the Vienna Convention on Consular Relations, concerning, inter alia, notification to consular authorities of the detention of their citizens.

DOCUMENT 14: THE VIENNA CONVENTION ON CONSULAR RELATIONS (EXCERPTED)

The States Parties to the present Convention,

Recalling that consular relations have been established between peoples since ancient times,

Having in mind the Purposes and Principles of the Charter of the United Nation concerning the sovereign equality of States, the maintenance of international peace and security, and the promotion of friendly relations among nations,

Considering that the United Nations Conference on Diplomatic Intercourse and Immunities adopted the Vienna Convention on Diplomatic Relations which was opened for signature on 18 April 1961,

Believing that an international convention on consular relations, privileges and immunities would also contribute to the development of friendly relations among nations, irrespective of their differing constitutional and social systems,

Realizing that the purpose of such privileges and immunities is not to benefit individuals but to ensure the efficient performance of functions by consular posts on behalf of their respective States,

Affirming that the rules of customary international law continue to govern matters not expressly regulated by the provisions of the present Convention,

Have agreed as follows:

Article 2
Establishment of Consular Relations

1. The establishment of consular relations between States takes place by mutual consent.
2. The consent given to the establishment of diplomatic relations between two States implies, unless otherwise stated, consent to the establishment of consular relations.

Article 5
Consular Functions

Consular functions consist in:

e. helping and assisting nationals, both individuals and bodies corporate, of the sending State;

i. subject to the practices and procedures obtaining in the receiving State, representing or arranging appropriate representation for nationals of the sending State before the tribunals and other authorities of the receiving State, for the purpose of obtaining, in accordance with the laws and regulations of the receiving State, provisional measures for the preservation of the rights and interests of these nationals, where, because of absence or any other reason, such nationals are unable at the proper time to assume the defence of their rights and interests;

Article 36
Communication and Contact with Nationals of the Sending State

1. With a view to facilitating the exercise of consular functions relating to nationals of the sending State:

a. consular officers shall be free to communicate with nationals of the sending State and to have access to them. Nationals of the sending State shall have the same freedom with respect to communication with and access to consular officers of the sending State;

b. if he so requests, the competent authorities of the receiving State shall, without delay, inform the consular post of the sending State if, within its consular district, a national of that State is arrested or committed to prison or to custody pending trial or is detained in any other manner. Any communication addressed to the consular post by the person arrested, in prison, custody or detention shall also be forwarded by the said authorities without delay. The said authorities shall inform the person concerned without delay of his rights under this sub-paragraph;

c. consular officers shall have the right to visit a national of the sending State who is in prison, custody or detention, to converse and correspond with him and to arrange for his legal representation. They shall also have the right to visit any national of the sending State who is in prison, custody or detention in their district in pursuance of a judgment. Nevertheless, consular officers shall refrain from taking action on behalf of a national who is in prison, custody or detention if he expressly opposes such action.

The rights referred to in paragraph 1 of this Article shall be exercised in conformity with the laws and regulations of the receiving State, subject to the proviso, however, that the said laws and regulations must enable full effect to be given to the purposes for which the rights accorded under this Article are intended.

DOCUMENT 15: FACTS ABOUT THE DEATH PENALTY (UPDATED JANUARY 14, 2011), BY THE DEATH PENALTY INFORMATION CENTER.

1015 18ᵗʰ Street NW, Suite 704
Washington, DC 20036
Phone: (202) 289 - 2275
Fax: (202) 289 - 7336
Email: dpic@deathpenaltyinfo.org
http://www.deathpenaltyinfo.org

DEATH PENALTY INFORMATION CENTER

Facts about the Death Penalty
Updated January 14, 2011

STATES WITH THE DEATH PENALTY (35)

Alabama	Florida	Louisiana	New Hampshire	South Dakota	
Arizona	Georgia	Maryland	North Carolina	Tennessee	
Arkansas	Idaho	Mississippi	Ohio	Texas	
California	Illinois	Missouri	Oklahoma	Utah	- plus
Colorado	Indiana	Montana	Oregon	Virginia	U.S. Gov't
Connecticut	Kansas	Nebraska	Pennsylvania	Washington	U.S. Military
Delaware	Kentucky	Nevada	South Carolina	Wyoming	

STATES WITHOUT THE DEATH PENALTY (15)

Alaska	Massachusetts	New Mexico*	Vermont	- plus
Hawaii	Michigan	New York	West Virginia	District of Columbia
Iowa	Minnesota	North Dakota	Wisconsin	
Maine	New Jersey	Rhode Island		

*Two inmates remain on death row in NM.

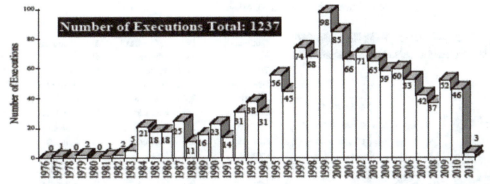

Number of Executions Total: 1237

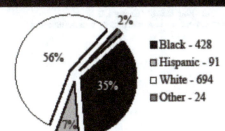

Race of Defendants Executed

2%
56%
35%
7%

- Black - 428
- Hispanic - 91
- White - 694
- Other - 24

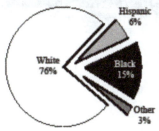

Race of Victim in Death Penalty Cases

Hispanic 6%
White 76%
Black 15%
Other 3%

Over 75% of the murder victims in cases resulting in an execution were white, even though nationally only 50% of murder victims generally are white.

Recent Studies on Race

- In 96% of the states where there have been reviews of race and the death penalty, there was a pattern of either race-of-victim or race-of-defendant discrimination, or both. (Prof. David Baldus report to the ABA, 1998).

- 98% of the chief district attorneys in death penalty states are white; only 1% are black. (Prof. Jeffrey Pokorak, Cornell Law Review, 1998).

- A comprehensive study of the death penalty in North Carolina found that the odds of receiving a death sentence rose by 3.5 times among those defendants whose victims were white. (Prof. Jack Boger and Dr. Isaac Unah, University of North Carolina, 2001).

- A study in California found that those who killed whites were over 3 times more likely to be sentenced to death than those who killed blacks and over 4 times more likely than those who killed Latinos. (Pierce & Radelet, Santa Clara Law Review 2005).

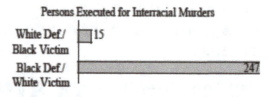

Persons Executed for Interracial Murders

| White Def./ Black Victim | 15 |
| Black Def./ White Victim | 247 |

Innocence

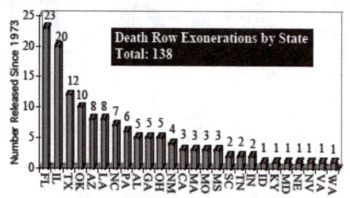

Death Row Exonerations by State
Total: 138

Since 1973, over 130 people have been released from death row with evidence of their innocence. (Staff Report, House Judiciary Subcommittee on Civil & Constitutional Rights, Oct. 1993, with updates from DPIC).

From 1973-1999, there was an average of 3.1 exonerations per year. From 2000-2007, there has been an average of 5 exonerations per year.

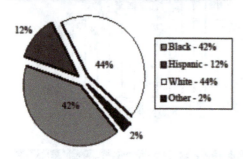

Race of Death Row Inmates

- ■ Black - 42%
- ■ Hispanic - 12%
- □ White - 44%
- ■ Other - 2%

DEATH ROW INMATES BY STATE: January 1, 2010

California	697	S. Carolina	63	Connecticut	10
Florida	398	Mississippi	61	Kansas	10
Texas	337	Missouri	61	Utah	10
Pennsylvania	222	U.S. Gov't	59	Washington	9
Alabama	201	Arkansas	42	U.S. Military	8
Ohio	168	Kentucky	35	Maryland	5
N. Carolina	167	Oregon	32	S. Dakota	3
Arizona	135	Delaware	19	Colorado	3
Georgia	106	Idaho	17	Montana	2
Tennessee	90	Indiana	15	New Mexico	2
Louisiana	85	Virginia	15	Wyoming	1
Oklahoma	84	Illinois	15	N. Hampshire	1
Nevada	78	Nebraska	11	**TOTAL**	**3261**

Race of Death Row Inmates and Death Row Inmates by State Source: NAACP LDF "Death Row, U.S.A." (January 1, 2010)
When added, the total number of death row inmates by state is slightly higher because some prisoners are sentenced to death in more than one state.

NUMBER OF EXECUTIONS BY STATE SINCE 1976

	Total	2010	2011		Total	2010	2011
Texas	464	17	0	Illinois	12	0	0
Virginia	108	3	0	Nevada	12	0	0
Oklahoma	96	3	2	Utah	7	1	0
Florida	69	1	0	Tennessee	6	0	0
Missouri	67	0	0	Maryland	5	0	0
Georgia	48	2	0	Washington	5	1	0
Alabama	50	5	1	Nebraska	3	0	0
N. Carolina	43	0	0	Pennsylvania	3	0	0
S. Carolina	42	0	0	Kentucky	3	0	0
Ohio	41	8	0	Montana	3	0	0
Louisiana	28	1	0	Oregon	2	0	0
Arkansas	27	0	0	Connecticut	1	0	0
Arizona	24	1	0	Idaho	1	0	0
Indiana	20	0	0	New Mexico	1	0	0
Delaware	14	0	0	Colorado	1	0	0
California	13	0	0	Wyoming	1	0	0
Mississippi	13	3	0	South Dakota	1	0	0
				US Gov't	3	0	0

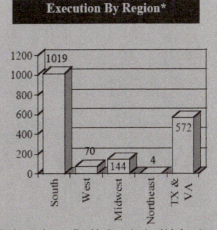

Execution By Region*

*Federal executions are listed in the region in which the crime was committed.

DEATH SENTENCING

The number of death sentences per year has dropped dramatically since 1999.

Year	1994	1995	1996	1997	1998	1999	2000	2001	2002	2003	2004	2005	2006	2007	2008	2009	2010
Sentences	313	313	315	268	294	277	224	159	166	152	140	139	123	120	119	112	112*

Source: Bureau of Justice Statistics: "Capital Punishment 2009." *Projected, based on DPIC's research

JUVENILES
• In 2005, the Supreme Court in *Roper v. Simmons* struck down the death penalty for juveniles. 22 defendants had been executed for crimes committed as juveniles since 1976.

MENTAL DISABILITIES
• *Intellectual Disabilities:* In 2002, the Supreme Court held in *Atkins v. Virginia* that it is unconstitutional to execute defendants with 'mental retardation.'
• *Mental Illness:* The American Psychiatric Association, the American Psychological Association, the National Alliance for the Mentally Ill, and the American Bar Association have endorsed resolutions calling for an exemption of the severely mentally ill.

WOMEN
•There were 61 women on death row as of January 1, 2010. This constitutes 1.9% of the total death row population. 12 women have been executed since 1976. (NAACP Legal Defense Fund, January 1, 2010)

DETERRENCE
• According to a survey of the former and present presidents of the country's top academic criminological societies, 88% of these experts rejected the notion that the death penalty acts as a deterrent to murder. (Radelet & Lacock, 2009)

• Consistent with previous years, the 2009 FBI Uniform Crime Report showed that the South had the highest murder rate. The South accounts for over 80% of executions. The Northeast, which has less than 1% of all executions, again had the lowest murder rate.

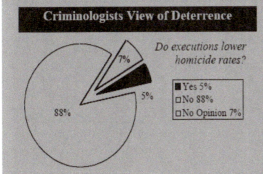

Criminologists View of Deterrence

Do executions lower homicide rates?

■ Yes 5%
□ No 88%
□ No Opinion 7%

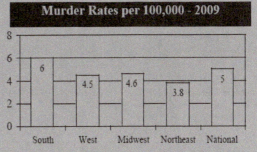

Murder Rates per 100,000 - 2009

1761

EXECUTIONS SINCE 1976 BY METHOD USED

1063	Lethal Injection	36 states plus the US government use lethal injection as their primary method. Some
157	Electrocution	states utilizing lethal injection have other methods available as backups. Though New
11	Gas Chamber	Mexico abolished the death penalty in 2009, the act was not retroactive, leaving two
3	Hanging	prisoners on death row and its lethal injection protocol intact.
3	Firing Squad	

FINANCIAL FACTS ABOUT THE DEATH PENALTY

• The California death penalty system costs taxpayers $114 million per year beyond the costs of keeping convicts locked up for life. Taxpayers have paid more than $250 million for each of the state's executions. (L.A. Times, March 6, 2005)

• In Kansas, the costs of capital cases are 70% more expensive than comparable non-capital cases, including the costs of incarceration. (Kansas Performance Audit Report, December 2003).

• In Maryland, an average death penalty case resulting in a death sentence costs approximately $3 million. The eventual costs to Maryland taxpayers for cases pursued 1978-1999 will be $186 million. Five executions have resulted. (Urban Institute 2008).

• The most comprehensive study in the country found that the death penalty costs North Carolina $2.16 million per execution *over* the costs of sentencing murderers to life imprisonment. The majority of those costs occur at the trial level. (Duke University, May 1993).

• Enforcing the death penalty costs Florida $51 million a year above what it would cost to punish all first-degree murderers with life in prison without parole. Based on the 44 executions Florida had carried out since 1976, that amounts to a cost of $24 million for each execution. (Palm Beach Post, January 4, 2000).

• In Texas, a death penalty case costs an average of $2.3 million, about three times the cost of imprisoning someone in a single cell at the highest security level for 40 years. (Dallas Morning News, March 8, 1992).

PUBLIC OPINION

• A 2010 poll by Lake Research Partners found that a clear majority of voters (61%) would choose a punishment other than the death penalty for murder, including life with no possibility of parole with restitution to the victim's family (39%), life with no possibility of parole (13%), or life with the possibility of parole (9%)

• A 2009 poll commissioned by DPIC found police chiefs ranked the death penalty last among ways to reduce violent crime. The police chiefs also considered the death penalty the least efficient use of taxpayers' money.

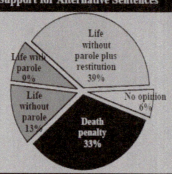

Support for Alternative Sentences

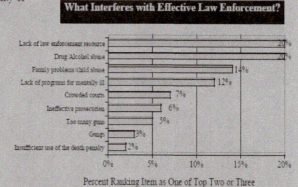

What Interferes with Effective Law Enforcement?

Percent Ranking Item as One of Top Two or Three

The Death Penalty Information Center has available more extensive reports on a variety of issues, including:
"The Death Penalty in 2009: Year-End Report" (December 2009)
"Smart on Crime: Reconsidering the Death Penalty in a Time of Economic Crisis" (October 2009)
"The Death Penalty in 2008: A Year End Report" (December 2008)
"A Crisis of Confidence: Americans' Doubts About the Death Penalty" (2007)
"Blind Justice: Juries Deciding Life and Death with Only Half the Truth" (2005)
"Innocence and the Crisis in the American Death Penalty" (2004)
"International Perspectives on the Death Penalty: A Costly Isolation for the U.S." (1999)
"The Death Penalty in Black & White: Who Lives, Who Dies, Who Decides" (1998)
"Innocence and the Death Penalty: The Increasing Danger of Executing the Innocent" (1997)
"Killing for Votes: The Dangers of Politicizing the Death Penalty Process" (1996)
"Twenty Years of Capital Punishment: A Re-evaluation" (1996)
"With Justice for Few: The Growing Crisis in Death Penalty Representation" (1995)
"On the Front Line: Law Enforcement Views on the Death Penalty" (1995)
"The Future of the Death Penalty in the United States: A Texas-Sized Crisis" (1994)

APPENDIX P: OPINION PIECES AND NEWS ON HUMAN RIGHTS IN THE U.S. AND THE INTERNATIONAL COMMUNITY

The purpose of this Appendix is to present different American voices and opinions about human rights from various U.S. perspectives. This is not meant to show the full variety of American perspectives, as there are too many to present in the space available. These are random examples of how people view the American government and U.S. policy and practice of human rights, whether domestically or abroad.

The views expressed in these articles do not necessarily reflect the views of the author.

Documents

DOCUMENT 1: NAVAJO TRIBE BLASTS U.S. HUMAN RIGHTS TRACK RECORD

By Alysa Landry, *The Daily Times*
Posted: 10/18/2010 11:27:42 PM MDT

FARMINGTON—The U.S. consistently has failed to protect the Navajo Nation and its people, the Navajo Human Rights Commission stated in its official response to the U.S. human rights record.

The response will be read next month in Geneva, Switzerland, in front of 192 dignitaries of the United Nations Human Rights Council. The reading comes as part of the U.N. Universal Periodic Review of its members on human rights obligations.

The U.S. is up for review this year. The country's report to the U.N. was made public Aug. 23.

The Navajo Human Rights Commission's response commends the U.S. State Department for recognizing the "virtue" of indigenous people and sovereign government, but it also states "The U.S. fails to meet its human rights obligations to indigenous peoples. These transgressions need to be accounted for."

The commission's response points out failures in three main categories: the failure to protect sacred or religious sites, the forced relocation of Navajo mandated by federal legislation, and rights of the Navajo to self-determination.

"It is unacceptable that a nation that claims to be an advocate for protecting human rights objects to the recognition of indigenous human rights as it pertains to religious and cultural beliefs," the response states.

"The U.S. restricted property rights and interest in the lands of the Diné and Hopi peoples without their free, prior and informed consent and thereby imposing a foreign system of property valuation. (Relocates and their descendants) are now denied the opportunity to learn, participate and pass on the Diné traditional Life Way," it states.

The response also includes questions the Navajo Human Rights Commission is requesting the U.N. Human Rights Council to ask of the U.S.

Those questions include:

- Why are the rights of indigenous peoples to "freely profess a religious faith and to manifest and practice it both in public and in private" not protected by U.S. federal legislations?

- Why doesn't the U.S. engage in true nation-to-nation dialogue with the Diné people to develop an effective mechanism consistent with the international standard of "free, prior and informed consent" to address Indian land claims and forced relocation?
- Why do the U.S.' laws and policies oppress indigenous nations' inherent rights to self-determination and sovereignty of Diné peoples over their lands, resources, water and minerals?
- When will the U.S. endorse the U.N. Declaration on the Rights of Indigenous Peoples?

"As the original inhabitants of the U.S., we have a long history of human right abuse and we can make our comment on the UPR of the U.S. from a standpoint of firsthand experience," Navajo Human Rights Commission Chairman Duane "Chili" Yazzie said. Yazzie is expected to attend the Geneva conference next month.

Alysa Landry: alandry@daily-times.com © Copyright 2010 Farmingham Daily News. Media News group | P.O.Box 450 | Farmington , NM 87499 | 505.325.4545.

DOCUMENT 2: REPUBLICAN CONGRESSMAN TROUBLED BY OBAMA'S LACK OF 'VOICE' ON HUMAN RIGHTS

Source: http://www.energypublisher.com/article.asp?id=3712
Monday, July 26, 2010

Rep. Frank Wolf (R-VA), co-chair of the Tom Lantos Human Rights Commission and a long-time advocate for human rights around the world, delivered a major speech on the House floor urging the Obama Administration to "find its voice" on human rights. During the Bush Administration it was not uncommon for Wolf to press the president and the State Department to be more outspoken on human rights. In December 2008, Wolf spoke at length on the House floor about various "missed opportunities" on human rights and a failure on the part of the Bush Administration to "consistently apply their rhetoric." However, as Wolf noted last night, the Obama Administration has struggled even to "find its voice when it comes to the promotion and protection of basic human rights and religious freedom."

Among the countries Wolf mentioned in his remarks were Sudan, China, Vietnam, North Korea, Iraq, Egypt and Morocco. He specifically highlighted the struggles of different faith communities including Uighur Muslims, Tibetan Buddhists, Ahmadi Muslims, Coptic Christians and Baha'is.

In addition, Wolf noted troubling developments within the State Department which threatened to "institutionalize the marginalization of these core issues." He also called on Congress to "stand in the gap" when the administration fails to advocate for those around the world whose voices have been silenced.

Wolf acknowledged that there are multiple dimensions to America's bilateral relations with countries around the globe, but said if the United States of America cannot be relied upon to speak out on behalf of the vulnerable and oppressed, then it is indeed a dark day for millions around the world yearning to breathe the sweet air of freedom.

"Where the administration fails to find its voice, Congress must stand in the gap," Wolf said. "For decades human rights enjoyed bipartisan support in this body. Now I fear these issues have fallen victim to bipartisan apathy.

"America must stand up for the ideals upon which our own experiment in self-governance was founded," Wolf continued.

"America must strike out against injustice, whatever form it takes. America must believe that even the mightiest walls of oppression can tumble and work toward that end. . . . will the administration accept this charge? Can this president find his voice? Will 'ripples of hope' once again infuse America's foreign policy?"

Below is the complete text of Wolf's remarks.

"On April 21, New York Times columnist Nicholas Kristof authored a piece that closed with the following words: 'If President Obama is ever going to find his voice on Sudan, it had better be soon.'

"Two weeks after the article ran I wrote the president, and I submit a copy of the letter for the Record, putting forth a number of recommendations in the hopes of salvaging the administration's languishing Sudan policy. My concerns echoed those voiced by six respected NGOs who the week prior had run an ad in The Washington Post and Politico calling for Secretary Clinton and Ambassador Rice to exercise 'personal and sustained leadership on Sudan' in the face of a 'stalemated policy' and waning U.S. credibility as a mediator.

"Sadly, Kristof's assessment can be applied elsewhere around the world. It seems that President Obama and the administration as a whole have struggled to find its voice when it comes to the promotion and protection of basic human rights and religious freedom.

"These most cherished ideals, which are at the very heart of the American experiment, have time and again been sidelined in this administration's foreign policy. This is a grievous mistake which has dire implications for the world's dissidents and democrats who yearn for freedom and look to America to be their advocate.

"Looking back to Sudan, a nation I first visited in 1989, and most recently in 2004 when Senator Sam Brownback and I were the first congressional delegation to go to Darfur, I remain deeply concerned that the country is headed for a resumption of civil war if the U.S. fails to exert the necessary leadership.

"While there were certainly times that I was critical of the Bush Administration's policies, it is indisputable that he and former Special Envoy John Danforth were instrumental in securing, after two and half years of negotiations, the Comprehensive Peace Agreement (CPA), which brought about an end to the brutal 20-year civil war in which more than 2 million perished, most of whom were civilians.

"A recent New York Times column by author Dave Eggers and Sudan activist John Prendergast titled, 'In Sudan, War is Around the Corner,' spoke to this reality. The pair wrote: 'Shortly after George W. Bush entered the White House, he decided he would put the full diplomatic leverage of the U.S. to work in ending this war, one of the bloodiest conflicts of the 20th century. He succeeded.'

"Eggers and Prendergast rightly noted that when the South is given the opportunity to vote for independence in January, as guaranteed by the CPA, the conventional wisdom is that they will waste no time in severing ties with Khartoum. This shouldn't come as a surprise considering that President Bashir remains at the helm in Khartoum. Long an indicted war criminal, he was earlier this month also officially charged by the International Criminal Court with orchestrating genocide in Darfur. Bashir's murderous aims in Darfur are not without precedent.

"With just six months to go, Khartoum persists in dragging its feet—undermining and stalling the process at every turn. Furthermore, the deeply flawed April elections do not bode well for the fate of a free, fair and timely referendum process. Failure to deliver on the long-awaited promise of a respectable referendum could have grave implications. While some of the administration's rhetoric has improved of late, notably during Vice President Biden's trip to Africa, we have yet to see the administration apply real consequences to Khartoum.

"In fact, most Sudan watchers would agree that we have seen little to no evidence, since the administration's release of their Sudan policy, that they have any intention of utilizing sticks. Rather, they appear to be relying exclusively on carrots.

"A July 14 Associated Press article titled, 'Promises, Promises: U.S. Fails to Punish Sudan,' described the administration's track record on Sudan this way: 'The words of the Obama administration were unequivocal: Sudan must do more to fight terror and improve human rights. If it did, it would be rewarded. If not, it would be punished. Nine months later, problems with Sudan have grown worse. Yet the administration has not clamped down. If anything, it has made small conciliatory gestures.'

"Eggers and Prendergast, in their New York Times piece, close with a chilling warning as it relates to the months ahead in Sudan: 'This is President Obama's Rwanda moment, and it is unfolding now, in slow motion. It is not too late to prevent the coming war in Sudan, and protect the peace we helped build five years ago.'

"President Obama and his advisers need not rely on the warnings of those in the advocacy community and on Capitol Hill when it comes to the high stakes in Sudan in the days ahead. Rather they can simply look to the Annual Threat Assessment of the U.S. Intelligence Community, which recently predicted that over the next five years, '... a new mass killing or genocide is most likely to occur in Southern Sudan'—more so than any other country.

"A welcomed step toward preserving the tenuous peace would be to provide South Sudan the air defense system that the Government of Southern Sudan (GOSS) requested and President Bush reportedly approved in 2008. This defensive capability would help neutralize Khartoum's major tactical advantage, a virtual necessity in light of the scorched earth tactics and antanov bombers that have marked their genocidal campaigns of the past and would make peace and stability more likely following the referendum vote.

"During the campaign for the presidency, then candidate Obama said 'Washington must respond to the ongoing genocide and the ongoing failure to implement the CPA with consistency and strong consequences.' These words still ring true today. And yet, apart from a recent National Security Council statement expressing support for 'international efforts to bring those responsible for genocide and war crimes in Darfur to justice,' we have seen an administration and a president struggling to find its voice on this most pressing human rights issue. Special Envoy Gration, at a recent event on Capitol Hill, reportedly went so far as to say that the genocide charges against Bashir will make his job harder.

"Sudan is not an anomaly. Consider China, a country where human rights, religious freedom and civil society continue to be under fierce attack by the country's ruling communist party.

"From the outset, this administration chose to marginalize human rights in the context of U.S.-China bilateral relations. On her first trip to Asia, Secretary of State Clinton was downright dismissive of human rights concerns saying that 'those issues can't interfere' with economic, security or environmental concerns.

"A firestorm of criticism ensued. Human rights organizations were rightly dismayed. How had impassioned advocacy for the dignity of every person been relegated to a position of mere interference? And this in spite of Obama campaign promises to 'be frank with the Chinese" and "press them to respect human rights.'

"In China we again see an administration which seems unable to find its voice on human rights. A glance at the news from the last several weeks alone makes it painfully clear that that voice—the voice which speaks out on behalf of those enduring tremendous persecution and oppression at the hands of their own government—has never been more necessary.

"A July 5 Associated Press (AP) story, reported that Yu Jue, 'a best-selling author and fierce critic of the Communist Party was taken into custody by the police on Monday for reasons that were unclear . . .'

"The AP reported on July 15 that 'dozens of blogs by some of China's most outspoken users have been abruptly shut down while popular Twitter services appear to be the newest target in government efforts to control social networking.'

"Veteran dissident Liu Xianbin, an original signatory of Charter 08, a historic pro-democracy manifesto, was arrested by Chinese authorities on June 27 on suspicion of 'inciting subversion of state power.'

"July also marks the one-year anniversary of the deadly suppression of Uighur protestors last summer in the northwest of China. China's beleaguered Uighur Muslim community continues to face severe repression in the aftermath of the violence. According to multiple independent news sources, authorities reportedly installed 40,000 security cameras throughout the city in anticipation of the one-year anniversary.

"Carl Gershman, president of the National Endowment for Democracy, authored a piece in The Washington Post on the occasion of the anniversary. He highlighted a report by the Uighur Human Rights Project aptly titled, 'Can Anyone Hear Us?' which documents 'the firing on protesters that led to hundreds of deaths, as well as mass beatings, the arbitrary detention of thousands and a 10-month communications shutdown that cut off the region from the outside world.'

"Gershman closes his piece with the following charge: 'The U.S. and the international community should also support the Uighurs' three-month-old call for an independent international investigation into the events of last July and the opening of a meaningful dialogue with Chinese authorities. Uighur voices have been crying in the wilderness. It's time to listen.'

"It is indeed time to listen. It is also time to add America's voice to the chorus of voices within China pressing for greater freedoms and basic human rights.

"Just last week I had the honor of meeting with two courageous Chinese human rights lawyers visiting the U.S. for legal training and to brief policymakers on the situation facing those defending rule of law in China. These lawyers often choose to represent, at their own peril, those human rights activists, house church leaders, bloggers etc. who face persecution in the form of trumped up charges and the absence of due process. The lawyers said quite pointedly that their lives improve, and those of their cohorts in prison or facing other pressures by the Chinese government, when the West speaks out for their plight and raises their cases by name.

"This sentiment is nothing new. I remarked that they are China's Sakarovs and Solzhenitsyns. Similarly these giants in the cause of freedom time and again recounted how their lives in the gulags improved when the West and President Reagan championed their cause and challenged the lies that were at the foundation of the Soviet system.

"It seems this administration has forgotten the lessons of history to the detriment of China's young democrats.

"In their annual Freedom in the World Report, the NGO Freedom House documented a litany of abuses perpetrated by the Chinese government and then made the following observation: 'While these acts of repression are disturbing, so is the absence of protest from the democratic world. When the Soviet Union arrested a dissident or suppressed religious expression, it drew widespread condemnation by figures ranging from heads of state to trade unions leaders, as well as by human rights organizations and prominent humanitarians. China's current actions, by contrast, elicit little more than boilerplate criticism, and just as often they provoke no response whatsoever.'

"Elsewhere in Asia we see an administration seeming to align itself with the oppressor over the oppressed. Look at Vietnam. On July 19, AFP reported that Kurt Campbell, assistant secretary of State for East Asian Affairs said 'as I look at all the friends in Southeast Asia, I think we have the greatest prospects in the future with Vietnam.'

"This is a strange affinity to have with a government that our own State Department said 'increased its suppression of dissent, arresting and convicting several political activists' during the reporting period of the 2009 Country Report on Human Rights Practices.

"The State Department's report continues: 'several editors and reporters from prominent newspapers were fired for reporting on official corruption and outside blogging on political topics. Bloggers were detained and arrested under vague national security provisions for criticizing the government and were prohibited from posting material the government saw as sensitive or critical. The government also monitored e-mail and regulated or suppressed Internet content . . . The government utilized or tolerated the use of force to resolve disputes with a Buddhist order in Lam Dong and Catholic groups with unresolved property claims . . .'

"Today Secretary Clinton is in Vietnam for ASEAN meetings. Initial news reports indicate that she raised human rights concerns in her meeting with the Foreign Minister and afterwards with journalists. However, a New York Times story today pointed out that the timing of her comments on these sensitive issues 'suggested that she wanted to make her point and move on.' If the administration is truly concerned about human rights and religious freedom in Vietnam, they would take the concrete step of placing Vietnam back on the Countries of Particular Concern (CPC) list, as has been recommended by the bipartisan U.S. Commission on International Religious Freedom (USCRIF) and the U.S. House of Representatives.

"Leonard Leo, chair USCIRF, rightly points out that Vietnam's human rights record has only improved when its 'feet were held to the fire.' Leo continued, 'but once Vietnam, with U.S. help, joined the World Trade Organization in 2007, religious freedom and human rights advocates have experienced waves of arrests,' Leo said. Waves of arrests from our 'friend' in Southeast Asia?

"Or consider North Korea. Without question, this country is one of the darkest places on the globe. More than 200,000 North Koreans—including children—are being held in political prison camps. It is estimated that between 400,000 and one million people have died in these camps, having been worked to death or starved to death.

"Last summer, an op-ed in the Wall Street Journal featured a quote from a North Korean refugee woman who said 'if I had a chance to meet with President Obama, I would first like to tell him how North Korean women are being sold like livestock in China and, second, to know that North Korean labor camps are hell on earth.'

"However, because North Korea possesses nuclear weapons and threatens not only to use them against neighboring countries but also to share nuclear weapons technology with such rogue states as Burma and Syria, the international community, the U.S. included, has tended to downplay or outright ignore the horrendous human rights abuses in North Korea in the interest of trying to negotiate through the so-called six-party talks an end to its nuclear program.

"But nothing has been achieved by these negotiations. And the recent sinking of the South Korean ship has stalled efforts to revive six-nation talks. Even in the face of North Korea's nuclear ambitions it is inexcusable that its abhorrent human rights record is relegated to the back burner and that the North Korea Freedom Act has not been fully implemented. Why has the administration had so little to say about those trapped in 'hell on earth'?

"Looking to the Middle East we again see an administration whose advocacy on behalf of persecuted peoples has been sorely lacking.

"A February 6 ABC News story opened with the following observation: 'Across the Middle East, where Christianity was born and its followers once made up a sizable portion of the population, Christians are now tiny minorities.'

"This is perhaps no more true than in Iraq. With the exception of Israel, the Bible contains more references to the cities, regions and nations of ancient Iraq than any other country.

"Tragically Iraq's ancient Christian community is facing extinction. The U.N. High Commission for Refugees estimates that some 250,000 to 500,000 Christians have left the country since 2003, or about half the Christian population.

"While I have appreciated Ambassador Chris Hill's commitment to this issue during his time as U.S. ambassador, and while I believe that Michael Corbin, the deputy assistant secretary of State who is charged with working on Iraqi minorities issues cares deeply about this issue, I see a continued unwillingness at the highest levels of the State Department to acknowledge and ultimately address the challenges facing these ancient faith communities.

"In an April 2009 column in the Wall Street Journal, Daniel Henninger summed it up this way: 'Candidate Obama last fall sent a letter to Condoleezza Rice expressing 'my concern about the safety and well-being of Iraq's Christian and other non-Muslim religious minorities.' He asked what steps the U.S. was taking to protect 'these communities of religious freedom.' Candidate Obama said he wanted these groups represented in Iraq's governing institutions. Does President Obama believe these things?'

"I have long advocated both during the previous administration and in the current administration, for the U.S. to adopt a comprehensive policy to address the unique situation of these defenseless minorities. I have pressed for a high-level human rights representative at the U.S. embassy in Baghdad. Such an approach is critical, with the U.S. presence in Iraq drawing down and our bilateral relations now governed by a 'Strategic Framework Agreement.'

"Among other things, we must be actively engaging the government of Iraq to press for adequate security at places of worship and ensure minority representation in local police units. These are just some of the steps that could be taken to assist in the preservation of these ancient faith communities. We have a moral obligation to do so. I was reminded of this again last week while meeting with a visiting high-level delegation of Iraqi bishops. Their impassioned pleas must not be ignored.

"Turning to Egypt, Eli Lake pointed out in a July 18 Washington Times piece that, 'the Obama administration ended support for a small fund operated by the U.S. Embassy in Cairo that supported groups promoting Egyptian democracy and that bypassed any clearance from the Egyptian government.'

"Ellen Bork, director of democracy and human rights at the Foreign Policy Initiative, summarized the situation well in a recent Weekly Standard piece, writing 'doing something for democracy in Egypt would require a policy reversal in Washington. .... since the end of the Bush administration and the beginning of the Obama administration, there has been retreat-including a cut in funding for democracy programs and acquiescence to an Egyptian veto over which groups may receive U.S. funds.'

"Ironically, U.S. support for democracy promotion in Egypt is dwindling at a time when the people of Egypt are increasingly dissatisfied with the current regime. A Washington Post story yesterday reported that 'a protest in Alexandria last month was attended by 4,000 people—a high number in Egypt, where many people are afraid to join demonstrations.'

"Lorne Craner, president of the International Republican Institute, echoed these sentiments about the administration's human rights and democracy promotion policy in Egypt and elsewhere around the world, in recent testimony before the House Committee on Foreign Affairs. He said 'a lack of strong, consistent leadership from the top of the administration . . . has become apparent to the bureaucracy; one result is the cutting or slowing of funding for democracy programming in countries such as Belarus, Cuba, Egypt, Iran, North Korea, Venezuela and Zimbabwe. Another consequence is that our embassies abroad are providing less diplomatic support on human rights and democracy. Asked about the U.S. position on democracy in Egypt, our Ambassador to Cairo praises the country's press freedoms.'

"Those yearning for greater freedoms in Egypt are not alone in facing the ire of their government. So, too, Egypt's Coptic Christian community faces increasing hardship.

"USCIRF, in its recently released annual report, described a deteriorating situation for this community. USCIRF found that 'the reporting period marked a significant upsurge in violence targeting Coptic Orthodox Christians. The Egyptian government has not taken sufficient steps to halt the repression of and discrimination against Christians and other religious believers, or, in many cases, to punish those responsible for violence or other severe violations of religious freedom. This increase in violence, and the failure to prosecute those responsible, fosters a growing climate of impunity.'

"Even though our own State Department has concluded that the last three years have been marked by a decline in religious freedom conditions in Egypt, there has been not significant change in U.S. policy.

"Elsewhere in the region, Morocco is actually an example where American citizens, many of whom are people of faith, are facing a hostile government. Over the last four months dozens of American citizens and scores of other foreign nationals have been deported and denied re-entry into the Kingdom of Morocco for allegedly proselytizing.

"Authorities have refused to turn over any evidence or offer any explanation of the charges. Among the individuals who were deported or denied reentry were businessmen, educators, humanitarian and social workers, many of whom had resided in Morocco for over a decade in full compliance with the law. Additionally, those deported were forced to leave the country within two hours of being questioned by authorities, leaving everything behind.

"Over the past several weeks, I have met with and heard from scores of Moroccan Christians. Many feel that their voices have long been silenced that that these events highlight some of the pressures they experience.

"On March 19, I wrote to the U.S. ambassador to Morocco, Sam Kaplan, sharing my intent to meet the Moroccan ambassador to the U.S., and urging Ambassador Kaplan to 'convey to the government of Morocco that members of Congress are watching these events closely and the outcome could negatively affect our bilateral relations.' I have also spoken with Ambassador Kaplan on several occasions and shared with him my deep disappointment that the U.S. embassy and the State Department have not been more publicly outspoken on behalf of these American citizens.

"It is the primary responsibility of the U.S.' embassies to defend and advocate for U.S. citizens and interests abroad.

"Unfortunately, the Moroccan government has been utterly unwilling to compromise. Perhaps they think they don't need to given the number of high-powered lobbyists, including several former members of Congress, they have on retainer. If that is the case, they are sorely mistaken. I have urged the Millennium Challenge Corporation (MCC) to suspend the five-year compact with Morocco which is worth $697.5 million. The MCC awards compacts on the basis of 17 key indicators of eligibility, six of which fall under the category of 'ruling justly.' However, recent events raise serious questions regarding the Moroccan government's willingness to abide by the principles outlined in the MCC indicators.

"A recent Wall Street Journal op-ed rightly pointed out that during a time of economic hardship 'U.S. taxpayers won't tolerate financing governments that mistreat Americans solely because of their religion.'

"Can the administration not even find its voice when it comes to the rights of U.S. citizens abroad being trampled?

"I've been assured that the State Department is raising the matter privately with the Moroccan Government. Frankly, this is insufficient. The manner and the means by which we raise concerns of this nature with foreign governments communicate a whole host of unspoken messages. Do we simply have a private meeting with the ambassador and ask him to look into the matter? Or does the Department's Press Secretary issue a statement expressing deep concern? Or better yet, does President Obama call the King of Morocco and make it clear that treating American citizens this way will not be tolerated? Each approach has distinct undertones which highlight the level of priority and seriousness that the U.S. government places on a particular issue. Privately raising the issue with Moroccan government officials is a far cry from what we need to be doing publicly.

"Even as the administration is struggling to find his voice on human rights, changes within the State Department threaten to institutionalize the marginalization of these core issues.

"The State Department's International Religious Freedom (IRF) Office had been without ambassadorial leadership, as is required by law, for more than 18 months. After increasing pressure from Congress and religious freedom advocacy groups, Obama named Suzan Johnson Cook to this post in June. She has not yet been confirmed.

"With a void in senior leadership at the IRF office, I have been increasingly alarmed by reports that the office is being subsumed into the Bureau of Democracy, Human Rights and Labor.

"Tom Farr, the first director of the U.S. State Department Office of International Religious Freedom, described what is happening this way in a Washington Post online column: 'The ambassador will not report directly to the secretary of state as do other ambassadors at large (all of whom are experts in their fields). The staffers who reported to predecessors will not report to Johnson Cook should she be confirmed. The position will be emasculated, in direct contravention of the legislation that created it.'

"In a May 25 letter to Assistant Secretary for Democracy, Human Rights and Labor (DRL) Michael Posner, I raised these concerns in detail. I submit a copy of the letter for the record.

"If the changes described by Farr move forward this could potentially violate U.S. law and break with 10 years of established practice under previous administrations, both Democratic and Republican. The Ambassador-at-Large position was established under the International Religious Freedom Act of 1998

(IRFA), of which I was the primary author, to promote religious freedom abroad. The legislation specifically states that 'there is established within the Department of State an Office on International Religious Freedom that shall be headed by the Ambassador-at-Large for International Religious Freedom.'

"Considering the importance of religious freedom to U.S. foreign policy and human rights promotion, I am alarmed by the possibility that DRL could be removing supervisory control from the Ambassador-at-Large over the Office of International Religious Freedom.

"These reported changes combined with the long ambassadorial vacancy do not bode well for the Bahai leader imprisoned in Iran's notorious prisons, or for the Ahmadi Muslim in Pakistan subject to officially sanctioned discrimination and persecution. Who will be their advocate?

"The IRF Office is but one example of internal changes at the State Department. The congressionally mandated Office to Monitor and Combat Anti-Semitism, headed by a special envoy, only has a single dedicated staff person. During the Bush administration there were 3-5 employees at various points. An April 2010 CNN story featured the findings of a study released on the eve of Holocaust Remembrance Day, which found that the number of anti-Semitic incidents more than doubled from 2008 to 2009. At a time when anti-Semitism is on the rise globally, the Special Envoy is relying almost exclusively on the already stretched thin IRF office for her staffing needs, therefore making it more difficult for the IRF office to fulfill its Congressional mandate.

"If the old adage 'personnel is policy' is true, then you could surmise that the absence of necessary personnel is itself a shift in policy priorities.

"There are staff vacancies elsewhere at the State Department that are deeply troubling. On June 24, I wrote Secretary of State Clinton about the Office of the Special Coordinator for Tibetan Issues. I submit the letter for the Record. I was prompted to write the letter in part because it had come to my attention that there was only one person working in the office.

"Congress codified the position of the Special Coordinator for Tibetan Issues as part of the Tibetan Policy Act of 2002. Not long after the establishment of the office, Congress approved language directing that the office 'consist of three professional full-time staff members and additional support staff, as needed, in addition to the special coordinator.' The current inadequate staffing levels, at that point 17 months into the administration, were troubling and at odds with congressional intent.

"Further, the congressionally mandated Report on Tibet Negotiations, which is due to Congress by March 31 of each year, has not yet been submitted. These developments or lack thereof send a message about the priority this administration is placing on Tibet. That message is not inconsistent with a message the White House sent last fall in declining to meet with the Dalai Lama when he was visiting Washington—the first time since 1991 that the Nobel Prize recipient and spiritual leader was not afforded a meeting with the president of the U.S.

"In closing, the complexities of foreign policy do not escape me. I am well aware that there are multiple dimensions to our bilateral relations with countries around the globe. But if the United States of America cannot be relied upon to speak out on behalf of those whose voices have been silenced, then it is indeed a dark day for millions around the world yearning to breathe the sweet air of freedom.

"Where the administration fails to find its voice, Congress must stand in the gap. For decades human rights enjoyed bipartisan support in this body. Now I fear these issues have fallen victim to bipartisan apathy.

"Too often, we underestimate the power of our words, or worse yet, the power of our silence.

"The late Robert Kennedy, speaking in 1966 Cape Town, South Africa, to a gathering of students committed to challenging the injustice of apartheid, famously said 'each time a man stands up for an ideal, or acts to improve the lot of others, or strikes out against injustice, he sends forth a tiny ripple of hope, and crossing each other from a million different centers of energy and daring those ripples build a current which can sweep down the mightiest walls of oppression and resistance.'

"America must stand up for the ideals upon which our own experiment in self-governance was founded. America must strike out against injustice, whatever form it takes. America must believe that even the mightiest walls of oppression can tumble and work toward that end.

"The hour is late and the stakes are high. Will the administration accept this charge? Can this president find his voice? Will 'ripples of hope' once again infuse America's foreign policy?"

DOCUMENT 3: HUMAN RIGHTS ADVOCATES PRESENT PLAN OF ACTION TO OBAMA ADMINISTRATION

By Freedom House, Human Rights First and Other Human Rights Advocates
Monday, February 22, 2010
Urge President to prioritize freedom of expression and association, support human rights defenders

Washington, DC—Freedom House, Human Rights First and dozens of human rights advocates from 27 countries today released the U.S.-specific portion of a Plan of Action to advance global human rights. The plan, which comes just days after the group met with President Obama and senior administration officials at the White House, includes a recommendation that the U.S. prioritize support for human rights defenders and independent media through the protection of freedom of expression and association in U.S. foreign policy. The recommendations for the U.S. government, formulated during the 2010 Human Rights Summit held in Washington, DC last week, form part of a larger plan of action for all governments and multi-lateral institutions to be released in the days ahead.

The 2010 Human Rights Summit, hosted by Human Rights First and Freedom House, brought together dissidents and human rights advocates from around the globe – including Iran, Uganda, Taiwan, Egypt, Russia, and Venezuela—with U.S. policy makers, officials from other democratic governments, and human rights and freedom of expression activists. During their meeting with President Obama, summit participants provided a first-hand account of the "on the ground" situation for human rights defenders, highlighted ways in which U.S. policy has impacted their work, and put forward ideas for improving upon these policies in the protection of fundamental freedoms.

"Human rights defenders work every day, often at great personal risk, to bring about positive, lasting change within their societies. By challenging injustice and raising awareness about human rights, these local activists aim to create a more secure world, one in which all people can live in freedom and dignity," said Human Rights First President and CEO Elisa Massimino. "The U.S. shares this goal and has pledged to support these courageous activists in their work. Our job is to make sure that U.S. policy is designed to deliver on that promise. The summit's recommendations spell out what more the U.S. can do to stand with those fighting to advance freedom everywhere."

Among the recommendations released today are calls for the U.S. to formulate a strategy to promote freedom of expression in countries where it is under threat and fulfill its pledge to make Internet freedom an international priority, to engage with other countries in order to counter government initiatives that threaten freedoms of association and expression in multilateral bodies, and to provide direct support to human rights defenders to participate in multilateral, regional and sub-regional human rights mechanisms. A more complete list follows this release.

"It was important for the President to have heard first hand from those who are on the front lines in order for the administration to develop a set of policies that truly address the global assault on freedom of expression and association," said Jennifer Windsor, executive director of Freedom House. "The meeting with the defenders reinforced the idea that bi-lateral talks between the U.S. and other countries by any government agency must carry a consistent message on human rights if we hope to strengthen our defense of fundamental freedoms around the world."

The summit's format combined working groups and participatory discussions about current threats to freedom of expression and association and the role that governments must play in the defense of these freedoms. In addition to the action plan, the summit gave government officials the opportunity to hear from activists engaged in front-line struggles for freedom and democracy. A group of the advocates will remain in Washington, DC this week to meet with officials from various government agencies to present the plan of action.

For more information about the summit visit www.humanrightssummit.org. To schedule interviews with summit participants, please contact Human Rights First's Brenda Bowser Soder (bowsersoderb@humanrights-first.org, 202-370-3323) or Freedom House's Mary McGuire (mcguire@freedomhouse.org, 202-747-7035).

2010 Washington Human Rights Summit
Plan of Action
Headline Action Points for the U.S. Government

Human rights defenders from more than two dozen countries met in Washington between February 17–19, 2010 and produced the following action plan in two parts: these headline action points for the U.S. government; and a fuller Plan of Action directed to the U.S. government, other governments, multilateral organizations and civil society organizations.

Introduction

Recognizing that its human rights practices have a far-reaching global impact, the U.S. government must abide by its commitments to safeguard universal human rights. The U.S. should prioritize support for and protection of human rights defenders in its foreign policy by emphasizing the promotion of the basic freedoms of expression and association through its policies and activities around the world.

To that end the U.S. government should:

Policy Formulation

- Ensure that advancing human rights, including the protection of the freedoms of association and expression, are operationalized through a National Security Presidential Directive or some comparable mechanism, and properly resourced.
- Ensure that the promotion of freedoms of association and expression are included in a national foreign assistance strategy.
- Strengthen the U.S. Guiding Principles on Non-Governmental Organizations (issued in 2006) by developing them into action guidelines for embassies, missions and other U.S. diplomatic representatives around the world.
- Formulate a strategy to promote freedom of expression in countries where it is under threat and fulfill its pledge to make Internet freedom an international priority.
- Facilitate, support and strengthen engagement by independent civil society organizations in regional and sub-regional multilateral bodies.
- Combat terrorism and violent extremism by promoting more human rights, not less.

Diplomatic Engagement

- Ensure that consistent human rights and democracy messages are conveyed in bilateral discussions at all levels and in all areas.
- When establishing bi-lateral structures to deal with human rights issues, include local civil society activists in their development and functioning.
- In countries where freedoms of association and expression are curtailed, ensure that embassies and missions have a plan of action for supporting independent civil society organizations (CSOs), media and human rights defenders. This includes, but is not limited to:
  - Convening regular meetings and building relationships with human rights defenders and journalists to show support for their work and remaining engaged in their efforts;
  - Monitoring trials of human rights defenders.
- Engage with other countries in order to counter government initiatives that threaten freedoms of association and expression in multilateral bodies.
- Lead multilateral efforts to promote a single Internet and end censorship.

Foreign assistance

- Ensure that the integrity and independence of U.S. government assistance is maintained. In those countries where restrictions exist on providing international aid to independent CSOs, the U.S. government should devise strategies for assisting civil society, and should register its objections with the host country's government. The U.S. government should not acquiesce to the demands of other governments to vet or restrict U.S. foreign assistance to CSOs.
- Remove onerous U.S. conditions on foreign assistance that jeopardize freedom of association and undermine CSOs.
- Provide direct support to human rights defenders to participate in multilateral, regional and sub-regional human rights mechanisms.

http://www.humanrightsfirst.org/2010/02/22/Human-Rights-Advocates-Present-Plan-of-Action-to-Obama-Administration/

DOCUMENT 4: EMPTY PROMISES? OBAMA'S HESITANT EMBRACE OF HUMAN RIGHTS

By: Kenneth Roth

Published in: *Foreign Affairs*

February 24, 2010

Obama's refusal to end the use of military commissions and detention without trial risks perpetuating the spirit of Guantánamo even after the physical facility has been shut.

After eight years of the Bush administration, with its torture of suspected terrorists and disregard for international law, Barack Obama's victory in the November 2008 U.S. presidential election seemed a breath of fresh air to human rights activists. Obama took office at a moment when the world desperately needed renewed U.S. leadership. In his inaugural address, Obama immediately signaled that, unlike Bush, he would reject as false "the choice between our safety and our ideals."

Obama faces the challenge of restoring the U.S.' credibility at a time when repressive governments—emboldened by the increasing influence of authoritarian powers such as China and Russia—seek to undermine the enforcement of international human rights standards. As he put it when accepting the Nobel Peace Prize, the U.S. cannot "insist that others follow the rules of the road if we refuse to follow them ourselves." His Nobel speech in Oslo also affirmed the U.S. government's respect for the Geneva Conventions. "Even as we confront a vicious adversary that abides by no rules," Obama argued, "I believe the United States of America must remain a standard bearer in the conduct of war. That is what makes us different from those whom we fight. That is a source of our strength."

When it comes to promoting human rights at home and abroad, there has undoubtedly been a marked improvement in presidential rhetoric. However, the translation of those words into deeds remains incomplete.

AN INCOMPLETE REVERSAL

Obama moved rapidly to reverse the most abusive aspects of the Bush administration's approach to fighting terrorism. Two days after taking office, he insisted that all U.S. interrogators, including those from the CIA, abide by the stringent standards adopted by the U.S. military in the wake of the Abu Ghraib debacle. He also ordered the shuttering of all secret CIA detention facilities, where many suspects "disappeared" and were tortured between 2001 and 2008. Finally, he promised to close the detention center at Guantánamo Bay, Cuba, within a year.

But it is not enough for the government to stop using torture; perpetrators must also be punished. The Obama administration has so far refused to investigate and prosecute those who ordered or committed torture—a necessary step to prevent future administrations from committing the crime. While in office, as he did during the campaign, Obama has repeatedly spoken of wanting to "look forward, not back." And although Attorney General Eric Holder has launched a "preliminary review" of interrogators who exceeded orders, he has until now refrained from prosecuting those who ordered torture or wrote the legal memos justifying it. This lets senior officials—arguably those who are most culpable—off the hook.

Meanwhile, Obama's one-year deadline for closing Guantánamo has slipped because of congressional opposition and the complexity of deciding how to handle the cases of more than 200 detainees. The real issue, however, is less when Guantánamo will close than how. Human Rights Watch and other nongovernmental organizations (NGOs) have urged the administration to prosecute detainees in regular federal courts, repatriate them, or resettle them in safe countries willing to accept them. However, the White House has insisted on maintaining two other options: prosecuting suspects before military commissions or continuing to hold them indefinitely without charge or trial.

The Obama administration's military commissions would avoid the most problematic aspect of the Bush administration's commissions—the power to introduce at trial statements obtained through coercion and abuse. But the Obama commissions, as approved by Congress, continue to suffer from a lack of independence (their judges are military officers, who must report to superiors in the chain of command), controversy about the offenses they cover (some are not clearly war crimes or were not clearly criminal at the time they were committed), and untested rules of procedure (unlike regular courts or even courts-martial, which have well-established procedures, the rules for military commissions are being constructed largely from scratch). These due process shortcomings are likely to keep the public and the press focused on the fairness of the trials accorded suspects, rather than the gravity of their alleged crimes.

Obama has also tried to distinguish himself from Bush in his approach to detaining suspects without charge or trial. The new administration has abandoned Bush's claim of inherent executive authority and relied instead on an interpretation of Congress' 2001 authorization to use military force against al Qaeda, the Taliban, and associated groups. But both approaches still permit the detention of suspects not captured on a traditional battlefield, such as in Afghanistan. That is a controversial approach because it permits U.S. soldiers or law enforcement officials to indefinitely detain suspected terrorists anywhere in the world without regard to the due process standards of the U.S. or any other country.

Obama's refusal to end the use of military commissions and detention without trial risks perpetuating the spirit of Guantánamo even after the physical facility has been shut.

STREET CRED

The Bush administration had difficulty encouraging foreign leaders to respect human rights because of its perceived arrogance, hypocrisy, and unilateralism. Since taking office, Obama has worked hard to restore U.S. credibility.

Obama's speeches in Accra, Cairo, Moscow, Oslo, and Shanghai have been a key vehicle for promoting a renewed U.S. human rights agenda. Rather than merely preaching abstract principles, Obama has drawn examples from the U.S.' checkered history and his own life story to encourage other nations to respect human rights. The humility in this approach avoids Bush's hectoring tone and places the U.S. squarely within the community of nations as a country that, like others, struggles to respect human rights and benefits when it does so.

In Accra, in a rebuke to President Bill Clinton's embrace of authoritarian African leaders in the 1990s, Obama observed, "Africa doesn't need strongmen, it needs strong institutions," such as "strong parliaments; honest police forces; independent judges; an independent press; a vibrant private sector; a civil society." However, Obama has not put sustained pressure on such U.S. allies as Paul Kagame of Rwanda or Meles Zenawi of Ethiopia to reform their increasingly authoritarian rule. Forceful U.S. condemnations have been largely limited to such pariahs as Robert Mugabe of Zimbabwe, Omar al-Bashir of Sudan, and the military junta in Guinea.

In Cairo, Obama rejected Bush's attempt to justify the invasion of Iraq as an exercise in democracy promotion, declaring that "no system of government can or should be imposed by one nation on any other." But he insisted nonetheless that the U.S. remains committed "to governments that reflect the will of the people." He stressed the importance of principled conduct even when it works against short-term U.S. interests, suggesting that, unlike Bush, he would accept an electoral victory by Egypt's Islamist opposition group, the Muslim Brotherhood.

Frustrating as that comment might have been to the government of Egyptian President Hosni Mubarak, Obama has generally shown too much deference to his hosts. He has not publicly criticized U.S. allies in the Middle East that violate democratic principles, nor is there any evidence that he has privately encouraged these authoritarian governments to move in a more democratic direction. For example, Washington has promised Cairo that there will be no human rights conditions placed on U.S. economic assistance to Egypt and has acquiesced in the Egyptian government's demand that all funds from the U.S. Agency for International Development earmarked for NGOs go only to those groups that comply with the Mubarak government's onerous restrictions. Obama's desire to maintain close relations with Mubarak, especially in the hope that he might assist in resolving the Israeli-Palestinian conflict, seems to have taken precedence over the human rights principles Obama articulated in his Cairo speech.

In Moscow, Obama met with civil-society representatives and praised the vital role they play in Russian society. He explained that criticisms and tough questions from U.S. civil-society organizations help him make better decisions and strengthen the U.S.—a bold statement in a country where NGOs monitoring human rights or promoting government accountability are routinely harassed. Yet his administration has not applied sustained pressure on the Russian government to stop trying to silence leaders of NGOs. Nor has Obama warned Russian leaders that serious abuses, such as the brazen murders of activists and journalists fighting human rights abuses in the North Caucasus, could damage the bilateral relationship.

Similarly, in China, Obama followed in the footsteps of successive U.S. presidents by downplaying the importance of human rights in favor of promoting trade, economic ties, and diplomatic cooperation. Before a handpicked audience of "future Chinese leaders" in Shanghai, he spoke of the U.S.' journey up from slavery and the struggles for women's and workers' rights, making clear that the U.S., too, has a far-from-perfect human rights record. He affirmed the U.S.' bedrock belief "that all men and women are created equal, and possess certain fundamental rights." However, in a question-and-answer session, he seemed to suggest that China's draconian "great firewall" on the Internet was a reflection of different "traditions," rather than demanding that it be torn down. That remark led to a storm of criticism from Chinese bloggers, and Obama left the country appearing to be in thrall to Chinese economic power and barely interested in risking anything to protect the rights of the 1.3 billion Chinese still living under a dictatorship.

In a speech at Georgetown University a few weeks later, Secretary of State Hillary Clinton justified this approach as "principled pragmatism," and administration officials have spoken privately of building up political capital to press China on human rights in the future. But there is no such pressure today. From Clinton's February 2009 statement that human rights "can't interfere" with other U.S. interests in China to Obama's refusal to meet with the Dalai Lama in October, Washington has consistently failed to confront China's authoritarian rulers on questions of religious and political freedom.

MULTILATERALISM LITE

During the 2008 election campaign, Obama promised to replace Bush's notorious unilateralism with a greater commitment to cooperation, alliance building, and engagement with adversaries. One early symbol of this new approach was the decision to reverse Bush's policy and authorize U.S. participation in the UN Human Rights Council—an important step toward trying to salvage that troubled institution. The 47-member council has been dominated by authoritarian governments since its inception in June 2007. Its members have incessantly criticized Israel and have generally seemed more concerned with protecting abusive leaders than condemning them for human rights violations.

But the positive step of joining the council was significantly offset in September, when Washington distanced itself from a council-sponsored report—written by the respected South African jurist Richard Goldstone—that accused Israel (as well as Hamas) of war crimes during its December 2008-January 2009 invasion of the Gaza Strip and called for the perpetrators to be brought to justice. Washington's strong criticism of the report called into question Obama's commitment to the impartial application of human rights principles to friends and foes alike. The move was particularly unfortunate because the report broke new ground for the council by criticizing an Israeli adversary, Hamas. Obama had it right in Oslo, when he said that "only a just peace based on the inherent rights and dignity of every individual can truly be lasting." Unfortunately, he has not yet applied that insight to Israel.

The Obama administration has also taken a more positive approach to international law than the wary and often hostile Bush administration did. Accelerating a trend that began in the late Bush years, Obama has actively supported the work of the International Criminal Court, especially in Darfur and the Democratic Republic of the Congo, as well as, more recently, in Kenya. For the first time, U.S. officials have participated as observers in deliberations about the tribunal's future.

The U.S. is also embracing certain UN human rights treaties, after an eight-year hiatus. It signed the new Convention on the Rights of People with Disabilities. In October, when Israeli Prime Minister Benjamin Netanyahu suggested that the laws of war should be amended to make it easier for states to fight irregular armed groups, Susan Rice, the U.S. ambassador to the United Nations, pushed back by reaffirming Washington's commitment to the Geneva Conventions—a position that Obama himself reiterated in Oslo.

Yet there have been limits to Obama's commitment to international law. His administration has sent mixed signals about a 1997 treaty banning antipersonnel land mines, first announcing that it would not sign the treaty and then saying that a policy review was still ongoing, even though the U.S. has not used, produced, or exported these weapons in the 12 years since the treaty was established. The administration has so far failed to seize this easy opportunity to embrace an important multilateral treaty. Similarly, the administration has not yet joined many of its NATO allies in endorsing the 2008 Convention on Cluster Munitions, which bans the use of these indiscriminate weapons, even though the U.S. military has not used them since 2003 and recognizes the danger they pose to civilians. And although the Obama administration has declared that it plans to ratify the UN Convention on the Elimination of All Forms of Discrimination Against Women, it has not pressed for Senate ratification of it, nor has it pressed for Senate ratification of the UN Convention on the Rights of the Child. The U.S. has the dubious distinction of being the only country other than Somalia not to have ratified the children's rights treaty and finds itself in the unenviable company of only Iran, Nauru, Somalia, Sudan, and Tonga when it comes to the treaty on women's rights.

DESTRUCTIVE ENGAGEMENT

Obama has rightfully rejected Bush's policy of dealing with repressive governments mainly by refusing to talk to them. His new approach has been most visible in Myanmar (also called Burma) and Sudan, where U.S. envoys have increased communication with senior officials without abandoning pressure on their governments to curb repression. In the case of Sudan, despite some mixed signals, the administration has managed to engage the government on the importance of curbing violence in Darfur and southern Sudan without speaking directly with President Bashir, who has been indicted as a war criminal.

In Central Asia, however, this emphasis on engaging authoritarian regimes has yielded disappointing results. In the highly repressive nations of Turkmenistan and Uzbekistan, where the dominant U.S. concern is sustaining military supply lines into neighboring Afghanistan, the Obama administration has refrained from publicly articulating specific human rights concerns. It has limited itself instead to general statements about U.S. support for democracy and the rule of law while stressing U.S. respect for the sovereign prerogatives of these countries' autocratic leaders. The administration has also largely squandered the opportunity to push for reform in Kazakhstan, despite the fact that its repressive government was particularly susceptible to pressure in the months before it assumed the rotating chairmanship of the Organization for Security and Cooperation in Europe.

In Afghanistan, Obama administration officials recognized from the outset that abusive and corrupt warlords linked to President Hamid Karzai's government were fueling the Taliban's popularity throughout the country. After Karzai's tainted electoral victory in August, the administration pushed his government to distance itself from some officials with blood on their hands or ill-gotten gains in their pockets. However, it is not yet clear whether Washington is prepared to sever its own ties with some of these tainted officials, such as the president's younger brother, Ahmed Wali Karzai, a powerful figure in Kandahar who is reportedly on the CIA payroll despite being connected to drug traffickers. Nor is there any indication that U.S. Special Forces will abandon the abusive militia they have hired in provinces such as Herat and Uruzgan.

Across the border in Pakistan, the Obama administration has been providing conditional military aid to the elected government—a more principled approach than its predecessor's, which unconditionally supported the autocratic rule of General Pervez Musharraf. Washington also accepted the reinstatement of ousted Supreme Court Chief Justice Iftikhar Chaudhry, even though his constitutional rulings and his revival of corruption charges could imperil President Asif Ali Zardari, a U.S. partner. Still, Obama has not taken up the cases of thousands of people who disappeared during Musharraf's rule. Nor has he pushed for human rights abusers from the Pakistani military, including Musharraf himself, to be held accountable.

Closer to home, in Latin America, Obama has cooperated with regional allies far more than his predecessor did. Unlike Bush, who tacitly accepted the 2002 coup attempt against Venezuela's Hugo Chávez, Obama was quick to join regional allies in condemning the ouster of Honduran President Manuel Zelaya last June and calling for his reinstatement—even if the administration did not adequately pressure the de facto government to accept Zelaya's return.

The White House has rightly deferred consideration of a much-sought-after free-trade agreement with Colombia, whose government has failed to dismantle the highly abusive paramilitary forces responsible for the murder of hundreds of trade unionists and others. Genuinely dismantling those paramilitary forces, and holding their leaders and accomplices accountable, should be a prerequisite to any free-trade agreement. At the same time, however, Obama has continued the misguided Bush-era policy of certifying the Colombian military's compliance with the human rights standards necessary to receive U.S. military aid—despite an ongoing atmosphere of impunity for the soldiers and officers responsible for widespread extrajudicial executions.

Obama has similarly fallen short in Mexico, where the U.S. government promised to contribute $1.35 billion over several years to the government for equipment and training to combat drug trafficking. Roughly 15 percent of these funds are dependent on Mexico's compliance with certain human rights requirements, including bringing military abuses under the jurisdiction of civilian courts. Mexico has utterly failed to meet that requirement, but the State Department has nevertheless allowed a portion of these funds to be delivered. All of this calls into question Obama's commitment to curbing military abuses and ending official impunity south of the border.

WALKING THE WALK

From a human rights perspective, there is no doubt that the Obama White House has done better than the Bush administration. As one would expect from so eloquent a president, Obama has gotten the rhetoric largely right. The challenge remains to translate poetic speeches into prosaic policy—and live up to the principles he has so impressively articulated. Making that shift will not be easy, but the consistent application of human rights principles is essential if Washington is to redeem its reputation and succeed in promoting the global values that Obama rightly believes are the key to prosperity and stability throughout the world.

DOCUMENT 5: US-TARGETED-BY-HUMAN-RIGHTS-ABUSERS-AT-ITS-UNIVERSAL-PERIODIC-REVIEW

Published on November 5, 2010
by Brett Schaefer and Steven Groves WebMemo #3050

The U.S. underwent a three-hour review of its human rights record before the United Nations Human Rights Council (HRC) on November 5 under that body's Universal Periodic Review (UPR). As predicted the farcical nature of the process was immediately apparent as serial human rights violators Cuba, Venezuela, Iran, Russia, China, Sudan, and North Korea queued up to lecture the U.S. on its human rights lapses and instruct it on how to improve its observance of the human rights that those countries routinely deny their own citizens.

The HRC ignored the Alice in Wonderland nature of the U.S. review and acted as if it were indeed conducting a serious human rights review. While this treatment was inevitable, the U.S. grist for the mill was in its UPR report Ultimately, the primary problem is the decision by the Obama Administration to legitimize the HRC through U.S. membership, which has given the council and its farcical UPR process undue credibility. The Obama Administration was mistaken to believe it could improve the HRC from within and should instead press for fundamental reforms at the mandatory review of the council next year.

The Obama Administration's Wrongheaded Decision to Join the Human Rights Council

The HRC was created in 2006 to replace the U.N. Commission on Human Rights, a body that had failed to hold governments accountable for violating basic human rights and fundamental freedoms. During negotiations to establish the HRC, many basic reforms and standards to ensure that the new council would not simply be a repeat of the commission did not receive sufficient support in the General Assembly. As a result, the HRC has been no better—and in some ways, worse—than the commission it replaced.

Anticipating this outcome, the Bush Administration decided not to seek a seat at the Geneva-based council and distanced itself from the council's proceedings except in instances of—deep national interest. The Obama Administration reversed this policy, arguing that the U.S. would be able to improve the HRC from within. Unfortunately, the performance of the HRC with the U.S. as a member has been virtually indistinguishable from its performance absent U.S. membership.

The Flawed UPR

The council's UPR was created to hold the human rights practices of every country open for public examination and criticism. Under the UPR, countries are supposed to self-assess their human rights records with input from civil society and submit a report to the HRC. That report—combined with submissions from NGOs and information from independent U.N. human rights experts, human rights treaty bodies, and other U.N. human rights bodies—is used as the basis for the UPR, which culminates in a three-hour dialogue in the Human Rights Council between the state under review and the other U.N. member states.

Unfortunately, past UPR sessions have featured countries like China, Cuba, Iran, and North Korea offering false reports to the council, laughably affirming their commitment to fundamental human rights and freedoms. These patently dishonest reports were accepted at face value and approved by the majority of member states in the council. Indeed, these countries received relatively little criticism during their reviews.

By contrast, the U.S. was roundly criticized during its review earlier today in Geneva. Countries resentful of the U.S. and its practice of criticizing their human rights records gamed the system to paint the U.S. as one of the world's worst human rights violators, with Cuba circulating an advance—sign-up sheet to allow U.S. critics to dominate the two hours reserved for country statements on America's record. The results were predictable:

- Cuba demanded an end to the "blockade against Cuba," which it described as a "crime of genocide" and a violation of the human rights and freedoms of Cubans, U.S. citizens, and third-party states. Cuba also accused the U.S. of harboring "terrorists" responsible for the "deaths of more than 3,000 Cubans" and sanctioning and committing war crimes and torture.

- Venezuela likewise demanded that the U.S. end the "infamous blockade of Cuba," abolish the death penalty, abrogate U.S. law that "permits slavery as a punishment," remove limits on freedom of expression, and cease spying on its own citizens. It also accused the U.S. of treating its agricultural workers as slaves and accused the U.S. of xenophobia, war crimes, terrorism, and other human rights violations.

- Russia congratulated the Obama Administration for efforts taken to eliminate "some of the most odious violations of human rights which were committed in the war on terrorism" and bring those responsible for torture in secret detention centers and Guantánamo to justice and pay compensation to the victims. It also demanded that the U.S. prohibit the death penalty.

- Iran condemned the U.S. and expressed its deep concern over the "extensive and systematic violation [of human rights] by the U.S. government at both national and international levels." It called on the U.S. to prohibit torture, close Guantánamo, halt serious violations of human rights, bring domestic legislation into compliance with international human rights standards, stop violating the freedoms of its citizens, try its "war criminals," end child prostitution, and adopt legislation to ban "Islamophobia."

- China voiced concern over "gaps" in U.S. law preventing full protection of human rights and the failure of the U.S. to ratify all human rights treaties. It specifically condemned the tendency toward "excessive use of force" by U.S. law enforcement and widespread discrimination against minorities and immigrants.

- Nicaragua asserted that the U.S. "since its very origin, [has] used force indiscriminately as the central pillar of its policy of conquest and expansion and causing death and destruction. Latin America has been one of the victims of this genocide caused by military dictatorships imposed and sustained by the U.S." Nicaragua then stated that the U.S. "pretends to be the guardian of human rights in the world but, in reality, is "the one which most systematically violates human rights." Nicaragua went on to demand that the U.S. abolish the death penalty, compensate Nicaragua for the acts of "terrorism" committed by the U.S. under President Reagan, and assume responsibility for the global warming consequences of capitalism.

- North Korea condemned "systematic and widespread human rights violations committed by the United States of America at home and abroad," including torture and illegal extrajudicial killings by U.S. troops. It also demanded that the U.S. abolish the North Korean Human Rights Act because it represents a "flagrant breach" of North Korea's sovereignty and violates the dignity and rights of the North Korean people.

- Sudan urged the U.S. to ratify all of the core international human rights treaties, branded Guantánamo as a violation of human rights and called for its closure, called for the end of the U.S. practice of registering the entry and exit of citizens of 25 countries from the Middle East and North Africa as discriminatory racial profiling, and demanded the end of the sanctions against the Sudanese government for genocide in Darfur.

The audacity of these countries in accusing the U.S. of human rights violations is staggering. While the U.S. is not perfect, it is as respectful and observant of human rights as any state sitting on the HRC and far superior to these countries that perpetrate serious, widespread violations of human rights daily. But to hear comments during the UPR, one would think that the U.S. was the worst human rights abuser on the planet.

American Self-Flagellation

The U.S. is not blameless for its treatment at the council. Although the U.S. self-assessment generally defends America's strong record in preserving human rights, including a robust defense of the U.S. Constitution as the basis for and protection of human rights in the U.S., it also provided ample fodder for those bent on using the UPR to deflect criticism of their own human rights records or assert a false moral equivalency between themselves and the U.S. on human rights.

For instance, the report inappropriately disparages Arizona's immigration law. Unsettled domestic legal issues such as immigration should be presented, if at all, impartially within international forums like the UPR, especially when such issues are complex and controversial. Obviously, countries were quick to capitalize on this as evidence of America's discrimination toward Hispanics and immigrants, both legal and illegal.

Another paragraph in the U.S. report demonstrates the type of self-flagellation that the HRC expects of the U.S.:

We are not satisfied with a situation where the unemployment rate for African Americans is 15.8%, for Hispanics 12.4%, and for whites 8.8%, as it was in February 2010. We are not satisfied that a person with disabilities is only one fourth as likely to be employed as a person without disabilities. We are not satisfied when fewer than half of African-American and Hispanic families own homes while three quarters of white families do. We are not satisfied that whites are twice as likely as Native Americans to have a college degree.

This paragraph's emphasis on group rights and achieving "equality of results" rather than only "equality of opportunity" is consistent with the HRC's flawed view of the nature of human rights and what member states are obligated to guarantee to their citizens.

Fundamental Reform Needed

Regrettably, the Administration's decision to elevate and legitimize the deeply flawed HRC through U.S. engagement and membership gives the UPR process similar credibility. It is imperative that the Administration pursue reforms in the 2011 review of the council to make the HRC and the UPR process a focused and powerful weapon in improving observance of fundamental human rights and freedoms. This starts with establishing strong membership criteria for the council.

Failure to achieve reforms in the 2011 review should lead Congress to again withhold a proportional amount of the U.S. contribution to the U.N. that supports the work of the council and serves as a stark reminder of the need to create an alternative arbiter of international human rights outside of the U.N. system.

Brett D. Schaefer is Jay Kingham Fellow in International Regulatory Affairs and Steven Groves is Bernard and Barbara Lomas Fellow in the Margaret Thatcher Center for Freedom, a division of the Kathryn and Shelby Cullom Davis Institute for International Studies, at The Heritage Foundation.

DOCUMENT 6: INDEPENDENCE FOR US TERRITORIES? WHAT ABOUT HAWAII?

By Leon Kaulahao Siu

UN Geneva, Switzerland, 25 August 2010

In the process of offering independence to its territories, the US needs to admit to its 1959 deception and allow a fresh chance for Hawaii to exercise self-determination. Without much fanfare, the U.S. has been conducting educational campaigns in the "US territories" of American Samoa, Guam, Puerto Rico and the US Virgin Islands, to inform the people about the options they have with regard to the future governance of their territories. Among the options being offered is independence.

Is this opportunity being offered to Hawaii also? Apparently no. So why not? After World War II when the United Nations was formed, it adopted a policy and procedures for helping colonies become independent nations. The colonies of the victors and those of the vanquished, were designated "Non-Self-Governing Territories" (NSGT). Each NSGT was assigned a sort of guardian/benefactor/trustee/administrator from the winning side (US, Great Britain, France, Russia, Netherlands, Belgium, etc.).

Under the UN Charter and the policies developed by the UN Special Committee on Decolonization, the trustee nations were to help stabilize, prepare and build the NSGTs' capacity for self-government. When that capacity was reached, the trustee nation would inform the people about the options available to them: 1) remain as a "territory" of the trustee nation; 2) become fully integrated into the trustee nation (such as becoming a "state" of the US); or 3) become a self-governing, independent sovereign nation. The designation of 'free association' falls into the category of independence. After considering these options, the people would hold a referendum and choose which they preferred. That is the exercise of "self-determination."

So, with regard to the NSGTs assigned to the US (the US calls them "US territories"), American Samoa, Guam, and the US Virgin Islands, the US has apparently deemed them ready to exercise their right to selfdetermination and recently began the process to prepare the people to choose what form of governing status and/or relationship they wish to adopt. [note: Puerto Rico which was removed as an NSGT and made a "commonwealth" of the US in 1957, has invoked the decolonization process. The outcome of their last referendum held in 1998 was to maintain the status quo.]

Historically the process of decolonization has not been smooth. In many cases, violent, bloody conflicts arose, particularly in Africa and Asia. NSGTs (former colonies) eager for "self-determination" took up arms against colonial powers who were reluctant to give up control. Then there were the conflicts amongst internal factions, some still raging today, even after independence. However peaceful or messy, in general, the process worked, bringing the dependent status of former colonies in Africa, Southeast Asia, the Pacific and so forth into that of independent nations. Today over 40 former NSGTs are full-fledged members of the United Nations.

Undoubtedly the most stellar performer in post-World War II reconstruction was the U.S. America's role in the reconstruction of the defeated Axis Powers of Japan, Germany and Italy, along with much of wartorn Europe, was a monumental feat of magnanimity and grace. America was a major force behind the formation of the United Nations to ensure that there could be a peaceful forum for settling international disputes, providing humanitarian aid and . . . decolonization.

In most respects, America's role in decolonization was also commendable. The Pacific Trust Territories of Micronesia was a huge NSGT assigned to the US to administer. In the 1980s under the stewardship of the U.S., several independent nations emerged out of the Trust Territories: the Federated States of Micronesia, the Republic of the Marshall Islands, the Republic of Kiribati, the Republic of Palau. All chose a form of independence involving a compact of free association with the US.

With the example of Micronesia and the present preparations for American Samoa, Guam, Puerto Rico and the US Virgin Islands underway, the US appears to have acted responsibly in the spirit of the UN Charter and its mandate for decolonization.

But America also has serious skeletons in its closet regarding decolonization. In many instances America got involved in backing colonial powers (its WWII allies) in resisting independence movements in Africa, the Middle East and Asia. In South-East Asia America even assumed the colonial role after the Vietnamese defeated the French at Diem Bien Phu.

There are also flaws within the picture being projected today of the American altruism for freedom through decolonization. What is really behind the sudden prospect of making the four remaining US territories into independent nations? Three of those territories have been held by the US since the Spanish American War 112 years ago, and the US has consistently claimed them to be, and treated them as, US-owned territories. Here's what I think is happening.

This November (2010) is the U.S.' turn to present its Universal Periodic Report (UPR) to the UN Human Rights Commission. This is an extremely significant report and, of course, the US wants to show it is performing well under UN human rights parameters, as well as in the areas of decolonization and self-determination. So, American Samoa, Guam, Puerto Rico and the US Virgin Islands are each being duly courted with the prerequisite preparations for self-determination and paraded before the UN as candidates for decolonization. All this to bolster the US' image with regard to human rights.

Why the sudden interest by the US in promoting self-determination? I believe the US is trying to deflect attention from the growing commotion over Hawaiian independence, especially since the issue is finally beginning to gain traction around the world. The US is trying to mask a deception it engineered in 1959, 'pulling the wool' over the eyes of the Hawaiian and American people, and under the noses of the UN. And the reason for that was to hide the grand deception of the illegal "annexation" of Hawaii in 1898, which resulted from the illegal invasion and usurpation of the sovereign independent nation of Hawaii in 1893. In other words, the US is trying to conceal a monumental 117-year-long fraud, the most recent manifestation of which took place under the UN's watch when the US made Hawaii a "state" in 1959.

You see, after World War II Hawaii was included on the UN list of Non Self-Governing Territories (NSGT). Alaska too! It's true! Apparently whoever compiled the UN list considered Hawaii and Alaska not integrated into the US and listed Hawaii and Alaska as NSGTs to be prepared for decolonization and self-determination, just like the Micronesian islands, the African and Asian colonies. So what happened? Why was there no educational program in Hawaii to inform Hawaiians or in Alaska to inform the Alaskans of the self-determination options as required by the UN Charter? Why did the US not even mention to Hawaiians or Alaskans the option for independence?

It was simply because the US was unwilling to give up Hawaii and Alaska—Hawaii for its militarily strategic location and Alaska for its vast natural resources. To avoid a required assessment (progress report) on the status of NSGTs due in 1960, the US hurriedly bundled Hawaii and Alaska together and made them into "states" of the U.S. in 1959, then reported to the UN to remove Hawaii and Alaska from the NSGT list prior to the 1960 assessment. The UN never questioned or monitored the US "statehood" process. The UN simply accepted and adopted the deceptive report filed by the US, not aware that every one of the requirements for decolonization had been ruthlessly violated and co-opted by the US. And certainly the people of Hawaii and Alaska were kept completely in the dark by the US' machinations.

The US is very worried about their November Universal Periodic Report to the Human Rights Commission. The US State Department has been trying to cover their bases, kissing up to the Native Americans and Native Alaskans by visiting their reservations and inviting their leaders to "consultations" at the White House and fawning over "indigenous rights" at the UN. The US knows that any one of the Native American nations could lower the boom on the US for human rights violations, so like consummate politicians on the campaign trail they are shaking hands and kissing babies. The US state department, and departments of the interior, health, education, etc. have mounted their dog and pony show, going out of their way to tell Indians that their grievances have been heard and "Will all be addressed soon. Give us a little more time. Trust us."

But most worrisome to the US is the onerous Hawaii situation. The US is terrified that the numerous violations of international law and the perpetration of fraud by the U.S. with regard to Hawaii, will come home to roost. They are fearful that the question of Hawaiian independence will be brought up at the UPR. In particular, they are scared that they will be asked what UN decolonization procedures and what international laws were followed in 1959 in making Hawaii and Alaska states. Were Hawaii and Alaska provided the opportunity like all other NSGTs for independence?

To answer questions pertaining to Hawaii, the US is going say that Hawaiian issues lie within the domestic purview and policies of the US. They will portray the pending legislation, "the Akaka bill" (that offers federal recognition as an indigenous U.S. tribe; a still-to-be congress-determined tribal governing entity; a still-to-be-determined tribal land base; native Hawaiian entitlement programs, etc.) as their vehicle for addressing the issue of "self-determination" regarding the Native Hawaiian people. But they will not be able to skirt the issue of decolonization because the remedy to the problem of Hawaii's special situation lies not in the realm of domestic policy of the US, it is in the realm of international law.

If the question of decolonization of Hawaii is raised at the UN UPR, the US will be hard-put to respond. If they say Hawaii became integrated as a state of the US in 1959, they would become vulnerable to questions of why the rudimentary self-determination procedures were not followed. They won't be able to claim ignorance. Their proper handling of the Trust Territories of the Pacific (Micronesia) and the preparations currently underway regarding American Samoa, Guam, Puerto Rico and the US Virgin Islands, demonstrate that the US fully understands the procedures. Therefore, the mishandling of Hawaii (and Alaska) can only be construed as deliberate and willful violations by the US to deprive and deny Hawaiians (and Alaskans) of their fundamental human rights.

What would the repercussions be? First, the US "statehood" status of Hawaii and Alaska would be rendered null and void. An action based on fraud cannot be entertained as being lawful. Next, Alaska and Hawaii would revert to the list of NSGTs where both Hawaiians and Alaskans can then exercise true self-determination.

This would be relatively simple for Hawaii. Prior to the US takeover in 1893, the Hawaiian Kingdom was a free, progressive, independent, sovereign nation with numerous treaties and over 90 diplomatic legations all over the world. The unlawful takeover by the U.S. did not extinguish Hawaii's sovereign character nor its independent stature. It just robbed Hawaiians of the ability to exercise their national prerogatives. The U.S.' fraudulent claim to Hawaii, backed by its sheer military might, the imposition and enforcement of US domestic law, has been the singular deterrent to the Hawaiians' ability to function as a lawful nation.

We believe that with the intervention of the international community and with the international community monitoring closely, the U.S. will relent and take the right and honorable course to step aside and allow the Hawaiian people to reactivate the lawful Hawaiian Kingdom government, reinstate the lands to the nation and restore their ability to function as free people and self-determine the direction and future of their country.

Alaska's predicament is similar, but its path to resolution is different in many respects.

The point is, in the process of offering independence to its four remaining non-self-governing territories, the US needs to own up to the fraud it perpetrated 1959 (and continued since) and provide a fresh chance for Hawaii and Alaska to exercise self-determination. If America is at all interested in doing the right thing, this would be the right thing to do.

Leon Kaulahao Siu is the Minister of Foreign Affairs for the Hawaiian Kingdom.

ForeignAffairs@HawaiianKingdom.ws

DOCUMENT 7: THE U.N. AND HUMAN RIGHTS: MORE THAN POLITICS

Human Rights, Managing Global Change, United Nations
Ted Piccone, Senior Fellow and Deputy Director, Foreign Policy
Emily Alinikoff, Senior Research Assistant, Foreign Policy
The Brookings Institution
DECEMBER 08, 2010—

Sixty-two years ago this week, thanks to U.S. leadership, the Universal Declaration of Human Rights was adopted, launching a set of principles and tools that has made the world safer for American values. Yet, the United Nations human rights system continues to take some serious flack in U.S. domestic politics. It is time to take another look from the perspective of human rights defenders on the ground.

Originally created under Eleanor Roosevelt's leadership to help deter repetition of World War II atrocities, the U.N.'s human rights work fell victim to Cold War rivalries. Even after the fall of the Berlin Wall, a growing number of states with bad human rights records sought seats to shield themselves from scrutiny while simultaneously attacking U.S. and Israeli human rights records, drawing heavy criticism here at home. As a result, and despite some achievements, the old Commission on Human Rights was abolished in 2006 and replaced by a new Human Rights Council, including a new peer review process that all states undergo once every four years. Disappointed by the results, the Bush administration disengaged entirely from the new body. President Obama, on the other hand, saw value in returning to the council and trying to strengthen it from within.

Now, as Republicans prepare to run the House of Representatives, expect to see criticism of the council's work on human rights move up a notch or two. Opponents of the Obama administration's engagement policy say it's time to call it quits and withdraw from the council after just two years of U.S. membership. They bristle to see the U.S. face peer examination of its human rights record by such states as Cuba and Iran, for example, even as they and other states like China and Russia submit to unprecedented exposure themselves. This myopic focus misses the mark. As governments take stock of the council's first five years, it is crucial to consider how this body actually promotes and protects human rights for the victims it is designed to defend, instead of focusing solely on the political machinations in Geneva.

One of the council's primary yet undervalued instruments of human rights promotion is its independent experts who investigate human rights situations on the ground and report back to the U.N. Currently, more than forty of these independent experts are working on human rights themes like the prevention of torture, violence against women, freedom of religion, and freedom of expression. An additional eight individuals examine violations in specific countries like North Korea, Sudan, Burma, and Cambodia.

To fulfill their mandates they conduct field visits to meet with victims, advocates, and government officials; send communications of alleged abuses to governments; issue press statements to call public attention to the problems they witness; and write reports to document their work. These prolific workers, though appointed by the council with input from states and nongovernmental organizations, serve as unpaid volunteers who perform this job on top of their other professional activities. From 2004–08, these experts recorded over 9,000 communications to governments regarding alleged human rights abuses. In 2009 alone, they conducted 73 field visits to 51 countries and prepared more than 150 reports. They have created a remarkable and underutilized public record of human rights policies and abuses from around the globe.

While critics are busy focusing on how many human rights abusers were elected to the council, these experts are in the field defending their victims and thousands of others. In Afghanistan, a U.N. independent expert discovered a prison where women detainees were forced to raise their children without adequate nutrition or healthcare. He secured regular doctor visits and increased the prison's budget allocation for food. In Indonesia, a special rapporteur discovered a secret agreement with Malaysia that allowed Indonesian workers to be treated like property, with no ownership over their national identity documents. He persuaded them to toss out the agreement to the immediate benefit of thousands of migrant workers. In Bahrain, prisoners arrested for peaceful protest were released by a pardon after several special rapporteurs sent a joint communication on their behalf. In Egypt, police officers were tried and prosecuted for torturing someone to death, a result demanded by the U.N.'s independent experts. As we document in the report "Catalysts for Rights," the list goes on and on.

For those who favor the Obama administration's strategy of engaging the council, supporting and strengthening these independent experts is a no brainer. For those opposed to the council, backing these experts is a tactical way to ensure an international spotlight stays not only on the human rights violations committed by the worst states but on whether these states cooperate with the U.N. human rights system to begin with. This is important because the record of a state's cooperation with the council is an official criterion for membership on the body, a point that needs to be enforced.

The evidence shows that cooperation by states with the council is uneven, at best. From 2004–08, states failed to respond to 50% of communications from the independent experts and took steps to address allegations in only 18% of cases. These figures vary notably across regional and political groups. Countries in Western and Eastern Europe had considerably better response rates, around 66%, while countries in Africa responded only 30% of the time. In terms of allowing country visits, more than 80% of states in Western and Eastern Europe have issued standing invitations to all the council's independent experts, while only 10% of countries in Asia and Africa allow the same access. Improving state cooperation with these experts should be a top priority going forward.

As a proactive and constructive player in Geneva, the U.S. has real opportunities to push for additional reforms at the council that will translate into protection of victims on the ground. Rather than walk away to let the spoilers take the reins, the U.S. should stay engaged by focusing on strengthening and supporting what we know works. That means making cooperation with the independent experts a serious criterion for membership on the council, expanding resources for their work, and establishing a system for following up on their recommendations so they can continue to save lives and promote the universal values that make the world safer.

Source: http://www.brookings.edu/opinions/2010/1208_human_rights_piccone.aspx

---

DOCUMENT 8: AMERICA'S INTERESTS AND THE U.N.

John Bolton
Former U.S. Ambassador to the United Nations
April 2008 IMPRIMIS

JOHN BOLTON is a senior fellow at the American Enterprise Institute. From August 2005 to December 2006, he served as the U.S. Permanent Representative to the United Nations, and for four years prior to that he was Undersecretary of State for Arms Control and International Security. Ambassador Bolton has a B.A. from Yale College and a J.D. from Yale Law School, where he was editor of the *Yale Law Journal*. He has written for several publications, including the *Wall Street Journal*, the *Washington Post*, and the *Weekly Standard*, and is the author of the recent book, *Surrender is Not an Option: Defending America at the United Nations and Abroad.*

The following is adapted from a speech delivered at a Hillsdale College National Leadership Seminar in Phoenix, Arizona, on February 11, 2008.

Jeane Kirkpatrick was frequently asked why the U.S. didn't simply withdraw from the U.N., and her answer was, "Because it's more trouble than it's worth." The fact is that the U.N., at times, can be an effective instrument of American foreign policy. Of course, to say this is heretical to the real devotees of the U.N., for whom the U.N. shouldn't be an instrument of anyone's foreign policy. But the fact is that everybody who participates in the U.N.—all of the 192 member governments, all of the non-governmental organizations, and all of the civil servants in the U.N. secretariats—try to advance their own interests. The only entity that gets criticized for that, needless to say, is the U.S. government.

Although I want to talk about some of the U.N.'s failings in the international security area, I first want to mention an issue that doesn't get as much attention, but which in many respects is more troubling and affects American interests in ways that could have a profound impact well into the future. This is what our friends in Europe call "norming."

"Norming" is the idea that the U.S. should base its decisions on some kind of international consensus, rather than making its decisions as a constitutional democracy. It is a way in which the Europeans and their left-wing friends here and elsewhere try and constrain U.S. sovereignty. You can see how disastrous this would be just by looking at the geography of the floor of the U.N. General Assembly. Look out at the representatives of the 192 governments spread out over the floor and you wonder where the U.S. even is. Well, we're there somewhere. But the fact is that we're sitting with a majority of countries that have no traditions or understanding of liberty. The argument of the advocates of "norming" is "one nation, one vote." That sounds very democratic: Who could object to that? But its result would be very *anti*-democratic. As an illustration of this, a friend of mine once went to a conference on international law and heard a professor from a major European university say, "The problem with the U.S. is its devotion to its Constitution over international norms."

We have controversial issues within the U.S.—issues that we debate, and over which reasonable people can disagree. But these controversies should be resolved through our political process, according to our Constitution, just as other countries can resolve their controversies as they see fit. Take, for example, the question of the death penalty. This is a matter about which many people feel very strongly, both for and against. We've just seen New Jersey repeal the death penalty. At the federal level, procedures have been reformed to meet objections from the Supreme Court, so that the death penalty can be handed out in appropriate cases. Opinions on the subject change constantly as we debate in the U.S. whether we should have a death penalty and, if so, under what circumstances. But at the U.N. this debate is closed; the death penalty has been ruled out. The new Secretary-General of the U.N., Ban Ki-moon, comes from South Korea—where they still have the death penalty—and last year, during his first few months in office, he remarked that this question is for each government to decide for itself. Upon saying this, he was all but subjected to articles of impeachment for failing to realize that the U.N. had already decided that question for all countries.

As I say, I think it's perfectly legitimate to debate the death penalty from either side. But it is inconceivable to me that anyone can seriously argue—as advocates of "norming" do—that the death penalty violates international standards of human rights, when in a democratic society like ours we are debating it.

Another issue on which "norming" is brought to bear is gun control. In 2001, the U.N. had a conference about international trafficking in small arms and light weapons—weapons that flow into conflict zones and pose a risk to U.N. peacekeepers. The idea was to discuss methods to deal with this threat. But the discussion turned out to have nothing to do with small arms and light weapons in African or Asian civil wars. Instead it was about gun control in the U.S., with advocates of "international norms" pressing for the prohibition of private ownership of firearms of any sort. The U.S. delegation made it clear that while we were concerned about the illicit flow of weapons into conflict areas, we were not going to sign on to any international agreement that prohibited private ownership of guns. I explained that we had a Constitution that precluded any such restrictions. This was treated as an entirely specious notion.

These are the kind of "norming" exercises by which foreign governments hope, over time, to build up a coral reef of U.N. resolutions and pronouncements that can be used to manipulate U.S. policy.

Although the U.N. is perfectly capable of passing resolutions about the death penalty and gun control—not to mention smoking—it has proved utterly incapable, even after 9/11, of agreeing to a definition of terrorism that would enable it to denounce terrorism. The U.N. is incapable of doing this, even to this day, because several member governments think there is good terrorism and bad terrorism. It is inconceivable, in my judgment, that the U.N. will ever be able to agree upon a definition of terrorism that's not complete pablum—and therefore utterly useless.

So in all the areas where the U.N. shouldn't be involved—issues best left to sovereign countries—it is very successful in passing judgment, especially when it can spit in the eye of the U.S. But in the one area where the U.N. could be of most use in promoting international peace, it has failed completely. So much for "norming."

Attempts at Reform

We, as Americans, are pretty practical people. We like to solve problems. I think that's the way most Americans approach the United Nations. So we have looked for ways to make the U.N. work better. But virtually every serious effort to reform it over the years has failed.

Let me give you a couple of examples. Most of us are familiar with the oil-for-food scandal—the mismanagement and corruption that accompanied the efforts to provide humanitarian assistance to the Iraqi people after the first Iraq War. Even Kofi Annan, the previous Secretary-General, recognized that this scandal caused grave damage to the U.N.'s reputation. Thus he brought in Paul Volcker, former chairman of the Federal Reserve Board, to investigate and propose reforms. One of Volcker's most important findings was that the oil-for-food scandal was not a unique incident—that it represented flaws endemic to the entire U.N. system. So Volcker proposed a whole series of reforms, chief among them being effective outside auditing of U.N. programs. We worked hard with other governments to get these reforms adopted by the General Assembly. Months and months of negotiation led to a vote by the U.N. Budget Committee, and the reforms were rejected by a margin of about two to one.

Let me repeat this for emphasis: The U.N. Budget Committee voted two to one against effective outside auditing of U.N. programs. This tells you pretty much everything you need to know about how the U.N. operates. And I should add that the countries voting in favor of these reforms contribute over 90 percent of the U.N.'s budget, whereas the countries voting against them contribute under ten percent.

We engaged in another reform effort to fix the U.N. Human Rights Commission—a body that everybody in Europe, and even Secretary-General Annan, admitted was a stain on the U.N.'s reputation. It spends most of its time defending human rights abusers and passing resolutions critical of the U.S. and Israel. We proposed a series of procedural reforms that would have changed the membership of the Human Rights Commission in a way to rid it of the worst human rights offenders. But the third world countries, led by Russia and China, adamantly refused to consider these reforms. One by one, our European friends allowed them to be dropped, so that the reform package got smaller and smaller. I knew that the effort was completely lost when it couldn't even be agreed that governments under sanctions by the Security Council for gross abuses of human rights or support for terrorism would be prohibited membership on the new Human Rights Council. At that point I recommended to the Secretary of State that we vote against the resolution. But ultimately the new Council was created with only four countries voting against it—the U.S., Israel, and our other two close allies, Palau and the Marshall Islands.

The Europeans criticized us at the time for giving up on reform, and my response was that it is foolish to put lipstick on a caterpillar and call it a butterfly. But in the end the Europeans cared less about reforming the Human Rights Commission than bludgeoning the U.S. into being more submissive to the U.N. So they expressed outrage at us, rather than at the countries that had rejected real reform. Subsequently, even the editorial boards of the *New York Times* and the *Washington Post*—neither of them conservative supporters of the Bush administration—called the new Human Rights Council even worse than its predecessor.

What I concluded following my 16 months as ambassador—and based on my work in the U.N. system dating back to my earliest service in the Reagan administration—was that efforts at marginal or incremental reform of the U.N. are doomed to failure. Instead, I believe that we should focus on one issue: changing the arrangement by which financing of the U.N. is mandatory.

Under the current system, the U.S. pays 22 percent of the cost of most U.N. agencies, and 27 percent of peacekeeping costs. We are far and away the largest contributor, and every year Congress pays the bill as apportioned by the General Assembly. My revolutionary reform principle would be this: The U.S. should pay for what it wants and insist that it get what it pays for. This would break up the entitlement mentality at the U.N. and foster an organization that is both more transparent and more effective.

Unfulfilled Promise

International peace and security was the objective that motivated the founders of the U.N. after World War Two. And it is precisely here that the U.N.'s promise has been least fulfilled during its 60-plus years of existence. During the half-century of the Cold War, the U.N. was fundamentally irrelevant to the great struggle between liberty and tyranny due to the make-up of the Security Council and the veto power held by the Soviet Union and, later, by the People's Republic of China. Since the end of the Cold War, many people have thought it possible that the U.N. could play a more important role in world affairs. These hopes have been completely dashed.

Take the present case of Darfur. Acts of genocide have been committed by the government of Sudan against the people of the region, and unspeakable brutality has gone on for over three years. Yet the Security Council has been incapable of inserting a U.N. peacekeeping force. Why is that? In part, it is because China has given protective cover to the Sudanese government. And why does China do this? Because it has a large and growing demand for energy and wants oil and natural gas leases in Sudan. Thus the genocidal government of Sudan has stood down the entire U.N. Security Council for years.

Or consider the case of Iraq. In the aftermath of Iraq's invasion of Kuwait in 1990 and the subsequent expulsion of Iraqi forces by the U.S.-led coalition, we and Saddam Hussein agreed to a cease-fire based on a number of conditions expressed in various Security Council resolutions. Saddam Hussein ignored those resolutions. Leaving aside the issue of weapons of mass destruction, there's no doubt that he failed to comply with the cease-fire resolution and other key resolutions of the Security Council. Yet when President Bush suggested that the Security Council take its own resolutions seriously, he was rebuffed. This is a perfect example of the U.N. being willing to talk but not act.

What is the lesson learned when unlawful governments are the subject of repeated resolutions by the Security Council and yet suffer no consequences for ignoring them? We find the consequences played out now in two direct threats to the U.S. and to international order: the nuclear weapons programs of North Korea and Iran. And, as in the days of the Cold War, the U.N. is fundamentally irrelevant in the face of these grave threats to world peace.

I'm sure all of you recall the Israeli Air Force raid last September that destroyed a major facility in Syria. It turned out to be a nuclear facility that was being constructed with the assistance of North Korea, quite possibly financed by Iran. This reminds us of the real threats we face, of the ineffectiveness of the U.N., and of the importance of U.S. military power and foreign policy.

There is one point of view here in America—a view given expression during the 2004 presidential campaign by Senator Kerry—holding that American foreign policy should meet some kind of "global test." By this way of thinking, America needs, in effect, to demonstrate the legitimacy of its foreign policy decisions by getting the approval of the U.N. Security Council or some other international body. The same suggestion will no doubt surface again this year, in the run-up to the November election. In the 21st century, then—just as in the 20th—the political decisions we make here in the U.S. will be much more significant than those made at the U.N.

DOCUMENT 9: U.S. GETS HUMAN RIGHTS ADVICE FROM THE WORLD

By Mary Shaw
30 November, 2010
Countercurrents.org

On November 5, the U.S. had its first-ever formal evaluation under the Universal Period Review process before the United Nations Human Rights Council (UNHRC). This process was established in 2006 to periodically review the human rights records of UN member states. But the George W. Bush administration apparently thought it was above this sort of thing.

As a result of this year's process, on November 10, the UNHRC issued a report of its findings and recommendations from the U.S. review. Most obvious were recommendations that the U.S. ratify several international human rights conventions and treaties that we have not yet formally endorsed. To no surprise, our use of torture and racial profiling, and the obvious culture of xenophobia apparent in our national discourse, also figured prominently in the feedback.

Below are some key excerpts from the report's recommendations on how the U.S. can improve its human rights standing in the world. The recommending nation appears in parenthesis after each item.

92.1. Ratify without reservations the following conventions and protocols: CEDAW; the ICESCR; the Convention on the Rights of the Child; the Convention on the Rights of Persons with Disabilities; the International Convention on the Protection of the Rights of All Migrant Workers and Members of Their Families; the International Convention for the Protection of All Persons from Enforced Disappearance; the Statute of the International Criminal Court; those of the ILO; the United Nations Declaration on Indigenous Peoples, and all those from the Inter-American Human Rights System (Bolivarian Republic of Venezuela) [with similar recommendations by France, Russia, Spain, Canada, Japan, and several other nations];

92.51. Comply with its international obligations for the effective mitigation of greenhouse gas emissions, because of their impact in climate change (Bolivarian Republic of Venezuela);

92.56. Repeal the norms that limit freedom of expression and require journalists to reveal their sources, under penalty of imprisonment (Bolivarian Republic of Venezuela);

92.66. Enact a federal crime of torture, consistent with the Convention, and also encompassing acts described as 'enhanced interrogation techniques' (Austria);

92.67. Take legislative and administrative measures to address a wide range of racial discrimination and inequalities in housing, employment and education (Democratic People's Republic of Korea);

92.68. Take legislative and administrative measures to ban racial profiling in law enforcement (Democratic People's Republic of Korea);

92.70. Take appropriate legislative and practical measures to improve living conditions through its prisons systems, in particular with regard to access to health care and education (Austria);

92.75. End the blockade against Cuba2 (Cuba); Put an end to the infamous blockade against Cuba (Bolivarian Republic of Venezuela); Lift the economic, financial and commercial blockade against Cuba, which affects the enjoyment of the human rights of more than 11 million people (Plurinational State of Bolivia);

92.81. Take the necessary measures in favor of the right to work and fair conditions of work so that workers belonging to minorities, in particular women and undocumented migrant workers, do not become victims of discriminatory treatment and abuse in the work place and enjoy the full protection of the labour legislation, regardless of their migratory status (Guatemala);

92.82. Adopt a fair immigration policy, and cease xenophobia, racism and intolerance to ethnic, religious and migrant minorities (Bolivarian Republic of Venezuela);

92.85. Formulate goals and policy guidelines for the promotion of the rights of indigenous peoples and cooperation between government and indigenous peoples (Finland);

92.88. Invite United Nations Special Rapporteurs to visit and investigate Guantánamo Bay prison and U.S. secret prisons and to subsequently close them (Islamic Republic of Iran);

92.122. Abolish the death penalty and in any event, establish a moratorium as an interim measure towards full abolition (Australia); Abolish capital punishment and, as a first step on that road, introduce as soon as practicable a moratorium on the execution of death sentences (Hungary); That steps be taken to set federal and state-level moratoria on executions with a view to abolish the death penalty nationwide (Norway);

. . . and much more.

It is a good sign that the U.S. chose to submit itself to this level of scrutiny. However, good intentions will mean nothing if the Obama administration does not follow through on these constructive recommendations from its partners in the world community.

Talk is cheap. Rhetoric is cheap. The world wants action. And the world wants some positive change that we can all believe in.

Are we strong enough as a nation to comply? Sadly, I shall not hold my breath.

Mary Shaw is a Philadelphia-based writer and activist, with a focus on politics, human rights, and social justice. She is a former Philadelphia Area Coordinator for the Nobel-Prize-winning human rights group Amnesty International, and her views appear regularly in a variety of newspapers, magazines, and websites. Note that the ideas expressed here are the author's own, and do not necessarily reflect the opinions of Amnesty International or any other organization with which she may be associated. E-mail: mary@mary-shawonline.com

DOCUMENT 10: BUSH ADMITS HE APPROVED WATERBOARDING

By R. Jeffrey Smith
THE WASHINGTON POST

In his new memoir, former president says his reply was "Damn right," when asked if CIA could waterboard detainee.

Human rights experts have long pressed the administration of former President George W. Bush for details of who bore ultimate responsibility for approving waterboarding of CIA detainees, the simulated drownings that many legal experts say was illicit torture.

In his memoir due out Tuesday, Bush makes clear that he personally approved the use of that coercive technique against alleged Sept. 11 plotter Khalid Sheik Mohammed, an admission the human rights experts say could one day have legal consequences for him.

In his book, titled "Decision Points," Bush recounts being asked by the CIA whether it could proceed with waterboarding Mohammed, who Bush said was suspected of knowing about still-pending terrorist plots against the U.S. Bush writes that his reply was "Damn right," and he states that he would make the same decision again to save lives, according to someone close to Bush who has read the book.

Bush previously had acknowledged endorsing what he described as the CIA's "enhanced" interrogation techniques—a term meant to encompass irregular, coercive methods—after Justice Department officials and other top aides assured him they were legal. "I was a big supporter of waterboarding," Vice President Dick Cheney acknowledged in a TV interview in February.

The Justice Department later repudiated some of the underlying legal analysis for the CIA effort. But Bush told an interviewer a week before leaving the White House that "I firmly reject the word 'torture,'\ u2009" and he reiterates that view in the book.

Since the 2003 waterboarding of Mohammed and similar interrogations of two other CIA detainees in 2002 and 2003, the intelligence agency has forsworn the technique, which involves pouring water onto someone's face while strapped to a board, to convince them they will shortly drown.

President Barack Obama and Attorney General Eric Holder have both said waterboarding is an act of torture proscribed by international law. But the Obama administration hasn't sought to punish former Bush administration officials for approving it.

Georgetown University law professor David Cole, a long-standing critic of Bush's interrogation and detention policies, called prosecution unlikely. "The fact that he did admit it suggests he believes he is politically immune from being held accountable," Cole said. "But politics can change.

STATESMAN.COM http://www.statesman.com/news/nation/bush-admits-he-approved-waterboarding-1019060.html

Appendix Q: Human Rights Education

The purpose of this Appendix is to give the reader a glimpse of the international level activity regarding human rights education in a political realm in which the U.S. participates.

Since the early 1990s the international community, pushed primarily by NGOs and other civil society actors, moved to get education about human rights brought into the mainstream of both formal and informal education in all countries of the world. The idea was that if people were educated in international human rights they would be more likely to respect the human rights of each other, and be better able to demand that their own government comply with its international human rights obligations.

The U.N. General Assembly adopted a resolution which declared 1995 to 2004 to be the "U.N. Decade for Human Rights Education" and hoped that states would reply by adding human rights to school curricula and elsewhere at age appropriate levels. I am not aware of the U.S. either taking action in response to this resolution to promote human rights education, or requesting states or local education departments to do so.

At the end of the "Decade" the U.N. decided by resolution, to set up a program entitled the World Programme for Human Rights Education (WPHRE). Its first educational focus was on primary education. The Evaluation of that Programme is Document 3 below. In 2010 it changed its focus to higher education and on human rights training programmes for teachers and educators, civil servants, law enforcement officials and military personnel at all levels. See Document 2 below.

In early 2010, the Human Rights Council set up an advisory council with the task of elaborating a Declaration on Human Rights education documents. As this book went to press, there is a draft Declaration elaborated. It is Document 1 below.

A few NGOs and academic institutions are active in trying to bring human rights education to the U.S.

In regard to the state's duty to provide human rights education, see Primary Document 40: Declaration on the Right and Responsibility of Individuals, Groups and Organs of Society to Promote and Protect Universally Recognized Human Rights and Fundamental Freedoms, paragraphs 14-16. That Declaration is not legally binding but has substantial political authority.

The subject of human right education should not be confused with the subject of the specific human right to receive an education, such as found in article 26 of the UDHR.

The following documents are a few of those involving the international level movement towards human rights education, including in the U.S.

The reader is advised to check the appropriate websites at the U.N. and U.S. level to see the present status of these documents.

An excellent source of human rights education information, curricula, and distance learning courses on human rights is the Human Rights Education Associates, whose website is: http://www.hrea.org/

Documents

DOCUMENT 1: DRAFT U.N. DECLARATION ON HUMAN RIGHTS EDUCATION

English version of January 29, 2010
Advisory Committee of the Human Rights Council Recommendation 4/2.
Draft United Nations declaration on human rights education and training
The Human Rights Council Advisory Committee,

Bearing in mind the mandate set out in Human Rights Council resolution 6/10 of 28 September 2007 requesting the Advisory Committee to prepare a draft declaration on human rights education and training, as well as Human Rights Council resolution 10/28 of 27 March 2009,

Recalling its recommendations 1/1 of 14 August 2008, 2/1 of 30 January 2009, and 3/3 of 7 August 2009 on the work of the drafting group on human rights education and training, as well as the preparatory documents submitted by the rapporteur of the drafting group,

Welcoming the particularly high response to the questionnaire sent by the drafting group to all stakeholders, who provided the drafting group with a wealth of information for its work,

Welcoming the contribution of the various stakeholders to the debate, including at the seminar on a draft United Nations declaration on human rights education and training, held in Marrakech, Morocco, on 16 and 17 July 2009, which was attended by the Chairperson and rapporteur of the drafting group,

Expressing its gratitude for the steadfast support of the States members of the Platform for Human Rights Education and Training,

Highlighting the active participation of national human rights institutions at each stage of the collective debate,

Expressing its satisfaction with the continued work of the drafting group, and particularly the draft declaration submitted by the special rapporteur of the drafting group in document A/HRC/AC/4/3,

Desiring to pursue the close cooperation with the United Nations, the United Nations Educational, Scientific and Cultural Organization and other relevant international and regional organizations in the work in progress,

Taking due note of the in-depth discussions on the draft declaration during the interactive debate at the fourth session of the Advisory Committee, as well as the further work carried out by the drafting group at the same session,

1. *Endorses* the draft declaration on human rights education and training annexed to this recommendation, as revised;
2. *Transmits* the draft declaration to the Human Rights Council for consideration at its thirteenth session, in accordance with the request contained in Human Rights Council resolutions 6/10 and 10/28;
3. *Recommends* that the draft declaration be disseminated widely and encourages further initiatives by the various stakeholders to promote collective consultations on the draft declaration;
4. *Expresses the hope* that the rapporteur of the drafting group on human rights education and training, Mr. Decaux, will be able to participate in the discussions of the Human Rights Council on the draft declaration submitted to it;
5. *Recommends* that the drafting group be kept informed of the follow-up to the work of the Human Rights Council and that it might be involved, in appropriate ways, in the ongoing debate and in the work of awareness-raising in the area of human rights education and training.

Annex

Proposed draft declaration on human rights education and training, as revised by the rapporteur of the drafting group of the Human Rights Council Advisory Committee

[The General Assembly]

Bearing in mind Article 13 of the Charter of the United Nations, which charges the General Assembly with "promoting international co-operation in the ... cultural,[and] educational ... fields, and assisting in the realization of human rights and fundamental freedoms for all without distinction as to race, sex, language, or religion",

Recalling the Universal Declaration of Human Rights, which sets "a common standard of achievement for all peoples and all nations, to the end that every individual and every organ of society, keeping this Declaration constantly in mind, shall strive by teaching and education to promote respect for these rights and freedoms and by progressive measures, national and international, to secure their universal and effective recognition and observance",

Drawing on article 26 of the Universal Declaration of Human Rights, which affirms in paragraph 1 that "everyone has the right to education" and stipulates in paragraph 2 that "education shall be directed to the full development of the human personality and to the strengthening of respect for human rights and fundamental freedoms",

Reaffirming that, as set out in the Universal Declaration of Human Rights, the International Covenant on Economic, Social and Cultural Rights and other human rights instruments, States are required to ensure that education is directed to the strengthening of respect for human rights and fundamental freedoms,

Aware of the international commitments of States under the various universal and regional human rights treaties and various international instruments,

Aware, in particular, of the Vienna Declaration and Programme of Action adopted on 25 June 1993 by the World Conference on Human Rights, which addresses the implementation of the right to education both as a right inherent in the dignity of the human person and as a means of promoting and ensuring respect for all human rights,

Stressing that the World Conference on Human Rights called on "all States and institutions to include human rights, humanitarian law, democracy and rule of law as subjects in the curricula of all learning institutions", stating that "human rights education should include peace, democracy, development and social justice, as set forth in international and regional human rights instruments, in order to achieve common understanding and awareness with a view to strengthening universal commitment to human rights",

Taking into account the progress made in the United Nations Decade for Human Rights Education (1995–2004) and the World Programme for Human Rights Education through the implementation of the plan of action for the first phase (2005–2007), which was extended to 2009, and the launch of a new phase of the World Programme for the period 2010–2014,

Encouraging the effective implementation of the goals set for 2015 in the Millennium Declaration, including equal access for girls and boys to all levels of education,

Recalling the Declaration on the Right and Responsibility of Individuals, Groups and Organs of Society to Promote and Protect Universally Recognized Human Rights and Fundamental Freedoms,

Bearing in mind the numerous initiatives undertaken within the framework of the United Nations, the United Nations Educational, Scientific and Cultural Organization and other international and regional organizations, as well as at the domestic level by public authorities and civil society organizations,

Recalling the 2005 World Summit Outcome, in which Heads of State and Government supported "the promotion of human rights education and learning at all levels, including through the implementation of the World Programme for Human Rights Education", and encouraged all States "to develop initiatives in this regard",

Recalling General Assembly resolution 60/251 establishing the Human Rights Council, in particular paragraph 5 (a), on the importance of human rights education and learning,

Recalling General Assembly resolution 62/171 and Human Rights Council resolution 12/4 relating to human rights education and training,

Desiring to strengthen the efforts undertaken and to encourage awareness and a collective commitment by all stakeholders, by providing a coherent and practical overview of the guiding principles that should govern the effective provision of human rights education and training for all, without distinction,

Motivated by the desire to send a strong signal to the international community about the fundamental importance of human rights education and training in the promotion and protection of human rights,

Hereby declares:

I. Definitions and principles

1. Human rights education and training comprises all educational, training, information and learning activities aimed at promoting a universal culture of human rights.

2. The right to human rights education and training is a fundamental right inherent in the dignity of the human person and is intimately related to the effective enjoyment of all human rights, in accordance with the principles of universality, indivisibility and interdependence of human rights.

3. Human rights education and training concerns all levels — preschool, primary, secondary and university — and all forms of education, training and learning, whether in a public or private, formal, informal or non-formal setting. It includes vocational training, particularly the training of trainers, continuing education, popular education, and public information and awareness activities.

4. Human rights education and training is an essential component of the right to education for all, as recognized in both the international and regional framework and the domestic law of different States. It is related to the full implementation of the right to education, particularly free compulsory primary education, and the

widespread provision of basic education for all, including for illiterate persons, as well as to the development of secondary education, including technical and vocational education, and higher education.

5. Human rights education and training should be based on the principles of the Universal Declaration of Human Rights and other relevant instruments, with the aim of:

(a) Raising awareness of human rights, including international, regional and national standards, principles, legislation and applicable guarantees;

(b) Pursuing the realization of all human rights;

(c) Developing a universal culture of human rights, in which everyone is aware of their own rights and duties in respect of the rights of others, and promoting the development of the individual as a responsible member of a free, peaceful, pluralist and tolerant society;

(d) Ensuring equal opportunities, through access for all to a quality education, without any discrimination; and

(e) Ensuring that education is developed in a spirit of participation, inclusion and responsibility that addresses both the content and the methods.

6. Human rights education and training is based on the principle of equality, particularly equality between girls and boys and between women and men, including in access to school, in accordance with the Millennium Development Goals.

7. Human rights education and training should take full account of vulnerable groups, including persons with disabilities, persons living in poverty, foreigners and migrants, by ensuring effective access to basic education, as well as to human rights education, in order to eliminate the causes of exclusion or marginalization and to enable everyone to exercise all their rights effectively.

8. Human rights education and training should also take into consideration the specific expectations of indigenous peoples, as well as those of persons from national or ethnic, religious and linguistic minorities.

9. Human rights education and training is an ongoing process that begins at school or preschool age and that concerns all ages, all situations and all parts of society.

10. Human rights education and training should embrace and enrich the diversity of civilizations, religions, cultures and traditions, which contribute to the universality of human rights.

11. Human rights education and training should use languages and methods suited to the target groups and should take into account the basic needs of the population, stressing the interdependence of all human rights so as to become a development tool.

12. Human rights education and training is closely related to the implementation of freedom of expression and the right to information. It should promote access for all to, and the participation of everyone in the development of, the media, including the press, radio and television, and the strengthening of the educational function of these different media.

13. Human rights education and training should embrace the possibilities of the digital age so as to encourage the development of new educational forums, with a view to achieving true equality in access to information and communications technologies.

14. Human rights education and training involves close links between schools, families, local communities and society as a whole, so as to create a favourable environment for the promotion and protection of human rights.

15. Human rights education and training contributes to the prevention of human rights violations and aims to eradicate domestic violence, particularly against women and girls, and other forms of social violence such as violence in schools, as well as discrimination, stereotyping and hate speech.

II. Implementation measures at the country level

16. The State has primary responsibility in respect of the right to human rights education and training. The State has not only an obligation to respect the right to human rights education and training, but also an obligation to achieve progressively the full realization of this right by all appropriate means, including particularly the adoption of legislative measures. It has an obligation to incorporate universal standards in its legislation and to pursue actively policies to fulfill its commitments in the area of human rights education and training, through its institutions and officials.

17. The State also has an obligation to protect and implement human rights education and training, by setting out the legal framework for the action of other public or private entities, including schools and universities, ensuring the professional training of trainers, establishing minimum guarantees and promoting best practices, particularly in the areas of non-discrimination and true equality.

18. The State has a particular responsibility for ensuring the effective enjoyment of the right to human rights education and training by vulnerable groups, by mobilizing its resources according to the criteria of accessibility, acceptability, adequate funding and suitability of the education and training.

19. The State also has responsibility for the initial and continuing professional training of its own officials, including judges, police officers, prison guards and all law enforcement officers. It should also ensure adequate training for members of its armed forces and uniformed services, including in international humanitarian law and international criminal law. It should also concern itself with private personnel acting on behalf of the State.

20. All members of the educational community, including educational institutions and teachers, pupils and students, as well as their families, have an important role to play in helping to better realize the right to human rights education and training through their own initiatives or through joint projects with the public authorities.

21. Human rights education and training, which is an important factor in democratization and knowledge-sharing, must be supported by a strong political will, as clearly demonstrated by an overall implementation strategy and the mobilization of human and financial resources, with specific commitments and goals.

22. The full implementation of such a strategy, drawn up on the basis of the country's needs and priorities, implies effective inter-ministerial coordination and the establishment of specialized administrative bodies.

23. The development and strengthening of national human rights institutions should enable them to play a particularly useful leading role in raising awareness and mobilizing all public and private actors, as well as, where necessary, a coordinating and evaluation role.

24. The conception, implementation and monitoring of this strategy should involve all stakeholders, including civil society bodies, by promoting, where appropriate, multi-stakeholder coalitions.

25. Human rights education and training requires the mobilization of the public authorities, particularly local authorities, and all organs of society, civil society and the private sector. The various actors of civil society, religious institutions, community associations, non-governmental organizations, trade unions, professional associations, youth workers and pupils' parents also have a vital role to play.

Companies, especially multinational companies, cultural institutions and industries, the media and new media should assume their full responsibility in the area of human rights education and training.

26. Human rights education and training must be seen as a long-term exercise; its effective implementation will require progressive and continuous efforts aimed at achieving long-term goals.

27. Human rights education and training should aim for the participation of every person and the strengthening of their capabilities, taking into account different economic, social and cultural circumstances, while promoting local initiatives in order to encourage ownership of the common goal of the fulfilment of all human rights for all.

28. An ongoing assessment of action taken at the national level is vital to the effectiveness of human rights education and training, and requires the establishment of specific goals and quantitative and qualitative indicators.

29. Progress in human rights education and training is nurtured by the initial and in service training of teachers at all educational levels and by theoretical and practical research in the fields of education and teaching methods, as well as international human rights law, thanks to cooperation and networking among specialized institutes and research centres, with a view to producing a definition of common concepts and teaching methods.

30. Particular care must be taken to guarantee the academic freedoms and protect the human rights of those responsible for human rights education and training, in their role as human rights defenders, whether in the formal, informal or non-formal sector.

31. Human rights education and training should draw on the cultural and traditional riches of different countries. The arts, including the theatre, music, the graphic arts and audio-visual works, should be encouraged as a means of training and raising awareness in the field of human rights.

32. Human rights education and training is a matter of communication. As such, it should feature prominently in the field of new technologies, through awareness campaigns suited to a networked world.

III. Implementation measures at the international level

33. The United Nations should promote human rights education and training for its civil and military personnel. It has a special responsibility in crisis situations to make human rights education and training a priority in its peace building and State reconstruction programmes, including in respect of the rule of law and a democratic culture.

34. International and regional organizations should promote human rights education and training for their civil and military personnel. They should, in their sphere of responsibility, include human rights education and training in their activities and cooperation programmes.

35. International non-governmental organizations also have an important role to play in human rights education and training, both internally, with regard to their membership, and in their programmes in the field.

36. International cooperation at the multilateral and bilateral levels, including decentralized cooperation, should support and reinforce national efforts through incentives and pilot schemes, as an extension of the World Programme for Human Rights Education.

37. The full implementation of human rights education and training, as well as of the right to education itself, requires complementary international, regional, national and local efforts, with a constant focus on coordination, coherence, synergies and interdependence.

38. International follow-up to the full implementation of human rights education and training entails the universal ratification of the international human rights instruments and the implementation of a true mainstreaming process by the competent bodies and mechanisms.

39. The treaty-monitoring bodies should, inter alia, adopt general comments on human rights education and training, if they have not already done so, and systematically highlight human rights education and training in the list of issues submitted to States parties and in their concluding observations.

40. Human rights education and training should also be given due prominence in the universal periodic review of the Human Rights Council, as well as in the guidelines on the information required and in the commitments and recommendations made. The process could be strengthened by involving experts in progress assessments.

41. An international centre for human rights education and training could also be set up to facilitate and coordinate the implementation and monitoring of the present Declaration.

42. The establishment of a voluntary international fund for human rights education and training should help finance initiatives and innovative projects in the field.

43. International or national goodwill ambassadors, celebrities, artists and sports men and women can also make a useful contribution to the promotion of a culture of human rights among very different audiences.

Adopted by consensus
8th meeting
29 January 2010

DOCUMENT 2: U.N. GENERAL ASSEMBLY RESOLUTION ON WORLD PROGRAMME FOR HUMAN RIGHTS EDUCATION
UNITED NATIONS

A

General Assembly	Distr.
HUMAN RIGHTS COUNCIL	GENERAL
Twelfth session	A/HRC/RES/12/4*
Agenda item 3	4 December 2009
	Original: ENGLISH

PROMOTION AND PROTECTION OF ALL HUMAN RIGHTS, CIVIL, POLITICAL, ECONOMIC, SOCIAL AND CULTURAL RIGHTS, INCLUDING THE RIGHT TO DEVELOPMENT
Resolution adopted by the Human Rights Council**
12/4. World Programme for Human Rights Education

The Human Rights Council,

*Re-issued for technical reasons.
**The resolutions and decisions adopted by the Human Rights Council will be contained in the report of the Council on its twelfth session (A/HRC/12/50), chap. I.

Reaffirming the fact that States are duty-bound, as stipulated in the Universal Declaration of Human Rights and the International Covenant on Economic, Social and Cultural Rights and in other international human rights instruments, to ensure that education is aimed at strengthening the respect of human rights and fundamental freedoms,

Recalling General Assembly resolutions 43/128 of 8 December 1988, by which the Assembly launched the World Public Information Campaign on Human Rights, 59/113 A of 10 December 2004, 59/113 B of 14 July 2005 and 60/251 of 15 March 2006, in which the Assembly decided, inter alia, that the Council should promote human rights education and learning, and Commission on Human Rights resolution 2005/61 of 20 April 2005 and Subcommission for the Promotion and Protection of Human Rights resolution 2006/19 of 24 August 2006, on the World Programme for Human Rights Education, structured in consecutive phases,

Recalling also Council resolutions 6/9 of 28 September 2007 on the development of public information activities in the field of human rights, 6/24 of 28 September 2007, in which the Council extended to December 2009 the first phase of the World Programme focusing on primary and secondary school systems, 9/12 of 24 September 2008, in which the Council established among the human rights voluntary goals the adoption and implementation of programmes of human rights education in all learning institutions, and 10/3 of 25 March 2009, on consultation on the focus of the second phase of the World Programme,

Recalling further that the World Programme is structured on an ongoing series of consecutive phases, intended as a comprehensive process, including formal and informal education and training, and that Member States should continue the implementation of human rights education in primary and secondary school systems, while taking the necessary measures to implement the World Programme according to its new focus,

1. *Takes note* of the report of the United Nations High Commissioner for Human Rights on the consultation on the focus of the second phase of the World Programme for Human Rights Education (A/HRC/12/36);

2. *Decides* to focus the second phase of the World Programme on human rights education for higher education and on human rights training programmes for teachers and educators, civil servants, law enforcement officials and military personnel at all levels;

3. *Encourages* States that have not yet taken steps to incorporate human rights education in the primary and secondary school system to do so, in accordance with the Plan of Action of the first phase of the World Programme;

4. *Requests* the Office of the United Nations High Commissioner for Human Rights to prepare, within existing resources, in cooperation with relevant intergovernmental organizations, in particular the United Nations Educational, Scientific and Cultural Organization (UNESCO) and non-governmental actors, consult States on and submit for consideration to the fifteenth session of the Human Rights Council (September 2010), a plan of action for the second phase of the World Programme (2010–2014), keeping in mind that it shall be properly structured, formulated in realistic terms, with an indication of at least minimum action, and including provisions to support activities undertaken by all actors;

5. *Recommends* that the Secretary-General ensure that an adequate component of United Nations assistance, to be provided at the request of Member States to develop their national systems of promotion and protection of human rights, is available to support human rights education;

6. *Reminds* Member States of the need to prepare and submit their national evaluation reports on the first phase of the World Programme to the United Nations Inter-Agency Coordinating Committee on Human Rights Education in the School System by early 2010;

7. *Requests* the Coordinating Committee to submit a final evaluation report of the implementation of the first phase of the World Programme, based on national evaluation reports, in cooperation with relevant international, regional and non-governmental organizations, to the General Assembly at its sixty-fifth session;

8. *Decides* to consider this issue at its fifteenth session under the same agenda item.

30th meeting
1 October 2009
[Adopted without a vote.]

DOCUMENT 3: FINAL EVALUATION OF THE IMPLEMENTATION OF THE FIRST PHASE OF THE WORLD PROGRAMME FOR HUMAN RIGHTS EDUCATION

UNITED NATIONS	A/65/322
General Assembly	Distr.:
Sixty-fifth session	GENERAL
Item 69 (b) of the provisional agenda*	24 August 2010
	Original: ENGLISH
	10-49311 (E) 200910

PROMOTION AND PROTECTION OF HUMAN RIGHTS: HUMAN
RIGHTS QUESTIONS, INCLUDING ALTERNATIVE APPROACHES
FOR IMPROVING THE EFFECTIVE ENJOYMENT OF HUMAN RIGHTS
AND FUNDAMENTAL FREEDOMS
FINAL EVALUATION OF THE IMPLEMENTATION OF THE FIRST
PHASE OF THE WORLD PROGRAMME FOR HUMAN
RIGHTS EDUCATION

Report of the United Nations Inter-Agency Coordinating Committee on
Human Rights Education in the School System, as submitted by the Office of the
High Commissioner for Human Rights

Summary

The present report is submitted in response to Human Rights Council resolution 12/4, in which the Council requested the United Nations Inter-Agency Coordinating Committee on Human Rights Education in the School System to submit to the General Assembly a final evaluation report, based on national evaluation reports, on the implementation of the first phase of the World Programme for Human Rights Education. The report finds that the 76 Member States which provided national evaluation reports are taking some measures to integrate human rights education in their school systems. There is particularly notable progress in making human rights education part of national curricula. There are also a number of national initiatives in terms of policy and action to foster a culture of respect for human rights in daily school life. Certain gaps in implementation remain, which suggests the need for a more comprehensive and systematic approach at the national level. Accordingly, Member States are encouraged to consolidate progress further by continuing implementation in line with the guidance provided by the plan of action.

Contents

Page

I. Introduction
A. Background information

1. The General Assembly, in resolution 59/113 A of 10 December 2004, proclaimed the World Programme for Human Rights Education as a global initiative structured in consecutive phases, intended to advance the implementation of human rights education programmes in all sectors. The first phase of the World Programme covered the period 2005-20091 and focused on integrating human rights education in the primary and secondary school systems.

2. In resolution 59/113 B of 14 July 2005, the Assembly adopted the plan of action for the first phase of the World Programme (A/59/525/Rev.1), which proposes a concrete strategy and practical guidance for implementing human rights education nationally.2 The Assembly, inter alia, encouraged all States to develop initiatives within the World Programme and, in particular, to implement, within their capabilities, the plan of action; and appealed to relevant organs, bodies or agencies of the United Nations system, as well as all other international and regional intergovernmental and non-governmental organizations, within their respective mandates, to promote and technically assist, when requested, the national implementation of the plan of action.

3. The plan of action was developed by a broad group of education and human rights practitioners from all continents. It seeks to promote a holistic, rights-based approach to the education system that includes both "human rights through education", ensuring that all the components and processes of education—including curricula, materials, methods and training—are conducive to the learning of human rights, and "human rights in education", ensuring that the human rights of all members of the school community are respected. Human rights education activities should convey fundamental human rights values, such as equality and non-discrimination, while affirming the interdependence, indivisibility and universality of these principles. At the same time, activities should be practical, relating human rights to learners' real-life experience and enabling them to build on human rights principles found in their own cultural context.

4. The plan of action recognizes the diversity of country contexts and the varying possibilities for integrating human rights education into school systems. It highlights the following five components which support the implementation of human rights education at the national level: policies; policy implementation; the learning environment; teaching and learning processes and tools; and education and professional development of teachers and other education personnel. The plan of action includes an appendix entitled "Components of human rights education in the primary and secondary school systems", which provides further guidance on how each of these components can be implemented and proposes good practice based on successful experiences from around the world as well as studies and research.

Relevant actors are urged to strive towards gradual and progressive implementation.

The components are addressed in greater detail in subsequent sections of the present report.

5. In paragraph 26 of the plan of action, it is suggested that national implementation of the plan of action take place in four stages: analysis of the current situation of human rights education in the school system; setting priorities and developing a national implementation strategy; implementing and monitoring; and evaluating. In paragraph 27, Member States are encouraged to undertake at least the first two stages during the first phase of the World Programme, as well as initial implementation of planned activities.

6. The United Nations Inter-Agency Coordinating Committee on Human Rights Education in the School System was established in September 2006, in accordance with the plan of action, to facilitate coordinated United Nations support for the national implementation of the plan of action during the first phase. The Office of the High Commissioner for Human Rights (OHCHR) has provided the secretariat for the Coordinating Committee.

B. Mandate for the evaluation

7. The plan of action calls for an evaluation of action undertaken during the first phase of the World Programme (2005–2009). Paragraph 49 states that each country will undertake an evaluation of actions implemented under the plan of action, taking into consideration progress made in legal frameworks and policies, curricula, teaching and learning processes and tools, revision of textbooks, teacher training, improvement of the school environment and other areas. The Member States will be called upon to provide their final national evaluation report to the Coordinating Committee. Paragraph 51 provides that the Coordinating Committee will prepare a final evaluation report based on national evaluation reports, in cooperation with relevant international, regional and non-governmental organizations. The report will be submitted to the General Assembly.

8. The Human Rights Council, in its resolution 12/4 of 1 October 2009, reminded Member States to submit their national evaluation reports to the Coordinating Committee by early 2010 and requested the Coordinating Committee to submit a final evaluation report of the implementation of the first phase of the World Programme, based on national evaluation reports, in cooperation with relevant international, regional and non-governmental organizations, to the General Assembly at its sixty-fifth session. Accordingly, the present evaluation report takes stock of reported progress during the first phase against the objectives set out in the plan of action.

C. Evaluation methodology

9. The evaluation methodology was discussed by the Coordinating Committee at its meetings of February and December 2009. It was agreed that it would be carried out through a documentary review of primary and secondary sources of information on national initiatives carried out during the first phase.

10. The primary sources of information are the national evaluation reports which were sent in reply to an evaluation questionnaire developed by the Coordinating Committee and distributed by OHCHR in early 2010 to the 192 States Members of the United Nations.4 As at 21 July 2010, OHCHR had received 76 responses; the list of countries having submitted national evaluation reports is contained in annex I to the present report. Many countries provided detailed answers and supplementary documents. Some countries, such as Albania, Mexico, Senegal and Zimbabwe, reported having involved a range of stakeholders in the production of the report. Cambodia noted that it had deployed a comprehensive methodology involving sampling; data collection and assessment on the ground; reporting by provincial departments; analysis and discussion by various heads of departments at national level; drafting and finalization by the central education department; and final approval by top leaders. The national reports were mainly compiled by ministries of education; in some countries, other offices dealing with external affairs, human rights, finance and justice were involved or even took the lead. External stakeholders such as non-governmental organizations, youth representatives and others were rarely involved in producing the national reports.

11. The evaluation also takes into account information contained in a variety of secondary sources submitted by Governments to the United Nations in the period 2005–2010, namely:

(a) Other correspondence received from Governments on national human rights education initiatives in the context of the World Programme, including replies to letters from OHCHR/UNESCO and the Coordinating Committee;

(b) Correspondence from Governments concerning the implementation of the International Year of Human Rights Learning;

(c) Replies from Governments to the questionnaire of the Human Rights Council advisory committee on the draft United Nations declaration on human rights education and training;

(d) Governments' common core documents;

(e) National reports submitted to the Working Group on the Universal Periodic Review.

12. The replies to the evaluation questionnaires were analysed in detail; the consistency in structure made it possible to make cross comparisons and to identify global trends and common challenges among Governments. The present report is therefore very largely based on the data contained in the national evaluation reports. It gives examples of national initiatives drawn from this body of information, which are intended to be illustrative and are by no means exhaustive. The secondary sources of information were, by contrast, more variable; they addressed different types of issues to varying levels of depth, making a detailed comparative analysis less feasible or appropriate. Accordingly, this second body of information was consulted only for countries that did not submit national evaluation reports (the list of those countries is contained in annex II to the present report). This dual approach enables the evaluation report to give a sense of global progress while focusing more deeply on specific issues and the experiences of individual countries which responded to the questionnaire.

13. No governmental information was available on approximately 60 countries. It may well be that these countries are taking measures related to human rights education; however, this report is not making any comments or drawing any conclusions about them.

14. The evaluation had recourse to over 200 documents, between primary and secondary sources, and there were various methodological issues to consider in the handling of this volume of information of differing quality and content. The national evaluation reports varied considerably: they were sometimes incomplete or ambiguous, e.g. containing conflicting or multiple replies to the same question or lacking in clarity owing to

language, handwritten scripts or limited information. Some countries did not follow the questionnaire structure in their answers; others reported future plans rather than an assessment of progress to date. Three subnational reports were received from one Government, reflecting the decentralized competence for education matters.

15. In order to bring some consistency and to report against the plan of action as comprehensively as possible, the analysis was organized according to each of the five components of the plan of action. The questions in the evaluation questionnaire were divided up as follows:

(a) Component one, on policies, includes an analysis of questions 10, 13, 14,15, 16, 18, 23 and 25;

(b) Component two, on policy implementation, includes an analysis of questions 11, 12 and 22;

(c) Component three, on the learning environment, includes an analysis of questions 17, 19, 20 and 21;

(d) Component four, on teaching and learning processes and tools, includes an analysis of questions 24 and 26;

(e) Component five, on education and professional development of school personnel, includes an analysis of questions 27, 28, 29 and 30.

16. The analysis keeps to this structure and aims as far as possible to report information as it was provided by Governments. An effort was made not to move information around to answer different questions from those intended by the respondent.

17. Finally, it is important to stress that the present report, in accordance with the plan of action and as reiterated by the Human Rights Council, is based on national evaluation reports provided by Member States. It is an analysis of official information provided in those self-assessments; it is not an independent verification or assessment of the information provided or of the quality of the actions taken.

II. Action at the national level

A. Policies

18. The first component of the plan of action, policies, involves "developing in a participatory way and adopting coherent educational policies, legislation and strategies that are human rights-based, including curriculum improvement and training policies for teachers and other educational personnel" (para. 18 (a)).

Human rights and educational policies

19. All 76 responding Governments state that they have educational policies which promote human rights education. Of these, 57 report having policies which explicitly refer to human rights, the right to education and rights-based approaches to the education system. These commitments are integrated in a range of legal and policy frameworks such as constitutions, education laws and legislation and policies related to specific topics such as child protection, disability, gender equality, domestic violence, sexual harassment and minority rights.

20. Some countries like El Salvador and Uruguay make specific reference in their policies to human rights education. Nicaragua has a specific law on the teaching of human rights and the Constitution. In Austria, there are decrees on education for democratic citizenship and human rights education. A number of other Member States report similar policy commitments but a closer examination of supporting documents finds that the term "human rights" is often not used explicitly. They refer to subjects like civic education, citizenship education, peace education, multicultural education and education for sustainable development, under which human rights issues are said to be addressed. Germany cites recommendations of the Standing Conference of Ministers of Education and Cultural Affairs on education for democratic citizenship, education for sustainable and global development and intercultural education which have been transformed into land law.

21. Some countries have refined their human rights education policies after reviewing their implementation. Norway developed its first plan of action on human rights in 2000 and is now making fundamental changes to its education laws in response to feedback received from civil society actors who identified the fragmented implementation of human rights education as a challenge.

22. Regional human rights education initiatives may support a coordinated policy approach at the national level. The Arab Plan for Education on Human Rights has been taken up by Iraq, Oman, Qatar and others. In Europe, Norway established the European Wergeland Centre in cooperation with the Council of Europe, with a view to offering support to European States on education for intercultural understanding human rights and democratic citizenship. Tunisia collaborates with organizations like the Arab Institute for Human Rights (*Institut arabe des droits de l'Homme*) and the Centre of Arab Women for Training and Research.

Human rights in the school curriculum

23. The plan of action calls for the integration of human rights education in the school curriculum. Most Member States seem to have focused on this course of action. Numerous Governments including Australia, Barbados, Chile, Côte d'Ivoire, Indonesia, Namibia, Zambia and others report that human rights education is integrated in the national curriculum and in educational standards. A few countries teach human rights as a stand-alone subject but many integrate human rights as across-cutting issue, most often in subjects such as citizenship, civic education and social studies, but also in other disciplines such as law, religion, life skills, ethical and moral education, environment, health and physical education and others.

24. In Costa Rica, human rights, democracy and peace is one of the four crosscutting transversal axes of the curriculum, seen as part of daily learning and experience. The Russian Federation has adopted a dual approach, teaching human rights and the rights of the child as a single subject as well as integrating them in other subjects, such as social sciences or law, as confirmed by a study undertaken in 2007–2008. A related survey found that 93 per cent of students felt their school studies covered human rights and the rights of the child. A study in Egypt by the National Council for Human Rights found that Arabic language and social studies courses in the fourth year of primary school took human rights into account. In Thailand, human rights appears in three subject areas: the social, religious and culture subject area, which covers child rights, human rights standards and mechanisms and the Universal Declaration on Human Rights; the health and physical education subject area, which covers topics such as consumer protection and freedom from sexual abuse; and the occupational and technologies subject area, which addresses the right to work. The Syrian Arab Republic has developed a national curriculum integrating principles and values related to human rights, including women's rights, in diverse subjects in primary and secondary education.

25. The majority of countries state that "human rights" is a compulsory subject and only one country reported it to be a completely optional course of study. Among the countries that reported it to be mandatory, Portugal said that it was compulsory for elementary school pupils (6 to 15 years of age); the civic education course explicitly provides for human rights education and there is a mandatory training module for students of 10 to 11 years of age referred to as "Citizenship and security" which approaches security issues from a human rights perspective. Human rights education as part of the national curriculum is also obligatory in Hungary and in Malaysia where it is part of subjects such as civics and citizenship education, moral education and Islamic education taught at both primary and secondary level. Some countries make it optional at certain stages of the school career and mandatory at others.

26. Governments gave detailed responses about the number of hours of study devoted to these curricular subjects. In most countries at least one or two hours a week are allocated to subjects which include human rights. However, it is not clear how extensively human rights are integrated into those subjects, what is being studied and how much actual time is spent on human rights. Cuba was one of the few countries to provide details showing the inclusion of specific human rights topics in its general curriculum. In addition, reference has been made to a number of extra-curricular human rights activities, for example, the "Human Rights Olympics" organized in Slovakia since 1997, which involve secondary school students in a nationwide annual competition testing their knowledge and essay-writing skills. In the Philippines, the Government has extended human rights education to the non-formal sector in order to reach out-of-school youth.

27. The national evaluation reports mention that the course content is being adapted to the needs of pupils of differing ages and abilities. Ukraine has methodologies that progressively tackle the complexity of human rights as students become older. In Chile, human rights education takes a comprehensive and staggered approach which addresses human rights issues step by step, starting from class-level activities to promote peace and tolerance among young children, and moving to the study of human rights violations committed during the military regime for older students. In France, there is a multifaceted programme which looks at notions of individual and collective responsibility. Human rights education starts from looking at concrete situations and turns to analysing how human rights can respond to these situations; it also includes awareness of major human rights documents. Some countries like El Salvador and Italy integrate human rights education into early childhood learning and nursery/kindergarten level through age appropriate activities.

28. On the issue of which institutions have the authority to develop, approve and change the curriculum, Governments invariably answered that the Ministry of Education gives final approval. In some States, authority is given to an independent body in which the Ministry of Education is one stakeholder among others. In Costa Rica, for example, the Higher Education Council comprised of various ministries, representatives of universities, secondary and primary schools, teachers and provincial boards approves the curriculum. In Cyprus,

the Committee of Experts for the development of a new curriculum has held structured consultations with interested stakeholders such as teachers' unions as well as parent and student associations. In Madagascar, the Ministry of National Education and the National Council of Education in partnership with eight national directorates for private education approve the curriculum. In some countries, regional organizations have influence in the development, approval and changing of curricula; Guyana reports that the Caribbean Examination Council plays this role with the approval of its member countries.

Policies concerning textbooks development

29. The development of policy guidelines for writing or revising textbooks that reflect human rights principles is an important contribution to human rights education. The majority of Governments (39 out of 76) said that they had such guidelines; two explicitly said that they did not, the rest did not respond clearly. In Jordan, a matrix of human rights, culture of peace and common universal values was prepared by Jordanian human rights experts to act as a reference for curriculum planners and textbook writers. In Peru, the Government took the approach of defining key principles on which such texts should be based, such as multiculturalism, equality and inclusion. In Cambodia, human rights education is incorporated in textbooks within the "Life skills" teaching framework; the same applies to Gambia. The Philippines reports that the Department of Education has issued criteria for assessing whether texts are free from ideological, religious, racial and gender prejudices. Responses to this question from other countries sometimes suggested that guidance may be somewhat limited, e.g. one country referred only to gender equality.

30. Only a minority of Governments responding to the evaluation questionnaire (21 out of 76) could confirm that textbooks had been developed in accordance with specific guidelines. El Salvador cites specific textbooks used in the school system which cover human rights, including national and international laws. Thailand is one of a small number of countries to have carried out a review of textbooks in order to identify gaps requiring attention. There seem to be very few Governments which produce textbooks themselves; one example is the Education Centre for Research and Development which is the sole public body in Lebanon with the authority to issue textbooks related to civic education. Most Governments appear only to set curriculum guidelines, which are not always mandatory, and then allow commercial companies, private authors, civil society groups, schools and others to develop textbooks on their own. The process of approval seems to vary considerably; the Czech Republic has a certification process while others take a more informal approach. Governments like Norway and the United Kingdom of Great Britain and Northern Ireland give schools the autonomy to choose their own materials, making it inappropriate for the Government to set tight guidelines on textbook content.

Policies concerning the learning environment

31. The plan of action promotes human rights practice in all aspects of school life. Few countries could provide details of national or subnational policies that promote a human rights approach to school governance, management, disciplinary procedures, inclusion policies and other regulations and practices affecting school culture and access to education. The replies tend to make ad hoc reference to general policies already mentioned such as child protection, inclusion, gender equity, non-discrimination, coexistence, violence, child-friendly schools and so on. There were nonetheless some examples of these types of issues being addressed. Gambia, Spain and others state that these issues are covered by school management manuals. In Mauritius, the school management manual also applies to the private sector education. Slovenian schools have a school education plan and a school code of conduct.

Policies concerning teacher training

32. The overall approach to teacher training seems ad hoc. There are only a few examples of a comprehensive policy on teacher training in accordance with the plan of action. A fair number of countries (15) did not respond at all or said they had no such policy. A recurrent reason relates to the issue of academic freedom, independence and institutional autonomy for higher education establishments. Norway, for example, says that the Government may not instruct such institutions on the content of teaching and research but can set a national curriculum for certain subjects; from 2010, future graduates will cover child rights from a national and international perspective. The Philippines reports that a 1998 Department of Education order provides for the training of teachers to become human rights teachers.

Final observations

33. Overall, an analysis of primary source information shows that all 76 respondent Governments have reported policy-level commitments with regard to human rights education to some degree; the secondary source information analysis shows that approximately 32 additional countries have relevant policy statements

in place. The fact that in many cases human rights education is said to be covered by related subjects, such as peace education, democratic citizenship education, civic education, education for sustainable development or life skills education, or as a cross-curricular issue, makes it difficult to draw firm conclusions on how far human rights principles are embodied in educational policies. Efforts made to integrate human rights education into national curricula seem particularly encouraging, while other policy areas seem to be overlooked, in particular as far as teacher training is concerned.

B. Policy implementation

34. The second component of the plan of action, policy implementation, refers to "planning the implementation of the above-mentioned educational policies by taking appropriate organizational measures and by facilitating the involvement of all stakeholders" (para. 18 (b)).

Overall national human rights education strategies and plans

35. The plan of action recommends the elaboration and dissemination of a comprehensive national implementation strategy with regard to human rights education in the school system. Nearly all Governments report having a national implementation strategy on human rights education, not necessarily developed in the context of the World Programme; only very few say that they have no strategy at all—sometimes because their federal political structures preclude the possibility of overall national planning. Examples of comprehensive national initiatives include Burkina Faso, which developed a strategy on the promotion and protection of human rights in 2008. In Guatemala, the peace accords set out the need to develop a national civic education programme for democracy and peace, which promotes human rights, the renewal of political culture and the peaceful resolution of conflicts. The implementation plan involved assessing needs, conducting forums and surveys and the provision of training to educators by the national human rights institution (*Procuraduría de los Derechos Humanos*). Tunisia established a National Commission on Human Rights Education in April 1996 presided over by the Ministry of Education, to be in charge of putting in place a related national strategy.

Under Jordan's human rights education plan, the National Commission for Education, Culture and Science has been appointed as a liaison between the Ministry of Education and other national organizations; it focuses on coordination arrangements, curriculum development, training and collaboration with bodies such as the National Centre of Human Rights. In Qatar, a supreme committee was formed comprising both national ministries and UNESCO to supervise child rights education in schools; it has developed a national action plan to provide educational guides for teachers which align international principles with Islamic culture. Croatia has a comprehensive national human rights education programme which was developed in the second half of the 1990s under the auspices of the National Human Rights Education Committee established by the Government. Morocco has made a major effort to integrate human rights education into the curriculum, programmes and manuals and raises awareness about its national programme on occasions such as Human Rights Day, International Children's Day and International Women's Day.

36. A majority of countries report that human rights education is included either fully or partially in national plans and strategies on human rights, the fight against racism and discrimination, gender equality, poverty reduction, primary and secondary education, education for all and education for sustainable development. The national evaluation reports provide examples of countries taking this approach. In Costa Rica, human rights education is dealt with in the context of programmes related to violence in schools, the participation of students and relations with the wider community, gender equality and the rights of disabled persons. In New Zealand, human rights education is dealt with in the context of the rights of minority and indigenous groups, resulting in a curriculum document which was developed with the full participation of indigenous groups and which addresses their interests.

In Switzerland, human rights education is part of the national plan for education for sustainable development (2007–2014), while in the United Kingdom (Scotland), the Government is providing over £9 million in funding during the period 2008–2011 to organizations tackling racist attitudes and working to improve the lives of ethnic minority communities through, among others, education initiatives.

III. Conclusions and recommendations

63. In paragraph 27 of the plan of action, Member States were encouraged to undertake, as a minimum action in the first phase, the first two stages of national implementation of the World Programme for Human Rights Education, i.e. a situation analysis (stage one) and the setting of priorities and development of a national implementation strategy (stage two). The majority of Member States have confirmed that they are now, by and large, implementing human rights education programmes.

64. Some Governments acknowledge that the World Programme has played a role in facilitating progress at the national level. Several countries find it to be an important influence, including Algeria, Jordan and Venezuela (Bolivarian Republic of), which say that it was an important spur to national action. A few countries report activities specifically aimed at promoting the World Programme, for instance Côte d'Ivoire held a seminar at the official launch of national activities on the World Programme, and Greece reports featuring information about the World Programme on the Ministry of Education's website. However, a number of countries report not to have used this international framework as an opportunity to increase implementation of human rights education in their school systems; national action appears to have been occurring somewhat independently of the proclamation of the World Programme.

65. There continue to be challenges in national implementation. Among the commonly identified gaps are the absence of explicit policies and detailed implementation strategies for human rights education and the lack of systematic approaches to the production of materials, the training of teachers and the promotion of a learning environment which fosters human rights values. The decentralization of political structures and/or education provision in a number of countries further complicates the implementation of a centralized model.

66. The Coordinating Committee makes the following recommendations to Governments wishing to take further steps to implement human rights education in the school system:

(a) Take stock of national progress as measured against the detailed guidance provided in the plan of action in order to identify gaps, possible strategies and good practice;

(b) Review the following issues which have been identified in the present report to see if they are relevant to the national context and require attention: (i) Overall review of the status of human rights education in the primary and secondary school system and development of a comprehensive implementation strategy, taking into consideration the guidance proposed by the plan of action; (ii) And specifically, among other issues, the need for educational policy commitments explicitly referring to the human rights framework; development and implementation of policies on teacher training which make human rights education part of mandatory teacher qualification requirements; review of the national curricula to clarify how and to what extent human rights education is dealt with, including through integration of human rights in other subjects which are assumed to address them; and allocation of funding to human rights education as an identifiable item in the context of national education budgets;

(c) Make greater use of the human rights education materials and tools developed by national, regional and international institutions and organizations within or beyond the context of the World Programme, including information technology platforms, as a way of addressing resource issues at the national level such as the lack of funding, education and learning materials and specifically teacher-training materials, and in order to draw inspiration from other national practices;

(d) Take steps to ensure that private education providers are also integrating human rights education into their services;

(e) Participate in international and regional initiatives with regard to policy and programme development in the area of human rights education.

67. By establishing the open-ended World Programme for Human Rights Education, and more recently by launching a new international initiative concerning the development of a United Nations declaration on human rights education and training, the international community has reaffirmed its long-term commitment to pursue human rights education, which was already embodied in many international instruments. Although significant steps have been taken, progress remains uneven when considered from a global perspective. The World Programme's first phase has nevertheless provided an opportunity for focusing the attention of the international community on the importance of human rights education in the school system.

68. While the World Programme now transitions to its second phase (2010-2014) with a new focus on a variety of different sectors (i.e. higher education, teachers and educators, civil servants, law enforcement officials and military personnel), work on primary and secondary-level education needs to continue. Governments are encouraged to build on existing achievements, consolidate them and exert sustained efforts to advance human rights education in the school system as a holistic process concerning many areas of action, including educational policies, policy implementation measures, the learning environment, teaching and learning processes and tools and education and professional development of teachers and other education personnel. The plan of action for the first phase of the World Programme continues to constitute a significant guidance tool in this area, and the open-ended World Programme remains a common collective framework

for action as well as a platform for cooperation between Governments and all other relevant stakeholders; its potential, in terms of enhancing national action towards the building of a universal culture of human rights, needs to be further exploited.
[Footnotes Omitted]

Annex I
List of Governments that responded to the evaluation questionnaire[a]

Albania
Algeria
Angola
Argentina
Australia
Austria
Barbados
Belarus
Belgium
Bolivia (Plurinational State of)
Burkina Faso
Cambodia
Chile
Colombia
Costa Rica
Côte d'Ivoire
Cuba
Cyprus
Czech Republic
Democratic Republic of the Congo
Egypt
El Salvador
Estonia
France
Gambia
Germany
Greece
Guatemala
Guyana
Honduras
Hungary
Indonesia
Iraq
Israel
Japan
Jordan
Kazakhstan
Kuwait
Lebanon

Lithuania
Madagascar
Malaysia
Malta
Mauritania
Mauritius
Mexico
Monaco
Montenegro
Morocco
Namibia
New Zealand
Nicaragua
Norway
Oman
Paraguay
Peru
Philippines
Portugal
Qatar (submissions from two different entities)
Russian Federation
Senegal (submission from two different entities)
Serbia
Slovakia
Slovenia
Spain
Sudan
Switzerland
Syrian Arab Republic
Thailand
Turkey
United Kingdom of Great Britain and Northern Ireland (separate submissions from England, Scotland and Northern Ireland)
Ukraine
Uruguay
Venezuela (Bolivarian Republic of)
Zambia
Zimbabwe

Annex II

List of Governments that submitted information on national human rights education initiatives in contexts other than the preparation of the present report.

Information on human rights education in countries whose Governments did not respond to the final evaluation questionnaire was also taken into account in the preparation of the present report. This information was found in various secondary sources as noted in the introduction to the report.

Afghanistan
Armenia
Azerbaijan
Brunei Darussalam
Bulgaria
Burundi
Cameroon
Cape Verde
Canada
Chad
China
Croatia
Denmark
Dominican Republic
Ecuador
Equatorial Guinea
Ethiopia
Finland
India
Indonesia
Gabon
Georgia
Guinea
Iceland
Italy
Kyrgyzstan
Lao People's Democratic Republic
Latvia
Lesotho

Liberia
Libyan Arab Jamahiriya
Liechtenstein
Luxembourg
Mongolia
Mozambique
Netherlands
Niger
Pakistan
Panama
Poland
Republic of Korea
Republic of Moldova
Romania
Rwanda
Samoa
Saudi Arabia
Singapore
South Africa
Sri Lanka
Sweden
The former Yugoslav Republic of Macedonia
Timor-Leste
Togo
Trinidad and Tobago
Tunisia
Turkmenistan
Uzbekistan

APPENDIX R: YOUR HUMAN RIGHTS UNDER THE INTERNATIONAL BILL OF HUMAN RIGHTS

Your Human Rights Under the International Bill of Rights is a complete list of your human rights found in three of the main historical international human rights instruments, transposed into second person declaratory statements, e.g. "You have the right to life."

©H. Victor Condé 2003

THE FOLLOWING are the substantive human rights which you hold which are found in the first three of the four following international human rights instruments which comprise the <u>International Bill of Rights</u>:
- Universal Declaration of Human Rights (UDHR)
- International Covenant on Economic, Social and Cultural Rights (ICESCR)
- International Covenant on Civil and Political Rights (ICCPR)
- Optional Protocol to the International Covenant on Civil and Political Rights (ICCPR-OP)

(Some sources include the Second Optional Protocol to the ICCPR, abolishing the death penalty, as one of the human rights instruments which form the International Bill of Rights. Because this is not generally accepted this instrument will not be reflected in the following list of human rights).

YOUR SUBSTANTIVE HUMAN RIGHTS

You have the right to the exercise of all the following rights without discrimination based on your race, religion, color, sex, language, political or other opinion, national/social origin, property, birth/ other status.

You have the right to life.

You have the right to liberty and security of person.

You have the right to be free from slavery and forced labor.

You have the right to be free from torture, cruel, inhuman, or degrading treatment or punishment.

You have the right to recognition as a legal person before the law.

You have the right to equal protection (equality) of the law.

You have the right to access to effective domestic legal remedies for human rights violations.

You have the right to be free from arbitrary arrest or detention.

You have the right to a fair public hearing/trial before a competent, independent, impartial judiciary.

You have the right to be presumed innocent against criminal charges and to all procedural due process rights.

You have the right to be free from retroactive (*ex post facto*) criminal laws, and from double jeopardy.

You have the right, if detained, to be treated with humanity (humanely) and with respect for your human dignity.

You have the right to be free from interference with privacy, home, and family.

You have the right to be free from imprisonment for the inability to pay debts.

You have the right to freedom of movement, choice of residence, and to leave a country.

You have the right to seek asylum from persecution.

You have the right to have a nationality.

You have the right to own property.

You have the right, as a man and a woman of marriageable age, to marry and have (found) a family.

You have the right, if you are in motherhood or a childhood, to special protection.

You have the right, if you are an alien, to freedom from arbitrary expulsion from a country.

You have the right to freedom of thought, conscience and religion.

You have the right to freedom of expression, opinion, and the press.

You have the right to freedom from propaganda advocating war, or inciting national, racial or religious hatred.

You have the right to free assembly and association.

You have the right to participate in the political life of the society.

You have the right, if you are a member of an ethnic, religious, or linguistic minority, to enjoy your own culture, use your own language and practice your own religion.

You have the right to an adequate standard of living, including housing, clothing, and food.

You have the right to the highest attainable standard of physical and mental health
You have the right to an education.
You have the right to social security.
You have the right to work, under just and favorable conditions.
You have the right to form and participate in trade unions.
You have the right to participate in the cultural life of your society.
You have the right to enjoy the benefits of scientific progress.
You have the right as a "peoples" to self determination (to determine your own political status; pursue economic and cultural development and use your own natural wealth and resources).
You have the right to a social and international order necessary to allow you to realize these rights.
You have the right to adequate rest and leisure.

[In situations of armed conflict you would have legal protection under human rights law and also under international humanitarian law.] And remember: for every human right their correlative duties that everyone must fulfill in order for human rights to be realized.

BIBLIOGRAPHY

Prepared by Trezlen D. Drake, JD, MLIS
Reference and International/Comparative Law Librarian, New York Law School

TERMINOLOGY

Amnesty International. *Amnesty International Handbook*. 7th ed. New York: Amnesty International Publications, 1992.

Bledsoe, R., and B. Boczek. *The International Law Dictionary*. Santa Barbara, CA: ABC-CLIO, 1987.

Condé, H. Victor. *A Handbook of International Human Rights Terminology*. 2nd ed. Lincoln: University of Nebraska Press, 2005.

Forsythe, David P. Ed. Encyclopedia of Human Rights. New York: Oxford University Press, 2009.

Gibson, J. *Dictionary of International Human Rights Law*. Lanham, MD: Scarecrow Press, 1996.

Lawson, E., ed. *Encyclopedia of Human Rights*. 2d. ed. New York: Taylor & Francis, 1997.

Parry, C., and J. Grant. *Encyclopaedic Dictionary of International Law*. 3d. ed. New York: Oxford University Press, 2009.

Plano, A., and R. Olton. *The International Relations Dictionary*. 4th ed. Santa Barbara, CA: ABC-CLIO, 1990.

Robertson, D. *A Dictionary of Human Rights*. 2d. ed. Florence, KY: Routledge, 2004.

Ziring L., J. Plano, and R. Olton. *International Relations: A Political Dictionary*. 5th ed. Santa Barbara, CA: ABC-CLIO, 1995.

GENERAL HUMAN RIGHTS

Amnesty International. *Amnesty International Report*. London: Amnesty International Publications, 1962–2010. (annual).

Amnesty International Report 2010. New York: Amnesty International USA, 2010.

_____. *The Universal Declaration of Human Rights 1948–1988*. New York: Amnesty International USA, 1988.

An-Na'im, Abdullah A. *Human Rights in Cross-Cultural Perspectives: A Quest for Consensus*. Philadelphia: University of Pennsylvania Press, 1995.

Austin, Clark S., Rita Cantos Cartwright, and Andrea S. Hoberman. *The Human Rights Education Project: Tools for the Activist*. San Diego, CA: Erini Publishing, 2000.

Claude, R. P., and B. H. Weston, eds. *Human Rights in the World Community*. 3d ed. Philadelphia: University of Pennsylvania Press, 2006.

Donnelly, J. *International Human Rights: Dilemmas in World Politics*. 3d ed. Boulder, CO: Westview Press, 2006.

Donnelly, J. *Universal Human Rights in Theory and Practice*. 2nd ed. Ithaca: Cornell University Press, 2003.

Universal Human Rights in Theory and Practice. 2d ed. Ithaca: Cornell University Press, 2002.

Dunne, Tim, and Nicholas J. Wheeler, eds. *Human Rights in Global Politics*. Cambridge: Cambridge University Press, 1999.

Forsythe, David P. *Human Rights and Peace: International and National Dimensions*. Lincoln: University of Nebraska Press, 1994.

Human Rights and World Politics. 2d ed. Lincoln: University of Nebraska Press, 1989.

Glendon, M. A. *Rights Talk: The Impoverishment of Political Discourse*. New York: The Free Press, 1993.

Hannum, Hurst, ed. *Guide to International Human Rights Practice*. 4th ed. New York: Transnational Publishers, 2004.

Hesse, Carla Alison, and Robert Post, eds. *Human Rights in Political Transitions: Gettysburg to Bosnia.* New York: Zone Books, 1999.
Koh, Harold H., and R. C. Slye. *Deliberative Democracy and Human Rights.* New Haven: Yale University Press, 2007.
Laqueur, W., and B. Rubin, eds. *The Human Rights Reader.* Rev. sub. ed. New York: Plume, 1990.
Primus, Richard A. *The American Language of Rights.* Cambridge: Cambridge University Press, 2004.
Ratner, Stephen, Jason Abrams, and James Bischoff. *Accountability for Human Rights Atrocities in International Law: Beyond the Nuremberg Legacy.* 3d ed. Oxford: Oxford University Press, 2009.

U.S. RELATED PUBLICATIONS

American Civil Liberties Union. *International Civil Liberties Report.* Los Angeles: American Civil Liberties Union, 1992–(annual).
American Law Institute. "Restatement of the Law, Third, The Foreign Relations Law of the United States." St. Paul, MN: American Law Institute, 1987–.
Amnesty International. *Betraying the Young: Children in the U.S. Justice System.* New York: Amnesty International USA, 1998.
"Rights for All: Human Rights in the United States of America: An Amnesty International International Briefing." London: Amnesty International, 1998.
United States of America—Rights for All. London: Amnesty International, 1998.
Forsythe, David P., ed. *The United States and Human Rights: Looking Inward and Outward.* Lincoln: University of Nebraska Press, 2008.
Human Rights First. *Human Rights and U.S. Foreign Policy: Report and Recommendations.* New York: Human Rights First, 11992.
The Reagan Administration's Record of Human Rights in 1983–1989. New York: Human Rights First.
Human Rights Watch, ed. *Justice in the Balance: Recommendations for an Independent and Effective International Criminal Court.* New York: Human Rights Watch, 1998.
Prison Conditions in the United States. New York: Human Rights Watch, 1991.
Kly, Y. N. *International Law and the U.S. Human Rights Foreign Policy.* Clarity Press, 1993.
Mittal, Anuradha and Peter Rosset. *America Needs Human Rights.* Hayward, CA: Institute for Food & Development Policy/Food First Books, 1999.
Smith, Christopher H., ed. *U.S./China Relations and Human Rights: Is Constructive Engagement Working?* DIANE, 1999.
Steinmetz, Sara. *Democratic Transition and Human Rights: Perspectives on U.S. Foreign Policy.* New York: State University of New York Press, 1994.
Stephens, Beth, Judith Chomsky, Jennifer Green, Paul Hoffman, and Michael Ratner. *International Human Rights Litigation in U.S. Courts.* 2d rev. ed. Boston: Martinus Nijhoff Publishers, 2008.
Wronka, Joseph. *Human Rights and Social Policy in the 21st Century: A History of the Idea of Human Rights and Comparison of the United Nations Universal Declaration of Human Rights with United States Federal and State Constitutions.* Milburn, NJ: University Press of America, 1998.

U.S. GOVERNMENT DOCUMENTS AND LEGISLATION

Congressional Quarterly Weekly Report. Washington, DC: Congressional Quarterly Inc., 1956–
Country Reports on Human Rights Practices for 2006, Vols. I & II. Washington, DC: U.S. Government Printing Office, 2008.
Country Reports on Human Rights Practices for 2007, Vols I & II. Washington, DC: U.S. Government Printing Office, 2008.
Critique: Review of the Department of State's Country Reports on Human Rights Practices for 1982. New York: Lawyers' Committee for Human Rights and Human Rights Watch, 1983–. (The annual is also called *Critique of DOS Country Reports;* beginning in 1990 the critique became the project of the Lawyers' Committee alone.)
International Human Rights Law Group. *U.S. Legislation Relating Human Rights to U.S. Foreign Policy.* 4th ed. Buffalo, NY: W. S. Hein, 1991.

OTHER COUNTRY REPORTS

Amnesty International Country Reports (http://www.amnesty.org/en/library/).

Freedom House Freedom in the World Reports (http://www.freedomhouse.org/template.cfm?page=15).

Human Rights Watch, World Report (http://www.hrw.org/). (Current and previous World Reports dating back to 1989 can be found under the "Publications" tab.

International Committee of the Red Cross Annual Report (http://www.icrc.org/). (Reports for 2004–2009 can be found under the "Info Resources" tab.)

International Women's Rights Action Watch, IWRAW Country Reports (http://www1.umn.edu/humanrts/iwraw/shadowreports.html).

UNDP Human Development Reports (http://hdr.undp.org/en/).

UNHCR Public Information Section Country Profiles (http://www.unhcr.org/cgi-bin/texis/vtx/home). (Select country in "Browse by Country" drop down menu.)

UNICEF State of the World's Children (http://www.unicef.org/apublic).

U.S. Dept. of State Country Reports on Human Rights Practices (http://www.state.gov/g/drl/rls/hrrpt/). (Contains Human Rights Reports from 1999 to present.)

U.S. Dept. of State Country Reports on Human Rights Practices (http://www.state.gov/www/global/human_rights/hrp_reports_mainhp.html). (Contains Human Rights Reports from 1993–1999).

WRITENET Country Papers (http://www.unhcr.org/refworld/publisher/WRITENET.html).

RELATED LAW REVIEW ARTICLES

Bassiouni, C. "Human Rights in the Context of Criminal Justice: Identifying International Procedural Protections and Equivalent Protections in National Constitutions." *Duke Journal of Comp. and International Law* 3 (Spring, 1993): 235–297.

Bayefsky, A., and Joan Fitzpatrick. "International Human Rights Law in U.S. Courts: A Comparative Perspective." *Michigan Journal of International Law* (Fall 1992): 1–89.

Bilder, Richard. "Integrating International Human Rights Law into Domestic Law." *Houston Journal of International Law* 4 (1981): 1.

Burke, K., S. Coliver, C. De La Vega, and S. Rosenbaum. "Application of International Human Rights Law in State and Federal Courts." *Texas International Law Journal* 18 (1981): 291.

Fitzpatrick, Joan. "The Future of the Alien Tort Claims Act of 1789: Lessons from *In Re Marcos* Human Rights Litigation." *St. John's Law Review* 67: 491–521.

Ginger, Ann F. "Human Rights and Peace Law in the U.S." *Temple International and Comp. Law Journal* 6 (Spring 1992): 25–53.

Nanda, Ved P. "The United States Reservation to the Ban on the Death Penalty for Juvenile Offenders: An Appraisal under the International Covenant on Civil and Political Rights." *DePaul Law Review* 42 (1993): 1311.

Neier, Aryeh. "Political Consequences of the United States Ratification of the International Covenant on Civil and Political Rights." *DePaul Law Review* 42 (1993): 1209.

Posner, E. "Climate Change and International Human Rights Litigation: A Critical Appraisal." *U. Penn Law Review* 155 (2007): 1925.

Quigley, John. "Criminal Law and Human Rights: Implications of the United States Ratification of the International Covenant on Civil and Political Rights." *Harvard Human Rights Journal* 6 (1993): 59.

Zimmerman, T. "Prospects for Economic, Social, and Cultural Rights under U.S. Law." *Whittier Law Review* 14 (1993): 549–577.

LAW JOURNALS

The Columbia Human Rights Law Review (HRLR). New York: Columbia University School of Law.

Harvard Human Rights Journal (Harv. Hum. Rts. J.). Cambridge, MA: Harvard Law School.

Human Rights Law Journal (H.R.L.J.). Kehl/Strasbourg: N. P. Engel Publishers, 1983–.

Human Rights Quarterly (Hum. Rts. Q.). Baltimore, MD: Johns Hopkins University Press, 1981–.

New York Law School Journal of Human Rights (N.Y.L. Sch. J. Hum. Rts.). New York: New York Law School, 1987–.

TEXTS OF HUMAN RIGHTS INSTRUMENTS

General

Center for the Study of Human Rights. *Twenty-Four Human Rights Documents*. New York: Columbia University, 1992.

Human Rights: A Compilation of International Instruments. New York: United Nations Centre for Human Rights, 2003.

Human Rights Documents: Compilation of Documents Pertaining to Human Rights. Washington, DC: U.S. Government Printing Office, 1983.

International Legal Materials (I.L.M.). Washington, DC: American Society of International Law, 1962–.

Lillich, Richard B., ed. *International Human Rights Instruments: A Compilation of Treaties, Agreements and Declarations of Special Interest to the United States*. 2d ed. Buffalo, NY: W. S. Hein, 1990–.

Symonides, J. and Volodin, V. *UNESCO'S Standard-Setting Instruments, Major Meetings and Publications*. Paris: UNESCO, 1996.

Law of Armed Conflict

International Committee of the Red Cross. *The Geneva Conventions of August 12, 1949*. Geneva: International Committee of the Red Cross, 1995.

———. *Protocols Additional to the Geneva Conventions of August 12, 1949*. Rev. ed. Geneva: International Committee of the Red Cross, 2010.

Roberts, A., and R. Guelff, eds. *Documents on the Laws of War*. 2d ed. Oxford: Clarendon Press, 2000.

Fleck, D. *The Handbook of International Humanitarian Law*. 2d ed. Oxford: Clarendon Press 2008.

Organization of American States

Basic Documents Pertaining to Human Rights in the Inter-American System. Washington, DC: General Secretariat, Organization of American States, 2010. OAS/Ser.L/V/I.4 rev. 13.

Buergenthal, T., and R. Norris, eds. *Human Rights: The Inter-American System*. Dobbs Ferry, NY: Oceana Publications, 1982–.

Organization for Security and Cooperation in Europe

Bloed, Arie. *From Helsinki to Vienna: Basic Documents of the Helsinki Process*. 1990.

"Conference on Security and Cooperation in Europe: Final Act." *Dept. of State Bulletin* 73: 323–350; I.L.M. 14: 1292–1325. Washington, DC: Government Printing Office, 1975.

Kavass, I., and J. Granier, eds. *Human Rights, the Helsinki Accords, and the United States: Selected Executive and Congressional Documents*, 9 vols. Reprint ed. Buffalo, NY: W. S. Hein, 1982.

Weissbrodt, D. and Hoffman, M. *Selected International Human Rights Instruments and Bibliography for Research in International Human Rights Law*. 4th ed. Cincinnatti: Anderson Publications, 2009

STATUS OF TREATIES

Marie, J. B. "International Instruments Relating to Human Rights/Classification and Status of Ratifications as of 1 January 1999." *Human Rights Law Journal* 20, no. 1–3 (30 July 1999).

Treaties in Force: A List of Treaties and Other International Agreements of the United States in Force. Washington, DC: U.S. Government Printing Office, 1929–.

United Nations Educational, Scientific and Cultural Organization, The Division of Human Rights and Peace. *Human Rights: Major International Instruments, Status as of 31 May 2010*. New York: UNESCO, 2010 (annual).

WEBSITE TEXT SOURCES

Bayefsky (www.Bayefsky.com).

University of Minnesota Human Rights Library (http://www.umn.edu/humanrts/). These documents can be accessed by subject matter (http://www1.umn.edu/humanrts/instree/ainstls2.htm) or instrument list (http://www1.umn.edu/humanrts/instree/ainstls1.htm).

United Nations High Commissioner for Human Rights (http://www.ohchr.org/EN/Library/Pages/Finding UNHumanRights.aspx).

INTERNET SITES

American University, Washington College of Law, WWW, Center for Human Rights and Humanitarian Law (http://www1.umn.edu/humanrts/bibliog/BIBLIO.htm) .

Department of State Foreign Affairs Network (http://dosfan.lib.uic.edu/ERC/index.html).

Electronic Information System for International Law (http://www.eisil.org/). (Electronic Library for American Society for International Law (ASIL).)

HuriSearch (http://www.hurisearch.org/). (The human rights search engine sponsored by HuriDocs.org.)

Inter-American Commission on Human Rights (http://www.cidh.oas.org).

Inter-American Court of Human Rights (http://www.corteidh.or.cr/index.cfm?&CFID=487586&CFTOKEN=78136649).

Law Library of Congress' Global Legal Information Network (http://www.glin.gov/search.action).

Organization of American States (http://www.oas.org).

United Nations, Dag Hammarskjöld Library. *United Nations Documentation: Research Guide on Human Rights* (http://www.un.org/Depts/dhl/resguide/spechr.htm). There is also a specialized research guide on international law (http://www.un.org/Depts/dhl/resguide/ specil.htm).

United Nations, High Commissioner for Human Rights (http://www.ohchr.org/).

United Nations, Human Rights Instruments (http://www.ohchr.org/EN/Library/Pages/FindingUNHuman Rights.aspx).

United Nations, Other Human Rights Documents (http://www.ohchr.org/EN/Library/Pages/HRGuide.aspx).

United Nations, Treaty Bodies Database (http://www.ohchr.org/EN/HRBodies/Pages/HumanRightsBodies.aspx).

United States House of Representatives Internet Law Library (http://www.lawguru.com/ilawlib/).

United States Department of State, Human Rights, Treaty Reports (http://www.state.gov/g/drl/hr/treaties/index/htm./)

United States Department of State, Human Rights, Universal Periodic Review (http://www.state.gov/g/drl/hr/upr/index.htm./)

United States Department of State, Treaties in Force (http://www.state.gov/s/l/treaty/tif/index.htm).

University of California at Berkeley Human Rights Center, *Bibliographies on Issues in Human Rights* (http://globetrotter.berkeley.edu/humanrights/bibliographies.html).

Weissbrodt, David, and Marci Hoffman. "Bibliography for Research on International Human Rights Law." *Minnesota Journal of Global Trade* 6 (1997): 200. (http://www1.umn.edu/humanrts/bibliog/BIBLIO.htm).

TEXTBOOKS

Alston, P., Ryan Goodman and Henry J. Steiner. *International Human Rights in Context: Law, Politics and Morals.* 3d ed. Oxford: Oxford University Press, 2007.

Buergenthal, T., Dinah Shelton, and David Stewart. *International Human Rights in a Nutshell.* 4th ed. St. Paul: West, 2009.

Buergenthal, T. R., T. Norris, and D. Shelton. *Protecting Human Rights in the Americas: Selected Problems.* 4th ed. Arlington, VA: N. P. Engel, 1995.

Henkin, L., G. Neuman, D. Orentlicher, and D. Leebron. *Human Rights* Casebook Series. New York: Foundation Press, 1999.

Martin, F., et al. *International Human Rights Law and Practice: Cases, Treaties and Materials.* The Hague: Kluwer Law International, 1997.

Newman, F., and D. Weissbrodt. *International Human Rights: Law, Policy and Process.* 2d ed. Albany: LexisNexis/Matthew Bender, 2009.

Van Schaak, B, and Slye, R. *International Criminal Law and its Enforcement, Cases and Materials.* 2d ed. New York: Foundation Press, 2010.

HUMAN RIGHTS ORGANIZATIONS

Amnesty International (http://www.amnesty.org/)

Coalition for an International Criminal Court (CICC) (http://www.igc.org/icc)

Human Rights First [formerly known as Lawyers' Committee for Human Rights] (http://www.humanrightsfirst.org/)

Human Rights Watch (http://www.hrw.org/)

HUMAN RIGHTS EDUCATION

Amnesty International Human Rights for Children Committee. *Human Rights for Children: A Curriculum for Teaching Human Rights to Children Aged 3–12*. Alameda, CA: Hunter House, 1992.

Andreopolis, George, and Richard P. Claude, eds. *Human Rights Education: Conceptual and Practical Challenges*. Philadelphia: University of Pennsylvania Press, 1996.

Au, Wayne, Bill Bigelow, and Stan Karp. *Rethinking Our Classrooms: Teaching for Equality and Justice Vol 1*. Rev. ed. Milwaukee, WI: Rethinking Schools, Ltd., 2007.

Bigelow, Bill. *Rethinking Our Classrooms: Teaching for Equality and Justice Vol. 2*. Milwaukee, WI: Rethinking Schools, Ltd., 2001.

Elliot, Roanne. *We: Lessons on Equal Worth and Dignity*. Minneapolis, MN: The United Nations Assoc. of Minnesota. 1992. (A middle school curriculum.)

Condé, H. *Human Rights Education: The Ultimate Sanction*. 10 Trinity Law Review, No. 1, Fall 2000.

Flowers, N., ed. *Human Rights Here and Now: Celebrating the Universal Declaration of Human Rights*. Minneapolis, MN: Human Rights Educators' Network, Human Rights USA, and the Stanley Foundation. 1998.

Gonzalez, Susan. *We: Lessons on Equal Worth and Dignity*. Minneapolis, MN: The United Nations Assoc. of Minnesota, 1997. (An elementary school curriculum.)

Hatch, Virginia. *Human Rights for Children: A Manual for Activities for Elementary Schools*. Washington, DC: Human Rights for Children Committee, 1991.

Human Rights Education: The Fourth R. Minneapolis, MN: Amnesty International USA, 1994–.

Nuñez, Lucia. *An Agenda for Peace: The Role of the United Nations*. Menlo Park, CA: Stanford Program on International and Cross-Cultural Education. 1995. (A curriculum guide, secondary to adult).

O'Brien, Edward, Elenor Greene, and David McQuoid-Mason. *Human Rights for All*. Minneapolis, MN: West Educational Publishing USA, 1996. (A high school curriculum.)

Reardon, Betty. *Educating for Human Dignity: Learning about Rights and Responsibilities*. Pennsylvania Studies in Human Rights. Philadelphia: University of Pennsylvania Press, 1995.

Shiman, David. *Teaching Human Rights*. Denver, CO: Center for Teaching International Relations Publications, University of Denver, 1993.

This is My New Home. Minneapolis, MN: Human Rights Center, University of Minnesota. (K-12 Human Rights Curriculum.)

United Nations. "ABC, Teaching Human Rights: Practical Activities for Primary and Secondary Schools." New York: United Nations, 2004.

INDEX

A

Abdelfattah Amor's report, 773–784

Abraham Lincoln's Emancipation Proclamation, 83

Abrams vs. United States, 581

Abu Ghraib prison issue, 48, 135, 427, 484–487, 1020

Accessibility (Principle), 153–154

Accession (To Treaty), 200

Accountability/accountable, 1–2

Activist, 111–112

Acton, Lord, 182

Adarand Constructors, Inc. vs. Pena, 360, 409, 546

Adarand Constructors, Inc. vs. Perla, 360

Administrative detention, 9

Administrative Procedure Act, 396

Admissibility
  criteria or grounds of, 2
  definition, 2
  filing of complaints, 2
  at international level, 3
  Optional Protocol, 2

Advice and consent of U.S. Senate, 3–4

Advocacy, 111
  civil society, 115
  of national, racial or religious hatred, 9, 86, 102
  victim, 251
  women's human rights, 267–268

Affirmative action, 365, 409, 509, 526, 565, 586, 594, 601, 766
  controversies, 4–5
  definition, 4
  programs, 360, 362, 412, 546, 683
  significance, 4–5

Affirmative asylum, 393–394

African Charter on Human and Peoples' Rights, 20

Age Discrimination Act of 1975, 420

Aggression, 41
  Rome Statute, 952

Aggressive crimes, 41

Aid conditionality, 5

Alabama vs. Shelton, 397

Alaskan Eskimos, 127, 129

Ali, Shaheen Sardar, 126

Aliens, 220
  state responsibility for injury to, 228

Alien Tort Claims Act (ATCA), 5–6, 81

Alien Tort Statute (ATS), 470

Al Qaeda, 30–31, 66–68, 70, 72, 168, 179, 190, 204, 234, 237–238, 367, 802
  summary of unlawful belligerent acts committed by, 477–478

Alston, Phillip, 231
  Alternative Forms, 1172
  Article 1, 148–149, 293
  Article 2-7, 293
  Article 3, 10, 155
  Article 5, 36, 48
  Article 7, 70
  Article 8, 59
  Article 8-21, 294
  Article 9, 155
  Article 10, 78
  Article 12, 142
  Article 14, 10
  Article 22-30, 295
  Article 29.1, 62
  Articles 1, 2, 7, 10, 16, 91
  preamble, 293

American-Arab Anti-Discrimination Committee (ADC), 544

American Bill of Rights, 14

American Convention on Human Rights (ACHR), 6, 835–846
  Protocol II to abolish the death penalty, 851–852
  Protocol of San Salvador, 846–851

American Declaration on the Rights and Duties of Man (ADHR), 6, 832–835

American Indian Religious Freedom Act (AIRFA), 589, 779

American Indians, 127, 358–359, 500, 520, 522, 526, 557, 564, 568, 570–572, 574, 579, 587, 779, 996–997, 1001

American Servicemen's Protection Act, 144

Americans with Disabilities Act of 1990 (ADA), 56, 362, 376, 409, 565

Ameziane vs. USA, 32, 229

Amin, Idi, 44

Amnesty International, USA, 6–7, 45
  Human Rights Education program, 578
  program to prevent torture, 1021
  report on alleged abuses in prisons, 471

Amnesty International Educators Network, 578

Annan, U.N. Secretary General Kofi, 109

Anti-Ahmadiya blasphemy laws, 86

Anti-blasphemy legislation, 86

Anti-Defamation League (ADL), 544, 549

Anti-Semitism, 7–8, 986

Anti-Terrorism and Effective Death Penalty Act of 1996 (AEDPA), 387, 398, 777, 1027

Apartheid, 8, 217, 327, 329, 510–511, 547, 601, 661, 744, 747, 750, 758, 875, 921, 943

Apprendi vs. New Jersey, 396

Arbitrary arrest, 8–9, 294, 299, 303, 411, 668, 704, 807, 834, 837, 985, 1097

Archaeological Resources Protection Act, 589

Argersinger vs. Hamlin, 397

ABOUT THE AUTHOR

H. Victor Condé is an international human rights lawyer and educator based in California and Europe. He holds a Juris Doctor from UC Davis Law School, an MA in International Human Rights, and LLM in International and Comparative Human Rights Law from the Univ. of Essex, and holds the Diplôme in International and Comparative Human Rights and Humanitarian Law from the International Institute of Human Rights in Strasbourg, France. He served as professor of human rights and humanitarian law at Trinity Law School in California, and lectured at the International Institute of Human Rights, the University of California at Irvine, and the Catholic University of Brussels and has served as a human rights legal consultant to NGOs and to the O.S.C.E . He is a member of the California and Hawaii Bars.